Intellectual Property and Antitrust Handbook

SECTION OF
ANTITRUST
LAW

Defending Liberty
Pursuing Justice

This volume should be officially cited as:

ABA SECTION OF ANTITRUST LAW,
INTELLECTUAL PROPERTY AND ANTITRUST HANDBOOK (2007)

Cover design by ABA Publishing.

Printed in the United States of America.

ISBN: 1-59031-866-8
ISBN13: 978-1-59031-866-9
Library of Congress Control Number is on file with the Library of Congress.

Discounts are available for books ordered in bulk. Special consideration is given to state bars, CLE programs, and other bar-related organizations. Inquire at ABA Publishing, American Bar Association, 321 N. Clark St., Chicago, Illinois 60610.

07 06 05 04 03   5 4 3 2 1

www.ababooks.org

CONTENTS

FOREWORD

The American Bar Association Section of Antitrust Law is pleased to publish the *Intellectual Property and Antitrust Handbook*.

The *Handbook* is intended to serve as an introduction and general guide to the application of the federal antitrust laws to intellectual property. It explores in detail the antitrust issues that arise from the acquisition, licensing, and enforcement of patents, copyrights, trademarks, and other forms of intellectual property, as well as developments in patent, copyright, and intellectual property law from the standpoint of economics and competition policy. This book provides practical guidance in this area, particularly in light of recent private and government enforcement activity.

The Section of Antitrust Law is grateful to editor Sean P. Gates and his team of contributing authors, each of whom dedicated many hours to the preparation of the *Intellectual Property and Antitrust Handbook*, under the leadership of Mark S. Popofsky, Chair of the Intellectual Property Committee of the Section of Antitrust Law.

We hope that this *Handbook* will be helpful to those who practice in this important and ever-changing field.

March 2007   Joseph Angland
                                        Chair, Section of Antitrust Law
                                          American Bar Association
                                                    2006-2007

PREFACE

The Intellectual Property Committee of the Section of Antitrust Law is pleased to present this *Handbook* on one of the most interesting and complex subjects facing antitrust practitioners: the intersection of antitrust and intellectual property law. Long viewed as in conflict, today's antitrust practitioners, courts, and agencies now generally recognize that antitrust and intellectual property laws are complementary, as they both seek to promote consumer welfare by increasing competition and innovation.

This book is the product of the hard work of numerous individuals. We owe special thanks to Sean P. Gates, who was responsible for marshalling the work of numerous drafters into a unified whole and has worked tirelessly to see this project through to completion. Section Chair Joseph Angland went above and beyond the call of duty to review and improve the entire manuscript prior to publication. David H. Evans, Christopher B. Hockett, and Richard G. Parker of the Section Council also provided valuable support and guidance on the *Handbook*. We also wish to thank Gregory F. Wells and Robin L. Moore of the Section's Books and Treatises Committee for their efforts in reviewing and editing the manuscript. In addition, we wish to that the following individuals who contributed their time and expertise to the drafting of this *Handbook*:

Edward G. Biester, III
Tanya K. Dumas
Thomas B. Ensign
Andrew J. Ewalt
Bree Hann
Adam C. Hemlock
Rajesh James
Sarah Kay Johnson
William J. Kolasky
Gail F. Levine
Robert A. Milne
Robin Moore

Thomas M. Morrow
M. Howard Morse
Philip B. Nelson
Charles P. Reichmann
Scott D. Russell
Marc G. Schildkraut
Michelle H. Seagull
Scott A. Sher
Robert D. Stoner
Kenneth M. Vorrasi
Hill B. Wellford

Finally, the book could not have been completed without the hard work of numerous people at Bingham McCutchen LLP, especially Kathleen Caulfield, Manami Elwell, Trenia Jones, James Mountain, Felix Otchere, and Erika Tillery.

We hope that you find the *Intellectual Property & Antitrust Handbook* to be a valuable resource.

March 2007   Mark S. Popofsky
Chair, Intellectual Property Committee
Section of Antitrust Law
American Bar Association
2006-2007

CHAPTER I

INTRODUCTION

The intellectual property and antitrust laws both seek to increase consumer welfare through greater competition and innovation. Intellectual property laws foster competitive innovation through the award of exclusivity for a limited time during which an inventor can exploit the innovation. The antitrust laws, on the other hand, encourage competition—including competition to innovate—by restricting exclusionary behavior and limiting rivals' ability to coordinate their conduct. While the antitrust and intellectual property laws are complementary to the extent that they both promote competition over the long term, the two regimes are sometimes at odds in the short term.

A. Overview of Intellectual Property and Antitrust Law

Chapter II examines the nature and interface of the intellectual property and antitrust laws. The chapter explains the different types of intellectual property. It then describes the purposes of the antitrust laws. And it then gives an overview of the intellectual property-antitrust interface.

That interface is shaped by the nature of intellectual property rights. Article I, Section 8, Clause 8 of the U. S. Constitution provides that Congress shall have the power "[t]o promote the progress of science and useful arts, by securing for limited times to authors and inventors the exclusive right to their respective writings and discoveries."[1] From this foundation, the intellectual property regime of the United States has grown. Today, there are four primary types of intellectual property rights: (1) copyrights, which protect original "works of authorship," such as music, books, and software; (2) trade secrets, which guard secret proprietary information, such as customer lists, product formulas, and business plans; (3) trademarks, which defend trade names and symbols used by businesses to identify their products and services; and (4) patents, which safeguard new and useful inventions and processes.

The antitrust laws act as a competitive governor on the exercise of all property rights, including intellectual property rights. Section 1 of the Sherman Act prohibits agreements that reduce competition without producing offsetting efficiency benefits, and Section 2 of the Sherman

---

1.   U.S. CONST. art. 1, § 8, cl. 8.

Act makes it unlawful for a firm (1) to monopolize, (2) to attempt to monopolize, or (3) to conspire to monopolize a relevant market.[2] The influence of the antitrust laws on the exercise of intellectual property rights is perhaps most evident in the types of restrictions that intellectual property holders can impose on licensees. Antitrust concerns can also arise in other areas, including cross-licensing and patent pooling arrangements, refusals to license, infringement litigation, and mergers.

B. Historical Tension Between Antitrust and Intellectual Property Laws

Chapter III addresses the historical treatment of intellectual property issues in antitrust cases.

Intellectual property owners entered the 20th century largely uninhibited by the restraining influence of the (then) decade-old Sherman Act. Early court decisions routinely held that the free exercise of intellectual property rights took precedence over the newly-enacted antitrust laws.[3] In the years following, however, there were increasing calls to curb abusive practices by patent holders. The courts initially responded to this movement by developing the doctrine of patent misuse,[4] but by the 1930s and 1940s, courts finally began to recognize that the anticompetitive misuse of a patent also could violate the antitrust laws.[5]

As the sanctity of intellectual property rights waned during the 1940s, 1950s, and 1960s, courts and the antitrust laws, which were gaining prominence, grew increasingly hostile toward attempts by owners of intellectual property to extend their rights beyond the scope of the intellectual property. This evolution is exemplified in two Supreme Court cases, decided almost 20 years apart, involving the same two parties and virtually identical conduct: *Automatic Radio Manufacturing v. Hazeltine Research*[6] and *Zenith Radio Corp. v. Hazeltine Research.*[7] In *Automatic Radio*, the Supreme Court upheld a royalty scheme that required the licensee to make payments based on the total number of

---

2.   15 U.S.C. §§ 1, 2.

3.   *See, e.g.*, Strait v. Harrow, 51 F. 819 (N.D.N.Y. 1892).

4.   Motion Picture Patents Co. v. Universal Film Mfg., 243 U.S. 502, 515 (1917).

5.   Carbice Corp. v. Am. Patents Dev., 283 U.S. 27 (1931); Morton Salt v. G. S. Suppiger Co., 314 U.S. 488 (1942).

6.   Automatic Radio Mfg. v. Hazeltine Research, 339 U.S. 827 (1950).

7.   Zenith Radio Corp. v. Hazeltine Research, 395 U.S. 100 (1969).

radio units it produced, regardless of whether the product included the relevant patent, on the basis that it was a reasonable and convenient method of fixing a royalty because it saved the parties from having to determine whether each product actually included the licensed technology. Twenty years later, however, the Supreme Court struck down an identical royalty provision between the same parties on the grounds that the licensor was extending its rights beyond the scope of the patent because the license might require the licensee to make royalty payments on products that did not incorporate the licensed technology.

The nadir of intellectual property rights arguably arrived in 1970 when the Antitrust Division of the U. S. Department of Justice announced the "Nine No-No's" of intellectual property licensing. In releasing the Nine No-No's, the DOJ asserted that it would challenge as per se unlawful any licensing agreement that (1) conditioned a license on the purchase of unpatented materials, (2) required the licensee to grant back subsequent improvements to the licensor, (3) restricted the resale of a licensed product, (4) restricted a licensee's ability to deal in products outside the scope of the patent, (5) restricted a licensor's ability to grant additional licenses to third parties, (6) required a licensee to take a mandatory package license, (7) included royalty provisions not reasonably related to the licensee's sales, (8) imposed restrictions on a licensee's use of a product made by a patented process, and (9) set minimum resale price provisions for the licensed products.[8]

Intellectual property rights regained prominence in the 1980s and 1990s. The election of Ronald Reagan to the White House in 1980 ushered in a new generation eager to implement Chicago School economic policies. The 1980s also saw the establishment of the Federal Circuit Court of Appeals to develop a uniform patent law. Over the next decade, the Department of Justice and Federal Trade Commission abandoned the per se treatment of most intellectual property licensing restraints identified in the "Nine No-No's" and, in 1995, released the joint *Antitrust Guidelines for the Licensing of Intellectual Property.*[9] The 1995 *Intellectual Property Guidelines* recognized, among other things,

---

8. *See* Bruce B. Wilson, Dep. Ass't Att'y Gen., Remarks Before the Fourth New England Antitrust Conference, Patent and Know-How License Agreements: Field of Use, Territorial, Price and Quantity Restrictions (Nov. 6, 1970).

9. *See* U.S. DEP'T OF JUSTICE & FED. TRADE COMM'N, ANTITRUST GUIDELINES FOR THE LICENSING OF INTELLECTUAL PROPERTY (Apr. 6, 1995) (hereinafter INTELLECTUAL PROPERTY GUIDELINES), *reprinted in* 4 Trade Reg. Rep. (CCH) ¶ 13,132 *and* Appendix 1 to this Handbook.

that (1) licensing is generally procompetitive, (2) intellectual property rights do not necessarily convey market power, and (3) the antitrust laws should be applied to intellectual property in a manner consistent with how they are applied to other forms of property.

C. The Economics of Intellectual Property

Chapter IV reviews the foundations of the economic theories underlying the intellectual property laws and analyzes their implications for antitrust policy and the licensing of intellectual property.

In order to provide an incentive to innovate, the intellectual property laws grant a period of exclusivity to innovators who develop new ideas and products. The grant of exclusivity is designed to compensate for the fact that, unlike other forms of property, intellectual property can be readily misappropriated: an imitator can easily copy an innovator's new idea. Absent the protection of the intellectual property laws, innovation could be discouraged because imitators would quickly introduce products based on an innovator's ideas, depriving the innovator of financial reward.

Another aspect of the intellectual property regime that encourages innovation is the obligation to disclose an idea publicly in exchange for a period of exclusivity. As a result of the requirement that innovators publicly disclose new ideas in order to reap the benefit of exclusivity, other innovators have an opportunity to review details regarding an idea and make subsequent improvements to the original concept or product. Such cumulative innovation provides long-term benefits to society in the form of progressive improvements to products and services.

D. Antitrust Analysis of Agreements Involving Intellectual Property

Chapter V examines why certain intellectual property agreements raise antitrust concerns. In assessing whether a specific intellectual property licensing restriction is likely to prompt antitrust concerns, the first step is determining whether the agreement is horizontal or vertical in nature. Put another way, does the license agreement restrict competition that would have existed in the absence of the license?[10] The characterization of a license agreement as horizontal or vertical frequently is important because the well-recognized efficiencies associated with many vertical licensing agreements merit analysis under

---

10. *Id.* § 3.3.

the rule of reason. Conversely, horizontal licensing agreements are treated more skeptically and often prompt greater scrutiny, even in circumstances where the licensing arrangement escapes per se analysis.

Identifying whether an arrangement is horizontal or vertical, however, is not always a straightforward exercise, especially where a license is used to settle an infringement lawsuit. In such situations, it may be difficult to establish whether, but for the license, the parties to the agreement would have been competitors because either the licensee's original technology did not actually infringe the licensor's intellectual property, or the licensee could have designed around the licensor's intellectual property with reasonable effort. Further complicating this analysis is the uncertainty regarding whether the burden of proof on these issues resides with the parties to the agreement or with the enforcement agencies or private plaintiffs.

With the exception of a few types of restrictive agreements, such as naked price-fixing arrangements, horizontal market allocations, concerted refusals to deal, and tying arrangements, most intellectual property licensing agreements are likely to be analyzed under the rule of reason regardless of whether they are characterized as horizontal or vertical in nature.[11] Under the rule of reason, the license, including any collateral restraints, will be evaluated to determine, on balance, (1) whether the agreement is procompetitive, (2) whether any collateral restraints associated with the license are likely to have an anticompetitive effect and, if so, (3) whether the restraint is reasonably necessary to achieve the procompetitive benefits of the licensing agreement.

1. Price and Output

Agreements among competitors that restrict price and output are a primary focus of the antitrust laws. Thus, in most contexts, such restraints among competitors are condemned as per se illegal. In certain circumstances, however, where the agreement on price or output is so intertwined with the operation of an otherwise lawful and efficiency-enhancing joint venture or intellectual property licensing arrangement, the enforcement agencies and courts are more likely to accept an ancillary restraint on price or output as being reasonably necessary to the broader, procompetitive agreement. For example, in *Broadcast Music v. CBS*,[12] the Supreme Court held that a blanket copyright license offered

---

11.   *Id.* § 3.4.
12.   Broad. Music v. CBS, 441 U.S. 1, 23 (1979).

by a joint venture which fixed the price of copyrighted music owned by its members was not subject to per se treatment because the new blanket license generated substantial efficiencies and an "agreement on price [was] necessary to market the [blanket license]."[13] Such ancillary restraints on price or output are more likely to be held lawful in situations where (1) the broader agreement generates significant cost efficiencies, and (2) the participants to the agreement retain the right to separately negotiate licenses with third parties for the intellectual property that each has contributed to the joint arrangement.

Vertical licensing arrangements that restrict a licensee's price or output are generally viewed with less skepticism than their horizontal equivalents. Most courts that have addressed output restraints in vertical licensing agreements have held that an intellectual property owner can contractually limit the quantity of licensed products that a licensee is permitted to produce under the license.[14] Similarly, to the extent that it has been addressed under the rule of reason, courts and the enforcement agencies generally have permitted a licensor to impose maximum resale price restraints on licensed products sold by a licensee.[15]

In contrast, minimum resale price maintenance effected through licensing agreements is an area of continuing ambiguity. Despite the rule outside of the intellectual property context that vertical price maintenance is per se illegal, in *United States v. General Electric*, the Supreme Court held that GE did not violate Section 1 of the Sherman Act by fixing the resale price of products sold under license.[16] Subsequent decisions, however, have limited and distinguished the *General Electric* rule.[17] And the antitrust agencies maintain that it is per se illegal for a licensor to fix the minimum resale price for licensed products sold by a licensee.[18]

---

13. *Id.* at 23.

14. *See, e.g.*, Atari Games v. Nintendo of Am., 897 F.2d 1572 (Fed. Cir. 1990).

15. *See* State Oil Co. v. Khan, 522 U.S. 3 (1997); R. Hewitt Pate, Acting Ass't Att'y Gen., Address Before the Am. Intellectual Property Law Ass'n (Jan. 24, 2003).

16. United States v. Gen. Elec. Co., 272 U.S. 476 (1926).

17. *See, e.g.*, United States v. Line Material, 333 U.S. 287, 307-13 (1948) (rule not applicable to restriction in sublicenses to patents involved in cross-licensing agreement).

18. INTELLECTUAL PROPERTY GUIDELINES, *supra* note 9, § 5.2; *see, e.g.*, R. Hewitt Pate, Acting Ass't Att'y Gen., Address Before the Am. Intellectual Property Law Ass'n (January 24, 2003).

2. *Field of Use, Geographic, and Customer Provisions*

Generally, restraints concerning a licensee's permitted field of use and territorial or customer restrictions are acceptable in vertical licensing arrangements. As with most vertical restraints, field of use, territorial, and customer restrictions are analyzed under the rule of reason.[19] Such restrictions generally are justified as an incentive for the licensee to invest in the commercialization and distribution of products incorporating the licensed intellectual property and to develop additional applications for the licensed property within the field of use, geographic area, or customer class that has been assigned to the licensee.

3. *Exclusive Dealing*

Exclusive dealing or "tie-out" restraints in vertical licensing agreements are analyzed under the rule of reason.[20] In assessing the likely competitive effect of such a restraint, the key factors that a court or enforcement agency likely would consider are (1) the duration of the exclusive arrangement, (2) the justification for the exclusivity, and (3) the percentage of the market likely to be foreclosed by the agreement. Absent a high rate of foreclosure, however, exclusive dealing restraints are unlikely to be deemed unlawful.

4. *Tying/Package License*

A tying agreement is "an agreement by a party to sell one product on the condition that the buyer also purchases a different (or tied) product, or at least agrees that he will not purchase that product from any other supplier."[21] While some courts have held that tying is per se illegal, most courts and the enforcement agencies typically apply a rule of reason analysis to tying arrangements. The enforcement agencies also have stated that they likely would challenge a tying arrangement where "(1) the seller has market power in the tying product, (2) the arrangement has an adverse effect on competition in the relevant market for the tied

---

19. *See, e.g., In re* Yarn Processing Patent Validity Litig., 541 F.2d 1127, 1135 (5th Cir. 1976); Carter v. Variflex, 101 F. Supp. 2d 1261, 1265-66 (C.D. Cal. 2000).
20. INTELLECTUAL PROPERTY GUIDELINES, *su pra* note 9, § 5.4.
21. Eastman Kodak Co. v. Image Technical Servs., 504 U.S. 451, 461 (1992).

product, and (3) efficiency justifications for the arrangement do not outweigh the anticompetitive effects."[22]

In the context of intellectual property, a tying arrangement is likely to take one of two forms, either (1) the licensor requires the licensee to purchase a separate product or service from the licensor as a condition of obtaining a license, or (2) the licensor offers only a package that covers multiple pieces of intellectual property instead of offering individual licenses for specific pieces of intellectual property. In either circumstance, the courts and enforcement agencies are likely to examine whether there are sufficient procompetitive economic justifications for the restraint before challenging the licensing provision. If the licensor has market power in the tying product and the justifications are found to be inadequate to offset the potential anticompetitive effects in the tied product market, such tying arrangements or package licenses are likely to be deemed unlawful.

5. Royalty Requirements

While the misuse doctrine in intellectual property law limits intellectual property owners' discretion concerning the amount or structure of royalties charged to licensees, the antitrust laws do not impose any significant restrictions on a licensor's ability to charge whatever royalties the market will bear. This issue was addressed, at least in dicta, in *Brulotte v. Thys Co.*, where Justice Harlan observed in his dissenting opinion that excessive royalties are unlikely to support a finding of an antitrust violation.[23] In that case, the Supreme Court controversially held that agreements that require a licensee to make royalty payments beyond the expiration of a patent are unenforceable under the misuse doctrine, but the Court did not hold or suggest that such a provision would violate the antitrust laws. Moreover, the Court's holding in *Brulotte*, as well as other lower court holdings that post-expiration royalty clauses are invalid, have endured a great deal of criticism on the basis that "charging royalties beyond the term of the patent does not lengthen the patentee's monopoly; it merely alters the timing of royalty payments."[24] As a consequence, it appears unlikely that such provisions would be deemed unlawful under the antitrust laws.

---

22.   INTELLECTUAL PROPERTY GUIDELINES, *supra* note 9, § 5.3 (footnote omitted).
23.   Brulotte v. Thys Co., 379 U.S. 29, 39 (1964) (Harlan, J., dissenting).
24.   *See, e.g.*, Scheiber v. Dolby Labs., 293 F.3d 1014, 1018 (7th Cir. 2002).

6. *Grantbacks*

A grantback requires a licensee to grant the licensor the right to any improvements to the technology developed by the licensee. The courts and enforcement agencies acknowledge that grantbacks can have procompetitive effects, and, as such, should be evaluated under the rule of reason.[25] Such grantbacks can have an anticompetitive effect, however, to the extent that they reduce a licensee's incentive to engage in research and development. Among the many factors that a court or enforcement agency is likely to assess in analyzing whether a grantback is likely to have an adverse effect on competition are (1) whether the licensor has market power in the relevant market, (2) whether the licensee has sufficient incentive to innovate despite the grantback, and (3) whether the licensee has the freedom to license its improvements to third parties.[26]

7. *Miscellaneous Restraints*

Other vertical restraints, including non-assert clauses (which preclude licensees from asserting that a licensor is infringing any of the licensee's intellectual property) and no-challenge clauses (which restrict a licensee's ability to subsequently challenge the validity of a licensor's intellectual property), are generally evaluated under the rule of reason. Such provisions are unlikely to be held unlawful by a court or challenged by an enforcement agency, unless (1) the licensor possesses market power, and (2) the clause is shown either to discourage innovation or to reinforce the licensor's position in the market in which the licensor possesses market power.

8. *Cross-Licensing and Patent Pools*

Cross-licenses and patent pools grant each of the parties to the agreement a right to use the other's intellectual property. These arrangements are often procompetitive because they clear blocking positions without the expense and uncertainty of litigation and permit firms to integrate additional technologies into their own products and

---

25. INTELLECTUAL PROPERTY GUIDELINES, *supra* note 9, § 5.6.
26. *Id.* § 5.6.

services.[27]   By their nature, however, cross-licenses and patent pools usually involve an agreement among competitors.   Nevertheless, provided an agreement is not a device for allocating markets and/or fixing prices, such arrangements are ordinarily analyzed by the enforcement agencies and courts under the rule of reason.[28]

In assessing whether a cross-license or patent pool would create market power and reduce competition, the agencies and courts have examined the extent to which the patents involved relate to competing, complementary, or blocking technologies as well as other factors, including: (1) whether the agreement is limited to essential or blocking patents, (2) the terms of any royalty scheme, (3) whether the agreement contains a grantback provision that might discourage innovation, and (4) whether the agreement is exclusive or the parties maintain the right to license their intellectual property to other parties.

9. Patent Settlements

As in other areas of law, settlements are generally recognized as an efficient means to resolve patent disputes.   In some circumstances, however, patent settlements between actual or potential competitors can have an anticompetitive effect on consumers. Any attempt to determine whether a patent settlement violates the antitrust laws is complicated by the uncertainty concerning the validity of the underlying intellectual property right.   Much of the recent attention regarding intellectual property settlements has been focused on "reverse payment" patent settlements in the pharmaceutical industry, under which the patent holder grants a license and pays royalties to the challenger.   Some commentators assert that a patent holder's willingness to make reverse payments only reflects a desire to avoid the uncertainty and risk of litigation, while others have argued that these reverse payments suggest that the disputed underlying intellectual patent right is weak or invalid and that such settlements are illegally perpetuating monopolies.[29]

---

27.   Carl Shapiro, *Navigating the Patent Thicket: Cross Licenses, Patent Pools, and Standard-Setting, in* INNOVATION POLICY AND THE ECONOMY (2001).

28.   In *In re Summit Technology Inc. & VISX Inc.*, No. 9286 (FTC March 24, 1998), a cross-license between competing laser eye surgery firms was found to violate § 1 of the Sherman Act because it eliminated competition between the firms.

29.   *See, e.g.*, Carl Shapiro, *Antitrust Analysis of Patent Settlements Between Rivals*, 17 ANTITRUST 70 (2003)

The case law in this area is mixed. In *In re Cardizem CD Antitrust Litigation*, the Sixth Circuit Court of Appeals held that the reverse payment settlements in that case were a per se violation of the antitrust laws.[30]   The FTC also has challenged several such arrangements, including a patent settlement between Schering-Plough and Upsher-Smith and American Home Products that allegedly delayed the introduction of generic versions of a brand name drug manufactured by Schering-Plough.[31] The Eleventh Circuit Court of Appeals, however, set aside the FTC's order and upheld the validity of the settlement.[32]   The court held that whether a reverse payment settlement violated Section 1 depended on "(1) the scope of the exclusionary potential of the patent; (2) the extent to which the agreements exceed that scope; and (3) the resulting anticompetitive effects."[33]   Similarly, the Second Circuit in *In re Tamoxifen Citrate Antitrust Litigation*,[34] held that a non-sham reverse payment settlement does not violate Section 1 unless the exclusionary effects of the settlement exceed the scope of the patent. The cases seem to reflect the lack of consensus that exists regarding the appropriate balance between a firm's ability to exercise its intellectual property rights and vigorous enforcement of the antitrust laws.

E.   Unilateral Conduct Involving Intellectual Property

Chapter VI describes the antitrust treatment of unilateral conduct involving intellectual property. This chapter focuses on two issues: an intellectual property holder's refusal to license and abusive enforcement by an intellectual property holder.

It is widely recognized that intellectual property owners generally do not have any obligation to license their intellectual property to others.[35] Courts also have observed, however, that a unilateral refusal to license "may raise antitrust concerns when the refusal is directed against competition and the purpose is to create, maintain, or enlarge a monopoly."[36] The Ninth Circuit and Federal Circuit examined the scope of a dominant firm's duty to license to rivals in *Image Technical Services*

---

30.   *In re* Cardizem CD Antitrust Litig., 332 F.3d 896, 908 (6th Cir. 2003).
31.   *In re* Schering-Plough, FTC Dkt No. 9297 (March 30, 2001).
32.   Schering-Plough v. FTC, 402 F.3d 1056 (11th Cir. 2005).
33.   *Id.* at 1066.
34.   466 F.3d 187 (2d Cir. 2006).
35.   35 U.S.C. § 271(d)(4).
36.   Intergraph Corp. v. Intel Corp., 195 F.3d 1346, 1358 (Fed. Cir. 1999).

v. Eastman Kodak Co. [37] and *In re Independent Service Organizations Antitrust Litigation.* [38]

In *Image Technical Services*, the Ninth Circuit held that Kodak's refusal to sell patented parts for its copiers to independent service organizations was an unlawful attempt under Section 2 of the Sherman Act to leverage its monopoly over Kodak parts in order to gain a monopoly over the servicing of Kodak equipment. In *Independent Service Organizations*, the Federal Circuit took a radically different approach in analyzing similar conduct by Xerox. The Federal Circuit held that Xerox's refusal to sell patented parts for its copiers to independent service organizations did not violate the antitrust laws and that, "in the absence of any indication of illegal tying, fraud in the Patent and Trademark Office, or sham litigation, the patent holder may enforce the statutory right to exclude others from making, using, or selling the claimed invention free from liability under the antitrust laws." The language in both *Image Technical Services* and *Independent Service Organizations* has prompted sharp criticism from commentators who argue that the rationales of each decision are too narrow or too broad, depending upon the author's view of the circumstances in which owners of intellectual property rights have a duty to license to third parties. [39]

Antitrust issues also arise in the enforcement of intellectual property rights. Inequitable conduct in the procurement or enforcement of a patent by a firm with market power also may violate the antitrust laws. In *Walker Process Equipment v. Food Machinery & Chemical Corp.*, [40] the Supreme Court held that fraudulent procurement of a patent by a firm with market power could give rise to a claim under Section 2 of the Sherman Act. Similarly, although the *Noerr-Pennington* doctrine generally exempts efforts to petition the government through litigation, enforcement of a patent obtained in good faith, but subsequently known to be invalid or not infringed by a firm with market power, is also subject to scrutiny under Section 2 of the Sherman Act. Such suits can be found to violate the antitrust laws where (1) the litigation is found to be objectively baseless, and (2) the litigation was filed by the firm with

---

37.   Image Technical Servs. v. Eastman Kodak Co., 125 F.3d 1195 (9th Cir. 1997).

38.   203 F.3d 1322, 1327 (Fed. Cir. 2000).

39.   *See infra*, Chapter VI, note 1 (compiling literature)

40.   382 U.S. 172 (1965).

market power to use the courts "as an anticompetitive weapon" against rivals.[41]

F. Mergers Involving Intellectual Property

Chapter VII examines the relevance of intellectual property in assessing whether a merger may substantially lessen competition. Just as with acquisitions of other classes of property, acquisitions involving intellectual property and mergers of firms that hold intellectual property portfolios are subject to scrutiny under Section 7 of the Clayton Act. A unique and controversial aspect of merger enforcement in industries where companies compete to develop intellectual property is the notion of innovation markets. An innovation market consists of the research and development directed to particular new or improved goods or processes, and the close substitutes for that research and development. In an innovation market, no one buys or sells anything; rather, firms expend resources that might lead to the introduction of new products at some future time.

Advocates of the innovation market theory argue that "delineating innovation markets can be a valuable instrument for evaluating the effects of merger-induced structural changes on the incentives for research and development and the resulting pace of industrial innovation."[42] Critics have skeptically suggested that, compared to the reliability of applying the *Merger Guidelines*[43] to mergers involving existing products, the ability of enforcement agencies to identify mergers that would harm innovation markets is very low.[44]

Nevertheless, throughout the 1990s, the DOJ and the FTC sought to block an increasing number of mergers where one party to the merger was an active participant in a relevant market and the other was at least

---

41. *See* Prof'l Real Estate Investors v. Columbia Pictures Indus., 508 U.S. 49, 50 (1993).
42. Richard J. Gilbert & Steven C. Sunshine, *Incorporating Dynamic Efficiency Concerns in Merger Analysis: The Use of Innovation Markets*, 63 ANTITRUST L.J. 569, 570 (1995).
43. U.S. DEP'T OF JUSTICE AND FED. TRADE COMM'N, HORIZONTAL MERGER GUIDELINES (Apr. 2, 1992), *reprinted in* 4 Trade Reg. Rep. (CCH) ¶ 13,104.
44. Dennis W. Carlton, *Antitrust Policy Toward Mergers When Firms Innovate: Should Antitrust Recognize the Doctrine of Innovation Markets?*, Testimony before the Federal Trade Commission Hearings on Global and Innovation-Based Competition (Oct. 25, 1995).

perceived to be a likely entrant due to its research and development activities, and where, due to the merging parties' intellectual property activities and portfolios, the firms were among the few (or only) likely potential entrants into a product market that did not yet exist. In *Genzyme Corporation/Novazyme Pharmaceuticals*, however, the FTC closed its investigation of the only two firms conducting work relating to a drug therapy for a particular disease.[45]   The FTC's investigation focused on the transaction's potential impact on the pace and scope of research.   In writing the Commission's opinion, Chairman Muris advocated a conservative approach to the use of innovation market analysis in merger enforcement. Commentators have both applauded and criticized the FTC's decision not to intervene in this case.

Other issues that focus attention on intellectual property rights during the course of merger investigations include claims by one of the merging firms that its future competitive significance would be reduced due to the invalidity or unenforceability of its intellectual property, the role of intellectual property as a barrier to entry, and the use of intellectual licensing remedies to resolve competitive concerns in a transaction.

G. Litigation Issues in Intellectual Property Antitrust Cases

Chapter VIII addresses practical issues in the litigation of intellectual property antitrust cases.

The Court of Appeals for the Federal Circuit was created in the 1980s to develop a uniform patent law. With limited exceptions, the Federal Circuit has exclusive jurisdiction over any case that includes a claim arising under patent law, even if the case also includes non-patent related claims.   Although Congress made clear that "broader subject matter jurisdiction is [not] intended for this court,"[46] the Federal Circuit now routinely exercises jurisdiction over non-patent matters, including antitrust claims.

The Federal Circuit's position on whether regional circuit law or Federal Circuit law should govern non-patent matters, including antitrust claims, has evolved dramatically since the court was created in 1982. Initially, the Federal Circuit elected to apply the law of the regional circuits to non-patent claims.   More recently, the Federal Circuit has increasingly applied its own law to non-patent claims.

45.   Genzyme Corp. Acquisition of Novazyme Pharm., FTC File No. 021-0026 (closing of investigation announced Jan. 13, 2004).
46.   S. Rep. No. 97-275, *reprinted in* 1982 U.S.C.C.A.N. 11, 14.

H. Counseling

Chapter IX profiles the practical issues that are likely to arise as practitioners assess the antitrust risks associated with the exercise of intellectual property rights. Counseling firms through the intersection of intellectual property and antitrust laws is among an antitrust lawyer's greatest challenges. Good counsel depends on good information. A counselor's main source of information is generally the client. The chapter therefore identifies the key issues, puts those issues in practical terms, and provides thought provoking sample questions for the practitioner to ask the client.

CHAPTER II

OVERVIEW OF INTELLECTUAL PROPERTY AND ANTITRUST LAW

The intersection of intellectual property law and antitrust law is delimited by the nature and purpose of each body of law. It is therefore important to start with these principles in the analysis of the antitrust treatment of the use of intellectual property. The difficult questions arise when the nature and purpose of one set of laws seem to conflict with those of the other.

A. Nature of the Intellectual Property Laws

Intellectual property is the collective term for a group of intangible property rights—primarily patents, copyrights, trademarks, and trade secrets—that give their owners a legal stake in the fruits of their creativity and reputation. Broadly speaking, patents cover inventions, copyrights cover expressive works of authorship, trademarks cover words and designs that indicate source, sponsorship, or quality, and trade secrets cover confidential business information. Each right protects a different aspect of intangible property and is an independent right; none of these rights is a subset of the others. The ultimate goal of the intellectual property system is to reward creative effort with the promise of exclusive or near-exclusive rights—whether to profits, recognition, or both—to encourage innovation, which ultimately benefits consumers and society at large.[1]

Intellectual property is similar to other types of property in that each right gives its owner the ability to exclude others, and each right can be transferred via license (leased) or assignment (sold) for the owner's profit. However, intellectual property differs from tangible property in that multiple users, whether ten, a thousand, or a million, can use a given item of intellectual property at the same time. Also, while it may be expensive to create the first product unit of an intellectual asset, the intellectual property portion of that product (as distinguished from any tangible embodiment, such as the binding of a copyrighted book or the metal in a patented machine) can be reproduced indefinitely at essentially zero cost.

---

1.   Mazer v. Stein, 347 U.S. 201, 219 (1954).

Free riding—when a subsequent user benefits from the innovation of an intellectual property creator without compensating that creator or otherwise permitting the creator to recoup its investment—is a particular hazard with intellectual property because of its low marginal cost of reproduction. Intellectual property law, at its simplest, prevents free riding, or at least limits it to levels that do not discourage innovation. The intellectual property laws may be thought of as ways to devise artificial, legal barriers against this form of theft, and by doing so, to preserve incentives to innovate.

The Constitutional mandate for the protection of intellectual property[2] strikes a balance between intellectual property owners and the general public by encouraging and rewarding a creator's innovation, but also ensuring varying degrees of rights of use for the public. Intellectual output not covered by the intellectual property laws, or creations with expired rights, become part of the "public domain," a catchall term for anything that the public may use without needing an intellectual property owner's permission. The interplay of intellectual property rights and the public domain is the central tension of intellectual property law and is the subject of frequent debate, and occasional action, by Congress.[3]

---

2. The public policy basis of the intellectual property laws finds its primary source in the Constitution, which empowers Congress "[t]o promote the Progress of Science and useful Arts, by securing for limited Times to Authors and Inventors the exclusive Right to their respective Writings and Discoveries." U.S. CONST. art. 1, § 8, cl. 8. This clause casts private rights in light of a public goal—"progress"—and tempers those rights further by recognizing them only for "limited times." The terms "writings" and "discoveries" are generally interpreted as equivalent to modern day copyrights and patents, respectively. *See generally* Eldred v. Ashcroft, 537 U.S. 186, 192-93 (2003) (referring to U.S. CONST. art. 1, § 8, cl. 8 as the "Copyright and Patent Clause").

3. For example, in 1998, Congress extended the term of copyright protection—not merely for future works, but for existing ones as well—in the Copyright Term Extension Act, Pub. L. 105-298, §§ 102(b) and (d), 112 Stat. 2827-28 (amending 17 U.S.C. §§ 302, 304). The Supreme Court concluded that in doing so, Congress acted within its powers under the Copyright and Patent Clause. *Eldred*, 537 U.S. at 194.

1. Types of Intellectual Property

a. Patents

A patent is a government-recognized right to an invention or discovery.[4] The owner of a patent has the exclusive right to "practice" the patent—make, use, offer to sell, sell, or import a product or service embodying the invention—within the United States.[5] There are three types of patents: utility patents; plant patents; and design patents. Utility patents—by far the most common type—may be obtained for any new and useful process, machine, composition of matter, or useful improvement thereof.[6] Plant patents may be obtained for certain new varieties of plants that the applicant has discovered and asexually reproduced.[7] Utility and plant patents are awarded for a term of 20 years measured from the date of filing.[8] Design patents may be obtained for any new, original, and ornamental design for an article of manufacture (i.e., a physical good), and are awarded for a term of 14 years measured from the date the patent is granted.[9] Patents are governed exclusively by federal law, codified as amended in the Patent Act of 1952.[10]

Patents are obtained by a process known as patent prosecution. If an inventor wishes to seek a patent, the inventor (or, more commonly, the inventor's assignee) files an application with the U. S. Patent and Trademark Office (PTO).[11] The PTO grants a patent when an inventor can show five things: an invention fits one of the general categories of patentable subject matter; it has not been preceded in identical form in

---

4.   *See, e.g.*, 35 U.S.C. § 101.
5.   *Id.* § 271.
6.   *Id.* § 101.
7.   *Id.* § 161.
8.   *Id.* §§ 154-157, 163.
9.   *Id.* §§ 171-173. A design patent is similar in some ways to a trademark, but with narrower coverage, stricter and more expensive application requirements, different remedies for infringement, and a limited duration of the right. *See id.* §§ 171-173.
10.   35 U.S.C. §§ 1-373.
11.   *See* www.uspto.gov/main/patents.htm. The PTO keeps the application confidential until 18 months after filing, in most circumstances, or until it issues the patent, whichever comes first. 35 U.S.C. § 122. Under previous law, patent applications were confidential until a patent issued. The change in the law was meant as a partial solution to the problem of "submarine patents," patents that "surface" long after industry adopts and develops sunk cost around the relevant technology.

the public "prior art"; it is useful; it represents a nontrivial extension of what was known; and the application discloses and describes the invention in such a way as to enable others to make and use the invention.[12]

A PTO patent examiner focuses primarily on novelty (the invention was not previously known) and nonobviousness (to a person skilled in the particular field, the invention was not an obvious solution to the problem it solves). During the prosecution phase, the applicant and examiner may identify and debate relevant prior art, consisting of other patents and prior publications. If the prior art anticipates (discloses) the invention or makes it obvious, no patent will issue.[13]

A U.S. patent is not extraterritorial. Thus, a creator must file separate applications in each foreign state or region (e.g. European Patent Office) in which it desires protection. Or, a creator that is a resident or national of a contracting state to the Patent Cooperation Treaty, of which the United States is a party, can file an international application that, essentially, acts as an application in every other contracting state.[14]

The United States differs from most other countries in that it follows a "first to invent" rule under which a first inventor receives the exclusive right to obtain a patent and can enforce that patent even against other inventors who make the discovery independently of any reliance on the first inventor's work. In contrast, most other nations follow a "first to file" rule, and there is a lively debate in the United States as to whether to abandon "first to invent."[15]

If an invention is patentable, the PTO will issue a patent. The patent consists of a title for the invention, the background of the invention, a brief summary of the invention, a description of the invention which distinguishes this invention from others, and claims. Claims are a set of numbered statements that distinctly claim the subject matter regarded as the invention. The patent will also include described drawings of the invention (when necessary), and a sworn oath.[16]

---

12. 35 U.S.C. §§ 101 (utility), 102 (novelty), 103 (nonobviousness), and 112 (enablement).
13. *See generally* 35 U.S.C. §§ 102-103.
14. Patent Cooperation Treaty, June 19, 1970, 28 U.S.T. 7645.
15. *See generally* James E. White, *The U.S. First-to-Invent System, the Mossinghoff Conclusion, and Statistics,* 85 J. PAT. & TRADEMARK OFF. SOC'Y 357 (April 2003) (comparing these rules and discussing a vigorous debate over the economic merits of each).
16. Issued patents and published applications are searchable online via the PTO website. The PTO's entire file of the application is known as the

Patent rights are entirely dependent on the issuance of a patent. The rights, however, are negative in that they do not grant an affirmative right to do anything except instigate a lawsuit against one who impermissibly uses the patented subject matter, otherwise known as patent infringement.

In a patent infringement action, an issued patent enjoys a statutory presumption of validity,[17] which may only be rebutted by clear and convincing evidence.[18] This presumption is based on the examination process leading to the issuance of a patent, which is rigorous. The U.S. system stands in contrast to patent regimes of most other nations, including those of Europe, where patents are issued under a registration-and-notice system (which does not include a rigorous examination) and do not benefit from a strong presumption of validity.

Patents are effective through the duration of their terms.[19] Their lives can be shortened, however, through an adverse reexamination by the PTO,[20] a judicial finding of invalidity,[21] or a judicial finding of unenforceability due to inequitable conduct.[22]

---

file history or "file wrapper." Photocopies of the file wrapper can be obtained from the PTO for a small fee.

17.   35 U.S.C. § 282.
18.   *E.g.*, Nystrom v. Trex Co., 374 F.3d 1105, 1117 (Fed. Cir. 2004).
19.   In 1995, the United States began to allow provisional applications for patents, which give the filer a less-expensive means of securing a priority date in anticipation of filing a nonprovisional application within the following 12 months. This allows a creator to be first to file in foreign jurisdictions, and still have time to prepare the often formidable U.S. patent application. A provisional filing can extend the 20-year term as much as 12 months. *See* 35 U.S.C. § 111(b). Under the provisions of 35 U.S.C. § 119(e), the corresponding non-provisional application benefits creators three ways: (1) patentability is evaluated as though filed on the earlier provisional application filing date, (2) the resulting publication or patent is treated as a reference under 35 U.S.C. § 102(e) as of the earlier provisional application filing date, and (3) the 20-year patent term is measured from the later nonprovisional application filing date.
20.   At any time during the enforceability of a patent (the patent term plus the six years under the statute of limitations for bringing an infringement action), any person may file a request for the PTO to conduct a new examination of any claim of the patent on the basis of prior art, which that person states to be pertinent and applicable to the patent and believes to have a bearing on the patentability of the invention. *See* 37 C.F.R. § 1.501. The request must be in writing and must be accompanied by payment of a reexamination request filing fee as set forth in 37 C.F.R.

b. Copyrights

A copyright is a form of protection for tangible "original works of authorship" including literary, dramatic, musical, artistic, and certain other intellectual works, both published and unpublished.[23] Ideas and facts are not copyrightable, but the creator's particular expression, such as the selection and arrangement of ideas and facts, may be copyrightable.[24] A copyrightable work must exhibit a "modicum of originality"[25] and be fixed in a "tangible medium of expression."[26] For example, an unchoreographed and unrecorded dance or jazz improvisation is not copyrightable because it is unfixed. In contrast, a child's original drawing for nursery school garners the full force of U.S. copyright protection the instant it appears on paper, as long as it meets the very low standard for creativity.

A copyright owner has the exclusive right to reproduce, prepare derivative works, distribute, and in some cases perform or display its copyrighted material.[27] Copyrights are governed exclusively by federal law, codified as amended as the Copyright Act of 1976.[28] Expressive

---

§ 1.20(c). The PTO may grant the request for reexamination only if a substantial new question of patentability is present with regard to at least one patent claim.

21.   *See, e.g.,* Medrad, Inc. v. MRI Devices, 401 F.3d 1313, 1321-22 (Fed. Cir. 2005) (finding patent invalid due to anticipation by prior art).

22.   "[I]nequitable conduct includes affirmative misrepresentation [during prosecution before the PTO] of a material fact, failure to disclose material information, or submission of false material information, coupled with an intent to deceive," and must be proven by clear and convincing evidence. Molins PLC v. Textron, Inc., 48 F.3d 1172, 1178 (Fed. Cir. 1995).

23.   17 U.S.C. § 102.

24.   *See generally* Feist Publ'ns v. Rural Tel. Serv., 499 U.S. 340 (1991) (copyright action by publisher of telephone listings dismissed, despite evidence that rival's listings had been copied wholesale from publisher's original work; listings were factual and therefore not protected by copyright law).

25.   The standard of originality is low, but it does exist. *Id.*

26.   17 U.S.C. § 102(a). For a discussion of ephemeral copies, particularly in computer programming, see MAI v. Peak Computing, 991 F.2d 511 (9th Cir. 1993).

27.   17 U.S.C. § 106.

28.   17 U.S.C. §§ 101-1332.

works that are unfixed, or otherwise do not meet the elements required for copyright protection, may be protected by state laws.[29]

Under the "doctrine of independent creation,"[30] copyright only protects against copying, and a copyright creator cannot object if a third party independently creates a new work that is similar, or even identical, to the original. If a second work is created independently, both creators have a protected copyright. This contrasts sharply with the "first to invent" rule under U.S. patent law.

No formalities are required for a copyrightable work to garner protection. A copyright springs into being the moment that a work is created and fixed into any medium of tangible expression (e.g. written down or recorded). Copyrights are created by function of the Copyright Act and "registration is not a condition of copyright protection."[31] However, registration is required before a copyright owner can sue to enforce its copyright.[32] In addition, a properly displayed copyright notice ("author," ©, or "creation year") will preclude a defendant from claiming "innocent infringement" in mitigation of actual or statutory damages.[33]

The Copyright Office at the U. S. Library of Congress administers the copyright system.[34] To register a copyright, an author must submit a short registration form, a fee, and an appropriate "deposit copy" of the work to the Copyright Office. Registration may occur at any time during the life of a work. So long as the applicant observes the formalities of this process, the Copyright Office registration procedure is largely clerical, meaning that the Copyright Office generally does not attempt, for example, to determine whether the deposited work is truly original or otherwise appropriate for copyright protection. For this reason, a copyright registration is only prima facie evidence of the validity of the

---

29. *E.g.*, Estate of Hemingway v. Random House, 23 N.Y.2d 341, 244 N.E.2d 250, 296 N.Y.S.2d 771 (1968).
30. *E.g.*, Moore v. Kulicke & Soffa Indus., 318 F.3d 561, 573 (3d Cir. 2003).
31. 17 U.S.C. § 408(a).
32. *See id.* §§ 411, 501. There is a split of authority as to whether a copyright owner can initiate an infringement suit before receiving a completed registration. *Compare* Apple Barrel Prods. v. Beard, 730 F.2d 384, 386-87 (5th Cir. 1984) (pending registration confers jurisdiction for suit under 17 U.S.C. § 411(a)) *with* Corbis Corp. v. Amazon.com, 351 F. Supp. 2d 1090, 1111-12 (W.D. Wash. 2004) (pending registration does not confer federal jurisdiction over a copyright claim) (collecting cases and discussing split of authority on this issue).
33. 17 U.S.C. § 401(d).
34. *See* www.copyright.gov.

copyright, and the evidentiary weight accorded to the registration during an infringement suit is left to the discretion of the trial court.[35] Nevertheless, registration accords significant benefits because it: (1) preserves a deposit copy to serve as proof that the work existed as of the day of the filing; (2) entitles a copyright owner to statutory damages for each instance of infringement of not less than $750 or more than $30,000 per work if a violation is not willful, and as much as $150,000 if a violation is willful;[36] and (3) entitles a prevailing copyright owner to attorneys' fees.[37] The availability of these increased remedies provides an incentive for some copyright owners to register early, rather than waiting to register after an infringement is discovered.

Copyright duration can be difficult to calculate. For works created after 1977, copyright protection lasts the life of the author (if known) plus an additional 70 years. For institutional and anonymous authors, the term is 120 years after creation or 95 years after first publication (whichever comes first).[38] Special rules apply when the creation meets the "work for hire" criteria.[39] Terms for works created before 1977 differ due to multiple amendments to the Copyright Act of 1976 and its predecessors.[40]

The exclusive rights granted by copyright protection are subject to several important restrictions developed by case law or listed as

---

35. 17 U.S.C. § 410(c). This contrasts with patent law, where the prima facie evidence of validity created by an issued patent can only be rebutted by clear and convincing evidence. *E.g., Nystrom*, 374 F.3d at 1117.
36. 17 U.S.C. § 504(c).
37. 17 U.S.C. § 412. Statutory damages and attorneys' fees are also available for infringement occurring after first publication of a work but before registration, if registration is made subsequent to the infringement but within three months of the work's first publication. 17 U.S.C. § 412(2).
38. 17 U.S.C. § 302.
39. 17 U.S.C. §§ 101 & 201(b). The employer is considered the author of a "work for hire" and receives copyright protection for 95 years from publication or 120 years from creation, whichever is less. If the work is made by an employee with in the scope of her employment, it is a work for hire. For independent contractors, only works that are commissioned for use as a contribution to a collective work, part of a motion picture or other audiovisual work, a translation, a supplementary work, a compilation, an instructional text, a test, answer material for a test, or an atlas may be a work for hire. And the parties must expressly agree, in writing, that the work shall be considered a work made for hire.
40. *See* 17 U.S.C. § 304; *see also* Copyright Term Extension Act, *supra* note 3, and §§ 102(b) and (d).

"limitations" in the Copyright Act.[41]   For instance, copyright does not apply to names, titles, or slogans.[42]   Nor will it protect useful aspects of pictorial, graphic, or sculptural works.[43]   An example of a limitation is fair use, a term of art defined in detail by the act.[44]   Fair use is an affirmative defense and is narrower than popularly believed. Fair use permits some minimal copying without the owner's permission, but it generally limits such copying to brief, partial, noncommercial, or parody uses.[45]

Another limitation to copyright law is the "merger doctrine." [46]   The merger doctrine prevents a creator from asserting exclusive rights over works that express the only method for explaining an idea. This doctrine prevents copyright law from limiting public use of a system, process, or ultra-necessary way to express an idea—i.e., instances where the idea and the expression merge. For example, ledger forms that express a method for keeping tax records are not copyrightable,[47] nor are functional features such as centered headings and underlined software program names,[48] as well as such necessary expressions of ideas as "caution wet paint."

Portions of the Copyright Act also proscribe rules for assessing compulsory licenses on large-scale video and audio transmissions—for instance, cable television retransmissions and satellite signals.[49]   The Act also provides sui generis protection for semiconductor chips[50] and boat hulls.[51]

---

41.   *See* 17 U.S.C. §§ 107-112, 117, 119, 121, 122, 512, 906, 907.
42.   Copyright Office Circular No. 34. Copyright Office Compendium II, § 202.021.
43.   17 U.S.C. § 101. "Useful article" is an article having intrinsic utilitarian function that is not merely to portray the appearance of the article or to convey information.
44.   17 U.S.C. § 107.
45.   *See id.* (listing factors to be considered in fair use).
46.   Baker v. Selden, 101 U.S. 99 (1879).
47.   Aldrick v. Remington Rand, Inc. 52 F. Supp. 732 (N.D. Tex. 1942).
48.   Mfrs. Techs., v. Cams, Inc., 706 F. Supp. 984 (D. Conn. 1989) (denying protection to elements that represent a narrow range of possibilities).
49.   17 U.S.C. § 111 (cable television), §§ 114, 115 (digital audio trans- missions), § 118 (public broadcasting), § 119 (satellite retransmissions), and §§ 1001-1010 (digital audio tape devices).
50.   17 U.S.C. §§ 900 *et seq.*
51.   17 U.S.C. §§ 1301-1310.

c.   Trademarks

A trademark is an identifier that distinguishes the source, sponsorship, or quality of the goods or services of one party from those of others.[52] Virtually any word, phrase, or design, or in some cases even color, sound, or distinctive packaging, can serve as a trademark so long as the mark serves to indicate a specific source or quality. Trademark rights apply to trade marks (brands of goods), trade names (names of businesses), service marks (brands of services), collective marks (marks that indicate membership in a group), and certification marks (marks that indicate a particular quality but not a particular source, e.g., "PG-13" for movies or "UL LISTED"[53] for appliances), among others. Modern practice refers to all of these collectively as "trademarks," or simply "marks." The owner of a registered mark has the exclusive right to use that mark in commerce,[54] and the owner of a mark may sue to prevent false designations of origin, false descriptions, dilution, and certain other conduct.[55] Trademarks are governed by the federal Lanham Act (also known as the Trademark Act)[56] and by the statutory and common law of many states.

Trademarks are somewhat different from other intellectual property rights in that they have an explicit trade regulation and consumer protection function. A trademark creates value not only for its owner, who has the incentive to develop and benefit from its business reputation (known by the trademark term "goodwill"), but also for consumers, who look for trademarks as a way of lowering their search costs by accepting a mark as a proxy for source or quality. Trademarks permit consumers to identify and rely upon business reputation, thereby avoiding the need for detailed inspection of each good or service they plan to purchase. While the trademark owner reaps a benefit, it also incurs an obligation: a

---

52.   *See* 15 U.S.C. § 1127.
53.   When discussing trademarks in a legal setting, particularly in court pleadings, it is common practice to write a word trademark in all capital letters (e.g., DISNEY or ENJOY COKE). This practice helps to emphasize that a word mark generally conveys rights in all uses of word, regardless of capitalization, font, or stylization of the lettering.
54.   15 U.S.C. § 1115(a).
55.   15 U.S.C. § 1125.
56.   15 U.S.C. §§ 1051-1141n.

trademark owner must maintain the source- and/or quality-identifying nature of its mark, or trademark rights will be lost.[57]

Under the Lanham Act, trademark rights arise automatically whenever a person or business develops goodwill in a mark and uses that mark in interstate commerce. Trademark owners also have the option of registering a trademark with the PTO and some states.[58] The process of obtaining a federally registered trademark is known as trademark prosecution. The applicant must submit a facsimile of the mark, a designation of goods and services, and a filing fee. If the mark is already in use, the applicant must submit specimens of the use in U.S. commerce; otherwise, the applicant must file an "intent-to-use" application. The PTO's trademark examiner reviews the application for trademark subject matter, potential conflict with other registered marks, and suitability of the goods and services description. If appropriate, the PTO issues an intent-to-register decision for the mark in one or more International Classes (so called because they reflect an international standard).[59] If the application was filed as intent-to-use, the applicant then has a period of months to submit a specimen, after which the mark will issue as registered. If filed as already in use, the mark will issue as registered after a short publication period. Unlike patents, all phases of the trademark application are public.[60]

A federal trademark registration confers substantial benefits. Primarily, it provides nationwide rights, meaning the exclusive right to use a mark in the full United States. If a trademark owner sues to enforce these rights, registration confers a presumption of validity and increased ability to seek damages and injunctive relief. Registrations must be renewed at intervals of years that vary according to how long the mark has been registered, but there is no limit to the number of renewals; in that sense, the term of a registered mark is potentially perpetual.

---

57. For example, if a trademark becomes generic (becomes the common word for an item, and fails to connote a particular manufacturer), even a registered trademark can be cancelled. 15 U.S.C. § 1064(3); *see* Kellogg Co. v. Nat'l Biscuit Co., 305 U.S. 111, 122 (1938) (finding trademark for "shredded wheat" cereal had become generic).
58. Federal registrations provide rights as to the nation as a whole, while state registrations provide rights only within a state; for this reason, the great majority of trademark applications are filed only in the federal system.
59. 37 C.F.R. § 6.1.
60. As with patents, the entire trademark prosecution file is called the file history or "file wrapper" and photocopies can be obtained from the PTO for a small fee.

Renewals require the submission of a maintenance fee and specimens of use in commerce. A registration will be cancelled automatically if not renewed.

For unregistered marks[61] (including those for which registration has been cancelled), trademark rights continue indefinitely so long as a mark continues to serve its function of indicating source or quality. Unlike copyrights and patent rights, unregistered trademark rights do not expire after a set term.

A trademark owner is not legally required to set off its mark with special capitalization, typeface, a general trademark symbol (™), or a registered trademark symbol (®) to protect the rights, but doing so helps call attention to the source-identifying nature of trademarks.

Compared to patents and copyrights, trademark rights are more vulnerable to being lost to the public domain. Because generic terms (which serve as the common, nonspecific description of a good or service) cannot be trademarked, if a previously trademarked term is permitted to become generic, all rights in that term will evaporate—even if the mark has been registered.[62] Non-use of a mark for three years, coupled with an apparent intent not to resume use, is prima facie evidence of abandonment.[63] If a good or service that the trademark indicates is discontinued, so also is the trademark.[64] And failure to exercise control over certain types of marks,[65] or to maintain standards of quality over any mark, is also grounds for loss of the right. Unlike owners of patents and copyrights, trademark owners do not have the option to ignore their property and leave it unused. To preserve their rights, trademark owners must use the property in commerce and zealously guard the goodwill embodied by their marks.

---

61. Unregistered marks are sometimes called "common law marks," for historical reasons, but this terminology is misleading in light of the modern federal statute's protection of marks regardless of registration. *See* 15 U.S.C. § 1125(a)-(c).
62. *See* 15 U.S.C. §§ 1052(e), 1064(3), 1065(4).
63. 15 U.S.C. § 1127.
64. *But see* Robert C. Denicola, *Institutional Publicity Rights: An Analysis of the Merchandising of Famous Trade Symbols*, 62 N.C. L. Rᴇᴠ. 603 (1983).
65. *See* 15 U.S.C. § 1064(5) (discussing maintenance of certification marks).

d. Trade Secrets and Know-How

State systems of intellectual property protection exist to protect intellectual output that does not meet the criteria of the three federal schemas. Some provisions, like California's Astaire Celebrity Image Protection Act[66] serve to protect specific industries. But others, like the widely adopted trade secret statutes, apply to a broad range of industries. Forty-two states have enacted some form of the Uniform Trade Secrets Act (UTSA), which permits the owner of a trade secret to prevent its misappropriation.[67] Although theft of trade secrets is sometimes prosecuted as mail fraud, wire fraud, or another federal crime, trade secrets as a matter of intellectual property are governed exclusively by various state laws.

States generally define a trade secret to be any information that derives independent economic value from not being generally known or readily ascertainable by proper means and is the subject of reasonable efforts to maintain its secrecy.[68] The UTSA will protect any information as long as it is capable of being commercially valuable.[69] In order to claim trade secret protection, states usually require that a business entity take reasonable steps to prevent its trade secrets from being disclosed to the general public.[70] For example, these steps could be restricted access to buildings, passwords on databases, or contractual protection.

A trade secret is not lost merely because it is shared with business partners, so long as the sharing occurs within reasonable limits, such as under the protection of nondisclosure agreements.[71] To avoid abrogation of trade secret protection, these nondisclosure agreements must be

---

66. Cal. Civ. Code § 3344.1 (1999).
67. Uniform Trade Secrets Act §§ 1-2 (as amended 1985), 14 U.L.A. 437-38, 449 (1990).
68. *Id.*
69. *E.g.*, Sunset Energy Fleet v. N.Y. Dep't of Env. Conserv., 285 A.D.2d 865, 867, 728 N.Y.S.2d 279, 281 (N.Y. App. 2001) ("A trade secret is defined as any formula, pattern, process or compilation of information that is not published or divulged and which gives an advantage over competitors who do not have access to such data." (citation and quotation omitted)).
70. *See, e.g.*, Mabrey v. SandStream, Inc., 124 S.W.3d 302, 310 (Tex. App. 2003) (key factor in determining existence of a trade secret is "the extent of measures taken to safeguard the secrecy of the information").
71. *See generally* Disclosure of Trade Secret as Abandonment of Secrecy, 92 A.L.R.3d 138 § 5.

reasonable and observed. Protection does not depend on any particular number of persons who know the information; instead, protection turns on the question of whether the information derives value from the fact that it is not generally known within an industry.

The secrecy requirement in trade secret law is to insure that no one claims intellectual property protection for information commonly known in a trade or industry, i.e., "know-how." Trade secret is a concept related to, but separate from, "know-how."[72] Know-how is a catchall term used to describe generalized knowledge of manufacturing processes, industry customs, customer preferences, or similar nonspecific information necessary to the running of a successful business.

Trade secrets are protected indefinitely so long as they remain secret. When information that was formerly a trade secret becomes generally known or easily discoverable within an industry, absent any other intellectual property protection, it becomes part of the public domain.

Trade secret protection may apply to information that is patentable or copyrightable; for example, firms often treat their patent applications as trade secrets during the initial, 18-month confidentiality period of a patent filing. Trade secret protection also can extend to information that cannot be subject to copyright or patent protection, such as customer lists and other factual, noninnovative information. Note, however, that a trademark cannot be a trade secret: the value of a trademark derives from its ability to indicate source or quality in the minds of consumers, so it is impossible to have an item of property function both as a trade secret and as a mark.

2. Obtaining and Enforcing Intellectual Property Rights

Each form of intellectual property permits its owner to exclude others from reproducing and commercializing the property.[73] These exclusive rights, however, are subject to many important limitations. For example, members of the general public (including the intellectual property owner's competitors) are permitted to make certain fair use of copyrights[74] and fair descriptive use of trademarks,[75] and there is also a

---

72.   Collins & Aikman Corp. v. Compo Indus., Civ. A. No. 6098, 1982 WL 17804, at *14 (Del. Ch. 1982) (collecting cases).

73.   *E.g.*, 35 U.S.C. § 271(a), (d) (patent); 17 U.S.C. § 106 (copyright); 15 U.S.C. § 1115(a) (trademark); Uniform Trade Secrets Act, *supra* note 67, § 2.

74.   17 U.S.C. § 107.

75.   15 U.S.C. § 1115(b)(4).

limited right to make research use of patents.[76] Moreover, intellectual property is generally expressed as a negative right, meaning that intellectual property owners only have the power to prevent others from profiting and are not necessarily guaranteed the right to profit, themselves.

Unauthorized use of intellectual property is generally known as infringement or misappropriation. Federal patent, copyright, and trademark laws permit intellectual property owners to seek damages and injunctive relief. Knowing and willful violations may trigger enhanced damages, punitive damages, and payment of attorneys' fees. State trade secret laws and some federal economic espionage acts provide similar remedies, depending upon applicable statutes or common law precedent.

Infringement litigation arising under the Patent Act takes place exclusively in federal courts as a matter of federal question jurisdiction.[77] Once a patent has issued, the patent's owner can sue for infringement against any person who practices the patent within the United States, actively induces such infringement, or contributes to such infringement.[78] The first major stage of a patent suit is determining the scope of the patent claims. In this proceeding, called a "Markman hearing," the judge decides, as matter of law, what aspects of an invention the patent claims cover.[79] A jury will then decide if the allegedly infringing product does, in fact, utilize the subject matter protected in the patent's claims. By statute, the patent owner's damages shall be "adequate to compensate for the infringement, but in no event less than a reasonable royalty ... together with interest and costs."[80] If the patent owner elects to pursue the statutory minimum of a reasonable royalty, the damage phase of a trial often involves expert testimony as to a series of factors used to

---

76. 35 U.S.C. § 271(e)(1).
77. 28 U.S.C. § 1338(a). The Supreme Court has held, however, that federal courts do not have exclusive jurisdiction over patent-related counterclaims that do not arise out of the facts of a plaintiff's well-pleaded complaint. Holmes Group v. Vornado Air Circulation Sys., 535 U.S. 826, 830 (2002).
78. 35 U.S.C. § 271. Contributory infringement occurs, for example, when a person sells or imports into the United States a component of a patented machine, knowing the same to be especially adapted for use in the infringement of a patent. 35 U.S.C. § 271(c).
79. Markman v. Westview Instruments, 52 F.3d 967 (Fed. Cir. 1995) (en banc), *aff'd*, 517 U.S. 370 (1996).
80. 35 U.S.C. § 284.

calculate the royalty.[81]   Alternatively, the patent owner may elect to pursue lost profits,[82] generally proven through the *Panduit* test.[83]   The accused infringer may defend on various grounds, including noninfringement, invalidity (the patent should not have issued because it was anticipated or obvious), lack of enablement, failure to disclose best mode, or misconduct in obtaining the patent from the PTO. The patent owner benefits at trial from a statutory presumption of validity,[84] which may only be rebutted by clear and convincing evidence.[85]   The Federal Circuit has exclusive jurisdiction over patent appeals.[86]

Infringement litigation arising under the Copyright Act also takes place exclusively in federal courts as a matter of federal question jurisdiction.[87]   Once a copyright is registered, or in some circuits as soon as an application has been filed,[88] a copyright owner may sue for infringement against any person who copies or imports a copy of a protected work[89] or, in some cases, any person who contributes to, actively induces, or is vicariously responsible for such conduct by

---

81.   *See, e.g.*, Dow Chem. v. Mee Indus., 341 F.3d 1370, 1382 (Fed. Cir. 2003) (citing Georgia-Pacific Corp. v. United States Plywood, 318 F. Supp. 1116, 1120 (S.D.N.Y. 1970)).

82.   The word "profits" does not appear in 35 U.S.C. § 284 but the Supreme Court has found that lost profits are included in the types of "pecuniary loss" available under that section.   Aro Mfg. v. Convertible Top Replacement Co., 377 U.S. 476, 507 (1964).

83.   *See* Panduit Corp. v. Stahlin Bros. Fibre Works, 575 F.2d 1152, 1156 (6th Cir. 1978) (factors are (1) demand for the patented product, (2) absence of acceptable noninfringing substitutes, (3) patent owner's capacity to meet demand, and (4) amount of profit patent owner would have made by meeting such demand).   The Federal Circuit modified the test in 1989, permitting the patent owner to estimate lost profits through a market share calculation and noting that *Panduit* is not the exclusive test for lost profits.   State Indus. v. Mor-Flo Indus., 883 F.2d 1573, 1575-79 (Fed. Cir. 1989).

84.   35 U.S.C. § 282.

85.   *E.g.*, Nystrom v. Trex Co., 374 F.3d 1105, 1117 (Fed. Cir. 2004).

86.   35 U.S.C. § 141, 28 U.S.C. § 1295(a)(1).

87.   28 U.S.C. § 1338(a), 17 U.S.C. § 301(a). However, the rule in *Holmes Group* would deprive federal courts of exclusive jurisdiction to hear copyright counterclaims.

88.   *See supra* note 32, *comparing Apple Barrel Prods.*, 730 F.2d at 386-87 *with Corbis Corp.*, 351 F. Supp. 2d at 1111-12 (discussing split of authority on this issue).

89.   17 U.S.C. § 501.

another party.[90]   A copyright registration provides a prima facie presumption of validity[91] and the availability of statutory damages.[92] Defenses to copyright infringement include invalidity, independent creation, or permitted use under the various limitations to copyright. Appeal is taken to the federal appellate circuit in which the district court resides.

Trademark infringement litigation takes place in federal court as a matter of federal question jurisdiction (regarding federal trademark rights)[93] or diversity jurisdiction (regarding state trademark rights).[94] Claims for violation of state trademark rights may also be brought in state courts. Technically, the Lanham Act reserves the term "trademark infringement" for registered marks[95] and provides a remedy for false designations of origin and unfair competition regarding unregistered marks;[96] however, as a practical matter, trademark practitioners and the courts refer to both types of legal claims as infringement. In general, the plaintiff in a trademark infringement lawsuit must prove that the defendant's use of the plaintiff's mark (or a substantially similar mark) is likely to confuse consumers as to source, sponsorship, or quality. Owners of "famous marks," which meet a higher standard of source indication, may sue for the dilution of the mark where the defendants' actions lead to the mark's blurring or tarnishment.[97] The Lanham Act also provides a remedy against "cybersquatting," the practice of registering an Internet domain name that uses another's registered mark or otherwise creates confusion.[98]   Defenses in trademark litigation include invalidity (usually an assertion of genericism or abandonment), the registrant's fraud on the PTO, the defendant's use in a manner that

---

90. *See generally* Metro-Goldwyn-Meyer Studios v. Grokster Ltd., 125 S. Ct. 2764, 2774-80 (2005) (discussing history of vicarious liability claims under copyright law and finding that distributor of "peer-to-peer" software could be liable under such claims due to its users' direct infringement of copyrighted digital media properties).
91. 17 U.S.C. § 410(c).
92. *Id.* § 504(c).
93. 28 U.S.C. § 1331.
94. *Id.* § 1332.
95. 15 U.S.C. § 1114.
96. *See id.* § 1125(a)-(b).
97. 15 U.S.C. § 1125(c).
98. *Id.* § 1125(d).

existed prior to a federal registration ("use priority"),[99] and lack of significant confusion, among others. Litigation often involves evidence of actual consumer confusion (e.g., customer complaints for the wrong product) or the use of a survey to measure consumer confusion, with the minimum level of actionable confusion generally set at 20 percent of consumers.[100] Appeal is taken to the federal appellate circuit in which the district court resides.

Litigation of trade secret infringement usually takes place in state courts as a state law matter or in federal courts as a matter of diversity jurisdiction, although federal question jurisdiction may attach for certain federal economic espionage claims.[101] Depending on the law involved, the plaintiff generally must begin by proving that the property at issue is truly a trade secret; the protectable nature of the information is not presumed.[102] If the plaintiff meets that burden, it must also prove that the defendant obtained and/or disseminated the information in an unauthorized and unlawful manner, such as theft or trespassing. Defenses in trade secret litigation may include assertions of authorized use or independent discovery. Courts are particularly likely to award preliminary and permanent injunctive relief in trade secret cases, since failure to grant relief could cause the secrecy (and therefore the value) of the information to evaporate.

B. Nature of the Antitrust Laws

1. Social Welfare and Consumer Welfare

While the Constitution clearly provides that the primary purpose of intellectual property laws are to promote progress for the benefit of the general public, the primary beneficiary of the antitrust laws is not so transparent. Clearly, the purpose of the antitrust laws is to protect and

---

99.   *See generally* 15 U.S.C. § 1115(b) (defenses to otherwise-incontestable trademarks).

100.   *See, e.g.,* Nabisco, Inc. v. PF Brands, 191 F.3d 208 (2d Cir. 1999), *abrogated on other grounds in* Moseley v. V Secret Catalogue, Inc., 537 U.S. 418 (2003). *But see* Nartron Corp. v. STMicroelectronics, 305 F.3d 397 (6th Cir. 2002) (overwhelming evidence of consumer confusion obviated need for consumer survey).

101.   *See generally* Economic Espionage Act of 1996, 18 U.S.C. §§ 1831-1839.

102.   *See* PepsiCo, Inc. v. Redmond, 54 F.3d 1262, 1269 (7th Cir. 1995) (elements are the "existence of any trade secrets" and "likelihood that [defendant] would compromise those secrets").

encourage competition between rivals.[103] But debate exists as to whether antitrust law should seek only to maximize consumer welfare or if it should pursue total social welfare, meaning the wealth of producers and consumers in combination. Competition authorities generally claim to pursue the former, while economists usually advocate the latter as the appropriate "lodestar" for antitrust analysis.[104] The distinction can prove to be ambiguous, given that "all economic exchange involves parties that are at one and the same time both buying and selling from one another."[105] Nevertheless, the distinction can cause tension when performing antitrust analysis of intellectual property transactions.

a. Implications of Welfare Tests for Antitrust and Intellectual Property Analysis

A total social welfare focus, which considers economic benefits to both consumers and producers, would find procompetitive benefits in a merger that results in fixed cost savings but does not result in lower prices. In comparison, a consumer welfare focus would only find procompetitive rationale in a transaction that decreased consumer prices, for whatever reason.[106] In practice, however, the distinction between consumer and total social welfare is seldom dispositive in an antitrust case. Commentators have noted that the two concepts are related— everyone, even a producer, is eventually a consumer as well—and that courts and antitrust enforcers sometimes use these concepts in an imprecise fashion[107] or apply a hybrid test as is used[108] in the agencies' *Merger Guidelines*.[109]

---

103. Orson, Inc. v. Miramax Film Corp., 79 F.3d 1358, 1368 n.10 (3d Cir. 1996) (collecting cases) (quoting Cont'l T.V. v. GTE Sylvania, Inc., 433 U.S. 36, 52 n.19 (1977) ("Interbrand competition ... is the primary concern of antitrust law.")).

104. *See* Kenneth Heyer, *A World of Uncertainty: Economics and the Globalization of Antitrust*, 72 ANTITRUST L.J. 375, 402 n.33 (2005).

105. *Id.*

106. *See generally* Oliver E. Williamson, *Economics as an Anti-Trust Defense: The Welfare Trade-Offs*, 58 AM. ECON. REV. 18, 21-23 (1968). In contrast, a pure consumer welfare focus might permit or encourage monopsonization (buyer cartels or the exercise of consumer market power), even if that conduct were to reduce producer surplus more than it benefits consumers as a whole. Heyer, *supra* note 104, at 402 n.33.

107. *See* Daniel J. Gifford & Robert T. Kudrle, *Rhetoric & Reality in the Merger Standards of the United States, Canada, and the European Union*, 72 ANTITRUST L.J. 423, 430-31 (2005) (citing ROBERT H. BORK,

Economic literature generally views intellectual property protection as maximizing total social welfare, not consumer welfare.[110] All else being equal, a total social welfare standard likely will result in a higher level of intellectual property protection than a consumer welfare standard.[111] As a result, if antitrust enforcement were to focus only on maximizing the welfare of current consumers of a product in question, a conflict could arise between antitrust and intellectual property goals. For example, consumer welfare might increase in the short term if antitrust policy were to prohibit owners of existing patents from fully exercising their market power. But would consumers (and society as a whole) benefit over time, given that, if this prohibition remained in effect for future patents, there would be a decreased incentive to conduct research to create new patented technology?

Such conflicts between antitrust and intellectual property welfare analysis may be avoided, or at least minimized, by incorporating innovation incentives and the benefits of long-term dynamic competition into the analysis. In theory, innovation incentives (such as enforceable intellectual property rights) allow producers to harvest a portion of consumers' surplus in the short term, yet increase consumers' surplus in the long term via new and improved goods and services. While this theory rests on a number of assumptions,[112] these assumptions are generally taken to be satisfied and, indeed, provide the intellectual underpinning for having a system of intellectual property protection at all.[113] Nevertheless, there remain difficult questions as to precisely how much intellectual property protection to provide, and where and how to

---

THE ANTITRUST PARADOX: A POLICY AT WAR WITH ITSELF 105-115 (1978)).

108. Gifford & Kudrle, *supra* note 107, at 451-52 (collecting commentary).

109. See *infra* note 136 and accompanying text.

110. James Langenfeld & Wenqing Li, *Intellectual Property and Agreements to Settle Patent Disputes: The Case of Settlement Agreements with Payments from Branded to Generic Manufacturers*, 70 ANTITRUST L.J. 777, 786-87 (2003) (citing William M. Landes & Richard A. Posner, *An Economic Analysis of Copyright Law*, 18 J. LEGAL STUD. 325 (1989)).

111. *Id.* at 787.

112. For example, the theory assumes that (1) innovation incentives lead to increased innovation; (2) additional innovations, in the aggregate, increase efficiency; and (3) at least some benefits from new or improved goods and services accrue to consumers.

113. The Copyright and Patent Clause, U.S. CONST. art. 1, § 8, implies that the Constitution accepts these assumptions. See *supra* note 1.

draw the line against protection that generates too little dynamic innovation incentive relative to the static cost of higher prices in the short run. Crafting such rules is obviously difficult; nevertheless, it is the ultimate welfare goal of antitrust and intellectual property law.

2. The Central Role of Market Power in Antitrust Analysis

a. The Definition of Market Power

Market power is defined as the ability to profitably and persistently raise prices beyond the level one would expect in a competitive market.[114] In its most extreme form, market power confers the ability to set a monopoly price, defined as the price at which a producer maximizes its surplus independently of any concern over competition. A firm with market power will not necessarily seek its maximum monopoly price;[115] therefore, the mere fact that a firm has *not* chosen a maximum monopoly price cannot, by itself, serve as proof of a lack of market power.[116] But a firm with market power will generally set prices higher than a firm without, leaving a smaller surplus in the hands of consumers.

---

114. Eastman Kodak Co. v. Image Technical Servs., 504 U.S. 451, 464 (1992) ("Market power is the power to force a purchaser to do something that he would not do in a competitive market. It has been defined as the ability of a single seller to raise price and restrict output." (quotations omitted)) (quoting Jefferson Parish Hosp. Dist. No. 2 v. Hyde, 466 U.S. 2, 14 (1984)); Fortner Enters. v. United States Steel, 394 U.S. 495, 503 (1969); *see also* United States v. Microsoft Corp., 253 F.3d 34, 51 (D.C. Cir. 2001) ("The Supreme Court defines monopoly power as 'the power to control prices or exclude competition.' More precisely, a firm is a monopolist if it can profitably raise prices substantially above the competitive level.") (quoting United States v. E.I. du Pont de Nemours & Co., 351 U.S. 377, 391 (1956)); 2A PHILLIP E. AREEDA & DONALD F. TURNER, ANTITRUST LAW ¶ 501, at 85 (1995).
115. It is important to recognize that a monopoly price is not an unlimited price: even a monopolist will find that as it raises prices, customers will purchase less of the product.
116. *Microsoft*, 253 F.3d at 57 ("a price lower than the short-term profit-maximizing price is not inconsistent with possession or improper use of monopoly power."); *cf.* Berkey Photo v. Eastman Kodak Co., 603 F.2d 263, 274 (2d Cir. 1979) ("[I]f monopoly power has been acquired or maintained through improper means, the fact that the power has not been used to extract [a monopoly price] provides no succor to the monopolist.").

Neither market power nor possession of an outright monopoly is illegal, by itself.[117] Market power that arises through superior products, business acumen, or historical accident is not a violation of the antitrust statutes, since it would make little sense for the law to first encourage aggressive competition but then penalize the competitor who wins.[118] Instead, antitrust law prohibits anticompetitive conduct and agreements.[119] Without market power, however, most attempts at anticompetitive conduct would fail: driving a firm's chief rivals out of business, or colluding or merging with these rivals, would not permit a firm to raise prices if still more rivals exist, or if barriers to the marketplace are so low that a small increase in price would cause competitors to enter. Therefore, although it is not *sufficient* to prove a violation of the antitrust laws, market power is a *necessary condition* to a finding of most kinds of anticompetitive conduct.[120] Market power serves as a screen to focus antitrust law on practices that are likely to have anticompetitive effects. Market power inquiry helps to identify transactions or unilateral conduct that likely will result in anticompetitive effects in the future, determine whether ambiguous business practices could have resulted in anticompetitive effects in the past, and judge whether efficiencies have been or will be passed on to consumers.[121]

---

117. *See* Verizon Communs. v. Law Offices of Curtis V. Trinko, 540 U.S. 398, 407 (2004); *Microsoft*, 253 F.3d at 58.
118. *See* United States v. Grinnell Corp., 384 U.S. 563, 571 (1966); *see also* United States v. Aluminum Co. of Am., 148 F.2d 416, 430 (2d Cir. 1945) (Hand, J.) ("The successful competitor, having been urged to compete, must not be turned upon when he wins.").
119. *See Microsoft*, 253 F.3d at 58 ("[T]o be condemned as exclusionary, a monopolist's act must have an 'anticompetitive effect.' That is, it must harm the competitive *process* and thereby harm consumers. In contrast, harm to one or more *competitors* will not suffice. The [Sherman Act] directs itself not against conduct which is competitive, even severely so, but against conduct which unfairly tends to destroy competition itself." (emphasis in original)) (quoting Spectrum Sports v. McQuillan, 506 U.S. 447, 458 (1993)).
120. *Id.* at 51 ("While merely possessing monopoly power is not itself an antitrust violation, it is a necessary element of a monopolization charge." (citations omitted)).
121. *See generally* Michael S. McFalls, *The Role and Assessment of Classical Market Power in Joint Venture Analysis*, 66 ANTITRUST L.J. 651, 657-58 (1998); Frank H. Easterbrook, *The Limits of Antitrust*, 63 TEX. L. REV. 1, 17-18 (August 1984).

A party making an antitrust claim can prove market power by direct evidence. Where evidence indicates that a firm has in fact controlled prices or excluded competition, the existence of market power may be clear.[122] Direct evidence, however, is rarely available, so courts generally rely on circumstantial evidence of market power. The primary method of introducing such circumstantial evidence is an inference derived from a seller's predominant share of the market.[123]

b. Market Power and Market Structure

To demonstrate market power by circumstantial evidence, a plaintiff must undertake a multi-step technical analysis of the market's structure: (1) define a relevant market; (2) show that the defendant possesses a dominant share of that market; and (3) show that there are significant barriers to entry and that existing competitors lack the capacity to increase their output in the short run, so that the threat of entry or greater competitive output does not constrain the seller's price.[124] The plaintiff bears the burden of proof for all portions of this analysis.

A relevant market consists of two elements: a product market and a geographic market.[125] A product market consists of all products that consumers would consider to be substitutes for one another, given some reasonable variation in price.[126] Where an increase in the price of one product leads to an increase in demand for another, both products should be included in the product market. In economic terms, the outer boundaries of a product market are determined by the interchangeability of use or the cross-elasticity of demand between the product and its

---

122. Rebel Oil Co. v. Atl. Richfield Co., 51 F.3d 1421, 1434 (9th Cir. 1995); *see also* FTC v. Indiana Fed'n of Dentists, 476 U.S. 447, 460-61 (1986) (using direct proof to show market power in Sherman Act § 1 action for unreasonable restraint of trade); Republic Tobacco v. N. Atl. Trading, 381 F.3d 717, 737 (7th Cir. 2004) ("[I]f a plaintiff can show the rough contours of a relevant market, and show that the defendant commands a substantial share of the market, then direct evidence of anticompetitive effects can establish the defendant's market power—in lieu of the usual showing of a precisely defined relevant market and a monopoly market share.").

123. *Eastman Kodak*, 504 U.S. at 464; *Microsoft*, 253 F.3d at 51.

124. Image Technical Servs. v. Eastman Kodak Co., 125 F.3d 1195, 1202 (9th Cir. 1997); *see also Microsoft*, 253 F.3d at 52.

125. FTC v. Tenet Health Care, 186 F.3d 1045, 1052 (8th Cir. 1999).

126. Brown Shoe Co. v. United States, 370 U.S. 294, 325 (1962).

substitutes. A geographic market is defined using a similar substitution test: it is the area in which consumers can practically turn for alternative sources of the product and in which the antitrust defendant faces competition. A properly defined relevant market includes potential suppliers (sometimes called "feasible entrants") who could readily enter the market and offer consumers a suitable alternative to the defendant's goods in response to a given increase in price.[127]

Once the relevant market is established, the antitrust plaintiff must show that the defendant has a dominant share. There is no absolute percentage that serves as a dominant share. As a first approximation, the courts of appeal generally require market shares of at least 50 to 60 percent.[128] The size of the defendant's market share is the primary factor in determining whether market power exists,[129] but it is by no means the only one. Firms with shares as low as 20 percent have been found to possess market power in an appropriate case.[130] Germane factors include consumer demand, pricing trends, and sales practices in the industry.[131]

If a plaintiff can prove that the defendant possesses a potentially dominant share of a relevant market, the final step is to show that as the defendant raises prices, competitors will not be willing or able to siphon off enough customers to make the defendant's price increase unprofitable. This may occur where the industry is operating at near capacity and competitors lack the ability to increase their output in the short run or when the defendant, alone or in combination with others, has devised strategies for excluding rivals. "In evaluating monopoly power, it is not market share that counts, but the ability to *maintain* market share."[132]

Courts and economics scholars have devised various methods for evaluating market structure as a proxy for market performance, often

---

127. *Tenet Health Care*, 186 F.3d at 1052.
128. United States v. Dentsply Int'l, 399 F.3d 181, 187 (3d Cir. 2005) ("Absent other pertinent factors, a share significantly larger than 55% has been required to establish[] prima facie market power."); *Tenet Health Care*, 186 F.3d at 1052 n.10 ("Market shares of less than 60% are generally not sufficient to create an inference of monopoly power.").
129. *Dentsply*, 399 F.3d at 187.
130. Toys "R" Us v. FTC, 221 F.3d 928, 937 (7th Cir. 2000) (defendant had market power with 20% share of toys sold in the United States, given its success in effectuating a boycott).
131. *Id.*
132. *Id.* at 188-89 (quoting United States v. Syufy Enters., 903 F.2d 659, 665-66 (9th Cir. 1990)).

focusing on "market concentration," which measures the aggregate market shares of firms in order to reflect the extent to which the largest market participants control supply. Although there is cross-fertilization between market power analyses under the several areas of antitrust law, market concentration analysis has developed primarily in the context of merger reviews.[133] The two market concentration tools in widest use are concentration ratios and the Herfindahl-Hirschman Index (HHI). Concentration ratios measure the proportion of a market accounted for by a given number of the leading firms, typically the top two, four, or eight firms. Early cases and Department of Justice practice cited concentration ratios as the preferred method,[134] but beginning with the 1982 *Merger Guidelines*[135] and continuing to the 1992 *Merger Guidelines* as revised in their current form,[136] the enforcement agencies adopted the HHI as the principal measure of market concentration. The HHI is calculated by summing the squares of the individual market shares of the firms in the market, resulting in a single figure between zero (an atomistic market) and 10,000 (a 100 percent share, squared—a perfect monopoly).[137] The process of squaring gives larger weight to larger shares. The resulting single HHI number is useful as a measurement by itself or as a comparator to an expected number to be derived from potential entry, exit, or merger by market participants. But again, high concentrations are not themselves indications of market power. They merely raise an inference, with the ultimate question of ability to maintain market share being a question for a finder of fact.

The courts' and agencies' focus on market share analysis implies a premise that more concentration generally leads to less procompetitive conduct. Whether this premise holds true for innovation—the specific

---

133. *See infra* § B.3.c.
134. *See, e.g.*, United States v. Black & Decker Mfg., 430 F. Supp. 729, 748-49 n. 38 (D. Md. 1976) (rejecting HHI as untested); U.S. DEP'T OF JUSTICE, MERGER GUIDELINES §§ 4, 5, 33 Fed. Reg. 23,442 (1968), *reprinted in* 4 Trade Reg. Rep. (CCH) ¶ 13,101.
135. U.S. DEP'T OF JUSTICE, MERGER GUIDELINES § III, 47 Fed. Reg. 28493 (1982), *reprinted in* 4 Trade Reg. Rep. (CCH) ¶ 13,102.
136. U.S. DEP'T OF JUSTICE AND FED. TRADE COMM'N, HORIZONTAL MERGER GUIDELINES (Apr. 2, 1992), *reprinted in* 4 Trade Reg. Rep. (CCH) ¶ 13,104 *and* U.S. DEP'T OF JUSTICE & FED. TRADE COMM'N, REVISION TO SECTION 4 OF HORIZONTAL MERGER GUIDELINES, *reprinted in* 72 Antitrust & Trade Reg. Rep. (BNA) 359 (1997) [collectively, hereinafter HORIZONTAL MERGER GUIDELINES].
137. *Id.*

type of presumptively procompetitive conduct that the intellectual property laws attempt to encourage—is an open question. Some commentators have argued that empirical evidence does not support an assumption that increased concentration leads to decreased research and development spending or inventive output; to the contrary, firms in a concentrated market may be larger and more able to engage in risky development efforts that lead to greater, more dynamic advances over time.[138]   And it must be remembered that increased research and development spending does not necessarily lead to greater consumer welfare, since welfare is a function not only of innovation, but of efficiency, pricing decisions, and other factors that may not move in lockstep with research efforts. Perhaps for these reasons, the agencies have been cautious when applying market concentration analysis to so-called innovation markets.

3. Types of Conduct Subject to Antitrust Scrutiny

Broadly speaking, three types of conduct may give rise to antitrust scrutiny: concerted action; exclusionary unilateral action; and mergers or merger-like combinations.   The antitrust laws and the enforcement agencies[139] do not treat these types of conduct equally.

a. Concerted Action: Agreements that Unreasonably Restrain Trade

Concerted action is generally analyzed under Section 1 of the Sherman Act, which states that "[e]very contract, combination in the form of trust or otherwise, or conspiracy, in restraint of trade or commerce among the several States, or with foreign nations, is declared to be illegal."[140]   The Supreme Court has recognized that Section 1 should not be read literally to prohibit all types of restraints of trade—which could encompass virtually any contracting activity—but, instead, should render unlawful only those restraints of trade that unreasonably restrict competition.[141]   Therefore, all concerted action cases must at a minimum contain proof of: (1) the existence of a contract, combination,

---

138.   *E.g.*, Richard T. Rapp, *The Misapplication of the Innovation Market Approach to Merger Analysis*, 64 ANTITRUST L.J. 19, 26-36 (Fall 1995).

139.   *See infra* § B.4.a, discussing the hierarchy of enforcement used by the Department of Justice.

140.   15 U.S.C. § 1.

141.   Standard Oil Co. v. United States, 221 U.S. 1, 58 (1911); *see also* Cal. Dental Ass'n v. FTC, 526 U.S. 756, 769-81 (1999).

or conspiracy among two or more separate entities that (2) unreasonably restrains trade and (3) affects interstate or foreign commerce.[142] Proof that a restraint is unreasonable is the crux of this test. To determine whether a restraint is unreasonable, courts traditionally apply one of two methods of analysis, depending on the nature of the agreement at issue: "per se" analysis or "rule of reason" (discussed in the next section).

Antitrust law distinguishes between horizontal and vertical restraints of trade.[143] Horizontal restraints are those established by agreements between actual or potential competitors; they directly affect interbrand competition. Vertical restraints are those established by agreements between firms at different levels of a market, such as between a manufacturer and its distributors; they tend to affect decisions made within a brand, sometimes called intrabrand competition.[144] Although both are examples of concerted action under Section 1, horizontal agreements have a higher risk of reducing competition between rivals, whereas vertical agreements are more likely to involve mere allocation of tasks to the most efficient actors within a production stream. Accordingly, courts are more likely to find horizontal restraints unreasonable or per se unlawful.[145]

Note that under Section 1, parallel behavior—competitors engaging in identical actions—is legal if it does not rise to the level of concerted action. Even conscious parallelism or oligopolistic price coordination does not violate Section 1 so long as competitors arrive at their price-setting decisions truly independently.[146] But Section 1 does not require a formal agreement or even direct evidence of concerted action: an agreement may be inferred from "direct or circumstantial evidence" that tends to "exclude the possibility of independent action" and "reasonably

---

142. *E.g.*, Orr v. Bank of Am., 285 F.3d 764, 782 (9th Cir. 2002); Maric v. St. Agnes Hosp., 65 F.3d 310, 313 (2d Cir. 1995).

143. For further discussion of vertical versus horizontal relationships, see *infra* § X.C.

144. *GTE Sylvania*, 433 U.S. at 51-57.

145. *See id. Compare* White Motor v. United States, 372 U.S. 253, 263 (1963) (noting horizontal restraints frequently are "naked restraints of trade with no purpose except stifling of competition"), *with* Bus. Elecs. Corp. v. Sharp Elecs. Corp., 485 U.S. 717, 735-36 (1988) ("a vertical restraint is not illegal per se unless it includes some agreement on price or price levels").

146. Brooke Group v. Brown & Williamson Tobacco, 509 U.S. 209, 227 (1993).

tends to prove ... a conscious commitment to a common scheme designed to achieve an unlawful objective."[147]

(1) Per Se vs. Rule of Reason

Per se analysis applies a presumption of unreasonableness, and hence illegality, for certain categories of restraints that are assumed to be virtually devoid of procompetitive justifications or efficiency-enhancing effects. For example, the law treats naked horizontal price fixing[148] and market allocation agreements among competitors[149] as per se illegal because they are likely to lead to competitive harm and have no plausible procompetitive justification. While it may be possible to imagine situations where such practices improve competitiveness, efficiency, and welfare, such situations would be rare and would not justify the substantial burden of requiring antitrust plaintiffs to prove unreasonableness in all such cases. There is a significant benefit to the marketplace in having a bright line rule to deter such conduct. Therefore, where per se activity is proven, most courts will find liability automatically and will not entertain an efficiencies-based defense.[150]

Rule of reason treatment, in contrast, requires an evaluation of a restraint's effect on competition in a relevant market.[151] This is an effects-based test that looks past a restraint's structure to determine "market impact," meaning the ultimate impact of the restraint on "competitive conditions."[152] Under the rule of reason, the party challenging an alleged restraint has the initial burden of proving that the restraint has injured or is likely to injure competition. If the plaintiff can prove injury to competition, the burden shifts to the defendant to prove that the alleged restraint serves a legitimate, procompetitive purpose. The court will then examine whether there are less anticompetitive

---

147. Monsanto Co. v. Spray-Rite Serv. Corp., 465 U.S. 752, 768 (1984).
148. Arizona v. Maricopa County Med. Soc'y, 457 U.S. 332, 354 (1982); Catalano, Inc. v. Target Sales, 446 U.S. 643, 650 (1980) (per curiam).
149. Palmer v. BRG of Ga., 498 U.S. 46, 49-50 (1990) (per curiam); United States v. Topco Assocs., 405 U.S. 596, 608 (1972).
150. *See Palmer*, 498 U.S. at 49-50.
151. Nat'l Soc'y of Prof'l Eng'rs v. United States, 435 U.S. 679, 692 (1978).
152. *Id.*

means to achieve those anticompetitive purposes.[153] A "full-blown rule of reason analysis"[154] can be difficult and time consuming.

Per se and rule of reason analysis have converged to some degree in recent years. In the late 1970s, Supreme Court decisions began to emphasize the need to exercise caution in applying the per se rule to restraints that appeared to fall within a traditionally-proscribed category if anticompetitive effects of the practice were not immediately obvious.[155] In the Court's words, the per se rule is a "demanding standard" and "departure from the rule-of-reason standard must be based upon demonstrable economic effect rather than ... upon formalistic line drawing."[156] The Court instructed that before applying per se treatment, courts should examine "whether the practice facially appears to be one that would always or almost always tend to restrict competition and decrease output, ... or instead one designed to 'increase economic efficiency and render markets more rather than less competitive.'"[157] The Court observed that the two standards overlap at the margin: "there is no bright line separating per se from Rule of Reason analysis."[158] The Court also created an in-between test involving a truncated rule of reason analysis, sometimes known as "quick look," to be applied when a practice is not within the traditional list of per se activities but "where the great likelihood of anticompetitive effects can be easily ascertained."[159] "It would be somewhat misleading ... to say the 'quick look' is just a new category of analysis intermediate in complexity between 'per se' condemnation and full-blown 'rule of reason' treatment, for that would suggest the [Supreme Court] has moved from a dichotomy to a trichotomy, when in fact it has backed away from any reliance upon fixed categories and toward a continuum."[160] The trend appears to be a

---

153. *See, e.g.*, United States v. Visa U.S.A., Inc., 344 F.3d 229, 238 (2d Cir. 2003).

154. *See, e.g., Cal. Dental*, 526 U.S. at 763.

155 *See, e.g.*, Broad. Music v. CBS, 441 U.S. 1, 18-21 (1979) (declining to apply per se rule to issuing of blanket licenses by joint venture of copyright holders; despite the fact that the practice could be described as price fixing, it could also be described as creating a new product that served as an efficient, procompetitive alternative to multiple individual licensing).

156. *GTE Sylvania*, 433 U.S. at 50, 58-89.

157. *Broad. Music*, 441 U.S. at 21.

158. NCAA v. Bd. of Regents, 468 U.S. 85, 104 n.26 (1984).

159. *Cal. Dental*, 526 U.S. at 770.

160. Polygram Holding v. FTC, 416 F.3d 29, 35-36 (D.C. Cir. 2005).

narrowing of the per se category and a skepticism about applying per se treatment in situations other than price fixing, market allocation, and their equivalents.[161]

b.   Unilateral Action: Exclusionary Conduct

Unilateral action is generally analyzed under Section 2 of the Sherman Act.[162] Such conduct falls under the theories "monopolization" and "attempted monopolization." Monopolization and attempted monopolization are different theories but they share many elements of proof with each other and with concerted-action claims under Section 1.

The elements of a monopolization claim are: (1) the possession of monopoly power in a relevant market and (2) the willful acquisition or maintenance of that power, as distinguished from growth or development of monopoly power as a consequence of a superior product, business acumen, or historical accident.[163] The possession element is relatively straightforward: monopoly power is the ability to control market prices or exclude competition[164] and, as in Section 1 cases, may be shown by direct or circumstantial evidence, including by market structure analysis.[165] The willful acquisition or maintenance element is a more difficult concept.

To prove the willfulness element of the monopolization test, early cases required a plaintiff to prove that monopoly was a probable result of the defendant's actions, as opposed to a situation that was "thrust upon" the defendant.[166] This reasoning fell out of favor as courts recognized that, under such a test, a firm with monopoly power might violate

---

161.   *See generally* ABA SECTION OF ANTITRUST LAW, ANTITRUST LAW DEVELOPMENTS 50-58 (5th ed. 2002).

162.   15 U.S.C. § 2. Other antitrust laws governing unilateral conduct exist, including the Robinson-Patman Act (codified in pertinent part at 15 U.S.C. § 13 (governing price discrimination)) and the Federal Trade Commission Act, 15 U.S.C. § 45. For simplicity and because courts have largely merged analysis under such other statutes with that under the Sherman Act, this section focuses on § 2.

163.   *Grinnell*, 384 U.S. at 570-71.

164.   *E.I. du Pont de Nemours Co.*, 351 U.S. at 391. Courts are not consistent in distinguishing monopoly and market power—some decisions state that the terms are synonymous. *E.g.*, U.S. Anchor Mfg. v. Rule Indus., 7 F.3d 986, 994 n.12 (11th Cir. 1993).

165.   *See supra* § B.2.b.

166.   *See, e.g.*, Am. Tobacco v. United States, 328 U.S. 781, 786-87 (1946).

Section 2 by pursuing normal, potentially procompetitive commercial conduct.[167]   More recent decisions generally have held that the acquisition or maintenance of monopoly need not be wholly involuntary or passive; however, courts seldom have attempted to articulate general principles for distinguishing pro- and anticompetitive conduct in this area.   Instead, courts have recognized that making such distinctions is inherently case specific and requires "the most subtle of economic judgments about particular business practices."[168]   Courts have developed a terminology that describes unlawful conduct as "exclusionary" or "predatory," while finding that the law protects conduct having a "legitimate business purpose."   Many commentators have criticized this terminology as conclusory and unhelpful.[169]   One antitrust enforcer has observed that "[t]he all-purpose, one-sentence, universal test for Section 2 liability is a 'holy grail' that may never be precisely located."[170]

The Supreme Court explained in *Aspen Skiing Co. v. Aspen Highlands Skiing Corp.* that "[i]f a firm has been 'attempting to exclude rivals on some basis other than efficiency,' it is fair to characterize its behavior as predatory."[171]   "'Thus, "exclusionary" comprehends at the most behavior that not only (1) tends to impair the opportunities of

---

167. *Compare* United States v. Aluminum Co. of Am. (*Alcoa*), 148 F.2d 416 (2d Cir. 1945) (suggesting that normal commercial conduct could violate § 2 if its effect is to enhance firm's market position), *with Syufy Enters.*, 903 F.2d at 668 (Ninth Circuit observed that *Alcoa*'s suggestion that a supplier can illegally monopolize a market simply by being efficient "has been questioned by just about everyone who has taken a close look at it").

168. Goldwasser v. Ameritech Corp., 222 F.3d 390, 397 (7th Cir. 2000).

169. *See, e.g.*, Herbert Hovenkamp, *Exclusion and the Sherman Act*, 72 U. CHI. L. REV. 147, 149-51 (2005); Einer Elhauge, *Defining Better Monopolization Standards*, 56 STAN. L. REV. 253, 257-92 (2003).

170. R. Hewitt Pate, Ass't Att'y Gen., Antitrust Div., U.S. Dep't of Justice, The Common Law Approach and Improving Standards for Analyzing Single Firm Conduct, Remarks Before the Thirtieth Annual Conference on International Antitrust Law and Policy at Fordham University 8 (Oct. 23, 2003).

171. 472 U.S. 585, 605 (1985) (quoting ROBERT H. BORK, THE ANTITRUST PARADOX at 138) (finding that where an owner of three ski resorts had no valid business reason for discontinuing its participation in a jointly offered interchangeable six-day "all-Aspen" lift ticket, refusal of that owner to cooperate with its smaller competitor could form the basis for a § 2 claim). In a more recent case, the Court noted that the *Aspen Skiing* decision is "at or near the outer boundary of Section 2 liability." *Trinko*, 540 U.S. at 399.

rivals, but also (2) either does not further competition on the merits or does so in an unnecessarily restrictive way."[172] Or, in slightly different words, exclusionary conduct "'is conduct, other than competition on the merits or restraints reasonably "necessary" to competition on the merits, that reasonably appears capable of making a significant contribution to creating or maintaining monopoly power."'[173] Although this test bears some similarity to the rule of reason test under Section 1, courts generally do not apply the term "rule of reason" to Section 2 cases.

The Department of Justice and the FTC, in a brief giving the agencies' views on a petition for certiorari to the Supreme Court, recently attempted to further synthesize the willfulness element of the test for monopolization. The agencies stated that "[c]onduct is 'exclusionary' or 'predatory' in antitrust jurisprudence if the conduct would not make economic sense for the defendant but for its elimination or softening of competition."[174] At the merits stage of the briefing, the agencies narrowed their proposed test by making clear that they advocated it "[i]n the context of an alleged refusal to assist a rival," and leaving open the question of whether they would apply it to all Section 2 conduct.[175] The Supreme Court declined to address either formulation.[176]

The Supreme Court explained in *Spectrum Sports v. McQuillan* that the offense of attempted monopolization requires proof: (1) that the defendant has engaged in predatory or anticompetitive conduct with (2) a specific intent to monopolize and (3) a dangerous probability of achieving monopoly power.[177] The same principles used to distinguish

---

172. *Id.* at 605 n.32 (quoting 3 PHILLIP AREEDA & DONALD TURNER, ANTITRUST LAW at 78 (1978)).

173. Barry Wright Corp. v. ITT Grinnell Corp., 724 F.2d 227, 230 (1st Cir. 1983) (Breyer, J.) (quoting 3 PHILLIP AREEDA & DONALD TURNER, ANTITRUST LAW at 83 (1978)); Town of Concord v. Boston Edison Co., 915 F.2d 17, 21 (1st Cir. 1990) (same); *see also* Stearns Airport Equip. v. FMC Corp., 170 F.3d 518, 522, 525 (5th Cir. 1999) (referring to "the inquiry demanded by *Aspen*—whether competition is or is not on the merits").

174. Brief for the United States and the Fed. Trade Comm'n as Amici Curiae, Verizon Communs. v. Law Offices of Curtis V. Trinko, 2002 WL 32354606 at *10 (2003).

175. Brief for the United States and the Fed. Trade Comm'n as Amici Curiae Supporting Petitioner, Verizon Communs. v. Law Offices of Curtis V. Trinko, 2003 WL 21269559 at **7, 15 (2003).

176. *Trinko*, 540 U.S. 398 (2004).

177. 506 U.S. 447, 456 (1993); *Microsoft*, 253 F.3d at 80.

aggressive competition from predation in monopolization cases apply for attempt claims. Unlike monopolization, attempt requires proof that the defendant had a "specific intent to destroy competition or build monopoly."[178]

Section 2 also prohibits a conspiracy to monopolize, which requires: (1) the existence of a combination or conspiracy; (2) an overt act in furtherance of the conspiracy; (3) specific intent to monopolize; and (4) causal antitrust injury.[179] It is unclear whether courts should add the "dangerous probability" element of attempt claims to proof of conspiracy claims.[180] Several appellate cases have declined to do so.[181] Regardless of whether "dangerous probability" is an explicit element of the test, the concept of a conspiracy may by its very nature imply a test of feasibility and illegality. It would be an odd result for a conspiracy to violate Section 2 if the completed enterprise sought by the conspirators would have been lawful.[182]

Four[183] of the practices most commonly challenged as exclusionary under Section 2 are predatory pricing (uneconomic pricing used to drive rivals from a market, at which time the monopolist expects to recoup its losses); vertical agreements that foreclose competition; anticompetitive litigation; and refusals to deal.[184] Of these, the last three are of particular concern to intellectual property holders, as discussed *infra* at Chapter VI.

---

178. Times-Picayune Publ'g v. United States, 345 U.S. 594, 626 (1953); *see also Spectrum Sports*, 506 U.S. at 456 (specific intent to monopolize required for an attempt claim).

179. Paladin Assocs. v. Mont. Power, 328 F.3d 1145, 1158 (9th Cir. 2003) (citing United States v. Yellow Cab Co., 332 U.S. 218, 224-25 (1947)).

180. The Supreme Court has not addressed conspiracy to monopolize since issuing its decision in *Spectrum Sports*, which added the "dangerous probability" element to attempt claims. 506 U.S. at 456.

181. *E.g.*, Freeman v. San Diego Ass'n of Realtors, 322 F.3d 1133, 1154 (9th Cir. 2003); U.S. Anchor Mfg. v. Rule Indus., 7 F.3d 986, 1001 (11th Cir. 1993).

182. *See* Williams v. 5300 Columbia Pike Corp., 891 F. Supp. 1169, 1175 (E.D. Va. 1995) ("a conspiracy to monopolize must be ... *somehow* rationally directed to the exclusion of competitors" (emphasis in original)).

183. The viability of a fifth common theory, monopoly leveraging (monopoly power in one market used to gain a competitive advantage in another market), has been vitiated by the Supreme Court's recent decision in *Trinko*, 540 U.S. at 415 n.4.

184. *See* ANTITRUST LAW DEVELOPMENTS, *supra* note 161, at 246-97 (discussing these and other common monopolization theories).

c.   Mergers

(1) Applicable Statutes

The competitive effects of mergers and acquisitions are principally governed by Section 7 of the Clayton Act, which prohibits such transactions "where in any line of commerce or in any activity affecting commerce in any section of the country, the effect of such acquisition may be substantially to lessen competition, or to tend to create a monopoly."[185]   Mergers and acquisitions may also be challenged as restraints of trade or monopolization under Sections 1 and 2 of the Sherman Act, as a violation of the prohibition against "unfair methods of competition" under Section 5 of the Federal Trade Commission Act,[186] or under various state unfair competition laws.

The Hart-Scott-Rodino Antitrust Improvements Act of 1976 (known generally as HSR or Section 7A) requires merging parties to file a notification with the Department of Justice and the Federal Trade Commission for merger activity that meets certain statutory transaction-price thresholds, and to wait a prescribed time period before consummating the transaction.[187]   Of particular interest to intellectual property lawyers, the Commission has concluded that exclusive licenses are HSR-reportable under some circumstances.[188]

---

185.   15 U.S.C. § 18.

186.   15 U.S.C. § 45.

187.   15 U.S.C. § 18a.   This premerger notification procedure permits the enforcement agencies to evaluate the likely competitive effects of a combination and, if necessary, demand changes to the transaction or challenge the practice before those effects take place, and thereby avoid the need to unwind a merger after the fact.   Under 2000 amendments to § 7A, the Federal Trade Commission publishes an annual notice of the premerger notification filing threshold.   In 2005, the threshold for the most frequently applicable portion of § 7A was set at a merger transaction value of $53.1 million.   *See* 70 Fed. Reg. 5020-01 (Jan. 31, 2005), *setting threshold applicable to* 15 U.S.C. 18a(a)(2)(b)(i).

188.   ABA SECTION OF ANTITRUST LAW, PREMERGER NOTIFICATION PRACTICE MANUAL 38 (3d ed. 2003).   The Commission has stated its views on many common merger questions via its informal opinion process, some results of which are reported in this manual.

(2) General Overview of Merger Concerns

Like the other conduct discussed in this chapter, mergers can have either pro- or anticompetitive effects. A merger can be procompetitive if it allows firms to eliminate redundant functions, enter new markets, or otherwise enhance efficiency. A merger can be anticompetitive if it increases the combined entity's power to raise prices or restrain output for a significant period of time.[189] Consequently, the principal concern with mergers under the antitrust laws is the creation or enhancement of market power. As a proxy for market power,[190] merger analysis typically focuses on the degree to which a merger would increase concentration in a relevant market, particularly in markets that already are highly concentrated. "Two to one" mergers (the premerger market has two significant competitors, the postmerger market has only one, meaning a monopoly) are rarely permissible, three to two mergers receive great scrutiny, four to three mergers are more likely to pass muster, and so on. An increase of concentration draws scrutiny because it may permit the merged entity unilaterally to maintain supracompetitive prices or because it may permit the remaining firms to coordinate their actions, whether explicitly or implicitly, to achieve the same result. Although conscious parallelism is not illegal under the Sherman Act's Section 1, an increased likelihood of conscious parallelism may violate the Clayton Act's Section 7.

There are two basic types of mergers and therefore two, slightly different types of merger analysis. Horizontal mergers—those between competitors—directly increase concentration by decreasing the number of market participants. Horizontal mergers draw the closest antitrust scrutiny because they pose the most direct risk of permitting a single firm to possess market power, particularly when such a merger eliminates the acquiring firm's closest rival,[191] and of permitting remaining firms to exercise collective market power by collusion or parallel conduct. Mergers between potential competitors raise the same issues, though perhaps not to so immediate a degree. Vertical mergers do not directly increase concentration; however, they still may facilitate collusion and they may lead to "vertical foreclosure," a type of exclusive effect whereby companies A and B merge and the competitor of company A

---

189. HORIZONTAL MERGER GUIDELINES, *supra* note 136, § 0.1.

190. *See supra* § B.2.b.

191. *See generally* Michael L. Weiner, *Explaining New Theories of Unilateral Effects*, 11 ANTITRUST 4 (Spring 1997).

suffers when it loses independent supplier or customer access to company B. The Supreme Court has expressed concern over vertical foreclosure because "by foreclosing the competitors of either party from a segment of the market otherwise open to them, the arrangement may act as a clog on competition, which deprives rivals ... of a fair opportunity to compete."[192]

The enforcement agencies' *Merger Guidelines* are a succinct resource for an overview of merger concerns and analysis.[193] While the *Guidelines* recognize the congressional intent that merger enforcement should "interdict competitive problems in their incipiency," they also state that merger law should "avoid unnecessary interference with the larger universe of mergers that are either competitively beneficial or neutral."[194]

4. Enforcement of Antitrust Laws

a. Federal and State Governmental Enforcement

Only the Department of Justice can bring federal criminal antitrust claims. Otherwise, the Department, the Federal Trade Commission,[195] and the states generally share authority under the antitrust laws. To avoid duplication of civil investigations, the federal agencies have established a "clearance" procedure to decide which will investigate a particular matter, particularly regarding mergers.[196] Both federal agencies coordinate to a less formal degree with state governmental parties, which may have standing under federal or state law.

---

192. Brown Shoe Co. v. United States, 370 U.S. 294, 323-24 (1962) (quotation omitted).
193. HORIZONTAL MERGER GUIDELINES, *supra* note 136. For commentary and analysis, *see generally* ABA SECTION OF ANTITRUST LAW, MERGERS AND ACQUISITIONS: UNDERSTANDING THE ANTITRUST ISSUES (2d ed. 2004).
194. HORIZONTAL MERGER GUIDELINES, *supra* note 136, § 0.1.
195. Both the Department and the Commission have the authority to enforce the Clayton Act. The Commission does not have direct authority to enforce the Sherman Act. Instead, it has direct authority to enforce the Federal Trade Commission Act, 15 U.S.C. § 45. Under § 5 of the FTC Act, that authority extends to conduct violating the "antitrust laws," which in turn includes the Sherman Act's civil provisions; therefore, the Department's and Commission's civil authority is largely the same.
196. For a description of the clearance process, see 4 Trade Reg. Rep. (CCH) ¶ 9,565.05 (1993).

In matters of policy, dealings with foreign governments, and amicus briefs to the Supreme Court, the agencies typically collaborate to produce a joint statement of their position on the law. The Department and the Commission have issued numerous public statements of their enforcement policies, including a series of jointly-authored guidelines.[197] Among these are the 1995 *Antitrust Guidelines for the Licensing of Intellectual Property.*[198]

The Department's Antitrust Division has recently emphasized a hierarchy of antitrust enforcement under which it focuses on cartels, mergers, and unilateral exclusionary conduct, in that order.[199] The Division describes criminal cartel enforcement as its "core priority."[200] This "hierarchy" should not be seen as a decision to focus on cartel enforcement at the expense of mergers, collaborations, and unilateral conduct; instead, the Division intends only to signal that it will move more cautiously in the latter areas, to avoid false positives in cases where it is more "difficult to distinguish between harmful exclusionary conduct and beneficial hard-nosed competition."[201]

(1) Criminal Enforcement by the Department of Justice

Criminal enforcement of the antitrust laws does not play a significant role at the intersection of competition and intellectual property policy. The Department of Justice has jurisdiction to bring criminal enforcement

---

197. *See, e.g.,* Policy Statements and Guidelines, *available at* http://www.usdoj.gov/atr/public/guidelines/guidelin.htm.
198. *See* U.S. DEP'T OF JUSTICE & FED. TRADE COMM'N, ANTITRUST GUIDELINES FOR THE LICENSING OF INTELLECTUAL PROPERTY (April 6, 1995) (hereinafter INTELLECTUAL PROPERTY GUIDELINES), *reprinted in* 4 Trade Reg. Rep. (CCH) ¶ 13,132 *and* Appendix 1 to this Handbook.
199. R. Hewitt Pate, Ass't Att'y Gen., Antitrust Div., U.S. Dep't of Justice, Int'l Cartel Enforce., Remarks before the 2004 Int'l Cartel Network Cartels Workshop (Nov. 21, 2004), *at* http://www.usdoj.gov/atr/public/speeches/206428.pdf. The Federal Trade Commission has made no similar statement; however, this is not surprising, given that the Commission does not have the legal authority to bring criminal cases against cartels.
200. R. Hewitt Pate, Ass't Att'y Gen., Antitrust Div., U.S. Dep't of Justice, Securing the Benefits of Global Competition, Remarks before the Tokyo Am. Cent. (Sept. 10, 2004), *available at* http://www.usdoj.gov/atr/public/speeches/205389.pdf.
201. *Id.* at 15.

matters under both Sections 1 and 2 of the Sherman Act;[202] however, the vast majority of criminal cases involve allegations of per se violations of Section 1 (such as price fixing, bid rigging, market allocation, or collaborations typical of cartels) and the Department has a longstanding policy of pursuing criminal indictment only where it believes it can prove a clear, purposeful violation of law.[203] The Department often brings criminal cases against companies operating in patent-intensive high technology industries, but the intellectual property aspects of the case tend to be irrelevant—the Department's focus is on price fixing and the like, regardless of whether the relevant product contains patented technology.[204]

(2) Civil Enforcement by the Department of Justice and Federal Trade Commission

The Department and Commission use similar procedures for initiating civil nonmerger investigations. Agency staff may open an

---

202. 15 U.S.C. §§ 1-2. Section 3 of the Robinson-Patman Act also provides criminal jurisdiction. 15 U.S.C. § 13a.
203. *See* Gary R. Spratling, Dep. Ass't Att'y Gen., Antitrust Div., U.S. Dep't of Justice, Transparency in Enforcement Maximizes Cooperation from Antitrust Offenders, Remarks before the Fordham Corporate Law Inst. 26th Annual Conf. on International Antitrust Law and Policy (Oct. 15, 1999), *available at* www.usdoj.gov/atr/public/speeches/3952.pdf. The ABA Section of Antitrust Law has noted the "paucity" of criminal prosecutions under other theories and has suggested that Congress consider deleting criminal liability provisions outside § 1. ABA SECTION OF ANTITRUST LAW, REPORT OF THE SECTION OF ANTITRUST LAW OF THE ABA TO THE ANTITRUST MODERNIZATION COMMISSION 8-9 (Sept. 30, 2004) ("For various reasons, the chance of any future criminal enforcement activity under the [Robinson-Patman Act] is highly implausible and ... probably inadvisable.... Although there is no evidence of misuse, given the paucity of criminal Section 2 cases, the [Antitrust Modernization] Commission may wish to consider adjusting [Section 2] as well as any other antitrust statutes with criminal penalties that have not been used in the modern era."), *available at* http://www.abanet.org/antitrust/comments/2004/Comments ModernizationCommission.pdf.
204. *See, e.g.*, Press Release, Dep't of Justice, Korean Company—Hynix—Agrees to Plead Guilty to Price Fixing and Agrees to Pay $185 Million Fine for Role in DRAM Conspiracy (Apr. 21, 2005), *available at* http://www.usdoj.gov/atr/public/press_releases/2005/208655.htm.

investigation based on customer complaints, competitor complaints, inquiries by Congress or other government departments, news reports or other publicly available information, or leads developed through unrelated agency work. To challenge a practice, the Department must file a lawsuit in federal district court, with appeals being to the circuit in which the district court sits. The Commission employs a very different process. If the Commission seeks a temporary restraining order or preliminary injunction, it must file suit in district court; otherwise, Commission staff initiate a claim before an administrative law judge employed by the Commission. Appeals of the administrative trial are made to the five Commissioners themselves, who are not required to show the same degree of deference to the trial result as would a federal appellate court. The Commissioners may produce a formal opinion, issuing a judgment or remanding the matter for further administrative litigation. The respondent (but not the Commission's petitioning staff) can appeal the Commissioners' decision directly to any circuit court where the challenged practice occurred or where the respondent resides or does business.[205]

The Department and Commission employ largely the same procedures for merger and acquisition review as for nonmerger investigations, with the notable exception that they open the vast majority of merger and acquisition investigations through the HSR premerger notification process,[206] rather than in response to complaints. In addition to preventing anticompetitive combinations at inception, the agencies may sue in the case of a consummated transaction and can seek the remedy of unwinding a business combination. Suits against consummated transactions, however, are relatively rare.

(3) Business Review Letters and Advisory Opinions

The Department and the Commission have the ability to review proposed conduct at the request of industry. The Department is prohibited from stating a pure advisory opinion but can issue a "business review letter" to a firm that requests such a letter for proposed (not ongoing) conduct.[207] The Commission's procedure is more flexible, permitting Commission staff to issue various types of business guidance, some of which may be for ongoing conduct or compliance with an

---

205. 15 U.S.C. § 45(c).
206. *See supra* § B.3.c.
207. 28 C.F.R. § 50.6.

existing enforcement order; however, formal "advisory opinions" are only available for proposed conduct.[208]

(4) Civil and Criminal Enforcement by the States

All fifty states and the District of Columbia have enacted consumer protection statutes of general applicability. Because such laws are similar to the Federal Trade Commission Act, practitioners often refer to the statutes collectively as the "little FTC Acts" and rely on Commission precedent when interpreting them. Most authorize a state agency, usually the state attorney general, to bring civil and sometimes criminal suits for injunctive relief and damages, whether on behalf of aggrieved consumers or the state itself. Almost all state consumer protection statutes provide private rights of action for damages and attorneys' fees and some authorize injunctive relief and class action procedure.

State agencies also have the option of directly enforcing several federal antitrust laws. States and their political subdivisions are considered "persons" for purposes of securing relief under the federal antitrust laws and may sue for damages and injunctive relief in their own capacities[209] or as parens patriae, on behalf of their citizens.[210] A particular role for state enforcement relates to the Supreme Court's decision *Illinois Brick Co. v. Illinois*,[211] which held that indirect purchasers can seek injunctive relief but not damages under federal law. Nineteen states and the District of Columbia have enacted laws—known as "*Illinois Brick* repealer statutes"—that specifically permit indirect purchasers to recover damages for state antitrust law violations.[212]

In recent decades, state attorneys general have become more aggressive in bringing antitrust suits in both state and federal court. Many Department of Justice and Federal Trade Commission lawsuits involve state attorneys general as coplaintiffs. In fact, the federal agencies have an informal policy of deferring to state enforcement where anticompetitive conduct primarily affects only one or a small number of states. Each federal agency maintains a permanent liaison with the state attorneys general to consider such issues; however, there is no formal clearance procedure as there is between the Department and the Commission.

---

208.   16 C.F.R. §§ 1.1-1.6.
209.   15 U.S.C. § 4.
210.   15 U.S.C. § 15.
211.   431 U.S. 720 (1977).
212.   *See* ANTITRUST LAW DEVELOPMENTS, *su pra* note 161, at 811-12.

b. Private Antitrust Litigation

Neither the Federal Trade Commission Act[213] nor the Sherman Act provides directly for private rights of action. The Clayton Act, however, authorizes a suit for damages by "any person … injured in his business or property by reason of anything forbidden in the antitrust laws."[214] As a result, a violation of Sherman Act Sections 1 and 2 regarding concerted or unilateral conduct, Clayton Act Section 7 regarding mergers, or other federal antitrust laws forms the basis for a private antitrust suit under federal law.

A private plaintiff under the federal antitrust laws must prove "antitrust injury," meaning injury that is causally linked to the antitrust violation and that is "of the type the antitrust laws were meant to prevent,"[215] rather than simply an "injur[y] that may conceivably be traced to an antitrust violation."[216] If a plaintiff establishes liability and antitrust injury, it may recover treble damages, costs of suit, and attorneys' fees.[217] The calculation of antitrust damages is complex and usually involves the use of expert economic testimony.[218]

Private damages actions under state antitrust laws are highly variable. Most state unfair competition laws permit enhanced damages, such as doubling or trebling the plaintiff's economic loss, but the enhancement is sometimes left to the discretion of the court or to a showing of willfulness or other additional scienter. Most state unfair competition laws permit the recovery of costs and attorneys' fees as a matter of course.[219]

As in any federal civil litigation, a litigant may bring a class action for antitrust violations under Federal Rule of Civil Procedure 23. Many states have similar class action provisions. Private antitrust lawsuits in federal court often are an amalgam of class action practice, federal claims, and state claims, and may rely on a presumption of liability due

213. Holloway v. Bristol-Myers Corp., 485 F.2d 986, 997 (D.C. Cir. 1973).
214. 15 U.S.C. § 15(a).
215. Atl. Richfield Co. v. USA Petroleum, 495 U.S. 328, 334 (1990).
216. *Standard Oil*, 405 U.S. at 263 n.14.
217. 15 U.S.C. § 15. Under the 2004 amendments to the Sherman Act, standards development organizations have been exempted from treble damages liability. *Id.*
218. *See generally* ANTITRUST LAW DEVELOPMENTS, *supra* note 161, at 873-82.
219. *See generally id.* at 812-13.

to a previous successful enforcement action by the Department, the Commission, or a state agency.

C. The Interface Between Intellectual Property and Antitrust

In the early history of the competition laws, intellectual property law and antitrust were sometimes viewed as opposing doctrines under the rubric that intellectual property grants monopoly power, whereas antitrust exists to take monopolies away. With the maturation of case law and antitrust economics, policy makers recognized that neither portion of this rubric was correct as a matter of economic analysis. Intellectual property creates exclusive rights but this exclusivity does not equate with the economic concept of market power; a patent, for example, may be worthless because the invention claimed by the patent has no commercial market or has so many substitutes—whether public domain methods or other patents—that it provides no competitive advantage. And antitrust does not exist to destroy market power or even to preserve any particular competitor; instead, modern antitrust law only applies liability to anticompetitive conduct and agreements, and it attempts to look past the form of transactions to predict their ultimate effect on consumer welfare.

Although antitrust and intellectual property are no longer seen as opponents, tensions continue to exist at the intersection of these bodies of law. The following chapters address such tensions in detail. What follows here is a brief introduction to certain particularly prominent and recurring issues.

Does antitrust carve out special rules for intellectual property? In their *Intellectual Property Guidelines*,[220] the Department of Justice and Federal Trade Commission formally recognized that the intellectual property and antitrust laws are complements.[221] These laws "share the

---

220. INTELLECTUAL PROPERTY GUIDELINES, *supra* note 198; *see also* ABA SECTION OF ANTITRUST LAW, THE FEDERAL ANTITRUST GUIDELINES FOR THE LICENSING OF INTELLECTUAL PROPERTY ORIGINS AND APPLICATIONS (2d ed. 2002) (hereinafter ABA LICENSING GUIDELINES) (collecting case law and analysis).

221. INTELLECTUAL PROPERTY GUIDELINES, *supra* note 198, § 1.0 (citing Atari Games v. Nintendo of Am., 897 F.2d 1572, 1576 (Fed. Cir. 1990) ("[T]he aims and objectives of patent and antitrust laws may seem, at first glance, wholly at odds. However, the two bodies of law are actually complementary, as both are aimed at encouraging innovation, industry and competition.")).

common purpose of promoting innovation and enhancing consumer welfare."[222]   The agencies stated that for purposes of antitrust analysis, intellectual property should in general be treated the same as any other type of property.[223]   Courts have reached the same conclusion.   In a famous passage in its *Microsoft* decision, the D.C. Circuit rejected the idea that special antitrust rules might exist regarding intellectual property rights:

> The company claims an absolute and unfettered right to use its intellectual property as it wishes: "[I]f intellectual property rights have been lawfully acquired," it says, then "their subsequent exercise cannot give rise to antitrust liability."   That is no more correct than the proposition that use of one's personal property, such as a baseball bat, cannot give rise to tort liability. As the Federal Circuit succinctly stated: "Intellectual property rights do not confer a privilege to violate the antitrust laws." [224]

In another famous quote, the Supreme Court explained that "[t]he patent laws which give a ... monopoly on making, using, or selling the invention are in pari materia with the antitrust laws and modify them pro tanto."[225]   Such quotes are useful but operate at a level of generality that may frustrate the antitrust practitioner.   Clearly, the unique statutory rights and inherent characteristics of intellectual property must be factored into antitrust analysis, but the same might also be said of any other type of statutory or property right.   Modern U.S. antitrust analysis is already performed on a fact-intensive, case-by-case basis (such as the rule of reason); therefore, factoring in the impact of intellectual property rights can be done without doing violence to core antitrust concepts.

Refusals to deal and "essential facilities."   There has been much recent debate as to whether the mere refusal to license intellectual property can serve as an antitrust violation.[226]   This debate largely centers

---

222.   *Id.*
223.   *Id.* § 2.1 ("The Agencies apply the same general antitrust principles to conduct involving intellectual property as they apply to conduct involving any other form of tangible or intangible property.").
224.   *Microsoft*, 253 F.3d at 63 (citation to brief omitted) (citing *In re* Indep. Serv. Orgs. Antitrust Litig. (*CSU*), 203 F.3d 1322, 1325 (Fed. Cir. 2000)).
225.   Simpson v. Union Oil Co., 377 U.S. 13, 24 (1964) (internal quotation omitted).
226.   *E.g.*, A. Douglas Melamed, *Exclusionary Conduct Under the Antitrust Laws: Balancing, Sacrifice, and Refusals to Deal*, 20 Berkeley Tech. L.J. 1247 (2005) (collecting cases and scholarship).

on patent rights and often involves the attempt to describe economically important patents as "essential facilities," meaning property rights so vital to competition in a particular market that their absence effectively forecloses entry.[227] The Ninth Circuit came close to recognizing the essential facilities concept when it found that the refusal to license photocopier patents to independent copy-service firms could support an antitrust claim.[228] The Federal Circuit rejected the concept, that refusing to license a patent could result in antitrust liability, in a later case involving nearly identical facts.[229]

The viability of the essential facilities doctrine, if such can be described as a doctrine, is unsettled with respect to intellectual property rights. The Supreme Court's 2004 *Trinko* decision did not express an explicit view on the essential facilities concept but cited with approval a leading article critical of it.[230] The Department, citing *Trinko* and the rights granted by the Patent Act itself,[231] concluded in its 2004 *Intellectual Property Task Force Report* that "an intellectual property owner's decision not to license its technology to others cannot violate the

---

227. *See generally* Paul D. Marquardt & Mark Leddy, *The Essential Facilities Doctrine and Intellectual Property Rights: A Response to Pitofsky, Patterson, and Hooks*, 70 ANTITRUST L.J. 847 (2003).
228. Image Technical Servs. v. Eastman Kodak Co., 125 F.3d 1195, 1209 (9th Cir. 1997).
229. *CSU*, 203 F.3d 1322.
230. *Trinko*, 540 U.S. at 410-11, 415 (citing Phillip E. Areeda, *Essential Facilities: An Epithet in Need of Limiting Principles*, 58 ANTITRUST L.J. 841 (1989)). In addition, Justice Breyer in an earlier case noted that the Court has "never adopted" the essential facilities doctrine. AT&T Corp. v. Iowa Util. Bd., 525 U.S. 366, 428 (1999) (concurring opinion).
231. R. Hewitt Pate, Ass't Att'y Gen., Antitrust Div., U.S. Dep't of Justice, Competition and Intellectual Property in the United States: Licensing Freedom and the Limits of Antitrust, Remarks before the 2005 European Union Competition Workshop at 4-5 (June 3, 2005) ("[T]he argument is that there must therefore be *some* circumstance in which the unilateral, unconditional refusal to license a patent must constitute an antitrust violation. With a single much-criticized exception, this is an argument that has never found support in any U.S. legal decision. At this point in the development of U.S. law, it is safe to say that this argument is without merit."), *available at* http://www.usdoj.gov/atr/public/speeches/209359.htm.

antitrust laws."[232]   The Department has recognized that right to refuse to license is not unlimited: according to the Department, attempts to "extend an intellectual property right beyond its legal limits" remain the proper subject of enforcement inquiry.[233]   The meaning of "beyond ... legal limits," if that becomes the test for refusals to deal, is anything but clear. The right to refuse to license is sufficiently complex that it merits a substantial portion of a chapter (Chapter VI) in this book.

The problem of uncertain rights.   Perhaps the most difficult problem at the intellectual property-antitrust intersection involves uncertain intellectual property rights. All property rights are subject to attack as to ownership and rights of use (even real estate law has provisions for quiet-title lawsuits and demands for an easement) but intellectual property is particularly subject to uncertainty because its boundaries are entirely legal fictions, not physical barriers that can be seen and touched. Courts have shown a willingness to find intellectual property unenforceable; for example, one study noted that roughly half of all litigated patents are found to be invalid.[234] Some commentators have even suggested that patents could be analyzed not as full legal rights, but as "probabilistic" ones.[235]

Uncertainty over an intellectual property right's enforceability makes antitrust analysis difficult because of the latter's focus on effects. A typical effects-based antitrust analysis seeks to determine the impact of conduct by comparing outcomes in the actual versus the "but-for" world (the world that would have existed but for the conduct).[236] Imagine competitors A and B, where A invents a new technology, receives a patent, and licenses the technology to B on the condition that B must not sell in A's home territory. If the patent is enforceable (A could have won an infringement suit against B), the license has no anticompetitive effect; in fact, the license may actually permit more market entry than if A

232.   U.S. DEP'T OF JUSTICE, REPORT OF THE DEP'T OF JUSTICE'S TASK FORCE ON INTELLECTUAL PROPERTY 41 (2004), *available at* http://www.cybercrime.gov/IPTaskForceReport.pdf.
233.   *Id.*
234.   John R. Allison & Mark A. Lemley, *Empirical Evidence on the Validity of Litigated Patents*, 26 AM. INTELLECTUAL PROPERTY L. ASS'N Q.J. 185, 205 (1998); *see also* Carl Shapiro, *Patent System Reform: Economic Analysis & Critique*, 19 BERKELEY TECH. L.J. 1017, 1028-29 (2004) (collecting scholarship).
235.   Mark Lemley & Carl Shapiro, *Probabilistic Patents*, 19 J. OF ECON. PERSPECTIVES 75 (2005).
236.   For further discussion of the importance of but-for analysis, see Ch. IX.

simply kept the patent to itself. But if the patent is not enforceable (A
could not have sued under the patent successfully against B), the conduct
would appear to nakedly allocate territory between horizontal
competitors, a per se violation of Sherman Act Section 1. What if—as is
frequently the case—reasonable minds could differ as to whether the
patent can be enforced? Must antitrust law simply assume that all
patents are valid, until proven otherwise in a court of law?

Neither the agencies nor the courts have found a simple solution to
the problem of uncertain intellectual property rights. The Federal Trade
Commission dealt with this problem in *In re Schering-Plough Corp.*,[237]
when it challenged a patent-litigation settlement in which the alleged
infringer of a pharmaceutical patent agreed to exit the market and
abandon its patent-invalidity allegations in exchange for a $60 million
cash "reverse" payment (reverse in the sense that one ordinarily would
expect a settling infringer to pay, not be paid).[238] The Commission
identified such a payment as a "red flag" of potential anticompetitive
behavior[239] and held that it was unnecessary to evaluate the validity and
enforceability of the patent[240] because, under the facts of the case, the
payment could only have been meant to effectively purchase
noncompetition.[241] In effect, the Commission ruled that exclusion of a
competitor in a disputed patent infringement case would be a legal result
if obtained via court injunction but constituted a violation of the
competition laws when secured through a private contract with a cash
quid pro quo.[242] While courts may consider such reasoning to be
aggressive,[243] the decision is notable for the Commission's willingness to
avoid the uncertain-rights question. The Department has not brought a
similar case.

---

237. Opinion of the Commission, Dkt. No. 9297 (Dec. 8, 2003), *available at*
http://www.ftc.gov/os/adjpro/d9297/031218commissionopinion.pdf,
vacated sub nom. Schering-Plough Corp. v. FTC, 402 F.3d 1056, 1076
(11th Cir. 2005), *cert. denied*, 126 S. Ct. 2929 (2006).
238. *Id.* at 4.
239. *Id.* at 29.
240. *Id.* at 35.
241. *Id.* at 9, 79.
242. *See id.*
243. The Commission's decision was vacated in *Schering-Plough Corp. v. FTC*, 402 F.3d 1056, 1076 (11th Cir. 2005), *cert. denied*, 126 S. Ct. 2929 (2006). The Eleventh Circuit held that the competitive effect of the settlement agreement could not be evaluated without analyzing the strength of the underlying patent. *Id.* at 1065-66.

Product design and exclusionary conduct. If a company has some right to refuse to deal in its intellectual property, is that right affected by its decision to design its product in a predatory way? The Department confronted this question in *United States v. Microsoft.*[244] The Department proved that Microsoft, a computer operating system manufacturer, had anticompetitively maintained its monopoly position in operating systems by imposing license restrictions that required computer original equipment manufacturers (OEMs) to configure "desktop" software in a way that disadvantaged rivals.[245] The Department also proved that Microsoft committed exclusionary conduct when it integrated its Internet browser with the operating system in order to reduce use of a rival browser.[246]

The *Microsoft* case has not ushered in a wave of cases challenging product design as anticompetitive. Moreover, during the remedies phase of the case, the Department accepted a consent order that, despite the demands of some co-plaintiffs and public parties, did not require Microsoft to reverse the "commingling" of the operating system and browser or to disclose such programs' full source code.[247] On those parties' appeal, the D.C. Circuit affirmed the consent order. The court expressed great reluctance to insert itself into product design decisions, stating, for example, that Microsoft should not be required to divulge application program interface source code because "[t]he effect upon Microsoft's incentive to innovate would be substantial; not even the broad remedial discretion enjoyed by the district court extends to the adoption of provisions so likely to harm consumers."[248] In doing so, the court echoed the Department's arguments in favor of the consent decree.[249] The plaintiffs were left to the remedy of money damages in

---

244. United States v. Microsoft Corp., 253 F.3d 34 (D.C. Cir. 2001); *see also* http://www.usdoj.gov/atr/cases/ms_index.htm (collecting pleadings, settlement, and public comment materials).
245. *Id.* at 60-64.
246. *Id.* at 65. The District of Columbia Circuit called this a "product integration" theory and, though it upheld liability in part, emphasized that "[a]s a general rule, courts are properly very skeptical about claims that competition has been harmed by a dominant firm's product design changes." *Id.*
247. Massachusetts v. Microsoft Corp., 373 F.3d 1199, 1207-08 (D.C. Cir. 2004).
248. *Id.* at 1219.
249. Brief of the United States, United States v. Microsoft Corp., No. 03-5030 (Aug. 6, 2003) at 36 ("appellants' incorrect remedial theory ... would

related civil suits. The Microsoft case seems to signal that both the Department and the courts (or at least the D.C. Circuit) are highly sensitive to the effects of antitrust remedies on innovation incentives, a theme that has gained increasing prominence in subsequent speeches by Department officials.[250]

"Fixing" intellectual property law through the use of antitrust? Both federal enforcement agencies have resisted the call to "fix" perceived flaws in the intellectual property system through use of the antitrust laws. The Department has noted that the legislature, via the intellectual property laws, has struck a balance between the rights of intellectual property owners, the rights of consumers, and concerns for a competitive marketplace, and that while "this may or may not be the correct balance[,] nevertheless, it is the one the legislature has chosen."[251] The Commission undertook a major study of the competitive effect of the patent laws, and although it noted that "failure to strike the appropriate balance between competition and patent law and policy can harm innovation,"[252] it recommended changes to the patent laws rather than a shift in antitrust analysis.[253] Neither agency appears interested in using antitrust to attack intellectual property rights in a direct way.

Some tension may always exist between the exclusive-rights regimes of intellectual property rights and the open-market policies underlying antitrust law. This is not surprising, given that the Supreme Court has noted such tensions even within the intellectual property laws themselves.[254] But on two bedrock principles—the complementarity of antitrust and intellectual property law and the lack of a broad intellectual property-based exemption from antitrust—there is no serious dispute in the United States. Intellectual property is simply one of many factors to

---

require sowing Microsoft's fields with salt"), *available at* http://www.usdoj.gov/atr/cases/f201200/201212.htm#IIIB4.

250. *E.g.*, Makan Delrahim, Dep. Ass't Att'y Gen., Antitrust Div., U.S. Dep't of Justice, Forcing Firms to Share the Sandbox: Compulsory Licensing of Intellectual Property Rights and Antitrust, Address before the British Inst. of Int'l and Comparative Law (May 10, 2004), *available at* http://www.usdoj.gov/atr/public/speeches/203627.pdf.
251. Pate, Licensing Freedom and the Limits of Antitrust, *supra* note 231, at 3.
252. FED. TRADE COMM'N, TO PROMOTE INNOVATION: THE PROPER BALANCE OF COMPETITION AND PATENT LAW AND POLICY 3 (2003), *at* http://www.ftc.gov/os/2003/10/innovationrpt.pdf.
253. *Id.* at 4-17 (summarizing recommendations).
254. Bonito Boats v. Thunder Craft Boats, 489 U.S. 141, 162 (1989).

be considered in the fact-intensive, effects-based analysis of unilateral conduct, concerted action, and mergers and acquisitions under modern U.S. antitrust practice.

CHAPTER III

THE HISTORICAL TREATMENT OF INTELLECTUAL PROPERTY ISSUES IN ANTITRUST CASES

Over the years, courts and the antitrust enforcement agencies have taken a number of different approaches regarding the extent to which antitrust law may impact the enforcement and licensing of intellectual property. During the first 40 years after the passage of the Sherman Act, courts generally treated the activities of intellectual property owners with a great deal of deference. That changed during the middle half of the 20th century, as courts began to develop theories of per se illegality with regard to many types of licensing restrictions. The enforcement agencies followed this trend, as illustrated by the creation of the infamous "Nine No-No's" during the late 1960s and early 1970s, which identified nine specific licensing activities that the Department of Justice deemed to be per se unlawful. However, during the late 1970s and early 1980s, the economic effects of licensing restrictions received more detailed examination, and courts and the agencies began to view antitrust and intellectual property law as being complementary to each other. This regime continues today, though recent decisions by the Court of Appeals for the Federal Circuit have created a quiet but growing concern that that very influential court may be developing a view that awards primacy to intellectual property law over antitrust law.

A. From Per Se Legality to Rule of Reason: 1890-1931

The enactment of the Sherman Act[1] in 1890 had little immediate impact on intellectual property owners. The judicial attitude toward the conduct of patent holders prevailing at the time is well expressed in an influential decision from the Sixth Circuit Court of Appeals often referred to as "the Button-Fastener Case."[2] This decision gave great

---

1. 26 Stat. 209, 15 U.S.C. §§ 1-7. Section 1 of the Sherman Act applies to actions taken by two or more persons or entities acting in concert. Section 2 applies to conduct by a single economic actor and prohibits both monopolization and attempted monopolization.
2. Heaton-Peninsular Button-Fastener Co. v. Eureka Specialty Co., 77 F. 288 (6th Cir. 1896) ("the Button-Fastener Case") (overruling defendants' demurrer to a complaint asserting that defendants' sale of fasteners for

deference to patent holders, and for more than 20 years thereafter it figured prominently in Supreme Court opinions rejecting challenges to patentees' conduct in licensing and asserting their patents. Relying on the rationale set forth in the Button-Fastener Case, the Supreme Court issued decisions in cases such as *E. Bement & Sons v. National Harrow*[3] and *Henry v. A.B. Dick Co.*[4] that upheld the rights of patent holders to use their patents in ways that might now be held to be anticompetitive. Under this regime, provided the patentee did not try to use a patented invention to contravene the police power of a state,[5] he would encounter few antitrust limitations in exploiting his patent. Emboldened, patentees began to overreach in the manner in which they licensed and enforced their patents, and in time the Court became willing to reconsider the extraordinary deference that these early cases established.

The Button-Fastener Case, decided scarcely six years after passage of the Sherman Act, upheld a tying arrangement in which the sale of a patented button-fastening machine was conditioned upon the requirement that the purchaser also must buy from the patentee the unpatented fasteners to be used with the machine. The patentee sold its patented machines to shoe dealers at cost, intending to profit from the sale of the unpatented fasteners.[6] When a competitor began selling fasteners to shoe dealers for use in the machines, the patentee sued for contributory infringement, and the dispute ultimately reached the Sixth Circuit.[7] Asking "upon what authority are we to circumscribe the exercise of the

---

use with the patented machine constituted contributory patent infringement). The author of the Button-Fastener decision was Circuit Judge Horace H. Lurton, who later served on the U.S. Supreme Court from 1909-1914, and who would author the majority opinion in the *Henry v. A.B. Dick* case, *infra*, in 1912.

3.   186 U.S. 70 (1902).

4.   224 U.S. 1 (1912).

5.   *See* Patterson v. Kentucky, 97 U.S. 501 (1878) (holding that the existence of a patent on an improved burning oil did not authorize the patentee to continue selling patented oil in violation of order of state inspector, who condemned the oil as unsafe); Vannini v. Paine, 1 Har. 65 (Del. 1832) (declining to permit patentee to enforce patent on method of conducting lotteries, in view of then-extant Delaware law criminalizing operation of a lottery).

6.   *Heaton-Peninsular Button-Fastener Co.*, 77 F. at 289.

7.   *Id.* The district court sustained the defendant's demurrer, and dismissed the complaint; the patentee appealed to the Sixth Circuit. *Id.* at 288.

privileges awarded a patentee,"[8] the Sixth Circuit declined to find the patentee's conduct violative of public policy:

> The monopoly in the unpatented staple results as an incident from the monopoly in the use of complainant's invention, and is therefore a legitimate result of the patentee's control over the use of his invention by others. Depending, as such a monopoly would, upon the merits of the invention to which it is a mere incident, it is neither obnoxious to public policy, nor an illegal restraint of trade.[9]

The Button-Fastener Case reflected the prevailing attitude toward patent rights, and a lengthy quotation from the case figured prominently in the first antitrust challenge to a patent license to come before the Supreme Court—*E. Bement & Sons v. National Harrow Co.*[10]

National Harrow was a patent pool that controlled the vast majority of domestic manufacturing and sales of float spring tooth harrows. The pool fixed the prices at which a pool member could sell products made under the National Harrow license.[11] Bement, a licensee, was alleged to have violated certain license agreements, and National Harrow brought suit for liquidated damages and to compel specific performance.[12] Bement defended by asserting that the pool and its license agreements violated the Sherman Act.[13]

The Court disagreed. After quoting extensively from the Button-Fastener Case, the Court stated:

> [T]he general rule is absolute freedom in the use or sale of rights under the patent laws of the United States. The very object of these laws is monopoly, and the rule is, with few exceptions, that any conditions which are not in their very nature illegal with regard to this kind of property, imposed by the patentee and agreed to by the licensee for the right to manufacture or use or sell the article, will be upheld by the

---

8.   *Id.* at 294 (finding caution to be "[e]specially ... applicable when we sit in judgment upon the limitations which a patentee may put upon the use of his invention").

9.   *Id.* at 296.

10.   186 U.S. 70 (1902).

11.   *Id.* at 72.

12.   *Id.* at 71.

13.   *Id.* at 75-76.

courts. The fact that the conditions in the contracts keep up the monopoly or fix prices does not render them illegal.[14]

The Court admitted that its prior decisions had held the Sherman Act applicable to any and all restraints of commerce, regardless of the reasonableness of the restraint. Nonetheless, the Court held that such restraints were distinguishable from those that a patentee may impose when licensing a patented invention, and decided that the Sherman Act

> clearly does not refer to that kind of a restraint of interstate commerce which may arise from reasonable and legal conditions imposed upon the assignee or licensee of a patent by the owner thereof, restricting the terms upon which the article may be used, and the price to be demanded therefor. Such a construction of the act, we have no doubt, was never contemplated by its framers.[15]

Ten years after *Bement*, the Court again afforded great deference to a patentee's licensing practices in deciding the case of *Henry v. A.B. Dick Co.*[16] The facts in *A.B. Dick* were not unlike those in the Button-Fastener Case. The plaintiff sold a patented mimeograph machine with a label on it stating that the machine had been sold with the license restriction that only the plaintiff's stencil paper, ink, and other supplies could be used with it. The defendant sold a can of ink to an owner of one of the machines with knowledge of the license agreement and that the ink would be used with the patented machine. The plaintiff then brought suit, alleging that this conduct constituted contributory patent infringement.

The Court agreed. Justice Horace Lurton—the author of the Sixth Circuit's opinion in the Button-Fastener Case—authored the opinion. Emphasizing that the rights of a patentee amounted to a monopoly derived from the Constitution itself,[17] and that in *Bement* the Court had sanctioned the price-fixing arrangement employed by the National Harrow's patent pool,[18] the Court held that the license restrictions were

---

14.   *Id.* at 91.
15.   *Id.* at 92.
16.   224 U.S. 1 (1912).
17.   *Id.* at 27 (describing the patent statute as "a statute creating and protecting a monopoly. It is a true monopoly, one having its origin in the ultimate authority, the Constitution.").
18.   *Id.* at 31. Of the price-fixing agreement in *Bement*, Justice Lurton wrote:

lawful. To the Court, only Congress had the power to restrain a patentee's conduct in making use of its patent:

> It must not be forgotten that we are dealing with a constitutional and statutory monopoly.... We are not at liberty to say that the Constitution has unwisely provided for granting a monopolistic right to inventors, or that Congress has unwisely failed to impose limitations upon the inventor's exclusive right of use. And if it be that the ingenuity of patentees in devising ways in which to reap the benefit of their discoveries requires to be restrained, Congress alone has the power to determine what restraints shall be imposed. As the law now stands it contains none, and the duty which rests upon this and upon every other court is to expound the law as it is written.[19]

A.B. Dick could be called the high-water mark of judicial deference toward patentees. One consequence of the Court's decision was that it dramatically increased the degree to which patentees attempted to control markets for staple and nonstaple goods through the use of conditional patent licenses.[20] Another consequence, however, was that it spurred congressional action. Two years after *A.B. Dick*, Congress enacted Section 3 of the Clayton Act,[21] partially in response to the *A.B. Dick* decision.[22] Section 3 prohibits the use of restrictions in leases or contracts for sale that prevent the lessee/purchaser from using the supplies or commodities of the competitors of the lessor/seller, if the

---

> If the stipulation in an agreement between the patentees and dealers in patented articles, which, among other things, fixed a price below which the patented articles should not be sold, would be a reasonable and valid condition, it must follow that any other reasonable stipulation, not inherently violative of some substantive law, imposed by a patentee as part of a sale of a patented machine, would be equally valid and enforceable.
>
> *Id.*

19. *Id.* at 35.
20. Dawson Chem. v. Rohm & Haas Co., 448 U.S. 176, 191 (1980) (evaluating the impact of *A.B. Dick*).
21. 38 Stat. 731, 15 U.S.C. § 14.
22. IBM v. United States, 298 U.S. 131, 137 (1936) (citing the *A.B. Dick* decision as a factor motivating the enactment of § 3 of the Clayton Act); *Dawson Chem.*, 448 U.S. at 191 n.10 (same).

restriction may substantially lessen competition or tend to create a monopoly.[23]

The Court's attitude toward intellectual property changed as well after *A.B. Dick*, and in coming years patentees would no longer receive the near-absolute deference they previously had enjoyed. Shortly after *A.B. Dick*, the Court upheld a lower court decision breaking up a patent pooling arrangement that established a standard royalty for licenses under the pooled patents and fixed the prices at which preferential discounts could be offered.[24] In another case, the Court decided that a patentee could not license its patent so as to fix the price at which a patented article could be resold by its purchaser.[25] Each time, the Court resisted overruling *A.B. Dick*, until 1917, when the Court took up the Motion Picture Patents case.

In *Motion Picture Patents Co. v. Universal Film Mfg. Co.*,[26] the Motion Picture Patents Company conditionally licensed its patented movie projection equipment upon the requirement that only its own unpatented films could be used with the projector. Upon learning that a competitor, Universal, had sold two of Universal's films to one of Motion Picture Patents' licensees for use with the licensed projector, Motion Picture Patents sued Universal for contributory patent infringement.

The Court's approach in *Motion Picture Patents* differed markedly from its approach in prior cases. Rather than defer to the patentee's discretion in exploiting its constitutionally-sanctioned monopoly, the Court instead emphasized that the monopoly has discernible limits, i.e., the "scope of every patent is limited to the invention described in the

---

23.   38 Stat. 731, 15 U.S.C. § 14. Professor Areeda notes that "[a]lthough Sherman Act § 1 covers tying, the practice was not focused on until Clayton Act § 3 was enacted in 1914." 17 PHILLIP E. AREEDA & HERBERT HOVENKAMP, ANTITRUST LAW 462 n.4 (2004).

24.   Standard Sanitary Mfg. v. United States, 226 U.S. 20, 49 (1912) ("the Bathtub Case") (stating that "[r]ights conferred by patents are indeed very definite and extensive, but they do not give any more than other rights a universal license against positive prohibitions" such as the Sherman Act).

25.   Bauer v. O'Donnell, 229 U.S. 1, 14-16 (1913) (distinguishing *A.B. Dick* on the ground that it involved "a qualified sale for less than value for limited use with other articles only," and *Bement* on the ground that it was a state law contract dispute that did not involve construction of the patent statute).

26.   243 U.S. 502 (1917).

claims contained in it, read in light of the specification."[27]   Accordingly, in determining whether the use of Motion Picture Patents' projectors with a competitor's film in violation of the license agreement constituted infringement, the Court looked to the claims of the patent to determine its scope.

The patent's claims covered a portion of a mechanism that enabled film to be fed through the projector uniformly and accurately, without causing the film to wear prematurely. No claim covered the film to be fed through the projector or any other material to be used with it. In contrast, the license agreement was unconcerned with the mechanism covered by the patent's claims, but rather, was entirely concerned with the films to be fed through it.[28]

The Court rejected the suggestion that a patentee could validly restrict the use of a patented machine to use with unpatented supplies (e.g., film) that are not part of the patented machine itself. Such a restriction:

> is invalid because such a film is obviously not any part of the invention of the patent in suit; because it is an attempt, without statutory warrant, to continue the patent monopoly in this particular character of film after it has expired, and because to enforce it would be to create a monopoly in the manufacture and use of moving picture films, wholly outside of the patent in suit and of the patent law as we have interpreted it.[29]

In view of the clear conflict with *A.B. Dick*, the Court acknowledged that the *A.B. Dick* decision was overruled.[30]

With the *Motion Picture Patents* decision, intellectual property owners no longer could make use of their inventions in a way that exceeded the scope of the patent's claims. Patent holders seeking to license and enforce their patents would be forced to contemplate the

---

27.   *Id.* at 510 (comparing the scope of a patent to the description of real property in a deed, "which sets the bounds to the grant which it contains").
28.   *Id.* at 512 (stating that the license "attempts a restriction upon the use of the supplies only, and it cannot ... be termed a restriction upon the use of the machine itself").
29.   *Id.* at 518.
30.   *Id.* The Court did not, however, overrule *Bement*, the continuing vitality of which later was affirmed in *United States v. General Electric*, 272 U.S. 476, 493 (1926).

limitations that might be placed on their activities by antitrust law,[31] the strictures of which the Court in *Standard Oil* had determined were to be enforced according to the rule of reason.[32]

B. From Rule of Reason to Per Se Illegality and Nine No-No's: 1931-1979

After *Motion Picture Patents*, the pendulum began to swing toward greater antitrust enforcement.[33] This shift is seen most notably in the Nine No-No's and reflects an overall shift in antitrust law, as the Court began to hold many types of restrictions to be per se illegal. Contemporaneously, the widespread mistrust of patents led to the emergence of the patent misuse doctrine, which provided a means to halt enforcement of patents in cases where a patent holder's conduct was somehow objectionable.

1. The Emergence of the Per Se Rule

By the early 1940s, the Court had adopted the view that a patent should be presumed to confer market power without a detailed

---

31.   Indeed, in *United States v. United Shoe Machinery Corp.*, 247 U.S. 32 (1918), the Department of Justice challenged a package-license for shoe-making machinery. The Department's challenge rested on the grounds that the patentee forced licensees to accept something they did not want, and also served to foreclose licensees from contracting with suppliers of substitute machinery. Applying a rule of reason analysis, the Court ultimately rejected the government's argument, deciding that the licensees had been free to decline to take licenses from the patentee. The case marked the Supreme Court's first application of the Sherman Act to a conditional patent license. *See* Charles F. Rule, *Patent-Antitrust Policy: Looking Back and Ahead*, 59 ANTITRUST L.J. 729, 734 (1991).

32.   Standard Oil Co. of N.J. v. United States, 221 U.S. 1, 66 (1910).

33.   A notable exception is *United States v. General Electric*, 272 U.S. 476 (1926), in which patentee General Electric was permitted to fix the selling price of lightbulbs made by Westinghouse under GE's patents. The Court stated that the licensing condition fell "reasonably within the reward which the patentee by the grant of the patent is entitled to secure." *Id.* at 489. The Court did not clearly explain how it arrived at this view. In later years, *General Electric* would be limited, but never overruled. *See* Rule, *supra* note 31, at 733 (opining that "anyone following the General Electric case does so at his risk").

examination of market conditions.[34] In *International Salt Co. v. United States*,[35] the Court applied this presumption and held a tying arrangement to be illegal, even though the patent holder faced significant competition.

The government alleged that the International Salt Company violated Section 1 of the Sherman Act and Section 3 of the Clayton Act by leasing its patented machines only to lessees that agreed to use International Salt's unpatented salt.[36] The government obtained summary judgment, and International Salt appealed.[37] Before the Court, International Salt argued that the summary judgment was improper because it precluded determination of factual issues as to whether the licensing restrictions were reasonable under the Sherman Act, or substantially lessened competition or tended to create a monopoly in salt under the Clayton Act.[38] The Court disagreed, finding no factual issue to be resolved, and it held the tie to be per se unlawful because it limited competition in the market for salt.[39] As the Court explained, "it is unreasonable, per se, to foreclose competitors from any substantial market."[40]

International Salt was followed by *Northern Pacific Railway Co. v. United States*,[41] in which the government alleged that "preferential routing" clauses in a railroad's sales and leases of land violated the Sherman Act. The clauses required the purchaser or lessee to ship over the railroad's lines all items produced or manufactured on the sold or leased land, so long as the railroad's rates were equal to those of competing carriers.[42] Citing *Standard Oil*, the Court noted that Sherman Act violations generally were evaluated under the rule of reason.[43] However, the Court went on to state:

> [T]here are certain agreements or practices which because of their pernicious effect on competition and lack of any redeeming virtue are conclusively presumed to be unreasonable and therefore illegal without elaborate inquiry as to the precise harm they have caused or the

---

34. Rule, *supra* note 31, at 736.
35. 332 U.S. 392 (1947).
36. *Id.* at 393.
37. *Id.*
38. *Id.* at 396.
39. *Id.*
40. *Int'l Salt*, 332 U.S. at 396.
41. 356 U.S. 1 (1958).
42. *Id.* at 3.
43. *Id.* at 5.

business excuse for their use. This principle of *per se* unreasonableness not only makes the type of restraints which are proscribed by the Sherman Act more certain to the benefit of everyone concerned, but it also avoids the necessity for an incredibly complicated and prolonged economic investigation into the entire history of the industry involved, as well as related industries, in an effort to determine at large whether a particular restraint has been unreasonable—an inquiry so often wholly fruitless when undertaken.[44]

Examples of practices expressly identified by the Court as meriting per se treatment included price fixing, division of markets, group boycotts, and tying arrangements.[45] The Court went on to find that the preferential routing clauses at issue constituted tying arrangements that were illegal per se.[46]

In *United States v. Arnold Schwinn & Co.*,[47] the Court condemned vertical territorial and customer restraints as per se unlawful. Schwinn, a franchisor, assigned each of its wholesale distributors a specific territory within the United States, and required each to sell (1) only within their respective territories and (2) only to Schwinn franchisees.[48] Evaluating these restraints, the Court articulated a bright-line rule of per se illegality for vertical restrictions, stating that "[u]nder the Sherman Act, it is unreasonable without more for a manufacturer to seek to restrict and confine areas or persons with whom an article may be traded after the manufacturer has parted with dominion over it."[49] Although the Court seemed to have rejected a per se rule for vertical restrictions four years earlier,[50] the *Schwinn* Court did not discuss any reasons for this apparent change of course.

Consistent with the Court's broad application of the per se rule, the Department of Justice indicated on a number of occasions, during the late 1960s and early 1970s, that it viewed certain licensing practices as being sufficiently restrictive to constitute antitrust violations and put industry

---

44. *Id.*
45. *Id.* (citing *International Salt* for the proposition as to tying arrangements).
46. *Northern Pac. Ry. Co.*, 356 U.S. at 7-8.
47. 388 U.S. 365 (1967).
48. *Id.* at 371.
49. *Id.* at 379. The Court noted, however, that if the manufacturer retained title of the goods in question throughout the distribution chain until it reached the ultimate purchaser, the same territorial restraint would receive rule of reason treatment, rather than per se treatment. *Id.* at 379-80.
50. White Motor v. United States, 372 U.S. 253 (1963).

on notice that the Department would challenge these practices as per se unlawful. Nine patent licensing practices that the Department viewed as anticompetitive were singled out, and famously became known as the "Nine No-No's."[51] These practices included:

(1) requiring a licensee to purchase unpatented materials from the licensor;

(2) requiring a grantback of any patent that issued to the licensee after the execution of the licensing arrangement;

(3) restricting a purchaser of a patented product in the resale of that product;

(4) restricting a licensee's freedom to deal in products or services falling outside the scope of the patent;

(5) agreeing to refrain from granting further licenses to any other person without the licensee's consent;

(6) engaging in mandatory package licensing;

(7) conditioning the license upon the payment of royalties in an amount not reasonably related to the licensee's sales of products covered by the patent;

(8) restricting a licensee's sales of products made by the use of a patented process; and

(9) requiring a licensee to adhere to any specified or minimum price with respect to the licensee's sale of licensed products.[52]

The No-No's arose at roughly the height of per se enforcement[53] at a time when vertical territorial restraints were treated as unlawful per se and patents were presumed to confer monopolies upon their owners.[54]

---

51.   *See, e.g.*, Remarks of Bruce B. Wilson, Dep. Ass't Att'y Gen., Antitrust Div., before Annual Joint Meeting of Michigan State Bar Antitrust Law Section and Patent, Trademark, and Copyright Section, Detroit, Michigan, *reprinted in* 4 Trade Reg. Rep. (CCH) ¶ 13,126 (Sept. 21, 1972).

52.   *See id.*

53.   Edward G. Biester, III, *Finding Reason Through Extremes: From Nine No-No's to Patent "Immunity,"* 3 ANTITRUST AND INTELLECTUAL PROPERTY 26 (2002).

54.   *Id.* at 27; *see also* Sheila F. Anthony, *Antitrust and Intellectual Property Law: From Adversaries to Partners*, 28 AIPLA Q.J. 1, 5 (2000) (stating that the conduct prohibited by the No-No's "was suspect because courts and agencies still tended to infer market power from the existence of a

Though the No-No's ultimately fell from favor, they were not wholly without benefit. Each rule was easily comprehensible and facilitated antitrust counseling. As one commentator put it, "One drafting a license agreement in 1970 considering whether to include a grantback clause could just say no."[55] Nonetheless, the benefits afforded by the rules were outweighed by the degree that they inhibited procompetitive behavior.

Though the Agencies actively pursued enforcement of the Nine No-No's during the 1960s and 1970s, they did not always succeed in persuading courts of the per se illegality of these practices.[56] By the early 1980s, the Agencies had all but ceased active enforcement of these prohibitions.[57]

2. Evolution of the Patent Misuse Doctrine

In parallel with these changes in the antitrust treatment of intellectual property, the courts developed the patent misuse doctrine. This doctrine offers a means to limit a patentee's use of its patent rights separate and apart from antitrust laws.[58] Unlike an antitrust claim, patent misuse is not an affirmative claim giving rise to monetary damages.[59] Rather, patent misuse is a defense to a claim of patent infringement and a defense in breach of contract cases where a licensor seeks recovery of royalties unpaid under a license agreement. Also in contrast to an antitrust claim, a defendant may invoke the patent misuse doctrine even if the defendant was not itself harmed by the alleged misuse. The defendant need only

---

patent, without weighing the significance of substitutes for the patented technology or product").

55.   Biester, *supra* note 53, at 26.

56.   Rule, *supra* note 31, at 737 (stating that "despite rhetoric about the 'Nine No-No's,' the Department of Justice was spectacularly unsuccessful in pursuing some of those theories in the courts," and contending that efforts to enforce the Nine No-No's "did not prove to be a good investment of resources, regardless of one's view of current policy or past policy").

57.   *Id.* (identifying *United States v. Studiengesellschaft Kohle*, 670 F.2d 1122 (D.C. Cir. 1981) as the last significant agency action regarding the Nine No-No's).

58.   B. Braun Med. v. Abbott Labs., 124 F.3d 1419 (Fed. Cir. 1997).

59.   *Id.* at 1428 (noting that "patent misuse simply renders the patent unenforceable," and adding that "the defense of patent misuse may not be converted to an affirmative claim for damages simply by restyling it as a declaratory judgment counterclaim").

show that the patentee misused the patent against any entity,[60] and the defense renders the patent unenforceable until such time as the patentee cures its misuse. Moreover, the misuse doctrine is not limited to the patent context. Recently, an increasing number of copyright cases have involved assertions of copyright misuse.[61]

Motion Picture Patents is credited with originating the doctrine of patent misuse,[62] though the doctrine would not acquire that name until the 1940s. The *Motion Picture Patents* Court's denial of relief to the patentee emphasized the impropriety of the patentee's attempt to exceed the scope of the patent, thereby impermissibly extending the rights awarded it by the patent grant. Subsequent cases in the 1920s and 1930s gave the Court additional opportunities to apply the principles set forth in *Motion Picture Patents*.

In *Carbice Corp. v. American Patents Device Corp.*,[63] the Court upheld the dismissal of a suit for contributory patent infringement brought by a patentee and its exclusive licensee seeking to enjoin a

---

60. Thus a patentee's efforts to enforce its patent may be thwarted with far less proof under the patent misuse doctrine than under antitrust law. As Professor Areeda notes, "[t]he central policy question that has emerged is whether conduct that can be roughly analogized to conduct condemned by antitrust may be condemned as a patent misuse without the proofs necessary to establish an antitrust violation." 17 PHILLIP E. AREEDA & HERBERT HOVENKAMP, ANTITRUST LAW 462 n.4 (2004).

61. *See, e.g.*, Lasercomb Am., Inc. v. Reynolds, 911 F.2d 970 (4th Cir. 1990) (deciding that "the rationale of *Morton Salt* in establishing the misuse defense applies to copyrights"). In addition to the Fourth Circuit, other Circuit Courts of Appeal have applied the copyright misuse defense to hold a plaintiff's copyright unenforceable. *See, e.g.*, Alcatel USA v. DGI Tech., 166 F.3d 772 (5th Cir. 1999); Practice Mgmt. Info. v. AMA, 121 F.3d 516 (9th Cir. 1997), *as amended* Jan. 9, 1998. Still other courts of appeals have recognized the existence of a copyright misuse defense. *See, e.g.*, Video Pipeline v. Buena Vista Home Entm't, 342 F.3d 191 (3d Cir. 2003); DSC Communs. v. Pulse Communs., 170 F.3d 1354 (Fed. Cir. 1999); Bateman v. Mnemonics, Inc., 79 F.3d 1532 (11th Cir. 1996); Data Gen. Corp. v. Grumman Sys. Support Corp., 36 F.3d 1147 (1st Cir. 1994); United Tel. v. Johnson Publ'g, 855 F.2d 604 (8th Cir. 1988).

62. Though English cases involving the "abuse of patents" may be found that date back to the 1600s. HERBERT HOVENKAMP ET AL., IP AND ANTITRUST § 1.3 (2005 Supp.) (citing "the case of Mompesson and Mitchell, who were stripped of their patents and imprisoned for abusing the patent granted to them in the early part of the seventeenth century").

63. 283 U.S. 27 (1931).

competitor from selling unpatented dry ice for use in the refrigerated transportation packages covered by the patent. The patent claim included both the transportation package *and* the dry ice; in other words, though dry ice by itself was unpatented, the patent covered a transportation package that used dry ice.[64] *Carbice* did not therefore present precisely the same question as *Motion Picture Patents*. Unpatented film in *Motion Picture Patents* was merely used with a patented apparatus, whereas the unpatented dry ice in *Carbice* comprised a part of the patented transportation package.[65] But this distinction did not move the Court. Rather, because the *Carbice* plaintiffs sought to profit not from sales of the patented transportation packages, but from sales of unpatented supplies, the Court found *Motion Picture Patents* to be directly on point and denied relief.[66]

Similarly, in *Leitch Manufacturing v. Barber Co.*,[67] the Court declined to find contributory infringement by the seller of an unpatented emulsion for use by road builders practicing the plaintiff's patented process for curing road surfaces. Notably, *Leitch* did not involve an express license restriction or even an express license at all. Rather, the patentee refrained from suing road builders who purchased the unpatented emulsion from the patentee, but where a road builder purchased the emulsion from the patentee's competitors, the patentee sued the competing seller for contributory infringement.[68] The Court noted this distinction but dismissed it as insignificant, stating that "[e]very use of a patent as a means of obtaining a limited monopoly of unpatented material is prohibited," regardless of the method chosen by the patentee for seeking to obtain such unauthorized monopoly.[69]

The modern patent misuse doctrine was first articulated a few years later, in 1942, when the Court decided *Morton Salt Co. v. Suppiger Co.*[70] In contrast to the cases preceding *Morton Salt*, the majority of which involved the question of whether the patentee could enforce the patent to enjoin a competitor from selling an unpatented product for use with the

---

64.   *Id.* at 29-30.
65.   *Id.* at 33 (reciting the patentee's attempts to distinguish *Motion Picture Patents*).
66.   *Id.* at 31-32. The Court analogized the plaintiffs' attempt to monopolize the market for unpatented dry ice to the type of conduct found to violate the Sherman Act in the *Bathtub* case. *Id.* at 34.
67.   302 U.S. 458 (1938).
68.   *Id.* at 460-61.
69.   *Id.* at 463.
70.   314 U.S. 488 (1942).

patented invention, *Morton Salt* involved a plaintiff seeking to enforce its patent on a salt dispensing machine against a manufacturer of another machine that was alleged to infringe the plaintiff's patent. The wrinkle in the case was that the patentee leased its machine only to those who also purchased unpatented salt from the patentee.[71] To the Court, this raised the question whether the patentee could be permitted, under principles of equity, to enforce a patent that was being used to restrain competition in the market for unpatented salt.[72] Invoking the equitable doctrine of "unclean hands," the Court refused to permit the patent to be enforced "at least until it has been made to appear that the improper practice has been abandoned and the consequences of the misuse of the patent have been dissipated."[73]

In a companion case, *B.B. Chemical Co. v. Ellis*,[74] the Court made it clear that misuse did not permanently impair enforcement of a patent. Rather, once the patentee halted the activity constituting misuse, the patent again could be enforced.[75]

The modern patent misuse doctrine reached its zenith in 1944, in the *Mercoid* cases.[76] The patent in *Mercoid* covered a hot air furnace control system that included an unpatented combustion switch.[77] The patentee, Mid-Continent, had granted Minneapolis-Honeywell an exclusive license under the patent, including the right to sublicense others to practice the patented invention, in exchange for royalty payments to be based solely on Minneapolis-Honeywell's sales of the unpatented combustion switch.[78] Minneapolis-Honeywell only granted the right to install the patented control systems to those who purchased the unpatented switch

71. *Id.* at 491.
72. *Id.* at 490.
73. *Id.* at 493. The Court's view of the anticompetitive effects of the patentee's conduct differed from that of the court below, the Seventh Circuit Court of Appeals, which had held that the patentee had not been conclusively shown to have used its patent in a manner that substantially lessened competition or that tended to create a monopoly in salt tablets. G.S. Suppiger Co. v. Morton Salt Co., 117 F.2d 968, 972 (7th Cir. 1941).
74. 314 U.S. 495 (1942).
75. *Id.* at 498.
76. Mercoid Corp. v. Mid-Continent Inv., 320 U.S. 661 (1944); Mercoid Corp. v. Minneapolis-Honeywell Regulator, 320 U.S. 680 (1944).
77. 320 U.S. at 663-64 (describing the "Cross" patent, and noting that the combustion switch, while a part of the patented combination, was itself unpatented).
78. *Id.* at 663.

from it and used the switch in the control system.[79]   Notably, the
unpatented switch had no practical or commercial value apart from its
use as part of the patented control system.[80]   Any entity that purchased
the unpatented switch from a supplier other than Minneapolis-Honeywell
would have therefore done so only for the purpose of committing
infringement by installing the patented control system without license
from Mid-Continent or Minneapolis-Honeywell.

Mercoid also manufactured and sold unpatented switches for use in
the patented control system.[81]   Mid-Continent and Minneapolis-
Honeywell sued Mercoid, alleging that Mercoid's sale of the unpatented
switch for use in the patented system constituted contributory infringement.[82]   The Court assumed that Mercoid was indeed a contributory
infringer.[83]   But it refused to permit the enforcement of the patent against
Mercoid, holding that the actions of Mid-Continent and Minneapolis-
Honeywell constituted patent misuse,[84] because they were attempting to
restrain the market for the unpatented combustion switch,[85] which the
Court deemed beyond their rights as patentee and exclusive licensee.

Mercoid created a great deal of dissatisfaction that ultimately led to
three separate attempts to lobby Congress to limit the use of the patent
misuse doctrine. These efforts succeeded with the inclusion in the Patent
Act amendments of 1952 of Sections 271(c) and (d), by which Congress
sought to effectively reverse *Mercoid* and limit the patent misuse
doctrine.[86]

Section 271(c) provides that the sale of articles (other than staple
articles capable of substantial noninfringing use) that are a material part

---

79.   *Id.*
80.   *Id.* at 664.
81.   *Id.*
82.   *Id.* at 662.
83.   *Id.* at 668 (noting "we assume for the purposes of this case that Mercoid
       was a contributory infringer"); *id.* at 664 ("And we may assume that
       Mercoid did not act innocently. Indeed, the Circuit Court of Appeals said
       that it could find no use for the accused devices [the combustion
       switches] other than in the Cross combination patent.").
84.   *Id.* at 668.
85.   *Id.* at 667.
86.   *See Dawson Chem.*, 448 U.S. at 235 (White, J., dissenting) ("Congress
       enacted § 271 for the express purpose of reinstating the doctrine of
       contributory infringement as it had been developed by decisions prior to
       Mercoid, and of overruling any blanket invalidation of the doctrine that
       could be found in the *Mercoid* opinions." (quotation omitted)).

of a patented invention for use in infringing the patented invention constitutes contributory infringement when the sale is made with knowledge that the article will be used in committing infringement. Section 271(c) therefore prevents a patentee from controlling staple goods used in a patented invention without need for resort to the doctrine of patent misuse.[87]

Section 271(d) also limits the patent misuse doctrine. That section exempts the following activities from constituting misuse:

(1) deriv[ing] revenue from acts which if performed by another without [the patentee's] consent would constitute contributory infringement of the patent;

(2) licens[ing] or authoriz[ing] another to perform acts which if performed without [the patentee's] consent would constitute contributory infringement of the patent; and

(3) [seeking] to enforce ... patent rights against infringement or contributory infringement.[88]

Accordingly, Section 271(d) clarifies that a patentee can make and sell nonstaple goods for use in the patented invention, while excluding others from doing so without the patentee's license or authorization.

Congress became active again in 1988, enacting the Patent Misuse Reform Act,[89] which further limited the patent misuse doctrine. The legislation provides that the refusal to license a patent does not constitute misuse nor does the refusal to use any rights to the patent.[90] Moreover, tying or package licensing is not misuse unless the patentee is shown to have market power in the market for the tying patent or the tying patented product—i.e., market power is not presumed.[91]

Following the enactment of the Patent Misuse Reform Act and the issuance of several decisions of the Court of Appeals for the Federal Circuit that imposed additional requirements for a finding of patent

---

87. *Id.* at 200-01.
88. 35 U.S.C. § 271(d). The provision in § 271(d)(3) thus reined in the expansive reading given to the *Mercoid* cases by lower courts in decisions such as *Stroco Products v. Mullenbach*, 67 U.S.P.Q. 168, 170 (S.D. Cal. 1944), which had held that even the filing of a suit alleging contributory infringement could constitute patent misuse on the theory that such suit sought to restrain trade in unpatented materials.
89. 35 U.S.C. § 271(d)(4)-(5).
90. *Id.* § 271(d)(4).
91. *Id.* § 271(d)(5).

misuse,[92] the defense has become increasingly difficult to sustain, and commentators have remarked upon the existence of a "fundamental shift" away from the doctrine over the past 30 years.[93]

C. The Modern Era: 1980 to Present

Beginning with the Supreme Court's decision in *Continental T.V. v. GTE Sylvania Inc.*,[94] it became clear that the era of widespread condemnation of licensing restrictions as per se illegal was approaching its end. Though certain licensing restrictions, such as price fixing, still may be per se unlawful, courts and the enforcement agencies currently employ rule of reason analysis to a far greater degree than in the past. This is attributable in part to a great deal of economic research that demonstrated that patents and other forms of intellectual property do not necessarily confer market power. The trend has been to view intellectual property and antitrust as being complementary, as both bodies of law serve to benefit society by promoting competition. The actions of the enforcement agencies have mirrored this trend, as perhaps best exemplified by the promulgation in 1995 of the agencies' joint *Antitrust Guidelines for the Licensing of Intellectual Property*.[95] In recent years, however, concerns have developed that this period of relative harmony may be unsettled by Federal Circuit jurisprudence suggesting, at least in dicta, that that court may view intellectual property as prevailing over antitrust law when the laws conflict.

1. The View from the Courts: Harmonizing the Two Bodies of Law or a Return to Intellectual Property Trumping Antitrust?

a.   Vertical Restraints and the Rule of Reason

In *Sylvania*, the Supreme Court reconsidered the harsh rule it had laid down in *Schwinn*. Sylvania sold televisions directly to a select

---

92.   *See, e.g., In r e* Indep. Serv. Org. Antitrust Litig., 203 F.3d 1322 (Fed. Cir. 2000).

93.   HOVENKAMP, *supra* note 62, at 3.2.

94.   433 U.S. 36 (1977).

95.   U.S. DEP'T OF JUSTICE & FED. TRADE COMM'N, ANTITRUST GUIDELINES FOR THE LICENSING OF INTELLECTUAL PROPERTY (April 6, 1995) (hereinafter INTELLECTUAL PROPERTY GUIDELINES), *reprinted in* 4 Trade Reg. Rep. (CCH) ¶ 13,132 *and* Appendix 1 to this Handbook.

group of franchised retailers.[96] It limited the number of franchises it granted in a particular area and required its franchisees to sell Sylvania products only from the franchised location.[97] Continental, a franchisee, notified Sylvania of Continental's intent to transfer Sylvania products from one city to a new warehouse in another city.[98] Sylvania cancelled Continental's franchise, and a dispute ensued in which Continental alleged that Sylvania's franchise agreements violated Section 1 of the Sherman Act.[99] The Court found the case indistinguishable from *Schwinn* and thus was compelled to decide whether *Schwinn* should be overruled.[100]

In contrast to the approach taken in *Schwinn*, the *Sylvania* Court recognized that vertical restraints were capable of being used for procompetitive purposes. For example, vertical restrictions could be used by manufacturers entering a new market to encourage retailers to make capital and labor investments, which would improve the distribution of the new manufacturer's products.[101] The Court also noted that a more established manufacturer could use vertical restraints to encourage retailers to promote the manufacturer's products with greater energy or to provide facilities to service and repair the products.[102]

The Court therefore held that vertical restraints in general, and Sylvania's restraints specifically, do not necessarily have a "pernicious effect on competition" or "lack any redeeming virtue" as would be required to deem them unlawful per se.[103] Accordingly, the Court overruled *Schwinn* and decided that vertical restraints be analyzed under the rule of reason.[104]

Sylvania was an extremely important decision for the antitrust treatment of intellectual property. The case had a profound impact on the manner in which many types of intellectual property licensing restrictions would be analyzed, given that many licensing transactions have a significant vertical component. The influence of the Court's premise that a variety of procompetitive purposes may serve to motivate

---

96.   *Id.* at 38.
97.   *Id.*
98.   *Id.* at 39.
99.   *Id.* at 40.
100.   *GTE Sylvania*, 433 U.S. at 46.
101.   *Id.* at 55.
102.   *Id.*
103.   *Id.* at 58.
104.   *Id.* at 58-59.

a licensor to use vertical restraints[105] may be found throughout the current agency guidelines.

b. Common Objectives of Antitrust and Intellectual Property Law:
    Complementary Laws Designed to Stimulate or Protect Innovation

In the modern era, antitrust and intellectual property are harmonized to a greater degree than in the past. Indeed, the Federal Circuit has recognized this on a number of occasions. In *Loctite Corp. v. Ultraseal Ltd.*,[106] the court emphasized that "the patent system ... serves a very positive function in our system of competition, *i.e.*, the encouragement of investment-based risk. By so doing, it encourages innovation and its fruits: new jobs and new industries, new consumer goods and trade benefits."[107] This meshed well with antitrust law, the court noted, stating that "because the underlying goal of the antitrust laws is to promote competition, the patent and antitrust laws are complementary."[108]

The Federal Circuit echoed this theme in its decision in *Atari Games Corp. v. Nintendo of America, Inc.*,[109] stating that the "aims and objectives of patent and antitrust laws may seem, at first glance, wholly at odds. However, the two bodies of law are complementary, as both are aimed at encouraging innovation, industry and competition."[110]

c. Antitrust Limited by Intellectual Property Law:
    The Federal Circuit Response

Having recognized in *Loctite* and *Atari* the similarities between the objectives of antitrust law and intellectual property law, the Federal Circuit nonetheless has proceeded to issue decisions in recent years suggesting that, in some circumstances, antitrust law may be limited by intellectual property law.

For example, in *Nobelpharma AB v. Implant Innovations, Inc.*,[111] the court held that it would apply Federal Circuit law in considering the

---

105. Willard K. Tom & Joshua A. Newberg, *Antitrust and Intellectual Property: From Separate Spheres to Unified Field*, 66 ANTITRUST L.J. 167, 194-95 (1997).

106. 781 F.2d 861 (Fed. Cir. 1985).

107. *Id.* at 876-77.

108. *Id.* at 877.

109. 897 F.2d 1572 (Fed. Cir. 1990).

110. *Id.* at 1576.

111. 141 F.3d 1059 (Fed. Cir. 1998).

conduct element of a monopolization claim arising under Section 2 of the Sherman Act.[112] This decision reversed the court's history of applying regional circuit law in deciding antitrust claims.[113] The court based its decision to apply its own case law on the ground that the challenged conduct, the enforcement of a patent allegedly procured by the commission of fraud on the Patent Office, clearly implicated the court's own exclusive jurisdiction over appeals in patent cases.[114]

In another case, the Federal Circuit used expansive dicta that articulated a seemingly narrow perception of the limits that antitrust law may place on a patentee's freedom to use its intellectual property rights. In *In re Independent Service Organizations Antitrust Litigation*,[115] the Federal Circuit considered an antitrust action brought by CSU, L.L.C. against Xerox, in which CSU, an entity in the business of servicing Xerox equipment, alleged that Xerox's refusal to sell or license replacement parts or diagnostic equipment to CSU or other independent service organizations violated the Sherman Act.[116] The court noted the absence of any reported decisions imposing antitrust liability for a unilateral refusal to sell or license a patent,[117] and held that Xerox neither was obligated to sell or license its patented parts nor did it violate antitrust laws by declining to do so.[118]

More controversial than the result of the case was the language employed by the court in arriving at its decision:

> In the absence of any indication of unlawful tying, fraud on the Patent and Trademark Office or sham litigation, the patent holder may enforce the statutory right to exclude others from making, using or selling the claimed invention free from any liability under the antitrust laws.[119]

This language has been criticized as excessively deferential to an intellectual property owner's exercise of its statutory rights.[120]

---

112. *Id.* at 1067.
113. *See, e.g.,* Cygnus Thera. Sys. v. Alza Corp., 92 F.3d 1153, 1161 (Fed. Cir. 1996).
114. *Nobelpharma,* 141 F.3d at 1067.
115. 203 F.3d 1322 (Fed. Cir. 2000).
116. *Id.* at 1324.
117. *Id.* at 1326.
118. *Id.* at 1328.
119. *Id.* at 1327.
120. Robert Pitofsky, *Challenges of the New Economy: Issues at the Intersection of Antitrust and Intellectual Property,* 68 ANTITRUST L.J. 913, 921-22 (2001) (characterizing the decision as placing "extremely

Reviewing the case, former Federal Trade Commission Chairman Robert Pitofsky identified at least four examples of conduct that courts or the antitrust enforcement agencies previously have deemed to constitute antitrust violations, but that might fall outside the three exceptions articulated in *In re Independent Service Organizations*:

(1) a patentee's refusal to license its patent unless a purchaser agrees to refrain from purchasing from a potential competitor of the patentee;

(2) a patent owner, conspiring with downstream licensees, terminates the license previously granted to another licensee whose pricing was undercutting the other licensees;

(3) a patent pooling arrangement provides two potential competitors with the right to select the other's licensees; and

(4) a patent owner fraudulently induces a standard-setting body to adopt a standard that requires use of the patentee's product, then refuses to license the patent or licenses only at excessively high royalty rates.[121]

In *Unitherm Food Systems v. Swift Eckrich, Inc.*,[122] the Federal Circuit framed the issue before the court by using language that again could be read to suggest a view that patents may be only narrowly limited by antitrust strictures. The patentee in *Unitherm* had, after issuance of its patent, sent letters to users of equipment sold by Unitherm, threatening to enforce the patent against them.[123] Unitherm and one of the purchasers of its equipment brought a declaratory judgment suit against the patentee, alleging that the patent claims were invalid and unenforceable based upon certain prior art activities, including a prior demonstration of the invention by Unitherm to the

---

narrow limits on a virtually unfettered right of a patent holder to refuse to deal in order to achieve an anticompetitive objective"); Peter Boyle, Penelope Lister, & J. Clayton Everett, *Antitrust Law at the Federal Circuit: Red Light or Green Light at the IP-Antitrust Intersection?*, 69 ANTITRUST L.J. 739, 751 (2002) (finding that "the clear, overarching message" from the case "is that intellectual property rights trump the antitrust laws").

121.   Pitofsky, *supra* note 120, at 922-23.

122.   375 F.3d 1341 (Fed. Cir. 2004), *rev'd on other grounds*, 126 S. Ct. 980 (2006).

123.   *Id.* at 1344-45.

patentee, all occurring before the patentee filed its patent application.[124] The court agreed that the patent was invalid and unenforceable,[125] and further decided that the patentee's conduct constituted *Walker Process* fraud.[126] However, in evaluating the *Walker Process* claim, the court repeatedly characterized the issue in terms of whether or not the patentee's "antitrust immunity" could be stripped away by virtue of the patentee's conduct.[127] Commentators reviewing the *Unitherm* decision have noted that the issue could have been phrased differently—perhaps in terms that harmonized patent law and antitrust law—and thus could have avoided introducing additional confusion regarding the Federal Circuit's perception of the balance between antitrust and the rights of intellectual property owners.[128]

2. The View from the Agencies: Abandoning Nine No-No's; Embracing the Antitrust Guidelines for the Licensing of Intellectual Property

By the late 1980s, the Department of Justice had all but repudiated the Nine No-No's.[129] As noted earlier, the No-No's had arisen at a time when vertical territorial restraints were treated as unlawful per se, and patents were presumed to confer market power.[130] After the Court's decision in *Sylvania*, and concomitant with a growing recognition that

---

124. *Id.* at 1345.
125. *Id.* at 1354.
126. *Id.* at 1355-62.
127. *See, e.g., Unitherm,* 375 F.3d at 1355 (stating that if the patentee were shown to have procured the patent through the commission of fraud on the Patent Office, it "would lose its exemption from the antitrust laws"); *id.* at 1356 ("As a general rule, behavior conforming to the patent laws oriented towards procuring or enforcing a patent enjoys immunity from the antitrust laws."); *id.* at 1357 ("Federal Circuit antitrust law centers on a single critical question: What behavior by the patentee in procuring or in enforcing a patent can strip the patentee of antitrust immunity?").
128. James B. Kobak, Jr. & Robert P. Reznick, *Antitrust Liability for Statements About Intellectual Property: Unocal, Unitherm, and New Uncertainty,* 19 ANTITRUST 87, 90-91 (2004) ("For many antitrust lawyers, speaking in terms of stripping away an absolute immunity is an unusual way of framing these issues.... The Federal Circuit approach implies a potential far-reaching immunity for patents that is nowhere stated in the Patent Act or the Constitution ....").
129. Rule, *supra* note 31, at 732.
130. Biester, *supra* note 53, at 27.

the mere issuance of a patent did not automatically provide its owner with monopoly power, support for the No-No's eroded.[131]   Moreover, the agencies came to adopt the view that intellectual property licensing restrictions could be used to promote economic efficiency.[132]

In 1995, the Department of Justice and the Federal Trade Commission jointly issued *Antitrust Guidelines for the Licensing of Intellectual Property*.[133] The *Guidelines* do not have the force of law, and bind neither courts nor the agencies themselves. As a practical matter, however, the agencies are unlikely to challenge a license agreement that complies with the *Guidelines*, and courts often cite the *Guidelines* as persuasive authority on the antitrust legality of patent licenses.[134]

The *Guidelines* articulate three general principles: (1) the agencies view licensing arrangements as generally procompetitive;[135] (2) the agencies regard the use of intellectual property rights as being governed by the same antitrust principles that govern the use of other property rights;[136] and (3) the agencies do not presume that intellectual property creates market power.[137]

Under the *Guidelines*, the agencies will determine whether a licensing restraint merits rule of reason or per se treatment by evaluating whether the particular restraint is likely to contribute to an efficiency-enhancing integration of economic activity.[138] If the restraint appears

---

131. *Id.*
132. Rule, *supra* note 31, at 732.
133. INTELLECTUAL PROPERTY GUIDELINES,*su pra* note 95.
134. Adam Hemlock and Jennifer Wu, *U.S. Antitrust Implications of Patent Licensing*, 52 FED. LAWYER 39 (2005).
135. INTELLECTUAL PROPERTY GUIDELINES, *supra* note 95, § 2.0 (identifying the three general principles); *id.* § 2.3 ("By potentially increasing the expected returns from intellectual property, licensing also can increase the incentive for its creation and thus promote greater investment in research and development.").
136. *Id.* § 2.1 ("As with other forms of private property, certain types of conduct with respect to intellectual property may have anticompetitive effects against which the antitrust laws can and do protect. Intellectual property is thus neither particularly free from scrutiny under the antitrust laws, nor particularly suspect under them.").
137. *Id.* § 2.2 ("Although the intellectual property right confers the right to exclude with respect to the *specific* product, process or work in question, there will often be sufficient actual or potential close substitutes for such product, process, or work to prevent the exercise of market power.").
138. *Id.* § 3.4.

unlikely to lead to such integration, and the restraint is of a type that previously has been given per se treatment,[139] the agencies will challenge the restraint as being per se unlawful.[140]

The *Guidelines* also create a "safety zone" for certain licensing restrictions.   Section 4.3 states that the agencies generally will not challenge a restriction in an intellectual property license that is not facially anticompetitive, provided that the licensor and its licensees collectively represent no more than 20 percent of each relevant market that is significantly affected by the restriction in question.[141]   Moreover, the fact that a licensing restraint may fall outside the safety zone does not automatically render it anticompetitive; to the contrary, the *Guidelines* recognize the likelihood that the vast majority of licenses that do not fall within the safety zone nonetheless may be procompetitive.

The *Guidelines* also usefully set forth the agencies' views as to the type of analysis they may apply to certain specific licensing arrangements and restraints. Horizontal restraints often will receive rule of reason treatment, though certain restraints such as price fixing, market or customer allocation, output-reduction agreements, and certain group boycotts may be challenged as per se unlawful.[142] The *Guidelines* clarify that resale price maintenance in the intellectual property context will continue to receive per se treatment.[143]   The *Guidelines* describe the agencies' view of tying arrangements and clarify that the agencies recognize that proper analysis of tying arrangements requires consideration of both anticompetitive effects and procompetitive efficiencies that may occur as a result of the tie-in. The *Guidelines* go on to state that a tying arrangement is likely to be challenged by the agencies if (1) the seller has market power in the relevant market, (2) the tying arrangement adversely affects competition in the relevant market for the tied product, and (3) the anticompetitive effects of the tie are not outweighed by the efficiencies brought about by the tie.[144]

---

139. *Id.* (specifically identifying "naked price fixing, output restraints and market division among horizontal competitors, as well as certain group boycotts and resale price maintenance" as falling within this group).

140. *Id.* § 3.4.

141. *Id.* § 4.3 (stating that the safety zone "does not apply to those transfers of intellectual property rights to which a merger analysis is applied").

142. *Id.* § 5.1.

143. *Id.* § 5.2.

144. *Id.* § 5.3.

Regarding exclusive dealing[145] and grantbacks,[146] the agencies will continue to employ rule of reason analysis.[147] The *Guidelines* touch on cross-licensing and pooling arrangements, and indicate that the agencies recognize that these restraints are capable of procompetitive and anticompetitive effects.[148] Where either a cross-licensing or a pooling arrangement is used to accomplish naked price fixing or market division, the agencies will challenge such conduct as per se illegal; otherwise, the agencies will analyze the arrangement under the rule of reason.[149]

D. Conclusion

In the modern era, antitrust law and intellectual property law appear to have been harmonized to a greater degree than ever before. Moreover, the promulgation of the *Guidelines* provides both intellectual property and antitrust law practitioners with a significant degree of certainty as to the manner in which to analyze the restrictions in an intellectual property license. The enforcement agencies and courts currently make greater use of rule of reason analysis, in recognition of the procompetitive benefits that may be created through many types of vertical and horizontal restraints. The wild card appears to be the dicta employed by the Federal Circuit in a number of recent opinions, which could give rise to concerns that the court may be willing to return to a regime in which intellectual property again has primacy over antitrust law. Antitrust decisions by this court merit particularly close attention in the future.

---

145. Exclusive dealing restrictions prevent the licensee from using competing technologies. *See* INTELLECTUAL PROPERTY GUIDELINES, *supra* note 95, § 5.4.
146. *Id.* § 5.6.
147. *Id.* § 5.4 (exclusive dealing); § 5.6 (grantbacks).
148. *Id.* § 5.5.
149. *Id.*

CHAPTER IV

THE ANTITRUST ECONOMICS OF INTELLECTUAL PROPERTY

A. Introduction

Economic analyses of intellectual property typically involve theoretical and empirical studies of the connection between intellectual property rights and market performance. While these analyses often start with the general premise that innovative effort is stimulated by allowing innovators to obtain legally protected property rights to the product of their innovative efforts, economists have long recognized that this is just a starting point. As is explained more fully below, economists have come to recognize that the performance of markets can vary dramatically because of the complicated relationships between market structure and innovative effort and between existing property rights and incentives to pursue additional innovative effort.

Because antitrust law often calls for economic evaluations of the performance implications of particular market structures and the interaction of these market structures and contractual relationships that govern the use of intellectual property, antitrust analyses often require a rigorous examination of the complicated economic relationships that involve innovation. For example, as has long been recognized by both economists and legal scholars, there can be a conflict between promoting competition to maximize current output from society's existing resources (static efficiency) and maximizing output over time (dynamic efficiency) because the promotion of dynamic efficiency may require that innovators be given exclusive rights, such as patents, that reduce static efficiency.

Economists have come to recognize that when studying the economic relationships between market structure and market perform-ance when innovation is important, it can be important to distinguish between different types of innovation. In particular, economists distinguish between "process" innovation and "product" innovation. The former involves changes in the production process (which are designed to reduce the costs associated with producing a given product). The latter involves changes in the product itself (e.g., add new attributes or improve the quality of existing attributes). Less than a fourth of all U.S. industrial research and development (R&D) expenditures are devoted to

93

cost-saving ("process") developments. The rest is focused on product development and improvement.[1]

Economists have identified a number of fundamental characteristics of innovations and the innovative process that are helpful when considering competition policies that may affect innovative performance. These characteristics include:

(1)   Innovation is a process that proceeds through different stages. Stages that are commonly recognized by economists include invention, entrepreneurship, investment, development, and diffusion.[2] The capabilities necessary to meet the challenges raised during the different stages vary;

(2)   Innovation can be expensive, especially in the later stages;[3]

(3)   Much innovative activity is privately funded, although public funding plays an important role in some R&D efforts;[4]

(4)   Successful innovation is not certain—there is often a random component.[5] The risk of innovation can cause society to underinvest in innovative efforts.[6] However, at some point

1.   FREDERICK SCHERER, INNOVATION AND GROWTH 88 (1984).
2.   "Invention is the act or insight by which a new and promising technical possibility is worked out (at least mentally, and usually also physically) in its essential, most rudimentary form. Development is the lengthy sequence of detail-oriented technical activities, including trial-and-error testing, through which the original concept is modified and perfected until it is ready for commercial introduction. The entrepreneurial function involves deciding to go forward with the effort, organizing it, obtaining financial support, and cultivating the market. Investment is the act of risking funds for the venture.... [D]iffusion (or imitation) is the process by which an innovation comes into widespread use as one producer after another follows the pioneering firm's lead." FREDERICK SCHERER & DOUGLAS ROSS, INDUSTRIAL MARKET STRUCTURE AND ECONOMIC PERFORMANCE 616-17 (1990).
3.   SCHERER & ROSS, *su pra* note 2, at 619.
4.   For a discussion of federally funded programs, *see* Burnett & Scherer, *The Weapons Industry,* in THE STRUCTURE OF AMERICAN INDUSTRY (Walter Adams, ed., 8th ed. 1990).
5.   SCHERER & ROSS, *su pra* note 2, at 618.
6.   "[W]e expect a free enterprise economy to under invest in invention and research (as compared to the ideal) because it is risky, because the product can be appropriated only to a limited extent, and because of increasing returns to use. This under investment will be greater for more basic research." Kenneth J. Arrow, *Economic Welfare and the Allocation*

during the process, the riskiness of the innovation effort may decline significantly because more is known about the requirements to fully implement the innovation and the likely market acceptance of the innovation;[7]

(5)   The risk of innovative efforts varies across projects, and thus industries;[8]

(6)   The level of innovative activity varies across industries and firms. Historically, much of the industrial innovative activity has been concentrated in manufacturing firms.[9] The importance of manufacturing sector to R&D is particularly striking when one recognizes that the manufacturing sector contributes a relatively small percentage (less than 20 percent) of the gross domestic product;[10]

(7)   A relatively small portion of R&D expenditures (less than 5 percent) are for basic R&D (original investigations for the advancement of scientific knowledge, without specific commercial objectives). Much of this basic R&D is done by university, non-profit, and government labs.[11]   In fact, historically more than 50 percent of the basic R&D has been done by academic and non-profit labs and more than 20 percent has been done by government labs;[12]

(8)   Introduction of a successful innovation may require access to complementary capabilities or intellectual property. Supporting inventions may be required before the original innovation is technically or economically viable;[13]

---

of Resources for Invention, in THE RATE AND THE ALLOCATION OF RESOURCES FOR INVENTION 619 (Richard R. Nelson, ed., 1962).

7.   SCHERER & ROSS, *su pra* note 2, at 618-619.

8.   Edwin Mansfield, *Patents and Innovation: An Empirical Study*, 32 MGMT. SCI. 56 (1986).

9.   "The manufacturing sector conducts 97 percent of all industrial R&D and hence is the prime mover in generating technological progress. Among 238 U.S. manufacturing industries in 1977, the median industry devoted 0.8 percent of sales to company-financed R&D." SCHERER & ROSS, *supra* note 2, at 615.

10.   U.S. GOV'T PRTG. OFF., THE ECONOMIC REPORT OF THE PRESIDENT, (2002).

11.   SCHERER & ROSS, *supra* note 2, at 616;   Ronald E. Shrieves, *Market Structure and Innovation: A New Perspective*, 26 J. INDUS. ECON. 329 (1978).

12.   SCHERER & ROSS, *su pra* note 2, at 616.

13.   *Id.* at 618.

(9)   Inventions by one industry often must be accepted by another industry before consumers benefit.[14]   Indeed, studies have shown that innovative ideas often come from outside of the firm that implements them;[15] and

(10) Innovations vary with respect to the cost others incur to replicate and/or take advantage of the invention.   In some cases, it may be hard for others to free ride on the inventors' efforts, while in other situations it may be quite easy.

Given the importance of innovation and the fact that, if innovative ideas are not protected, there may be little incentive to undertake innovative efforts, it is not surprising that governmental policies, such as patent law, have been developed to provide at least transitory protection of an inventor's intellectual property. Part B of this Chapter, explores in more detail the rationales for patent protection, including a discussion of the optimal length/breadth of patents. It also reviews the "patent race literature," which focuses on the issue of whether patent rights in combination with certain industry structures may stimulate firms to expend too many resources on innovation. The section concludes with an overview of the empirical literature that assesses the extent to which patents are important to the stimulation of innovative activity.

Part C of this Chapter provides an overview of the economics literature that has explored the nature of relationships between market structure and innovative activity. As this review indicates, economists have long debated the nature of the relationship between innovation and market structure. Some economists have argued that innovation is a form of competition and, as a result, a market structure that encourages price competition is also likely to encourage innovation. Other economists, often citing the early work of Joseph Schumpeter, have argued that large firms, perhaps in concentrated markets, are more likely to support innovation than smaller firms.[16] Still other economists have argued that fundamental characteristics of the technology, along with other structural characteristics of the market, simultaneously interact to shape the nature of innovative activity and market structure.

---

14.   *Id.* at 616.

15.   James M. Utterback, *Innovation and the Diffusion of Technology*, 183 SCIENCE 620 (1974).

16.   JOSEPH SCHUMPETER, CAPITALISM, SOCIALISM, AND DEMOCRACY 106 (1942).

Part D of this Chapter provides an overview of three of the most important issues related to the economics of intellectual property. First, there is a discussion of the role of the patent system in preventing free-riding and encouraging the socially optimal level of innovation. A second topic is the role of transactions costs in the creation and licensing of intellectual property, particularly in the context of licensing where there is cumulative innovation. A final and related topic concerns the implications of overlapping patent rights, often called patent thickets. Important types of transactions costs emerging in this context are the "complements" and "hold-up" problems. Possible solutions to these problems such as cross-licensing and patent pools are suggested.

Part E of this chapter offers brief policy conclusions.

B. Intellectual Property and Innovation

1. Rationales for Patent Protection

There are four principal benefits or rationales of patent protection that are discussed in the literature. These rationales are: "Invention Motivation," "Invention Dissemination," "Invention Commercialization," and "Orderly Cumulative[17] Development of Invention."[18] These rationales are sometimes conflicting, or at least create conflicting issues. More importantly, the context of the innovation process presumed in the different rationales can be very different. Thus, it is not surprising that the theoretical and empirical work on optimal patents that is reviewed in this section has conflicting conclusions—depending on the particular patent rationale and underlying innovation context that lie beneath each model.

We will discuss each of the four rationales for patent protection in turn. It is helpful to understand the different perspectives provided by these four theories when considering the theoretical and empirical work that has been done on optimal patent life.

---

17. Cumulative innovation refers to a situation where subsequent innovations are dependent on preceding innovations. Noncumulative innovation is present when innovations occur in isolation, so the ability to proceed with an innovation is not dependent on others (e.g., because there are no blocking property rights).

18. We have adopted the rubric presented in Roberto Mazzoleni & Richard R. Nelson, *Economic Theories about the Benefits and Costs of Patents*, 32 J. ECON. ISS. 1031 (1998). These concepts are widely recognized.

a.   Theory 1—Invention Motivation

Economists have long recognized that patent protection can encourage innovation by increasing the returns from innovative activity. Absent patent protection, innovators cannot appropriate the full benefits of their innovation; some of the benefits go to "free riders" without payment.   Patent protection is said to restore appropriability and internalize externalities.   Note that the assumption here is that inventors cannot gain the full benefit of innovation by using a new product or process while keeping the relevant information secret to prevent rapid imitation.   Further, the "invention motivation" theory of patenting is generally couched in terms of invention as a one-time event, not a cumulative process whereby inventions build on each other.   Thus, increases in appropriability unambiguously increase innovation since, under this rationale, there is no offsetting retardation of later innovation that could result if follow-on innovation is deterred by the presence of a patent on the pioneering innovation.

There are costs associated with encouraging invention through patent protection.   Because patents restrict access to completed innovations and may allow the exercise of market power, there can be static costs to patent protection even under Theory 1.   Moreover, if we relax the assumptions of Theory 1, there can be dynamic costs, when extending the life of the first-mover's patent beyond the time period necessary to elicit the innovative activity by the first-mover deters innovation by others.   In addition, it is not always the case that more, or swifter, innovation is socially desirable.   For example, more invention may not be desirable if it results in wasteful patent races to be the first successful inventor.   Because of these offsetting potential costs to patent protection, there is an implied "optimal" patent duration and breadth that attempts to balance these factors.   Much of the theoretical literature on optimal patent protection attempts to explore this balancing.[19]

b.   Theory 2—Invention Dissemination

Economists have also considered whether patents may encourage the wider use of inventions.   They have recognized that patents may encourage dissemination of inventions because, absent patent protection,

---

19.   *See* discussion *infra*, §§ B, C, and D; *see also* Jerry R. Green & Suzanne Scotchmer, *On the Division of Profit in Sequential Innovation*, 26 RAND J. ECON. 20, 20-33 (1995).

inventors would be more likely to rely on secrecy to obtain their innovation rewards. Secrecy would both limit information flows to follow-on inventors and would discourage licensing of the innovation, both of which can benefit society. Unlike the first theory, where patenting is seen more as *restricting* the use of an invention, this theory stresses that patenting brings about *wider* dissemination. However, dissemination of the technology may be consistent with increased profits (and thus an increased incentive to innovate) when the patent holder earns royalties from the dissemination of the technology.[20]

Theory 2 is likely to have the most applicability when (a) the inventor by himself cannot exploit all uses of the invention and (b) secrecy would otherwise be effective in enabling the inventor to reap at least some returns. Some studies suggest that this is the case for many *process* innovations.[21] In these cases, to the extent that patents facilitate licensing, they increase the reward for disclosure relative to secrecy, and facilitate wider use. By contrast, for *product* (sometimes called "apparatus") innovations where secrecy may be less effective in the first instance as a means of appropriating returns, patents may do less to encourage disclosure.[22]

c. Theory 3—Invention Commercialization

Patents may induce development and commercialization of initial inventions that have little or no value in their initial form but need further development to be commercially valuable. More specifically, patents can facilitate exclusive licensing to entities who would invest in necessary development work. They can also induce initial inventors to become entrepreneurs.

---

20. The decision of whether to patent or not is discussed in Green & Scotchmer, *supra* note 19, and N. T. Gallini, *Patent Policy and Costly Imitation.* 23 RAND J. ECON. 52 (1992); *see also* James J. Anton, & Dennis A. Yao, *Little Patents and Big Secrets: Managing Intellectual Property,* 35 RAND J. OF ECON. 1 (2004) (modeling patenting not as a discrete decision and allowing firms to decide how much is the optimal amount that should be disclosed and how much kept secret).

21. *See, e.g.,* Richard C. Levin et al., *Appropriating the Returns from Industrial Research and Development,* BROOKINGS PAPERS ON ECON. ACTIVITY 783 (1987) (survey conducted by a group of Yale economists).

22. Patent lawyers often refer to these "product" innovations as "apparatus" innovations.

The need for patent protection to encourage firms to commercialize inventions is central to recent debates over whether patents should be granted for inventions that were developed through the use of government funds. The Bayh-Dole Act of 1980 gave universities and government labs patent rights even when their work has been supported by government funding. The rationale behind the Bayh-Dole Act is that, absent patent protection, key inventions would not be exploited because firms would not find it to be profitable to invest funds in the commercialization of the product because others would be able to free-ride on this investment. Opponents of Bayh-Dole have argued that there is no reason that patents cannot be taken out on subsequent development work or that the results of such development work cannot be undertaken in ways that offer other protections from free-riding. For example, a number of studies indicate that a simple head start on commercialization can yield large profits on a new product and that secrecy often can protect effectively new process technology used by the commercial developer.[23] If this is the case, a firm that commercializes the invention does not need a patent on the original invention to profit from commercialization of the product.

d.   Theory 4—Orderly Cumulative Development of Innovation[24]

Comprehensive, enforceable patents may encourage the orderly development of technologies that are inspired by an initial insight with strong follow-on or cumulative potential.[25] When an initial invention is likely to serve as the basis for a number of follow-on ("cumulative") inventions, an orderly, perhaps sequential, innovative effort can be

---

23.   *See, e.g.*, Levin, *supra* note 21; Mansfield, *supra* note 8; Wesley Cohen *Empirical Studies of Innovative Activity*, in HANDBOOK OF THE ECONOMICS OF INNOVATION AND TECHNOLOGICAL CHANGE 188-264 (P. Stoneman, ed., 1995).

24.   Theory 4 differs from Theory 3 in that, instead of positing that the initial invention has only one commercial product at the end of the invention process, the initial discovery or invention is seen as opening up a whole range of follow-on developments or inventions. Such a cumulative framework tends to set up a much richer set of theoretical modeling possibilities that is missing from the noncumulative framework underlying, in particular, Theory 1.

25.   These types of inventions are sometimes called "broad prospects" in acknowledgement of their cumulative potential.

significantly more efficient than a more haphazard approach.[26] In such a situation, it can be the case that broad patent rights that go to the pioneer innovator may facilitate the efficient development of the full range of follow-on possibilities by controlling the licensing terms and avoiding duplicative efforts. Furthermore, broad patent rights in a cumulative innovation environment can foster frontier innovation by giving the innovator the rights to develop or collect royalties from follow-on discoveries.

Economists have suggested that in markets where sequential innovation is likely, it may be efficient to grant the prospect-opening inventor sufficiently broad patent rights that the inventor has an incentive to create what has been termed "broad shoulders" for following innovations to stand on.[27] Moreover, it has been argued that the creation of "broad shoulders" is only possible by preventing, through broad patent protection, duplicative R&D that closely mimics the patent holder's patent.[28] However, economists have also recognized that broad patent protection, while needed to maximize the incentive to create "broad shoulders" at the initial stage, might also hinder inventive activity at later stages if efficient licensing opportunities prove to be hard to transact and follow-on innovation is hindered because of the resulting overreaching threat of infringement.[29]

---

26. *See* Suzanne Scotchmer, *Standing on the Shoulder of Giants: Cumulative Research and Patent Law,* 5 J. ECON. PERSP. 29, 29-41 (1991).
27. *Id.*
28. The inefficiencies that arise from duplicative efforts have been addressed in different frameworks. For an early study *see* Edmund W. Kitch, *The Nature and Function of the Patent System,* 20 J. L. & ECON. 265 (1977).
29. In Carmen Matutes, Pierre Regibeau, & Katharine Rockett, *Optimal Patent Design and the Diffusion of Innovations,* 27 RAND J. ECON. 60 (1996), the authors address the need for early disclosure while preserving the incentives to innovate.

2. *Optimal Patent Length/Breadth Literature—Non-Cumulative Framework*[30]

A significant portion of the economics literature that analyzes the optimal length and breadth of patents employs a static or noncumulative perspective.[31] This literature essentially comes out of a Theory 1 framework of appropriability; i.e., it is primarily concerned with providing the best incentive mechanism to develop a primary invention that has no follow-ons. In this literature, there is a tradeoff between providing adequate incentive for the inventor to innovate and the static efficiency loss associated with the monopoly power that may be conferred by the patent (assuming that there are no effective substitutes for the patent).

The literature on optimal patent life is generally connected to Nordhaus and Scherer.[32] This literature has been extended by Gilbert and Shapiro, Klemperer, and others to consider both optimal patent life and breadth simultaneously.[33] This latter literature chooses a combination of breadth and patent length that minimizes the welfare loss associated with a specific degree of innovation incentive.

Klemperer considers two kinds of welfare loss in a differentiated product model: (1) reductions in the consumption of the (patented)

---

30. The summary of the theoretical and empirical literature on optimal patent length provided here has particularly benefited from an earlier survey in Adam B. Jaffe, *The U.S. Patent System in Transition: Policy Innovation and the Innovation Process,* 29 RES. POL'Y 531 (1997). Jaffe surveys the major changes in patent policy and practice that have occurred over the last two decades and reviews some of the theoretical and empirical literature that bears on the expected effects of changes in patent policy on innovation.

31. When patents are noncumulative, the economic analysis is simplified because it does not reflect the connections between innovative efforts that exist in a more dynamic market environment where innovative efforts can build on each other.

32. WILLIAM D. NORDHAUS, INVENTION, GROWTH, AND WELFARE: A THEORETICAL TREATMENT OF TECHNOLOGICAL CHANGE (1969); F.M. Scherer, *Nordhaus's Theory of Optimal Patent Life: A Geometric Reinterpretation,* 62 AM. ECON. REV. 422 (1972).

33. Richard Gilbert & Carl Shapiro, *Optimal Patent Length and Breadth,* 21 RAND J. ECON. 106 (1990). The "breadth" of a patent refers to the range of applications that are covered by the patent. "Broad" patents cover more applications than "narrow" patents. Patent "scope" is often used synonymously with patent "breadth."

preferred product by switching to less-preferred products that are beyond the patent scope and so are sold competitively; and (2) simply not consuming the entire product class at all due to noncompetitive prices of the (preferred) patented product.[34] He concludes that if the reduction in consumption of the preferred product through substitution is the larger expected effect of extending patent breadth, then an optimal patent policy would be wider patents of shorter length (to eliminate inefficient shifts among closely substitutable products). He also finds that if simply not consuming the product at all is the larger expected effect of extending patent breadth, then an optimal patent policy would be more narrow patents of greater length (to eliminate the efficiency from not consuming). Gilbert and Shapiro's model,[35] since it is a homogeneous product model,[36] only recognizes the inefficiency connected with not consuming the product in question due to higher prices. Accordingly, their model generally finds that long-lived patents of narrow breadth are superior (again, to eliminate the inefficiency of not consuming).

Maintaining this framework of discrete innovations, Takalo proposes a stylized model that reconciles the earlier contradictory predictions regarding optimal patent breadth and length.[37] In particular, Takalo finds that if the marginal rate of substitution between patent length and breadth is larger on the incentive to innovate than on social welfare, an optimal patent has minimum life and maximum breadth. Conversely, maximum length is optimal if the marginal rate of substitution is larger on social welfare.

Gans and King extend Klemperer, Gilbert, and Shapiro's work by factoring into the analysis the timing of the innovation.[38] In this model the costs of the innovation vary over time. Contrary to Gilbert and Shapiro's results, in a model that adds the costs associated with timing, the optimal patent policy (which also has the best timing) has broader patents of finite length.

34. Paul Klemperer, *How Broad Should the Scope of Patent Protection Be?*, 21 RAND J. ECON. 113 (1990).
35. Gilbert & Shapiro, *supra* note 33.
36. Homogeneous products are products that are not distinguishable in the eyes of a consumer. In contrast, differentiated products differ in the eyes of a consumer.
37. Tuomas Takalo, *On the Optimal Patent Policy*, 14 FINNISH ECON. PAPER 33 (2001).
38. Joshua S. Gans & Stephen P. King, *Patent Length and the Timing of Innovative Activity*, IPRIA Working Paper (2005).

3. Patent Race Literature

A second strand of literature that analyzes the relationship between patents and innovation is the literature on patent races and "over fishing."[39]   When investment opportunities are public knowledge, multiple firms will have the opportunity to invest in innovation. In this environment, an optimal patent policy must take into account the strategic interaction between firms competing to develop the innovation. More competition is not necessarily efficient: firms might duplicate investments by entering races or engage in overinvestment.

The patent race literature calls into question one of the implicit assumptions underlying Theory 1. The strictest version of Theory 1 presumes that potential inventors work on *diverse and noncompeting ideas,* and thus that more inventive effort, and more inventors, means more useful inventing. Theory 1 takes on a different look if, instead, competition in R&D is allowed and firms are presumed to be *focused on a single research alternative* or a set of closely connected ones. In this latter setting, the patent race models point to a number of reasons why the increase in total inventive effort induced by the lure of a patent is not necessarily an unambiguous plus. If inventors perceive that *other* inventors are in the game, the expected returns will depend not simply on whether they achieve an invention, but on whether they achieve it *first.* Thus, patent protection may result in an outcome where firms invest their resources at a faster rate than the social optimum,[40] and too many firms will race toward the same inventive goal (or fish in a still limited "pool" of invention prospects).

Of course, this outcome will be less likely in industries where there is a wider menu of potential noninfringing ideas, such that different firms will pursue different approaches. In these industries broader patents will not deter innovative efforts since there is room for alternative noninfringing advancements. For this reason, some have suggested that an optimal patent policy ought to be *industry-specific,* allowing, for

---

39.   Early patent race models are found in Glen L. Loury, *Market Structure and Innovation,* 93 Q. J. ECON. 395 (1979) and Partha Dasgupta & Joseph E. Stiglitz, *Industrial Structure and the Nature of Innovative Activity,* 90 ECON. J. 266 (1980), which also analyzes "over fishing" models, as does Yoram Barzel, *Optimal Timing of Innovation,* 50 REV. ECON. & STAT. 348 (1968).

40.   Since economists have found that the social rate of return to R&D is often higher than the private rate of return, there may still be too little R&D even when there are patent races.

example, broad patent protection for industries such as the computer industry or telecommunications with many fertile, noncompeting ideas, but limiting patent breadth in certain other industry categories.

Denicolo has specifically attempted to extend the analysis of the optimal patent breadth-length mix to the case of a patent race where there is R&D competition.[41] Denicolo observes that the optimal patent breadth literature of Gilbert and Shapiro and Klemperer take the socially desired R&D investment as pre-specified and study the efficient way (least deadweight loss) to incentivize firms to invest in R&D of exactly that amount.[42] By contrast, Denicolo attempts to takes into account the effect of R&D competition itself on the incentive to innovate and, therefore, on the optimal patent breadth. Denicolo concludes that the more inefficient is R&D competition (in the sense that it spurs patent races), the broader and shorter patents should be. The reason is that inefficient R&D is less likely to be promoted by broad patents that limit competition.

Judd, Schmedders, and Yeltekin focus on identifying the optimal rules of a patent race and, in particular, what is the best combination of prize and accomplishment to grant the patent.[43] The optimal mix depends on the specifics of the model, but the model shows that, unless efficiency costs are low, patent races foster innovation and maximize social welfare.

4. Optimal Patent Length/Breadth Literature— Cumulative Framework

Another important strand of literature is that connected to the determination of optimal patent breadth in a world such as that posited in Theory 4, where there is cumulative innovation, i.e., a multistage process of inventions, changes to these initial inventions, and improvement. In this framework, an optimal patent policy is concerned both with providing the best incentive mechanism to develop a primary invention as well as to assure incentives for secondary follow-on inventions. When an innovation can be subject to successive improvements, the incentives of the initial inventor will depend on the potential to share the benefits

---

41. Vincenzo Denicolo, *Patent Races and Optimal Patent Breadth and Length*, 44 J. OF INDUS. ECON. 249 (1996).

42. Gilbert & Shapiro, *supra* note 33.

43. Kenneth L. Judd, Karl Schmedders & Sevin Yeltekin, *Optimal Rules for Patent Races. A Revised Version*, CMS-EMS Discussion Papers No. 1343 (August 2003).

from follow-on innovations. To the extent that the patent protection for the primary invention controls the development of the follow-on invention, the patent may become an instrument for orderly development of more innovation.

Kitch views this as a problem of optimal coordination among different researchers working on related technologies.[44] Without coordination, there is likely to be wasteful duplication of effort and possibly over-investment as firms try to be the first to break through. Kitch argues that granting broad patent rights to the initial pioneering inventor as a technology initially develops will rationalize the development process. Development will not stop, however, since the pioneering inventor would have an incentive to include in the development process other potential inventors with additional ideas or capabilities via licensing or other contractual arrangements.

Later work has increasingly emphasized the incentives of the potential follow-on inventors.[45] In this line of research, patent scope of the original invention is measured as the magnitude of improvement represented by a follow-on invention before it is either granted its own patent or held to infringe the original invention. For example, Green and Scotchmer show that in the case of sequential innovation where the follow-on innovations compete with the primary innovation, there could be inadequate incentive to invest in basic research.[46] According to Green and Scotchmer, an optimal patent policy will reduce this inefficiency by transferring profit to the first-generation innovators. Other literature in this line also confirms Kitch's view that broad patents should be granted to initial inventions that form the basis for a cumulative development line.[47] The intuition behind this result is that, absent a broad patent which allows the capture of positive externalities, the incentive to create broad "shoulders" for other inventors to stand on is socially inadequate. Scotchmer has even argued in some contexts that "second-generation"

44.   Edmund W. Kitch, *The Nature and Function of the Patent System*, 20 J. LAW & ECON. 265 (1977).

45.   *See, e.g.,* Scotchmer, *supra* note 26; Suzanne Scotchmer, *Protecting Early Innovators: Should Second-Generation Products Be Patentable*, 27 RAND J. ECON. 322 (1996) [hereinafter "*Early Innovators*"]; Green & Scotchmer, *supra* note 19; Howard F. Chang, *Patent Scope, Antitrust Policy, and Cumulative Innovation*, 26 RAND J. ECON. 34 (1995); Ted O'Donoghue et al., *Patent Breadth, Patent Life, and the Pace of Technological Progress*, 7 J. ECON. & MGMT. STRATEGY 1 (1998).

46.   Green & Scotchmer, *supra* note 19.

47.   Kitch, *supra* note 44.

products should not be patentable at all.[48]   This result, however, seemingly depends on the assumption that the trajectory of innovation is known, such that the first innovator will have an ex ante incentive to license its technology to the second whenever it is optimal to do so under terms that do not prevent the development of second-generation invention. Others have pointed out that this assumption may not be tenable in some situations given the uncertainty of future innovation paths. If the ex ante licensing assumption is not tenable, then there may be situations, particularly when we are dealing with inventions that are likely to spawn many fertile lines of subsequent cumulative invention, that infringing second-generation products will not be developed.

Hopenhayn and Mitchell explore how an optimal patent policy should take into account the fact that inventions differ in the extent to which they are likely to generate cumulative inventions and the speed with which they are likely to do so.[49] For example, if an innovation leads to multiple and rapid improvements, an initial innovation effort will likely require greater initial rewards (i.e., broader patents) in order to recover the value of the investment before the invention becomes rapidly obsolete. On the other hand, this broad patent protection might not be necessary when secondary improvements take place at a slower rate. Hopenhayn and Mitchell demonstrate how overall innovation incentives can be improved if patentees are offered a "menu" of combinations of patent duration and patent scope or breadth. Allowing patentees to choose different types of patents with different durations and different legal rights incentivizes them to reveal private knowledge regarding the fertility of their inventions and the likely speed of follow-on. This enables a better balance between the incentives of the initial and subsequent inventors than can be achieved with uniform patent scope.

It should be noted that Cornelli and Schankerman suggest in a slightly different context that patent policy should take account of the heterogeneity of innovation.[50] While Hopenhayn and Mitchell concentrate on heterogeneity between *innovations* in their future prospects, Cornelli and Schankerman consider optimal patent policy when R&D productivity differs across *firms*. They believe high R&D-productivity firms should receive greater patent protection than lower

---

48.   *Early Innovators,s upra* note 45.
49.   Hugo A. Hopenhayn & Matthew F. Mitchell, *Innovation Variety and Patent Breadth*, 32 RAND J. ECON. 152 (2001).
50.   Francesca Cornelli & Mark Schankerman, *Patent Renewal and R&D Incentives*, 30 RAND J. ECON. 197 (1999).

productivity firms. Since firm type is not observable they propose to use patent renewal fees as a mechanism to differentiate patent lives: firms with more valuable innovations will be willing to pay additional fees in order to renew the patent and extend the patent life.

Virtually all the systematic empirical work that has been done on the effects of patents has been guided by Theory 1, since it explores whether patents appear to provide an incentive to invent through increasing the effectiveness of appropriability. There have been several interview or survey studies that have explored the perceived importance of patents as a means of enabling firms to profit from their inventions, all of which have explored inter-industry differences.[51]

All of the empirical work in this area has come basically to the same conclusion—that patents are a particularly important inducement to invention in only a few industries. In pharmaceuticals, for example, patents seem to be an important part of the inducement for R&D. However, in industries like semiconductors and computers, the advantages that come with a head start—including setting up production, sales and service structures, and moving down the learning curve—were judged much more effective than patents as an inducement to R&D. In some of these industries, the respondents said that imitation was innately time-consuming and costly, even if there were no patent protection. In others, it was said that technology was moving so fast that patents were pointless. In any event, the empirical literature on appropriability certainly shows that there appear to be some industries where patents play a much smaller role than other forces in shaping the pattern of innovation. When we are looking at patent policy, we have to do so within the context of understanding how means other than patents induce invention and related activities. These other means include government grants and contracts, strong first-mover advantages, and rapid technological change.

There have also been several studies of the effects of different degrees of patent scope on invention. First, there are two studies *across countries*. Kortum and Lerner studied the significant increase in

---

51.   *See, e.g.*, Levin, *supra* note 21; Mansfield, *supra* note 8; Wesley M. Cohen, Richard R. Nelson, & John P. Walsh, *Protecting Their Intellectual Assets: Appropriability Conditions and Why U.S. Manufacturing Firms Patent (or Not)*, NBER Working Paper No. 7552 (2000).

patenting in the U.S. since the mid-1980s.[52] They looked at four possible explanations—the creation of the Court of Appeals for the Federal Circuit viewed as favorable for the scope of patent protection; favorable changes in the regulatory system; the development of new areas such as biotech and information technology; and increases in research productivity—and concluded that stronger patent protection and increased scope did not explain the surge in patenting; rather the main factor was judged to be an increase in the productivity of the research process. Sakakibara and Brandsetter estimate the impact of an apparent increase in the scope of Japanese patent protection starting in 1988, when Japan converted to a system much like that of the U.S. in which a single patent can have multiple claims.[53] They find no evidence of an increase in inventive activity, either in terms of overall R&D spending by Japanese firms or the number of innovations produced by Japanese firms in the US.

Nor is there compelling industry evidence on the effectiveness of changes in patent scope. Hall and Ziedonis analyzed the semiconductor industry, which is characterized by rapid technological change and cumulative innovation.[54] They did not find that stronger patent protection since the 1980s was driving the innovation effort or output of firms in the semiconductor industry. They found that patenting in this industry is driven by patent portfolio races aimed either to ensure access to technology and not be "held up" by rival patenting of the same technology, or to strengthen bargaining power when negotiating the access to other technology. Ziedonis found that this type of defensive patenting is stronger when markets of technology are more fragmented (i.e., the ownership of external technologies is fragmented).[55] More fragmented ownership increases the hold-up risk and defensive patenting can help avoid delays. Building on the work of Hall and Ziedonis,

52. Samuel Kortum & Josh Lerner, *Stronger Protection or Technological Revolution: What is Behind the Recent Surge in Patenting?*, 48 CARNEGIE-ROCHESTER SERIES ON PUBLIC POLICY, 247 (1998).
53. Mariko Sakakibara & Lee Branstetter, *Do Stronger Patents Induce More Innovation? Evidence From the 1988 Japanese Patent Law Reforms*, 32 RAND J. ECON. 77 (2001).
54. Bronwyn H. Hall & Rosemarie Ham Ziedonis, *The Patent Paradox Revisited: An Empirical Study of Patenting in the U.S. Semiconductor Industry, 1979-1995*, 32 RAND J. ECON. 101 (2001).
55. Rosemarie Ham Ziedonis, *Don't Fence Me In: Fragmented Markets for Technology and the Patent Acquisition Strategies of Firms*, 50 MGMT. SCI. 804 (2004).

Bessen and Hunt found a similar growth on the propensity for software patents.[56] After controlling for factors such as R&D expenses, this growth is explained by both changes in the patent law, which have made software patents more cost effective, and strategic patenting. They also found that this greater propensity did not in turn trigger greater investment in R&D.

In related research that helps explain the surge in patenting in the United States during the past decade, Sanyal and Jaffe confirmed the significance of the invention rate itself on driving patenting.[57] In addition they found evidence that relaxing the standards for patenting, and thereby increasing the likelihood of success at the patent office, increases patenting.

Other research examines the impact of the strength of patents on R&D and innovation from different angles. In a country-level study, Kanwar and Evenson found a positive correlation between the strength of intellectual property rights and R&D investment.[58] Their data correspond to 29 countries over a 20 year period. Finally, one study, by Merges and Nelson, presents evidence on how patent scope affects innovation in a cumulative setting.[59] Based on case studies of several important historical technologies, Merges and Nelson question the theoretical literature advocating broad patent protection for pioneering innovators in the context of cumulative innovation. The analytical basis for the disagreements is that Merges and Nelson believe that ex ante uncertainty and disagreement among competitors about which lines of development will be most fruitful makes licensing agreements or other such coordination mechanisms unlikely and/or ineffective. Examining the historical development of electrical lighting, automobiles, airplanes, and radio, they argue that the assertion of strong patent positions and disagreements about patent rights inhibited the broad development of the

56.   J. Bessen & R. M. Hunt, *An Empirical Look at Software Patents*, *Federal Reserve Bank of Philadelphia Working Paper* No. 03-17 (2004).

57.   P. Sanyal & A. B. Jaffe, *Peanut Butter Patents versus the New Economy: Does the Increased Rate of Patenting Signal More Invention or Just Lower Standards?* mimeo (2004).

58.   Sunil Kanwar & Robert E. Evenson, *Does Intellectual Property Protection Spur Technological Change?* 55 OXFORD ECON. PAPERS 235 (2003); *see also* Michael L. Katz & Janusz A. Ordover, *R&D Cooperation and Competition*, BROOKINGS PAPERS ON ECON. ACTIVITY, Special Issue, 137 (1990).

59.   Robert P. Merges & Richard R. Nelson, *On the Complex Economics of Patent Scope*, 90 COLUM. L. REV. 839 (1990).

technologies rather than aiding subsequent development. Johnson and Popp also examined the effect of patents on future innovation.[60] The American Inventors Protection Act of 2000 introduced changes that make patents public sooner—18 months after application. Opponents argue that these changes reduce the secrecy protections and facilitate imitation; proponents argue that more efficient innovation will take place as duplication is reduced. Employing U.S. patent data between 1976 and 1996, Johnson and Popp found that larger patents that take longer to be approved are cited more and hence are more likely to be affected by this change in legislation. However, the authors acknowledge that, in an environment of cumulative innovation, these changes should benefit society as a whole despite some inventors being worse off.

The theoretical literature on patent races and patent menus also lacks sufficient empirical evidence. Lerner studied patent race theory in the hard drive industry, finding that the leading firm is not the firm that innovates the most.[61] Cockburn and Henderson, however, did not find evidence of patent races in the pharmaceutical industry, with little correlation among firms' research investments.[62]

C. Market Structure and Innovation

This section focuses on the economics literature that relates market structure to innovation. In particular, it reviews economics literature that analyzes how market structure can affect innovation. The section not only identifies factors that may cause innovation to increase in competitive markets, but also considers the possibility that large firms in concentrated markets may undertake more innovative efforts. In addition, it considers the possibility that innovation and concentration levels are jointly determined by fundamental characteristics of the market, such as technological opportunities. This review surveys both theoretical and empirical literature.

---

60. Daniel K. N. Johnson & David Popp, *Forced Out of the Closet: The Impact of the American Inventors Protection Act on the Timing of Patent Disclosure*, 34 RAND J. ECON. 96 (2003).
61. Josh Lerner, *An Empirical Exploration of a Technology Race*, 28 RAND J. ECON. 228 (1997).
62. Iain Cockburn & Rebecca Henderson, *Racing to Invest? The Dynamics of Competition in Ethical Drug Discovery* 3 J. ECON. & MANAGEMENT STRATEGY 481 (1994).

1. Competition and Potential Competition Can Increase Innovative Activity

Economists have constructed theoretical models that indicate incentives associated with outperforming rivals can encourage competitive firms to innovate. In some cases, it is the lure of supranormal returns that encourages competitive firms to innovate. In others, innovative activity is promoted by the possibility that rivals will take customers, threatening the firm's long-run existence. In contrast, firms that are insulated from competitive pressures may chose a "quiet life"[63] and not undertake aggressive R&D programs.

In early work analyzing how the incentive to innovate varies across market structures, Arrow presented models in which a monopolist's incentive to innovate is always less than competitors' incentive to innovate.[64] His work uses a model in which the innovator licenses all firms that wish to use a cost-reducing innovation and that are willing to pay a royalty. Once the royalty is paid, all firms engage in perfect competition. In Arrow's model, which ignores the difficulties of appropriating the information generated by innovative efforts, a monopolist takes into account preinnovation profits and produces less output, which means that the monopolist will earn fewer incremental profits from process innovation.

Economists have expanded on this early work by studying the relationship between innovative activity and market structure in other game theoretic models.[65] For example, using a completely symmetric, Cournot-duopoly,[66] new product game,[67] economists have shown that, in

---

63. As Hicks commented, "The best of all monopoly profits is a quiet life," which implies that insulation from competition may lead to inefficient production and higher costs. J. R. Hicks, *Annual Survey of Economic Theory: The Theory of Monopoly*, 3 ECONOMETRICA 1 (1935).

64. Arrow, *supra* note 6, at 619.

65. Game theoretic models are models that predict market outcomes based on assumptions about the competitive interactions of firms. These competitive interactions are modeled by making behavioral assumptions about the firm strategies and the market outcomes that result when particular combinations of strategies are selected.

66. The Cournot model is an economic game in which the players each assume that the other players will maintain the output levels they produced in the previous period. A Cournot-duopoly is a Cournot game with two competing firms (players).

equilibrium,[68] both firms undertake more R&D than they would in the absence of rivalry.[69] Some economists argue that an uncooperative outcome to such games is particularly likely because competitors tend to overestimate their own R&D abilities and underestimate the capabilities of rivals.[70] Cooperative behavior (which includes both tacit and explicit collusion) is also less likely when R&D involves secret competitive activity which complicates the detection and punishment of cheating on a collusive outcome. Moreover, it has also been shown that an increase in the number of symmetric rivals can accelerate R&D, at least to some point.[71] However, if the number of rivals is too large, it may be that the returns from R&D that an individual firm can capture are viewed as too small to justify R&D (both because of the sharing of the rents among more firms and because the size of the rents that are to be shared is reduced due to increased price competition), causing firms to do no R&D.[72]

Yi extended Arrow's analysis to models that assume Cournot competition.[73] He found that for process innovation, if the innovation is not drastic (i.e., results in lower costs such that the firm's monopoly price is below the cost of incumbent firms), the benefit of a small process innovation decreases with the number of firms under certain conditions. Intuitively this is because the benefit of a process innovation is correlated with output of the firm, which declines as the number of firms increases. Since output increases with the lower price resulting from the innovation, it is also intuitive that the result depends on the elasticity of demand. For constant elasticity of demand, the benefit of a small innovation may increase or decrease with the number of firms up to and including three firms, but will decrease with more firms thereafter. These results hold for innovations up to the size of "almost drastic."[74]

67. A new product game is a game in which at least one player has the option of introducing a new product.
68. Equilibrium occurs when no market actor has an incentive to change its behavior given the actions of the other market actors.
69. SCHERER & ROSS, *su pra* note 2, at 634.
70. William Fellner, *The Influence of Market Structure on Technological Progress*, 65 Q. J. ECON. 556-77 (1951).
71. SCHERER & ROSS, *su pra* note 2, at 636.
72. *Id.* at 636-37.
73. Sang-Seung Yi, *Market Structure and Incentives to Innovate: The Case of Cournot Oligopoly*, 65 ECON. LETTERS 379 (1999).
74. An innovation is defined to be drastic if the innovating firm's monopoly price is below the other firms' marginal costs.

Boone generalized the results to include a parametric measure of the intensity of competition with Bertrand[75] and Cournot competition as special cases. Boone considers firms with differing costs.[76] He also assumes that the number of firms is determined endogenously by the cost history and the intensity of competition. The model uses three firms located in a triangle. Intensity of competition is measured by the inverse of travel cost. Boone assumes that the value paid by the highest bidder is positively correlated with the speed of technological progress. The discount factor is assumed to be constant across firms. In his model, the intensity of competition determines whether the lowest cost firm will purchase the innovation and at what value. He finds that under his assumptions, in weakly competitive industries with a stream of small innovations, a small rise in competition may reduce the speed of technological progress. He also finds that if competition is intense and innovations lead to major changes in technology, small increases in competition may speed innovation because the leader is under pressure to innovate as a failure to innovate would cause the leader to lose its competitive advantage.

As is explained in more detail above in the analysis of patent races, firms that perceive competition for technical opportunities may have a strong incentive to innovate. However, firms that see that they are behind in an innovation race may slow down their R&D efforts since they perceive that there are fewer returns from such an effort.[77]

Economists have shown that the threat of competition may lead to more innovation by incumbents, relative to potential entrants.[78] For example, Gilbert and Newbery have shown that, under certain conditions, incumbents will have a greater marginal incentive to invest in

---

75.   Bertrand competition is an economic game in which competitors all assume that the other competitors will charge the same price that they charged in the previous period. It differs from Cournot competition because it focuses on prices as the competitive variable, rather than quantities (which Cournot competitors assume will not change between periods).

76.   Jan Boone, *Intensity of Competition and the Incentive to Innovate*, 19 INT'L J. INDUS. ORG. 705 (2001).

77.   *See, e.g.*, F. M. Scherer, *Market Structure and the Employment of Scientists and Engineers*, 57 AM. ECON. REV. 524-31 (1967); Gene M. Grossman & Carl Shapiro, *Dynamic R&D Competition*, 97 ECON. J. 372-87 (1987).

78.   For a discussion of this literature, see also JEAN TIROLE, THE THEORY OF INDUSTRIAL ORGANIZATION 394-99 (1994).

R&D than will entrants when entry is a serious threat.[79] This encourages preemptive patenting, leading to industries that tend to remain monopolized by the same firm. The monopolist will preemptively invest in R&D if the cost is less than the profits it would earn by preventing entry.[80]

Extending the work of Gilbert and Newbery, Reinganum assumed that the inventive process is stochastic rather than deterministic.[81] As a result of this changed assumption, Reinganum found that an incumbent will invest less on a given project than will a potential entrant. In the Reinganum model, the incumbent firm receives a flow of profits while it is in the process of innovating. The greater the investments that the firm makes in R&D, the sooner its existing product will be replaced and the shorter will be the period of time during which it receives the profit flow from its existing product. The incumbent effectively replaces its existing product with a more profitable product. Since an entrant profits from the results of its R&D, but has nothing in the market that will be displaced by the new product, the entrant has a greater marginal incentive to invest in R&D than does the incumbent.

Lin extended the Reinganum model using a two-stage game.[82] Firms compete in the first stage, then engage in a patent race. Firms behave so as to soften rivals' incentive for future R&D. The result is an equilibrium price that is higher than in the standard duopoly models and a slower pace of innovation than the standard duopoly equilibrium outcome. Coordination of R&D (e.g., through the formation of a joint venture by the competitors) eliminates the R&D threat and permits the standard duopoly outcome to be obtained. The results hold for both Cournot and Bertrand models. The welfare effects are ambiguous, depending on the degree of wasteful R&D in the patent race and the effect of the reduced product market price from cooperation.

---

79. Richard J. Gilbert & David M. G. Newbery, *Preemptive Patenting and the Persistence of Monopoly*, 72 AMER. ECON. REV. 514 (1982).
80. One key assumption in this work is that the date of an invention is a deterministic function of the time path of expenditures.
81. Jennifer F. Reinganum, *Uncertain Innovation and the Persistence of Monopoly*, 83 AMER.E CON. REV. 741 (1983). An inventive process that is "stochastic" has a random (uncertain) component to it. In contrast, a deterministic process is perfectly predictable given knowledge of the underlying behavioral relationships.
82. Ping Lin, *Product Market Competition and R&D Rivalry*, 58 ECON. LETTERS 105 (1998).

Harris and Vickers extend the Gilbert and Newbery model by distinguishing two kinds of patent races.[83]   A "standard race" is one in which a price is awarded to the first player to reach the finish line. In an "asymmetrical race" a prize is awarded if someone reaches the finish line, but it is also true that one player loses something of value if one of his rivals reaches the finish line (and as a result this player is content if nobody wins). Harris and Vickers model asymmetrical races, since they believe that this provides insights into patent races in which an incumbent firm's principal, if not sole, concern is preventing potential rivals from entering its market.   They found that in a model of an asymmetrical race the challenger is often deterred from making an effort to win the race because strategic interactions are such that incumbents would outdo any reasonable effort by the challenger. Moreover, to deter the challenger, the incumbent often does not need to complete the patent itself.   On the other hand, there are some situations in which the challenger does proceed and cross the finish line first. Nonetheless, they concluded that among the strategic advantages that an incumbent firm might enjoy in patent races (especially when the parties begin far from the finish line) is the possibility that the incumbent will benefit from a result in which no one wins the patent race. Moreover, they suggest that this strategic advantage may underlie the persistence of market power in some markets.[84]

Katz and Shapiro considered the possibility that a firm might benefit from its rival's innovation.[85]   In their model, each firm separately compares the profits that it would earn assuming no innovation with the profits that it would earn should it be the innovator and with the profits it would earn if a competitor does the innovating. The authors note that when patents are not perfect, and the innovation is not essential to survival, imitation might occur. If a firm can imitate its rival quickly, effectively, and at low cost, it may benefit from a discovery made by a competitor. Even when patents are so strong that imitation is impossible, licensing may allow a firm to profit from a rival's innovation. For minor innovations, Katz and Shapiro found that the industry leader will typically be the innovator, whether or not imitation and licensing are feasible. In markets where patent protection is strong, they found that

---

83.   Christopher Harris & John Vickers, *Patent Races and the Persistence of Monopoly*, 33 J. INDUS. ECON. 461 (1985).

84.   *Id.* at 477.

85.   Michael L. Katz & Carl Shapiro, *R&D Rivalry with Licensing or Imitation*, 77 AMER. ECON. REV. 402 (1987).

major innovations will be made by industry leaders. But if imitation is easy, the innovators will be smaller firms or entrants.

Boone noted that an individual company's response to competitive pressure will depend on its own cost level relative to those of its opponents.[86] As a result, the effects of competitive pressure on the innovation response of firms will differ across firms. Because of this, any study that tries to find a single innovation response for all firms in an industry will be flawed. An increase in competitive pressure may raise some firms' incentives to innovate, but decrease those of other firms. Also, Boone showed that an increase in competitive pressure cannot increase incentives for both fundamental research and development at the industry level. In Boone's model, an increase in competition cannot increase overall efficiency in the market and also increase the number of new products introduced into the market.

Bonanno and Haworth examined two questions with regard to the effect of competition on innovation.[87] First, they considered whether cost-reducing innovations are positively or negatively correlated with the intensity of competition. Second, they analyzed what factors might be important to a firm when deciding whether to engage in process (cost-reducing) innovation or product (quality-improving) innovation.

To address the first question, they considered two industries that were identical except that one has Cournot competition and the other had Bertrand competition. They assumed that the industry characterized by Cournot competition was less competitive, because this process leads to lower output and higher prices. The authors found that any given cost reduction increased profits more in the case of Cournot competition than in the case of Bertrand competition. Thus, they concluded that there are cost-reducing innovations that would be pursued under Cournot that would not be pursued under the more competitive Bertrand scenario.

With respect to the second question, Bonanno and Haworth found that the degree of competition in a market does affect the choice between process and product innovation.[88] A firm with a high-quality product is more likely to go for product innovation if it is a Bertrand competitor,

---

86. Jan Boone, *Competitive Pressure, Selection and Investments in Develop-ment and Fundamental Research*, Working Paper, The Netherlands: Tilburg University, Department of Economics (1998).

87. Giacomo Bonanno & Barry Haworth, *Intensity of Competition and the Choice between Product and Process Innovation*, 16 INT'L J. INDUS. ORG. 495 (1996).

88. The results are likely to be dependent on the particular models that were employed and may not be present in more general models.

and process innovation if it is a Cournot competitor. In a Bertrand regime, a cost reduction has a negative strategic effect that leads to more competition so that the new equilibrium following process innovation would lower prices for both firms. Product innovation will lead to a price increase for the innovator, but might either increase or decrease the price of the other firm. A firm with a low-quality product is more likely to go for process innovation if it is a Bertrand competitor, but will prefer product innovation if it is a Cournot competitor. Process innovation by the firm with a low-quality product has negative strategic effects, so the innovator and the competitor will both lower their prices. Product innovation by the firm with the low-quality product would potentially have positive strategic effects, since it shifts the innovator's reaction curve up.[89]

2. Innovation by Large Firms in Concentrated Markets

The conclusion that competitive market structure will lead to dynamic efficiency has been challenged by a number of economists. Schumpeter is most often cited as the originator of the view that atomistic firms operating in competitive markets may not be as dynamically efficient as a larger firm operating in a more concentrated market.[90] Specifically, Schumpeter concludes, "What we have got to accept is that it [the large-scale establishment or unit of control] has come to be the most powerful engine of progress and ... long-run expansion of total output ... through this strategy which looks so restrictive when viewed in the individual case and from the individual point of time."[91]

Schumpeter's argument has been interpreted in two slightly different ways. First, it could be that large firms are more innovative than smaller firms. Second, it could be that firms in concentrated industries undertake more innovation. While both theories may be consistent, there are differences, and they have spawned somewhat different empirical tests of the "Schumpeter Hypothesis."

Economists have developed a number of situations in which a large firm in a concentrated industry may have an incentive to invest more heavily in innovative activity than a smaller firm in a less concentrated industry. Some of these explanations are based on the premise that

---

89. Bonano & Haworth, *supra* note 87, at 495-510.
90. SCHUMPETER, *supra* note 16.
91. *Id.*

innovative activity is less costly for large firms. Other explanations are based on the belief that large firms may obtain more benefits from innovative efforts.

The principal basis for believing that large firms may have lower innovation costs is that there are significant economies of scale in the innovative process.[92] Economies of scale in the innovation process may be generated in three ways. First, firms that undertake large amounts of R&D may be able to employ more specialized resources, reducing the marginal costs of innovation. Second, to the extent that innovation involves significant fixed costs, large-scale firms will face smaller average total costs because they can average the fixed costs of their innovative effort over a greater level of output.[93] Third, large firms may be able to support a larger portfolio of R&D efforts, increasing the likelihood that it will develop an improved product or process, which makes large-scale innovation efforts less risky.[94]

The costs of innovative activity may also be smaller for large firms if the cost of investment capital is lower. As a result, some economists have hypothesized that large firms will undertake more innovation because they have access to inexpensive capital. In some cases, economists have argued that inexpensive capital is generated internally. Specifically, it is argued that monopolistic profits are used to fund increased innovative activities.[95] However, others have argued that large firms face lower capital costs in capital markets.[96]

Economists have identified a number of factors that may increase the benefits of innovation to large firms in concentrated markets relative to smaller firms. First, large firms may obtain a larger total benefit from a process innovation that lowers production costs because a given percentage decline in costs will lead to greater cost savings when it is applied to a larger number of units of production.[97] Second, a large firm may be more likely to benefit from an innovative effort because it is more likely to be diversified into a number of different products, which

---

92. SCHERER & ROSS, *su pra* note 2, at 652.
93. William M. Cohen & Steven Klepper, *A Reprise of Size and R&D*, 106 ECON. J. 925, 926 (1996).
94. SCHERER & ROSS, *su pra* note 2, at 652.
95. "One hypothesis is that profits accumulated through the exercise of monopoly power are a key source of funds to support costly and risky innovation." *Id.* at 630.
96. *Id.* at 652.
97. A. Long, *Firm Size and Efficient Entrepreneurial Activity: A Reformulation of Schumpeter Hypothesis*, 88 J. POL. ECON. 771, 771-82 (1980).

will increase the likelihood that a discovery will be applicable to one of its businesses.[98] Third, large firms may be able to market new products more effectively, increasing the value of new product development to them, which encourages innovative activity.[99]

a. Empirical Studies of the Relationship between Market Concentration or Firm Size and Innovation

As indicated above, Schumpeter led economists to two hypotheses: (1) large firms are more likely to undertake innovation than small firms and (2) higher levels of innovative activity are more likely to be observed in concentrated industries.[100]   This section considers the numerous empirical studies economists have done to test the two "Schumpeterian hypotheses."

Summary data on R&D activity provides some support for Schumpeter's hypotheses. Historically, large enterprises have performed a significant share of formal R&D (e.g., firms with more than 10,000 employees performed more than 80 percent of formal R&D).[101] As the figure shows, large firms continue to perform a significant share of the R&D. However, as the figure also shows, smaller firms have performed an increasing share in recent years. Moreover, it has long been the case that small firms have performed a significant share of R&D.   For example, Jewkes, Sawers, and Stillerman review 70 important 20th century inventions and find that only 24 had their origins in industrial research laboratories.[102]

---

98.   "[A] monopoly may create superior incentives to invent [because] appropriability may be greater under monopoly than under competition." *See* Arrow, *supra* note 6; *see also* SCHERER & ROSS, *su pra* note 2, at 659. However, there is limited empirical support for this proposition. *See, e.g.,* John T. Scott, *Firm versus Industry Variability in R&D Intensity,* in R&D PATENTS & PRODUCTIVITY 233 (Z. Griliches, ed., 1984); William M. Cohen, Richard C. Levin & David C. Mowery, *Firm Size and R&D Intensity: A Reexamination,* 35 J. INDUS. ECON. 543 (1987). However, larger firms do appear to do more basic R&D. *See, e.g.,* Albert N. Link & James E. Long, *The Simple Economics of Basic Scientific Research: A Test of Nelson's Diversification Hypothesis,* 30 J. INDUS. ECON. 105 (1981).

99.   SCHERER & ROSS, *su pra* note 2, at 652.

100.   SCHUMPETER, *supra* note 16.

101.   SCHERER & ROSS, *su pra* note 2, at 654.

102.   JOHN JEWKES, DAVID SAWERS, & RICHARD STILLERMAN, THE SOURCES OF INVENTION (1969).

Large Firms Fund Most R&D, But Small Firm R&D Has Been Increasing Faster

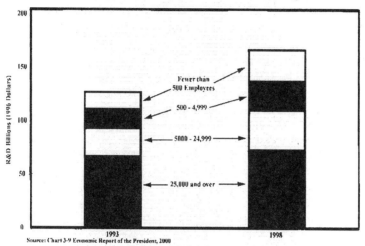

Source: Chart 3-9 Economic Report of the President, 2000

In an effort to test the two Schumperterian hypotheses, economists have undertaken numerous statistical studies that have attempted to control for the myriad of factors that affect innovation besides firm size and market concentration. These studies have been reviewed by a number of economists.[103] As a result, rather than reproducing an exhaustive review of the literature, this section identifies key findings, focusing on more recent findings. The discussion distinguishes between relationships between firm size and innovation and market concentration and innovation, since the economics literature has focused on both relationships.

---

103. *See generally* SCHERER & ROSS, *supra* note 2, at 613-60; MORTON I. KAMIEN & NANCY L. SCHWARTZ, MARKET STRUCTURE AND INNOVATION (1982); WILLIAM BALDWIN & JOHN T. SCOTT, MARKET STRUCTURE AND TECHNOLOGICAL CHANGE (1987); Wesley Cohen & Richard Levin, *Empirical Studies of Innovation and Market Structure*, in HANDBOOK OF INDUSTRIAL ORGANIZATION 1059-1107 (R. Schmalensee & R. D. Willig eds., 1989); Cohen, *supra* note 23.

b. Firm Size and Innovation

Economists have found a positive relationship between firm size and the likelihood that a firm performs R&D.[104] While early work was based on somewhat limited data,[105] more recent work that allows one to control for industry effects (i.e., to control for other industry characteristics that might affect the performance of R&D) has confirmed the basic relationship.[106]

Early studies found that R&D rose more than proportionately with firm size. However, these studies did not control for industry effects and thus may have reported biased statistics.[107] Subsequent work, most notably by Scherer, suggested that innovation increases more than proportionately with firm size only up to some size level. This view was the consensus view during the 1980s.[108] More recent work suggests that "R&D rises monotonically with firm size, and proportionately beyond some modest firm size threshold."[109] In addition, economists have often found that R&D varies "closely with firm size within industries, with size typically explaining over half of its variation."[110] As a result, economists increasingly came to believe that "large firms did not possess

---

104. For a contrary view, see Jacob Schmookler, *Bigness, Fewness, and Research*, 67 J. POL. ECON. 628-32 (1959).
105. Henry H. Villard, *Competition, Oligopoly and Research*, 66 J. POL. ECON. 483-97 (1958); Richard R. Nelson & Sidney G. Winter (1978) *Forces Generating and Limiting Concentration Under Schumpeterian Competition*, BELL J. ECON. 9, 524-48 (1978).
106. John Bound et al., *Who Does R&D and Who Patents?*, in R&D PATENTS AND PRODUCTIVITY 21-54 (Zvi Griliches, ed., 1984); Cohen, Levin & Mowery, *supra* note 98. For a general discussion of the use of the FTC's line of business data to study structural relationships, such as the concentration-margin relationship, see Michael Salinger, *The Concentration-Margins Relationship Reconsidered*, in BROOKINGS PAPERS ON ECONOMIC ACTIVITY 287-335 (1990).
107. Illustrative of these early studies are Ira Horowitz, *Firm Size and Research Activity*, 28 S. ECON J. 298-301 (1962) and D. Hamberg, *Size of Firm, Oligopoly and Research: The Evidence*, 30 CAN. J. ECON. & POL. SCI. 62-75 (1964).
108. *See, e.g.*, SCHERER & ROSS, *supra* note 2; MORTON I. KAMIEN & NANCY L. SCHWARTZ, MARKET STRUCTURE AND INNOVATION (1982).
109. Cohen, *supra* note 23.
110. *Id.*

any advantages in R&D competition."[111] Specifically, "studies not only confirmed that large firms do not conduct a disproportionate amount of R&D relative to size but also indicated that large firms actually generate fewer innovations per dollar of R&D than smaller firms, which has been widely interpreted as reflecting a disadvantage of size."[112]

More recent work by Cohen and Klepper suggests that some modification of the previously existing consensus may be in order.[113] Specifically, they report evidence that increased size may be associated with increased R&D (and more productive R&D) because firms with larger business units can spread the costs associated with R&D over greater sales revenues. In addition, they found that, "for the firms in the FTC data set, the close relationship between R&D and size appears to be due principally to business unit [subsidiary or division level] rather than corporate level factors."[114] In a related study, Cohen and Klepper found that the relationship between firm size and innovation is stronger for process innovations than for product innovations.[115] They cautioned, however, that their findings did not indicate that large firms are the

---

111. WESLEY M. Cohen & Steven Klepper, *Firm Size and the Nature of Innovation within Industries: The Case of Process and Product R&D*, 78 REV. ECON. & STAT. 232 (1996).

112. *Id.* Other studies done during this time period found that interindustry differences in R&D intensity have a much more significant effect on the level of R&D than differences in the size of firms within an industry. *See, e.g.*, Cohen, Levin, & Mowery, *supra* note 98. Economists have also looked at the relationship between firm size and R&D intensity. For example, based on an analysis of FTC line of business data, a study concluded:

> [O]verall firm size has a very small, statistically insignificant effect on business unit R&D intensity when either fixed industry effects or measured industry characteristics are taken into account. Business unit size has no effect on the R&D intensity of business units that perform R&D, but it affects the probability of conducting R&D. Business unit and firm size jointly explain less than one percent of the variance in R&D intensity; industry effects explain nearly half the variance.

Cohen, Levin, & Mowery, *supra* note 98.

113. Cohen & Klepper, *supra* note 93.

114. *Id.* at 938.

115. Cohen & Klepper, *supra* note 111.

engines of economic growth, nor did they indicate that there are no disadvantages to large size.

c. Market Concentration and Innovation

Economists have explored how today's market structure affects the level of innovation.[116] As Scherer and Ross point out, "[m]ost studies for the United States and other leading nations reveal a positive correlation between concentration and industry R&D/sales ratios, or cruder proxies of these ratios."[117] However, there are some contrary results. For example, a few studies have found that that concentration is negatively associated with R&D.[118]

In related work, Greer and Rhoades found that market power as measured by concentration is positively correlated with productivity changes.[119] However, the inclusion of R&D expenditures in the equation eliminated the explanatory power (statistical significance) of market concentration. Some have interpreted this result as indicating that "the chain of causation appears to run from higher R&D spending, which is correlated with seller concentration, to higher productivity growth."[120]

While most studies have focused on a linear relationship between market concentration and innovation, Scherer found that there may be a

---

116. Schumpeter was also concerned with how the incentive to innovate was related to ex post market structure (and associated market power). There has been substantially less research on this issue. *See* Almarin Phillips, *Patents, Potential Competition, and Technical Progress*, 56 AM. ECON. REV. 301-10 (1966) (discussing this possibility).

117. SCHERER & ROSS, *supra* note 2, at 646; *See also* WILLIAM L BALDWIN & JOHN T. SCOTT, MARKET STRUCTURE AND TECHNOLOGICAL CHANGE (1987).

118. *See, e.g.*, Oliver Williamson, *Innovation and Market Structure*, 73 J. POL. ECON. 67 (1965); BARRY BOZEMAN & ALBERT LINK, INVESTMENTS IN TECHNOLOGY: CORPORATE STRATEGIES AND PUBLIC POLICY ALTERNATIVES (Praeger, ed., 1983); A. Mukhopadhyary, *Technological Progress and Change in Market Concentration in the U.S.*, 52 S. ECON. J. 141 (1985).

119. Douglas F. Greer & Stephen A. Rhoades, *Concentration and Productivity Changes in the Long and Short Run*, 43 S. ECON. J. 1031 (1976); *See also* Louis Amato, J. Michael Ryan, & Ronald P. Wilder, *Market Structure and Dynamic Performance in the U.S. Manufacturing*, 47 S. ECON. J. 1105 (1981).

120. SCHERER & ROSS, *su pra* note 2, at 645.

nonlinear relationship.[121]   Specifically, it is possible that innovation increases with concentration up to some point and then declines. This finding has been replicated by others.[122]

Some early work by economists suggested that innovation might have deconcentrating effects.[123]   Subsequent work has suggested that innovation and entry are sometimes associated with each other.[124] Granger causality tests performed by Geroski suggest that entry may cause innovation, rather than vice versa.[125]   Similarly, others have found that innovation may be associated with the growth of smaller firms or entry, which may lead to lower concentration in innovative markets.[126] Moreover, Gort and Konakayama found that entry rates were higher than exit rates in the early stages of major product developments, which suggests that product innovation can have a deconcentrating effect.[127] However, Geroski observes that the presence of significant industry fixed effects implies that other structural characteristics of markets may simultaneously determine both innovation and entry.[128]

Numerous economists have observed that the results that relate concentration to innovation are sensitive to industry characteristics.[129] For example, Scott and Levin et al. found that the addition of variables that controlled for differences in company characteristics and industry characteristics eliminated the statistical significance of concentration as

---

121. F. M. Scherer, *Market Structure and the Employment of Scientists and Engineers*. 57 AM. ECON. REV. 524 (1967).
122. *See, e.g.*, Scott, *supra* note 98; Richard C. Levin et al., *R&D Appropriability, Opportunity, and Market Structure: New Evidence on Some Schumpeterian Hypotheses*, 75 AM. ECON. REV. 20 (1985).
123. J. Blair, *Technology and Size*, 38 AM. ECON. REV. 121 (1948).
124. *See, e.g.*, P. A. Geroski, *Innovation, Technological Opportunity, and Market Structure*, 42 OXFORD ECON. PAPERS 586 (1990); P. A. Geroski, *Entry and the Rate of Innovation*, 1 ECON. INNOVATION & NEW TECH. 203 (1991); P. A. GEROSKI, MARKET DYNAMICS & ENTRY (1991).
125. Granger causality tests are statistical tests that are designed to test for causal relationships between economic variables in a statistical study.
126. A. Mukhopadhyary, *Technological Progress and Change in Market Concentration in the U.S.*, 52 S. ECON. J. 141 (1985).
127. Michael Gort & Akira Konakayama, *A Model of Diffusion in the Production of an Innovation*, 72 AM. ECON. REV. 1111 (1982).
128. *See infra* § D for a discussion of the simultaneous determination of innovation and market concentration.
129. *See* articles reviewed in Cohen, *supra* note 23, at 195.

an explanation for variations in innovative activity,[130] suggesting that the statistical significance that was observed in some regressions may be a statistical artifact of statistical relationships involving fundamental industry characteristics.[131]

3. Fundamental Structural Characteristics of Technology May Determine Market Structure and Innovative Activity

Economists have recognized that both concentration and R&D efforts may be simultaneously determined by other market characteristics. Specifically, it may be that "the market structure affecting R&D decisions is not given, but endogenously determined by technology and competition."[132]

A number of economists have explored the relationship between innovation and concentration by using multi-equation models in which concentration and R&D are both simultaneously determined by other factors.[133] When performed, statistical tests support the view that both

---

130.   Richard C. Levin, Wesley M. Cohen, & David C. Mowery, *R&D Appropriability, Opportunity, and Market Structure: New Evidence on Some Schumpeterian Hypotheses*, 75 AM. ECON. REV. 20 (1985). Concentration was included in these regressions in two forms: expenditures and expenditures squared. The coefficients on both of these variables were insignificant when company and industry effects were included in the regressions. Regressions are statistical tests that are designed to estimate statistical relationships between variables. Statistical relationships are revealed in regression coefficients that are produced by the statistical test. When the statistical test is done properly, the regression coefficients can be interpreted to identify the likely direction and statistical significance of the relationships between the variables.

131.   Scott, *supra* note 98; Levin, Cohen & Mowery, *supra* note 130.

132.   SCHERER & ROSS, *supra* note 2, at 642.

133.   *See, e.g.*, Stephen Farber, *Buyer Market Structure and R&D Effort: A Simultaneous Equations Model*, 62 R. ECON. STAT. 336 (1981); B. Wahlroos & M. Backstrom, *R&D Intensity with Endogenous Concentration: Evidence for Finland*, 7 EMPIRICAL ECON. 13 (1982); R. Connolly & M. Hirschey, *R&D, Market Structure, and Profits: A Value-Based Approach*, 66 R. ECON. STAT. 682 (1984); Richard C. Levin & Peter C. Reiss, *Tests of a Schumpeterian Model of R&D and Market Structure, in* R&D PATENTS AND PRODUCTIVITY 175 (Z. Griliches ed. 1984); and R. Levin et al., *R&D Appropriability, Opportunity, and*

innovation and concentration are simultaneously determined.[134]   As a result, some have concluded that "[r]ecent empirical works suggests that R&D intensity and market structure are jointly determined by technology, the characteristics of demand, the institutional framework, strategic interaction and chance."[135]

One of the market characteristics that may simultaneously shape both market structure and innovation is the set of technological opportunities that firms face. Specifically, if rich technological opportunities mean that an innovator may not be able to retain significant rents because others will develop competing innovations, one may not see as much innovative activity in unconcentrated markets where there are rich technological opportunities as one sees in more concentrated markets.[136] In a study that uses levels of innovative activity at one point in time to control for technological opportunities in the industry at other points in time, it was observed that higher seller concentration was associated with less innovation.[137] Some have concluded that "interindustry differences in technological opportunity, however measured, have much greater power in explaining varying R&D or innovation intensities than differences in such market structure indices as concentration."[138]

D. Economic Aspects of Intellectual Property and Licensing

1. Free-Riding

As discussed above, the granting of intellectual property rights is often viewed as preventing free-riding on the efforts of innovators, thus preserving the incentive to innovate. Free-riding occurs when economic actors cannot recoup their fixed investments because economic agents

---

Market Structure: New Evidence on Some Schumpeterian Hypotheses, 75 AM. ECON. REV. 20 (1985).

134. Simulation models also support this view. *See, e.g.,* Richard R. Nelson & Sidney G. Winter, *Forces Generating and Limiting Concentration Under Schumpeterian Competition*, 9 BELL J. ECON. 524 (1978).

135. George Symeonidis, *Innovation, Firm Size and Market Structure: Schumpeterian Hypotheses and Some New Themes*, 27 OECD ECON. STUDIES 35 (1996).

136. SCHERER, *supra* note 1, at 88; William S. Comanor, *Market Structure, Product Differentiation, and Industrial Research*, 81 Q. J. ECON. 639 (1967).

137. P. A. Geroski, *Innovation, Technological Opportunity, and Market Structure*, 42 OXFORD ECON. PAPERS 586 (1990).

138. SCHERER & ROSS, *su pra* note 2, at 648.

that have not made those investments are nonetheless able to use the fruits of those investments to compete with the innovator.[139] If the fruits of innovation are available for all to enjoy without sufficient compensation, the incentive to create will be attenuated or lost. The patent system is often seen as a means of preventing such free-riding and restoring the proper incentive to innovate.

This rationale for the patent system is sometimes also expressed in terms of the internalization of externalities or the provision of "public goods." There are some goods which, once produced, can be enjoyed by all, even those that don't pay for them, at no or little additional marginal cost. National defense is a prototypical example. For goods of this type, the public benefit from producing these goods exceeds what private individuals, taken together, are willing to pay, i.e., there is a positive externality from production of these goods. As a result, absent either government production or other institutions/policies that further incentivize private production, there will be insufficient production of such goods. Innovations that can be quickly copied have some of the characteristics of a public good. Absent some mechanism to "exclude" imitators or prevent copying, the private return to creative effort will be insufficient to call forth a socially optimal level of innovation.

Certain aspects of these views have been recently challenged. In particular, Lemley has stated that all free-riding need not be prevented by an optimal patent system.[140] Rather, society should be unconcerned about free-riding on the efforts of intellectual property creators except to the extent that curbing free-riding is necessary to encourage the socially optimal degree of creativity. According to Lemley, the socially optimal degree of creativity, in turn, will occur as long as creators are allowed to cover their average fixed costs of innovation—there is no need to allow potential creators to reap all the benefits of their innovations. This view stems from Lemley's underlying observation that the externalities

139. Free-riding occurs in many economic contexts. For example, a shoe manufacturer might invest in providing point-of-sale service for potential customers of its shoes. If potential customers are able to partake of this service and then buy their shoes for a lower price elsewhere where no such service is given, this free ride will prevent the shoe manufacturer from recouping his fixed investment in point-of-sale service. Accordingly, absent some institution or business practice that prevents or limits such free-riding, shoe suppliers will not be able to profitably provide such point-of-sale service.

140. Mark A. Lemley, *Property, Intellectual Property, and Free Riding*, 83 TEX. L. REV. 1031 (2005).

associated with the use of intellectual property are positive, unlike the usual case with real property. In the case of real property, one person's use of property diminishes another person's ability to use it (i.e., there are negative externalities), and if property rights are not granted to one entity, too much use will occur resulting in the oft-quoted "tragedy of the commons." By contrast, Lemley argues, the use of intellectual property results in positive externalities, since one person's use does not diminish another's ability to use it, and the process of cumulative innovation can enhance the intellectual property. Accordingly, the challenge with intellectual property is to only discourage free-riding (and internalize what are largely positive externalities) to the extent necessary to allow creators of intellectual property to capture sufficient returns to recoup investment. The goal need not be to eliminate all free-riding.

Others disagree with this characterization. Duffy, for example, argues that intellectual property and real property should be treated similarly, and that the elimination of free-riding (rather than the ex post recovery of costs) should accordingly be the proper goal of an intellectual property regime.[141] Duffy points out that what is important to innovation incentives is the ex ante return on investment, not the ex post return. Since most innovation efforts fail, the average ex post return needs to substantially exceed full cost recovery. Furthermore, Duffy observes that if policy makers knew the socially optimal level of investment in intellectual property, they could set up the intellectual property regime to yield, on average, full cost recovery. But since policymakers don't know the optimal level of investment in intellectual property, a full cost standard such as Lemley proposes is likely to lead to underinvestment in intellectual property relative to a regime that attempts to eliminate free-riding and give innovators the full private benefit of their innovation.

In the context of cumulative innovation, there are further positive externalities from innovation that must be internalized if innovation incentives of the initial innovator are to be optimized. That is because innovation by the initial creator creates downstream opportunities that are socially desirable. As discussed above, one potential method of internalization is the issuance of broad patents which allow the initial innovator to capture downstream profits made possible by the upstream innovation. But broad patents may also inhibit downstream innovation, particularly when there are uncertain innovation paths, and ex ante

---

141. John F. Duffy, *Intellectual Property Isolationism and the Average Cost Thesis*, 83 TEX. L. REV. 1077 (2005).

licensing to potential downstream innovators is problematic due to high transactions costs.

2. *Transactions Costs*

Transactions costs[142] enter into both the creation and licensing of intellectual property. The need for an intellectual property system can, at its core, be characterized as a matter of transactions costs. Demsetz, for example, postulated that property rights would not arise where external effects were of such small significance, relative to transactions costs, that it would not pay anyone to take them into account.[143] By the same token, in situations where transactions costs are small relative to potential gains from internalizing externalities, property rights would tend to be vested and voluntary exchange would internalize externalities and eliminate free-riding. That is one of the goals of the property rights vested by the patent system, as discussed above.

Even after property rights are initially vested in creators through the patent system, there are transactions costs related to the licensing (or, more generally, transfer) of intellectual property. Intellectual property creators are unlikely to be able to reap the full commercial value of their innovations absent combination of this intellectual property with complementary factors of production, such as manufacturing, distribution, and possibly further downstream intellectual property. Licensing, cross-licensing, or otherwise transferring intellectual property can facilitate such combination with complementary factors, yielding benefits both to developers of intellectual property (in terms of increased profits) as well as consumers (through cost/price reductions and new products).[144] Yet there are also significant transactions costs associated with such licensing.

---

142. Transactions costs are the cost of consummating an economic transaction, including information costs, bargaining costs, and accounting for risk.
143. Harold Demsetz, *Towards a Theory of Property Rights*, 57 AM. ECON. REV. PAPER & PROC. 351 (1967). An example would be the benefit that a well-maintained flower garden provides to the neighborhood. It is unlikely that these external benefits will be internalized given their small magnitude relative to the transactions costs of vesting property rights and arranging individual neighbor compensation to the garden owner.
144. *See* U.S. DEP'T OF JUSTICE & FED. TRADE COMM'N, ANTITRUST GUIDELINES FOR THE LICENSING OF INTELLECTUAL PROPERTY (April 6, 1995) (hereinafter INTELLECTUAL PROPERTY GUIDELINES), *reprinted in* 4 Trade Reg. Rep. (CCH) ¶ 13,132 *and* Appendix 1 to this Handbook,

These transaction costs are fundamentally associated with the future-oriented and uncertain nature of intellectual property. There is uncertainty as to the value of the intellectual property,[145] the future innovation path, as well as the identification of the set of potential licensees, all of which inhibit the bargaining process for licenses. There is also the potential for leakage of unprotected know-how ("appropriability hazard") in a licensing contract.[146] To the extent that these transactions costs are significant, licensing that would otherwise be economic may not fully occur. As was suggested above, these bargaining impediments to licensing are particularly likely in the context of cumulative innovation where first innovators with broad patent rights might not have sufficient *ex ante* incentive to license to numerous potential "second-generation" developers of follow-on lines of innovation.

Transactions costs of licensing intellectual property are likely to be greater than transactions costs involving use of real property. Because most intellectual property lacks a physical locus, it is often hard to define the boundaries of what exactly is being transferred in a license. Intellectual property often has "fuzzy boundaries" not found in real property, since the quality of some issued patents is poor and the true validity and extent of property rights conferred by a patent may sometimes only be ascertained through lengthy and expensive legal proceedings.[147] Further, since intellectual property can be appropriated simply by being copied, preserving one's property rights upon licensing

---

§ 2.3. The *Guidelines* recognize that restrictive licensing practices can mitigate transactions costs in technology markets, with positive welfare effects.

145. *See* Robert P. Merges & Richard R. Nelson, *On Limiting or Encouraging Rivalry in Technical Progress: The Effect of Patent Scope Decisions*, 25 J. ECON. BEH. & ORG. 1 (1994).

146. *See, e.g.*, Joanne E. Oxley, *Institutional Environment and the Mechanism of Governance: The Impact of Intellectual Property Protection on the Structure of Inter-Firm Alliances*, 38 ECON. BEH. & ORG. 283 (1999); *see also* Ashish Arora, *Contracting for Tacit Knowledge: The Provision of Technical Services in Technology Licensing Contracts*, 50 J. DEV.E CON. 233 (1996).

147. *See* Deepak Somaya & David J. Teece, *Combining Patented Inventions in Multi-invention Products: Transactional Challenges and Organizational Choices*, Working Paper at 15-17 (August 2, 2001); *see also* Robert P. Merges, *As Many As Six Impossible Patents Before Breakfast: Property Rights for Business Concepts and Patent System Reform,* 14 BERKELEY TECH. L.J. 577 (1999).

can be difficult. Finally, the ability to easily copy intellectual property also makes it readily divisible, such that the same property can be licensed to many licensees, increasing transactions costs.[148]

Transactions costs in connection with intellectual property licensing are likely to be particularly significant in a cumulative innovation setting where large numbers of (potentially overlapping) patents are potentially infringed by a given product.[149] In this situation, it is difficult for a potential market participant/licensee to determine which technologies legitimately bear on the product in question and who the relevant patent holders are. It is also costly and time-consuming to determine which patents are legitimate or important, and which are not, as well as the value contributed by any individual patent. Moreover, it is difficult to determine which currently unissued patents might be in the pipeline, only to materialize later, or to determine which new technologies might have to be considered in commercialization. Once relevant patent holders are located, there can be problems with each one holding out for maximum monopoly rents, presenting the problem of royalty stacking.[150] These difficulties caused by overlapping patent rights raise the transactions costs of licensing and in some situations can deter socially efficient licensing and cause underutilization of scarce intellectual property resources.

3. Thickets and the Dilemma of the Anti-Commons

The strategic and welfare implications of overlapping patent rights faced by those seeking to commercialize new products has recently received increased attention under the rubric of "navigating the patent thicket" and the "dilemma of the anti-commons." Two important types of transactions costs that can affect the path of licensing and innovation emerge in this context. First is the complements problem. Second is the hold-up problem.

A patent thicket is said to exist when the process of cumulative innovation results in a web of overlapping intellectual property rights that a company must "hack" its way through in order to commercialize a

---

148. These points are made in Richard A. Posner, *Transaction Costs and Antitrust Concerns in the Licensing of Intellectual Property,* 4 THE JOHN MARSHALL REV. INTELL. PROP. LAW 325 (2005).
149. Such situations are rapidly becoming the norm in certain technological fields, such as biotechnology and semiconductors.
150. *See* DAVID J. TEECE, MANAGING INTELLECTUAL CAPITAL 208-09 (2000).

new product or technology.[151] Effectively, in order to introduce a new product, the company is initially in the position of needing to identify and negotiate a royalty with each person who claims a patent right. Often, there are multiple essential or "blocking" patents which are complementary rather than competing in nature, and separate royalties on each of these patents must be negotiated. Some of these patents may take years to work their way through the Patent and Trademark Office (PTO), and can surface as "submarine" patents to catch an unwary downstream innovator. Many of these problems are believed to be exacerbated by the tendency of the PTO to issue too many problematic patents,[152] some of which are overly broad. With cumulative innovation and multiple blocking patents producing a patent thicket, stronger patent rights can end up stifling, not encouraging, innovation.

The problem of patent thickets derives from the classic complements problem in economic theory. Cournot showed that a manufacturer of brass who had to purchase key complementary inputs of copper and zinc from separate monopolists would pay higher input prices and charge a higher brass price than if a single monopolist controlled both the copper and zinc inputs, either selling those inputs to brass producers or producing the brass itself.[153] Analogously, when multiple firms control complementary patents each of which is essential to produce a new product, there is an inherent inefficiency in that patent royalties will tend to build up or stack up,[154] in addition to the high transactions costs of bargaining with each of several patent monopolists. This has become a particular problem in industries such as semiconductors where thousands of patents are issued each year and manufacturers are at risk for infringing multiple patents with a single product.

---

151. *See* Carl Shapiro, *Navigating the Patent Thicket: Cross Licenses, Patent Pools, and Standard Setting*, in INNOVATION POLICY AND THE ECONOMY (Adam Jaffe, Joshua Lerner & Scott Stern, eds., 2001).

152. For example, many patents cover products or processes already widely used when the patent issued, increasing the difficulty of inventing around. *See id.* at 3.

153. For a description of Cournot's work on complements, as well as modern extensions, see Carl Shapiro, *Theories of Oligopoly Behavior*, in HANDBOOK OF INDUSTRIAL ORGANIZATION 330-414 (Richard Schmalensee & Robert Willig, eds., 1989).

154. Shapiro has shown that if N firms control patents that are essential for the production of a given product, and if these N firms independently set their licensing fees, the resulting markup on that product is N times the monopoly mark up. Shapiro, *supra* note 153, at 331-32.

The complements problem has also been discussed in terms of creating the opposite economic problem from the well-known "tragedy of the commons," which refers to the fact that a resource (such as the atmosphere or ocean) can be overused if it is not protected by property rights.[155] In contrast, it has been pointed out that when there are multiple blocking patents in the context of cumulative innovation, there may be too many gatekeepers protecting the upstream intellectual property, which can lead to underutilization of this resource by downstream practitioners and resulting reduced incentive to invest in R&D. Heller and Eisenberg have called such potential underutilization stemming from excessive property rights "the tragedy of the anticommons."[156] They are particularly concerned about this problem in the biomedical research context, where they believe there are too many concurrent patents issued (on such items as gene fragments) such that downstream researchers are unable to procure a complete set of licenses and may be forced to divert resources to less promising projects.[157] In addition, an anticommons can result through the use of reach-through license agreements (RTLAs) or similar license-stacking mechanisms on patented research tools. An RTLA gives the owner of a patented invention rights in subsequent downstream discoveries, often through a royalty on sales. While RTLAs have certain advantages for both downstream researchers/producers and patent holders,[158] they may also lead to an anticommons problem as upstream owners stack overlapping and inconsistent claims on potential downstream producers.[159] Particularly where the prospects of success

---

155. "A resource is prone to overuse in a tragedy of the commons when too many owners each have a privilege to use a given resource and no one has a right to exclude another." Michael A. Heller & Rebecca S. Eisenberg, *Can Patents Deter Innovation? The Anticommons in Biomedical Research*, 280 SCIENCE 698 (1998).
156. "A resource is prone to underuse in a 'tragedy of the anticommons' when multiple owners each have a right to exclude others from a scarce resource and no one has an effective privilege of use." *Id.* at 698.
157. *Id.* at 699.
158. RTLAs can help downstream producers/researchers with limited funds to use patented research tools right away but defer payment until the research produces commercially successful products. Patent holders benefit in that they may prefer a chance to achieve larger, but uncertain, payoffs from downstream commercial success rather than certain upfront fees. Heller & Eisenberg, *supra* note 155, at 699.
159. *Id.*

downstream are uncertain, or the expected commercial value is small, the parties may fail to bargain past the anticommons.

A potential solution to the problem of complementary patents and royalty stacking is that patent holders can (1) cross-license among themselves so they can each produce the final product and/or (2) create a package license or patent pool to sell to third parties.[160] A cross-license is simply an agreement between two or more patent-holding companies that grants each the right to practice the other's patents. It is often royalty-free, particularly when patent portfolios among the firms are balanced. Therefore, issues of royalty stacking are moot. Cross-licenses can have the additional benefit that they largely protect the cross-licensing firms from infringement suits by each other, reducing the risk of further R&D investment.[161] A patent pool or package license can also be used to obviate the complements problem. Under a patent pool, an entire group of patents is licensed as a package, usually to anyone willing to pay the associated royalties. Such a pool license can lead both to higher combined profits for the licensors as well as a lower combined price for the patents than if they were licensed individually, since there is no stacking of monopoly royalties.[162] Importantly, for these cross-licensing or patent pooling arrangements to provide these benefits without significant offsetting costs in terms of reduced competition, it is generally agreed that only complementary patents should be included.

A related transactions costs problem in a cumulative innovation setting can occur when downstream researchers or producers are subject to hold up by upstream patent holders enjoying (potentially) broad patent protection.[163] This situation emerges in particular if there are long delays between filing and issuance of patents, and downstream producers make sunk investments during this time frame. In these situations, downstream producers take significant risks when they invest in further product development, lest they get caught in a web of unforeseen patents of

---

160. A similar solution has emerged with respect to copyrights. For example, in the music industry, copyright collectives have evolved to facilitate licensing transactions so that broadcasters and other producers may readily obtain permission to use numerous copyrighted works helped by different owners.

161. T. Randolph Beard & David L. Kaserman, *Patent Thickets, Cross Licensing, and Antitrust*, 47 ANTITRUST BULL. 355 (2002)

162. Shapiro, *supra* note 153, at 331-32.

163. If patent grants are narrow, downstream firms can relatively easily invent around a patent and therefore likely have sufficient bargaining to prevent hold up.

unknown and potentially broad scope.[164] If the downstream manufacturer has already designed its product and sunk investment in large-
scale production before relevant patents issue, he is in a much weaker
negotiating position if approached by the patent holder and threatened
with an infringement suit. At this point, redesign of the product to avoid
infringing patents may be very expensive, and the downstream producers
may be forced into paying large royalties. The transactions costs
associated with such hold up situations, as well as the likelihood of high
royalty payments, can also inhibit downstream innovation.[165]

The potential solution to the hold up problem is quite difficult, since
it involves fundamental aspects of reform of the patent system. Any
solution would likely have to consider: (a) better information at an earlier
stage about patents likely to issue; (b) the ability of interested parties to
challenge, either before or after issuance, certain patents at the PTO
before they are given a presumption of validity by the courts;[166] and (c)
the creation of intervening rights to protect downstream firms that
become exposed to infringement claims by virtue of patent
continuations.[167]

E. Conclusion

Economic analysis of intellectual property reveals the difficulty of
drawing simple conclusions as to the efficacy of particular patent policy
or antitrust policy initiatives on innovative performance. This partly
stems from the underlying different and potentially conflicting rationales
for patent protection that have been discussed in the literature, both
theoretical and empirical. To the extent these theories of patent

---

164. Potential patent holders and their investors also operate under uncertainty,
for example trying to raise capital on the basis of amorphous rights
preserved by patent filings.
165. *See* Shapiro, *supra* note 153.
166. *See* Robert D. Stoner, *Proposed Reforms in the U.S. Patent Regime to
Combat Patents That Stifle Competition*, in 5 ANTITRUST AND
INTELLECTUAL PROPERTY 36-37 (2004).
167. Continuations are those patent applications that seek additional broader
claims during or after the examination process where the original
application is granted or rejected. Such rights would shelter inventors
and users that infringe a patent only because of claim amendments
following a continuation, provided that the sheltered products or
processes are developed or used before the amended claims are
published. *See* Stoner, *supra* note 166, at 32-34.

protection differ (as portrayed in this chapter), so will the patent policy implications emanating from those theories. As just one example, different theories of patent protection yield different conclusions as to the efficacy of broad versus narrow patent protection. A further confounding factor is that there is no clearly delineated understanding of the relationship between market structure (or firm size) and innovation. In certain situations, both high and low market concentration can spur innovation. That implies that in promoting innovation, antitrust levers, like patent policy levers, must be pulled with caution. Finally, there are additional complicating factors, such as the role of transactions costs, in formulating an antitrust policy toward intellectual property protection. In order to offset problems like patent thickets emanating from transactions costs, patent pooling and cross-licensing may, in many situations, provide a solution whose potential benefits outweigh any costs in terms of reduced competition.

CHAPTER V

ANTITRUST ANALYSIS OF INTELLECTUAL
PROPERTY AGREEMENTS

Often times, the value of intellectual property may only be realized when the property is combined with complementary resources. A patent covering a new device is worthless unless combined with the manufacturing capacity to produce the device. Since intellectual property holders do not always have the necessary resources to exploit their property, the integration of intellectual property with the appropriate complementary resources is often accomplished through agreements between firms. In other words, agreements involving intellectual property can be markedly procompetitive. Yet such agreements may also involve terms or parties that result in anticompetitive effects and, therefore, raise antitrust concerns. This chapter explores the line between pro- and anticompetitive intellectual agreements.

A. General Antitrust Principles Applied to Intellectual Property Agreements

The most comprehensive source of guidance regarding the antitrust principles applicable to intellectual property agreements are the *Antitrust Guidelines for the Licensing of Intellectual Property* issued by the Department of Justice and the Federal Trade Commission in 1995.[1] The *Intellectual Property Guidelines* set forth a well-accepted analytical framework for the antitrust implications of these types of agreements and are therefore an excellent starting point. The following sections therefore focus on the *Guidelines*, supplemented by antitrust case law.

In assessing restraints in licensing arrangements, however, it is also important to consider intellectual property misuse doctrines. In 1969, the Supreme Court noted in *Zenith Radio Corp. v. Hazeltine Research*,[2] that the existence of patent misuse does not necessarily embody "the

---

1. *See* U.S. DEP'T OF JUSTICE & FED. TRADE COMM'N, ANTITRUST GUIDELINES FOR THE LICENSING OF INTELLECTUAL PROPERTY (April 6, 1995) (hereinafter INTELLECTUAL PROPERTY GUIDELINES), *reprinted in* 4 Trade Reg. Rep. (CCH) ¶ 13,132 *and* Appendix 1 to this Handbook.
2. 395 U.S. 100 (1969).

ingredients of a violation of either § 1 or § 2 of the Sherman Act."[3] But since the *Zenith* case, the trend has been toward requiring a showing of adverse effects on competition in a relevant market to establish misuse, and therefore the distinctions between antitrust and misuse have blurred.[4] The misuse and antitrust doctrine remain distinct, with distinct elements and different remedies.[5] Case law involving misuse defenses, however, has become increasingly important in evaluating potential antitrust issues.   This case law is discussed in later sections—in addition to antitrust case law and the *Guidelines*—when relevant to specific types of licensing arrangements.

1. Distinguishing Between Vertical and Horizontal Arrangements

In analyzing whether an agreement unlawfully restrains trade, the courts, economists, and enforcement agencies recognize distinctions between vertical and horizontal agreements and restraints.   The characterization of a restraint as horizontal or vertical generally depends on the relationship of the parties to the agreement imposing the restraint.[6]

---

3.   *Id.* at 140.
4.   *See* Mallinckrodt, Inc. v. Medipart, Inc., 976 F.2d 700 (Fed. Cir. 1992); Windsurfing Int'l, v. AMF, Inc., 782 F.2d 995, 1001-02 (Fed. Cir. 1986) ("To sustain a misuse defense involving a licensing arrangement not held to have been per se anticompetitive by the Supreme Court, a factual determination must reveal that the overall effect of the license tends to restrain competition unlawfully in an appropriately defined relevant market"); USM Corp. v. SPS Techs., 694 F.2d 505, 510-14 (7th Cir. 1982) (analyzing discriminatory royalties under antitrust principles and holding that there was no patent misuse).
5.   *See* Virginia Panel Corp. v. Mac Panel Co., 133 F.3d 860, 868-74 (Fed. Cir. 1997) ("[V]iolation of the antitrust laws, in this case section 2 of the Sherman Antitrust Act, ... requires more exacting proof than suffices to demonstrate patent misuse."); *cf.* Nobelpharma v. Implant Innovations, 141 F.3d 1059, 1068-71 (Fed. Cir. 1998) (discussing the distinctions between equitable defense in infringement action of inequitable conduct and *Walker Process* "fraud" that might support an affirmative antitrust claim).
6.   *See* Bus. Elecs. Corp. v. Sharp Elecs. Corp., 485 U.S. 717, 730 & n.4 (1988) ("Restraints imposed by agreement between competitors have traditionally been denominated as horizontal restraints, and those imposed by agreement between firms at different levels of distribution as vertical restraints.").

As described in Section 3.3 of the *Intellectual Property Guidelines*, the agencies' antitrust analysis of intellectual property licensing arrangements "examines whether the relationship among the parties to the arrangement is primarily horizontal or vertical in nature, or whether it has substantial aspects of both."[7] Distinguishing between vertical (complementary) and horizontal (competitive) relationships is more difficult in analyzing relationships between parties to intellectual property licensing arrangements than in considering levels of manufacture and distribution of goods.

This is because the analysis turns on whether the parties might compete but for the agreement. The agencies "will ordinarily treat a relationship between a licensor and its licensees, or between licensees, as horizontal when they would have been actual or likely potential competitors in a relevant market in the absence of the license."[8] According to the *Guidelines*, "[a] firm will be treated as a likely potential competitor if there is evidence that entry by that firm is reasonably probable in the absence of the licensing arrangement."[9] The analysis becomes complicated because firms may be horizontal competitors with respect to certain markets (e.g., a goods market) yet in a vertical relationship with respect to the licensed intellectual property. For instance, firms could be competitors in the market for farm equipment but in a vertical relationship with regard to an emissions control technology used in farm equipment and patented by one of the firms.[10]

An arrangement is vertical when complementary factors are combined by parties who are not competitors, such as: (a) when the licensor's business is limited to research and development and it licenses to manufacturers; (b) when the licensor is "a component manufacturer owning intellectual property rights in a product that the licensee manufactures by combining the component with other inputs"; or (c) when the licensor manufactures products and licensees operate primarily in distribution and marketing.[11] Vertical restraints, therefore, are

---

7. INTELLECTUAL PROPERTY GUIDELINES, *supra* note 1, § 3.3.
8. *Id.* § 3.3 ("Horizontal and Vertical Relationships").
9. *Id.* § 3.1 n.14.
10. *See, e.g., id.* & Ex. 5.
11. *Id.* § 3.3. As illustrated in Example 1 to § 2.3 of the *Guidelines*, a company that develops a new software program for inventory management with wide application in the health care field might license such software in an arrangement imposing field of use and territorial limitations. Assuming the licensees are not actual or likely potential

restraints imposed by a firm at one level of the market structure or distribution chain on a firm at another level, such as restrictions a manufacturer might place on its distributors in a distribution agreement.[12]

Distinguishing between horizontal and vertical relationships and restraints informs the analysis of potential harm to competition.[13] Although the existence of a purely vertical relationship does not assure that there are no anticompetitive effects,[14] horizontal restraints are more likely than vertical restraints to raise competitive concerns. In fact, certain categories of restraints may be per se unlawful as horizontal restraints, while they would be judged under the rule of reason as vertical restraints.[15]

---

competitors of the licensor, the parties are in a vertical relationship and the restraints would likely be analyzed as vertical restraints.

12.   *See* Cont'l T.V. v. GTE Sylvania Inc., 433 U.S. 36, 54-55 (1977). According to the *Guidelines*, "[a] licensing arrangement has a vertical component when it affects activities that are in a complementary relationship, as is typically the case in a licensing arrangement." INTELLECTUAL PROPERTY GUIDELINES, *supra* note 1, § 3.3; *see also id.* § 2.3, Example 1 (vertical customer and territorial restraints in a licensing arrangement would typically not raise significant competitive concerns).

13.   *See* Willard K. Tom & Joshua A. Newberg, *Antitrust and Intellectual Property: From Separate Spheres to Unified Field,* 66 ANTITRUST L.J. 167, 203-08 (1997) (discussion of vertical/horizontal distinctions in connection with United States v. Pilkington plc, Civ. No. 94-345 (D. Ariz. Complaint filed May 25, 1994), and United States v. Gen. Elec. Co., CV No. 96-121-M-CCL (D. Mont. Complaint filed Aug. 1, 1996)).

14.   INTELLECTUAL PROPERTY GUIDELINES,*su pra* note 1, § 3.3.

15.   State Oil Co. v. Khan, 522 U.S. 3, 22 (1997) (vertical maximum price restraints are subject to the rule of reason); *see also GTE Sylvania*, 433 U.S. at 57 (overruling *Schwinn* and holding that vertical non-price restraints may facilitate interbrand competition and are subject to the rule of reason). Although the terminology and legal framework is different in the European Union, these distinctions are also illustrated in the EU's Technology Transfer Block Exemption Regulation ("TTBER"), Commission Regulation (EC) No. 772/2004 of 27 April 2004 on the application of Article 81(3) of the Treaty to categories of technology transfer agreements, and associated Guidelines on the Application of Article 81 of the EC Treaty to Technology Transfer Agreements ("EU Guidelines"). Certain categories of restraints are categorized as hardcore restrictions, and thus not exempted pursuant to the TTBER, in a technology transfer between competing "undertakings" (i.e., organizations), while the same restraints may be exempt from the proscriptions of Article 81 under the TTBER in a technology transfer

This distinction recognizes that licensing of intellectual property enhances consumer welfare by allowing integration of the intellectual property with complementary factors of production, such as manufacturing facilities, distribution systems, and other intellectual property.[16] Restraints in intellectual property licensing, including field-of-use restraints and territorial restraints, exclusivity, and other types of restraints are often procompetitive, as they allow the owner of the intellectual property to deploy it most efficiently in combination with particular assets of others that add value in various contexts.[17]

In contrast to the permissive approach to vertical restraints in licensing arrangements, the agencies perceive that "antitrust concerns may arise when a licensing arrangement harms competition among entities that would have been actual or likely potential competitors in a relevant market in the absence of the license (entities in a 'horizontal relationship')."[18] But the existence of a horizontal relationship between the parties to a license agreement "does not, in itself, indicate that the arrangement is anticompetitive."[19]

As attested in the preamble to and the substance of the 2000 *Competitor Collaboration Guidelines*,[20] the courts and the agencies recognize that many types of collaborations between competitors are procompetitive.[21] Indeed, the National Cooperative Research and

---

between non-competing firms. *Compare* TTBER Art. 4, § 1 *with id.* § 2. *See also* EU Guidelines ¶¶ 26-33, ¶¶ 77-95 (agreements between competitors); ¶¶ 96-106 (agreements between non-competing undertakings).

16. INTELLECTUAL PROPERTY GUIDELINES,*su pra* note 1, §§ 2.0(c), 2.3.
17. *Id.*
18. *Id* § 3.1.
19. *Id.* § 3.3.
20. U.S. DEP'T OF JUSTICE & FED. TRADE COMM'N, ANTITRUST GUIDELINES FOR COLLABORATIONS AMONG COMPETITORS (2000) (hereinafter COMPETITOR COLLABORATION GUIDELINES), *reprinted in* 4 Trade Reg. Rep. (CCH) ¶ 13, 161.
21. *See* Preamble, COMPETITOR COLLABORATION GUIDELINES ("In order to compete in modern markets, competitors sometimes need to collaborate. Competitive forces are driving firms toward complex collaborations to achieve goals such as expanding into foreign markets, funding expensive innovation efforts, and lowering production and other costs. Such collaborations often are not only benign but procompetitive … [A] perception that antitrust laws are skeptical about agreements among actual or potential competitors may deter the development of procompetitive collaborations."); *see also* Addamax Corp. v. Open

Production Act of 1993 provides limited protections against application of the per se rule, and, with notification filings to the federal government, against treble damages, in connection with certain types of cooperative efforts.[22]

Nevertheless, some horizontal restraints, including price fixing, output restrictions, allocation of territories or customers, and certain group boycotts, are subject to per se proscription.[23] Horizontal restraints that are not subject to per se proscription are still more likely to draw antitrust scrutiny than most vertical restraints, and some may be subject to truncated or quick-look rule of reason analysis.[24]

2. Enforcement Agency Policies

The *Guidelines* describe the framework of analysis performed by the agencies in examining potential anticompetitive effects of restraints in

---

Software Found., 152 F.3d 48, 51 (1st Cir. 1998) (rule of reason applied to ancillary restraint in software collaboration).

22. Nat'l Cooperative Research and Production Act of 1993, as amended, 15 U.S.C. §§ 4301-4305.

23. INTELLECTUAL PROPERTY GUIDELINES, *supra* note 1, §§ 3.4, 5.1; *see also* COMPETITOR COLLABORATION GUIDELINES, *supra* note 20, § 1.2 (listing per se categories: "agreements among competitors to fix prices or output, rig bids, or share or divide markets by allocating customers, suppliers, territories, or lines of commerce"). For an example of a horizontal restraint in an otherwise vertical licensing arrangement challenged as per se unlawful, *see* United States v. Gen. Elec. Co., CV-96-121-M-CLL, 1997 U.S. Dist. LEXIS 5089 (D. Mont. Mar. 18, 1997) (covenant not to compete in license agreement). In the *GE* case, the DOJ obtained a consent decree prohibiting GE from enforcing non competition clauses in end-user licenses with hospitals for GE-developed diagnostic software and other tools and manuals used in servicing GE's medical imaging equipment. *Id.* (final judgment Jan. 11, 1999).

24. INTELLECTUAL PROPERTY GUIDELINES, *supra* note 1, § 3.4. In *In re Schering-Plough Corp.*, (Dec. 8, 2003), the FTC determined that it was unnecessary to prove a relevant market in a full-blown rule of reason analysis based on direct evidence of anticompetitive effects, but the Eleventh Circuit panel disagreed with the FTC's analysis, focusing on the need to address whether there would have been any adverse effect on competition absent a patent settlement in light of the unresolved issue whether the party to the settlement infringed valid claims of the patent. *Compare In re* Schering-Plough Corp., Docket No. 9297, 2003 F.T.C. LEXIS 187, *29-60 (2003), *with* Schering-Plough Corp. v. FTC, 402 F.3d 1056, 1072-76 (11th Cir. 2005), *cert. denied*, 126 S. Ct. 2929 (2006).

intellectual property license arrangements. As summarized in section 3.4 of the *Guidelines* ("Framework for Evaluating Licensing Restraints"), most restraints are evaluated under the rule of reason, although there are certain situations in which the agencies might challenge a restraint under *per se* rules or may conclude under a truncated analysis that a restraint either has no likely anticompetitive effects or, conversely, that it has likely anticompetitive effects and no valid efficiency justification.

The history and evolution of the governing legal standards in the courts and the enforcement policies and legal and economic theories of the United States enforcement agencies are traced in Chapter III. Early policies (including the *per se* proscriptions of the "Nine No-No's") included presumptions that patents or other types of intellectual property necessarily give their owners a monopoly or power in a market relevant for purposes of the antitrust laws.[25] These policies underwent a significant change in 1988, when the DOJ issued its *Antitrust Guidelines for International Operations*.[26] Pursuant to those *Guidelines*, the DOJ policy was to analyze restrictions in an intellectual property license under the rule of reason "unless the underlying transfer of technology is a sham."[27] A license would be regarded as a "sham" if the parties were demonstrably "not interested in transferring intellectual property rights, but rather [were] using the license to disguise their effort to restrict output or raise price in some market other than the market for the intellectual property."[28]

The government's enforcement policies as they stood in 1995 were set forth in the *Intellectual Property Guidelines*. The *Guidelines* continue in force and provide guidance and insights as to how the agencies will analyze antitrust issues in the licensing of intellectual

---

25. The Supreme Court clarified in *Illinois Tool Works v. Independent Ink*, 126 S. Ct. 1281, 1293 (2006), that there is no such presumption of market power from the mere existence of a patent, even for purposes of a tying claim.

26. *See* U.S. DEP'T OF JUSTICE, A NTITRUST ENFORECEMENT GUIDELINES FOR INTERNATIONAL OPERATIONS (1988), reprinted in 4 Trade Reg. Rep (CCH) 13,109 (hereinafter 1988 INTERNATIONAL ANTITRUST GUIDELINES). *See, e.g., id.* § 3.6 (Intellectual Property Licensing Arrangements), Cases 10 (Vertical Restraints in a Patent License), 11 (Exclusive Patent Cross Licenses with Grantbacks), and 12 (Know-How Technology Transfer Agreement with Exclusive Territories).

27. *Id.* § 3.62.

28. *Id.* n.131.

property.[29]   The 2000 *Competitor Collaboration Guidelines* reaffirmed several aspects of the analysis in the *Guidelines*.[30]

   Promoting   Innovation   and   Enhancing   Consumer   Welfare. According to the *Guidelines,* "The intellectual property laws and the antitrust laws share the common purpose of promoting innovation and enhancing consumer welfare."[31]   The *Guidelines* embody three general

---

29.   The *Guidelines* acknowledge that the licensing of intellectual property is often international, and its analysis applies equally to domestic and international licensing arrangements. *Id.* § 2.1.   Nevertheless, the United States agencies do not purport to speak for those charged with the enforcement of foreign laws. *Id.* § 2.3, Example 1, n.13 ("These Guidelines do not address the possible application of the antitrust laws of other countries to restraints such as territorial restrictions in international licensing arrangements").   In 2004, following criticism of prior rules, the European Commission released an amended TTBER, together with associated guidelines, that adopted an economics-driven approach to intellectual property antitrust and moved the EU and the United States enforcement policies closer.   Commission Regulation (EC) No. 772/2004 of 27 April 2004 on the application of Article 81(3) of the Treaty to categories of technology transfer agreements, and Guidelines on the Application of Article 81 of the EC Treaty to Technology Transfer Agreements; *see also* Guidelines for Patent and Know-how Licensing Agreements Under the Antimonopoly Act of Japan (July 30, 1999), *available at* http://www.jftc.go.jp/e-page/legislation/ama/patentandknow-how.pdf.   However, differences persist in various international legal frameworks, enforcement policies, and presumptively permissible and impermissible conduct.   That is a topic beyond the scope of this handbook, but the laws and guidelines of foreign competition authorities should be consulted to the extent licensing arrangements may have significant effects in markets in jurisdictions outside the United States.

30.   By way of example, the *Competitor Collaboration Guidelines* pick up where the *Guidelines* left off in adopting and articulating the law of ancillary restraints and joint venture analysis under which restraints otherwise considered per se unlawful might be reviewed instead under the rule of reason and found to be procompetitive to the extent that they are reasonably necessary to allow the parties to achieve the procompetitive benefits of an efficiency-enhancing integration of economic activity. COMPETITOR COLLABORATION GUIDELINES, *supra* note 20, § 3.

31.   INTELLECTUAL PROPERTY GUIDELINES, *supra* note 1, § 1.0 ("The intellectual property laws provide incentives for innovation and its dissemination and commercialization by establishing enforceable property rights for the creators of new and useful products, more efficient processes, and original works of expression.   In the absence of

principles: (a) for the purpose of antitrust analysis, the agencies regard intellectual property as being essentially comparable to any other form of property; (b) the agencies do not presume that intellectual property creates market power in the antitrust context; and (c) the agencies recognize that intellectual property licensing allows firms to combine complimentary factors of production and is generally procompetitive.[32]

The agencies apply the same general antitrust principles to conduct involving intellectual property that they apply to conduct involving any other form of intangible property. Intellectual property is "neither particularly free from scrutiny under the antitrust laws, nor particularly suspect under them."[33]

Market Power. The *Guidelines* acknowledge that there will often be sufficient actual or potential substitutes for a particular product, process, or work subject to exclusive rights to prevent the intellectual property holder's exercise of market power.[34] Thus, the agencies "will not presume that a patent, copyright, or trade secret necessarily confers market power upon its owner."[35] In 2006, over ten years after the *Guidelines*, the Supreme Court removed any doubt about this issue in *Illinois Tool Works v. Independent Ink*,[36] holding that the courts should not presume market power merely based upon the existence of a patent, even for purposes of tying cases.

---

intellectual property rights, imitators could more rapidly exploit the efforts of innovators and investors without compensation. Rapid imitation would reduce the commercial value of innovation and erode incentives to invest, ultimately to the detriment of consumers. The antitrust laws promote innovation and consumer welfare by prohibiting certain actions that may harm competition with respect to either existing or new ways of serving consumers."). *See* Kiwanee Oil v. Bicron Corp., 416 U.S. 470, 480 (1974); Atari Games Corp. v. Nintendo of Am., 897 F.2d 1572, 1576 (Fed. Cir. 1990) (the patent and antitrust laws are both "aimed at encouraging innovation, industry and competition").

32.   INTELLECTUAL PROPERTY GUIDELINES, *supra* note 1, § 2.0 (General Principles).

33.   *Id.* § 2.1 (Standard Antitrust Analysis Applies to Intellectual Property).

34.   *Id.* § 2.2; *see also* Potlach Corp. v. Innovations, Inc., 1976-2 Trade Cas. (CCH) ¶ 61,014 (N.D. Ill. 1976) ("The patented construction is interchangeable with others, not owned by Plaintiff, used for the identical purpose. The relevant market would therefore include all of these similar constructions ... In this larger market Plaintiff's market share is not substantial enough to constitute monopoly power....").

35.   INTELLECTUAL PROPERTY GUIDELINES, *supra* note 1, § 2.2.

36.   126 S. Ct. 1281 (2006).

The *Guidelines* further state that any market power that is, in fact, conferred by a patent or other intellectual property "does not by itself offend the antitrust laws."[37] Nor, according to the *Guidelines*, "does such market power impose on the intellectual property owner an obligation to license the use of that property to others."[38] Nevertheless, market power associated with intellectual property could be unlawfully acquired, or even if lawfully acquired and maintained, "would be relevant to the ability of an intellectual property owner to harm competition through unreasonable conduct in connection with such property."[39]

Procompetitive Benefits of Licensing. The *Guidelines* recognize the procompetitive benefits of licensing, which "can facilitate integration of the licensed property with complementary factors of production" and "lead to more efficient exploitation of the intellectual property, benefiting consumers through the reduction of costs and the introduction of new products," and in the long run "promote greater investment in research and development."[40]

The *Guidelines* expressly recognize that field of use, territorial, and other limitations on intellectual property licenses may be procompetitive, and that licensing "may promote the coordinated development of technologies that are in a blocking relationship."[41] They recognize that intellectual property derives value from combination with comple-

---

37.   INTELLECTUAL PROPERTY GUIDELINES, *supra* note 1, § 2.2 & n.11 (citing United States v. Grinnell Corp., 384 U.S. 563, 571 (1966), and United States v. Aluminum Co. of Am., 148 F.2d 416, 430 (2d Cir. 1945) (Sherman Act is not violated by the attainment of market power solely through "superior skill, foresight and industry")).

38.   *Id.* § 2.2; *see also id.* § 3.1 ("The Agencies will not require the owner of intellectual property to create competition in its own technology.").

39.   *Id.* § 2.2; *see* United States v. Microsoft Corp., 253 F.3d 34, 63 (D.C. Cir. 2001) (suggesting that the argument that exercise of lawfully acquired copyright protection cannot give rise to antitrust liability "is no more correct than the proposition that use of one's personal property, such as a baseball bat, cannot give rise to tort liability"). *Compare In re* Indep. Serv. Orgs. Antitrust Litig., 203 F.3d 1322, 1325 (Fed. Cir. 2000) ("Intellectual property rights do not confer a privilege to violate the antitrust laws."), *with id.* at 1327 ("In the absence of any indication of illegal tying, fraud in the Patent and Trademark Office, or sham litigation, the patent holder may enforce the statutory right to exclude others from making, using, or selling the claimed invention free from liability under the antitrust laws.").

40.   INTELLECTUAL PROPERTY GUIDELINES, *supra* note 1, § 2.3.

41.   *Id.*

mentary factors of production, including "manufacturing and distribution facilities, workforces, and other items of intellectual property."[42] Often it is most efficient to contract with others for such complementary factors, to sell rights to the intellectual property, or to enter joint venture arrangements for its development.[43]

Antitrust Concerns in Licensing Arrangements. In antitrust analysis, the agencies will "focus on the actual effects of the arrangement, not on its formal terms."[44] Among potential antitrust concerns are restraints that divide up goods markets among firms that would have otherwise competed using different technologies,[45] arrangements that merge two of only a few research and development operations in a field,[46] and acquisitions of intellectual property that lessen competition in a relevant market.[47]

The agencies "will not require the owner of intellectual property to create competition in its own technology."[48] The *Guidelines* note, however, that "antitrust concerns may arise when a licensing arrangement harms competition among entities that would have been actual or likely potential competitors in a relevant market in the absence of the license (entities in a 'horizontal relationship')."[49] For example, a restraint in a licensing arrangement may harm such competition if it: (1) facilitates market division or price-fixing; (2) forecloses access to, or significantly raises the price of, an important input in a relevant market; or (3) facilitates coordination to increase price or reduce output.[50]

Markets Affected by Licensing Arrangements: Goods, Technology, and Innovation Markets. Section 3.2 of the *Guidelines* addresses markets affected by licensing arrangements. Licensing arrangements raise concerns "if they are likely to affect adversely the prices, quantities, qualities, or varieties of goods or services either currently or potentially available."[51] If the competitive effects cannot adequately be assessed within relevant markets for goods and services, the agencies may also

42.   *Id.*
43.   *Id.*
44.   *Id.* § 3.1 (Nature of the Concerns).
45.   *Id.* at Ex. 7.
46.   *Id.* §§ 3.1 & 3.2.3.
47.   *Id.* §§ 3.1 & 5.7.
48.   *Id.* § 3.1.
49.   *Id.* § 3.1.
50.   *Id.*
51.   *Id.* § 3.2.

examine effects on markets for technology, or even "innovation" markets relating to research and development efforts.[52]

A restraint in a licensing arrangement may have competitive effects in final or intermediate markets for goods or services made or provided using the intellectual property,[53] "or it may have effects upstream, in markets for goods [or services] that are used as inputs, along with the intellectual property, to the production of other goods [or provision of other services]."[54] In general, the agencies "will approach the delineation of relevant market and the measurement of market share in the intellectual property area as in Section 1 of the *U.S. Department of Justice and Federal Trade Commission Horizontal Merger Guidelines*."[55]

When intellectual property rights are marketed separately from the products in which they are used, the agencies may analyze competitive effects in a market for the licensed technology and its close substitutes.[56] Those close substitutes may include both alternative technologies and

---

52. *Id.* §§ 3.2.2 & 3.2.3.
53. The *Guidelines* include services in their definition of the term "goods," so that, unlike the statutory language of § 3 of the Clayton Act or § 2 of the Robinson-Patman Act, references to goods in the *Guidelines* does not exclude, but rather includes, services.
54. INTELLECTUAL PROPERTY GUIDELINES, *supra* note 1, § 3.2.1 (Goods Markets).
55. Id. § 3.0 (citing U.S. DEP'T OF JUSTICE AND FED. TRADE COMM'N, HORIZONTAL MERGER GUIDELINES (Apr. 2, 1992) (hereinafter 1992 HORIZONTAL MERGER GUIDELINES), *reprinted in* 4 Trade Reg. Rep. (CCH) ¶ 13,104). The 1992 *Horizontal Merger Guidelines* employ a "hypothetical monopolist" test, incrementally adding potential substitutes to a narrowly-defined core product, until it is determined that a hypothetical monopolist over that product and its substitutes could profitably impose a small but significant (5%) and nontransitory increase in price. This test only accounts for demand-side substitution, and supply-side substitution must be accounted for in the identification of present and possible prospective participants in any market.
56. INTELLECTUAL PROPERTY GUIDELINES,*su pra* note 1, § 3.2.2 (Technology Markets). *But see id.* n.19 ("Intellectual property is often licensed, sold, or transferred as an integral part of a marketed good. An example is a patented product marketed with an implied license permitting its use. In such circumstances, there is no need for a separate analysis of technology markets to capture relevant competitive effects.").

goods or services competing with those that are produced with the intellectual property under examination.[57]

The agencies also may assess competitive effects in an "innovation market" relating to research and development.[58] An innovation market consists of the research and development directed to particular new or improved goods or processes and close substitutes, including research and development, technology, and goods and services.[59] Although the *Guidelines* speak to potential adverse effects of a licensing arrangement in an innovation market, enforcement activity with respect to innovation markets has focused on mergers, and generally those in the pharmaceutical industry where the R&D for a drug usually takes several years, and new products are subject to regulatory examination.[60]

---

57. *Id.* at Ex. 2 & n.18 ("the owner of a process for producing a particular good may be constrained in its conduct with respect to that process not only by other processes for making that good, but also by other goods that compete with the downstream good and by the processes used to produce those other goods"). Example 2 demonstrates that combining two competing technologies in a bona fide joint venture is not necessarily anticompetitive as long as there are sufficient remaining competing technologies or goods to constrain pricing. It also suggests a methodology for defining "technology markets" similar to the hypothetical monopolist test utilized in the 1992 *Horizontal Merger Guidelines* with respect to goods markets, and a flexible approach to evaluating market shares. *See id.* at Ex. 2 & n.20.

58. *Id.* § 3.2.3 (Research and Development: Innovation Markets).

59. *Id.*

60. *Id.* § 3.2.3 ("A licensing arrangement may have competitive effects on innovation that cannot be adequately addressed through the analysis of goods or technology markets"), Example 3 (addressing hypothetical cross-license by two firms specializing in advanced metallurgy of future patents relating to development of a new component for aircraft jet turbines), and Example 4 (addressing hypothetical joint venture under which three of largest manufacturers of plastic bottles would combine research and development efforts on rapidly biodegradable plastic for bottles, granting exclusive rights to patents and know-how to the three parties to the joint venture, which would be subject to analysis similar to analysis of other types of joint ventures between competitors). Research and development (and certain production) joint ventures are subject to rule of reason analysis and, if notifications are filed, protected against treble damages, under the National Cooperative Research and Production Act of 1993 (NCRPA), as amended, 15 U.S.C. §§ 4301-05. Pursuant to the 2004 amendments to the NCRPA, certain activities of standard development organizations may also be subject to such protections.

***Modes of Analysis and Framework for Evaluating Licensing
Restraints.*** As noted above, the agencies' analysis of licensing restraints
depends to some extent on whether the parties are in a vertical or a
horizontal relationship.[61]   As summarized in section 3.4 of the
Guidelines, "[i]n the vast majority of cases, restraints in intellectual
property licensing arrangements are evaluated under the rule of reason."

Under the rule of reason, the agencies initially inquire whether the
restraint is likely to have anticompetitive effects.[62] If it is likely to have
such effects, they will consider "whether the restraint is reasonably
necessary to achieve procompetitive benefits that outweigh those
anticompetitive effects."[63] The discussion of "Procompetitive Benefits of
Licensing" in section 2.3 of the *Guidelines* discussed above provides
examples of how intellectual property is integrated with complementary
factors of production to enhance efficiency.   General principles
concerning the agencies' evaluation of licensing arrangements under the
rule of reason are set forth in part 4 of the *Guidelines*, which is discussed
further below.

The *Guidelines* identify the following restraints that may be treated
as unlawful per se without an elaborate inquiry into likely competitive
effect: "naked price-fixing, output restraints, and market division among
horizontal competitors, as well as certain group boycotts and resale price
maintenance."[64]   The agencies may challenge restraints falling within
these categories under per se rules unless the restraint "can be expected
to contribute to an efficiency-enhancing integration of economic
activity."[65] The *Guidelines* acknowledge that licensing arrangements
generally do "promote such integration because they facilitate the
combination of the licensor's intellectual property with complementary

---

61.   INTELLECTUAL PROPERTY GUIDELINES, *su pra* note 1, § 3.3.
62.   *Id.* §§ 3.4 & 4.1.
63.   *Id.* § 3.4 (citing part 4 of the *Guidelines* and FTC v. Indiana Fed'n of
       Dentists, 476 U.S. 447 (1986); NCAA v. Bd. of Regents, 468 U.S. 85
       (1984); Broad. Music v. CBS, 441 U.S. 1 (1979); and 7 PHILLIP E.
       AREEDA, ANTITRUST LAW § 1502 (1986)).
64.   INTELLECTUAL PROPERTY GUIDELINES, *supra* note 1, § 3.4 (citing FTC v.
       Superior Court Trial Lawyers Ass'n, 493 U.S. 411, 433 (1990); Nat'l
       Soc'y of Prof'l Eng'rs v. United States, 435 U.S. 679, 692 (1978)).
65.   *Id.* § 3.4 ("If there is no efficiency-enhancing integration of economic
       activity and if the type of restraint is one that has been accorded per se
       treatment, the Agencies will challenge the restraint under the per se rule.
       Otherwise, the Agencies will apply a rule of reason analysis") (citing
       Broad. Music, 441 U.S. at 16-24).

factors of production owned by the licensee."[66]   A restraint "may further such integration by, for example, aligning the incentives of the licensor and the licensees to promote the development and marketing of the licensed technology, or by substantially reducing transactions costs."[67]

The analysis of the *Guidelines* is reflected in the *Competitor Collaboration Guidelines*.   Section 3 of the *Competitor Collaboration Guidelines* further articulates how the agencies may treat a restraint that might be characterized as per se unlawful in other contexts as subject to rule of reason analysis to the extent that it is reasonably related to an efficiency-enhancing integration of economic activity and is reasonably necessary to achieve the procompetitive benefits of that efficiency-enhancing integration.[68]   This same general analysis is reflected in (or at least anticipated by) the analysis of potential anticompetitive effects and justification for restraints in section 4.2 of the *Guidelines*, without express notation of inclusion and exclusion from per se rules dependent upon the ancillary nature of the restraint.   As noted in section 5.1 of the *Guidelines*, "[a]s in the case of joint ventures among horizontal competitors, licensing arrangements among such competitors may promote rather than hinder competition if they result in integrative efficiencies."[69]

The *Guidelines* acknowledge that "[a]pplication of the rule of reason generally requires a comprehensive inquiry into market conditions."[70]   However, the agencies may apply a truncated rule of reason analysis to reach favorable or unfavorable conclusions regarding a restraint.   For example, if the agencies conclude that a restraint has no likely anticompetitive effects, "they will treat it as reasonable, without an elaborate analysis of market power or the justifications for the restraint."[71]   On the other end of the spectrum, "if a restraint facially appears to be of a kind that would always tend to reduce output or increase prices, and the restraint is not reasonably related to efficiencies, the Agencies will likely challenge the restraint without an elaborate analysis of particular industry circumstances."[72]

---

66.   *Id.* § 3.4.
67.   *Id.*
68.   COMPETITOR COLLABORATION GUIDELINES, *supra* note 20, § 3.2.
69.   INTELLECTUAL PROPERTY GUIDELINES, *su pra* note 1, § 5.1.
70.   *Id.* § 3.4.
71.   *Id.* § 3.4.
72.   *Id.* § 3.4 (citing FTC v. Indiana Fed'n of Dentists, 476 U.S. 447, 459-60 (1986), and NCAA v. Bd. of Regents, 468 U.S. 85, 109 (1984)).

The *Guidelines* note that the FTC's approach to a truncated rule of reason is detailed in *Massachusetts Board of Registration in Optometry*,[73] and that "the FTC uses the analytical category of 'inherently suspect' restraints to denote facially anticompetitive restraints that would always or almost always tend to decrease output or increase prices, but that may be relatively unfamiliar or may not fit neatly into traditional per se categories."[74] Under this approach, "asserted efficiency justifications for inherently suspect restraints are examined to determine whether they are plausible and, if so, whether they are valid in the context of the market at issue."[75]

Agencies' Evaluation of Licensing Arrangements Under the Rule of Reason. In analyzing anticompetitive effects under the rule of reason, the agencies will consider issues of market structure, coordination, and foreclosure as described in section 4.1.1 of the *Guidelines*, and issues involving exclusivity as discussed in section 4.1.2 of the *Guidelines*. Only if they conclude that a restraint is likely to have an anticompetitive effect in a relevant market will they assess efficiencies and justifications, as discussed in section 4.2 of the *Guidelines*.

As discussed above, the agencies' analysis of restraints in licensing arrangements depends on whether the parties are in a horizontal or vertical relationship. As explained the *Guidelines*, a horizontal restraint in a licensing agreement "may increase the risk of coordinated pricing, output restrictions, or the acquisition or maintenance of market power" or the risk "of retarding or restricting the development of new or improved goods or processes."[76] The potential for competitive harm may depend on market factors, such as the degree of concentration, barriers to entry, and the likely demand and supply responses to changes in price in relevant markets.[77]

The agencies will analyze whether a vertical restraint harms competition at either the level of the licensor or the licensee, for example by foreclosing competitors' access to important inputs or facilitating

---

73. 110 F.T.C. 549, 604 (1988).

74. INTELLECTUAL PROPERTY GUIDELINES, *supra* note 1, § 3.4, n.27.

75. *Id.* § 3.4, n.28 (citing *Mass. Bd.*, 110 F.T.C. at 604). *See generally* PolyGram Holding v. FTC, 416 F.3d 29, 39 (D.C. Cir. 2005) (affirming order based on truncated analysis); *In re* N. Texas Physicians, FTC Docket No. 9312 (Dec. 1 2005) (available at http://www.ftc.gov/os/adjpro/d9312/index.htm).

76. INTELLECTUAL PROPERTY GUIDELINES, *supra* note 1, § 4.1.1.

77. *Id.* (citing 1992 HORIZONTAL MERGER GUIDELINES, *supra* note 55, §§ 1.5, 3).

coordination on price or limitations of output.[78]   According to the *Guidelines*, "[t]he risk of anticompetitively foreclosing access or increasing competitors' costs is related to the proportion of the markets affected by the licensing restraint; other characteristics of the relevant markets, such as concentration, difficulty of entry, and the responsiveness of supply and demand to changes in price in the relevant markets; and the duration of the restraint."[79]

Vertical restraints may create risks of facilitating horizontal coordination to raise prices or reduce output in a relevant market, especially in markets that are concentrated and difficult to enter.[80]   Even though prevalent parallel restraints may create some concerns in some contexts, the agencies recognize that the use of similar restraints may be common and procompetitive in an industry and similar or parallel restraints may contribute to efficient exploitation of the licensed property.[81]

Efficiencies and Justifications.   The agencies only consider efficiencies and justifications if they conclude based on market factors described in section 4.1 that a restraint has, or is likely to have, an anticompetitive effect in a relevant market.[82]

The agencies consider whether a restraint is reasonably necessary to achieve procompetitive efficiencies, including consideration of practical and significantly less restrictive alternatives:

---

78.   *Id.*
79.   *Id.* ("A licensing arrangement does not foreclose competition merely because some or all of the potential licensees in an industry choose to use the licensed technology to the exclusion of other technologies. Exclusive use may be an efficient consequence of the licensed technology having the lowest cost or highest value.").
80.   *Id.* ("For example, if owners of competing technologies impose similar restraints on their licensees, the licensors may find it easier to coordinate their pricing. Similarly, licensees that are competitors may find it easier to coordinate their pricing if they are subject to common restraints in licenses with a common licensor or competing licensors.").
81.   *Id.; cf. E.I. du Pont de Nemours & Co. v. FTC*, 729 F.2d 128, 142 (2d Cir. 1984) (vacating Commission order barring the use of most-favored-nations clauses that had been used by each competitor in the industry).
82.   INTELLECTUAL PROPERTY GUIDELINES, *supra* note 1, § 4.2 ("if the agencies conclude, upon an evaluation of the market factors described in section 4.1, that a restraint in a licensing arrangement is unlikely to have an anticompetitive effect, they will not challenge the restraint").

If it is clear that the parties could have achieved similar efficiencies by means that are significantly less restrictive, then the Agencies will not give weight to the parties' efficiency claim. In making this assessment, however, the Agencies will not engage in a search for a theoretically least restrictive alternative that is not realistic in the practical prospective business situation faced by the parties.[83]

As discussed in section 4.2 of the *Guidelines*, if the restraint is reasonably necessary to achieve procompetitive efficiencies, the agencies will balance the procompetitive efficiencies and the anticompetitive effects to determine the probable net effect on competition in each relevant market. Although section 4 of the *Guidelines* discusses "General Principles Concerning the Agencies' Evaluation of Licensing Arrangements under the Rule of Reason," the analysis in section 3.2 of the subsequent *Competitor Collaboration Guidelines* confirms that this ancillary restraint analysis would likely be applied by the agencies in determining whether an otherwise per se unlawful restraint should be governed by the rule of reason, in addition to how it might fare under that rule of reason analysis.

The agencies may be inclined to challenge a restraint with anticompetitive effects when the duration of the restraint "clearly exceeds the period needed to achieve the procompetitive efficiency."[84] All of these evaluations depend on market context.[85]

Antitrust "Safety Zone." The *Guidelines* establish in section 4.3 an antitrust "safety zone," which confirms that the agencies would not

83. *Id.* The *Competitor Collaboration Guidelines* also note that an agreement (or restraint) may be "reasonably necessary" without being essential. COMPETITOR COLLABORATION GUIDELINES, *supra* note 20, § 3.2 ("In making this assessment ... the Agencies consider whether practical, significantly less restrictive means were reasonably available when the agreement was entered into, but do not search for a theoretically less restrictive alternative that was not practical given the business realities.").

84. INTELLECTUAL PROPERTY GUIDELINES, *supra* note 1, § 4.2 ("The effective duration of a restraint may depend on a number of factors, including the option of the affected party to terminate the arrangement unilaterally and the presence of contract terms (e.g., unpaid balances on minimum purchase commitments) that encourage the licensee to renew a license agreement.").

85. *Id.* ("A restraint that may be justified by the needs of a new entrant, for example, may not have a procompetitive efficiency justification in different market circumstances. *Cf.* United States v. Jerrold Elec., 187 F. Supp. 545 (E.D. Pa. 1960), *aff'd per curiam*, 365 U.S. 567 (1961).").

challenge a restraint absent extraordinary circumstances when certain conditions are met.[86]

First, as described in section 4.3 of the *Guidelines*, in order to qualify for a safety zone, a restraint must not be "facially anticompetitive." Facially anticompetitive restraints are those "that normally warrant per se treatment, as well as other restraints of a kind that would always or almost always tend to reduce output or increase prices."[87] The *Guidelines* include among restraints that normally warrant per se treatment: "naked price-fixing, output restraints, and market divisions among horizontal competitors, as well as certain group boycotts and resale price maintenance."[88]

Second, for the safety zone to apply, "the licensor and its licensees collectively [may] account for no more than twenty percent of each relevant market significantly affected by the restraint."[89] The applicability of the safety zone is "determined by reference only to goods markets unless the analysis of goods markets alone would inadequately

---

86. *Id.* § 4.3 ("The safety zone is designed to provide owners of intellectual property with a degree of certainty in those situations in which anticompetitive effects are so unlikely that the arrangements may be presumed not to be anticompetitive without an inquiry into particular industry circumstances.").

87. *Id.* § 4.3 n.30. The *Guidelines* reference *Massachusetts Board of Registration in Optometry*, 110 F.T.C. 549, 604 (1988), as providing details about the approach of the FTC in using "the analytical category of 'inherently suspect' restraints to denote facially anticompetitive restraints that would always or almost always tend to decrease output or increase prices, but that may not fit neatly into the traditional per se categories." INTELLECTUAL PROPERTY GUIDELINES, *supra* note 1, § 3.4. Nevertheless, since the *Guidelines* were issued in April 1995, the Supreme Court has limited, rather than expanded, the categories of restraints that are viewed as per se unlawful or inherently anticompetitive. *See, e.g.,* State Oil Co. v. Khan, 522 U.S. 3, 11 (1997); Cal. Dental Ass'n v. FTC, 526 U.S. 756, 780 (1999).

88. INTELLECTUAL PROPERTY GUIDELINES, *supra* note 1, § 3.4. Notably absent are tying arrangements. *See id.* § 5.3.

89. *Id.* § 4.3. Reliance on a "safety zone" thus depends on market definition, which may be difficult to establish with any degree of reliability and cost-effectiveness, depending on the context. Nevertheless, when the parties to licenses are clearly smaller players in a large or unconcentrated market, consideration of the safety zone may be useful in avoiding the need for further analysis.

address the effects of the licensing arrangement on competition among technologies or in research and development."[90]

Pursuant to section 4.3 of the *Guidelines*, "[i]f an examination of the effects on competition among technologies or in research and development is required, and if market share data are unavailable or do not accurately represent competitive significance," then criteria other than market shares may establish a safety zone. In such situations, aside from facially anticompetitive restraints, the safety zone applies, as to technology markets, when "there are four or more independently controlled technologies in addition to the technologies controlled by the parties to the licensing arrangement that may be substitutable for the licensed technology at a comparable cost to the user."[91] As to innovation markets, there must be "four or more independently controlled entities in addition to the parties to the licensing arrangement [that] possess the required specialized assets or characteristics and the incentive to engage in research and development that is a close substitute of the research and development activities of the parties to the licensing agreement."[92]

Licensing arrangements are not presumed to be unlawful merely because they fall outside the safety zone. Rather, arrangements falling outside the safety zone are analyzed by the agencies as described above in the previous section, and as outlined in parts 3 to 5 of the *Guidelines*. As noted in section 4.3 of the *Guidelines*, "it is likely that the great majority of licenses falling outside the safety zone are lawful and procompetitive."

---

90.   *Id.* As further noted in § 4.3, "[t]he status of a licensing arrangement with respect to the safety zone may change over time." *Id.* The agencies' determination regarding a safety zone "is based on the factual circumstances at the time of the conduct at issue," which may be the transaction giving rise to the restraint or the subsequent implementation of the restraint. *Id.* & n.32; *see also* COMPETITOR COLLABORATION GUIDELINES, *supra* note 20, § 2.4 ("The Agencies assess the competitive effects of a relevant agreement as of the time of possible harm to competition, whether at formation of the collaboration or at a later time, as appropriate.").

91.   INTELLECTUAL PROPERTY GUIDELINES,*supra* note 1, § 4.3.

92.   *Id.* § 4.3. In comparison, the more recent § 4.3 of the *Competitor Collaboration Guidelines* provides for a safety zone in an innovation market where there are three or more such independently controlled research efforts in addition to those of the collaboration, as opposed to the "four or more" of the *Guidelines*.

3. Evidentiary Burdens and Presumptions

The *Guidelines* have no direct legal or regulatory force, but seek to reflect both enforcement policy and, with limited exceptions, the contours of the federal antitrust laws as established by the courts in interpreting the broadly drafted proscriptions of the federal antitrust statutes. The discussion of evidentiary burdens and presumptions below focuses on those interpretations by the courts, noting aspects reflected in the *Guidelines*.

The Antitrust Plaintiff's Burden of Proof. Included in the principles embodied in the *Guidelines* are the principles that standard antitrust analysis applies to intellectual property, and that intellectual property is "neither particularly free from scrutiny under the antitrust laws, nor particularly suspect under them."[93] Standard antitrust analysis under the Sherman Act encompasses over 100 years of standards, burdens, and presumptions that have waxed and waned with developing legal and economic theories and knowledge.[94]

In *Illinois Tool Works v. Independent Ink*[95] the Supreme Court recently put an end to any presumption of market power based on the mere existence of a patent, even in tying cases. Without such a presumption, it is clear that traditional antitrust principles and burdens of proof are applied in cases involving intellectual property.

The burdens and presumptions applicable to claims under Section 1 of the Sherman Act may be summarized as follows. First, the burden is generally on the plaintiff asserting a violation of Section 1 of the Sherman Act to establish: (1) a contract, combination in the form of a trust or otherwise, or conspiracy between or among two or more parties; (2) that unreasonably restrains trade; and (3) affects interstate or foreign commerce.[96]

---

93. INTELLECTUAL PROPERTY GUIDELINES, *supra* note 1, § 2.1.
94. This Chapter addresses intellectual property agreements that raise antitrust concerns. Unilateral conduct raising antitrust concerns is addressed in Chapter VI. Nevertheless, license agreements, naturally subject to § 1 of the Sherman Act because by their very nature they comprise "agreements," may also raise antitrust concerns that may be addressed by § 2 of the Sherman Act depending on the circumstances. *See, e.g.*, United States v. Microsoft Corp., 253 F.3d 34, 64 (D.C. Cir. 2001) (§ 2 violation found and upheld on appeal based on exclusive dealing, even where § 1 claim with respect to the same conduct failed).
95   126 S. Ct. 1281 (2006).
96. *See* Tunis Bros. v. Ford Motor Co., 952 F.2d 715, 722 (3d Cir. 1991).

Generally, in analyzing licensing arrangements, the first element (an agreement between two parties) would be established by the existence of a license agreement between two independently controlled entities. The interstate commerce element is satisfied if the activity in question "substantially and adversely affects interstate commerce."[97]

Thus, the main issue in a Section 1 challenge of an agreement involving the licensing of intellectual property is the broad consideration of whether the agreement "unreasonably" restrains trade. Section 1 claims in general are subject to the rule of reason.[98] Where a claim is governed by the rule of reason, the burden is on the plaintiff to allege and prove that the overall effect of the restraints in an agreement is harmful to competition in a market that is relevant for purposes of the antitrust laws.[99]

Proof of harm to competition typically first requires a plaintiff to establish the contours of the relevant product or service market and geographic market in which competition occurs.[100] Second, a plaintiff must establish that the defendant or conspirators exercise market power and adversely affect competition in the relevant market.[101]

Market power is generally defined as "the ability to maintain prices above, or output below, competitive levels for a significant period of

---

97. Hosp. Bldg. v. Trs. of Rex Hosp., 425 U.S. 738, 743 (1976); *see also* Summit Health v. Pinhas, 500 U.S. 322, 329 (1991); McLain v. Real Estate Bd., 444 U.S. 232, 241-42 (1980).

98. *See* Bus. Elecs. Corp. v. Sharp Elecs. Corp., 485 U.S. 717, 726 (1988) ('there is a presumption in favor of a rule-of-reason standard").

99. *See generally* Chicago Bd. of Trade v. United States, 246 U.S. 231, 238 (1918) (all agreements restrain trade and § 1 proscribes only those restraints that unreasonably restrict competition).

100. *See* ABA SECTION OF ANTITRUST LAW, ANTITRUST LAW DEVELOPMENTS at 67, 589-90 (5th ed. 2002) ("Without defining the relevant market, there is no meaningful context within which to assess the restraint's competitive effects.") (citing cases); *see also* Walker Process Equip. v. Food Mach. & Chem. Corp., 382 U.S. 172, 178 (1965) ("without a definition of the market there is no way to measure a defendant's ability to lessen or destroy competition").

101. United States v. Visa USA, 344 F.3d 229, 238 (2d Cir. 2003) ("As an initial matter, the government must demonstrate that the defendant conspirators have 'market power' in a particular market for goods or services.... Next, the government must demonstrate that within the relevant market, the defendants' actions have had substantial adverse effects on competition, such as increases in price, or decreases in output or quality.").

time."[102]   The exercise of market power may be established by direct evidence or through expert testimony on market shares in a relevant market, coupled with economic analysis as to why such market shares may warrant an inference of market power in light of market structure, barriers to entry, and other factors. [103]

If the plaintiff meets its burden, at least according to some courts, "the burden of production shifts to the defendants, who must provide a procompetitive justification for the restraint."[104]   In assessing such justifications, the courts or fact-finders may assess the extent to which the restraint is reasonably necessary to achieve the procompetitive justification and the extent to which such objectives may be achieved through less restrictive means.[105]

In addition, a private plaintiff in a civil action seeking injunctive relief or damages pursuant to the Clayton Act[106] for injury to its business or property by reason of a violation of the Sherman Act must establish standing[107] and antitrust injury.[108]

---

102.   INTELLECTUAL PROPERTY GUIDELINES, *supra* note 1, § 2.2 (Intellectual Property and Market Power). Section 2.2 further notes (in footnote 9) that market power "can be exercised in other economic dimensions, such as quality, service, and the development of new or improved goods and services."

103.   *See* ABA SECTION OF ANTITRUST LAW, ANTITRUST EVIDENCE HAND-BOOK 167-70 (2d ed. 2002); ANTITRUST LAW DEVELOPMENTS, *supra* note 100, at 589-90.

104.   *Visa USA,* 344 F.3d at 238; *see also* PolyGram Holding v. FTC, 416 F.3d 29, 39 (D.C. Cir. 2005) (failure to establish valid procompetitive justification for restraint).

105.   *Visa USA*, 344 F.3d at 238 ("If the defendants [provide a procompetitive justification], the government must prove either that the challenged restraint is not reasonably necessary to achieve defendants' procompetitive justifications, or that those objectives may be achieved in a manner less restrictive of free competition.").

106.   Treble damages and costs including a reasonable attorney's fee are provided for in § 4 of the Clayton Act, 15 U.S.C. § 15, and injunctive relief against threatened loss or damage from a violation of the antitrust laws is provided for in § 16 of the Clayton Act, 15 U.S.C. § 26.

107.   *See* Associated Gen. Contractors v. Cal. State Council of Contractors, 459 U.S. 519, 529 (1983).

108.   *See* Atl. Richfield Co. v. USA Petroleum, 495 U.S. 328, 334 (1990); Cargill, Inc. v. Montfort of Col., Inc., 479 U.S. 104, 110 (1986); Brunswick Corp. v. Pueblo Bowl-O-Mat, 429 U.S. 477, 486 (1977).

The burdens and presumptions may be very different with respect to a claim that is subject to per se proscription than one subject to full rule of reason analysis. In between, the agencies and the courts may apply truncated or quick look rule of reason analysis that blurs some of those distinctions.[109] Some types of per se claims may require a plaintiff asserting such claims to establish exercise of market power,[110] which also may make the burdens and presumptions in a per se case more similar to than different from a rule of reason case.

For the past thirty years the Supreme Court has mostly contracted rather than expanded categories of restraints or agreements that are per se unlawful under the antitrust laws.[111] Nevertheless, there are still certain types of restraints and agreements that may be treated as per se unlawful, and as to which the plaintiff may assert that proof of relevant market and anticompetitive effect is not required. Generally, per se treatment is more likely to be applied to horizontal restraints, as opposed to vertical restraints.

For example, horizontal price-fixing, price-related restraints, output restrictions, territorial restraints, customer restraints, and group boycotts may be subject to per se proscription. If a restraint that might otherwise be characterized as per se unlawful is reasonably related to an efficiency-enhancing integration of economic activity it would be subject to the rule of reason.[112]

---

109. *See, e.g.*, PolyGram Holding v. FTC, 416 F.3d 29, 34-35 (D.C. Cir. 2005) (opining that rule of reason, quick look, or truncated rule of reason and per se rules should be viewed as a continuum, not three distinct analyses into which categories of cases should be slotted); *see also In re N. Tex. Physicians*, FTC Docket No. 9312 (Dec. 1 2005) (available at http://www.ftc.gov/os/adjpro/d9312/index.htm).
110. *See Polygram Holding*, 416 F.3d at 34-35. For example, as to group boycott claims, see *Northwest Wholesale Stationers v. Pacific Stationery & Printing*, 472 U.S. 284, 296 (1985). As to tying claims, see *Jefferson Parish Hospital District No. 2 v. Hyde*, 466 U.S. 2, 13-29 (1984) (no per se tying claim where plaintiff could not establish market power in the tying market).
111. *See infra* Chapter III.
112. *See* NCAA v. Bd. of Regents, 468 U.S. 85, 101-103 (1984); Rothery Storage & Van Co. v. Atlas Van Lines, 792 F.2d 210 (D.C. Cir. 1986); *see also* Texaco, Inc. v. Dagher, 126 S. Ct. 1276, 1280-81 (2006) (referencing the ancillary restraints doctrine, and finding that an agreement between the owners of a lawful joint venture with respect to the pricing of the joint venture's products is not a per se violation of § 1 of the Sherman Act).

B. Licensing Restraints That Raise Antitrust Issues

The analytical concepts discussed above play out in the analysis of specific licensing restraints. This section discusses common restraints and their antitrust implications.

1. Price and Output Restraints

Naked horizontal price fixing agreements[113] and agreements to restrict output or supply[114] are subject to per se proscription under Section 1 of the Sherman Act. As noted in sections 3.4 and 5.1 of the *Guidelines*, the per se analysis applies to intellectual licensing restrictions that effect these types of agreements.[115]

Vertical price fixing is generally treated as per se unlawful,[116] with the exception of vertical *maximum* price agreements, which are subject to the rule of reason.[117] Again, these concepts apply to licensing restraints. As stated in section 5.2 of the *Guidelines*, quoting *Dr. Miles*, "[r]esale price maintenance is illegal when 'commodities have passed into the

---

113. United States v. Trenton Potteries Co., 273 U.S. 392, 397-98 (1927).
114. *See* FTC v. Superior Court Trial Lawyers Ass'n, 493 U.S. 411, 423 (1990); *see also NCAA*, 468 U.S. at 101-110 (noting that horizontal price and output restraints are typically per se unlawful, but applying the rule of reason and finding violation in the context of a collegiate sports league); United States v. Socony-Vacuum Oil, 310 U.S. 150, 216 (1940) (agreement to purchase excess product has the same effect as an agreement to raise or maintain prices).
115. INTELLECTUAL PROPERTY GUIDELINES,*su pra* note 1, §§ 3.4, 5.1.
116. *See* United States v. Univis Lens Co., 316 U.S. 241, 252-53 (1942); *see also* Standard Sanitary Mfg. v. United States, 226 U.S. 20, 41-51 (1912) (combination of manufacturers to limit terms of sale and fix prices of finished goods manufactured using patented machines and to require jobbers to sign agreements to adhere to resale pricing under the umbrella of terms for licensing of certain patents violated the Sherman Act); Dr. Miles Med. v. John D. Park & Sons, 220 U.S. 373, 408 (1911) (network of agents selling medicine manufactured under secret formula at fixed prices was in reality a resale distribution network and price fixing was illegal resale price maintenance).
117. State Oil Co. v. Khan, 522 U.S. 3, 18-19 (1997) (overruling Albrecht v. Herald Co., 390 U.S. 145 (1968), and holding that vertical maximum price fixing is subject to the rule of reason). Any reference to or reliance on *Albrecht* in § 5.2 of the *Guidelines*, issued in 1995, is obviously superseded by the 1997 decision in *State Oil*.

channels of trade and are owned by dealers."[118]	The *Guidelines* further
state, "consistent with the principles set forth in section 3.4, the Agencies
will enforce the per se rule against resale price maintenance in the
intellectual property context."[119]	In support of this policy, the agencies
note that "[i]t has been held per se illegal for a licensor of an intellectual
property right in a product to fix a licensee's *resale* price of that
product."[120]

A narrow exception to the per se rule against vertical minimum price
agreements is set forth in the Supreme Court's 1926 opinion in *United
States v. General Electric.*[121]	In that case, the Court noted that a patentee
could choose to grant a license to make and use, without granting a
license to sell.[122]	When the patentee chooses to grant a license to sell,
and also continues to sell the patented product itself, the Court found it
appropriate to allow the patentee to prohibit the licensee from
undercutting profit maximizing monopoly pricing anticipated by the
grant of the exclusive rights in the patent.[123]	Thus, the restraint on the
licensee's sale price was not unlawful as long as the restriction applied
only to the first sale of the patented article.[124]

118.	INTELLECTUAL PROPERTY GUIDELINES, *supra* note 1, § 5.2 (quoting *Dr.
Miles*, 220 U.S. at 408).
119.	*Id.* § 5.2.
120.	*Id.* (citing United States v. Univis Lens Co., 316 U.S. 241 (1942); Ethyl
Gas. Corp. v. United States, 309 U.S. 436 (1940)).
121.	272 U.S. 476 (1926).
122.	*Id.* at 490.	The current version of the Patent Act also includes the
additional exclusive right to offer for sale. 35 U.S.C. § 271(a) ("whoever
without authority makes, uses, offers to sell or sells any patented
invention within the United States or imports into the United States any
patented invention during the term of the patent therefore, infringes the
patent").
123.	*Id.* at 490 ("When the patentee licenses another to make and vend, and
retains the right to continue to make and vend on his own account, the
price at which his licensee will sell will necessarily affect the price at
which he can sell his own patented goods.	It would seem entirely
reasonable that he should say to the licensee, 'Yes, you may make and
sell articles under my patent, but not so as to destroy the profit that I wish
to obtain by making them and selling them myself.' He does not thereby
sell outright to the licensee the articles the latter may make and sell, or
vest absolute ownership in them.	He restricts the property and interest
the licensee has in the goods he makes and proposes to sell.").
124.	*Id.* at 485-91.	The Court distinguished both *Dr. Miles* and *Standard
Sanitary Manufacturing Co. v. United States*, 226 U.S. 20 (1912), on the

Subsequent decisions have limited the application of the *General Electric* decision to its facts; i.e, a situation in which a patent holder licenses a single licensee to manufacture and sell patented products in competition with the licensee. In *Ethyl Gasoline Corp. v. United States*,[125] the holder of the patent for lead additives to improve performance of gasoline in automotive engines imposed strict controls on refiners licensed under the patents, and on jobbers who purchased from refiners and sold to the public.   The patent laws did not shield this conduct from the antitrust laws, as the patentee effectively sought to control pricing of a commodity after the sale from the licensed refiners to the licensed jobbers.[126] In the words of the Court, "conspicuous among such controls which the Sherman law prohibits and the patent law does not sanction is the regulation of prices and the suppression of competition among the purchasers of the patented articles."[127]

In *United States v. Univis Lens Co.*,[128] the licensor sold patented bifocal lens blanks to licensees, which used the blanks to make finished eyeglass lenses.   The Court held that with the first sale of the patented lens blanks pursuant to a royalty, the patentee lost any right to fix a price charged by others for the finished lenses, and its downstream licensing scheme which did so constituted unlawful price fixing.[129]

The courts have also refused to apply *General Electric* when multiple manufacturers are involved in parallel licensing agreements such that the patent holder effectively sets industry-wide resale prices.[130] In addition, lower courts have refused to allow a patentee to impose price

---

ground that they involved attempts "to control the trade in the articles sold and fasten upon purchasers, who had bought at full price and were complete owners, an obligation to maintain resale prices." *Id.* at 488.
125. 309 U.S. 436 (1940).
126. *Id.* at 452-59.
127. *Id.* at 452.
128. 316 U.S. 241 (1942).
129. *Id.* at 246-54.
130. *See* United States v. New Wrinkle, 342 U.S. 371, 379 (1952); United States v. United States Gypsum Co., 333 U.S. 364, 389 (1948) ("industry-wide license agreements, entered into with knowledge on the part of licensors and licensees of the adherence of others, with the control over prices and methods of distribution through the agreements and the bulletins, were sufficient to establish a prima facie case of conspiracy"); United States v. Masonite Corp., 316 U.S. 265, 279 (1942); *see also* United States v. Paramount Pictures, 334 U.S. 131, 143 (1948) (following *Gypsum* with respect to resale price maintenance in copyright licenses for motion picture admissions).

controls over a product that does not fall within the scope of the patent claims.[131]

In *United States v. Line Material Co.*,[132] the Court held that cross-licenses for blocking patents that established the price at which the licensees and sublicensees could sell the patented product were per se unlawful, and not protected under *General Electric*, which involved only a single patentee.[133]   Some lower courts have interpreted these subsequent decisions to limit *General Electric* to situations that involve only one manufacturing licensee.   For example, the Third Circuit stated in *Newburgh Moire Co. v. Superior Moire Co.*,[134] "we think that the patent laws were not intended to empower a patentee to grant a plurality of licenses, each containing provisions fixing the price at which the licensee might sell the product or process to the company, and that, if a plurality of licenses are granted, such provisions therein are prohibited by the antitrust laws."[135]

In *Lucas Arts v. Humongous Entertainment*,[136] LucasArts licensed a software tool to Humongous, which Humongous used to develop video games. The license prohibited Humongous for three years from selling any video game developed with the licensed software tool to distributors other than LucasArts for less than 75 percent of the six month rolling

---

131.   *See* United States v. Gen. Elec. Co., 82 F. Supp. 753, 813-16 (D.N.J. 1949); United States v. Gen. Elec. Co., 80 F. Supp. 989, 1005 (S.D.N.Y. 1948) ("[T]here can be no jurisdiction for fixing the price of an unpatented product. A patentee may not employ his patent to restrain trade beyond the scope of his grant.").

132.   333 U.S. 287 (1948).

133.   *Id.* at 311 ("While the *General Electric* case holds that a patentee may, under certain conditions, lawfully control the price the licensee of his several patents may charge for the patented device, no case of this Court has construed the patent and anti-monopoly statutes to permit separate owners of separate patents by cross-licenses or other arrangements to fix the prices to be charged by them and their licensees for their respective products."); *see also In re* Yarn Processing Patent Validity Litig., 541 F.2d 1127, 1135-36 (5th Cir. 1976).

134.   237 F.2d 283 (3d Cir. 1956).

135.   *Id.* at 293-94. *But see* Westinghouse Elec. Corp. v. Bulldog Elec. Prods. Co., 179 F.2d 139. 143 (4th Cir. 1950) ("There is no reason, however, why [the patentee] should be restricted to a price maintenance agreement with a single licensee, as argued by Bulldog, and the reasoning which permits licensing by grantees of patents and price maintenance provisions in maintenance contracts is clearly to the contrary.").

136.   870 F. Supp. 285 (N.D. Cal. 1993).

average wholesale price at which such products are resold to North American retailers.[137] The district court, relying on *General Electric*, found that this price restraint in a copyright license agreement was neither per se unlawful price-fixing, nor violated the antitrust laws because it was "reasonably adapted to secure pecuniary reward for the [LucasArts' lawful] monopoly."[138]

The situation is different when the licensor merely sets a minimum royalty or sets the royalty rate for sublicenses. The Supreme Court's opinions in *Univis Lens* and *Ethyl Gasoline* discussed above establish that a patentee may be found liable for per se unlawful price fixing by obtaining agreements to fix the prices of patented goods in sales transactions after the first sale. According to at least some lower court opinions, however, there is no per se unlawful price fixing where a licensor merely establishes royalties based on the licensee's sublicenses or sales of protected goods,[139] or restricts the pricing or sets the royalty rate of sublicenses to be granted in advance of the first sale of a product incorporating the intellectual property.[140]

---

137. *Id.* at 287.
138. *Id.* at 289.
139. Gen. Cinema v. Buena Vista Distrib., 681 F.2d 594 (9th Cir. 1982) (no price-fixing where films were licensed to a theater with the theater establishing ticket prices, and with royalties to the licensor based on a percentage of the higher of: (1) actual ticket sales prices or (2) a minimum price for the purpose of calculating the royalty); Kingray, Inc. v. NBA, 188 F. Supp. 2d 1177, 1190-91 (S.D. Cal. 2002) (NBA contract with DIRECTV gave DIRECTV the right, in its sole discretion, to set prices for NBA game package service, but required DIRECTV to account to the NBA based on the higher of: (1) actual sales price; or (2) a "deemed" sales price established by the NBA, falls within the rule of *General Cinema* that "a contract giving a distributor discretion to set the price for product but requiring the distributor to pay the manufacturer a set percentage or minimum price as a royalty does not constitute price fixing"); Columbia Pictures v. Coomer, 99 F. Supp. 481, 482-83 (E.D. Ky. 1951) (distinguishing *Paramount Pictures* as a nationwide conspiracy and stating that "license contracts for the exhibition of copyrighted motion pictures, containing price maintenance provisions for admission to such exhibitions, with nothing more to condemn them, are reasonable and normally adapted to secure to the copyright owner the pecuniary reward to which he is entitled under his copyright monopoly and are not in violation of the Sherman Act not otherwise illegal").
140. *See* Congoleum Indus. v. Armstrong Cork Co., 366 F. Supp. 220, 228 (E.D. Pa. 1973) ("[D]efendant contends that [the license provision] which

Horizontal restraints are different. Unless a horizontal price or output restraint in a license is reasonably necessary to achieve an efficiency-enhancing integration of economic activity, the agencies would likely challenge such a restraint under the per se rule.[141] For example, the FTC challenged the cross-licensing of laser eye surgery technology between the only two companies approved by the FDA to offer such technology, when the per-procedure royalty was such a high portion of the total cost of the surgery that the licensing effectively served to fix prices for the surgery procedure.[142]

---

limits the royalty rate Inmont can charge to sublicensees designated by Congoleum, is illegal per se ... but has not supported its argument with a single decision that has held it unlawful for a patentee to set royalty rates in licenses and sublicenses or any reason why this provision in this license is anticompetitive."); *id.* at 231 ("The defendant also contends that it was illegal per se to set the royalty rate for the wall covering portion of the sublicense from Inmont to W.R. Grace & Co. (Grace). Again, Armstrong has failed to set forth any reason why this agreement is anticompetitive in nature or effect, and the Court finds no basis to support a conclusion of patent misuse."); *see also* Wis. Music Network v. Muzak Ltd., 5 F.3d 218 (7th Cir. 1993) (National account pricing imposed on local franchisees was not per se unlawful vertical price fixing). Depending on the product and the license, there may be disputes over what constitutes the first sale and what type of restraints may be imposed through licensing in advance of the first sale where a physical product is transferred for a price from one party to another in advance of retail sale or use. *Compare* Mallinckrodt, Inc. v. Medipart, Inc., 976 F.2d 700, 708-09 (Fed. Cir. 1992) (where neither price-fixing nor tying were at issue, "single use only" restriction on patented medical device was subject to the rule of reason and not per se misuse as a post-sale restraint), *with* Straus v. Victor Talking Mach., 243 U.S. 490, 494-501 (1917) ("license contracts" pursuant to which Victor dealers were authorized to distribute machines and convey licenses to unlicensed members of the general public only after receipt of a "royalty" of not less than $200 from the end user and subject to a "License Notice" providing that title to the machine remained in Victor but that use was licensed through the expiration of the last applicable patent "is in substance and in fact a mere price fixing scheme").

141. INTELLECTUAL PROPERTY GUIDELINES,*su pra* note 1, § 3.4.
142. *See* Summit Tech. and VISX, Inc., FTC Docket No.9286 (complaint Mar. 24, 1998), *available at* http://www.ftc.gov/os/caselist/d9286.htm (competitive impact statement regarding consent decree, Aug. 21, 1998). Summit and VISX defended their arrangement as clearing potentially blocking patents.

The presence of an efficiency-enhancing integration, however, may change the analysis. One example of a horizontal price agreement subject to the rule of reason is *Broadcast Music v. CBS*,[143] in which the Supreme Court held that blanket licensing of musical composition copyrights was not a naked restraint of trade with no purpose except stifling of competition, "but rather accompanies the integration of sales, monitoring, and enforcement against unauthorized copyright use."[144] The Court further concluded that "a bulk license of some type is a necessary consequence of the integration necessary to achieve these efficiencies, and a necessary consequence of an aggregate license is that its price must be established."[145]

In the context of joint ventures, price restraints that limit the independent pricing of the participants of the joint venture may be condemned under either the per se rule or a quick look rule of reason when they are not reasonably necessary to achieve the efficiency-enhancing integration of economic activity.[146] The Supreme Court determined in *Texaco, Inc. v. Dagher*,[147] however, that uniform pricing within the joint venture of brands contributed to the joint venture is not per se unlawful.

Output or quantity restrictions in cross-licenses between competitors, however, are per se unlawful, as established by the Supreme Court in *Hartford Empire v. United States*.[148] On the other hand, vertical output restraints or quantity limitations in license agreements are generally subject to the rule of reason, and generally upheld as reasonable restraints.[149]

---

143.   441 U.S. 1 (1979).
144.   *Id.* at 20.
145.   *Id.* at 21.
146.   Polygram Holding v. FTC, 416 F.3d 29 (D.C. Cir. 2005).
147.   126 S. Ct. 1276 (2006).
148.   323 U.S. 386 (1945).
149.   *See* Atari Games Corp. v. Nintendo of Am., 897 F.2d 1572, 1578 (Fed. Cir. 1990) (citing United States v. E.I. Du Pont de Nemours & Co., 118 F. Supp. 41 (D. Del. 1953), *aff'd on other grounds*, 351 U.S. 377 (1956); United States v. Parker-Rust-Proofing Co., 61 F. Supp. 805 (E.D. Mich. 1945); Aspinall Mfg. v. Gill, 32 F. 697 (C.C.D.N.J. 1887)); *see also* Ethyl Corp. v. Hercules Powder Co., 232 F. Supp. 453, 460 (D. Del. 1963).

2. Territorial Restrictions

A territorial restriction is a covenant limiting the geographic area in which one or more parties can sell products or otherwise conduct activity authorized by the agreement in certain limited areas.[150] As described by the Supreme Court in *Business Electronics Corp. v. Sharp Electronics Corp.*,[151] "[r]estraints imposed by agreement between competitors have traditionally been denominated as horizontal restraints, and those imposed by agreement between firms at different levels of distribution as vertical restraints."[152]

Horizontal territorial restraints are typically treated as per se unlawful[153] unless such restraints are ancillary to an efficiency-enhancing integration of economic activity.[154] In contrast, vertical territorial restraints are always subject to the rule of reason, and, under that analysis, are often upheld as a lawful means of providing incentives for the locally authorized distributor or dealer (or licensee) to promote and service the brand.[155]

The *Guidelines* note that "field-of-use, *territorial,* and other limitations on intellectual property licenses may serve procompetitive ends by allowing the licensor to exploit its property as efficiently and

---

150. *See* ANTITRUST LAW DEVELOPMENTS, *supra* note 100, at 152 (5th ed. 2002) ("Territorial ... restrictions limit a distributor's freedom by prohibiting it from selling outside an assigned territory ... thereby restraining intrabrand competition.").
151. 485 U.S. 717 (1988).
152. *Id.* at 730 & n.4. *See infra* Chapter VI.A.1.
153. *See* United States v. Topco Assocs., 405 U.S. 596, 607-08 (1972); United States v. Sealy, Inc., 388 U.S. 350, 354 (1967); Timken Roller Bearing Co. v. United States, 341 U.S. 593, 598 (1951); *see also* Palmer v. BRG of Ga., 498 U.S. 46, 49 (1990) (per curiam) (market allocation agreements "are anticompetitive regardless of whether the parties split a market within which they both do business or whether they merely reserve one market for one and another for the other").
154. *See* Rothery Storage & Van Co. v. Atlas Van Lines, 792 F.2d 210, 229 (D.C. Cir. 1986); *see also* United States v. Ecast, Inc., Civil No. 1:05-cv-01754 (D.D.C. Sept. 2, 2005) (Complaint, Proposed Final Judgment and Competitive Impact Statement) (invoking rule of reason rather than per se rule in challenge of horizontal territorial restraint related to agreement to jointly produce and distribute a product).
155. *See* Cont'l T.V., v. GTE Sylvania Inc., 433 U.S. 36, 54-55 (1977); *see also* Atari Games Corp. v. Nintendo of Am., 897 F.2d 1572, 1578 (Fed. Cir. 1990).

effectively as possible."[156] Among the procompetitive benefits of these types of licensing restrictions acknowledged in the *Guidelines* are the following:

> These various forms of exclusivity can be used to give a licensee an incentive to invest in the commercialization and distribution of products embodying the licensed intellectual property and to develop additional applications for the licensed property. The restrictions may do so, for example, by protecting the licensee against free-riding on the licensee's investments by other licensees or by the licensor. They may also increase the licensor's incentive to license, for example, by protecting the licensor from competition in the licensor's own technology in a market niche that it prefers to keep to itself.[157]

The *Guidelines* illustrate the agencies' policy in Example 1, which discusses licenses of a hypothetical company that developed new copyrighted software for inventory management with wide application in the health field. The hypothetical licensing program includes field of use and territorial limitations, with some licensees permitted to use the software only in hospitals, and others only in group medical practices. Different royalties are charged for different uses, and each licensee is permitted to use the software only in specified portions of the United States and specified foreign countries. Assuming that none of the licensees are actual or likely potential competitors of the licensor in the sale of inventory management software, and absent provisions preventing or discouraging licensees from developing, using, or selling any other software, or from competing in any other good or service, the licensing arrangement is merely a subdivision of the licensor's intellectual property among different fields of use and territories. Such an arrangement "does not appear likely to harm competition among entities that would have been actual or likely potential competitors if [the licensor] had chosen not to license the software program," and thus the agencies would be unlikely to object to this arrangement.[158]

This analysis is bolstered by the Patent Act. Section 261 of the Patent Act provides express statutory authority for a patentee to "grant and convey an exclusive right under his application for patent, or patents,

---

156. INTELLECTUAL PROPERTY GUIDELINES, *supra* note 1, § 2.3 (emphasis added).
157. *Id.*
158. *Id.*, Ex. 1.

to the whole or any specified part of the United States."[159]   The Ninth
Circuit, in *Brownell v. Ketcham Wire & Manufacturing Co.*,[160]
considered contentions by the government that a license under certain
United States patents that granted exclusivity in the United States and
proscribed sale or export outside the United States was a division of
markets that violated the Sherman Act.[161]   Relying on the statutory
provision of section 261, and noting that "[e]xclusive territorial licenses
granted under patents are old in the law," the Ninth Circuit held that the
licensee's agreement not to sell or export patented articles to any foreign
country was merely a lawful agreement to abide by the terms of the
license granted, and that the agreement of the licensor not import
patented articles into the United States was merely a lawful exclusive
license.[162]   Thus,   the licensing   agreement   was   not   illegal   or
unenforceable under the antitrust laws.

Some courts have relied on the statutory provisions of section 261 of
the Patent Act and broad language in cases such as *Brownell* to suggest
that territorial restraints in patent license agreements do not violate the
Sherman Act as a matter of law.[163]   To the extent such restraints are

---

159.   35 U.S.C. § 261. In *Ethyl Gasoline Corp. v. United States*, 309 U.S. 436,
       456 (1940), the Supreme Court confirmed that a patentee "may grant
       licenses to make, use or vend, restricted in point of space or time, or with
       any other restriction upon the exercise of the granted privilege, save only
       that by attaching a condition to his license he may not enlarge his
       monopoly and thus acquire some other which the statute and the patent
       together did not give." *See* Bement v. Nat'l Harrow Co., 186 U.S. 70, 92-
       93 (1902).

160.   211 F.2d 121, 128-30 (9th Cir. 1954).

161.   *Id.* at 125, 128-30. As the court noted, "[i]t is clear that agreements to
       divide a market are violations of the antitrust laws (citing Addyston Pipe
       & Steel v. United States, 175 U.S. 211 (1899); Cont'l Wall Paper v. Louis
       Voight & Sons, 212 U.S. 227 (1909)). But these cases do not concern the
       exercise of a patent monopoly." *Id.* at 128. Outside the patent licensing
       context, the Supreme Court has held restraints including territorial
       restraints proscribing foreign trade by prohibiting import and export
       implementing a trademark licensing per se unlawful. *See* Timken Roller
       Bearing Co. v. United States, 341 U.S. 593, 598 (1951); *see also* United
       States v. Bayer Co., 135 F. Supp. 65, 68 (S.D.N.Y. 1955). *But see* Clorox
       Co. v. Sterling Winthrop, 117 F.3d 50, 55-56 (2d Cir. 1997) (no per se
       illegal restraint in trademark license).

162.   211 F.2d at 128-30.

163.   Miller Insituform v. Insituform of N. Am., 605 F. Supp. 1125, 1130-31
       (M.D. Tenn. 1985) (granting motion to dismiss) ("The Court holds that,

subject to antitrust scrutiny, it would be pursuant to the rule of reason.[164]
The D.C. Circuit held that territorial restraints on the sale of non-patented
products made pursuant to a license under a process patent are governed
by the rule of reason.[165]

Vertical restraints in license agreements have been successfully
challenged when the restraints were not imposed by the patentee as part
of its unilaterally imposed licensing scheme to maximize the patentee's
profits, but rather at the request of licensees to limit competition with
other licensees.[166]

---

as a matter of law, a patent licensor's use of geographic restrictions in a
sublicensing scheme to divide territories into ones of primary or exclusive
jurisdiction constitutes a lawful application of the rights derived from a
patent grant."), *aff'd*, 830 F.2d 606 (6th Cir. 1987); United States v.
Parker-Rust-Proof Co., 61 F. Supp. 805, 812 (E.D. Mich. 1945) ("The
owner of a patent has a right . . . to limit the territory in which the
licensee may operate under the patent . . ."); *see also* Becton, Dickinson
& Co. v. Eisele & Co., 86 F.2d 267, 269 (6th Cir. 1936). The district
court in *Miller Insituform* suggested that the express language of the
Patent Act was addressed only to assignments of exclusive rights, but that
the same reasoning should apply to licenses, while acknowledging that
some commentators disagreed on that point. 605 F. Supp. at 1130-31.

164. Atari Games Corp. v. Nintendo of Am., 897 F.2d 1572, 1578 (Fed. Cir.
1990) (citing both *Continental T.V.* (rule of reason applicable to vertical
non-price restraints) and *Brownell* (export restraints in a patent license are
lawful by statute) in rejecting per se challenge to export restraints).

165. *See* United States v. Studiengesellschaft Kohle, 670 F.2d 1122, 1133
(D.C. Cir. 1981); *see also* Robintech, Inc. v. Chemidus Wavin, Ltd., 628
F.2d 142, 147 (D.C. Cir. 1980).

166. Int'l Wood Processors v. Power Dry, 792 F.2d 416, 429 (4th Cir. 1986)
("Where, as here, the principal exclusive licensor conspired with others
holding the patent rights, financial advisors, and a licensee under the
patent, to create a new corporate structure which would control the patent
and licensing rights and would eliminate competition from all other
uncontrolled licensees, the new patent holder endangered competition in
the market for the patent by attempting to obtain from the licensees the
lost right to exclude."); Mannington Mills v. Congoleum Indus., 610 F.2d
1059, 1071-73 (3d Cir. 1979) ("the patent system has no interest in
permitting the patentee's monopoly to be used as a screen for the
maintenance of a horizontal cartel at the licensee level"); United States v.
CIBA Geigy Corp., 508 F. Supp. 1118, 1148 (D.N.J. 1976); United States
v. Crown Zellerbach Corp., 141 F. Supp. 118, 127-28 (N.D. Ill. 1956)
("By serving the interests of [licensee] Crown and not of [patentee]

Similarly, territorial restraints involving actual or likely competitors in the absence of the license may be construed, depending on the circumstances, as a sham license or one whose main aim and effect is to allocate markets among competitors.[167] Example 7 of the *Guidelines* illustrates that a license for a process that is not an improvement over existing technologies and that is not, in fact, utilized by licensees would likely be challenged as per se unlawful if the patentee manufacturing the product which is the output of the process signs up competing manufacturers to exclusive territories, and each agrees not to sell outside its territory. On the other hand, if the process is an improvement over existing processes there may be an efficiency-enhancing integration of economic activity, any territorial restraints may be assessed under the rule of reason.[168]

3. Customer Restrictions

A customer restriction is a covenant that limits the customers to whom one or more parties to a contract can sell certain products or technologies licensed. Like territorial restraints, customer restrictions are

---

ALSCO, the agreement presents a genuine and triable issue under the Sherman Act.")

167. *Crown Zellerbach Corp.*, 141 F. Supp. at 126; United States v. Nat'l Lead, 63 F. Supp. 513, 527 (S.D.N.Y. 1945), *aff'd*, 332 U.S. 319 (1947). In *United States v. American National Can & KMK Maschinen AG*, Civ. No. 96-01458 (D.D.C. 1996), 61 Fed. Reg. 34,862 (1996), the DOJ alleged that the defendants essentially divided the already concentrated markets for laminated tubes, laminated tube-making equipment and laminated tube-making technology by KMK's sale of certain assets to ANC pursuant to which KMK stopped selling laminated tubes in North America, and gave ANC an exclusive license to use its laminated tube-making technology and an exclusive right to buy its laminated tube-making equipment in North America. In *In re FMC Corp. and Asahi Chemical Industry Co.*, FTC File No. 981-0237, Docket C 3935 (Dec. 21, 2000) (*available at* http://www.ftc.gov/os/caselist/c3935.htm), the FTC alleged that an exclusive trademark license from FMC to Asahi giving Asahi exclusive rights to use FMC's trademark in Japan and the Asia Pacific region in connection with a particular pharmaceutical product also formed the foundation for an undocumented understanding that FMC would not sell that pharmaceutical in Japan or Asia Pacific and that Asahi would not sell the pharmaceutical in the United States or Europe.

168. INTELLECTUAL PROPERTY GUIDELINES, *supra* note 1, Ex. 7.

generally viewed as per se unlawful in the horizontal context, unless ancillary to an efficiency-enhancing integration of economic activity.[169] As vertical restraints in a license, however, customer restrictions are generally subject to the rule of reason, and are often seen as having valid procompetitive justifications in the context of a patentee maximizing the value and utilization of its patent.[170]

By way of example, courts have permitted licenses restricting sales to customers licensed under other patents[171] or to licensees under specific claims of a patent.[172] When competition is restrained after the first sale of the patented article, however, attempts to impose restraints on resale may be subject to challenge.[173]

4. Field of Use Restrictions

A field of use restriction is a covenant that limits the industries or uses for which a licensed invention may be employed. For example, a patentee might grant a license to one licensee only for consumer

---

169. *See* United States v. Topco Assocs., 405 U.S. 596, 611-12 (1972) (territorial and customer restraints deemed horizontal preventing members of supermarket cooperative from selling brand outside territory or to other retailers were per se unlawful); Rothery Storage & Van Co. v. Atlas Van Lines, 792 F.2d 210, 229 (D.C. Cir. 1986) (restraints ancillary to an efficiency-enhancing integration of economic activity are subject to the rule of reason).

170. Territorial restraints and customer restraints are subject to similar analysis, as both are generally considered per se unlawful market allocation in the horizontal context, but are subject to the rule of reason in the vertical context. *See* INTELLECTUAL PROPERTY GUIDELINES, *supra* note 1, § 2.3 and Example 1 (quoted above in section on territorial restraints); *In re* Yarn Processing Patent Validity Litig., 541 F.2d 1127, 1135 (5th Cir. 1976) (license to manufacture patented machines restricting sales to those licensed by the patentee to use them fell within the statutory rights of the patentee and did not comprise unlawful post-sale restraints); *see also* Westinghouse Elec. & Mfg. v. Cutting & Washington Radio Corp., 294 F. 671, 672-73 (2d Cir. 1923) (enforcing license limiting sale to three classes of customers).

171. Deering, Milliken & Co. v. Temp-Resisto Corp., 160 F. Supp. 463, 478-82 (S.D.N.Y. 1958), *aff'd in part and rev'd in part*, 274 F.2d 626 (2d Cir. 1960).

172. SCM Corp. v. RCA, 318 F. Supp. 433, 457-58 (S.D.N.Y. 1970).

173. *See* United States v. Univis Lens Co., 316 U.S. 241, 251-52 (1942); Ethyl Gas. Corp. v. United States, 309 U.S. 436, 453 (1940).

applications of an invention and grant a license to another licensee limited to industrial application of the same invention. A license for a limited field of use, like other types of licenses, might be exclusive or non-exclusive.

In section 2.3 of the *Guidelines*, the agencies acknowledge that "[f]ield-of-use ... limitations on intellectual property licenses may serve procompetitive ends by allowing the licensor to exploit its property as efficiently and effectively as possible," and that such restrictions "may also increase the licensor's incentive to license, for example, by protecting the licensor from competition in the licensor's own technology in a market niche that it prefers to keep to itself."[174] Field of use restrictions are a long-standing method for licensors to derive value from their intellectual property, and for licensees to commercialize innovations in a more efficient manner.

In 1938, the Supreme Court confirmed the legality of field-of-use restraints in patent licenses in *General Talking Pictures v. Western Electric*.[175] *General Talking Pictures* involved seven patents "for inventions in vacuum tube amplifiers which have been used in wire and radio telephony, talking motion pictures, and other fields."[176] The patent owner, AT&T, licensed the patents to a subsidiary for use in the commercial field, which included talking picture equipment for theaters. Another licensee had a license "expressly confined to the right to manufacture and sell the patented amplifiers for radio amateur reception, radio experimental reception, and home broadcast reception," and was found liable for infringement by providing amplifiers for use in theaters. The Supreme Court held the restrictions lawful in affirming the judgment of infringement, citing precedent supporting the proposition that "[p]atent owners may grant licenses extending to all uses or limited to use in a defined field."[177] It categorized field of use restrictions as proper exploitation of the patents, rather than improper attempts to extend the "patent monopoly."[178]

Courts have generally followed *General Talking Pictures* in rejecting antitrust challenges to field-of-use restraints in license agreements.[179]

---

174. INTELLECTUAL PROPERTY GUIDELINES, *supra* note 1, § 2.3.
175. 304 U.S. 175, *aff'd on reh'g*, 305 U.S. 124 (1938).
176. *Id.* at 176.
177. *Id.* at 181.
178. *Id.*; *see also* 305 U.S. at 127.
179. B. Braun Med. v. Abbott Labs., 124 F.3d 1419, 1426 (Fed. Cir. 1997) ("field of use restrictions ... are generally upheld ... and any anti-competitive effects they may cause are reviewed in accordance with the

Field of use restraints on sales of an unpatented product manufactured using a process patent are subject to the rule of reason.[180]
In *Mallinckrodt, Inc. v. Medipart, Inc.*,[181] the Federal Circuit reviewed Supreme Court jurisprudence authorizing licensing restrictions on sale or use. It concluded that although price restraints or tying after the first sale may be per se unlawful under some Supreme Court authority, vertical nonprice restrictions (such as the single use requirement for the radiation treatment devices at issue in *Mallinckrodt*) should be governed by the rule of reason:

> Should the restriction be found to be reasonably within the patent grant, i.e., that it relates to the subject matter within the scope of the patent claims, that ends the inquiry. However, should such inquiry lead to the conclusion that there are anticompetitive effects extending beyond the patentee's statutory right to exclude, these effects do not automatically impeach the restriction. Anticompetitive effects that are not per se violations of law are reviewed in accordance with the rule of reason.[182]

In 1997, the Federal Circuit reaffirmed application of the rule of reason to vertical non-price restrictions in *B. Braun Medical v. Abbott Laboratories*.[183] In *Braun*, the Federal Circuit reaffirmed that, although unconditional sale of a patented device exhausts the patentee's right to control the purchaser's use thereafter, the exhaustion doctrine does not apply to an expressly conditioned sale or license. According to the Federal Circuit, the key inquiry "under this fact-intensive doctrine" is

---

rule of reason"); United States v. Studiengesellschaft Kohle, 670 F.2d 1122, 1133 (D.C. Cir. 1981); Armstrong v. Motorola, Inc., 374 F.2d 764, 774 (7th Cir. 1967); Automatic Radio Mfg. v. Hazeltine Research, 176 F.2d 799, 802-03 (1st Cir. 1949), *aff'd*, 339 U.S. 827 (1950); Turner Glass Corp. v. Hartford-Empire Co., 173 F.2d 49, 53 (7th Cir. 1949); Smith Int'l v. Kennametal, Inc., 621 F. Supp. 79, 88-89 (N.D. Ohio 1985); United States v. CIBA Geigy Corp., 508 F. Supp. 1118, 1149-51 (D.N.J. 1976); Bela Seating Co. v. Poloron Prods., 297 F. Supp. 489, 503-04, 509-10 (N.D. Ill. 1968), *aff'd*, 438 F.2d 733 (7th Cir. 1971); Reliance Molded Plastics v. Jiffy Prods., 215 F. Supp. 402, 405, 408-09 (D.N.J. 1963), *aff'd per curiam*, 337 F.2d 857 (3d Cir. 1964); Benger Lab. v. R.K. Laros Co., 209 F. Supp. 639, 648-49 (E.D. Pa. 1962), *aff'd per curiam*, 317 F.2d 455 (3d Cir. 1963).
180. *Studiengesellschaft Kohle*, 670 F.2d at 1133.
181. 976 F.2d 700 (Fed. Cir. 1992).
182. *Id.* at 708.
183. 124 F.3d 1419 (Fed. Cir. 1997).

whether by imposing the condition, the patentee has impermissibly broadened the physical or temporal scope of the patent grant with anticompetitive effect. It noted that using a patent which conveys market power in a relevant market "to restrain competition in an unpatented product or employing the patent beyond its 17-year term" are two common examples of such impermissible broadening. In contrast, "field of use restrictions (such as those at issue in [*Braun*]) are generally upheld ... and any anticompetitive effects they may cause are reviewed in accordance with the rule of reason."

In *Monsanto Co. v. McFarling*,[184] the Federal Circuit held that the Sherman Act did not prevent a patentee holding exclusive rights over genetically-engineered soybean seeds from restricting use of the seeds to growing crops for harvest and sale and proscribing retention of second generation seeds for replanting. McFarling argued that this restriction conditioned the initial purchase of the seeds (the tying product) on the purchase of a fresh supply of seeds (the tied product) in subsequent years. However, the license did not require McFarling to buy anything from Monsanto in future years. Because Monsanto's patents covered the seeds grown from the seeds sold, the use restrictions were within the scope of Monsanto's patents and, accordingly, were lawful use restraints.

5. *Veto Rights on Additional Licenses/Sublicenses*

An intellectual property owner may assign rights in the property or grant exclusive[185] or nonexclusive licenses.[186] Such assignments or licenses may include or exclude the right to grant sublicenses. Antitrust concerns arise where the parties to contractual arrangements concerning patent rights who are competitors effectively prevent anyone from licensing others without their mutual consent.

---

184. 302 F.3d 1291 (Fed. Cir. 2002) (preliminary injunction); 363 F.3d 1336 (Fed. Cir. 2004), *cert. denied*, 125 S. Ct. 2956 (2005).

185. For example, § 261 of the Patent Act, 35 U.S.C. § 261, provides:

> Applications for patent, patents, or any interest therein, shall be assignable in law by an instrument in writing. The applicant, patentee, or his assigns or legal representatives may in like manner grant and convey an exclusive right under his application for patent, or patents, to the whole or any specified part of the United States.

186. Waterman v. Mackenzie, 138 U.S. 252, 255 (1891).

In particular, licensing arrangements that provide nonexclusive licensees with veto rights on additional licenses or sublicenses raise antitrust concerns. Indeed, several cases in the 1950s, two of which were affirmed by the Supreme Court, held agreements with such characteristics to be per se unlawful.[187] In 1951, in *United States v. Besser Manufacturing Co.,*[188] the district court found per se unlawful an agreement pursuant to which a key patent for manufacturing concrete blocks was licensed to the two leading competitors, with each of them given the right to preclude further licenses and restricting the patentee from granting additional licenses unless both consented. As the Court stated:

> It may well be that an exclusive license to one party would be valid, but here the patentees have joined hands with the two largest competitors in the industry and by terms of their agreement have virtually made it impossible for others to obtain rights under those patents. The contract even gives [those two largest competitors] the power to restrict competition—present and future—by requiring their joint consent before licensing others. It is this combination requiring collective action that primarily invalidates the agreement. We believe it clear that the parties intended this contract to be a means whereby control of the industry could be acquired and competition eliminated. For what reason would [these competitors] want the consent of the other before approving a license suggested by the patentees?[189]

---

187. Mason City Tent & Awning v. Clapper, 144 F. Supp. 754, 765-66 (W.D. Mo. 1956); United States v. Krasnov, 143 F. Supp. 184, 198 (E.D. Pa. 1956), *aff'd per curiam*, 355 U.S. 5 (1957); United States v. Besser Mfg. Co., 96 F. Supp. 304, 312 (E.D. Mich. 1951), *aff'd*, 343 U.S. 444 (1952); *see also* United States v. Nat'l Lead Co., 63 F. Supp. 513, 524 (S.D.N.Y. 1945), *aff'd*, 332 U.S. 319 (1947) ("where there is a refusal to license (or refusal to license except on specified conditions which would extend the patent monopoly) which is the product of agreement or conspiracy, on the part of the owners of competing patents, I believe, the law is offended to the same extent as the law is violated when several combine and agree not to do business with a particular customer or class of customers").
188. 96 F. Supp. 304 (E.D. Mich. 1951), *aff'd*, 343 U.S. 444 (1952). The court in *Besser* also found a § 2 violation, as Besser subsequently secretly bought up its competitor's stock and designated board members, effectively exercising control over entities collectively deemed to hold a monopoly.
189. *Id.* at 311.

Similarly, in 1956 the district court in *United States v. Krasnov*[190] addressed an agreement providing for licensee veto of further licenses in an agreement establishing cross-licenses between the two largest U.S. competitors in the manufacture and sale of furniture slip covers. Before the agreement, the principal patent at issue had been controlled by one of the two major competitors and challenged by the other. Under the agreement, consent of both was required for further licenses, and the parties shared the expenses of enforcing the patent against third parties. The court held that where the owner of the patent, its assignee, and the assignee's licensee—including "the two dominant manufacturers in the trade"—bind themselves to a situation where no one "can create any rights under the patent in any other person without the consent of the other two," the evil struck down in *Besser* exists, "namely, (1) veto power over licensing rights granted to a licensee and (2) the contractual arrangement which created the power to restrict competition by requiring joint consent before others could be licensed."[191]

A third case from the 1950s, *Mason City Tent & Awning Co. v. Clapper*,[192] involved an agreement resolving patent interference proceedings among three inventors and their assigns with respect to patent applications relating to tractor covers. The three patent applicants agreed to license each other before detailed settlement discussions and disclosure of information on priority dates. At the conclusion of discussions, the applicants agreed that one inventor had priority as to the main patentable invention, a second one had priority as to a more narrow patentable invention, and the third was not entitled to any patent.[193] The two patentees agreed not to grant further licenses without consent of all parties, and all parties agreed not to grant sublicenses without the consent of all parties.[194] This arrangement was construed by the court to allow a nonexclusive licensee, with no direct rights in any patent or under the

---

190. 143 F. Supp. 184 (E.D. Pa. 1956), *aff'd*, 355 U.S. 5 (1957).
191. *Id.* at 201-02.
192. 144 F. Supp. 754 (W.D. Mo. 1956); *see also* Clapper v. Original Tractor Cab Co., 165 F. Supp. 565, 576-77 (S.D. Ind. 1958) (involving same agreement and explaining reasons why court concluded that "[a]n agreement by a patentee which gives a non-exclusive licensee a veto power in the selection of other licensees is invalid according to Sherman Act standards, Sections 1 and 2"), *aff'd in part and rev'd in part on other grounds*, 270 F.2d 616 (7th Cir. 1959).
193. 144 F. Supp. at 758.
194. *Id.* at 759.

Patent Act, to restrain competition.[195] The court held that "an agreement by a patentee which gives a nonexclusive licensee a veto power in the selection of other licensees" was per se unlawful.[196]

More recent cases on different facts have tended toward the application of the rule of reason to such restraints, at least where the restraints are not accompanied by a broad spectrum of unlawful conduct. For example, in *Moraine Products v. ICI America*,[197] the court addressed an agreement under which the patentee had granted a license exclusive in the United States except as to it and one other company. Since this license did not grant the right to issue sublicenses, but rather granted exclusivity except as to the patentee and one other competitor, it created a situation in which it would take the agreement of the competing patentee and licensee to allow anyone else a license under the patent. The court refused to apply the per se rule of *Besser* and *Krasnov* to strike down this arrangement, distinguishing the "exclusive" license with no right to grant sublicenses from the "nonexclusive" license with the right to veto sublicenses, and declined to accept arguments that exclusive licenses were per se lawful. Instead, it remanded for analysis of the arrangement under the rule of reason.[198]

---

195.   *Id.* at 766-67.
196.   *Id.* at 767.
197.   538 F.2d 134 (7th Cir. 1976); *cf.* Mannington Mills v. Congoleum Indus., 610 F.2d 1059, 1072-73 (3d Cir. 1979) (citing *Besser* in reversing summary judgment and allowing discovery on remand regarding alleged Sherman Act violations by patentee allegedly conspiring with licensees to restrain competition by terminating license; "we think that a patentee's termination of a licensee, in concert with competing licensees, is not entitled to an antitrust exemption ... [as] [w]here the patentee's anticompetitive conduct is undertaken after a number of non-exclusive licenses have been granted and in concert with competing licensees ... there is a greater risk that the restriction is designed not to reward the patent monopoly, but to increase the licensee's reward.").
198.   538 F.2d at 138-46. The court noted in applying the rule of reason that *Besser* and *Krasnov* cited in support of per se illegality of arrangement at issue each "involved a broad spectrum of anticompetitive conduct on the part of the defendants." *Id.* at 139-40; *see also* Polysius Corp. v. Fuller Co., 709 F. Supp. 560, 577-79 (E.D. Pa.) (restraints not per se unlawful and not proven to be unlawful under the rule of reason), *aff'd without opinion*, 889 F.2d 1100 (Fed. Cir. 1989); Malco Mfg. Co. v. Nat'l Connector Corp., 151 U.S.P.Q. (BNA) 255, 263 (D. Minn. 1966), *aff'd in part and rev'd in part*, 392 F.2d 766 (8th Cir. 1968); United States v. Singer Mfg. Co., 205 F. Supp. 394, 428-30 (S.D.N.Y. 1962) (discussing

In *Cook, Inc. v. Boston Scientific Corp.*,[199] Judge Posner examined the situation of a patentee's "coexclusive" license of exclusive patent rights for coating stents with medication to two competing firms, which precluded further licenses or sublicenses without the consent of both licensees and the patentee.   The court suggested that "coexclusive licenses were a natural compromise," as the patentee would prefer to hedge bets on which licensee might fare better with FDA approval and in the marketplace in light of the two firms' different coating methods, while recognizing that some degree of exclusivity would be necessary to induce the licensees' investment in obtaining FDA approval and marketing the coated stent product and treatment.[200]   The court noted that "there is no argument that [the patentee] would have violated antitrust law or been guilty of patent misuse had it granted an exclusive, nonassignable license."[201]   Reasoning from that point, the court stated it therefore could not "see how [the patentee's] action in granting two

---

limitations and non-applicability of per se proscription of *Besser, Krasnov,* and *Mason City* to facts presented), *rev'd on other grounds*, 374 U.S. 174 (1963). *But see* PrimeTime 24 Joint Venture v. NBC, 219 F.3d 92, 102-03 (2d Cir. 2000) (suggesting that in the context of licensing of copyrights, a horizontal concerted refusal to deal could be per se unlawful).

199.   333 F.3d 737 (7th Cir. 2003).

200.   *Id.* at 739-41.

201.   *Id.* at 740-41 ("The compromise [of the coexclusive license] might be undone by assignment or sublicensing. Suppose Cook fell behind BSC in the race to develop an approved and marketable paclitaxel-coated stent and tried to recover the lead by assigning its license to a firm with greater resources or other advantages that would enable it to overtake BSC. The effect would be to confront the latter with more competition than it had reckoned on when it took out its license from Angiotech. Hence the bar on assignment without the permission of the other licensee (plus Angiotech, though that is not a factor here). Although competition is generally a good thing, there is no argument that Angiotech would have violated antitrust law or been guilty of patent misuse had it granted an exclusive, nonassignable license. And so we cannot see how Angiotech's action in granting two licenses and forbidding the licensees to increase the number of competitors by means of assignment or sublicensing could raise an antitrust or patent-misuse issue. Notice that the licenses do not forbid the acquisition of the licensee by another firm—to which as an affiliate the licensee could grant a sublicense without obtaining the permission of the other parties to the contract with Angiotech—that might be a more formidable competitor of the other licensee.").

licenses and forbidding the licensees to increase the number of competitors by means of assignment or sublicensing could raise an antitrust or patent misuse issue."[202]

In summary, older cases, including two affirmed without opinions or substantive comment by the Supreme Court, apply per se proscription to agreements granting competing nonexclusive licensees veto rights over additional licenses. There is conflicting subsequent case law applying the rule of reason and suggesting that those cases may be limited to their facts, which included substantial additional anticompetitive conduct accompanying the licensing arrangement, as well as findings of market power. Any agreement in which competitors must agree before allowing additional competitors to license the patent may raise antitrust concerns, especially if the patent is one that provides substantial market power in a relevant market. However, there may be situations, particularly with respect to exclusive licenses, in which at least some such restraints may be justified.

6. Exclusivity in Licensing Arrangements

There are two types of exclusivity that may raise antitrust concerns in licensing arrangements: exclusive licensing and exclusive dealing.[203]

a. Exclusive Licensing

Exclusive licensing refers to the granting of licenses "which restrict the right of the licensor to license others and possibly also to use the technology itself."[204] Although the ambiguity in this definition may reflect some ambiguity in common usage, an exclusive license typically

---

202. *Id.* at 740-41; *see also Moraine Prods.*, 538 F.2d at 140-41 (discussing that a Dec. 16, 1975 letter, signed by Acting Assistant Attorney General Bruce B. Wilson, explained that "although the Antitrust Division generally believes that an agreement among the licensor and its prospective licensees to limit the number of licenses is probably anticompetitive, the [Salk] Institute has shown that such a limitation is the least anticompetitive way to develop somastostatin [a drug to treat diabetes and other diseases] on reasonable terms," i.e., limiting initial licensing to five nonexclusive licensees, two in the US and three in Europe for the first three years of sales, where Salk had been unable to obtain license agreements with qualified and interested firms without such a limitation).

203. INTELLECTUAL PROPERTY GUIDELINES, *su pra* note 1, §§ 4.1.2, 5.4.

204. *Id.* § 4.1.2.

refers to one in which the licensor gives up its right to practice the invention as well as the right to grant additional licenses. A patentee may grant exclusive licenses for a limited territory or field of use. A license in which the licensor retains the right to practice the invention, but gives up the right to grant additional licenses, may be referred to as a license with partial or limited exclusivity.

The Patent Act expressly provides that the patentee or its assigns may "grant and convey an exclusive right under his application for patent, or patents, to the whole or any specified part of the United States."[205] For over 100 years, courts have recognized the rights of a patentee to grant assignments and exclusive and nonexclusive licenses.[206]

A nonexclusive license is simply an agreement not to sue for infringement, and vests no title or right to sue others for infringement in the licensee.[207] The *Guidelines* note that "[a] non-exclusive license of intellectual property that does not contain any restraints on the competitive conduct of the licensor or the licensee generally does not present antitrust concerns even if the parties to the license are in a horizontal relationship, because a non-exclusive license normally does not diminish competition that would occur in its absence."[208]

---

205.   35 U.S.C. § 261.

206.   *See* Waterman v. Mackenzie, 138 U.S. 252, 255 (1891); *see also* Zenith Radio Corp. v. Hazeltine Research, 395 U.S. 100, 135-36 (1969) ("The law ... recognizes that [a patentee] may assign to another his patent, in whole or in part, and may license others to practice his invention"); Bement v. Nat'l Harrow Co., 186 U.S. 70, 88-89 (1902) ("An owner of a patent has the right to sell it or to keep it; to manufacture the article himself or to license others to manufacture it; to sell such article himself or to authorize others to sell it").

207.   *See* Gen. Talking Pictures v. W. Elec. Co., 304 U.S. 175, 181, *aff'd on reh'g*, 305 U.S. 124 (1938); De Forest Radio Tel. & Tel. v. United States, 273 U.S. 236, 242 (1927); *Waterman*, 138 U.S. at 255; U.S. Philips Corp. v. Int'l Trade Comm'n, 424 F.3d 1179, 1189 (Fed. Cir. 2005), *cert. denied sub nom.* Princo Corp. v. U.S. Philips Corp., 126 S. Ct. 2899 (2006).

208.   INTELLECTUAL PROPERTY GUIDELINES, *supra* note 1, § 4.1.2. However, "the Agencies will focus on the actual practice and its effects, not on the formal terms of the arrangement," and "[a] non-exclusive license may have the effect of exclusive licensing if it is structured so that the licensor is unlikely to license others or to practice the technology itself." *Id.*; *see, e.g.*, United States v. S.C. Johnson & Son, Competitive Impact Statement, Civil No. 94-50249 (N.D. Ill.), 59 Fed. Reg. 43,859, 43,863 n.4 (Aug. 25, 1994).

An exclusive license generally "may raise antitrust concerns only if the licensees themselves or the licensor and its licensees, are in a horizontal relationship."[209] The *Guidelines* note that "[t]he antitrust principles that apply to a licensor's grant of various forms of exclusivity to and among its licensees are similar to those that apply to comparable vertical restraints outside the licensing context, such as exclusive territories and exclusive dealing."[210]

Generally, the mere grant of an exclusive license, even between competitors, does not, without more, violate the antitrust laws or constitute misuse.[211] Even where the licensor and licensee are

---

209. INTELLECTUAL PROPERTY GUIDELINES, *supra* note 1, § 4.1.2 ("Examples of arrangements involving exclusive licensing that may give rise to antitrust concerns include cross-licensing by parties collectively possessing market power (*see* section 5.5), grantbacks (*see* section 5.6), and acquisitions of intellectual property rights (*see* section 5.7)"). Example 8 in the *Guidelines* illustrates that when an inventor lacking the ability to bring a product to market itself grants an exclusive license to a firm that does not currently sell a competing product or have access to competing technology, the grant of an exclusive license does not affect competition between the licensor and licensee.

210. *Id.*

211. *See* Virtue v. Creamery Package Mfg., 227 U.S. 8, 36-37 (1913) ("the Disbrow Company, by its contract with the Owatonna Company, did nothing more than confirm or enlarge the rights which the Owatonna Company had obtained, by the contract of 1893, and conveyed to it the exclusive right in the patents for certain named royalties. This was no violation of law."); Baxter Int'l v. Abbott Labs., 315 F.3d 829, 830-31 (7th Cir. 2003); Genentech, Inc. v. Eli Lilly & Co., 998 F.2d 931, 949 (Fed. Cir. 1993) ("the grant of an exclusive license is a lawful incident of the rights to exclude provided by the Patent Act"); United States v. Studiengesellschaft Kohle, 670 F.2d 1122, 1127 (D.C. Cir. 1981); United States v. Westinghouse Elec., 648 F.2d 642, 647 (9th Cir. 1981); Levi Case Co. v. ATS Prods., 788 F. Supp. 428, 431-32 (N.D. Cal. 1992); SCM Corp. v. Xerox Corp., 463 F. Supp. 983, 1005-06 (D. Conn. 1978) ("The grant of an exclusive license from Battelle to Xerox pursuant to the 1948 agreement, as reconfirmed in the 1951 agreement and extended to worldwide rights, was entirely lawful when made."); United States v. E.I. duPont de Nemours & Co., 118 F. Supp. 41, 224 (D. Del. 1953) ("As owner of these patents, duPont had right to grant an exclusive license and under the cases such a license in no way violates the provisions of the Sherman Act"), *aff'd*, 351 U.S. 377 (1956); *cf.* Miller Insituform v. Insituform of N. Am., 830 F.2d 606, 607-09 (6th Cir. 1987) (unilateral termination of sublicense does not violate Sherman Act as the patentee

competitors, the grant of an exclusive license may be nothing more than the valid exercise of a statutory right, unless there is further evidence of an anticompetitive conspiracy or there are other circumstances present that might support an antitrust claim.[212] Antitrust concerns may arise where the licensees or the licensor and the licensee would be actual or potential competitors but for the exclusive license, and the exclusive license facilitates the exercise of market power.[213]

---

can control the power to exclude competition); Sheet Metal Duct v. Lindab Inc., 55 U.S.P.Q.2d (BNA) 1480, 1484 (E.D. Pa. 2000) ("It is not misuse of patent rights for a patentee to deal only with those with whom it pleases .... Lindab has the right as a patentee to sell its product exclusively to Midstates at whatever price it chooses.").

212. *See* Moraine Prods. v. ICI Am., 538 F.2d 134, 138-45 (7th Cir. 1976) (remanding for rule of reason analysis a challenge of an exclusive license that precluded further licenses or sublicense without consent of all parties); *see also* Smith Int'l v. Kennametal, Inc., 621 F. Supp. 79, 89-90 (N.D. Ohio 1985) (contractual arrangements under which co-owner of patent granted exclusive license to the other co-owner and then signed up as an exclusive distributor for a particular territory and agreed to purchase requirements of patented product from licensor should be treated as a lawful agreement between co-owners of patent and a vertical exclusive territorial agreement and exclusive dealing arrangements subject to the rule of reason). *Compare* E. Bement & Sons v. Nat'l Harrow Co., 186 U.S. 70, 94-95 (1902) (early case allowing competitor patent pool to grant an exclusive license for one specific design to one of the participants), *with* United States v. Singer Mfg. Co., 374 U.S. 174, 193 (1963) (exclusive licensing between and among competitors as part of agreement to prevent Japanese competition violated the Sherman Act). Although the district court originally refused to dismiss a Sherman Act § 1 challenge of a licensing arrangement creating "coexclusive" licensees who could not assign or sublicense in *Cook, Inc. v. Boston Scientific Corp.*, 2002 U.S. Dist. LEXIS 17331, 2002-1 Trade Cas. (CCH) ¶ 73,626 (N.D. Ill. Feb. 28, 2002), the Court of Appeals found nothing anticompetitive in that arrangement. 333 F.3d 737, 739-41 (7th Cir. 2003).

213. *See* United States v. Am. Nat'l Can Co., 1996-2 Trade Cas. (CCH) ¶ 71,641, 1996 U.S. Dist. LEXIS 19895 (D.D.C. 1996) (exclusive license between competitors viewed by DOJ as anticompetitive agreement eliminating potential competition at all levels where the licensor gave up the right to sell its technology and equipment in North America to others in exchange for exclusivity from the licensee); United States v. S.C. Johnson & Son, 1995-1 Trade Cas. (CCH) ¶ 70,884, 1994 U.S. Dist. LEXIS 20797 (N.D. Ill. 1994). *But see* United States v. Westinghouse

b. Exclusive Dealing

Exclusive dealing "arises when a license prevents or restrains the licensee from licensing, selling, distributing, or using competing technologies."[214] Exclusive dealing may foreclose competition in some respects, but may enhance competition and consumer welfare in others:

> Such restraints may anticompetitively foreclose access to, or increase competitors' costs of obtaining important inputs, or facilitate coordination to raise price or reduce output, but they also may have procompetitive effects. For example, a licensing arrangement that prevents the licensee from dealing in other technologies may encourage the licensee to develop and market the licensed technology or specialized applications of that technology.[215]

As noted above, the *Guidelines* provide that "[t]he fact that intellectual property may in some cases be misappropriated more easily than other forms of property may justify the use of some restrictions that might be anticompetitive in other contexts."[216]

Elec., 648 F.2d 642, 647 (9th Cir. 1981) ("Westinghouse has done no more than license some of its patents and refuse to license others ... The right to license that patent, exclusively or otherwise, or to refuse to license at all, is "the untrammeled right" of the patentee ... In short, in granting MELCO and MHI some licenses but not others, Westinghouse did no more than employ means "normally and reasonably adapted to secure pecuniary reward for the (patent) monopoly.").

214. INTELLECTUAL PROPERTY GUIDELINES, *supra* note 1, § 4.1.2 ("Exclusivity may be achieved by an explicit exclusive dealing term in the license or by other provisions such as compensation terms or other economic incentives"); *see also id.* § 5.4.

215. *Id.* § 4.1.2.

216. *Id.* For example, in licensing know-how and trade secrets, a covenant restricting competition, or at least a covenant that shifts the burden of proof to the licensee to establish that it has not used the licensor's know-how and trade secrets in competing, may be reasonable. *See* Eli Lilly & Co. v. Zenith Goldline Pharm., 172 F. Supp. 2d 1060, 1065-67 (S.D. Ind. 2001) (denying cross motions for summary judgment and requiring trial on contentions of a conspiracy through exclusive dealing to restrict the supply of cefaclor for the U.S. market, where agreement prohibited supply to third parties unless ACS-Dobfar could establish to Lilly's satisfaction that Lilly's know-how was not used was viewed as evidence of an attempt to establish reasonable restraints).

As illustrated in Example 8 of the *Guidelines*, where an inventor and its licensee are not actual or likely potential competitors in the manufacture or sale of the pertinent products or in the sale or development of the pertinent technology, a license that bars the licensee from selling competing products is "unlikely ... to harm competition by anticompetitively foreclosing access, raising competitors' costs of inputs, or facilitating anticompetitive pricing [where] the relevant product market is unconcentrated, the exclusive dealing restraint affects only a small proportion of the outlets for distribution of [pertinent] products, and entry is easy."[217]

In *Tampa Electric Co. v. Nashville Coal Co.*,[218] the Supreme Court made clear that exclusive dealing arrangements were evaluated under the rule of reason, and the FTC reached a similar conclusion in 1982 in *Beltone Electronics Corp.*[219] Consistent with Supreme Court and FTC precedent, Section 5.4 of the *Guidelines* explains that in "determining whether an exclusive dealing arrangement is likely to reduce competition in a relevant market, the Agencies will take into account the extent to which the arrangement (1) promotes the exploitation and development of a licensor's technology and (2) anticompetitively forecloses the exploitation and development of, or otherwise constrains competition among, competing technologies."[220]

The Agencies may take into account "the degree of foreclosure in the relevant market, the duration of the exclusive dealing arrangement, and other characteristics of the input and output markets, such as concentration, difficulty of entry, and the responsiveness of supply and demand to changes in price in the relevant markets."[221] In evaluating potential procompetitive effects, the Agencies consider "the extent to which a restraint encourages licensees to develop and market the licensed technology (or specialized applications of that technology), increases licensors' incentives to develop or refine the licensed technology or otherwise increases competition and enhances output in a relevant market."[222]

Although exclusive dealing arrangements are governed by the rule of reason, older cases had found per se patent misuse where a license

---

217. INTELLECTUAL PROPERTY GUIDELINES, *supra* note 1, Ex. 8.
218. 365 U.S. 320 (1961).
219. 100 F.T.C. 68 (1982).
220. INTELLECTUAL PROPERTY GUIDELINES, *supra* note 1, § 5.4.
221. *Id.*
222. *Id.*

required a licensee to refrain from dealing in competitive products.[223] At least two courts have held, however, that the 1988 Patent Misuse Reform Act provisions requiring a showing of market power for tying misuse applies not only to tie-in arrangements, but also to "tie-outs," which prohibit dealing in competitive products.[224]

The antitrust analysis of exclusive dealing, thus, may turn on an assessment of the competitive impact of the restriction. Where there are no barriers to entry, or where alternative channels of distribution or supply of competing products or technologies preclude a finding of significant foreclosure of competition, the foundation for an exclusive dealing claim is typically not present.[225] As with assessment of any restraint under the rule of reason, obvious less restrictive alternatives may be pertinent to assessments of whether a restraint is reasonable.[226]

Older cases, however, suggest that foreclosure of competition for a relatively small percentage of the market (at least for a significant

---

223. Berlenbach v. Anderson & Thompson Ski Co., 329 F.2d 782, 784-85 (9th Cir. 1964); McCullough v. Kammerer Corp., 166 F.2d 759, 761-62 (9th Cir. 1948); Nat'l Lockwasher Co. v. George K. Garrett Co., 137 F.2d 255, 257 (3d Cir. 1943); Krampe v. Ideal Indus., 347 F. Supp. 1384 (N.D. Ill. 1972); *see also* Zenith Radio Corp. v. Hazeltine Research, 395 U.S. 100, 136 (1969) (per se misuse to condition license "on the licensee's agreement to purchase, use or sell, or not to purchase use or sell, another article of commerce not within the scope of his patent monopoly"). In addition, courts have found copyright misuse where licenses prohibit the licensee from developing or promoting competing computer programs. *See* Practice Mgmt. Info. Corp. v. Am. Medical Ass'n, 121 F.3d 516, 520 (9th Cir. 1997); Lasercomb Am. v. Reynolds, 911 F.2d 970, 979 (4th Cir. 1990).

224. *See* Texas Instruments v. Hyundai Elecs. Indus., 49 F. Supp. 2d 893, 914 (S.D. Tex. 1999); Recombinant DNA Tech. Patent & Contract Litig., 850 F. Supp. 769, 777 (S.D. Ind. 1994).

225. *See* Concord Boat Corp. v. Brunswick Corp., 207 F.3d 1039, 1059 (8th Cir. 2000) (finding that exclusive dealing claim was not viable, among other reasons, because of lack of evidence of barriers to entry). Economic incentives, as opposed to absolute restraints, might support an exclusive dealing claim, but the plaintiff's burden of proof of foreclosure in such situations is difficult to meet. *See id.*; *see also* Monsanto Co. v. Scruggs, 342 F. Supp. 2d 568, 580-81 (N.D. Miss. 2004) (finding that the financial incentive agreements "do not foreclose competition in a substantial share of the relevant product market(s)").

226. *See* Eli Lilly & Co. v. Zenith Goldline Pharm., 172 F. Supp. 1060, 1065-67 (S.D. Ind. 2001).

duration) could sustain a Sherman Act Section 1 or Clayton Act Section 3 exclusive dealing claim.[227] Following the Supreme Court's opinions in *Jefferson Parish Hospital District No. 2 v. Hyde*,[228] and other authority suggesting that exclusive dealing can be procompetitive and market power cannot be established based on foreclosure of less than 30 percent of a relevant market, more recent cases tend to find no basis for Section 1 exclusive dealing claims unless the percentage of the market foreclosed is significantly in excess of 30 percent.[229]

In *United States v. Microsoft*,[230] the Court of Appeals held that exclusive dealing could constitute exclusionary conduct to support a Sherman Act Section 2 claim without the showing of the same nature or degree of foreclosure that would be required to establish a Section 1 violation. The court agreed with the government's contention that "a monopolist's use of exclusive contracts, in certain circumstances, may give rise to a § 2 violation even though the contracts foreclose less than the roughly 40% or 50% share usually required in order to establish a § 1 violation."[231] It found that "Microsoft's deals with the [internet access providers] clearly have significant effect in preserving its monopoly; they help keep usages of Navigator below the critical level necessary for Navigator or any other rival to pose a real threat to Microsoft's monopoly."[232]

---

227. *See* FTC v. Brown Shoe Co., 384 U.S. 316, 320-21 (1966) (a significant number of outlets foreclosed); Standard Oil Co. v. United States, 337 U.S. 293, 305 (1949) (foreclosure of 6.7 percent); Twin City Sportserv. v. Charles O. Finley & Co., 676 F.2d 1291, 1298-1308 (9th Cir. 1982) (foreclosure of 24% of market with 10-year contracts).

228. 466 U.S. 2 (1984); *see also id.* at 45 (O'Connor, J., concurring).

229. *See Concord Boat*, 207 F.3d at 1059 ("The boat builders failed to produce sufficient evidence to demonstrate that Brunswick had foreclosed a substantial share of the stern drive engine market through anticompetitive conduct."); U.S. Healthcare v. Healthsource, Inc., 986 F.2d 589, 596 (1st Cir. 1983) (25 percent foreclosure not unlawful).

230. 253 F.3d 34 (D.C. Cir. 2001).

231. *Id.* at 70.

232. *Id.* at 68-71. The court also rejected Microsoft's general claim that its copyright entitled it to impose unlimited restrictions on the ability of original equipment manufacturers to alter the Windows boot-up sequence, which would have permitted OEMs to delete Microsoft's Internet Explorer in favor of competing browsers not bundled with Windows. *Id.* at 63. The court held, however, that the license prohibition against causing any user interface other than the Windows desktop to launch automatically was not a basis for liability because this restraint

Exclusive dealing contracts of shorter duration are less problematic that those of longer duration. Some courts have suggested that contracts for less than a year or those terminable at will or on relatively short notice are at least presumptively lawful.[233] However, in one recent case in which there were no written contractual arrangements, but rather a terminable course of dealing with distributors that knew they would be terminated by the supplier of 70 to 80 percent of the products in the relevant market if they carried a competitive product, the court held that this exclusivity supported Section 2 liability. In *United States v. Dentsply International, Inc.*,[234] the Third Circuit held that distributors were effectively locked into exclusive dealing arrangements with Dentsply even though they were not subject to long term contracts.[235] Together, *Microsoft* and *Dentsply* suggest that exclusive dealing as exclusionary conduct to support Sherman Act Section 2 liability may raise more significant issues in certain circumstances than traditional rule of reason exclusive dealing claims under Section 1 of the Sherman Act or Section 3 of the Clayton Act.

7. Tying

Tying arrangements may be judged under a variety of antitrust theories.[236] They may be treated as per se unlawful or subject to the rule of reason. Moreover, they may be analyzed under Section 1 of the Sherman Act, Section 3 of the Clayton Act[237] or Section 5 of the FTC

---

was justified by Microsoft's legitimate interest in preventing a substantial alteration of its copyrighted work. *Id.*

233. Roland Mach. v. Dresser Indus., 749 F.2d 380, 395 (7th Cir. 1984) (contracts terminable in less than a year are presumptively lawful); *see also* FTC v. Motion Picture Adver. Serv., 344 U.S. 392, 396 (1953) (permitting exclusive agreements of a year or less); *U.S. Healthcare*, 986 F.2d at 596 (contracts terminable in less than a year held lawful).

234. 399 F.3d 181 (3d Cir. 2005).

235 *Id.* at 191-92. Dentsply was alleged to have controlled 70-80% of artificial teeth sales for the past ten years, and its distributors were prohibited from dealing in competitors' goods. Although the district court found for the defendant on all claims, including Sherman Act §§ 1 and 2 claims and Clayton Act § 3 claims, the Department of Justice only proceeded on § 2 claims on appeal and prevailed.

236. *See* Ill. Tools Works v. Indep. Ink, 126 S. Ct. 1281, 1286 (2006) (four different rules of law have supported challenges to tying arrangements).

237. Section 3 of the Clayton Act addresses tying in the context of the sale of "goods, wares, merchandise, machinery, supplies, or other commodities,

Act, and may establish a basis for a Sherman Act Section 2 claim. In addition, tying may establish a basis for patent or copyright misuse.[238]

As the Supreme Court noted in *Illinois Tool Works v. Independent Ink*,[239] "[o]ver the years ... this Court's strong disapproval of tying arrangements has substantially diminished," such that "[r]ather than relying on assumptions, in its more recent opinions the Court has required a showing of market power in the tying product."[240] To establish a per se tying violation under Section 1 of the Sherman Act or Section 3 of the Clayton Act, the plaintiff generally must prove: (1) two separate products or services are involved,[241] (2) there is a sale or

---

whether patented or unpatented," and thus, unlike § 1 of the Sherman Act and § 5 of the FTC Act, does not apply to services or intangible property. Marts v. Xerox, Inc., 77 F.3d 1109, 1113 n.6 (8th Cir. 1996) (warranties are services not subject to § 3); Wilson v. Mobil Oil, 940 F. Supp. 944, 954 (E.D. La. 1996) ("Here the tying product, a trademarked franchise, is not a commodity, and plaintiffs have therefore failed to state a claim under Section 3 of the Clayton Act."). Section 3 of the Clayton Act expressly addresses conditions placed on sales and leases of patented machinery. *See, e.g.*, United Shoe Mach. Corp. v. United States, 258 U.S. 451, 462 (1922) ("Congress has undertaken to deny the protection of patent rights to such covenants as come within the terms of the Clayton Act, and if the statute is constitutional, the sole duty of the court is to enforce it in accordance with its terms.").

238. As noted in the *Guidelines*, "[p]ackage licensing—the licensing of multiple items of intellectual property in a single license or in a group of related licenses—may be a form of tying arrangement if the licensing of one product is conditioned upon the acceptance of a license of another, separate product." INTELLECTUAL PROPERTY GUIDELINES, *supra* note 1, § 5.3 (citing United States v. Paramount Pictures, 334 U.S. 131, 156-58 (1948) (copyrights)). Nonetheless, this section addresses general tying law and principles as applied to tying in license agreements. Package licensing is addressed below as is pooling of patents.

239. 126 S. Ct. 1281 (2006).

240. *Id.* at 1286; *see also id.* at 1287 (noting the shift in the Court between Fortner Enters. v. United States Steel Corp., 394 U.S. 495, 498-99 (1969) (*Fortner I*) ("arrangements of this kind are illegal in and of themselves, and no specific showing of unreasonable competitive effect is required") and United States Steel Corp. v. Fortner Enters., 429 U.S. 610, 622 (1977) (*Fortner II*) (failure of proof of market power was fatal to tying claim)).

241. Eastman Kodak Co. v. Image Technical Servs., 504 U.S. 451, 462 (1992); Jefferson Parrish Hosp. Dist. No.2 v. Hyde, 466 U.S. 2, 21-22 (1984); *Fortner I*, 394 U.S. at 497-98; N. Pac. Ry. v. United States, 356 U.S. 1, 5-

agreement to sell one product or service conditioned on the purchase of another,[242] (3) the seller has sufficient economic power in the market for the tying product to enable it to restrain trade in the market for the tied

---

6 (1958). In tying cases involving intellectual property there may be complex issues regarding whether bundled products or services are efficiency-enhancing integrated technological improvements. *Compare* United States v. Microsoft Corp, 147 F.3d 935 (D.C. Cir. 1998) (recognizing that improvements to integrated software may benefit consumers), *with* C.R. Bard, Inc. v. M3 Sys., 157 F.3d 1340, 1382-83 (Fed. Cir. 1998) (evidence was sufficient to support jury finding of exclusionary conduct where there was evidence that modifications that prevented use of competing biopsy needles with guns were adopted to impede competition as opposed to being adopted for safety or palpable technological improvements).

242. *N. Pac. Ry.*, 356 U.S. at 6 n.4 ("where the buyer is free to take either product by itself there is no tying problem"); *Jefferson Parrish*, 466 U.S. at 12 n.17; Virginia Panel Corp. v. MAC Panel Co., 133 F.3d 860, 870-71 (Fed. Cir. 1997) (neither threats to limit or void warranties, nor aborted negotiation of a proposed license agreement that would have required purchase of unpatented staple goods comprised an unlawful tie); Medtronic MiniMed v. Smiths Med. MD, 371 F. Supp. 2d 578, 585-86 (D. Del. 2005); Applera Corp. v. MJ Research, 309 F. Supp. 2d 293, ,294 (D. Conn. 2004) (factual issues for trial on whether there was coercion in multiple patent licensing); *see also* Paladin Assocs. v. Mont. Power Co., 328 F.3d 1145, 1156 (9th Cir. 2003) (affirming summary judgment for defendant where plaintiff failed to provide sufficient evidence of coercion); Highland Capital v. Franklin Nat'l Bank, 350 F.3d 558, 568 (6th Cir. 2003) (affirming summary judgment for defendant in Bank Holding Company Act tying claim for lack of sufficient proof of coercion or "conditioning" sale of one item on purchase of the other); Six W. Retail Acquisition v. Sony Theatre Mgmt., 97 Civ. 5499 (LAP), 2004 U.S. Dist. LEXIS 5411, at *22 (S.D.N.Y. Mar. 30, 2004) (evidence that some theaters would pay for less desirable films to preserve favorable relationships with Sony was "a far cry from evidence of a distributor's actually conditioning access to one film on an exhibitor's taking a less-desired film"); Moccio v. Cablevision Sys., 208 F. Supp. 2d 361, 375 (E.D.N.Y. 2002) (no unlawful tying where customers were not required to purchase premium cable channels).

product,[243] and (4) a not insubstantial amount of interstate commerce in the tied product is affected.[244]

There is a disputed fifth element. The *Guidelines* and certain lower court cases suggest that it is important to consider effects on competition in the tied market before condemning such practices as unlawful.[245] If there is no basis for a per se tying claim, there still may be a tying claim under the rule of reason.[246]

There are a number of cases in the lower courts that suggest that the per se rule should not be applied to technological integration with demonstrable efficiencies, or to products and markets where there are arguably benefits from tying and the industry is one in which the economics and technology have not been thoroughly examined by the

243. *See* Ill. Tool Works v. Indep. Ink, 126 S. Ct. 1281, 1292-93 (2006); *Jefferson Parrish*, 466 U.S. at 27; *Fortner II*, 429 U.S. at 620-22; Times-Picayune Publ'g v. United States, 345 U.S. 594, 613-14 (1953); Allen-Myland, Inc. v. IBM, 33 F.3d 194, 200 (3d Cir. 1994).

244. *See Jefferson Parrish*, 466 U.S. at 15-16; United States v. Loew's, Inc., 371 U.S. 38, 49 (1962).

245. INTELLECTUAL PROPERTY GUIDELINES, *supra* note 1, § 5.3. *See* ANTITRUST LAW DEVELOPMENTS, *supra* note 100, at 205-06 & nn.1167-76 & at 177-78 (5th ed. 2002) ("Judicial analysis of tying arrangements has undergone important adjustments in the past twenty years ... Although the Supreme Court continues to classify some tying arrangements as per se violations, the test courts now use to determine whether the per se rule should be applied to a particular arrangement increasingly resembles a rule of reason inquiry . . . ."). *Compare* Hack v. President & Fellows of Yale Coll., 237 F.3d 81, 86 (2d Cir. 2000) ("We have required allegations and proof of five specific elements before finding a tie illegal: first, a tying and a tied product; second, evidence of actual coercion by the seller that forced the buyer to accept the tied product; third, sufficient economic power in the tying product market to coerce purchaser acceptance of the tied product; fourth, anticompetitive effects in the tied market; and fifth, the involvement of a "not insubstantial" amount of interstate commerce in the 'tied' market."), *with* Brokerage Concepts v. U.S. Healthcare, 140 F.3d 494, 511 (3d Cir. 1998) ("no inquiry need be made into the actual prevailing market conditions"). *See also* CTUnify, Inc. v. Nortel Networks, No. 03-6157, 115 Fed Appx. 831, 2004 U.S. App. LEXIS 24211 (6th Cir. Nov. 18, 2004) (not for publication) (no antitrust injury to allow suit for tying where complaint failed to allege anticompetitive effects in the tied product market).

246. *See* United States v. Microsoft Corp., 253 F.3d 34, 84-97 (D.C. Cir. 2001) (en banc); Town Sound & Custom Tops v. Chrysler Motors Corp., 959 F.2d 468, 482 (3d Cir. 1992) (en banc).

courts.[247] Other cases suggest that a tying claim may not be viable where the evidence establishes that the allegedly tied products can only be sold as a single product.[248] Furthermore, although justifications are typically irrelevant in assessing per se claims, courts have considered justifications for ties, including quality control, operability, and customer satisfaction, in determining whether to apply a per se proscription.[249]

a. The Agencies' Approach to Intellectual Property Tying Claims

The *Guidelines* suggest that the Agencies would evaluate an intellectual property tying case under a rule of reason analysis.[250] According to the *Guidelines*, "[a]lthough tying arrangements may result in anticompetitive effects such arrangements can also result in significant

---

247 . *See Microsoft*, 253 F.3d at 84-97; United States v. Microsoft Corp., 147 F.3d 935, 943-44 (D.C. Cir. 1998); Cal. Computer Prods. v. IBM, 613 F.2d 727, 745 (9th Cir. 1979); Berkey Photo v. Eastman Kodak Co., 603 F.2d 263, 273 (2d Cir. 1979); *see also* Caldera, Inc. v. Microsoft Corp., 72 F. Supp. 2d 1295, 1327 (D. Utah 1999) (recognizing principle but denying summary judgment for defendant in light of factual dispute on integration question).

248. Ricoh Co. v. Nashua Corp., 1999 U.S. App. LEXIS 2672 (Fed. Cir. Feb. 18, 1999) (unpublished opinion); *see also* Fortner Enters. v. United States Steel Corp., 394 U.S. 495, 509 (1969).

249. *See* United States v. Jerrold Elecs., 187 F. Supp. 545, 556-57 (E.D. Pa. 1960) (tie to establish integrated system and warranties justified for limited time in beginning of new industry to ensure proper functioning of complex equipment), *aff'd per curiam,* 365 U.S. 567 (1961); *see also* Dehydrating Process Co. v. A.O. Smith Corp., 292 F.2d 653, 656-57 (1st Cir. 1961) (tie of patented device and patented products necessary to address customer dissatisfaction was not an unlawful tie). In condemning tying arrangements as per se unlawful, the Supreme Court has noted that supplies tied to leases of patented machines were not validly justified for quality control or functionality. *See* Int'l Salt Co. v. United States, 332 U.S. 392, 397-98 (1947) ("Of course, a lessor may impose on a lessee reasonable restrictions designed in good faith to minimize maintenance burdens and to assure satisfactory operation."); IBM v. United States, 298 U.S. 131, 139-40 (1936) ("Appellant is not prevented from proclaiming the virtues of its own cards or warning against the danger of using, in its machines, cards which do not conform to its necessary specifications, or even from making its leases conditional upon the use of cards which conform to them.").

250. INTELLECTUAL PROPERTY GUIDELINES,*su pra* note 1, § 5.3.

efficiencies and procompetitive benefits."[251] Furthermore, section 5.3 of the *Guidelines* states that "[t]he agencies would be likely to challenge a tying arrangement if: (1) the seller has market power in the tying product, (2) the arrangement has an adverse effect on competition in the relevant market for the tied product, and (3) efficiency justifications for the arrangement do not outweigh the anticompetitive effects."[252]

b. Historical Case Law Approach to Intellectual Property Tying Claims

The history of tying law as it relates to intellectual property is full of twists that reflect changing theories and a significant interplay between the Supreme Court and Congress.   Older cases in which a patent is equated with a "monopoly" regardless of competition and relevant markets, tend to condemn tying as anticompetitive or an attempt to extend the "patent monopoly" to unpatented goods.

In 1912, in *Henry v. A.B. Dick Co.*,[253] the Supreme Court permitted tying the sale of unpatented ink to the sale of a patented mimeograph machine as a form of metering the use of the machine as a payment measure for use of the patented device.

In 1914, Congress enacted the Clayton Act, including Section 3, which made it unlawful "to lease or make a sale or contract for sale of goods, wares, merchandise, machinery, supplies, or other commodities, whether patented or unpatented . . . on the condition, agreement, or understanding that the lessee or purchaser thereof shall not use or deal in the goods, wares, merchandise, machinery, supplies, or other commodities of a competitor or competitors of the lessor or seller, where the effect . . . may be to substantially lessen competition or tend to create a monopoly in any line of commerce."[254]   In 1917, invoking the "public policy" of Section 3 of the Clayton Act, the Supreme Court overruled *Henry v. A.B. Dick Co.* in *Motion Picture Patents Co. v. Universal Film Manufacturing Co.*[255]

Motion Picture Patents involved a patent for improvements to movie projectors allowing feeding the film "with a regular, uniform and accurate movement and so as not to expose the film to excessive strain or wear."[256]   The license allowing manufacture of the machines required

---

251. *Id.*
252. *Id.*
253. 224 U.S. 1 (1912).
254. 15 U.S.C. § 14.
255. 243 U.S. 502 (1917).
256. *Id.* at 505.

that machines be sold with the condition that they only be used to exhibit the licensor's leased films (which were under patent, but the patent on which expired).[257] The Supreme Court affirmed decrees finding this restriction invalid, noting that:

> the practice adopted . . . proves that under color of its patent the owner intends to and does derive its profit, not from the invention on which the law gives it a monopoly but from the unpatented supplies with which it is used and which are wholly without the scope of the patented monopoly, thus in effect extending the power to the owner of the patent to fix the price to the public of the unpatented supplies as effectively as he may fix the price on the patented machine.

In 1922, in *United Shoe Machinery Corp. v. United States*,[258] the Supreme Court expressly applied the Clayton Act to find unlawful, as tending to create a monopoly, the conduct of United Shoe Machinery, which supplied 95 percent of the machines used to make shoes. At issue were a series of restraints and penalties which, along with the implied threat of termination, effectively prevented the use of competing machines.[259]

About ten years later, in 1931, the Court in *Carbice Corp. v. American Patents Development Corp.*,[260] refused to allow the owner of a patent for a refrigerated transportation package using dry ice to pursue an action for contributory liability for infringement based on the sale of dry ice with the knowledge that it would be used with infringing packages. The Court perceived that allowing such a suit would effectively allow the holder of the patent to secure a "monopoly" over dry ice even though it did not invent dry ice and the claims of its patent did not preclude others from manufacturing or selling dry ice.[261]

In 1936, in *IBM Corp. v. United States*,[262] the Court held that leases for patented tabulating machines, which required the use of lessor's perforated cards in the machines, violated Section 3 of the Clayton Act.[263]

---

257. *Id.* at 506.
258. 258 U.S. 451 (1922).
259   *Id.* at 457.
260. 283 U.S. 27 (1931).
261   *Id.* at 33-34.
262. 298 U.S. 131 (1936).
263   *Id.* at 135-37.

In 1938, in *Leitch Manufacturing Co. v. Barber Co.,*[264] the Court confronted another case like *Carbice* involving claims of contributory infringement, but this time in the context of a method or process patent covering a method for applying bituminous emulsion to aid in curing wet concrete for roads. The Court refused to allow the suit against a competing supplier of bituminous emulsion, because the patent only covered a method utilizing that emulsion, not the emulsion itself.[265]

In 1942, the Court refused to enforce a patent against a direct infringer based on tying in *Morton Salt Co. v. G.S. Suppinger Co.*[266] Prior cases had merely limited the contributory infringement doctrine. The Court in *Morton Salt*, however, refused to enforce the patent against a direct infringer, combining the equitable doctrine of unclean hands with antitrust policy to establish what is now generally referred to as patent misuse.[267] Then, in 1947, in *International Salt Co. v. United States,*[268] the Court held that leases of patented machines utilizing salt requiring the purchase of salt supplies from lessor violated Section 3 of the Clayton Act and Section 1 of the Sherman Act.[269]

Similarly, tying involving copyrights was held per se unlawful by the Supreme Court in 1948 in *United States v. Paramount Pictures*[270] and in 1962 in *United States v. Loew's, Inc.*[271] Lower courts have also recognized a copyright misuse doctrine similar to the patent misuse doctrine.[272]

In 1944, the Supreme Court decided two cases involving unpatented switches that were components of combination patents for heating systems. In the first, *Mercoid Corp. v. Mid-Continent Investment Co.,*[273] the Court addressed claims under a combination patent for a heating system with three main elements: a motor driven stoker for feeding fuel to the combustion chamber of the furnace, a room thermostat for

264.   302 U.S. 458 (1938).
265   *Id.* at 463-64.
266.   314 U.S. 488 (1942); *see also* B.B. Chem. Co. v. Ellis, 314 U.S. 495, 498-99 (1942).
267   314 U.S. at 492.
268.   332 U.S. 392 (1947).
269   *Id.* at 397-98.
270.   334 U.S. 131, 143 (1948).
271.   371 U.S. 38, 49-50 (1962).
272.   *E.g.*, Lasercomb Am. v. Reynolds, 911 F.2d 970 (4th Cir. 1990) (copyright misuse in license terms preventing licensees from developing or assisting in developing competing software).
273.   320 U.S. 661 (1944).

controlling the feeding of the fuel, and a combustion stoker switch to prevent extinguishment of the fire.[274] The patent owner (Mid-Continent) and its exclusive licensee (Minneapolis-Honeywell) did not make or sell the full heating systems, but rather Minneapolis-Honeywell sold only the combustion stoker switches and provided an implied license over the use of the invention with the sale of the switch which was a part of the combination. Mid-Continent sued Mercoid for contributory infringement for making and selling unpatented combustion stoker switches for use in systems employing the patented combination, and Mercoid counterclaimed asserting violation of the antitrust laws. The Supreme Court held that there could be no action for contributory infringement for sale of an unpatented article even if it was a component of the combination patent and even if it had no uses outside of the patented system, and remanded to allow further consideration of the antitrust counterclaim.[275]

The second case, *Mercoid Corp. v. Minneapolis-Honeywell Regulator Co.*,[276] involved another combination patent on heating systems involving several switches, and an attempt to enjoin Mercoid from selling the unpatented component. The Court suggested that the antitrust laws, not the patent laws controlled:

> [A]n unpatented part of a combination patent is no more entitled to monopolistic protection than any other unpatented device. For ... a patent on a combination is a patent on the assembled or functioning whole, not on the separate parts. The legality of any attempt to bring unpatented goods within the protection of the patent is measured by the anti-trust laws not by the patent law.... [T]he effort here made to control competition in this unpatented device plainly violates the anti-trust laws, even apart from the price-fixing provisions of the license agreements. It follows that petitioner is entitled to be relieved against the consequences of those acts. It likewise follows that respondent may not obtain from a court of equity any decree which directly or indirectly helps it to subvert the public policy which underlies the grant of its patent.[277]

In 1952, Congress superseded the *Mercoid* cases by statute. In the Patent Act of 1952, Congress added § 271(b), which provided that those who induce infringement are liable for patent infringement, and § 271(c),

---

274. *Id.* at 664.
275. *Id.* at 666-72.
276. 320 U.S. 680 (1944).
277 *Id.* at 684.

which established a statutory contributory infringement claim against those who supply goods, such as those at issue in the *Mercoid* cases, that have no use other than one which infringes a patent.[278] It also added § 271(d)(1)-(3), which provide that:

> No patent owner otherwise entitled to relief for infringement or contributory infringement of a patent shall be denied relief or deemed guilty of misuse or illegal extension of the patent right by reason of his having done one or more of the following: (1) derived revenue from acts which if performed by another without his consent would constitute contributory infringement of the patent; (2) licensed or authorized another to perform acts which if performed without his consent would constitute contributory infringement of the patent; (3) sought to enforce his patent rights against infringement or contributory infringement.[279]

In 1980, in *Dawson Chemical Co. v. Rohm & Haas Co.*,[280] the Court held that "the provisions of § 271(d) effectively confer upon a patentee, as a lawful adjunct of his patent rights, a limited power to exclude others from competition in non-staple goods."[281] Accordingly, the Court held that it was not misuse for the holder of a process patent to license only those who purchased the herbicide used in the process from it and to sue others for contributory infringement for selling the herbicide which had no use outside the process claimed in the patent. Thus, notwithstanding the older Supreme Court cases discussed above, tying involving a non-staple good is not misuse.[282]

---

278.   35 U.S.C. § 271(c) ("Whoever offers to sell or sells within the United States or imports into the United States a component of a patented machine, manufacture, combination or composition, or a material or apparatus for use in practicing a patented process, constituting a material part of the invention, knowing the same to be especially made or especially adapted for use in an infringement of such patent, and not a staple article or commodity of commerce suitable for substantial noninfringing use, shall be liable as a contributory infringer.").

279   *Id.* § 271(d)(1)-(3).

280.   448 U.S. 176 (1980).

281.   *Id.* at 201.

282.   *See* Hodosh v. Block Drug, 833 F.2d 1575, 1579 (Fed. Cir. 1987); Senza-Gel Corp. v. Seiffhart, 803 F.2d 661, 670-71 (Fed. Cir. 1986); Polysius Corp. v. Fuller Co., 709 F. Supp. 560, 575 (E.D. Pa. 1989).

c.   No Presumption of Market Power in Tying Claims Involving Patents

Generally, the plaintiff in a tying case must prove that the defendant had market power in the tying product in order to establish per se unlawful tying.[283] The Supreme Court, in *Jefferson Parrish Hospital District No.2 v. Hyde*,[284] suggested that market power in the tying market could not be established based on market share where the party allegedly applying the tie had less than a 30 percent market share.[285]

One of the general principles embodied in the *Guidelines* is that the existence of intellectual property rights does not give rise to a presumption of market power, and this principle is applied by the agencies with respect to tying issues.[286] This principle, however, is not ingrained in older case law.

Per se condemnation of tying related to intellectual property stems in part from older cases viewing the patent or copyright grant as a "monopoly" without regard to competing technologies or products.[287] The presumption of market power from a patent articulated in older cases was recited by a divided Supreme Court in *Jefferson Parish* (a case which did not itself involve intellectual property): "if the Government has granted the seller a patent or similar monopoly over a product, it is fair to presume that the inability to buy the product elsewhere gives the

---

283.   United States Steel Corp. v. Fortner Enters., 429 U.S. 610, 622 (1977); *see also* Jefferson Parrish Hosp. Dist. No. 2 v. Hyde, 466 U.S. 2, 17-18 (1984) ("When, however, the seller does not have either the degree or the kind of market power that enables him to force customers to purchase a second, unwanted product in order to obtain the tying product, an antitrust violation can be established only by evidence of an unreasonable restraint on competition in the relevant market.").

284.   466 U.S. 2 (1984).

285   *Id.* at 16.

286.   INTELLECTUAL PROPERTY GUIDELINES, *supra* note 1, §§ 2.0 & 5.3 ("The Agencies will not presume that a patent, copyright or trade secret necessarily confers market power upon its owner.").

287.   *See, e.g.,* Int'l Salt Co. v. United States, 332 U.S. 392, 397 (1947); *see also* Standard Oil Co. v. United States, 337 U.S. 293, 307 (1949) ("[a] patent, . . . although in fact there may be many competing substitutes for the patented article, is at least prima facie evidence of [market] control [of the tying device]."); IBM v. United States, 298 U.S. 131, 136 (1936) (condemning tying of unpatented cards to patented machines under § 3 of the Clayton Act).

seller market power."[288] The Court further described how tying through patents has typically been treated as unlawful:

> Any effort to enlarge the scope of the patent monopoly by using the market power it confers to restrain competition in the market for a second product will undermine competition on the merits in that second market. Thus, the sale or lease of a patented item on condition that the buyer make all his purchases of a separate tied product from the patentee is unlawful.[289]

In 1988 Congress amended Section 271(d) of the Patent Act to limit the presumption of market power, at least as to defenses of patent misuse to infringement claims:

> No patent owner ... shall be denied relief or deemed guilty of misuse or illegal extension of the patent right by reason of ... (5) condition[ing] the license of any rights to the patent or the sale of the patented product on the acquisition of a license to rights in another patent or purchase of a separate product, unless, in view of the circumstances, the patent owner has market power in the relevant market for the patent or patented product on which the license or sale or conditioned.[290]

The Supreme Court in *Illinois Tool Works v. Independent Ink*[291] overruled any precedent that had suggested that market power was to be presumed based merely on the existence of a patent, noting that "Congress, the antitrust enforcement agencies, and most economists have all reached the conclusion that a patent does not necessarily confer market power on the patentee."[292] Thus, the Court held that "in all cases

---

288. *Jefferson Parish*, 466 U.S. at 16.
289. *Id.*
290. 35 U.S.C. § 271(d); *see* Lockformer Co. v. PPG Indus., 264 F. Supp. 2d 622, 629 (N.D. Ill. 2003) (parties asserting tying patent misuse failed to meet burden of production of evidence to establish market power). The Federal Circuit in *Independent Ink v. Illinois Tool Works* held that this provision protected patentees against misuse defenses in the absence of proof of market power, but that it did not supersede cases suggesting that a patent creates a presumption of market power for purposes of a tying antitrust violation. 396 F.3d 1342, 1349 n.7 (Fed. Cir. 2005); *see* Grid Sys. Corp. v. Texas Instruments, 771 F. Supp. 1033, 1044 n.2 (N.D. Cal. 1991).
291. 126 S. Ct. 1281 (2006).
292. *Id.* at 1293.

involving a tying arrangement, the plaintiff must prove that the defendant has market power in the tying product."[293]

d. Technological Integration as Tying

Another area of continuing debate, as demonstrated by *C.R. Bard, Inc. v. M3 Systems,*[294] a split decision in favor of an antitrust plaintiff, is whether technological integration and product design changes should give rise to antitrust liability. At issue in *Bard* were two patents for "devices for taking samples of body tissue for biopsy purposes, wherein a biopsy needle firing device or 'gun' mechanically injects a biopsy needle assembly into the core body tissue."[295]   In Bard's patent infringement suit against M3, the jury found both patents invalid and not infringed. M3 contended, among its counterclaims, that Bard improperly modified its biopsy gun to prevent its competitors' non-infringing, flangeless needles from being used in Bard's guns.[296] The jury found that "there was a relevant product market for replacement needles for fully automated reusable biopsy guns, that Bard had monopoly power in that market, and that it had acquired or maintained its monopoly power in that market through restrictive or exclusionary conduct." According to the court, the evidence was sufficient to support the jury's verdict that Bard enjoyed monopoly power in the market for replacement needles and maintained that position "by exclusionary conduct, to wit, modifying its patented gun in order to exclude competing replacement needles."[297]

Bard contended that it modified its biopsy gun to make it easier to load and unload, and the dissent argued vigorously that the courts should not interfere with or allow antitrust claims to be predicted upon improvements to products.[298] The majority held, however, that "there was substantial evidence that Bard's real reasons for modifying the gun were to raise the cost of entry to potential makers of replacement needles, to make doctors apprehensive about using non-Bard needles, and to preclude the use of 'copycat' needles."[299]

---

293. *Id.*
294. 157 F.3d 1340 (Fed. Cir. 1998).
295. *Id.* at 1346.
296. *Id.* at 1382 (Bryson, J., concurring in part and dissenting in part).
297. *Id.*
298. *Id.* at 1367-74.
299. *Id.* at 1382 ("One internal Bard document showed that the gun modifications had no effect on gun or needle performance; another internal document showed that the use of non-Bard needles in the gun

204 Intellectual Property and Antitrust Handbook

In 1998 the Court of Appeals for the District of Columbia Circuit, in a split 2 to 1 panel decision, held that a 1995 Consent Decree against Microsoft did not support a preliminary injunction granted by the district court to prevent Microsoft from tying its web browser software to its operating systems software.[300] The Court of Appeals interpreted the Consent Decree, which permitted Microsoft to develop integrated products, "as permitting any genuine technological integration, regardless of whether elements of the integrated package are marketed separately."[301] The Court further held that an "integrated product" is:

> a product that combines functionalities (which may also be marketed separately and operated together) in a way that offers advantages unavailable if the functionalities are bought separately and combined by the purchaser.[302]

The Court stated that the test for integration "comes down to the question of whether its integrated design offers benefits when compared to a purchaser's compilation of corresponding stand-alone function-alities."[303] The Court held that a "court's evaluation of a claim of integration must be narrow and deferential."[304] It held that on the record before it, Microsoft "clearly met the burden of ascribing facially plausible benefits to its integrated design as compared to an operating system combined with a stand-alone browser such as Netscape's Navigator."[305]

'could not possibly result in injury to either the patient or the physician.'"). By way of contrast, see *Medtronic MiniMed v. Smiths Medical MD*, 371 F. Supp. 2d 578 (D. Del. 2005), in which the court granted summary judgment for the patentee on antitrust counterclaims where there was no evidence of abuse of patents in patentees move away from traditional industry locking apparatus between patented insulin pump and infusion sets, the shift to a new locking system did not preclude others from selling infusion sets compatible with the patentees system, and the counterclaimant lacked standing as it did not even attempt or intend to produce infusion sets compatible with the patentee's pumps and locking system. *Id.* at 588-89.

300.   United States v. Microsoft Corp., 147 F.3d 935 (D.C. Cir. 1998).
301   *Id.* at 948.
302   *Id.*
303   *Id.* at 949.
304   *Id.* at 949-50.
305   *Id.* at 950.

When the later-filed *Microsoft* case came before the District of Columbia Circuit en banc in 2001,[306] the court reiterated that the Supreme Court has classified tying as per se unlawful, yet, according to the court, "the sort of tying arrangement attacked here is unlike any the Supreme Court has considered."[307] The court noted that the Supreme Court tying cases did not address a situation where "the tied good [was] physically and technologically integrated with the tying good."[308] Although the court held that per se treatment was inappropriate, it rejected the overly deferential standard of integration from its earlier panel decision as contrary to prevailing antitrust doctrine. Nevertheless, it noted that there was not enough experience with software bundling cases to condemn such practices per se, and that doing so arguably could stunt innovation. First, since firms without market power also bundled platform software, the practice could be presumed to have some efficiency advantages. Second, "because of the pervasively innovative character of platform software markets, tying in such markets may produce efficiencies that courts have not previously encountered."[309] Thus, the court directed reconsideration on remand of the tying claims under the rule of reason, but limited its judgment to the tying arrangement before it "where the tying product is software whose major purpose is to serve as a platform for third-party applications and the tied product is complimentary software functionality."[310] The court further suggested that, under the rule of reason, the government would have to establish adverse competitive effect in the tied product market.[311]

In *McFarland v. Monsanto Co.*,[312] the Federal Circuit considered a patent misuse challenge and antitrust counterclaim asserting that the licensing scheme for patented genetically engineered seeds that were designed to work with certain herbicides was unlawful tying. Monsanto required that end user licenses only allow the seeds to be used for a single season's planting and restrained the users of the seeds from redistributing or saving any patented seed or crop from the seeds for replanting.[313] McFarling contended that Monsanto "impermissibly tied an unpatented product to a patented product," specifically that "by

---

306. United States v. Microsoft Corp., 253 F.3d 34 (D.C. Cir. 2001) (en banc).
307. *Id.* at 90.
308. *Id.*
309. *Id.* at 93.
310. *Id.* at 95.
311. *Id.*
312. 363 F.3d 1336 (Fed. Cir. 2004).
313. *Id.* at 1339.

prohibiting seed-saving, Monsanto has extended its patent on the gene technology to include an unpatented product—the germplasm—or God-made soybean seed which is not within the terms of the patent."[314] The Federal Circuit declined to view the case as a permissible field of use restraint on the first generation seeds, as argued by Monsanto, but rather found that the purported tie relating to second generation seeds did not exceed the scope of the patent, as the second generation seeds read on the patent claims just as the first generation seeds did, so that restraints on the second generation seeds were merely restraints within the scope of the patents.[315]

8. Package Licensing

Package licenses bundle the right to use multiple pieces of a single firm's intellectual property into one licensing agreement. For example, a research-and-development company might offer to radio manufacturers a package license for all of its patents used in manufacturing radios.[316]

Licensors sometimes prefer to offer package licenses as a way to reduce transaction costs associated with negotiating separate licenses for each piece of intellectual property in their portfolios. When a licensee is likely to use an unknown amount of the licensor's intellectual property, package licenses can also reduce monitoring and enforcement costs. If a patentee owned 100 patents related to different aspects of radio manufacturing, and it licensed only three of them to a radio manufacturer, the patentee would have to examine each of the manufacturer's products to ensure that none infringed any of the 97 unlicensed patents. A package license to all 100 patents, however, avoids any need to distinguish between licensed and unlicensed patents and guarantees that the licensor would not need to bring an infringement action.

Despite these cost-saving possibilities, which can benefit licensees as much as licensors, a potential licensee may seek to negotiate a license for

---

314. *Id.* at 1341.
315. *Id.* at 1342; *see also* Monsanto Co. v. Swann, 308 F. Supp. 2d 937, 942 (E.D. Mo. 2003) (no tying under similar licenses where purchaser of one-season's seed was not obligated to purchase seed for any subsequent seasons).
316. Although this section focuses on package licensing of patent rights, similar questions may arise when copyrights or trademarks are packaged, as when a franchisor licenses a franchisee to use all of its trademarks in a fast-food restaurant.

some smaller amount of intellectual property, at a lower price than the package license. To return to the above example, suppose that 30 of the patentee's 100 patents related to AM frequencies and the other 70 patents related to FM frequencies. If the radio manufacturer had developed or acquired other non-infringing, AM-related technology, it might seek to license only the 70 FM-related patents from the patentee. If the patentee refused to offer the FM-only license or if the patentee offered the FM-only license at the same, or a relatively close, price as the license covering all 100 patents, the radio manufacturer might claim that the package license was an improper tying arrangement that violated Section 1 of the Sherman Act and/or provided a defense to a patent infringement action as an act of patent misuse.[317]

Regardless of whether a package license is challenged through an antitrust suit or a misuse defense, courts typically focus on whether the license improperly "ties" unwanted intellectual property rights to other intellectual property that the licensee desires. As discussed above, a tying arrangement is "an agreement by a party to sell one product [the tying product] only on the condition that the buyer also purchases a different (or tied) product, or at least agrees that he will not purchase that product from any other supplier."[318] Thus, in the earlier example, the radio manufacturer would argue that the patentee tied the unwanted AM-

---

317. 5 U.S.C. § 1 (2000). A licensee might also argue that a package license violated § 3 of the Clayton Act, if the package involved the transfer of goods to which intellectual property rights are attached. *See* 15 U.S.C. § 14 (2000) (forbidding the conditioning of the sale of "goods, wares, merchandise, machinery, supplies, or other commodities" in certain circumstances); *see also* 1 HERBERT HOVENKAMP ET AL., IP AND ANTITRUST: AN ANALYSIS OF ANTITRUST PRINCIPLES APPLIED TO INTELLECTUAL PROPERTY LAW § 22.2 (2005). Moreover, the FTC might claim that the package license violates § 5 of the FTC Act. *See* 15 U.S.C. § 45(a)(1) (2000) ("Unfair methods of competition in or affecting commerce, and unfair or deceptive acts or practices in or affecting commerce, are declared unlawful."). Whatever statute underlies the challenge, a court is likely to apply a similar analysis. *See* ANTITRUST LAW DEVELOPMENTS, *supra* note 100, at 179 & n.997 (5th ed. 2002) (collecting cases).

318. N. Pac. Ry. Co. v. United States, 356 U.S. 1, 5-6 (1958) (footnote omitted); *see also* INTELLECTUAL PROPERTY GUIDELINES, *supra* note 1, § 2.1 (explaining that agencies "apply the same general antitrust principles to conduct involving intellectual property that they apply to conduct involving any other form of tangible or intangible property").

related patents (the "tied product") to the attractive FM-related patents (the "tying product").

As discussed above, the Supreme Court has long held that tying arrangements are illegal per se,[319] and recent appellate decisions establish the following four elements of a per se violation: (1) the tying product and the tied product are separate; (2) the sale of the tying product is conditioned on buying of the tied product; (3) the seller has economic power in the market for the tying product; and (4) the arrangement affects a not insubstantial amount of interstate commerce in the tied product.[320] At least the first three of these elements raise unique issues in the context of package licenses.[321]

Antitrust law treats tying and tied products as separate if there are "two distinguishable product markets" for them.[322] When two (or more) patents are necessary to create any product for which there is demand, the patents are not considered separate products and licensing them as a package will not constitute a per se violation of antitrust laws.[323] Still, the nature of intellectual property sometimes complicates the separate-product analysis because ideas novel enough to receive intellectual property protection often are so innovative that no market for them has yet formed. For example, when Microsoft began integrating its Internet Explorer browser into its Windows operating system (OS), there was considerable uncertainty about whether the combined browser-OS was a new product or whether the browser and OS were separate products.[324]

---

319. *See* Jefferson Parish Hosp. Dist. No. 2 v. Hyde, 466 U.S. 2, 9 (1984) ("It is far too late in the history of our antitrust jurisprudence to question the proposition that certain tying arrangements pose an unacceptable risk of stifling competition and therefore are unreasonable 'per se.'").

320. *See, e.g.*, United States v. IBM, 163 F.3d 737, 741 (2d Cir.1998) (citing Eastman Kodak Co. v. Image Technical Servs., 504 U.S. 451, 462-64 (1992)); Data Gen. Corp. v. Grumman Sys. Support Corp., 36 F.3d 1147, 1178-79 (1st Cir. 1994).

321. In considering the fourth element, courts have looked to absolute dollar amounts to determine whether a "not insubstantial" amount of commerce has been affected. Since the Supreme Court found a $60,800 effect on interstate commerce to be sufficient, *United States v. Loew's, Inc.*, 371 U.S. 38, 49 (1962), this element rarely goes unsatisfied. *See* ANTITRUST LAW DEVELOPMENTS, *supra* note 100, at 204.

322. *Jefferson Parish,* 466 U.S. at 21.

323. Int'l Mfg. v. Landon, Inc., 336 F.2d 723, 729 (9th Cir. 1964).

324. *See* United States v. Microsoft Corp., 253 F.3d 34, 84-95 (D.C. Cir. 2001) (declining to condemn browser-OS tie as illegal per se in view of the

Implicit in the word "tying" is the requirement that sale of the tied product must be conditioned on—that is, "tied to"—purchase of the tying product. When a package license is challenged as an illegal tie, the licensee will not be able to demonstrate the necessary conditioning unless it has requested that the licensor offer a separate license for the desired "tying" property[325] and the licensor has refused to grant such a license.[326] Even if the licensor goes through the motions of granting licenses for subsets of its intellectual property, the pricing of those smaller licenses may establish tying. Returning again to the radio manufacturer, if the patentee charged the same price for a package license covering all 100 patents that it charged for an FM-only license (or if the patentee offered only a miniscule discount), a court could find that the sale of the FM-related patents were conditioned on the sale of the AM-related patents.

In addition to separate products and conditioning, a per se tying claim requires proof of the seller's economic power in the market for the tying product.[327] This, of course, can no longer be presumed merely because the tying involves intellectual property.[328]

If a package license does not satisfy all four of the elements that would require its per se condemnation as a tying arrangement, courts will undertake a rule of reason analysis, balancing the license's anticompetitive effects against any procompetitive justifications.[329] Package licensing may harm competition by foreclosing a seller of an intellectual property right that competes with one of the rights in the package from effectively licensing that right to a package licensee.

---

novelty of the issue, but strictly limiting the holding to the facts of the case).

325. *See* Shea v. Blaw-Knox Co., 388 F.2d 761 (7th Cir. 1968) (rejecting misuse defense where patentee had been willing to offer individual license, but infringer had never requested one).

326. *Cf.* Zenith Radio Corp. v. Hazeltine Research, 395 U.S. 100, 133-35 (1969) (finding that there was conditioning—and thus patent misuse—when licensor refused to grant separate licenses to its patents).

327. Precedent requires a showing of market power to make out an affirmative per se antitrust claim of tying. *See supra* note 7 and accompanying text. In the context of patent misuse, however, a statute requires a demonstration of market power to establish illegal tying under either a per se or a rule of reason theory. *See* 35 U.S.C. § 271(d)(5).

328. *See* Ill. Tool Works v. Indep. Ink, 126 S. Ct. 1281 (2006).

329. *See, e.g., Jefferson Parish*, 466 U.S. at 29-31 (employing abbreviated rule of reason analysis after concluding that challenged practice was not a per se violation).

Suppose, for example, that one of the patents in Hazeltine's package license of radio-related patents covers a noise-reduction technology substantially similar to an alternative technology covered by a patent that Dolby would like to license. Radio manufacturers would need a license to use only one of the competing noise-reduction technologies, and if Hazeltine included the patent on its technology in a package license that manufacturers are already purchasing, manufacturers might be less likely to license Dolby's technology. If this were to cause Dolby to go out of business, it might give Hazeltine even greater power in the market for noise-reduction technology. On the other hand, package licensing can also have procompetitive effects; it reduces transaction, monitoring, and enforcement costs, as described above.[330]

A recent Federal Circuit decision, *U.S. Philips Corp. v. International Trade Commission*,[331] appears to signal a more receptive approach to package licensing arrangements. Philips owned patents to technology used in manufacturing recordable and rewritable compact discs ("CDs"), and it licensed all of its patents as a package, not individually. The package license required licensees to pay royalties based on the number of CDs produced, regardless of how many patents the licensee actually used. When several foreign licensees stopped paying royalties, Philips filed a complaint with the International Trade Commission (ITC) alleging that the licensees were importing CDs that infringed on its patents. The licensees asserted a misuse defense to the infringement charge, claiming that Philips had improperly forced them to take licenses on patents that were not necessary to the manufacture of CDs ("nonessential patents") as a condition of licensing the necessary (or "essential") patents. Finding that the package license was a per se illegal tying arrangement (and alternatively that it was an unreasonable restraint of trade), an administrative law judge declined to enforce Philip's patents, and the ITC affirmed that result. The Federal Circuit reversed and remanded the case for further proceedings.

Although the ITC had condemned Philips's package license as a tying arrangement, the Federal Circuit rejected the notion that the license was illegal per se. In particular, the court emphasized the procompetitive benefits of package licenses—including the reduction of transaction,

---

330. *See* INTELLECTUAL PROPERTY GUIDELINES, *supra* note 1, § 2.3 (describing procompetitive benefits of licensing).

331. 424 F.3d 1179 (Fed. Cir. 2005), *cert. denied sub nom.* Princo Corp. v. U.S. Philips Corp., 126 S. Ct. 2899 (2006).

administrative, and monitoring costs[332]—to distinguish patent-patent ties from the patent-product ties that the Supreme Court had treated as illegal per se.[333] The court also expressed concern about a rule that would not enforce any patents included in a package license covering both essential and non-essential patents. It reasoned that, if technological innovation rendered non-essential one of the formerly essential patents covered by the package license, all of the licensed patents would become unenforceable due to misuse, even though the package license would have been perfectly valid when the parties agreed to it.[334] The court also held that Philips's package license did not condition the sale of desired patents on the purchase of unwanted patents because the license was "simply a promise not to sue for infringement" and licensees were neither forced to use any of Philips's technology nor precluded from using competitors' products.[335]

Prior to the Federal Circuit's decision in *Philips*, most treatises on intellectual property law suggested that a package license that included both essential and non-essential patents would constitute patent misuse unless the patentee were willing to license the essential and non-essential separately if the licensee so desired.[336] *Philips* rejects this wooden approach in favor of an approach that requires a closer examination of the business reasons for the package license and its likely effects.

---

332. *See U.S. Philips*, 424 F.3d at 1192-93.
333. *Id.* at 1187-89 (distinguishing United States v. Paramount Pictures, 334 U.S. 131 (1948), and United States v. Loew's, Inc., 371 U.S. 38 (1962)).
334. *Id.* at 1196-97.
335. *Id.* at 1189-90.
336. *See, e.g.*, 6 DONALD S. CHISUM, CHISUM ON PATENTS § 19.04[3][c], at 19-468 (2005) ("[A] policy of mandatory or coercive package licensing under which the patent owner refuses to license patents separately normally will constitute misuse because it is a species of tying arrangement."); J. THOMAS MCCARTHY, MCCARTHY'S DESK ENCY-CLOPEDIA OF INTELLECTUAL PROPERTY 307 (2d ed. 1995) ("Only if the licensee takes the package because of the patentee's 'coercion' in a nonnegotiable 'take all or none' position would package licensing raise the danger of being patent misuse or an antitrust violation by a tie-in of unwanted patents to the desired patents in the package."); 8 ERNEST BAINBRIDGE LIPSCOMB III, LIPSCOMB'S WALKER ON PATENTS § 28:27, at 312 (3d ed. 1989) ("Whatever may be the asserted reason or justification of the patent owner, if he compels a licensee to accept a package of patents or none at all, he employs one patent as a lever to compel the acceptance of a license under another. Equity will not countenance such a result.").

9. Royalty-Related Restrictions

An intellectual property owner has a great deal of discretion in establishing royalty rates and structures, but there are certain areas that may implicate antitrust or misuse. The Supreme Court stated in *Brulotte v. Thys Co.*[337] that "[a] patent empowers the owner to exact royalties as high as he can negotiate with the leverage of that monopoly."[338]   A particularly high royalty may inhibit use of the invention, but it is up to the patentee to decide whether and at what price to grant licenses to maximize its return on its investment in the intellectual property.[339]   At the same time, in *Brulotte*, the Court held that postexpiration royalties are per se unlawful, based on the limited duration of the patent right, as set forth in the Constitution and the Patent Act.[340]

a.   Royalties Based on Total Sales or Sales of Noninfringing Goods

The bases for royalty payments—i.e., whether the payment is premised solely on sales of patented items or patented as well as related

---

337.   379 U.S. 29 (1964); *see also* United States v. Gen. Elec. Co., 272 U.S. 476, 491 (1926).

338.   *Id.* at 33; *see also In re* Indep. Serv. Org. Antitrust Litig., 964 F. Supp. 1479 (D. Kan. 1997) (allegedly excessive prices not misuse), *aff'd*, 203 F.3d 1322 (Fed. Cir. 2000); Carter-Wallace, Inc. v. United States, 449 F.2d 1374, 1382-83 (Ct. Cl. 1971); LaSalle St. Press v. McCormick & Henderson, Inc., 445 F.2d 84, 95 (7th Cir. 1971); W.L. Gore & Assocs. v. Carlisle Corp. 381 F. Supp. 680, 700-01 (D. Del. 1974) ("Charging what the market will bear is what the patent grant is all about."), *aff'd in part, rev'd in part*, 529 F.2d 614 (3d Cir. 1976).   Although the Seventh Circuit suggested that excessive and oppressive royalty rates may be patent misuse in reversing an injunction in *American Photocopy Equipment v. Rovico, Inc.*, 359 F.2d 745 (7th Cir. 1966), on remand the trial court both found that the royalties at issue were not excessive and stated that the patentee had the right to set whatever royalty rate it might chose, in a decision that was affirmed by the Seventh Circuit.   Am. Photocopy Equip. v. Rovico, Inc., 257 F. Supp. 192, 199-201 (N.D. Ill. 1966), *aff'd*, 384 F.2d 813 (7th Cir. 1967).

339.   "If the patentee sets his price higher than the profit-maximizing level, he will sell less patented product and receive lower profits." *W.L. Gore & Assocs.*, 381 F. Supp. at 701.   In effect, the courts recognize that the holder of exclusive rights may price as a monopolist would, or even higher.

340.   379 U.S. at 30-34 (citing U.S. CONST. art. I, § 8, and 35 U.S.C. § 154).

non-infringing sales—may raise misuse concerns. In 1950, in *Automatic Radio Manufacturing Co. v. Hazeltine Research,*[341] the Supreme Court held that calculation of royalties based upon total sales, as opposed to sales of only patented articles, was not per se misuse. Hazeltine Research had a portfolio of 570 patents and 200 patent applications relating to the manufacture of radio broadcasting apparatus. It licensed them to Automatic Radio Manufacturing and others, pursuant to a nonexclusive license requiring payment of royalties based on a small percentage of the manufacturer's selling price of radio broadcast machines, subject to a minimum annual royalty of $10,000. Automatic Radio contended that "that the license agreement [could not] be enforced because it is a misuse of patents to require the licensee to pay royalties based on its sales, even though none of the patents are used."[342] The Court affirmed the lower court's summary judgment in favor of the licensor:

> We cannot say that payment of royalties according to an agreed percentage of the licensee's sales is unreasonable. Sound business judgment could indicate that such payment represents the most convenient method of fixing the business value of the privileges granted by the licensing agreement.... [T]here is in this royalty provision no inherent extension of the monopoly of the patent.[343]

Nearly twenty years later, Hazeltine's licensing policies came before the Supreme Court again, this time with a different result. In *Zenith Corp. v. Hazeltine Research,*[344] the Court held that "conditioning the grant of a patent license upon payment of royalties on products which do not use the teaching of the patent does amount to patent misuse."[345] The practice, if abused, could be seen as using the "leverage" of the patent "to control or limit the operations of the licensee."[346]

Crucial to the different result according to the Court was evidence of coercion in *Zenith* that was absent in *Automatic Radio,* as the Court in *Zenith* found that "patent misuse inheres in a patentee's insistence on a

---

341. 339 U.S. 827 (1950).
342. *Id.* at 830. The Court found it unnecessary in light of its holding to address the contentions of a factual dispute as to whether the products at issue actually would or would not have infringed. *Id.* at 833 & n.6.
343. *Id.* at 834.
344. 395 U.S. 100 (1969).
345. *Id.* at 135.
346. *Id.* at 136.

percentage-of-sales royalty, regardless of use, and his rejection of licensee proposals to pay only for actual use."[347] The Court in *Zenith* confirmed that it agreed with the reasoning and result in *Automatic Radio*, noting that the "record and oral argument in *Automatic Radio* disclose no basis for the conclusion that Automatic Radio was forced into accepting the total-sales royalty rate by [Hazeltine's] use of its patent leverage."[348] It explained that "[i]f convenience of the parties rather than patent power dictates the total-sales royalty provision, there are no misuse of the patents and no forbidden conditions attached to the license."[349] As with a tying claim, there is no unlawful forcing without coercion.

The distinction between royalty arrangements that are forced versus those that are for the convenience of the parties has continued. For instance, the DOJ obtained a Consent Judgment against Microsoft in 1995 to preclude Microsoft's practice of establishing long term agreements with OEMs requiring that royalties be paid based on the OEMs' total sales of processors, regardless of whether Microsoft's operating system software was included in the sale.[350] The DOJ contended that this practice effectively precluded competing operating system providers from making inroads against Microsoft, as the OEMs would not want to pay two royalties for a chip that did not contain Microsoft's operating system. In *Engel Industries v. Lockformer Co.*,[351] in contrast, the Federal Circuit found no misuse where the licensee chose to pay royalties based on a non-staple good used in the patented system that was the subject of the patent, and the agreement recited that it was for the convenience of the parties.[352]

---

347. *Id.* at 139; *see also* United States v. United States Gypsum Co., 333 U.S. 364 (1948) (royalty provision covering patented and unpatented goods supported price-fixing claims).

348. *Zenith*, 395 U.S. at 138 n.29.

349. *Id.* at 138 ("The Court's opinion in *Automatic Radio* did not deal with the license negotiations which spawned the royalty formula at issue and did not indicate that HRI used its patent leverage to coerce a promise to pay royalties on radios not practicing the learning of the patent.").

350. United States v. Microsoft Corp., C.A. No. 94-5694 (D.D.C.), *available at* http://www.usdoj.gov/atr/cases/ms_index_licensing.htm. For further discussion on the allegations and settlement in this matter see *United States v. Microsoft Corp.*, 56 F.3d 1448 (D.C. Cir. 1995).

351. 96 F.3d 1398 (Fed. Cir. 1996).

352. *See also* W. Elec. Co. v. Stewart-Warner Corp., 631 F.2d 333, 339 (4th Cir. 1980) (rejecting claims of alleged misuse "by basing royalties on the

b. Preissuance Royalties

Computing royalties over a period prior to the issuance of a patent generally does not raise the same level of antitrust concerns as computing royalties over the postexpiration period, which has been held to be per se misuse.[353] The Supreme Court considered this issue in 1979 in *Aronson v. Quick Point Pencil.*[354] In *Aronson*, the inventor of a keyholder granted Quick Point the exclusive right to make and sell keyholders covered by the inventor's patent application. The royalty was to be five percent of the selling price of the keyholders, and the obligation to pay the royalty applied prior to issuance of any patent. However, if no patent was issued within five years, the agreement provided for a reduced royalty of 2.5 percent of sales "so long as [Quick Point] continue[d] to sell same."[355]

No patent was ever issued, the royalty was reduced to 2.5 percent, and eventually, after $7 million in sales over 14 years, Quick Point sought to declare the license invalid on the grounds that any state contract law that might otherwise provide for enforcement of the agreement to pay royalties was pre-empted by federal patent law and policy.[356] The Court noted, however, that enforcement of the agreement

---

sales of the finished semiconductor devices instead of the fair market value of the chips" because "such a method is simply more convenient because it is much easier to ascertain the selling price of the finished product than the fair market value of one of its components"); Applera Corp. v. MJ Research, 349 F. Supp. 2d 321 (D. Conn. 2004) (license not found to have been "conditioned" on total sales, since alternatives were offered and rejected); Bayer AG v. Housey Pharm., 228 F. Supp. 2d 467, 468-71 (D. Del. 2002) (no misuse in royalties based on sales of products developed using patent for method of research, or in the alternative a lump sum based on licensee's research and development budget, where license recited that method of computing royalties was for the convenience of the parties, and there was no evidence offered that alternative royalties were proposed or rejected); Miller Insituform v. Insituform of N. Am., 605 F. Supp. 1125, 1133-34 (M.D. Tenn. 1985) (rejecting challenge of royalty of 8 percent of total contract price which includes the costs of preparatory and finishing work, labor, and nonpatented materials), *aff'd*, 830 F.2d 606 (6th Cir. 1987).

353. *Brulotte*, 379 U.S. at 32-34.
354. 440 U.S. 257 (1979).
355. *Id.* at 259.
356. The licensee relied on cases in which the Supreme Court has held that state law may not forbid the copying of an idea in the public domain which does not meet the requirements for federal patent protection.

216   *Intellectual Property and Antitrust Handbook*

"merely requires Quick Point to pay the consideration which it promised in return for the use of a novel device which enabled it to pre-empt the market."[357] Its holding in *Lear, Inc. v. Adkins*,[358] that a licensee could challenge the validity of a patent and that a licensee who establishes invalidity was excused from the obligation to pay royalties, was not applicable where no patent issued and the parties contractually accounted for the possibility that the patent would never issue. In addition, since there was no patent, the concerns of extension of exclusive rights for a limited time applicable in declaring postexpiration royalties to be per se misuse in *Brulotte* did not apply to excuse Quick Point from the perpetual royalty obligations it agreed to in the event that a patent did not issue. The Court thus noted that the facts presented did not "require us to draw the line between what constitutes abuse of a pending application and what does not."[359]

The Patent Act expressly recognizes the right to assign patent applications and grant exclusive rights under an application.[360] The law recognizes the right of the owner of a patent application to license the use of trade secrets,[361] and information in an unpublished patent application

---

Compco Corp. v. Day-Brite Lighting, 376 U.S. 234 (1964); Sears, Roebuck & Co. v. Stiffel Co., 376 U.S. 225 (1964). In addition, it relied on *Lear, Inc., v. Adkins*, 395 U.S. 653 (1969), in which the Court rejected licensee estoppel in patent cases, and held that a continuing obligation to pay royalties after a patent was declared invalid would be contrary to "the strong federal policy favoring the full and free use of ideas in the public domain." *Id.* at 674. Further, it relied on *Brulotte*, in which the Court held that postexpiration royalties were per se misuse. 379 U.S. at 32-34. *See Aronson*, 440 U.S. at 260-65.

357. 440 U.S. at 264.
358. 395 U.S. 653 (1969).
359. *Aronson*, 440 U.S. at 265 ("No doubt a pending patent application gives the applicant some additional bargaining power for purposes of negotiating a royalty agreement. The pending application allows the inventor to hold out the hope of an exclusive right to exploit the idea, as well as the threat that the other party will be prevented from using the idea for 17 years.").
360. 35 U.S.C. § 261 ("Applications for patent, patents, or any interest therein, shall be assignable in law by an instrument in writing. The applicant, patentee, or his assigns or legal representatives may in like manner grant and convey an exclusive right under his application for patent, or patents, to the whole or any specified part of the United States.").
361. *See* Painton & Co. v. Bourns, Inc., 442 F.2d 216, 224 (2d Cir. 1971) ("In thousands of contracts businessmen have divulged such secrets to

may be a trade secret. The practical reality that it may take several years for a patent to issue, and the policy of encouraging prompt commercial exploitation of inventions, together point to preissuance sales royalties as reasonable and procompetitive absent extraordinary circumstances.[362]

c. Double Royalties and Exhaustion

As a general matter, the first authorized sale of a patented product in commerce exhausts the rights of the patentee with respect to that particular product.[363] Thus, an issue of potential misuse may arise to the extent that a patentee seeks to extract "double royalties" from such a first sale and from a subsequent sale.[364] In *PSC Inc. v. Symbol Technologies*,[365] a district court applied the rule of reason and granted summary judgment in favor of an alleged infringer's misuse defense, finding that the collection of double royalties at separate levels of distribution constituted an unreasonable restraint on competition. The court found that collecting royalties from one licensee on patented scan engines and from another licensee on integrated terminals with scan engines from the first licensee, violated the patent exhaustion doctrine, under which the authorized sale of a patented product places that product

competitors, dealing at arms-length and well able to protect themselves, on the faith that mutually acceptable provisions for payment, for the preservation of confidentiality, and for the return of the secret information on termination or default will be enforced by the courts.").

362. For an example of a refusal to apply the reasoning of *Brulotte* to characterize royalties on pre-patent-issuance sales as an unlawful extension of the "patent monopoly," see *Congoleum Industries v. Armstrong Cork Co.*, 366 F. Supp. 220, 234-35 (E.D. Pa. 1973) ("The rationale of the *Brulotte* decision is not applicable in this instance where the license agreement was in conjunction with an invention that had not become the basis of a patent monopoly and which had not entered the public domain"), *aff'd*, 510 F.2d 334 (3d Cir. 1975).

363. Intel Corp. v. ULSI Sys. Tech., 995 F.2d 1566, 1568 (Fed. Cir. 1993) ("an authorized sale of a patented product places that product beyond the reach of the patent"); *see also* Unidisco, Inc. v. Schattner, 824 F.2d 965, 968 (Fed. Cir. 1987) (the exhaustion or first sale doctrine applies to the sale of a product manufactured by a licensee acting pursuant to a license).

364. *See generally* Cyrix Corp. v. Intel Corp., 846 F. Supp. 522, 539 (E.D. Tex.) (a purpose of the patent exhaustion doctrine is "preventing patentees from extracting double recoveries for an invention"), *aff'd* 42 F.3d 1411 (Fed. Cir. 1994).

365. 26 F. Supp. 2d 505 (W.D.N.Y. 1998).

beyond the reach of the patent.[366] The court also found that the collection of double royalties had strong anticompetitive effects in the market for scan engines, because manufacturers of hand-held laser scanners and integrated terminals had to pay twice for the same license.[367]

Generally, once a patented item is sold with the authorization of the patentee, restrictions may not be placed on subsequent purchasers or users.[368] However, the patentee may lawfully limit the scope of the field of use,[369] and there is authority for licensing the use of patented devices even after sale based on the separate licensing of the exclusive rights to make, use or sell the invention.[370]

In *Mallinckrodt, Inc. v. Medipart, Inc.,*[371] the Federal Circuit upheld the sale of a patented medical device for delivery of radioactive or therapeutic material in aerosol mist form to the lungs of a patient, subject to a notice of restricted limitation to a single use. As long as the restriction is reasonably within the patent grant, the Federal Circuit held that this type of field of use restraint is permissible.[372]

d.   Discriminatory Royalties

As a general matter, the antitrust laws do not mandate that a patentee charge all licensees the same price. Charging different royalties to different licensees is not grounds to establish misuse or an antitrust violation, in the absence of some unique evidence to establish

---

366.   *Id.* at 510.
367.   26 F. Supp. 2d at 510-11.
368.   *See* Mallinkrodt, Inc. v. Medipart, Inc., 976 F.2d 700, 706-07 (Fed. Cir. 1992) (discussing Adams v. Burke, 84 U.S. (17 Wall.) 453, 457 (1873)); *see also* Intel Corp. v. ULSI Sys. Tech., 995 F.2d 1566, 1568 (Fed. Cir. 1993).
369.   *See* Gen. Talking Pictures Corp. v. W. Elec., 304 U.S. 175, *aff'd on reh'g,* 305 U.S. 124 (1938).
370.   *See In re* Yarn Processing Patent Validity Litig., 541 F.2d 1127 (5th Cir. 1976); Duplan Corp. v. Deering Milliken, Inc., 444 F. Supp. 648, 671-72 (D.S.C. 1977), *aff'd in part and rev'd in part,* 594 F.2d 979 (4th Cir. 1979); *see also Mallinckrodt,* 976 F.2d at 703-07 (discussing Adams v. Burke and the long line of cases related to restrictions on use).
371.   976 F.2d 700 (Fed. Cir. 1992).
372.   *Id.* at 708; B. Braun Med. v. Abbott Labs., 124 F.3d 1419, 1426-27 (Fed. Cir. 1997).

anticompetitive effects,[373] such as limiting competition with an affiliate of the licensor in a downstream market as in the so-called "Shrimp Peeler Cases"[374] in the mid-1960s. The Shrimp Peeler Cases involved challenges to the leasing of patented shrimp peeling machines to canners in the Gulf Coast at one rate, while the same type of machine was leased to canners in the Northwestern region at double that rate. The patentee held an interest in a Gulf Coast canner. The FTC and private litigants contended that applying the different royalty rates provided an unfair advantage in the downstream market for canned shrimp by limiting price competition from shrimp canned in the Northwest The Fifth Circuit affirmed the FTC's finding that the rate structure in this context comprised an unfair method of competition under Section 5 of the FTC Act.[375] District courts in Alaska and Washington found that the licensing scheme constituted patent misuse.[376]

Subsequent cases, however, have generally rejected any requests to read these cases broadly to imply that discriminatory royalties alone are grounds to establish misuse or an antitrust violation. For example, in *Akzo N.V. v. Intenational Trade Commission,*[377] the Federal Circuit affirmed a finding of the ITC that prices that varied by end use are not per se unlawful and that the failure to establish anticompetitive effect was fatal to contentions that the differentiated royalty scheme violated the antitrust laws. In particular, the court noted that royalties varied for different uses had procompetitive effects by increasing the volume of patented materials sold.[378]   Similarly, in *USM Corp. v. SPS*

---

373. *See* Standard Oil Co. v. United States, 283 U.S. 163, 179 (1931); Akzo N.V. v. Int'l Trade Comm'n, 808 F.2d 1471 (Fed. Cir. 1986); USM Corp. v. SPS Techs., 694 F.2d 505 (7th Cir. 1982).

374. Grand Caillou Packing, 65 F.T.C. 799 (1964), *aff'd in part and rev'd in part sub nom.* LaPeyre v. FTC, 366 F.2d 117 (5th Cir. 1966).

375. 366 F.2d at 121 ("There is abundant evidence in the record to support the Commission's conclusion that Peelers' leasing procedure is innately discriminatory and anti-competitive in its effect, and that in circumstances of the instant case, the refusal to treat the Northwest and the Gulf Coast shrimp canners on equal terms has substantially and unjustifiably injured competition in the shrimp canning industry").

376. Laitram Corp. v. King Crab, Inc., 244 F. Supp. 9 (D. Alaska), *modified,* 245 F. Supp. 1019 (1965); Peelers Co. v. Wendt, 260 F. Supp. 193 (W.D. Wash. 1966).

377. 808 F.2d 1471 (Fed. Cir. 1986).

378. *Id.* at 1489 ("Contrary to Akzo's position that Du Pont's pricing system is anti-competitive and an unreasonable restriction on use and resale, the

Technologies,[379] the Seventh Circuit held that discriminatory royalties could not establish misuse absent a showing of anticompetitive effects "in the market of the patentee's customers."[380]   The license at issue required USM "to remit to SPS 25 percent of any royalties it obtains by sublicensing SPS's patent, except that if USM should happen to sublicense any of four companies that SPS had previously licensed directly USM must remit 75 percent of the royalties obtained from the (sublicensees)."[381]   Judge Posner, writing for the Seventh Circuit, noted that findings of misuse are generally guided by the same principles of analysis of competitive effects as antitrust violations.[382]   The court noted that differentials in price are not treated as inherently anticompetitive either under the Robinson-Patman Act or the Sherman Act, and that

---

Commission found and the record establishes that Du Pont's value-in-use pricing has the pro-competitive effect of increasing the volume of aramid fibers that are sold."); *see also* USM Corp. v. SPS Techs., 694 F.2d 505 (7th Cir. 1982); Carter-Wallace, Inc. v. United States, 449 F.2d 1374 (Ct. Cl. 1971) (refusing to strike discriminatory royalty misuse defense, but striking defenses based on assertions that lower royalty rates to certain licensees for certain combination drug uses); Bela Seating Co. v. Poloron Prod., 438 F.2d 733, 738 (7th Cir. 1971) ("Where ... there were rational bases upon which Bela could refuse to grant Poloron a license on the same terms as it granted [another] license, there is no invidious discrimination so as to offend the antitrust law.").

379.   694 F.2d 505 (7th Cir. 1982).
380.   *Id.* at 513; *see also In re* Indep. Serv. Orgs. Antitrust Litig., 964 F. Supp. 1479, 1491 (D. Kan. 1997) ("CSU also claims that Xerox charged higher prices to self-servicers (customers who self service their copiers and printers) than ISOs.   Of course, inherent in Xerox's patent grant is the right to license its product to some and not to others.... Thus, *Xerox has the right to price its patented products at different prices to different customers.*") (emphasis added), *as modified*, 989 F. Supp. 1131, 1139 ("A patent holder's right to price its patented products at different prices to different customers is inherent in the patent grant."), *aff'd*, 203 F.3d 1322 (Fed. Cir. 2000).
381.   *Id.* at 510. Sharing of royalties for sublicenses is generally subject to the rule of reason.   Standard Oil Co. v. United States, 283 U.S. 163 (1931); *see also* Congoleum Indus. v. Armstrong Cork Co., 366 F. Supp 220 (E.D. Pa. 1973), *aff'd* 510 F.2d 334 (3d Cir. 1975).   Where royalties shared are a particularly high percentage of the costs of production, however, royalty sharing arrangements may be subject to contentions that the arrangement comprises unlawful price-fixing.   *See In re* Yarn Processing Patent Validity Litig., 541 F.2d 1127 (5th Cir. 1976).
382.   694 F.2d at 510-12.

USM had made no effort to prove the elements of any antitrust violation.[383] The court observed that the Shrimp Peeler Cases had been criticized, and also found those cases distinguishable because USM failed to show any "competitive effects in the market of the patentee's customers."[384]

Discrimination in price in the sales of commodities that adversely affects competition in any line of commerce may be unlawful under the Robinson-Patman Act.[385] The Robinson-Patman Act does not apply to transactions involving only intangible property, and thus has been held inapplicable to intellectual property licensing.[386] The Robinson-Patman Act may be implicated in sales of patented goods, even with respect to a contract providing exclusive distribution rights.[387]

---

383. *Id.* at 512.
384. *Id.* at 513.
385. 15 U.S.C. § 13(a).
386. Innomed Labs v. Alza Corp., 368 F.3d 148, 161 n.3 (2d Cir. 2004) ("contracts that explicitly grant a license to exploit the intellectual property contained in a commodity have been viewed as primarily concerned with intangible rights, and are therefore not covered by the Act"); LaSalle St. Press v. McCormick & Henderson, Inc., 293 F. Supp. 1004, 1006 (N.D. Ill. 1968) (contract providing license to use a patented process to manufacture a product is a contract for an intangible right, not a commodity), *aff'd in part and rev'd in part*, 445 F.2d 84 (7th Cir. 1971); KMG Kanal-Muller-Gruppe Int'l v. Inliner U.S.A., 1999-2 Trade Cas. (CCH) ¶ 72,628, at 85,641, 1999 U.S. Dist. LEXIS 13895 (S.D. Tex. 1999).
387. *Innomed Labs*, 368 F.3d at 161-62 ("There is no evidence that Congress intended that some distribution contracts would be exempted from the [Robinson-Patman] Act simply because the purchaser bought not only the commodity but also the right to distribute it on an exclusive or semi-exclusive basis... The existence of patented elements within the transferred product does not alter this conclusion... A product that is patented, or that contains patented elements, remains a commodity for purposes of the Robinson-Patman Act..."). The Second Circuit explained that once the authorized first sale of a patented product has taken place, subsequent sales of that product through the distribution chain are not impacted by exclusive rights under the patent, and the purchaser of the patented goods "has not also received the right to exploit the patent itself in any way." *Id.* (citing Jazz Photo Corp. v. Int'l Trade Comm'n, 264 F.3d 1094, 1102 (Fed. Cir. 2001) ("The fact that an article is patented gives the purchaser neither more nor less rights of use and disposition.")). Thus, according to the Second Circuit, "contracts that do not explicitly transfer any intangible patent rights to the buyer in addition to the product

The potential anticompetitive effects of discriminatory royalties have also been an issue in situations involving standard setting and patent pools. Many standard setting organizations require participants to license patents infringed by the standard on reasonable and nondiscriminatory terms. To the extent that the establishment of the standard enhances the value of the intellectual property, some argue that it is reasonable to require licensing at a level that would have been "reasonable" before the standard was adopted.[388] Consent decrees addressing alleged anticompetitive conduct with respect to patents may require nondiscriminatory licensing. Patent pools may also provide for reasonable and nondiscriminatory licensing to alleviate any competitive concerns that may arise from the collective conduct of pool participants, although it also may be appropriate for those contributing intellectual property to the pool to receive favorable royalty rates.

e.   Postexpiration Royalties

As noted above, the Supreme Court held in *Brulotte v. Thys, Inc.*[389] that agreements providing for postexpiration royalties constitute per se patent misuse.[390] In *Brulotte*, the patentee owned patents relating to hop-picking machines, and also sold the patented machines. The patentee also issued licenses for use of the machines, with a royalty of the greater for each season of $500 per hop-picking season or $3.33 per 200 pounds of dried hops harvested by the machine. The relevant patents expired in 1957, but the licenses required royalties beyond that date, and continued

---

itself are commodities contracts... [C]ontracts that transfer the exclusive right to distribute a patented product, without more, are covered by the Robinson-Patman Act as a matter of law." *Id.*

388.   *See generally* Daniel G. Swanson & William J. Baumol, *Reasonable and Nondiscriminatory (RAND) Royalties, Standards Selection, and Control of Market Power*, 73 ANTITRUST L.J. 1, 10-14 (2005); Chairman Deborah Platt Majoras, Recognizing the Procompetitive Potential of Royalty Discussions in Standard Setting, Stanford Univ. Sept. 23, 2005, at 7 ("joint ex ante royalty discussions that are reasonably necessary to avoid hold up do not warrant per se condemnation").

389.   379 U.S. 29 (1964).

390.   379 U.S. at 30-34; *see* Virginia Panel Corp. v. MAC Panel Co., 133 F.3d 860, 869 (Fed. Cir. 1997). By way of contrast, trade secret licenses have been enforced to require payment of royalties long after trade secrets have fallen into the public domain. *See* Warner-Lambert Pharm. v. Reynolds, 178 F. Supp. 655 (S.D.N.Y. 1959), *aff'd*, 280 F.2d 197 (2d Cir. 1960).

to restrain assignment or removal of the machines from Yakima County where they were placed. Although the state courts had enforced the licenses as to payments accruing both before and after the expiration of the patents, the Supreme Court reversed "insofar as [the judgment below] allows royalties to be collected which accrued after the last of the patents incorporated into the machines had expired."[391]

Following *Brulotte*, lower courts have refused to enforce provisions for royalties for postexpiration use of a patented invention with certain variations, depending on circuit law or the facts of the case. As a general rule, a requirement to pay postexpiration royalties will not be enforced where the language of the agreement supports a court's conclusion that the royalties effect an extension of the patent exclusivity beyond the term of the patent.[392]

---

391. 379 U.S. at 30; *see also id.* at 31 ("The Supreme Court of Washington held that in the present case the period during which royalties were required was only 'a reasonable amount of time over which to spread the payments for the use of the patent'. . . . But there is intrinsic evidence that the agreements were not designed with that limited view ....").

392. *See, e.g.*, Meehan v. PPG Indus., 802 F.2d 881 (7th Cir. 1986) (agreement entered prior to issuance of patent that failed to differentiate pre- and postexpiration royalties could not be enforced as to postexpiration royalties on basis of trade secret royalties where the agreement provided for royalties for use of the trade secrets for only 10 years (less than the life of a patent) in the event no patent issued); Boggild v. Kenner Prods., 776 F.2d 1315 (6th Cir. 1985) (refusing to require payment of postexpiration royalties where parties entered license agreement before patent issued, but with expectation of patent issuing); Pitney Bowes, Inc. v. Mestre, 701 F.2d 1365, 1370-73 (11th Cir. 1983) (hybrid trade secret and patent license with no differentiation between pre- and postexpiration royalties was per se misuse under *Brulotte*); Modrey v. Am. Gage & Mach., 478 F.2d 470, 474-75 (2d Cir. 1973) (contention of misuse in license providing postexpiration royalties "does not affect the appellee's claim to the royalty payment here involved, one due long before the expiration of the patent"); Veltman v. Norton Simon, Inc., 425 F. Supp. 774 (S.D.N.Y. 1977); *see also* Rocform Corp. v. Acitelli-Standard Concrete Wall, 367 F.2d 678, 681 (6th Cir. 1966) (refusing to enforce a patent through a requested injunction based on misuse in an agreement providing for postexpiration royalties); Ar-Tik Sys. v. Dairy Queen, 302 F.2d 496, 510 (3d Cir. 1962); Shields Jetco v. Torti, 314 F. Supp. 1292 (D.R.I. 1970).

In *Scheiber v. Dolby Laboratories*,[393] the defendant allegedly induced the patent holder to provide in the license agreement for lower royalties through the expiration of a Canadian patent which expired two years later than his last United States patent, and then refused to pay according to the terms it had requested.[394]   Judge Posner, writing for the court, expressed disagreement with the per se misuse rule under *Brulotte*, as he had done 20 years earlier in *USM Corp. v. SPS Technologies*,[395] suggesting that the agreement could not extend patent exclusivity, as neither the license terms nor the patent could be applied as against third parties postexpiration, and that the longer the royalties were amortized, the lower the annual royalties the patentee would be able to charge for use of the invention.[396]   However, the court acknowledged that it was the Supreme Court's prerogative to overrule its precedent,[397] and the Supreme Court denied a petition for certiorari.[398]

Significantly, the Supreme Court noted in *Brulotte* that it was not confronted with a case in which multiple patents were licensed and at least one patent was still in force.[399]   Accordingly, courts have typically declined to find misuse where at least one licensed patent is still in force,

---

393.   293 F.3d 1014 (7th Cir. 2002).
394.   *Id.* at 1016. Both *Scheiber* and *Meehan v. PPG Industries*, 802 F.2d 881 (7th Cir. 1986), provide examples in which the courts have refused to allow level royalties through the date of expiration of a foreign patent, where all applicable United States patents have expired. Although the Court in *Scheiber* suggested that "*Brulotte* involved an agreement licensing patents that expired at different dates, just like this case; the cases are indistinguishable." 293 F.3d at 1017. Other courts, however, have refused to apply the per se rule of *Brulotte*, where multiple patents are licensed with level royalties through the date of the last to expire and in situations, which seemed to apply to *Scheiber*, where there is no coercion.
395.   694 F.2d 505, 510-11 (7th Cir. 1982).
396.   *Scheiber*, 293 F.3d at 1017-18.
397.   *Id.* at 1018-19.
398.   537 U.S. 1109 (2003). In *Engineered Products Co. v. Donaldson Co.*, 313 F. Supp. 2d 951, 993-97 (N.D. Iowa 2004), the court denied a motion in limine to exclude evidence of misuse based on postexpiration royalties while expressing doubt over whether it was factually supported. The jury rejected the misuse defense. 330 F. Supp. 2d 1013, 1021 (N.D. Iowa 2004), *aff'd*, 2005 U.S. App. LEXIS 18828 (Fed. Cir. 2005) (unpublished).
399.   379 U.S. at 32 (distinguishing Automatic Radio Mfg. v. Hazeltine Research, 339 U.S. 827 (1950)).

and there is no evidence of coercive tying or where there are differential royalties with a higher royalty during the life of one or more patents, coupled with reduced postexpiration royalties on account of remaining unexpired patents or know-how or trade secrets licensed simultaneously.[400]

An interesting twist on the subject of postexpiration royalties was presented in *Bayer AG v. Housey Pharmaceuticals*,[401] which involved patents relating to research methods used by pharmaceutical companies, rather than the end product drugs. The patentee offered two types of licenses. One type required payment of a running royalty based on sales of pharmaceutical products discovered using the invention. The other was for the payment of a lump sum based on the licensee's research and development budget.[402] An alleged infringer asserted several theories of

---

400. *Compare* Hull v. Brunswick Corp., 704 F.2d 1195 (10th Cir. 1983) (refusal to renegotiate package license by individual patents which would have been inefficient and impractical was not misuse despite level royalty for package through date of last patent to expire), Well Surveys v. Perfo-Log, 396 F.2d 15, 17-18 (10th Cir. 1968) ("If the *Rocform* decision is taken as holding that a package license, including both important and unimportant patents, is misuse per se when there is no diminution in royalty, or provision for termination, after expiration of an important patent, we respectfully disagree... The relative importance of the patents has no significance if a licensee is given the choice to take a patent alone or in combination on reasonable terms. Freedom of choice is the controlling question."), Sunrise Med. HHG v. AirSep Corp., 95 F. Supp. 2d 348, 458 (W.D. Pa. 2000) ("There is also subsequent authority, however, that the royalty rate need not diminish as patents included in a package license expire, as long as the licensee is not coerced"), *and* A.C. Aukerman Co. v. R.L. Chaides Constr., 29 U.S.P.Q.2D (BNA) 1054, 1058 (N.D. Cal. 1993) ("*Brulotte* has been held inapplicable to package licensing agreements containing expired patents if the licensee was not coerced to enter the arrangement"), *with* Am. Securit Co. v. Shatterproof Glass Corp., 268 F.2d 769, 777 (3d Cir. 1959) (finding coerced package license with level royalties through date of last patent to expire was misuse), *and* Duplan Corp. v. Deering Milliken, Inc., 444 F. Supp. 648, 697-99 (D.S.C. 1977) (following *Am. Securit* with respect to coerced level royalties through expiration date of last patent to expire) *aff'd in part and rev'd in part*, 594 F.2d 979 (4th Cir. 1979). *But see Rocform*, 367 F.2d at 680-82 (affirming finding of patent misuse even in absence of coercive tying where there was a level royalty through the last patent to expire and no termination clause).
401. 228 F. Supp. 2d 467 (D. Del. 2002).
402. *Id.* at 468-69.

patent misuse, including an assertion that the royalty structure imposed a requirement of royalty payments beyond the term of the patents. Although certain running royalty licenses provided for royalties on sales of products subsequent to the expiration of the patents, the court granted summary judgment for the patentee on this misuse claim because, unlike in *Brulotte*, "the royalties to be paid after the expiration of the patent are for the use of the subject invention prior to the expiration of the patent."[403] Although this case may have unique applicability to licenses of method patents with a long delay between the use of the method and the licensee's realization of a profit on the fruits of that use, it is consistent with a narrow reading of *Brulotte* in which postexpiration payments are barred only when it is apparent on the face of the license agreement that they are attributed to postexpiration use of the invention.[404]

10. Grantbacks

Provisions in license agreements that require the licensee to grant intellectual property rights in any improvements or related technology back to the licensor are referred to as "grantback" clauses.

Grantbacks may be a valid means of furthering licensing and dissemination of technology, while relieving the licensor of risks that, in allowing others to use its technology, it will facilitate development of intellectual property rights by licensees that may preclude it from remaining at the forefront of use of its own technology.[405] As further explained in the *Guidelines:*

> Grantbacks can have procompetitive effects, especially if they are nonexclusive. Such arrangements provide a means for the licensee and the licensor to share risks and reward the licensor for making possible

---

403. *Id.* at 472-73.
404. *See also* Gilson v. Rainin Instrument, 2005 U.S. LEXIS 7754 (W.D. Wis. 2005) (finding that royalties beyond the expiration date of a patent were not based upon use of the expired patent).
405. INTELLECTUAL PROPERTY GUIDELINES, *supra* note 1, § 5.6 ("A nonexclusive grantback allows the licensee to practice its technology and license it to others. Such a grantback provision may be necessary to ensure that the licensor is not prevented from effectively competing because it is denied access to improvements developed with the aid of its own technology. Compared with an exclusive grantback, a non-exclusive grantback, which leaves the licensee free to license improvements technology to others, is less likely to have anticompetitive effects.").

further innovation based on or informed by the licensed technology, and both promote innovation in the first place and promote the subsequent licensing of the results of the innovation.[406]

On the other hand, according to the *Guidelines*, grantbacks may adversely affect competition "if they substantially reduce the licensee's incentives to engage in research and development and thereby limit rivalry in innovation markets."[407]

Three Supreme Court cases from the 1940's illustrate antitrust concerns with respect to grantbacks, and particularly exclusive grantbacks. In *Hartford-Empire Co. v. United States*,[408] the Court addressed remedies after affirming lower court findings of a conspiracy to restrain competition through a series of agreements concerning patents related to glass manufacturing machines. The agreements included options to acquire any related patents the licensees might receive or acquire.[409] These options furthered the conspiring licensors' ability to control markets through coordination of their extensive patent portfolios. The Court therefore affirmed the injunction against the enforcement of license provisions providing "that improvements by the licensee on machinery leased and sold shall become the property of the lessor" and those providing "that rights to improvements and inventions covering licensed machinery or processes or methods shall become the exclusive property of the lessor or vendor."[410]

Two years later, in 1947, the Supreme Court determined in *Transparent-Wrap Machine Corp. v. Stokes & Smith Co.*[411] that the inclusion in a license of a provision requiring the licensee to assign improvement patents to the licensor was not per se illegal and unenforceable.[412] The Court declined to extend the reasoning of tying cases to this context, and found arguments that incentives to innovate might be compromised inapplicable to the case presented. The Court noted that its refusal to hold grantbacks per se unlawful "does not mean

---

406. *Id.*; *see also* Transparent-Wrap Mach. v. Stokes & Smith Co., 329 U.S. 637, 646 (1947) (upholding agreement where "any improvement patent can be put to immediate use and exploited for the account of the licensee.").
407. *Id.*
408. 323 U.S. 386 (1945).
409. *Id.* at 396-98.
410. *Id.* at 422-24.
411. 329 U.S. 637 (1947).
412. *Id.* at 645-48.

that the practice ... has immunity under the anti-trust laws."[413]   For example, it noted that grantbacks could permit firms to accumulate multiple patents to solidify a monopoly.[414]

The third Supreme Court case involving grantbacks was *United States v. National Lead Co.*[415]   Like *Hartford-Empire*, in *National Lead* the Supreme Court affirmed findings of antitrust violations relating to patent pooling agreements and considered the appropriate remedies. One provision of the decree issued by the district court was that the compulsory licensing ordered in the decree could "at the option of the licensor, be conditioned upon the reciprocal grant of a license by the applicant, at a reasonable royalty, under any and all patents covering titanium pigments or their manufacture, now issued or pending, or issued within five years from the date of this decree, if any, owned or controlled by such applicant."[416]   The Supreme Court held that imposing this condition was within the discretion of the district court, noting that without it a party receiving the benefit of the compulsory licensing could "simply change places with du Pont in becoming the dominant factor in the industry under this extraordinary advantage of being able to take everything for itself and keeping everything it has."[417]

The balancing suggested by the Supreme Court cases was carried over into the *Guidelines*, which confirm that the agencies will evaluate a grantback under the rule of reason.[418]   In assessing grantbacks, the agencies focus on potential adverse effects of reducing incentives to innovate as well as potential beneficial effects of increasing incentives to disseminate technology:

> An important factor in the Agencies' analysis of a grantback will be whether the licensor has market power in a relevant technology or innovation market. If the Agencies determine that a particular grantback provision is likely to reduce significantly licensee's

---

413.   329 U.S. at 647-48.
414.   *See Transparent-Wrap*, 329 U.S. at 646-48 (*"Hartford-Empire Co. v. United States*, 323 U.S. 386, 324 U.S. 570, dramatically illustrates how the use of a condition or covenant in a patent license that will assign improvement patents may give rise to violations of the anti-trust laws."); *see also* Kobe v. Dempsey Pump Co, 198 F.2d 416 (10th Cir. 1952) (accumulation of patents may violate the antitrust laws).
415.   332 U.S. 319 (1947).
416.   332 U.S. at 328-30 n.4 (Decree ¶ 7).
417.   *Id.* at 360
418.   INTELLECTUAL PROPERTY GUIDELINES, *su pra* note 1, § 5.6.

incentives to invest in improving the licensed technology, the Agencies will consider the extent to which the grantback provision has offsetting pro-competitive effects, such as (1) promoting dissemination of licensees' improvements to a licensed technology, (2) increasing the licensors' incentives to disseminate the licensed technology, or (3) otherwise increasing competition and output in a relevant technology or innovation market. See Section 4.2. In addition, the Agencies will consider the extent to which grantback provisions in the relevant markets generally increase licensors' incentives to innovate in the first place.[419]

These concerns often arise in the context of patent pools.[420] In patent pooling business review letters issued between 1997 and 2002, the DOJ cleared grantback provisions in connection with its broader approval of pooling of patents essential to practice industry standards.[421] These pools (which involved major competitors) were carefully constructed to limit the pooled patents to those "essential" (under various definitions) to practicing industry standards, with procedural protections to prevent spillover anticompetitive effects. Thus, they do not necessarily test the limits of lawful grantbacks, but they do provide some insights.

For example, the MPEG-2 grantback provision required the licensee to grant any of the Licensors and other "Portfolio" licensees a non-exclusive worldwide license or sublicense, on fair and reasonable terms and conditions, on any "Essential Patent" that it has the right to license or sublicense. In approving the pooling arrangement, the DOJ noted that it did not view this grantback provision as anticompetitive:

> Its scope, like that of the license itself, is limited to Essential Patents. It does not extend to mere implementations of the standard or even to improvements on the essential patents. Rather, the grantback simply

---

419. *Id.*
420. *Id.* § 5.5 (citing cases) ("a pooling arrangement that requires members to grant licenses to each other for current and future technology at minimal cost may reduce the incentives of its members to engage in research and development because members of the pool have to share their successful research and development and each of the members can free ride on the accomplishments of other pool members").
421. MPEG-2 Business Review Letter (June 26, 1997); DVD Business Review Letter (Philips, Sony & Pioneer) (Dec 16, 1998); DVD Business Review Letter (Hitachi, Matsushita, Mitsubishi, Time Warner, Toshiba and Victor) (June 10, 1999); 3G Patent Platform Business Review Letter (Nov. 12, 2002).

obliges licensees that control an Essential Patent to make it available to all, on a nonexclusive basis, at a fair and reasonable royalty, just like the Portfolio patents. This will mean that any firm that wishes to take advantage of the cost savings afforded by the Portfolio license cannot hold its own essential patents back from other would-be manufacturers of MPEG-2 products. While easing, though not altogether clearing up, the holdout problem, the grantback should not create any disincentive among licensees to innovate. Since the grantback extends only to MPEG-2 Essential Patents, it is unlikely that there is any significant innovation left to be done that the grantback could discourage. The grantback provision is likely simply to bring other Essential Patents into the Portfolio, thereby limiting holdouts' ability to exact a supracompetitive toll from Portfolio licensees and further lowering licensees' costs in assembling the patent rights essential to their compliance with the MPEG-2 standard.

In applying a rule of reason analysis to grantback provisions, among the factors that the courts may consider, are:

(1) the relevant market, market power and the extent of competition in the market for the technology;[422]

(2) the scope and duration of the grantback;[423]

---

422. *Compare* Santa Fe-Pomeroy, Inc. v. P & Z Co., 569 F.2d 1084, 1101-02 (9th Cir. 1978) ("The district court found that there were many competitive, alternative methods of subterranean foundation construction … Although the Doughty process has been widely accepted, it by no means has a monopoly on foundation wall construction."), *and* United States v. E.I. duPont de Nemours & Co., 118 F. Supp. 41, 224-25 (D. Del. 1953) (no antitrust violation without market power), *aff'd*, 351 U.S. 377 (1956), *with* United States v. Gen. Elec. Co., 82 F. Supp. 753, 815-16 (D.N.J. 1949) (finding that GE "regimented an industry by, among other things, its acquisition of patents to perpetuate a control over the incandescent electric lamp long after its basic patents expired to maintain a dominant position rendering it possible for it to eliminate competition and maintain an industrial monopoly of the type recognized by the *Transparent-Wrap* case to be an eventuality violative of the anti-trust laws").

423. *Compare Santa Fe-Pomeroy*, 569 F.2d at 1101 (finding no violation of the rule of reason where "the grant-back was limited in time and subject matter to the duration of the BARTD contract, and therefore had no restrictive or 'chilling' effect on any improvements devised during the performance of non-BARTD projects"), *and* E.I. duPont, 118 F. Supp. at 41, 224 (grantback agreements limited to the field of the moisture-proof

(3) whether the grantback is royalty free and whether improvements are sublicensed royalty free;[424] and

(4) the extent to which pooling arrangements in conjunction with grantbacks impede competition and innovation.[425]

Many cases hold that in the absence of proof of related antitrust violations or anticompetitive effects, the grantback of a nonexclusive license does not violate the antitrust laws or constitute misuse.[426] Exclusive grantbacks also have been upheld in several cases where they

---

cellophane patent licensed did not enhance duPont's market power), *aff'd*, 351 U.S. 377 (1956), *with* Duplan Corp. v. Deering Milliken, Inc., 444 F. Supp. 648, 700 (D.S.C. 1977) (requirement that a licensee assign patents broader than those of licensor enhanced and extended monopoly of the licensed patent), *aff'd in part and rev'd in part*, 594 F.2d 979 (4th Cir. 1979), *and* United States v. Nat'l Lead Co., 63 F. Supp. 513, 524 (S.D.N.Y. 1945) (beyond mere cross-licensing, pooling agreements were found unlawful where they "applied to patents not yet issued and to inventions not yet imagined. They applied to commerce beyond the scope of any patents. They extended to a time beyond the duration of any then-existing patent... They embraced acknowledgement of patent validity with respect to patents not issued, nor applied for, and concerning inventions not yet conceived."), *aff'd*, 332 U.S. 319 (1947).

424. Int'l Nickel Co. v. Ford Motor Co., 166 F. Supp. 551, 565-66 (S.D.N.Y. 1958) (rejecting misuse contentions based on grantback provisions where improvements were sub-licensed royalty free to all licensees, and finding that in such circumstances, the "net effect may well be to increase rather than to decrease competition").

425. United States v. Associated Patents, 134 F. Supp. 74, 82 (E.D. Mich. 1955) (in pooling arrangement, outside parties were foreclosed from obtaining improvement licenses in fields reserved for pool members, and technological developments were discouraged by restrictions on parties rights to use and license improvements), *aff'd mem. sub nom.* Mac Inv. Co. v. United States, 350 U.S. 960 (1956); United States v. Besser Mfg. Co., 96 F. Supp. 304, 310-11 (E.D. Mich. 1951) (pooling with rights to future patents and improvements in exclusive cross-license with veto rights over any additional licensees violated antitrust laws).

426. *See, e.g.*, Binks Mfg. Co. v. Ransburg Electro-Coating Corp., 281 F.2d 252, 259 (7th Cir. 1960); Lightwave Tech. v. Corning Glass Works, 1991 U.S. Dist. LEXIS 543, 19 U.S.P.Q.2d 1838 (S.D.N.Y. Jan. 18, 1991); Barr Rubber Prods. v. Sun Rubber Co., 277 F. Supp. 484, 506 (S.D.N.Y. 1967), *aff'd in part and rev'd in part*, 425 F.2d 1114 (2d Cir. 1970); Well Surveys v. McCullough Tool, 199 F. Supp. 374, 395 (N.D. Okla. 1961), *aff'd*, 343 F.2d 381 (10th Cir. 1965).

have been applied in competitive markets and are limited in duration and scope.[427] Cases in which grantbacks are condemned as unlawful tend to present situations where grantbacks are used in conjunction with accumulation of patents in pools or otherwise that facilitate monopolization, market allocation, price fixing, or other anticompetitive coordination among competitors.[428]

11. Non-Assert Clauses

A licensor may request that a licensee agree not to assert certain intellectual property rights as a condition of the licensor's providing a license to its rights, effectively inviting a cross-license. Nonexclusive, consensual cross-licenses and grantbacks are tools that firms can employ to eliminate and avoid blocking patent situations. However, in an action against Intel in the 1990s, the FTC alleged that Intel had monopoly power over general purpose microprocessors and purportedly used that power to effectively prevent Digital Equipment, Compaq and Intergraph from enforcing their own intellectual property rights, effectively alleging coercion of a compulsory, royalty-free cross-license. In settling the FTC proceedings, Intel ultimately agreed to continue to provide its proprietary information to the affected parties who declined Intel's proposed cross-

---

427. *See, e.g., Santa Fe-Pomeroy*, 569 F.2d at 1101-02 (many competitive alternatives); Zajicek v. KoolVent Metal Awning Corp., 283 F.2d 127, 131-32 (9th Cir. 1960); Swofford v. B & W, Inc., 251 F. Supp. 811, 820-21 (S.D. Tex. 1966), *aff'd*, 395 F.2d 362 (5th Cir. 1968); Sperry Prods. v. Aluminum Co. of Am., 171 F. Supp. 901, 936-38 (N.D. Ohio 1959) ("no attempt has been made to show any adverse economic consequences arising from the 'grant backs'"), *aff'd in part and rev'd in part*, 285 F.2d 911 (6th Cir. 1960). *But see* Duplan Corp. v. Deering Milliken, Inc., 444 F. Supp. 648, 700 (D.S.C. 1977) (requirement that a licensee assign patents covering a broader scope than those of the licensor enhanced and extended monopoly), *aff'd in part and rev'd in part*, 594 F.2d 979 (4th Cir. 1979).

428. *See, e.g., Hartford-Empire*, 323 U.S. 386 (1945); United States v. Aluminum Co. of Am., 91 F. Supp. 333, 410 (S.D.N.Y. 1950); *General Elec.*, 82 F. Supp. at 815-16 (grantbacks held illegal in connection with broad monopolization); United States v. Gen. Elec. Co., 80 F. Supp. 989, 1005-06 (S.D.N.Y. 1948) (grantbacks held illegal in conjunction with price-fixing).

licenses, but reserved the right to stop doing so if those parties sought to enjoin Intel with respect to its microprocessors.[429]

12. No-Challenge Clauses

The doctrine of "licensee estoppel" had been applied prior to 1969 to prevent a licensee from accepting the benefits of a patent license, and then challenging the validity of a licensed patent. Similarly, license agreements may contain "no-challenge" clauses, creating a contractual covenant to the same effect. In *Lear, Inc. v. Adkins*,[430] the Supreme Court reviewed over a century's worth of its decisions relating to "licensee estoppel," concluded that federal law and policy dictated that patent licensees cannot be estopped from challenging the validity of a patent, and overruled authority to the contrary.[431]

---

429. Copies of the Complaint, the Agreement Containing Consent Order, and Analysis of Consent Order to Aid Public Comments may be viewed on the FTC's web site. *See In re* Intel Corp, FTC Dkt. No. 9288 (Complaint filed Aug. 3, 1999), *available at* http://www.ftc.gov/os/caselist/d9288.htm; *see also* Intergraph Corp. v. Intel Corp., 195 F.3d 1346, 1360-62 (Fed. Cir. 1999) (reversing the district court's rulings regarding coerced reciprocity).

430. 395 U.S. 653 (1969).

431. *Id.* at 671. On a slightly different issue, as the Lear Court noted "[i]t is generally the rule that licensees may avoid further royalty payments, regardless of the provisions of their contract, once a third party proves that the patent is invalid." *Id.* At 667. The licensee may be held liable for unpaid royalties that accrued before the patent was held invalid. In *Lear*, the licensee, Lear, had repudiated the agreement before the patent issued. *Id.* at 659-60. The Federal Circuit has held that *Lear* should not be read to allow a licensee to pursue a declaratory judgment unless it ceases payment of royalties or otherwise materially breaches the license agreement such that it may then have a reasonable apprehension of being sued. *See Studiengesellschaft Kohle M.B.H. v. Shell Oil Co.*, 112 F.3d 1561, 1566-68 (Fed. Cir. 1997) (holding that a licensee "cannot invoke the protection of the *Lear* doctrine until it (i) actually ceases payment of royalties, and (ii) provides notice to the licensor that the reason for ceasing payment of royalties is because it has deemed the relevant claims to be invalid"). In contrast, the Second Circuit stated in *Warner-Jenkinson Co. v. Allied Chemical Corp.*, 567 F.2d 184, 187 (2d Cir. 1977), "[a]ddressing the question whether a patent licensee must actually withhold royalty payments before he can challenge validity, we conclude—as have most courts who have considered the issue—that such repudiation of the licensing agreement should not be precondition to

A license provision barring a licensee from contesting validity or requiring the payment of royalties pending any determination of invalidity may be unenforceable, but the courts have been reluctant to find that such clauses comprise misuse.[432] At least one court has rejected direct application of *Lear* to copyright licenses,[433] and another has held

---

suit." In *Gen-Probe v. Vysis*, 359 F.3d 1376 (Fed. Cir. 2004), the Federal Circuit held that a licensee that has not materially breached the license agreement, for example, pursuant to the terms quoted above from *Studiengesellschaft Kohle*, was protected by the agreement from suit for infringement and did not have a reasonable apprehension of suit to support a declaratory judgment action. In *MedImmune, Inc. v. Genentech, Inc.*, 127 S. Ct. 764 (2007), however, the Supreme Court abrogated *Gen-Probe*, holding that a patent licensee is not required to terminate or breach a license agreement before seeking declaratory relief.

432. For example, in *Bayer AG v. Housey Pharmaceuticals*, 228 F. Supp. 2d 467, 473-74 (D. Del. 2002), the license agreement provided that the licensee was not estopped from contesting the validity or enforceability of the patents, but that the licensor reserved the right to terminate the license if a validity challenge were made, and that the licensee agreed to pay royalties over the pendency of the challenge. The court noted that at least the provision regarding payment of royalties may be precluded by *Lear*, citing *Cordis Corp. v. Medtronic Inc.*, 780 F.2d 991, 995 (Fed. Cir. 1985) ("The holding of *Lear* ... prevents the affirmative enforcement by the licensor of the royalty payment provisions of the license agreement while the patent's validity is being challenged by the licensee."). *See generally Lear*, 395 U.S. at 673 ("The decisive question is whether overriding federal policies would be significantly frustrated if licensees could be required to continue to pay royalties during the time they are challenging patent validity in the courts."). Nevertheless, the court held that "[t]he inclusion of a provision in a license agreement that is unenforceable under *Lear* ... does not constitute patent misuse." *Id.* at 474 (citing Panther Pumps & Equip. v. Hydrocraft, Inc., 468 F.2d 225, 232 (7th Cir. 1972); Wallace Clark & Co. v. Acheson Indus., 401 F. Supp. 637, 640 (S.D.N.Y. 1975), *aff'd*, 532 F.2d 846 (2d Cir. 1976); Congoleum Indus. v. Armstrong Cork Co., 366 F. Supp. 220, 233 (E.D. Pa. 1973), *aff'd*, 510 F.2d 334 (3d Cir. 1975)). *But see* Bendix Corp. v. Balax, Inc., 471 F.2d 149, 158 (7th Cir. 1972) (no-contest clause in license agreement binding after termination of agreement might conceivably constitute misuse).

433. The Seventh Circuit has held that no-contest clauses in copyright licensing agreements may be valid where the issue of "copyrightability" is present and that the *Lear* decision did not apply to copyrights. *See* Saturday Evening Post Co. v. Rumbleseat Press, 816 F.2d 1191 (7th Cir. 1987). *But see* Twin Books Corp. v. Walt Disney Co., 877 F. Supp. 496 (N.D. Cal. 1995) (distinguishing *Rumbleseat*, applying *Lear* in a

that shrink-wrap licenses in which licensees agree not to engage in otherwise permissible reverse engineering are not precluded by the Copyright Act.[434] As to trademark licenses, licensee estoppel generally continues to be applied by the courts, except, according to the Second Circuit, in the context of certification marks.[435]

The courts have reached varied results on the extent to which licensee estoppel still applies after *Lear* with respect to license agreements entered in settlement of litigation.[436] The res judicata effect of consent judgments entered in settlement of litigation that acknowledge validity and infringement may provide greater protection against future challenges than a settlement agreement acknowledging validity or a general "dismissal with prejudice" of a declaratory judgment claim filed in response to, or in anticipation of, an infringement action.[437]

---

copyright licensing case), *rev'd on other grounds*, 83 F.3d 1162 (9th Cir. 1996).

434. Bowers v. Baystate Tech., 320 F.3d 1317, 1323-26 (Fed. Cir. 2003).
435. *See* Idaho Potato Comm'n v. M&M Produce Farm & Sales, 335 F.3d 130 (2d Cir. 2003) (citing numerous cases applying licensee estoppel in the trademark context, but refusing, based on *Lear*, to apply licensee estoppel as to a challenge of a certification mark); *see also* Windsurfing Int'l v. AMF, Inc., 782 F.2d 995 (Fed. Cir. 1986) (agreement not to contest the validity of a trademark license found not a misuse).
436. *Compare* Hemstreet v. Spiegel, Inc., 851 F.2d 348, 350 (Fed. Cir. 1988) (enforcing terms of a litigation settlement agreement under which the licensee expressly agreed to make payments "as they become due notwithstanding that said patents-in-suit may be held invalid and/or unenforceable in any other proceeding at a later date"), *and* Ransburg Elector-Coating Corp. v. Spiller & Spiller, Inc., 489 F.2d 974, 978 (7th Cir. 1973) (enforcing agreement for installment payments for use of invention prior to settlement date even though product at issue was subsequently held not to infringe patent), *with* Warner-Jenkinson Co. v. Allied Chem., 567 F.2d 184, 187-88 (2d Cir. 1977) (licensee was not estopped from litigating the validity of a patent by provisions making a license agreement in settlement of prior litigation non-terminable as to the first two years of royalty payments), *and* Massillon-Cleveland-Akron Sign Co. v. Golden State Adver., 444 F.2d 425, 427 (9th Cir. 1971) ("We think the rationale of *Lear* requires us to hold that the covenant ... in the settlement agreement ... not to contest the validity of [the] patent, is void on its face and unenforceable.").
437. *See* Foster v. Hallco Mfg., 947 F.2d 469 (Fed. Cir. 1991); Am. Equip. v. Wikomi Mfg., 630 F.2d 544, 548 (7th Cir. 1980) (giving res judicata effect to consent decree acknowledging both validity and infringement); Wallace Clark & Co. v. Acheson Indus., 532 F.2d 846, 849 (2d Cir. 1976)

C. Cross-Licenses and Patent Pools

Cross-licenses and patent pools are agreements by which multiple owners of intellectual property license each other and possibly third parties. Cross-licenses involve two or more intellectual property owners that license their rights to each other. Cross-licenses are often on a royalty-free basis, although they can also involve cash or other in-kind payments. The term "patent pool" is generally used to describe an arrangement whereby two or more intellectual property owners "pool" their rights and offer them in a package to third parties.[438] A patent pool may be administered by the rights owners, or by a separate entity to which the rights to license are assigned.[439] Licenses offered by ASCAP,

---

(same); Schlegel Mfg. Co. v. USM Corp., 525 F.2d 775 (6th Cir. 1975); Glasstech, Inc. v. AB Kyro Oyo, 11 U.S.P.Q.2d (BNA) 1703 (N.D. Ohio 1989) (*Lear* "cannot be interpreted so broadly as to condone a kind of gamesmanship, wherein an alleged infringer, after employing the judicial system for months of discovery, negotiation and sparring, abandons its challenge of validity, executes a license in settlement, and then repudiates the license and seeks to start the fight all over again in the courts"). *But see* Kaspar Wire Works, v. Leco Eng'g & Mach., 575 F.2d 530 (5th Cir. 1978) (a consent judgment dismissing a declaratory judgment action "with prejudice" accompanied by equivocal oral statements of intent made to the court did not preclude subsequent challenge of validity of patent at issue); Crane Co. v. Aeroquip Corp., 504 F.2d 1086, 1092 (7th Cir. 1974) ("Defendant was within its rights to test validity after entering into the consent judgment of validity."); Kray v. Nat'l Distillers & Chem., 502 F.2d 1366, 1368-69 (7th Cir. 1974) (where licensee, in settling prior litigation, agreed not to contest the validity of the patent, and the court thereafter "dismissed the action with prejudice (even though the parties had requested that the dismissal be entered without prejudice)," the licensee was not estopped from challenging the validity of the patent).

438.	Some older court decisions used the term "patent pool" to refer to arrangements whereby the licensors licensed their rights to each other but not third parties. *See, e.g.*, Hartford-Empire Co. v. United States, 323 U.S. 386 (1945); Gen. Talking Pictures Corp. v. W. Elec. Co., 304 U.S. 175 (1938).

439.	*See, e.g.*, Kobe, Inc. v. Dempsey Pump Co., 198 F.2d 416 (10th Cir. 1952); Baker-Cammack Hosiery Mills v. Davis Co., 181 F.2d 550 (4th Cir. 1950); United States v. Vehicular Parking, Ltd., 54 F. Supp. 828 (D. Del. 1944); Letter from Joel I. Klein, Acting Ass't Att'y Gen., Antitrust Div., Dep't of Justice, to Garrard R. Beeney, Esq. (Dec. 16, 1998), *available at* www.usdoj.gov/atr/public/busreview/2121.htm [hereinafter

BMI and other performing rights organizations under copyrights held by thousands of composers and music publishers are commonly referred to as "blanket licenses."[440] Cross-licenses and patent pools are distinguishable from "package licenses," which are licenses from a single party under multiple patents or copyrights.[441]

1. Statutes Implicated by Cross-Licenses and Patent Pools

Sections 1 and 2 of the Sherman Act have been applied to cross-licenses and patent pools.[442] Cross-licensing agreements have also been challenged under Section 5 of the FTC Act.[443]

The Supreme Court has recognized that cross-licenses and patent pools are appropriately evaluated under the rule of reason, except when the arrangement's only apparent purpose is price fixing,[444] or is a sham for an agreement that would otherwise warrant per se treatment.[445] The federal agencies have stated that agreements falling under per se proscription include horizontal output restraints, market division among

---

3C DVD Letter]; Letter from Joel I. Klein, Ass't Att'y Gen., Antitrust Div., Dep't of Justice, to Carey R. Ramos, Esq. (June 10, 1999), *available at* www.usdoj.gov/atr/public/busreview/2485.htm [hereinafter 6C DVD Letter].

440.   *See, e.g.*, Broad. Music v. CBS, 441 U.S. 1, 5 (1979).
441.   *See, e.g.*, Zenith Radio Corp. v. Hazeltine Research, 395 U.S. 100, 104 (1969) (patentee offered "standard package license" under all domestic patents principally in radio and television field).
442.   *See, e.g.*, United States v. Line Material Co., 333 U.S. 287 (1948) (holding that cross-licensing agreement constituted unlawful price-fixing in violation of § 1); United States v. Gen. Elec. Co., 82 F. Supp. 753 (D.N.J. 1949) (violation of Section 2 of the Sherman Act through the use of patent pools and cross-licensing agreements).
443.   *See, e.g.*, *In re* Summit Tech. Inc, No. 9286, 63 Fed. Reg. 46,453 (FTC Sept. 1, 1998) (Aid to Public Comment) (Federal Trade Commission alleged illegal horizontal restraint that combined competing patents and set prices for eye surgery equipment, in violation of § 5 of FTC Act).
444.   *Line Material*, 333 U.S. at 315.
445.   United States v. New Wrinkle, Inc., 342 U.S. 371, 377 (1952); *Intellectual Property Guidelines* § 3.4 (1995) ("In some cases, however, the courts conclude that a restraint's 'nature and necessary effect are so plainly anticompetitive' that it should be treated as unlawful per se, without an elaborate inquiry into the restraint's likely competitive effect.") (*citing* FTC v. Superior Court Trial Lawyers Ass'n, 493 U.S. 411, 433 (1990)); Nat'l Soc'y of Prof'l Eng'rs v. United States, 435 U.S. 679, 692 (1978).

horizontal competitors, certain group boycotts, and resale price maintenance (other than maximum resale price maintenance).[446]

The Supreme Court applied the rule of reason in a Section 1 case against the blanket licenses offered by ASCAP and BMI, where copyright owners that were actual and potential competitors jointly set the license royalty rates.[447] The court held that the per se rule was not applicable because the blanket license "is not a 'naked restraint of trade with no purpose except stifling of competition.'"[448] Rather, the blanket license "accompanies the integration of sales, monitoring, and enforcement against unauthorized copyright use."[449] The challenged price restraints were a "necessary consequence" of this procompetitive arrangement, and thus the rule of reason was the appropriate standard.[450]

Cross-licenses and patent pools may violate Section 2 of the Sherman Act when they impermissibly serve to create or maintain monopoly power in a relevant market.[451] When courts have found Section 2 liability based on participation in a cross-licensing or patent pooling arrangement, such cases usually involve other anticompetitive conduct. For example, the Tenth Circuit found a Section 2 violation in *Kobe, Inc. v. Dempsey Pump Co.*,[452] where patent owners created a closed patent pool that acquired every significant patent in the field of hydraulic pumps for oil wells, and then enforced those patents against actual and potential competitors.

2. Analysis of Cross-Licenses and Patent Pools Under the Rule of Reason

Courts have considered a variety of factors in evaluating the legality of cross-licenses and patent pools under the rule of reason, including the

---

446. INTELLECTUAL PROPERTY GUIDELINES,*supra* note 1, § 3.4.
447. Broad. Music v. Columbia Broad. Sys., 441 U.S. 1 (1979).
448. *Id.* at 20 (*quoting* White Motor Co. v. United States, 372 U.S. 253, 263 (1963)).
449. *Id.*
450. *Id.* at 21.
451. *See, e.g.*, United States v. Singer Mfg. Co., 374 U.S. 174 (1963) (cross-license arrangement, along with other conduct, formed basis of § 2 liability); Duplan Corp. v. Deering Milliken, Inc., 444 F. Supp. 648, 682 (D.S.C. 1977) (cross-licensing of textile machinery patents formed partial basis for finding of § 2 violation), *rev'd in part on other grounds*, 594 F.2d 979 (4th Cir. 1979).
452. 198 F.2d 416 (10th Cir. 1952).

nature of the intellectual property involved, the licensors' market power in affected relevant markets, exclusivity, and quantity restrictions.

a. The Nature of the Intellectual Property Involved

A cross-license or patent pool is less likely to raise antitrust concerns if it is comprised solely of blocking, complementary, or essential patents. A patent is "blocking" when it cannot be practiced without infringing another patent, and thus the patents are not competitive with one another.[453] "Complementary" patents do not "block" each other, but their combination enables the efficient practice of a technology, use of a process, or manufacture of a good.[454] "Essential" patents or copyrights are rights that are necessarily infringed when conforming to a technical standard.[455]

(1) Blocking Patents

Courts and the agencies have recognized that a legitimate purpose for a cross-license or patent pool is the exchange of blocking patents.[456] In

---

453. Standard Oil Co. v. United States, 283 U.S. 163, 171 n.5 (1931) ("A patent may be rendered quite useless, or 'blocked,' by another unexpired patent which covers a vitally related feature of the manufacturing process."); *Intellectual Property Guidelines* § 2.3 ("An item of intellectual property 'blocks' another when the second cannot be practiced without using the first."). Copyrights can also block each other when one or more of the works is a "derivative work." *See* 17 U.S.C. § 101.

454. *Line Material*, 333 U.S. at 357 ("We have here complementary patents each of which alone is commercially of little value, but both of which, together, spell commercial success for the product.").

455. *See* U.S. Philips Corp. v. Int'l Trade Comm'n, 424 F.3d 1179, 1194 (Fed. Cir. 2005), *cert. denied sub nom.* Princo Corp. v. U.S. Philips Corp., 126 S. Ct. 2899 (2006); 3C DVD Letter, *supra* note 439; 6C DVD Letter, *supra* note 439.

456. *Standard Oil*, 283 U.S. at 171 n.5; Carpet Seaming Tape Licensing Corp. v. Best Seam Inc., 616 F.2d 1133, 1142 (9th Cir. 1980); Int'l Mfg. v. Landon, Inc., 336 F.2d 723 (9th Cir. 1964); Cutter Labs. v. Lyophile-Cryochem Corp., 179 F.2d 80 (9th Cir. 1949); Boston Sci. v. Schneider AG, 983 F. Supp. 245 (D. Mass. 1997); *see* INTELLECTUAL PROPERTY GUIDELINES, *supra* note 1, § 5.5; FED. TRADE COMM'N, TO PROMOTE INNOVATION: THE PROPER BALANCE OF COMPETITION AND PATENT LAW AND POLICY ch. 2, at 31-32 (Oct. 2003) [hereinafter, FTC, COMPETITION

Standard Oil Co. v. United States,[457] the government alleged that the defendant oil companies violated Section 1 of the Sherman Act by cross-licensing their blocking patents on the process of "cracking" gasoline. The Supreme Court applied the rule of reason to the agreements,[458] and held the agreements lawful. "If the available advantages are upon on [sic] reasonable terms to all manufacturers desiring to participate, such interchange may promote rather than restrain competition."[459]

In some industries, such as semiconductors, firms may require access to hundreds of patents to produce a single product.[460] Many of these properties overlap, with each patent blocking several others. This tends to create a patent thicket—that is, a "dense web of overlapping intellectual property rights that a company must hack its way through in order to actually commercialize new technology."[461] Patent thickets often result from defensive patenting and compiling of large patent portfolios to use as bargaining chips to obtain access to others' overlapping intellectual property rights.[462] Patent pools and cross-licensing may permit parties to clear a patent thicket, thus increasing efficiency and encouraging output.

(2) Complementary Patents

Complementary patents do not necessarily block each other's use, but rather combine efficiently to advance the practice of the relevant technology. In *Baker-Cammack Hosiery Mills v. Davis Co.,*[463] the defendants in a patent infringement suit countered with an antitrust claim, alleging that plaintiffs unlawfully restrained competition by pooling patents related to the process of producing women's stockings. The Fourth Circuit rejected the counterclaim, holding that "the patents [were] complementary rather than competitive."[464] Most manufacturers

---

AND PATENT LAW], *available at* http://www.ftc.gov/os/2003/10/innovationrpt.pdf.
457. 283 U.S. 163 (1931).
458. *Id.* at 175.
459. *Standard Oil,* 283 U.S. at 171.
460. FTC, COMPETITION AND PATENT LAW, *supra* note 456, at 28.
461. Carl Shapiro, *Navigating the Patent Thicket: Cross Licenses, Patent Pools, and Standard-Setting, in* 1 INNOVATION POLICY AND THE ECONOMY 119, 120 (Adam Jaffe et. al. eds., 2001).
462. FTC, COMPETITION AND PATENT LAW, *supra* note 456, at 28.
463. 181 F.2d 550, 569 (4th Cir. 1950).
464. *Id.* at 570.

chose to use both patents simultaneously, and the product manufactured by simultaneous use was "recognized as a superior article by the trade."[465] Further, the patents were licensed on reasonably fair terms that did not prevent competitors from utilizing the technology.[466] As with blocking patents, the agencies have recognized the potential procompetitive benefits of licensing complementary patents.[467]

(3) Essential Patents

Patent pools are often established for the purpose of licensing the rights that are required to comply with a technical standard. For example, a group of companies that participated in the establishment of the DVD technical standards established the 6C DVD patent pool, which licenses patents that are "essential" to practice the DVD standard specifications.[468] The licensing of essential patents through a patent pool can have procompetitive benefits, such as reducing transaction costs by combining several licensing transactions into one, enhancing the value of licensors' patents by ensuring that each licensors' patents will not be blocked by the others, avoiding the "unpleasant surprise" of licensees discovering an additional license is required, and grouping licenses so the price reflects the worth of the technology.[469]

Several patent pools that were subject to DOJ business review letters have taken a similar approach to the definition of "essential patent." The MPEG-2 pool defines an essential patent as "any Patent claiming an apparatus and/or a method necessary for compliance with the MPEG-2 Standard under the laws of the country which issued or published the Patent."[470] The 3C and 6C DVD patent pools also define "essential" as

---

465. *Id.*
466. *Id.*
467. INTELLECTUAL PROPERTY GUIDELINES,*su pra* note 1, § 5.5.
468. 6C DVD Letter, *supra* note 439. A Licensor's patent is "essential," and thus subject to the commitments in the MOU, if it is "necessarily infringed," or "there is no realistic alternative" to it, "in implementing the DVD Standard Specifications." *Id.*
469. U.S. Philips Corp. v. Int'l Trade Comm'n, 424 F.3d 1179, 1192-93 (Fed. Cir. 2005), *cert. denied sub nom.* Princo Corp. v. U.S. Philips Corp., 126 S. Ct. 2899 (2006); 3C DVD Letter, *supra* note 439; 6C DVD Letter, *supra* note 439.
470. *See* Letter from Joel I. Klein, Acting Ass't Att'y Gen., Antitrust Div., Dep't of Justice, to Garrard R. Beeney, Esq. (June 26, 1997), *available at*

including such "technically" essential patents, but those pools also
include patents claiming technologies for which "there is no realistic
alternative" in implementing the DVD Standard Specifications," i.e.,
patents that are "commercially essential."[471] The MPEG and DVD pools
retained an independent expert to determine which of the patents held by
the pool members are essential for internal royalty allocation purposes.[472]

In *U.S. Philips Corp. v. International Trade Comm'n*,[473] several
manufacturers of DVD discs alleged that Philips had tied essential and
nonessential patents in the CD-R/RW patent pool, thus misusing the
patents. The Federal Circuit stated that "[p]atents within a patent
package can be regarded as 'nonessential' only if there are
'commercially feasible' alternatives to those patents."[474] The *Philips*
court held that the inclusion of non-essential patents in a patent pool is
not per se patent misuse and rejected the interveners' contention that the
relevant patents were nonessential, noting the absence of evidence that
any licensee or potential licensee had asked to have the patents removed
from the license, or that any product manufacturer had ever expressed a
preference for the allegedly alternative technology.[475] The court
ultimately held that Philips had not misused its patents via tying.

b.   Market Power of Licensors

An second important factor in evaluating a cross-license or patent
pool arrangement under the rule of reason is whether the licensors
collectively hold market power in an affected relevant market (including
the market for the licensed technology, as well as the markets for any
downstream products).

---

www.usdoj.gov/atr/public/busreview/1170.htm [hereinafter MPEG LA
Letter].

471.   3C DVD Letter, *supra* note 439; 6C DVD Letter, *supra* note 439.

472.   3C DVD Letter, *supra* note 439; 6C DVD Letter, *supra* note 439.

473.   424 F.3d 1179 (Fed. Cir. 2005), *cert. denied sub nom.* Princo Corp. v.
U.S. Philips Corp., 126 S. Ct. 2899 (2006).

474.   *Id.* at 1194 (*citing* Int'l Mfg. v. Landon, 336 F.2d 723, 729 (9th Cir.
1964)).

475.   *Id.*at 1195-97; *see also* Minebea Co. v. Papst, 444 F. Supp. 2d 68, 213-14
(D.D.C. 2006) (package licensing of essential hard disk drive patents with
nonessential ones was not per se patent misuse); Globespanvirata, Inc. v.
Texas Instruments., 2006-1 Trade Cas. (CCH) ¶ 75,229, at 104,724
(D.N.J. 2006) (rejecting tying claim based on package licensing of
essential patents for practicing standardized technology with nonessential
patents).

In *United States v. Krasnov*,[476] the court held that a cross-licensing arrangement between slip-cover manufacturers with combined market power violated Sections 1 and 2 of the Sherman Act. The arrangement (1) restricted defendants from licensing others without mutual consent; (2) allocated customers; (3) established prices to be charged by the licensors; and (4) required licensors to determine jointly the institution and maintenance of infringement suits.[477] In holding that the agreement violated the Sherman Act, the court placed great emphasis on the fact that the "defendants were the two largest competitors in the industry and dominated it dollar-wise."[478] The court found that defendants' dominant market power allowed them to use the licensing agreement to control prices and exclude competitors.[479]

Reflecting a similar view, the *Intellectual Property Guidelines* state that "[i]n general, exclusion from a pooling or cross-licensing arrangement among competing technologies is unlikely to have anticompetitive effects unless (1) excluded firms cannot effectively compete in the relevant market for the good incorporating the licensed technologies and (2) the pool participants collectively possess market power in the relevant market."[480]

c. Exclusivity

Whether a cross-license or patent pool restricts the intellectual property owners from licensing outside of the arrangement can be relevant to its legality. In *Buffalo Broadcasting v. ASCAP*,[481] the Second Circuit held that a copyright blanket license was not a "restraint of trade" for purposes of Section 1 of the Sherman Act because individual licenses under the blanket-licensed copyrights were a "realistic" alternative. The court explained that the "only valid test" for whether the individual program license was "too costly" to be a realistic alternative is whether the royalty for the individual license, "in an objective sense," was higher than the value of the rights obtained.[482]

---

476. 143 F. Supp. 184 (E.D. Pa. 1956).
477. *Id.* at 189.
478. *Id.* at 199.
479. *Id.*
480. INTELLECTUAL PROPERTY GUIDELINES, *supra* note 1, § 5.5.
481. 744 F.2d 917 (2d Cir. 1984).
482. *Id.* at 926.

In *Matsushita Electrical Industrial Co. v. Cinram International*,[483] the district court applied *Buffalo Broadcasting* to the DVD 6C patent pool, and held that the pool did not violate the Sherman Act. The court examined the history of the licensors' individual negotiations (including the royalty rates at which those licenses were offered) and concluded that individual licensing of the pooled patents was a commercially viable alternative to the pool license, and was not mere "lip-service."[484]

Another consideration in determining the legality of a cross-license or patent pool is the extent to which such an arrangement is open to additional licensees.[485] While cross-licensing arrangements and patent pools are not required to open their arrangements to all parties, exclusion of licensees may have anticompetitive effects. For instance, in *Zenith Radio Corp. v. Hazeltine Research*,[486] where patent pool licensors for television and radio equipment selectively refused to license Zenith, the Supreme Court held that such conduct violated Section 1.[487] The DVD patent pools have contractually committed to grant pool licenses on a nondiscriminatory basis to all interested parties.[488]

d. Price Restrictions

Several courts have struck down cross-license and patent pool arrangements on the ground that the agreements restricted the prices at which the parties sold the licensed goods.[489] In *United States v. Line Materials*,[490] the relevant cross-licenses set price floors at which the licensee could sell the patented electrical devices. The defendants argued that such provisions were lawful based on *United States v. General Electric*,[491] which held that it is reasonable for a patent owner that itself manufactures the patented product to establish the price at which a licensee sells the product. However, the *Line Materials* Court distinguished *General Electric* because it did not involve cross-licenses.

---

483. 299 F. Supp. 2d 370 (D. Del. 2004).
484. *Id.* at 379.
485. INTELLECTUAL PROPERTY GUIDELINES, *supra* note 1, § 5.5.
486. 395 U.S. 100 (1969).
487. *Id.* at 132.
488. 3C DVD Letter, *supra* note 439; 6C DVD Letter, *supra* note 439.
489. United States v. Line Material Co., 333 U.S. 287 (1948); United States v. Holophane, 119 F. Supp. 114 (S.D. Ohio 1954); United States v. Vehicular Parking, 54 F. Supp. 828 (D. Del. 1944).
490. 333 U.S. 287 (1948).
491. 272 U.S. 476 (1926).

"It is not the cross-licensing to promote efficient production which is unlawful.... The unlawful element is the use of the control that such cross-licensing gives to fix prices."[492] In *United States v. Holophane Co.,*[493] the court found illegal a series of patent license agreements that allocated markets among sellers of prismatic glasswear.

3. Other Antitrust Implications of Cross-Licensing and Patent Pools

a. Tying Intellectual Property

Patent pools are susceptible to tying claims in the same manner as licenses granted by a single patentee. In *U.S. Philips Corp. v. International Trade Commission,*[494] the Federal Circuit reversed the ITC's finding that Philips and other members of the CD-R/RW pool had misused their patents by allegedly tying essential and nonessential patents. Most notably, the court held that the rule of reason was the appropriate test, rather than the per se rule.[495] In *Globespanvirata Inc. v. Texas Instruments,*[496] a district court relied on *Philips* in holding that the rule of reason should govern the plaintiff's tying claims under Section 1. The court rejected plaintiff's argument that *Philips* was distinguishable as a case about patent misuse rather than antitrust violations, noting that the *Philips* court observed that "the analysis of tying arrangements in the context of patent misuse is closely related to the analysis of tying arrangements in antitrust law."[497] In *Wuxi Multimedia v. Koninklijke Philips Electronics,*[498] the court granted defendants' motion to dismiss claims of unlawful tying of essential and nonessential patents.

b. Restrictions that Impede Innovation

Courts and the agencies will examine whether a cross-licensing or patent pooling arrangement will have a negative effect on innovation. For example, in the 1970s the U.S. automobile industry defended itself against claims that cross-licensing agreements related to pollution-

---

492. *Line Material,* 333 U.S. at 315.
493. 119 F. Supp. 114 (S.D. Ohio 1954)
494. 424 F.3d 1179 (Fed. Cir. 2005), *cert. denied sub nom.* Princo Corp. v. U.S. Philips Corp., 126 S. Ct. 2899 (2006).
495. *Id.* at 1193.
496. No. 03-2854, 2006 WL 543155 (D.N.J. March 3, 2006).
497. *Id.* at *9 (*citing U.S. Philips Corp.,* 424 F.3d at 1185).
498. No. 04cv1136, 2006 U.S. Dist. LEXIS 9160 (S.D. Cal. Jan. 5, 2006).

limiting technology.[499]   The *Guidelines* note that pooling arrangements can have procompetitive effects in innovation markets by exploiting economies of scale and integrating complementary capabilities of the pool members.[500]   Further, the *Guidelines* state that such arrangements are likely to cause competitive problems "only when the arrangement includes a large fraction of the potential research and development in an innovation market."[501]

A cross-license or patent pool that prevents competitors from challenging arguably invalid patents,[502] or prevents practitioners from trying to invent around blocking patents, may also chill innovation.[503]   In *Summit Tech.*,[504] the FTC settled through consent agreement allegations that a pooling arrangement between eye surgery patent holders was a horizontal restraint of trade.   The pool gave the firms veto power over decisions to license the pooled patents to any other licensees, and to set a fee for each surgical procedure performed by their sublicensees. According to the complaint, the pool reduced or eliminated competition between its two participants with respect to selling the surgical equipment and licensing the technology, it deterred entry, and resulted in a raised cost of using the technology.[505]

---

499. United States v. Auto. Mfrs. Ass'n, 307 F. Supp. 617 (C.D. Cal. 1969), *aff'd*, City of New York v. United States, 397 U.S. 248 (1970); *In re* Multidist. Vehicle Air Pollution, 367 F. Supp. 1298 (C.D. Cal. 1973).
500. INTELLECTUAL PROPERTY GUIDELINES,*supra* note 1, § 5.5.
501. *Id.*
502. *See generally In re* Summit Tech. & VISX, Inc., No. 9286 (FTC Aug. 21, 1998) (Analysis Of Proposed Consent Order To Aid Public Comment), *available at* http://www.ftc.gov/os/1998/9808/d09286ana.htm; *see also In re* Summit Tech. & VISX, Inc., No. 9286 (FTC Aug. 21, 1998) (Agreement Containing Consent Order To Cease And Desist As To Summit Tech.), *available at* http://www.ftc.gov/os/1998/9808/d09286suagr.htm; *In re* Summit Tech., Inc. & VISX, Inc., No. 9286 (FTC Aug. 21, 1998) (Agreement Containing Consent Order To Cease And Desist As To VISX, Inc.), *available at* http://www.ftc.gov/os/1998/9808/d09286viagr.htm; Summit and VISX Settle FTC Charges of Violating Antitrust Laws (Aug. 21, 1998), *available at* http://www.ftc.gov/opa/1998/9808/sumvisx.htm.
503. FTC, COMPETITION AND PATENT LAW, *supra* note 456, at 31-32.
504. *In re* Summit Tech., No. 9286, 63 Fed. Reg. 46,453 (Sept. 1, 1998) (Aid to Public Comment).
505. *In re* Summit Tech., No. 9286, ¶¶ 25-28 (FTC Mar. 24, 1998) (Administrative Complaint), *available at* http://www.ftc.gov/os/1998/03/summit.cmp.htm.

c. Dispute Settlements

Parties to patent litigation often enter into cross-licenses a part of settling their claims. The settlement of patent litigation, in itself, is not an antitrust violation, including when such settlements result in a cross-license.[506] However, settlement cross-licenses with price or other restraints can violate Section 1 of the Sherman Act.

D. Settlements of Intellectual Property Disputes

Antitrust issues in settlements of intellectual property disputes may arise in a number of contexts. But a spate of more recent cases has evaluated intellectual property settlements against the backdrop of the Drug Price Competition and Patent Term Restoration Act of 1984, more commonly known as the Hatch-Waxman Act.[507] This section explores these cases and the ramifications this body of cases may have outside of the Hatch-Waxman context.

1. The Problem Presented by Intellectual Property Disputes

According to some commentators, some settlements of intellectual property disputes may result in greater market power and more exclusion than would result if the parties had continued to litigate. Mark Lemley and Carl Shapiro, for example, posit that "[t]here is no reason to assume that bargaining between the monopolist and the potential entrant to maximize their joint profits will lead to a socially optimal settlement. Indeed, the incumbent monopolist and the potential entrant will quite probably achieve an anticompetitive settlement, at least in the absence of antitrust rules limiting the manner in which they can resolve their dispute."[508] The reason is that the monopoly profits are greater than the joint profits that would result from competition between the patent holder and alleged infringer. Hence, the patent holder can use some of the difference between the monopoly and more competitive outcome to induce the alleged infringer to accept the monopoly outcome or something close to it. Such a settlement would deprive consumers of the

---

506. *See* Standard Oil Co. v. United States, 283 U.S. 163 (1931); Duplan Corp. v. Deering Milliken, Inc., 444 F. Supp. 648, 682 (D.S.C. 1977); Proctor & Gamble Co. v. Paragon Trade Brands, 61 F. Supp. 2d 102 (D. Del. 1996).
507. 21 U.S.C. § 355.
508. Mark A. Lemley & Carl Shapiro, *Probabilistic Patents*, 19 J. ECON. PERSPECTIVE 75, 91 (2005).

competition they would have obtained through litigation. Thus, "even a weak patent can be used as a fig leaf for an agreement not to compete."[509] Using antitrust to thwart such settlements is appropriate, under this theory, because patent invalidation benefits consumers.

One relevant question is whether this is a widespread problem. In one sense, it is difficult to tell because there is no data showing how many disputes are resolved without litigation. Only 1.5 percent of patents are ever litigated.[510] Only .1 percent of patents are the subject of judicial trials.[511] These data show that an overwhelming majority of patent disputes are settled. Shapiro would thus advise using the antitrust law to prevent any such settlement that leads to lower expected consumer surplus than would arise from ongoing litigation.[512]

Almost all of the recent cases, however, have involved settlements in the Hatch-Waxman context where the patent holder offers the alleged infringer net consideration, sometimes referred to as a reverse payment, to settle the patent dispute. In return, the alleged infringer agrees to either remain off the market for the life of the patent or to split the remaining life of the patent.[513] Where the patent life is split, it is not split in the colloquial sense, with one party practicing the patent for part of the patent life and the other party practicing the patent for the remainder. Rather, the patent holder continues to practice the patent for the entire patent life while the infringer enters the market at a later date, but prior to the patent's expiration. For example, a patent might have ten years left and the settlement might permit the alleged infringer to enter five years from the date of the settlement, splitting the patent "fifty-fifty." At the extreme, a settlement may "split" the patent life 100-0. In this case the reverse payment is sometimes called an exit payment.

The antitrust issue concerning intellectual property settlements that include reverse payments is that it is difficult to know if the reverse payment and delayed entry were a legitimate means of settling a patent dispute and protecting a patent holder's right to exclude others from the

---

509. *Id.*
510. *Id.* at 79.
511. *Id.*
512. Carl Shapiro, *Antitrust Limits to Patent Settlements*, 34 RAND J. ECON. 391, 407-08 (2003)
513. *See* FED. TRADE COMM'N, GENERIC DRUG ENTRY PRIOR TO PATENT EXPIRATION 23-34 (July 2002) (hereinafter FTC GENERIC DRUG STUDY), *available at* http://www.ftc.gov/ os/2002/07/genericdrugstudy.pdf (setting out statistics concerning settlements involving "brand" payments that split the patent life at Table 3-3).

market or if the reverse payment was, in reality, an agreement among horizontal competitors pursuant to which one would stay off the market in return for a share of the monopoly profits the other would enjoy.

2. The Hatch-Waxman Act

The Hatch-Waxman Act[514] is intended to speed the entry of generic drugs, which benefits consumers due to the lower prices of generic drugs relative to their brand counterparts. In furtherance of this goal, the Hatch-Waxman Act offers a means for generic versions of established pharmaceuticals to enter the market without going through the full testing required for new drugs.

To begin the process of generic entry, an applicant must file an Abbreviated New Drug Application (ANDA).[515] If there is a patent covering the brand name drug, that patent should be listed in an FDA publication entitled, "Approved Drug Products with Therapeutic Equivalence," commonly referred to as the "Orange Book." The Hatch Waxman Act requires that the ANDA applicant report the reason its entry would not infringe the patent(s) listed in the Orange Book. For instance, the patent(s) may have expired.

The cases that have generated litigation are those where the applicant certifies that the relevant patent is invalid or that the generic drug will not infringe the patent.[516] Such a certification of noninfringement or invalidity is known as a Paragraph IV Certification. To encourage generic drug companies to challenge patents that may be invalid or design around patents covering brand name drugs, the Hatch-Waxman Act provides a 180-day exclusivity period as against other generic drugs to the first generic applicant to file a Paragraph IV Certification.

Once the ANDA filer has made a Paragraph IV Certification, the patent holder may file an infringement suit. If it does so within forty-five days of receiving notice, the patent holder obtains an automatic stay

---

514. 21 U.S.C. § 355.
515. This discussion is derived from the more extended discussion of the Hatch-Waxman Act in the FTC GENERIC DRUG STUDY, *supra* note 513, at 4-8.
516. In both of these cases, the erstwhile entrant is asserting that the generic is outside the scope of a validly granted patent. In the case of invalidity, the generic entrant asserts the scope of the incumbent's patent is zero, while a claim of non-infringement concedes that the incumbent's patent does cover some range in intellectual property space but that the metes and bounds of the patent do not include the generic formulation.

preventing the generic from entering the market. The stay may last up to 30 months from the receipt of the notice. Because of the stay, the patent litigation will occur (or at least start) before the generic can enter the market.[517] This contrasts sharply with the more typical situation where a patent holder sues an alleged infringer already in the market and allegedly practicing the patented technology.

3. Are Reverse Payments Reverse?

A starting point for considering the competitive nature of payments that flow from a patent holder to an alleged infringer is assessing whether they are different in kind from other settlements of intellectual property disputes. Some commentators have called payments from the patent holder to the alleged infringer a "reverse payment" because this is not deemed the normal flow of net consideration to resolve a patent dispute (i.e. normally, to the extent there is a monetary settlement, the alleged infringer pays damages to the patent owner). These commentators argue that a reverse payment results in a settlement that is better for the patent holder and worse for consumers than the expected outcome of the litigation.[518]

---

517. The Hatch-Waxman Act was a compromise designed to meet opposing concerns of innovator and generic companies. On the one hand, innovator drug companies filed for patent protection on their innovations years before the patented drug finally obtained FDA approval for use. Studies in the 1980s concluded that pharmaceutical patents had effective lives of no more than 8-10 years because of the time needed to clear the FDA review process. On the other side, under applicable Supreme Court decisions, generic drug companies could not, in effect, begin establishing generic equivalence until the incumbent's patent expired and then needed to replicate many of the studies the incumbent had already performed.

518. Articles critical of reverse payments include Shapiro, *supra* note 512, at 407-08; Herbert Hovenkamp, Mark Janis, & Mark A. Lemley, *Anticompetitive Settlements of Intellectual Property Disputes*, 87 Minn. L. Rev. 1719, 1762 (2003); David Balto, *Pharmaceutical Patent Settlements: The Antitrust Risks*, 55 Food & Drug L.J. 321 (2000); Jeremy Bulow, *The Gaming of Pharmaceutical Patents,* Stanford Research Paper No. 1804 (May 2003); Keith Leffler & Cristofer Leffler, *Patent Litigation Settlements: Payment by the Patent Holder Are Anticompetitive and Should Be Per Se Illegal*, Res. in Law & Econ. (forthcoming), *available at* http://faculty.washington.edu/kleffler/Research.html.

Others, however, have concluded that so-called reverse payments are not actually reverse because the Hatch-Waxman regime alters the parties' negotiating positions. In *In re Ciprofloxacin Hydrochloride Antitrust Litigation*,[519] for example, the court explained that in the Hatch-Waxman context, the alleged infringer generally has not entered the market. By comparison, in the more traditional context, the infringer has entered and, if found to infringe, might have to pay substantial damages. In the example provided by the *Cipro* court, the patent holder can prove damages of $100 million if it prevails. The parties settle before trial with a $40 million settlement to the patent holder and with the infringer agreeing to exit the market for the life of the patent. According to the court, this amounts to an implicit net payment to the infringer of $60 million to stay off the market.[520]

Commentators have reached the same conclusion.[521] The alleged infringer can obtain only competitive profits if it prevails in litigation. On the other hand, it will pay damages based on the patent holder's "monopoly" profits if it loses. Under many conditions, the alleged infringer is willing to forgo potential competitive profits to avoid the risk of much higher damages even if it believes it will prevail in the patent suit. The patent holder is likewise willing to forgo some or all of the damages because it can make even more if the alleged infringer exits the market. Under the circumstances, the alleged infringer has a means of escaping the damage award by enhancing the patent holder's expectations of monopoly profits. The alleged infringer will give up the likelihood that it will be able to compete and the patent holder will give up the possibility of damages. The alleged infringer will avoid paying damages and the patent holder will continue to enjoy its monopoly. Thus, one may argue that the same logic that condemns reverse payments would condemn almost any settlement where the alleged infringer agreed to compromise on its ability to use the allegedly infringing technology even if no money changed hands.[522]

---

519. 261 F. Supp. 2d 188 (E.D.N.Y. 2003).
520. *Id.* at 252; *see Valley Drug*, 344 F.3d at 1309. For an example of such a settlement, see *Refrigerating Co. v. Kold-Hold Mfg. Co.*, 185 F.2d 809, 812 (6th Cir. 1950).
521. *See* Marc G. Schildkraut, *Patent-Splitting Settlements and the Reverse Payment Fallacy*, 71 ANTITRUST L.J. 1046-48 (2004); David A. Crane, *Exit Payments in Settlement of Patent Infringement Lawsuits: Antitrust Rules and Economic Implications*, 54 Fla. L. Rev. 747, 775-76 (2002).
522. Schildkraut, *supra* note 521.

**4. Approaches to Reconciling Intellectual Property and
     Antitrust in the Context of Dispute Settlements**

A patent holder has the right to exclude others from making, using or
selling the patent holder's valid patented invention.[523]   The antitrust laws
accommodate this statutory right.[524]   A restriction on the use of a patent
does not typically constitute an antitrust violation, unless it both (1)
meets the requirements for such violation and (2) is outside the scope of
the patent grant.[525]   Accordingly, the holder of a valid patent may grant
licenses that are "restricted in point of space or time, ... [so long as he
does] not enlarge his monopoly."[526]   Thus, if the patent holder has a valid
and infringed patent, an agreement that excludes the infringer in whole or
in part could not be unlawful.   As the Supreme Court explained in
NYNEX Corp. v. Discon, Inc.,[527] outside the intellectual property context,
"behavior [that] hurt[s] consumers" is not unlawful if the "consumer
injury naturally flowed ... from the exercise of market power that is
lawfully in the hands of a monopolist."

But patents do not always trump antitrust law.   Hovenkamp, Janis,
and Lemley would divide cases involving both patents and antitrust into
three categories.   In one category, the presence or absence of a patent is
irrelevant because the practice is clearly not illegal under the antitrust
laws and the case could be dismissed without delving into the merits of
the patent.   At the other extreme, the restriction is clearly beyond the
scope of the intellectual property right, so that such rights are irrelevant
to the antitrust analysis.   It is only the middle set of cases that must be
decided on intellectual property grounds—where the agreement would
not violate the antitrust laws if the exercise of market power is within the
scope of the patent but would do so if the exercise is beyond the patent's

523.   35 U.S.C. §§ 154, 271(a); *see also* United States v. United Shoe Mach.
       Corp., 247 U.S. 32, 57 (1917) ("[A patent's] strength is in the restraint,
       the right to exclude others from the use of the invention, absolutely or on
       the terms the patentee chooses to impose.").
524.   Simpson v. Union Oil Co., 377 U.S. 13, 24 (1964) ("The patent laws ...
       are in *pari materia* with the antitrust laws and modify them *pro tanto*.");
       INTELLECTUAL PROPERTY GUIDELINES,*su pra* note 1, §§ 1.0, 2.1, 3.1.
525.   Monsanto Co. v. McFarling, 302 F.3d 1291, 1298 (Fed. Cir. 2002)
       (emphasis added) (citing Gen. Talking Pictures Corp. v. W. Elec. Co.,
       305 U.S. 124, 127 (1938)).
526.   Ethyl Gas. Corp. v. United States, 309 U.S. 436, 456 (1940).
527.   525 U.S. 128, 136 (1998).

scope.[528] An example of this middle category of cases is *Standard Oil Co. v. United States*[529] where the Supreme Court approved the appointment of a special master to determine whether the patents contributed to a pool actually blocked one another.[530]

Similarly, not all settlements of intellectual property disputes are unlawful. According to a leading antitrust treatise:

> Our legal system encourages all firms, including those with conflicting intellectual property claims, to settle their differences out of court. In the case of conflicting intellectual property rights, these settlements often take the form of ... market division or field-of-use agreements ... As a result, at least some settlement agreements raise significant antitrust issues and some would be illegal per se if created in the absence of a genuine intellectual property dispute... Nevertheless, assuming a genuine dispute, the outcome of even a settlement agreement producing a per se antitrust violation might be no more anticompetitive than the outcome of litigation. A judgment establishing the validity of a rival's claim might [leave the rival] with a monopoly.[531]

As a result of this insight, the courts have historically taken a rather tolerant view of intellectual property settlements.[532]

More recently, however, commentators and courts are split with regard to how much tolerance is appropriate. Two proposed approaches require the court to estimate the outcome of the underlying patent dispute and then use that estimate as a basis for judging whether the settlement violates the antitrust laws. A third approach is for the court to assume that the parties to the dispute are in the best position to calibrate the likely success of the patent holder's claim. To the extent the parties agree to split the remaining life of the patent, such a settlement should be viewed as reflecting the parties' position with regard to the strength of

---

528. Hovenkamp et al., *supra* note 518, at 1727-28.
529. 283 U.S. 163 180-81 (1931).
530. Hovenkamp et al., *supra* note 518, at 1735.
531. 12 HERBERT HOVENKAMP, ANTITRUST LAW ¶ 2046, at 262-63 (1999) ("Settlements Resolving Intellectual Property Disputes")
532. *Id.*; *see also* Hutzler Bros. v. Sales Affiliates, 164 F.2d 260, 267 (4th Cir. 1947) ("We cannot attach ... any ulterior motives, or any improper conduct, to plaintiffs in connection with the agreed settlement with Bohemen in the interference proceedings. Had the interference proceedings been prosecuted to final judgment, this would have unquestionably delayed the granting of the patent in suit.").

the patent claim. A reverse payment, under this theory, is a red flag because it arguably delays what would otherwise be the agreed upon generic entry date. A fourth approach is to treat the patent as presumptively valid and, therefore, if the lawsuit was not a sham, any settlement would be lawful so long as it was within the scope of the patent rights.

a. The Conventional Approach

To determine whether the settlement is more anticompetitive than the outcome of litigation requires examining the scope of the patent (or other intellectual property). If the exercise of market power were inside the scope of the patent, the exercise would be lawful; if outside the scope, it would be illegal.

One approach to determining the scope of a patent is by a preponderance of the evidence. This is the approach adopted by the *Intellectual Property Guidelines*. The *Guidelines* state that firms are horizontal competitors only when they "would have been *actual* or *likely* potential competitors in a relevant market in the absence of a license."[533] Under the *Guidelines,* where it is likely that a patent excludes a firm's entry, it is simply *not* a potential competitor.[534] The *Collaboration Guidelines* take the same approach.[535]

This approach is most clearly set out in Example 5 of the *Guidelines.* There, AgCo, a manufacturer of farm equipment, develops a new patented technology and licenses it to FarmCo, another farm equipment manufacturer. Under Example 5, it is likely that any improved emissions control technology that FarmCo could develop would infringe AgCo's patent. The *Guidelines* conclude:

> FarmCo is not a likely potential competitor of AgCo in the relevant market because, even if FarmCo could develop an improved emission control technology, *it is likely* that it would infringe AgCo's patent. This means that the relationship between AgCo and FarmCo with

533. INTELLECTUAL PROPERTY GUIDELINES, *supra* note 1, § 3.3 (emphasis added).
534. *See id.* § 5.5.
535. COMPETITOR COLLABORATION GUIDELINES, *supra* note 20, at n.6 (2000); *see also* "Analysis to Aid Public Comment," *In re* Abbott Labs. and Geneva Pharms., at 3-4 ("[a] firm is a potential competitor if there is evidence that entry by that firm is reasonably probable in the absence of the agreement at issue.").

regard to the supply and use of emissions control technology is vertical.[536]

Applying the *Guidelines'* approach to a settlement of patent litigation is straightforward. If, in a settlement, the holder of a patent paid an alleged infringer to settle by exiting and staying out of the market for the duration of the patent term, we would ask whether the alleged infringer would have been able to remain in the market and compete but for the settlement. If it is reasonably probable that the alleged infringer would have been able to continue competing, the alleged infringer is an actual or at least potential competitor and there would be a horizontal relationship between the alleged infringer and the patent holder. Under these conditions, the settlement might be an unlawful market division agreement. On the other hand, if it were reasonably probable that the alleged infringer would not be able to continue to compete, the settling parties would not have been in a horizontal relationship and it is unlikely that the antitrust laws would have been violated.[537]

A criticism of the *Guidelines* standard is that it may prevent parties from settling cases with weak patents. Consider a case where the patent holder believes it has only a 40 percent chance of prevailing. Being risk averse, it settles the case without net consideration by accepting 30 percent of the patent life. Although it would not violate the welfare standard, this settlement arguably violates · the *Guidelines* standard because the patent holder is likely to lose the patent litigation, the alleged infringer is a potential entrant, the parties are in a horizontal relationship, and the settlement appears to be per se unlawful.[538]

On the other hand, if the patent holder has a 51 percent chance of prevailing, the *Guidelines* standard would permit the patent holder to pay the alleged infringer to stay out of the market until the patent expires. Based on the preponderance of the evidence, the alleged infringer is not a potential entrant and the parties are not in a horizontal relationship.

b.   Welfare Criteria Approach

An alternative approach is to use welfare criteria to analyze the settlement. This approach relies on the observation that a patent may be viewed as a *probabilistic* property right. What the patent grant actually

---

536.   INTELLECTUAL PROPERTY GUIDELINES, *supra* note 1, Ex. 5 (emphasis added).
537.   *See* Schildkraut, *supra* note 521, at 1050-52.
538.   *See id.* at 1054-57.

gives the patent holder is the right to sue to prevent others from infringing the patent. Nothing in the patent grant guarantees that the patent holder will be able to exclude rivals who are allegedly infringing, at least without a court order.[539] Thus, patent holders do not have a property right, at least without litigation, to the flow of income that would result from an ironclad patent claim. Consumers, on the other hand, have a "property right" to the "competition that would have prevailed, on average, had the two parties litigated the patent dispute to a resolution in the courts."[540] Under this approach, that "the proposed settlement [must] generate at least as much surplus for consumers as they would have enjoyed had the settlement not been reached and the dispute instead [were] resolved through litigation."[541]

Under the welfare standard, the court must finely calibrate the likelihood of entry. Thus, if the patent holder has an 80 percent chance of prevailing in the patent litigation but the parties settle by splitting the patent life 90-10, the welfare standard would be violated. Similarly, under the welfare standard, members of a patent pool must calibrate their license fee to the odds that the patents are actually blocking.[542] If there were a 90 percent chance that the patents were blocking, the pool members could charge a much higher fee than if there were a 50 percent chance that the patents were blocking. It would be up to the courts to determine if the license fee had been properly calibrated.

A criticism of the welfare standard is that it departs from the traditional civil burden of proof. Instead of the preponderance of the evidence, the welfare standard requires calibrating rights based on the probabilistic strength of the patent litigation. In the world of civil litigation, outcomes are usually binary, either you are liable for breaching the contract or you are not. If the jury concludes it is 60 percent likely that the defendant trespassed, the defendant would generally have to pay

539. Shapiro, *supra* note 512, at 395, 396.
540. *Id.* at 396; *see* Keith Leffler & Christofer Leffler, *The Probabilistic Nature of Patent Rights: In Response to Kevin McDonald,* 17 ANTITRUST 77 (2003).
541. Shapiro, *supra* note 512, at 393. Because, when the parties are risk neutral, the earliest date the patentee is willing to offer the entrant *and* the latest date the entrant is willing to accept is the expected mean date under litigation, Shapiro's standard of comparison for the settlement is the expected litigation result. Setting aside litigation cost savings, there is only one possible settlement when the settlement involves only time of entry.
542. *Id.* at 408-10.

all of the damages for the trespass; if it is 30 percent likely, the defendant pays nothing.[543]

Civil antitrust cases have typically followed the same path.[544] In a merger subject to Section 7 of the Clayton Act, for instance, a party typically can acquire a firm that is not a horizontal competitor, so long as it is unlikely that firm would have entered the acquirer's market.[545] Under the welfare standard, by comparison, a small chance of entry, say 10 percent, would result in condemnation of the merger unless there are countervailing efficiencies.[546]

Finally, a criticism of any approach that requires the court to delve into the merits of the underlying patent dispute, whether under the *Guidelines* standard or welfare standard, is that such an approach invites an antitrust suit that covers the same controversy the parties thought they had just settled.[547] As the Second Circuit commented in the *In re*

---

543. For a discussion of the incompatibility between probabilistic rights and traditional standards of proof, see Kevin McDonald, *Hatch-Waxman Patent Settlements and Antitrust: On "Probabilistic" Patent Rights and False Positives*, ANTITRUST, Spring 2003, at 72; Schildkraut, *supra* note 521, at 1049-52; *see also* Gideon v. Johns-Manville Sales, 761 F.2d 1129, 1137 (5th Cir. 1985 ("[p]ossibility alone cannot serve as the basis for recovery."); Youst v. Longo, 729 P.2d 728, 741 (Cal. 1987); Restatement (Second) of Torts § 433B cmt. (1965). There are a few lower court decisions in the area of mass torts where the possibilities were sufficient to award damages. In these cases, the courts simply allocated the damages among the defendants, although it could not be determined which defendant was the cause of harm to individual plaintiffs. *See* Sindell v. Abbott Labs., 607 P. 2d 924 (Cal. 1980); Morton v. Abbott Labs., 538 F. Supp 593 (M.D. Fla. 1982); Starling v. Seaboard Coast Line, 533 F. Supp. 183 (S.D. Ga. 1982).
544. *See* McDonald, *supra* note 543, at 72 (citing Associated Gen. Contractors v. Cal. State Council of Carpenters, 459 U.S. 519, 534, n.30 (1983)).
545. FTC v. Atl. Richfield Co., 549 F.2d 289, 294-95 (4th Cir. 1977) (requiring "clear proof" that the acquiring firm would have entered the market); Tenneco, Inc. v. FTC, 689 F.2d 346, 352 (2d Cir. 1982) (requiring evidence that the acquiring firm "would likely" have entered the market).
546. *See* Schildkraut, *supra* note 521, at 1050.
547. Schildkraut offers an example where an alleged infringer is likely, but not certain, to prevail in litigation. Nevertheless, the infringer's expected loses from continued litigation are greater than its expected gains from litigation: the monopoly profits lost by the patent holder and the potential concomitant damages are greater than the potential competitive profits

Tamoxifen Citrate Antitrust Litigation,[548] "there is no legal requirement that parties litigate an issue fully for the benefit of others."[549] Moreover, as Judge Posner pointed out in *Asahi Glass*, forcing such litigation may not maximize welfare because firms may be reluctant to challenge patents if their settlement options, in the event of an infringement suit, are reduced.[550]

c.   Reverse Payments as a Red Flag

As an alternative to estimating the outcome of the underlying intellectual property dispute, another approach is to look at the terms of the settlement to assess whether the agreement is anticompetitive. For instance, Shapiro observes that, "[i]n the simple model, a naked cash payment flowing from the patent holder to the challenger (in excess of avoided litigation costs) is a clear signal that the settlement is likely to be anticompetitive. Presumably, the patent holder would not pay more than avoided litigation costs unless it believed that it was buying later entry than it expects to face through the litigation alternative."[551] Similarly, according to Hovenkamp, Janis, and Lemley, "if a pioneer pays a generic to delay entry, the likelihood is that the delay does not in fact represent the expected outcome of litigation, but rather has been biased toward later entry by the payment."[552]

Formally, under this theory, the analysis begins with an assessment of the patent holder's "reservation date" for entry in the settlement negotiations—the earliest date at which the incumbent would be willing to allow the alleged infringer to enter the market rather than litigate. Any settlement that delays that entry would be anticompetitive.   Thus, suppose both the patent holder and alleged infringer correctly believe that the patent holder has a 70 percent chance of prevailing.   The patent

---

available to the alleged infringer if it prevails. The parties thus settle with a split of the patent life that favors the patent holder and a split of the expected damages that favors the alleged infringer.   This is unlawful under the *Guidelines* standard because the litigants are in a horizontal relationship and the patent split is a per se unlawful market division. The alleged infringer must litigate to its expected bankruptcy. *See id.* at 1055.

548.   466 F.3d 187, 215 (2d Cir. 2005).
549.   Slip Op. at 59.
550.   Asahi Glass Co. v. Pentech Pharm., 289 F. Supp. 2d 986, 994 (N.D. Ill. 2003).
551.   Shapiro, *supra* note 512, at 408.
552.   Hovenkamp et al., *supra* note 518, at 1762.

holder, however, makes a lump sum payment to the alleged infringer as part of the settlement of the litigation, inducing the alleged infringer to exit the market and to not re-enter until the patent has expired. According to those critical of reverse payments, this is a violation of law because consumers have received less competition than they might expect from litigation: the consumers lost the 30 percent chance that the alleged infringer would prevail in the patent litigation.

An explanation of this form of analysis can be found in the Commission's opinion in *In re Schering-Plough Corp.*[553] In that case, the Federal Trade Commission applied a rule of reason analysis to two patent settlements entered into by Schering with generics that had filed ANDAs that claimed that they did not infringe Schering's patent. In the settlement that received the most attention from the Commission, Schering and the alleged infringer had split the patent life, with the generic agreeing not to enter until about half of the remaining patent term had expired. The Commission alleged that the split of the patent life had been engineered through a reverse payment. Schering and the generic denied this, arguing that the consideration Schering paid to the generic was for a series of cross licenses to technology owned by the generic. After the Administrative Law Judge dismissed the complaint, the Commission reversed.

The Commission found that the restraints were not inherently suspect and thus required a fact-based analysis of actual and likely market effects. Under this rule of reason analysis, the Commission first found price effects because generic entry had offered consumers an opportunity to buy the pharmaceutical at issue at a lower price. If the generic had entered earlier, consumers would have had a cheaper option earlier.

This raised the question of whether consumers would have had the cheaper option earlier but for the settlement. Schering asserted that it had presented evidence that it would have prevailed in the patent dispute.[554] If Schering's position were correct, under the *Guidelines* approach, this would mean that the generic was not a potential entrant and there could be no unlawful horizontal relationship.

The Commission rejected this approach without discussing the *Guidelines*, concluding that it was not "necessary ... to embark on an

553. FTC Dkt. No. 9297, 2003 F.T.C. LEXIS 187 (Dec. 18, 2003), *available at* http://www.ftc.gov/os/adjpro/d9297/ 031218commissionopinion.pdf.

554. *See, e.g.*, Appeal Brief of Respondent Schering-Plough Corp., FTC Docket No. 9297 (Sept. 30, 2002), *available at* http://www.ftc.gov/os/adjpro/d9297/020930schering-ploughappealbrief.pdf.

inquiry into the merits of the underlying patent dispute when resolving antitrust issues in patent settlements."[555] The parties had settled at a time when they did not know who would have prevailed. It was the evaluation at the time of settlement that was important according to the Commission. And, it was impossible at that time to know whether the settlement was within the scope of the patent. Consequently, it was the settlement agreement and not the patent that prevented earlier generic entry. In other words, the settlement agreement could be unlawful irrespective of the potential or actual scope of Schering's patent. That is, by settling Schering lost the right to assert that its patent precluded the generic entry at issue.

The Commission, therefore, focused on the payment. First, the Commission concluded that the consideration paid to the generic was not, or at least was not entirely, for a cross license received in return. If all the consideration had been for the cross license, it would have posed no problem, according to the Commission, because such a settlement without a reverse payment would merely reflect the parties' compromise of their competing litigation assessments. The reverse payment however "raised ... a red flag" requiring further inquiry.[556]

The Commission inquiry of this red flag began by asking why Schering would pay the generic to settle. According to the Commission, "[a]bsent proof of other offsetting considerations, it is logical to conclude that the quid pro quo for the payment was an agreement by the generic to defer entry beyond the date that represented an otherwise reasonable litigation compromise."[557] That is, but for the payment, there would have been a better settlement for consumers.[558] Moreover, the Commission seemed to suggest that it is up to respondents to prove other offsetting considerations.

Another case treating reverse payments with skepticism is *In re Cardizem CD Antitrust Litigation*,[559] where the Sixth Circuit held that an

---

555. *Id* at 31.
556. *Schering Plough*, Commission Opinion, supra note 553, at 29.
557. *Id.* at 26.
558. According to the Commission: "[W]e ... focus on the effects that Schering's payment to [the generic] was likely to have on the generic entry date which the parties would otherwise have agreed to in settlement." "[W]e ... look at the agreement as of the time it was made to determine whether it was 'unreasonable,' *i.e.*, whether it likely delayed generic entry beyond the date that would have been provided in a differently crafted settlement." *Id.*
559. 332 F.3d 896, 908 (6th Cir. 2003).

interim settlement was a per se market division agreement. In that case, the generic drug company had filed an ANDA and the pioneer drug company commenced a patent suit. Under the interim settlement, the generic company agreed that it would not sell the generic version of the drug until it had obtained a final, nonappealable judgment in its favor in the patent suit or the pioneer company had licensed the drug to a third party. The pioneer agreed to pay the generic $10 million per quarter and additional money that depended on the outcome of the patent litigation. The court found that the agreement was a horizontal market allocation and thus a per se violation of the Sherman Act. The court concluded that the settlement could not be characterized as merely an attempt to enforce patent rights because the pioneer drug company had bolstered the effectiveness of the patent by paying a competitor to stay off the market.

One criticism of treating reverse payments as a red flag is that such a payment should not be presumed to show an anticompetitive intent.[560] For instance, Robert Willig and John Bigelow offered several different conditions under which a patent holder might make a reverse payment without anticompetitive intent. Indeed, the reverse payment might be necessary to achieve a settlement that would be better for consumers than the outcome of litigation.[561]

The first rationale offered by Willig and Bigelow, which has also been noted by several courts, is that a risk averse patent holder[562] might

---

560. Robert D. Willig & John P. Bigelow, *Antitrust Policy Towards Agreements that Settle Patent Litigation,* 49 ANTITRUST BULL. 655, 659-60 (2004).

561. *Id.* For graphic representations of Willig and Bigelow's analysis, see Schildkraut, *supra* note 521, at 1057-67.

562. "A person is risk-averse when the displeasure from losing a given amount of income is greater than the pleasure from gaining the same amount of income... In terms of the utility concept that we analyzed ... risk aversion is the same as diminishing marginal utility of income. Being risk-averse implies that the gain in utility achieved by getting an extra amount of income is less than the loss in utility from losing the same amount of income." PAUL A. SAMUELSON & WILLIAM D. NORDHAUS, ECONOMICS 207 (17th ed. 2001). As Paul Samuelson explained: "People are generally risk-averse, preferring a sure thing to uncertain levels of consumption...." *Id.* at 207. Kenneth Arrow has similarly concluded: "From the time of Bernoulli on, it has been common to argue that (a) individuals tend to display aversion to the taking of risks, and (b) that risk aversion in turn is an explanation for many observed phenomena in the economic world." Kenneth J. Arrow, *The Theory of Risk Aversion, in* ESSAYS IN THE THEORY OF RISK-BEARING 90 (1974). Professor Scherer

be willing to pay to reach a settlement that is no better (or even worse) than the likely results of litigation. Such risk aversion is like paying for an insurance policy against a loss that is not expected but which could be catastrophic.[563] Other reasons for why there may be a gap between the patent holder and the alleged infringer that can only be spanned by a reverse payment is that the alleged infringer may be unduly optimistic about its chances of prevailing; or, it may be cash strapped and willing to litigate unless it receives some payment; or the alleged infringer may need cash to overcome a problem of information asymmetries.[564]

Take the example of two litigants negotiating a dispute in 2005 over a patent that expires in 2015. The patent holder believes it has a 50 percent chance of winning, and would certainly be willing to settle without a payment that allows the alleged infringer into the market in 2010. Assuming that the patent holder is correct about the chances it would prevail in court, such a settlement is as beneficial to consumers as continuing the litigation. It satisfies the welfare test because it leads to the same consumer surplus that would arise from ongoing litigation.[565]

But if a risk-averse patent holder is unable to convince the alleged infringer to accept the 2010 entry date, the patent holder might be willing to agree to an earlier date to eliminate the uncertainty of litigation.

---

has observed, "[o]nly the decision maker who attaches no significance whatsoever to avoiding risk will always choose alternatives with the highest best-guess payoffs. And such managers, empirical studies suggest, are rare." F.M. SCHERER, INDUSTRIAL MARKET STRUCTURE AND ECONOMIC PERFORMANCE 30 (2d ed. 1980); *see also* RICHARD E. CAVES, MULTINAT'L ENTERPRISE AND ECONOMIC ANALYSIS 26 (1982) ("[T]he argument against risk-avoiding diversification by the MNE [MultiNat'l enterprise] is likely to fail... Another objection is that the business manager himself faces nondiversifiable risks if his company does badly... Those managers who run enterprises ... may simply have room to pursue a number of personal goals, including risk avoidance...."). Jeremy Bulow, however, argues that risk aversion in large publicly traded companies should be very small and easily hedged. Jeremy Bulow, *The Gaming of Pharmaceutical Patents*, Stanford Research Series, Research Paper No. 1804, May 2003, at 32. Shapiro has similar doubts about the risk aversion of large companies but does seem to acknowledge that this might not be important because the managers may be risk averse even if the company is risk neutral. Shapiro, *supra* note 512, at 407, 408.

563. *See* Schildkraut, *supra* note 521, at 1061; Crane, *supra* note 521, at 762.
564. *See* Willig & Bigelow, *supra* note 560, at 667-73; Schildkraut, *supra* note 521, at 1061-63.
565. Shapiro, *supra* note 512, at 407-08.

Suppose, however, there is no date that the parties can agree on that will settle the litigation. While the patent holder insists on 2009, the alleged infringer insists on 2008. Under such circumstances, a reverse payment can sometimes bridge the gap. This is possible because delaying the time of entry has a different value to the litigants but money may have the same value to them. The time is worth more to the patent holder than to the alleged infringer because the revenue from the patent is most likely higher with a single firm in the market than with two firms in the market. Thus, in the above example, the parties might settle for a lump sum cash payment to the alleged infringer and entry by the alleged infringer in July 2009.[566] Without the lump sum payment, the parties may be unable to reach a settlement.

In *Schering Plough*, the Commission acknowledged that "a pioneer may be willing to pay some money to bridge the gap in expectations" if "the generic challenger is more optimistic about the litigation outcome than the pioneer."[567] The Commission, however, did not consider evidence on this point.

Another criticism of treating reverse payments as a red flag is that it places a great deal of weight on the intent of one of the settling parties. That is, the reverse payment is used as evidence that the patent holder intended to get a better split of the patent life in the settlement than it expected to obtain in litigation. Yet, even if reverse payments could be interpreted as proving an anticompetitive intent, courts repeatedly have rejected evidence of anticompetitive intent as a substitute for evidence of anticompetitive effects.[568] While a risk neutral patent holder may think it will do better in settlement than in litigation, it may simply be wrong. According to Judge Posner and the Second Circuit, the private thoughts of a patent holder are not the key issue in an antitrust case evaluating the settlement of a patent dispute.[569] According to Willig and Bigelow, a risk neutral patent holder could be unduly pessimistic about the true odds of

---

566. *See* Schildkraut, *supra* note 521, at 1061-63.
567. *Schering Plough*, Commission Opinion at 38.
568. *See, e.g.*, Brooke Group v. Brown & Williamson Tobacco, 509 U.S. 209, 224 (1993); Spectrum Sports v. McQuillan, 506 U.S. 447, 459 (1993); Levine v. Central Fla. Med. Affiliates, 72 F.3d 1538, 1552 (11th Cir. 1996); SCFC ILC, Inc. v. Visa USA, 36 F.3d 958, 970 (10th Cir. 1994); U.S. Healthcare v. Healthsource, 986 F.2d 589, 596 (1st Cir. 1993); *Schachar*, 870 F.2d at 400.
569. Asahi Glass Co. v. Pentech Pharm., 289 F. Supp. 2d 986, 993 (N.D. Ill. 2003); *In re* Tamoxifen Citrate Antitrust Litig., 466 F.3d 187, 210-11 (2d Cir. 2006).

prevailing in litigation, while the alleged infringer has an unduly optimistic view of its chances of success. The parties may only be able to bridge the gap between their perspectives by a payment to the alleged infringer. This payment could result in a settlement that is better for consumers than the likely outcome of litigation.[570]

As the arguments have developed, the views of some commentators who favored treating reverse payments as red flags have softened. For instance, Lemley and Shapiro wrote a more recent article where they argued against per se condemnation. They recommended that evidence of a reverse payment ought to shift the burden of proof to the defendant to show that the reverse payment was not an anticompetitive device.[571]

Others, however, have not changed their view. For example, while not rejecting the theoretical premises of Willig and Bigelow, Keith and Cristofer Leffler continue to press for per se illegality of reverse payments because they believe that there is rarely a need for reverse payments to settle patent litigation. Typically they find that the gap between the patent holder and alleged infringer can be closed by a cross-licensing agreement and such a settlement will result in a better outcome for consumers.[572]

d.   The Evolving Sham Standard

Several courts have rejected the view that reverse payments should be viewed suspiciously, concluding that a settlement does not violate the antitrust laws so long as the parties were settling a legitimate intellectual property dispute and the settlement was within the potential scope of the patent.

In *Valley Drug v. Geneva Pharmaceuticals*,[573] for example, the Eleventh Circuit concluded that the settlement should be compared to the potential scope of the patent. *Valley Drug* involved two agreements

---

570.   Willig & Bigelow, *supra* note 560, at 673; Schildkraut, *supra* note 521, at 1065-67.
571.   Mark A. Lemley & Carl Shapiro, *Probabilistic Patents*, 19 J. OF ECON. PERSPECTIVE 75, 93, n.19 (2005)
572.   Keith Leffler & Cristofer Leffler, *Patent Litigation Settlements: Payments By The Patent Holder Are Anticompetitive And Should Be Per Se Illegal*, available at http://faculty.washington.edu/kleffler/Research.html; Keith Leffler & Cristofer Leffler, *The Probabilistic Nature of Patent Rights: In Response to Kevin McDonald*, 17 ANTITRUST 77 (2003).
573.   344 F.3d 1294 (11th Cir. 2003).

covering Hatch-Waxman patent litigation between a pioneer pharmaceutical manufacturer and a generic manufacturer. When the generic filed its ANDA, it alleged the invalidity of the pioneer's patent. The pioneer promptly sued, preventing the generic from entering the market for 30 months. The generic manufacturer, however, had filed an ANDA related to both tablets and capsules and the pioneer had mistakenly failed to sue over the capsules, meaning that there was no automatic 30-month stay precluding the generic from introducing its capsule formulation before the validity of the pioneer's patent could be decided by the court. To prevent entry of the generic capsule pending the outcome of the litigation, the pioneer sought a preliminary injunction.

Before the court ruled on the preliminary injunction, the parties entered into an interim settlement, in which the generic manufacturer agreed not to market either its tablet or capsule until final judicial resolution of the patent suit. In return, the pioneer agreed to pay the generic a lump sum every month until the district court decided the merits of the patent dispute.

Valley Drug also addressed a second agreement between the same pioneer and a second generic manufacturer relating to the same pharmaceutical. The pioneer again alleged infringement of its patents and the generic claimed that the pioneer had improperly listed the patents in the FDA's Orange Book after the generic had filed its ANDA. Under the settlement, the generic manufacturer agreed not to market its generic product until another generic entered the market with a non-infringing product or until one of the patents involved expired. In exchange, the pioneer agreed to a series of payments to the generic.

The district court condemned the agreement as a per se market allocation.[574] The Court of Appeals reversed because the district court failed to consider the potential exclusionary power of the patent. If the pioneer had a right to exclude competitors based on its patent, "it is not obvious that competition was limited more than that lawful degree by paying potential competitors for their exit."[575] The court observed that, given the large profits at stake, the payment might be the product of the pioneer's risk aversion rather than a lack of faith in its patents. The court added that in a Hatch-Waxman suit the pioneer had no ability to bargain by compromising on damages because the generic was not yet in the market generating potential damages. Hence, the pioneer had to bargain

---

574. *In re* Terazosin Hydrochloride Antitrust Litig., 164 F. Supp. 2d 1340 (S.D. Fla. 2000).

575. 344 F.3d at 1309.

with something else—a reverse payment.[576] The court did acknowledge, however, that very large payments might show a lack of faith in the patent.

In this case, the pioneer's patents were later invalidated. Based on this fact, the plaintiffs argued that the settlements could not possibly be within the exclusionary power of the patents. The court, however, said that the settlements could not be condemned on the basis of such 20/20 hindsight. Instead, the lower court had to judge the settlements at the time the parties entered into them. The court was concerned that using hindsight would unduly restrict settlement agreements of patent disputes, which would undermine the incentive structure of the patent law.

Another case that strongly supports the sham standard, albeit in dicta, is Seventh Circuit Court Judge Richard Posner's district court opinion in *Asahi Glass*, which issued just weeks after *Valley, Drug*.[577] In *Asahi,* the pioneer had sued a generic manufacturer for infringement. The settlement of this suit allowed the generic manufacturer to distribute the generic version of its drug in Puerto Rico, but in the remainder of the United States only when another version of the generic appeared on the market. Asahi, the maker of the active ingredient in the pharmaceutical at issue, sued the settling parties, alleging that the settlement was a market division agreement. Asahi's antitrust claim was dismissed for lack of standing.

As alternative grounds for reaching the same disposition, Judge Posner began by noting that settlements are favored as a matter of judicial policy. He then observed that a third party "should not . . . haul the parties to the settlement over the hot coals of antitrust litigation" unless the circumstances of the settlement were suspicious.[578]

Taking aim at the argument that reverse payments are anti-competitive, Judge Posner observed that if the patent were valid and infringed, it would exclude to the same extent as the reverse payment. Moreover, "any settlement agreement can be characterized as involving compensation to the defendant, who would not settle unless he had something to show for the settlement." Thus, if the courts condemned

---

576. *See also In re* Ciprofloxacin Hydrochloride Antitrust Litig., 261 F. Supp. 2d 188 (S.D.N.Y. 2003) (noting that Hatch-Waxman scheme "affects the parties' relative risk assessment and explains the flow of settlement funds and their magnitude").

577. Asahi Glass Co. v. Pentech Pharm., 289 F. Supp. 2d 986 (N.D. Ill. 2003).

578. *Id.* at 992.

reverse payments, "we shall have no more patent settlements."[579] This "would reduce the incentive to challenge patents by reducing the challenger's settlement options should he be sued for infringement."[580]

Thus, for Judge Posner, the focus ought to be on whether the patent was almost certainly invalid or not infringed, not on whether the settlement included a reverse payment. Citing to the sham litigation test in *Professional Real Estate Investors v. Columbia Pictures Industries,*[581] Judge Posner would permit antitrust challenges to patent settlements to go forward only if the infringement suit was "objectively baseless." The patent holder's subjective motivation would be irrelevant.[582]

The Eleventh Circuit weighed in again by reversing the Federal Trade Commission's opinion condemning Schering Plough's settlements. The court noted that the Commission failed to consider the scope of Schering's patent and had instead focused on the reverse payment as the determining factor.

The court chastised the Commission's "low threshold of demonstrating the anticompetitive nature of the agreements"[583] under its rule of reason analysis. And then observed that "[d]espite the appearance that it openly considered [the respondents'] procompetitive affirmative defense, the Commission immediately condemned the settlements because of their absolute anticompetitive nature, and discounted the merits of the patent litigation."[584] The court then observed that neither the rule of reason nor per se analysis was appropriate. Rather, the antitrust analysis of the settlement must focus on the (1) scope of the exclusionary potential of the patent, (2) the extent the agreements exceed that scope, and (3) the anticompetitive effects if the scope were exceeded.[585]

The court first noted that there was no allegation that the infringement suits were shams.[586] Thus, the question was whether the challenged agreements restricted competition beyond the scope of the patent. With regard to the Commission's concern about reverse payments, the court cited *Standard Oil Co. v. United States*[587] for the

---

579. *Id.* at 994.
580. *Id.*
581. 508 U.S. 49 (1993).
582. 289 F. Supp. 2d at 993.
583. 402 F.3d at 1065.
584. *Id.*
585. *Id.* at 1066.
586. *Id.* at 1068.
587. 283 U.S. 163, 170-71 n. 5 (1931).

proposition that parties to a patent dispute may exchange consideration to settle,[588] noting the general policy favoring the settlement of litigation. Turning to the Commission's conclusion that there would have been a better settlement for consumers but for the payments, the court noted that there was no record evidence supporting the Commission's conclusion. Furthermore, the court rejected the Commission's use of logic in lieu of substantial evidence. "We are not sure," the court observed, "where this 'logic' derives from."[589]   The court, citing to expert testimony in the record, noted that ancillary agreements might be the only avenue to settlement.

The *Schering* court next explained that the risks were different in Hatch-Waxman litigation because the generic manufacturer had not entered the market and it therefore did not face the possibility of enormous damages for infringement.   Thus, the court opined, the Commission's logic would result in condemnation of any settlement where damages were compromised:

> [U]nder the Commission's analysis, such a settlement would be a violation of the antitrust law because the infringer reaped the benefit of the patentholder's partial surrender of damages.   Like the reverse payments at issue here, 'such a rule would discourage any rational party from settling a patent case because it would be an invitation to antitrust litigation.'[590]

This, according to the court, was not the "suitable accommodation" between antitrust and the patent system that the Eleventh Circuit had in mind in *Valley Drug*.

Ultimately, the court, like the Commission, did not undertake an analysis to determine whether the generic manufacturers would have infringed Schering's patent. Unlike the Commission, however, the court concluded that because the settlements fell within the protection of Schering's patent, they were not illegal.[591]

The case that most thoroughly analyzed the trade offs among competing standards was the Second Circuit's decision, *In re Tamoxifen Citrate Antitrust Litigation*.[592] In this case, the pioneer lost its validity

---

588.   402 F.3d at 1072.
589.   *Id.* at 1073.
590.   *Id.* at 1074 (quoting *In re* Ciprofloxacin Hydrochloride Antitrust Litig., 261 F. Supp. 2d 188, 251 (E.D.N.Y. 2003)).
591.   *Id.* at 1074.
592.   466 F.3d 187 (2d Cir. 2006).

claim at the district court level. The parties settled while the appeal was pending, with the generic receiving payments and agreeing not to enter with its own generic version of the pharmaceutical until the pioneer's patent had expired. The pioneer also licensed the generic to re-sell, under its own label, the product manufactured by the branded company. The Federal Circuit vacated the district court's judgment of invalidity after the settlement. Thereafter, three other manufacturers filed ANDAs seeking to offer their own generic equivalent of the same pharmaceutical. The branded company successfully defended its patent in court on each occasion.

The Second Circuit began with an acknowledgement that the possession of a valid patent did not give the patent holder any exemption from the Sherman Act beyond the limits of the patent monopoly.[593] But it also noted that courts must try to encourage the settlement of litigation.[594] The court was concerned not only about dissuading settlements, but that such discouragement would heighten the uncertainty surrounding patents and might delay innovation.[595]

Like the court in *Asahi Glass* and in *Valley Drug*, the Second Circuit noted that it was impossible to know at the time of settlement what would have happened in the litigation. And, the court thought it ill advised to speculate about the outcome on appeal unless there was something more at play.[596]

It also noted, as other courts had, that the reverse payment in the Hatch Waxman context was no different from the compromise of damages in the ordinary patent suit where the alleged infringer was already in the market.[597] Citing *Valley Drug* and *Asahi Glass*, the court concluded that such a payment did not make an otherwise lawful settlement unlawful.[598]

Thus, the court adopted a sham rule. Unless the lawsuit was objectively baseless, a settlement within the scope of the patent would be

---

593. *Id.* at 202 (citing United States v. Singer Mfg. Co., 374 U.S. 174, 196-97 (1963)).
594. *Id.* at 202-03.
595. *Id.* at 203.
596. *Id.*
597. *Id.* at 207 & n. 20 (citing *Cipro II*, 261 F. Supp. 2d at 252, *Asahi Glass*, 289 F. Supp 2d at 994, and Daniel A. Crane, *Ease over Accuracy in Assessing Patent Settlements*, 88 MINN. L. REV. 698, 700 (2004)).
598. *Id.* at 206 (citing *Valley Drug*, 344 F.3d at 1309 and *Asahi Glass*, 289 F. Supp. 2d at 994).

lawful whether facilitated by a payment or not.[599] According to the court, a settlement should violate the antitrust law only when it was entered into in bad faith or was otherwise utilized as a part of a scheme to restrain trade. Any other rule, the court opined, would require patent holders to litigate each threat to its patent to final judgment.[600]

While a reverse payment alone might not, therefore, be sufficient to condemn a settlement agreement, the court asked whether it was possible that an excessive reverse payment might be suspicious.[601] The court concluded, "that the suspicion abates upon reflection." So long as the patent litigation is not a sham, "the patent holder is seeking to arrive at a settlement in order to protect that to which it is presumably entitled: a lawful monopoly."[602]

Of course, a payment larger than the generic's profits might "betray a fatal disbelief in the validity of the patent or the likelihood of the infringement."[603] But the court doubted the wisdom of effectively invalidating the patent based on the patent holder's fear of losing. The court agreed with Judge Posner, that the private thoughts of a patent holder are not at issue in an antitrust case.[604] And in any event, simply making a payment did not indicate a disbelief in a patent's strength, as a risk averse patent holder might pay simply to settle: "there is always some risk of loss that the patent holder might wish to insure against by settling."[605]

The court recognized that its rule would allow patent holders to use reverse payments to retain monopolies protected by weak patents.[606] But if the patent was really weak, the court thought that buying off one challenger would just attract other challengers looking to be bought off. Eventually, the patent holder will have no monopoly profits left with which to pay the parade of challengers.[607] As the dissent pointed out, however, in the Hatch Waxman context each challenger's entry would be delayed for 30 months by the statutory scheme. This could deny consumers competition for a considerable period.

---

599. *Id.* at 203 (citing *Duplan Corp.*, 540 F.2d at 1220).
600. *Id.* at 212-13.
601. *Id.* at 209-10.
602. *Id.*
603. *Id.*
604. *Id.* at 210.
605. *Id.*
606. *Id.* at 211.
607. *Id.*

5. Court-Approved Settlements

One way litigants might avoid the uncertainty attendant to any settlement is to seek court approval of the settlement. The *Noerr Pennington* doctrine may protect the parties entering into a court ordered settlement. *Noerr* shields parties attempting to influence officials regardless of their intent.[608] This includes attempts to influence the judiciary.[609] There are exceptions to the immunity, most notably where the petition effort is a sham: an attempt to obtain an anticompetitive effect through the use of the process rather than the outcome of the process.[610] Further, unethical and deceptive practices in the judicial process might strip litigants of their antitrust immunity.[611] Accordingly, and assuming the patent litigation is not a sham, litigants obtaining court approval of their settlement, more than just a dismissal, may be within the immunity afforded by *Noerr*.[612]

In *MedImmune, Inc., v. Genentech, Inc.,*[613] the Federal Circuit shed some light on the scope of the immunity. The underlying dispute was an interference proceeding. After over seven years, the Board of Patent Appeals and Interferences decided in the favor of the senior party. The junior party, Genentech, objecting to the decision, then filed an action in federal court. The district court urged the parties to resolve the priority issue through mediation. With the help of a mediator, the parties reached agreement, where the parties agreed that the junior party was entitled to priority and agreed to a cross license that included a formula to share royalties. The district court entered judgment on the parties' resolution

---

608. United Mine Workers v. Pennington, 381 U.S. 657, 670 (1965); E. R.R. Presidents Conference v. Noerr Motor Freight, 365 U.S. 127 (1961).
609. California Motor Transp. v. Trucking Unlimited, 404 U.S. 508, 510-11 (1972).
610. *Noerr*, 365 U.S. at 144.
611. Allied Tube & Conduit v. Indian Head, Inc., 486 U.S. 492, 499-500 (1988); Walker Process Equip. v. Food Mach. & Chem. Corp., 382 U.S. 172, 178 (1965).
612. In Mark L. Kovner, Colin R. Kass, & Avery W. Gardiner, *Applying the Noerr Doctrine to Pharmaceutical Patent Litigation Settlements,* 71 ANTITRUST L. J. 609, 622 & n.42 (2003), the authors argue that the *Noerr* doctrine protects settlements even if they are not court approved, citing *Columbia Pictures Industries v. Professional Real Estate Investors,* 944 F.2d 1525, 1528 (9th Cir. 1991), *aff'd on other grounds,* 508 U.S. 49 (1993), and several other cases.
613. 427 F.3d 958 (Fed. Cir. 2005), *cert. granted,* 126 S. Ct. 1329 (2006).

of the issue of priority and directed the Patent Trademark Office to vacate its prior decision, revoke the patent of the senior party, and issue a patent to the junior party. Rather than simply following the district court judgment, the Board stated that the senior patent was cancelled by operation of law when the district court order became final. The Board also asked the patent examiner to review the patent on any grounds not involving judicial review. After further examination, the patent was issued, eleven years after the inception of the interference.

The plaintiff, MedImmune, was licensed under the Genentech patent. After the issuance of that patent, Genentech advised MedImmune that one of its products was subject to royalties under the license. MedImmune objected and filed for a declaratory judgment, requesting that the patent was invalid or unenforceable. One of the plaintiff's claims was that the settlement among the defendants was collusive. The district court dismissed the antitrust challenge under the *Noerr-Pennington* doctrine because the "restraint upon trade or monopolization is the result of a valid governmental action, as opposed to private action" and therefore "enjoy[s] absolute immunity from antitrust liability for the anti-competitive restraint."[614]

The Federal Circuit went further, concluding that it did not even have to reach the *Noerr-Pennington* issue. First, the court opined that antitrust challenges to patent interference settlements can discourage settlements.[615] Further, citing to the *Intellectual Property Guidelines*, the court rejected the per se or presumptive standard of illegality as contrary to both precedent and policy. The court then stated that the joint communications to a court in the terms of settlement and a joint petition to the PTO to implement the court's judgment "are not actions that would be prohibited or tainted absent immunization by *Noerr-Pennington*."[616] The court similarly held that the filing of the judgment in the PTO and the joint filing by the parties to the judgment did not require *Noerr* protection either. Thus, it appears that for the Federal Circuit a settlement that is enforced by court order is simply not a combination in restraint of trade.

---

614. 2003 U.S. Dist. LEXIS 23443, at *15 (C.D. Cal. Dec. 24, 2003)
615. 427 F.3d at 966.
616. *Id.* at 967.

CHAPTER VI

ANTITRUST ANALYSIS OF UNILATERAL CONDUCT BY INTELLECTUAL PROPERTY OWNERS

This chapter focuses on unilateral conduct in the exploitation of intellectual property that has come under Section 2 scrutiny. In particular, the chapter discusses: (1) the antitrust issues presented by unilateral refusals to license or sell intellectual property, and (2) the circumstances in which the unilateral enforcement of intellectual property rights will be subject to antitrust scrutiny.

A. Refusal to License or Sell Intellectual Property

Do the antitrust laws impose an obligation upon intellectual property holders, at least under certain circumstances, to license or otherwise deal their intellectual property? The question has not been squarely addressed by the U.S. Supreme Court, but, as discussed below, has been the subject of a split among the federal courts of appeals and intense debate among commentators.[1]

---

1. The literature in this area includes: Carl Shapiro, *Patent System Reform: Economic Analysis and Critique*, 19 BERKELEY TECH. L.J. 1017 (2004) ("Shapiro"); Jonathan I. Gleklen, *Per Se Legality for Unilateral Refusals to License IP Is Correct as a Matter of Law and Policy*, Antitrust Source, July 2002 ("Gleklen I"); Jeffrey K. MacKie-Mason, *Counterpoint: Antitrust Immunity for Refusals to Deal in (Intellectual) Property Is a Slippery Slope*, Antitrust Source, July 2002, at 3 ("MacKie-Mason"); A. Douglas Melamed & Ali M. Stoeppelwerth, *The CSU Case: Facts, Formalism and the Intersection of Antitrust and Intellectual Property Law*, 10 GEO. MASON L. REV. 407 (2002) ("Melamed"); R. Hewitt Pate, *Refusals to Deal and Intellectual Property Rights*, 10 GEO. MASON L. REV. 429 (2002) ("Pate"); Peter M. Boyle et al., *Antitrust Law at the Federal Circuit: Red Light or Green Light at the IP-Antitrust Intersection*, 69 ANTITRUST L.J. 739 (2002) ("Boyle et al."); Daniel J. Gifford, *The Antitrust/Intellectual Property Interface: An Emerging Solution to an Intractable Problem*, 31 HOFSTRA L.R. 363 (2002) ("Gifford"); Michael A. Carrier, *Unraveling the Patent-Antitrust Paradox*, 150 U. PA.L. REV. 761 (2002) ("Carrier"); Mark D. Whitener, Statement, submitted in connection with May 1, 2002 Session FTC-DOJ Hearings, *available at* http://www.ftc.gov/opp/intellect/020501

Section 2 monopolization requires proof of both monopoly power and predatory or exclusionary acts in the acquisition or maintenance of

---

whitener.pdf ("Whitener"); Jonathan Gleklen, *Antitrust Liability for Unilateral Refusals to License Intellectual Property: Xerox and Its Critics*, submitted in connection with May 1, 2002 Session FTC-DOJ Hearings, *available at* http://www.ftc.gov/opp/intellect/020501gleklen. pdf ("Gleklen II"); Ashish Arora, *Refusals to License: A Transaction-Based Perspective*, submitted in connection with May 1, 2002 Session of FTC-DOJ Hearings, *available at* http://www.ftc.gov/opp/intellect/ 020501aroral.pdf ("Arora"); 3 PHILLIP E. AREEDA & HERBERT HOVENKAMP, ANTITRUST LAW ¶ 709 (2d ed. 2002) ("AREEDA & HOVENKAMP"); Robert Pitofsky, *Challenges of the New Economy: Issues at the Intersection of Antitrust and Intellectual Property*, 68 ANTITRUST L.J. 913 (2001) ("Pitofsky"); David McGowan, *Innovation, Uncertainty, and Stability in Antitrust Law*, 16 BERKELEY TECH. L.J. 729 (2001) ("McGowan II"); James B. Kobak, Jr., *The Federal Circuit as a Competition Law Court*, 83 J. PAT. & TRADEMARK OFFICE SOC'Y 527 (2001) ("Kobak"); Michelle M. Burtis & Bruce H. Kobayashi, *Why an Original Can Be Better Than a Copy: Intellectual Property, the Refusal to Deal, and ISO Antitrust Litigation*, 9 SUP. CT. ECON. REV. 143 (2001) ("Burtis & Kobayashi"); Mark W. Patterson, *When Is Intellectual Property Intellectual? The Leveraging Problem*, 73 S. CAL. L. REV. 1133 (2000) ("Patterson"); B. Zorina Kahn, *Symposium on Antitrust and Intellectual Property: Federal Antitrust Agencies and Public Policy Toward Antitrust and Intellectual Property*, 9 CORNELL J.L. & PUB. POL'Y 133 (1999) ("Kahn"); David McGowan, *Networks and Intention in Antitrust and Intellectual Property*, 24 J. CORP. L. 485 (1999) ("McGowan I"); Marina Lao, *Unilateral Refusals to Sell or License Intellectual Property and the Antitrust Duty to Deal*, 9 CORNELL J.L. & PUB. POL'Y 193 (1999) ("Lao I"); Charles L. Freed, *Antitrust and the Duty to License Intellectual Property—Can Manufacturers Be Compelled to Deal with ISOs?*, 14 ANTITRUST 33 (1999) ("Freed"); Ronald W. Davis, *What Are the Limitations on "Throwing Your Weight Around" Using Intellectual Property Rights?*, 13 ANTITRUST 47 (1999) ("Davis"); Willard J. Tom & Joshua A. Newberg, *Antitrust and Intellectual Property: From Separate Spheres to Unified Field*, 66 ANTITRUST L.J. 167 (1997) ("Tom & Newberg"); Richard Calkins, *Patent Law: The Impact of the 1988 Patent Misuse Reform Act and* Noerr-Pennington *Doctrine on Misuse Defenses and Antitrust Counterclaims*, 38 DRAKE L. REV. 175 (1989) ("Calkins").

that power.[2] If a holder of intellectual property does not possess monopoly power in a properly defined relevant market, it cannot be liable for monopolization under Section 2.[3] The mere possession of a patent or copyright does not, without more, confer monopoly power.[4]

---

2. United States v. Grinnell Corp., 384 U.S. 563, 576 n.7 (1966); United States v. Paramount Pictures, 334 U.S. 131, 173 (1948); United States v. Griffith, 334 U.S. 100, 106 (1948); *see also* ABA SECTION OF ANTITRUST LAW, ANTITRUST LAW DEVELOPMENTS 246-52 (5th ed. 2002).
3. Possession of monopoly power is not required to establish an attempt to monopolize; rather, a "dangerous probability" of achieving monopoly power through predatory or exclusionary means and with a specific intent to monopolize is required. *See, e.g.*, Spectrum Sports v. McQuillan, 506 U.S. 447 (1993); ANTITRUST LAW DEVELOPMENTS, *supra* note 2, at 299-308. Courts generally assess "dangerous probability" by reference principally to market shares in the relevant market, together with other factors such as entry barriers. *See id.* at 302-08. Where market share is low, courts are unlikely to find a dangerous probability of monopolization; where it is higher, they are more likely to so find. *See id.* Generally speaking, courts rarely find a "dangerous probability" of success when the defendant's market share is under 30%; they sometimes do when it is between 30% and 50%; and they often do when it exceeds 50%. *See id.*
4. *See, e.g.*, Ill. Tool Works v. Indep. Ink, 126 S. Ct. 1281 (2006); Jefferson Parish Hosp. Dist. No. 2. v. Hyde, 466 U.S. 2, 37 n.7 (1984) (O'Connor, J., concurring) ("A common misconception has been that a patent ... suffice[s] to demonstrate market power... [A] patent holder has no market power in any relevant sense if there are close substitutes for the patented product."); N. Pac. Ry. Co. v. United States, 356 U.S. 1, 10 n.8 (1958) ("Of course it is common knowledge that a patent does not always confer a monopoly over a particular commodity."); C.R. Bard, Inc. v. M3 Sys., 157 F.3d 1340, 1368 (Fed. Cir. 1998) ("It is not presumed that the patent-based right to exclude necessarily establishes market power in antitrust terms."); Abbott v. Brennan, 952 F.2d 1346, 1354 (Fed. Cir. 1991) (possession of patent and market advantages thus gained do not establish antitrust market power); A.I. Root Co. v. Computer/Dynamics, Inc., 806 F.2d 673, 676 (6th Cir. 1986) ("[W]e reject any absolute presumption of market power for copyright[ed] or patented product[s]."); USM Corp. v. SPS Techs., 694 F.2d 505, 511 (7th Cir. 1982) (Posner, J.) ("[O]f course, not every patent confers market power..."); U.S. DEP'T OF JUSTICE & FED. TRADE COMM'N, ANTITRUST GUIDELINES FOR THE LICENSING OF INTELLECTUAL PROPERTY (April 6, 1995) (hereinafter INTELLECTUAL PROPERTY GUIDELINES), *reprinted in* 4 Trade Reg. Rep. (CCH) ¶ 13,132 *and* Appendix 1 to this Handbook.

While the possession of monopoly power is of significant concern, that element is often not at issue. Instead, the case law in this area tends to focus on whether the refusal to deal satisfies the "willful acquisition or maintenance" element.

1. Refusals to Deal in General: Strong but Rebuttable Presumption That Even Monopolists May Choose with Whom They Will Deal Free of Antitrust Liability

Antitrust cases involving unilateral refusals to deal intellectual property arise in the context of a broader jurisprudence concerning refusals to deal. A brief overview of that broader jurisprudence, with particular emphasis on *Verizon Communications v. Law Offices of Curtis V. Trinko*, the Supreme Court's most recent pronouncement on refusals to deal is an important starting point.

In *Trinko*, the Supreme Court wrote that, in general, the Sherman Act "does not restrict the long recognized right of [a] trader or manufacturer engaged in an entirely private business, freely to exercise his own independent discretion as to parties with whom he will deal."[6] According to the Court, however, "[t]he high value that we have placed on the right to refuse to deal with other firms does not mean that the right

---

5. 540 U.S. 398 (2004). For commentary on *Trinko*, see, for example, Robert A. Skitol, *Correct Answers to Large Questions About* Verizon v. Trinko, Antitrust Source, May 2004 ("Skitol"); Andrew I. Gavil, *Exclusionary Distribution Strategies by Dominant Firms: Striking a Better Balance*, 72 ANTITRUST L.J. 3 (2004) ("Gavil"); Jeff Cashdan et al., *Hitting the Section 2 'Refresh' Button for In-House Counsel Following* Trinko, Antitrust Source, July 2004, at 14 ("*Trinko* ABA Seminar"); Janet L. McDavid & Mary Anne Mason, *The 'Trinko' Decision*, Nat'l L. J., Feb. 16, 2004, at 16 ("McDavid & Mason"); Eleanor Fox, *The Trouble with* Trinko, Paper Presented at ABA Antitrust Section Spring Meeting April 1, 2004 ("Fox"), *available at* www.abanet.org/antitrust/committees/communication/; Neal R. Stoll & Shepard Goldfein, *'Trinko II': When Refusing to Deal with Competitor Is Monopoly Act*, 231 N.Y.L.J., Mar. 16, 2004, at 3 ("Stoll & Goldfein"); and Matthew L. Cantor, *Is "Trinko" the Last Word on a Telephone Monopolist's Duty to Deal?*, 231 N.Y.L.J., May 19, 2004, at 4 ("Cantor").

6. *Trinko*, 540 U.S. at 408 (quoting United States v. Colgate & Co., 250 U.S. 300, 307 (1919)) (internal quotation marks omitted).

is unqualified. Under certain circumstances, a refusal to cooperate with rivals can constitute anticompetitive conduct and violate Section 2."[7]

But the Court emphasized that it has been "very cautious" in recognizing exceptions to the general rule that even monopolists are free to decide with whom to deal:[8]

> Firms may acquire monopoly power by establishing an infrastructure that renders them uniquely suited to serve their customers. Compelling such firms to share the source of their advantage is in some tension with the underlying purpose of antitrust law, since it may lessen the incentive for the monopolist, the rival, or both to invest in those economically beneficial facilities. Enforced sharing also requires antitrust courts to act as central planners, identifying the proper price, quantity, and other terms of dealing—a role for which they are ill-suited. Moreover, compelling negotiation between competitors may facilitate the supreme evil of antitrust: collusion.[9]

Trinko involved an alleged refusal by Verizon, an incumbent monopoly local telephone service provider, to provide AT&T access to its systems and support operations in a manner sufficient to allow AT&T to compete effectively with Verizon as a local service provider in Verizon's service area. Verizon was obligated to provide such support pursuant to the Telecommunications Act of 1996.[10] The plaintiff—an end-consumer of AT&T's local services filing suit on behalf of a putative class of all such consumers—alleged that Verizon's refusal to cooperate constituted, among other things, a violation of Section 2.

The Court focused on whether Verizon's alleged failure to cooperate satisfied the "willful acquisition or maintenance" element of Section 2.[11] At the outset of its analysis the Court stated that:

---

7.   *Id.* (quoting Aspen Skiing Co. v. Aspen Highlands Skiing Corp., 472 U.S. 585, 601 (1985)) (internal quotation marks omitted).

8.   *Id.*

9.   *Id.* at 407-08. Some commentators have criticized the Court's "central planner" comment as encouraging courts "to abdicate the obviously critical role they play in maintaining effective competition. " Gavil, *supra* note 5, at 50; *see also, e.g.,* Fox, *supra* note 5, at *2-3.

10. 47 U.S.C. § 202(a).

11. The Court also found, as a threshold matter, that the 1996 Telecommunications Act did not foreclose plaintiff's antitrust claim; the Act's "savings clause" specifically preserves claims that satisfy existing antitrust standards. *Trinko,* 540 U.S. at 407.

The mere possession of monopoly power, and the concomitant charging of monopoly prices, is not only not unlawful; it is an important element of the free-market system. The opportunity to charge monopoly prices—at least for a short period—is what attracts "business acumen" in the first place; it induces risk taking that produces innovation and economic growth. To safeguard the incentive to innovate, the possession of monopoly power will not be found unlawful unless it is accompanied by an element of anticompetitive conduct.[12]

The Court's discussion thereafter centered on distinguishing Verizon's conduct from that of the defendant in *Aspen Skiing Co. v. Aspen Highlands Skiing Corp.*,[13] which is "the leading case for § 2 liability based on refusal to cooperate with a rival."[14]

In *Aspen Skiing*, the defendant (Ski Company) owned three of the four ski mountains in the Aspen, Colorado area, and for years had cooperated with the owner of the fourth (Highlands) in issuing a joint, multi-day, all-area ski ticket. After demanding that Highlands accept a smaller share of the total revenue, Ski Company cancelled the program and refused to reinstate it except on terms that Highlands deemed unacceptable. In addition, Ski Company refused various efforts by Highlands to recreate the four-mountain pass for its customers, including an offer by Highlands to buy, at retail prices, tickets for Ski Company's mountains on behalf of Highlands' customers. The Supreme Court upheld a jury verdict that Ski Company's refusal to deal violated Section 2 of the Sherman Act.[15]

---

12. *Id.*
13. 472 U.S. 585 (1985).
14. *Trinko*, 540 U.S. at 408.
15. *Aspen Skiing*, 472 U.S. at 595-99. The issue of whether Ski Company actually possessed monopoly power in a properly defined market was not presented to the Supreme Court. Many have questioned whether "downhill skiing services in Aspen, Colorado" was a properly defined relevant market, given the availability of other elite ski areas in the region and around the world, as well as the availability of other forms of vacation recreation. *See, e.g.*, Frank H. Easterbrook, *On Identifying Exclusionary Conduct*, 61 NOTRE DAME L. REV. 972, 972-73 (1986); Dennis W. Carlton, *A General Analysis of Exclusionary Conduct and Refusal to Deal—Why* Aspen *and* Kodak *Are Misguided*, 68 ANTITRUST L.J. 659, 678 n.34 (2001) ("Carlton") (pointing out that "if the four mountains constitute[d] a relevant market, then the joint venture [was] a

After characterizing *Aspen Skiing* as "at or near the outer boundary of Section 2 liability,"[16] the *Trinko* Court identified the following aspects of Ski Company's conduct that led to a finding of liability:

(1) Ski Company had abandoned a course of business that it had voluntarily commenced years earlier;

(2) Ski Company had willingly entered into the course of dealing with Highlands and pursued it for some time, which suggested that it had been profitable;

(3) Ski Company steadfastly persisted in its abandonment of a "presumably profitable" course of dealing with Highlands, which, to the Court, suggested "a willingness to forsake short-term profits to achieve an anticompetitive end," namely, the elimination of Highlands as a viable competitor;[17] and

(4) Ski Company was unwilling to resume the program even if compensated at the *retail* price for its tickets, which further suggested that it was foregoing profits by refusing to deal with Highlands. As the Court put it, "[Ski Company] turned down a proposal to sell at its own retail price, suggesting a calculation that its future monopoly retail price would be higher."[18] This, according to the Court, "revealed a distinctly anticompetitive bent."[19]

The Court found Ski Company's prior, "presumably profitable," collaboration with Highlands significant because it "shed ... light upon

---

merger to monopoly," which should have created its own antitrust concerns).

16.   *Trinko*, 540 U.S. at 399.

17.   *Id.* at 409.

18.   *Id.* In the context of predatory pricing, the Supreme Court adopted a recoupment theory akin to that described by the Court in the language quoted above. In *Brooke Group v. Brown & Williamson Tobacco*, 509 U.S. 209, 222 (1993), the Court held that in order to succeed on a predatory pricing theory, a plaintiff would have to show, among other things, "a dangerous probability" that the defendant would "recoup[] its investment in below-cost prices." *Id.* at 224. According to the Court, the essence of the violation is the elimination of competitors in the short run so as to be able to reap monopoly profits in the long run. *See, e.g.,* Cargill, Inc. v. Monfort of Colo., Inc., 479 U.S. 104, 117 (1986). *See generally* ANTITRUST LAW DEVELOPMENTS,*su pra* note 2, at 256-69.

19.   *Trinko*, 540 U.S. at 409.

the *motivation* of its refusal to deal,"[20]—that is, whether the refusal was "prompted not by competitive zeal but by anticompetitive *malice*."[21]

The *Trinko* Court ultimately found Verizon's alleged conduct distinguishable from that of Ski Company in that (1) there was no prior course of dealing (voluntary or otherwise) between Verizon and AT&T, and Verizon's prior conduct could "therefore … shed[] no light upon the *motivation* of its refusal to deal";[22] and (2) the course of dealing at issue in *Trinko* was not voluntary, but rather compelled by the 1996 Telecommunications Act; thus there was no reason to infer that Verizon was foregoing an otherwise profitable arrangement in refusing to cooperate with AT&T. "Verizon's reluctance to interconnect at the cost-based rate of compensation available under [the 1996 Telecommunications Act] tells us nothing about dreams of monopoly."[23]

The *Trinko* Court stated that its holding would be unchanged "even if [it] considered to be established law the 'essential facilities' doctrine crafted by some lower courts."[24] Under the doctrine, courts have imposed upon monopolists a duty to provide reasonable access to "facilities under the monopolist's control and without which one cannot

---

20. *Id.* (emphasis added). Ski Company apparently never offered any efficiency-based justification for its refusal to deal with Highlands, e.g., that Highlands was free-riding on Ski Company's customer base and/or that channeling more customers onto the three Ski Company mountains would have allowed Ski Company to achieve economies of scale. *Aspen Skiing*, 472 U.S. at 608.

21. *Id.* (emphasis added). This language has led some to question whether the Court meant to make the legality of a refusal to deal depend on the monopolist's subjective "malice" or "anticompetitive bent." For further discussion of this view, *see, e.g.,* Adam Candeub, Trinko *and Re-Grounding The Refusal To Deal Doctrine*, 66 U. PITT. L. REV. 821, 854 (2005).

22. *Trinko*, 540 U.S. at 409 (emphasis added).

23. *Id.* Having found that Verizon's alleged conduct did not violate existing § 2 standards, the Court found no reason to add Verizon's conduct to "the few existing exceptions from the proposition that there is no duty to aid competitors," particularly in light of the regulatory structure imposed by the 1996 Telecommunications Act, which was "designed to deter and remedy anticompetitive harm." *Id.* at 399.

24. *Id.* The Second Circuit's opinion below had found that plaintiffs had stated a claim against Verizon under the "essential facilities" doctrine. Law Offices of Curtis V. Trinko v. Bell Atl. Corp., 305 F.3d 89, 107-08 (2d Cir. 2002).

effectively compete."[25] The theory has been applied, for example, in requiring AT&T to provide rival long distance carrier MCI "interconnection" access to the AT&T long distance telephone network.[26] Citing an article by a leading commentator highly critical of the essential facilities doctrine,[27] the *Trinko* Court stated that "[w]e have never recognized such a doctrine . . . and we find no need either to recognize it or to repudiate it here."[28] The Court noted that, even if viable, the essential facilities doctrine requires the "unavailability of access to the 'essential facilities.'"[29] The 1996 Telecommunications Act compels access as a matter of statute, therefore "mak[ing] it unnecessary to impose a judicial doctrine of forced access."[30] The *Trinko* Court also

---

25. *Id.* at 107.
26. *See* MCI Communs. Corp. v. AT&T, 708 F.2d 1081, 1132 (7th Cir. 1983). The Seventh Circuit stated four elements for an essential facilities claim: "(1) control of the essential facility by a monopolist; (2) a competitor's inability practically or reasonably to duplicate the essential facility; (3) the denial of the use of the facility to a competitor; and (4) the feasibility of providing the facility." *Id.* at 1132-33; *see also, e.g.*, ANTITRUST LAW DEVELOPMENTS, *supra* note 2, at 278-84 (discussing authority); WILLIAM C. HOLMES, INTELLECTUAL PROPERTY AND ANTITRUST LAW § 6.07 (2004) ("HOLMES").
27. *See* Phillip Areeda, *Essential Facilities: An Epithet in Need of Limiting Principles*, 58 ANTITRUST L.J. 841 (1989).
28. *Trinko*, 540 U.S. at 410-11.
29. *Id.* at 411.
30. *Id.* The Court's comments concerning the essential facilities doctrine may signal its intent to limit the doctrine severely, if not to repudiate it altogether. *See, e.g.*, Pocono Invitational Sports Camp v. NCAA, 317 F. Supp. 2d 569, 587 n.23 (E.D. Pa. 2004) (noting *Trinko* "calls the use of the [essential facilities] doctrine into question except in the most extreme cases."). *But cf.* MetroNet Servs. v. Qwest Corp., 383 F.3d 1124 (9th Cir. 2004) (court dismissed essential facilities theory on narrow ground that the regulatory regime provided access; no suggestion that *Trinko* had rejected the doctrine altogether); Applera Corp. v. MJ Research, 349 F. Supp. 2d 338, 347 n.6 (D. Conn. 2004) (declining to dismiss an essential facilities theory; noting only that "the Supreme Court [in *Trinko*] has neither recognized nor repudiated the essential facilities doctrine"); Nobody In Particular Presents, Inc. v. Clear Channel Communs., 311 F. Supp. 2d 1048, 1110-14 (D. Colo. 2004) (denying defense motion for summary judgment on essential facilities claim; no suggestion that doctrine was rejected by *Trinko*).

Some have argued that the essential facilities doctrine should not in any event apply to "facilities" that are protected by intellectual property. To

rejected the theory of "monopoly leveraging," another rationale embraced by the Court of Appeals below.[31] Following *Trinko*, a number of courts have dismissed refusal-to-deal claims brought against incumbent local telephone providers and other regulated defendants.[32]

The impact of *Trinko* on refusals to deal in respect of intellectual property remains unclear. For example, under *Trinko*, will a refusal to deal concerning intellectual property be immune from Section 2 liability except upon a showing that the refusal represented a sacrifice of short-term profits for long-term monopoly gains?[33] Will holders of intellectual

---

hold otherwise, they argue, would dampen the incentive to innovate. HERBERT HOVENKAMP, MARK D. JANIS & MARK LEMLEY, IP AND ANTITRUST: AN ANALYSIS OF ANTITRUST PRINCIPLES APPLIED TO INTELLECTUAL PROPERTY LAW § 13 at 13-16 (2005) ("HOVENKAMP IP"); Abbott B. Lipsky & J. Gregory Sidak, *Essential Facilities*, 51 STAN. L. REV. 1187, 1219 (1999).

31.   *Trinko*, 540 U.S. at 415 n.4.   Under monopoly leveraging theory, some courts had found that a monopolist could be liable under Section 2 for using its monopoly power in one market to gain a competitive advantage in another market, even where it did not threaten to monopolize that second market. *See, e.g.*, Berkey Photo v. Eastman Kodak Co., 603 F.2d 263, 275 (2d Cir. 1979). In *Trinko*, however, the Supreme Court held that "[t]o the extent the Court of Appeals dispensed with a requirement that there be a 'dangerous probability of success' in monopolizing a second market, it erred." 540 U.S. at 415 n.4.

32.   *See, e.g.*, Covad Communs. v. BellSouth Corp., 374 F.3d 1044 (11th Cir. 2004); *MetroNet*, 383 F.3d 1124; Levine v. BellSouth Corp., 302 F. Supp. 2d 1358 (S.D. Fla. 2004); N.Y. Mercantile Exch. v. Intercont'l Exch., 323 F. Supp. 2d 559 (S.D.N.Y. 2004). *But see* Am. Cent. E. Tex. Gas v. Union Pac. Res. Group, No. 02-41010, 2004 WL 136091 (5th Cir. Jan. 27, 2004) (unpublished) (upholding arbitral decision that pipeline owner's refusal to deal amounted to a violation of Section 2 notwithstanding *Trinko*).

33.   *Compare MetroNet*, 383 F.3d at 1134 (relying on *Trinko*; summary judgment for defendant in refusal-to-deal case where defendant's conduct "[did] not entail a sacrifice of short-term profits for long-term gain"), *with* Creative Copier Servs. v. Xerox Corp., 344 F. Supp. 2d 858, 866-67 (D. Conn. 2004) (rejecting argument that claim must be dismissed for lack of allegations that company refusing to deal had sacrificed short-term profits: "[N]owhere in *Trinko* did the Court indicate that a complaint should be dismissed if it fails to recite the magic words 'no short-term profit.'"), *and Nobody In Particular Presents*, 311 F. Supp. 2d at 1112-14 (refusal-to-deal claim survived summary judgment where defendant alleged to have changed a long-standing practice, "sacrific[ing] short-

property that terminate existing license arrangements be subject to greater risk of Section 2 liability than holders that refuse to enter any arrangement at all?[34] Will the motives for refusals to license intellectual property be scrutinized for evidence of "anticompetitive conduct"?[35] Or will owners of intellectual property be free to refuse to license regardless

---

term gains in hopes of destroying [competitors] and reaping long-term monopolistic profits"). *See also Trinko* ABA Seminar, *supra* note 5, at 4 (remarks of Herbert Hovenkamp) ("A unilateral refusal to deal will not be actionable [under *Trinko*] unless you can show that the defendant gave up short run profits in order to injure or exclude the rival who has requested the dealing. "); McDavid & Mason, *supra* note 5 (*Trinko* "leaves open the question of what other kinds of conduct short of a sacrifice of short-term profits would be sufficient to condemn a monopolist's behavior as predatory ..."); Skitol, *supra* note 5, at 3 ("*Trinko* might ... mean ... that a monopolist's showing that its conduct maximized short-term profits ... will always thus be a dispositive defense to any Section 2 claim."); Simon Genevaz, *Against Immunity for Unilateral Refusals to Deal in Intellectual Property: Why Antitrust Law Should Not Distinguish Between IP & Other Property Rights*, 19 BERKELEY TECH. L.J. 741, 780-81 (2004) ("Genevaz") (arguing that *Trinko* does not preclude methods other than "sacrifice" test to show anticompetitive intent in refusal-to-deal cases).

34.   The Eleventh Circuit has held that "*Trinko* now effectively makes the unilateral termination of a voluntary course of dealing a *requirement* for a valid refusal-to-deal claim under *Aspen.*" *Covad*, 374 F.3d at 1049 (emphasis added) (following *Trinko* and dismissing refusal-to-deal and essential facilities claims by Internet service provider alleging incumbent local phone company failed to provide reasonable access); *see also* Z-Tel Communs. v. SBC Communs., 331 F. Supp. 2d 513, 527 (E.D. Tex. 2004) (noting *Covad* statement regarding "requirement" of prior voluntary course of dealing; denying dismissal on basis that defendant local phone company allegedly had voluntarily dealt with entities similar to plaintiff before enactment of Telecommunications Act of 1996); 3 AREEDA & HOVENKAMP, *supra* note 1, ¶ 773(g), at 199-200 (Supp. 2004) ("[T]he [*Trinko*] Court made the existence of a previous voluntary relationship very close to dispositive."). *But cf. Creative Copier Servs.*, 344 F. Supp. 2d at 867-68 (applying *Trinko* to dismiss refusal-to-deal claim; "it cannot be that any time an owner of intellectual property offers a free license of that property, the antitrust laws preclude the owner from ever charging for a license in the future").

35.   *See, e.g.*, Morris Communs. v. PGA Tour, 364 F.3d 1288, 1294-95 (11th Cir. 2004) (post-*Trinko*; Court requires refusal-to-deal defendant to show "legitimate business purpose," rebuttable by showing "pretext").

of their motives? Will the level of regulation affecting the intellectual property at issue influence antitrust risk for refusals to license?[36]

In *Schor v. Abbott Laboratories*,[37] the court considered the impact of *Trinko* in the context of a monopoly leveraging claim involving a patented drug product. The court dismissed plaintiffs' claims on the pleadings and observed that monopoly leveraging, "presupposes anticompetitive conduct," and that "not all conduct that hurts competitors is anticompetitive or a violation of the antitrust laws."[38] The case did not involve an outright refusal to license or sell a patented product, but rather an allegation that a patentee disadvantaged competitors by substantially increasing the price of its patented drug product to competitors for use in a combination therapy, while not reflecting such a price increase in its own combination product. An end purchaser accused the patentee of thereby leveraging its patent exclusivity on the individual drug product to the detriment of competition in the combination market. After noting the Supreme Court's reference to monopoly leveraging in *Trinko*, the court wrote, "[t]here is sparse case law regarding if or how the monopoly leveraging theory applies to conduct by a patentee, and what little case law there is does not concern a price increase by a patent holder."[39] The court nevertheless found it "appropriate to analogize refusal to deal cases with the price increases at issue here because if a patentee has the right to refuse to sell its product altogether, it has the right to raise the price."[40] The court ultimately held that the patentee, by virtue of its patent rights, did have the right to refuse to sell altogether,[41] and therefore the price increase could not be viewed as "anticompetitive conduct."[42] The court

---

36. *See In re* Remeron Antitrust Litig., 335 F. Supp. 2d 522, 530-31 (D.N.J. 2004) (declining to hold that regulated nature of prescription drug industry warranted antitrust caution: "'[Under *Trinko*] when there is nothing built into the regulatory scheme which performs the antitrust function, the benefits of antitrust are worth its sometimes considerable disadvantages.'").

37. No. 05-C-1592, 2005 WL 1653606 (N.D. Ill. July 12, 2005).

38. *Id.* at *5.

39. *Id.* The court also noted that the patents held by defendant also covered the combination of its drug with other products and therefore covered both the single product and the combination markets.

40. *Id.*

41. In this regard, the Court principally relied on the Federal Circuit's decision in *Xerox. See infra* § A.2.b(2) (for discussion of *Xerox*).

42. In contrast, in *Service Employees International Union Health & Welfare Fund v. Abbott Laboratories*, No. C 04-4203 CW, 2005 WL 528323

held that "a patentee's exercise of its statutorily granted market power does not constitute a Sherman Act violation, even if such conduct affects a second market."[43]

2. Refusals to Deal in Intellectual Property: A Split Over Whether the Presumption of Free Choice Is Rebuttable

Even prior to *Trinko*, courts that addressed refusals to deal in the context of intellectual property generally agreed that there is a presumption that a holder of intellectual property should not face antitrust liability for unilaterally refusing to license that property.[44] The courts, however, disagree on whether and, if so, under what circumstances, the presumption may be rebutted. The effect of *Trinko* on these two lines of cases remains unresolved.

a. Antitrust Limits on Intellectual Property Rights: The View That a Refusal to License Can Be the Basis for Antitrust Liability in Certain Limited Circumstances

This section (1) examines the leading cases—*Data General Corp. v. Grumman Systems Support Corp.*[45] and *Image Technical Services v. Eastman Kodak Co.*[46]—holding that unilateral refusals to license intellectual property can, in limited circumstances, form the basis for antitrust liability, and (2) examines other authorities that arguably support this view.

(N.D. Cal. Mar. 2, 2005), the court confronted the same allegations of monopoly leveraging (same defendant, same drug product) and declined to dismiss the complaint. The court relied on *Image Technical Services v. Eastman Kodak Co.*, 125 F.3d 1195 (9th Cir. 1997) ("*Kodak II*"), for the proposition that plaintiff had adequately alleged a monopoly leveraging claim. *Id.* at *3. The court further held that "defendant's assertion that its patents preclude liability under federal antitrust law is not persuasive." *Id.* For further discussion of *Kodak II*, see subsection A.2.a(1), below.

43. *Schor*, 2005 WL 1653606, at *7.
44. *See infra* § A.2.a, A.2.b (discussing cases).
45. 36 F.3d 1147 (1st Cir. 1994).
46. 125 F.3d 1195 (9th Cir. 1997).

(1) Data General and Kodak II

In *Data General*, the First Circuit, considering a refusal to deal certain copyrighted software, established a strong but rebuttable presumption that refusals to license intellectual property are not actionable under Section 2. The court held that "while exclusionary conduct can include a monopolist's unilateral refusal to license a copyright, an author's desire to exclude others from use of its copyrighted work is a presumptively valid business justification for any immediate harm to consumers."[47] The court explained that, while it was not holding "that an antitrust plaintiff can never rebut this presumption," rebuttal would be possible only in "rare cases" in which "imposing antitrust liability is unlikely to frustrate the objectives of the Copyright Act."[48] According to the court, the objective of the Copyright Act is to encourage innovation and creativity:

> [I]n passing the Copyright Act, Congress ... made an empirical assumption that allowing copyright holders to collect license fees and exclude others from using their works creates a system of incentives that promotes consumer welfare in the long term by encouraging investment in the creation of desirable artistic and functional works of expression.[49]

---

47.   36 F.3d at 1187. According to the court, a unilateral refusal to deal is prima facie exclusionary only if there is "evidence of *harm* to the competitive process," as opposed to individual competitors. *Id.* at 1183. Where this is shown, the defendant can rebut the plaintiff's *prima facie* case by showing a "valid business justification" for the refusal, that is, "countervailing *benefits* to the competitive process." *Id.* The court noted that "pursuit of efficiency and quality control might be legitimate competitive reasons for an otherwise exclusionary refusal to deal, while the desire to maintain a monopoly market share or thwart the entry of competitors would not." *Id.* As noted above, however, when the refusal to deal involves copyrights, the First Circuit applied a presumption of business justification.

48.   *Id.* at 1187 n.64.

49.   *Id.* at 1186-87. In this connection, the court noted that "one reason why the Copyright Act fosters investment and innovation is that it may allow the author to earn monopoly profits by licensing the copyright to others or reserving the copyright for the other's exclusive use." *Id.* at 1184. Thus, in order to accomplish such long-term objectives, "at least in a particular market and for a particular period of time, the Copyright Act tolerates

The *Data General* court did not explain how a plaintiff could show, in a particular "rare" case, that the objectives of the Copyright Act would not be threatened by penalizing a copyright holder for a refusal to license. The court did suggest that the presumption might be rebutted if a defendant's copyrights had been acquired "in any unlawful manner."[50] But the court rejected plaintiff's reliance on the fact that, by refusing to license its diagnostic software, Data General had reversed a long-standing practice of assisting plaintiff to participate in the aftermarket for servicing Data General's computer equipment. The court explained that, unlike the Supreme Court in *Aspen Skiing*, it was "unable to view [defendant's] market practices in both competitive and noncompetitive conditions"; Data General "ha[d] always been a monopolist in the [relevant] market, and competitive conditions ha[d] never prevailed."[51] Accordingly, the First Circuit concluded that "it would not be 'appropriate to infer' from [Data General's] change of heart that its former policies 'satisfy consumer demand in free competitive markets.'"[52]

In *Kodak II*,[53] the Ninth Circuit adopted what it characterized as a modified version of the *Data General* "rebuttable presumption" test.[54] The plaintiffs in *Kodak II* were independent service organizations ("ISOs") that competed with Kodak to provide maintenance and repair service for the copiers Kodak manufactured. After a period in which parts for the Kodak equipment were generally available to ISOs, Kodak restricted the ISOs' ability to procure replacement parts, thus making it difficult for them to compete in the service market. Plaintiffs alleged that Kodak had (1) illegally tied sales of parts for its copiers to maintenance and repair services for such copiers and (2) monopolized the service market for Kodak equipment by refusing to sell replacement parts to

---

behavior that may harm both consumers and competitors." *Id.* at 1184-85.

50.   *Id.* at 1188.
51   *Id.*
52.   *Id.* (quoting Aspen Skiing Co. v. Aspen Highlands Skiing Corp., 472 U.S. 585, 603 (1985)); *see also* Storage Tech. v. Custom Hardware Eng'g & Consulting, 2006-2 Trade Cas. (CCH) ¶ 75,434, at 106,049-50 (D. Mass. 2006) (granting summary judgment on § 2 claims premised upon defendant's refusal to license or to provide access to copyrighted code).
53.   125 F.3d 1195 (9th Cir. 1997).
54.   *Id.* at 1218.

ISOs. After the district court granted summary judgment to Kodak, the case eventually made its way to the Supreme Court.[55]

The Supreme Court reversed. The Court's principal holding was that, despite the fact that Kodak did not possess monopoly power in the sale of photocopy equipment, it could possess such power in the aftermarkets for replacement parts and service for its own copiers. In essence, the Court found that, having made the decision to purchase a Kodak copier, customers could be considered "locked in" to Kodak parts and service. Given the cost of major photocopy equipment, customers might not be able easily to switch to substitutes if the price of Kodak parts and service got too high.[56] With respect to the refusal-to-deal claim, the Supreme Court, citing *Aspen Skiing*, stated that "a firm can refuse to deal with its competitors. But such a right is not absolute; it exists only if there are legitimate competitive reasons for the refusal."[57] The Supreme Court found that plaintiff had presented evidence that Kodak had used its dominance over replacement parts to diminish competition in the service market and that there was a fact dispute concerning Kodak's business justifications for its actions.[58] Notably, the issue of the patents and copyrights that Kodak held on certain of its parts was not raised by Kodak.

The case was tried to a jury on remand, which reached a verdict for the plaintiff ISOs. Kodak appealed to the Ninth Circuit and raised the question whether its desire to exploit its patents and copyrights could serve as a valid business justification for its refusal to deal with the ISOs.[59] The Ninth Circuit's answer, citing *Data General*, was a qualified "yes":

> Given the interplay of the antitrust and intellectual property laws ... Kodak's contention that its refusal to sell its parts to ISOs was based on

---

55.   Eastman Kodak Co. v. Image Technical Servs., 504 U.S. 451 (1992) ("*Kodak I*").
56.   *Id.* at 473-83.
57.   *Id.* at 483 n.32.
58.   *Id.* at 482-86. For criticism of the *Kodak* I and *Aspen* decisions, see Carlton, *supra* note 15, which argues that *Aspen* penalized *change*, creating incentive for firms to shy away from potentially efficient collaborations, and that *Kodak I* overlooked that, even if forced to deal with ISOs, Kodak was free to manipulate competition through its pricing of replacement parts over which it had discretion. *Id.* at 676.
59.   Plaintiff did not pursue its tying claim at trial. *Kodak II*, 125 F.3d at 1201.

its reluctance to sell its patented or copyrighted parts was a presumptively legitimate business justification. Kodak may assert that its desire to profit from its intellectual property rights justifies its conduct, and the jury should presume that this justification is legitimately procompetitive.[60]

"Nonetheless," the court held, "this presumption is rebuttable."[61] While the *Data General* court only identified one means to rebut the presumption—that the intellectual property had been obtained in an "unlawful manner"—the Ninth Circuit held that "the presumption may also be rebutted by evidence of *pretext*."[62]   The Ninth Circuit acknowledged that evidence concerning Kodak's "subjective motivation" to "beat the competition," or even its "hostility to competitors," would not by itself establish pretext.[63]   Instead, according to the court, "[e]vidence regarding the state of mind of Kodak employees may show pretext, when such evidence suggests that the proffered business justification played no part in the decision to act."[64]

The court therefore held that the jury's verdict was supported by substantial evidence that Kodak's intellectual property justification was pretextual, i.e., that a desire to protect its intellectual property rights was not the real reason for its refusal to deal with the ISOs. Significantly, although Kodak refused to sell thousands of parts to the ISOs, only 65 were patented and fewer than all were copyrighted. The court drew a sharp distinction between the case before it "concerning a blanket refusal that included protected and unprotected products" and cases where the refusal involved *only* protected products.[65]   Moreover, Kodak's parts manager testified that "patents did not cross [his] mind" at the time Kodak instituted its policy of refusing to deal parts.[66]

---

60.   *Id.* at 1219 (citation omitted).
61.   *Id.*
62.   *Id.* (emphasis added).
63.   *Id.*
64.   *Id.*
65.   *Id.* (citing Miller Insituform, Inc. v. Insituform of N. Am., Inc., 830 F.2d 606, 607 (6th Cir. 1987); United States v. Westinghouse Elec., 648 F.2d 642, 647 (9th Cir. 1981); SCM Corp. v. Xerox Corp., 645 F.2d 1195, 1197 (2d Cir. 1981)).
66.   *Id.* at 1219. Despite its finding that the jury instructions inadequately addressed Kodak's intellectual property rights, the Ninth Circuit found the error harmless in light of the evidence of pretext. *Id.* Freed, *supra* note 1, criticizes this conclusion as "based on a seemingly superficial review of the evidence." *Id.* at 33-34.

In reaching its conclusion that a rebuttable presumption was appropriate, the Ninth Circuit considered a number of factors:

(1) *The Right to Exclude Conferred by Copyrights.* With respect to the copyrights, the court acknowledged that the federal copyright laws "grant[] to the copyright owner the exclusive right to distribute the protected work."[67] This includes the right to "'refrain from vending or licensing.'"[68] Just as patent law tolerates similar restrictions with respect to patents, copyright law tolerates near-term restrictions on competition in copyrighted works to foster the long-term goal of "stimulat[ing] artistic creativity for the general public good."[69]

(2) *The Right to Exclude Conferred by the Patent Laws.* The court also acknowledged that "[p]atent laws 'reward the inventor with the power to exclude others from the making, using, or selling [of a patented] invention in the United States.'"[70] Thus, "a patent amounts to a permissible monopoly over the protected work."[71] "The right to license [a] patent, exclusively or otherwise, or to refuse to license at all, is the *'untrammeled right'* of the patentee."[72] The court also noted that the patent laws are designed to encourage innovation, thus benefiting the public "from the faster introduction of inventions, and the resulting increase in market competition."[73]

67. *Kodak II*, 125 F.3d at 1215 (citing 17 U.S.C. § 106).
68. *Id.* (quoting Data Gen. Corp. v. Grumman Sys. Support Corp., 36 F.3d 1147, 1186 (1st Cir. 1994)).
69. *Id.*
70. *Id.* at 1214 (quoting SCM Corp. v. Xerox Corp., 645 F.2d 1195, 1203 (2d Cir. 1981)).
71. *Id.* at 1215 (citing Zenith Radio Corp. v. Hazeltine Research, 395 U.S. 100, 135 (1969)).
72. *Id.* at 1215 (emphasis added) (quoting United States v. Westinghouse Elec., 648 F.2d 642, 647 (9th Cir. 1981)).
73. *Id.* at 1214-15. Some have argued the standard assumption that the granting of rights to exclude serves to enhance the long-term incentives to innovate may not always hold true. For example, when one firm gains exclusive access to a crucial technology, or acquires a substantial portfolio of blocking patents, the incentive of rivals to innovate in related areas may decrease. MacKie-Mason, *supra* note 1, at 3; Carl Shapiro, *Navigating the Patent Thicket: Cross Licenses, Patent Pools and Standard Setting*, Remarks Before Nat'l Bureau on Economic Research

(3) *1988 Amendments to the Patent Act.* The Ninth Circuit noted that, in 1988, Congress amended the Patent Act to provide that "[n]o patent owner otherwise entitled to relief for infringement ... of a patent shall be denied relief or be deemed guilty of misuse or illegal extension of the patent right by reason of ... [the patent owner's] refus[al] to license or use any rights to the patent."[74] In *Data General*, the First Circuit suggested that the amendment "may even herald the prohibition of all antitrust claims ... premised on a refusal to license a patent."[75] The Ninth Circuit, disagreeing with such a broad interpretation, stated that "[t]he amended statutory language does not compel this result" in part because it was merely "intended to codify existing law."[76] The court did allow that "[t]he amendment ... indicate[s] congressional intent to protect the core patent right of exclusion."[77]

(4) *Limits on the General Right to Exclude.* While acknowledging the strong support in law and policy for the "right of a patent or

---

Seminar: Innovation Policy and the Economy (Apr. 2000), *available at* http://www.haas.berkeley.edu/~shapiro/thicket.pdf ("With cumulative innovation and multiple blocking patents, stronger patent rights can have the perverse effect of stifling, not encouraging, innovation."); Transcript at 24-25, FTC Hearings on Global and Innovation-Based Competition (Oct. 12, 1995) (Dkt./Case No. P951201) (remarks of Joseph Stiglitz) (wrong to assume "that the broader the patent rights are, the better it is for innovation, and that isn't always correct, because we have an innovation system in which one innovation builds on another. If you get monopoly rights down at the bottom, you may stifle competition that uses those patents later on . . . so the breadth and utilization of patent rights can be used not only to stifle competition, but also have adverse effects in the long run on innovation."), *available at* http://www.ftc.gov/opp/ global/GC101295.htm; Lao I, *supra* note 1, at 215-18 (surveying sources suggesting lack of strong link between patent protection and degree of innovation).

74. 35 U.S.C. § 271(d).
75. Data Gen. Corp. v. Grumman Sys. Support Corp., 36 F.3d 1147, 1187 (1st Cir. 1994). *See generally* Calkins, *supra* note 1, at 196-200 (discussing 1988 amendments).
76. *Kodak II*, 125 F.3d at 1215 n.7.
77. *Id.*; *see also* Grid Sys. v. Tex. Instruments, 771 F. Supp. 1033, 1037 n.2 (N.D. Cal. 1991) (finding that the 1988 amendments relate "only to patent misuse," not antitrust).

copyright holder to refuse to sell or license protected work,"[78] the Ninth Circuit held that "[t]his basic right of exclusion does have limits."[79]   For example, as noted, a patent or copyright confers no protection from antitrust liability if it was unlawfully acquired.[80]   Nor does intellectual property provide protection if the owner attempts to extend exclusivity beyond the grant of the patent or copyright in question or engages in collusive activity such as price fixing, market allocation, or the like.[81]

The Ninth Circuit drew support for its conclusion that unilateral refusals to license intellectual property are not immune from antitrust scrutiny from footnote 29 of the Supreme Court's decision in *Kodak I*. In that footnote, the Supreme Court wrote that it had "held many times that [monopoly] power gained through some natural and legal advantage, *such as a patent, copyright* or business acumen can give rise to liability if a 'seller exploits his dominant position in one market to expand his empire into the next.'"[82]   The Ninth Circuit in *Kodak II* interpreted footnote 29 as stating "that a monopolist who acquires a dominant position in one market through patents and copyrights may violate Section 2 if the monopolist exploits that dominant position to enhance a monopoly in another market."[83]   Footnote 29, however, appears in the Supreme Court's discussion of plaintiff's *tying* claims (brought under Section 1 of the Sherman Act), not in its treatment of Section 2.   The Ninth Circuit was not troubled by this fact, noting that "the Section 2 discussion frequently refers back to the Section 1 discussion, and the Court's statement ... is broad enough to cover monopoly leveraging under Section 2."[84]

78.	*Id.*
79.	*Id.* at 1216.
80.	*Id.*; *see also, e.g., Data Gen.*, 36 F.3d at 1186; SCM Corp. v. Xerox Corp., 645 F.2d 1195, 1208-09 (2d Cir. 1981). *See generally infra* § B.1 (discussion of antitrust treatment of fraudulently obtained patents).
81.	*Kodak II*, 125 F.3d at 1216-17; *see also, e.g.,* 3 AREEDA & HOVENKAMP, *supra* note 1, ¶ 709(b).
82.	*Kodak I*, 504 U.S. at 479 n.29 (emphasis added).
83.	*Kodak II*, 125 F.3d at 1215-16.
84.	*Id.* at 1216; *accord* MacKie-Mason, *supra* note 1, at 6. *But see* CSU, LLC v. Xerox Corp. (*In re* Indep. Serv. Orgs. Antitrust Litig.), 203 F.3d 1322, 1327 (Fed. Cir. 2000) ("*Xerox*") (disagreeing with Ninth Circuit and concluding that footnote 29 does not pertain to § 2 analysis); Gleklen I, *supra* note 1, at 7-8 (same).

(2) Other Authority

Although the *Data General* and *Kodak II* rulings are the most direct articulations of a standard that allows for antitrust liability for purely unilateral refusals to license intellectual property, there is support for the proposition elsewhere.

- *United States v. Microsoft.* In the *Microsoft* case (which did not focus on a pure refusal to license, but rather on Microsoft's refusal to license except on terms it dictated), the district court wrote that "copyright law does not give Microsoft blanket authority to license (or refuse to license) its intellectual property as it sees fit."[85] On appeal, the District of Columbia Circuit rejected as frivolous Microsoft's argument that "'[I]f intellectual property rights have been lawfully acquired ... their subsequent exercise cannot give rise to antitrust liability.'"[86] According to the Court, "[t]hat [argument] is no more correct than the proposition that use of one's personal property, such as a baseball bat, cannot give rise to tort liability."[87]

- *DOJ/FTC Intellectual Property Guidelines.* The 1995 U.S. Department of Justice and FTC Antitrust Guidelines for the Licensing of Intellectual Property state that, while antitrust does not "impose on [an] intellectual property owner an obligation to license that property to others," the agencies "apply the same general antitrust principles to conduct involving intellectual property that they apply to any other form of property."[88] According to the *Guidelines*, "[i]ntellectual property is ... neither particularly free from scrutiny under the antitrust laws, nor particularly suspect under them."[89] The *Guidelines* also suggest

85.   United States v. Microsoft Corp., No. CIV. A. 98-1232 (TPJ), 1998 WL 614485, at *15 (D.D.C. Sept. 14, 1998).

86.   United States v. Microsoft Corp., 253 F.3d 34, 63 (D.C. Cir. 2001).

87.   *Id.* It is worth noting that in the next sentence, the D.C. Circuit cited with approval *Xerox*, in which, as discussed in § A.2.b(2), (3), below, the Federal Circuit held that unilateral refusals to license valid intellectual property rights are justified without regard to the motivation for the refusal. *See id.* (citing *Xerox*, 203 F.3d 1322, 1325 (Fed. Cir. 2000)).

88.   INTELLECTUAL PROPERTY GUIDELINES,*su pra* note 4, § 2.1.

89.   *Id.;se e also id.* § 2.0 ("for the purpose of antitrust analysis, the Agencies regard intellectual property as being essentially comparable to any other form of property.").

that while monopoly power can be obtained lawfully through intellectual property, such power "would be relevant to the ability of an intellectual property owner to harm competition through unreasonable conduct in connection with such property."[90]

In a 2001 brief opposing *certiorari* in the *Xerox* matter,[91] the United States indicated that it would not support a rule "that a refusal to sell or license property protected by a valid patent may never be the basis of an antitrust violation except in the circumstances of an illegal tying arrangement."[92] Moreover, in the government's view:

[A] lawful monopolist [by virtue of intellectual property or otherwise] could properly be held liable under § 2 for a refusal to deal only if it ha[s] monopoly power *and* if its refusal to deal sacrificed profit available from exercising that monopoly power in order to exclude competition and thereby to create additional market power—only if, in other words, it sought to ... "exclude rivals on some basis other than efficiency."[93]

---

90.   *Id.* § 2.2. In the 1970s, the antitrust enforcement agencies were hostile toward the exercise of intellectual property rights, developing a list of prohibited practices that came to be known as the "Nine No-No's." As reflected, for example, in the INTELLECTUAL PROPERTY GUIDELINES, *supra* note 4, the Agencies' attitude toward intellectual property has changed dramatically. *See, e.g.*, Tom & Newberg, *supra* note 1 (discussing contrast between earlier periods and post-Guidelines period).

91.   CSU, LLC v. Xerox Corp. (*In re* Indep. Serv. Orgs. Antitrust Litig.), 203 F.3d 1322 (Fed. Cir. 2000) (discussed in detail *infra* § A.2.b(2)).

92.   Brief for the United States as Amicus Curiae at *7, CSU, LLC v. Xerox Corp., 2001 WL 34135314 (Sup. Ct. 2001) (No. 00-62) ("*Amicus Curiae Brief*").

93.   *Id.* at *8 (quoting Aspen Skiing Co. v. Aspen Highlands Skiing Corp., 472 U.S. 585, 605 (1985)). Other intellectual property regimes use compulsory licensing to limit patent holders' market power in the event of non-use. For example, the European Commission's Proposal for a Regulation on the Community Patent, which is intended to reflect the philosophy of Member States, would empower the Commission to grant a compulsory license in response to "defense patenting," *i.e.*, when a patent holder refuses to use a patent for more than three years after it has issued. *See* Sandra Schmieder, *Scope of Biotechnology Inventions in the United States and in Europe—Compulsory Licensing, Experimental Use and Arbitration: A Study of the Patentability of DNA-Related Inventions with*

b. Intellectual Property Rights As Inviolate: The View That a Refusal to License Cannot Be the Basis for Antitrust Liability

In contrast to *Kodak II*, there is substantial authority for the proposition that unilateral refusals to license bona fide intellectual property cannot form the basis of antitrust liability. This section (1) reviews certain early authority on this issue; (2) examines the Federal Circuit's decision in *CSU, LLC v. Xerox Corp. (In re Independent Service Organization Antitrust Litigation)* ("*Xerox*"),[94] in which the court disagreed with the Ninth Circuit's analysis in *Kodak II*; and (3) discusses cases decided after *Xerox.*

(1) Early Authority

The Supreme Court has long referred to the valid exercise of patent rights as an exception to the operation of the antitrust laws. Thus, in *Simpson v. Union Oil Co. of California*,[95] the Supreme Court referred to the exercise of patent rights as an exception to the antitrust laws: "The patent laws which give a 17-year monopoly on 'making, using or selling the invention' are *in pari materia* with the antitrust laws and modify them *pro tanto*."[96] In *Dawson Chemical v. Rohm & Haas Co.*,[97] the Court held that the "essence" of the patent grant is the "right to exclude others from profiting by the patented invention" and that "[c]ompulsory licensing is a rarity in our patent system."[98] In *United States v. United*

Special Emphasis on the Establishment of an Arbitration Based Compulsory Licensing System, 21 SANTA CLARA COMPUTER & HIGH TECH. L.J. 163, 169-70, 215 (2004).

94. 203 F.3d 1322 (Fed. Cir. 2000).
95. 377 U.S. 13 (1964).
96. *Id.* at 24 (English translation: "The patent laws ... relate to similar subject matter as the antitrust laws and modify those laws to that extent."); *see also, e.g.*, Precision Instrument Mfg. v. Auto. Maint. Mach., 324 U.S. 806, 811 (1945) (A patent "is an exception to the general rule against monopolies."). More generally, the Supreme Court has held that conduct specifically permitted by federal law cannot be deemed a violation of the antitrust laws. *See, e.g.*, United States v. Rock-Royal Co-Op, 307 U.S. 533, 560 (1939) (pricing authorized by agricultural cooperative statute).
97. 448 U.S. 176 (1980).
98. *Id.* at 215. It should be noted that courts sometimes order compulsory licensing to remedy the effects of other anticompetitive conduct, for example patent pools or other collusive conduct that has been adjudged to violate the Sherman Act. *See, e.g.*, United States v. Glaxo Group, 410

Shoe Machinery Co. of New Jersey,[99] the Court held that asserting patent rights "within the field covered by the patent law is not an offense against the Anti-Trust Act" and that an intellectual property owner "necessarily has the power of granting ... [a license] to some and withholding it from others."[100]   In *Continental Paper Bag v. Eastern Paper Bag*,[101] the Court noted that patents accord their owners "complete monopoly," and that their "exclusive right to make, use, and vend" their inventions is "so explicitly given and so complete that it would seem to need no further explanation than the word of the statute."[102]   As to copyrights, the Court held that "the owner of [a] copyright, if he pleases, may refrain from vending or licensing and content himself with simply exercising the right to exclude others from using his property."[103]

The lower courts followed suit.   In *SCM Corp. v. Xerox Corp.*,[104] Xerox was accused of violating Section 2 in part by virtue of its refusal to license its patents for plain paper copying.   The Second Circuit rejected plaintiff's contention that a unilateral refusal to license a patent should be treated as any other refusal to deal by a monopolist.[105]

U.S. 52, 64 (1973); United States v. Besser Mfg., 96 F. Supp. 304, 314 (E. D. Mich. 1951); United States v. Imperial Chem. Indus., 105 F. Supp. 215 (S.D.N.Y. 1952); *see also* 3 AREEDA & HOVENKAMP, *supra* note 1, ¶ 710.

99.   247 U.S. 32 (1918).

100.   *Id.* at 57, 58; *see also* Lewis Blind Stitch Match Co. v. Premium Mfg, 163 F. 950, 954 (8th Cir. 1908) ("[A] patentee is under no obligation to use or place upon the market a device or machine embodying his invention.").

101.   210 U.S. 405 (1908).

102.   *Id.* at 423-24; *see also, e.g.*, Hartford-Empire Co. v. United States, 323 U.S. 386, 417 (1945) ("[A] defendant hereafter acquiring a patent can[] ... elect to use it himself and refuse to license it, or to retain it and neither use nor license it.   These are options patent owners have always enjoyed."); E. Bement & Sons v. Nat'l Harrow Co., 186 U.S. 70, 94 (1902) (patent owner free to license some but not others); United States v. Am. Bell Tel. Co., 167 U.S. 224, 250 (1897) (An inventor "is [the] one who has discovered something of value.   It is his absolute property ... and he may insist upon all the advantages and benefits which the statute promises."); Extractol Process v. Hiram Walker & Sons, 153 F.2d 264, 268 (7th Cir. 1946) ("The patentee is the sole judge of the licensee he shall select, to make, to sell, or to use his patented article.   Patentee's reasons for selection of its licensee are of no concern to others").

103.   Fox Film Corp. v. Doyal, 286 U.S. 123, 127 (1932).

104.   645 F.2d 1195 (2d Cir. 1981).

105.   *Id.* at 1204.

According to the court, "[w]here a patent holder ... merely exercises his 'right to exclude others from making, using or selling the invention,' ... by refusing unilaterally to license his patent ... such conduct is expressly permitted by the patent laws."[106] The court did not discuss the possibility that a unilateral refusal to license nonetheless might be subject to antitrust liability if the refusal was based on something other than the patent owner's desire to profit from its intellectual property rights.[107] Instead, the Court held that "a patent holder is permitted to maintain his patent monopoly through conduct permissible under the patent laws."[108]

In *United States v. Westinghouse Electric*,[109] the Ninth Circuit, citing *SCM,* reached a similar result in a refusal to license case:

In advancing its [refusal to license] theory ... the government argues that an antitrust violation may be found where a patent holder does

---

106. *Id.*; *see also, e.g.*, Schering-Plough, Corp. v. FTC, 402 F.3d 1056, 1067 (11th Cir. 2005) ("[A] patent holder does not incur antitrust liability when it chooses to exclude others from its patented work."), *cert. denied*, 126 S. Ct. 2929 (2006); Unitherm Food Sys. v. Swift Eckrich, Inc., 375 F.3d 1341, 1356 (Fed. Cir. 2004) ("As a general rule, behavior conforming to the patent laws oriented towards procuring or enforcing a patent enjoys immunity from the antitrust laws."), *rev'd on other grounds*, 126 S. Ct. 980 (2006); Glass Equip. Dev. v. Besten, Inc., 174 F.3d 1337, 1343-44 (Fed. Cir. 1999) ("A patent owner who brings a lawsuit to enforce the statutory right to exclude others from making, using or selling the claimed invention is exempt from the antitrust laws, even though such a suit may have an anticompetitive effect."); Chisolm-Ryder Co. v. Mecca Bros., No. CIV-68-179, 1982 WL 1950, at *4 (W.D.N.Y. Dec. 31, 1982) (patent monopoly is "outside of the antitrust laws and its exercise within the patent grant is not violative thereof").
107. *See Kodak II*, 125 F.3d 1195, 1219 (9th Cir. 1997) (discussing such a requirement).
108. *SCM*, 645 F.2d at 1204. In *W.L. Gore & Associates v. Carlisle Corp.*, 529 F.2d 614 (3d Cir. 1976), the patent holder was accused of demanding exorbitant royalties in exchange for a license. *Id.* at 622-23. Rejecting a claim that this amounted to patent misuse, the court stated that the "general rule" is that "a patent empowers the owner to exact royalties as high as he can negotiate with the leverage of that monopoly." *Id.* at 623 (citing Brulotte v. Thys Co., 379 U.S. 29, 33 (1964)). The court went on to hold that "a royalty demand which is so high as to preclude acceptance of a license offer is, after all, not appreciably different from a refusal to license on any terms. The right to refuse to license is the essence of a patent holder's right under the patent law." *Id.*
109. 648 F.2d 642 (9th Cir. 1981).

precisely that which the patent laws authorize. Westinghouse has done no more than to license some of its patents and refuse to license others.[110]

According to the court, "[t]he right to license [a] patent, exclusively or otherwise, or to refuse to license at all, is the 'untrammeled right' of the patentee."[111]   The only exception noted by the court was where the patentee obtained the patent through "deliberate fraud," engaged in tying, or sought royalties on unpatented products.[112]

In *Miller Insituform, Inc. v. Insituform of North America*,[113] the Sixth Circuit, following *SCM* and *Westinghouse*, held that "a patent holder who lawfully acquires a patent cannot be held liable under Section 2 of the Sherman Act for maintaining the monopoly power he lawfully acquired by refusing to license the patent to others."[114]   The court also held that termination of a license was equally within the patentee's discretion: "by terminating the sublicense ... appellee merely exercised his power to exclude others from using [the patented invention], as was its right under 35 U.S.C. § 154. In so doing, it did not violate Section 2 of the Sherman Act."[115]

---

110.   *Id.* at 647.
111.   *Id.* The Ninth Circuit referenced this passage from *Westinghouse* in its *Kodak II* decision. *Kodak II*, 125 F.3d at 1215. The *Kodak II* court also cited *Westinghouse* for the proposition that it could find "no reported case in which a court has imposed antitrust liability for a unilateral refusal to sell or license a patent or copyright." *Id.* at 1216.   Despite its own statement in *Westinghouse* that patent holders enjoy an "untrammeled" right to refuse licenses, the Ninth Circuit in *Kodak II* held only that "*some* weight be given to the intellectual property rights of the monopolist" in "[h]armonizing antitrust monopoly theory with the monopolies granted by intellectual property law." *Id.* at 1217 (emphasis added).
112.   *Id.*
113.   830 F.2d 606 (6th Cir. 1987).
114.   *Id.* at 609.
115.   *Id.; see, e.g.*, Intergraph Corp. v. Intel Corp., 195 F.3d 1346, 1362 (Fed. Cir. 1999) (although decision turned on lack of competition between plaintiff computer makers and defendant chip manufacturer, Federal Circuit held that the market power sometimes conferred by patents does not "impose on the intellectual property owner an obligation to license the use of that property to others"); Cygnus Therapeutics Sys. v. ALZA Corp., 92 F.3d 1153, 1160 (Fed. Cir. 1996), *overruled on other grounds by* Nobelpharma AB v. Implant Innovations, 141 F.3d 1059 (Fed. Cir. 1998); Wahpeton Canvas Co. v. Bremer, 958 F. Supp. 1347 (N.D. Iowa

(2) *The Federal Circuit's Decision in Xerox*

The line of cases came to a head in the Federal Circuit's decision in *Xerox*.[116] The facts of the *Xerox* case were similar to those facing the Ninth Circuit in *Kodak II*: Xerox, a manufacturer of photocopiers,

1997) (summary judgment for patentee who selectively refused to sell patented aftermarket parts); Boston Sci. v. Schneider Europe AG, 983 F. Supp. 245, 269 (D. Mass. 1997) ("The patent is itself a government grant of monopoly and is therefore an exception to usual antitrust rules."); Axis, S.p.A. v. Micafil, Inc., 870 F.2d 1105 (6th Cir. 1989) (no antitrust claim for refusal to license patents; patentee "under no obligation to license"; refusal-to-deal claim dismissed); Crucible Inc. v. Stora Kopparbergs Bergslags, A.B., 701 F. Supp. 1157, 1162 (W.D. Pa. 1988) (citing *SCM*; "because the patents were lawfully acquired, the court concludes that Crucible's refusal to license (conduct permissible under the patent laws) does not trigger any liability under the antitrust laws."); GAF Corp. v. Eastman Kodak Co., 519 F. Supp. 1203, 1233 (S.D.N.Y. 1981) ("Kodak's unilateral refusal to license internally developed patents may not trigger liability under the patent laws."); Gates Learjet Corp. v. Magnasync Craig Corp., 339 F. Supp. 587, 601 (D. Colo. 1972) ("A patentee need not license anyone."); USM Corp. v. SPS Techs., 694 F.2d 505, 513 (7th Cir. 1982) ("[T]he essence of the patent grant is to allow the patentee to exclude competition in the use of the patented invention or ... to license competitors only on such terms as he sees fit.").

Also, in *In re E.I. du Pont de Nemours & Co.*, 96 F.T.C. 653 (1980), the Federal Trade Commission found "no authority for the proposition that DuPont should have licensed its technology," absent evidence that it "used unreasonable means to acquire its know-how, or that it joined with others in preventing access by competitors." *Id.* at 48-49. According to the Commission, "imposition of a duty to license might serve to chill the very kind of innovative process that led to DuPont's cost advantage." *Id.* at 49.

Cases involving copyrights have reached similar results. *See, e.g.*, Tricom, Inc. v. Elec. Data Sys., 902 F. Supp. 741, 743 (E.D. Mich. 1995) (rejecting antitrust claim; "Under patent and copyright law, EDS may not be compelled to license its proprietary software to anyone."); Advanced Computer Servs. v. MAI Sys., 845 F. Supp. 356, 370 (E.D. Va. 1994) (termination of licensing arrangement not an antitrust violation: "MAI is legally entitled to enforce its copyrights and prevent . . . infringement."); Corsearch, Inc. v. Thomson & Thomson, 792 F. Supp. 305, 322 (S.D.N.Y 1992) ("Under the copyright laws, the copyright owner has a right to license the use of its intellectual property and to terminate or limit that use in such manner as it deems appropriate.").

116. 203 F.3d 1322 (Fed. Cir. 2000).

instituted a policy of refusing to sell replacement parts to Independent Service Organizations against which Xerox competed in the service market. The ISOs sued, alleging that Xerox's refusal to sell violated Section 2 of the Sherman Act by unlawfully extending its monopoly power over replacement parts into the service market.[117] Unlike Kodak in the Ninth Circuit case, all of the Xerox replacement parts at issue were covered by patents or copyrights.[118]

Despite the similar factual scenarios, the Federal Circuit came to a conclusion contrary to that of the Ninth Circuit. The court began its analysis by noting that, while "[i]ntellectual property rights do not confer a privilege to violate the antitrust laws," the antitrust laws "do not negate the patentee's right to exclude others from patent property."[119] The court held that "[i]n the absence of any indication of illegal tying, fraud in the Patent and Trademark Office, or sham litigation, the patent holder may enforce the statutory right to exclude others from making, using or selling of the claimed invention free from liability under the antitrust laws."[120] "[W]e therefore will not inquire into [the patent holder's] subjective motivation for exerting his statutory rights, even though his refusal to sell or license his patented invention may have an anticompetitive effect, so long as that anticompetitive effect is not illegally extended beyond the statutory patent grant."[121]

The court also held that it is plaintiff's burden to show that one of the "exceptional situations" exists, e.g., tying, fraud, or sham enforcement.[122] And, even where plaintiff has met this burden, "he must then also prove the elements of the Sherman Act violation"—for example, that the patent holder possesses monopoly power in a properly defined market.[123]

With respect to copyrights, the court reached an analogous result. The court endorsed the conclusion of the *Data General* court that "an author's desire to exclude others from the use of its copyrighted work is

117. After a settlement agreement was reached in the case, one ISO plaintiff, Copier Servicing Unlimited, opted out of the agreement and pursued the claims.
118. *Xerox*, 203 F.3d at 1324-25.
119. *Id.* at 1325.
120. *Id.* at 1327.
121. *Id.* at 1327-28.
122. *Id.* at 1328.
123. *Id.*

a presumptively valid business justification for any immediate harm to consumers" arising from a refusal to license.[124]

The Federal Circuit rejected the notion, espoused by the Ninth Circuit in *Kodak II*, that a showing of "pretext" could overcome the presumption that a refusal to license intellectual property is justified. With respect to patents, the court stated that "[w]e see no more reason to inquire into the subjective motivation of Xerox in refusing to sell or license its patented works than we found in evaluating the subjective motivation of a patentee in bringing suit to enforce that same right."[125] With respect to copyrights, the court disapproved of the Ninth Circuit's allowing the jury to "second guess the subjective motivation of the copyright holder in asserting its statutory rights to exclude ... without properly weighing the presumption of legitimacy in asserting its rights under the copyright laws."[126] The court labeled the Ninth Circuit's "pretext" exception as "in reality a significant departure from the First Circuit's [*Data General*'s] central premise that rebutting the presumption would be an uphill battle and would only be appropriate in ... rare cases."[127]

The Federal Circuit also rejected the Ninth Circuit's conclusion that footnote 29 in the Supreme Court's opinion in *Kodak I* suggested that patent or copyright holders could face Section 2 liability for refusals to deal that resulted in a dominant position in a second market. The Federal Circuit held that the footnote signaled no such intention because, as presented to the Supreme Court, the case against Kodak was essentially a tying case under Section 1 in which no patents had been asserted in defense of the claims against Kodak. According to the court, "properly viewed within the framework of a tying case, the footnote can be interpreted as restating the undisputed premise that the patent holder cannot use his statutory right to refuse to sell patented parts to gain a

---

124. *Id.* at 1329 (citing Data Gen. Corp. v. Grumman Sys. Support Corp., 36 F.3d 1147, 1187 (1st Cir. 1994)).
125. *Id.* at 1327.
126. *Id.* at 1329.
127. *Id.*; *see also, e.g.*, Applera Corp. v. MJ Research, 349 F. Supp. 2d 338, 354 (D. Conn. 2004) ("The nature of a patent grant is exclusionary ... What is relevant in cases at the intersection of patent and antitrust law is whether conduct somehow exceeds the scope of the patent grant, and where ... this question is answered in the negative, there is no sound basis for inquiring into the patent holder's subjective motivation for exerting his statutory rights.").

monopoly in a market *beyond the scope of the patent.*"[128]   Indeed, the
court stated that "absent exceptional circumstances, a patent may confer
the right to exclude competition altogether in more than one antitrust
market."[129]

Plaintiff filed a petition for *certiorari* with the U.S. Supreme Court,
urging the Court to resolve the conflict in approach between the Ninth
and the Federal Circuits. The Court requested briefing from the Solicitor
General to express the views of the United States, which recommended
that the Court not hear the case. While acknowledging the apparent
circuit conflict, the government argued that the Federal Circuit's decision
need not be read as "making patent holders immune from liability under
Section 2 in all circumstances," noting that the Federal Circuit in *Xerox*
had acknowledged that efforts by the patent holder to exceed the scope of
the patent grant, e.g., through tying, were not immune from liability.[130]
The government also noted that he did not read the Federal Circuit as
saying that tying was the only method by which a patent holder might
improperly seek to exceed the scope of the patent grant, and therefore be
subject to antitrust liability for such efforts.[131] The government took no
express position on the disagreement between the Ninth and the Federal
Circuits on the role of "intent" evidence.[132] Rather, he observed that if
the Ninth Circuit in *Kodak II* had been confronted with an antitrust claim
based on a refusal to deal only patented or copyrighted parts (as in
Xerox) it might have reached a different result. The government
concluded that, in light of what it termed the "considerable uncertainty"
about the scope of both *Xerox* and *Kodak II*, the Supreme Court should
"allow these difficult issues to percolate further in the courts of
appeals."[133]

---

128.   *Xerox*, 203 F.3d at 1327.
129.   *Id.* at 1327.
130.   *Amicus Curiae Brief,s upra* note 92, at *8.
131.   *Id.* at *9.
132.   *Id.* at *10.
133.   *Id.* at *11.

(3) Post-Xerox Decisions

Several courts have examined the *Xerox* opinion.[134] In *Townshend v. Rockwell International*,[135] the defendant in a patent infringement case involving 56K modem technology advanced an antitrust counterclaim. The alleged infringer claimed that the patent holder had fraudulently caused the patented technology to be adopted as an industry standard and had thereafter made the patents available for licensing to competitors only on the condition that they cross-license their technology to the patent holder. The court dismissed the antitrust claims, holding that, "because a patent owner has the legal right to refuse to license his or her patent on any terms, the existence of a predicate condition to a license agreement cannot state an antitrust violation."[136] Citing *Xerox* the court wrote, "Given that a patent holder is permitted under the antitrust laws to completely exclude others from practicing his or her technology, the Court finds that 3Com's submission of proposed licensing terms with which it was willing to license does not state a violation of the antitrust laws."[137]

In *Intergraph Corp. v. Intel Corp.*,[138] Intel was accused of refusing to give preferred access to its patented microprocessor technologies to a computer equipment manufacturer so long as that manufacturer continued to pursue infringement litigation against Intel. After the Federal Circuit held that the plaintiff could not pursue a claim that Intel had attempted to monopolize the computer equipment market (in which it did not compete),[139] the district court on remand rejected plaintiff's attempt to pursue a claim that Intel's refusal to deal on preferred terms constituted an antitrust violation in the *microprocessor* market. In denying this effort, largely on the ground that it was precluded by the

---

134. At least one court has declined to extend the *Xerox* opinion's reasoning to refusals to deal *trade secrets*. Telecomm Tech. Servs. v. Siemens Rolm Communs., 150 F. Supp. 2d 1365, 1370 (N.D. Ga. 2000) ("The [Xerox] court, which addressed only copyrighted and patented works, expressly held that refusal to deal was within the scope of those statutory rights. There is no analogous statutory right regarding trade secrets."), *aff'd on other grounds*, 388 F.3d 820 (11th Cir. 2004).
135. No. C99-0400SBA, 2000 WL 433505 (N.D. Cal. Mar. 28, 2000).
136. *Id.* at *8.
137. *Id.*
138. 88 F. Supp. 2d 1288 (N.D. Ala. 2000).
139. Intergraph Corp. v. Intel Corp., 195 F.3d 1346, 1362 (Fed. Cir. 1999).

Federal Circuit's earlier decision, the district court wrote concerning its view of the significance of the *Xerox* decision:

> In [*Xerox*] the Federal Circuit held that "in the absence of any indication of illegal tying, fraud in the Patent & Trademark Office, or sham litigation, the patent holder may enforce the statutory right to exclude . . . free from liability under the antitrust laws." Intergraph has not claimed that Intel is guilty of any of the disqualifying factors set out in [*Xerox*]. Thus, if anything, the [*Xerox*] case removes any remaining ambiguity concerning the impact of the [Federal Circuit's] *Intergraph* decision on plaintiffs' maintenance of monopoly claims in this Court.[140]

The Federal Circuit affirmed the district court's decision.[141]

In *Schor v. Abbott Laboratories*,[142] discussed in section A.1, above, the court granted Abbott's motion to dismiss and found that "the *Xerox* court's reasoning ... represents a sounder approach to a patentee's antitrust liability than the Ninth Circuit's opinion in *Kodak II*."[143] The court "agree[d] with the Federal Circuit's suggestion ... that a patent holder is not liable for an antitrust violation for refusing to sell or license a patented product within the scope of the patent grant, and that this immunity is not limited to a single market."[144] Thus, according to the court, "if the product is encompassed within the patent claims, the Sherman Act does not limit the patent holder's refusal to license or sell that item, or limit the patent holder's right to charge a higher price, in any market."[145]

In *Applera Corp. v. MJ Research*,[146] a refusal to deal involving intellectual property was considered in light of the Supreme Court's decision in *Trinko*. In a counterclaim, MJ Research ("MJ") contended

---

140. *Intergraph*, 88 F. Supp. 2d at 1293.
141. 253 F.3d 695 (Fed. Cir. 2001).
142. No. 05-C-1592, 2005 WL 1653606 (N.D. Ill. July 12, 2005).
143. *Id.* at *7.
144. *Id.* at *8.
145. *Id.* Abbott's patents also applied "in both markets to cover [the booster drug's] use in conjunction with drugs manufactured and sold by third parties." *Id. But see* Serv. Employees Int'l Union Health & Welfare Fund v. Abbott Labs., No. C 04-4203 CW, 2005 WL 528323 (N.D. Cal. Mar. 2, 2005) (same claim asserted by different plaintiff; district court refused to dismiss complaint and held that plaintiff stated viable monopoly leveraging claim under *Kodak II*).
146. 349 F. Supp. 2d 338 (D. Conn. 2004).

that Applera had refused to allow MJ to distribute end-user licenses for its patents (which covered automated performance of certain nucleic acid amplification), and that Applera had refused to sell end-user licenses to MJ for its own internal use. The court held that the Federal Circuit's decision in *Xerox* "controlled," and that Applera's unilateral refusal to license MJ or to allow MJ to serve as its agent to distribute end-user licenses was not subject to antitrust liability.[147] The court cited *Trinko* for the proposition that, "[a]s a general matter, the Sherman Act 'does not restrict the long recognized right of [a] trader or manufacturer engaged in an entirely private business, freely to exercise his own independent discretion as to parties with whom he will deal.'"[148]

The court rejected MJ's attempt to invoke *Aspen Skiing*'s focus on the change in long-standing practices as a basis for liability. The court found that "the change in policy to which MJ refers is not one of Applera's sudden refusal to license MJ after a prior history of licensing."[149] Instead, Applera had shifted from a licensing regime focusing on certain key reagents, as to which MJ had *not* been a licensee, to a regime focusing on the performance of the patented process, as to which MJ *could* have been a licensee.[150] Moreover, the Court distinguished *Aspen* on the ground that it did not involve intellectual property:

> [G]iven that *Aspen Skiing* was not concerned with the intersection of patent and antitrust law, and the Supreme Court's later caution [in *Trinko*] that *Aspen Skiing* represents the "outer boundary" of Sherman Act Section 2 liability ... this Court declines to read *Aspen Skiing* so expansively to cover the refusal to license situation at issue here.[151]

In *Telecomm Technical Services v. Siemens Rolm, Inc.*,[152] the court followed *Xerox* in a case involving allegations by ISOs that a maker of telephone switching equipment had refused to deal patented and

---

147. *Id.* at 347-48.
148. *Id.* at 346-47.
149. *Id.* at 348.
150. *Id.*
151. *Id.* at 348 n.9. The *Applera* court also rejected MJ's argument based on an essential facilities theory, largely on the ground that the *Xerox* case controlled since patents were involved. As to *Trinko*, the court merely noted that "The Supreme Court has neither recognized nor repudiated the essential facilities doctrine." 349 F. Supp. 2d at 347 n.6.
152. 150 F. Supp. 2d 1365 (N.D. Ga. 2000).

copyrighted parts to them, inhibiting their ability to compete in the service market for such equipment. Although it initially denied defendant's motion for summary judgment, the court reconsidered its ruling in light of the Federal Circuit's subsequent decision in *Xerox*. The court held that the manufacturer's refusal to sell patented or copyrighted parts could not be an antitrust violation (under the holding of *Xerox*) but that its refusal to sell parts or license software *not* protected by intellectual property could be a violation.[153]   Ultimately, the court dismissed the claim because plaintiff was unable to segregate the effects of the refusal as to unprotected products from those that were protected.[154]

The Eleventh Circuit affirmed on other grounds.[155]   The Eleventh Circuit acknowledged the conflict among the circuits on refusals to deal involving intellectual property, noting that "this question lies at the intersection of intellectual property law and antitrust law and presents a difficult and increasingly important issue."[156]   The court deemed it unnecessary to reach the "difficult" issue, however, "because there is no evidence of any harm to equipment owners, completely independent of any patents Siemens may have on these parts."[157]   The court observed that equipment owners could order replacement parts themselves and then ask an ISO to install them or provide an ISO with a letter of agency, allowing the ISO to purchase parts on behalf of the equipment owner.[158] As to the refusal to license certain copyrighted operating system software, the court found that the software performed no diagnostic or repair function and thus "[did] not give [the manufacturer] a competitive advantage in the *service* market."[159]

---

153.   *Id.* at 1369-70.

154.   *Id.* at 1374.

155.   The district court believed that the Federal Circuit would have jurisdiction over the appeal. *Id.* at 1368.   After the district court's decision, however, the Supreme Court issued its opinion in *Holmes Group v. Vornado Air Circulation Systems*, 535 U.S. 826 (2002), holding that the Federal Circuit does not have jurisdiction over appeals unless a patent issue is raised on the face of the initial complaint.

156.   *Telecom Tech. Servs.*, 388 F.3d at 826, 827 n.7.

157.   *Id.* at 827.

158.   *Id.* at 827-28.

159.   *Id.* at 828; *see also, e.g.*, Valley Drug v. Geneva Pharms., 344 F.3d 1294, 1304-05 (11th Cir. 2003) (citing *Xerox* for proposition that "a patentee can choose to exclude everyone from producing the patented article or can choose to be the sole supplier itself").

c. Debate Over *Xerox* and *Kodak II*

The tension between the approaches adopted by the Federal Circuit in *Xerox* and the Ninth Circuit in *Kodak II* has elicited extensive commentary.[160] Commentary has focused on (1) whether, aside from fraudulent procurement, sham enforcement, or collusion, a unilateral refusal to deal intellectual property should ever be subject to antitrust scrutiny, and if so, (2) the role subjective intent should play in the antitrust analysis of such refusals to deal.

(1) The extent to which rights conferred by the patent and copyright laws confer antitrust immunity.

Commentators have debated whether *Kodak II* takes adequate account of the rights conferred by the patent and copyright laws and, conversely, whether *Xerox* confers unwarranted blanket immunity to holders of intellectual property.

(A) THE COMPETING POLICIES OF THE ANTITRUST AND
        INTELLECTUAL PROPERTY LAWS

Critics of *Kodak II* proceed from the premise that, in order to stimulate innovation and long-term competition, intellectual property laws confer the right to exclude others from the protected material. Absent fraudulent procurement, sham enforcement, or collusion, they argue, a unilateral decision not to license is merely the exercise of that basic right to exclude and should therefore enjoy absolute immunity from antitrust consequences.[161]

---

160. At least one article takes the position that "the purported conflict" between *Xerox* and *Kodak II* "is largely illusory." Burtis & Kobayashi, *supra* note 1, at 143.

161. *See, e.g.*, 3 AREEDA & HOVENKAMP, *supra* note 1, ¶ 706b1, at 220; Gleklen I, *supra* note 1, at 2-3, 10; Pate, *supra* note 1 (unconditional, unilateral refusals to license intellectual property should not violate antitrust laws irrespective of subjective intent); McGowan I, *supra* note 1, at 493 ("In patent cases, the right to engage in pure exclusion is all but absolute."); *see also, e.g.*, Dawson Chem. v. Rohm & Haas Co., 448 U.S. 176, 215 (1980) ("the right to exclude others from profiting by the patented invention" is "essence" of patent); Cont'l Paper Bag v. E. Paper Bag, 210 U.S. 405, 429 (1908) (holding that the ability to exclude competitors is "the very essence of the right conferred by the patent"); Genentech, Inc. v. Eli Lilly & Co., 998 F.2d 931, 949 (Fed. Cir. 1993)

Critics of the Ninth Circuit's opinion point out that, to the degree a duty to license is found to exist under the court's pretext analysis, the court will be required to establish the price and terms of the compelled license, and then to monitor changes over time.[162] Such a "regulatory" role has long been deemed inappropriate for courts, including by the Supreme Court in *Trinko*.[163] And any requirement that licensing be extended on "reasonable" terms could impinge on the patent or copyright owner's freedom to recover monopoly profits from the covered work.[164] Others have argued that imposing compulsory licensing "reduces the

---

(right to select licensees not a restraint of trade); Miller Insituform, Inc. v. Insituform of N. Am., Inc., 830 F.2d 606, 609 (6th Cir. 1987) (refusal to license cannot be § 2 violation); SCM Corp. v. Xerox Corp., 645 F.2d 1195, 1204, 1206 (2d Cir. 1981) ("No court has ever held that the antitrust laws require a patent holder to forfeit the exclusionary power inherent in his patent the instant his patent monopoly affords him monopoly power over a relevant product market."); United States v. Westinghouse Elec., 648 F.2d 642, 647 (9th Cir. 1981) (approving *SCM* formulation; patentee has "untrammeled right" to refuse to license; antitrust violation may not be found "where a patent holder does precisely that which the patent laws authorize"); W.L. Gore & Assocs. v. Carlisle Corp., 529 F.2d 614, 623 (3d Cir. 1976) ("right to refuse to license is the essence of the patent holder's right"); Schor v. Abbott Labs., No. 05-C-1592, 2005 WL 1653606, at *6-8 (N.D. Ill. July 12, 2005) (rejecting *Kodak II*'s analysis and finding that patent grant permits patentee to sell, or not, within the scope of the patent's coverage); Intergraph Corp. v. Intel Corp., 88 F. Supp. 2d 1288, 1292 (N.D. Ala. 2000) ("[T]he antitrust laws do not negate the patentee's right to exclude others from patent property."). The Copyright Act gives analogous rights to copyright owners. 17 U.S.C. § 106; *see also, e.g.*, Stewart v. Abend, 495 U.S. 207, 229 (1990); Fox Film Corp. v. Doyal, 286 U.S. 123, 127 (1932) ("The owner of [a] copyright, if he pleases, may refrain from vending or licensing and content himself with simply exercising the right to exclude others from using his property."); *Data Gen.*, 36 F.3d at 1184-85 ("[T]he Copyright Act fosters investment and innovation . . . [by] allow[ing] the author to earn monopoly profits by licensing the copyright to others or reserving the copyright for the author's exclusive use.").

162.   *See, e.g.*, 3 AREEDA & HOVENKAMP, *supra* note 1, ¶ 709b1, at 220.
163.   *See, e.g.*, Verizon Communs. v. Law Offices of Curtis V. Trinko, 540 U.S. 398, 414-15 (2004); MetroNet Servs. v. Qwest Corp., 383 F.3d 1124, 1133-34 (9th Cir. 2004); Covad Communs. v. BellSouth Corp., 374 F.3d 1044, 1051 (11th Cir. 2004); RICHARD A. POSNER, ANTITRUST LAW 242-44 (2d ed. 2001) ("POSNER").
164.   Gleklen I, *supra* note 1, at 5-6.

incentives of rival firms to innovate their own solutions to the monopolist's patents. The results perpetuate the patentee as a kind of price-regulated utility, contrary to the purposes of the antitrust laws."[165]

By contrast, critics of *Xerox* have expressed concern that limiting antitrust liability to cases involving fraud, sham litigation, or collusion grants dominant firms with intellectual property portfolios carte-blanche to deny access to rivals of key inputs or facilities regardless of competitive impact.[166] If the *Xerox* holding applied literally, these critics

---

165. 3 AREEDA & HOVENKAMP, *supra* note 1, ¶ 709b1, at 220.
166. Pitofsky, *supra* note 1, at 920 ("[T]he [*Xerox*] Court reached its decision in sweeping language that exalts patent and copyright rights over other considerations and throws into doubt the validity of previous lines of authority that attempted to strike a balance between intellectual property and antitrust."); Gleklen II, *supra* note 1, at 10-13 (responding to Pitofsky critique of *Xerox*); Melamed, *supra* note 1, at 409-10, 425 (blanket immunity creates antitrust exemption not clearly articulated by Congress and inconsistent with Supreme Court's move away from rigid formalistic "rules"); Genevaz, *supra* note 33, at 741-71; Suzzette Rodriguez Hurley, *Failing to Balance Patent Rights and Antitrust Concerns: The Federal Circuit's Holding in In Re* Independent Services Organizations Antitrust Litigation, 13 FED. CIR. B.J. 475, 493 (2003-2004) (*Xerox* holding "not only overly broad, but it could also have significantly negative effects on the notions of free market competition that drive our economy"); Kobak, *supra* note 1, at 537 (Federal Circuit in *Xerox* "upset the balance between IP and antitrust so thoughtfully struck in places such as the IP Guidelines"); Patrick H. Moran, *The Federal and Ninth Circuits Square Off: Refusals to Deal and the Precarious Intersection Between Antitrust and Patent Law*, 87 MARQ. L. REV. 387, 422 (2003) (*Xerox* "goes too far to protect patent holders by extending immunity from antitrust laws beyond what Congress intended"); Carrier, *supra* note 1, at 764 (Making "action within the scope of the patent ... automatically be immune from antitrust scrutiny ... 'solves' the patent-antitrust conflict only by according priority to the patent laws. This purported solution amounts to an assumption that the increase in welfare from safeguarding the patentee's right to exclude will always outweigh the increase that would have resulted from antitrust's enhanced competition.").
More broadly, the Federal Circuit has been accused of favoring patent rights over antitrust considerations in its jurisprudence. *See, e.g.*, Boyle et al., *supra* note 1, at 741 ("[S]everal in the antitrust community perceive the [Federal Circuit] as giving undue deference to intellectual property considerations."); Kobak, *supra* note 1, at 527 (The Federal Circuit "has taken a grudging view of antitrust ... principles and a broad view of the

argue, Microsoft would be free to refuse to license its copyrighted operating system for whatever reason, regardless of the effect on competition—a view rejected by the D.C. Circuit.[167] Likewise, a monopolist over an electrical distribution system would be able to exclude competitors regardless of competitive effect, so long as it secured patents or copyrights on its system.[168]

Critics of *Xerox* do not advocate wholesale imposition of antitrust liability for unilateral refusals to license intellectual property. Rather, they argue that, consistent with the general law concerning refusals to deal, antitrust liability should be imposed only rarely.[169] Among other things, this is because unilateral refusals rarely permit a monopolist to earn monopoly profits beyond what it would be able to earn otherwise. Moreover, there often are legitimate efficiency reasons for monopolists to refuse to deal with particular rivals or customers.[170]

Blanket immunity for unilateral refusals to deal intellectual property, however, is said to violate the Supreme Court's warning that "exemptions from the [Sherman Act] are strictly construed and strongly

'rights' of patent holders to enforce ... [or] refuse to license ... their patents.").

167.   *See, e.g.*, United States v. Microsoft Corp., 253 F.3d 34, 63 (D.C. Cir. 2001) (rejecting argument that if intellectual property rights were lawfully obtained their subsequent exercise cannot give rise to antitrust liability; such contention "is no more correct than the proposition that use of one's personal property, such as a baseball bat, cannot give rise to tort liability").

168.   *See* Melamed, *supra* note 1, at 424 ("[S]ome unilateral refusals to deal are very anticompetitive and damaging. The AT&T case was, after all, a refusal-to-deal case. There is no reason to think that AT&T should have been permitted to engage in the conduct at issue there if only the interfaces used by MCI to connect with AT&T's network had been patented.") (referring to MCI Communs. Corp. v. AT&T, 708 F.2d 1081, 1132 (7th Cir. 1983)); MacKie-Mason, *supra* note 1, at 8 ("What if Aspen had a patented gear mechanism in its ski lifts? Suppose Otter Tail Power had patents on parts in its electric transformers (which it refused to use to wheel power)?"); Genevaz, *supra* note 33, at 765-66. *But see* Gleklen I, *supra* note 1, at 9 (asserting that "at the extreme every refusal to grant a bare IP license can be characterized as a tying arrangement").

169.   *See, e.g.*, MacKie-Mason, *supra* note 1, at 9; Melamed, *supra* note 1, at 419-20; *see also* Kobak, *supra* note 1, at 541 (*Xerox* was "wrongfully decided as a matter of orthodox antitrust law.").

170.   *See, e.g.*, Melamed, *supra* note 1, at 420.

disfavored."[171]   Critics of *Xerox* argue that the Patent and Copyright Acts contain no explicit antitrust immunity or exemption.   They reject the notion that the "rights to exclude" embedded in the Patent and Copyright Acts constitute exemptions from antitrust liability for exercising those rights. The rights to exclude found in the intellectual property laws, they argue,[172] are no different than those inherent in most forms of property, which are not subject to antitrust immunity.[173]

---

171.   Square D Co. v. Niagara Frontier Tariff Bureau, 476 U.S. 409, 421 (1986).

172.   *See, e.g.*, MacKie-Mason, *supra* note 1, at 3-4 (rights to exclude found in intellectual property are "standard instances of property law in general"); Genevaz, *supra* note 33, at 758-62 (arguing that intellectual property and other property should be treated as equals). *But see, e.g.*, Simpson v. Union Oil Co., 377 U.S. 13, 24 (1964) ("The patent laws ... are in *pari materia* with the antitrust laws and modify them *pro tanto.*"); Gleklen I, *supra* note 1, at 6-7 (arguing that other forms of property may not be as absolute as intellectual property, one example being that traditional property may be subject to the common law of easements); Melamed, *supra* note 1, at 422-23 (noting that, unlike tangible property, intellectual property "can be replicated at little or no marginal cost," but finding insufficient empirical data to justify a "safe harbor" for intellectual property); POSNER, *supra* note 163, at 246 ("Intellectual property is often expensive to create but once created the cost of making additional copies usually is low, dramatically so in the case of software.").

173.   *See, e.g.*, Kaiser Aetna v. United States, 444 U.S. 164, 176 (1979) (right to exclude others is "one of the most essential sticks in the bundle of rights that are commonly characterized as property"); Cont'l Paper Bag v. E. Paper Bag, 210 U.S. 405, 425 (1908) ("patents are property, and entitled to the same rights and sanctions as other property"); Consol. Fruit Jar Co. v. Wright, 94 U.S. 92, 96 (1896) ("A patent for an invention is as much property as a patent for land.   The right rests on the same foundation, and is surrounded and protected by the same sanctions."); 35 U.S.C. § 261 ("patents shall have the attributes of personal property"); INTELLECTUAL PROPERTY GUIDELINES, *supra* note 4, §§ 2.0-2.1 ("The Agencies regard intellectual property as being essentially comparable to any other form of property."). *But see* INTELLECTUAL PROPERTY GUIDE-LINES, *supra* note 4, § 2.1 ("[I]ntellectual property is [not] in all respects the same as any other form of property.   Intellectual property has important characteristics, such as ease of misappropriation, that distinguish it from many other forms of property. These characteristics can be taken into account by standard antitrust analysis, however, and do not require the application of fundamentally different principles."); Gleklen I, *supra* note 1, at 6-7; POSNER,*s upra* note 163, at 246.

(B) CONCERNS OVER CONDITIONAL LICENSING.

Critics of *Xerox* have expressed particular concern over the prospect that granting blanket antitrust immunity for unilateral refusals to deal intellectual property would allow monopolists to achieve tying-like results on a purely unilateral basis through *conditional* licensing—i.e., a unilateral decision to license potential invention *A* only to those willing to buy unpatented product *B*.[174] In a brief opposing *certiorari* in *Xerox,* the Solicitor General expressed concern that a patent holder not be excused from antitrust liability in circumstances where "the patent holder, although not engaging in an express tying arrangement like that alleged in *Kodak*, had nonetheless sought to accomplish a similar result by restricting the sale or license of its patented product to those customers who had also demonstrated their willingness to purchase from it another product or service over which it did not have a lawful monopoly."[175]

---

174. *See, e.g.*, 3 AREEDA & HOVENKAMP, *supra* note 1, ¶ 709c1 ("A willingness to license conditioned on the licensee's supplying a product or intellectual property right in return is governed by ordinary legal principles governing reciprocity arrangements."); Pate, *supra* note 1, at 434-38 (reading *Xerox* as being limited to unilateral, unconditional refusals to deal; conditional refusals should be subject to antitrust scrutiny); Boyle et al., *supra* note 1, at 739 (same); MacKie-Mason, *supra* note 1, at 7-8 (no economic distinction between tying and certain types of conditional refusals); Pitofsky, *supra* note 1, at 922-23 ("An approach that starts from the point that a patent holder does not have to sell or license its patent to anyone, and proceeds from that unchallenged assumption to the rule that it therefore can condition its sales or licenses in any way it sees fit (with tie-in sales as the sole antitrust exception), would be an unwise and unfortunate departure from the traditional approach in this area."); Melamed, *supra* note 1, at 425 (not clear how *Xerox* Court would deal with a firm unilaterally announcing "that it will license patented product A only to firms that also buy B from it"); Benjamin Klein & John Shepard Wiley, *Competitive Price Discrimination as an Antitrust Justification for Intellectual Property Refusals to Deal*, 70 ANTITRUST L.J. 599, 601 (2003) ("Klein & Wiley") (pointing out that "as a practical matter, it may be difficult to distinguish between unilateral and conditional refusals in terms of economic effect.").

175. *Amicus Curiae Brief, supra* note 92, at *8; *see also* Ethyl Gas. Corp. v. United States, 309 U.S. 436, 456 (1940) ("[A patentee] may grant licenses to make, use or vend, restricted in point of space or time, or with

Commentators have suggested that the Solicitor General's concern has been realized on at least two occasions: In *Townshend v. Rockwell International Corp.*[176] and *Intergraph Corp. v. Intel Corp.*[177] (both discussed in subsection A.2.b(3), above), the courts relied on *Xerox* to find conditional refusals to license immune from antitrust liability.[178] The district court's holding in the latter case has been criticized as failing to recognize the allegedly conditional nature of Intel's refusal to deal with Intergraph,[179] and because the "district court did not appear to take into account the Federal Circuit's further statement [in *Xerox*] that a court could inquire into the intent of the intellectual property holder (and thus potentially challenge) conduct resulting in an anticompetitive effect that illegally extends beyond the statutory patent grant."[180]

Consistent with this critique, *Xerox* supporters discount the possibility that the Federal Circuit would find conditional refusals to deal immune from antitrust scrutiny. They note that *Xerox* did not involve such facts and that the Federal Circuit's opinion acknowledged the "undisputed premise that the patent holder cannot use his statutory right to refuse to sell patented parts to gain a monopoly in a market *beyond the scope of the patent.*"[181] Moreover, in a decision issued several years

---

any other restriction upon the exercise of the granted privilege, save only that by attaching a condition to his license he may not enlarge his monopoly and thus acquire some other which the statute and the patent together did not give.").

176 No. C99-0400SBA, 2000 WL 433505 (N.D. Cal. Mar. 28, 2000).

177 88 F. Supp. 2d 1288 (N.D. Ala. 2000), *aff'd*, 253 F.3d 695 (Fed. Cir. 2001).

178. *See, e.g.*, Pitofsky, *supra* note 1, at 923; Pate, *supra* note 1, at 435-37.

179. *See* Pate, *supra* note 1, at 435-36.

180. *Id.* at 435.

181. *Xerox*, 203 F.3d at 1327 (Fed. Cir. 2000); *see, e.g.*, Pate, *supra* note 1, at 434-35 (*Xerox* does not "preclude antitrust claims where it can be demonstrated that the defendant has attempted to use his right to refuse to license or sell his patented parts in order to gain a monopoly in a market beyond the scope of the patent."); 3 AREEDA & HOVENKAMP, *supra* note 1, ¶ 709b2, at 230 (Federal Circuit in *Xerox* rightly held that "the simple refusal to license a patent ... is not an antitrust violation, regardless of the patentee's power or state of mind. By contrast, a conditional refusal—that is, an offer to license conditioned on price fixing, tying, reciprocity, exclusive dealing, or another trade restraint—can be an antitrust violation when the requirements for that particular restraint have been met."); McGowan II, *supra* note 1, at 740 ("Antitrust should not penalize unilateral refusals to license technology but should

after *Xerox*, the Federal Circuit made clear that a patentee's antitrust immunity is "hardly absolute" and that it could not "enumerate the full range of activities capable of effecting a [patentee's] loss of immunity."[182]

(C) THE ROLE OF SUBJECTIVE INTENT IN THE ANTITRUST ANALYSIS OF
     REFUSALS TO DEAL INTELLECTUAL PROPERTY.

Supporters of *Xerox* also point out that the decision avoids having liability turn on subjective intent,[183] a quagmire into which critics of *Kodak II* contend that that decision must necessarily wade. Despite the Ninth Circuit's suggestion that evidence of a "desire to best the competition" or of "hostility to competitors" does not show pretext,[184] critics argue *Kodak II*'s pretext standard boils down to an inquiry as to the "real motive" for the refusal. As one commentator put it, "[the Ninth Circuit's test] purports to make the refusal-to-license question rest on the monopolist's intent, distinguishing between the 'intent to protect one's intellectual property rights,' which is valid, from the 'intent to create or maintain a monopoly,' which is not."[185] But many have argued that

---

review conditional refusals generally under the rule of reason"); Gleklen I, *supra* note 1, at 8-9 (arguing that exception for conditional refusals to license has no support in case law).

182. Unitherm Food Sys. v. Swift Eckrich, Inc., 375 F.3d 1341, 1356-57 (Fed. Cir. 2004), *rev'd on other grounds*, 126 S. Ct. 980 (2006).

183. *See, e.g.*, Pate, *supra* note 1, at 438-40; Boyle et al., *supra* note 1, at 750-52.

184. *Kodak II*, 125 F.3d 1195, 1219 (9th Cir. 1997); *see also, e.g.*, Ocean State Physicians Health Plan v. Blue Cross & Blue Shield, 883 F.2d 1101, 1113 (1st Cir. 1989) (A "desire to crush a competitor, standing alone, is insufficient to make out a violation of the antitrust laws."); Olympia Equip. Leasing v. W. Union Tel., 797 F.2d 370, 379 (7th Cir. 1986) ("If conduct is not objectively anticompetitive, the fact that it was motivated by hostility to competitors ... is irrelevant."); Pate, *supra* note 1, at 439 ("In most cases, the intent to create a monopoly anticompetitively cannot be distinguished from the intent to do so competitively.").

185. 3 AREEDA & HOVENKAMP, s*upra* note 1, ¶ 709b2, at 222-25; *see also, e.g.*, Gifford, *supra* note 1, at 409 ("When it made the defendant's subjective motivation the critical issue, the Ninth Circuit departed from the trend towards more objective standards in antitrust generally and in the antitrust/intellectual property interface particularly."); Herbert Hovenkamp, *Symposium: Intellectual Property Rights and Federal Antitrust Policy*, 24 J. CORP. L. 477, 480 (1999) ("The Ninth Circuit opinion's incoherence and lack of regard for both the Patent Act and

attempting to make such a distinction is impossible. Perhaps most fundamentally, there is often no difference between protecting intellectual property rights and creating or maintaining a monopoly: asserting such rights may inevitably exclude competition and generate monopoly power.[186] Some have argued that permitting an inquiry into the subjective intent of the patent or copyright holder is inconsistent with the Supreme Court's holding in *Professional Real Estate Investors, Inc. v. Columbia Pictures Industries*[187] There, the Supreme Court held that efforts to enforce a copyright, not found to be objectively baseless, cannot give rise to antitrust liability regardless of the copyright owner's intent.[188]

---

controlling precedent has made it an easy target of critics, while most courts have ignored or rejected it."). *But see* Genevaz, *supra* note 33, at 768 (describing intent test in refusal-to-deal cases as "not subjective but objective").

186. 3 AREEDA & HOVENKAMP, *supra* note 1, ¶ 709b2, at 222; Melamed, *supra* note 1, at 426 (intent test "is based on a false dichotomy because the very purpose of intellectual property law is to permit the holder to reap the benefits of exclusive enjoyment, even if that means charging monopoly prices to customers and not sharing the property with rivals"); Gleklen I, *supra* note 1, at 9 (same); Boyle et al., *supra* note 1, at 750 ("An intellectual property owner's right to exclude, including the right to refuse to license or sell protected products, does not depend on the IP owner having an altruistic motive for exercising its right."); Pate, *supra* note 1, at 438-41 ("Introducing a 'pretext' standard into the calculus of determining legitimate business justifications injects subjectivity into what ought to be an objective inquiry into the competitive effects of a business arrangement."); Patterson, *supra* note 1, at 1157 ("It is not fruitful to ask if the owner's 'intent' is to exploit its intellectual property; in a subjective sense, it always is."); Whitener, *supra* note 1, at 5-7 ("absurd" to make refusal-to-deal analyses depend on subjective intent); McGowan I, *supra* note 1, at 491-92, 516-24 (criticizing *Kodak II* for considering subjective intent). *But see, e.g.*, Skitol, *supra* note 5, at 6 (questioning whether Supreme Court's focus on intent in *Trinko* lends support to Ninth Circuit's analysis in *Kodak II*).

187. 508 U.S. 49 (1992) (sometimes referred herein after as *"PRE"*).

188. *Id.* at 64; *see, e.g.*, 3 AREEDA & HOVENKAMP, *supra* note 1, ¶ 709b2, at 223-24; Gleklen I, *supra* note 1, at 9; *see also, e.g.*, *Xerox*, 203 F.3d at 1327-28 ("We see no more reason to inquire into the subjective motivation of Xerox in refusing to sell or license its patented works than we found in evaluating the subjective motivation of a patentee in bringing suit to enforce that same right [as addressed in *PRE*].").

Some have suggested, however, that the Supreme Court's decision in *Trinko* expanded the role of intent evidence in refusal-to-deal cases, effectively ratifying the pretext standard of *Kodak II*. One commentator, for instance, has asserted that, because the *Trinko* Court focused on anticompetitive intent, the decision "gives implicit support to the pretext test for unilateral refusals to deal in intellectual property."[189]

Outside the intellectual property context, some recent precedents support this notion: The Fifth Circuit recently opined that *Trinko* requires that "courts ... be careful in determining that a business's refusal to deal is based on anticompetitive *motives* versus a valid business strategy."[190]   Further, in *Morris Communications Corp. v. PGA Tour, Inc.*[191]—a decision issued after the Supreme Court's ruling in *Trinko*—the Eleventh Circuit relied upon *Kodak II* to endorse a pretext standard in

189.   Genevaz, *supra* note 33, at 758, 781; *see id.* at 780-83 (arguing that *Trinko* reiterates intent as a requirement in refusals to deal intellectual property and implicitly supports pretext test); *see also* Skitol, *supra* note 5, at 4 ("[E]ven in cases that involve longtime refusals, rather than discontinuance or changed policies, the opinion can be read as requiring some inquiry into intent."); Stoll & Goldfein, *supra* note 5 ("*Trinko* appears to represent a significant change in the requirements for satisfying the intent element of a § 2 claim that involves a refusal to deal."); *Trinko* ABA Seminar, *supra* note 5, at 14 (remarks of Mark Whitener) ("Unfortunately ... the [*Trinko*] Court went on to link [its conclusion that Ski Company had sacrificed short-term profits in the likely expectation of later monopoly profits] to a search for anticompetitive *intent*, asking whether the defendant's actions were prompted by competitive zeal or anticompetitive malice ...   But this and several other portions of the decision suggest that the Court is looking for a malicious purpose of the conduct, for the intent behind the conduct."); Fox, *supra* note 5, at 4 n.11 (Court found significant whether "positive action is prompted by 'competitive zeal' or 'anticompetitive malice'").

190.   Am. Cent. E. Tex. Gas v. Union Pac. Res. Group, No. 02-41010, 2004 WL 136091, at *9 (5th Cir. Jan. 27, 2004) (unpublished) (emphasis added) (affirming an arbitral finding in a refusal-to-deal case based in part on evidence of the defendant's subjective intent).   The Court also found significant the fact that, unlike *Trinko*, which involved a heavily regulated industry, the defendant was subject to no regulatory oversight to safeguard competition. *See also* A.I.B. Express v. FedEx Corp., No. 03 Civ. 8087 SAS, 2004 WL 2526293, at *6 (S.D.N.Y. Nov. 8, 2004) (relying on *Trinko*; finding allegations that defendant terminated an allegedly profitable relationship sufficient to plead "anticompetitive bent").

191.   364 F.3d 1288 (11th Cir. 2004).

a refusal-to-deal case. While the product to which plaintiff sought access—the PGA golf tour's "real time" tournament scoring system—was not copyrighted, the court did note that the product was made possible only through the PGA's effort and investment.[192] The Eleventh Circuit stated that "a company may deal or refuse to deal with whomever it pleases," so long as it does not have a "*purpose* to create or maintain a monopoly."[193] If a defendant having monopoly power advances a "legitimate business purpose" for a refusal, according to the Eleventh Circuit, "the burden shifts to the plaintiff to show that the proffered business justification is pretextual."[194] The court found that the PGA's justification of wishing to avoid "free riding" by the plaintiff was not pretextual and affirmed the grant of summary judgment to the PGA.

The conflict between the approaches of the Ninth and Federal Circuits remains unresolved, and the impact of *Trinko* on this conflict remains unclear. Not surprisingly, many commentators advocate approaches to the refusal to deal question that differ from the analyses of both the Ninth and the Federal Circuits.[195] The Supreme Court's decision

192. *Id.* at 1298.
193. *Id.* at 1294-95 (emphasis added).
194. *Id.* at 1295-96 (citing *Kodak II*).
195. *See, e.g.*, Melamed, *supra* note 1, at 423-27 (proposed guiding principle: "one may enjoy the fruits of her lawfully obtained [intellectual] property, including whatever monopoly profits that property enables her to earn, but she may not sacrifice such profits strategically, by using that property in ways that serve no legitimate purpose (*i.e.*, one that neither benefits consumers nor promotes efficiency) in order to create additional market power."); Boyle et al., *supra* note 1, at 760 ("If the patented or copyrighted component is the thing that makes the IP owner's product essential for effective competition [and is not tangential thereto], the IP owner should be entitled to deny its competitors access to the product ...."); Carrier, *supra* note 1, at 761 (surveying various academic proposals for dealing with IP-antitrust interface; proposes a standard under which the degree of antitrust intervention is calibrated by the degree and nature of innovation in particular industries); Genevaz, *supra* note 33, at 771-72 (proposing "rule of reason" inquiry for refusals to deal intellectual property; presumptive validity of refusal to deal overcome "when the anticompetitive effects of the exclusion from the intellectual property outweigh the pro-competitive ones"); McGowan II, *supra* note 1, at 740 (intellectual property claims should be evaluated based on total surplus, not simply consumer surplus); Patterson, *supra* note 1, at 1155-60 ("When an intellectual property owner selectively sells or licenses its property in a way that bears no relation to potential

in *Trinko*, however, at the very least makes clear that a monopolist will be required to deal with competitors only in very narrow circumstances, even where intellectual property is not involved.[196] It is safe to say therefore that *Trinko* does not favor the *Kodak II* approach.[197]

B. Unilateral Enforcement of Intellectual Property Rights

The unilateral *enforcement* of intellectual property rights also may be subject to antitrust scrutiny. "As a general rule, behavior conforming to the patent laws oriented towards procuring or enforcing a patent enjoys immunity from the antitrust laws."[198] As in the context of unilateral

purchasers' or licensees' uses of protected aspects of that property... [there] should be no special exemption from the antitrust laws;" proposing to require intellectual property owners to show that the market power they have acquired in a secondary market flows directly from their intellectual property); Gleklen II, *supra* note 1, at 13-15 (responding to Patterson); Klein & Wiley, *supra* note 174, at 641 (arguing that refusals by equipment manufacturers to deal with ISOs can be justified by a "competitive price discrimination" theory); Jonathan B. Baker, *Competitive Price Discrimination: The Exercise of Market Power without Anticompetitive Effects (Comment on Klein & Wiley)*, 70 ANTITRUST L.J. 643 (2003); Benjamin Klein & John Shepard Wiley, *Market Power in Economics and in Antitrust: Reply to Baker*, 70 ANTITRUST L.J. 655 (2003); Lao I, *supra* note 1, at 194-95 (arguing against absolute immunity for refusals to deal intellectual property; imposing limited duty to deal intellectual property may enhance, rather than deter, innovation); Arora, *supra* note 1, at 2 (proposing cost-benefit analysis based on theory of "disproportionate leverage").

196. *See supra* § A.1. (for details on *Trinko*).

197. *Trinko* ABA Seminar, *supra* note 5, at 6 (*Trinko* "overrule[d] the Ninth Circuit's decision in [*Kodak II*]" because the Court found "very important" the "plaintiff's absolute inability to provide the good [as to which dealing was requested] itself"; in *Kodak II*, by contrast, "there was no showing that, with respect to most of the aftermarket parts in that case, the plaintiffs could not procure or produce them for themselves.").

198. Unitherm Food Sys. v. Swift Eckrich, Inc., 375 F.3d 1341, 1356 (Fed. Cir. 2004), *rev'd on other grounds*, 126 S. Ct. 980 (2006); *see also, e.g.*, Simpson v. Union Oil Co., 377 U.S. 13, 24 (1964) ("The patent laws ... are in *pari materia* with the antitrust laws and modify them *pro tanto*."); *Xerox*, 203 F.3d 1322, 1328 (Fed. Cir. 2000) ("[T]he owner of the copyright, if [it] pleases, may refrain from vending or licensing the content [itself] with simply exercising the right to exclude others from using [its] property.").

refusals to license, however, there are exceptions to the general rule and unilateral enforcement efforts can give rise to antitrust liability in certain narrow situations.

The three major areas in which enforcement efforts have resulted in antitrust liability being imposed upon intellectual property owners are (1) when the enforcement of intellectual property was obtained through fraud on the patent office (so-called *Walker Process*[199] fraud cases); (2) attempts to enforce intellectual property in bad faith (so-called *Handgards*[200] cases);[201] and (3) in certain circumstances, concealing

---

199. Walker Process Equip. v. Food Mach. & Chem. Corp., 382 U.S. 172 (1965).
200. Handgards, Inc. v. Ethicon, Inc., 601 F.2d 986 (9th Cir. 1979) (*"Handgards I"*); Handgards, Inc. v. Ethicon, Inc., 743 F.2d 1282 (9th Cir. 1984) (*"Handgards II"*).
201. The literature in respect of *Walker Process* and bad faith enforcement claims includes: Timothy J. Muris, *Clarifying the State Action and* Noerr *Exemptions*, 27 HARV. J.L. & PUB. POL'Y 443 (2004); Gavil, *supra* note 5; S.W. O'Donnell, *Unified Theory of Antitrust Counterclaims in Patent Litigation*, 9 VA. J.L. & TECH. 8 (2004) ("O'Donnell"); James B. Kobak, Jr. & Robert P. Reznick, *Antitrust Liability For Statements About Intellectual Property:* Unocal, Unitherm, *and New Uncertainty*, 19 ANTITRUST 87 (2004) ("Kobak & Reznick"); Marina Lao, *Reforming the* Noerr-Pennington *Antitrust Immunity Doctrine*, 55 RUTGERS L. REV. 965 (2003) ("Lao II"); David A. Balto & Andrew M. Wolman, *Intellectual Property and Antitrust: General Principles*, 43 IDEA 395 (2003); Lisa Wood, *In Praise of the* Noerr-Pennington *Doctrine*, 18 ANTITRUST 72 (2003) ("Wood"); Gifford, *supra* note 1; David M. Young, *Strategic Responses to 'Sham Litigation' Claims in Patent Infringement Suits*, 9 No. 15 Andrews Intell. Prop. Litig. Rep. 3 (2002); Joseph Kattan, *Antitrust Implications: Disclosures and Commitments to Standard-Setting Organizations*, 16 ANTITRUST 22 (2002) ("Kattan"); William K. Tom, *Editor's Note, Symposium: The Federal Circuit and Antitrust*, 69 ANTITRUST L.J. 627 (2002); Carrier, *supra* note 1; David R. Steinman & Danielle S. Fitzpatrick, *Antitrust Counterclaims in Patent Infringement Cases: A Guide to* Walker Process *and Sham-Litigation Claims*, 10 TEX. INTELL. PROP. L.J. 95 (2001) ("Steinman"); James R. Atwood, *Securing and Enforcing Patents: The Role of* Noerr/Pennington, 83 J. PAT. & TRADEMARK OFF.S OC'Y 651 (2001); James B. Kobak, Jr., *The Doctrine That Will Not Die:* Nobelpharma, Walker Process, *and the Patent-Antitrust Counterclaim*, 13 ANTITRUST 47 (Fall 1998); James B. Kobak, Jr., Professional Real Estate Investors *and the Future of Patent-Antitrust Litigation:* Walker Process *and* Handgards *meet* Noerr-Pennington, 63 ANTITRUST L.J. 185 (1994) ("Kobak PRE"); Kevin J. Arquit, *Patent*

intellectual property from a standard-setting organization and subsequently enforcing that intellectual property against standard-compliant products.

1. *Walker Process Fraud Claims*

a.   The *Walker Process* Decision

In *Walker Process Equipment v. Food Machinery & Chemical Corp.*,[202] the Supreme Court held that the maintenance and enforcement of a patent obtained by fraud on the Patent and Trademark Office ("PTO") may form the basis of an action under Section 2 of the Sherman Act.[203] In reaching this result, the Court emphasized that patents are "an exception to the general rule against monopolies and to the right to access to a free and open market."[204] Because patents are "affected with a public interest,"[205] however, the Court found that patents procured by fraud would not benefit from the antitrust exception:

> Walker's counterclaim alleged that Food Machinery obtained the patent by knowingly and willfully misrepresenting facts to the Patent Office. Proof of this assertion would be sufficient to strip Food Machinery of its exemption from the antitrust laws.[206]

The Court noted that "[t]his conclusion applies with equal force to an assignee who maintains and enforces the patent with knowledge of the patent's infirmity."[207] The Court warned, however, that "Food Machinery's good faith would furnish a complete defense. This includes an honest mistake as to the effect of [the alleged withheld information] upon patentability—so called 'technical fraud.'"[208]

In a concurring opinion, Justice Harlan elaborated on this point:

Abuse and the Antitrust Laws, 59 ANTITRUST L.J. 739 (1991); Calkins, *supra* note 1.
202.   382 U.S. 172 (1965).
203.   *Id.* at 173.
204.   *Id.* at 177 (quoting Precision Instrument Mfg. v. Auto. Maint. Mach., 324 U.S. 806, 816 (1945)) (internal quotation marks omitted).
205.   *Id.* at 177.
206.   *Id.*
207.   *Id.* at 177 n.5.
208.   *Id.* at 177.

It is well also to recognize the rationale underlying this decision, aimed of course at achieving a suitable accommodation in this area between the differing policies of the patent and antitrust laws. To hold, as we do, that private suits may be instituted ... to recover damages for Sherman Act monopolization knowingly practiced under the guise of a patent procured by deliberate fraud, cannot well be thought to impinge upon the policy of the patent laws to encourage inventions and their disclosure. Hence, as to this class of improper patent monopolies, antitrust remedies should be allowed room for full play. On the other hand, to hold, as we do not, that private antitrust suits might also reach monopolies practiced under patents that for one reason or another may turn out to be voidable under one or more of the numerous technicalities attending the issuance of a patent, might well chill the disclosure of inventions through the obtaining of a patent because of fear of the vexations or punitive consequences of treble-damage suits.[209]

The *Walker Process* Court also made clear that simply establishing fraud on the PTO is not sufficient to impose antitrust liability; the plaintiff also must prove the other elements of a Section 2 claim.[210]

While directed at patents, *Walker Process* has served as the basis for antitrust claims relating to copyrights allegedly obtained by fraud.[211]

---

209. *Id.* at 179-80 (Harlan, J., concurring).
210. *Walker Process*, 382 U.S. at 177-80. These other elements will be discussed below. *See infra* § B.1.d(2).
211. *See, e.g.*, Nat'l Flood Servs. v. Torrent Techs., 2006 U.S. Dist. LEXIS 34196, at *27 (W.D. Wash. 2006); Re-Alco Indus. v. Nat'l Ctr. for Health Educ., 812 F. Supp. 387 (S.D.N.Y. 1993) (attempted monopolization case based on enforcement of invalid copyright; claim dismissed for inadequate allegations of relevant market); Michael Anthony Jewelers v. Peacock Jewelry 795 F. Supp. 639, 645-50 (S.D.N.Y. 1992) (*Walker Process*-style claim in connection with fraudulent procurement and enforcement of copyright survives motion to dismiss); Knickerbocker Toy Co. v. Winterbrook Corp., 554 F. Supp. 1309, 1321 (D.N.H. 1982) ("Fraudulent procurement of a copyright by means of knowing and willful misrepresentations to the Copyright Office may strip a copyright holder of its exemption from the antitrust laws" citing *Walker Process*; allegations of market power inadequate); Vogue Ring Creations v. Hardman, 410 F. Supp. 609, 616 (D.R.I. 1976) (accepting concept of *Walker Process*-style claim for fraudulent procurement of copyright registration, but finding insufficient proof of bad faith); *But see* HOVENKAMP IP, *supra* note 30, § 11.1 n.4 (asserting that "*Walker Process* claims do not apply to copyright, unregistered trademark and

b.	*Walker Process* Cases in Practice

The lower courts, echoing Justice Harlan's concurrence in *Walker Process*, have made abundantly clear that the patentee should be stripped of its immunity and exposed to antitrust liability only in situations of egregious conduct. As the Federal Circuit has held:

> Neither the bringing of an unsuccessful suit to enforce patent rights, nor the effort to enforce a patent that falls to invalidity, subjects the suitor to antitrust liability.... [T]he patentee must have the right of enforcement of a duly granted patent, unencumbered by punitive consequences should the patent's validity ... not survive litigation. The law recognizes a presumption that the assertion of a duly granted patent is made in good faith.... [T]his presumption is overcome only by affirmative evidence of bad faith.[212]

In *Cataphote Corp. v. DeSoto Chemical Coatings, Inc.*,[213] the Ninth Circuit emphasized the stringent standard for establishing fraud sufficient to trigger antitrust liability:

> The road to the Patent Office is so tortuous and patent litigation is usually so complex, that "knowing and willful fraud" as the term is used in *Walker*, can mean no less than clear, convincing proof of intentional fraud involving affirmative dishonesty, "a deliberately planned and carefully executed scheme to defraud ... the Patent Office." Patent fraud cases prior to *Walker* required a rigorous standard of deceit.... *Walker* requires no less.[214]

---

trade secret cases because no government agency issues the intellectual property right in question. Thus, for purposes of intellectual property, *Walker Process* is a doctrine that effectively applies only in patent cases."); *cf.* Clipper Express v. Rocky Mountain Motor Tariff Bureau, 690 F.2d 1240, 1260-61 (9th Cir. 1982) (holding that the *Walker Process* doctrine is not limited to patents, but applies in any case involving "fraudulent furnishing of false information to an agency in connection with an adjudicatory proceeding").

212.	C.R. Bard, Inc. v. M3 Sys., 157 F.3d 1340, 1369 (Fed. Cir. 1998); *see also, e.g.*, HOLMES, *supra* note 26, § 15.03, at 15-27 ("The courts have consistently given a very narrow construction to the type of fraud that will support an antitrust claim.").

213.	450 F.2d 769 (9th Cir. 1971).

214.	*Id.* at 772.

Similarly, in *C.R. Bard, Inc. v. M3 Systems, Inc.*,[215] the Federal Circuit wrote:

> Deceptive intent is not inferred simply because information was in existence that was not presented to the examiner; and indeed, it is notable that in the usual course of patent prosecution, many choices are made, recognizing the complexity of inventions, the virtually unlimited sources of information, and the burdens of patent examination.[216]

Walker Process fraud is viewed as a more serious offense than inequitable conduct and is held to a higher standard.[217] "Inequitable

---

215. 157 F.3d 1340 (Fed. Cir. 1998).

216. *Id.* at 1365; *see also, e.g.*, N. Telecom, Inc. v. Datapoint Corp., 908 F.2d 931, 939 (Fed. Cir. 1990) (discussing ease with which routine patent examination may be portrayed as tainted conduct); Hewlett-Packard Co. v. Bausch & Lomb, Inc., 882 F.2d 1556, 1563 (Fed. Cir. 1989) ("[A]n extremely high level of misconduct, actual fraud, is necessary to sustain a *Walker Process* antitrust claim ... [W]hen a party seeks to collect monetary damages from a patentee because of alleged violations of the antitrust laws, it is appropriate to require a higher degree of misconduct for that damage award than when a party asserts only a defense to an infringement claim.").

217. *See, e.g.*, Nobelpharma AB v. Implant Innovations, 141 F.3d 1059, 1069-70 (Fed. Cir. 1998) ("Inequitable conduct in fact is a lesser offense than common law fraud."). Inequitable conduct—based on the doctrine of unclean hands—represents conduct that, while not as egregious as *Walker Process* fraud, nevertheless makes a patent invalid or unenforceable. *See, e.g.*, FMC Corp. v. Hennessy Indus., 836 F.2d 521, 523 n.3 (Fed. Cir. 1987) ("'Inequitable conduct' may render a patent unenforceable, but differs from the 'fraud' required to support a *'Walker Process'* type antitrust claim."). Inequitable conduct requires proof that a patent applicant failed to disclose to the PTO material information known to him or submitted material information he or she knew to be false. *See, e.g.*, Merck & Co. v. Danbury Pharmacal, Inc., 873 F.2d 1418, 1420 (Fed. Cir. 1989); FMC Corp. v. Manitowoc Co., 835 F.2d 1411, 1415 (Fed. Cir. 1987); DONALD S. CHISUM, CHISUM ON PATENTS § 19.03 (2001) ("CHISUM") (extensive treatment of inequitable conduct); *see also Nobelpharma*, 141 F.3d at 1070 (materiality defined (for applications prosecuted prior to 1992) as information that would have been "*important* to the patentability of a claim by a reasonable examiner") (emphasis added); Stark v. Advanced Magnetics, 119 F.3d 1551, 1556 (Fed. Cir. 1997). To qualify as "inequitable," the misrepresentation or omission must have been made with an "intent to deceive." *See, e.g.*, Kingsdown

conduct is ... an equitable defense in a patent infringement action and serves as a shield, while a more serious finding of fraud potentially exposes a patentee to antitrust liability and thus serves as a sword."[218]

Accordingly, "a finding of *Walker Process* fraud requires higher threshold showings of both intent and materiality than does a finding of inequitable conduct."[219]

The Federal Circuit recently urged the regional circuits to follow its law on the conduct necessary to strip a patentee of antitrust immunity, although there is no guarantee that they will. It is important, therefore, that Federal Circuit and regional circuit law be consulted.[220]

Med. Consultants v. Hollister, Inc., 863 F.2d 867, 876 (Fed. Cir. 1988); CHISUM, *supra*, § 19.03[4].

218. *Nobelpharma*, 141 F.3d at 1070; *see also* CHISUM, *supra* note 217, § 19.03[6][e] ("When a party relies on fraudulent procurement as a sword (antitrust liability) rather than as a shield (invalidity or unenforceability), the party must make a greater showing of scienter. The party also must make a greater showing of materiality.").

219. *Nobelpharma*, 141 F.3d at 1070-71. While inequitable conduct (not rising to the level of *Walker Process* fraud) cannot support a claim under Section 2, the antitrust enforcement agencies have taken the position that such conduct *may* contravene § 5 of the FTC Act. *See* INTELLECTUAL PROPERTY GUIDELINES, *supra* note 4, § 6; *see also In re* VISX, Inc., No. 9286, 1999 WL 33577396 (FTC May 27, 1999) (rejecting inequitable conduct allegations brought pursuant to § 5 of the FTC Act); *In re* Am. Cyanamid Co., 72 FTC 623, 684-85 (1967), *aff'd sub. nom.* Charles Pfizer & Co. v. FTC, 401 F.2d 574 (6th Cir. 1968).

220. As the Federal Circuit put it, "[i]f the resolution of the [*Walker Process*] dispute rests, in part, upon a determination of whether or not a patentee's behavior stripped it of its antitrust exemption, the appellate court hearing the matter will have to decide whether to apply Federal Circuit law or risk disturbing 'Congress's goal of ensuring patent-law uniformity' by applying its own law." Unitherm Food Sys. v. Swift Eckrich, Inc., 375 F.3d 1341, 1355 n.3 (Fed. Cir. 2004) (citation omitted) (quoting Holmes Group v. Vornado Air Circulation Sys., 535 U.S. 826, 827 (2002)), *rev'd on other grounds*, 126 S. Ct. 980 (2006). Thus, according to the court, "the determination of *which* actions can cause a patentee or a patent applicant to lose the general protection of the patent law and to risk liability for damages is clearly an issue unique to the patent law—and therefore inappropriate for resolution under the potentially varying interpretations of the regional circuits." *Id.* at 1357.

Most district courts have followed the Federal Circuit's decision on choice of law. *See, e.g., In re* Ciprofloxacin Hydrochloride Antitrust Litig., No. 1:00MDL1383DGT, 2005 WL 736604, at *25 (E.D.N.Y. Mar.

c.   The Elements of a *Walker Process* Fraud Case

Broadly speaking, the following elements must be established to make out a private *Walker Process* monopolization claim:

(1) the patentee intentionally committed fraud on the PTO by misrepresenting or omitting material facts in the course of prosecuting the patent application;
(2) the patentee utilized the fraudulently procured patent to exercise monopoly power in a properly defined relevant antitrust market;

31, 2005) (Federal Circuit law will decide issue of "whether conduct in procuring or enforcing a patent is sufficient to strip a patentee of its immunity from the antitrust laws") (quoting *Nobelpharma*, 141 F.3d at 1068); *In re* Terazosin Hydrochloride Antitrust Litig., 335 F. Supp. 2d 1336, 1357 (S.D. Fla. 2004) (same); *In re* Relafen Antitrust Litig., 346 F. Supp. 2d 349, 363, 365-67 (D. Mass. 2004) (applying Federal Circuit law); Doran v. Purdue Pharma, 324 F. Supp. 2d 1147, 1151 (D. Nev. 2004) (same); Applera Corp. v. MJ Research, 303 F. Supp. 2d 130, 133 n.11 (D. Conn. 2004) (same); PennPac Int'l v. Rotonics Mfg., No. 99-CV-2890, 2001 WL 569264, at *5 n.3 (E.D. Pa. May 25, 2001) ("Federal Circuit law applies to all antitrust claims premised on the bringing of a patent infringement suit. It follows that antitrust claims premised on notice given to infringers is also governed by Federal Circuit law.") (citation omitted); Warner Lambert Co. v. PurePac Pharm., No. Civ. A. 98-02749 (JCL), 2000 WL 34213890, at *6 (D.N.J. Dec. 22, 2000) (same); Travelers Express v. Am. Express Integrated Payment Sys., 80 F. Supp. 2d 1033, 1042 (D. Minn. 1999) (same); Victus, Ltd. v. Collezione Europa U.S.A., Inc., 26 F. Supp. 2d 772, 779 n.4 (M.D.N.C. 1998) ("The law of the Federal Circuit will control the question of whether conduct in enforcing a patent infringement suit is sufficient to strip a patentee of its immunity from antitrust laws. However ... the law of the [regional circuit] will still control the resolution of issues involving other elements of antitrust law.") (citation omitted); Moore N.A. v. Poser Bus. Forms, No. 97-712, 2000 WL 1480992, at *5-6 (D. Del. Sept. 29, 2000). *But see* Schor v. Abbott Labs., No. 05-C-1592, 2005 WL 1653606, at *6 (N.D. Ill. July 12, 2005) (court holds it is not bound by Federal Circuit law on whether patentee should be stripped of antitrust immunity over alleged monopoly leveraging; court nonetheless finds Federal Circuit authority persuasive and elects to follow it); *cf.* Spotless Enters. v. Carlisle Plastics, 56 F. Supp. 2d 274, 285 n.11 (E.D.N.Y. 1999) (criticizing the Federal Circuit's choice-of-law rule as creating a conundrum for district courts).

(3) the party asserting the *Walker Process* fraud claim suffered or is threatened with injury to its business or property, and otherwise has standing to sue under Section 4 or 16 of the Clayton Act; and

(4) the party asserting the claim suffered reasonably quantifiable damages.[221]

Element (1), fraud, must be established with clear and convincing evidence.[222] The "antitrust" elements, (2) through (4), must be shown by a preponderance of the evidence.[223]

---

221. *Unitherm*, 375 F.3d at 1358; CHISUM, *supra* note 217, § 19.03[6][e]; ALD (5th), *supra* note 2, at 1041.

222. *See, e.g.*, *Unitherm*, 375 F.3d at 1360 (in *Walker Process* case, "clear and convincing circumstantial evidence" required); Oetiker v. Jurid Werke GmbH, 671 F.2d 596, 600 (D.C. Cir. 1982) ("A finding that a patent was procured by fraud [sufficient to give rise to an antitrust violation] must be based on 'clear, unequivocal and convincing' evidence."); *see also* N. Telecom v. Datapoint Corp., 908 F.2d 931, 939 (Fed. Cir. 1990) ("Given the ease with which a relatively routine act of patent prosecution can be portrayed as intended to mislead or deceive, clear and convincing evidence of conduct sufficient to support an inference of culpable intent is required.").

223. *See* 4 LEONARD B. SAND, ET AL., MODERN FEDERAL JURY INSTRUCTIONS ¶ 81.02, at 81-35 (2005) (Form Instruction 81-10 requiring proof of antitrust elements by a preponderance of the evidence). Moreover, as a matter of pleading, the fraud must be alleged with particularity pursuant to Fed. R. Civ. P. 9(b). Defendants often succeed in having *Walker Process* cases dismissed on the pleadings for failure to meet this standard. *See, e.g.*, Versatile Plastics v. Sknowbest! Inc., 247 F. Supp. 2d 1098 (E.D. Wis. 2003) (court dismissed antitrust damage claim arising from patent infringement notice letters; complaint failed to allege facts necessary to establish bad faith, such as knowledge of individuals allegedly involved in fraudulent conduct); Bristol-Myers Squibb Co. v. IVAX Corp., 77 F. Supp. 2d 606, 613 (D.N.J. 2000) (*Walker Process* counterclaims fall short of "pleading standards mandated by the federal rules"); Imp. Sys. Int'l v. Lee, No. 90 Civ. 6896 (MEL), 1992 WL 77613 (S.D.N.Y. Mar. 20, 1992) (*Walker Process* claim did not allege fraud with detail sufficient to satisfy Rule 9(b)); Kash 'N Gold, Ltd. v. Samhill Corp., No. 90 Civ. 1097 (MJL), 1990 WL 196089, at *1, 3 (S.D.N.Y. Nov. 29, 1990) (*Walker Process* claim dismissed for lack of specificity; noting that Rule 9(b) permits "malice, intent, knowledge and other condition of mind" to be averred generally, but that "'circumstances must be pleaded that provide a factual foundation for otherwise conclusory

For an attempt to monopolize, elements (1), (3) and (4) must be established, together with showings that the patentee's use of the tainted patent created a dangerous probability of achieving monopoly power and that the patentee possessed a specific intent to monopolize.[224]

The elements are considered below.

(1) The "Fraud" Elements

In *Unitherm Food Systems v. Swift Eckrich, Inc.*,[225] the Federal Circuit explained that "*Walker Process* fraud is a variant of common law fraud," and that the elements of common law fraud should be applied in *Walker-Process* cases.[226] The fraud elements are as follows:

(1) a representation of a material fact, (2) the falsity of that representation, (3) the intent to deceive or, at least, a state of mind so reckless as to the consequences that it is held to be the equivalent of intent (scienter), (4) a justifiable reliance upon the misrepresentation by the party deceived which induces him to act thereon, and (5) injury to

allegations of scienter'" (quoting Stern v. Leucadia Nat'l Corp., 844 F.2d 997, 1004 (2d Cir. 1988))); Papst Motoren GmbH & Co. KG v. Kanematsu-Goshu (U.S.A.) Inc., 629 F. Supp. 864, 871-72 (S.D.N.Y. 1986) (conclusory assertions of "fraud" cannot satisfy particularity requirement; no allegations of relevant market); Jordan v. N.Y. Mercantile Exch., 571 F. Supp. 1530, 1542 n.4 (S.D.N.Y. 1983) (applying Rule 9(b)'s pleading requirement to allegations of bad faith); Erie Tech. Prods. v. JFD Elec. Components, 198 U.S.P.Q. 179, 186 (E.D.N.Y. 1978) (dismissing *Walker Process* claim; no allegation of relevant market); Raines v. Switch Mfg., No. C-96-2648 DLJ, 1997 WL 578547, at *4-5 (N.D. Cal. July 28, 1997) (applying Rule 9 and holding that antitrust plaintiff must "provide some factual basis for the allegation that [the patentee] knew the patent was invalid or unenforceable"). *But see, e.g.,* True Position, Inc. v. Allen Telecom, No. 01-823 GMS, 2003 U.S. Dist. LEXIS 881, at *18 (D. Del. Jan. 21, 2003); Rolite, Inc. v. Wheelabrator Envtl. Sys., 958 F. Supp. 992, 1005 (E.D. Pa. 1997) (finding plaintiff stated fraudulent omission claim with sufficient particularity); Ryan-House v. GlaxoSmithKline plc, No. 2:02 CV 442, slip op. (E.D. Va. Mar. 12, 2004) (motion to dismiss *Walker Process* claim denied).

224. *Nobelpharma*, 141 F.3d at 1070; *see also* CHISUM, *supra* note 217, § 19.03[6][e].
225. 375 F.3d 1341 (Fed. Cir. 2004), *rev'd on other grounds*, 126 S. Ct. 980 (2006).
226. *Id.* at 1358.

the party deceived as a result of his reliance on the mis-representation.[227]

(A) MATERIALITY

To be material, the misrepresentation or omission must be sufficiently important "that the patent would not have issued but for the misrepresentation or omission."[228] This showing of but-for causation is necessary because a *Walker Process* case is "an action to correct an anticompetitive market effect" and "[f]raud on the PTO cannot produce such an anticompetitive market effect unless the PTO would not have issued the patent but for the patentee's misrepresentation or omission."[229]

---

227. *Id.* at 1358-59.
228. *See, e.g.*, *Nobelpharma*, 141 F.3d at 1070-71; *see also, e.g.*, *Unitherm*, 375 F.3d at 1355 (*Walker Process* claimant must show that "the [subject] patent issued because [the patentee] defrauded the PTO"); C.R. Bard, Inc. v. M3 Sys., 157 F.3d 1340, 1365 (Fed. Cir. 1998) ("To establish culpability any omission must be of a fact material to patentability that ... did mislead the examiner into taking favorable action that would not otherwise have been taken."); Brunswick Corp. v. Riegel Textile Corp., 752 F.2d 261, 265 (7th Cir. 1984) (holding that the "invention sought to be patented must not be patentable"). The "but-for" test for materiality generally is evaluated on an objective basis. *See, e.g.*, JULIAN O. VON KALINOWSKI ET AL., ANTITRUST LAWS AND TRADE REGULATION § 73.03[1][a][i], at 73-23 (2004) ("VON KALINOWSKI") (The argument "that objective materiality must be demonstrated to create an antitrust claim arising out of fraudulent procurement seems far more compelling [than a subjective test]."); HOLMES, *supra* note 26, § 15.03, at 15-31 to 15-32; CHISUM, *su pra* note 217, § 19.03[6][e].
229. HOVENKAMP IP, *supra* note 30, at 11-11. There can be no actionable fraud if the information in question was submitted to the PTO or it can be shown that the patent examiner otherwise was aware of the information. For example, the withheld information may have been discovered through independent research by the patent examiner. The Federal Circuit has held that "[w]hen a reference was before the examiner, whether through the examiner's search or the applicant's disclosure, it cannot be deemed to have been withheld from the examiner." Molins PLC v. Textron, Inc., 48 F.3d 1172, 1185 (Fed. Cir. 1995) (internal quotation marks omitted).
   Sometimes the material is disclosed to the examiner in a related application rather than in the one under scrutiny. *See, e.g.*, Akron Polymer Container v. Exxel Container, 148 F.3d 1380, 1384 (Fed. Cir. 1998) (deceitful intent could not be found where patent applicant failed to disclose material information in one application, where it had disclosed

By contrast, in assessing inequitable conduct, information is deemed material (for patents prosecuted prior to 1992) if a reasonable examiner merely would have considered it "important" in deciding whether to grant a patent; for patents prosecuted after 1992, "materiality" is defined as information which would establish "a *prima facie* case of unpatentability," or that would refute or contradict a position taken by the applicant on the patentability (or lack thereof) of the subject matter in question.[230]

Walker Process fraud may be accomplished through affirmative misrepresentations or omissions. This is because omissions can be as "reprehensible as misrepresentations."[231] Thus, "if the evidence shows that the asserted patent was acquired by means of either a fraudulent misrepresentation or a fraudulent omission and that the party asserting the patent was aware of the fraud when bringing suit, such conduct can expose a patentee to liability under the antitrust laws."[232]

Walker Process defendants routinely argue that plaintiffs cannot show with clear and convincing evidence that, had the examiner been on

---

the information in a related application being handled by a *different* examiner); *In re* VISX, Inc., No. 9286, 1999 WL 33577396 (FTC May 27, 1999) (dismissing count for fraud on PTO and stating that "evidence in the record confirms that if two patent applications are pending at the same time before the same examiner, it is not necessary to cite the references from either application in the other application, because the same examiner has both applications before him, and will be aware of 'what is going on' in both applications"). *But see* Monsanto Co. v. Rohm & Haas Co., 456 F.2d 592, 600 (3d Cir. 1972) (holding that a patent examiner cannot be charged with knowledge of previous applications pending before him); Armour & Co. v. Swift Co., 466 F.2d 767, 779 (7th Cir. 1972) (holding that "the applicant has the burden of presenting the Examiner with a complete and accurate record"); U.S. PATENT & TRADEMARK OFFICE, MANUAL OF PATENT EXAMINING PROCEDURE § 2004.09 (8th ed. 2004) ("Do not assume that an examiner will necessarily remember, when examining a particular application, other applications which the examiner is examining, or has examined.").

230.   37 C.F.R. § 1.56(b); *see, e.g.*, Dayco Prods. v. Total Containment, Inc., 329 F.3d 1358, 1362 (Fed. Cir. 2003).

231.   *Nobelpharma*, 141 F.3d at 1070; *see also, e.g.*, HOVENKAMP IP, *supra* note 30, at 11-11 ("[T]he most common and insidious forms of fraud on the PTO are not affirmative statements, but the failure to disclose information, such as prior art references the PTO is unlikely to find on its own or information about the patentee's own commercial activities.").

232.   *Nobelpharma*, 141 F.3d at 1070.

notice of the full facts, he or she would have rejected the application. In light of the heavy burden placed on plaintiffs, defendants are often successful in this effort.[233]

(B)   FALSITY

Falsity may consist of a misrepresentation, omission, or misleading statement made in the procurement of a patent.[234] In *Unitherm*, for example, the patentee failed to disclose material information concerning prior art.[235] The duty of candor explicitly prohibits the making of a materially false statement or failing to disclose a material fact in a patent application. [236]

---

233. *See, e.g.*, Hewlett-Packard Co. v. Bausch & Lomb, Inc., 882 F.2d 1556, 1563 (Fed. Cir. 1989); E.I. du Pont de Nemours & Co. v. Berkley & Co., 620 F.2d 1247, 1275 (8th Cir. 1980) (describing materiality as plaintiff's "heavy burden"); *In re Clark*, 522 F.2d 623, 628 (C.C.P.A. 1975); Fuji Photo Film Co. v. Jazz Photo Corp., 173 F. Supp. 2d 268, 276-77 (D.N.J. 2001) (granting summary judgment to defendant where there was insufficient evidence that alleged omissions before PTO were either intentional or material); Miller Pipeline v. British Gas PLC, 69 F. Supp. 2d 1129, 1136 (S.D. Ind. 1999) ("little or no evidence showing . . . alleged misrepresentation was material and that the patent office relied upon it."); Scripto-Tokai Corp. v. Gillette Co., No. CV-91-2862-LGB(JRX), 1994 WL 746072, at *11-12 (C.D. Cal. Sept. 9, 1994) (summary judgment granted in light of failure to show that omissions in patent prosecutions were material); Jack Winter, Inc. v. Koratron Co., 375 F. Supp. 1, 67 (N.D. Cal. 1974) (plaintiff could not establish materiality of alleged misrepresentations); Erie Tech. Prods. v. JFD Elec. Components, 198 U.S.P.Q. 179, 185-86 (E.D.N.Y. 1978) (no allegation of materiality).
234. *See, e.g., Nobelpharma*, 141 F.3d at 1070-71 (stripping patentee of immunity from antitrust liability upon a finding of substantial evidence of omission of prior art); Arcade, Inc. v. Minn. Mining & Mfg., 1 F.3d 1253 (Fed. Cir. 1993) (affirming that misrepresentation of test data and failure to disclose affidavit supported jury's finding of antitrust violation).
235. Unitherm Food Sys. v. Swift Eckrich, Inc., 375 F.3d 1341, 1359 (Fed. Cir. 2004), *rev'd on other grounds*, 126 S. Ct. 980 (2006).
236. 37 C.F.R. § 10.22(a) (2003); Hycor Corp. v. Schlueter Co., 740 F.2d 1529, 1538 (Fed. Cir. 1984) (warning that "[t]he highest standards of honesty and candor on the part of applicants in presenting such facts to the [PTO] are ... necessary elements in a working patent system. We would go so far to say they are essential."); *see also, e.g.*, Armour & Co.

(C) THE INTENT TO DECEIVE

According to the Federal Circuit, the "intent to deceive" element of a *Walker Process* claim "is the most difficult to prove."[237] The intent required has been described variously as "intentional fraud involving affirmative dishonesty"[238] and "a deliberately planned and carefully executed scheme."[239] Merely negligent, or even grossly negligent, misstatements or omissions generally will not support a finding of fraudulent intent sufficient to establish an antitrust claim.[240]

---

v. Swift Co., 466 F.2d 767, 779 (7th Cir. 1972) (holding that, in light of burdens on the "busy [e]xaminer," applicant must submit "complete and accurate record" in support of patent application).

237. *Unitherm,* 375 F.3d at 1360.

238. Cataphote Corp. v. DeSoto Chem. Coatings, 450 F.2d 769, 772 (9th Cir. 1971).

239. *Id.*

240. "Applicants for patents do not engage in fraudulent conduct when they make honest mistakes in judgment concerning the information material to consideration of their applications" or deviate slightly from the proper standard of care. Digital Equip. v. Diamond, 653 F.2d 701, 715 (1st Cir. 1981); *see also* Am. Hoist & Derrick Co. v. Sowa & Sons, 725 F.2d 1350, 1368 (Fed. Cir. 1984) ("[W]e emphasize that a specific intent, greater than an intent evidenced by gross negligence or recklessness, is an indispensable element."). "It is well established that a patent attorney's erroneous judgment or even gross negligence is not sufficient to give rise to an inference of intent to deceive." TRW Fin. Sys. v. Unisys Corp., 835 F. Supp. 994, 1011 (E.D. Mich. 1993) (citing Halliburton Co. v. Schlumberger Tech., 925 F.2d 1435, 1441-43 (Fed. Cir. 1991)). The Sixth Circuit, in an unpublished opinion, held that "mistakes resulting from inadvertence or ignorance of the law of trademarks do not give rise to liability for fraud [against the PTO]." Brenton Prod. Enters. v. Motion Media, No. 96-6044, 1997 WL 603412, at *3 (6th Cir. Sept. 30, 1997) (citing Schwinn Bicycle Co. v. Murray Ohio Mfg., 339 F. Supp. 973, 983 (M.D. Tenn. 1971)) (finding no fraud against PTO where statements of plaintiff's officers could "reasonably be construed to have resulted from inadvertence or ignorance of the applicable law of trademarks"). On the other hand, in another unpublished opinion, the Federal Circuit stated that ignorance of the law in the context of inequitable conduct, "while perhaps relevant to good faith, does not relieve . . . the possibility of inferred intent." Jack Frost Labs. v. Physicians & Nurses Mfg., Nos. 96-1114, 96-1430, 96-1543, 1997 WL 592814, at *6 (Fed. Cir. Sept. 23, 1997); *see also, e.g.,* Kingsdown Med. Consultants v. Hollister, Inc., 863 F.2d 867, 876 (Fed. Cir. 1988) ("[A] finding that particular conduct amounts to

Some courts have found the requisite intent lacking where the allegedly omitted disclosure was admitted in another application. In the context of omissions, the Federal Circuit has held that, "for an omission such as a failure to cite a piece of prior art to support a finding of *Walker Process* fraud, the withholding of the reference must show evidence of fraudulent intent. A mere failure to cite a reference to the PTO will not suffice."[241] For example, in *Kimberly-Clark Corp. v. Johnson & Johnson Co.*,[242] the applicant failed to disclose certain prior art in an application, but did disclose such art to the same examiner in a related application filed within three months of the other. The Federal Circuit reversed a finding of invalidity due to inequitable conduct stating that the prior patent was not being concealed from the examiner given that it was disclosed in one of the applications and the court refused to read "any nefarious purpose in the failure to disclose it in the [other] application."[243]

Since direct proof of fraudulent intent is rarely available, the patent applicant's scienter may be inferred from circumstantial evidence. "Intent need not be proven by direct evidence; it is most often proven by a showing of acts, the natural consequences of which are presumably intended by the actor. Generally, intent must be inferred from the facts and circumstances surrounding the applicant's conduct."[244] Thus, *Walker Process* fraud can be shown where "clear and convincing circumstantial

'gross negligence' does not of itself justify an inference of intent to deceive."); Argus Chem. v. Fibre Glass-Evercoat Co., 812 F.2d 1381, 1385 (Fed. Cir. 1987) (something "greater than an intent evidenced by gross negligence or recklessness" required for a *Walker Process* claim of attempt to monopolize). *But see Cataphote*, 450 F.2d at 772 (suggesting that "gross negligence" might be sufficient); Litton Indus. Prods. v. Solid State Sys., 755 F.2d 158, 166 n.18 (Fed. Cir. 1985) (applying Ninth Circuit law; suggesting same).

241.	Nobelpharma AB v. Implant Innovations, Inc., 141 F.3d 1059, 1071 (Fed. Cir. 1998).

242.	745 F.2d 1437, 1456 (Fed. Cir. 1984).

243.	*Id.*; *see, e.g.*, Dayco Prods. v. Total Containment, Inc., 329 F.3d 1358, 1366 (Fed. Cir. 2003) (finding that the "requisite intent [for inequitable conduct] could not be inferred because the patentee did 'disclose the existence of the [second] application to the [first] application's examiner, and thus put the PTO on notice of the copendency of the two applications'").

244.	*Unitherm*, 375 F.3d at 1360 (Fed. Cir. 2004) (quoting Molins PLC v. Textron, Inc., 48 F.3d 1172, 1180-81 (Fed. Cir. 1995)) (internal quotation marks omitted).

evidence establishes that, at the very least, [the patentee] exhibited 'a state of mind so reckless as to the consequences that it is held to be the equivalent of intent.'"[245]

However, "given the ease with which a relatively routine act of patent prosecution can be portrayed as intended to mislead or deceive, clear and convincing evidence of conduct sufficient to support an inference of culpable intent is required.... While intent to deceive the PTO may be found as a matter of inference from circumstantial evidence, circumstantial evidence cannot indicate merely gross negligence."[246] Moreover, "clear and convincing evidence must prove that an applicant had the specific intent to accomplish an act that the applicant ought not to have performed, viz., misleading or deceiving the PTO." [247]

The Supreme Court held in *Walker Process* that the patentee's "good faith" would "furnish a complete defense" to a claim of monopolization stemming from fraud on the PTO.[248] "This includes an honest mistake as to the effect of [the allegedly withheld information] upon patentability— so-called 'technical fraud.'"[249] Accordingly, to the degree the patentee is able to show good faith, honest mistake or even negligence, he or she should succeed in defeating a *Walker Process* fraud claim.[250]

---

245. *Id.* at 1360 (quoting *In re* Spalding Sports Worldwide, Inc., 203 F.3d 800, 807 (Fed. Cir. 2000)). Early cases from the Federal Circuit and other jurisdictions implied direct evidence of intent might be a requirement in a *Walker Process* case. *See, e.g.*, Scripto-Tokai Corp. v. Gillette Co., No. CV-91-2862-LGB(JRX), 1994 WL 746072, at *11 (C.D. Cal. Sept. 9, 1994) (requiring "deliberate intent to deceive" to establish *Walker Process* claim); Papst Motoren GmbH & Co. KG v. Kanematsu-Goshu (U.S.A.) Inc., 629 F. Supp. 864, 870 (S.D.N.Y. 1986) (same).

246. *Unitherm*, 375 F.3d at 1360 (quoting Molins PLC v. Textron, Inc., 48 F.3d 1172, 1180-81 (Fed. Cir. 1995)) (internal quotation marks omitted).

247. *Id.*

248. Walker Process Equip. v. Food Mach. & Chem. Corp., 382 U.S. 172, 177 (1965); *see also, e.g.*, C.R. Bard, Inc. v. M3 Sys., 157 F.3d 1340, 1365 (Fed. Cir. 1998). Good faith is an absolute defense to the charge of common law fraud."); CHISUM, *supra* note 217, § 19.03[4] ("A good faith mistake does not constitute fraud or inequitable conduct.").

249. *Walker Process*, 382 U.S. at 177.

250. *See, e.g.*, *C.R. Bard*, 157 F.3d at 1368 (evidence of several alleged misstatements or omissions in patent prosecution—including incorrectly naming inventors, not supplying samples of product, failing to provide to PTO additional material provided to Food and Drug Administration, failing to disclose certain related patents and co-pending patents, and not disclosing all evidence with respect to the on-sale issue—were *not*

sufficient to support a jury's finding of *Walker Process* liability); Cabinet Vision v. Cabinetware, 129 F.3d 595 (Fed. Cir. 1997); Argus Chem. v. Fibre Glass-Evercoat Co., 812 F.2d 1381 (Fed. Cir. 1987); CVD, Inc. v. Raytheon Co., 769 F.2d 842, 849 (1st Cir. 1985); Litton Indus. Prods. v. Solid State Sys., 755 F.2d 158, 166-67 (Fed. Cir. 1985) ("Wholly inadvertent errors or honest mistakes, which are caused by neither fraudulent intent nor by the patentee's gross negligence, do not constitute the requisite level of intent."); Oetiker v. Jurid Werke GmbH, 671 F.2d 596, 600 (D.C. Cir. 1982) ("A good faith judgment not to cite prior art to the PTO, even if erroneous, cannot be fraud." Evidence showed good faith belief that withheld information would not influence PTO decision on patentability.); *Handgards I*, 601 F.2d 986, 996 (9th Cir. 1979); Deere v. Heaston, 593 F.2d 956, 960 (10th Cir. 1979) (evidence showed good faith belief that withheld information would not influence PTO decision on patentability); Cataphote Corp. v. DeSoto Chem. Coatings, 450 F.2d 769, 772-73 (9th Cir. 1971) (evidence of patentee's good faith belief in correctness of his disclosure decisions defeated claim of fraud); Bendix Corp. v. Balax, Inc., 421 F.2d 809 (7th Cir. 1970); Fuji Photo Film Co. v. Jazz Photo Corp., 173 F. Supp. 2d 268, 276-77 (D.N.J. 2001) (granting summary judgment to defendant where there was insufficient evidence that alleged omissions before PTO were either intentional or material); Miller Pipeline v. British Gas PLC, 69 F. Supp. 2d 1129, 1136-40 (S.D. Ind. 1999) (insufficient evidence of intent to deceive examiner); Baxa Corp. v. McGaw, Inc., 996 F. Supp. 1044, 1050 (D. Colo. 1997) (granting summary judgment on *Walker Process* claim for lack of evidence of bad faith), *aff'd without op.*, 185 F.3d 883 (Fed. Cir. 1999); *Scripto-Tokai*, 1994 WL 746072, at *11-12 (plaintiff could not overcome patentee's showing of good faith basis for disclosure decisions); *In re* Recombinant DNA Tech. Patent & Contract Litig., 874 F. Supp. 904, 914-15 (S.D. Ind. 1994) (university's representation that nonexclusive license appeared unattractive and request that federal agency grant exclusive license for patents resulting from agency-funded research not actionable as fraud on agency); TRW Fin. Sys. v. Unisys Corp., 835 F. Supp. 994, 1013-15 (E.D. Mich. 1993) (*Walker Process* claim subject to summary judgment for failure to overcome evidence of patentee's good faith); *Papst Motoren*, 629 F. Supp. at 870 ("*Walker* and its progeny emphasize that to sustain [defendant's] antitrust counterclaim, 'deliberate fraud' is required: 'there must be allegations and proof of knowing, willful and intentional acts of misrepresentation to the Patent Office.'"); Jack Winter, Inc. v. Koratron Co., 375 F. Supp. 1, 67 (N.D. Cal. 1974) (*Walker Process* plaintiff could not show bad faith); Erie Tech. Prods. v. JFD Elec. Components Corp., 198 U.S.P.Q. 179, 185-86 (E.D.N.Y. 1978) (no allegations of deliberate fraud).

The courts have often said that the level of intent necessary to establish *Walker Process* fraud is greater than that necessary to establish inequitable conduct.[251] But the distinction between the intent necessary to show inequitable conduct and that necessary to show *Walker Process* fraud is not always apparent in practice.[252] For example, inequitable conduct requires an "intent to deceive."[253] In *Walker Process* cases, courts have referred to "deceptive intent,"[254] and "affirmative dishonesty,"[255] phrases which, on their face, provide no clear differentiation from the "intent to deceive" required for inequitable conduct. Moreover, courts have held that *indirect* proof of intent—such as a reckless disregard for the truth—may be sufficient in both the inequitable conduct and the *Walker Process* contexts.[256] In *Cataphote*, the Ninth Circuit even suggested that "gross negligence" might be adequate to establish a *Walker Process* claim.[257] The Federal Circuit, in

---

251. *See, e.g.*, Nobelpharma AB v. Implant Innovations, 141 F.3d 1059, 1070-71 (Fed. Cir. 1998); *C.R. Bard*, 157 F.3d at 1364; *Baxa*, 996 F. Supp. at 1048-49; Minn. Mining & Mfg. v. Research Med., 691 F. Supp. 1305, 1309-10 (D. Utah 1988) (*Walker Process* fraud requires greater showing of scienter and materiality than inequitable conduct requires); CHISUM, *supra* note 217, § 19.03[6][e] (antitrust claim based on fraudulent procurement requires higher showings of scienter and materiality than for inequitable conduct asserted as a defense).
252. *See* HOVENKAMP IP, *supra* note 30, § 11.2(c), at 11-9 ("It is not entirely clear whether the standard of intent in a *Walker Process* claim is higher than the standard required to prove inequitable conduct."); VON KALINOWSKI, *supra* note 228, § 73.03[1][a][ii], at 73-26 ("Beyond [the] rather loose standards [set out in the cases], the courts have not established any clear-cut guidelines to measure the quality of conduct that will demonstrate the necessary intent.").
253. *See, e.g.*, Kingsdown Med. Consultants v. Hollister, Inc., 863 F.2d 867, 876 (Fed. Cir. 1988) ("intent to deceive" necessary for finding of inequitable conduct); Molins PLC v. Textron, Inc., 48 F.3d 1172, 1181 n.11 (Fed. Cir. 1995) (same); CHISUM, *su pra* note 217, § 19.03[4] ("Since *Kingsdown*, the Federal Circuit has steadily adhered to the intent to deceive requirement for inequitable conduct.").
254. *See, e.g.*, *Nobelpharma*, 141 F.3d at 1070-71.
255. *Cataphote*, 450 F.2d at 772.
256. *See, e.g.*, Lipman v. Dickinson, 174 F.3d 1363, 1370 (Fed. Cir. 1999) (inequitable conduct); Unitherm Food Sys. v. Swift Eckrich, Inc., 375 F.3d 1341, 1360 (Fed. Cir. 2004) (*Walker Process* fraud), *rev'd on other grounds*, 126 S. Ct. 980 (2006); CHISUM, *su pra* note 217, § 19.03[4].
257. 450 F.2d at 772.

certain early decisions (when it applied regional circuit law to *Walker Process* cases), made similar statements. For example, in *Litton Industrial Products*, the Federal Circuit, applying Ninth Circuit law, wrote:

> Wholly inadvertent errors or honest mistakes, caused by neither fraudulent intent *nor by patentee's gross negligence*, do not constitute the requisite level of intent ... This level of intent for *Walker Process* actions, where inequitable conduct ... is used offensively for recovering damages, apparently corresponds to the level of intent required under Federal Circuit case law for asserting inequitable conduct defensively to render a patent unenforceable.[258]

One point of apparent differentiation between the treatment of inequitable conduct and *Walker Process* fraud is that "unlike a finding of inequitable conduct ... a finding of *Walker Process* fraud may not be based on an equitable balancing of lesser degrees of materiality and intent."[259] As one commentator observed, however, "where the information withheld . . . on the patent application is found to possess a high degree of materiality sufficient to support a conclusion that a reasonable patentee should have known about the matter, the patentee will face a difficult burden in attempting to establish good faith or

---

258. *Id.* at 166 n.18 (emphasis added). This view appears to have been rejected as a matter of Federal Circuit law. *See, e.g., Kingsdown*, 863 F.2d at 876 ("[A] finding that particular conduct by patent applicant amounts to 'gross negligence' does not of itself justify an inference of intent to deceive."); *see also* Argus Chem. v. Fibre Glass-Evercoat Co., 812 F.2d 1381, 1385 (Fed. Cir. 1987) (something "greater than an intent evidenced by gross negligence or recklessness" required for a *Walker Process* claim of attempt to monopolize). Thus, the *Litton* holding (purporting to apply Ninth Circuit law) may be of dubious value in light of the Federal Circuit's present view, expressed for the first time in *Nobelpharma*, that Federal Circuit law should apply to the question of whether conduct in prosecution of a patent is sufficient to strip a patentee of its immunity from the antitrust laws. *See Nobelpharma*, 142 F.3d at 1067.

259. *Nobelpharma*, 141 F.3d at 1070-71; *cf.* Baxter Int'l v. McGaw, Inc., 149 F.3d 1321, 1327 (Fed. Cir. 1998); Kolmes v. World Fibers Corp., 107 F.3d 1534, 1541 (Fed. Cir. 1997); CHISUM, *supra* note 217, § 19.03[4] n.7 ("In determining whether an inference of intent can be drawn from circumstantial evidence, it is proper to consider the degree of materiality of the information.").

negligent mistake."[260] Another treatise has suggested that there is little value in attempting precisely to distinguish the respective showings of intent necessary for *Walker Process* fraud and inequitable conduct:

> The patent laws require proof of "intent to deceive" by clear and convincing evidence to demonstrate inequitable conduct. We think such proof will generally also suffice to show "intentional fraud" under the *Walker Process* standard. Most of the disputes in the case law result not from the application of different standards but from the uncertainty inherent in inferring intention from indirect evidence. The patent law will not permit such an inference from mere "gross negligence" on the part of the patentee. This limitation, coupled with the clear and convincing evidence requirement and the fact that the ultimate aim is to find evidence of intent to deceive, is enough to ensure that the courts in *Walker Process* cases are in fact focused on distinguishing truly intentional conduct from mere carelessness.[261]

It seems clear that, in some rough manner, courts look for a higher level of culpability for *Walker Process* fraud than for inequitable conduct. No bright line test has been developed to delineate the difference. In the end, the inquiry is highly fact specific.

In *Nobelpharma AB v. Implant Innovations, Inc.*,[262] the Federal Circuit affirmed a jury verdict of *Walker Process* fraud based on a finding that the withheld material would have caused the examiner to disallow the patent (thus making the omission highly material) coupled with evidence of the inventors' apparent awareness of the relevance of the withheld information.[263] The evidence disclosed that the inventors were aware of critical prior art (a book, authored by one of the inventors, disclosed the prior art) and had initially included references to it in their application, but that the inventors' patent agent deleted the references before submission to the PTO. The agent claimed that he could not

260. VON KALINOWSKI, *supra* note 228, § 73.03[1][a][ii], at 73-27; *see also, e.g.*, Rohm & Haas Co. v. Crystal Chem. Co., 722 F.2d 1556, 1571 (Fed. Cir. 1983) ("While direct proof of intent to mislead is normally absent ... proof of the actual state of mind of the applicant ... is not required" where the materiality of the misrepresentation is clear.); Rohm & Haas Co. v. Dawson Chem., 635 F. Supp. 1211 (S.D. Tex. 1986) (considering antitrust claim: "Fraud on the Patent Office may be determined only by a careful balancing of intent *in light of* materiality.") (emphasis added).
261. HOVENKAMP IP, *supra* note 30, § 11.2c, at 11-10.
262. 141 F.3d 1059 (Fed. Cir. 1998)
263. *Id.* at 1071-72.

recall why the book had been omitted, but testified that if he had viewed the book as material he would have disclosed it. The Federal Circuit found that the jury was entitled to infer the requisite intent based on the failure to disclose such critical material.[264]

Similarly, in *Unitherm*, the patentee did not disclose to the PTO the fact that essentially the same invention (a browning process for precooked meats) had been developed by the alleged infringer (Unitherm) several years before the patentee filed his application with the PTO. This fact was material because, had the patent examiner been aware of it, the application would have been rejected under the "prior on-sale bar"[265] or prior "public use"[266] doctrine. The Court found that fraudulent intent could be inferred from the following facts: (1) a colleague of the putative inventor had attended several demonstrations given by Unitherm of its browning process approximately four years before the putative inventor filed his application; (2) this colleague made a report of the demonstrations to a group of co-workers, including, "to the best of his recollection," the putative inventor; (3) the putative inventor himself attended a presentation concerning Unitherm's process; (4) Unitherm faxed directly to the putative inventor drawings and schematics of its browning process approximately two years before the patent application was filed; and (5) there was other evidence that the patentee was aware that Unitherm had made sales of its browning process more than one year prior to the subject application.[267] The Court found that the jury was entitled to disbelieve the patentee's claim that there was legitimate confusion over what "golden brown" meant in the

---

264. *Id.* at 1072.
265. *Unitherm*, 375 F.3d at 1361. The "prior on-sale bar" doctrine provides that "a party's placing of the product of a method invention on sale more than a year before that party's application filing date must act as a forfeiture of any right to the grant of a valid patent on the method to that party." D.L. Auld v. Chroma Graphics, 714 F.2d 1144, 1148 (Fed. Cir. 1983); *see also* 35 U.S.C. § 102(b) ("A person shall be entitled to a patent unless the invention was ... on sale in this country, more than one year prior to the date of the application for patent in the United States.").
266. "Public use is use by the inventor, or by a person who is not under any limitation, restriction, or obligation of secrecy to the inventor." ROBERT L. HARMON, PATENTS AND THE FEDERAL CIRCUIT 74-75 (3d ed. 1994).
267. 375 F.3d at 1360-61. While the Federal Circuit upheld the jury's verdict with respect to fraud, it reversed the overall result because Unitherm had presented insufficient evidence of monopoly power. *Id.* at 1363-66.

Unitherm browning process.[268]   The Federal Circuit held that it was reasonable for the jury to believe that the putative inventor "was fully aware that his 'invention' was precisely the Unitherm process that [Unitherm's representative] had been trying to sell ... since 1993," and that the putative inventor "intended to deceive the PTO by claiming that he was 'the original and first inventor' ... when he knew that he was not."[269]

In contrast, the Ninth Circuit Court of Appeals found the requisite intent to defraud lacking in *Cataphote*.[270]   Although the district court invalidated the patent because the product had been placed in public use and on sale more than one year prior to the patent application, the district court held that Cataphote, the patentee, did not knowingly and willfully misrepresent to the PTO that the invention disclosed in its application had not been in public use for more than one year prior to the filing.[271] The Ninth Circuit affirmed, stating that "patent fraud proscribed by *Walker* is extremely circumscribed."[272]   The Ninth Circuit found that Cataphote could reasonably have believed that in light of the continued experimentation during the year prior to filing the "limited volume of sales" would not constitute prior use sufficient to invalidate the patent.[273] Moreover, the court stated that "[w]hile reliance on counsel's advice does not conclusively establish good faith," the opinion of counsel that there was no patent violation and his recommendation to file the application were factors to be considered when weighing the reasonableness of Cataphote's belief that it had a patentable product.[274]

Despite evidence of several alleged misstatements or omissions in the patent prosecution, the Federal Circuit found no clear intent to deceive in *C.R. Bard, Inc. v. M3 Systems*.[275]   M3 Systems alleged that Bard made numerous material misrepresentations before the PTO. These included naming incorrect inventors; failing to provide the examiner with actual samples of the device, relevant articles, and materials submitted to

268.   *Id.* at 1361.
269.   *Id.*
270.   450 F.2d 769 (9th Cir. 1971).
271.   *See id.* at 772-73.
272.   *Id.* at 772.
273.   *See id.* at 772-73.
274.   *Id. But cf. In re* Relafen Antitrust Litig., 346 F. Supp. 2d 349, 365-66 (D. Mass. 2004) (despite self-serving testimony of good faith mistake, court found fact issue on intent where documents showed patentee felt it had "put one over" on the PTO in getting the patent issued).
275.   157 F.3d 1340 (Fed. Cir. 1998).

the Food and Drug Administration; and failing to disclose related and co-pending patents and all evidence with respect to the sale of a first-generation device.[276] The Federal Circuit found that these "asserted flaws" in patent prosecution, taken together or separately, did not constitute substantial evidence of fraud and reversed the jury's verdict.[277] The court reasoned that Bard's failure to provide the examiner with actual models, but with descriptions instead, and its correction of inventorship to include joint inventors, supplied evidence neither that Bard had deceptive intent nor that the examiner was deceived.[278]

Given the high level of scienter required to establish *Walker Process* fraud, the possibility that the entity actually enforcing the patent may be several steps removed from the alleged fraud presents issues in such cases.[279] For example, inventors frequently are corporate employees and assign their patents to their employers, and such employers, in turn, enforce the patents. Usually counsel, rather than the inventor, actually handles the patent prosecution before the PTO. In such situations, counsel may literally have provided the false statement to the PTO (or withheld material information), with or without the knowledge of the inventor and/or decision-makers at the ultimate corporate assignee.

The Federal Circuit considered such issues in *Unitherm*. In that case, the inventor had assigned the patent to his corporate employer. The court first held that the inventor (Prem Singh) was responsible for the omission of material information to the PTO. The court relied on the patent law requirement that the inventor submit an oath or declaration attesting that he or she is the first inventor of the claimed subject matter and that he or she is aware of no reason why the requested patent should not issue.[280]

---

276. *See id.* at 1365.
277. *See id.* at 1367.
278. *See id.* at 1366-67.
279. Such issues are *not* presented in inequitable conduct cases. If inequitable conduct is found to have occurred, the patent is deemed unenforceable regardless of its current owner. Frank's Casing Crew & Rental Tools v. PMR Techs., 292 F.3d 1363, 1376-77 (Fed. Cir. 2002) (affirming finding that current licensee's patent rights were unenforceable due to inequitable conduct by patentee in patent prosecution); Hewlett-Packard Co. v. Bausch & Lomb, Inc., 746 F. Supp. 1413, 1414-15 (N.D. Cal. 1990) (finding inequitable conduct by patentee and holding patent unenforceable by purchaser of patent), *aff'd*, 925 F.2d 1480 (Fed. Cir. 1991).
280. *Unitherm*, 375 F.3d at 1359; *see also* 37 C.F.R. §§ 1.41(2), 1.63, 1.51(a)(2). As the Supreme Court has held, patent applicants have "an uncompromising duty to report to [the PTO] all facts concerning possible

Although plaintiff had offered no direct evidence proving that Singh "actually made the material misrepresentation," i.e., that he had completed the PTO attestation, the court "nevertheless presume[d] that Singh, the named inventor and applicant, must have reviewed the specification and signed the required declaration before the application was filed."[281] This would seem to make Singh liable even if counsel, rather than Singh himself, failed to make the requisite disclosures.[282]

The court acknowledged that, without more, its presumption concerning the attestation "would hold only Singh himself liable for the material misrepresentation."[283] But the court found that additional factors warranted finding Singh's employer, ConAgra, liable for the misrepresentation as well. First, it was undisputed that "both Singh and numerous ConAgra colleagues and supervisors knew of the [omitted prior art]."[284] Second, without regard to the knowledge of colleagues and superiors at ConAgra, the court held that agency principles would serve to make ConAgra responsible for its employee's fraud: "The undisputed facts surrounding Singh's patent application demonstrate that he filed it as an employee of ConAgra, to whom he assigned it. These same facts establish ConAgra's potential liability for any damages arising from Singh's misstatements."[285]

(D) JUSTIFIABLE RELIANCE BY THE PARTY DECEIVED

The Federal Circuit in *Unitherm* held that "[t]he best evidence of the fourth [fraud] element [reasonable reliance] ... is that the PTO issued the patent."[286] This element is closely related to the standard of materiality. If the patent would not have issued absent the misrepresentation or

---

fraud or inequitableness underlying the applications at issue." *Precision Instrument Mfg. v. Auto. Maint. Mach.*, 324 U.S. 806, 818 (1945).

281. *Unitherm*, 375 F.3d at 1359.
282. *Id.*; *see Crystal Semiconductor v. Opti, Inc.*, No. 97-CA-026, 1999 WL 33457762, at *11 (W.D. Tex. Apr. 29, 1999) (court unwilling to grant Vice President of company patent immunity from inequitable conduct based on argument that he was not "substantially involved" in the preparation or prosecution of patent and did not fit into definition set forth in 37 C.F.R. § 1.56).
283. *Unitherm*, 375 F.3d at 1359.
284. *Id.*
285. *Id.*
286. *Id.* at 1361.

omission, the materiality standard is met and the PTO necessarily relied upon the misrepresentation or omission.[287]

(E) INJURY TO THE PARTY DECEIVED BY THE FRAUD

According to the Federal Circuit, "injury to the PTO and to the public that it serves, arises as a matter of course whenever the other four [fraud] elements are met."[288] This is because "[a] patent by its very nature is affected with a public interest. The far-reaching social and economic consequences of a patent, therefore, give the public a paramount interest in seeing that patent monopolies spring from backgrounds free from fraud or other inequitable conduct.... Where fraud is committed, injury to the public through a weakening in the Patent System is manifest."[289]

(2) The Antitrust Elements

As noted above, the finding of fraud sufficient to strip the patentee of its antitrust immunity "mark[s] only the beginning of the antitrust inquiry, not its end point."[290] The Supreme Court in *Walker Process* stated that:

> To establish monopolization or attempt to monopolize a part of trade or commerce under § 2 of the Sherman Act, it would then be necessary [after showing fraud] to appraise the exclusionary power of the illegal patent claim in terms of the relevant market for the product involved. Without a definition of that market, there is no way to measure [the defendant's] ability to lessen or destroy competition.[291]

287. As discussed above in the context of *Unitherm*, in the case of omissions, the PTO is deemed to rely on the misrepresentation implicit in the declaration or oath that each inventor must submit pursuant to 37 C.F.R. §§ 1.63 and 1.51(a)(2). *See Unitherm*, 375 F.3d at 1359.
288. *Id.* at 1361.
289. *Id.* (citing Norton v. Curtis, 433 F.2d 779, 796 (C.C.P.A. 1970)).
290. *Unitherm*, 375 F.3d at 1355.
291. Walker Process Equip. v. Food Mach. & Chem. Corp., 382 U.S. 172, 177 (1965); *see also* Spectrum Sports v. McQuillan, 506 U.S. 447 (1993) (*Walker Process* requires appraisal of exclusionary power of fraudulently obtained patent in terms of relevant market for product involved).

For example, as the Court noted, "[t]here may be effective substitutes for the [patented device] which do not infringe the patent. This is a matter of proof, as is the amount of damages suffered by the [excluded competitor]."[292]

(A) PREDATORY OR EXCLUSIONARY CONDUCT

Section 2 requires a showing that the defendant monopolist engaged in predatory or exclusionary conduct to obtain, maintain or enhance its monopoly power.[293] If a patentee actually brings suit to exclude competitors based on a fraudulently-obtained patent, such enforcement would qualify as exclusionary conduct;[294] overt threats to sue may be

---

292. *Walker Process*, 382 U.S. at 178. Attempt to monopolize claims also require a showing of a specific intent to monopolize. If the *Walker Process* defendant is shown to have an intent to defraud the PTO sufficient to strip it of its antitrust immunity and is shown to have enforced (or threatened to enforce) its ill-gotten patent, the specific intent to monopolize may be established. *See, e.g., Handgards I*, 601 F.2d 986, 993 n.13 (9th Cir. 1979) ("The requisite intent to monopolize may be inferred from [a] finding of bad faith."); Nobelpharma AB v. Implant Innovations, 141 F.3d 1059, 1070 (Fed. Cir. 1998) (failure to cite prior art in a patent application, a fraudulent omission, coupled with evidence of fraudulent intent will expose a patentee to liability under the antitrust laws); Kearney & Trecker Corp. v. Giddings & Lewis, Inc., 452 F.2d 579 (7th Cir. 1971) (specific intent found where patent procured in violation of conflict of interest principles); *see also* ALD (5th), *supra* note 2, at 1047-48 (where patent known to be invalid is nonetheless enforced through litigation, "the specific intent requirement to support a Section 2 attempt to monopolize claim exists because the patentee instituted or maintained the litigation in bad faith, *i.e.*, with knowledge of the invalidity of the patent").
293. *See Walker Process*, 382 U.S. at 177; *Spectrum Sports*, 506 U.S. at 455-56.
294. *See* Rohm & Haas Co. v. Dawson Chem., 635 F. Supp. 1211, 1218 (S.D. Tex. 1986) ("[T]he offense which is sanctioned by the antitrust laws is not the fraudulent procurement of a patent in circumstances that create monopoly power but the bringing of groundless suits for patent infringement."); Kobak & Reznick, *supra* note 201, at 90 ("[T]he true gravamen of [a *Walker Process*] violation is not simply obtaining the patent but enforcing it with knowledge of the fraud."). The Federal Circuit in *Nobelpharma* also held that "the plaintiff in the patent infringement suit must ... have been aware of the fraud when bringing suit." 141 F.3d at 1069.

found to constitute sufficient "enforcement" as well.[295]   On the other hand, merely acquiring a patent, even if by fraud, should not generally be deemed exclusionary unless accompanied by some actual or threatened enforcement activity.[296]

---

295. *See, e.g.*, Glass Equip. Dev. v. Besten, Inc., 174 F.3d 1337, 1343 (Fed. Cir. 1999) (letters threatening infringement litigation can be actionable so long as plaintiff can show that the underlying patent was fraudulently procured or that the threatened lawsuit was a sham); Bourns, Inc. v. Raychem Corp., 331 F.3d 704 (9th Cir. 2003) (threatened enforcement of fraudulently procured patents sufficient to make out *Walker Process* claim; claim ultimately failed for lack of antitrust injury); Baxa Corp. v. McGaw, Inc., 996 F. Supp. 1044, 1049 (D. Colo. 1997); Northlake Mktg. & Supply v. Glaverbel S.A., 861 F. Supp. 653, 661 (N.D. Ill. 1994) ("instituting a suit (or directly threatening such a suit)" are required). *But cf.* Oetiker v. Jurid Werke GmbH, 671 F.2d 596, 600-02 (D.C. Cir. 1982) (mild letters from small patentee to large company, Volkswagen, not accompanied by any actual enforcement action, insufficient threat of enforcement); K-Lath v. Davis Wire Corp., 15 F. Supp. 2d 952, 963-64 (C.D. Cal. 1998) (letter stating company had strong presumption of validity and enforceability of patent and that company reserved its rights to enforce patent did not equate to threat of enforcement); Indium Corp. of Am. v. Semi-Alloys, Inc., 566 F. Supp. 1344, 1347-48 (N.D.N.Y. 1983) (no threat of enforcement despite company's suits against three industry competitors and license offer letter to plaintiff), *aff'd*, 781 F.2d 879, 883 (Fed. Cir. 1986).

296. *See, e.g.*, *Unitherm*, 375 F.3d at 1358 ("[I]f the patentee has done nothing but obtain a patent in a manner that the plaintiff believes is fraudulent, the courts lack jurisdiction to entertain ... a *Walker Process* claim."); FMC Corp. v. Manitowoc Co., 835 F.2d 1411, 1418 n.16 (Fed. Cir. 1987) ("Mere procurement of a patent, whatever the conduct of the applicant in the procurement, cannot without more affect the welfare of the consumer and cannot in itself violate the antitrust laws."); Goss Int'l Ams. v. MAN Roland, Inc., 2006 U.S. Dist. LEXIS 36386, at *10 (D.N.H. 2006) (holding that the enforcement element of a *Walker Process* claim may be satisfied by warning letters); *Cygnus Therapeutic*, 92 F.3d at 1161 (district court properly granted summary judgment dismissing plaintiff's *Walker Process* antitrust claim because patentee-defendant had not threatened to enforce its patent), *overruled on other grounds by Nobelpharma*, 141 F.3d 1059; Brunswick Corp. v. Riegel Textile Corp., 752 F.2d 261, 265 (7th Cir. 1984); *Oetiker*, 671 F.2d 596; *Handgards I*, 601 F.2d at 993 (no *Walker Process* claim established where plaintiff did not contend that defendant sought to enforce fraudulently obtained patent); *K-Lath*, 15 F. Supp. 2d at 964 (dismissing *Walker Process* claim

The Federal Circuit addressed the level of enforcement necessary to support an antitrust claim in the *Unitherm* case.[297] In *Unitherm*, rather than bring its antitrust claim as a counterclaim to a patent infringement action, as is usually the case,[298] the claimant (Unitherm) brought a declaratory judgment action seeking a ruling that the patent in question was invalid together with an antitrust claim under a *Walker Process* theory.

The defendant argued that because it had not enforced the patent against Unitherm, and thus had not attempted to exclude competition, it could not be liable for monopolization or attempting to monopolize. The Federal Circuit noted that, while "strictly speaking a *Walker Process* claim is premised upon the *enforcement* of a patent procured by fraud on the patent office," a plaintiff "may bring a Declaratory Judgment action of invalidity ... even in the absence of overt enforcement actions."[299] The court held that, "as a matter of Federal Circuit antitrust law, the standards we have developed for determining jurisdiction in a Declaratory Judgment Action of patent invalidity also define the minimum level of 'enforcement' necessary to expose the patentee to a *Walker Process* claim."[300] Under this standard, the Federal Circuit looks to the "totality of the circumstances" in assessing whether a patentee's actions have created a reasonable apprehension that it will enforce its patent. Absent overt enforcement activity by the patentee, "if the

---

for lack of "threat or reasonable apprehension of an infringement suit"); Silva v. Mamula, Civ. No. 93-5618, 1994 WL 66070, at *2 (E.D. Pa. Feb. 24, 1994) (mere acquisition of patent by fraud is insufficient to satisfy requirements of § 2: "it is the use of that patent in illegal antitrust behavior that gives rise to liability"); *Northlake Mktg. & Supply*, 861 F. Supp. at 658 (dismissing *Walker Process* claim because plaintiff failed to present sufficient evidence that defendant, an exclusive licensee, had threatened to enforce patent), *amended*, No. 92 C 2732, 1994 U.S. Dist. LEXIS 13990 (N.D. Ill. Sept. 29, 1994); Struthers Scientific & Int'l v. Gen. Foods, 334 F. Supp. 1329, 1332 (D. Del. 1971).

297. *Unitherm*, 375 F.3d at 1341; *see also* Hydril Co. v. Grant Prideco, L.P., 385 F. Supp. 2d 609 (S.D. Tex. 2005) (applying Federal Circuit law, not Fifth Circuit law, to determine whether antitrust plaintiff had alleged level of enforcement activity required to support a *Walker Process* claim).

298. *See, e.g., Nobelpharma*, 141 F.3d at 1068 (*Walker Process* claims are "typically raised as a counterclaim by a defendant in a patent infringement suit").

299. *Unitherm*, 375 F.3d at 1357-58.

300. *Id.* at 1358.

circumstances warrant, a reasonable apprehension may be formed in the absence of any communication from [patentee] to [the potential infringer]."[301]

---

301. *Id.* In addition to a reasonable apprehension of suit, the Federal Circuit held in *Indium Corp. of America v. Semi-Alloys, Inc.*, 781 F.2d 879 (Fed. Cir. 1986), that a declaratory judgment plaintiff must show that it "'has actually produced the accused device' or 'has prepared to produce such a device.'" *Id.* at 883 (quoting Jervis B. Webb Co. v. S. Sys., Inc., 742 F.2d 1388, 1398-99 (Fed. Cir. 1984)). The court emphasized that the reasonable apprehension test is objective, not subjective. *See id.* In that case, the court found that declaratory judgment jurisdiction had not been established despite evidence that the patentee had sued two other parties for infringement of the patents several years earlier, had offered plaintiff a licensing agreement and had engaged in other allegedly intimidating behavior. *Id.* at 883. In other cases, the Federal Circuit has found reasonable apprehension to be shown based on such factors as (1) related litigation, *see, e.g.*, Arrowhead Indus. Water v. Ecolochem, Inc., 846 F.2d 731, 737 (Fed. Cir. 1988) (bringing suit against third party "evidenced not only an intent but a willingness and capacity to employ litigation in pursuit of its patent rights"); Vanguard Research v. Peat, Inc., 304 F.3d 1249 (Fed. Cir. 2002) (even though patent holder repeatedly stated that it did not intend to sue competitor for patent infringement, patent holder exhibited willingness to protect that technology by filing earlier lawsuit alleging misappropriation of trade secrets and by informing competitor's clients that competitor was using patent holder's technology without license); Shell Oil Co. v. Amoco Corp., 970 F.2d 885, 888 (Fed. Cir. 1992) ("[r]elated litigation may be evidence of a reasonable apprehension"); Goodyear Tire & Rubber v. Releasomers, Inc., 824 F.2d 953 (Fed. Cir. 1987) (patent holder's maintenance of state court action regarding manufacturer's alleged misappropriation of certain trade secrets related to patented process placed manufacturer in reasonable apprehension of suit for patent infringement); or (2) correspondence expressing an intent to enforce patent rights by litigation, even where the letter "skillfully skirt[s] an express charge of infringement." *See, e.g.*, *Arrowhead Indus. Water*, 846 F.2d at 737-38; *see also* EMC Corp. v. Norand Corp., 89 F.3d 807, 815 (Fed. Cir. 1996) (finding reasonable apprehension requirement satisfied where letter referred to patentee's "inclination to 'turn the matter over to' [patentee's] litigation counsel 'for action,' and urged a 'preliminary business discussion,' 'perhaps avoiding this matter esca-lating into a contentious legal activity'").

(B) MONOPOLY POWER

Even if a plaintiff succeeds in stripping the patentee of its antitrust exemption through a showing of fraud, the plaintiff must still show that the ill-gotten patent allowed the defendant to exercise monopoly power or that there is a dangerous possibility that the defendant will gain monopoly power.[302] That requires the usual inquiry for direct or indirect evidence of monopoly power.[303] Failure to establish monopoly power has resulted in the dismissal of *Walker Process* cases, even ones where fraud had been shown.[304]

---

302. *See, e.g.*, *Walker Process*, 382 U.S. at 177-78.
303. *See, e.g.*, ANTITRUST LAW DEVELOPMENTS, *supra* note 2, at 233-46 (for more comprehensive treatment); 2A AREEDA & HOVENKAMP, *supra* note 1, ¶¶ 501-22, at 89-179 (same).
304. *See, e.g.*, *Unitherm*, 375 F.3d 1341 (despite finding fraud sufficient to strip patentee of antitrust immunity under *Walker Process*, plaintiff failed to establish relevant market or otherwise show monopoly power); Technicon Instruments v. Alpkem Corp., 866 F.2d 417, 421 (Fed. Cir. 1989); Hennessy Indus. v. FMC Corp., 779 F.2d 402, 405 (7th Cir. 1985); Am. Hoist & Derrick Co. v. Sowa & Sons, 725 F.2d 1350, 1366-67 (Fed. Cir. 1984); Mayview Corp. v. Rodstein, 620 F.2d 1347, 1356 (9th Cir. 1980) (*Walker Process* "required that the aggrieved party establish the traditional elements of a violation of § 2, which include, inter alia, an analysis of the relevant markets and an examination of the exclusionary power of the illegal patent claim ... Mayview adduced no 'hard evidence' on the relevant geographic, product or customer markets, and ... there was no evidence on the degree of market control."); Acme Precision Prods. v. Am. Alloys Corp., 484 F.2d 1237 (8th Cir. 1973) (antitrust counterclaim rejected for failure to establish relevant market, despite evidence of fraud); Agrashell, Inc. v. Hammons Prods., 479 F.2d 269 (8th Cir. 1973); Augustine Med. v. Mallinckrodt, Inc., No. 01-387-SLR, 2003 U.S. Dist. LEXIS 6079, at *26 (D. Del. Apr. 9, 2003) (granting motion for summary judgment that plaintiff did not violate § 2 in enforcement of patent because, even if plaintiff were stripped of its antitrust immunity by reason of *Walker Process* fraud, defendant failed to establish antitrust elements); Barry Fiala, Inc. v. Arthur Blank & Co., No. 2:02cv2282, 2003 U.S. Dist. LEXIS 2609 (W.D. Tenn. Feb. 19, 2003) (*Walker Process* counterclaims failed to define relevant market or to assert that plaintiff had dangerous probability of achieving monopoly power); Woodjoy Enters. v. Wise Cracker, Inc., No. Civ.A.3:98-CV-0560, 2002 WL 1878862 (N.D. Tex. Aug. 12, 2002) (granting summary judgment to defendant where plaintiff offered insufficient evidence of defendant's monopoly power or intent to deceive PTO); B.V. Optische Industrie De

(C) STANDING/ANTITRUST INJURY

A private antitrust plaintiff must show antitrust standing to pursue a claim.[305] In addition to showing that the alleged misconduct in fact caused it injury (a basic standing requirement in all tort cases), an antitrust plaintiff must also show "antitrust injury;" that is, injury "of the type the antitrust laws were intended to prevent and that flows from that which makes defendant's acts unlawful."[306] Put differently, the plaintiff's injury must arise from a *competition-reducing* aspect of the claimed illegal conduct. Thus, for example, in *Brunswick Corp. v. Pueblo Bowl-O-Mat, Inc.,*[307] the Supreme Court barred a challenge by a bowling alley to a merger that, if blocked, would allow the only other bowling alley in town to go out of business. There was no antitrust injury because, if successful in its claim, plaintiff would have faced less

---

Oude Delft v. Hologic, Inc., 909 F. Supp. 162 (S.D.N.Y. 1995) (dismissing complaint for failure to plead a relevant market); Re-Alco Indus. v. Nat'l Ctr. for Health Educ., 812 F. Supp. 387 (S.D.N.Y. 1993) (dismissing attempted monopolization claim based on enforcement of invalid copyright because plaintiff did not adequately allege a relevant product market); Knickerbocker Toy Co. v. Winterbrook Corp., 554 F. Supp. 1309 (D.N.H. 1982) (*Walker Process*-style claim involving fraudulently procured copyright dismissed for lack of adequate allegations of market power); Colortronic Reinhard & Co. v. Plastic Controls, Inc., 496 F. Supp. 259 (D. Mass. 1980) (while proof of fraud was clear, proof of market power was insufficient); Reinke Mfg. Co. v. Sidney Mfg. Corp., 446 F. Supp. 1056, 1067 (D. Neb. 1978) ("Defendant made no effort to establish the relevant geographic or product markets or the effect on the market of the Reinke patent monopoly."), *aff'd on other grounds*, 594 F.2d 644 (8th Cir. 1979); Mitsubishi Elec. Corp. v. IMS Tech., 44 U.S.P.Q.2d 1904 (N.D. Ill. 1997) (*Walker Process* claim failed for lack of sufficient market power allegation); Erie Tech. Prods. v. JFD Elec. Components Corp., 198 U.S.P.Q. 179 (E.D.N.Y. 1978) (dismissing *Walker Process* claim; no allegation of relevant market).

305. Detailed treatment of standing and antitrust injury is beyond the scope of this Handbook. For more detail, see, e.g., Ronald W. Davis, *Standing on Shaky Ground: The Strangely Elusive Doctrine of Antitrust Injury*, 70 ANTITRUST L.J. 697 (2003); ALD (5th), *supra* note 2, at 838-69; Sean P. Gates, *California Antitrust: Standing Room for the Wrongfully Discharged Employee?*, 47 Hastings L.J. 509, 516-25 (1996).

306. Atl. Richfield Co. v. USA Petroleum, 495 U.S. 328, 334 (1990); *see also, e.g.*, Brunswick Corp. v. Pueblo Bowl-O-Mat, Inc., 429 U.S. 477, 489 (1977).

307. 429 U.S. 477 (1977)

rather than more competition. Similarly, in *Brunswick Corp. v. Riegel Textile Corp.*,[308] the plaintiff brought a *Walker Process*-style claim, but the relief sought was that the patent in question be transferred to plaintiff.[309] Setting aside the fact that a *Walker Process* case cannot be predicated on procurement of a *valid* patent, the Seventh Circuit noted the lack of antitrust injury, pointing out that, from the standpoint of competition, "it is a matter of indifference whether Riegel or Brunswick exploits a [patent] monopoly of antistatic yarn."[310]

To establish antitrust injury in the *Walker Process* context, a plaintiff would have to show that, in the absence of the wrongfully-issued patent, competition would have been enhanced, i.e., more competitors, lower prices. For a competitor-plaintiff to show injury in fact, it would have to show that it would have been willing and able to come to market with a competing product.[311] As the Seventh Circuit put it in *Xechem, Inc. v. Bristol-Myers Squibb Co.*,[312] the antitrust plaintiff alleging unlawful exclusion must "show that (and when) it would have entered the market in the absence of anticompetitive practices."[313] *Walker Process* claims

---

308. 752 F.2d 261 (7th Cir. 1984).
309. *See id.* at 267.
310. *Id.*; *see also* Eastman Kodak Co. v. Goodyear Tire & Rubber, 114 F.3d 1547 (Fed. Cir. 1997) (no antitrust injury where plaintiff "would have suffered the same injury regardless of who had acquired and enforced the patent against it"). *But see, e.g.*, Fishman v. Estate of Wirtz, 807 F.2d 520 (7th Cir. 1986) (holding competition for monopoly protected by the antitrust laws).
311. *See, e.g.*, Bubar v. Ampco Foods, 752 F.2d 445, 450 (9th Cir. 1985); HOVENKAMP IP, *supra* note 30, § 11.2(f) at 11-14; *see also, e.g.*, Bristol-Myers Squibb Co. v. Ben Venue Labs., 90 F. Supp. 2d 540 (D.N.J. 2000) (*Walker Process* plaintiffs need not be entirely ready to enter market where patentee's actions triggered bar to FDA regulatory approval to market competing generic drug).
312. 372 F.3d 899 (7th Cir. 2004).
313. *Id.* at 902; *see also, e.g.*, Bourns, Inc. v. Raychem Corp., 331 F.3d 704, 711 (9th Cir. 2003) ("Only an actual competitor or one ready to be a competitor can suffer antitrust injury."); Andrx Pharm. v. Biovail Corp. Int'l, 256 F.3d 799, 819 (D.C. Cir. 2001) (court permitted plaintiff to show that, absent anticompetitive conduct, it would have come to market sooner); Brotech Corp. v. White Eagle Int'l Tech. Group, No. Civ. A. 03-232, 2004 WL 1427136, at *6-7 (E.D. Pa. June 21, 2004) (same); *In re* Wellbutrin SR/Zyban Antitrust Litig., 281 F. Supp. 2d 751, 757 (E.D. Pa. 2003) (same); Novo Nordisk of N. Am. v. Genentech, Inc., 885 F. Supp. 522, 524-25 (S.D.N.Y. 1995) (same).

have failed where plaintiffs have been unable to show such but-for readiness.[314]

Customers constitute another category of potential private plaintiff. A few courts have held that customers do not have standing to bring antitrust actions against patentees for *Walker Process* fraud—at least where the patentee has not sought to enforce its patent against the customers and there is no reasonable basis for fearing such enforcement. As the court held in *In re Remeron Antitrust Litigation*:[315]

> *Walker Process* and its progeny involve antitrust counterclaimants who were potential or actual competitors in patent infringement suits. In this case, [antitrust] [p]laintiffs, as direct purchasers, neither produce [the patented drug product] nor would have done so; moreover, plaintiffs may not now claim standing to bring a *Walker Process* claim by donning the cloak of a Clayton Act monopolization claim.[316]

Similarly, in *In re Ciprofloxacin Hydrochloride Antitrust Litigation*,[317] the court noted a "serious question" whether customer plaintiffs had standing to assert *Walker Process* claims.[318] On the other hand, a number of cases alleging *Walker Process* theories on behalf of customers have proceeded with no standing question raised.[319] Assuming

---

314. *See, e.g., Bourns,*3 31 F.3d at 711-12 (no standing where plaintiff was not prepared to manufacture product covered by patent); Indium Corp. of Am. v. Semi-Alloys, Inc., 781 F.2d 879, 882 (Fed. Cir. 1986) (same); *Brunswick,* 752 F.2d at 266-68 (no standing where no consumer interest is harmed); *Silva,* 1994 WL 66070, at *3 (no antitrust injury where parties against whom allegedly unlawful infringement suit was brought were not competitors of patent holder; no claim that new competitors would enter). In *Bourns,* a divided Ninth Circuit panel held that a *Walker Process* plaintiff does not have standing where it had not yet entered the market at the time defendant threatened to enforce its patents. The dissent argued all that need be shown is that plaintiff was a *potential* competitor and had a genuine intent and preparedness to enter the market absent the fraudulently obtained patents. *See Bourns,* 331 F.3d at 713 (Pregerson, J., concurring in part and dissenting in part).

315. 335 F. Supp. 2d 522 (D.N.J. 2004).

316. *Id.* at 529.

317. No. 1:00MNL1383DGT, 2005 WL 736604 (E.D.N.Y. Mar. 31, 2005).

318. *Id.* at *27.

319. *See, e.g., In re* Relafen Antitrust Litig., 360 F. Supp. 2d 166 (D. Mass. 2005) (denying summary judgment against customer-plaintiffs' *Walker Process* claim); *In re* Terazosin Hydrochloride Antitrust Litig., 335 F. Supp. 2d 1336, 1336 (S.D. Fla. 2004) (purchaser plaintiffs pursuing

they are not barred as a matter of law, customer-plaintiffs would have to establish that, absent the antitrust violation, competition would have been more vigorous. In the *Walker Process* context, consumer plaintiffs would have to show that if the fraudulent patents had not issued, more sellers would have been competing in the relevant market, leading to lower prices.[320] Given the exacting burden of proof, *Walker Process* cases "are usually not successful."[321] On the other hand, parties asserting such claims sometimes do succeed, at least in defeating motions for summary judgment.[322]

Walker Process and sham theories; standing not questioned); *In re* Buspirone Antitrust Litig., 210 F.R.D. 43 (S.D.N.Y. 2002) (certifying class of direct purchasers pursuing claims that manufacturer filed sham patent claims against competing manufacturers); *see also* Chemi SpA v. GlaxoSmithKline, 356 F. Supp. 2d 495 (E.D. Pa. 2005) (rejecting claim that potential supplier to excluded manufacturers lacked antitrust standing); HOVENKAMP IP, *supra* note 30, § 10.5, at 10-24 ("Customers are indeed the favored class of antitrust plaintiffs.").

320. Customer plaintiffs also must deal with issues of remoteness, including the complexity of apportioning damages along complex chains of distribution. The Supreme Court has held that only direct purchasers from antitrust violators may sue for overcharge damages under § 4 of the Clayton Act. *See* Kansas v. Utilicorp United, Inc., 497 U.S. 199, 218 (1990) ("[W]e might allow indirect purchasers to sue only when, by hypothesis, the direct purchaser will bear no portion of the overcharge and otherwise suffer no injury."); Ill. Brick Co. v. Illinois, 431 U.S. 720, 736-47 (1977) (precluding indirect purchasers from "seeking to recover on their pass-on theory"). A number of states, however, by statute or case law, permit indirect purchasers to sue for damages under state analogues to the Sherman Act. *See generally* ABA SECTION OF ANTITRUST LAW, STATE ANTITRUST PRACTICE AND STATUTES (3d ed. 2004).

321. HOVENKAMP IP, *supra* note 30, § 11.2(f), at 11-14.1; HOLMES, *supra* note 26, § 15.03, at 15-24 (noting that *Walker Process* cases "have almost always failed"); Steinman, *supra* note 201, at 99 n.22.

322. *See, e.g.*, Nobelpharma AB v. Implant Innovations, 141 F.3d 1059, 1059 (Fed. Cir. 1998) (affirming award of damages to *Walker Process* fraud claimant against patentee of technology for bone tissue implants); Kearney & Trecker Corp. v. Cincinnati Milacron, Inc., 562 F.2d 365 (6th Cir. 1977) (affirming finding of antitrust liability for fraudulent procurement of patents on automatic tool changers); *In re* Relafen Antitrust Litig., 346 F. Supp. 2d 349, 364-67 (D. Mass. 2004) (*Walker Process* claims survive summary judgment); Bristol-Myers Squibb Co. v. Ben Venue Labs., 90 F. Supp. 2d 540, 540 (D.N.J. 2000) (denying summary judgment on *Walker Process* fraud claims brought by generic

2. Bad Faith Litigation

Whereas *Walker Process* involves a patent holder that has enforced a patent known to be invalid because it was fraudulently obtained, *Handgards* involves a patent holder that seeks to enforce a patent knowing that the patent is either invalid (for a reason other than fraud on the patent office) or not infringed.[323] The gravamen of both types of actions is enforcement, or at least threatened enforcement, of intellectual property that is known by its owner to be invalid or not infringed. From

---

drug manufacturers against pioneer drug manufacturer regarding procurement of patent on cancer drug); Buehler AG v. Ocrim, S.p.A., 836 F. Supp. 1291 (N.D. Tex. 1992) (denying motion for summary judgment with respect to monopolization claims for fraudulent procurement and enforcement of patent covering design of feed gates in grain rolling mills); Conceptual Eng'g Assocs. v. Aelectronic Bonding, 714 F. Supp. 1262 (D.R.I. 1989) (awarding damages for monopolization of market for automatic fusion welding apparatus based on knowing maintenance and enforcement of invalid patents); Rohm & Haas Co. v. Dawson Chem., 635 F. Supp. 1211 (S.D. Tex. 1986) (denying summary judgment motions directed at Walker Process fraud claims relating to patents on herbicides).

A patentee found to have committed *Walker Process* fraud faces treble damages, reimbursement of plaintiff's costs and attorney's fees, as well as the imposition of an injunction. Beyond that, fraud or inequitable conduct in the procurement of a patent can lead to a wide array of additional consequences, including the following: (1) antitrust enforcement actions by the Department of Justice or Federal Trade Commission, *see, e.g.*, United States v. Markham, 537 F.2d 187 (5th Cir. 1976); (2) a government suit seeking cancellation, *see, e.g.*, United States v. Am. Bell Tel. Co., 128 U.S. 315 (1888); (3) a judicial finding of invalidity or unenforceability, including for related patents or claims, *see, e.g.*, Keystone Driller v. Gen. Excavator, 290 U.S. 240 (1933); (4) attorney's fees, *see, e.g.*, Monolith Portland Midwest Co. v. Kaiser Aluminum & Chem., 407 F.2d 288 (9th Cir. 1969); (5) securities liability, *see, e.g.*, CHISUM, *supra* note 217, § 19.03[6][g]; (6) disgorgement of royalties, *see, e.g.*, Lear, Inc. v. Adkins, 395 U.S. 653 (1969); (7) loss of attorney-client and work product protections, *see, e.g.*, Environ Prods. v. Total Containment Inc., No. 95-4467, 1996 WL 494132 (E.D. Pa. Aug. 22, 1996); and (8) PTO disciplinary action against registered attorneys or agents, *see, e.g.*, Kingsland v. Dorsey, 338 U.S. 318 (1949).

323. The patentee could, for example, become aware that the patented technology was actually in public use, of a mistake by the examiner in the course of the prosecution, aware of disabling facts after the patent issued, or of facts that a particular product in fact does not infringe its patent.

an antitrust perspective, it should not matter why the intellectual property is invalid or not infringed, just that the owner knows this to be the case and, nevertheless, has sought to enforce the patent to anticompetitive ends.[324]

A major issue in *Handgards* cases is that, as a general matter, intellectual property holders are entitled to enforce their presumptively valid rights through litigation.[325]   The courts agree that intellectual property holders should not be subject to treble damage antitrust liability simply because they lose an infringement case.[326]   Such a result would

---

324.   *See, e.g.*, HOVENKAMP IP, *supra* note 30, § 11.1, 11-3.

325.   *See, e.g.*, Atari Games Corp. v. Nintendo of Am., 897 F.2d 1572, 1576 (Fed. Cir. 1990) ("Congress has specifically granted patent owners the right to commence a civil suit in order to protect their inventions."); Colortronic Reinhard & Co. v. Plastic Controls, 668 F.2d 1, 9 (1st Cir. 1981); *Handgards I*, 601 F.2d 986, 993 (9th Cir. 1979) ("[p]atentees must be permitted to test the validity of their patents"); HOVENKAMP IP, *supra* note 30, § 11.1, at 11-2 ("[L]itigation of valid intellectual property rights against infringers is not only permitted, but indeed is critical to the success of the intellectual property system.").

326.   *See, e.g.*, Prof'l Real Estate Investors v. Columbia Pictures Indus., 508 U.S. 49, 61 n.5 (1993) (courts should not engage in post-hoc reasoning that unsuccessful lawsuits must have been baseless); Walker Process Equip. v. Food Mach. & Chem. Corp., 382 U.S. 172, 180 (1965) (Harlan, J., concurring) (permitting antitrust liability based on a showing of mere invalidity "might well chill the disclosure of inventions through the obtaining of a patent because of fear of the vexations or punitive consequences of treble-damage suits"); C.R. Bard, Inc. v. M3 Sys., 157 F.3d 1340, 1369 (Fed. Cir. 1998) ("The patentee must have the right of enforcement of a duly granted patent, unencumbered by punitive consequences should the patent's validity or infringement not survive litigation."); Valley Drug v. Geneva Pharms., 344 F.3d 1294, 1308 (11th Cir. 2003) ("Patent litigation is too complex and the results too uncertain for parties to accurately forecast whether enforcing the exclusionary right. . . will expose them to treble damages if the patent immunity were destroyed by the mere invalidity of the patent."); Asahi Glass Co. v. Pentech Pharms., 289 F. Supp. 2d 986, 992-93 (N.D. Ill. 2003) (Posner, J.) ("A firm that has received a patent from the Patent Office (and not by fraud...) and thus enjoys the presumption of validity that attaches to an issued patent ... is entitled to defend the patent's validity in court, to sue alleged infringers, and to settle with them, whatever its private doubts, unless a neutral observer would reasonably think either that the patent was almost certain to be declared invalid, or the defendants were almost

vitiate the incentives to innovation and creativity that the patent and copyright laws seek to foster.[327]

This section discusses the criteria that courts have developed for determining when enforcement of intellectual property is done in bad faith and thus stripped of antitrust immunity. Such criteria must necessarily reflect the need to protect legitimate petitioning activity (as reflected in the *Noerr-Pennington* doctrine) as well as the rights inherent in the grant of intellectual property. We first consider the *Noerr-Pennington* doctrine and the scope of the immunity it confers.

a.   The Scope of *Noerr-Pennington* Immunity in Respect
     of Litigation and Related Activities

(1) Noerr-Pennington and Litigation Efforts

In *California Motor Transport Co. v. Trucking Unlimited*,[328] the Supreme Court ruled that petitioning the courts by bringing lawsuits is covered by the *Noerr-Pennington* doctrine. There the Court held that "[t]he right of access to the Courts is indeed ... one aspect of the right to petition."[329] Accordingly, "groups with common interests may ... without violating the antitrust laws, use ... agencies and courts to advocate their causes and points of view respecting resolution of their business and economic interests vis-à-vis their competitors."[330]   The Court

---

certain to be found not to have infringed it, if the suit went to judgment.").

327. *See, e.g.*, *Walker Process*, 382 U.S. at 180 (Harlan, J. concurring); *Valley Drug*, 344 F.3d at 1307-08 ("Patent law ... serves the interests of consumers by protecting invention against prompt imitation in order to encourage more innovation than would otherwise occur.").

328. 404 U.S. 508 (1972).

329. *Id.* at 510.

330. *Id.* at 510-11; *see also, e.g.*, *Prof'l Real Estate*, 508 U.S. at 57 (stating that in *Cal. Motor Transport*, "we extended *Noerr* to 'the approach of citizens ... to administrative agencies ... and to courts'" (quoting *Cal. Motor Transp.*, 404 U.S. at 510)); *USS-POSCO Indus. v. Contra Costa County Bldg. & Constr. Trades Council*, 31 F.3d 800, 810 (9th Cir. 1994) ("The *Noerr-Pennington* doctrine provides broad antitrust protection for those who 'petition the government for a redress of grievances.' This protection extends to lobbying of government officials and petitioning of administrative agencies and courts." (citations omitted) (quoting *City of Columbia v. Omni Outdoor Adver.*, 499 U.S. 365, 379 (1991)); *Westmac, Inc. v. Smith*, 797 F.2d 313, 315 (6th Cir. 1986) ("The right to petition,

couched its decision principally in terms of First Amendment considerations:

> [I]t would be destructive of rights of association and of petition to hold that groups with common interests may not, without violating the antitrust laws, use the channels and procedures of state and federal agencies and courts to advocate their causes and points of view respecting resolution of their business and economic interests vis-à-vis their competitors.[331]

Although the Court held that *Noerr* immunity extended to litigation, courts have reasoned that the scope of immunity granted to efforts to adjudicate is less broad than that granted to efforts to influence the legislative process. The rationale for a broader scope for efforts to influence legislative action comes from the greater protections traditionally afforded the political efforts of citizens to influence the legislative process. As the Court explained, "a publicity campaign directed at the general public, seeking legislation or executive action, enjoys antitrust immunity even when the campaign employs unethical and deceptive methods. But *in less political arenas*, unethical and deceptive practices can constitute abuses of administrative or judicial processes that may result in antitrust violations."[332]

---

upon which the [*Noerr*] doctrine is based, extends to all departments of government, and therefore governs the access of citizens to courts and administrative agencies.") (citation omitted); MCI Communs. Corp. v. AT&T, 708 F.2d 1081, 1153 (7th Cir. 1983) ("The Court in *California Motor Transport* ... extended *Noerr-Pennington* to administrative and adjudicatory proceedings."); *In re* Relafen Antitrust Litig., 360 F. Supp. 2d 166, 178 (D. Mass. 2005) ("[I]nitiating and prosecuting a patent infringement action [is] the type of petitioning activity generally protected by the Noerr-Pennington doctrine.").

331. *Cal. Motor Transp.*, 404 U.S. at 510-11. Despite the language of *Cal. Motor Transp.*, FTC staff members have taken the position that the *Noerr-Pennington* doctrine may not apply to Section 5 of the FTC Act (a principal provision employed by the Commission in its enforcement activities). *See, e.g.*, John T. Delacourt, Ass't Dir., FTC Office of Policy Planning, *The FTC's* Noerr-Pennington *Task Force: Restoring Rationality to Petitioning Immunity*, Antitrust, Summer 2003, at 36 ("Delacourt I") ("The *Noerr* doctrine derives from a statutory construction of the Sherman Act, rather than from a constitutional construction of the First Amendment right to petition.").

332. Allied Tube & Conduit v. Indian Head, Inc., 486 U.S. 492, 499-500 (1988) (emphasis added).

(2) Noerr-Pennington and Litigation-Related Activities

The majority of the courts of appeals now hold that *Noerr-Pennington* immunity may apply to pre-litigation threats to sue depending on the circumstances of the case. Immunity depends largely on the extent to which pre-litigation acts, such as sending letters threatening litigation, are related to potential non-frivolous litigation as opposed to baseless threats intended to interfere with the recipient's business relationships.[333] In adopting this position, courts have largely employed reasoning expressed by the Fifth Circuit:

---

333. *See, e.g.*, Primetime 24 Joint Venture v. NBC, 219 F.3d 92, 100 (2d Cir. 2000); Glass Equip. Dev. v. Besten, Inc., 174 F.3d 1337, 1349 (Fed. Cir. 1999) (*Noerr* protection accorded "actual and threatened infringement suits" unless "sham" could be shown); McGuire Oil v. Mapco, Inc., 958 F.2d 1552, 1560 (11th Cir. 1992) (holding that threats of litigation are protected under *Noerr*); CVD, Inc. v. Raytheon Co., 769 F.2d 842, 850-51 (1st Cir. 1985) (holding that "the threat of unfounded trade secrets litigation in bad faith is sufficient to constitute a cause of action under the antitrust laws"); Coastal States Mktg. v. Hunt, 694 F.2d 1358, 1367 (5th Cir. 1983) (holding that threat letters are protected under *Noerr*); ICOS Vision Sys. Corp. v. Scanner Techs. Corp., 2006 U.S. Dist. LEXIS 13847, at *13 (S.D.N.Y. 2006) (holding that the sending of infringement letters enjoys *Noerr* protection if objectively reasonable and done in good faith); Applera Corp. v. MJ Research, 303 F. Supp. 2d 130, 131-35 (D. Conn. 2004) (letters threatening infringement action protected by *Noerr* doctrine); B&G Plastics v. E. Creative Indus., 269 F. Supp. 2d 450, 454 (S.D.N.Y. 2003) ("'[S]ending letters threatening court action ... [is] entitled to immunity to the same extent as the related litigation.'" (quoting Matsushita Elecs. v. Loral Corp., 974 F. Supp. 345, 359 (S.D.N.Y. 1997)); Versatile Plastics v. Sknowbest! Inc., 247 F. Supp. 2d 1098, 1103-06 (E.D. Wis. 2003) (granting defendants' motion to dismiss and holding that infringement notice letters in patent action are protected under *Noerr* doctrine as step taken to secure party's rights in future litigation); E-Z Bowz, L.L.C. v. Prof'l Prod. Research, No. 00 Civ. 8670, 2003 WL 22068573, at *28 (S.D.N.Y. Sept. 5, 2003); PennPac Int'l v. Rotonics Mfg., No. 99-CV-2890, 2001 WL 569264, at *6 (E.D. Pa. May 25, 2001) (letters threatening infringement action protected by *Noerr* doctrine); Avery Dennison Corp. v. Acco Brands, No. CV-99-1877DT(MCX), 2000 WL 986995, at *22-23 (C.D. Cal. Feb. 22, 2000) (letters warning of copyright infringement protected under *Noerr*); Miller Pipeline v. British Gas, 69 F. Supp. 2d 1129, 1138 (S.D. Ind. 1999) (litigation threat letters subject to *Noerr* immunity); *Matsushita Elecs.*, 974 F. Supp. at 359 (party was entitled to immunity where it sent out

Given that petitioning immunity protects joint litigation, it would be absurd to hold that it does not protect those acts reasonably and normally attendant upon effective litigation. The litigator should not be protected only when he strikes without warning. If litigation is in good faith, a token of that sincerity is a warning that it will be commenced and a possible effort to compromise the dispute. This is the position taken by most of the courts that have considered the question.[334]

From a public policy perspective, protecting pre-litigation threats to the same degree as actual litigation encourages communication between potential litigants and allows for pre-suit settlement.[335] As one commentator has explained, "*Noerr* protects the right to petition the government. Although a mere threat directed at one's competitor to sue or to seek administrative relief does not involve or 'petition' the government, it would be anomalous and socially counterproductive to protect the right to sue but not the right to threaten suit."[336]

When the prelitigation threat relates to patents, patentees are presumed to have the right to communicate concerning potential infringement. Such a right is based on both *Noerr* principles and the patent grant.[337] As the Federal Circuit has written:

"A patentee that has a good faith belief that its patents are being infringed violates no protected right when it so notifies infringers." . . . Accordingly, a patentee must be allowed to make its rights known to a

---

letters on same day it filed complaint which court found "not only attendant to litigation that wasn't frivolous or baseless, but also represented a reasonable attempt to expedite the resolution of that litigation"); Thermos Co. v. Igloo Prods., No. 93 C 5826, 1995 WL 842002, at *4-5 (N.D. Ill. Sept. 27, 1995) (*Noerr* immunity extended to cease-and-desist letters sent to alleged infringers); *cf.* Zenith Elecs. Corp. v. Exzec, Inc., 182 F.3d 1340, 1353 (Fed. Cir. 1999) (holding that, based on both the patent grant itself and *Noerr*, patentee "has the right to ... enforce its patent and that includes threatening alleged infringers with suit").

334. Coastal States Mktg. v. Hunt, 694 F.2d 1358, 1367 (5th Cir. 1983).
335. *See id.*
336. 1 AREEDA & HOVENKAMP,*su pra* note 1, ¶ 205e, at 237-38.
337. *See, e.g.*, Globetrotter Software v. Elan Computer Group, 362 F.3d 1367, 1377 (Fed. Cir. 2004) (stating that "decision to permit state-law tort liability for only objectively baseless allegations of infringement rests on both federal [patent laws] and the First Amendment").

potential infringer so that the latter can determine whether to cease its allegedly infringing activities, negotiate a license if one is offered, or decide to run the risk of liability and/or the imposition of an injunction.[338]

Moreover, where the product is not clearly marked as patented, patent law requires that a notice of infringement be sent in order to collect damages in a subsequent infringement action.[339] According to the Patent Act, such a notice "shall specify the patented process alleged to have been used and the reasons for a good faith belief that such process was used. The patent holder shall include in the notification such information as is reasonably necessary to explain fairly the patent holder's belief."[340]

In *Globetrotter Software v. Elan Computer Group*,[341] the Federal Circuit held that both *Noerr* immunity and preemption by federal patent laws applied to state common law claims asserted against a patentee in connection with letters and e-mails threatening infringement proceedings.[342] The *Globetrotter* court held that because Globetrotter was exercising its federal patent rights in sending the e-mail and letters, "The federal patent laws preempt state laws that impose tort liability for a patent holder's good faith conduct in communications asserting infringement of its patent and warning about potential litigation."[343] In order to avoid preemption, "bad faith must be alleged and ultimately proven, even if bad faith is not otherwise an element of the tort claim."[344]

---

338. Va. Panel Corp. v. MAC Panel Co., 133 F.3d 860, 869 (Fed. Cir. 1997) (quoting Mallinckrodt, Inc. v. Medipart, Inc., 976 F.2d 700, 709 (Fed. Cir. 1992)); *see also* Virtue v. Creamery Package Mfg., 227 U.S. 8, 37-38 (1913) ("Patents would be of little value if infringers of them could not be notified of the consequences of infringement, or proceeded against in the courts. Such action, considered by itself, cannot be said to be illegal.").

339. *See* 35 U.S.C. § 287(a).

340. *Id.* § 287(b)(5)(B).

341. 362 F.3d 1367 (Fed. Cir. 2004).

342. *See id.* at 1370.

343. *Id.* at 1377; *see also In re* Relafen Antitrust Litig., 346 F. Supp. 2d 349, 359 n.3 (D. Mass. 2004) (state claims subject to *Noerr* protection because they "implicated significant First Amendment and patent law concerns").

344. *Globetrotter*, 362 F.3d at 1379; *see also* Zenith Elecs. Corp. v. Exzec, Inc., 182 F.3d 1340, 1355 (Fed. Cir. 1999) (state tort claims asserted in response to patent enforcement letters "can survive federal preemption only to the extent that those claims are based on a showing of 'bad faith'

The court also noted that "our sister circuits, almost without exception, have applied the *Noerr* protections to pre-litigation communications."[345]

The courts, however, are not unanimous on this issue. In *Cardtoons, L.C. v. Major League Baseball Players Ass'n*,[346] the Tenth Circuit held that *Noerr* immunity does not apply to pre-litigation threats. In *Cardtoons*, the major league baseball players association had sent letters to the plaintiff threatening litigation if the plaintiff continued to produce trading cards that featured caricatures of active major league players.[347] Although the district court and a Tenth Circuit panel initially held that *Noerr* immunity protected such threats, the Tenth Circuit reversed on rehearing en banc. The en banc court reasoned that "[a] letter from one private party to another private party simply does not implicate the right to petition, regardless of what the letter threatens."[348]

Courts have reached differing results about whether certain other non-judicial acts related to litigation, such as sending letters to alleged patent infringers' customers and/or issuing press releases to publicize a litigation, should also receive *Noerr* immunity. Some courts have been reluctant to expand immunity to pre-litigation activity indirectly connected to a future litigation, expressing the view that letters threatening customers have little, if anything, to do with the type of petitioning protected by the First Amendment.[349] Indeed, as one treatise

---

action in asserting infringement," even if "bad faith is not otherwise an element of the tort claim").

345. *Globetrotter*, 362 F.3d at 1376 (citing Coastal States Mktg. v. Hunt, 694 F.2d 1358, 1367 (5th Cir. 1983); McGuire Oil v. Mapco, Inc., 958 F.2d 1552, 1560 (11th Cir. 1992); A.D. Bedell Wholesale v. Philip Morris, Inc., 263 F.3d 239, 252-53 (3d. Cir. 2001); Primetime 24 Joint Venture v. NBC, 219 F.3d 92, 100 (2d Cir. 2000)).

346. 208 F.3d 885 (10th Cir. 2000) (en banc).

347. *See id.* at 886-87.

348. *Id.* at 892. Three judges dissented from the en banc ruling in *Cardtoons*, writing: "The majority's ruling encourages, nay demands, more litigation; it requires intellectual property owners to bypass the post office on the way to the court house and avoid the letter carrier in a rush to get to the process server. Today's decision ignores the reality of intellectual property law, in which the enforcement of legal rights, and thus the invocation of the litigation process, is customarily commenced by a cease-and-desist letter." 208 F.3d at 894 (Lucero, J., joined by Brorby, and Briscoe, J.J., dissenting).

349. *See, e.g.*, Rodime PLC v. Seagate Tech., 174 F.3d 1294, 1307 (Fed. Cir. 1999) (refusing to apply *Noerr* immunity to Rodime's tortious interference claim based on Seagate's contacts with Rodime's potential

observed, "[s]tatements to the media or to industry trade groups are sufficiently far removed from the act of petitioning—and are not necessary to facilitate the act—that it makes little sense to cloak them in *Noerr* immunity."[350] Nevertheless, a number of courts have found that *Noerr* protects competitors' threatening letters to customers[351] and

---

licensees because such contacts "had nothing to do with petitioning the government"); eBay Inc. v. Bidder's Edge Inc., No. C-99-21200 RMW, 2000 WL 1863564, at *2 (N.D. Cal. July 25, 2000) (holding that eBay, which had sued Bidder's Edge for copyright infringement, could not rely on *Noerr* immunity to protect its conduct in contacting third-party publishers and demanding that they cease running Bidder's ads); Laitram Mach. v. Carnitech A/S, 901 F. Supp. 1155, 1161 (E.D. La. 1995) (holding that *Noerr* did not protect "the sending of three letters to Laitram's customers, informing them that Laitram's shrimp cooking machine incorporated trade secrets from its own patent and infringed on the Florida corporation's shrimp cooking machine patent"); Johnson v. ConVey/Keystone, Inc., 856 F. Supp. 1443 (D. Or. 1994); Oahu Gas Serv. v. Pac. Res., 460 F. Supp. 1359, 1386 (D. Haw. 1978) (refusing to afford "threats of lawsuits against potential [c]ustomers" *Noerr-Pennington* immunity).

350. HOVENKAMP IP, *supra* note 30, § 11.3(b)(5), at 11-30.
351. Globetrotter Software v. Elan Computer Group, 362 F.3d 1367, 1377-80 (Fed. Cir. 2004) (letters and e-mails to customer of alleged infringer protected under *Noerr* doctrine); Melea Ltd. v. Quality Models, 345 F. Supp. 2d 743, 758 (E.D. Mich. 2004) ("Plaintiffs are immune from liability because the Plaintiffs' letters proposed a potential lawsuit to Defendant's customers. Therefore, the *Noerr-Pennington* doctrine bars Defendant's counterclaim for tortious interference with a business relationship arising from Plaintiffs' letters to Defendant's customers."); Alexander Binzel Corp. v. Nu-Tecsys Corp., No. 91 C 2092, 2000 WL 310304, at *3 (N.D. Ill. Mar. 24, 2000) ("Most courts to consider the issue have extended *Noerr-Pennington* immunity to shield non-judicial acts that are "reasonably and normally attendant upon protected litigation."); Matsushita Elecs. v. Loral Corp., 974 F. Supp. 345, 359 (S.D.N.Y. 1997) (extending immunity to infringement warning letters sent to customers of defendants). *But see Laitram Mach.*, 901 F. Supp. at 1161 (*Noerr* does not protect "the sending of three letters to Laitram's customers, informing them that Laitram's shrimp cooking machine incorporated trade secrets from its own patent and infringed on the Florida corporation's shrimp cooking machine patent."); *Oahu Gas Serv., Inc.*, 460 F. Supp. at 1386 (refusing to afford "threats of lawsuits against potential [c]ustomers" *Noerr* immunity).

general publicity efforts[352] so long as such acts relate to a non-sham litigation.[353]

Courts generally hold that those who sponsor or fund litigation brought by others are subject to *Noerr* protection in respect of that litigation.[354]

---

352. *See, e.g.*, Zenith Elecs. Corp. v. Exzec, Inc., 182 F.3d 1340, 1353 (Fed. Cir. 1999) ("[F]ederal patent law bars the imposition of liability under federal or state law for publicizing a patent in the marketplace unless the plaintiff can show that patent holder acted in bad faith."); Aircapital Cablevision, Inc. v. Starlink Communs. Group, 634 F. Supp. 316, 325-26 (D. Kan. 1986) ("[T]he underlying litigation was not 'sham'; therefore, the attendant publicity is protected by Noerr-Pennington."); B&G Plastics v. E. Creative Indus., 269 F. Supp. 2d 450, 470-71 (S.D.N.Y. 2003).

353. Where a patentee sends warning letters to an alleged patent infringer's customers, the alleged infringer can assert a claim or counterclaim for trade libel or product disparagement under the Lanham Act. 15 U.S.C. § 1125(a). The Federal Circuit has held that "before a patentee can be held liable [under the Lanham Act] for marketplace activity in support of its patent, and thus deprived of the right to make statements about potential infringement of its patent, the marketplace activity must have been undertaken in bad faith." *Zenith Elecs.*, 182 F.3d at 1347-48; *see also, e.g.*, Golan v. Pinzel, 310 F.3d 1360, 1371 (Fed. Cir. 2002). Depending on its nature and method of dissemination, a "cease-and-desist" or other form of warning letter may not be a "commercial advertisement or promotion" within the meaning of the Lanham Act. 15 U.S.C. § 1125(a); Coastal Abstract Serv. v. First Am. Title Ins. Co., 173 F.3d 725, 734 (9th Cir. 1999); Avery Dennison Corp. v. Acco Brands, No. CV-99-1877DT(MCX), 2000 WL 986995, at *7-8 (C.D. Cal. Feb. 22, 2000) (finding letters from attorney to customers of alleged trademark infringer did not qualify as "commercial advertising or promotion"). In order to demonstrate bad faith, the Federal Circuit requires a threshold showing that the statements were objectively baseless. *See, e.g.*, *Globetrotter*, 362 F.3d at 1375-76

354. *See, e.g.*, Baltimore Scrap Corp. v. David J. Joseph Co., 237 F.3d 394, 401 (4th Cir. 2001) ("The First Amendment freedoms of petitioning and association protect groups who for whatever reason want to contribute to a lawsuit openly or to stand apart from public view while another party files a lawsuit."); Amarel v. Connell, 102 F.3d 1494, 1519 (9th Cir. 1997) (*Noerr* protection available to "surreptitious[]" sponsors of litigation); Liberty Lake Inv. v. Magnuson, 12 F.3d 155, 158 (9th Cir. 1993) (*Noerr* immunity extended despite fact that defendant had solicited "straw plaintiffs" to pursue litigation); Opdyke Inv. v. City of Detroit, 883 F.2d

3. Other "Petitioning" arising in the Intellectual Property Context

Courts have held that certain purely ministerial interactions with government entities do not constitute "petitioning" of the sort implicating First Amendment concerns. For example, the act of listing a pharmaceutical patent in the FDA's so-called Orange Book has been held not to constitute protected petitioning because the FDA performs no review of the propriety of such listings.[355] Thus, in the *Buspirone* litigation,[356] the court held that an "[Orange Book] listing is much more like the filing of a tariff than the kind of conduct through which private parties seek to influence governmental decision making and that has been traditionally immunized under the *Noerr-Pennington* doctrine."[357]

1265, 1273 (6th Cir. 1989) (same); Wilmorite, Inc. v. Eagan Real Estate, 454 F. Supp. 1124, 1133 (N.D.N.Y. 1977) (same); *cf.* E. R.R. Presidents Conference v. Noerr Motor Freight, 365 U.S. 127, 142 (1961) (lobbying activity sponsored by railroads, but carried out by others, held immune from antitrust liability). *But see In re* Burlington N., Inc., 822 F.2d 518, 531 (5th Cir. 1987) (third party sponsors of litigation *not* entitled to *Noerr* immunity if they would have lacked "an interest ... sufficient to support a reasonable claim of standing" had they brought the suit in their own names), *called into doubt by* Prof'l Real Estate Investors v. Columbia Pictures Indus., 508 U.S. 49, 55 n.3 (1993).

355.   Listing a patent in the Orange Book requires generic companies seeking approval of bioequivalent versions of the patented drug to the make certain certifications with respect to the patent. *See* 21 U.S.C. § 355(j)(2)(A)(vii). If the applicant seeks to market its generic before expiration of the listed patent, it must send a notice to the patent owner certifying its good faith belief that the patent is invalid or will not be infringed by the proposed generic product. *See id.* § 355(j)(2)(B). If the patent owner files an infringement action within 45 days of receiving the certification, an automatic 30-month stay of FDA's approval of the generic is triggered, regardless of the merits of the patent suit. *See id.* § 355(j)(5)(B). The 30-month stay acts as a statutory bar to generic competition. Recent legislative amendments limit patent owners to a single 30-month stay for a given drug product. *See, e.g.*, Medicare Prescription Drug Improvement and Modernization Act of 2003, § 1101, Pub. L. No. 108-173, tit. XI, 117 Stat. 2066 (2003).

356.   *In re* Buspirone Patent Litig., 185 F. Supp. 2d 363 (S.D.N.Y. 2002).

357.   *Id.* at 373. Here the court relied upon the Second Circuit's decision in *Litton Systems v. AT&T*, 700 F.2d 785 (2d Cir. 1983). In that case, the Second Circuit found that the filing of an "interface" tariff with the FCC did not constitute petitioning activity where the FCC performed no immediate review of the submission before it took effect. The court

According to the court "it is critical to distinguish between activities in which the government acts or renders a decision only after an independent review of the merits of a petition and activities in which the government acts in a merely ministerial or non-discretionary capacity in direct reliance on the representations made by private parties."[358]

Some defendants have argued that Orange Book listing nevertheless is entitled to protection because of its linkage to patent litigation in the pharmaceutical industry. In the *Buspirone* litigation, the court also rejected the patentee drug company's argument that its listing of a patent in the Orange Book was "inextricably bound up with its subsequent patent infringement suits" and therefore akin to pre-litigation threat letters.[359] The court held that "[the patentee's] listing activity was ... distinct from its litigation both analytically and as a practical matter. [The patentee] could have listed the ... patent in the Orange Book without subsequently bringing infringement suits against [the generic companies], and [the patentee] could have brought these suits without relying on its Orange Book listing."[360] By choosing to proceed with litigation under the Orange Book listing, the patentee received "a number of additional automatic benefits," including the 30-month stay of FDA

---

found that AT&T was able to exclude competition simply by the act of filing tariffs, not as the result of any affirmative governmental determination. *Id.* at 795, 807. Such conduct was found not to be entitled to *Noerr* immunity. *Id.*; *see also, e.g.*, Ticor Title Ins. v. FTC, 998 F.2d 1129, 1138 (3d Cir. 1993) (collective rate filing does not constitute petitioning); City of Kirkwood v. Union Elec., 671 F.2d 1173, 1181 (8th Cir. 1992); Lao II, *supra* note 201, at 1004-07, 1019-20 (only petitioning that involves an element of "persuasion" should be protected by *Noerr* doctrine).

358. *In re Buspirone*, 185 F. Supp. 2d at 369; *see also, e.g.*, Organon, Inc. v. Mylan Pharm., 293 F. Supp. 2d 453, 458-59 (D.N.J. 2003) (holding that because the FDA's action in listing a patent in the Orange Book "was not an independent governmental determination, but rather a purely ministerial function," *Noerr* immunity did not apply); Warner Lambert Co. v. PurePac Pharm., No. Civ. A. 98-02749 (JCL), 2000 WL 34213890, at *7 (D.N.J. Dec. 22, 2000) (where "alleged deceit and fraudulent conduct is directed at a regulatory agency which does not conduct independent investigations," *Noerr*-protected petitioning not involved); Muris, *supra* note 201, at 453-56 (arguing that ministerial "petitioning" not worthy of *Noerr* protection).
359. *In re Buspirone*, 185 F. Supp. 2d at 372.
360. *Id.*

approval of the generic drug.[361] In contrast, however, a number of other courts have gone on to hold that Orange Book listing alone did not create antitrust liability.[362]

4. Conduct that Vitiates Noerr-Pennington Immunity

The seminal cases dealing with potential antitrust liability for the bad faith enforcement of intellectual property rights that have *not* been obtained by fraud are the *Handgards* decisions from the Ninth Circuit.[363] There, Handgards accused Ethicon of pursuing a series of patent infringement actions against it in bad faith as part of an overall scheme to monopolize the market for heat-treated plastic gloves. Handgards presented evidence at trial that Ethicon knew that its patents were invalid at the time it initiated its infringement actions.[364] The Ninth Circuit held that a claim for attempted monopolization under Section 2 of the Sherman Act could be premised on the pursuit of patent infringement litigation "in bad faith, that is, with knowledge that the patents, though

361. *Id. But see In re* Relafen Antitrust Litig., 346 F. Supp. 2d 349, 359 n.3 (D. Mass. 2004) (declining to hold Orange Book listing not protected, finding that "[the patentee's] initiation and prosecution of patent infringement suits to be the more direct cause of the complained-of generic delay").
362. *See, e.g.*, Twin City Bakery Workers & Welfare Fund v. Astra AB, 207 F. Supp. 2d 221 (S.D.N.Y. 2002) (finding that while not immune from antitrust laws, listing patent in Orange Book did not violate Sherman Act because party did so well before patent expired; by contrast, defendant in *Buspirone* made Orange Book filing day before patent filing); *Organon*, 293 F. Supp. 2d at 459 (finding that even though *Noerr* immunity did not apply, Organon had "reasonable basis" to list its patent in Orange Book).
363. *See Handgards I*, 601 F.2d 986 (9th Cir. 1979); *Handgards II*, 743 F.2d 1282 (9th Cir. 1984).
364. The evidence was that Ethicon had learned by the time the infringement action was underway that the real inventor was not the individual identified on the patent (an Ethicon employee). Rather than dropping the lawsuit, Ethicon fabricated interrogatory responses to convey the impression that its employee was the first inventor. The evidence also showed that Ethicon knew that the same invention had been on sale more than one year prior to the date it filed its patent application, thus making the subject matter unpatentable under the prior on-sale bar doctrine. *See supra* § B.2.

lawfully obtained, were invalid."[365] The court held that "[p]atentees must be permitted to test the validity of their patents in court through actions against alleged infringers.... On the other hand, infringement actions initiated and conducted in bad faith contribute nothing to the policies of either the patent law or the antitrust law."[366]

The Ninth Circuit required bad faith to be shown with clear and convincing evidence.[367] The court viewed this high standard of proof to be an adequate deterrent against frivolous antitrust claims that, if allowed to proliferate, could deter patent incentives. According to the court, the lower "preponderance" standard "might well chill" legitimate patent enforcement efforts "'because of fear of the vexations or punitive consequences of treble-damages suits.'"[368] The court also held that its bad faith standard, if established by the evidence, would be sufficient to constitute a "sham" that would strip the patentee of its *Noerr-Pennington* immunity. As the court put it:

> We believe that *Handgards I* established a standard that embodies both the *Noerr-Pennington* immunity and the sham exception. There we held that "the jury should be instructed that a patentee's infringement suit is presumptively in good faith and that this presumption can be rebutted only by clear and convincing evidence [of bad faith]." The good faith presumption affords the equivalent of *Noerr-Pennington* immunity while the requirement of bad faith easily affords the equivalent of the sham exception.[369]

---

365. *Handgards I*, 601 F.2d at 994. The Ninth Circuit made this holding after the first trial of Handgards' antitrust claim—which resulted in a jury verdict for Handgards (*Handgards I*). Despite holding that there was no bar to Handgards pursuing such an antitrust claim, the Ninth Circuit reversed and remanded due to certain inadequacies in the jury instructions. The case was retried, resulting in another jury verdict for Handgards. The result of the second trial was appealed; the Ninth Circuit reaffirmed its basic holding in *Handgards I* and upheld the jury's verdict in the second trial. *Handgards II*, 743 F.2d at 1300.

366. *Handgards I*, 601 F.2d at 993.

367. *Id.* at 996.

368. *Id.* (quoting Walker Process Equip. v. Food Mach. & Chem. Corp., 382 U.S. 172, 180 (1965) (Harlan, J., concurring)).

369. *Handgards II*, 743 F.2d at 1294-95 (citation omitted) (quoting *Handgards I*, 601 F.2d at 996).

In *Professional Real Estate Investors v. Columbia Pictures Industries,*[370] the Supreme Court addressed directly the circumstances in which
a claim for sham litigation would be justified, at least where the litigation
or other underlying conduct did not involve fraud or misrepresentation.
In that case, Columbia Pictures sued Professional Real Estate Investors
("PRE") for copyright infringement based on its use of rented videodiscs
in rooms of one of the resort hotels it operated. Columbia alleged that,
since the rooms were open to the public, playing the discs in the rooms
constituted a prohibited "public performance" of the copyrighted
movies.[371] PRE counterclaimed under Section 2 of the Sherman Act,
accusing Columbia of attempted monopolization.[372]

The district court held that the rentals and subsequent replay in hotel
rooms were not a public performance and issued summary judgment
against Columbia. The Ninth Circuit affirmed.[373] On remand for
consideration of PRE's antitrust counterclaim, the district court granted
summary judgment to Columbia after concluding that (i) although
Columbia lost its infringement claim, it was "expecting a favorable
judgment" when it filed its lawsuit, (ii) the substantive issue had not been
easy to resolve, and (iii) the Ninth Circuit had some difficulty resolving
the case.[374] On appeal, the Ninth Circuit rejected PRE's argument that
"subjective intent in bringing the suit was a question of fact precluding
entry of summary judgment."[375] Rather, the Ninth Circuit concluded,
Columbia's "probable cause" to bring the suit ruled out any sham as a
matter of law: "a suit brought with probable cause does not fall within
the sham exception to the *Noerr-Pennington* doctrine."[376]

The Supreme Court affirmed, rejecting PRE's proposal that a sham
litigation may be identified based solely on the antitrust defendant's
subjective intent to cause anticompetitive harm to the plaintiff. To the
contrary, the Court held that "litigation cannot be deprived of [*Noerr*]

---

370. 508 U.S. 49 (1993).
371. *Id.* at 53.
372. *Id.* at 52. The Supreme Court noted that, because PRE was attempting to
      establish a service of supplying movies for in-room use at hotels, "PRE
      therefore competed with Columbia not only for the viewing market [at
      the resort in question] but also for the broader market for in-room
      entertainment services at hotels." *Id.*
373. *See id.* at 53.
374. *Id.*
375. *Id.* at 54.
376. *Id.*

immunity as a sham unless the litigation is objectively baseless."[377] Where the lawsuit is not objectively baseless, the fact that the suit may be brought for an anticompetitive purpose is immaterial. In so holding, the Court outlined a two-part test for determining what constitutes sham litigation. First, "the lawsuit must be objectively baseless in the sense that no reasonable litigant could realistically expect success on the merits."[378] According to the Court, "If an objective litigant could conclude that the suit is reasonably calculated to elicit a favorable outcome, the suit is immunized under *Noerr*, and an antitrust claim premised on the sham exception must fail."[379] Second, and only if the first prong is satisfied, a court should examine the litigant's "subjective motivation" focusing on "whether the baseless lawsuit conceals 'an attempt to interfere directly with the business relationships of a competitor.'"[380]

However, the Court expressly stated that it was not deciding "whether and, if so, to what extent *Noerr* permits the imposition of antitrust liability for a litigant's fraud or other misrepresentations."[381]

---

377. *Id.* at 51.
378. *Id.* at 60.
379. *Id.* The Federal Circuit has held that objective baselessness must be shown with clear and convincing evidence. *See, e.g.*, Mitek Surgical Prods. v. Arthrex, Inc., 230 F.3d 1383, 1383 (Fed Cir. 2000) (unpublished); Nobelpharma AB v. Implant Innovations, 141 F.3d 1059, 1064 (Fed. Cir. 1998).
380. *Prof'l Real Estate*, 508 U.S. at 60-61. The Court rejected PRE's argument that subjective intent should control in part by reference to the objectives of the copyright laws: "[T]o condition a copyright upon a demonstrated lack of anticompetitive intent would upset the notion of copyright as a 'limited grant' of 'monopoly privileges' intended simultaneously 'to motivate the creative activity of authors' and 'to give the public appropriate access to their work product.'" *Id.* at 64 (quoting Sony Corp. of Am. v. Universal City Studios, 464 U.S. 417, 429 (1984)).

The Court also did not adopt the Seventh Circuit approach set forth in *Grip-Pak, Inc. v. Illinois Tool Works, Inc.*, 694 F.2d 466 (7th Cir. 1982), under which *Noerr* immunity is denied if "'the stakes, discounted by the probability of winning, would be too low to repay the investment in litigation.'" *See Prof'l Real Estate*, 508 U.S. at 55 n.3 (quoting *Grip-Pak*, 694 F.2d at 472). Later in the opinion, however, the *PRE* Court suggested that such considerations might be relevant to the subjective motivation prong of the test it adopted. *Id.* at 65-66.
381. *Id.* at 61 n.6.

Applying the test in the case before it, the Court found that Columbia's copyright infringement suit could not be viewed as objectively baseless: there was a legitimate dispute concerning Columbia's "public performance" argument and "any reasonable copyright holder in Columbia's position could have believed it had some chance of winning."[382]

The *PRE* Court reminded antitrust plaintiffs that even if they satisfy both prongs of the sham litigation test, they must still prove a "substantive antitrust violation."[383]   While proof of a sham deprives an antitrust defendant of immunity, it does not establish antitrust liability.[384] Thus, to impose antitrust liability arising from sham litigation, a court must find that: (1) the litigation was objectively baseless;[385] (2) the action was brought in bad faith; and (3) all required aspects of an antitrust violation are shown.[386]

a.   Are *Walker Process* and *Handgards*-type Antitrust
     Claims Subject to the *PRE* Test?

The lower courts have struggled with the issue of whether *Walker Process* or *Handgards*-type plaintiffs are required to satisfy the *PRE* two-part test *in addition* to the basic elements of the respective claims. The Supreme Court specifically declined to decide "whether and, if so, to what extent *Noerr* permits the imposition of antitrust liability for a litigant's fraud or other misrepresentations."[387]   The Court did note, however, that "misrepresentations, condoned in the political arena, are not immunized when used in the adjudicatory process."[388]   Since *PRE*, the lower courts have therefore been confronted with the question of whether there is a stand-alone "misrepresentation" exception to *Noerr* immunity.

In *Nobelpharma*, the Federal Circuit held that sham litigation under the *PRE* standard and *Walker Process* "provide *alternative* legal grounds

---

382.   *Id.* at 65.
383.   *Id.* at 61.
384.   *Id.*
385.   *Id.* at 51.
386.   *See id.* at 60; Walker Process Equip. v. Food Mach. & Chem. Corp., 382 U.S. 172, 178 (1965). *See generally supra* § B.1.c. (discussion of the antitrust elements).
387.   *Prof'l Real Estate*, 508 U.S. at 61 n.6.
388.   *Id.*

on which a patentee may be stripped of its immunity from the antitrust laws; both legal theories may be applied to the same conduct."[389] The court thus observed that "[t]he Supreme Court [in *PRE*] saw no need to merge these separate lines of cases and neither do we."[390] "Each provides its own basis for depriving a patent owner of immunity from the antitrust laws; either or both may be applicable to a particular party's conduct in obtaining and enforcing a patent."[391] The court held that "if the ... elements of *Walker Process* fraud, as well as the other criteria for antitrust liability, are met, such liability can be imposed without the additional sham inquiry required under [the *PRE* case]."[392]

In *Liberty Lake Investments v. Magnuson*,[393] the Ninth Circuit rejected the contention that, if abuse in the litigation process could be shown, e.g., misrepresentations, then "under footnote 6 of the *Professional Real Estate Investors* opinion it is unnecessary even to reach its two-part test."[394] *Liberty Lake* involved allegedly fraudulent environmental challenges to a real estate development; the developer alleged that the defendant had engaged in tactics that amounted to fraud and misrepresentation, including soliciting straw parties to serve as

---

389. Nobelpharma AB v. Implant Innovations, 141 F.3d 1059, 1071 (Fed. Cir. 1998) (emphasis added).

390. *Id.*

391. *Id.*

392. *Id.* At least one commentator has stated that fraud must be viewed as a separate exception to *Noerr* immunity due to the Supreme Court's holding in the *Walker Process* case. Lao II, *supra* note 201, at 977-78 (because instituting patent infringement litigation is petitioning judiciary, "unless Food Machinery's fraud took it outside the reach of *Noerr*, its infringement action would have had to be immune"). *See generally supra* § B.1 (detailed discussion of *Walker Process*). Others have argued that *Walker Process* fraud should be viewed as a species of sham claim. *See, e.g.*, HOVENKAMP IP, *supra* note 30, § 11.1, at 11-3; Lao II, *supra* note 201, at 976-78; O'Donnell, *supra* note 201, at 45, 59 ("[T]here is no meaningful reason for having a distinct *Walker Process* fraud claim, even if it is within the ambit of sham litigation; both *Walker Process* and *Handgards* sham cases arise from the attempted enforcement of an invalid patent; both claims potentially involve invalidation due to misconduct before the PTO."); Atwood, *supra* note 201, at 655 ("[T]he Court's holding in *Walker Process* could easily have been framed in terms of something akin to a sham or misrepresentation exception.").

393. 12 F.3d 155 (9th Cir. 1993).

394. *Id.* at 158.

plaintiffs, paying said plaintiffs' legal fees, and failing to communicate settlement overtures to the straw plaintiffs. The developer claimed that these tactics "ma[d]e the litigation sham without regard to the objective merit of the lawsuit or its proponents' motivation."[395] The Ninth Circuit held that "[r]ead in context with the entire *Professional Real Estate Investors* opinion, footnote 6 does not obviate application of the Court's two-part test for determining sham litigation *in the absence of proof* that a party's knowing fraud upon, or its intentional misrepresentations to, the court deprive the litigation of its legitimacy."[396]

In reaching its result, the court noted that "[i]n a case involving a fraudulently-obtained patent, that which immunizes the predatory behavior from antitrust liability (the patent) is, in effect a nullity because of the underlying fraud."[397] Thus, the court seemed to suggest that, where a patent was obtained by fraud and/or where a litigant made knowing misrepresentations to a court, the two-part *Professional Real Estate* test would not apply.

In *Hydranautics v. FilmTec Corp.*,[398] a case alleging sham litigation on the basis of a fraudulently-obtained patent, the Ninth Circuit considered whether the above dicta in *Liberty Lake* concerning fraudulently-obtained patents was "good law," and concluded that "it [was], at least where the fraud is intentional."[399] The court noted that the holdings in *PRE* and *Liberty Lake* "[left] open the question of whether an infringement action based on a fraudulently obtained patent is objectively baseless."[400] The *Hydranautics* court held, however, that "where the plaintiff obtained the patent by intentional fraud or was an assignee who knew of the patent's infirmity" such plaintiff "would not demonstrate probable cause for a patent infringement suit," i.e., would not show an objective basis for the suit.[401] Because the antitrust plaintiff there had alleged facts in its complaint that, if proven, would establish that the defendant patentee had obtained its patent by fraud, the case could not be dismissed on the pleadings.

The Federal Trade Commission recently ruled that "deliberate misrepresentations that substantially affect the outcome of a proceeding

---

395. *Id.* The court found no evidence of such fraudulent conduct or intentional misrepresentations on the record before it.
396. *Id.* at 159 (emphasis added).
397. *Id.*
398. 70 F.3d 533 (9th Cir. 1995).
399. *Id.* at 538.
400. *Id.*
401. *Id.*

or so infest its core to deprive the proceeding of legitimacy may not, in appropriate circumstances, qualify for *Noerr-Pennington* protection."[402] In *In re Union Oil Co. of California ("Unocal")*,[403] the FTC alleged that Unocal had violated Section 5 of the FTC Act by making various misrepresentations and omissions in a rulemaking proceeding before the California Air Resources Board ("CARB")—a state administrative entity charged with promulgating standards for the production of certain low emission gasoline in the state of California. Unocal allegedly misrepresented that the technology it urged CARB to adopt would be freely available and not subject to patent protection or enforcement. Only later, after its proposed technology was adopted in the regulations and the industry had spent billions to comply with the regulations, did Unocal announce that it held patents over the technology and intended to enforce them. The FTC held that, in the context of misrepresentations, *PRE*'s focus on whether "a litigant seeks to use the outcome rather than the process" to achieve an anticompetitive result makes little sense:

> [T]he very purpose of making the misrepresentation likely *is* to obtain the desired outcome. To treat this intention as dispositive is to shelter petitioning *because* of its anticompetitive goals. Indeed, granting protection to intentional misrepresentations would create perverse incentives to lie, in abuse of judicial and administrative processes.[404]

---

402. *In re* Union Oil Co., 138 F.T.C. 1 (2004). In mid-2001, the FTC established an internal task force, one objective of which was to identify opportunities to promote "an independent misrepresentation exception [to the *Noerr* doctrine]" that would stand "separate and distinct from the 'sham' exception set forth in [*PRE*]." Press Release, Fed. Trade Comm'n, FTC Chairman Muris Outlines Agency's Positive Agenda (Dec. 10, 2002), *available at* http://www.ftc.gov/opa/2002/12/handler. htm; *see also* Delacourt I, *supra* note 331, at 36-37 (task force charged with exploring "a broad range of potential *Noerr* exceptions" in light of perceived "creeping expansion" of *Noerr* immunity); Wood, *supra* note 201, at 72; John T. Delacourt, *Protecting Competition by Narrowing Noerr: A Reply*, Antitrust, Fall 2003, at 77 ("Delacourt II"); Lao II, *supra* note 201, at 1020-24 (advocating a misrepresentation exception to *Noerr* immunity).

403. *In re* Union Oil Co., 138 F.T.C. 125 (initial decision issued Nov. 25, 2003).

404. *Union Oil*, 138 F.T.C. at 47.

The FTC thus held that:

> [M]isrepresentation can warrant denial of *Noerr-Pennington* protection, pursuant either to a separate doctrinal exception or a variant of the sham exception. We hold, however, that false petitioning loses *Noerr-Pennington* protection only in limited circumstances, such as when the petitioning occurs outside the political arena; the misrepresentation is deliberate, factually verifiable, and central to the outcome of the proceeding or case; and it is possible to demonstrate and remedy this effect without undermining the integrity of the deceived governmental entity. In addition, we emphasize that, even if *Noerr-Pennington* considerations do not protect the false petitioning, no liability arises under the FTC, Sherman, or Clayton Acts unless that conduct is anticompetitive.[405]

The Commission identified several factors it viewed as important in drawing the political/non-political distinction, including the governmental entity's expectations of truthful representations of fact from petitioners, the governmental entity's discretion in rendering a decision, and the extent of necessary reliance by the governmental entity on the petitioner's factual allegations.[406] The Commission held that the staff's complaint against Unocal satisfied these standards and reinstated the complaint.[407]

---

405. *Id.* at 78-79.
406. *Id.* at 51-57.
407. Some commentators have criticized the FTC's decision as imposing overly ambiguous standards that inject significant uncertainty into the scope of *Noerr* protection. Kobak & Reznick, *supra* note 201, at 87. For more on lack of disclosure to standard setting organizations, *see, e.g.*, Kattan, *supra* note 201. Cases outside of the intellectual property context have split on the issue of whether there is a misrepresentation exception to *Noerr* immunity. *See, e.g.*, Baltimore Scrap Corp. v. David J. Joseph Co., 237 F.3d 394, 402 (4th Cir. 2001) ("[W]e need not reach the question of whether a fraud exception to *Noerr-Pennington* still exists after [*PRE*]," but if it did, it would apply "only to the type of fraud that deprives litigation of its legitimacy."); Armstrong Surgical Ctr. v. Armstrong County Mem. Hosp., 185 F.3d 154, 160 (3d Cir. 1999) (stating that there is "doubt on whether [a misrepresentation] exception exists under any circumstances"); Cheminor Drugs v. Ethyl Corp., 168 F.3d 119, 123 (3d Cir. 1999) (no separate misrepresentation exception; objective baselessness evaluated without regard to misrepresentation, unless the misrepresentation "infected the core of [the petitioner's] claim and the government's resulting actions"); Kottle v. Nw. Kidney Ctrs., 146

On a practical level, in light of the stringent requirements of *Walker Process* and *Handgards*, plaintiffs succeeding on such claims would have a good chance of also meeting the *PRE* test, thus rendering the issue of *Noerr*'s application somewhat academic.[408]

b. Establishing Objective Baselessness

The Court in *PRE*[409] explained the objective baselessness requirement in terms of both the common law tort of wrongful civil proceedings[410] and Rule 11 of the Federal Rules of Civil Procedure.[411] As to the former, the Court held that "[t]he existence of probable cause to institute legal proceedings precludes a finding that an antitrust defendant has engaged in sham litigation." [412] According to the Court, "[t]he notion of probable cause, as understood and applied in the common law tort of wrongful civil proceedings ... requires no more than a 'reasonabl[e] belie[f] that there is a chance that [a] claim may be held valid upon adjudication.'"[413] In short, so long as a party could reasonably believe it "had some chance of winning" its suit, it will not be stripped of *Noerr* immunity.[414] "Under our decision today ... a proper probable cause determination irrefutably demonstrates that an antitrust plaintiff has not

---

F.3d 1056, 1060-61 (9th Cir. 1998) (holding that misrepresentation made in quasi-judicial proceeding would not be subject to immunity if it was so egregious as to "deprive the litigation of its legitimacy"); St. Joseph's Hosp. v. Hosp. Corp. of Am., 795 F.2d 948, 955 (11th Cir. 1986) (hospital's misrepresentations to a government agency "do not enjoy *Noerr* immunity"); Whelan v. Abell, 48 F.3d 1247, 1255 (D.C. Cir. 1995) (holding that, "[h]owever broad the First Amendment right to petition may be, it cannot be stretched to cover petitions based on known falsehoods").

408. *See* Hydranautics v. FilmTec Corp., 70 F.3d 533, 537 (9th Cir. 1995); HOVENKAMP IP, *supra* note 30, § 11.2, at 11-7.

409. 508 U.S. 49 (1993).

410. *See, e.g.*, 2 DAN B. DOBBS, THE LAW OF TORTS § 436 (2001) (general discussion of tort of wrongful civil proceedings).

411. *See, e.g.*, 5A CHARLES ALAN WRIGHT & ARTHUR R. MILLER, FEDERAL PRACTICE AND PROCEDURE § 1335 (3d ed. 2004) (general discussion of standards for Rule 11 cause of action).

412. Prof'l Real Estate Investors v. Columbia Pictures Indus., 508 U.S. 49, 62 (1993).

413. *Id.* at 62-63 (quoting Hubbard v. Beatty & Hyde, Inc., 343 Mass. 258, 262, 178 N. E. 2d 485, 488 (1961) (internal quotation marks omitted)).

414. *Id.* at 65.

proved the objective prong of the sham exception and that the defendant is accordingly entitled to *Noerr* immunity."[415]   One district court found that a suit could not be viewed as objectively baseless where, "[although] hypertechnical, [the plaintiff's position] passed the 'straight face' test."[416]

Where, as in the litigation between PRE and Columbia Pictures, "there is no dispute over the predicate facts of the underlying legal proceeding" and the relevant law is in an "unsettled" condition, the probable cause requirement would "plainly" be met, according to the Supreme Court.[417] The Court also noted that where the predicate facts of the underlying lawsuit are not disputed, "a court may decide probable cause as a matter of law."[418]

The Court also held that a claim would have an objective basis, and therefore maintain its *Noerr* protection, if "at the very least" it "was

---

415. *Id.* at 63.
416. *In re* Terazosin Hydrochloride Antitrust Litig., 335 F. Supp. 2d 1336, 1359 (S.D. Fla. 2004).
417. *Prof'l Real Estate*, 508 U.S. at 63-65. Where the predicate facts of the underlying lawsuit are disputed, then the fact-finder must resolve the disputed facts. In an intellectual property context, there may be fact disputes concerning such issues as whether material information was withheld from the PTO; whether the patentee came into possession of facts suggesting invalidity prior to bringing the infringement action; and, whether before bringing suit, the patentee conducted an investigation adequate to satisfy Rule 11. *See, e.g.*, *In re* Relafen Antitrust Litig., 346 F. Supp. 2d 349, 360-62 (D. Mass. 2004) (although underlying patent suit resolved, "'the facts tending to establish the existence or want of existence of probable cause' were disputed, [including] ... the facts that 'appeared to [the defendants] when they filed their petition'" (quoting Nelson v. Miller, 227 Kan. 271, 277, 607 P.2d 438 (1980), and Stewart v. Sonneborn, 98 U.S. 187, 195 (1879)). *But see, e.g.*, Am. Home Prods. v. Johnson & Johnson, No Civ. A. 91-5594, 1994 WL 46522, at *1 (E.D. Pa. Feb. 15, 1994) (holding that "the question of objective[] baseless[ness] was a mixed one of fact and law involving patentee's knowledge that was properly submitted to the jury"). *Compare* FilmTec Corp. v. Hydranautics, 67 F.3d 931 (Fed. Cir. 1995) (holding antitrust claim could be dismissed; since underlying lawsuit was successful at district court level, the claim could not be deemed objectively baseless as a matter of law), *with* Hydranautics v. FilmTec Corp., 70 F.3d 533, 533 (9th Cir. 1995) (same facts; holding antitrust claim could not be dismissed as a matter of law where antitrust plaintiff claimed that success at district court level stemmed from fraud and misrepresentation).
418. *Prof'l Real Estate*, 508 U.S. at 63.

based on an objectively 'good faith argument for the extension, modification or reversal of existing law.'"[419] Here, the Court cited Rule 11 of the Federal Rules of Civil Procedure, which provides in part that:

> By presenting to the court ... a pleading, written motion, or other paper, an attorney ... is certifying that to the best of the person's knowledge, information and belief, *formed after an inquiry reasonable under the circumstances*—(1) it is not being presented for any improper purpose ... (2) the claims, defenses, and other legal contentions therein are warranted by existing law ... [and] (3) the allegations and other factual contentions have evidentiary support.[420]

The Court warned that, "when the antitrust defendant has lost the underlying litigation, a court must 'resist the understandable temptation to engage in *post hoc* reasoning by concluding' that an ultimately unsuccessful 'action must have been unreasonable or without foundation.'"[421]

In the patent context, there is a presumption that an infringement action is brought in good faith, and merely losing a patent case, without more, will not strip a patentee of its antitrust immunity. As the Federal Circuit has held, "the patentee must have the right of enforcement of a duly granted patent, unencumbered by punitive consequences should the patent's validity or infringement not survive litigation."[422]

---

419. *Id.* at 65 (quoting Fed. R. Civ. P. 11).
420. Fed. R. Civ. P. 11 (emphasis added). In his concurring opinion, Justice Souter wrote that the Court's reference to Rule 11 was not meant to "signal the importation [into the objective baselessness inquiry] of every jot and tittle of the law of attorney sanctions." *Prof'l Real Estate*, 508 U.S. at 67 (Souter, J., concurring).
421. 508 U.S. at 61 n.5 (quoting Christiansburg Garment Co. v. Equal Employ. Opp. Comm'n, 434 U.S. 412, 421-22 (1978)).
422. C.R. Bard, Inc. v. M3 Sys., 157 F.3d 1340, 1369 (Fed. Cir. 1998); Brooks Furniture Mfg. v. Dutailier Int'l, 393 F.3d 1378, 1382 (Fed. Cir. 2005) ("There is a presumption that the assertion of infringement of a duly granted patent is made in good faith."); Q-Pharma, Inc. v. Andrew Jergens Co., 360 F.3d 1295, 1304 (Fed. Cir. 2004) ("A patent owner who brings suit for infringement, without more, is generally exempt from the antitrust laws."); *see also, e.g.*, PennPac Int'l v. Rotonics Mfg., No. 99-CV-2890, 2001 WL 569264, at *6 (E.D. Pa. May 25, 2001) (noting presumption of patent validity in applying sham test to infringement action); Mitek Surgical Prods. v. Arthrex Inc., 21 F. Supp. 2d 1309, 1317 (D. Utah 1998) ("[A] litigant may only proceed with antitrust

In applying the first prong of the *PRE* test, a suit cannot be deemed objectively baseless if it was successful on the merits.[423] In *PRE* itself, the Court noted that "[a] winning lawsuit is by definition a reasonable effort at petitioning for redress and therefore not a sham."[424] Going

---

counterclaims which are based upon the filing of a lawsuit if it 'pierces' the presumption that a patent infringement suit is brought in good faith.").

423.   Courts that have considered the question generally agree that the objective baselessness test should be applied to a suit as a whole, rather than to individual claims. Thus, even if a particular cause of action is baseless, a litigant generally will not be stripped of *Noerr* immunity if the balance of its suit has merit. *See, e.g.*, Eden Hannon & Co. v. Sumitomo Trust & Banking, 914 F.2d 556, 565 (4th Cir. 1990); Matsushita Elecs. v. Loral Corp., 974 F. Supp. 345, 357 n.20 (S.D.N.Y. 1997); Boston Sci. v. Schneider Europe AG, 983 F. Supp. 245, 272-73 (D. Mass. 1997) ("I doubt that the sham litigation exception to the *Noerr-Pennington* doctrine applies to independent claims as opposed to an entire suit."); Dentsply Int'l v. New Tech. Co., No. 96-272 MMS, 1996 U.S. Dist. LEXIS 19846 (D. Del. Dec. 19, 1996); HOVENKAMP IP, *supra* note 30, § 11.3(b)(2), at 11-21 ("[C]ourts have generally focused on the suit itself rather than the cause of action as the right unit of measure ... This conclusion comports with the principles of *Noerr* to the extent that the addition of a baseless claim to a meritorious suit does not significantly change the competitive relationship of the parties.").

It has been pointed out, however, that where the impact of a particular cause of action is dramatic (e.g., where a party is named as a defendant only with respect to the baseless cause of action), "it may make more sense to use the cause of action rather the lawsuit as a whole as the unit of measure for objective baselessness." HOVENKAMP IP, *supra* note 30, § 11.3(b)(2), at 11-21; *see also* Intel Corp. v. Via Tech, No. C99 03062-WHA, 2001 WL 777085, at *5-6 (N.D. Cal. Mar. 20, 2001) (holding that whether existence of non-sham counts in multiple-count action provides *Noerr* immunity is open question).

424.   *Prof'l Real Estate*, 508 U.S. at 61 n.5; *see also* A Fisherman's Best, Inc. v. Recreational Fishing Alliance, 310 F.3d 183, 191, 194 (4th Cir. 2002) (sham exception inapplicable because "[a] successful effort to influence governmental action 'certainly cannot be characterized as a sham'"); FilmTec Corp. v. Hydranautics, 67 F.3d 931, 937-38 (Fed. Cir. 1995) (citing Boulware v. Nev. Dep't of Human Res., 960 F.2d 793, 799 (9th Cir. 1992)) ("Had FilmTec ultimately prevailed in its infringement suit, Hydranautics would have a difficult time establishing that FilmTec's suit was a sham." However, the court also noted that "The actual outcome of that suit, although instructive, is not determinative: 'The Court hearing the antitrust claim must make its own assessment of the objective merits of the predicate suit.'"); *Eden Hannon*, 914 F.2d at 565 ("If a litigant can

further, one court has defined "victory" as the plaintiff securing the relief it sought in the case, even if through voluntary concessions by the defendant: "[T]he Court cannot agree ... that a plaintiff who has filed suit and receives the relief sought (*e.g.*, monetary compensation, a change in conduct, etc.) could only have been deemed to have 'won' under *PRE* if it continued to litigate the case and received a favorable judgment from the Court."[425] Courts have also held that a claim that survives a summary judgment motion by the defendant cannot be deemed objectively baseless.[426]

---

persuade a neutral judge or jury that it is entitled to legal relief from the conduct of another based upon the law and facts, that suit cannot be a sham under the *Noerr-Pennington* doctrine."); *In re* Terazosin Hydrochloride Antitrust Litig., 335 F. Supp. 2d 1336, 1357 (S.D. Fla. 2004) ("A winning lawsuit is by definition ... not a sham."); *see also* Allied Tube & Conduit v. Indian Head, Inc., 486 U.S. 492, 502 (1988) ("The effort to influence governmental action in this case certainly cannot be characterized as a sham given the actual adoption of the 1981 Code into a number of statutes and local ordinances."); Bayou Fleet v. Alexander, 234 F.3d 852, 862 (5th Cir. 2000) (competitor's successful lobbying efforts before municipal zoning officials to restrict plaintiff's business expansion efforts were protected behavior despite allegations of improper anticompetitive intent; "because [the defendant] achieved favorable results," its efforts were "by definition, reasonable"); *In re* Burlington N., Inc., 822 F.2d 518, 528 (5th Cir. 1987) (holding that "success on the merits does not necessarily preclude an antitrust plaintiff from proving that the defendant's earlier litigation activities were sham," but that "an antitrust plaintiff attempting to base liability on successful petitioning must overcome a strong inference that *Noerr-Pennington* applies").

425. *In re Terazosin*, 335 F. Supp. 2d at 1358 n.13.

426. *See, e.g.*, Beckman Instruments v. LKB Produkter AB, 892 F.2d 1547, 1551 (Fed. Cir. 1989) ("In particular, we find it difficult to agree that the inequitable conduct defense was 'baseless' when it survived a motion for summary judgment and was rejected only after findings were made on disputed facts."); Nobelpharma AB v. Implant Innovations, 930 F. Supp. 1241, 1255 (N.D. Ill. 1996) (claim not objectively baseless where court denied motion for summary judgment on same claim), *aff'd*, 141 F.3d 1059 (Fed. Cir. 1998); Gen-Probe, Inc. v. Amoco Corp., 926 F. Supp. 948, 958 (S.D. Cal. 1996) ("A denial of summary judgment means that the nonmoving party has produced enough evidence that a rational jury could find in its favor. A party with sufficient evidence to support a jury finding in its favor has probable cause to bring a lawsuit."); Organon, Inc. v. Mylan Pharm., 293 F. Supp. 2d 453, 461 (D.N.J. 2003) (infringement action not objectively baseless where substantially the same claim

On the other hand, in *Hydranautics v. FilmTec Corp.*, the Ninth Circuit held that a plaintiff may win its suit at the district court level, but still be found to have asserted an objectively baseless claim, if that victory was procured by fraud:

> [*PRE*] explains that "probable cause" to institute legal proceedings, in the sense in which the phrase is used in tort suits for malicious prosecution of civil claims, establishes that the litigation is not "objectively baseless." At common law, a reversed judgment for the plaintiff in the first action usually is not conclusive as to probable cause in the malicious prosecution action, *where the judgment was obtained by fraud.*[427]

Thus, according to the court, "if the patent was obtained by intentional fraud ... then a reversed judgment based upon that fraud, where the plaintiff obtained the patent by intentional fraud or was an assignee who knew of the patent's infirmity, would not demonstrate probable cause for a patent infringement suit."[428]

---

survived summary judgment in three other cases); Skinder-Strauss Assocs. v. Mass. Continuing Legal Educ., 870 F. Supp. 8, 11 (D. Mass. 1994) ("If, on the other hand, Skinder survives a summary judgment motion or the court concludes that the suit was not objectively meritless, then Skinder is entitled to judgment in its favor on the [antitrust] counterclaims and no further proceedings are needed."); Harris Custom Builders v. Hoffmeyer, 834 F. Supp. 256, 261-62 (N.D. Ill. 1993) (action sufficient to survive summary judgment cannot be a sham).

427. Hydranautics v. FilmTec Corp., 70 F.3d 533, 538 (9th Cir. 1995) (emphasis added).

428. *Id.* at 539; *see also FilmTec Corp.*, 67 F.3d at 938 ("[A] preliminary success on the merits does not necessarily preclude a court from concluding that litigation was baseless."); Whelan v. Abell, 48 F.3d 1247, 1255-56 (D.C. Cir. 1995) (fact that Maryland Securities Commission issued order to show cause did not bar antitrust plaintiff from showing that underlying allegations were sham; Maryland commission may not have made any independent "probable cause" determination, and in any event, plaintiff had no opportunity to contest the order to show cause before it was issued by the commission); *In re Burlington*, 822 F.2d at 528; *In re* Relafen Antitrust Litig., 360 F. Supp. 2d 166, 182 (D. Mass. 2005) (rejecting "SmithKline's assertion that its survival of summary judgment, without more, compelled the conclusion that its claim was not objectively baseless"); Warner Lambert Co. v. PurePac Pharm., No. Civ. A. 98-02749 (JCL), 2000 WL 34213890, at *5 (D.N.J. Dec. 22, 2000) ("[D]enial of summary judgment ... in and of itself, cannot deem liti-

In *In re Relafen Antitrust Litigation*,[429] the defendant patent holder argued that, because it survived summary judgment in the underlying patent case, its claim could not be deemed objectively baseless. The court rejected this argument in light of the plaintiffs' contention that affidavits upon which the district court relied in denying summary judgment were allegedly sham. The court, relying on authority from the First and Second Circuits, held that "[i]t is ... entirely possible that a baseless factual claim will survive a motion for summary judgment, particularly where an attorney prepares an affidavit for a client stating a material fact for which there is no basis."[430] Since the evidence before the court on the underlying summary judgment motion allegedly "was undermined by matters not properly before the court on the ... motion, including the credibility of the affiant and the weight of contrary evidence," the court held that the summary judgment result could not settle the question of objective baselessness.[431]

The *Relafen* court, however, also declined to accept the antitrust plaintiffs' contention that, because the patentee lost the underlying case (after a trial), plaintiffs should receive summary judgment on objective baselessness. Plaintiffs relied on *Theofel v. Farey-Jones*,[432] in which the Ninth Circuit held that the trial court in the underlying litigation may make findings "tantamount to a finding that [the litigant's] conduct was objectively baseless."[433] The *Relafen* court held that, although the underlying trial court found the patentee's witnesses to be incredible (describing them as "generally unconvincing" and "transparently disingenuous"), it did not "clearly and convincingly" find patentee's

---

gation objectively reasonable without specific examination of the basis for denial of summary judgment."); Brotech Corp. v. White Eagle Int'l Techs. Group, No. Civ.A. 03-232, 2003 WL 22797730, at *4 (E.D. Pa. Nov. 18, 2003) (mere denial of motion to dismiss underlying infringement suit not sufficient to establish probable cause for *PRE* purposes).

429. 346 F. Supp. 2d 349 (D. Mass. 2004).
430. *Id.* at 363 (citing Calloway v. Marvel Entm't Group, 854 F.2d 1452, 1473 (2d Cir. 1988)); *see also* Media Duplication Servs. v. HDG Software, 928 F.2d 1228, 1240 n.10 (1st Cir. 1991) ("[S]uccessful opposition to a summary judgment motion does not always conclusively establish the reasonableness of the claim in question.").
431. *In re Relafen*, 346 F. Supp. 2d at 363.
432. 359 F.3d 1066 (9th Cir. 2004).
433. *Id.* at 1079.

position "indefensible 'on its face.'"[434] Absent such a clear indication, the court relied on the Supreme Court's warning in *PRE* that courts should "resist the understandable temptation to ... conclud[e] that an ultimately unsuccessful action must have been unreasonable or without foundation."[435] The court also cited the Supreme Court's decision in *Stewart v. Sonneborn*,[436] which recognized that probable cause may present a jury issue "when the question of the defendants' belief of the facts relied upon to prove want of probable cause is involved."[437]

The *Relafen* court also noted that, because every judicial determination that a patent is invalid for anticipation requires a finding that "a prior reference described the claimed invention to a person of ordinary skill in the art," such a finding cannot serve as conclusive evidence of objective baselessness (as the plaintiffs had argued).[438] To so hold would expose every patentee who unsuccessfully litigated such a claim to a purely intent-based test for sham litigation, a result the court viewed as inconsistent with the teaching of *PRE*.[439]

Sometimes it will be sufficiently clear from the underlying court decision that a losing plaintiff had a significant basis for its claim. In such situations, courts (including the Supreme Court in *PRE*), have ruled as a matter of law that a claim was not objectively baseless. As the District of Columbia Circuit Court put it in *Covad Communications Co. v Bell Atlantic Corp.*:[440]

> Our review of the patent court's opinions convinces us that Bell Atlantic's case against Covad was not objectively baseless. Bell

---

434. *In re Relafen*, 346 F. Supp. 2d at 364.
435. *Id.* (citing Prof'l Real Estate Investors v. Columbia Pictures Indus., 508 U.S. 49, 50 n.5 (1993)).
436. 98 U.S. 187 (1879).
437. *Id.* at 194; *see also* Boulware v. Nev. Dep't of Human Res., 960 F.2d 793, 799 (9th Cir. 1992) ("Both the initial success on the merits and the subsequent reversal are relevant to the [objective baselessness] inquiry but neither factor is determinative."); Victus, Ltd. v. Collezione Europa U.S.A., 26 F. Supp. 2d 772, 779-84 (M.D.N.C. 1998) (fact that patentee lost case on summary judgment could not show objective baselessness where there was reasonable uncertainty in the law).
438. *In re Relafen*, 346 F. Supp. 2d at 364.
439. *Id.*
440. 398 F.3d 666 (D.C. Cir. 2005).

Atlantic advanced reasonable arguments that each court went to some lengths to reject.[441]

As noted above, in *PRE* the Court analogized objective baselessness to the standard under Rule 11. Thus, where it can be shown that a claim did not satisfy Rule 11, it would likely be deemed objectively baseless. In the patent context, it has been held that to satisfy Rule 11 a patentee must make a reasonable inquiry as to whether the target of the suit in fact infringed the patent; infringement actions should not be commenced on the mere suspicion of infringement.[442] Accordingly, the adequacy of a patentee's pre-suit investigation can become a subject of inquiry in assessing objective baselessness.[443]

As these cases make apparent, establishing objective baselessness is very difficult.[444] The difficulty is perhaps heightened in patent cases

---

441. *Id.* at 677; *see also* Novell, Inc. v. CPU Distrib., Civ. A. No. H-97-2326, 2000 U.S. Dist LEXIS 9952 (S.D. Tex. May 12, 2000) (despite prior adverse district court ruling on similar issue, claim not objectively baseless where issue complex); Mitek Surgical Prods. v. Arthrex Inc., 21 F. Supp. 2d 1309, 1317-18 (D. Utah 1998) (objective baselessness not shown simply because patentee lost infringement case; issues were "subtle and complex"); *In re* Circuit Breaker Antitrust Litig., 984 F. Supp. 1267, 1274 (C.D. Cal. 1997) (suit not objectively baseless despite success of affirmative defenses asserted against it).

442. *See, e.g.*, Q-Pharma, Inc. v. Andrew Jergens Co., 360 F.3d 1295, 1300-02 (Fed. Cir. 2004); View Eng'g v. Robotic Visions Sys., 208 F.3d 981, 986 (Fed. Cir. 2000); Judin v. United States, 110 F.3d 780, 784-85 (Fed. Cir. 1997). *But see* Vista Mfg. v. Trac-4, Inc., 131 F.R.D. 134, 138 (N.D. Ind. 1990) (no "general rule that Rule 11 requires an infringement plaintiff to examine the defendant's product in all instances").

443. *See, e.g.*, Glaverbel Societe Anonyme v. Northlake Mktg. & Supply, 45 F.3d 1550 (Fed. Cir. 1995) (no bad faith where patentee conducted prelitigation tests and alleged infringer did not unequivocally deny infringement); PennPac Int'l v. Rotonics Mfg., No. 99-CV-2890, 2001 WL 569264, at *6 (E.D. Pa. May 25, 2001) (granting summary judgment for antitrust defendant because pre-suit investigation showed suit was not a sham); Hoffman-LaRoche, Inc. v. Genpharm, Inc., 50 F. Supp. 2d 367, 380 (D.N.J. 1999) (denying motion to dismiss sham counterclaim where counterclaimant alleged lack of reasonable investigation of infringement before suit filed).

444. *See, e.g.*, Herbert R. Northrup & Augustus T. White, *Construction Union Use of Environmental Regulation to Win Jobs: Cases, Impact and Legal Challenges*, 19 HARV. J.L. & PUB. POL'Y 55, 95 (1995) ("[I]n *Professional Real Estate Investors v. Columbia Pictures*, the Supreme

because patents undergo a review process with the PTO before issuing. As one treatise put it, patent owners thus "are entitled to a legal presumption that their intellectual property rights are valid, and that presumption should ordinarily give them probable cause to believe those rights are in fact valid."[445] As discussed above, such a presumption would be rebutted only where the patentee enforced the patent with knowledge that it was obtained by fraud or otherwise was invalid. Lesser forms of patent misconduct, such as inequitable conduct[446] or patent misuse,[447] generally do not strip the patentee of its antitrust

---

Court had determined that, to demonstrate a 'sham,' an antitrust plaintiff must demonstrate that the proceeding was 'objectively baseless' in the sense that no reasonable litigant could realistically expect success on the merits ... The plaintiff will rarely be able to make such a showing."); David T. Pritikin and Bruce M. Zessar, *The Sham Litigation Doctrine in Patent Litigation: The Nexus Between Bad Faith Enforcement of Patent Rights and the Antitrust Laws*, 414 PLI/Pat 661, 684 (1995) ("While Walker Process and Handgards claims were rarely successful prior to PRE ... PRE has provided courts with a ready basis to summarily dismiss such claims.").

445. HOVENKAMP IP, *supra* note 30, ¶ 11.3(b)(2), at 11-20

446. As discussed in section B.1.b, above, in the patent context, it has been held that conduct qualifying as inequitable conduct (rendering the patent invalid) is not sufficient to make out a case under § 2 unless it rises to the level of common law fraud. *See, e.g.*, FMC Corp. v. Manitowoc Co., 835 F.2d 1411, 1417-18 (Fed. Cir. 1987); Korody-Colyer Corp. v. Gen. Motors, 828 F.2d 1572, 1578 (Fed. Cir. 1987); Argus Chem. v. Fibre Glass-Evercoat Co., 812 F.2d 1381, 1384-85 (Fed. Cir. 1987); Am. Hoist & Derrick Co. v. Sowa & Sons, 725 F.2d 1350, 1368 (Fed. Cir. 1984); Al-Site Corp. v. Opti-Ray Inc., 28 U.S.P.Q.2d 1058, 1061-62 (E.D.N.Y. 1993) (noting that although omitted prior art was not material for purposes of defendant's antitrust counterclaim, it was material for purposes of its inequitable conduct defense). The *Intellectual Property Guidelines* state, "Inequitable conduct before the Patent and Trademark Office will not be the basis of a section 2 claim unless the conduct also involves knowing and willful fraud and the other elements of a section 2 claim are present." INTELLECTUAL PROPERTY GUIDELINES, *supra* note 4, § 6.

447. Patent misuse is a defense to an infringement claim "and relates generally to the use of [otherwise valid] patent rights to obtain or to coerce an unfair commercial advantage." C.R. Bard, Inc. v. M3 Sys., 157 F.3d 1340, 1372 (Fed. Cir. 1998). According to the Federal Circuit, "[p]atent misuse relates primarily to a patentee's actions that affect competition in unpatented goods or that otherwise extend the economic effect beyond

immunity. From 1993 (the year *PRE* was decided) to 2004, there does not seem to be a single reported case of a *Handgards*-type sham litigation claim succeeding on the merits.[448]

c. Establishing Anticompetitive Intent

Under *PRE*, the need to inquire into a litigant's subjective motivation is necessary only where objective baselessness has been established. Given that objective baselessness is very difficult to show, courts seldom reach the subjective intent prong of the *PRE* test.

In *PRE* the Supreme Court held that, "under this second part of our definition of sham, the court should focus on whether the baseless lawsuit conceals 'an attempt to interfere directly with the business relationships of a competitor,' ... through the 'use [of] the governmental *process*, as opposed to the *outcome* of that process—as an anticompetitive weapon.'"[449] The Court also suggested that the following factors might be relevant to the subjective prong of the test: "whether [the antitrust defendant] was indifferent to the outcome of the merits of the [allegedly sham] lawsuit, whether any damages ... would justify [the antitrust defendant's] investment in the suit, or whether [the

---

the scope of the patent grant." *Id.* The types of conduct that have been held to constitute misuse in certain circumstances include enforced package licensing, price restraints, royalty terms extending beyond the patent grant, and tying. *See, e.g.*, ABA SECTION OF ANTITRUST LAW, INTELLECTUAL PROPERTY MISUSE/LICENSING AND LITIGATION (2000) (for detail on misuse); CHISUM, *supra* note 217, § 19.04[3] (same). The Federal Circuit has held that "[p]atent misuse is viewed as a broader wrong than antitrust violation because of the economic power that may be derived from the patentee's right to exclude. Thus misuse may arise when the conditions of antitrust violation are not met." *C.R. Bard*, 157 F.3d at 1372 (citing *Zenith Radio*, 395 U.S. at 140-41). Mere enforcement of one's patent rights does not constitute misuse: "It is not patent misuse to bring suit to enforce patent rights not fraudulently obtained." *Id.* at 1373.

448. *See also* HOVENKAMP IP, *supra* note 30, ¶ 11.3(b)(4), at 11-23 to 11-24 (finding no such successful cases between 1993 and 2000).

449. Prof'l Real Estate Investors v. Columbia Pictures Indus., 508 U.S. 49, 60-61 (1993) (emphasis added) (quoting E. R.R. Presidents Conference v. Noerr Motor Freight, 365 U.S. 127, 144 (1961), and City of Columbia v. Omni Outdoor Adver., 499 U.S. 365, 380 (1991)).

antitrust defendant] had decided to sue primarily for the benefit of collateral injuries inflicted through the use of legal process."[450]

Assuming the *PRE* test even applies in *Walker Process* and *Handgards*-type claims,[451] it seems likely that courts would impose similarly stringent intent requirements in applying the "subjective" prong of the test. One commentator has written that, in the context of patent infringement suits, the second prong may have little use:

> The essence of a patent infringement suit is exclusion. To bring the suit without a basis in both fact and law is to intend in one of the most direct ways possible to interfere with a competitor's business. Yet this "baseless" invocation of the court's jurisdiction might still be found to be genuine under *PRE* in the sense that competitive harm was the normally expected outcome, not some collateral incident to it. At least in infringement litigation, it is far from clear why the second part of the test is necessary if all the other elements of a monopolization case are present and it is already established that plaintiff sought an injunction shutting down a competitor's business without, in the words of the *PRE* majority opinion, even a "'reasonabl[e] belie[f] that there is a chance that [a] claim may be held valid'" under the objective standard. Reasoning from first principles, one would think, that at least a strong inference of wrongful intent might be created by the showing of objective baselessness in a suit to enforce exclusionary rights. But *PRE* is an exclusionary rights case, and it says nothing about such an inference.[452]

Along similar lines, another commentator has written that the subjective prong essentially confers absolute immunity on litigation activity, especially in the patent infringement context:

> With respect to patent or copyright infringement suits that are alleged to be sham, the application of the subjective test makes [little] sense. By definition, a patent or copyright infringement suit is a suit for the exclusion of a competitor: if the intellectual property plaintiff wins, the infringer is excluded from competition. It is by winning an infringement suit that patent or copyright owners can most effectively exclude a competitor. Therefore, it is unlikely that these plaintiffs merely hope to interfere with a competitor's business through the process of

---

450. *Id.* at 65.
451. See *supra* § B.2.b(1) (for discussion of this issue).
452. Kobak PRE, *supra* note 201, at 207 (footnote omitted) (quoting *PRE*, 508 U.S. at 62-63 (quoting Hubbard v. Beatty & Hyde, Inc., 348 Mass. 258, 262, 178 N.E.2d 485, 488 (1961))).

litigation, rather than through a successful outcome. To insist on the second prong would mean that few infringement suits (even after being shown to be objectively baseless) would be considered "shams" because the intellectual property plaintiff usually hopes to prevail, in order to completely exclude the competitor.[453]

Others have complained about the indefiniteness of the subjective prong.[454]

Even if *PRE* does not apply, however, "[a] plaintiff has an especially difficult burden in the patent enforcement context because 'the law recognizes a presumption that the assertion of a duly granted patent is made in good faith; this presumption is overcome only by affirmative evidence of bad faith.'"[455] The courts in both *Walker Process* and *Handgards*-type cases have made clear that a stringent showing of intent is necessary—ranging from "intentional fraud involving affirmative dishonesty,"[456] to "a state of mind so reckless as to the consequences that it is held to be the equivalent of intent,"[457] to a "bad faith ... knowledge that the patents ... were invalid."[458] Mere negligence, even gross negligence, generally is not sufficient to establish the scienter requirement in such cases.[459] Clear and convincing evidence is required.[460] The Federal Circuit has held that "[p]atent rights are useful only if they can legally exclude others from the patented subject matter. That [the patentee] is a

---

453. Lao II, *supra* note 201, at 986-87.

454. *See, e.g.*, O'Donnell, *supra* note 201, at 27 ("The language [of the test] is exceedingly imprecise").

455. *In re* Terazosin Hydrochloride Antitrust Litig., 335 F. Supp. 2d 1336, 1365-66 (S.D. Fla. 2004) (quoting C.R. Bard, Inc. v. M3 Sys., 157 F.3d 1340, 1369 (Fed. Cir. 1998)); *see also, e.g.*, Brooks Furniture Mfg. v. Dutailier Int'l, 393 F.3d 1378, 1382 (Fed. Cir. 2005) ("There is a presumption that the assertion of infringement of a duly granted patent is made in good faith.").

456. Cataphote Corp. v. DeSoto Chem. Coatings, 450 F.2d 769, 772 (9th Cir. 1971).

457. Unitherm Food Sys. v. Swift Eckrich, Inc., 375 F.3d 1341, 1360 (Fed. Cir. 2004), *rev'd on other grounds*, 126 S. Ct. 980 (2006).

458. *Handgards I*, 601 F.2d 986, 994 (9th Cir. 1979).

459. *See, e.g.*, Am. Hoist & Derrick Co. v. Sowa & Sons, 725 F.2d 1350, 1358 (Fed. Cir. 1984) ("[W]e emphasize that a specific intent, greater than an intent evidenced by gross negligence or recklessness, is an indispensable element.").

460. *See, e.g.*, *Handgards I*, 601 F.2d at 996; *Unitherm*, 375 F.3d at 1360.

larger company than [the alleged infringer], that it has sued others, and that it was unwilling to grant a license, are not indicative of bad faith."[461]

d. Patterns of "Automatic" Petitioning

Another issue is whether the demanding two-part *PRE* test applies where the antitrust plaintiff asserts that the defendant engaged in a *series* of judicial or administrative proceedings without regard to the merits of any individual claim, but instead for the purpose of preventing or undermining competition. In *California Motor Transport*,[462] the Supreme Court wrote that:

> One claim, which a court or agency may think baseless, may go unnoticed; but a pattern of baseless repetitive claims may emerge which leads the fact-finder to conclude that the administrative and judicial processes have been abused.... [A]ctions of that kind cannot acquire immunity by seeking refuge under the umbrella of "political expression."[463]

The Court in *PRE* did not address whether, in a case of such allegedly repetitive anticompetitive litigation, it is necessary to establish the two-prong test for sham as to each suit or claim. The Ninth Circuit held this to be unnecessary in *USS-POSCO Industries v. Contra Costa County Building & Construction Trades Council*.[464] In that case, a non-union company alleged that local unions instituted approximately 29 frivolous lawsuits and administrative complaints for the purpose of

---

461. Brooks Furniture Mfg. v. Dutailier Int'l, 393 F.3d 1378, 1384 (Fed. Cir. 2005)

462. 404 U.S. 508 (1972).

463. *Id.* at 513; *see also* Otter Tail Power v. United States, 410 U.S. 366 (1973) (prosecution of series of baseless lawsuits to forestall competitively adverse regulatory decision and obtain or enhance monopoly power not immune from antitrust scrutiny).

464. 31 F.3d 800 (9th Cir. 1994). The FTC has taken the position that the "pattern" exception to *Noerr* should apply to any predatory pattern of invoking government process of any kind, not simply litigation: "Just as the repeated filing of lawsuits without regard to the merits ... warrants rejection of *Noerr* immunity," so too does the repeated filing of knowing and material misrepresentations to the PTO and FDA. Analysis to Aid Public Comment, *In re* Bristol-Myers Squibb Co., No. C-4076, at 11 (FTC Mar 7, 2003), *available at* http://www.ftc.gov/os/2003/03/bristolmyersanalysis.htm.

coercing employers into hiring union labor.[465]   The Ninth Circuit held that *PRE* "provides a strict two-step analysis to assess whether a single action constitutes sham petitioning."[466]

In the court's view, since *PRE* did not explicitly address the situation of repetitive lawsuits, the more relevant Supreme Court authority was *California Motor Transport.* In that case, the Supreme Court focused on whether the "legal filings [were] made, not out of a genuine interest in redressing grievances, but as part of a pattern or practice of successive filings undertaking essentially for purposes of harassment."[467] The Ninth Circuit thus held that there is no need to evaluate the merits of *each* claim in such cases. As the court put it, "even a broken clock is right twice a day."[468]   Nevertheless, the court did employ a kind of "big picture" objective baselessness test. Despite evidence of anticompetitive intent, the court found the union's activities to be protected because 15 of the 29 law suits had proven successful. According to the court, this was not a situation in which some of the lawsuits, "just as matter of pure chance" turned out to have merit.[469]   The court found that the unions' success in over half of the suits was dispositive:

> The fact that more than half of all the actions as to which we know the results turn out to have merit cannot be reconciled with the charge that the unions were filing lawsuits and other actions willy-nilly without regard to success. Given that the plaintiff has the burden in litigation, a batting average exceeding .500 cannot support [the antitrust plaintiff's] theory.[470]

---

465. *USS-POSCO Indus.*, 31 F.3d at 804.
466. *Id.* at 810-11.
467. *Id.* at 811.
468. *Id.*
469. *Id.*
470. *Id.* District courts applying *USS-POSCO* have evaluated the objective basis of individual claims even where a pattern of automatic petitioning is alleged. *See, e.g.*, Avery Dennison Corp. v. Acco Brands, No. CV-99-1877DT(MCX), 2000 WL 986995, at *22 (C.D. Cal. Feb. 22, 2000) ("Without any information regarding the merits of the lawsuits," impossible to determine if defendant engaged in a "pattern or practice of successive filings."); *In re* Circuit Breaker Antitrust Litig., 984 F. Supp. 1267, 1273 (C.D. Cal. 1997) (evaluating objective basis of multiple government petitions); *Gen-Probe*, 926 F. Supp. at 959 ("[U]nder either the *PRE* or the *USS-POSCO* test ... [plaintiffs] must demonstrate objective baselessness" of alleged sham suits.); *see also, e.g., In re*

In *Primetime 24 Joint Venture v. National Broadcasting Co.*,[471] however, the Second Circuit held that *Noerr-Pennington* immunity did not shield an alleged conspiracy among the four major television networks simultaneously to file with the FCC thousands of objections to the plaintiff's competing service, knowing that most of the objections lacked merit.[472] The court distinguished between a case in which a defendant brings a single lawsuit from one involving "a pattern or practice of successive filings undertaken essentially for purposes of harassment." In such cases, "[t]he relevant issue is whether the legal challenges 'are brought pursuant to a policy of starting legal proceedings without regard to the merits and for the purpose of injuring a market rival.'"[473]

On the other hand, some courts have applied the objective baselessness test in the context of multiple lawsuits.[474]   For instance,

---

Terazosin Hydrochloride Antitrust Litig., 335 F. Supp. 2d 1336, 1367 (S.D. Fla. 2004) (refusing to condemn alleged "series" of claims where success rate was 0.636); Livingston Downs Racing Ass'n v. Jefferson Downs, 192 F. Supp. 2d 519, 538-41 (M.D. La. 2001) (court analyzed merits of each lawsuit in alleged series of automatic petitioning).

471.   219 F.3d 92 (2d Cir. 2000).

472.   *Id.* at 99.

473.   *Id.* at 101 (quoting *USS-POSCO*, 31 F.3d at 811). Some courts have distinguished *Primetime 24* on the basis of the number of distinct claims filed against a single competitor: "The *Primetime 24* court held that thousands of statutory challenges against a single competitor to raise its expenses ... stated a claim for sham litigation.... Here, Abbott sued seven different generic companies, in seventeen separate lawsuits involving five different patents.... [T]his case does not cast the shadow of 'serial litigation' used to injure a single competitor that occurred in *Primetime 24*." *In re Terazosin*, 335 F. Supp. 2d at 1367 (citing Twin City Bakery Workers & Welfare Fund v. Astra Aktiebolag, 207 F. Supp. 2d 221, 224 n.2 (S.D.N.Y. 2002)); Marchan Eyewear v. Tura LP, No. 98 CV 1932 (SJ), 2002 WL 31253199, at *8 (E.D.N.Y. Sept. 30, 2002) (two lawsuits cannot constitute a pattern of "automatic petitioning").

474.   *See, e.g.,* Globetrotter Software v. Elan Computer Group, 362 F.3d 1367, 1377 (Fed. Cir. 2004) (applying *PRE* to a sham litigation claim premised on threats of infringement under three separate patents); Glass Equip. Dev. v. Besten, Inc., 174 F.3d 1337, 1343-44 (Fed. Cir. 1999) (applying *PRE* to two patent lawsuits and a series of allegedly sham threats); *In re Terazosin*, 335 F. Supp. 2d at 1366 n.26 ("Federal Circuit law, which governs this issue, applies the *PRE* objective/subjective test to claims of multiple patent infringement."); Applera Corp. v. MJ Research, 303 F. Supp. 2d 130, 133 (D. Conn. 2004) (rejecting application of *Primetime 24*

courts have held, in the patent context, that a patent holder may bring a series of claims alleging that multiple parties infringed the same patent. The mere fact that a patentee has brought essentially the same patent claim against multiple parties should not, without more, constitute a "series" of suits that lose *Noerr* protection without application of the two-part *PRE* test. For example, in *In re Terazosin*, the court held that "[a]lthough plaintiffs allege that the '207 lawsuits should be viewed as six separate actions, the '207 suits should be treated as one suit for purposes of this analysis because they all involved the same patent and the same underlying legal issue."[475]

5. Practical Issues In Walker Process and Bad Faith Litigation Cases

a. Heightened Pleading Standards in *Walker Process* Cases

In *Medimmune, Inc. v. Genentech, Inc.*,[476] the Federal Circuit affirmed that, "[l]ike all fraud-based claims, *Walker Process* allegations are subject to the pleading requirements of Fed. R. Civ. P. 9(b)."[477]

---

because Federal Circuit has applied *PRE* "even if the patent holder threatened more than one infringement suit"); Organon, Inc. v. Mylan Pharm., 293 F. Supp. 2d 453, 462 (D.N.J. 2003) (dismissing a sham litigation claim based on patent lawsuits against six generic manufacturers, relying on *PRE*); Moore U.S.A. v. Standard Register, 139 F. Supp. 2d 348, 358-59 (W.D.N.Y. 2001) (applying *PRE* standard to claim that four patent litigations were sham); Travelers Express v. Am. Express Integrated Payment Sys., 80 F. Supp. 2d 1033, 1042 (D. Minn. 1999) (when dealing with a series of lawsuits, "the appropriate inquiry is to determine whether each of the prior lawsuits was objectively baseless").

475. *In re Terazosin*, 335 F. Supp. 2d at 1360; *see, e.g., See* FED. TRADE COMM'N,G ENERIC DRUG ENTRY PRIOR TO PATENT EXPIRATION 19 (July 2002), *available at* http://www.ftc.gov/os/2002/07/genericdrugstudy.pdf ("it would be misleading simply to count the number of decisions in either party's favor, because several of the decisions may be related to the same patent"), *available at* http://www.ftc.gov/os/2002/07/genericdrugstudy.pdf; *see also Twin City Bakery*, 207 F. Supp. 2d at 224 n.2 ("It would be unreasonable to expect defendants to initiate litigation against only some of the generic-drug applicants they claim are infringing their patents.").

476. 427 F.3d 958 (Fed. Cir. 2005).

477. *Id.* at 22 (citing Vess v. Ciba-Geigy Corp. USA, 317 F.3d 1097, 1103-04 (9th Cir. 2003)); *see also* Miller Pipeline v. British Gas, 69 F. Supp. 2d 1129, 1135 (S.D. Ind. 1999); Grid Sys. v. Tex. Instruments, 771 F. Supp.

Accordingly, to plead a *Walker Process* claim, a plaintiff must plead the circumstances constituting the applicant's fraud on the PTO with particularity.

When the defendant enforcing a disputed patent is not the original patent applicant, however, courts have questioned whether "Rule 9(b) is applicable to the requirement—present [in such circumstances]—that the party 'enforce the patent with knowledge of the fraudulent manner in which it was obtained.'"[478]

b.   Pleading Issues Regarding *Noerr-Pennington*

The question has arisen whether *Noerr-Pennington* is an affirmative defense such that a patentee accused of sham litigation or *Walker Process* fraud must affirmatively assert the defense or otherwise risk waiving it. The Fourth Circuit has answered in the negative. Although it had previously characterized *Noerr-Pennington* as an affirmative defense,[479] the Fourth Circuit wrote in *IGEN International v. Roche Diagnostics*[480] that "[w]e are inclined to believe that the [underlying] litigation brought with it into this collateral proceeding ... a rebuttable presumption of *Noerr-Pennington* immunity, which Roche was not required to plead as an affirmative defense."[481] Similarly, in *McGuire Oil v. Mapco, Inc.*,[482] the Eleventh Circuit held that "*Noerr-Pennington* immunity is not merely an affirmative defense" and the party opposing its application bears the burden of "alleg[ing] facts sufficient to show that *Noerr-Pennington* immunity did not attach."[483]

By contrast, in *Bayou Fleet v. Alexander*,[484] the Fifth Circuit held that *Noerr-Pennington* is an affirmative defense, but that it is not waived if

---

1033, 1040 (N.D. Cal. 1991); Essential Commun. Sys. v. AT&T, 446 F. Supp. 1090, 1105 (D.N.J. 1978).

478.   Molecular Diagnostics Labs. v. Hoffmann-La Roche, Inc., No. 04-01649 (HHK), 2005 U.S. Dist. LEXIS 30142, at *31 (D.D.C. Dec. 1, 2005) (declining to resolve the question of Rule 9(b)'s applicability in these circumstances, and holding that, assuming that Rule 9(b) did apply, plaintiff had pleaded defendant's knowledge of the underlying fraud with sufficient particularity).

479.   *See* N.C. Elec. Membership Corp. v. Carolina Power & Light, 666 F.2d 50, 52 (4th Cir. 1981).

480.   335 F.3d 303 (4th Cir. 2003).

481.   *Id.* at 311.

482.   958 F.2d 1552 (11th Cir. 1992).

483.   *Id.* at 1558 n.9.

484.   234 F.3d 852 (5th Cir. 2000).

raised at a "pragmatically sufficient time"[485] and does not prejudice the other party. Given the differing views on the issue, it is clearly advisable to assert *Noerr-Pennington* immunity as an affirmative defense in *Walker Process* and sham claims.

In addition, some courts have imposed a "heightened pleading standard" on plaintiffs bringing *Handgards*-type sham litigation claims. These courts reason that more than notice pleading is required out of respect for the defendant's First Amendment rights, which might be "chilled" by bald threats of the imposition of treble-damage antitrust liability.[486] Thus, when pleading claims that could give rise to a claim (or defense) of *Noerr* immunity, the claimant should be mindful of providing adequate detail as to the factual basis for piercing such immunity.

On the other hand, one commentator has suggested that courts may be too lenient in permitting conclusory sham claims to proceed past the pleading stage: "Recent federal court decisions indicate judicial reluctance to restrain the prosecution of sham litigation counterclaims.... [D]espite the burdens that these counterclaims entail ... and even though few of these counterclaims ultimately succeed, courts seem reluctant to curtail their use."[487] Another treatise notes that "the conclusory allegation of sham is easy," and that such allegations "are unusually empty of meaning."[488] Rather than a "heightened" standard, the authors believe that basic notice pleading requires more than the parroting of buzzwords such as "sham": "[A]lthough it is not necessary to plead specific facts, mere boilerplate assertions of a sham should not be

---

485. *Id.* at 860.
486. *See, e.g.*, Hydro-Tech Corp. v. Sundstrand Corp., 673 F.2d 1171, 1177 n.8 (10th Cir. 1982); Franchise Realty Interstate Corp. v. San Francisco Local Joint Executive Bd., 542 F.2d 1076, 1082-83 (9th Cir. 1976); Or. Natural Res. Council v. Mohla, 944 F.2d 531, 533 (9th Cir. 1991); Elecs. for Imaging, Inc. v. Coyle, No. C 01-4853 MJJ, C 05-0619 MJJ, 2005 WL 1661958, at *6 (N. D. Cal. July 14, 2005); Letica Corp. v. Sweetheart Cup Co., 790 F. Supp. 702, 705 (E.D. Mich. 1992); Spanish Int'l Communs. v. Leibowitz, 608 F. Supp. 178 (S.D. Fla. 1985); Bethlehem Plaza v. Campbell, 403 F. Supp. 966 (E.D. Pa. 1975).
487. Young, *supra* note 201, at 5 (citing Jarrow Formulas v. Int'l Nutrition, 175 F. Supp. 2d 296, 310 (D. Conn. 2001); Knoll Pharm. v. TEVA Pharm. USA, No. 01 C 1646, 2001 WL 1001117 (N.D. Ill. Aug. 24, 2001); Moore U.S.A. v. Standard Register, 139 F. Supp. 2d 348, 359 (W.D.N.Y. 2001)).
488. 1 AREEDA & HOVENKAMP,*su pra* note 1, ¶ 207a, at 247-48.

sufficient to state a claim. The plaintiff must give the defendant and the court some notion of what legal concept he is relying upon and the sense in which defendant's actions are claimed to have constituted a sham. This is simply to insist that the plaintiff give the court and the defendant an idea of just what its claim is."[489]

c. Statute of Limitations

Private antitrust actions under Sections 4 and 16 of the Clayton Act must be "commenced within four years after the cause of action accrued."[490]   In general, a cause of action accrues when a defendant commits a prohibited act that injures a plaintiff's business.[491] The statute of limitations does not begin to run until damages are inflicted or reasonably ascertainable.[492]   For continuing violations, each act in furtherance of the continuing violation triggers a new limitations period.[493]

In the context of antitrust claims based on allegedly sham patent litigation, the question arises whether the claim accrues as of the commencement of the sham litigation or upon its resolution. The court in *Chemi SpA v. GlaxoSmithKline*[494] held the latter, reasoning that the Supreme Court in *PRE* analogized sham litigation with the tort of malicious prosecution, which claims do not accrue until the underlying litigation has terminated.[495]

---

489. *Id.* ¶ 207b, at 252.

490. 15 U.S.C. § 15b.

491. *See, e.g.,* Zenith Radio Corp. v. Hazeltine Research, 401 U.S. 321, 338 (1971); Concord Boat Co. v. Brunswick Corp., 207 F.3d 1039, 1051 (8th Cir. 2000); Johnson v. Nyack Hosp., 86 F.3d 8, 11 (2d. Cir. 1996); Higgins v. N.Y. Stock Exch., 942 F.2d 829, 832 (2d. Cir. 1991).

492. *See Zenith Radio,* 401 U.S. at 338-40.

493. *Id.* at 328; *accord* Hanover Shoe, Inc. v. United Shoe Mach. Corp., 392 U.S. 481, 502 n.15 (1968); O'Dell v. Gen. Motors, 122 F. Supp. 2d 721, 727 (E. D. Tex. 2000); *In re* Nine W. Shoes Antitrust Litig., 80 F. Supp. 2d. 181, 192 (S.D.N.Y. 2000).

494. 356 F. Supp. 2d 495 (E.D. Pa. 2005).

495. *Id.* at 499-500; *accord In re* Relafen Antitrust Litig., 286 F. Supp. 2d 56, 63-64 (D. Mass. 2003) ("Of course, the plaintiffs would not know that it was a sham suit [when the suit was filed] and, therefore, would be unable to plead any damages. To require such action would lead to the absurd result that vast numbers of potential antitrust plaintiffs would be required in every patent or business litigation to sue or intervene preemptively in those actions in the unlikely (but possible) event that the suit was filed

d. Attorney-Client Privilege

Powerful evidence of good faith in a *Walker Process* or sham litigation case can be that the patentee sought the opinion of counsel before commencing an infringement action, and counsel, after an adequate investigation, opined that there was some chance of success. Courts hold that bona fide opinions from counsel can show good faith, or the absence of bad faith, in such cases.[496]

Of course, deciding to rely on an "advice of counsel" defense waives the patentee's attorney-client privilege in this area.[497] As a general

---

fraudulently."); *see also* N. Trust Co. v. Ralston Purina Co., No. 94 C 4045, 1994 WL 605743, at *7 (N.D. Ill. Nov. 3, 1994) (statute of limitations ran from date of settlement of alleged sham infringement suit). *But see* Al George, Inc. v. Envirotech, 939 F.2d 1271, 1275 (5th Cir. 1991) (holding "that the last overt act in pursuance of the alleged conspiracy was Envirotech's filing of its patent-infringement suit in 1981").

496. *See, e.g.*, Int'l Star Class Yacht Racing Ass'n v. Tommy Hilfiger, U.S.A., 80 F.3d 749, 754 (2d Cir. 1996) ("[A]n infringer who 'acts in reasonable reliance on the advice of counsel' generally cannot be said to have acted in bad faith. Conversely, the failure to follow the advice of counsel given before the infringement must factor into an assessment of an infringer's bad faith.") (citing Sands, Taylor & Wood Co. v. Quaker Oats Co., 978 F.2d 947, 962 (7th Cir. 1992)); Electro Med. Sys. v. Cooper Life Scis., 34 F.3d 1048, 1056 (Fed. Cir. 1994) ("Possession of a favorable opinion of counsel is not essential to avoid a willfulness determination; it is only one factor to be considered, albeit an important one."); B&G Plastics v. E. Creative Indus., 269 F. Supp. 2d 450, 469-70 (S.D.N.Y. 2003) (bad faith not established, in part, because "[patentee] went so far as to consult with patent counsel before issuing [infringement warning] letter. While acting on advice of counsel is not dispositive of good faith, it certainly bolsters [such a claim]."); PennPac Int'l v. Rotonics Mfg., No. 99-CV-2890, 2001 WL 569264, at *6 (E.D. Pa. May 25, 2001) (sham litigation claim rejected where, inter alia, patentee obtained advice of counsel before sending letters threatening suit); TRW Fin. Sys. v. Unisys Corp., 835 F. Supp. 994, 1014-15 (E.D. Mich. 1993) (bad faith not shown where patentee's attorney prepared detailed opinion memorandum; "Although the court disagrees with [the attorney's] ultimate conclusion of validity of the patent, it is clear from the memo that much thought was given to the filing of the instant lawsuit, and that it was not frivolously filed for anticompetitive reasons.").

497. *See, e.g.*, Micron Separations, Inc. v. Pall Corp., 159 F.R.D. 361, 362 (D. Mass. 1995) (holding that production of opinion of counsel documents

matter, questions of waiver of attorney-client privilege and the scope of any such waiver "are not unique to patent law and are a matter of either state law, as to claims and defenses that arise under state law, or precedent from regional circuits."[498] Federal Circuit law, however, may apply to alleged waivers of attorney-client privilege respecting representations or omissions before the PTO, as waiver in these circumstances "implicates a substantive patent law issue," namely a patent's enforceability.[499]

Although courts have agreed that reliance on an advice-of-counsel defense results in a subject-matter waiver of the attorney-client privilege, they have disagreed as to the extent of the waiver for documents created after the infringement suit begins, such as trial preparation materials. Some courts find that the waiver "extends throughout the period of infringement, 'including up through trial.'"[500] Other courts hold that for documents created after commencement of the suit, a waiver exists for only those that contradict, or cast doubt upon, the opinion advice.[501]

---

constituted waiver of attorney-client privilege with respect to all information relating to same subject matter).
498. Chimie v. PPG Indus., 218 F.R.D. 416, 419 n.4 (D. Del. 2003).
499. Martin Marietta Materials v. Bedford Reinforced Plastics, 227 F.R.D. 382, 391-92 (W.D. Pa. 2005).
500. *See, e.g.*, Convolve, Inc. v. Compaq Computer, 224 F.R.D. 98, 104-05 (S.D.N.Y. 2004); *Micron Separations*, 159 F.R.D. at 362; AVEKA L.L.C. v. Mizuno Corp., 243 F. Supp. 2d 418, 423 (M.D.N.C. 2003) ("[B]ecause infringement is a continuing activity, the requirement to exercise due care and seek and receive advice is a continuing duty. Therefore, once a party asserts the defense of advice of counsel, this opens to inspection the advice received during the entire course of the alleged infringement. Consequently, the waiver of attorney-client privilege or work product protection covers all points of time, including up through trial.").
501. *See, e.g.*, BASF Aktiengesellschaft v. Reilly Indus., 283 F. Supp. 2d 1000, 1006 (S.D. Ind. 2003) (describing middle ground as reflecting fact that "a party should not be allowed to rely on self-serving statements while withholding damaging or contradictory information under the pretense of the attorney-client privilege," but also recognizing existence of "a higher standard for waiver of opinion work product for trial counsel"); *Micron Separations*, 159 F.R.D. at 362 (only those documents casting doubt on opinion of counsel must be produced).

Finally, some courts find the waiver ends once the infringement litigation begins.[502]

The waiver may not be limited to the advice given by opinion counsel. Since the waiver encompasses the subject matter of advice, some courts hold that all opinions received by the client must be revealed, even those opinions the client receives from attorneys other than opinion counsel.[503] Moreover, relying on an opinion of counsel can also result in a waiver of the attorney-work product privilege for the counsel preparing the opinion.[504] The potential of such a waiver has led some companies to hire separate counsel to offer the non-infringement opinion from the counsel who tries the case.[505] Accordingly, a decision to present such evidence must be made only after consideration of the likely implications of full discovery into attorney-client materials.

---

502. *See, e.g.*, Dunhall Pharms. v. Discus Dental, 994 F. Supp. 1202, 1206 (C.D. Cal. 1998) (holding that waiver of attorney-client privilege and work product privilege is limited to only those communications and documents created prior to suit); Carl Zeiss Jena GmbH v. Bio-Rad Labs., No. 98 Civ. 8012, 2000 WL 1006371, at *2 (S.D.N.Y. July 19, 2000); Kelsey-Hayes Co. v. Motor Wheel Corp., 155 F.R.D. 170, 172 (W.D. Mich. 1991).

503. *See AVEKA*, 243 F. Supp. 2d at 423.

504. The courts have generally split along two lines when determining the scope of work product protection waiver. *See generally* Chiron Corp. v. Genentech, Inc., 179 F. Supp. 2d 1182, 1188-89 (E.D. Cal. 2001) (collecting cases). Those courts that opt for a more limited waiver of work product protection reason that the advice of counsel defense only implicates the state of mind of the client. Therefore, unless the client actually reviewed the work product, there is no reason to require production of the materials. *See* Nitinol Med. Techs. v. AGA Med., 135 F. Supp. 2d 212 (D. Mass. 2000); Thorn EMI N. Am. v. Micron Tech., 837 F. Supp. 616, 620-21 (D. Del. 1993). Other courts have held that a broader work product waiver should apply in order to prevent attorneys from deliberately omitting damaging information from their opinion letters "in order to insulate their clients from a finding of willful infringement." Mosel Vitelic Corp. v. Micron Tech., 162 F. Supp. 2d 307, 312 (D. Del. 2000); *accord AVEKA*, 243 F. Supp. 2d at 424; Minn. Specialty Crops, Inc. v. Minn. Wild Hockey Club, 210 F.R.D. 673, 676-79 (D. Minn. 2002); Chiron Corp., 179 F. Supp. 2d at 1189.

505. *See, e.g., Convolve*, 224 F.R.D. at 107 (denying "plaintiffs' motion to compel discovery withheld on the basis of the work product privilege ... Seagate's trial counsel is not obligated to disclose any work product, uncommunicated to Seagate, relating to the subject matter of the opinions issued by Mr. Sekimura.").

Courts have held that a patentee will be deemed to have waived attorney-client privilege only if the patentee has taken an "affirmative step in the litigation to place the advice of the attorney in issue."[506] Acts short of such an affirmative step do not serve automatically to place the advice of counsel at issue and thereby waive the privilege.[507] Thus, courts have held that the mere assertion by a defendant that it pursued allegedly sham litigation in good faith, without more, does not entitle plaintiff to discovery of attorney-client material. In *PostX Corp. v. Secure Data In Motion, Inc.*,[508] for example, the antitrust plaintiff contended that the defendant's defense of good faith constituted an implied waiver of the attorney-client privilege, despite defendant's stipulation that it would not rely on privileged material in establishing its defense.[509] The court held that the privilege would not be deemed waived if the defendant was not seeking to use privileged material affirmatively. Plaintiff had argued that, notwithstanding the stipulation, defendant's witnesses (non-lawyer business executives) admitted that they could not separate their own "independent" thoughts about the merits of the litigation from discussions they had had with counsel.[510] Thus, according to plaintiff, the good faith defense was "so 'inextricably intertwined' with the advice of counsel that it automatically places attorney-client communications at issue."[511] The court rejected the argument:

> [I]t is difficult to conceive of a patent case in which opposing counsel could not extract the kind of deposition testimony given here and then argue implied waiver of all communications regarding the decision to bring suit. As [defendant] points out, if its assertions of good faith automatically resulted in waiver, patent infringement plaintiffs could never defend against antitrust counterclaims without relinquishing the attorney-client privilege for most or all of their pre-filing communications with counsel. Because [defendant] is not using the

---

506.   SmithKline Beecham Corp. v. Apotex Corp., No. 99-CV-4304, 2005 WL 2436662, at *3 (E.D. Pa. Sept. 28, 2005) (quoting Rhone-Poulenc Rorer, Inc. v. Home Indem. Co., 32 F.3d 851, 863 (3d Cir. 1995)) (internal quotation marks omitted).

507.   *See id.*

508.   No. C 02-04483, 2004 WL 2663518 (N.D. Cal. Nov. 20, 2004.).

509.   *Id.* at *4.

510.   *Id.*

511.   *Id.*

attorney-client privilege as a sword, it has not relinquished its use as a shield.[512]

Finally, where fraud is alleged, courts sometimes permit discovery of privileged material under the so-called crime-fraud exception.[513]

6. Liability for Concealing Intellectual Property from Standard-Setting Bodies

In certain circumstances, unilateral conduct by patent holders may give rise to antitrust liability where the patent holder withholds

512. *Id.* at *5.
513. *See, e.g.*, For Your Ease Only, Inc. v. Calgon Carbon Corp., No. 02 C 7345, 2003 WL 22889442, at *5 (N.D. Ill. Dec. 5, 2003) (holding that party seeking production had presented adequate evidence to establish that adversary intentionally concealed prior art from the U.S. PTO sufficient to allow discovery of privileged materials that were used in furtherance of that fraud); Nobelpharma AB v. Implant Innovations, 930 F. Supp. 1241, 1261 (N.D. Ill. 1996) (*Walker Process* counterclaim: holding privilege waived for patent attorney under crime-fraud exception); Monon Corp. v. Stoughton Trailers, 169 F.R.D. 99, 100 (N.D. Ill. 1996) (holding that Monon's failure to disclose material prior art and prior commercial sale of the patented invention warranted piercing of attorney-client privilege under the crime-fraud exception); Leybold-Heraeus Tech. v. Midwest Instrument, 118 F.R.D. 609, 615 (E.D. Wis. 1987) (ordering production of otherwise privileged documents because party seeking production had established *prima facie* case that its adversary had failed to disclose material prior art to U.S. PTO in consolidated patent and antitrust litigation). *But see In re* Spalding Sports Worldwide, 203 F.3d 800, 807 (Fed. Cir. 2000) (finding that party seeking to discover privileged materials had not made a sufficient showing of fraud under *Walker Process* standard to pierce privilege in connection with an invention record); Duplan Corp. v. Deering Milliken, Inc., 540 F.2d 1215, 1220 (4th Cir. 1976) (declining to pierce attorney-client privilege under crime-fraud exception in consolidated patent and antitrust litigation); Softview Computer Prods. v. Haworth, Inc., No. 97 Civ. 8815 KMWHBP, 2000 WL 351411, at *7-8 (S.D.N.Y. March 31, 2000) (holding that party seeking production had failed to make a *prima facie* showing of fraud under *Walker Process* standard in consolidated patent and antitrust action); Thermos Co. v. Starbucks Corp., No. 96 C 3833, 1999 WL 203818, at *4-5 (N.D. Ill. April 6, 1999) (no showing of *prima facie* fraud where party seeking discovery relied upon wholly conclusory statements).

information concerning relevant patents (or patent applications) from a standard-setting body, then, after the standard is adopted and has become entrenched, asserts such IP against entities producing standard-compliant products.[514]

In *In re Dell Computer Corp.*,[515] the Commission charged Dell Computer Corporation ("Dell") with violating the FTC Act in connection with alleged deception of the Video Electronics Standards Association ("VESA"). In 1992, Dell had become a member of VESA, a non-profit standards-setting association composed of virtually all major U.S. computer hardware and software manufacturers. Around the same time, VESA began the process of setting a design standard for a computer bus design, later to be known as the VESA Local Bus or "VL-bus."[516] In 1992, while Dell representatives sat as VESA members, VESA approved the VL-bus design standard. A year earlier, Dell had received a patent which, according to Dell, gave it "exclusive rights to the mechanical slot configuration used on the motherboard to receive the VL-bus card."[517] According to the FTC complaint, at no time prior to or after the VESA approval in 1992 did Dell disclose to the VESA the existence of this patent and in fact, a Dell representative certified that the proposed VL-bus design standard did not infringe on any trademarks, copyrights, or patents that Dell possessed. Some time later however, Dell informed

---

514. Where antitrust liability is found in the circumstances described, a possible penalty might be an order estopping the patent holder from asserting its patent against standard-compliant products. *See, e.g., In re* Dell Computer Corp., 121 F.T.C. 616 (May 20, 1996); Stambler v. Diebold, Inc., No. 85-CV-3014, 1988 WL 95479 (E.D.N.Y. Sept. 2, 1988) (holding that plaintiff was estopped from asserting its patent against standard-compliant products where it had remained silent as to the existence of the patent while participating in industry development of the standard), *aff'd* in 878 F.2d 1445 (Fed. Cir. 1989); Potter Instrument v. Storage Tech., Nos. 79-579-A, 79-626-A, 79-993-A, 79-994-A, 79-995-A, 1980 WL 30330 (E.D. Va. Mar. 25, 1980), *aff'd* on other grounds, 641 F.2d 190 (4th Cir. 1981) (holding that a plaintiff's intentional failure to disclose a patent it owned to a standard-setting body, in violation of the body's policy on patent disclosure, estopped the plaintiff from enforcing the patent).
515. *In re* Dell Computer Corp., 121 F.T.C. 616 (May 20, 1996).
516. A VL-bus is designed to carry information or instructions between the computer's central processing unit and the computer's peripheral devices such as a hard disk drive, a video display terminal, or a modem. *Id.* at 617.
517. *Id.*

certain VESA members who were manufacturing computers using the new design standard that they were violating Dell's exclusive rights. Although the case was resolved by way of consent order (without Dell admitting wrongdoing), the Commission took the position that Dell's conduct amounted to an unreasonable restraint of competition by, among other things, "chilling" willingness to participate in industry standard-setting efforts.[518]

In *Townshend v. Rockwell International*,[519] the court distinguished *Dell* and held that the defendants did not commit an antitrust violation by failing to disclose IP to a standard-setting body. At issue were attempts by Townshend and 3Com to procure industry standards which incorporated Townshend's patented modem technology. The situation in *Dell* was distinguished on the basis that:

(1) Townshend's patents were issued *after* the standard-setting body had adopted the standard in question, whereas in *Dell*, the patent owner had an issued patent at the time the standard-setting proceeding took place;[520]

(2) 3Com informed the standards body that Townshend had pending patent applications covering the modem technology, while the patent owner in *Dell* did not disclose the existence of the patent to the standards-setting organization;[521]

(3) In *Dell*, the FTC recognized that an industry standard which incorporates patented technology can confer market power in a market for *products* incorporating the industry standard. The FTC did not however, consider the issue of whether this standard conferred market power in a market consisting of *proprietary technology* (such as the market in *Townshend*);[522]

(4) There was no assertion in *Townshend* that the adoption of the industry standard in question prevented the development of proprietary technology that could otherwise be developed (and thus no evidence of the probability of monopolization in the market for the proprietary technology).[523] In *Dell* on the other

---

518. *Id.* at 618.
519. Townshend v. Rockwell Int'l, No. 99-0400, 2000 WL 433505 (N.D. Cal. Mar. 28, 2000).
520. *Id.* at *11.
521. *Id.*
522. *Id.* at *12.
523. *Id.* at *12-13.

hand, the standards-setting body was choosing among options, and there was a possibility that they could have adopted a standard which did not incorporate Dell's patent.[524]

The court in *Townshend* held that even if a patentee's nondisclosure influenced a standard-setting organization to adopt a standard, whatever market power arose from the adoption stemmed from the exclusionary power of the patents themselves. Therefore:

> [I]n the absence of allegations of market share in the technology market or allegations that the industry standard prevents the development of proprietary technology that could otherwise be developed, Conexant has not alleged that the alleged incorporation of Townshend's patents into the V.90 standard presents a dangerous probability of monopolization in the market for proprietary technology.[525]

Townshend was favorably cited in *Broadcom Corp. v. Qualcomm Inc.*[526] In *Broadcom*, the district court granted a motion to dismiss Section 2 claims that were predicated largely on allegations that Qualcomm (1) induced a standard-setting organization to adopt a standard that incorporated Qualcomm's patented technology by promising to license its technology on fair, reasonable and non-discriminatory terms, and (2) refused to honor its promise. The case thus did not involve deception as to the existence of patents, but allegations that a false promise was made to induce the adoption of a standard. The court held that Qualcomm's conduct did not injure or eliminate competition, explaining that competition would have been eliminated in the relevant market in any event as a natural byproduct of the standard-setting organization's decision to set a standard. According to the court, "[w]hile Qualcomm's behavior may have influenced how that [standard setting organization] would eliminate competition, it is the [organ-

---

524. *Id.* at *11.
525. *Id.* at *13. This reasoning has been criticized by commentators who have noted that, where standards are concerned, a substantial component of market power flows from the widespread adoption of the standard rather than the existence of the non-disclosed patent(s) alone (*see,* Hovenkamp IP, *supra* note 30, at 35-45).
526. Broadcom Corp. v. Qualcomm Inc., 2006 U.S. Dist. LEXIS 62090 (D.N.J. Aug. 31, 2006).

ization's] decision to set a standard ... not Qualcomm's 'inducement,' that results in the absence of competition."[527]

In *Unocal*,[528] the FTC reversed a decision by an ALJ and ruled that Unocal violated section 5 of the FTC Act through misrepresentations to the California Air Resources Board ("CARB"). Unocal allegedly had assured CARB it would not assert patent rights it held concerning automobile emissions research, while at the same time inducing CARB and other oil refiners to adopt reformulated gasoline standards that overlapped Unocal's patent claims. The Commission held that deliberate misrepresentation to a government body should fall outside the protection of the *Noerr-Pennington* doctrine. The FTC indicated that if such non-immune conduct resulted in anticompetitive effects, it might also incur liability under antitrust law, stating:

> [W]e emphasize that, even if Noerr-Pennington considerations do not protect the false petitioning, no liability arises under the FTC, Sherman or Clayton Acts unless the conduct is anticompetitive. These limitations will ensure, with a substantial margin for error, that the possibility of antitrust challenge will neither chill petitioning that merits protection nor undermine the decision-making functions of other governmental entities. This approach, moreover, will also help make certain that intentionally and egregiously false petitioning does not cause competitive injury.[529]

In *In re Rambus*,[530] the FTC found that Rambus, a developer of semiconductor memory technology, monopolized certain memory technology markets through a course of deceptive conduct involving its participation in the Joint Electronics Devices Engineering Council (JEDEC).[531] In coming to this conclusion, the Commission relied on Rambus's entire course of conduct:

527. The court acknowledged, however, that such conduct may give rise to claims under other legal theories. *Id.* at *27.
528. *Unocal*, FTC slip op., *supra* note 425; *see also supra* at B.2.b(1) (additional discussion of *Unocal*).
529. *Unocal*, FTC slip op., at *116.
530. *In re* Rambus, Inc., FTC Dkt. No. 9302 (F.T.C. Aug. 2, 2006), http://www.ftc.gov/os/adjpro/d9302/060802commissionopinion.pdf.
531. *Id.* at 3.

(1) Rambus had remained silent while other JEDEC members discussed and adopted technologies that became subject to Rambus's evolving patent claims;[532]

(2) Rambus voted and commented on technologies without revealing it was seeking patent coverage for them (despite language on the ballot calling for disclosure of relevant patents);[533]

(3) Rambus evaded direct questions from JEDEC members on its patent portfolio;[534]

(4) Rambus was engaged in a program of amending its patent applications to develop a patent portfolio that would cover JEDEC's standards, and used information gleaned from JEDEC to do this, without disclosing to JEDEC what it was doing (violating JEDEC policy which required members to reveal the existence of patents and patent applications that later might be enforced against those practicing the JEDEC standards);[535]

(5) Upon withdrawing from JEDEC, Rambus provided JEDEC with a list of its patents but omitted patent applications and the patent that it believed covered JEDEC's work.[536] After JEDEC's standards were implemented, Rambus began enforcing patent rights over aspects of JEDEC's standards.[537]

The Commission held that, taken together, this conduct amounted to a deceptive course of conduct in violation of section 5 of the FTC Act. According to the Commission, Rambus withheld information that would have been highly material to the standard-setting process within JEDEC, and in an atmosphere where JEDEC members expected disclosure.[538]

---

532. *Id.* at 66.
533. *Id.*
534. *Id.*
535. *Id.* at 67.
536. *Id.* at 66.
537. *Id.* at 5.
538. *Id.* at 68, 33 ("[W]e cannot stress too strongly, the importance we place on the fact that the challenged conduct occurred in the context of a standard-setting process in which members expected each other to act cooperatively"). Following the lead of the Federal Circuit's opinion in the related *Infineon* case, *Rambus, Inc. v. Infineon Techs.*, 318 F.3d 1081, 1098 (Fed. Cir. 2003), the FTC said it looked to the behavior, understandings and expectations of JEDEC members, including Rambus, to inform its understanding of the JEDEC environment, *id.* at 53. The Commission noted: Rambus's own documents and witnesses believed it

The Commission concluded that Rambus's conduct was calculated to mislead members into believing that Rambus neither had, nor was seeking, relevant patents that would be enforced against JEDEC-compliant products.[539] The FTC cited authority where courts had previously held that willful or intentional deception may constitute "exclusionary conduct" that would support a claim under section 2 of the Sherman Act.[540] The conduct was exclusionary because it contributed to the acquisition of monopoly power by distorting JEDEC's technology choices and undermining JEDEC members' ability to protect themselves against patent "hold-up."[541] In addition, other elements of section 2 were met in that Rambus's 90 percent share of the relevant market was enough to infer the existence of a monopoly power;[542] there was a causal link between Rambus's exclusionary conduct and its monopoly position (given the evidence that a properly-informed JEDEC may have selected a substitute technology);[543] and the industry became "locked in" to the JEDEC standards.[544]

---

should have disclosed its patent filings, *id.* at 53; other JEDEC participants testified that disclosure of relevant intellectual property was important for its standard setting process to work (so patentees could not later assert their patents and "hold up" the industry by charging higher royalties than could have been extracted before the standard was set), *id.* at 54; and there were "numerous" other examples of JEDEC members disclosing patents and applications relevant to the standards under consideration, *id.* at 57. The FTC concluded that together, JEDEC's policies and practices, as well as the actions of its member participants, provided the basis for the expectation that JEDEC standard-setting activity would be conducted co-operatively and members would not try to distort the process by acting deceptively in terms of the patents they possessed or expected to possess, *id.* at 66.

539. *Id.* at 68.
540. *Id.* at 29.
541. *Id.* at 68. In this context, "hold-up" means that Rambus would position itself to charge higher royalties than could have been extracted before the standard was set.
542. *Id.* at 73.
543. *Id.* at 77.
544. The FTC found that the industry was "locked in" to two particular standards (SDRAM and DDR SDRAM), but found no sufficient causal link between Rambus's exclusionary conduct and JEDEC's adoption of another type of standard (DDR2 SDRAM). *Id.* at 99. Once the market was locked in, Rambus would have the ability to extract large sums in payment royalties.

In addition to barring Rambus from making misrepresentations or omissions to standard-setting organizations, the FTC's Final Opinion and Order in the *Rambus* matter require Rambus to license its SDRAM and DDR SDRAM technology, sets maximum allowable royalty rates it can collect for the licensing, bars Rambus from collecting or attempting to collect more than the maximum allowable royalty rates from companies that may already have incorporated its DRAM technology, and requires Rambus to employ a Commission-approved compliance officer to ensure that Rambus's patents and patent applications are disclosed to industry standard-setting bodies in which it participates.[545] The Commission held that it has the remedial authority to order compulsory licensing, including royalty-free licensing, in appropriate circumstances.[546] According to the Commission, royalty-free compulsory licensing requires proof "that this form of relief is necessary to restore the competitive conditions that would have prevailed absent [the defendant's] misconduct.[547] The Commission further held that Complaint Counsel failed to meet this burden of proof because the evidence showed a realistic possibility that JEDEC would have adopted Rambus's technologies had Rambus agreed to license on reasonable and nondiscriminatory terms; thus, the Commission ordered that Rambus be limited to obtaining reasonable royalties.[548]

In short, antitrust liability may lie where participants in industry standard-setting bodies deliberately withhold patent information which they know is relevant, and do so in an environment which requires disclosure. Key considerations in establishing liability of the patent holder in these circumstances include:

(1) Whether the organization's rules or procedures require disclosure of the patent or patent application, or there is at least a reasonable expectation such information will be disclosed.[549] To

545. Opinion of the Commission on Remedy, *In re* Rambus, Inc., FTC Dkt. No. 9302 (F.T.C. Feb. 5, 2007), http://www.ftc.gov/os/adjpro/d9302/070205opinion.pdf.
546. *Id.* at 6-10.
547. *Id.* at 10.
548. *Id.* at 12-30.
549. In terms of the expectation of disclosure (irrespective of organization rules), *see, e.g.*, Indian Head, Inc. v. Allied Tube & Conduit, 817 F.2d 938 (2d Cir. 1987) *aff'd* 486 U.S. 492 (1966). In this case, a PVC manufacturer initiated a proposal before a private industry organization to extend the organization's code to approve its plastic conduit. In response,

withhold in such circumstances may constitute exclusionary conduct according to *Rambus*, as other members might infer no potential patent issues exists, and act accordingly. On the other hand, disclosure may not be required if there is no general expectation of disclosure or policy imposing it;[550]

(2) The entire course and pattern of the patent holder's conduct. The *Rambus* decision examined in detail all the facts surrounding Rambus's conduct while a member of JEDEC, as well as its continued course of conduct once it left the JEDEC membership. The holding might have been different for instance, had Rambus withdrawn from JEDEC as soon as it became aware that the standards under discussion might overlap with its patent applications;

(3) Whether the patent holder's failure to disclose its rights was conscious or deliberate. In *Rambus*, it was fairly clear that the patent and the standard overlapped and that Rambus was aware of this overlap and wished to exploit it for its own competitive advantage. Courts may be more hesitant to impute a deliberate deception on the part of a defendant where there is evidence the defendant believed in good faith that the patent would not cover the standard;

---

defendant, a steel pipe manufacturer, enlisted other steel makers in an effort to block the proposed PVC standard by packing the meeting with new members to vote against the proposal. The Second Circuit held that defendant's conduct constituted an antitrust violation (in terms of §1 Sherman Act). Although no organization rule had been violated, defendant "violated the integrity of the [organization's] procedures" and "subverted" the organization's standard-setting process for the purpose of achieving an anticompetitive result (the exclusion of PVC conduit from the marketplace). 817 F.2d at 947. The court stated, "We refuse to permit a defendant to use its literal compliance with a standard-setting organization's rules as a shield to protect such conduct from antitrust liability." 817 F.2d at 947.

550. *See, e.g.*, Symbol v. Proxim, No. Civ. 01-801-SLR, 2004 WL 1770290, at *8 (D. Del. July 28, 2004), where the District Court held that a patentee's failure to disclose its patent to the IEEE standards group governing WiFi technology was excused because the patentee committed to license the patent on reasonable and nondiscriminatory terms, and the organization did not require disclosure if the patentee committed to license all relevant patents. In addition, the facts surrounding the IEEE and its members suggested no general duty of disclosure.

(4) Causation must be proven. In other words, it must be proven that the standard-setting organization would not have adopted the standard in question but for the misrepresentation or omission, or at least that the choices available to the standard-setting body were distorted by the conduct of the patent holder; and

(5) The standard-setting organization's decision to adopt the standard must influence competition in the market. This is more likely when, for instance: the organization's members collectively have a dominant share of the market; past standards promulgated by the organization have dominated the market; only one standard can be selected; and the intellectual property owner is unwilling to license the undisclosed patent on reasonable and nondiscriminatory terms.[551]

In response to some of the potential hold-up problems that may arise in standard-setting organizations, some organizations have sought to adopt rules requiring participants to not only disclose intellectual property rights essential to the implement the standard developed by the organization, but to also disclose the specific licensing terms (rather than to simply offer RAND terms).[552]   For instance, in a Business Review Letter, the Department of Justice analyzed a proposal under which a patent holder would disclose its patents essential to implement a proposed standard and its "most restrictive licensing terms" for those patents.   Finding a rule of reason analysis appropriate, the Department explained that this rule could help avoid hold-up problems "by preserving the benefits of competition between alternative technologies that exist during the standard-setting process."[553]   The Department was not concerned about a potential artificial depression in licensing rates because the proposed rule did not allow joint negotiations.[554]   Other organizations have proposed allowing members to jointly negotiate royalty rates with an intellectual property holder before the standard has

---

551.   HOVENKAMP IP, *supra* note 30, at 35-45.

552.   *See, e.g.,* Letter from Thomas O. Barnett, Ass't Att'y Gen., to Robert A. Skitol (October 30, 2006), *available at* http://www.usdoj.gov/atr/public/busreview/219380.pdf.

553.   *Id.* at 9.

554.   *Id.*

been set.[555]   And the Chairman of the FTC has indicated that this type of rule may also be permissible under a rule of reason analysis.[556]

---

555. *See, e.g.*, "Recognizing the Procompetitive Potential of Royalty Discussions in Standard Setting," Remarks of Chairman Deborah Platt Majoras prepared for Standardization and the Law: Developing the Golden Mean for Global Trade at 6 (Sept. 23, 2005), http://www.ftc.gov/speeches/majoras/050923stanford.pdf.
556. *See id.* at 7 ("joint ex ante royalty discussions that are reasonably necessary to avoid hold up do not warrant per se condemnation").

CHAPTER VII

ANTITRUST ISSUES IN MERGERS INVOLVING INTELLECTUAL PROPERTY

A. Section 7 of the Clayton Act and Acquisitions of Intellectual Property

1. Overview of Section 7 of the Clayton Act

Both the Clayton Act and the Sherman Act apply to acquisitions of intellectual property. Section 7 of the Clayton Act generally prohibits mergers and acquisitions that substantially lessen competition or tend to create a monopoly.[1] The Antitrust Division of the Department of Justice ("DOJ") and the Federal Trade Commission ("FTC") exercise concurrent jurisdiction to challenge mergers, acquisitions, joint ventures, and other transactions under Section 7. Mergers and acquisitions may also be challenged as unreasonable restraints of trade under Section 1 of the Sherman Act[2] and as monopolization or attempted monopolization under Section 2 of the Sherman Act.[3] The FTC can also challenge transactions under Section 5 of the Federal Trade Commission Act, which prohibits "unfair methods of competition."[4]

The scope of Section 7 is quite broad. It encompasses a variety of acquisitions of stocks, assets, and partnership interests. Section 7, as originally enacted in 1914, only prohibited acquisitions of stock. In 1950, Congress amended Section 7 with the passage of the Celler-

---

1. 15 U.S.C. § 18. Section 7 of the Clayton Act provides in relevant part: "No person engaged in commerce shall acquire, directly or indirectly, the whole or any part of the stock or other share capital . . . of another person engaged in commerce ... where ... the effect of such acquisition may be substantially to lessen competition, or tend to create a monopoly." *Id.*
2. 15 U.S.C. § 1. Section 1 prohibits "[e]very contract, combination ... or conspiracy, in restraint of trade." *Id. See, e.g.,* United States v. First Nat'l Bank & Trust, 376 U.S. 665 (1964); United States v. Columbia Steel Co., 334 U.S. 495 (1948).
3. 15 U.S.C. § 2. Section 2 prohibits monopolization or attempted monopolization of a relevant market. *Id. See, e.g., Columbia Steel,* 334 U.S. at 495.
4. 15 U.S.C. § 45 ("Unfair methods of competition ... are hereby declared unlawful.").

Kefauver Antimerger Act to encompass asset acquisitions. Patents,[5] copyrights,[6] and trademarks[7] are considered assets for purposes of Section 7. An acquisition of an exclusive license to intellectual property is also considered an asset for the purpose of Section 7 analysis.[8]

The legal analysis used to assess the anticompetitive effects of acquisitions of intellectual property is standard merger analysis set forth in the DOJ/FTC *Horizontal Merger Guidelines* (*Merger Guidelines*)[9] and the *Antitrust Guidelines for the Licensing of Intellectual Property* (*Intellectual Property Guidelines*).[10] The *Merger Guidelines* set forth the analysis used to determine if a merger or acquisition is likely to have anticompetitive effects, such as increased prices, reduced output, or reduced innovation. This analysis requires consideration of market shares and changes in market concentration, the likelihood of unilateral anticompetitive effects or coordinated interaction, entry conditions, and efficiencies.

The *Intellectual Property Guidelines* provide explicitly that transfers of intellectual property are to be analyzed under standards set forth in the *Merger Guidelines*:

> Certain transfers of intellectual property rights are most appropriately analyzed by applying the principles and standards used to analyze mergers, particularly those in the 1992 Horizontal Merger Guidelines. The Agencies will apply a merger analysis to an outright sale by an

---

5. *See, e.g.*, SCM Corp. v. Xerox Corp., 645 F.2d 1195, 1205 (2d. Cir. 1981); Telectronics Proprietary v. Detronic, Inc., 687 F. Supp. 832, 844 (S.D.N.Y. 1988); United States v. Lever Bros. Co., 216 F. Supp. 887, 889 (S.D.N.Y. 1963);

6. *See, e.g.*, United States v. Columbia Pictures, 189 F. Supp. 153, 181-82 (S.D.N.Y. 1960).

7. *See, e.g.*, United States v. Lever Bros., 216 F. Supp. 887, 889 (S.D.N.Y. 1963).

8. *See, e.g.*, Record Club of Am. v. Capitol Records, 1971 Trade Cas. (CCH) ¶ 73,694, at 90,898 (S.D.N.Y. 1971); W. Geophysical Co. v. Bolt Assocs., 305 F. Supp. 1248, 1251 (D. Conn. 1969); *Columbia Pictures*, 189 F. Supp. at 181-82.

9. U.S. DEP'T OF JUSTICE AND FED. TRADE COMM'N, HORIZONTAL MERGER GUIDELINES (Apr. 2, 1992) (hereinafter 1992 HORIZONTAL MERGER GUIDELINES), *reprinted in* 4 Trade Reg. Rep. (CCH) ¶ 13,104.

10. U.S. DEP'T OF JUSTICE & FED. TRADE COMM'N, ANTITRUST GUIDELINES FOR THE LICENSING OF INTELLECTUAL PROPERTY (April 6, 1995) (hereinafter INTELLECTUAL PROPERTY GUIDELINES), *reprinted in* 4 Trade Reg. Rep. (CCH) ¶ 13,132 *and* Appendix 1 to this Handbook.

intellectual property owner of all of its rights to that intellectual property and to a transaction in which a person obtains through grant, sale, or other transfer an exclusive license for intellectual property (*i.e.*, a license that precludes all other persons, including the licensor, from using the licensed intellectual property). Such transactions may be assessed under section 7 of the Clayton Act, sections 1 and 2 of the Sherman, and section 5 of the Federal Trade Commission Act.[11]

2. *Acquisitions of Intellectual Property*

Intellectual property transfers that fall under the purview of the antitrust laws occur, principally, in two ways: (i) a company can transfer the ownership or control of intellectual property as part of the purchase of, or merger with, another company; or (ii) a company can acquire an exclusive license to specific intellectual property.

Obtaining a nonexclusive license to intellectual property is an acquisition of intellectual property, but the acquisition does not raise anticompetitive concerns unless the terms of the license, or the circumstances, render it a de facto exclusive license.[12] That is, the government and the courts will consider the actual practice and its effects and not just the formal terms of a licensing arrangement. Thus, a nonexclusive license may have the effect of exclusive licensing if it is structured so that the licensor is unlikely to license others or to practice the technology itself. On the other hand, a licensing arrangement will not be treated as exclusive merely because a party chooses to deal with a single licensee or because only a single licensee has chosen to take a license.[13]

---

11.   *Id.* § 5.7.
12.   *Id.* § 4.1.2.
13.   *See id.* The *Intellectual Property Guidelines* in fact contain a hypothetical example of a firm, Omega, on the verge of entering a pharmaceutical market granting a license to the incumbent monopolist in the market, Delta. In the hypothetical, the license is "nominally non-exclusive." Omega has, however, "rejected all requests by other firms to obtain a license ... despite offers by those firms of terms that are reasonable" in relation to those in the license to Delta. The *Guidelines* conclude that "[a]lthough Omega's license to Delta is nominally non-exclusive, the circumstances indicate that it is exclusive in fact." Moreover, Omega would be a likely potential competitor of Delta in the absence of the licensing arrangement, and thus the two firms are in a horizontal relationship in the relevant market, and the government would

In *United States v. S.C. Johnson & Son, Inc.*,[14] which was settled through a consent decree, the DOJ sued to block an arrangement between Bayer AG, a German company, and S.C. Johnson, the dominant U.S. insecticide maker.   The DOJ alleged that a nominally nonexclusive license for household insecticides was exclusive-in-fact since the licensor refused all other offers to license and refrained from using its technology itself. The DOJ alleged that Bayer was planning to enter the U.S. market but instead granted an effectively exclusive license for the active ingredient in its product to S.C. Johnson.[15] The DOJ further alleged that the arrangement reduced Bayer's incentive to compete in the manufacture and sale of household insecticides.[16] The complaint thus concluded that by purchasing some of the assets Bayer would have used in entering the market and obtaining an exclusive de facto license to Bayer's innovative active ingredient, S.C. Johnson effectively eliminated competition that could have helped drive down the price of household insecticides.[17]

a.   Accumulation of Patents

Accumulation of numerous internally developed patents can have the effect of extending or perpetuating control over the market for an original patented invention.[18] This is true whether the accumulated patents are novel improvements upon existing patents ("improvement patents") or cover products and processes complimentary to the original patented invention.   Where the accumulated patents do not confer monopoly power, or at least substantial market power, the accumulation of internally developed patents is unlikely to have anticompetitive consequences.

---

apply a merger analysis to the transaction since it involves the acquisition of a likely potential competitor. *Id.*, Example 11.

14.   United States v. S.C. Johnson & Son, 59 Fed. Reg. 43,859 (Aug. 25, 1994) (Competitive Impact Statement); *see also* United States v. S.C. Johnson & Son, 1995-1 Trade Cas. (CCH) ¶ 70,884 (N.D. Ill. 1994) (final judgment).

15.   *S.C. Johnson & Son*, 59 Fed. Reg. at 43,863.

16.   *Id.*

17.   *Id.*

18.   For these purposes, "internally developed" patents include those patents developed by a company's own employee or by an outside entity specifically retained to conduct research on behalf of the company where resulting intellectual property is assigned to the company.

Anticompetitive concerns may arise, however, if a monopolist accumulates a large internally developed patent portfolio that has the effect of extending its monopoly and raising barriers to entry. A monopolist's accumulation of numerous patents, even if less significant, in a particular field may diminish the possibility of competition from rival firms.[19]

---

19. 3 PHILLIP E. AREEDA & HERBERT HOVENKAMP, ANTITRUST LAW: AN ANALYSIS OF ANTITRUST PRINCIPLES AND THEIR APPLICATION, ¶ 704b (2d ed. 2002) [hereinafter AREEDA & HOVENKAMP]. Areeda and Hovenkamp explain:

> The more patents in a field possessed by the monopolist, the more difficult it becomes for anyone else to work in or to utilize patents in that field. Many new patents in the field will inevitably be improvements on existing patents. Because the improvements cannot be practiced without infringing the existing basic or prior improvement patents, only the monopolist (or its licensees) can use the new patents.... Each additional patent possessed by the monopolist lessens the possibility of competition from others. And the collection of minor improvement patents may extend the period of the monopolist's control beyond the legal life of its basic patents ... [A]lthough rivals or others might be able to 'invent around' the monopolist's patents, they may be discouraged from trying. Inventive effort might seem less likely to produce new basic patents than improvement patents that cannot be practiced without the monopolist's consent ... [On the other hand], the monopolist itself may have both the incentive and the resources to continue steady research and development. As a result ... the monopolist might find and patent the alternative methods for the products or processes of its field and thus perpetuate its power....

Id. Areeda and Hovenkamp assert that the accumulation of patents may create barriers to entry even when each patent is of little significance:

> [T]he monopolist's large and possibly growing hoard blanketing its field would confront any new producer with the substantial possibility of patent infringement litigation. And even if all the patents are relatively 'weak,' their sheer number threatens that one might be held valid and infringed. The potential newcomer may therefore feel compelled to make its peace with the monopolist before committing substantial investments to the field. Or it may not enter at all.

Nonetheless, no court has ever held that the creation of a large internally developed patent portfolio, without more, violates Section 2 of the Sherman Act. Where the company is a monopolist and does not practice the accumulated patents, mere acquisition of rights will not raise antitrust concerns. Indeed, the Supreme Court has said that "mere accumulation of patents, no matter how many, is not in and of itself illegal."[20]

b.   Acquisitions of Patents as part of a Monopolization Scheme

Assignments of patents have been held to violate the Sherman Act only where the assignment is part of a broader monopolization scheme or agreement among competitors to restrain trade. In the seminal case, *United States v. United Shoe Machinery*,[21] the DOJ brought suit in 1935, alleging antitrust violations from patent accumulations as well as mergers and leasing practices. The complaint alleged that United Shoe dominated the market for shoe production equipment in part through its more than 2,000 patents blocking entry. In fact, the vast majority of the patents—over 95 percent—flowed from in-house R&D efforts. The court found no antitrust violation, apart from United Shoe's leasing practices, and even concluded that United Shoe's position in the industry was the result of "superior skill, foresight and industry."[22] The court nonetheless questioned United Shoe's acquisitions of patents, suggesting its legitimate purposes could have been served by nonexclusive licenses. "Taking the further step of acquiring the patents ... buttressed United's market power [and] made it less likely that United would have competition."[23]

Other cases have found potential monopolization where the defendant combined acquisitions with other conduct. For instance, in *Kobe, Inc. v. Dempsey Pump Co.*,[24] the Tenth Circuit held that the acquisition, non-use, and enforcement of "every important patent" in the field, with a purpose to exclude competition, together with other anticompetitive acts, violated Section 2 of the Sherman Act. Similarly,

---

Id.
20.   Automatic Radio Mfg. v. Hazeltine Research, 339 U.S. 827, 834 (1950)
21.   United States v. United Shoe Mach. Corp., 110 F. Supp. 295 (D. Mass. 1953), *aff'd*, 347 U.S. 521 (1954).
22.   *Id.* at 344.
23.   *Id.* at 333.
24.   Kobe, Inc. v. Dempsey Pump Co., 198 F.2d 416 (10th Cir. 1952).

in *United States v. Singer Manufacturing Co.*,[25] the Supreme Court held that the transfer of a patent to facilitate bringing infringement actions as part of a broader monopolistic scheme also violated the Sherman Act.[26]

In *DiscoVision Associates v. Disc Manufacturing*,[27] a district court held that a firm's right to file patent applications was qualified, "subject to abuse and antitrust scrutiny," if the firm sought "to expand the monopoly granted by the patent laws by misuse, agreement, or accumulation." Given allegations that DiscoVision had done more than just accumulate patents, including engaging in dilatory and deceptive practices before the Patent and Trademark Office, the court denied a motion to dismiss the plaintiff's monopolization claims.

In *SCM Corp. v. Xerox Corp.*,[28] however, the Second Circuit made clear that mere procurement of patents would not violate Section 2. In that case, Xerox licensed key patents relating to plain paper office copiers nonexclusively from Battelle, a research and development think tank. At the same time, Xerox itself was accumulating a large internally generated patent portfolio. Subsequently, it acquired the Battelle patents outright, years before the first mass market plain paper copier had been sold—in other words, before the relevant product market existed.

SCM filed a private antitrust suit against Xerox, alleging that it had been excluded from the plain paper copier market due in large part to Xerox's patent estate. SCM alleged that, at the time of Xerox's acquisition of the Battelle patents, Xerox could have reasonably foreseen that it would create a monopoly. In fact, the Battelle patents did permit Xerox to obtain a monopoly in the market for plain paper copiers. One key aspect of SCM's case was its theory that Xerox's refusal to license patents to SCM constituted anticompetitive conduct in violation of Section 2 of the Sherman Act. The jury found for the plaintiff and awarded damages, after trebling, of $111 million. The district court reversed the damage award, but certified the matter for appeal before considering SCM's claim for equitable relief—a request for a court ordered license.

The Second Circuit went one step further than the district court and rejected the finding of liability as a matter of law, thereby also precluding

25.   United States v. Singer Mfg. Co., 374 U.S. 174 (1963).
26.   *Id.*; *see also* United States v. United States Gypsum Co., 333 U.S. 364 (1948); Hartford-Empire Co. v. United States, 323 U.S. 386 (1945).
27.   DiscoVision Assocs. v. Disc Mfg., 42 U.S.P.Q.2d (BNA) 1749 (D. Del. 1997).
28.   SCM Corp. v. Xerox Corp., 645 F.2d 1195 (2d Cir. 1981).

prospective relief (i.e., a compulsory license) as well as damages.[29] The court recognized that the role of investors in "both the inventive process and commercialization of inventions" is important and procompetitive, noting Xerox participated financially in both the inventive process by funding research at Battelle and the subsequent commercialization of xerography.[30] The court reasoned that the acquisition of patents from Battelle occurred at a time at which no plain paper copier market existed and Xerox "possessed no power whatsoever in even the inchoate market."[31] The Second Circuit concluded that "the procurement of a patent ... will not violate Section 2 even where it is likely that the patent monopoly will evolve into an economic monopoly."[32]

Because the patent laws expressly provide the patentee the right to exclude others, to subject a patentee that internally develops or lawfully acquires patents to antitrust liability where the patent portfolio subsequently blossoms into a monopoly would "unduly trespass upon the policies that underlie the patent law system."[33] The Second Circuit noted that Section 154 of the Patent Act confers on the patent owner the right to unilaterally refuse to license, and "where a patent has been lawfully acquired, subsequent conduct permissible under the patent laws cannot trigger any liability under the antitrust laws."[34] Thus, the court held that the owner of internally developed patents and/or lawfully acquired patents, even if a monopolist, was not required by Section 2 of the Sherman Act to license parties to compete.[35]

Historically, an owner of intellectual property acting unilaterally had an absolute right to refuse to license since the right to exclude is the essence of the patent right.[36] Following the *SCM v. Xerox* case, most courts have held that refusing to license internally developed and lawfully acquired intellectual property to would-be competitors was beyond the reach of the antitrust laws, even where the patent owner was a monopolist. For example, in *United States v. Westinghouse Electric*,[37] the Ninth Circuit said that "[no] court has ever held that the antitrust laws

29. *Id.* at 1197.
30. *Id.* at 1206 n. 9.
31. *Id.* at 1211.
32. *Id.* at 1206.
33. *Id.* at 1212.
34. *Id.* at 1206.
35. *Id.*
36. *See* Zenith Radio Corp. v. Hazeltine Research, 395 U.S. 100, 135 (1969); Cont'l Paper Bag Co. v. E. Bag Co., 210 U.S. 405, 425 (1908).
37. United States v. Westinghouse Elec., 648 F.2d 642 (9th Cir. 1981).

require a patent holder to forfeit the exclusionary power inherent in his patent the instant his patent monopoly affords him monopoly power."[38] And the First Circuit held that copyrights, even those that conferred a monopoly on its owner, should not be viewed as an "essential facility" which must be shared with competitors—with the possible exception of where such intellectual property was acquired by unlawful means. Rather, the court held that "the exercise of patent rights is a legitimate means by which a firm may maintain its monopoly power."[39]

In *Image Technical Services v. Eastman Kodak Co.*,[40] however, the Ninth Circuit cast doubt on the vitality of the Second Circuit's *SCM v. Xerox* decision. In *Kodak*, the Ninth Circuit held that the antitrust laws could be used to compel Kodak to license its (presumably internally developed) intellectual property to independent service organizations in order to enable them to compete with Kodak in servicing and supplying spare parts for Kodak equipment. The court, without expressly distinguishing *SCM v. Xerox*, seemed to reject its fundamental premise that antitrust liability cannot be based on conduct expressly permitted by the Patent Act. Instead, the Ninth Circuit held that the patent right merely provided the patentee with a presumptively valid "business justification" for refusing to license its intellectual property. Absent such business justification, unilateral conduct by the owner of intellectual property, including a refusal to sell or license, may violate the antitrust laws if it adversely affects competition. The court then found that the defendant's subjective intent to exclude competition from independent service organizations was the real reason for Kodak's conduct. Kodak's reliance on its intellectual property as a basis for refusing to license plaintiffs was therefore "pretextual" and, thus, Kodak's "business justification" disappeared. As a result, Kodak had a duty to license any actual or potential competitor. The Ninth Circuit acknowledged that it was not relying on the essential facilities doctrine and that it could "find no

---

38. *Id.* at 648 (quoting *SCM v. Xerox*, 645 F.2d at 1204).
39. Data Gen. Corp. v. Grumman Sys. Support Corp., 36 F.3d 1147, 1186 (1st Cir. 1994) (citing Barry Wright Corp. v. ITT Grinnell Corp., 724 F.2d 227, 230 (1st Cir. 1983)); *see* Cygnus Therapeutic Sys. v. Alza Corp., 92 F.3d 1153, 1161 (Fed. Cir. 1996); Miller Insituform, Inc. v. Insituform of N. Am., Inc., 830 F.2d 606, 609 (6th Cir. 1987), *cert. denied*, 484 U.S. 1064 (1987); Crucible, Inc. v. Stora Kopparbergs Bergslags AB, 701 F. Supp. 1157, 1162 (W.D. Pa. 1988) (refusal to license lawfully acquired patents cannot be antitrust violation).
40. Image Technical Servs. v. Eastman Kodak Co., 125 F.3d 1195 (9th Cir. 1997).

reported case in which a court has imposed antitrust liability for a unilateral refusal to sell or license a patent or copyright."[41]

The Federal Circuit explicitly rejected the Ninth Circuit's approach in *Kodak* and held that it is improper to consider the purpose or effect of a unilateral refusal to license intellectual property in *In re Independent Service Organizations Antitrust Litigation (Xerox)*.[42] The Federal Circuit held that absent illegal tying, fraud on the Patent and Trademark Office, or sham litigation, a patent owner may not be subjected to antitrust liability for its refusal to license its patents or sell patented parts (as in *Kodak*, presumably these patents were internally developed), regardless of the patentee's intent (subjective or otherwise) or any anticompetitive effect that refusal may have in related service markets. The plaintiffs in *Xerox* were independent service organizations providing maintenance and repair service for Xerox copiers. Xerox refused to sell spare parts or its copyrighted diagnostic software to plaintiffs. The plaintiffs alleged that this conduct violated the antitrust laws. The Federal Circuit disagreed, saying:

> We see no more reason to inquire into the subjective motivation of Xerox in refusing to sell or license its patented works than we found in evaluating the subjective motivation of the patentee in bringing suit to enforce that same right. In the absence of any illegal tying, fraud on the Patent and Trademark Office, or sham litigation, the patent holder may enforce the statutory right to exclude others from making, using or selling the claimed invention free from liability under the antitrust laws. We therefore will not inquire into his subjective motivation for exerting his statutory rights, even though his refusal to sell or license his patent invention may have an anticompetitive effect, so long as that anticompetitive effect is not illegally extended beyond the statutory patent grant. [43]

c.   Grantbacks

Another means of acquiring intellectual property rights is through grantbacks. A grantback is a provision in a patent license requiring the licensee to convey back to the licensor any improvement patent that the licensee may develop. Grantbacks may be either exclusive or nonexclusive. Nonexclusive grantbacks to licensors without market power raise few, if any, antitrust issues. A nonexclusive grantback

---

41.   *Id.* at 1216.
42.   203 F.3d 1322 (Fed. Cir. 2000).
43.   *Id.* at 1328-29.

fosters the legitimate procompetitive goal of permitting the licensor to practice improvements in order to fully compete with his licensees, while at the same time not limiting access to the improvements to third parties.

For example, in *United States v. National Lead Co.*,[44] the Supreme Court recognized that a licensor's insistence on a nonexclusive grantback to a licensee's improvements to the licensed technology was necessary to assure the licensor a right to continue to use his own technology.[45] Nonexclusive grantbacks to a licensor who is a monopolist have been held in some older cases, as part of a wider course of conduct, to violate Section 2 of the Sherman Act.[46] Nonetheless, most commentators today believe that nonexclusive grantbacks—even to monopolists—should be per se legal.[47]

Even exclusive grantbacks are judged under the rule of reason and may be lawful.[48] In *Transparent-Wrap Machine v. Stokes & Smith Co.*,[49] the Supreme Court held that a license requiring the licensee to assign any improvement patents to the licensor was not per se unlawful. The Court explained, "One who uses the patent to acquire another is not extending his patent monopoly to articles governed by the general law and as respects which neither monopolies nor restraints on trade are sanctioned. He indeed is using one legalized monopoly to acquire another legalized monopoly."[50]

Grantbacks may raise anticompetitive concern under Section 2 of the Sherman Act, especially if the licensor possesses substantial market power.[51] The most important factors to be considered in evaluating a grantback are whether the licensor has market power, whether the grantback is exclusive or nonexclusive, and whether the provision is likely to reduce the licensee's incentive to invest in improving the licensed technology, as well as the effect of the grantback on

---

44. United States v. Nat'l Lead Co., 332 U.S. 319 (1947).
45. *See id.* at 359-60.
46. *See* United States v. Imperial Chem. Indus., 105 F. Supp. 215 (S.D.N.Y. 1952) (systematic insistence on nonexclusive grantbacks constituted attempt to monopolize); United States v. Gen. Elec. Co., 82 F. Supp. 753, 768, 815-16 (D.N.J. 1949).
47. *See* 3 AREEDA & HOVENKAMP, *supra* note 19, ¶ 707f.
48. *See* INTELLECTUAL PROPERTY GUIDELINES, *supra* note 10, § 5.6.
49. Transparent-Wrap Mach. v. Stokes & Smith Co., 329 U.S. 637 (1947).
50. *Id.* at 644.
51. *See* Kobe, Inc. v. Dempsey Pump Co., 198 F.2d 416, 420 (10th Cir. 1952); Hartford-Empire Co. v. United States, 323 U.S. 386, 406-07 (1945).

dissemination of improvements and on licensors' incentives to innovate in the first place. Other relevant factors that courts have considered include whether the licensee retains the right to use improvements, whether the grantback precludes, permits, or requires the licensor to grant sublicenses, whether the grantback is limited to the scope of the licensed patents or covers inventions which would not infringe the licensed patent, the duration of the grantback, and whether the grantback is royalty free.[52]

B. Unique Hart-Scott-Rodino Issues Relating to Intellectual Property

The Hart-Scott-Rodino Antitrust Improvements Act of 1976 (HSR Act)[53] requires prior notification to the federal government of certain intellectual property licensing transactions, as well as transactions structured as acquisitions of intellectual property assets. The HSR Act generally requires premerger notification of voting securities or asset acquisitions that meet certain size-of-transaction tests.[54]

1. *Exclusive Licenses*

The FTC Premerger Office views exclusive intellectual property licenses as asset acquisitions. A license will be considered exclusive if any aspect of the license is exclusive, for instance, if it is exclusive in a particular territory or for a particular use. On the other hand, a license will be deemed nonexclusive if the licensor retains the unrestricted right to use the licensed intellectual property or to license it to others.[55]

The FTC Premerger Notification Office has extended this position to field-of-use exclusivity, so that if a license grants exclusivity for specific uses or exclusive territories, it may be considered an acquisition of an asset. To be treated as an acquisition, a license must be exclusive even against the grantor. The grant of a nonexclusive license is not an acquisition of an asset, since the grantor retains the right to use the intellectual property and/or grant additional licenses. While termination

---

52. *See, e.g.*, Santa Fe-Pomeroy Inc. v. P&Z Co., 569 F.2d 1084, 1101-02 (9th Cir. 1978).
53. 15 U.S.C. § 18a. The HSR Act is § 7A of the Clayton Act.
54. *See* 15 U.S.C. § 18a(a).
55. ABA SECTION OF ANTITRUST LAW, PREMERGER NOTIFICATION PRACTICE MANUAL, Interpretation No. 49 (2d ed. 1991) [hereinafter PREMERGER NOTIFICATION PRACTICE MANUAL 2D].

rights or march-in rights are not sufficient to render a license nonexclusive, "the grant of marketing and distribution rights, even if granted on an exclusive basis, does not constitute the acquisition of an asset."[56]

2. Valuation

The FTC requires that if the gross amount of royalty payments under an exclusive intellectual property license that are expected to be paid over the life of a license may be reasonably estimated, then the gross amount of the future royalties must be used for the valuation determination, not discounted to present value. But if the amount of future royalties is "too speculative to estimate reasonably," the acquiring person's board of directors or its delegee must determine the current fair market value of a fully paid-up license in good faith, within 60 days prior to notification or 60 days prior to consummation if no filing is required.[57]

The size of the transaction may be based upon the aggregate amount of future royalties (not discounted to present value) over the term of the license or a good faith estimate of fair market value if future royalties are speculative.[58] The staff position is that where aggregate royalties are determined (e.g., by a lump sum payment), or where a specified minimum royalty is agreed to, the aggregate sum should be treated as the acquisition price. Future payments of "interest" may be disregarded if separately identified in the license, but the FTC staff will not permit an attempt to designate a portion of future royalties as "interest" if such an amount is not so identified. That is, interest is not included in the size-of-transaction test, but installment payments cannot be revalued to reflect their present worth. The result is that if an agreement says "licensee will

56. ABA SECTION OF ANTITRUST LAW, PREMERGER NOTIFICATION PRACTICE MANUAL, Interpretation No. 29 (3d ed. 2003) [hereinafter PREMERGER NOTIFICATION PRACTICE MANUAL 3D].

57. PREMERGER NOTIFICATION PRACTICE MANUAL 3D, *supra* note 56, Interpretation No. 91; *see also* FED. TRADE COMM'N, VALUATION OF TRANSACTIONS REPORTABLE UNDER THE HART-SCOTT-RODINO ACT, *available at* http://www.ftc.gov/bc/hsr/hsrvaluation.htm (taking the position that the "acquisition price" is "determined" if the amount of consideration, including contingent future payments "can be reasonably estimated" and noting that "anticipated future payments are included at face value and cannot be discounted to present value").

58. *See* PREMERGER NOTIFICATION PRACTICE MANUAL 2D, *supra* note 55, Interpretation No. 129.

pay licensor $3 million annual royalties for 18 years," the transaction is reportable, whereas, if the agreement says "licensee will pay licensor $2.5 million per year in royalties, and $500,000 per year in interest for 18 years," the acquisition is not reportable. The fair market value of the license will control if it is greater than the aggregate of future payments.

C. Technology and Innovation Markets

1. The DOJ/FTC Intellectual Property Guidelines

The *Intellectual Property Guidelines* distinguish three types of markets that may be affected by intellectual property licensing arrangements: "If an arrangement may adversely affect competition to develop new or improved goods or processes, the Agencies will analyze such an impact either as a separate competitive effect in relevant goods or technology markets, or as a competitive effect in a separate innovation market."[59] These concepts have had their greatest impact on merger enforcement.

Goods markets are comprised of goods or services and are the markets with which antitrust has been traditionally concerned, such as markets for pharmaceuticals, computer chips, or computer services.[60] Technology markets are markets in which companies compete in the licensing of intellectual property. The FTC and DOJ will analyze the competitive effects in technology markets when rights to intellectual property are marketed separately from the products in which they are used.[61]

Innovation markets, sometimes called research and development, or R&D markets, are markets in which firms compete in research and development. The *Intellectual Property Guidelines* explain:

A licensing arrangement may have competitive effects on innovation that cannot be adequately addressed through the analysis of goods or technology markets. For example, the arrangement may affect the development of goods that do not yet exist. Alternatively, the arrangement may affect the development of new or improved goods or

---

59.   INTELLECTUAL PROPERTY GUIDELINES,*su pra* note 10, § 3.2.3.
60.   *Id.* § 3.2.1.
61.   *Id.* § 3.2.2.

processes in geographic markets where there is no actual or likely potential competition in the relevant goods.[62]

Just as a goods market consists of goods or services and close substitutes for such goods or services, an innovation market consists of "the research and development directed to particular new or improved goods or processes, and the close substitutes for that research and development."[63] Significantly, the FTC and DOJ have represented that they will "delineate an innovation market only when the capabilities to engage in the relevant research and development can be associated with specialized assets or characteristics of specific firms. Such specialized assets most often include physical assets, experience, production capability, and intellectual property."[64] According to the *Guidelines*, the agencies will not pursue an innovation market analysis if it cannot reasonably identify the firms with the required capability and incentive to engage in R&D.

2. Technology Markets

There have not been many actions brought by the enforcement agencies alleging anticompetitive effects in technology markets. In one leading case involving technology markets, *Montedison S.p.A.*,[65] the FTC alleged that a proposed joint venture of Montedison and Royal Dutch/Shell would lessen competition in licensing of polypropylene technology and polypropylene catalyst technology. The two firms accounted for only a modest share of polypropylene production, but the technologies controlled by the firms accounted for over 80 percent of completed and projected capacity additions, pursuant to technology licenses. The combined firm would also account for over 70 percent of all polypropylene capacity projected and recently built.[66] The final consent order required Shell to divest all of its polypropylene assets including its interest in the polypropylene technology and catalyst licensing business.[67]

Before approving Dow Chemical's acquisition of Union Carbide Corp. in 2001, the FTC similarly required Dow to divest and license

62. *Id.* § 3.2.3 (internal citations omitted).
63. *Id.*
64. *Id.*
65. *In re* Montedison S.p.A., 119 F.T.C. 676 (1995).
66. *Id.* at 681-82.
67. *Id.* at 694-700.

intellectual property for the production of polyethylene used in plastic products such as trash bags, stretch film and sealable food pouches, to BP Amoco, its former partner in developing the technology.[68] As in *Montedison*, this matter involved allegations that the merging firms' control over production technology would lead to anticompetitive effects both in the licensing of technology and in the market for the product. The FTC alleged that postmerger, two firms (Dow and Exxon working with Union Carbide) would control more than 50 percent of polyethylene sales, essentially all commercialized catalyst technology, and reactor process technology used in approximately 75 percent of installed capacity in the United States and Canada.[69]

The FTC order in *Dow/Union Carbide* remedied the alleged anticompetitive effects by (1) allowing BP, which had been working with Dow, to develop and license catalysts without being subject to patent claims; and (2) enabling Exxon to develop and license catalysts and reactor process technology independently of Dow. By allowing BP to offer catalysts in connection with licenses of its reactor technology, the FTC order is intended to preserve the viability of that technology.

3. Innovation Markets

Since 1995, the federal enforcement agencies have brought a number of innovation market cases involving products ranging from computer software and security equipment to cancer drugs and intravascular ultrasound catheters.[70] The antitrust agencies articulate three distinct

---

68.   See *In re* Dow Chem. & Union Carbide Corp., FTC Dkt. No. C-3999 (2001) (Decision and Order) (Dow/Union Carbide), *available at* http://www.ftc.gov/os/2001/02/dowuniondo.pdf.
69.   See *id.* (Complaint).
70.   See, *e.g.*, *In re* Johnson & Johnson, Inc., FTC File No. 051-0050 (consent agreement accepted for public comment Nov. 2, 2005); *In re* Amgen Inc. & Immunex Corp., FTC Dkt. No. C-4053 (consent order issued Sept. 3, 2002); *In re* Dow Chem. & Union Carbide Corp., FTC Dkt. No. C-3999 (Mar. 15, 2001); *In re* Glaxo Wellcome plc, FTC Dkt. No. C-3990 (Jan. 26, 2001); *In re* Valspar Corp., FTC Dkt. No. C-3995 (Jan 26, 2001); *In re* Novartis AG, FTC Dkt. No. C-3979 (Dec 15, 2000); *In re* Pfizer Inc. and Warner-Lambert Co., FTC Dkt. No. C-3957 (June 19, 2000); United States v. Miller Indus., Civ. No. 00-0305 (D.D.C. complaint filed Feb. 17, 2000); MacDermid, Inc., FTC Dkt. No. C-3911 (Feb. 4, 2000); *In re* Hoechst AG and Rhone-Poulenc S.A., FTC Dkt. No. C-3919 (Jan 18, 2000); *In re* RHI AG, FTC File No. 991-0281 (consent agreement accepted for public comment Dec. 30, 1999); *In re* Precision Castparts

competitive concerns in their innovation market cases: first, whether the arrangement or acquisition will negatively affect the diversity of research and development tracks, and inhibit the development of a variety of new, better or cheaper products; second, whether the arrangement or acquisition will negatively affect the pace of research and development, thereby delaying better or cheaper products; and third, whether the arrangement or acquisition will harm competition in post-innovation goods markets. These cases, for the most part, have involved mergers to monopoly or near monopoly with weak competitors and unilateral theories of competitive harm.

The agencies' focus on unilateral rather than coordinated interaction theories of harm in innovation market cases is likely driven by the difficulty of collusive behavior with regard to R&D. While collusion in R&D cannot be rejected out of hand in all circumstances, it seems unlikely—particularly in dynamic markets—where innovation market concerns have been raised most often. Reaching terms of coordination on the direction or pace of R&D with its multiple dimensions seems difficult, other than through a market division or a decision not to conduct any R&D. Moreover, the incentive to cheat is high, given the rewards to successful innovation. The ability to cheat undetected is also

---

Corp., FTC Dkt. No. C-3904 (Dec. 17, 1999); United States v. AlliedSignal Inc., Civ. No. 99-02959 (D.D.C. complaint filed Nov. 8, 1999); United States v. Compuware Corp., Civ. No. 99-02884 (D.D.C complaint filed Oct. 29, 1999); *In re* SNIA S.p.A., FTC Dkt. No. C-3889 (July 28, 1999); *In re* Rohm and Haas Co., FTC Dkt. No. C-3883 (July 13, 1999); *In re* Zeneca Group plc, FTC Dkt. No. C-3880 (June 7, 1999); *In re* Medtronic, Inc., FTC Dkt. No. C-3879 (June 3, 1999); *In re* Merck & Co., FTC Dkt. No. C-3853 (Feb. 18, 1999); *In re* Medtronic, Inc., FTC Dkt. No. C-3842 (Dec. 21, 1998); United States v. Halliburton Co., Civ. No. 98-2340 (D.D.C. complaint filed Sept. 29. 1998); *In re* Roche Holding, 125 F.T.C. 919 (1998); S.C. Johnson & Son, 125 F.T.C. 753 (1998); United States v. Lockheed Martin Corp., Civ. No. 98-00731 (D.D.C. complaint filed March 23, 1998); *In re* Automatic Data Processing, 124 F.T.C. 456 (1997); *In re* Cadence Design Sys., 124 F.T.C. 131 (1997); *In re* Mahle GmbH, 123 F.T.C. 1431 (1997); *In re* Baxter Int'l, 123 F.T.C. 947 (1997); *In re* Ciba-Geigy Ltd., 123 F.T.C. 842 (1997); *In re* Upjohn Co., 121 F.T.C. 44 (1996); *In re* Hoechst AG, 120 F.T.C. 1010 (1995); *In re* Glaxo plc, 119 F.T.C. 815 (1995); *In re* Montedison S.p.A., 119 F.T.C. 676 (1995); *In re* Sensormatic Elecs., 119 F.T.C 520 (1995); *In re* Wright Med. Tech., 119 F.T.C. 344 (1995); *In re* Boston Sci., 119 F.T.C. 344 (1995); *In re* Am. Home Prods., 119 F.T.C. 217 (1995).

high since innovation is often conducted in secret, at least in the absence of facilitating devices such as licenses serving as reporting mechanisms.[71] This is especially true of firms without any revenue stream from a current product on the market, such as firms developing new drugs, and in "winner take all" races or situations where there are substantial "first-mover" advantages. Senior DOJ officials have in fact noted, "though it is possible to have coordinated effects, [they] most often expect to see some type of unilateral effect."[72]

Sometimes cited as a precursor to innovation market theory, in 1990, the FTC challenged Roche Holding's investment in Genentech as likely to lessen competition in research and development in various biotech products.[73] In two markets, one of the firms was the market leader with a dominant market share; in the other market, the firms were developing alternative patented designs. In a third market, the firms were the most advanced in development and held significant patents and patent applications, but there was no existing product, creating, what at the time was dubbed, a "double potential competition" case.

Concrete proof that a merger in a potential competition case could inhibit an R&D market came in 1993 with a document in the DOJ's investigation of a proposed acquisition by ZF Friedrichshafen AG of General Motors' Allison transmission business. This investigation revealed that ZF believed that it could either compete with GM in the development of next generation transmissions or acquire GM's Allison business. The DOJ alleged that GM and ZF, which were actual or potential competitors in only a few small U.S. markets, were "direct

71. *See* HORIZONTAL MERGER GUIDELINES,*su pra* note 9, § 2.1
72. Constance K. Robinson, Leap-Frog and other Forms of Innovation: Protecting the Future for High-Tech and Emerging Industries Through Merger Enforcement, Before the American Bar Association (June 10, 1999), available at http://www.usdoj.gov/atr/public/speeches/2482.pdf. Two cases alleging innovation markets appear to suggest that there will be a reduction in innovation based on coordinated interaction. In both cases, the FTC challenged a merger involving two of three major competitors currently in a medical device market, manufacturing heart-lung machines in one case and defibrillators in the other. In each case, the FTC focused primarily on the likelihood of collusion on price. The FTC did, however, also allege that each merger would increase the likelihood that innovation would be reduced. *See In re* SNIA S.p.A., FTC Docket. No. C-3889 (July 28, 1999); Medtronic, Inc., FTC Docket No. C-3842 (Dec. 21, 1998).
73. *In re* Roche Holding, 119 F.T.C. 676 (1990)

horizontal competitors in technological innovation for the design, development, and production of medium and heavy automatic transmissions for commercial and military vehicles."[74] According to the DOJ, ZF's introduction of a technologically superior product spurred the Allison division to develop a new line of substantially improved transmissions. The DOJ alleged that ZF recognized it had to make a strong competitive response.[75]

The complaint alleged that the competition between GM and ZF resulted in "improved products, new products, lower costs of manufacture, and lower prices to consumers."[76] Significantly, product improvements benefited all customers, whether or not the transmissions were sold in markets where the firms were actual or potential competitors. The DOJ alleged, therefore, that the merger would lessen competition in a market for worldwide technological innovation in the design, development, and production of transmissions. It alleged that "under any measure, the proposed transaction would reduce the number of competitors in the Innovation Market from three to two," and alleged that the only other competitor was "less effective" because of its narrow focus on bus transmissions.[77] After the complaint was filed, the parties abandoned the transaction.

In its challenge to the merger of pharmaceutical companies Ciba-Geigy Ltd. and Sandoz Ltd. into Novartis AG, the FTC alleged the transaction would combine the two leaders in the field of gene therapy.[78] The FTC challenged the merger's effect on gene therapy R&D in four specific products. But the FTC also alleged markets of gene therapy technology and research and development, focusing broadly on the therapeutic technique, recognizing that no product had been approved or was expected to be approved for several years. In *Ciba/Sandoz*, the FTC feared a reduction in innovation due to the combination of the merging parties' patent estates. To resolve the FTC's concern, the parties entered

---

74.   United States v. Gen. Motors, Civ. No. 93-530 (D. Del. Nov. 16, 1993) (Complaint ¶ 35).
75.   The DOJ quoted one ZF document: "There are only two ways to counter the attack of Ally [Allison] against the European market and the rest of the world: a) Purchase Ally and b) Rethink and reschedule the Ecomat strategy in respect to cost and product line quickly and massively." *Id.* ¶ 37.
76.   *Id.* ¶ 35.
77.   *Id.* ¶ 43.
78.   *In re* Ciba-Geigy Ltd., 123 F.T.C. 842 (1997) (Ciba/Sandoz).

into a consent order agreeing to license their gene therapy patents to third parties at commercially reasonable rates.[79]

In *Ciba/Sandoz*, the FTC specifically alleged that the merging firms controlled intellectual property necessary to commercialize gene therapy products as well as other specialized assets—technological, manufacturing, clinical and regulatory know-how and manufacturing capability. By combining the two leaders, the FTC alleged that the merger was likely to lead to "a reduction in, delay of, or redirection of research and development tracks."[80]   Other firms were conducting research, but those firms expected to obtain licenses from or joint venture with either Ciba or Sandoz, or expected to challenge the validity of their intellectual property. The FTC claimed that the merged firm would have less of an incentive to license intellectual property rights or to collaborate with other companies. The agency also alleged that the merger would therefore "heighten barriers to entry by combining portfolios of patents and patent applications of uncertain breadth and validity, requiring potential entrants to invent around or declare invalid a greater array of patents"—creating a so-called "killer patent portfolio."[81]

The FTC's complaint against the merger of Hoechst AG and Rhone-Poulenc S.A. to form Aventis S.A. similarly insisted upon divestiture to resolve concerns from the combination of a firm with an approved drug and its closest R&D competitor. The FTC alleged a market of research, development, manufacture and sale of direct thrombin inhibitors, for the treatment of blood clotting diseases. [82]   According to the Commission's complaint, Hoechst was the only firm with FDA approval to sell such a product and Rhone-Poulenc was the only firm in the final stages of developing such a product.[83]   The agency's Analysis to Aid Public Comment makes clear that the firms were "each other's closest competitors" in the market.[84]   Thus, the FTC alleged the merger would "reduce innovation competition, among researchers and developers of direct thrombin inhibitor products, including the reduction in, delay of or redirection of research and development projects," and would increase

---

79.   For a more detailed discussion of this case, see *supra* Section C.3.
80.   *Ciba/Sandoz*, 123 F.T.C. at 851.
81.   *Id.* at 852.
82.   *In re* Hoechst AG & Rhone-Poulenc S.A., FTC Dkt. No. C-3919 (Jan. 18, 2000) (Complaint ¶ 5) (*Hoechst/Rhone-Poulenc*).
83.   *Id.* ¶ 9.
84.   *In re* Hoechst AG, 64 Fed. Reg. 71,141, 71,142 (Dec. 20, 1999) (Analysis to Aid Public Comment).

the merged firm's ability "to exercise market power unilaterally."[85]   As in *Ciba/Sandoz*, the FTC also alleged that the merger would increase barriers to entry "by combining portfolios of patents and patent applications."[86]

The most recent instance of the government alleging anticompetitive effects in innovation markets was the FTC's investigation of Genzyme's completed acquisition of Novazyme. In *Genzyme/Novazyme*, the FTC investigated whether anticompetitive effects would result in the research and development for the treatment of a rare disease known as Pompe.[87] At the time of the acquisition, Genzyme and Novazyme were the only two firms attempting to develop a treatment for Pompe.   After investigating for over two years, the Commission voted in 2004 to not file an administrative complaint and close its investigation.[88]

The Commissioners disagreed on the appropriate analytical framework to be used in assessing the competitive effects of the merger, and specifically differed on whether there should be a presumption of anticompetitive effect.   Chairman Muris recognized that the "Commission properly has been cautious in using innovation market analysis" because "economic theory and empirical investigations have not established a general causal relationship between innovation and

---

85.   *In re Hoechst/Rhone-Poulenc*, FTC Dkt. No. C-3919 (Complaint ¶ 16).

86.   *Id.*

87.   Because Pompe is a rare disease affecting less than 200,000 patients in the United States, R&D efforts to treat the disease is covered by the Orphan Drug Act of 1983. 21 U.S.C. §§ 360aa-ee. To incentivize the firms to develop drugs that treat rare diseases, such as Pompe, the Act grants any firm that develops a drug that treats the disease seven years of marketing exclusivity, in which the Food and Drug Administration will not approve another company's application to approve the "same drug" for seven years after the firm's drug is approved. *See* 21 U.S.C. § 360cc.

88.   By a 3-1-1 vote, the Commission decided to close the investigation. Chairman Muris issued a statement supporting closure of the investtigation. Although Commissioners Leary and Swindell joined Muris in voting to close the investigation, they did not join his statement and did write separately. Commissioner Thompson voted against closing the investigation and issued a dissenting statement. Because Commissioner Jones Harbour was appointed to the Commission during the latter stages of the investigation, she did not participate in the vote, but issued a statement on innovation markets. *See* FTC Press Release, FTC Closes its Investigation of Genzyme Corporation's 2001 Acquisition of Novazyme Pharmaceuticals, Inc. (Jan. 13, 2004), available at http://www.ftc.gov/opa/2004/01/genzyme.htm.

competition."[89] "A careful, intense factual investigation is necessary," Chairman Muris stated, "to distinguish between procompetitive and anticompetitive combinations of innovation efforts."[90] Chairman Muris explained:

> [N]either economic theory or empirical research supports an inference regarding the merger's likely effect on innovation (and hence patient welfare) based simply on observing how the merger changed the number of independent R&D programs. Rather, one must examine whether the merged firm was likely to have a reduced incentive to invest in R&D, and also whether it was likely to have the ability to conduct R&D more successfully.[91]

Chairman Muris found that the merger did not diminish the speed by which the firms would have innovated absent the merger because the evidence indicated that the firms were not in a "race to innovate."[92] Chairman Muris also found no evidence to support the theory that as a result of the merger Genzyme would delay (or even abandon) the Novazyme Pompe program if its Pompe program proved unsuccessful.[93]

In his dissenting statement, Commissioner Thompson stated that the "Genzyme / Novazyme merger constitutes a consummated merger to monopoly in the research and development of a highly specialized drug, and entry of a new market participant is not likely to replace the innovation competition eliminated by the merger."[94] Based on his review of the facts, "this merger to monopoly should be presumed anticompetitive under the *Horizontal Merger Guidelines*."[95] Commissioner Thompson noted that no such evidence was offered by Genzyme to rebut the presumption of anticompetitive effect, and

---

89.   Statement of Chairman Timothy J. Muris in the matter of Genzyme Corporation/Novazyme Pharmaceuticals, Inc., at 2-3 (citing in part FTC Staff Report, Anticipating the 21st Century: Competition Policy in the New High-Tech, Global Marketplace (May 1996)), available at http://www.ftc.gov/os/2004/01/murisgenzymestmt.pdf.
90.   *Id.* at 3 (internal citations omitted).
91.   *Id.*
92.   *Id.* at 11-12.
93.   *Id.* at 13-15.
94.   Statement of Commissioner Mozelle W. Thompson, Genzyme's Corporation's Acquisition of Novazyme Pharmaceuticals Inc., at 1, *available at* http://www.ftc.gov/os/2004/01/thompsongenzymestmt.pdf.
95.   *Id.* at 3.

therefore, a challenge by the Commission was warranted.[96]   He explained, "I see no compelling reason why innovation mergers should be exempt from the *Horizontal Merger Guidelines* or the presumption of anticompetitive effects for mergers to monopoly and other mergers as discussed therein."[97]

Although she did not participate in the vote, Commissioner Harbour separately stated, "Although one may question whether we have yet reached the point where a general presumption of anticompetitive effects in highly concentrated innovation markets is applicable, in the extreme case of a merger to monopoly that eliminates all competition and diversity in the innovation market, such a presumption seems appropriate."[98]

D. Acquisitions of Intellectual Property

1. *Horizontal versus Vertical Characterizations*

Horizontal acquisitions between a licensor and a licensee occur when the licensor and licensee "would have been actual or likely potential competitors in a relevant market in the absence of the license."[99]   A horizontal relationship between a licensor and a licensee is not per se anticompetitive.[100]   As the *Intellectual Property Guidelines* make clear, "In the vast majority of cases, restraints in intellectual property licensing arrangements are evaluated under the rule of reason."[101]

Like horizontal relationships, vertical relationships are also primarily analyzed under the rule of reason.[102]   "A licensing arrangement has a vertical component when it affects activities that are in a complementary relationship, as is typically the case in a licensing arrangement."[103]   As in analyses of acquisitions of other assets, vertical acquisitions of

---

96.   *Id.* at 1.

97.   *Id.* at 3.

98.   Statement of Commissioner Pamela Jones Harbour, Genzyme's Corporation's Acquisition of Novazyme Pharmaceuticals Inc., at 3, available at http://www.ftc.gov/os/2004/01/harbourgenzymestmt.pdf.

99.   INTELLECTUAL PROPERTY GUIDELINES, *su pra* note 10, § 3.3.

100. *Id.*

101. *Id.* § 3.4.

102. *Id.* § 3.4.

103. *Id.*

432   *Intellectual Property and Antitrust Handbook*

intellectual property will be examined for its affect on downstream markets.[104]

Another initial characterization that can have a significant effect on the analysis of a license under the *Intellectual Property Guidelines* is whether a license is exclusive or nonexclusive. An exclusive license may raise antitrust concern, according to the *Guidelines*, if licensees or the licensor and licensees are in a horizontal relationship. On the other hand, a nonexclusive license that does not restrain the competitive conduct of the parties involved generally does not present antitrust concerns. This applies even if the parties to the license are in a horizontal relationship, because the nonexclusive license normally does not diminish competition that would occur in its absence.[105]

2. The "Killer Patent Portfolio"

Of particular note when considering the affects on markets when intellectual property portfolios are merged is the creation of a "killer patent portfolio." As discussed earlier, this concept first came to light in 1975 when the FTC filed a complaint alleging that Xerox had monopolized the market for plain paper office copies. The complaint focused on Xerox's accumulation of a so-called "killer patent portfolio"[106] by both internal development and acquisition, as well as

---

104. *Id.* § 3.3.
105. *Id.* § 4.1.2.
106. According to Professor F.M. Scherer, then chief economist at the FTC, the heart and soul of the case was the "killer patent portfolio":

> [Xerox] had somewhere between 1,000 and 2,000 patents in the mid-1970's. They were adding to their portfolio at a rate of several hundred patents a year. They had the technology completely encircled, and a consideration that prompted our decision to intervene with compulsory licensing was that the 914 Copier was introduced in 1959. The case came for a decision in 1975. They had enjoyed 16 years of a spectacular patent monopoly. How long should a monopoly last? We intervened because we thought essentially that 17 years was what the law had in mind, 17 years was enough.... [T]he essence of the case was, frankly, social engineering. It was time to break open this monopoly and create competition.... The theory about acquisition and some of the price discrimination practices, and so forth, was fluff. The center of the case was the extension over time of the monopoly through patent accumulation.

unlawful marketing practices including alleged tying, exclusive dealing, price discrimination and restrictive licensing agreements.[107]   Xerox agreed to settle the matter by entering into a consent order requiring it to abandon the challenged marketing practices and to license its patents for a modest royalty.[108]

This case highlights the dilemma at the core of traditional Section 2 law: Should the antitrust laws prohibit or limit lawfully acquired monopolies such as those acquired by superior efficiency or technology? The harmful effects of these legitimately acquired monopolies are the same as the effects of monopolies achieved through unlawful conduct. But the antitrust laws recognize that punishing legitimately acquired monopolies can have an even greater anticompetitive effect by creating a disincentive for successful companies to compete aggressively.[109] So the antitrust laws tolerate, and even accept, lawfully acquired monopolies which do not engage in unlawful exclusionary conduct.   And while monopolies protected by patents (even lawfully acquired killer patent portfolios) may be more persistent, entrenched, and long-lived than most, there appears to be no principled reason for treating them differently.

The issue of a killer patent portfolio resurfaced at the FTC 25 years later, in the Ciba-Geigy merger with Sandoz discussed above.[110] Like the copier technology involved in the *SCM v. Xerox* case, gene therapy technology was in its early development stage and actual gene therapy products were years away from the marketplace. The FTC alleged that the acquisition would impede the development of products in the gene therapy innovation market. The FTC feared the creation of a killer patent portfolio in gene therapy by combining the merging parties' patent estates. To resolve the FTC's concern, the parties entered into a consent order agreeing to license their gene therapy patents to third parties at commercially reasonable rates.[111]

Roundtable Discussion on Competition Policy, Intellectual Property and Innovation Markets, in COMPETITION POLICY AND INTELLECTUAL PROPERTY RIGHTS IN THE KNOWLEDGE BASED ECONOMY 448-9 (R. Anderson & N. Gallini eds., 1998).

107. *In re* Xerox Corp., 86 F.T.C. 364 (1975).
108. *Id.*
109. *See, e.g.*, United States v. Aluminum Co. of Am., 148 F.2d 416, 430 (2d Cir. 1945); Berkey Photo, Inc. v. Eastman Kodak Co., 603 F.2d 263, 273 (2d Cir. 1979).
110. *Ciba-Geigy Ltd.*, *supra* note 78.
111. For a more detailed discussion of this case, see *supra* Section C.3.

As seen in the *Xerox* and *Ciba-Geigy* enforcement actions, a company's development and/or acquisition of a killer patent portfolio may be anticompetitive under different circumstances. First, a company may seek to maintain its monopoly over a product by acquiring patents on potential substitute products. This conduct enables the monopolist to preserve its monopoly by foreclosing future competition. A patent portfolio may also give rise to anticompetitive concern when a company acquires patents from another party that controls the only other way to implement a product's feature. Such an acquisition allows a company to "effectively extract all or most of the rents from the entire relevant market for the combined product produced by all the complementary features."[112]

E. Intellectual Property as a *General Dynamics* or Failing Firm Defense

1. *General Dynamics Defense*

Parties involved in mergers and acquisitions have relied upon the Supreme Court's precedent in *United States v. General Dynamics Corp.* to rebut presumptions relating to market shares and market concentration.[113] In *General Dynamics*, the DOJ challenged a merger between two coal producers, alleging that the transaction would result in a lessening of competition. The DOJ relied upon historical production statistics to assert that anticompetitive effects would likely result from the merger because the market would be concentrated. The parties argued in response that prior market shares were not representative of current or future market concentration and in fact may have overstated it. The Supreme Court rejected the DOJ's assertion, holding that one of the coal companies that lacked coal reserves had little competitive significance despite a large market share based on sales.[114] The Supreme Court found that "[e]vidence of past production does not, as a matter of logic, necessarily give a proper picture of a company's future ability to compete."[115]

Based on the *General Dynamics* precedent, merging parties have attacked assertions of high market concentration by arguing that

---

112. Willard K. Tom, *The 1975 Xerox Consent Decree: Ancient Artifacts and Current Tensions*, 68 ANTITRUST L.J. 967, 984 (2001).
113. United States v. Gen. Dynamics Corp., 415 U.S. 486 (1974).
114. *Id.* at 501.
115. *Id.*

historical market shares overstate future competitive significance. In *FTC v. National Tea Co.*, for example, the FTC alleged that a merger between two grocery store chains would substantially lessen competition.[116] Applying *General Dynamics*, the Eighth Circuit found that because one of the grocery store chains was experiencing distressed operations and performance, and its departure from the relevant market was imminent, present market shares did not accurately represent the firm's competitive significance.[117]

The opposite argument, however, is also asserted against proposed transactions in which market concentration is relatively weak. These arguments, so called reverse-*General Dynamics* cases, contend that historical market shares underestimate the future significance of competitors. For example, a company may not currently be significant in the market based on historical market shares, but may be quite significant in the future because of intellectual property it may own or control or have in development. Such intellectual property, while not having an immediate impact on competition in the relevant market, may be proven to enhance the future competitive significance of an otherwise insignificant party. Thus, when examining the competitive effects of proposed transaction, the government or parties to a merger may rely on *General Dynamics* to assert that intellectual property held by the merging parties over- or understate the parties' competitive significance in a relevant market.

For example, one may argue that a firm likely to lose an intellectual property infringement suit may lack the ability to compete in the future. This argument was made by the parties in the FTC's challenge to Boston Scientific's acquisition of Cardiovascular Imaging Systems, Inc. ("CVIS"). In January 1995, the FTC sued to block the acquisition, alleging that the two firms produced catheters used in the diagnosis and treatment of cardiovascular disease and that, if consummated, the transaction would substantially lessen competition.[118] The Boston Scientific-CVIS merger resulted, in part, to resolve ongoing patent infringement litigation between the companies.[119]

---

116. FTC v. Nat'l Tea Co., 603 F.2d 694 (8th Cir. 1979).
117. *Id.* at 700. The FTC argued that Nat'l Tea was attempting to establish a failing company defense, but the court rejected this argument. *Id.* at 700 n.8.
118. FTC v. Boston Sci., No. 95-00198 (D.D.C. Jan. 27, 1995) (Complaint ¶ 10).
119. FTC v. Boston Sci., No. 95-00198 (D.D.C. Jan. 27, 1995) (Mem. of P. &A. in Supp. of the FTC's Mot. for Prelim. Inj. at 40).

In defense of the merger, the parties argued that because CVIS was likely to prevail in the patent litigation against Boston Scientific, Boston Scientific's competitive position in the catheter market would be significantly diminished.[120] The FTC rejected this argument, noting that while Boston Scientific made that argument to the FTC, it had argued in the patent litigation that CVIS' patents were invalid and that CVIS was infringing one of Boston Scientific's patents.[121] FTC Complaint Counsel argued that "[t]he patent litigation [was] in its early states and the ultimate outcome [was] far from certain."[122] It then concluded that "there [was] no reason that the litigation must end in an adjudicated decision that would require Boston Scientific to exit the market."[123] Rather than forcing Boston Scientific to exit, the court hearing the patent suit could have found CVIS' patents invalid, or the parties might have reached a negotiated cross-license.[124]

2. Failing Company and Weakened Firm Defenses

The "failing company defense" is a judicially created defense to otherwise unlawful combinations under the Clayton Act. The Supreme Court first acknowledged the defense in *International Shoe Co. v. FTC*.[125] In holding that a merger between two shoe manufacturers would not substantially lessen competition under Section 7 of the Clayton Act, the Court stated that the Act was not violated because the acquired manufacturer faced "financial ruin."[126] The Court reasoned that such a defense should be available because of the social consequences of business failure (i.e., its affect on employees, shareholders, creditors, etc.) and the fact the anticompetitive effects would be less if acquired by a competitor than if the assets of the failing company exited the market altogether.[127]

The defense is expressly recognized in the *Merger Guidelines*.[128] The *Guidelines* provide that "a merger is not likely to create or enhance market power or to facilitate its exercise, if imminent failure . . . of one

---

120. *Id.*
121. *Id.*
122. *Id.*
123. *Id.*
124. *Id.*
125. Int'l Shoe Co. v. FTC, 280 U.S. 291 (1930).
126. *Id.* at 302-03.
127. *Id.* at 302.
128. *See* HORIZONTAL MERGER GUIDELINES, *su pra* note 9, § 5.0.

of the merging firms would cause the assets of that firm to exit the relevant market. In such circumstances, post-merger performance in the relevant market may be no worse than market performance had the merger been blocked and the assets left the market."[129]

The failing firm defense has not been yet applied in a reported merger involving intellectual property. In innovation markets, the defense would seem to apply as it does in goods markets. If a firm is failing, its R&D efforts are likely hindered. But in technology markets, intellectual property may still impact competition though its holder is failing.

F. Intellectual Property as a Barrier to Entry

Parties to a merger will often argue that the likely entry of new participants in the relevant market will reduce the likelihood that the merged firm will exercise market power or facilitate coordinated interaction. Barriers to entry are conditions in the marketplace that make entry into the relevant market more difficult or less likely, thereby reducing the likelihood that new firms will enter the market and discipline the merged firm that increases price or reduces output.

In *United States v. Baker Hughes Inc.*,[130] the DOJ appealed a district court's denial of a preliminary injunction against a merger based, in part, on the likelihood of actual and potential entry. On appeal to the D.C. Circuit, the DOJ argued that the parties must prove that entry was likely to be "quick and effective" in order to rebut the presumption of illegality from high market concentration.[131] The D.C. Circuit rejected the DOJ's proposed entry standard, stating that it imposed a burden of proof not found in, or supported by, case law or in the government's merger guidelines at the time.[132] The court also found the DOJ's standard too onerous because it would require defendants to prove that entry "will occur" when such evidence is "rarely available."[133] The DOJ's standard, moreover, ignored the fact that even the threat of entry by a firm that never enters the market can still stimulate competition in a concentrated market.[134]

---

129. *Id.*
130. United States v. Baker Hughes Inc., 908 F.2d 981 (D.C. Cir. 1990).
131. *Id.* at 987.
132. *Id.*
133. *Id.*
134. *Id.* at 988.

The *Merger Guidelines* provide that "[a] merger is not likely to create or enhance market power or to facilitate its exercise, if entry into the market is so easy that market participants, after the merger, either collectively or unilaterally could not profitably maintain a price increase above premerger levels."[135] Parties seeking to defend transactions on the grounds that entry will occur if prices are raised (or output restricted) after the merger is consummated must demonstrate that entry by other firms would be "timely, likely, and sufficient" to counteract the price increase (or output restraint).[136]

For the government to conclude that entry will deter postmerger anticompetitive effects, the parties must prove that entry: (1) will have a significant impact on price in the relevant market within two years from initial planning;[137] (2) will be profitable for firms at premerger prices;[138] and (3) will cause prices to fall to premerger levels.[139]

Intellectual property is an example of an entry barrier that can limit new firms from entering a particular market, increasing the likelihood of postmerger anticompetitive effects. Protection from intellectual property can be a firm's source of market power, particularly in high technology industries characterized by rapid innovation. In the DOJ's investigation of Borland International's acquisition of Ashton-Tate Corp., for example, the transaction combined the two largest suppliers of relational database management systems (RDBMS) software for personal computers, creating a combined market share of 60 percent.[140] The remainder of the market was comprised of smaller firms that primarily developed and marketed software compatible with Ashton-Tate's proprietary RDBMS software. In addition to a market structure with high concentration, Ashton-Tate was involved in ongoing copyright infringement litigation against one of its biggest RDBMS rivals. The DOJ alleged that the merger would result in a substantial increase in Borland's market power, in part, because Borland would control the intellectual property rights in RDBMS technology.[141] The parties resolved the DOJ's concerns by

135. *See* HORIZONTAL MERGER GUIDELINES, *supra* note 9, § 3.0
136. *See id.*
137. *Id.* § 3.2.
138. *Id.* § 3.3.
139. *Id.* § 3.4.
140. United States v. Borland Int'l, 56 Fed. Reg. 56,096, 56,098-99 (Oct. 31, 1991) (Competitive Impact Statement); *see also* United States v. Borland Int'l, 1992-1 Trade Cas. (CCH) ¶ 69,774 (N.D. Cal. 1992) (final judgment).
141. *Borland Int'l*, 56 Fed. Reg. at 56,098-99.

entering into a consent decree, requiring Borland to not enforce Ashton-Tate's intellectual property rights and settle the copyright infringement litigation, in an attempt to preserve competition in RDBMS software.[142]

G. Intellectual Property Combinations as an Efficiency

Efficiencies can play an important role in analyzing the competitive effects of mergers and acquisitions. Mergers can be efficient when they achieve cost savings for customers or consumers by combining and utilizing resources more cost-effectively. Efficiencies can be created, for example, when merging firms integrate their research and development resources or intellectual property portfolios to produce a superior product or increase the dissemination of new technology.

The *Merger Guidelines* were revised in 1997 to expressly include efficiencies in the competitive effects analysis of mergers and acquisitions. The *Merger Guidelines* recognize that "mergers have the potential to generate significant efficiencies by permitting a better utilization of existing assets, enabling the combined firm to achieve lower costs in producing a given quantity and quality than either firm could have achieved without the proposed transaction. Indeed, the primary benefit of mergers to the economy is their potential to generate such efficiencies."[143] Not all efficiencies are treated alike, however; the analysis under the *Merger Guidelines* only considers those efficiencies that are specific to the merger and that are verifiable.[144] Although not a defense to otherwise anticompetitive combinations, efficiencies are relevant to the extent they decrease the likelihood of postmerger coordinated interaction or unilateral exercises of market power.[145]

Efficiency arguments in support of a transaction may be difficult to prove in court. In *FTC v. H.J. Heinz Co.*,[146] for example, the FTC challenged the merger of Heinz and Beech-Nut, the second and third largest manufacturers of baby foods, in a market that was dominated by Gerber with an approximate 65 percent share. The parties argued that although the market was concentrated, the transaction would result in efficiencies that would reduce production costs and consequently place the merged firm in a better position to compete against Gerber.[147] The

---

142. *Id.* at 56,100-01.
143. HORIZONTAL MERGER GUIDELINES, *supra* note 9, § 4.
144. *Id.*
145. *Id.*
146. FTC v. H.J. Heinz Co., 246 F.3d 708, 711 (D.C. Cir. 2001).
147. *Id.* at 720-22.

D.C. Circuit rejected these efficiency arguments and remanded for entry of a preliminary injunction.   It stated that efficiencies could be a "defense" under Section 7 of the Clayton Act, but they would have to be "extraordinary" to rebut the government's proof of anticompetitive effects in a concentrated relevant market.[148]   The court also said that to be credited, the asserted efficiencies must be merger-specific, which the parties were unable to establish in this case.[149]

The Eleventh Circuit also found the merging parties' efficiency claims to be insufficient to rebut the government's prima facie case in *FTC v. University Health, Inc.*[150]   In this case, the court acknowledged that "in certain circumstances ... a defendant may rebut the government's prima facie case with evidence showing that the intended merger would create significant efficiencies in the relevant market."[151]   In asserting arguments that the transaction would generate efficiencies, the court held that the defendants "must demonstrate that the intended acquisition would result in significant economies and that these economies ultimately would benefit competition and, hence, consumers."[152]   The Eleventh Circuit ultimately found the parties' efficiency arguments to be too speculative and unsubstantiated to rebut the presumption of illegality based on high market concentration.[153]

Courts have also considered the standard of proof required to establish efficiency arguments in defense of a transaction. In *FTC v. Staples, Inc.*,[154] for example, the court rejected a clear and convincing standard, stating "the Court [does not] believe that the defendants must prove their efficiencies by 'clear and convincing evidence' in order for those efficiencies to be considered by the Court. That would saddle Section 7 defendants with the nearly impossible task of rebutting a possibility with certainty."[155] To rebut the government's case, the court stated that the defendants "must simply ... show[ ] that the Commission's evidence gives an inaccurate prediction of the proposed acquisition's probable effect."[156] Other courts held prior to *Staples* and the 1997 revisions to the *Merger Guidelines* that a clear and convincing

148.   *Id.* at 720.
149.   *Id.* at 721-22.
150.   FTC v. Univ. Health, 938 F.2d 1206 (11th Cir. 1991).
151.   *Id.* at 1222.
152.   *Id.* at 1223.
153.   *Id.* at 1223-24.
154.   FTC v. Staples, Inc., 970 F. Supp 1066 (D.D.C. 1997).
155.   *Id.* at 1089.
156.   *Id.*

standard was applicable to proof of efficiency claims from a proposed transaction.[157]

H. Licensing of Intellectual Property as a Remedy

Various remedies are available to resolve anticompetitive concerns resulting from a proposed transaction. One such remedy is to require the merging parties to sell off, or divest, certain assets to a third party in order to mitigate anticompetitive effects and preserve competition. Intellectual property is increasingly an asset that is required to be divested through means of an exclusive or sole license to remedy anticompetitive transactions. Many mergers and acquisitions, for example, in the pharmaceutical and software industries that raise anticompetitive concern are resolved through divestiture of intellectual property.

It is important, in this context, to distinguish between the types of licenses that can be required to divest intellectual property. A divestiture under an exclusive license authorizes the licensee, and only the licensee, to use the intellectual property rights transferred. An exclusive license is truly a divestiture because the merging parties no longer retain the right to use the intellectual property. Some divestitures, by contrast, require the parties to enter into a sole license with a third party, which transfers the intellectual property to the third party while permitting the merging parties to retain the right to also use the intellectual property. A divestiture of intellectual property under a nonexclusive license authorizes the third party to use the intellectual property, while also allowing the merging firms to license the intellectual property to others. Sole and nonexclusive licenses enable the third party to overcome a barrier to entry in the relevant market rather than seek to divest the merging parties of a competitive significant asset.

Some divestitures require the merging parties to license both of the parties' technologies. In Boston Scientific's acquisition of CVIS,[158] for example, the FTC alleged that the acquisition would combine the market leaders in the development, manufacturing, and marketing of IVUS catheters, resulting in a share of over 80% of the U.S. market.[159] To resolve the FTC's concerns, Boston Scientific agreed to license its and

---

157. *See, e.g.*, United States v. Rockford Mem'l Corp., 717 F. Supp. 1251, 1289 (N.D. Ill. 1989).
158. *See infra* Section E.1.
159. FTC v. Boston Sci., No. 95-00198 (D.D.C. Jan. 27, 1995) (Complaint ¶ 11).

CVIS' IVUS catheter technology to a third party, Hewlett-Packard Company.[160] The license granted to HP was nonexclusive and provided HP the right to exclusively sublicense the IVUS technology.[161] The FTC order stated that the purpose of the license was to "create an independent competitor in the development, production and sale of IVUS Catheters and to remedy the lessening of competition resulting from the [acquisition]."[162]

Other divestitures require the acquiring company to divest intellectual property owned or controlled by only one of the parties. In *Hoechst/Rhone-Poulenc*,[163] for example, the FTC alleged that the merger would lead to anticompetitive effects in the market for thrombin inhibitors, which are used to treat blood clotting diseases. The agency alleged that Hoechst was the only manufacturer of the inhibitors in the U.S., and Rhone-Poulenc was in the final development stage for its own inhibitor. To preserve competition in the research, development, and manufacturing of thrombin inhibitors, the FTC's consent order required the parties to transfer all of the intellectual property rights relating to Rhone-Poulenc's inhibitor in development to Novartis Pharma AG.[164]

160. *In re* Boston Scientific, 119 F.T.C. 549, 557-58 (1995).
161. *Id.*
162. *Id.* at 557.
163. *Hoechst/Rhone-Poulenc*, FTC Dkt. No. C-3919 (Complaint ¶¶ 9, 10).
164. *Id.* (Decision & Order at 7-8).

CHAPTER VIII

INTELLECTUAL PROPERTY ANTITRUST ISSUES IN LITIGATION

Litigation of intellectual property antitrust cases raises a number of unique issues. Due to the jurisdiction of the United States Court of Appeals for the Federal Circuit over certain types of patent claims, appellate jurisdiction and choice of law in intellectual property antitrust cases are often difficult issues. This chapter details the history, jurisdiction, and scope of Federal Circuit jurisdiction, and explores the difficult choice of law questions facing the Federal Circuit when adjudicating non-patent matters, such as antitrust claims. It also reviews choice of law issues raised when regional circuits and district courts adjudicate patent matters that may involve antitrust issues. Finally, this chapter discusses procedural issues that arise in intellectual property antitrust litigation, including when counterclaims are compulsory, the possibility of bifurcating discovery and trial, and available remedies.

A. Jurisdiction and Choice of Law in Intellectual Property Antitrust Disputes

The Federal Circuit was established in 1982 to create uniformity in patent law. Accordingly, the Federal Circuit applies its own precedent to patent law claims. However, the Federal Circuit's jurisdiction over non-patent claims, as well as the law applied to those claims, is not as clear. In the years following the creation of the Federal Circuit, the Supreme Court and Federal Circuit issued several opinions that delineated the Federal Circuit's jurisdiction. More recently, the Federal Circuit has clarified whether its own precedent, or that of the regional circuits, should govern its consideration of non-patent claims. At the same time, regional circuits and district courts face difficult choice of law questions when adjudicating patent counterclaims.

1. Jurisdiction: The Federal Circuit and the Regional Circuits

The Federal Circuit's appellate jurisdiction is exclusive for cases in which jurisdiction in the district court is based "in whole or in part" on 28 U.S.C. § 1338(a), the statute that gives district courts original jurisdiction over claims "arising under" patent law.[1] In all other cases, the regional circuits have exclusive jurisdiction in cases on appeal from the district courts. As a result of this split jurisdiction, the Federal Circuit is often called upon to determine whether it or the regional circuit is the appropriate court to hear a given appeal.

a.   Creation and Purpose of the Federal Circuit

In 1982, Congress enacted the Federal Courts Improvement Act ("FCIA"), which established the Court of Appeals for the Federal Circuit to, among other things, "improve the administration of the patent law by centralizing appeals in patent cases."[2] The creation of an appellate forum with nationwide jurisdiction over patent cases was expected to "increase doctrinal stability in the field of patent law."[3] Congress intended the Federal Circuit to be confined to the subject matter set forth in the FCIA.[4] Aware of the potential for the new court to address issues

---

1.   28 U.S.C. § 1295(a). Federal district courts exercise original jurisdiction over all civil actions "arising under" the federal patent, copyright, and trademark statutes. 28 U.S.C. § 1338(a). Claims based on an intellectual property license or contract do not "arise under" such statutes for purposes of federal subject matter jurisdiction. *See* Jim Arnold v. Hydrotech Sys., 109 F.3d 1567, 1572 (Fed. Cir. 1997) (recognizing the "well settled" principle that causes of action based on contract rights or the common law of torts do not arise under patent law); Schwarzkopf Dev. v. Ti-Coating, Inc., 800 F.2d 240, 244 (Fed. Cir. 1986) (claim based on failure to pay royalties under a patent license agreement arises out of state contract law, not the patent law). The Federal Trade Commission (FTC) can also exercise jurisdiction over patent and antitrust claims in the merger context. The FTC has determined that the FTC Act "confers broad power to prevent unfair methods of competition" and is not limited by the power granted to the Federal Circuit because 28 U.S.C. § 1338(a) "has no bearing on Commission jurisdiction." Opinion of the Commission, *In re* Union Oil Co., FTC Dkt. No. 9305, at 49, 51 (July 7, 2004) (overturning the Administrative Law Judge's decision that the FTC lacked jurisdiction because the claims involved patent questions).
2.   *See* S. Rep. No. 275, 97th Cong., at 2 (1982), *reprinted in* 1982 U.S.C.C.A.N. 11.
3.   *Id.* at 5, 1982 U.S.C.C.A.N. at 15. *See generally* Ronald S. Katz & Adam J. Safer, *Why is One Patent Court Deciding Antitrust Law for the Whole Country*, ALI-ABA Course of Study Materials, October 2000.
4.   In addition to patent appeals, the Federal Circuit also exercises exclusive jurisdiction over appeals of government claims from the United States Court of Federal Claims. *See* 28. U.S.C. § 1295(a)(3).

beyond this limited scope, Congress cautioned that "it is not the committee's judgment that broader subject matter jurisdiction is intended for this court."[5] Of particular concern were the jurisdictional considerations in patent antitrust cases, where parties were likely to engage in forum shopping by adding or dropping patent claims.[6] Notwithstanding these concerns, however, Congress left it to the Federal Circuit to interpret its own jurisdictional mandate in accordance with the goals of the FCIA and the concerns expressed in the Act's legislative history.[7] Consequently, the Federal Circuit has taken responsibility for deciding questions of its own jurisdiction on a case by case basis.[8]

b.   Jurisdiction of the Federal Circuit

(1) The Well-Pleaded Complaint Rule

As a general rule, the Federal Circuit has exclusive jurisdiction over any case that includes a claim "arising under" patent law, even if such case also includes one or more non-patent-related causes of action, such

---

5.   S. Rep. No. 275, 1982 U.S.C.C.A.N. at 14.
6.   *Id.* at 30 (warning against potential manipulation of appellate jurisdiction by litigants whose claims are predominately antitrust related).
7.   S. Rep. No. 275, 1982 U.S.C.C.A.N. at 30; *see also* Atari, Inc. v. JS&A, 747 F.2d 1422, 1428 (Fed. Cir. 1984) (en banc) (noting that Congress expected Federal Circuit to "formulate appropriate standards for determining jurisdiction in cases involving patent and non-patent claims in accordance with the objectives of the Act") (internal quotations omitted), *overruled on other grounds by* Nobelpharma AB v. Implant Innovations, Inc., 141 F.3d 1059 (Fed. Cir. 1998). As the *Atari* court noted, Congress anticipated the need for the Federal Circuit to determine the precise contours of its jurisdictional mandate, stating, "[s]hould questions legitimately arise respecting ancillary and pendent claims and for the direction of appeals in particular cases, the Committee expects the courts to establish, as they have in similar situations, jurisdictional guidelines respecting such cases." *Id.* (quoting H.R. Rep. No. 312, 97th Cong., 1st Sess. at 41).
8.   The Federal Circuit applies its own circuit law to determine whether its exclusive appellate jurisdiction is appropriate in a given case. *See* Woodard v. Sage Prods., 818 F.2d 841, 844 (Fed Cir. 1987) (en banc) (noting that Federal Circuit may look to regional circuits for guidance on jurisdictional issues but that "our decision to follow another circuit's interpretation of a common jurisdictional statute results from the persuasiveness of its analysis, not any binding effect").

as antitrust claims.[9] In *Christianson v. Colt Industries Operating Corp.*,[10] the Supreme Court ruled that a claim "arises under" patent law only if "a well-pleaded complaint establishes either that the federal patent law created the cause of action or that the plaintiff's right to relief necessarily depends on resolution of a substantial question of federal patent law, in that patent law is a necessary element of one of the well-pleaded claims."[11]   Although the antitrust claims asserted in *Christianson* arguably entailed determination of patent law, the Court held that it is not "necessarily sufficient that a well-pleaded claim alleges a single theory under which the resolution of a patent-law question is essential."[12] Rather, where an antitrust claim is supported by alternative theories in the complaint, patent law must be essential to *each* of those theories in order for Section 1338(a) jurisdiction to be proper.[13]

The well-pleaded complaint rule provides a method for determining whether an individual claim "arises under" the patent law such that exclusive jurisdiction over the claim lies with the Federal Circuit. However, the well-pleaded complaint rule alone does not define the proper scope of the Federal Circuit's jurisdiction, i.e., whether it extends to all issues in the case or only to the issues "arising under" patent law.[14]

---

9.   See *Atari*, 747 F.2d at 1428-40.
10.   486 U.S. 800 (1988).
11.   *Id.* at 808-09 (1988). The Court also held that "a case raising a federal patent-law defense does not, for that reason alone, 'arise under' patent law, 'even if the defense is anticipated in the plaintiff's complaint, and even if both parties admit the defense is the only question truly at issue in the case.'" *Id.* at 809 (quoting Franchise Tax Bd. of Cal. v. Constr. Laborers Vacation Trust, 463 U.S. 1, 14 (1983)).
12.   *Id.* at 810.
13.   *Id.* As the Court noted, "[t]he well-pleaded complaint rule ... focuses on claims, not theories, and just because an element that is essential to a particular theory might be governed by federal patent law does not mean that the entire monopolization claim 'arises under' patent law." *Id.* at 811 (internal citations omitted); *cf.* Uroplasty, Inc. v. Advanced Uroscience, Inc., 239 F.3d 1277, 1279-80 (Fed. Cir. 2001) (vacating district court judgment for lack of § 1338(a) jurisdiction where plaintiff's claims for trade secret misappropriation could be proved "without requiring the resolution of a substantial issue of patent law").
14.   See 1 HERBERT HOVENKAMP ET AL., IP AND ANTITRUST: AN ANALYSIS OF ANTITRUST PRINCIPLES APPLIED TO INTELLECTUAL PROPERTY LAW 5-6.1 (2005).

The Federal Circuit addressed this issue in *Atari, Inc. v. JS&A Group*.[15] In that case, Atari brought an action against JS&A in federal district court alleging patent infringement and contributory copyright infringement, among other federal and state law claims. The district court granted a preliminary injunction against JS&A based solely on Atari's contributory copyright infringement theory. In an effort to direct any appeal of the preliminary injunction to the Seventh Circuit, Atari requested, and the court granted, a separation of the single patent claim from the other claims in the complaint.[16] After JS&A filed its notice of appeal to the Federal Circuit, Atari moved to transfer the appeal to the Seventh Circuit.

The Federal Circuit denied Atari's motion to transfer, holding that Federal Circuit jurisdiction over the appeal was proper because the district court's jurisdiction was based "in whole or in part" on Section 1338(a).[17] The fact that the district court had separated the patent claim was deemed immaterial:

> The criteria for jurisdiction of the district court over a case are determined at the complaint stage, and a subsequent event such as the present separation order entered solely to direct appeals, that does not alter those criteria, cannot oust the appellate court of its potential jurisdiction over appeals from final decisions in that case.[18]

In other words, Federal Circuit jurisdiction "depends on the nature of the case brought in the district court, not the nature of the issues raised by the appeal."[19] In *Atari*, this meant that a single patent claim asserted in the complaint conferred Federal Circuit jurisdiction over all issues in

15. 747 F.2d 1422 (Fed. Cir. 1984) (en banc).
16. *Id.* at 1425.
17. *Id.* at 1429.
18. *Id.* at 1431-32.
19. 15A CHARLES ALAN WRIGHT, ARTHUR R. MILLER, EDWARD H. COOPER, FEDERAL PRACTICE AND PROCEDURE § 3903.1 (2d ed. 1992); *see also Atari*, 747 F.2d at 1429 ("[Congress] could have provided appellate jurisdiction in this court only over judgments entered on the patent claim. It did not. It designed and enacted a statute that provided jurisdiction in the court over appeals from decisions in 'cases' in which the district court's jurisdiction 'was based, in whole or in part, on Section 1338.'"); Abbott Labs. v. Brennan, 952 F.2d 1346, 1349-50 (Fed. Cir. 1991) ("[T]he direction of appeal to the Federal Circuit does not change during or after trial, even when the only issues remaining are not within our exclusive assignment.").

the case, regardless of the substantive law involved.[20] Because patent cases tend to generate antitrust counterclaims a significant number of the non-patent claims heard by the Federal Circuit concern issues of antitrust law.[21]

(2) The Scope of Federal Circuit Jurisdiction

Atari established a starting point for determining the scope of Federal Circuit jurisdiction, but the opinion left several questions unanswered.[22] The *Atari* court expressly declined to decide certain jurisdictional questions, such as whether Federal Circuit jurisdiction would be proper where patent and non-patent claims were consolidated into a single case or where patent claims drop out of a case before the appeal.[23]

In the years following *Atari*, the Federal Circuit provided guidance on some of these issues. In *Interpart Corp. v. Imos Italia*,[24] the court decided that its exclusive appellate jurisdiction was proper over an appeal from a final judgment in a case created by the consolidation of a complaint for patent infringement and a suit based on a non-patent claim.[25] A few years later, in *Korody-Colyer v. General Motors*,[26] the court exercised jurisdiction over an appeal from a Rule 54(b) judgment that raised antitrust issues but no patent issues. The patent claims in the

---

20.   To minimize the forum shopping opportunities that would arise from the exercise of Federal Circuit jurisdiction over non-patent issues, the Federal Circuit in *Atari* decreed that it would "apply the law of the involved circuit to issues over which it normally possessed no jurisdiction." 747 F.2d at 1436 n.2. Choice of law issues relating to intellectual property antitrust are discussed in Section A.2. *infra*.
21.   *See* Katz & Safer, *supra* note 3, at 2 ("Because patent and antitrust claims are often paired, and because the Federal Circuit has asserted exclusive jurisdiction over such paired claims, the Federal Court hears a disproportionate number of antitrust issues….")
22.   *See* WRIGHT, *supra* note 19, at 159 ("The [*Atari*] opinion was clearly calculated to establish the frame work for developing more detailed rules as future cases should present more specific and varied problems.").
23.   747 F.2d at 1429 (listing related jurisdictional issues not reached in the opinion).
24.   777 F.2d 678 (Fed Cir. 1985).
25.   *Id.* at 680-81. The Federal Circuit later extended this holding by exercising jurisdiction over a petition for mandamus seeking to overturn an order issued in a consolidated patent and antitrust case. *See In re Innotron Diagnostics*, 800 F.2d 1077, 1084 (Fed. Cir. 1986).
26.   828 F.2d 1572 (Fed. Cir. 1987).

case had already been decided by the district court and appealed to the Federal Circuit. In light of this experience, the Federal Circuit concluded that it was "best situated" to hear the antitrust related appeal.[27]

When the patent claims drop out of a case before a determination on the merits, the Federal Circuit will usually decline jurisdiction over any non-patent appeal.[28] In *Gronholz v. Sears, Roebuck & Co.*,[29] the patent claims originally alleged in the complaint were voluntarily dismissed by the plaintiff. The Federal Circuit refused to exercise jurisdiction over the non-patent issues, reasoning that, by voluntarily dismissing the patent claim, the plaintiff effectively amended his complaint.[30] Because the complaint no longer contained any claims "arising under" the patent law, Federal Circuit jurisdiction was improper.[31]

In contrast, Federal Circuit jurisdiction is proper over non-patent appeals where the patent allegations have been dismissed in an order having a res judicata effect.[32] In such cases, the dismissal constitutes an

---

27. *Id.* at 1574 (noting that interests of judicial economy were best served by continued Federal Circuit jurisdiction over the case). The court distinguished its earlier opinion, *USM Corp. v. SPS Techs.*, 770 F.2d 1035, 1037 (Fed. Cir. 1985), in which it transferred to the regional circuit an appeal on a separated antitrust phase of a patent-antitrust suit. USM was distinguishable because the regional circuit there, having heard two prior appeals, was in the best position to hear subsequent appeals from the same case. In addition, the separation of the issues in *USM* occurred before the Federal Circuit came into existence and, therefore, could not have been calculated to manipulate appellate jurisdiction.

28. *See* HOVENKAMP, *supra* note 14, at 5-12.

29. 836 F.2d 515 (Fed. Cir. 1987) ("Where … all patent claims and counter-claims are voluntarily dismissed in the district court, thus effectively amending the complaint to exclude patent claims, the Federal Circuit does not have exclusive jurisdiction over the appeal of the remaining nonpatent issues.").

30. *Id.* at 517-18.

31. *Id.* at 518; *see also* Chamberlain Group v. Skylink Techs., 381 F.3d 1178, 1189 (Fed. Cir. 2004) ("For the purposes of determining Federal Circuit jurisdiction, we do not differentiate between actual and constructive amendments; both divest us of jurisdiction if they eliminate all issues of patent law."); *cf.* Nilssen v. Motorola, Inc., 203 F.3d 782, 784-85 (Fed. Cir. 2000) (declining jurisdiction over an appeal raising only state law claims where the patent claims were dismissed without prejudice and with leave to re-file in a separate complaint).

32. *See* Zenith Elecs. Corp. v. Exzec, Inc., 182 F.3d 1340, 1346 (Fed. Cir. 1994) (holding that joint stipulation and order dismissing patent claims

adjudication of the claims on the merits, rather than an amendment of the complaint. Accordingly, the district court's Section 1338 jurisdiction over the case, and in turn, the Federal Circuit's jurisdiction, is undisturbed. [33]

(3) No Federal Circuit Jurisdiction Based Solely on Patent-Related Counterclaims

Until recently, the Federal Circuit took the position that its exclusive subject matter jurisdiction was appropriate even where the only patent-related cause of action asserted in a case was a patent counterclaim. In *AeroJet-General Corp. v. Machine Tool Works*,[34] the Federal Circuit held that a compulsory patent counterclaim in an action properly brought in a federal district court was sufficient to establish jurisdiction in the Federal Circuit, notwithstanding the fact that the district court's jurisdiction over the complaint itself was not based on Section 1338(a).[35] *AeroJet* left open the question of whether the court's holding would be the same with respect to a permissive counterclaim,[36] but the Federal Circuit answered this question in the affirmative several years later in *DCS Communications Corp. v. Pulse Communications*,[37] which extended Federal Circuit jurisdiction over cases involving any counterclaim arising under patent law, whether compulsory or permissive.[38]

In 2002, however, the Supreme Court rejected the Federal Circuit's broad interpretation of its jurisdictional mandate, holding in *Holmes*

---

with prejudice did not divest Federal Circuit of exclusive jurisdiction over remaining claims); *see also Chamberlain Group*, 381 F.3d at 1189-90 (discussing different jurisdictional effects of dismissals with and without prejudice and holding Federal Circuit jurisdiction proper where patent claims were dismissed using "without prejudice" language, but practical effect of dismissal was to alter legal status of the parties vis-à-vis patent claims).

33.   *Id.* at 1346. *But see* Denbicare U.S.A. v. Toys "R" Us, Inc., 84 F.3d 1143 (9th Cir. 1996) (holding that regional circuit jurisdiction was proper in appeal of nonpatent claims even though plaintiff's motion to dismiss its patent claim was opposed by defendant).

34.   895 F.2d 736 (Fed. Cir. 1990) (en banc).

35.   *Id.* at 739.

36.   *Id.*

37.   170 F.3d 1354 (Fed. Cir. 1999).

38.   *Id.* at 1359 (finding "no sufficient basis in the language or purpose of section 1295(a)(1) to distinguish between compulsory and permissive counterclaims" for purposes of determining Federal Circuit jurisdiction).

Group v. Vornado Air Circulation Systems[39] that a compulsory counterclaim for patent infringement does not, by itself, confer Federal Circuit jurisdiction. In that case, Holmes brought a non-patent claim against Vornado. Vornado's answer included a compulsory counterclaim for patent infringement. After the district court granted the injunction, Vornado appealed to the Federal Circuit and that court asserted jurisdiction on the basis of the patent issues raised in the counterclaims. Holmes petitioned the Supreme Court for certiorari to determine whether Federal Circuit jurisdiction over the appeal was proper. Largely relying on its decision in *Christianson*, the Supreme Court ruled that the Federal Circuit lacked jurisdiction in the case because the complaint did not assert any claim "arising under" federal patent law.[40] Vornado's patent counterclaim could not form the basis for "arising under" jurisdiction, because the *Christianson* well-pleaded complaint rule provides that "arising under" jurisdiction "must be determined from what necessarily appears in the plaintiff's statement of his own claim...."[41] Thus, after *Holmes*, the regional circuit courts exercise jurisdiction over appeals in cases where patent issues are implicated only in counterclaims.[42]

39.　535 U.S. 826 (2002).
40.　*Id.* at 834. The *Holmes* Court expressly left open the issue, also unaddressed in *Christianson*, of "whether the Federal Circuit's jurisdiction is fixed with reference to the complaint as initially filed or whether an actual or constructive amendment to the complaint raising a patent-law claim can provide the foundation for the Federal Circuit's jurisdiction." *Id.* at 829 n.1 (2002).
41.　*Id.* at 830 (citing *Christianson*, 486 U.S. at 809).
42.　*See, e.g.*, Telcomm Tech. Servs. v. Siemens Rolm Communs., 295 F.3d 1249 (Fed. Cir. 2002) (raising jurisdiction question *sua sponte* and ordering case transferred to Eleventh Circuit pursuant to *Holmes*); Medigene v. Loyola Univ., 41 Fed. Appx. 450 (Fed. Cir. 2002) (ordering appeal transferred to Seventh Circuit pursuant to *Holmes*). Similarly, a patent defense or counterclaim is insufficient to confer jurisdiction in a federal district court under section 1338(a). *See, e.g.*, Conroy v. Fresh Del Monte Produce, 325 F. Supp. 2d. 1049 (N.D. Cal. 2004) (remanding antitrust lawsuit alleging misuse of fraudulently obtained patents because complaint did not "arise under federal law" even if the defense of invalidity was anticipated in the complaint); R.F. Shinn Contractors v. Shinn, 1:01CV00750, 2002 U.S. Dist. LEXIS 25253 (M.D.N.C. Nov. 8, 2002) (remanding action to state court because, inter alia, patent infringement counterclaim was insufficient to support federal jurisdiction after *Holmes*).

2. *Choice of Law*

Pursuant to the "all issues" approach set forth in *Atari*, the Federal Circuit routinely exercises appellate jurisdiction over non-patent matters, including antitrust claims. The court's exercise of jurisdiction presents a special choice of law problem: when deciding substantive or procedural issues outside the scope of its statutorily defined exclusive jurisdiction, should the Federal Circuit apply the law of the regional circuit in which the case originated or should it interpret the law independently?

a. The Federal Circuit Choice of Law

The Federal Circuit has radically altered its position on the question of what body of law—regional circuit law or Federal Circuit law— should govern antitrust and other non-patent matters that come before it. In the early years of its existence, the Federal Circuit deferred to the law of the originating regional circuit on issues not within the scope of its exclusive jurisdiction.[43] The court's rationale seemed to be based on a combination of prudential concerns and notions of Congressional intent in crafting the FCIA.[44] As noted by the *Atari* court, the Federal Circuit's disregard of regional circuit jurisprudence in deciding questions of non-patent law would encourage the type of forum shopping that Congress cautioned against in the Act's legislative history.[45] Additionally, were the Federal Circuit to independently interpret substantive law outside the

---

43. *See* Cygnus Therapeutics Sys. v. Alza Corp., 92 F.3d 1153, 1161 (Fed. Cir. 1996) (applying Ninth Circuit law to plaintiff's *Walker Process* claim), *overruled by* Nobelpharma AB v. Implant Innovations, 141 F.3d 1059 (Fed. Cir. 1998); *Loctite*, 781 F.2d at 875 (applying Seventh Circuit law to Section 2 attempt to monopolize claim); Atari, Inc. v. JS&A Group, 747 F.2d 1422, 1439-40 (Fed. Cir. 1984) (en banc) (applying Seventh Circuit law to appeal from preliminary injunction against contributory copyright infringement); *Bandag*, 750 F.2d at 909 (applying Ninth Circuit law to trademark portion of appeal); Am. Hoist & Derrick Co. v. Sowa & Sons, 725 F.2d 1350, 1366 (Fed. Cir. 1984) (applying Ninth Circuit law to Sherman Act § 2 claim).

44. *See* HOVENKAMP, *supra* note 14, at 5-20.

45. 747 F.2d at 1439; *see also* S. Rep. No. 275, *reprinted in* 1982 U.S.C.C.A.N. at 30 ("[M]ere joinder of a patent claim in a case whose gravamen is antitrust should not be permitted to avail a plaintiff of the jurisdiction of the Federal Circuit in avoidance of the traditional jurisdiction and governing legal interpretations of a regional court of appeals.").

bounds of its exclusive jurisdiction, district courts would be faced with two distinct, and potentially conflicting, lines of precedent—one in the Federal Circuit and the other in the regional circuit with authority over the district court.[46]

Recent Federal Circuit decisions, however, have eroded the court's early choice of law rules in favor of expanded application of Federal Circuit law to non-patent claims—in particular, antitrust claims.[47]   In *Nobelpharma AB v. Implant Innovations*,[48] the court expressly overruled three of its own precedents by holding that Federal Circuit law would henceforth govern the question of "whether conduct in procuring or enforcing a patent is sufficient to strip a patentee of its immunity from the antitrust laws."[49]   Nobelpharma alleged that the defendant infringed a patent for Nobelpharma's dental implant.   The defendant asserted

---

46. *See* Panduit Corp. v. All States Plastic Mfg., 744 F.2d 1564, 1574 (Fed. Cir. 1984) (noting that practitioners and district judges in the regional circuit "should not be saddled with two different sets of requirements" depending on which court an appeal is taken to); *Atari*, 747 F.2d at 1439 ("It would be at best unfair to hold in this case that the district court, at risk of error, should have 'served two masters,' or that it should have looked, Janus-like, in two directions in its conduct of that judicial process.").

47. *See In re* Indep. Serv. Orgs. Antitrust Litig., 203 F.3d 1322, 1325 (Fed. Cir. 2000); *Nobelpharma*, 141 F.3d at 1067; Pro-Mold & Tool v. Great Lakes Plastics, 75 F.3d 1568, 1574-75 (Fed. Cir. 1996); *see also* Midwest Indus. v. Karavan Trailers, 175 F.3d 1356, 1358-59 (Fed. Cir. 1999) (holding that Federal Circuit law governs "questions involving the relationship between patent law and other federal and state law rights" and expressly overruling three precedents to the contrary); *see generally* Scott A. Stempel & John F. Terzaken III, *Symposium: The Federal Circuit and Antitrust: Casting a Long IP Shadow Over Antitrust Jurisprudence: The Federal Circuit's Expanding Jurisdictional Reach*, 69 ANTITRUST L.J. 711 (2002) (discussing how Federal Circuit expanded jurisdiction over substantive non-patent issues); Ronald S. Katz & Adam J. Safer, *Should One Patent Court be Making Antitrust Law for the Whole Country?*, 69 ANTITRUST L.J. 687, 691 (2002) (discussing the Federal Circuit's expanded jurisdiction and the problems it has created); Robert P. Taylor, *Twenty Years of the Federal Circuit: An Overview*, 716 PLI/Pat 9, 36 (2002) (noting that the Federal Circuit, at this point in time, has enough experience to adjudicate antitrust claims).

48. 141 F.3d 1059 (Fed. Cir. 1998).

49. *Id.* at 1068 ("Whether conduct procuring or enforcing a patent is sufficient to strip a patentee of its immunity from the antitrust laws is to be decided as a question of Federal Circuit law.").

defenses of patent invalidity and noninfringement, as well as a *Walker Process*-style antitrust counterclaim. The district court granted a directed verdict for the defendant on the patent issues and the jury found in the defendant's favor on the antitrust counterclaim. Nobelpharma appealed the judgments to the Federal Circuit, which affirmed. The remarkable aspect of the Federal Circuit's decision was its departure from its normal choice of law approach to antitrust claims. At the outset of the opinion, the Federal Circuit acknowledged that "[a]s a general proposition, when reviewing a district court's judgment involving federal antitrust law, we are guided by the law of the regional circuit."[50] However, the court also observed that Federal Circuit law, not the law of the regional circuits, governs issues that clearly involve the Federal Circuit's exclusive jurisdiction. The court then concluded that "whether a patent infringement suit is based on a fraudulently procured patent impacts our exclusive jurisdiction."[51] The court's rationale for reversing its choice of law approach to certain antitrust claims was apparently motivated by practical considerations. Noting that *Walker Process* claims are typically raised as counterclaims by defendants in patent infringement actions, the court concluded that it was "in the best position to create a uniform body of federal law on this subject and thereby avoid the danger of confusion [that] might be enhanced if this court were to embark on an effort to interpret the laws of the regional circuit."[52]

The new choice of law rule established in *Nobelpharma* applies not only to *Walker Process* claims, but also "to all antitrust claims premised on the bringing of a patent infringement suit."[53] However, elements of antitrust claims that are not unique to patent law, "such as relevant

---

50. *Id.* at 1067.
51. *Id.* at 1067; *see also* Unitherm Foods Sys. v. Swift Ekrich, Inc., 375 F.3d 1341, 1356 (Fed. Cir. 2004) ("The fundamental question of Federal Circuit antitrust law is whether or when a patentee's behavior in either procuring or enforcing a patent can give rise to antitrust liability."), *rev'd on other grounds*, 126 S. Ct. 980 (2006).
52. *Id.* at 1068 (internal quotation omitted).
53. *Id.* This holding required the Federal Circuit to overrule the contrary choice of law approach set forth in *Cygnus Therapeutics Systems v. Alza Corp.*, 92 F.3d 1153 (Fed. Cir. 1996), *Loctite Corp. v. Ultraseal, Ltd.*, 781 F.2d 861, (Fed. Cir. 1985), and *Atari, Inc. v. JS&A Group, Inc.*, 747 F.2d 1422 (Fed. Cir. 1984) (en banc). *Id.*

market, market power, damages, etc.," continue to be decided under regional circuit law.[54]

b. Regional Circuit Choice of Law

A major implication of the *Holmes* decision is that regional circuit courts increasingly will be called upon to adjudicate appeals involving a mix of patent and antitrust law issues.[55] In such cases, it is clear that in deciding the antitrust claims, each regional circuit is guided by its own

---

54. 141 F.3d at 1068; *see also Unitherm*, 375 F.3d at 1349 (noting that in a *Walker Process* case, regional circuit law governs general antitrust elements including antitrust standing, antitrust injury, market definition, and damages); C.R. Bard, Inc. v. M3 Sys., 157 F.3d 1340, 1367 n.7 (Fed. Cir. 1998) (observing that, under *Nobelpharma*, fraudulent procurement element of *Walker Process* claim is governed by Federal Circuit law, but other elements of claim are governed by regional circuit law). As a matter of policy, the Federal Circuit defers to regional circuit law in deciding procedural issues that are not unique to patent law. *See* Panduit Corp. v. All States Plastic Mfg., 744 F.2d 1564, 1574-75 (Fed. Cir. 1984) (applying regional circuit law to review of disqualification of counsel and noting that the policy of deferring to regional circuits on procedural matters serves "the intent and spirit of not only our enabling statute but also the general desire of the federal judicial system to minimize confusion and conflicts"). However, if a procedural issue bears "an essential relationship" to subject matter within the exclusive jurisdiction of the Federal Circuit, Federal Circuit law generally controls. *See* Biodex Corp. v. Loredan Biomed., Inc., 946 F.2d 850, 858-59 (Fed. Cir. 1991), (applying Federal Circuit law to question of whether jury findings of fact in patent trial may be reviewed on appeal in the absence of any post-verdict motion); Gardco Mfg. v. Herst Lighting Co., 820 F.2d 1209, 1212 (Fed. Cir. 1987) (holding that the question of whether Rule 42(b) separation of inequitable conduct issue for a nonjury trial held before a jury trial on validity and infringement "clearly implicates the jurisprudential responsibilities" of the Federal Circuit; therefore, regional circuit law does not control).

55. Within the first six months following *Holmes*, the Federal Circuit declined to exercise jurisdiction over three patent counterclaim appeals, dismissing one and transferring two back to other regional circuit courts. *See* Mattel, Inc. v. Lehman, 49 Fed. Appx. 889, 890 (Fed. Cir. 2002) (dismissing appeal pursuant to *Holmes*); *Telcomm Tech. Servs.*, 295 F.3d at 1251 (transferring case to Eleventh Circuit citing *Holmes*); Medigene v. Loyola Univ., 41 Fed. Appx. 450 (Fed. Cir. 2002) (transferring case to Seventh Circuit citing *Holmes*).

respective precedents. Less clear, however, is what body of law governs the patent counterclaims that come before the circuit courts of appeal as a result of *Holmes*.[56]

Before the creation of the Federal Circuit in 1982, the regional circuits routinely heard patent cases, establishing their own substantive patent law precedents. Because subsequent Federal Circuit patent decisions did not invalidate regional circuit precedents,[57] regional circuit patent law is technically still good law, and district courts within those circuits may feel bound to follow it.[58] Some commentators argue that preservation of uniformity in patent law—the principle reason for which the Federal Circuit was created—requires regional circuits to defer to Federal Circuit law when deciding patent counterclaims.[59] *Holmes*, however, may be interpreted as supporting the opposite approach.[60] In rejecting Federal Circuit jurisdiction over patent law counterclaims, Justice Scalia, writing for the majority, noted, "Our task here is not to determine what would further Congress's goal of ensuring patent uniformity, but to determine what the words of the statue must fairly be understood to mean."[61]   Justice Stevens, in a concurring opinion, was more frank: "[W]e have already decided that the Federal Circuit does not have exclusive jurisdiction over all cases raising patent issues.

---

56.   *See generally* Joseph Etra, Holmes v. Vornado: *A Radical Change in Appellate Jurisdiction*, 5 COLUM. SCI. & TECH. L. REV. 5 (2003/2004).
57.   No circuit court of appeals has the authority to overrule a decision of another circuit. *See* Seattle Audobon Soc'y v. Lyons, 871 F. Supp. 1291, 1313 (W.D. Wash. 1994) ("Differences among circuits are common, and the District of Columbia Circuit has no power to overrule another circuit's decision."); *see generally* Stephen L. Wasby, *Intercircuit Conflicts in the Courts of Appeals*, 63 MONT. L. REV. 119, 140 (2002) (discussing circuit splits and how courts of appeals often disagree with each other and need not follow each other's precedents).
58.   *See* Larry D. Thompson, Jr., *Adrift on a Sea of Uncertainty: Preserving Uniformity in Patent Law Post-Vornado Through Deference to the Federal Circuit*, 92 GEO. L.J. 523, 591 (2004) (arguing in favor of regional circuit deference to Federal Circuit patent law).
59.   *See id.* The Federal Circuit would most likely endorse this approach as well. In *Atari*, decided pre-*Holmes*, the court suggested that regional circuits making occasional patent decisions "may find the body of decisions of this court a useful reference, in light of the considerations here expressed concerning the burden of conflicting views on the district courts." *Atari*, 747 F.2d at 1440.
60.   *See generally* Etra, *supra* note 56.
61.   535 U.S. at 833.

Necessarily, therefore, other circuits will have some role to play in the development of this area of the law."[62]

A recent post-*Holmes* Eleventh Circuit decision suggests that the regional circuit courts will not simply defer to Federal Circuit precedent when deciding patent-related appeals. In *Telecom Technical Services v. Siemens Rolm Communications*,[63] the Eleventh Circuit expressly stated that a Federal Circuit precedent directly on point "only has persuasive authority."[64] The facts of *Telecom Technical Services* were substantially similar to those of the 2000 Federal Circuit case *In re ISO Antitrust Litigation*.[65] Both cases involved Section 2 monopoly claims asserted by independent service organizations (ISOs) against the makers of products the ISOs serviced for refusal to sell patented parts for those products. The district court in *Telecom Technical Services*, believing (correctly at the time) that any appeal in the case would go to the Federal Circuit and that the *In re ISO Antitrust Litigation* holding would be controlling, ultimately granted the defendant's motion for summary judgment on the antitrust claims.[66] While the appeal was pending in the Federal Circuit, however, the Supreme Court issued its decision in *Holmes* that patent counterclaims alone are insufficient to secure Federal Circuit jurisdiction. Because the patent issues in *Telecom Technical Services* were raised only in counterclaims, the Federal Circuit, transferred the case to the Eleventh Circuit pursuant to *Holmes*.[67] Noting the Federal Circuit's lack of jurisdiction over the appeal, the Eleventh Circuit concluded that the *In re ISO Antitrust Litigation* holding "now only has persuasive authority."[68]

---

62. *Id.* at 838-39 (citation omitted).
63. 388 F.3d 820 (11th Cir. 2004).
64. *Id.* at 826.
65. 203 F.3d 1322 (Fed. Cir. 2000). In *In re ISO*, a group of independent service organizations sued Xerox under § 2 of the Sherman Act, alleging that Xerox was establishing a monopoly for the servicing of its copiers by refusing to sell patented parts to ISOs. The Federal Circuit rejected this argument. *Id.* at 1324. The court held that "Xerox was under no obligation to sell or license its patented parts and did not violate the antitrust laws by refusing to do so." *Id.* at 1328.
66. 388 F.2d at 823-24. The district court had initially denied summary judgment, but reversed this ruling after the Federal Circuit issued its opinion in *In re ISO*. *See id.* at 825.
67. Telcomm Tech. Servs. v. Siemens Rolm Communs., 295 F.3d 1249, 1251 (Fed. Cir. 2002).
68. *Id.* at 826; *cf.* Schinzing v. Mid-States Stainless, Inc., No. 04-2535, 2005 U.S. App. LEXIS 14300, at *6 (8th Cir. July 15, 2005) (asserting

Although the antitrust issues in the case were ultimately decided on grounds other than those considered by the Federal Circuit in *In re ISO Antitrust Litigation*, the Eleventh Circuit showed no signs of deferring to the Federal Circuit on questions of patent law, treating the Federal Circuit precedent as just one of several relevant authorities.[69]

c. District Court Choice of Law

As a general rule, district courts hearing cases that involve both patent and non-patent claims apply Federal Circuit law to the former and regional circuit law to the latter.[70] This could change, however, if regional circuits begin to decide patent counterclaims with greater frequency, thus creating their own bodies of patent law. In a post-*Holmes* world, a district court deciding patent issues will have to choose between two possibly conflicting authorities: Federal Circuit precedent, which has governed patent claims in district courts for over twenty years, and the emerging patent law of its own circuit. Of course, if there is Supreme Court precedent on point, the district court is bound to defer to it. In most instances, however, district courts will be faced with a difficult choice of law question in patent cases.[71]

B. Procedural Issues in Intellectual Property Antitrust Cases

Courts are faced with several procedural issues in intellectual property antitrust cases. Courts must often determine whether an

---

jurisdiction, but deciding, without any explanation, to apply Federal Circuit law to the "substantive issues of patent law").

69. *Id* at 826-27 ("As a number of recent cases have observed, there is a tension between the protections offered by patent and antitrust laws.") (citing *In re ISO*, 203 F.3d 1322, 1325-26 (Fed. Cir. 2000); *Image Technical Servs. v. Eastman Kodak Co.*, 125 F.3d 1195, 1215 (9th Cir. 1997); *Data Gen. Corp. v. Grumman Sys. Support*, 36 F.3d 1147, 1187 (1st Cir. 1994)).

70. *See, e.g.*, Hampshire Paper Corp. v. Highland Supply, Civil No. 02-32-JD, 2002 U.S. Dist LEXIS 13566, at *3 (D. N.H. July 18, 2002) ("[T]he standard of review for a motion challenging subject matter jurisdiction with respect to patent claims is provided by the Federal Circuit, while the standard for determining subject matter jurisdiction as to the trademark claims is provided by the First Circuit.").

71. *Telecom* and *Schinzing* address this choice of law issue, but provide little actual guidance to district courts faced with this decision. No other cases offer any additional guidance.

antitrust counterclaim is permissive or compulsory under the Federal Rules of Civil Procedure because antitrust claims are often based on the same set of facts as the patents claims. In addition, courts must also decide whether the antitrust claims should be bifurcated from the patent claims at both the trial and discovery phases.

1.   When is an Antitrust Counterclaim Compulsory?

Antitrust counterclaims are commonly asserted in response to patent infringement actions. Whether an antitrust counterclaim is deemed compulsory in the underlying infringement suit depends on the type of claim asserted, as well as the circuit law that controls the issue. Despite early Supreme Court precedent on this question,[72] the circuit courts are split on whether antitrust claims are waived if not asserted in the underlying patent litigation.[73]

The distinction between a compulsory and permissive counterclaim is set forth in Rule 13 of the Federal Rules of Civil Procedure. Rule 13(a) requires a counterclaim against any opposing party to be asserted in the pleadings "if it arises out of the transaction or occurrence that is the subject matter of the opposing party's claim." Courts have liberally interpreted this language, holding that a counterclaim is compulsory where "a logical relationship exists between the claim and the counterclaim."[74]   Courts may determine the existence of a "logical relationship" between claims by considering whether many of the same factual and legal issues are involved, or whether the claims stem from the same basic dispute between the parties.[75] If a compulsory counterclaim is not asserted in the original lawsuit, it may not be raised in any subsequent action.

Antitrust claims relating to the wrongful obtainment or enforcement of patents often "arise out of the same transaction or occurrence" as the underlying patent infringement action.[76] Yet, in *Mercoid Corp. v. Mid-*

---

72.   Mercoid Corp. v. Mid-Continent Inv., 320 U.S. 661 (1944).

73.   *See infra* notes 83-89 and accompanying text for further discussion.

74.   Critical-Vac Filtration Corp. v. Minuteman Int'l, 233 F.3d 697, 699 (2d Cir. 2000); *see also* 6 CHARLES ALAN WRIGHT, ARTHUR R. MILLER, & MARY KAY KANE, FEDERAL PRACTICE & PROCEDURE § 1409 (2d ed. 1990).

75.   *See* Great Lakes Rubber Corp. v. Herbert Cooper Co., 286 F.2d 631, 634 (3d Cir. 1961).

76.   This is also true with respect to other forms of intellectual property. Court have held antitrust counterclaims to be compulsory in actions for

Continent Investment Co.,[77] the Supreme Court refused to apply Rule 13(a) to bar a patent-misuse-based antitrust counterclaim despite a prior patent infringement action in which the claim could have been raised.

Mercoid was an action for contributory infringement of a furnace system patent wherein the defendant, Mercoid, asserted an antitrust counterclaim alleging that Mid-Continent and its exclusive licensee had conspired to expand the monopoly of the patent in violation of the antitrust laws.[78] Mid-Continent argued that Mercoid was barred from asserting the counterclaim because it had failed to do so in a prior patent litigation involving the same parties.[79] The Supreme Court disagreed, holding that while a defendant typically would be barred from asserting any *defense* which might have been interposed in an earlier litigation, "it would not follow that this counterclaim for damages would likewise be barred. That claim for damages is more than a defense; it is a separate

---

trademark and copyright infringement. For cases dealing with trademark infringement, see *Harley-Davidson Motor v. Chrome Specialties*, 173 F.R.D. 250, 254 (E.D. Wisc. 1997) (granting motion to preliminarily enjoin antitrust action filed in another district because claims asserted therein were compulsory counterclaims in the present trademark infringement action); *Minnetonka, Inc. v. Sani-Fresh Int'l*, 103 F.R.D. 377, 379 (D. Minn. 1984) (granting motion to stay antitrust action on the grounds that claims asserted therein were compulsory counterclaims in prior filed trademark infringement suit). For cases dealing with copyright infringement, see *Static Control Components v. Dallas Semiconductor*, 1:02CV1057, 2003 U.S. Dist. LEXIS 12313, **35-36 (M.D.N.C. July 9, 2003) (magistrate judge recommended dismissal of plaintiff's antitrust claims finding that they were compulsory counterclaims in copyright infringement action pending in another district); Grumman Sys. Support Corp. v. Data Gen. Corp., 125 F.R.D. 160, 162 (N.D. Cal. 1988) (finding that "there is sufficient overlap between the factual underpinnings of the two actions to save a great deal of judicial resources" if litigated together); *see also* United Artists Corp. v. Masterpiece Prods., 221 F.2d 213, 216 (2d Cir. 1955) (finding a sufficient "logical relationship" between action for copyright infringement and counterclaim alleging conspiracy to deprive defendants of their rights where the infringement action was "one of a series of harassing maneuvers designed to interfere" with defendants' exercise of their rights).

77.   320 U.S. 661 (1944).
78.   *Id.* at 662.
79.   Mercoid was not a party to the earlier patent action, but it directed the defense on behalf of the individual homeowner who was sued by Mid-Continent.

statutory cause of action."[80] The Court seemed to assume, without discussion, that had Mercoid asserted its antitrust claim in the prior patent litigation, such claim would have been viewed as *permissive* under Rule 13(b), rather than compulsory under Rule 13(a).[81]

The so-called *Mercoid* "exception" has been widely criticized by courts and commentators, and its continuing validity is questioned.[82] A number of district and appellate courts, unimpressed with the reasoning behind *Mercoid*'s permissive counterclaim rule, have limited the holding to the specific facts of the case.[83] For example, in *Critical-Vac Filtration Corp. v. Minuteman International*,[84] the Second Circuit narrowly construed *Mercoid* by limiting its application to counterclaims arising out of patent misuse.[85] The Fourth Circuit, in *Burlington Industries v.*

---

80. 320 U.S. at 671.

81. *Id.* ("The fact that it might have been asserted as a counterclaim in the prior suit by reason of Rule 13(b) of the Rules of Civil Procedure . . . does not mean that the failure to do so renders the prior judgment res judicata as respects it.").

82. *See* Burlington Indus. v. Milliken & Co., 690 F.2d 380 (4th Cir. 1982) ("[T]he *Mercoid* decision has been read narrowly ... and its continuing validity is open to serious question."); Grumman Sys. Support Corp. v. Data Gen. Corp., 125 F.R.D. 160 (N.D. Cal. 1988) (noting that *Mercoid* "was immediately criticized by the commentators and its holding eroded by the lower courts with time"); Douglas v. Wis. Alumni Research Found., 81 F. Supp. 167 (N.D. Ill. 1948) ("A consideration of the nature of a compulsory counterclaim would appear to indicate certain inherent weaknesses in the rationale of the *Mercoid* decision."); HOVENKAMP, *supra* note 14, at, § 5.5 (arguing that the Supreme Court or Congress "should eliminate the *Mercoid* 'exception' and apply a standard Rule 13(a) analysis to antitrust claims").

83. *See, e.g.*, Lewis Mfg. v. Chisholm-Ryder Co., 82 F.R.D. 745 (W.D. Pa. 1979) (distinguishing *Mercoid* on the grounds that "Lewis was a named defendant which provided its own defense and is therefore different from *Mercoid* which was only defending a third party in the earlier action") (citations omitted).

84. 233 F.3d 697 (2d Cir. 2000).

85. *Id.* at 701-703; *see also* Eon Labs v. Smithkline Beecham, Corp., 298 F. Supp. 2d 175, 180-81 (D. Mass 2003) (following *Critical-Vac* and ruling that *Mercoid* exception did not apply to antitrust claims alleging enforcement of invalid patent); Rohm & Haas v. Biotech, 770 F. Supp. 928, 930-33 (D. Del. 1991) (noting that the *Mercoid* Court could not have envisioned application of its holding to claims for patent invalidity because Supreme Court did not recognize *Walker Process* style antitrust claim until twenty years later); USM Corp. v. SPS Techs., 102 F.R.D.

Milliken & Co.,[86] distinguished *Mercoid* on the grounds that, unlike the complaint before the court, "the complaint [in *Mercoid*] did not demand a declaratory judgment on the issue of the enforceability of the patents or of any license agreement under which those patents were licensed.[87]

Despite broad criticism, *Mercoid* has never been overruled and two circuit courts of appeals have acknowledged its continued validity.[88] In addition to positive treatment by the Ninth and Fifth Circuit, *Mercoid* has been cited favorably, but with little or no discussion of the force of its reasoning, by the Sixth, Eighth and First Circuits.[89]

167, 169-71 (N.D. Ill. 1984) (restricting *Mercoid* holding to its facts and rejecting contention that fraudulent procurement antitrust claim could not be construed as compulsory counterclaim under Rule 13(a)).

86.   690 F.2d 380, 398 (4th Cir. 1982).

87.   *Id.* at 398.

88.   *See* Tank Insulation Int'l v. Insultherm, Inc., 104 F.3d 83 (5th Cir. 1997) (recognizing *Mercoid* "exception"); Hydranautics v. FilmTec Corp., 70 F.3d 533 (9th Cir. 1995) (stating that "*Mercoid* leaves open the possibility of raising antitrust claims as permissive counterclaims in an infringement action").

89.   *See* Schlegel Mfg. v. USM. Corp., 525 F.2d 775, 778 (6th Cir. 1975) (quoting *Mercoid* without criticism); Agrashell, Inc. v. Hammons Prods., 479 F.2d 269, 287 (8th Cir. 1973) ("[*Mercoid*] indicates that cases such as this one involve permissive, not compulsory, counterclaims"); Fowler v. Sponge Prods., 246 F.2d 223, 227 (1st Cir. 1957) ("[T]he Supreme Court has clearly stated that a counterclaim for treble damages is permissive in nature so that failure to plead it in a prior patent suit does not bar a subsequent independent suit by him under the anti-trust laws."); *see also* Tindall v. Parks, No. 96-CIV. 7651(RPP), 1997 WL 473532, at *1 (S.D.N.Y. Aug. 19, 1997) (citing *Mercoid* for proposition that antitrust claims in which the gravamen is a patent infringement lawsuit initiated by counterclaim defendant are permissive counterclaims). The Third Circuit has affirmed without opinion a district court decision that an antitrust claim was a compulsory counterclaim in a prior patent infringement action. *See* Am. Packaging v. Golden Valley Microwave Foods, Civ. A. No. 94-1839, 1995 WL 262522, at *4 (E.D. Pa. May 1, 1995) (reading *Mercoid* "as going to the actual facts of that case" and finding it "inappropriate to read it in a way that extrapolates beyond those bounds"), *aff'd without op.*, No. 95-1386, 1996 U.S. App. LEXIS 12061 (3d Cir. Apr. 8, 1996). The Third Circuit reached the opposite conclusion, however, on the question of whether claims asserted in a patent infringement lawsuit were compulsory counterclaims in a pending antitrust case between the same parties. *See* Xerox Corp. v. SCM Corp., 576 F.2d 1057 (3d Cir. 1978) (finding that patent infringement litigation

The Federal Circuit has so far refrained from ruling definitively on the matter,[90] but there is some indication that it would not read the *Mercoid* exception broadly.[91]   In *Genentech, Inc. v. Regents of the University of California*,[92] the Federal Circuit held that the district court did not err in treating the university's proposed antitrust claims as compulsory counterclaims in the pending declaratory judgment action against the university asserting patent invalidity, unenforceability and noninfringement.[93]   In its opinion, the Federal Circuit acknowledged that "there is not unanimity among the circuits on this question as applied to antitrust counterclaims in patent infringement suits" and that the Supreme Court's statement on this issue in *Mercoid* "has occasioned varied application on particular facts."[94]

2. Severance of Antitrust Issues and Intellectual Property Issues

a.   Bifurcation of Antitrust Issues

Where a case involves both intellectual property and antitrust issues, courts routinely bifurcate the patent case from the antitrust claims

---

did not arise out of the same transaction or occurrence as the antitrust litigation "alleging major antitrust violations").

90.   *See* HOVENKAMP, *supra* note 14, at 5-58.1 (2005 Supplement). In *Nobelpharma*, the Federal Circuit observed that "[a]n antitrust claim premised on stripping a patentee of its immunity from the antitrust laws is *typically* raised as a counterclaim by a defendant in a patent infringement suit." 141 F.3d at 1067 (emphasis added). The court acknowledged the conflicting authority on whether such a counterclaim would be compulsory, without attempting to resolve the conflict. *Id.* at 1067 n.4.

91.   *See, e.g.,* Glitsch, Inc. v. Koch Eng'g, 216 F.3d 1382, 1386 (Fed. Cir. 2000) ("The Court's ruling [in *Mercoid*] was based on its determination that the public policy of preventing patent misuse outweighed the public policy underlying the doctrine of *res judicata*, at least as applied on the facts of that case.   But the balance that the Court struck between patent misuse and *res judicata* is wholly inapplicable in the quite different setting of this case.").

92.   143 F.3d 1446, 1456 (Fed. Cir. 1998), *vacated on other grounds*, 527 U.S. 1031 (1999).

93.   *Id.* at 1456 (noting that in deciding whether a counterclaim is compulsory "the court may give weight to the advantages of consolidation, efficiency, and expedition, in requiring that the issues arising from related facts be litigated in the same suit").

94.   *Id.*

pursuant to Federal Rule of Civil Procedure 42(b) or otherwise stay the antitrust claims until the patent rights are determined.[95] Bifurcation in intellectual property antitrust suits is generally "conducive to expedition and economy" [96] because resolution of the patent claims will often dispose of the related antitrust issues. For example, a finding of patent validity or enforceability in the first trial would likely negate antitrust counterclaims predicated on patent invalidity.[97] Similarly, a finding of

---

95. *See In re* Innotron Diagnostics, 800 F.2d 1077 (Fed. Cir. 1986) (recognizing the "now-standard practice of separating for trial patent issues and those raised in an antitrust counterclaim"); Ecrix Corp. v. Exabyte Corp., 191 F.R.D. 611, 614 (D. Colo. 2000) (granting motion to bifurcate patent infringement claim and antitrust and unfair competition claims for separate trials); Hunter Douglas, Inc. v. Comfortex Corp., 44 F. Supp. 2d 145, 157 (N.D.N.Y. 1999) (ordering three-phase trial with separate phases for patent liability, patent damages, and antitrust counterclaims, including patent misuse defense); Hewlett-Packard v. Genrad, Inc., 882 F. Supp 1141, 1158 (D. Mass. 1995) (exercising discretion to separate trial and discovery of patent issues from antitrust and unfair competition issues); Virginia Panel Corp. v. MAC Panel Co., 887 F. Supp. 880, 883-83 (W.D. Va. 1995) (separating patent infringement claims from defendant's patent misuse defense and antitrust counterclaims), *aff'd*, 133 F.3d 860 (Fed. Cir. 1997); Baxter Int'l v. Cobe Lab., No. 89 C 9460, 1992 WL 77665, at *5 (N.D. Ill. Apr. 7, 1992) (granting motion to sever and stay discovery and trial of antitrust counterclaim until after trial of patent claims to avoid unfair prejudice to plaintiff); *see also* M. Howard Morse, *Intellectual Property Licensing: The Intersection between Intellectual Property Rights and the Antitrust Laws*, 1355 PLI/Pat 947, 1012 (2003) (cases containing antitrust and patent claims are often bifurcated at trial or discovery).
96. Fed. R. Civ. P. 42(b).
97. *See* FMC Corp. v. Manitowoc Co., 835 F.2d 1411, 1417-18 (Fed. Cir. 1987) (plaintiff's failure to establish inequitable conduct "precludes a determination that it had borne its greater burden of establishing the fraud required to support its *Walker Process* [antitrust] claim"); ASM Am. v. Genus, Inc., No. 01-2190, 2002 U.S. Dist. LEXIS 1351, at *18-21 (N.D. Cal. Jan. 9, 2002) (holding that stay of antitrust claims "would promote an efficient resolution of the patent invalidity issues and substantially narrow or eliminate the antitrust claims as a result"); *Baxter Int'l, Inc.*, 1992 WL 77665, at *2 ("If, after trial of the patent issues, the court concludes that the [patent in issue] is enforceable, then most of [defendant's] antitrust counterclaim will be rendered moot."); United States Gypsum Co. v. Nat'l Gypsum Co., No. 89 C 7533, 1994 WL 74989, at *2 (N.D. Ill Mar. 10, 1994), *aff'd*, 74 F.3d 1209 (Fed. Cir.

patent infringement can prove that the patent owner's claim was not objectively baseless, and therefore does not provide a basis for the accused infringer's antitrust claims.[98]

In its leading decision on the issue of bifurcation, the Federal Circuit held that "[i]n deciding whether one trial or separate trials will best serve the convenience of the parties and the court, avoid prejudice, and minimize expense and delay, the major consideration is directed toward the choice most likely to result in a just final disposition of the litigation."[99] Pursuant to this guideline, some trial courts have exercised their discretion to deny bifurcation where, on the particular facts of the case, the patent and antitrust claims are "so intertwined as to preclude effective separation."[100] Such an overlap is common where the antitrust

---

1996) (deferring trial on antitrust issues because a finding of no inequitable conduct in procuring the patent would obviate need to adjudicate *Walker Process* claim).

98. *See, e.g., FilmTec Corp.*, 67 F.3d at 936 ("Obviously, if the patentee is successful in his infringement action, his suit is not baseless, and it cannot be a sham."); Warner Lambert Co. v. Purepac Pharm., Civ.A. 00-02053(JCL), 2000 WL 34213890, at *12 (D. N.J. Dec. 22, 2000) (outcome of patent infringement trial "may either support or eliminate [defendant's] claim that [plaintiff] filed an objectively baseless suit"); Hunter Douglas, Inc. v. Comfortex Corp., 44 F. Supp. 2d 145, 151-52 (N.D.N.Y. 1999) ("[I]f Hunter Douglas succeeds in its patent infringement action, a significant portion of Comfortex's proof relative to its § 2 claim would become irrelevant.").

99. *In re* Innotron Diagnostics, 800 F.2d 1077, 1084 (Fed. Cir. 1986).

100. *In re* Theodor Groz & Sohne, 972 F.2d 1352, 1352 (Fed Cir. 1992) (unpublished) (sustaining trial court order denying bifurcation, noting that "district courts may generally favor the separation of patent and antitrust issues for trial, as we recognized in *Innotron*, does not render every order refusing to sever such claims an abuse of discretion."); *see also* Affymetrix, Inc. v. PE Corp., 219 F. Supp. 2d 390, 398 (S.D.N.Y. 2002) (refusing to bifurcate trial "at this early stage in discovery" but limiting discovery to patent- and contract-related claims and those aspects of plaintiff's antitrust claims "directly related to defendants' alleged inequitable conduct and patent misuse"); Intel Corp. v. VIA Tech., No. C 99-03062, 2001 WL 777085, at *7 (N.D. Cal. Mar. 20, 2001), *aff'd*, 319 F.3d 1357 (Fed. Cir. 2003) (deferring decision on bifurcation for purposes of trial, but refusing to stay discovery on antitrust issues where antitrust claims were "prior in time" to patent claims in operative complaint).

claim is predicated on allegations that the patent was fraudulently procured by the patent owner.[101]

b. Bifurcation of Discovery

Discovery pertaining to antitrust claims is generally more complex and wide-ranging than discovery pertaining to patent issues.[102] The determination of relevant markets, market power, and subjective intent, among other proof, require costly economic and factual analysis. Thus, when a court orders separate trials on the patent and antitrust issues raised in a single lawsuit, it will often stay discovery relating to the antitrust claims until the patent dispute is resolved.[103] In making the determination of whether to stay discovery, courts will often look at whether the patent infringement and antitrust evidence overlap[104] and

---

101. *See, e.g.*, *Ecrix Corp.*, 191 F.R.D. at 614 (interests of judicial economy may be outweighed and a single trial ordered "when the claims overlap, generally when the antitrust claim is based on an accusation that the patent was initially fraudulently procured by the patent holder").

102. *See, e.g.*, *Innotron Diagnostics*, 800 F.2d at 1085 n.14.

103. *See* Simpson v. Stand 21 S.A., 32 U.S.P.Q. 2d 1848, 1850 (S.D. Ind. 1994) (ordering separate trial of patent issues before trial of non-patent counterclaims and third-party claims, and staying discovery pertaining to non-patent and third-party claims until after resolution of patent issues); CMI v. Verax Sys., 5 U.S.P.Q. 2d 1676, 1678 (W.D.N.Y. 1987) (severing antitrust and unfair competition counterclaims from patent infringement, invalidity and unenforceability action and staying "discovery on the antitrust and unfair competition causes of action until after trial of the infringement and other patent issues"); Components, Inc. v. W. Elec. Co., 318 F. Supp. 959, 967-68 (S.D. Me. 1970) (staying discovery on antitrust and misuse issues until after termination of the trial of the infringement and validity issues). *But see Innotron Diagnostics*, 800 F.2d at 1085 n.14 (discovery not stayed but setting additional fourteen months for discovery on antitrust issues), *Ecrix Corp.*, 191 F.R.D. at 614 (ordering separate trials but denying stay of discovery on antitrust claims because, *inter alia*, proceeding with discovery on both issues would "allow for a quick resolution of the antitrust trial, if it is required, as both parties will already have most of the information required").

104. *See Ecrix Corp.*, 191 F.R.D. at 614 ("There will be overlap in the patent infringement/antitrust evidence so discovery on both issues will be allowed to proceed.").

whether discovery on the antitrust issue would delay resolution of the patent claims[105]

C. Remedies in Intellectual Property Antitrust Cases

Damages in intellectual property antitrust cases may be awarded for the amount of "overcharge" the plaintiff paid in supracompetitive prices, or the amount it lost in profits. Alternatively, parties may sue for equitable relief to obtain compulsory licenses for the patents or other intellectual property that had been misused. The court may order the grant of compulsory licenses on a royalty-free basis, or may permit the patentee to collect reasonable royalties.

1. Private Actions for Damages

Antitrust damages are governed by Section 4 of the Clayton Act, which provides that any person injured by reason of an antitrust violation shall be entitled to "threefold the damages by him sustained, and the cost of suit, including a reasonable attorney's fee."[106] There are essentially two general categories of antitrust damages: overcharge injuries and lost profits.[107] Damages for most antitrust violations relating to intellectual property rights fall into one of these two categories.

"Overcharge injuries" are damages sustained by purchasers that pay a supracompetitive monopoly or cartel price due to the defendant's antitrust violation. These damages typically are measured by the difference between the amount the injured party was required to pay and the amount that would have been charged in a competitive market.[108] Private damages actions under federal antitrust laws are limited by the indirect purchaser rule, however, which bars recovery for purchasers who do not purchase directly from defendants.[109]

---

105. *See Stand 21*, 32 U.S.P.Q. 2d at 1850 (staying discovery of the antitrust counterclaims because such discovery could "substantially delay the resolution of the patent issues")
106. 15 U.S.C. § 15.
107. *See generally* HOVENKAMP, *su pra* note 14, § 6.3.
108. *See id.* at 6-21.
109. *See* Ill. Brick Co. v. Illinois, 431 U.S. 720 (1977). The indirect purchaser rule allows for exceptions where the intermediate purchaser is owned or controlled by either the plaintiff or the defendant, where the direct purchaser is a co-conspirator, and where the indirect purchases were

Damages suffered by competitors as a result of exclusionary practices, vertical restraints or other anticompetitive conduct are generally calculated based on a lost profits analysis, and are measured by the difference between the injured party's actual and "but for" profits.[110] Lost profits are the most common form of antitrust damages claimed by competitors and terminated firms.   An infringement defendant who prevails on an antitrust counterclaim might seek damages in the form of the cost (trebled) of defending the baseless lawsuit. However, courts are divided on the question of whether this measure of antitrust damages is appropriate.[111]   The Fifth, Seventh, Eight and Ninth Circuits have allowed recovery for triple the cost of defending against a baseless infringement action,[112] while the Second Circuit has denied such recovery.[113]

The statue of limitations period for a damages action brought under Section 4 of the Clayton Act is four years,[114] meaning the action must be filed within four years of the date on which the cause of action "accrued."[115]   In the case of antitrust claims predicated on an alleged sham litigation, the statute of limitations begins to run on the day the lawsuit was filed, and is not affected by the filing of any subsequent pleadings.[116]

---

made under pre-existing, fixed-quantity cost-plus contracts with the direct purchaser.

110.   *See* HOVENKAMP, *supra* note 14, at 6-21.

111.   *See id.* at 6-32.3.

112.   *See* Premier Elec. Constr. v. Nat'l Elec. Contractors Ass'n, 814 F.2d 358, 371-374 (7th Cir. 1987); Handgards, Inc. v. Ethicon, Inc. (Handgards I), 601 F.2d 986, 997 (9th Cir. 1979); Kearney & Trecker Corp. v. Cincinnati Milacron, 562 F.2d 365, 374 (6th Cir. 1977); Kobe, Inc. v. Dempsey Pump Co., 198 F.2d 416 (5th Cir. 1952).

113.   *See* Ansul Co. v. Uniroyal, 448 F.2d 872, 882-883 (2d Cir. 1971); *see also* Am. Infra-Red Radiant Co. v. Lambert Indus., 360 F.2d 977, 997 (8th Cir. 1966) ("[W]henever the patent litigation is initiated pursuant to a lawful purpose and there is no causal connection between the bringing of the action and the illegal conduct, the cost of the defense of the suit cannot become an element of damage which is tripled under the Clayton Act.").

114.   15 U.S.C. § 15b.

115.   Determining the date of accrual is a controversial matter in itself. For a discussion of the relevant case law, see generally 2 PHILLIP E. AREEDA & HERBERT HOVENKAMP, ANTITRUST LAW ¶ 320 (2d ed. 2000).

116.   *See* Pace Indus. v. Three Phoenix Co., 813 F.2d 234, 237 (9th Cir. 1987) ("We hold that where the alleged antitrust violation is the attempted

2. *Equitable Relief*

a. Compulsory Licensing

In some intellectual property antitrust cases, compulsory licensing may be an appropriate remedy for anticompetitive misuses of patents or other intellectual property. In *United States v. Glaxo Group*, the Supreme Court acknowledged that "[m]andatory selling on specified terms and compulsory patent licensing at reasonable charges are recognized antitrust remedies."[117] Compulsory licensing is designed to restore competition to an industry by allowing access to the defendant's intellectual property by competitors.[118] Its use as an antitrust remedy is justified when necessary to prevent against the continued monopolization or restraint of trade in an industry or market. Another reason for imposing compulsory licensing is that this remedy encourages the entry of new competitors into markets that previously had been closed as a result of illegal restraints. Under this theory, compulsory licensing provides access to something (intellectual property rights) formerly within the defendant's exclusive control, and as such, can be viewed as "akin to essential facility doctrine or refusal to deal law."[119]

---

enforcement of an illegal contract through judicial process, the initiation of judicial proceedings is the last overt act for purposes of the statute of limitations."); *see also* Al George, Inc. v. Envirotech, Corp., 939 F.2d 1271, 1274-75 (5th Cir. 1991) (following Pace and holding that last overt act in furtherance of conspiracy was filing of patent infringement suit); *In re* Relafen Antitrust Litig., 286 F. Supp. 2d 56, 61-62 (D. Mass. 2003) ("Continuing to litigate a sham lawsuit does not constitute a 'continuing violation' of the antitrust laws.").

117. 410 U.S. 52, 64 (1973) (overruling district court's refusal to impose compulsory licensing as antitrust remedy); *see also* Besser Mfg. v. United States, 343 U.S. 444, 447 (1952) ("[C]ompulsory patent licensing is a well-recognized remedy where patent abuses are proved in antitrust actions and it is required for effective relief.").

118. *See, e.g.*, United States v. United Shoe Mach. Corp., 110 F. Supp. 295, 351 (D. Mass. 1953), *aff'd*, 347 U.S. 521 (1954) ("[C]ompulsory licensing, on a reasonable royalty basis, is in effect a partial dissolution, on a non-confiscatory basis."); *see also* HOVENKAMP,*su pra* note 14, at 6-41.

119. HOVENKAMP, *supra* note 14, at 6-41; *see also* Data Gen. Corp. v. Grumman Sys. Support Corp., 761 F. Supp. 185, 194 (D. Mass. 1991), *aff'd*, 36 F.3d 1147 (1st Cir. 1994) (noting, in dicta, that compulsory

The Supreme Court first confronted a compulsory licensing remedy in *Hartford-Empire Co. v. United States*.[120] *Hartford-Empire* involved several glass manufacturers found to have conspired to obtain over 800 patents covering glass-making machinery and license these patents in a manner designed to exclude new entry into the market.[121] After finding antitrust violations, the district court entered a decree that called for mandatory royalty-free licensing of any present or future patent owned by the defendants.[122] On appeal, the Supreme Court sustained the judgment, but concluded that the compulsory licensing provisions in the decree "in effect confiscate considerable portions of the [defendants'] property ... [and] go beyond what is required to dissolve the combination and prevent future combinations of like character."[123] Notwithstanding this criticism, the Court did not dispose of the compulsory licensing remedy contained in the decree, holding instead that the decree's provisions "should be modified to permit the reservation of reasonable royalties" and should be limited to patents relating to the machinery involved in the antitrust violations.[124]

Despite the Supreme Court's endorsement of compulsory licensing in *Hartford-Empire* and its progeny,[125] district courts have been fairly

---

licensing is an appropriate remedy for successful essential facilities claim based on refusal to grant an intellectual property license).

120. 323 U.S. 386 (1945).
121. *Id.* at 392.
122. *Id.* at 413.
123. *Id.* at 414.
124. *Id.* at 417.
125. *See* United States v. Nat'l Lead Co., 332 U.S. 319 (1947) (upholding compulsory licensing decree but rejecting government's request to substitute royalty-free licensing for reasonable royalty licensing); Besser Mfg. v. United States, 343 U.S. 444 (1952) ("[C]ompulsory patent licensing is a well-recognized remedy where patent abuses are proved in antitrust actions and it is required for effective relief."); United States v. Gypsum Co., 340 U.S. 76 (1950) (upholding decree requiring compulsory licensing of all patents in gypsum products field, including future patents for a period to be determined by district court, on equal terms to all applicants). The Supreme Court revisited the issue of compulsory licensing in 1973 in *United States v. Glaxo Group*, 410 U.S. 52 (1973). There, the Court overruled the district court's refusal to impose compulsory licenses on a reasonable royalty basis, stating that appellate courts have "an obligation to intervene in this most significant phase of the case when necessary to assure that the relief will be effective." *Id.* at 64.

reluctant to use this antitrust remedy to dissipate the effects of intellectual property-related anticompetitive conduct.[126]   The vast majority of compulsory licenses have been imposed in the context of consent decrees, rather than litigated cases.[127] Compulsory licensing has also been imposed by the FTC in consent orders concerning alleged violations of Section 5 of the Federal Trade Commission Act.[128]

b.   Reasonable Royalties or Royalty-Free?

While the Supreme Court has approved the use of compulsory licensing as an antitrust remedy, the Court has yet to rule on the validity of royalty-free compulsory licensing.   The *Hartford-Empire* opinion conveyed the Court's hostility towards royalty-free licensing and public dedication of intellectual property.[129]   Two years later, however, the

---

126. Early examples of compulsory licensing requirements imposed as a consequence of antitrust litigation include *United Shoe Machinery*, 110 F. Supp. at 351 (imposing reasonable royalty compulsory patent licensing, among other remedies, after finding monopolization of shoe machinery trade); *United States v. General Instruments*, 115 F. Supp. 582, 591 (D. N.J. 1953) (refusing government's request for dedication of defendants' patents but imposing reasonable royalty licensing of current patents and patents obtained within five years); and *United States v. Imperial Chemical Industries.*, 105 F. Supp. 215, 226-27 (S.D.N.Y. 1952) (decreeing compulsory licensing of patents misused by defendants, but declining to impose compulsory licensing of defendants' future patents).

127. *See* HOVENKAMP, *supra* note 14, at 6-51.

128. *See In re* Xerox Corp., 86 F.T.C. 364 (1975) (entering consent order requiring royalty-free licensing of patents for office copiers); *In re* Eli Lilly & Co., 95 F.T.C. 538, 546-51 (1980) (entering consent decree requiring royalty-free licensing of certain patents for a period of five years). The FTC's power to require mandatory patent licensing to alleviate the effects of an antitrust violation was established in *In re American Cyanamid Co. v. FTC*, 363 F.2d 757 (6th Cir. 1966) (holding that FTC was authorized, where appropriate, to require compulsory licensing on a reasonable royalty basis); *see also* Decision and Order, *In re* Union Oil Co., FTC Dkt. No. 9305, at 3 (July 27, 2005) (FTC decision enforcing a consent order that prevents Chevron from enforcing or charging royalties for certain Union Oil patents that it would acquire through the merger).

129. 323 U.S. 386, 415 ("[I]f ... a defendant owns valid patents, it is difficult to say that, however much in the past such defendant has abused the rights thereby conferred, it must now dedicate them to the public."); *see also* United States v. Vehicular Parking, Ltd., 61 F. Supp. 656, 657 (D.

Court retreated from this position and proclaimed the issue undecided.[130] In *National Lead*, the Court denied the government's request for royalty-free licensing, but stated that "it may well be that reasonable royalties will be but nominal in value. Such royalties might be set at zero or some nominal rate. The conclusions, however, would depend on the facts of each case."[131]

Notwithstanding the Supreme Court's hints at possible acceptance of royalty-free licensing in *National Lead*, almost all courts that have imposed a compulsory licensing remedy in litigated cases have allowed reasonable royalties for the defendant.[132] There are several reasons why courts might be reluctant to order royalty-free licensing. First, antitrust remedies in civil suits are designed to be remedial, not punitive, and courts, therefore, might view royalty-free decrees and public dedication as unduly harsh.[133] Second, antitrust remedies should go no further than

---

Del. 1945) (rejecting government's interpretation of *Hartford-Empire* "that the court has power to mandate a royalty-free license where the patent has been used as an instrument in violation of the anti-trust laws").

130. *Nat'l Lead Co.*, 332 U.S. at 338 (denying Justice Department's request for royalty-free licensing "without reaching the question whether royalty-free licensing ... is permissible as a matter of law in any case").

131. *Id.* at 349.

132. *See, e.g.*, United States v. Singer Mfg. Co., 231 F. Supp 240, 244 (S.D.N.Y. 1964) (on remand from the Supreme Court, district court refused to impose decree requiring royalty-free licensing but ordered parties submit a proposed decree requiring reasonable royalty licensing); *Gen. Instruments*, 115 F. Supp. at 591 (recognizing that issue of royalty-free licensing was left open by the Supreme Court in *Hartford-Empire* but concluding that dedication of patents was not warranted under the specific circumstances of the case); *Imperial Chem.*, 105 F. Supp. at 223-24 ("To provide for the issuance of royalty free licenses with respect to any of these [valid] patents would be to destroy the total value of the patent. We find no statutory authority for decreeing such remedies."); *see also In re* Am. Cyanamid Co., 72 F.T.C. 623, 1967 FTC LEXIS 43, *150-52 (Sept. 29, 1967) (suggesting that royalty-free licensing may be an available remedy, but imposing relief that required licensing at a 2.5% royalty rate). *See generally* Lawrence Schlam, *Compulsory Royalty-Free Licensing as an Antitrust Remedy for Patent Fraud: Law, Policy, and the Patent-Antitrust Interface Revisited*, 7 CORNELL J.L. & PUB. POL'Y 467 (1998) (discussing legal and policy reasons supporting use of compulsory licensing).

133. *See Nat'l Lead Co.*, 332 U.S. at 338 (stating that the purpose of a decree in a civil proceeding "is effective and fair enforcement, not punishment").

reasonably necessary to restore competition to the industry.[134] In many cases, reasonable royalty licensing is adequate to correct the anticompetitive harm caused by intellectual property-related antitrust violations.

Very few district courts have ordered royalty-free compulsory licensing or dedication of patents to the public.[135] *United States v. General Electric*[136] is a notable example. In that case, a district court ordered the defendant to dedicate certain patents to the public without receiving any royalties in exchange.[137] Central to the court's holding was the fact that the lamp industry was completely dominated by a single firm with an "arsenal" of patents. The court was concerned that requiring GE's smaller competitors to bear the burden of reasonable royalties "could prove to be the very factor that would push them out of the competitive circle of the market."[138] Accordingly, dedication of the relevant patents was viewed as an "essential remedy" under the circumstances of the case.[139]

---

134. *See Imperial Chem,* 105 F. Supp. at 220 ("Only those provisions reasonably necessary to accomplish correction and adjustment of a dislocated competitive situation may be applied.").

135. *See, e.g.,* United States v. Greyhound Corp., 1957 Trade Cas. (CCH) ¶ 68,756, at 73,089 (N.D. Ill. 1957) (ordering dedication of existing patents); United States v. Gen. Elec. Co., 115 F. Supp. 835, 843-44 (D. N.J. 1953) (ordering dedication of existing patents); United States v. Am. Can Co., 1950-51 Trade Cas. (CCH) ¶ 62,679, at 63,972-73 (N.D. Cal. 1950) (ordering royalty-free compulsory licensing).

136. 115 F. Supp. 835 (D. N.J. 1953); *see also Compulsory Licensing of Patents by the Federal Trade Commission,* 59 Nw. U. L. Rev. 543 (1964-1965) (discussing how *General Electric* may signal beginning of trend towards royalty-free licensing, and noting the implications of such a trend).

137. *Id.* at 843-44.

138. *Id.* at 844.

139. *Id.*

In contrast, a rather large number of consent decrees have contained royalty-free compulsory licensing provisions,[140] including consent orders entered by the FTC.[141]

---

140. *See, e.g.*, United States v. Gen. Motors, 1965 Trade Cas. (CCH) ¶ 71,624 (E.D. Mich. 1965) (royalty-free licensing on existing patents; reasonable royalties on patents obtained within five years); United States v. Pitney-Bowes, Inc., 1959 Trade Cas. (CCH) ¶ 69,235 (D. Conn. 1959); United States v. RCA, 1958 Trade Cas. (CCH) ¶ 69,164 (S.D.N.Y. 1958) (royalty-free licensing on existing patents; reasonable royalties on future patents).

141. *See In re* Xerox Corp., 86 F.T.C. 364 (1975); *In re* Eli Lilly & Co., 95 F.T.C. 538 (1980).

CHAPTER IX

COUNSELING GUIDELINES FOR THE LICENSING OF INTELLECTUAL PROPERTY

The Antitrust Division of the Department of Justice and Federal Trade Commission *Antitrust Guidelines for the Licensing of Intellectual Property*[1] form the primary basis for advising clients on the antitrust boundaries of technology licensing, notwithstanding the fact that they are only persuasive authority in the courts.[2] To date, the *Intellectual Property Guidelines* are the most comprehensive source of law and policy regarding the appropriate antitrust principles to be applied when analyzing the legality of the licensing of intellectual property, and are frequently cited as authority. Other relevant authority includes some case law from lower courts that involves the appropriate antitrust principles to be applied in the context of intellectual property licensing. In addition, the agencies also respond to specific requests for guidance from the business community—through the DOJ's Business Review Letter and the FTC's Staff Advisory Opinion Letters process—detailing how they would evaluate and react to particular types of business conduct. Finally, counselors should be aware of case law that involves the sale of goods (as opposed to the licensing of intellectual property),

---

1. *See* U.S. DEP'T OF JUSTICE & FED. TRADE COMM'N, ANTITRUST GUIDELINES FOR THE LICENSING OF INTELLECTUAL PROPERTY (April 6, 1995) (hereinafter INTELLECTUAL PROPERTY GUIDELINES), *reprinted in* 4 Trade Reg. Rep. (CCH) ¶ 13,132 *and* Appendix 1 to this Handbook.

2. The *Intellectual Property Guidelines* reflect the enforcement position of the federal antitrust authorities, but they are not binding on the courts. Nonetheless, the Guidelines themselves are based primarily on existing case law and current economic thinking, making them persuasive authority and an informed source for counselors. *See* Yee Wah Chin & Kathryn E. Walsh, *Antitrust Counseling in Intellectual Property Licensing*, 832 PLI/Pat 267, 275 (June 2005); Richard J. Hoskins & Zubin P. Khambatta, *Antitrust Law and Intellectual Property Licensing: An Overview*, 806 PLI/Pat 449 (Oct. 2004). Also relevant to understanding the enforcement position of the agencies are the various mechanisms used to provide industry guidance, such as: speeches from the top ranking officials, studies from agencies' leading economists, policy statements regarding the negotiation and settlement of claims that fall short of litigation, and joint reports generated from investigative hearings into particular practices and hearings.

which also provides important guidance as to the appropriate antitrust framework to apply to the licensing of intellectual property. In sum, these sources should be considered collectively by the antitrust counselor. In this chapter, we rely most extensively on the *Intellectual Property Guidelines*, and note where case law authority diverges from the principles articulated in the *Intellectual Property Guidelines*.

At the most basic level, the *Intellectual Property Guidelines* instruct that antitrust counseling is inherently a fact-specific process, requiring attorneys to comprehend the substance of a licensing transaction.[3] To facilitate the process, the *Guidelines* outline a multi-step approach for effective counseling.

As an initial matter, counselors must identify the nature of the licensing restrictions associated with the transaction and how such restrictions affect the parties' relationship to one another and to other potential competitors.[4] This inquiry requires an examination of what anticompetitive effects potentially can arise from a particular arrangement, and in so doing, a determination of the level of antitrust scrutiny likely to be applied. For all but the most suspect of licensing practices, the absence of market power typically ends the need for further antitrust inquiry.[5] But where market power exists, or where the parties purport to have a compelling need for engaging in practices traditionally viewed as problematic, the counselor must evaluate the strength and legitimacy of the proffered business justifications and whether the procompetitive goals of the restraints can be accomplished by less restrictive means.[6] Finally, where licensing restrictions are reasonably necessary to advance valid business justifications yet present a risk of restraining competition, the counselor must assess of whether the arrangement will produce sufficient off-setting procompetitive effects to outweigh the potential for anticompetitive harm. More simply, the counselor must ask whether the procompetitive benefits of the license are unlikely to be realized but for the licensing restrictions.

A. Identifying and Understanding the Nature of the Restriction

By providing intellectual property owners with considerable discretion to structure their licensing schemes, the *Intellectual Property*

---

3.   INTELLECTUAL PROPERTY GUIDELINES,*su pra* note 1, § 1.0 & n.2.
4.   *See id.* §§ 3.3-3.4.
5.   *Id.* § 3.4.
6.   *Id.* §§ 3.4, 4.1-4.2, 5.1.

Guidelines embrace the notion that consumers can benefit greatly from a regulatory regime that facilitates the wide-scale dissemination of technology.[7] Through intellectual property licensing arrangements, technology can be broadly and quickly deployed. Moreover, a permissive licensing regime increases the likelihood that innovators will focus on their core competencies while entrusting their creations to those in the vertical chain with superior capabilities in production, use, marketing, and distribution.[8]

With these principles in mind, the *Intellectual Property Guidelines* allow innovators to take reasonable measures to protect and maximize the value of their intellectual property. For example, licensing restrictions can contribute to an efficiency-enhancing integration of complementary assets by "aligning the incentives of the ... licensees to promote the development and marketing of the licensed technology, or by substantially reducing transaction costs."[9] Other restrictions allow the innovator to license its technology to discrete geographies or narrow fields of use, thereby "increas[ing] the licensor's incentive to license ... by protecting the licensor from competition in the licensor's own technology in a market niche that it prefers to keep to itself."[10]

Although certain licensing restrictions are necessary to efficiently and effectively exploit intellectual property rights (which benefits consumers), in some cases, agreed-upon restrictions may restrain

---

7. In the United States, intellectual property owners are under no general obligation either to use their patent rights or license them to others. INTELLECTUAL PROPERTY GUIDELINES, *supra* note 1, § 2.2. (where intellectual property rights confer market power, such market power does not "impose on the intellectual property owner an obligation to license the use of that property to others"); 35 U.S.C. § 271(d) (unilateral refusal to deal will not be construed as patent misuse); *In re* Indep. Serv. Orgs. Antitrust Litig., 203 F.3d 1322 (Fed. Cir. 2000). *But see* Image Technical Servs. v. Eastman Kodak Co., 125 F.3d 1195 (9th Cir. 1997); Robert Pitofsky, Challenges of the New Economy: Issues at the Intersection of Antitrust and Intellectual Property, Remarks before the Am. Antitrust Inst. (June 15, 2000), *available at* http://www.ftc.gov/speeches/pitofsky/000615speech.htm.
8. *See* INTELLECTUAL PROPERTY GUIDELINES, *supra* note 1, §§ 1.0, 2.3; *see generally* FED. TRADE COMM'N, TO PROMOTE INNOVATION: THE PROPER BALANCE OF COMPETITION AND PATENT LAW AND POLICY (Oct. 2003), available at www.ftc.gov/os/2003/10/innovtionrpt.pdf.
9. INTELLECTUAL PROPERTY GUIDELINES,*su pra* note 1, § 3.4.
10. *Id.* § 2.3.

competition to the detriment of consumers.[11] Antitrust review of licensing arrangements must therefore begin by identifying the conditions upon which the parties have agreed to license technology. This identification is followed by an inspection of how the restrictions affect both the parties' relationship and competition more generally.

It is important to note that these counseling guidelines are only as good as the parties' contemporaneous documents or testimony reflecting the parties' intentions at the time they entered into their licensing arrangement. All too often, counselors present "facts" learned from the parties that contradict the documentary evidence within their ordinary course business files or facts that do not withstand cross-examination. Thus, the counselor must confirm with the client that the justification for any business arrangement, or the client's understanding of the market, is supported by the weight of existing evidence.

B. Characterizing the Licensing Relationship

1. The Impact of Characterization on Antitrust Analysis

The distinction between horizontal and vertical relationships is significant when analyzing intellectual property licensing arrangements; the parties' relationship to one another determines the potential harm to competition that can result from a particular arrangement. Characterization of the relationship is therefore a substantial first step in determining the appropriate legal standard for antitrust review.

When the parties are in a vertical relationship, antitrust law adopts a more permissive approach toward licensing restrictions.[12] The law recognizes that non-price restrictions (and maximum resale price restrictions) in purely vertical licenses are less likely to harm competition than restrictions in horizontal licenses.[13] An important exception to this general principle involves exclusive dealing arrangements that create a substantial degree of market foreclosure.[14] Additionally, antitrust

---

11.   *Id.* § 3.1.
12.   *See id.* §§ 3.4, 4.1; *see also* Cont'l T.V. v. GTE Sylvania Inc., 433 U.S. 36, 49 (1977).
13.   *See, e.g.,* State Oil Co. v. Khan, 522 U.S. 3, 15-18 (1997).
14.   INTELLECTUAL PROPERTY GUIDELINES, *supra* note 1, § 4.1.2, Ex. 8; *see also* United States v. Microsoft Corp., 253 F.3d 34, 68-71 (D.C. Cir. 2001).

concerns arise where a vertical restriction is likely to facilitate coordination among competitors.[15]

Technology arrangements between horizontal competitors are more likely to harm competition and, therefore, are at a greater risk of attracting antitrust scrutiny, even though they do not per se violate the antitrust laws.[16] The primary concern with horizontal arrangements is that they may be used to conceal or facilitate collusive behavior, such as agreements to maintain prices, restrict output, reduce innovation, or allocate markets.[17] Similarly, license restrictions among competitors may increase the likelihood that the companies will tacitly coordinate their strategic decisions.[18] The risk of such behavior depends upon market structure, including industry concentration, barriers to entry, and other characteristics that insulate incumbents from competition and allow market participants to exercise market power collectively.[19]

2. Distinguishing between Horizontal and Vertical Licenses

In the context of intellectual property licensing, the task of distinguishing between vertical and horizontal relationships is often more difficult than simply identifying whether the parties are manufacturers, distributors or resellers. Indeed, licensing parties occupying the same level of commerce (e.g., manufacturers) can stand in a vertical relationship, just as parties at opposite ends of the chain (e.g., manufacturers and resellers) can enter into an arrangement with horizontal implications. The key factor is whether the parties' arrangement integrates complementary factors of production or impacts a competitive or potentially competitive relationship.[20] Frequently, technology licenses exhibit aspects of both horizontal and vertical arrangements.[21]

---

15. INTELLECTUAL PROPERTY GUIDELINES, *su pra* note 1, § 4.1.1.
16. *Id.* § 3.3 ("existence of a horizontal relationship between [competitors] does not, in itself, indicate that the arrangement is anticompetitive").
17. *Id.* § 4.1.
18. *Id.* § 4.1.1.
19. *Id.*
20. *Id.* §§ 3.4, 4.1.1.
21. *See, e.g.*, Generac Corp. v. Caterpillar Inc., 172 F.3d 971 (7th Cir. 1999) (trademark license entered into as part of a distribution agreement where Caterpillar was both an upstream supplier of the trademark and downstream purchaser of finished product. After analyzing competition in both product markets, the agreement was found to be neither per se illegal nor unreasonably anticompetitive).

What is a Vertical Relationship? A vertical business arrangement allows parties to procure capabilities that they lack. Examples of purely vertical arrangements include licensing situations where: (1) one party focuses exclusively on the research and development of technologies, and the other focuses on using the technology to manufacture products or services; (2) two parties make component parts, both of which are inputs that help to create a larger finished product when combined; or (3) one party focuses exclusively on manufacturing products, and the other specializes in distribution, marketing or retail.

What is a Horizontal Relationship? Horizontal relationships, on the other hand, encompass arrangements between parties that compete for sales in a given product, technology, or innovation market. Horizontal relationships also include arrangements between parties that are likely to find themselves in a competitive posture in the future, even if they do not compete presently (i.e., potential competitors). As explained in the *Intellectual Property Guidelines*, a licensing relationship is treated as horizontal when the parties "would have been actual or likely potential competitors in a relevant market in the absence of the license."[22] Thus, a license that facially appears to be vertical can nevertheless be characterized as horizontal if one party is reasonably likely to enter the market of another.

How does antitrust treat the licensing of blocking technology? Where a licensing agreement involves a superior technology or blocking intellectual property rights, the licensing relationship between even direct competitors may be vertical. For example, if an intellectual property-protected technology is "far superior" to a competitor's technology, the relationship may be considered vertical, because the "far superior" technology is not a substitute for the inferior technology.[23] However, if the proprietor of the inferior technology is likely to develop an improvement that would allow it to eventually compete with the "superior" technology, the parties will be deemed to have a horizontal relationship by virtue of potential competition.[24]

Similarly, parties whose intellectual property rights are blocking "are not in a horizontal relationship with respect to those patents," because infringing intellectual property rights cannot be exploited in the absence of an agreement.[25] Thus, a licensing agreement used to clear blocking

22.   *See* Intellectual Property Guidelines, *supra* note 1, § 3.3.
23.   *See id.* § 3.3, Ex. 5.
24.   *See id.*
25.   *See id.* § 5.5, Ex. 10.

positions would be treated as complementary, and therefore, vertical, regardless of the similarity in the patents' intended application. However, the same would not be true if the parties' agreement lessens the likelihood that one of the parties will invent around the blocking position or successfully challenge the validity of the intellectual property rights alleged to be blocking.

Parties who seem to stand in a complementary relationship, however, will be deemed in a horizontal relationship if their license agreement is overly broad and restricts competition in other technology or innovation markets where the parties are actual or potential competitors. For example, parties would be considered in a horizontal relationship if their licensing agreement attempts to apply restrictions to all downstream products, including those that do not incorporate the licensed technology. The same would be true if a license attempts to cure a partial blocking position (i.e., for a particular use or narrow territory) with a broad set of restrictions that impedes competition in applications or geographies where no infringement concerns exist.

3. Questions a Counselor Must Ask when Characterizing the Relationship

The characterization of a licensing arrangement can be critically important in the assessment of whether an agreement poses potential antitrust risks. Because relationships between licensor and licensee can be complex, it is imperative that the counselor be well versed in the client's business. Engaging the parties in thorough dialogue about their intellectual property and licensing arrangements affords the best opportunity to identify potential issues at their inception. Counselors must consider three key areas: (1) are the technologies substitutes; (2) are the patents blocking; and (3) is one technology vastly superior. Below, we highlight questions that counselors should ask when making the determination as to the nature of the relationship between licensor and licensee.

Are the Technologies Substitutes?

- Do the parties own technologies that compete for sales in a particular process, design, or use?
- Does a well-defined group of customers or manufacturers view the technologies as functionally equivalent and interchangeable? If so, can such customers use either technology to accomplish

their goals?   Similarly, do the parties regularly compete for technology sales to these customers? If not, why?

- Are the technologies similarly priced? For those customers who view the technologies as functionally interchangeable, do large price differentials preclude a substantial portion from purchasing the more expensive technology?

- Is there a well-defined group of customers which does not view the technologies as substitutable?   In what ways, or for what uses, do the two technologies fundamentally differ?   Have the parties ever competed for technology sales to such customers for these particular uses?

- To the extent one party does not compete for specific customers or technology uses, is that party likely to develop a technology that will eventually compete on these bases?

- Do the parties compete for sales to end-users in downstream product markets? Here, the focus is on whether end-users view the finished products as functionally equivalent and substitutable, regardless of whether or not the goods incorporate competing technologies. If dealing in a patented product, do the parties' products compete in certain geographies or for particular non-infringing uses?

- If the parties do not currently compete in downstream product markets, is either party likely to enter the market with a competing product?

Is One Technology Vastly Superior?

- Is one technology vastly superior to the other? If so, does that superiority translate into an added level of function or consumer utility that renders the inferior technology incapable of competing for sales with a well-defined group of customers?

- To the extent the technology of one party is vastly superior to that of the other, is the proprietor of the inferior technology likely to develop a non-infringing improvement that will be either competitive or superior?

Do the Parties Own Blocking Positions?

- Do the intellectual property rights of the parties infringe upon one another, such that the parties are prohibited (i.e., blocked) from using or selling their technologies in the absence of a

license?   Are the parties completely blocked from practicing
their technologies, or are they able to compete in certain
geographies, or for particular non-infringing uses?

- Are the intellectual property rights at issue valid, meaning that
  the substance and scope of the claimed blocking positions is
  likely to withstand challenge during an infringement action?
- To the extent the parties claim to have blocking patents, is either
  party likely to design around the patents by developing a non-
  infringing technology? Similarly, to the extent that one or both
  parties have "weak" intellectual property rights, is either party
  likely to mount a successful challenge to the validity of the
  other's intellectual property rights?

C. Market Power within a Relevant Market

1. *Intellectual Property Guidelines Approach to Defining Market Power*

The *Intellectual Property Guidelines* define market power as "the
ability profitably to maintain prices above, or output below, competitive
levels for a significant period of time."[26] The *Guidelines* do not presume
that the mere possession of intellectual property necessarily confers
market power upon its owner.   This is because "there will often be
sufficient actual or potential close substitutes for such product, process,
or work to prevent the exercise of market power."[27]

2. *Three Possible Relevant Markets*

The *Intellectual Property Guidelines* identify three types of markets
that may be impacted by a licensing agreement: (1) goods and services
markets; (2) technology markets; and (3) research and development
markets.[28]   If the effects of licensing arrangements can be assessed
adequately within the relevant markets for the goods and services (either
final or intermediate) affected by the arrangements, the *Guidelines*
counsel limiting the analysis to the market for those goods or services,
which may be defined through the methods identified in Section 1 of the

---

26.   *Id.* § 2.2.
27.   *Id.*
28.   *See id.* § 3.2.

U.S. Department of Justice and Federal Trade Commission *Horizontal Merger Guidelines.*[29]

What is a technology market? When rights to intellectual property are marketed separately from the products in which they are used, the *Intellectual Property Guidelines* require an analysis of a separate technology market, consisting of the licensed intellectual property and its substitutes.[30] To date, the courts have not yet specified the process for defining technology markets,[31] however, the *Guidelines* instruct that we first look to objective evidence of market share. They will also include evidence of buyers' and market participants' assessment of the 'competitive significance' of participants in a technology market.[32] If such data is unavailable, the *Guidelines* assign comparably efficient competing technologies equal market shares. For new technologies, the *Guidelines* dictate that one should generally use the "best available information to estimate market acceptance over a two-year period, beginning with commercial introduction."[33]

What is an innovation market? Because a licensing arrangement may also have competitive effects on innovation that cannot be adequately addressed through the analysis of goods or technology markets, the *Intellectual Property Guidelines* extend its analysis to research and development or "innovation" markets.[34] Such markets consist of the R&D directed to a particular new or improved good or process, and close substitutes for that research and development, i.e., goods, technologies, or research efforts that significantly constrain the exercise of market power with respect to the relevant research and development.[35] In an innovation market, the *Guidelines* "base the market

---

29.   *Id.* § 3.2.1, n.17.
30.   *Id.* § 3.2.2, Ex. 2.
31.   For an excellent example of how the agencies would strive to prove the existence of a technology market in a civil non-merger litigation, see the complaint counsel's posttrial brief in *In re Union Oil Co. of California*, No. 9305, 2005 WL 906397, at *116 (F.T.C. Mar. 9, 2005) (alleging that Unocal monopolized the market for technology to make, use, and sell CARB-compliant summertime gasoline).
32.   INTELLECTUAL PROPERTY GUIDELINES, *supra* note 1, § 3.2.2, Ex. 2.
33.   *Id.*
34.   *Id.* § 3.2.3, Ex. 4; *see also* Christine A. Varney, Why Innovation Market Analysis Makes Sense, Remarks before the Antitrust 1995 Conference (Mar. 15, 1995), *available at* 1995 WL 112078, at *2-5 (outlining a construct for defining innovation markets).
35.   INTELLECTUAL PROPERTY GUIDELINES, *supra* note 1, § 3.2.3 & n.25.

shares of participants ... on their shares of identifiable assets or characteristics upon which innovation depends, on shares of research and development expenditures, or on shares of a related product."[36] In the absence of such information, the agencies will assign equal market shares to entities with "comparable capabilities and incentives to pursue research and development that is a close substitute" to the activities of the licensing parties.[37]

3. Counseling Questions Regarding the Determination of Market Power

Antitrust analysis often turns on market definition. Accordingly, it is imperative that counselors have a thorough understanding of the possible relevant market(s) that might be asserted, the market's permeability and contours, the market shares of market participants, and the relative difficulties surrounding entry. Once again, engaging the parties in dialogue over these issues is an indispensable means of gleaning the relevant information.

Which Market Should Be Analyzed? How these questions are answered will dictate whether the agreement affects a "goods" or a "technology" market.

- What is the nature of the market—is it a goods market, a technology market, or an R&D/innovation market?
- What is the best way to evaluate the market for the technology at issue in the parties' agreement? Is the technology sold primarily in the form of an intermediate good (e.g., a component input) or

---

36. *Id.* § 3.2.3. There are relatively few instances in which antitrust liability has been found in an innovation market. This may be because there is no consensus about whether or to what extent antitrust violations can occur in such markets. For example, in its most recent pronouncement on innovation markets, FTC Chairman Muris indicated that the Commission is especially cautious in using innovation market analysis because "economic theory and empirical investigations have not established a general causal relationship between innovation and comp-etition." Statement of Chairman Timothy J. Muris in the Matter of Genzyme Corporation/Novazyme Pharmaceuticals, Inc., File No. 021 0026 (Jan 13, 2004) (internal quotations and citation omitted), *available at* http://www.ftc.gov/os/2004/01/murisgenzymestmt.pdf, at 2.

37. INTELLECTUAL PROPERTY GUIDELINES,*su pra* note 1, § 3.2.3, Ex. 3.

as a final product? Or is the technology marketed separately from the products in which they are used (e.g., a process)?

What are the Boundaries of the Relevant Market? As in all analyses of relevant markets, counselors must determine which products/technologies compete in the relevant market.

- Who else in the market offers competing products or technology?
- If customers could no longer purchase the parties' products or technology, from where else can customers purchase viable substitutes? Are these alternative technologies or products comparable in terms of function, quality, reputation, and availability?
- Are there any other solutions capable of addressing the needs of customers and end-users?

What are the Parties' Market Shares? Market shares are a starting point for determining whether a party has "market power" in a relevant market.

- If dealing with products or services markets, what percentage of sales (in units and revenue) can be attributed to the parties both individually and combined?
- Are these market share estimates confirmed by internal company documents? What do industry experts and market analysts report for market shares?
- Are these market shares stable or volatile over recent years and quarters? Are they increasing or decreasing, and why?
- What are the market shares for the parties' closest competitors and which way are they trending?
- On the other hand, if the technology at issue is primarily sold on a stand-alone basis, how many other technology providers are in the market?
- How many offer comparatively efficient technologies (i.e., competitively viable)?
- Do the parties' internal documents confirm this view? What about industry experts?

- Has the number of technology market participants remained stable? If volatile, is the number of participants increasing or decreasing, and why?

Do the Parties Have Market Power? Of course, a market share determination is only the first step in determining whether a party has market power. Once market share has been determined, a counselor must take the next step of identifying whether the parties entering into the license agreement have "market power" by addressing the following questions:

- If either party imposes a significant and lasting price increase on the products or technology, how would customers react? Would the price increase prompt a substantial portion of new customers to purchase an alternate product or technology?
- If not, would the increase cause customers to delay their purchases in favor of an incumbent solution?
- To the extent there is a significant replacement business for the parties' products or technology, do existing customers have the ability to switch providers mid-stream?
- Is there a large installed base that is incompatible with competing technologies (i.e., locked-in customers)? How long would it take to switch providers and at what cost? Will these customers switch in response to a price increase?

What are Entry Conditions? The final inquiry in determining whether a party has lasting market power is to ascertain whether entry is likely. According to the *Intellectual Property Guidelines*, "easy entry" is a defense to a claim of market power. Thus, counselors should ask the following to determine whether entry is easy:

- Is it likely that a meaningful level of new entry will occur quickly (e.g., within two years) if the parties imposed a significant and lasting price increase?
- Are there companies in adjacent markets with the ability and motivation to enter the market? Can they quickly reposition resources?
- Are existing competitors likely to expand operations or develop a next generation product or technology?

- Are there companies in foreign markets with comparable products and technology? If so, are they blocked from entering the US market?
- What are entry conditions like for new entry?
- Is the market growing or profitable?
- Are there intellectual property or other legal barriers to entry (e.g., certification)? Must a new entrant have an established reputation, or operate at a minimum scale in order to make entry viable?
- How long would it take for a new entrant to develop and market a comparable or superior product, and at what cost?

D. The Applicable Antitrust Standard

1. Per se Violations—Market Power Irrelevant

Just as is the case with other forms of property, certain kinds of licensing agreements are per se violations of the antitrust laws regardless of the presence of market power. Thus, horizontal price-fixing resulting from agreements of competing intellectual property owners has been found unlawful.[38] Similarly, naked agreements between competitors that seek to divide markets[39] or restrain output[40] will be found illegal. Agreements among competitors that restrict licensing or give one competitor the right to veto another's strategic licensing decisions (e.g., pricing, marketing, output, innovation) will likewise be treated as per se illegal.[41] In the context of vertical price-fixing, the setting of minimum resale prices remains a per se violation.[42] Finally, it is possible that

---

38. United States v. New Wrinkle, Inc., 342 U.S. 371, 377 (1952).
39. *See, e.g.*, Engine Specialties v. Bombardier Ltd., 605 F.2d 1, 7-8 (1st Cir. 1979). But market allocation devices are not necessarily illegal in the patent context, indeed, territorial restrictions are specifically provided for by statute. *See* 35 U.S.C. § 261 (exempting territorial restrictions in a patent license within the U.S. from the antitrust laws).
40. Broad. Music v. CBS, 441 U.S. 1, 19-20 (1979).
41. Mannington Mills v. Congoleum Indus., 610 F.2d 1059, 1070 (3d Cir. 1979).
42. *New Wrinkle, Inc.*, 342 U.S. at 378-80. *But see* United States v. Gen. Elec. Co., 272 U.S. 476, 488-89 (1926).

restrictions that are devoid of an efficiency justification may be per se illegal as well.[43]

2. Rule of Reason—Market Power Matters

A rule of reason analysis weighs the procompetitive efficiencies of a given restraint against possible anticompetitive effects, necessarily engaging in a qualitative comparison.[44]   Thus, whether licensing restraints will be afforded per se or rule of reason treatment turns on "whether the restraint in question can be expected to contribute to an efficiency-enhancing integration of economic activity."[45]   Because licensing arrangements are thought generally to promote such integration, the "vast majority" of licensing agreements will be analyzed under the rule of reason.[46] It is only in those rare cases where there is no plausible efficiency-enhancing integration of economic activity and the type of restraint has been traditionally afforded per se treatment that rule of reason analysis will not apply.

Rule of reason analysis generally requires a comprehensive inquiry into market conditions.   However, under the *Intellectual Property Guidelines*, that inquiry may be significantly reduced in scope if the restraint likely has no anticompetitive effects.[47]   In such cases, the restraint may be deemed reasonable without an elaborate analysis of market power or the justifications for the restraint.

Conversely, a so-called quick-look analysis may be appropriate where a restraint appears to be "facially" of a kind that always or almost always results in increased prices or reduced output, and is not reasonably related to efficiencies.[48]   The *Guidelines* specifically cite the

---

43.   *See* Complaint, United States v. LSL Biotech., No. 00-529-TUC-RCC, ¶¶ 6, 42 (D. Ariz. Sept. 15, 2000) (DOJ alleged that the restraints in a joint venture were "not reasonably necessary to any legitimate joint activity," "not reasonably necessary" to the venture, and so overbroad as to scope and duration as to "constitute a naked restraint."), *available at* http://www.usdoj.gov/atr/cases/f6500/6503.pdf;   Complaint, United States v. The MathWorks, Inc., No. 02-888-A, ¶ 5 (E.D. Va. June 21, 2002), *available at* http://www.usdoj.gov/atr/cases/f11300/11369.pdf; *Gen. Elec.*, 272 U.S. at 483-85.
44.   *See* INTELLECTUAL PROPERTY GUIDELINES, *supra* note 1, § 4.2.
45.   *Id.* § 3.4 (citing *Broad. Music*, 441 U.S. at 16-24).
46.   INTELLECTUAL PROPERTY GUIDELINES,*su pra* note 1, § 3.4.
47.   *Id.*
48.   *Id.* § 3.4, n.27.

truncated rule of reason methodology adopted in *Massachusetts Board of Registration in Optometry.*[49] The feasibility of this flexible antitrust approach finds support in *California Dental Association v. FTC,* where the Supreme Court advised that "[t]he truth is that our categories of analysis of anticompetitive effect are less fixed than terms like 'per se,' 'quick look,' and 'rule of reason' tend to make them appear."[50] Rather, "there is generally no categorical line to be drawn between restraints that give rise to an intuitively obvious inference of anticompetitive effect and those that call for more detailed treatment. What is required, rather, is an enquiry meet for the case, looking to the circumstances, details, and logic of a restraint."[51]

3. Safe Harbors

In the application of the rule of reason, the *Intellectual Property Guidelines* establish an antitrust "safety zone."[52] This rule affords a degree of certainty to licensors and licensees contemplating entering into agreements.[53] The *Intellectual Property Guidelines* state that "[a]bsent extraordinary circumstances, the Agencies will not challenge a restraint in an intellectual property licensing arrangement in a goods or services market if (1) the restraint is not facially anticompetitive [i.e., a per se violation] and (2) the licensor and its licensees collectively account for

---

49.   *Id.* (citing 110 F.T.C. 549, 604 (1988)).

50.   526 U.S. 756, 779 (1999).

51.   *Id.* at 780-81; *see also* Polygram Holding v. FTC, 416 F.3d 29, 35-36 (D.C. Cir. 2005) (holding that the "legal framework ... devised [by the FTC] in *Mass. Board* ... is consistent with the Supreme Court's teaching ... in *California Dental*," and therefore an appropriate method of analysis for § 1 antitrust claims).

52.   *See* INTELLECTUAL PROPERTY GUIDELINES, *supra* note 1, § 4.3. These safety zones are reiterated in the *Competitor Collaboration Guidelines. See* U.S. DEP'T OF JUSTICE & FED. TRADE COMM'N, ANTITRUST GUIDELINES FOR COLLABORATIONS AMONG COMPETITORS (hereinafter COMPETITOR COLLABORATIONS GUIDELINES), *reprinted in* 4 Trade Reg. Rep. (CCH) ¶ 13,161 (2000).

53.   However, just because an agreement falls out outside of the safety zone does not mean that it will be found anticompetitive. This is because the safety zone is no substitute for analysis of the effects of a proposed restraint.

no more than *twenty percent* of each relevant market significantly affected by the restraint."[54]

The *Intellectual Property Guidelines* present a more nuanced analysis of whether the safety zone applies in technology and innovation markets. In a technology market where accurate market share information is unavailable, the *Guidelines* extend "safety zone" protection to licenses that are (1) not facially anticompetitive if (2) there are at least four independently controlled technologies that are substitutes for the technology subject to the licensing agreement. In innovation markets, the "safety zone" applies to licenses that are (1) not facially anticompetitive if (2) there are at least four independently controlled entities in addition to the parties to the licensing arrangement which "possess the required specialized assets or characteristics and the incentive to engage in research and development that is a close substitute of the research and development activities of the parties to the licensing agreement."[55]

Thus, to determine whether the parties fall within the antitrust safety zones established by the *Intellectual Property Guidelines*, one must ask the following questions:

(1) Do the parties collectively account for less than twenty percent of the relevant product markets?
(2) Are there at least four other competitively viable technologies available on the market?
(3) Is the licensing agreement free of any facially anticompetitive provisions, such as horizontal restraints on price, output, or group boycotts?

Such safety zones are not recognized expressly by the case law and, as a result, should not be relied upon by the antitrust counselor when facing private antitrust challenges to licensing regimes. However, as a practical matter, the case law rarely—if ever—would hold that a party with a 20 percent market share has "market power." As a result, in all likelihood, a licensing provision that was not facially anticompetitive implemented by parties without such market power would not be found by a court to violate the antitrust law.

---

54. INTELLECTUAL PROPERTY GUIDELINES, *supra* note 1, § 4.3 (emphasis added).
55. *Id.*

E. Business Justifications Underlying Restrictions

Where the analysis shows that a restraint is likely to have an anticompetitive effect, the next inquiry requires a counselor to determine whether the restraint is reasonably necessary to achieve procompetitive efficiencies.   If it is, the counselor must endeavor to "balance the procompetitive efficiencies and the anticompetitive effects to determine the probable net effect on competition in each relevant market."[56]

Among the factors that drive the analysis are whether the proffered justifications are cognizable (i.e., theoretically plausible and of a character that is likely to advance competitive efficiencies) and valid (i.e., whether in application they actually accomplish their asserted goal).[57] More importantly, the licensing restraints must be an appropriate and proportional remedy for thc parties' particular business concerns, which entails consideration of the "existence of practical and significantly less restrictive alternatives."[58] The existence of a less restrictive alternative lessens the impact of asserted efficiencies.[59] But the *Intellectual Property Guidelines* make clear that efficiency analysis must stay firmly grounded in commercial reality, eschewing "a search for a theoretically least restrictive alternative that is not realistic in the practical prospective business situation faced by the parties."[60]

In order to determine whether a particular business justification for an otherwise anticompetitive licensing arrangement will survive antitrust scrutiny, a counselor must be prepared to answer the following.

Is the Justification Necessary to the Licensing Arrangement? Because business justifications must *be* transaction specific, the counselor must be able to explain how the justification itself is necessary to achieve the goals of the arrangement.   Accordingly, the counselor

---

56.   *Id.* § 4.2.
57.   *Id.*; *see also In re* Polygram Holding, No. 9298, 2003 WL 21770765, at 13-14 (F.T.C. July 24, 2005), *aff'd,* Polygram Holding v. FTC, 416 F.3d 29 (D.C. Cir. 2005).
58.   INTELLECTUAL PROPERTY GUIDELINES,*su pra* note 1, § 4.2.
59.   *Id.*
60.   *Id.* This pragmatic approach has been adopted wholesale by the *Competitor Collaborations Guidelines*, and is mirrored in the case law. *See, e.g.*, Am. Motor Inns v. Holiday Inns, 521 F.2d 1230, 1249 (3d Cir. 1975) (stating that, in a rule of reason case, the existence of a less restrictive alternative is relevant but not determinative as the "[a]pplication of the rigid 'no less restrictive alternative' test ... would place an undue burden on the ordinary conduct of business").

must consider the business context of the transaction, and the rationale for the deal, as well as the business goals the parties seek to achieve by the arrangement.

Is the Justification Grounded in Business Reality? It is important to assess the degree to which the parties' thinking and business records support their proffered justifications. As a result, the parties' internal planning documents must support proffered business justifications.

How Restrictive is the Arrangement? Because the real world balancing of efficiencies and competitive effects can be difficult, assessing benefits against costs is often accomplished by examining whether less restrictive alternatives were available. Proper consideration of this question requires the counselor to understand the motivations for and contours of each contemplated restriction: Why are certain intellectual property rights and restrictions included in the transaction? What business concerns do the parties hope to cure and in what ways do they think incentive structures need to be realigned to the benefit of the licensing relationship? Are any concerns over free-riding and misappropriation well-founded and supported in the parties' documents?

What is the Anticipated Customer Response? Customer response is often a key factor in the antitrust analysis. Accordingly, thorough scrutiny of the basis of any possible negative consumer reaction is imperative: Which customers will complain about the deal? Are they made to purchase more intellectual property rights or products than desired? Have the parties considered other alternatives that will address customer concerns, without sacrificing the parties' business objectives?

What is the Effect on Competition? Antitrust laws are meant to protect competition, not competitors. Still, analysis of an arrangement's potential harm to particular competitors may sometimes serve as a proxy for assessing whether the arrangement may harm competition in general. Understanding the competitive dynamics in the relevant market therefore aids the antitrust analysis. Who are the competitors that may be affected by the deal? Would the deal result in the elimination of an actual or potential competitor? Will it handicap any rivals by raising their costs of production, distribution, or R&D? Does it foreclose a rival from accessing the market or a significant portion of end-users? If the proposed arrangement has the potential to harm competition, what offsetting efficiencies might the license accomplish that cannot be achieved in another way? Are there substantial efficiencies? Can they be accomplished by less restrictive means?

With these general principles in mind, we turn to the treatment of specific licensing restrictions.

F. Analyzing Particular Licensing Practices

Common licensing practices often raise antitrust issues. Effective counseling therefore requires the ability to identify these issues and develop the means to alleviate the concerns.

1. Royalties

The owner of intellectual property has the right to require royalty payments in exchange for licensing its rights, and may generally charge as high a rate as the market will bear, provided the royalty is related to the licensee's use of the intellectual property.[61]   Here, intellectual property owners want to consider issues such as: Are the intellectual property rights valid? Have they expired? Are the royalties keyed to goods or processes that use the licensed technology? The following are the primary questions that counselors must ask in deciding whether a particular royalty arrangement runs afoul of the antitrust laws.

Are Royalties Potentially Tied to Goods That Do Not Use the Licensed Technology? Typically royalty payments are based on criteria designed to measure utilization of the licensed intellectual property, though licensors are permitted to use reasonable proxy measures that ease the accounting process. As such, "total sales" provisions that require the payment of royalties for the sale of products not necessarily using the licensed technology are permissible if agreed to voluntarily for the convenience of the parties; however, antitrust liability can attach if the "total sales" provision was coerced through an exercise of market

---

61.   *See* Zenith Radio Corp. v. Hazeltine Research, 395 U.S. 100, 135 (1969) ("conditioning the grant of a patent license upon payment of royalties on products which do not use the teaching of the patent" is unlawful); *see also* Brulotte v. Thys Co., 379 U.S. 29, 33 (1964) ("A patent empowers the owner to exact royalties as high as he can negotiate" but "[t]he exaction of royalties for use of a machine after the patent has expired is an assertion of monopoly power in the post-expiration period when ... the patent has entered the public domain."); W. Elec. v. Stewart-Warner Corp., 631 F.2d 333, 339 (4th Cir. 1980) (reasonable to base a royalty on the sale price of the finished products where substantially all of the market value of the finished product was derived from the patented feature).

power.[62] Thus, intellectual property owners who posses market power are advised to consider the relative merits of less restrictive alternatives for calculating intellectual property utilization, particularly when there is a risk that a total sales provision may impact price or foreclose market opportunities.[63] As to whether a total sales provision has been coerced, the counselor must ask questions such as: Did the licensee propose a different arrangement? Does the licensee understand the terms? Are there more convenient ways to accurately calculate usage? Will the total sales provision results in over-billing or double billing if the licensee decides to purchase a competing product?

Do the Royalty Rates Differ by Licensee? Discriminatory royalties describe situations where various licensees are charged different royalty rates. They generally do not violate the antitrust laws (including the Robinson Patman Act[64]) or constitute patent misuse, unless the practice adversely affects competition in a relevant market.[65] Thus, counselors should consider whether the imposition of discriminatory royalties will either exclude smaller competitors from the market or place them at a significant competitive disadvantage due to higher costs.

Are Royalties Shared with Sub-Licensees? Licensing agreements that require licensees to share sub-license royalties with the patent owner are subject to rule of reason review.[66] Here, royalty sharing

---

62. *See* Engle Indus. v. Lockformer Co., 96 F.3d 1398, 1408-09 (Fed. Cir. 1996) (rejecting patent misuse claim based on royalties charged on unpatented components where licensee had a choice whether to buy components from licensor).

63. United States v. Microsoft Corp., 1995-2 Trade Cas. (CCH) ¶ 71,096, at 75,244 (D.D.C. Aug. 21, 1995) (The DOJ had previously charged that "per processor licenses discourage OEMs from licensing competing operating systems and/or cause OEMs to raise the price of PCs with a competing operating system to recoup the fee paid to Microsoft." *United States v. Microsoft Corp.*, 159 F.R.D. 318, 323 (D.D.C. 1995), *rev'd on other grounds*, 56 F.3d 1448 (D.C. Cir. 1995). The consent decree issued thereafter directed Microsoft to revise its method of calculating royalties owed for its operating system to a "per copy" basis from a "per processor" measure.).

64. *See, e.g.,* KMG Kanal-Muller-Gruppe Int'l v. Inliner U.S.A., 1999-2 Trade Cas. (CCH) ¶ 72,628, at 85,641 (S.D. Tex. May 13, 1999) (holding that the Robinson-Patman Act is inapplicable when commodities are not sold with a license).

65. *See* La Peyre v. FTC, 366 F.2d 117, 121-22 (5th Cir. 1966). *But see* USM Corp. v. SPS Techs., 694 F.2d 505, 515-14 (7th Cir. 1982).

66. Standard Oil Co. v. United States, 283 U.S. 163, 172-73 (1931).

arrangements should be agreed to upfront, and they should be reasonable relative to other costs.[67] In the absence of such precautions, the parties are at risk of having any after-the-fact revenue sharing arrangements condemned as a vertical agreement to set or stabilize resale prices. Similarly, failure to negotiate revenue allocations prior to contract formation undermines the perceived legitimacy of any business justification the parties may assert.   Finally, royalties that are disproportionately large relative to cost may appear to be minimum resale prices.

Are Royalties Being Charged on Invalid or Expired Intellectual Property?   Under the patent misuse doctrine, intellectual property owners generally are prohibited from collecting royalties beyond the expiration of the licensed intellectual property,[68] although this does not prohibit intellectual property owners from allowing licensees to satisfy payment obligations on a deferred schedule that extends beyond the life of the patent at issue.[69]   Similarly, the limitation on post-expiration royalties does not apply to package licenses where the parties agree voluntarily[70] to a royalty stream that does not diminish as individual patents expire.[71]   For example, in situations where the value of the packaged intellectual property rights are expected to increase in proportion with the technology's market acceptance, the parties might

67.   *In re* Yarn Processing Patent Validity Litig., 541 F.2d 1127, 1136-38 (5th Cir. 1976) (royalty sharing arrangement held to be an illegal price fixing agreement where the royalties are several times larger than other costs).
68.   *See* Bayer AG v. Housey Pharms., 169 F. Supp. 2d 328, 331 (D. Del 2001) ("Arrangement in which a patentee effectively extends the term of its patent by requiring post-expiration royalties constitutes *per se* patent misuse."), *aff'd*, 340 F.3d 1367 (Fed. Cir. 2003); *see also Brulotte*, 379 U.S. at 31 (same).
69.   In this situation, where intellectual property owners are willing to provide licensees with an extended time-frame for satisfying royalty obligations, intellectual property owners are advised to clearly articulate the method of calculating royalties owed (which must cease to accrue at patent expiration), as distinguished from the deferred repayment schedule.
70.   For an extended discussion of the factors courts consider in evaluating whether package licenses have been agreed to voluntarily or imposed through coercion, see *infra* notes 141-145 & accompanying text.
71.   *See* Sunrise Medical HHG, Inc. v. AirSep Corp., 95 F. Supp. 2d 348, 458, 413-14 (W.D. Pa. 2000) ("[T]he royalty rate need not diminish as patents included in a package license expire, as long as the licensee is not coerced," reasoning that conditioning a patent license on acquisition of rights in another patent is not illegal absent a showing of market power.).

expressly agree that the overall royalty rate should remain constant (rather than diminish) despite the expiration on certain individual patents.

Are There Information Firewalls When Accounting for Royalties Owed by a Competitor? Although royalty provisions (as well as profit or revenue sharing arrangements) are generally regarded as competitively neutral, the manner in which they are implemented and administered can create antitrust risk if the arrangement facilitates collusion between parties that compete at some level of commerce.[72] For example, price fixing or market allocation concerns can arise if the royalty accounting process requires parties who compete in downstream markets to share competitively sensitive information (e.g., marginal revenue per sale, cost structure, customer pipeline). To mitigate such risk, licensing parties that stand in a horizontal relationship are best advised to appoint a third party administrator to handle the flow of competitively sensitive data and/or develop compensation formulae that rely on aggregated cost and revenue figures which have been cleansed of customer specific information.

Do the Parties Contemplate Changing Their Royalty Rates Throughout the Relationship? Similarly, collusion can become a concern for parties who are brought into a horizontal relationship by virtue of a technology license, even if the underlying license relates solely to complementary technology. Consider a pooling arrangement where parties contribute complimentary technology to a joint venture for the purpose of developing a new product that each member intends to market independently. If the parties later agree to raise minimum royalty rates, after the finished good has entered the market,[73] then such an amendment may be viewed as an attempt to increase or stabilize prices, particularly if the royalties represent a significant portion of the product's overall cost structure.

---

72. *See* COMPETITOR COLLABORATIONS GUIDELINES, *supra* note 52, §§ 2.2, 3.31(b), 3.34 (e).

73. Note, the authority of an intellectual property owner under the patent laws to control the manufacture, use and sale of a patented product is exhausted by the first sale of the product by someone authorized to make sales. Once this occurs, efforts to resell or relicense a patented good are governed exclusively by standard antitrust principles. *See* Mallinckrodt, Inc. v. Medipart, Inc., 976 F.2d 700, 708 (Fed. Cir. 1992).

498 Intellectual Property and Antitrust Handbook

2. Resale Price Maintenance

As a general rule, agreements between parties that aim to set or stabilize minimum prices are per se unlawful, regardless of whether the parties stand in a horizontal or vertical position.[74] Although the Supreme Court, in *United States v. General Electric*,[75] seemingly carved out a narrow exception to allow vertical price fixing between patent licensees,[76] this safe harbor has been narrowed significantly by lower courts[77] and does not apply to the *resale* of a patented product separately from its manufacture, initial sale or use.[78] For these reasons, intellectual property owners are generally advised to rely on non-price restrictions if their business objectives require some measure of direct control over

---

74. *Id. But see* United States v. Gen. Elec. Co., 272 U.S. 476, 480-90 (1926) (upholding licensing arrangement obligating licensee manufacturer to use same consignment system and pricing structure as licensor); LucasArts Entm't v. Humongous Entm't, 870 F. Supp. 285, 288-89 (N.D. Cal. 1993) (reasoning that the statutory right to forbid sales entirely necessarily "includes the power to restrict the prices at which ... licensees may sell licensed materials").

75. 272 U.S. 476 (1926).

76. *Id.* at 490 (holding that a patent owner who personally manufactures and sells the patented product may lawfully condition a license to manufacture the product on the fixing of the first sale price of the patent product because the price "will necessarily affect" the price at which the patent owner can sell its own goods).

77. *See In re* Yarn Processing Patent Validity Litig., 541 F.2d 1127, 1136 (5th Cir. 1976) (*General Electric* does not apply "where two or more patentees fix the prices of products incorporating several independently owned patents"); Newburgh Moire Co. v. Superior Moire Co., 237 F.2d 283, 293-94 (3d Cir. 1956) (same); *see also* United States v. New Wrinkle, Inc., 342 U.S. 371, 378-80 (1952) (irrespective of the *General Electric* rule, antitrust law prohibits patentees from setting prices in concert with other licensees or patentees); Cummer-Graham Co. v. Straight Side Basket Corp., 142 F.2d 646, 647 (5th Cir. 1944) (*General Electric* does permit patent owner to fix prices of patented machines or processes).

78. Ethyl Gas. Corp. v. United States, 309 U.S. 436, 446-48 (1940) (patent owner who makes and sells a patented good to another licensee may not attempt to fix the resale price via license); B. Braun Med. v. Abbott Labs., 124 F.3d 1419, 1426 (Fed. Cir. 1997) ("As a general matter ... an uncon-ditional sale of a patented device exhausts the patentee' right to control the purchaser's use of the device thereafter."); *see also* United States v. Univis Lens Co., 316 U.S. 241, 243-45 (1942).

resellers of their patented products. In fact, some case law even supports the proposition that a patent owner may limit the quantity of patented products that a licensee may produce, irrespective of the well-understood inverse relationship between quantity and price.[79]   However, such practices are subject to rule of reason review, and the *Intellectual Property Guidelines* seemingly take a more hostile view toward quantity restrictions agreed to by parties that are actual or potential competitors.[80]

Intellectual property owners and manufacturers are best advised to do no more than suggest a resale price. Below, we set forth questions that an antitrust counselor should consider when examining whether parties to a license arrangement are going beyond the limitations on resale price control.

Is the Intellectual Property Owner Announcing That It Will Only Deal with Resellers Who Follow Suggested Prices, or Is the Intellectual Property Owner Taking Action to Influence the Resale Price of Its Licensees?   Although intellectual property owners are prohibited from dictating resale prices, they may decide unilaterally to terminate all dealings with licensees that do not follow suggested prices.[81]   In fact, intellectual property owners can broadly announce a uniform policy that they will only deal with resellers that follow suggested prices.[82] However, any attempt to influence a discounting licensee to raise (or stabilize) its resale prices through threats, coercion or retaliation will be treated as a per se illegal attempt to fix minimum prices, in violation of Section 1 of the Sherman Act.[83]   Thus, intellectual property owners who hope to use suggested prices to exert a certain level of negative control over downstream resale pricing must take care to avoid the three most common situations where the courts have inferred an illegal agreement to fix or stabilize prices.

Is the Intellectual Property Owner Threatening to Punish Discounting Resellers? Intellectual property owners are free to terminate

---

79.   *See* Atari Games v. Nintendo of Am., 897 F.2d 1572, 1578 (Fed. Cir. 1990) (in dicta, the court indicates that quantity restrictions in a patent license are not per se illegal); United States v. E.I. duPont de Nemours & Co., 118 F. Supp. 41, 226 (D. Del. 1953), *aff'd*, 351 U.S. 377 (1956).

80.   INTELLECTUAL PROPERTY GUIDELINES, *supra* note 1, § 3.4 (quantity restrictions are potentially per se unlawful).

81.   *See* United States v. Colgate & Co., 250 U.S. 300, 307 (1919); *see also* Bus. Elecs. Corp. v. Sharp Elecs. Corp., 485 U.S. 717, 723-24 (1988).

82.   *See Colgate & Co.*, 250 U.S. at 307; *see also Bus. Elecs.*, 485 U.S. at 723-24.

83.   *See* Monsanto Co. v. Spray-Rite Serv. Corp., 465 U.S. 752, 765 (1984).

discounting resellers, but they must be careful not to come to any agreement over price. For example, a warning from an intellectual property owner that it will terminate a reseller unless it raises prices that actually results in a higher price may raise an inference that the parties agreed to stabilize prices. Similarly, a licensor terminating a discounting reseller for not following suggested retail prices who soon thereafter enters into a new agreement with the same licensee at a higher price invites unwelcome inferences. In both cases, circumstantial evidence may be sufficient to establish that there was a meeting of the minds over price. To mitigate risk, a licensor should be advised to make termination decisions without providing threats or "second chances."

Is the Intellectual Property Owner Retaliating Against Discounting Resellers? Similarly, an intellectual property owner who sanctions a price-cutting reseller via reduced delayed or service as a means of securing higher resale prices incurs considerable risk that its actions will be construed as coercive tactics designed to secure an agreement over price.

Is the Intellectual Property Owner Engaging in Price Discussions with Its Licensees? Communications with resellers who are complaining about a particular price-cutting reseller can also be problematic, and raise a possible inference that the intellectual property owner is not acting unilaterally. In *Monsanto Co. v. Spray-Rite Serv. Corp.,*[84] a manufacturer's decision to terminate a price-cutting distributor was viewed as an effort to enforce an explicit price agreement between the manufacturer and the remaining distributors (i.e., the distributors who complained of the price-cutting), making the termination per se unlawful. Liability under the *Monsanto* decision is unlikely if the licensor establishes (and rigorously follows) a policy that it will not monitor resale pricing behavior, and will treat as unwelcome any reports from third parties concerning other resellers who may or may not be following suggested resale price policies. In practice, it is often difficult to establish such an arrangement, and as a result, a unilateral minimum resale pricing scheme often is fraught with potential difficulties, especially where the licensee channel is diverse and large, and often is in communication with the licensor.

Is the Intellectual Property Owner Setting Maximum Resale Pricing or Is the Maximum Resale Price Agreement Simply a Mechanism to Set the Actual Resale Price? Licensing provisions that establish price ceilings, above which licensees may not make sales, are

---

84.   465 U.S. 752 (1984).

evaluated under the rule of reason, and therefore are generally permissible, provided the price ceiling is not a price floor in disguise.[85] Again, this is a situation where substance trumps form, where the courts or Agencies can infer an agreement to set minimum prices, if the parties' behavior, communications, documents and parallel pricing behavior reveal coordination on price.

3. Non-Price Restrictions

Licensing arrangements often contain non-price restrictions, including provisions that limit the geographic area within which the licensed technology may be used or sold (i.e., "territorial restrictions"); the applications for which the technology may be used (i.e., "field of use restrictions"); and the class of customers to whom products using the licensed technology may be sold (i.e., "customer restrictions"). The *Intellectual Property Guidelines* recognize that such restrictions can result in procompetitive efficiencies and create incentives to license by "reducing transaction costs," "protecting the licensee against free-riding on the licensee's investments by other licensees or by the licensor," and "protecting the licensor from competition in the licensor's technology in a market niche that it prefers to keep to itself." [86]

Notably, the intellectual property laws provide a patentee with special immunities to impose non-price restraints on any licensee that manufactures a finished product using the patentee's technology.[87] However, these special protections are said to "exhaust" on resale, which includes any attempt by the patentee to sell or distribute finished goods that it personally manufactured.[88] For instance, limiting the territory of a patent license is explicitly permitted by statute,[89] though this statute offers no continuing protection after the "first sale" of a patented product, meaning traditional antitrust principles govern.[90] Thus, unless the patentee is willing to outsource its production technology to a

85. *See* State Oil Co. v. Khan, 522 U.S. 3 (1997).
86. INTELLECTUAL PROPERTY GUIDELINES,*su pra* note 1, §§ 5.5, 2.3.
87. *See* United States v. Gen. Elec. Co., 272 U.S. 476, 489 (1926); *see also New Wrinkle*, 342 U.S. at 378; INTELLECTUAL PROPERTY GUIDELINES, *supra* note 1, § 5.2, n.33.
88. United States v. Univis Lens Co., 316 U.S. 241, 250 (1942).
89. *See* 35 U.S.C. § 261.
90. *See, e.g., Adams v. Burke*, 84 U.S. 453, 456-57 (1873); *Univis Lens*, 316 U.S. at 250.

licensee/manufacturer, standard antitrust rules govern the resale restrictions.

Non-price restrictions are evaluated under the rule of reason, where the analysis focuses on whether the restrictions are likely to compromise current levels of competition by facilitating market allocation among actual or potential competitors.[91] Thus, non-price restrictions between horizontal competitors merit the most careful inquiry, whereas most vertical relationships are unlikely to cause great concern.

Counselors evaluating non-price restrictions must nonetheless examine the circumstances surrounding and contours of proposed restrictions. The following questions help identify restrictions that may be subject to challenge.

Is the Licensing Arrangement a Sham or Devoid of Any Legitimate Justification? A licensing arrangement will be struck down as per se illegal if it is found to be a "sham" or pretext for implementing a market division between competitors.[92] Otherwise, licenses containing non-price restrictions are subject to a rule of reason analysis.[93] Here, the greatest antitrust risk for intellectual property owners relates to a situation where the parties have no procompetitive justification for the non-price restriction.[94] In the absence of an off-setting justification, the analysis reduces to the simple question of whether the restriction is likely to lead to increased prices or reduced output within a relevant market.

91.	*See* Gen. Talking Pictures Corp. v. W. Elec. Co., 304 U.S. 175, 180-82 (1938) (field of use restrictions), *aff'd on reh'g*, 305 U.S. 124 (1938); Ethyl Gas. Corp. v. United States, 309 U.S. 436, 456 (1940) (territorial restrictions); *In re* Yarn Processing Patent Validity Litig., 541 F.2d 1127, 1135 (5th Cir. 1976) (customer restrictions); *see also* Atari Games Corp. v. Nintendo of Am., 897 F.2d 1572, 1578 (Fed. Cir. 1990) (quantity restrictions). *But see* INTELLECTUAL PROPERTY GUIDELINES, *supra* note 1, § 3.4 (classifying maximum output restrictions between parties in a horizontal relationship as potentially *per se* unlawful).

92.	*See* Complaint, United States v. Pilkington, Plc., No. Civ. A. CV 94-345, ¶¶ 19-25 (D. Ariz. May 25, 1994) (alleging territorial restriction applied to licensee's competing technology was a sham attempt to allocate markets among competitors, in violation of antitrust law), *available at* http://www.usdoj.gov/atr/cases/f0000/0014.pdf; *see also Pilkington*, 1994 WL 750645 (final judgment).

93.	*See* INTELLECTUAL PROPERTY GUIDELINES, *supra* note 1, § 3.4.

94.	*Id.* § 2.3 & Ex. 1; *see also* B. Braun Med. v. Abbott Labs., 124 F.3d 1419, 1426 (Fed. Cir. 1997).

Were the Restrictions Imposed Unilaterally, or at the Behest of Competing Resellers? Intellectual property owners that stand in a vertical relationship with a network of rival licensees must ensure that any desired non-price restrictions, such as exclusive territories or customer groups, are imposed unilaterally, rather than in consultation with other licensees.[95] As with resale price maintenance, the intellectual property owner must ensure that competing resellers are not the driving force behind restrictions which seek to eliminate intra-brand competition.

Is the Non-Price Restriction Overbroad? Antitrust law may condemn the use of non-price restrictions that are applied beyond the scope of the licensed technology if they affect substitute technologies that would otherwise compete for sales, but for the licensing arrangement.[96] Typically, such overly broad restrictions, which are evaluated under the rule of reason, are seen in field-of-use provisions, where the licensor attempts to limit a product's use after first sale, or where the restriction relates to uses beyond what is possible or covered from the licensed intellectual property.

4. Exclusive Licenses and Exclusive Dealing

An exclusive dealing arrangement is a vertical non-price restraint that precludes a licensee for a period of time from establishing a business relationship (i.e., licensing, selling, distributing, or using) with proprietors of competing technologies.[97] As with other vertical restraints, exclusive dealing is evaluated under the rule of reason.[98]

Whether a license includes a grant of exclusive or non-exclusive intellectual property rights can have a significant effect on the antitrust risk associated with a licensing arrangement. The foreclosure effects of exclusive dealing can extend beyond goods and technology markets, meaning intellectual property owners must also evaluate the likely competitive effects in innovation markets. For example, recently the Department of Justice demonstrated its concern that exclusive dealing

95. *See* Dr. Miles Med. v. John D. Park & Sons, 220 U.S. 373, 405-06 (1911); Int'l Wood Processors v. Power Dry, Inc., 792 F.2d 416, 429 (4th Cir. 1986).
96. *See, e.g.,* Va. Panel Corp. v. MAC Panel Co., 133 F.3d 860, 868 (Fed. Cir. 1997); United States v. Westinghouse Elec., 471 F. Supp. 532, 541 (N.D. Cal. 1978), *aff'd,* 648 F.2d 642 (9th Cir. 1981).
97. INTELLECTUAL PROPERTY GUIDELINES,*su pra* note 1, § 5.4.
98. *Id.* §§ 5.4, 4.1.2, & Ex. 8; *see also* Tampa Elec. v. Nashville Coal Co., 365 U.S. 320 (1961).

can stifle innovation and future competition when it forced two high-technology defense contractors to scale back the scope of their teaming agreement to products currently in production.[99] Before modification of the arrangement, the contractors had planned to jointly develop and produce night-vision products for current and future defense programs.[100] The Department would not allow such a comprehensive and forward looking agreement to close, fearful that it might preclude other contractors from working with the Department of Defense to develop the next generation of related products, thus threatening competition and continued innovation.[101]

In general, to determine whether exclusive dealing violates antitrust law, counselors should ask the following questions.

Is the Agreement Exclusive? The practical effect of the license will trump its form, meaning the counselor should independently examine whether a license is de facto exclusive even if nominally non-exclusive.[102] For example, an established history of dealing with only one licensee, without ever using the technology personally, or licensing it to others interested in obtaining the technology on similar terms, can be interpreted as a de facto exclusive license, in the absence of a valid explanation.[103]

What Is the Degree of Market Foreclosure Created by the Exclusive Arrangement? An exclusive license prohibits the grantor from granting others a license and precludes the licensor itself from using the intellectual property, at least in some field of use and some territory.[104] Thus, by its nature, exclusive dealing "forecloses" rivals and

---

99.   *See* DOJ Press Release, "Justice Department Requires Raytheon Company and DRS Technologies Inc. to Modify Agreement on Infrared Sights for Military Vehicles," (Aug. 20, 2003), *available at* http://www.usdoj.gov/atr/public/press_releases/2003/201234.pdf.
100.   *Id.*
101.   *Id.*
102.   *See* United States v. Dentsply Int'l, 399 F.3d 181, 193-94 & n.2 (3d Cir. 2005); *see also* INTELLECTUAL PROPERTY GUIDELINES, *supra* note 1, § 4.1.2.
103.   United States v. S.C. Johnson & Son, 1995-1 Trade Cas. (CHH) ¶ 70,884, at 73,875-76 (N.D. Ill. Nov. 8, 1994) (DOJ alleged that a nominally nonexclusive license for household insecticides was exclusive in fact since the licensor refused all offers to license and refrained from using its technology itself).
104.   An exclusive license will be treated as an acquisition of the intellectual property, and may be reportable under the Hart-Scott-Rodino Act if

new entrants from marketing their technologies to a particular licensee.[105] However, this does not automatically mean that such practices are suspect. After all, sufficient alternatives may exist for rival licensors to distribute their intellectual property. A counselor must determine the percentage of the market foreclosed by the exclusive arrangement. Do customers have sufficient access to alternatives? Generally, exclusive dealing arrangements that foreclose less than 50% of a relevant market are presumed lawful.[106]

What Is the Duration of Exclusivity? Generally, exclusive dealing arrangements that last less than one year are presumed lawful.[107] Beyond this measures, courts typically conduct a full blown rule of reason inquiry into market power, effects on competition, and the parties' procompetitive justifications.[108]

What Are the Justifications for Exclusivity and Are Those Justifications Supported by Sufficient Documentary Evidence? There are well-recognized economic benefits that flow from exclusive dealing

---

certain filing thresholds are met. *See* 16 C.F.R. § 801.10. If the licensor retains rights to use the intellectual property, the license is co-exclusive and will not be reportable under the Hart-Scott-Rodino Act. *Id.*

105. *See* Barry Wright Corp. v. ITT Grinnell Corp., 724 F.2d 227, 236 (1st Cir. 1983) ("virtually every contract to buy 'forecloses' or 'excludes' alternative sellers from some portion of the market, namely the portion consisting of what was bought").

106. *See* United States v. Microsoft Corp., 253 F.3d 34, 71 (D.C. Cir. 2001) (commenting that foreclosure of "roughly 40% or 50% share [of the downstream market is] usually required in order to establish a § 1 violation"); *see also* Jefferson Parrish Hosp. Dist. No. 2 v. Hyde, 466 U.S. 2, 44 (1984) (O'Connor, J., concurring) (found exclusive dealing lawful without detailed analysis at 30% foreclosure).

107. *See* Omega Envtl. v. Gilbarco, Inc., 127 F.3d 1157, 1163-64, 1172 (9th Cir. 1997) (a contract that ends or is terminable at one year is "presumptively lawful", and two years is eminently reasonable); *see also* Roland Mach. v. Dresser Indus., 749 F.2d 380, 394-95 (7th Cir. 1984) (one-year contracts presumptively legal); U.S. Healthcare v. Health-source, Inc., 986 F.2d 589, 596 (1st Cir. 1993) (termination on 30 days' notice normally a *de minimis* constraint). *But see Dentsply*, 399 F.3d at 181, 184 (irrelevant that contract can be canceled at-will and without penalty if economic incentives are such that exclusivity is likely to extend indefinitely).

108. *See* INTELLECTUAL PROPERTY GUIDELINES, *supra* note 1, §§ 4.1, 5.4; *see also Tampa Elec.*, 365 U.S. at 333; *Barry Wright Corp.*, 724 F.2d at 236-37.

arrangements, such as increased inter-brand competition, greater use of the licensed technology, and a more stable stream of royalties needed to fund additional investments.[109]   Further, "the fact that intellectual property may in some cases be misappropriated more easily than other forms of property, may justify the use of some restrictions that might be anti-competitive in other contexts."[110]   Thus, counselors should determine whether one of these justification formed the basis for the exclusive arrangement, and whether such justifications are supported by contemporaneous business documents.

5. *Grantbacks*

A grantback provision requires the licensee to convey back to the licensor (and possibly other licensees as well) the right to use improvements made to the licensed technology, and in some situations, the right to use certain new patents in related fields of use.[111]   Often the licensor has compelling business reasons for requiring grantback rights. Most notably, without the grantback, the licensor may have put the licensee in business and enabled the improvement, while at the same time, placing its own creation at risk of obsolescence.   Further, grantbacks provide licensors with a strong incentive to seek out licensees who are in a better position to improve further the licensor's core technology.[112]   As such, grantbacks are evaluated under the rule of reason[113] and generally deemed procompetitive when conducted on a nonexclusive basis.[114]

Significant antitrust issues can arise, however, when the grantbacks are exclusive, thus prohibiting the licensee from licensing the improvement to others. [115]   If exclusive, the next questions are whether

109.   *See* INTELLECTUAL PROPERTY GUIDELINES, *supra* note 1, § 4.1.2 & Ex. 8; *see also Jefferson Parish*, 466 U.S. at 45 (O'Connor, J., concurring) (detailing the economic benefits that accrue from long-term contracts that ensure stable supply, sales, and price stability).

110.   INTELLECTUAL PROPERTY GUIDELINES,*su pra* note 1, § 4.1.2.

111.   *Id.* §§ 4.1.2, 5.6.

112.   *See* Transparent-Wrap Mach. v. Stokes & Smith Co., 329 U.S. 637, 646-48 (1947).

113.   *See id.*; *see also* INTELLECTUAL PROPERTY GUIDELINES, *supra* note 1, § 5.6.

114.   *See, e.g.,* Binks Mfg. v. Ransburg Electro-Coating Corp., 281 F.2d 252, 259 (7th Cir. 1960).

115.   *See* INTELLECTUAL PROPERTY GUIDELINES, *supra* note 1, §§ 4.1.2, 5.6.

the licensee is also precluded from personally using the improvement, and at what cost, if any. The primary concern in these situations is that the arrangement will exclude a competitor or potential competitor from the market. Antitrust concerns are further heightened when the licensor has extracted grantback rights from a network of licensees, thus enabling the licensor to accumulate multiple patent rights and potentially co-opt a portion of the market.[116]

Ultimately, the anticompetitive implications of exclusive grantbacks, if any, are a function of the scope and duration of the grantback, market conditions, royalty structure, and the competitive relationship of the parties. Balancing these factors determines whether the grantback is likely to have the anticompetitive effect of broadening the scope of the patent or lengthening the period of monopoly. In this context, technology owners and counselors are advised to focus on two issues.

Does the Scope of the Exclusive Grantback Focus Narrowly on Improvements That Infringe the Licensor's Patent, or Do They Extend Broadly to Any Related Technology within a Wide Field?[117] Naturally, an all-encompassing grantback extending to non-infringing improvements poses the greatest concern, because it relieves the licensor from having to compete with an alternate technology. Similarly, if the duration of the exclusive grantback is not limited to the life of the underlying patent, then the licensor will effectively acquire control of the technology, through its use of the improvement, for a while longer.

Does the Grantback Obligation Lessen the Licensee's Incentives to Develop a Substitute Technology, and if So, Will the Arrangement Likely Extend or Maintain the Licensor's Market Power Beyond the Remaining Life of the Patent? Again, a grantback that dampens the incentive to compete could raise significant antitrust scrutiny. A grantback, for example, that provides that all improvements to a technology must be provided to the licensor dampens the licensee's incentive to compete, knowing that the licensee will not own the improvements to the technology exclusively.

---

116. *See Transparent-Wrap Mach.*, 329 U.S. at 643.
117. *See* Santa Fe-Pomeroy, Inc. v. P & Z Co., 569 F.2d 1084, 1101 (9th Cir. 1978) (grantback limited in time and subject matter "had no restrictive or 'chilling' effect on any improvements"); United States v. Besser Mfg., 96 F. Supp. 304, 310 (E.D. Mich. 1951) (purpose of unlawful agreements was "to make certain that these two giants of the industry didn't battle each other over patents any more"), *aff'd*, 343 U.S. 444 (1952).

Grantbacks that are appropriately and conscientiously structured and do not impose undue restrictions on licensees are unlikely to invite antitrust scrutiny.

6. Tying Agreements and Package Licensing

In the realm of intellectual property licensing, tying arrangements and the related practice of package licensing describe instances where the availability of a patent license (the tying item) is expressly conditioned upon the buyer's agreement to acquire a second, undesired item (the tied item or service).[118] Predictably, the primary antitrust concern with tying and package licensing is the potential to leverage the power associated with one patent to the detriment of competition in additional markets that lie beyond the patent's scope.[119] As a result, consumers can be made to buy unwanted products or technology, which can also function as a method of excluding rivals from the market.

a. Tying

Following settled antitrust law, a tying arrangement will be condemned as per se illegal if: (1) the tying and tied items are separate and distinct; (2) the seller "conditions" the sale of the tying item on the buyer's agreement to buy (or forbear from buying) the tied item; (3) the seller has market power in the market for the tying item; and (4) the tie affects a substantial amount of commerce in the tied item.[120] In addition, an intellectual property holder found to have tied in violation of the antitrust laws will also be found to have engaged in patent misuse.[121]

---

118. See INTELLECTUAL PROPERTY GUIDELINES, *supra* note 1, § 5.3.
119. *Id.*
120. See generally Jefferson Parish Hosp. Dist. No. 2 v. Hyde, 466 U.S. 2 (1984); *see also* Eastman Kodak Co. v. Image Technical Servs., 504 U.S. 451 (1992).
121. See 35 U.S.C. § 271(d)(5) (a tying arrangement amounts to patent misuse when it is shown that "the patent owner has market power ... for the patent or patented product on which the license or sale is conditioned"); *see also* Alcatel USA, Inc. v. DGI Techs., 166 F.3d 772, 793-94 (5th Cir. 1999) (holding that the plaintiff had misused its operating system copyright by licensing copyrighted software to customers for use only in conjunction with its microprocessor cards, which were not protected by patent or copyright).

Under the *Intellectual Property Guidelines*, however, a tying agreement is likely to be a violation only if "(1) the seller has market power in the tying product market, (2) the arrangement has had an adverse effect on competition in the relevant market for the tied product, and (3) efficiency justifications for the arrangement do not outweigh the anti-competitive effects."[122] In effect, the Agencies have adopted a rule of reason analysis, which places the *Guidelines* in conflict with the case law on this topic, which still treats tying as per se illegal, once the plaintiff establishes that the defendant had market power in the tying product.

Thus, when analyzing a proposed tie in a license agreement, a counselor should examine the following questions.

Is the Alleged Bundle Truly Comprised of Separate Items? Here, the counselor must determine whether the intellectual property license truly comprises separate items. The counselor should ask whether (1) there is separate consumer demand for the two products; (2) there are other market participants who unbundle the products; (3) there are vendors who sell only one of the two products; and (4) historically, the licensor unbundled the products, and only recently switched to conditioning the license of the tied item on the license of the tying item.

Notably, patents that are bundled together into a single package license will not be deemed "separate products" for purposes of tying or misuse analysis if each of constituent patents are so inter-related and interdependent that no separate demand exists for them individually.[123] Examples of such "single product" patent bundles may include patents that are blocking or patents that are "necessary and essential" to conform to an industry standard, manufacture a product, or fully develop a technology.[124] As the logic goes, if the bundled patents have no economic value or practical application outside of the bundle, then they are properly viewed as a single product.

---

122. INTELLECTUAL PROPERTY GUIDELINES, *supra* note 1, § 5.3 (footnotes omitted).

123. *See* Metromedia Broad. v. MGM/UA Entm't, 611 F. Supp. 415, 423-24 (C.D. Cal. 1985); *Microsoft*, 253 F.3d at 49.

124. *See, e.g.*, U.S. Philips Corp. v. Int'l Trade Comm'n, 424 F.3d 1179, 1196-97 (Fed. Cir. 2005), *cert. denied sub nom.* Princo Corp. v. U.S. Philips Corp., 126 S. Ct. 2899 (2006).

Is the Integration of the Two Items Sufficiently Seamless and Beneficial Such that the Combination in fact Constitutes a New and Improved Product? Most notably, in *United States v. Microsoft,*[125] the D.C. Circuit Court of Appeals recognized that applications sold as part of an operating system could be considered one "product." Analogously, if a licensor can demonstrate that the combination of two products represents a new and improved product that is sufficiently different from the two products previously sold separately from each other, that could eliminate liability for tying. Thus, a counselor should ask, for example, whether the bundle increased the combined product functionality in a manner that could be achieved only through the tie;[126] changed the safety profile of the two products by combining them (e.g., a specially-designed diagnostic tool included with a drug[127]); resulted in significant transaction-specific cost savings that were likely to be passed through to customers;[128] or proved necessary for brand management and quality control in connection with launching a new product.[129]

If not, Are There Business Justifications for the Tie? It is largely a "judge-specific" decision today as to how to weigh the justifications for a tie. Some courts engage in a full rule of reason analysis, while others require a far higher showing that the justification for the tie was so important that it fundamentally changed the nature of the product offered.[130] In the end, however, offering a valid business justification will serve to help a defendant in a tying case if it can prove "that means less restrictive than the tie-in were not feasible to achieve the desired

---

125.	253 F.3d 34 (D.C. Cir. 2001).
126.	*Id.* at 87.
127.	*But see In re* Sandoz Pharms., 115 F.T.C. 625 (1992) (consent order to cease and desist the practice of tying together a patented drug and garden-variety diagnostic testing services that were previously sold separately).
128.	Digital Equip. v. Uniq Digital Techs., 73 F.3d 756, 761-62 (7th Cir. 1996).
129.	United States v. Jerrold Elecs., 187 F. Supp. 545, 554-58 (E.D. Pa. 1960), *aff'd,* 365 U.S. 567 (1961); *see also* Mozart Co. v. Mercedes-Benz of N. Am., 833 F.2d 1342, 1348 n.5 (9th Cir. 1987); Dehydrating Process Co. v. A.O. Smith Corp., 292 F.2d 653, 655 (1st Cir. 1961).
130.	*Jerrold Elecs.,* 187 F. Supp. at 554-58; *see also Jefferson Parish,* 466 U.S. at 22 (applying *per se* tying rules only where "it is efficient" to offer the tied and tying products separately); Data Gen. Corp. v. Grumman Sys. Support Corp., 36 F.3d 1147, 1180-83 (1st Cir. 1994); *In re* Data Gen. Corp. Antitrust Litig., 490 F. Supp. 1089, 1101-02 (N.D. Cal. 1980).

protection."[131] Courts have accepted, with significant limitations, only a few justifications as sufficient to overcome a claim that a party has illegally tied its products together. The most commonly asserted business justifications are the need to protect good will, control quality, generate distribution synergies, and facilitate the introduction of a new product.[132]

Again, it is critically important for the counselor to ensure that these justifications reflect the business reality at the time the parties entered into the license. If the purported justification is not substantiated by documentary evidence, or by uncontroverted testimony, it will be subject to extreme criticism by courts or the agencies as a post hoc creation of counsel used to justify an otherwise illegal arrangement.

b. Package Licensing

Package licensing refers to an arrangement where an intellectual property owner grants a license to more than one patent to the same licensee at the same time.[133] Generally, package licenses are treated as efficient and procompetitive when agreed to voluntarily and for the convenience of the parties.[134] Package licensing can reduce transaction costs, minimize the risk of litigation between the licensing parties, and allow for an easier assessment of the value of the license technology.[135] However, as with tying, package licensing will raise antitrust concerns if the licensor exercises its economic power to "force" the licensee to purchase unwanted technology through the bundle. Such forced licensing may result in either increased prices or may serve to exclude

---

131. *See* Metrix Warehouse v. Daimler-Benz AG, 828 F.2d 1033, 1040 (4th Cir. 1987).
132. *See Mozart Co.*, 833 F.2d at 1348 n.5 (Mercedes required its dealers to obtain all repair and replacement parts only from it in order to prevent dealers from free-riding on the defendant's good will); *Dehydrating Process*, 292 F.2d at 655-56 (protecting good will); *Microsoft Corp.*, 253 F.3d at 87, 92-95 (facilitate new product introduction); *Jerrold Elecs.*, 187 F. Supp. at 554-58 (same).
133. *See* INTELLECTUAL PROPERTY GUIDELINES, *supra* note 1, § 5.3. Unlike patent pools, which encompass the intellectual property of multiple IP Owners, package licensing relates to the unilateral action of an IP owner to bundle multiple pieces of its intellectual property into a single agreement.
134. *See infra* notes 63-64, 69-71 & accompanying text.
135. *Id.*; *see also U.S. Philips Corp.*, 424 F.3d at 1192-93.

rivals offering competing technology to that provided in the forced package license bundle.[136]   Thus, when evaluating whether a package license comports with boundaries of antitrust law, a counselor must consider the following issues.

Has the Licensee Been "Forced" or "Coerced" into Purchasing the Packaged License? As a threshold matter, the notion of "forcing" or "coercion" begins with a determination of whether the licensor has market power over certain patents being packaged (e.g., the tying product). In addition to having market power, "forcing" also requires that the intellectual property owner to refrain from licensing the packaged patents separately.[137]   In essence, this inquiry mirrors the conditioning requi-rement from standard tying analysis. A counselor must ask, for example, whether the intellectual property owner has refused all reasonable requests to negotiate separate licenses for any subset of the packaged technology? Has the intellectual property owner expressly conditioned the availability of some patents on the purchase of the entire bundle? To the extent individual patent licenses are offered, can the entire patent bundle be purchased on equal or better terms? Finally, "forcing" must also entail some measure of anticompetitive consequences for the licensee, for example, purchasing unwanted products (or technology rights) or utilizing (or refrain from using) certain technology.[138]   Naturally, a licensee has not been "coerced" or disadvantaged if the package license advances the mutual interests of the parties or includes additional intellectual property rights free of charge and without commitment to use.[139]

Does the Package License Tie a Patent to a Product or to Another Patent? Traditionally, package licenses that result from an exercise of market power could be assailed under a per se theory of misuse or illegal

---

136.   *See* 35 U.S.C. § 271(d)(5); *see also* DiscoVision Assocs. v. Disc Mfg., 42 U.S.P.Q. 2d (BNA) 1749, 1758-59 (D. Del. 1997) (holding that allegations of economic coercion with respect to package licenses of technologies were sufficient, and impairment of competition did not require allegations that competitors failed to make competing sales in the tied markets).

137.   *See, e.g.,* Zenith Radio Corp. v. Hazeltine Research, 395 U.S. 100, 133-34 nn. 27-28 (1969); Automatic Radio Mfg. v. Hazeltine Research, 339 U.S. 827, 834 (1950); W. Elec. v. Stewart-Warner Corp., 631 F.2d 333, 338-39 (4th Cir. 1980); McCullough Tool v. Well Surveys, Inc., 343 F.2d 381, 408-09 (10th Cir. 1965).

138.   *U.S. Philips Corp.*, 424 F.3d at 1188-92.

139.   *Id.*

tying.[140]   However, the Federal Circuit recently has held that per se condemnation of package licensing should be limited where the package license includes the bundling of patents to products, where the court found the risk of foreclosure and anticompetitive harm is greatest.[141] On the other hand, licensing arrangements that are limited to bundled patents (or groups of patents) are more appropriately reviewed under the rule of reason, where all facts and circumstances are taken into account in order to determine if the package license is anticompetitive. This distinction is justified, according to the court, by the fact that a patent license is merely a "promise not to sue for infringement" and therefore does not compel its licensees to use all of is patents, thereby not interfering with any market for other patents.[142]   Thus, it is critically important for the counselor to consider exactly what the package comprises.

Does the Package License Include Both "Essential" and "Non-Essential" Intellectual Property?   For package licenses that involve patent bundling arrangements, the primary issue is whether the bundle includes "non-essential" technology.   In the context of patent misuse, "essential patents" are those deemed technically necessary to practice an industry standard, manufacture a ˈ product, or fully implement a technology, for which there are commercially viable substitutes.[143]   As a matter of law, package licenses that bundle essential technologies are procompetitive and consequently are immune from antitrust or patent misuse review.[144]   However, competitive concerns can arise once technological innovation and competitive entry render what was once "essential" technology at the inception of the package, a "non-essential" patent.[145]   When this occurs, the counselor must consider whether the package license allows the intellectual property owner to leverage any

---

140. *See, e.g.,* United States v. Paramount Pictures, 334 U.S. 131 (1948).

141. *U.S. Philips Corp.*, 424 F.3d at 1188-89.

142. *Id.*

143. Notably, for purposes of patent misuse, the term "essential" is broader than how the term is used by the agencies when evaluating patent pools. *See infra* notes 164-168 & accompanying text (explaining that the agencies have taken the position that "essential patents by definition have no substitutes; one needs license to each of them in order to comply with the standard").

144. *U.S. Philips Corp.*, 424 F.3d at 1194-96.

145. As further justification for rule of reason review of patent-to-patent package licenses, the *Philips* court indicated that the legality of an arrangement must be evaluated ex ante, based on the conditions in existence when the parties agreed to the license. *Id.* at 1196-97.

market power it may have in the essential patents to stabilize prices or reduce competition between substitute (i.e., non-essential) technologies.[146]

Do the Royalties Earned From the Package License Derive Exclusively from Valid and Essential Technology? Is a Package License Comparatively Efficient to Negotiating the Licenses Individually? When evaluating the competitive implications of a package license that includes essential and non-essential patents, the critical question is whether the there is any evidence that the non-essential patents are valuable, and if so, whether the royalties earned from the license are attributable to the non-essential technologies.[147] Stated differently, the counselor must ask whether there is any evidence that the essential patents would have been less expensive if negotiated on an individual basis?[148] If not, then the arrangement fails to cause cognizable harm, which according to the Federal Circuit is not surprising given "the reality that the value of any patent package is largely, if not entirely, based on the patents that are essential to the technology in question."[149]

7. Patent Pooling and Cross-Licensing

Patent pooling describes the situation where two or more parties grant licenses to use their respective intellectual property to each other or to a third party that sub-licenses the pooled technology to others.[150] In its most basic form, patent pooling entails a straightforward cross-license between two parties. In more complex arrangements, multiple patent owners contribute intellectual property rights to a pool, which may be administered by a third party as a part of (or in place of) an industry standard-setting organization.

Regardless of form or complexity, pooling arrangements can ease and expedite the full exploitation of technology, and therefore advance procompetitive ends, "by integrating complementary technologies, reducing transaction costs, clearing blocking positions, and avoiding costly infringement litigation."[151] As noted by the Supreme Court, the pooling of blocking patents by competitors is "frequently necessary" for

---

146. *Id.* at 1188-92.
147. *Id.* at 1189.
148. *Id.* at 1189-92.
149. *Id.* at 1191.
150. *See* INTELLECTUAL PROPERTY GUIDELINES, *supra* note 1, § 5.5.
151. *Id.*

technical advancement and is subject to a rule of reason analysis.[152] Likewise, where the efficiencies associated with a pooling arrangement make it possible to market a product that would not otherwise exist, the Court has also allowed pool members to impose restraints traditionally condemned as per se illegal, provided that the collateral restraints are no more burdensome than what is needed to accomplish the purpose of the pool.[153]

Notwithstanding the well-recognized benefits of cross-licensing and patent pooling, such arrangements can also create significant antitrust risk to the extent they decrease competition between technology contributors, dampen innovation, or restrict competition in downstream product markets.[154] Antitrust treatment of pooling arrangements has varied greatly over the years, resulting in some uncertainty over how the effects of such arrangements should be evaluated.[155] More recently, however, as the prevailing attitude toward intellectual property licensing has moderated, the *Intellectual Property Guidelines*, along with several subsequently issued business review letters, have evolved into the leading source of guidance in the field.[156] Here, the Agencies instruct that a pooling arrangement will likely be deemed anticompetitive, and therefore illegal, if it: (1) diminishes competition between contributing parties whose intellectual property rights would have been actual or

---

152. Standard Oil Co. v. United States, 283 U.S. 163, 171 (1931); *see also* Broad. Music v. CBS, 441 U.S. 1, 24 (1979).
153. *See Broad. Music*, 441 U.S. 1 (court allowed joint price setting within the pool, provided that contributing members retain the right to individually license their intellectual property outside the pool).
154. See INTELLECTUAL PROPERTY GUIDELINES,*su pra* note 1, § 5.5.
155. *See generally supra* § IV (Historical Treatment of Intellectual Property).
156. *See* Letter from Charles A. James, Ass't Att'y Gen., Antitrust Div., U.S. Dep't of Justice, to Ky P. Ewing, Esq. (Nov. 12, 2002) ("3G Business Review Letter"), *available at* http://www.usdoj.gov/atr/public/busreview/200455.pdf; Letter from Joel I. Klein, Ass't Att'y Gen., Antitrust Div., U.S. Dep't of Justice, to Carey R. Ramos, Esq. (June 10, 1999) ("DVD-6 Business Review Letter"), *available at* http://www.usdoj.gov/atr/public/busreview/2485.pdf; Letter from Joel I. Klein, Ass't Att'y Gen., Antitrust Div., U.S. Dep't of Justice, to Garrard R. Beeney, Esq. (Dec. 16, 1998) ("DVD-3 Business Review Letter"), *available at* http://www.usdoj.gov/atr/public/busreview/ 2121.pdf; Letter from Joel I. Klein, Acting Ass't Att'y Gen., Antitrust Div., U.S. Dep't of Justice, to Gerrard R. Beeney, Esq. (June 26, 1997) ("MPEG-2 Business Review Letter"), *available at* http://www.usdoj.gov/atr/public/busreview/1170.pdf.

Intellectual Property and Antitrust Handbook

potential competitors in the absence of the arrangement; (2) deters participants from engaging in or expanding their research and development operations; (3) adversely impacts competition in downstream product markets that incorporate the pooled technology through the unjustified exclusion of firms with competing technology; (4) embodies collective price or output restraints that do not contribute to an efficiency-enhancing integration of economic activity among the participants.[157] Recently, in *U.S. Philips Corp. v. International Trade Commission*,[158] the Federal Circuit found that Philips could offer licenses for a package of patents reading on the CD-R and CD-RW standards, even if the package included both essential and non-essential patents. The Court noted that package licensing can produce efficiencies not achievable through the licensing of individual patents, and suggested that in most cases package licenses will not be invalidated only because one or more of the patents included in a license is non-essential. To be safe, however, an antitrust counselor must consider the following.

What Is the Purpose of Pooling the Patents? In order to properly assess and mitigate the antitrust risk associated with the creation and administration of a pooling arrangement, technology owners and their counsel must clearly identify the fundamental purpose of the pool. Why do the parties seek to pool their intellectual property rights? Is this an effort to establish an industry standard? Are they endeavoring to create a particular good or service that they could not otherwise do, or at least not without incurring great expense? The answer to these questions explains the need for including certain patents in the pool or requiring particular licensing restrictions. Likewise, the parties' purpose provides the counselor with a foundation from which to determine the net competitive effects of the arrangement.

What Type of Intellectual Property Has Been Included in the Pool, and Why? With the purpose of the pool established, counselors must identify the intellectual property rights that are being contributed to the pool, and from whom. Here, the key question is whether the pool is comprised exclusively of complementary patents, or whether it also includes duplicative patents that are generally substitutable with one another. Patents are complementary if their value depends upon being used together, such as: improvements to a basic technology; component technologies of a standard; or blocking patents, where a patent cannot be

---

157. *See* INTELLECTUAL PROPERTY GUIDELINES, *supra* note 1, § 5.5.
158. 424 F.3d 1179 (Fed. Cir. Sept. 21, 2005), *cert. denied sub nom.* Princo Corp. v. U.S. Philips Corp., 126 S. Ct. 2899 (2006).

exploited without infringing on the rights of another. Frequently, a pool of complementary patents is the only practical way to exploit technologies and provide common access to multiple licensees.

As a general rule, patent pools should include only those complementary patents that are technically "essential" to practice a standard, manufacture a product, or fully implement a technology,[159] though additional patents can also be included if no realistically viable or "economically feasible alternatives exist."[160] Broadening the scope of the pool to include substitutable patents that are non-infringing (i.e., non-essential) creates the potential for eliminating competition between the substitute technologies, and reduces the incentive to develop alternate technologies. Therefore, if some of the pooled technologies are not complementary, then one must ask whether legitimate business justifications support their inclusion.[161] For example, can the non-essential technologies be fully used on a stand-alone basis, or must they be combined with technologies that are available *only* (i.e., on an exclusive basis) in the pool? Is there an alternate way to structure the pool that would allow the duplicative technologies to be removed, without compromising the overall business objective?[162] As demonstrated in the Department of Justice 3-G Business Review Letter, the inclusion of non-essential patents may be improper if the parties' business justification (for pooling essential technologies on an exclusive basis) is not sufficiently compelling to outweigh the resulting loss in competition from pooling the duplicative technologies.[163]

---

159. *See* DVD-3 Business Review Letter at 10, indicating that "[o]ne way to ensure that the proposed pool will integrate only complementary patent rights is to limit the pool to patents that are essential to compliance with the Standard Specifications. Essential patents by definition have no substitutes; one needs license to each of them in order to comply with the standard. At the same time, they are complementary to each other; a license to one essential patent is more valuable if the licensee also has licenses to use other essential patents.")

160. *See* DVD-6 Business Review Letter.

161. *See* DVD-3 Business Review letter; 3G Business Review Letter.

162. *See* DVD-3 Business Review letter; 3G Business Review Letter.

163. *See* 3G Business Review Letter at 2, where after considerable negotiation and restructurings, the DOJ allowed intellectual property owners, on a non-exclusive basis, to pool all technologies essential to the creation of a common platform for third-generation wireless communications. But the DOJ would not allow five competing (i.e., non-essential) communication standards to be included in the platform, even though the rival standards

By What Process Have the Parties Distinguished Essential from Non-Essential Patents? The degree to which patents are complementary, and whether they are valid, are primary factors in assessing the competitive implications of pooling.[164] Given the importance of this fact, parties must take steps to evaluate whether the purported rationale for pooling their intellectual property actually holds true. A bare assertion that patents are blocking will not deter inquiry into whether the parties are using a pool to shield invalid or substitute patents from competition.[165] Thus, parties must take steps to determine whether the patents are valid, blocking, essential, etc. For example, have the patents expired? Is there a commonly held belief in the industry that the blocking patents are invalid, such that competitors are unconcerned with the risk of an infringement action, and willing to practice the "blocked" technology in the absence of a license? Do any of the parties have the capability to easily design around a blocking position? With respect to patent claims that cover a particular component or process, do they necessarily correlate with the manufacture of an individual commercial product (i.e., are they essential)?

For these reasons, pool members are encouraged to hire an independent expert to determine the essentiality of the patents. In the DVD-6 Business Review Letter, for example, the Department of Justice accepted the parties' protocol for determining essentiality given that the expert's decision was conclusive and non-appealable and his compensation was not affected by the results of the analysis.[166]

What are the Terms that the Pooled Technologies Are Licensed to Pool Members and Third Parties? Patent pooling arrangements have the potential to affect competition in markets downstream or related to the technology and products directly incorporated into the pool. As such, counselors must consider who might be affected by the pool's pricing or access policies, particularly in related markets where pool members comprise a substantial share of sales. For example, does the royalty rate

---

were less valuable independent of the platform. Instead, the competing standards were provided equal access to the platform technologies, thus enabling the standards to form competing patent pools. *Id.*

164. *See* INTELLECTUAL PROPERTY GUIDELINES, *supra* note 1, §§ 3.3, Ex. 5; 5.5, Ex. 10.

165. *See* Complaint filed in *In re* Summit Tech., Inc. & VISX, Inc., FTC Docket No. 9286 (1998), *available at* http://www.ftc.gov/os/1998/03/summit.cmp.htm.

166. *See* DVD-6 Business Review Letter.

constitute a significant portion of the total cost of the products produced using the pooled technology? If so, then concerns arise over whether the licensors are using the pool to coordinate or stabilize downstream pricing.[167] Similar anticompetitive concerns arise where the licensors have a substantial share of a particular market and competitors are unable to procure a license to the underlying patents on equal terms. To mitigate against these types of antitrust risk, pools generally should offer licenses on terms that are fair, reasonable, and non-discriminatory.[168]

Does the Pool Inhibit Third Parties from Accessing the Pool? The ability of patent owners to license their patents outside the pool is a critical issue in the antitrust counseling process. Frequently pools adopt exclusivity restrictions designed to prevent their competitors from accessing any of pooled technologies. For example, the pool may hold an exclusive right to grant sub-licenses, or alternatively, patent owners may be required to receive the consent of pool members before licensing their technologies outside the pool. In either case, courts focus on whether the restrictions foreclose a competitor from practicing its patent in a relevant market, or inhibit development of competing technologies.

Patent pools are under no direct obligation to deal with all interested parties, though exclusionary policies that are not reasonably related to an efficiency-enhancing justification can be sanctioned if the pool participants collectively have market power and if the excluded firm cannot effectively compete in downstream product markets that incorporate the pooled technology.[169]

Additional antitrust concerns can arise when exclusionary rules are applied in conjunction with other suspect practices, such as the pooling of non-essential patents or inclusion of collateral price and non-price restrictions. As already mentioned, one of the deciding factors in both *BMI* and the 3-G Patent Platform was that individual patent owners were allowed to negotiate directly with non-participating licensees. In *BMI*,

---

167. *See* DVD-6 Business Review Letter (DOJ satisfied that a pooling arrangement between leading DVD manufacturers would not facilitate collusion in the production of DVD discs and DVD players because the overall production of manufacturing DVD products was likely to be much higher than the per-product pool royalty.).

168. *See* DVD-6 Business Review Letter (DOJ satisfied that a pooling arrangement between leading DVD manufacturers would not facilitate collusion in the production of DVD discs and DVD players because the overall production of manufacturing DVD products was likely to be much higher than the per-product pool royalty).

169. *See* INTELLECTUAL PROPERTY GUIDELINES, *supra* note 1, § 5.5.

this allowed licensees to purchase less than the full portfolio of pooled technology, where as in 3-G, the non-exclusive structure enhanced the competitive opportunities for alternative technologies.

Does the Pool Impose Grantback Obligations on Contributing Members? Mandatory grantback obligations imposed upon contributing members and licensees have the potential to decrease the incentive to innovate. Licensees have less incentive to invest in the development of superior (i.e., more competitive) technologies if they are required to share their rewards with the entire pool.[170] Significant foreclosure concerns can also arise if the licensee is required to make an exclusive grant of rights to the pool. Thus, if pool participants require grantback rights from licensees, the structure and scope of the obligation will have to be tailored to the justification and sufficiently procompetitive to compensate for any loss in potential competition. Generally, the three primary issues are: Is the grantback limited to essential patents? Is it non-exclusive? And will the licensee be provided fair compensation?

As a general rule, grantback obligations are acceptable if they are limited to improvements on essential patents and if they allow the licensee to earn compensation for making the grant to the pool. In this way, the procompetitive aspects of grantbacks are maintained, without disturbing the licensee's incentive to develop alternate (i.e., non-essential) technologies or non-infringing improvements. As with all other patents included within the pool, the licensee should be required to grant non-exclusive licenses to the essential patents on fair, reasonable and non-discriminatory terms.

How Do the Parties Plan to Administer the Creation and Operation of the Pool? Allowing an independent third party to administer a patent pool and negotiate licensing terms serves two beneficial purposes. First, where pooling arrangements require the free flow of competitively sensitive data in order to allocate royalty income, a third party administrator stands in a better position to maintain information firewalls between the participants, particularly where pool participants are actual or potential competitors outside the pool. Similarly, an independent administrator is well positioned to ensure that licenses are negotiated on fair, reasonable, and non-discriminatory terms.

---

170. *Id.*; *see also* United States v. Mfrs. Aircraft Ass'n, 1976-1 Trade Cas. (CCH) ¶ 60,810 (S.D.N.Y. Nov. 12, 1975) (final judgment dissolving cross-licensing arrangement); United States v. Auto. Mfrs. Ass'n, 1969 Trade Cas. (CCH) ¶ 72,907 (C.D. Cal. Oct. 29, 1969) (same), *modified by* 1982-83 Trade Cas. (CCH) ¶ 65,088 (C.D. Cal. Nov. 19, 1982).

ANTITRUST GUIDELINES FOR THE LICENSING OF INTELLECTUAL PROPERTY

**Antitrust Guidelines
for the Licensing
of Intellectual Property
Issued by the
U.S. Department of Justice***
**and the
Federal Trade Commission**

April 6, 1995

---

* These Guidelines supersede section 3.6 in Part I, "Intellectual Property Licensing Arrangements," and cases 6, 10, 11, and 12 in Part II of the U.S. Department of Justice 1988 Antitrust Enforcement Guidelines for International Operations.

1). Intellectual property protection and the antitrust laws

1.0 These Guidelines state the antitrust enforcement policy of the U.S. Department of Justice and the Federal Trade Commission (individually, "the Agency," and collectively, "the Agencies") with respect to the licensing of intellectual property protected by patent, copyright, and trade secret law, and of know-how.[1] By stating their general policy, the Agencies hope to assist those who need to predict whether the Agencies will challenge a practice as anticompetitive. However, these Guidelines cannot remove judgment and discretion in antitrust law enforcement. Moreover, the standards set forth in these Guidelines must be applied in unforeseeable circumstances. Each case will be evaluated in light of its own facts, and these Guidelines will be applied reasonably and flexibly.[2]

In the United States, patents confer rights to exclude others from making, using, or selling in the United States the invention claimed by the patent for a period of seventeen years from the date of issue.[3] To gain patent protection, an invention (which may be a product, process, machine, or composition of matter) must be novel, nonobvious, and useful. Copyright protection applies to original works of authorship

---

1.   These Guidelines do not cover the antitrust treatment of trademarks. Although the same general antitrust principles that apply to other forms of intellectual property apply to trademarks as well, these Guidelines deal with technology transfer and innovation-related issues that typically arise with respect to patents, copyrights, trade secrets, and know-how agreements, rather than with product-differentiation issues that typically arise with respect to trademarks.

2.   As is the case with all guidelines, users should rely on qualified counsel to assist them in evaluating the antitrust risk associated with any contemplated transaction or activity. No set of guidelines can possibly indicate how the Agencies will assess the particular facts of every case. Parties who wish to know the Agencies' specific enforcement intentions with respect to any particular transaction should consider seeking a Department of Justice business review letter pursuant to 28 C.F.R. § 50.6 or a Federal Trade Commission Advisory Opinion pursuant to 16 C.F.R. §§ 1.1B1.4.

3.   *See* 35 U.S.C. § 154 (1988). Section 532(a) of the Uruguay Round Agreements Act, Pub. L. No. 103-465, 108 Stat. 4809, 4983 (1994) would change the length of patent protection to a term beginning on the date at which the patent issues and ending twenty years from the date on which the application for the patent was filed.

embodied in a tangible medium of expression.[4] A copyright protects only the expression, not the underlying ideas.[5] Unlike a patent, which protects an invention not only from copying but also from independent creation, a copyright does not preclude others from independently creating similar expression. Trade secret protection applies to information whose economic value depends on its not being generally known.[6] Trade secret protection is conditioned upon efforts to maintain secrecy and has no fixed term. As with copyright protection, trade secret protection does not preclude independent creation by others.

The intellectual property laws and the antitrust laws share the common purpose of promoting innovation and enhancing consumer welfare.[7] The intellectual property laws provide incentives for innovation and its dissemination and commercialization by establishing enforceable property rights for the creators of new and useful products, more efficient processes, and original works of expression. In the absence of intellectual property rights, imitators could more rapidly exploit the efforts of innovators and investors without compensation. Rapid imitation would reduce the commercial value of innovation and erode incentives to invest, ultimately to the detriment of consumers. The antitrust laws promote innovation and consumer welfare by prohibiting certain actions that may harm competition with respect to either existing or new ways of serving consumers.

2). **General principles**

2.0 These Guidelines embody three general principles: (a) for the purpose of antitrust analysis, the Agencies regard intellectual property as

---

4.   *See* 17 U.S.C. § 102 (1988 & Supp. V 1993). Copyright protection lasts for the author's life plus 50 years, or 75 years from first publication (or 100 years from creation, whichever expires first) for works made for hire. *See* 17 U.S.C. § 302 (1988). The principles stated in these Guidelines also apply to protection of mask works fixed in a semiconductor chip product (*see* 17 U.S.C. § 901 *et seq.* (1988)), which is analogous to copyright protection for works of authorship.

5.   *See* 17 U.S.C. § 102(b) (1988).

6.   Trade secret protection derives from state law. *See generally Kewanee Oil Co. v. Bicron Corp.*, 416 U.S. 470 (1974).

7.   "[T]he aims and objectives of patent and antitrust laws may seem, at first glance, wholly at odds. However, the two bodies of law are actually complementary, as both are aimed at encouraging innovation, industry and competition." *Atari Games Corp. v. Nintendo of America, Inc.*, 897 F.2d 1572, 1576 (Fed. Cir. 1990).

being essentially comparable to any other form of property; (b) the Agencies do not presume that intellectual property creates market power in the antitrust context; and (c) the Agencies recognize that intellectual property licensing allows firms to combine complementary factors of production and is generally procompetitive.

a) Standard antitrust analysis applies to intellectual property

The Agencies apply the same general antitrust principles to conduct involving intellectual property that they apply to conduct involving any other form of tangible or intangible property. That is not to say that intellectual property is in all respects the same as any other form of property. Intellectual property has important characteristics, such as ease of misappropriation, that distinguish it from many other forms of property. These characteristics can be taken into account by standard antitrust analysis, however, and do not require the application of fundamentally different principles.[8]

Although there are clear and important differences in the purpose, extent, and duration of protection provided under the intellectual property regimes of patent, copyright, and trade secret, the governing antitrust principles are the same. Antitrust analysis takes differences among these forms of intellectual property into account in evaluating the specific market circumstances in which transactions occur, just as it does with other particular market circumstances.

Intellectual property law bestows on the owners of intellectual property certain rights to exclude others. These rights help the owners to profit from the use of their property. An intellectual property owner's rights to exclude are similar to the rights enjoyed by owners of other forms of private property. As with other forms of private property, certain types of conduct with respect to intellectual property may have anticompetitive effects against which the antitrust laws can and do protect. Intellectual property is thus neither particularly free from scrutiny under the antitrust laws, nor particularly suspect under them.

The Agencies recognize that the licensing of intellectual property is often international. The principles of antitrust analysis described in these Guidelines apply equally to domestic and international licensing

---

8.	As with other forms of property, the power to exclude others from the use of intellectual property may vary substantially, depending on the nature of the property and its status under federal or state law. The greater or lesser legal power of an owner to exclude others is also taken into account by standard antitrust analysis.

arrangements. However, as described in the 1995 Department of Justice and Federal Trade Commission Antitrust Enforcement Guidelines for International Operations, considerations particular to international operations, such as jurisdiction and comity, may affect enforcement decisions when the arrangement is in an international context.

b) Intellectual property and market power

Market power is the ability profitably to maintain prices above, or output below, competitive levels for a significant period of time.[9] The Agencies will not presume that a patent, copyright, or trade secret necessarily confers market power upon its owner. Although the intellectual property right confers the power to exclude with respect to the *specific* product, process, or work in question, there will often be sufficient actual or potential close substitutes for such product, process, or work to prevent the exercise of market power.[10] If a patent or other form of intellectual property does confer market power, that market power does not by itself offend the antitrust laws. As with any other tangible or intangible asset that enables its owner to obtain significant supracompetitive profits, market power (or even a monopoly) that is solely as consequence of a superior product, business acumen, or historic

---

9. Market power can be exercised in other economic dimensions, such as quality, service, and the development of new or improved goods and processes. It is assumed in this definition that all competitive dimensions are held constant except the ones in which market power is being exercised; that a seller is able to charge higher prices for a higher-quality product does not alone indicate market power. The definition in the text is stated in terms of a seller with market power. A buyer could also exercise market power (e.g., by maintaining the price below the competitive level, thereby depressing output).

10. The Agencies note that the law is unclear on this issue. *Compare Jefferson Parish Hospital District No. 2 v. Hyde*, 466 U.S. 2, 16 (1984) (expressing the view in dictum that if a product is protected by a patent, "it is fair to presume that the inability to buy the product elsewhere gives the seller market power") *with id.* at 37 n.7 (O'Connor, J., concurring) ("[A] patent holder has no market power in any relevant sense if there are close substitutes for the patented product."). *Compare also Abbott Laboratories v. Brennan*, 952 F.2d 1346, 1354-55 (Fed. Cir. 1991) (no presumption of market power from intellectual property right), *cert. denied*, 112 S. Ct. 2993 (1992) *with Digidyne Corp. v. Data General Corp.*, 734 F.2d 1336, 1341-42 (9th Cir. 1984) (requisite economic power is presumed from copyright), *cert. denied,* 473 U.S. 908 (1985).

accident@ does not violate the antitrust laws.[11] Nor does such market power impose on the intellectual property owner an obligation to license the use of that property to others. As in other antitrust contexts, however, market power could be illegally acquired or maintained, or, even if lawfully acquired and maintained, would be relevant to the ability of an intellectual property owner to harm competition through unreasonable conduct in connection with such property.

c) Procompetitive benefits of licensing

Intellectual property typically is one component among many in a production process and derives value from its combination with complementary factors. Complementary factors of production include manufacturing and distribution facilities, workforces, and other items of intellectual property. The owner of intellectual property has to arrange for its combination with other necessary factors to realize its commercial value. Often, the owner finds it most efficient to contract with others for these factors, to sell rights to the intellectual property, or to enter into a joint venture arrangement for its development, rather than supplying these complementary factors itself.

Licensing, cross-licensing, or otherwise transferring intellectual property (hereinafter "licensing") can facilitate integration of the licensed property with complementary factors of production. This integration can lead to more efficient exploitation of the intellectual property, benefiting consumers through the reduction of costs and the introduction of new products. Such arrangements increase the value of intellectual property to consumers and to the developers of the technology. By potentially increasing the expected returns from intellectual property, licensing also can increase the incentive for its creation and thus promote greater investment in research and development.

Sometimes the use of one item of intellectual property requires access to another. An item of intellectual property "blocks" another when the second cannot be practiced without using the first. For example, an improvement on a patented machine can be blocked by the patent on the machine. Licensing may promote the coordinated development of technologies that are in a blocking relationship.

---

11.   *United States v. Grinnell Corp.*, 384 U.S. 563, 571 (1966); *see also United States v. Aluminum Co. of America*, 148 F.2d 416, 430 (2d Cir. 1945) (Sherman Act is not violated by the attainment of market power solely through "superior skill, foresight and industry").

Field-of-use, territorial, and other limitations on intellectual property licenses may serve procompetitive ends by allowing the licensor to exploit its property as efficiently and effectively as possible. These various forms of exclusivity can be used to give a licensee an incentive to invest in the commercialization and distribution of products embodying the licensed intellectual property and to develop additional applications for the licensed property. The restrictions may do so, for example, by protecting the licensee against free-riding on the licensee's investments by other licensees or by the licensor. They may also increase the licensor's incentive to license, for example, by protecting the licensor from competition in the licensor's own technology in a market niche that it prefers to keep to itself. These benefits of licensing restrictions apply to patent, copyright, and trade secret licenses, and to know-how agreements.

Example 1[12]

Situation: ComputerCo develops a new, copyrighted software program for inventory management. The program has wide application in the health field. ComputerCo licenses the program in an arrangement that imposes both field of use and territorial limitations. Some of ComputerCo's licenses permit use only in hospitals; others permit use only in group medical practices. ComputerCo charges different royalties for the different uses. All of ComputerCo's licenses permit use only in specified portions of the United States and in specified foreign countries.[13] The licenses contain no provisions that would prevent or discourage licensees from developing, using, or selling any other program, or from competing in any other good or service other than in the use of the licensed program. None of the licensees are actual or likely potential competitors of ComputerCo in the sale of inventory management programs.

Discussion: The key competitive issue raised by the licensing arrangement is whether it harms competition among entities that would have been actual or likely potential competitors in the absence of the arrangement. Such harm could occur if, for example, the licenses

---

12. The examples in these Guidelines are hypothetical and do not represent judgments about, or analysis of, any actual market circumstances of the named industries.
13. These Guidelines do not address the possible application of the antitrust laws of other countries to restraints such as territorial restrictions in international licensing arrangements.

anticompetitively foreclose access to competing technologies (in this case, most likely competing computer programs), prevent licensees from developing their own competing technologies (again, in this case, most likely computer programs), or facilitate market allocation or price-fixing for any product or service supplied by the licensees. (*See* section 3.1.) If the license agreements contained such provisions, the Agency evaluating the arrangement would analyze its likely competitive effects as described in parts 3-5 of these Guidelines. In this hypothetical, there are no such provisions and thus the arrangement is merely a subdivision of the licensor's intellectual property among different fields of use and territories. The licensing arrangement does not appear likely to harm competition among entities that would have been actual or likely potential competitors if ComputerCo had chosen not to license the software program. The Agency therefore would be unlikely to object to this arrangement. Based on these facts, the result of the antitrust analysis would be the same whether the technology was protected by patent, copyright, or trade secret. The Agency's conclusion as to likely competitive effects could differ if, for example, the license barred licensees from using any other inventory management program.

3). Antitrust concerns and modes of analysis

a) Nature of the concerns

While intellectual property licensing arrangements are typically welfare-enhancing and procompetitive, antitrust concerns may nonetheless arise. For example, a licensing arrangement could include restraints that adversely affect competition in goods markets by dividing the markets among firms that would have competed using different technologies. *See, e.g.*, Example 7. An arrangement that effectively merges the research and development activities of two of only a few entities that could plausibly engage in research and development in the relevant field might harm competition for development of new goods and services. *See* section 3.2.3. An acquisition of intellectual property may lessen competition in a relevant antitrust market. *See* section 5.7. The Agencies will focus on the actual effects of an arrangement, not on its formal terms.

The Agencies will not require the owner of intellectual property to create competition in its own technology. However, antitrust concerns may arise when a licensing arrangement harms competition among entities that would have been actual or likely potential competitors[14] in a relevant market in the absence of the license (entities in a "horizontal relationship"). A restraint in a licensing arrangement may harm such competition, for example, if it facilitates market division or price-fixing. In addition, license restrictions with respect to one market may harm such competition in another market by anticompetitively foreclosing access to, or significantly raising the price of, an important input,[15] or by facilitating coordination to increase price or reduce output. When it appears that such competition may be adversely affected, the Agencies will follow the analysis set forth below. *See generally* sections 3.4 and 4.2.

b) Markets affected by licensing arrangements

Licensing arrangements raise concerns under the antitrust laws if they are likely to affect adversely the prices, quantities, qualities, or varieties of goods and services[16] either currently or potentially available. The competitive effects of licensing arrangements often can be adequately assessed within the relevant markets for the goods affected by the arrangements. In such instances, the Agencies will delineate and analyze only goods markets. In other cases, however, the analysis may require the delineation of markets for technology or markets for research and development (innovation markets).

i) Goods markets

A number of different goods markets may be relevant to evaluating the effects of a licensing arrangement. A restraint in a licensing arrangement may have competitive effects in markets for final or intermediate goods made using the intellectual property, or it may have effects upstream, in markets for goods that are used as inputs, along with the intellectual property, to the production of other goods. In general, for goods markets affected by a licensing arrangement, the Agencies will approach the delineation of relevant market and the measurement of

---

14. A firm will be treated as a likely potential competitor if there is evidence that entry by that firm is reasonably probable in the absence of the licensing arrangement.
15. As used herein, "input" includes outlets for distribution and sales, as well as factors of production. *See, e.g.*, sections 4.1.1 and 5.3-5.5 for further discussion of conditions under which foreclosing access to, or raising the price of, an input may harm competition in a relevant market.
16. Hereinafter, the term "goods" also includes services.

market share in the intellectual property area as in section 1 of the U.S. Department of Justice and Federal Trade Commission Horizontal Merger Guidelines.[17]

ii) Technology markets

Technology markets consist of the intellectual property that is licensed (the "licensed technology") and its close substitutes—that is, the technologies or goods that are close enough substitutes significantly to constrain the exercise of market power with respect to the intellectual property that is licensed.[18] When rights to intellectual property are marketed separately from the products in which they are used,[19] the Agencies may rely on technology markets to analyze the competitive effects of a licensing arrangement.

Example 2

Situation: Firms Alpha and Beta independently develop different patented process technologies to manufacture the same off-patent drug for the treatment of a particular disease. Before the firms use their technologies internally or license them to third parties, they announce plans jointly to manufacture the drug, and to assign their manufacturing processes to the new manufacturing venture. Many firms are capable of using and have the incentive to use the licensed technologies to manufacture and distribute the drug; thus, the market for drug

---

17.   U.S. Department of Justice and Federal Trade Commission, Horizontal Merger Guidelines (April 2, 1992) (hereinafter 1992 Horizontal Merger Guidelines). As stated in section 1.41 of the 1992 Horizontal Merger Guidelines, market shares for goods markets "can be expressed either in dollar terms through measurement of sales, shipments, or production, or in physical terms through measurement of sales, shipments, production, capacity or reserves."

18.   For example, the owner of a process for producing a particular good may be constrained in its conduct with respect to that process not only by other processes for making that good, but also by other goods that compete with the downstream good and by the processes used to produce those other goods.

19.   Intellectual property is often licensed, sold, or transferred as an integral part of a marketed good. An example is a patented product marketed with an implied license permitting its use. In such circumstances, there is no need for a separate analysis of technology markets to capture relevant competitive effects.

manufacturing and distribution is competitive. One of the Agencies is evaluating the likely competitive effects of the planned venture.

Discussion: The Agency would analyze the competitive effects of the proposed joint venture by first defining the relevant markets in which competition may be affected and then evaluating the likely competitive effects of the joint venture in the identified markets. (*See* Example 4 for a discussion of the Agencies' approach to joint venture analysis.) In this example, the structural effect of the joint venture in the relevant goods market for the manufacture and distribution of the drug is unlikely to be significant, because many firms in addition to the joint venture compete in that market. The joint venture might, however, increase the prices of the drug produced using Alpha's or Beta's technology by reducing competition in the relevant market for technology to manufacture the drug.

The Agency would delineate a technology market in which to evaluate likely competitive effects of the proposed joint venture. The Agency would identify other technologies that can be used to make the drug with levels of effectiveness and cost per dose comparable to that of the technologies owned by Alpha and Beta. In addition, the Agency would consider the extent to which competition from other drugs that are substitutes for the drug produced using Alpha's or Beta's technology would limit the ability of a hypothetical monopolist that owned both Alpha's and Beta's technology to raise its price.

To identify a technology's close substitutes and thus to delineate the relevant technology market, the Agencies will, if the data permit, identify the smallest group of technologies and goods over which a hypothetical monopolist of those technologies and goods likely would exercise market power—for example, by imposing a small but significant and nontransitory price increase.[20] The Agencies recognize that technology often is licensed in ways that are not readily quantifiable in monetary terms.[21] In such circumstances, the Agencies will delineate the relevant market by identifying other technologies and goods which buyers would substitute at a cost comparable to that of using the licensed technology.

---

20. This is conceptually analogous to the analytical approach to goods markets under the 1992 Horizontal Merger Guidelines. *Cf.* § 1.11. Of course, market power also can be exercised in other dimensions, such as quality, and these dimensions also may be relevant to the definition and analysis of technology markets.
21. For example, technology may be licensed royalty-free in exchange for the right to use other technology, or it may be licensed as part of a package license.

In assessing the competitive significance of current and likely potential participants in a technology market, the Agencies will take into account all relevant evidence. When market share data are available and accurately reflect the competitive significance of market participants, the Agencies will include market share data in this assessment. The Agencies also will seek evidence of buyers' and market participants' assessments of the competitive significance of technology market participants. Such evidence is particularly important when market share data are unavailable, or do not accurately represent the competitive significance of market participants. When market share data or other indicia of market power are not available, and it appears that competing technologies are comparably efficient,[22] the Agencies will assign each technology the same market share. For new technologies, the Agencies generally will use the best available information to estimate market acceptance over a two-year period, beginning with commercial introduction.

3.2.3 Research and development: innovation markets

If a licensing arrangement may adversely affect competition to develop new or improved goods or processes, the Agencies will analyze such an impact either as a separate competitive effect in relevant goods or technology markets, or as a competitive effect in a separate innovation market. A licensing arrangement may have competitive effects on innovation that cannot be adequately addressed through the analysis of goods or technology markets. For example, the arrangement may affect the development of goods that do not yet exist.[23] Alternatively, the arrangement may affect the development of new or improved goods or

---

22. The Agencies will regard two technologies as "comparably efficient" if they can be used to produce close substitutes at comparable costs.
23. *E.g., Sensormatic*, FTC Inv. No. 941-0126, 60 Fed. Reg. 5428 (accepted for comment Dec. 28, 1994); *Wright Medical Technology, Inc.*, FTC Inv. No. 951-0015, 60 Fed. Reg. 460 (accepted for comment Dec. 8, 1994); *American Home Products*, FTC Inv. No. 941-0116, 59 Fed. Reg. 60,807 (accepted for comment Nov. 28, 1994); *Roche Holdings Ltd.*, 113 F.T.C. 1086 (1990); *United States v. Automobile Mfrs. Ass'n*, 307 F. Supp. 617 (C.D. Cal. 1969), *appeal dismissed sub nom. City of New York v. United States*, 397 U.S. 248 (1970), *modified sub nom. United States v. Motor Vehicles Mfrs. Ass'n*, 1982-83 Trade Cas. (CCH) ¶ 65,088 (C.D. Cal. 1982).

processes in geographic markets where there is no actual or likely potential competition in the relevant goods.[24]

An innovation market consists of the research and development directed to particular new or improved goods or processes, and the close substitutes for that research and development. The close substitutes are research and development efforts, technologies, and goods[25] that significantly constrain the exercise of market power with respect to the relevant research and development, for example by limiting the ability and incentive of a hypothetical monopolist to retard the pace of research and development. The Agencies will delineate an innovation market only when the capabilities to engage in the relevant research and development can be associated with specialized assets or characteristics of specific firms.

In assessing the competitive significance of current and likely potential participants in an innovation market, the Agencies will take into account all relevant evidence. When market share data are available and accurately reflect the competitive significance of market participants, the Agencies will include market share data in this assessment. The Agencies also will seek evidence of buyers' and market participants' assessments of the competitive significance of innovation market participants. Such evidence is particularly important when market share data are unavailable or do not accurately represent the competitive significance of market participants. The Agencies may base the market shares of participants in an innovation market on their shares of identifiable assets or characteristics upon which innovation depends, on shares of research and development expenditures, or on shares of a related product. When entities have comparable capabilities and incentives to pursue research and development that is a close substitute for the research and development activities of the parties to a licensing arrangement, the Agencies may assign equal market shares to such entities.

---

24. *See* Complaint, *United States v. General Motors Corp.*, Civ. No. 93-530 (D. Del., filed Nov. 16, 1993).
25. For example, the licensor of research and development may be constrained in its conduct not only by competing research and development efforts but also by other existing goods that would compete with the goods under development.

Example 3

Situation: Two companies that specialize in advanced metallurgy agree to cross-license future patents relating to the development of a new component for aircraft jet turbines. Innovation in the development of the component requires the capability to work with very high tensile strength materials for jet turbines. Aspects of the licensing arrangement raise the possibility that competition in research and development of this and related components will be lessened. One of the Agencies is considering whether to define an innovation market in which to evaluate the competitive effects of the arrangement.

Discussion: If the firms that have the capability and incentive to work with very high tensile strength materials for jet turbines can be reasonably identified, the Agency will consider defining a relevant innovation market for development of the new component. If the number of firms with the required capability and incentive to engage in research and development of very high tensile strength materials for aircraft jet turbines is small, the Agency may employ the concept of an innovation market to analyze the likely competitive effects of the arrangement in that market, or as an aid in analyzing competitive effects in technology or goods markets. The Agency would perform its analysis as described in parts 3-5.

If the number of firms with the required capability and incentive is large (either because there are a large number of such firms in the jet turbine industry, or because there are many firms in other industries with the required capability and incentive), then the Agency will conclude that the innovation market is competitive. Under these circumstances, it is unlikely that any single firm or plausible aggregation of firms could acquire a large enough share of the assets necessary for innovation to have an adverse impact on competition.

If the Agency cannot reasonably identify the firms with the required capability and incentive, it will not attempt to define an innovation market.

Example 4

Situation: Three of the largest producers of a plastic used in disposable bottles plan to engage in joint research and development to produce a new type of plastic that is rapidly biodegradable. The joint venture will grant to its partners (but to no one else) licenses to all patent rights and use of know-how. One of the Agencies is evaluating the likely competitive effects of the proposed joint venture.

Discussion: The Agency would analyze the proposed research and development joint venture using an analysis similar to that applied to other joint ventures.[26] The Agency would begin by defining the relevant markets in which to analyze the joint venture's likely competitive effects. In this case, a relevant market is an innovation marketCresearch and development for biodegradable (and other environmentally friendly) containers. The Agency would seek to identify any other entities that would be actual or likely potential competitors with the joint venture in that relevant market. This would include those firms that have the capability and incentive to undertake research and development closely substitutable for the research and development proposed to be undertaken by the joint venture, taking into account such firms' existing technologies and technologies under development, R&D facilities, and other relevant assets and business circumstances. Firms possessing such capabilities and incentives would be included in the research and development market even if they are not competitors in relevant markets for related goods, such as the plastics currently produced by the joint venturers, although competitors in existing goods markets may often also compete in related innovation markets.

Having defined a relevant innovation market, the Agency would assess whether the joint venture is likely to have anticompetitive effects in that market. A starting point in this analysis is the degree of concentration in the relevant market and the market shares of the parties to the joint venture. If, in addition to the parties to the joint venture (taken collectively), there are at least four other independently controlled entities that possess comparable capabilities and incentives to undertake research and development of biodegradable plastics, or other products that would be close substitutes for such new plastics, the joint venture ordinarily would be unlikely to adversely affect competition in the relevant innovation market (*cf* section 4.3). If there are fewer than four other independently controlled entities with similar capabilities and incentives, the Agency would consider whether the joint venture would give the parties to the joint venture an incentive and ability collectively to reduce investment in, or otherwise to retard the pace or scope of,

---

26.   *See, e.g.,* U.S. Department of Justice and Federal Trade Commission, Statements of Enforcement Policy and Analytical Principles Relating to Health Care and Antitrust 20-23, 37-40, 72-74 (September 27, 1994). This type of transaction may qualify for treatment under the Nat'l Cooperative Research and Production Act of 1993, 15 U.S.C. §§ 4301-05.

research and development efforts. If the joint venture creates a significant risk of anticompetitive effects in the innovation market, the Agency would proceed to consider efficiency justifications for the venture, such as the potential for combining complementary R&D assets in such a way as to make successful innovation more likely, or to bring it about sooner, or to achieve cost reductions in research and development.

The Agency would also assess the likelihood that the joint venture would adversely affect competition in other relevant markets, including markets for products produced by the parties to the joint venture. The risk of such adverse competitive effects would be increased to the extent that, for example, the joint venture facilitates the exchange among the parties of competitively sensitive information relating to goods markets in which the parties currently compete or facilitates the coordination of competitive activities in such markets. The Agency would examine whether the joint venture imposes collateral restraints that might significantly restrict competition among the joint venturers in goods markets, and would examine whether such collateral restraints were reasonably necessary to achieve any efficiencies that are likely to be attained by the venture.

c) Horizontal and vertical relationships

As with other property transfers, antitrust analysis of intellectual property licensing arrangements examines whether the relationship among the parties to the arrangement is primarily horizontal or vertical in nature, or whether it has substantial aspects of both. A licensing arrangement has a vertical component when it affects activities that are in a complementary relationship, as is typically the case in a licensing arrangement. For example, the licensor's primary line of business may be in research and development, and the licensees, as manufacturers, may be buying the rights to use technology developed by the licensor. Alternatively, the licensor may be a component manufacturer owning intellectual property rights in a product that the licensee manufactures by combining the component with other inputs, or the licensor may manufacture the product, and the licensees may operate primarily in distribution and marketing.

In addition to this vertical component, the licensor and its licensees may also have a horizontal relationship. For analytical purposes, the Agencies ordinarily will treat a relationship between a licensor and its licensees, or between licensees, as horizontal when they would have been actual or likely potential competitors in a relevant market in the absence of the license.

The existence of a horizontal relationship between a licensor and its licensees does not, in itself, indicate that the arrangement is anticompetitive. Identification of such relationships is merely an aid in determining whether there may be anticompetitive effects arising from a licensing arrangement. Such a relationship need not give rise to an anticompetitive effect, nor does a purely vertical relationship assure that there are no anticompetitive effects.

The following examples illustrate different competitive relationships among a licensor and its licensees.

Example 5

Situation: AgCo, a manufacturer of farm equipment, develops a new, patented emission control technology for its tractor engines and licenses it to FarmCo, another farm equipment manufacturer. AgCo's emission control technology is far superior to the technology currently owned and used by FarmCo, so much so that FarmCo's technology does not significantly constrain the prices that AgCo could charge for its technology. AgCo's emission control patent has a broad scope. It is likely that any improved emissions control technology that FarmCo could develop in the foreseeable future would infringe AgCo's patent.

Discussion: Because FarmCo's emission control technology does not significantly constrain AgCo's competitive conduct with respect to its emission control technology, AgCo's and FarmCo's emission control technologies are not close substitutes for each other. FarmCo is a consumer of AgCo's technology and is not an actual competitor of AgCo in the relevant market for superior emission control technology of the kind licensed by AgCo. Furthermore, FarmCo is not a likely potential competitor of AgCo in the relevant market because, even if FarmCo could develop an improved emission control technology, it is likely that it would infringe AgCo's patent. This means that the relationship between AgCo and FarmCo with regard to the supply and use of emissions control technology is vertical. Assuming that AgCo and FarmCo are actual or likely potential competitors in sales of farm equipment products, their relationship is horizontal in the relevant markets for farm equipment.

Example 6

Situation: FarmCo develops a new valve technology for its engines and enters into a cross-licensing arrangement with AgCo, whereby AgCo licenses its emission control technology to FarmCo and FarmCo licenses its valve technology to AgCo. AgCo already owns an alternative valve technology that can be used to achieve engine performance similar to that using FarmCo's valve technology and at a comparable cost to consumers. Before adopting FarmCo's technology, AgCo was using its own valve technology in its production of engines and was licensing (and continues to license) that technology for use by others. As in Example 5, FarmCo does not own or control an emission control technology that is a close substitute for the technology licensed from AgCo. Furthermore, as in Example 5, FarmCo is not likely to develop an improved emission control technology that would be a close substitute for AgCo's technology, because of AgCo's blocking patent.

Discussion: FarmCo is a consumer and not a competitor of AgCo's emission control technology. As in Example 5, their relationship is vertical with regard to this technology. The relationship between AgCo and FarmCo in the relevant market that includes engine valve technology is vertical in part and horizontal in part. It is vertical in part because AgCo and FarmCo stand in a complementary relationship, in which AgCo is a consumer of a technology supplied by FarmCo. However, the relationship between AgCo and FarmCo in the relevant market that includes engine valve technology is also horizontal in part, because FarmCo and AgCo are actual competitors in the licensing of valve technology that can be used to achieve similar engine performance at a comparable cost. Whether the firms license their valve technologies to others is not important for the conclusion that the firms have a horizontal relationship in this relevant market. Even if AgCo's use of its valve technology were solely captive to its own production, the fact that the two valve technologies are substitutable at comparable cost means that the two firms have a horizontal relationship.

As in Example 5, the relationship between AgCo and FarmCo is horizontal in the relevant markets for farm equipment.

d) Framework for evaluating licensing restraints

In the vast majority of cases, restraints in intellectual property licensing arrangements are evaluated under the rule of reason. The Agencies' general approach in analyzing a licensing restraint under the rule of reason is to inquire whether the restraint is likely to have anticompetitive effects and, if so, whether the restraint is reasonably necessary to achieve procompetitive benefits that outweigh those anticompetitive effects. *See Federal Trade Commission v. Indiana Federation of Dentists*, 476 U.S. 447 (1986); *NCAA v. Board of Regents of the University of Oklahoma*, 468 U.S. 85 (1984); *Broadcast Music,*

Inc. v. Columbia Broadcasting System, Inc., 441 U.S. 1 (1979); 7 Phillip
E. Areeda, *Antitrust Law* § 1502 (1986). *See also* part 4.

In some cases, however, the courts conclude that a restraint's "nature
and necessary effect are so plainly anticompetitive" that it should be
treated as unlawful per se, without an elaborate inquiry into the restraint's
likely competitive effect. *Federal Trade Commission v. Superior Court
Trial Lawyers Association,* 493 U.S. 411, 433 (1990); *National Society of
Professional Engineers v. United States,* 435 U.S. 679, 692 (1978).
Among the restraints that have been held per se unlawful are naked
price-fixing, output restraints, and market division among horizontal
competitors, as well as certain group boycotts and resale price
maintenance.

To determine whether a particular restraint in a licensing
arrangement is given per se or rule of reason treatment, the Agencies will
assess whether the restraint in question can be expected to contribute to
an efficiency-enhancing integration of economic activity. *See Broadcast
Music,* 441 U.S. at 16B24. In general, licensing arrangements promote
such integration because they facilitate the combination of the licensor's
intellectual property with complementary factors of production owned by
the licensee. A restraint in a licensing arrangement may further such
integration by, for example, aligning the incentives of the licensor and
the licensees to promote the development and marketing of the licensed
technology, or by substantially reducing transactions costs. If there is no
efficiency-enhancing integration of economic activity and if the type of
restraint is one that has been accorded per se treatment, the Agencies will
challenge the restraint under the per se rule. Otherwise, the Agencies
will apply a rule of reason analysis.

Application of the rule of reason generally requires a comprehensive
inquiry into market conditions. (*See* sections 4.1-4.3.) However, that
inquiry may be truncated in certain circumstances. If the Agencies
conclude that a restraint has no likely anticompetitive effects, they will
treat it as reasonable, without an elaborate analysis of market power or
the justifications for the restraint. Similarly, if a restraint facially appears
to be of a kind that would always or almost always tend to reduce output
or increase prices,[27] and the restraint is not reasonably related to

---

27. Details about the Federal Trade Commission's approach are set forth in
Massachusetts Board of Registration in Optometry, 110 F.T.C. 549, 604
(1988). In applying its truncated rule of reason inquiry, the FTC uses the
analytical category of Ainherently suspect@ restraints to denote facially
anticompetitive restraints that would always or almost always tend to

efficiencies, the Agencies will likely challenge the restraint without an elaborate analysis of particular industry circumstances.[28] *See Indiana Federation of Dentists*, 476 U.S. at 459-60; *NCAA*, 468 U.S. at 109.

Example 7

Situation: Gamma, which manufactures Product X using its patented process, offers a license for its process technology to every other manufacturer of Product X, each of which competes world-wide with Gamma in the manufacture and sale of X. The process technology does not represent an economic improvement over the available existing technologies. Indeed, although most manufacturers accept licenses from Gamma, none of the licensees actually uses the licensed technology. The licenses provide that each manufacturer has an exclusive right to sell Product X manufactured using the licensed technology in a designated geographic area and that no manufacturer may sell Product X, however manufactured, outside the designated territory.

Discussion: The manufacturers of Product X are in a horizontal relationship in the goods market for Product X. Any manufacturers of Product X that control technologies that are substitutable at comparable cost for Gamma's process are also horizontal competitors of Gamma in the relevant technology market. The licensees of Gamma's process technology are technically in a vertical relationship, although that is not significant in this example because they do not actually use Gamma's technology.

The licensing arrangement restricts competition in the relevant goods market among manufacturers of Product X by requiring each manufacturer to limit its sales to an exclusive territory. Thus, competition among entities that would be actual competitors in the absence of the licensing arrangement is restricted. Based on the facts set forth above, the licensing arrangement does not involve a useful transfer of technology, and thus it is unlikely that the restraint on sales outside the designated territories contributes to an efficiency-enhancing integration of economic activity. Consequently, the evaluating Agency would be likely to challenge the arrangement under the per se rule as a horizontal

---

   decrease output or increase prices, but that may be relatively unfamiliar
   or may not fit neatly into traditional per se categories.

28.   Under the FTC's *Mass. Board* approach, asserted efficiency justifications
   for inherently suspect restraints are examined to determine whether they
   are plausible and, if so, whether they are valid in the context of the
   market at issue. *Mass. Board*, 110 F.T.C. at 604.

territorial market allocation scheme and to view the intellectual property aspects of the arrangement as a sham intended to cloak its true nature.

If the licensing arrangement could be expected to contribute to an efficiency-enhancing integration of economic activity, as might be the case if the licensed technology were an advance over existing processes and used by the licensees, the Agency would analyze the arrangement under the rule of reason applying the analytical framework described in this section.

In this example, the competitive implications do not generally depend on whether the licensed technology is protected by patent, is a trade secret or other know-how, or is a computer program protected by copyright; nor do the competitive implications generally depend on whether the allocation of markets is territorial, as in this example, or functional, based on fields of use.

4). General principles concerning the Agencies' evaluation of licensing arrangements under the rule of reason

a) Analysis of anticompetitive effects

The existence of anticompetitive effects resulting from a restraint in a licensing arrangement will be evaluated on the basis of the analysis described in this section.

i) Market structure, coordination, and foreclosure

When a licensing arrangement affects parties in a horizontal relationship, a restraint in that arrangement may increase the risk of coordinated pricing, output restrictions, or the acquisition or maintenance of market power. Harm to competition also may occur if the arrangement poses a significant risk of retarding or restricting the development of new or improved goods or processes. The potential for competitive harm depends in part on the degree of concentration in, the difficulty of entry into, and the responsiveness of supply and demand to changes in price in the relevant markets. *Cf.* 1992 Horizontal Merger Guidelines §§ 1.5, 3.

When the licensor and licensees are in a vertical relationship, the Agencies will analyze whether the licensing arrangement may harm competition among entities in a horizontal relationship at either the level of the licensor or the licensees, or possibly in another relevant market. Harm to competition from a restraint may occur if it anticompetitively forecloses access to, or increases competitors' costs of obtaining, important inputs, or facilitates coordination to raise price or restrict output.   The risk of anticompetitively foreclosing access or increasing competitors' costs is related to the proportion of the markets affected by the licensing restraint; other characteristics of the relevant markets, such as concentration, difficulty of entry, and the responsiveness of supply and demand to changes in price in the relevant markets; and the duration of the restraint.   A licensing arrangement does not foreclose competition merely because some or all of the potential licensees in an industry choose to use the licensed technology to the exclusion of other technologies.   Exclusive use may be an efficient consequence of the licensed technology having the lowest cost or highest value.

Harm to competition from a restraint in a vertical licensing arrangement also may occur if a licensing restraint facilitates coordination among entities in a horizontal relationship to raise prices or reduce output in a relevant market.   For example, if owners of competing technologies impose similar restraints on their licensees, the licensors may find it easier to coordinate their pricing.   Similarly, licensees that are competitors may find it easier to coordinate their pricing if they are subject to common restraints in licenses with a common licensor or competing licensors.   The risk of anticompetitive coordination is increased when the relevant markets are concentrated and difficult to enter.   The use of similar restraints may be common and procompetitive in an industry, however, because they contribute to efficient exploitation of the licensed property.

ii) Licensing arrangements involving exclusivity

A licensing arrangement may involve exclusivity in two distinct respects.   First, the licensor may grant one or more *exclusive licenses*, which restrict the right of the licensor to license others and possibly also to use the technology itself.   Generally, an exclusive license may raise antitrust concerns only if the licensees themselves, or the licensor and its licensees, are in a horizontal relationship.   Examples of arrangements involving exclusive licensing that may give rise to antitrust concerns include cross-licensing by parties collectively possessing market power (*see* section 5.5), grantbacks (*see* section 5.6), and acquisitions of intellectual property rights (*see* section 5.7).

A non-exclusive license of intellectual property that does not contain any restraints on the competitive conduct of the licensor or the licensee generally does not present antitrust concerns even if the parties to the license are in a horizontal relationship, because the non-exclusive license normally does not diminish competition that would occur in its absence.

A second form of exclusivity, *exclusive dealing*, arises when a license prevents or restrains the licensee from licensing, selling, distributing, or using competing technologies. *See* section 5.4. Exclusivity may be achieved by an explicit exclusive dealing term in the license or by other provisions such as compensation terms or other economic incentives. Such restraints may anticompetitively foreclose access to, or increase competitors' costs of obtaining, important inputs, or facilitate coordination to raise price or reduce output, but they also may have procompetitive effects. For example, a licensing arrangement that prevents the licensee from dealing in other technologies may encourage the licensee to develop and market the licensed technology or specialized applications of that technology. *See, e.g.*, Example 8. The Agencies will take into account such procompetitive effects in evaluating the reasonableness of the arrangement. *See* section 4.2.

The antitrust principles that apply to a licensor's grant of various forms of exclusivity to and among its licensees are similar to those that apply to comparable vertical restraints outside the licensing context, such as exclusive territories and exclusive dealing. However, the fact that intellectual property may in some cases be misappropriated more easily than other forms of property may justify the use of some restrictions that might be anticompetitive in other contexts.

As noted earlier, the Agencies will focus on the actual practice and its effects, not on the formal terms of the arrangement. A license denominated as non-exclusive (either in the sense of exclusive licensing or in the sense of exclusive dealing) may nonetheless give rise to the same concerns posed by formal exclusivity. A non-exclusive license may have the effect of exclusive licensing if it is structured so that the licensor is unlikely to license others or to practice the technology itself. A license that does not explicitly require exclusive dealing may have the effect of exclusive dealing if it is structured to increase significantly a licensee's cost when it uses competing technologies. However, a licensing arrangement will not automatically raise these concerns merely because a party chooses to deal with a single licensee or licensor, or confines his activity to a single field of use or location, or because only a single licensee has chosen to take a license.

Example 8

Situation: NewCo, the inventor and manufacturer of a new flat panel display technology, lacking the capability to bring a flat panel display product to market, grants BigCo an exclusive license to sell a product embodying NewCo's technology. BigCo does not currently sell, and is not developing (or likely to develop), a product that would compete with the product embodying the new technology and does not control rights to another display technology. Several firms offer competing displays, BigCo accounts for only a small proportion of the outlets for distribution of display products, and entry into the manufacture and distribution of display products is relatively easy. Demand for the new technology is uncertain and successful market penetration will require considerable promotional effort. The license contains an exclusive dealing restriction preventing BigCo from selling products that compete with the product embodying the licensed technology.

Discussion: This example illustrates both types of exclusivity in a licensing arrangement. The license is exclusive in that it restricts the right of the licensor to grant other licenses. In addition, the license has an exclusive dealing component in that it restricts the licensee from selling competing products.

The inventor of the display technology and its licensee are in a vertical relationship and are not actual or likely potential competitors in the manufacture or sale of display products or in the sale or development of technology. Hence, the grant of an exclusive license does not affect competition between the licensor and the licensee. The exclusive license may promote competition in the manufacturing and sale of display products by encouraging BigCo to develop and promote the new product in the face of uncertain demand by rewarding BigCo for its efforts if they lead to large sales. Although the license bars the licensee from selling competing products, this exclusive dealing aspect is unlikely in this example to harm competition by anticompetitively foreclosing access, raising competitors' costs of inputs, or facilitating anticompetitive pricing because the relevant product market is unconcentrated, the exclusive dealing restraint affects only a small proportion of the outlets for distribution of display products, and entry is easy. On these facts, the evaluating Agency would be unlikely to challenge the arrangement.

b) Efficiencies and justifications

If the Agencies conclude, upon an evaluation of the market factors described in section 4.1, that a restraint in a licensing arrangement is unlikely to have an anticompetitive effect, they will not challenge the restraint. If the Agencies conclude that the restraint has, or is likely to have, an anticompetitive effect, they will consider whether the restraint is reasonably necessary to achieve procompetitive efficiencies. If the restraint is reasonably necessary, the Agencies will balance the procompetitive efficiencies and the anticompetitive effects to determine the probable net effect on competition in each relevant market.

The Agencies' comparison of anticompetitive harms and procompetitive efficiencies is necessarily a qualitative one. The risk of anticompetitive effects in a particular case may be insignificant compared to the expected efficiencies, or vice versa. As the expected anticompetitive effects in a particular licensing arrangement increase, the Agencies will require evidence establishing a greater level of expected efficiencies.

The existence of practical and significantly less restrictive alternatives is relevant to a determination of whether a restraint is reasonably necessary. If it is clear that the parties could have achieved similar efficiencies by means that are significantly less restrictive, then the Agencies will not give weight to the parties' efficiency claim. In making this assessment, however, the Agencies will not engage in a search for a theoretically least restrictive alternative that is not realistic in the practical prospective business situation faced by the parties.

When a restraint has, or is likely to have, an anticompetitive effect, the duration of that restraint can be an important factor in determining whether it is reasonably necessary to achieve the putative procompetitive efficiency. The effective duration of a restraint may depend on a number of factors, including the option of the affected party to terminate the arrangement unilaterally and the presence of contract terms (e.g., unpaid balances on minimum purchase commitments) that encourage the licensee to renew a license arrangement. Consistent with their approach to less restrictive alternative analysis generally, the Agencies will not attempt to draw fine distinctions regarding duration; rather, their focus will be on situations in which the duration clearly exceeds the period needed to achieve the procompetitive efficiency.

The evaluation of procompetitive efficiencies, of the reasonable necessity of a restraint to achieve them, and of the duration of the restraint, may depend on the market context. A restraint that may be justified by the needs of a new entrant, for example, may not have a procompetitive efficiency justification in different market circumstances. *Cf. United States v. Jerrold Electronics Corp.*, 187 F. Supp. 545 (E.D. Pa. 1960), *aff'd per curiam*, 365 U.S. 567 (1961).

c) Antitrust "safety zone"

Because licensing arrangements often promote innovation and enhance competition, the Agencies believe that an antitrust "safety zone" is useful in order to provide some degree of certainty and thus to encourage such activity.[29]   Absent extraordinary circumstances, the Agencies will not challenge a restraint in an intellectual property licensing arrangement if (1) the restraint is not facially anticompetitive[30] and (2) the licensor and its licensees collectively account for no more than twenty percent of each relevant market significantly affected by the restraint.   This "safety zone" does not apply to those transfers of intellectual property rights to which a merger analysis is applied. *See* section 5.7.

Whether a restraint falls within the safety zone will be determined by reference only to goods markets unless the analysis of goods markets alone would inadequately address the effects of the licensing arrangement on competition among technologies or in research and development.

If an examination of the effects on competition among technologies or in research development is required, and if market share data are unavailable or do not accurately represent competitive significance, the following safety zone criteria will apply.   Absent extraordinary circumstances, the Agencies will not challenge a restraint in an intellectual property licensing arrangement that may affect competition in a technology market if (1) the restraint is not facially anticompetitive and (2) there are four or more independently controlled technologies in addition to the technologies controlled by the parties to the licensing arrangement that may be substitutable for the licensed technology at a comparable cost to the user.   Absent extraordinary circumstances, the Agencies will not challenge a restraint in an intellectual property licensing arrangement that may affect competition in an innovation market if (1) the restraint is not facially anticompetitive and (2) four or more independently controlled entities in addition to the parties to the licensing arrangement possess the required specialized assets or characteristics and the incentive to engage in research and development that is a close substitute of the research and development activities of the parties to the licensing agreement.[31]

---

29.   The antitrust "safety zone" does not apply to restraints that are not in a licensing arrangement, or to restraints that are in a licensing arrangement but are unrelated to the use of the licensed intellectual property.
30.   "Facially anticompetitive" refers to restraints that normally warrant per se treatment, as well as other restraints of a kind that would always or almost always tend to reduce output or increase prices. *See* section 3.4.
31.   This is consistent with congressional intent in enacting the Nat'l Cooperative Research Act. *See* H.R. Conf. Rpt. No. 1044, 98th Cong., 2d Sess., 10, *reprinted in* 1984 U.S.C.C.A.N. 3105, 3134B35.

The Agencies emphasize that licensing arrangements are not anticompetitive merely because they do not fall within the scope of the safety zone. Indeed, it is likely that the great majority of licenses falling outside the safety zone are lawful and procompetitive. The safety zone is designed to provide owners of intellectual property with a degree of certainty in those situations in which anticompetitive effects are so unlikely that the arrangements may be presumed not to be anticompetitive without an inquiry into particular industry circumstances. It is not intended to suggest that parties should conform to the safety zone or to discourage parties falling outside the safety zone from adopting restrictions in their license arrangements that are reasonably necessary to achieve an efficiency-enhancing integration of economic activity. The Agencies will analyze arrangements falling outside the safety zone based on the considerations outlined in parts 3-5.

The status of a licensing arrangement with respect to the safety zone may change over time. A determination by the Agencies that a restraint in a licensing arrangement qualifies for inclusion in the safety zone is based on the factual circumstances prevailing at the time of the conduct at issue.[32]

5). Application of general principles

5.0 This section illustrates the application of the general principles discussed above to particular licensing restraints and to arrangements that involve the cross-licensing, pooling, or acquisition of intellectual property. The restraints and arrangements identified are typical of those that are likely to receive antitrust scrutiny; however, they are not intended as an exhaustive list of practices that could raise competitive concerns.

a) Horizontal restraints

The existence of a restraint in a licensing arrangement that affects parties in a horizontal relationship (a "horizontal restraint") does not necessarily cause the arrangement to be anticompetitive. As in the case of joint ventures among horizontal competitors, licensing arrangements among such competitors may promote rather than hinder competition if they result in integrative efficiencies. Such efficiencies may arise, for example, from the realization of economies of scale and the integration

---

32. The conduct at issue may be the transaction giving rise to the restraint or the subsequent implementation of the restraint.

of complementary research and development, production, and marketing capabilities.

Following the general principles outlined in section 3.4, horizontal restraints often will be evaluated under the rule of reason. In some circumstances, however, that analysis may be truncated; additionally, some restraints may merit per se treatment, including price fixing, allocation of markets or customers, agreements to reduce output, and certain group boycotts.

Example 9

Situation: Two of the leading manufacturers of a consumer electronic product hold patents that cover alternative circuit designs for the product. The manufacturers assign their patents to a separate corporation wholly owned by the two firms. That corporation licenses the right to use the circuit designs to other consumer product manufacturers and establishes the license royalties. None of the patents is blocking; that is, each of the patents can be used without infringing a patent owned by the other firm. The different circuit designs are substitutable in that each permits the manufacture at comparable cost to consumers of products that consumers consider to be interchangeable. One of the Agencies is analyzing the licensing arrangement.

Discussion: In this example, the manufacturers are horizontal competitors in the goods market for the consumer product and in the related technology markets. The competitive issue with regard to a joint assignment of patent rights is whether the assignment has an adverse impact on competition in technology and goods markets that is not outweighed by procompetitive efficiencies, such as benefits in the use or dissemination of the technology. Each of the patent owners has a right to exclude others from using its patent. That right does not extend, however, to the agreement to assign rights jointly. To the extent that the patent rights cover technologies that are close substitutes, the joint determination of royalties likely would result in higher royalties and higher goods prices than would result if the owners licensed or used their technologies independently. In the absence of evidence establishing efficiency-enhancing integration from the joint assignment of patent rights, the Agency may conclude that the joint marketing of competing patent rights constitutes horizontal price fixing and could be challenged as a per se unlawful horizontal restraint of trade. If the joint marketing arrangement results in an efficiency-enhancing integration, the Agency would evaluate the arrangement under the rule of reason. However, the Agency may conclude that the anticompetitive effects are sufficiently apparent, and the claimed integrative efficiencies are sufficiently weak or not reasonably related to the restraints, to warrant challenge of the arrangement without an elaborate analysis of particular industry circumstances (*see* section 3.4).

b) Resale price maintenance

Resale price maintenance is illegal when "commodities have passed into the channels of trade and are owned by dealers." *Dr. Miles Medical Co. v. John D. Park & Sons Co.*, 220 U.S. 373, 408 (1911). It has been held per se illegal for a licensor of an intellectual property right in a product to fix a licensee's *resale* price of that product. *United States v. Univis Lens Co.*, 316 U.S. 241 (1942); *Ethyl Gasoline Corp. v. United States*, 309 U.S. 436 (1940).[33] Consistent with the principles set forth in section 3.4, the Agencies will enforce the per se rule against resale price maintenance in the intellectual property context.

c) Tying arrangements

A "tying" or "tie-in" or "tied sale" arrangement has been defined as "an agreement by a party to sell one product . . . on the condition that the buyer also purchases a different (or tied) product, or at least agrees that he will not purchase that [tied] product from any other supplier." *Eastman Kodak Co. v. Image Technical Services, Inc.*, 112 S. Ct. 2072, 2079 (1992). Conditioning the ability of a licensee to license one or more items of intellectual property on the licensee's purchase of another

---

33. But cf. *United States v. General Electric Co.*, 272 U.S. 476 (1926) (holding that an owner of a product patent may condition a license to manufacture the product on the fixing of the *first* sale price of the patented product). Subsequent lower court decisions have distinguished the *GE* decision in various contexts. *See, e.g., Royal Indus. v. St. Regis Paper Co.*, 420 F.2d 449, 452 (9th Cir. 1969) (observing that *GE* involved a restriction by a patentee who also manufactured the patented product and leaving open the question whether a non-manufacturing patentee may fix the price of the patented product); *Newburgh Moire Co. v. Superior Moire Co.*, 237 F.2d 283, 293-94 (3d Cir. 1956) (grant of multiple licenses each containing price restrictions does not come within the *GE* doctrine); *Cummer-Graham Co. v. Straight Side Basket Corp.*, 142 F.2d 646, 647 (5th Cir.) (owner of an intellectual property right in a process to manufacture an unpatented product may not fix the sale price of that product), *cert. denied*, 323 U.S. 726 (1944); *Barber-Colman Co. v. Nat'l Tool Co.*, 136 F.2d 339, 343B44 (6th Cir. 1943) (same).

item of intellectual property or a good or a service has been held in some cases to constitute illegal tying.[34] Although tying arrangements may result in anticompetitive effects, such arrangements can also result in significant efficiencies and procompetitive benefits. In the exercise of their prosecutorial discretion, the Agencies will consider both the anticompetitive effects and the efficiencies attributable to a tie-in. The Agencies would be likely to challenge a tying arrangement if: (1) the seller has market power in the tying product,[35] (2) the arrangement has an adverse effect on competition in the relevant market for the tied product, and (3) efficiency justifications for the arrangement do not outweigh the anticompetitive effects.[36] The Agencies will not presume that a patent, copyright, or trade secret necessarily confers market power upon its owner.

Package licensing—the licensing of multiple items of intellectual property in a single license or in a group of related licenses—may be a form of tying arrangement if the licensing of one product is conditioned upon the acceptance of a license of another, separate product. Package licensing can be efficiency enhancing under some circumstances. When multiple licenses are needed to use any single item of intellectual property, for example, a package license may promote such efficiencies. If a package license constitutes a tying arrangement, the Agencies will evaluate its competitive effects under the same principles they apply to other tying arrangements.

d) Exclusive dealing

In the intellectual property context, exclusive dealing occurs when a license prevents the licensee from licensing, selling, distributing, or using competing technologies. Exclusive dealing arrangements are evaluated under the rule of reason. *See Tampa Electric Co. v. Nashville Coal Co.,* 365 U.S. 320 (1961) (evaluating legality of exclusive dealing under section 1 of the Sherman Act and section 3 of the Clayton Act); *Beltone*

---

34. *See, e.g., United States v. Paramount Pictures, Inc.,* 334 U.S. 131, 156-58 (1948) (copyrights); *International Salt Co. v. United States,* 332 U.S. 392 (1947) (patent and related product).
35. *Cf.* 35 U.S.C. § 271(d) (1988 & Supp. V 1993) (requirement of market power in patent misuse cases involving tying).
36. As is true throughout these Guidelines, the factors listed are those that guide the Agencies' internal analysis in exercising their prosecutorial discretion. They are not intended to circumscribe how the Agencies will conduct the litigation of cases that they decide to bring.

Electronics Corp., 100 F.T.C. 68 (1982) (evaluating legality of exclusive dealing under section 5 of the Federal Trade Commission Act). In determining whether an exclusive dealing arrangement is likely to reduce competition in a relevant market, the Agencies will take into account the extent to which the arrangement (1) promotes the exploitation and development of the licensor's technology and (2) anticompetitively forecloses the exploitation and development of, or otherwise constrains competition among, competing technologies.

The likelihood that exclusive dealing may have anticompetitive effects is related, inter alia, to the degree of foreclosure in the relevant market, the duration of the exclusive dealing arrangement, and other characteristics of the input and output markets, such as concentration, difficulty of entry, and the responsiveness of supply and demand to changes in price in the relevant markets. (*See* sections 4.1.1 and 4.1.2.) If the Agencies determine that a particular exclusive dealing arrangement may have an anticompetitive effect, they will evaluate the extent to which the restraint encourages licensees to develop and market the licensed technology (or specialized applications of that technology), increases licensors' incentives to develop or refine the licensed technology, or otherwise increases competition and enhances output in a relevant market. (*See* section 4.2 and Example 8.)

e) Cross-licensing and pooling arrangements

Cross-licensing and pooling arrangements are agreements of two or more owners of different items of intellectual property to license one another or third parties. These arrangements may provide procompetitive benefits by integrating complementary technologies, reducing transaction costs, clearing blocking positions, and avoiding costly infringement litigation. By promoting the dissemination of technology, cross-licensing and pooling arrangements are often procompetitive.

Cross-licensing and pooling arrangements can have anticompetitive effects in certain circumstances. For example, collective price or output restraints in pooling arrangements, such as the joint marketing of pooled intellectual property rights with collective price setting or coordinated output restrictions, may be deemed unlawful if they do not contribute to an efficiency-enhancing integration of economic activity among the participants. *Compare NCAA* 468 U.S. at 114 (output restriction on college football broadcasting held unlawful because it was not reasonably related to any purported justification) *with Broadcast Music*, 441 U.S. at 23 (blanket license for music copyrights found not per se illegal because the cooperative price was necessary to the creation of a new product).   When cross-licensing or pooling arrangements are mechanisms to accomplish naked price fixing or market division, they are subject to challenge under the per se rule. *See United States v. New Wrinkle, Inc.*, 342 U.S. 371 (1952) (price fixing).

Settlements involving the cross-licensing of intellectual property rights can be an efficient means to avoid litigation and, in general, courts favor such settlements. When such cross-licensing involves horizontal competitors, however, the Agencies will consider whether the effect of the settlement is to diminish competition among entities that would have been actual or likely potential competitors in a relevant market in the absence of the cross-license. In the absence of offsetting efficiencies, such settlements may be challenged as unlawful restraints of trade. *Cf. United States v. Singer Manufacturing Co.*, 374 U.S. 174 (1963) (cross-license agreement was part of broader combination to exclude competitors).

Pooling arrangements generally need not be open to all who would like to join. However, exclusion from cross-licensing and pooling arrangements among parties that collectively possess market power may, under some circumstances, harm competition. *Cf. Northwest Wholesale Stationers, Inc. v. Pacific Stationery & Printing Co.*, 472 U.S. 284 (1985) (exclusion of a competitor from a purchasing cooperative not per se unlawful absent a showing of market power). In general, exclusion from a pooling or cross-licensing arrangement among competing technologies is unlikely to have anticompetitive effects unless (1) excluded firms cannot effectively compete in the relevant market for the good incorporating the licensed technologies and (2) the pool participants collectively possess market power in the relevant market. If these circumstances exist, the Agencies will evaluate whether the arrangement's limitations on participation are reasonably related to the efficient development and exploitation of the pooled technologies and will assess the net effect of those limitations in the relevant market. *See* section 4.2.

Another possible anticompetitive effect of pooling arrangements may occur if the arrangement deters or discourages participants from engaging in research and development, thus retarding innovation. For example, a pooling arrangement that requires members to grant licenses to each other for current and future technology at minimal cost may reduce the incentives of its members to engage in research and development because members of the pool have to share their successful research and development and each of the members can free ride on the accomplishments of other pool members. *See generally United States v. Mfrs. Aircraft Ass'n, Inc.*, 1976-1 Trade Cas. (CCH) ¶ 60,810 (S.D.N.Y. 1975); *United States v. Automobile Mfrs. Ass'n*, 307 F. Supp. 617 (C.D. Cal 1969), *appeal dismissed sub nom. City of New York v. United States*, 397 U.S. 248 (1970), *modified sub nom. United States v. Motor Vehicle Mfrs. Ass'n*, 1982-83 Trade Cas. (CCH) ¶ 65,088 (C.D. Cal. 1982). However, such an arrangement can have procompetitive benefits, for example, by exploiting economies of scale and integrating complementary capabilities of the pool members, (including the clearing of blocking positions), and is likely to cause competitive problems only when the arrangement includes a large fraction of the potential research and development in an innovation market. *See* section 3.2.3 and Example 4.

Example 10

Situation: As in Example 9, two of the leading manufacturers of a consumer electronic product hold patents that cover alternative circuit designs for the product. The manufacturers assign several of their patents to a separate corporation wholly owned by the two firms. That corporation licenses the right to use the circuit designs to other consumer product manufacturers and establishes the license royalties. In this example, however, the manufacturers assign to the separate corporation only patents that are blocking. None of the patents assigned to the corporation can be used without infringing a patent owned by the other firm.

Discussion: Unlike the previous example, the joint assignment of patent rights to the wholly owned corporation in this example does not adversely affect competition in the licensed technology among entities that would have been actual or likely potential competitors in the absence of the licensing arrangement. Moreover, the licensing arrangement is likely to have procompetitive benefits in the use of the technology. Because the manufacturers' patents are blocking, the manufacturers are not in a horizontal relationship with respect to those patents. None of the patents can be used without the right to a patent owned by the other firm, so the patents are not substitutable. As in Example 9, the firms are horizontal competitors in the relevant goods market. In the absence of collateral restraints that would likely raise price or reduce output in the relevant goods market or in any other relevant antitrust market and that are not reasonably related to an efficiency-enhancing integration of economic activity, the evaluating Agency would be unlikely to challenge this arrangement.

f) Grantbacks

A grantback is an arrangement under which a licensee agrees to extend to the licensor of intellectual property the right to use the licensee's improvements to the licensed technology. Grantbacks can have procompetitive effects, especially if they are nonexclusive. Such arrangements provide a means for the licensee and the licensor to share risks and reward the licensor for making possible further innovation based on or informed by the licensed technology, and both promote innovation in the first place and promote the subsequent licensing of the results of the innovation. Grantbacks may adversely affect competition, however, if they substantially reduce the licensee's incentives to engage in research and development and thereby limit rivalry in innovation markets.

A non-exclusive grantback allows the licensee to practice its technology and license it to others. Such a grantback provision may be necessary to ensure that the licensor is not prevented from effectively competing because it is denied access to improvements developed with the aid of its own technology. Compared with an exclusive grantback, a non-exclusive grantback, which leaves the licensee free to license improvements technology to others, is less likely to have anticompetitive effects.

The Agencies will evaluate a grantback provision under the rule of reason, *see generally Transparent-Wrap Machine Corp. v. Stokes & Smith Co.*, 329 U.S. 637, 645-48 (1947) (grantback provision in technology license is not per se unlawful), considering its likely effects in light of the overall structure of the licensing arrangement and conditions in the relevant markets. An important factor in the Agencies' analysis of a grantback will be whether the licensor has market power in a relevant technology or innovation market. If the Agencies determine that a particular grantback provision is likely to reduce significantly licensees' incentives to invest in improving the licensed technology, the Agencies will consider the extent to which the grantback provision has offsetting procompetitive effects, such as (1) promoting dissemination of licensees' improvements to the licensed technology, (2) increasing the licensors' incentives to disseminate the licensed technology, or (3) otherwise increasing competition and output in a relevant technology or innovation market. *See* section 4.2. In addition, the Agencies will consider the extent to which grantback provisions in the relevant markets generally increase licensors' incentives to innovate in the first place.

g) Acquisition of intellectual property rights

Certain transfers of intellectual property rights are most appropriately analyzed by applying the principles and standards used to analyze mergers, particularly those in the 1992 Horizontal Merger Guidelines. The Agencies will apply a merger analysis to an outright sale by an intellectual property owner of all of its rights to that intellectual property and to a transaction in which a person obtains through grant, sale, or other transfer an exclusive license for intellectual property (i.e., a license that precludes all other persons, including the licensor, from using the licensed intellectual property).[37] Such transactions may be assessed under section 7 of the Clayton Act, sections 1 and 2 of the Sherman Act, and section 5 of the Federal Trade Commission Act.

Example 11

Situation: Omega develops a new, patented pharmaceutical for the treatment of a particular disease. The only drug on the market approved for the treatment of this disease is sold by Delta. Omega's patented drug has almost completed regulatory approval by the Food and Drug Administration. Omega has invested considerable sums in product development and market testing, and initial results show that Omega's drug would be a significant competitor to Delta's. However, rather than enter the market as a direct competitor of Delta, Omega licenses to Delta the right to manufacture and sell Omega's patented drug. The license agreement with Delta is nominally nonexclusive. However, Omega has rejected all requests by other firms to obtain a license to manufacture and sell Omega's patented drug, despite offers by those firms of terms that are reasonable in relation to those in Delta's license.

Discussion: Although Omega's license to Delta is nominally nonexclusive, the circumstances indicate that it is exclusive in fact because Omega has rejected all reasonable offers by other firms for licenses to manufacture and sell Omega's patented drug. The facts of this example indicate that Omega would be a likely potential competitor of Delta in the absence of the licensing arrangement, and thus they are in a horizontal relationship in the relevant goods market that includes drugs for the treatment of this particular disease. The evaluating Agency would apply a merger analysis to this transaction, since it involves an acquisition of a likely potential competitor.

---

37. The safety zone of section 4.3 does not apply to transfers of intellectual property such as those described in this section.

6). Enforcement of invalid intellectual property rights

The Agencies may challenge the enforcement of invalid intellectual property rights as antitrust violations. Enforcement or attempted enforcement of a patent obtained by fraud on the Patent and Trademark Office or the Copyright Office may violate section 2 of the Sherman Act, if all the elements otherwise necessary to establish a section 2 charge are proved, or section 5 of the Federal Trade Commission Act. *Walker Process Equipment, Inc. v. Food Machinery & Chemical Corp.*, 382 U.S. 172 (1965) (patents); *American Cyanamid Co.*, 72 F.T.C. 623, 684-85 (1967), *aff'd sub. nom. Charles Pfizer & Co.*, 401 F.2d 574 (6th Cir. 1968), *cert. denied*, 394 U.S. 920 (1969) (patents); *Michael Anthony Jewelers, Inc. v. Peacock Jewelry, Inc.*, 795 F. Supp. 639, 647 (S.D.N.Y. 1992) (copyrights). Inequitable conduct before the Patent and Trademark Office will not be the basis of a section 2 claim unless the conduct also involves knowing and willful fraud and the other elements of a section 2 claim are present. *Argus Chemical Corp. v. Fibre Glass-Evercoat, Inc.*, 812 F.2d 1381, 1384-85 (Fed. Cir. 1987). Actual or attempted enforcement of patents obtained by inequitable conduct that falls short of fraud under some circumstances may violate section 5 of the Federal Trade Commission Act, *American Cyanamid Co., supra.* Objectively baseless litigation to enforce invalid intellectual property rights may also constitute an element of a violation of the Sherman Act. *See Professional Real Estate Investors, Inc. v. Columbia Pictures Industries, Inc.*, 113 S. Ct. 1920, 1928 (1993) (copyrights); *Handgards, Inc. v. Ethicon, Inc.*, 743 F.2d 1282, 1289 (9th Cir. 1984), *cert. denied*, 469 U.S. 1190 (1985) (patents); *Handgards, Inc. v. Ethicon, Inc.*, 601 F.2d 986, 992-96 (9th Cir. 1979), *cert. denied*, 444 U.S. 1025 (1980) (patents); *CVD, Inc. v. Raytheon Co.*, 769 F.2d 842 (1st Cir. 1985) (trade secrets), *cert. denied*, 475 U.S. 1016 (1986).

APPENDIX 2

ECONOMICS BIBLIOGRAPHY

Amato, Louis, Ryan, J. Michael, & Wilder, Ronald P. (1981). Market Structure and Dynamic Performance in U.S. Manufacturing. *Southern Economic Journal, 47*, 1105-1110.

Anderson, R. D. (1988). The Interface between Competition Policy and Intellectual Property in the Context of the International Trading System. *Journal of International Economic Law, 1*, 655-678.

Andewelt, R. B. (1984). Analysis of Patent Pools under the Antitrust Laws. *Antitrust Law Journal, 53*, 611-639.

Angelmar, R. (1985). Market Structure and Research Intensity in High-Technological-Opportunity Industries. *Journal of Industrial Economics, 34*, 69-79.

Anton, James J. & Yao, Dennis A. (2004). Little Patents and Big Secrets: Managing Intellectual Property, *RAND Journal of Economics, 35*, 1-22.

Aoki, R., & Hu, J. L. (1999). Licensing vs. Litigation: The Effect of the Legal System on Incentives to Innovate. *Journal of Economics and Management Strategy, 8*, 130-60.

Arora, A., & Gambardella, A. (1994). The Changing Technology of Technological Change: General and Abstract Knowledge and the Division of Innovative Labor. *Research Policy, 23*, 523-532.

Arora, Ashish, "Contracting For Tacit Knowledge: The Provision of Technical Services in Technology Licensing Contracts," 50 Journal of Development Economics 233-256 (1996).

Arrow, K. J. (1962). Economic Welfare and the Allocation of Resources for Invention. In R. R. Nelson (Ed.), *The Rate and Direction of Inventive Activity* (pp. 609-626). New York, NY: Princeton University Press.

Baker, J. B. (1995). Fringe Firms and Incentives to Innovate. *Antitrust Law Journal, 63*, 621-641.

Baldwin, William, & Scott, John T.. (1987). *Market Structure and Technological Change*. New York, NY: Harwood Academic Publishers.

557

Barzel, Yoram (1968). Optimal Timing of Innovation. *Review of Economic and Statistics, 50,* 348-355.

Bauer, J. M. (1997). Market Power, Innovation, and Efficiency in Telecommunications: Schumpeter Reconsidered. *Journal of Economic Issues, 31,* 557-565.

Beard, T R., & Kaserman, D.L., "Patent Thickets, Cross Licensing, and Antitrust," 47 The Antitrust Bulletin 355-357 (Summer-Fall 2002)

Besen, S. M., & Raskind, L. J. (1991). An Introduction to the Law and Economics of Intellectual Property. *Journal of Economic Perspectives,* 3-27.

Bessen, J., & Hunt, R.M., (2004), An Empirical Look at Software Patents, *Federal Reserve Bank of Philadelphia Working Paper* No. 03-17.

Blair, J. (1948). Technology and Size. *American Economic Review, 38,* 121-52.

Bloch, H. (2000). Schumpeter and Steindl on the Dynamics of Competition. *Journal of Evolutionary Economics, 10,* 343-353.

Bonanno, Giacomo, & Haworth, Barry (1996). Intensity of Competition and the Choice Between Product and Process Innovation. *International Journal of Industrial Organization, 16,* 495-510.

Boone, J., & van Dijk, T. (1998). Competition and Innovation. *De Economist, 146,* 445-461.

Boone, Jan (1998). Competitive Pressure, Selection and Investments in Development and Fundamental Research (Working Paper). The Netherlands: Tilburg University, Department of Economics.

Boone, Jan (2001). Intensity of Competition and the Incentive to Innovate. *International Journal of Industrial Organization, 19,* 705-726.

Bound, J., Cummins, C., Griliches, Z., Hall, B., & Jaffe, A. (1984). Who Does R&D and Who Patents? In Zvi Griliches (Ed.), *R&D Patents and Productivity* (pp. 21-54). Chicago, IL: The University of Chicago Press.

Bowman, W.S. (1973). *Patent and Antitrust Law: A Legal and Economic Appraisal.* Chicago: University of Chicago Press.

Bozeman, Barry, & Link, Albert (1983). Investments in Technology: Corporate Strategies and Public Policy Alternatives. New York, NY: Praeger.

Brodley, J. F. (1990). Antitrust Law and Innovation Cooperation. *Journal of Economic Perspectives, 4*, 97-112.

Brouwer, M. (1998). Firm Size and Efficiency in Innovation: Comment on van Dijk et al. *Small Business Economics, 11*, 391-393.

Burnett, and Scherer, (1990), The Weapons Industry, in Walter Adams, ed., The Structure of American Industry, eighth ed., Chapter 11, MacMillan Publishing.

Caballero-Sanz, F., Moner-Colonques, R., & Sempere-Monerris, J. J. (1998). Market Structure and R&D Joint Ventures: The Case of Product Innovations. *European Journal of Law and Economics, 5*, 51-66.

Cave, J. A. (1985). A Further Comment on Preemptive Patenting and the Persistence of Monopoly. *American Economic Review, 75*, 256-258.

Chang, Howard F. (1995). Patent Scope, Antitrust Policy, and Cumulative Innovation. *RAND Journal of Economics, 26*, 34-57.

Chen, Z., & Ross, T.W. (1999). Refusals to Deal and Orders to Supply in Competitive Markets. *International Journal of Industrial Organization, 17, 399-417.*

Choi, J. P. (1996). Preemptive R&D, Rent Dissipation, and the "Leverage Theory." *Quarterly Journal of Economics, 111*, 1153-1181.

Cockburn, Iain & Henderson, Rebecca (1994). Racing to Invest? The Dynamics of Competition in Ethical Drug Discovery. *Journal of Economics and Management Strategy, 3*, 481-519.

Cohen, Wesley (1995). Empirical Studies of Innovative Activity. In P. Stoneman (Ed.), *Handbook of the Economics of Innovations and Technological Change* (pp. 188-264). Cambridge, MA: Blackwell Publishers Ltd.

Cohen, Wesley M., & Klepper, Steven (1996). A Reprise of Size and R & D. *The Economic Journal, 106*, 925-951.

Cohen, Wesley M., & Klepper, Steven (1996). Firm Size and the Nature of Innovation within Industries: The case of process and product R&D. *Review of Economics and Statistics, 78*, 232-243.

Cohen, Wesley M., & Levin, Richard C. (1989). Empirical Studies of Innovation and Market Structure. In R. Schmalensee & R. D. Willig (Eds.), *Handbook of Industrial Organization*, (Volume II, (pp. 1059-1107)). Amsterdam: North-Holland

Cohen, W. M., Levin, R. C., & Mowery, D. C. (1987). Firm Size and R&D Intensity: A Re-Examination. *Journal of Industrial Economics, 35*, 543-565.

Cohen, Wesley M., Nelson, Richard R. and Walsh, John P. (2000), Protecting Their Intellectual Assets: Appropriability Conditions and Why U.S. Manufacturing Firms Patent (or Not), Working Paper No. 7552, National Bureau of Economic Research.

Comanor, William S. (1967). Market Structure, Product Differentiation, and Industrial Research. *Quarterly Journal of Economics, 81*, 639-657.

Connolly, R.A., & Hirschey, M. (1984). R&D, Market Structure, and Profits: A Value-Based Approach. *Review of Economics and Statistics, 66*, 682-86.

Cornelli, Francesca, & Schankerman, Mark (1999). Patent Renewal and R&D Incentives. *RAND Journal of Economics, 30*(2), 197-213.

Dasgupta, P., & Stiglitz, J. E. (1980). Uncertainty, Industrial Structure and the Speed of R&D, 1-28.

Dasgupta, Partha, & Stiglitz, Joseph E. (1980). Industrial Structure and the Nature of Innovative Activity. *Economic Journal, 90*, 266-293.

Dasgupta, P. (1986). The Theory of Technological Competition. In J. E. Stiglitz & G. F. Mathewson (Eds.), *New Developments in the Analysis of Market Structure* (pp. 519-550). Cambridge, MA: MIT Press.

Dasgupta, P., & Stiglitz, J. (1980). Uncertainty, Industrial Structure, and the Speed of R&D. *Bell Journal of Economics, 11*, 1-28.

Denicolo, V. (1996). Patent Races and Optimal Patent Breadth and Length. *Journal of Industrial Economics, 44*, 249-265.

Denicolo, Vincenzo, & Delbono, F. (1999). Monopoly, Competition, and the Speed of R&D. *International Review of Economics and Business, 46*, 35-43.

Demsetz, H., Towards a Theory of Property Rights, 57 Am. Econ. Rev. Paper & Proc 351-52 (1967)..

Dimasi, J. A., Grabowski, H. G., & Vernon, J. (1995). R&D Costs, Innovative Output and Firm Size in the Pharmaceutical Industry. *International Journal of the Economics of Business, 2*, 201-219.

Duffy, J.F., "Intellectual Property Isolationism and the Average Cost Thesis," 83 Tex. L. Rev. 1077, March 2005.

Farber, Stephen (1981). Buyer Market Structure and R&D Effort: A Simultaneous Equations Model. *Review of Economics and Statistics, 62*, 336-45.

Fellner, W. (1951). The Influence of Market Structure on Technological Progress. *Quarterly Journal of Economics, 65*, 556-577.

Fishman, A., & Rob, R. (1999). The Size of Firms and R&D Investment. *International Economic Review, 40*, 915-931.

Friedman, D. D., Landes, W. M., & Posner, R. A. (1991). Some Economics of Trade Secret Law. *Journal of Economic Perspectives, 5(1)*, 61-72.

Fritsch, M., & Meschede, M. (2001). Product Innovation, Process Innovation, and Size. *Review of Industrial Organization, 19*, 335-350.

Futia, C. A. (1980). Schumpeterian Competition. *Quarterly Journal of Economics, 94*, 675-695.

Gallini, N. T. (1992). Patent Policy and Costly Imitation. *RAND Journal of Economics, 23*, 52-63.

Gans, J. S., & Stern, S. (2000). Incumbency and R&D Incentives: Licensing the Gale of Creative Destruction. *Journal of Economics & Management Strategy, 9*, 485-511.

Gans, Joshua S. & King, Stephen P. (2005). Patent Length and the Timing of Innovative Activity. IPRIA Working Paper.

Geroski, P. A. (1990). Innovation, Technological Opportunity, and Market Structure. *Oxford Economic Papers, 42*, 586-602.

Geroski, P. A. (1991). Entry and the Rate of Innovation. *Economic Innovation and New Technology, 1*, 203-214.

Geroski, P. A. (1991). *Market Dynamics and Entry.* Cambridge, MA: Blackwell Publishers Ltd.

Gilbert, R. & Shapiro, C. (1990). Optimal Patent Length and Breadth. *Rand Journal of Economics, 21(1),* 106-112.

Gilbert, R., & Shapiro, C. (1997). Antitrust Issues in the Licensing of Intellectual Property: The Nine No-no's Meet the Nineties. *Brookings Papers on Economic Activity, Microeconomics,* 283-336.

Gilbert, R., & Tom, W. K. (2001). *Is Innovation King at the Antitrust Agencies? The Intellectual Property Guidelines Five Years Later.* Retrieved March 1, 2002 from the Economics Department at Washington University Web site: http://econwpa.wustl.edu:8089/eps/io/papers/0106/0106002.pdf

Gilbert, Richard J., & Newbery, David M. G. (1982). Preemptive Patenting and the Persistence of Monopoly. *American Economic Review,* 72, 514-526.

Gilbert, R.J., & Shapiro, C. (1996). An Economic Analysis of Unilateral Refusals to License Intellectual Property. *Proceedings of the National Academy of Sciences, 93,* 12749-12755. Retrieved April 17, 2002, from http://www.pnas.org/cgi/reprint/93/23/12749.pdf

Gilbert, R. J., & Sunshine, S. C. (1995). Incorporating Dynamic Efficiency Concerns in Merger Analysis: The use of innovation markets. *Antitrust Law Journal, 63,* 574-81.

Gort, Michael, & Konakayama, Akira (1982). A Model of Diffusion in the Production of an Innovation. *American Economic Review,* 72, 1111-1119.

Grabowski, H., & Vernon, J. (1996). Longer Patents for Increased Generic Competition in the US: The Waxman-Hatch Act After One Decade. *PharmacoEconomics Supplement, 10(2),* 110-123.

Green, Jerry R., & Scotchmer, S. (1995). On the Division of Profit in Sequential Innovation. *RAND Journal of Economics, 26,* 20-33.

Greenstein, S., & Ramey, G. (1998). Market Structure, Innovation and Vertical Product Differentiation. *International Journal of Industrial Organization, 16,* 285-311.

Greer, Douglas F., & Rhoades, Stephen A. (1976). Concentration and Productivity Changes in the Long and Short Run. *Southern Economic Journal, 43,* 1031-1044.

Grossman, Gene M., & Shapiro, Carl (1987). Dynamic R&D Competition. *Economic Journal, 97*, 372-387.

Hall, Bronwyn H., & Ziedonis, Rosemarie Ham (2001). The Patent Paradox Revisited: An Empirical Study of Patenting in the U.S. Semiconductor Industry, 1979-1995. *RAND Journal of Economics, 32*(1), 101-128.

Hamberg, D. (1964). Size of Firm, Oligopoly, and Research: The Evidence. *Canadian Journal of Economics and Political Science, 30*, 62-75.

Hamdouch, A., & Samuelides, E. (2000). *Innovation and Competition in IT Service Industries* (Working Paper). France: University of Paris, Maison des Sciences Economiques.

Harris, Christopher, & Vickers, John (1985). Patent Races and the Persistence of Monopoly. *Journal of Industrial Economics, 33(4)*, 461-481.

Michael A. Heller and Rebecca S. Eisenberg, "Can Patents Deter Innovation? The Anticommons in Biomedical Research," 280 Science 698 (1998)

Hicks, J. R. (1935). Annual Survey of Economic Theory: The Theory of Monopoly. *Econometrica, 3*, 1-20.

Hoerner, R. J. (1984). Patent Misuse. *Antitrust Law Journal, 53*, 641-662.

Hopenhayn, Hugo A. & Mitchell, Matthew F. (2001). Innovation Variety and Patent Breadth. *RAND Journal of Economics*, 32, 1, 152-166.

Horowitz, Ira (1962). Firm Size and Research Activity. *Southern Economic Journal, 28*, 298-301.

Jaffe, Adam B. (1997). The U.S. Patent System in Transition: Policy Innovation and the Innovation Process. *Research Policy, 29*, 531-57.

Jensen, R., & Thursby, M. (1996). Patent Races, Product Standards, and International Competition. *International Economic Review, 37*, 21-49.

Jewkes, John, Sawers, David, & Stillerman, Richard (1969). *The Sources of Invention*. New York, NY: W. W. Norton.

Johnson, Daniel K. N. and Popp, David, (2003), Forced Out of the Closet: the Impact of the American Inventors Protection Act on the Timing of Patent Disclosure, *Rand Journal of Economics*, 34, 1, 96-112.

Jorde, T. M., & Teece, D. J. (1990). Innovation and Cooperation: Implications for Competition and Antitrust. *Journal of Economic Perspectives, 4,* 75-96.

Jorde, T. M., & Teece, D. J. (1993). Rule of Reason Analysis of Horizontal Arrangements: Agreements Designed to Advance Innovation and Commercialize Technology. *Antitrust Law Journal, 61,* 579-619.

Judd, Kenneth L., Schmedders, Karl & Yeltekin, Sevin (2003). Optimal Rules for Patent Races. A Revised Version (August 2003) of CMS-EMS Discussion Papers No. 1343.

Kahkonen, Anssi T., (2003). An Experimental Investigation of Patent Menu Policy.

Kamien, Morton I., & Schwartz, Nancy L. (1982). *Market Structure and Innovation.* Cambridge: Cambridge University Press.

Kanwar, Sunil & Evenson, Robert E., (2003), Does Intellectual Property Protection Spur Technological Change? *Oxford Economic Papers,* 55, 2, 235-264.Katz, M. & Ordover, J. (1990). R&D cooperation and competition. *Brookings Papers on Economic Activity, Special Issue,* 137-191.

Katz, Michael L., & Shapiro, Carl (1987). R&D Rivalry with Licensing or Imitation. *American Economic Review, 77,* 402-420.

Kitch, Edmund W. (1977). The Nature and Function of the Patent System. *Journal of Law and Economics, 20, 265-290.*

Kitson, M., & Michie, J. (1998). *Markets, Competition and Innovation* (Working Paper No. 84). UK: University of Cambridge, ESRC Centre for Business Research.

Klemperer, Paul (1990). How Broad Should the Scope of Patent Protection Be? *RAND Journal of Economics, 21*(1), 113-130.

Kortum, Samuel, & Lerner, Josh (1998). Stronger Protection or Technological Revolution: What is Behind the Recent Surge in Patenting? *Carnegie-Rochester Series on Public Policy, 48,* 247-304.

Kristiansen, E. G., & Thum, M. (1997). R&D Incentives in Compatible Networks. *Journal of Economics, 65,* 55-78.

Kristiansen, E. G. (1998). R&D in the Presence of Network Externalities: Timing and Compatibility. *RAND Journal of Economics, 29*, 531-547.

Leahy, D., & Neary, J. P. (1997). Public Policy Towards R&D in Oligopolistic Industries. *American Economic Review, 87*, 642-662.

Lee, T., & Wilde, L. L. (1980). Market Structure and Innovation: A Reformulation. *Quarterly Journal of Economics, 94*, 429-436.

Lemley, M. A. (1997). The Economics of Improvement in Intellectual Property Law. *Texas Law Review, 75*, 989-1084.

Lemley, M.A. "Property, Intellectual Property, and Free Riding," 83 Tex. L. Rev. 1031, March 2005.

Lerner, J. (1994). The Importance of Patent Scope: An Empirical Analysis. *RAND Journal of Economics, 25*, 319-333.

Lerner, Josh, (1997). An Empirical Exploration of a Technology Race. *RAND Journal of Economics*, 28, 2, 228-247

Levin, Richard C., Cohen, Wesley M., & Mowery, David C. (1985). R&D Appropriability, Opportunity, and Market Structure: New Evidence on Some Schumpeterian Hypotheses. *American Economic Review, 75*, 20-24.

Levin, R. C., Klevorick, A. K., Nelson, R. R., & Winter, S. G. (1987). Appropriating the Returns from Industrial Research and Development. *Brookings Papers on Economic Activity, 3*, 783-820.

Levin, Richard C., & Reiss, Peter C. (1984). Tests of a Schumpeterian Model of R&D and Market Structure. In Z. Griliches (Ed.), *R&D Patents and Productivity* (pp. 175-208). Chicago, IL: The University of Chicago Press.

Levin, R. C., & Reiss, P. C. (1988). Cost Reducing and Demand-Creating R&D with Spillovers. *RAND Journal of Economics, 19*, 538-556.

Lin, Ping (1998). Product Market Competition and R&D Rivalry. *Economics Letters, 58*, 105-111.

Link, A. N. (1980). Firm Size and Efficient Entrepreneurial Activity: A Reformulation of the Schumpeter Hypothesis. *Journal of Political Economy, 88*, 771-782.

Link, Albert N., & Long, James E. (1981). The Simple Economics of Basic Scientific Research: A Test of Nelson's Diversification Hypothesis. *Journal of Industrial Economics, 30*, 105-109.

Lippman, S.A., & McCardle, K. F. (1987). Dropout Behavior in R&D Races with Learning. *RAND Journal of Economics, 18*(2), 287-295.

Loury, G. L. (1979). Market Structure and Innovation. *Quarterly Journal of Economics, 93*, 395-410.

Love, J. H., & Roper, S. (1999). The Determinants of Innovation: R&D, Technology Transfer and Networking Effects. *Review of Industrial Operation, 15*, 43-64.

Lunn, J. (1986). An Empirical Analysis of Process and Product Patenting: A Simultaneous Equation framework. *Journal of Industrial Economics, 34*, 319-330.

Lunn, J., & Martin, S. (1986). Market Structure, Firm Structure, and Research and Development. *Quarterly Review of Economics and Business, 26*, 31-44.

Mansfield, Edwin (1986). Patents and Innovation: An Empirical Study. *Management Science, 32*, 173-181.

Martin, S. (2000). *Competition Policy for High Technology Industries.* (Discussion Paper). The Netherlands: Tinbergen Institute.

Matutes, Carmen, Regibeau, Pierre, & Rockett, Katharine (1996). Optimal Patent Design and the Diffusion of Innovations. *RAND Journal of Economics, 27,* 60-83.

Mazzoleni, Roberto, & Nelson, Richard R. (1998). Economic Theories about the Benefits and Costs of Patents. *Journal of Economic Issues, 32*(4), 1031-1052.

McFetridge, D. G., & Rafiguzzaman, M. (1986). The Scope and Duration of the Patent Right and the Nature of Research Rivalry. In J. Palmer (Ed.), *The Economics of Patents and Copyrights* (91-120). Greenwich, CT: JAI Press.

McGahan, A., & Silverman, B. S. (2001). How Does Innovative Activity Change as Industries Mature? *International Journal of Industrial Organization, 19*, 1141-60.

Merges, R., "As Many As Six Impossible Patents Before Breakfast: Property Rights for Business Concepts and Patent System Reform," 14 Berkeley Technology Law Journal 577-615 (1999).

Merges, R., & Nelson, R. (1990). On the Complex Economics of Patent Scope. *Columbia Law Review, 90*(4), 839-916.

Merges, Robert P., & Nelson, Richard R., "On Limiting or Encouraging Rivalry in Technical Progress: The Effect of Patent Scope Decisions," 25 Journal of Economic Behavior and Organization 1-24 (1994)

Mukhopadhyary, A. (1985). Technological Progress and Change in Market Concentration in the U.S., 1963-77. *Southern Economic Journal, 52,* 141-9.

National Bureau of Economic Research. (1997). *The Enforcement of Intellectual Property Rights: A Survey of the Empirical Literature* (Working Paper No. 6296). Cambridge, MA: Lanjouw, J. O., & Lerner, J.

National Bureau of Economic Research. (1998). *The Allocation of Publicly-Funded Biomedical Research* (Working Paper No. 6601). Washington, DC: Lichtenberg, F. R.

National Bureau of Economic Research. (1999). *Damages and Injunctions in the Protection of Proprietary Research Tools* (Working Paper No. 7086). Cambridge, MA: Schankerman, M., & Scotchmer, S.

National Bureau of Economic Research. (1999). *The U.S. Patent System in Transition: Policy Innovation and the Innovation Process* (Working Paper No. 7280). Cambridge, MA: Jaffe, A.B.

National Bureau of Economic Research. (1999). *The Patent Paradox Revisited: Determinants of Patenting in the U.S. Semiconductor Industry, 1980-94* (Working Paper No. 7062). Cambridge, MA: Hall, B.H., & Ham. R.

National Bureau of Economic Research. (2001). *Protecting their Intellectual Assets: Appropriability Conditions and Why U.S. Manufacturing Firms Patent (or not)* (Working Paper No. 7552). Cambridge, MA: Cohen, W.M., & Walsh, J.

Nelson, Richard R., & Winter, Sidney G. (1978). Forces Generating and Limiting Concentration under Schumpeterian Competition. *Bell Journal of Economics, 9,* 524-48.

568   *Intellectual Property and Antitrust Handbook*

Nordhaus, William D. (1969). *Invention, Growth, and Welfare: A Theoretical Treatment of Technological Change.* Cambridge, MA: MIT Press

O'Donoghue, Ted (1998). A Patentability Requirement for Sequential Innovation. *RAND Journal of Economics, 29(4)*, 654-679.

O'Donoghue, T., Schotchmer, S., & Thisse, J. F. (1998). Patent Breadth, Patent Life, and the Pace of Technological Progress. *Journal of Economics and Management Strategy, 7(1)*, 1-32.

Ordover, J. A. (1984). Economic Foundations and Considerations in Protecting Industrial and Intellectual Property. *Antitrust Law Journal, 53*, 503-518.

Ordover, J. A. (1991). A Patent System for Both Diffusion and Exclusion. *Journal of Economic Perspectives, 5*(1), 43-60.

Organization for Economic Co-Operation and Development. (1996). *Innovation, Firm Size and Market Structure: Schumpeterian Hypotheses and Some New Themes* (Working Paper No. 161). Paris, France: Symeonidis, G.

Oxley Joanne E., "Institutional Environment and the Mechanism of Governance: The Impact of Intellectual Property Protection on the Structure of Inter-Firm Alliances," 38 Journal of Economic Behavior and Organization 283-309 (1999).

Phillips, Almarin (1966). Patents, Potential Competition, and Technical Progress. *American Economic Review, 56*, 301-310.

RAND Corporation and Brookings Institution Study. (1967). *Technology, Economic Growth, and Public Policy.* Washington, DC: Nelson, R., Peck, M., & Kalachek, E.

Rapp, R. T. (1995). The Misapplication of the Innovation Market Approach to Merger Analysis. *Antitrust Law Journal, 64*(1), 19-47.

Raut, L. K. (2001). *Firm's R&D Behavior Under Rational Expectations* (Working Paper). Cal State at Fullerton.

Reinganum, Jennifer F. (1983). Uncertain Innovation and the Persistence of Monopoly. *American Economic Review, 83*, 741-748.

Reinganum, J. F. (1985). Innovation and Industry Evolution. *Quarterly Journal of Economics, 10*, 81-99.

Sakakibara, Mariko, & Branstetter, Lee (2001). Do Stronger Patents Induce More Innovation? Evidence from the 1988 Japanese Patent Law Reforms. *RAND Journal of Economics, 32*(1), 77-100.

Salinger, Michael (1990). The Concentration-Margins Relationship Reconsidered. *Brookings Papers on Economic Activity. Microeconomics, 1990,* 287-335.

Sanyal, P. & Jaffe, A. B., (2004), Peanut Butter Patents Versus the New Economy: Does the Increased Rate of Patenting Signal More Invention or Just Lower Standards?, mimeo

Scherer, F. M. (1965). Firm Size, Market Structure, Opportunity, and the Output of Patented Inventions. *American Economic Review, 55,* 1097-1125.

Scherer, F. M. (1967). Market Structure and the Employment of Scientists and Engineers. *American Economic Review, 57,* 524-531.

Scherer, F. M. (1972). Nordhaus's Theory of Optimal Patent Life: A Geometric Reinterpretation. *American Economic Review, 62,* 422-427.

Scherer, F. M. (1980). *Industrial Market Structure and Economic Performance.* Chicago, IL: Rand McNally.

Scherer, F.M. (1984). *Innovation and Growth.* Cambridge, MA: MIT Press.

Scherer, F. M., Harhoff, D., & Kukies, J. (2000). Uncertainty and the Size Distribution of Rewards from Innovation. *Journal of Evolutionary Economics, 10,* 175-200.

Scherer, F.M., & Ross, D. (1990). *Industrial Market Structure and Economic Performance.* Boston, MA: Houghton Mifflin.

Schmitz Jr., J. A. (1989). Imitation, Entrepreneurship, and Long-Run Growth. *Journal of Political Economy, 97*(3), 721-739.

Schmookler, Jacob (1959). Bigness, Fewness, and Research. *Journal of Political Economy, 67,* 628-632.

Schumpeter, J. (1942). *Capitalism, Socialism and Democracy.* New York, NY: Harper.

Scotchmer, Suzanne (1991). Standing on the Shoulders of Giants: Cumulative Research and Patent Law. *Journal of Economics Perspectives, 5*(1), 29-41.

Scotchmer, Suzanne (1996). Protecting Early Innovators: Should Second-Generation Products be Patentable. *RAND Journal of Economics, 27,* 322-331.

Scott, John T. (1984). Firm Versus Industry Variability in R&D Intensity. In Z. Griliches (Ed.), *R&D Patents and Productivity* (pp. 233-248). Chicago, IL: The University of Chicago Press.

Shapiro, C., & Willig, R. D. (1990). On the Antitrust Treatment of Production Joint Ventures. *Journal of Economic Perspectives, 4,* 113-130.

Shapiro C., "Navigating the Patent Thicket: Cross Licenses, Patent Pools, and Standard Setting," *in Innovation Policy and the Economy, Volume I,* Adam Jaffe, Joshua Lerner, and Scott Stern, eds., MIT Press, 2001

Sheremata, W. A. (1997). Barriers to Innovation: A Monopoly, Network Externalities, and the Speed of Innovation. *Antitrust Bulletin, 42,* 937-972.

Shrieves, Ronald E. (1978). Market Structure and Innovation: A New Perspective. *Journal of Industrial Economics, 26,* 329-347.

Sobel, G. (1984). The Antitrust Interface with Patents and Innovation: Acquisition of Patents, Improvement Patents and Grant-Backs, Non-Use, Fraud on the Patent Office, Development of New Products and Joint Research. *Antitrust Law Journal, 53,* 681-711.

Spence, M. (1986). Cost Reduction, Competition and Industry Performance. In J.E. Stiglitz, & G.F. Mathewson (Eds.), *New Developments in the Analysis of Market Structure.* (pp. 475-518). Cambridge, MA: MIT Press.

Stoner, R.D., "Proposed Reforms in the U.S. Patent Regime to Combat Patents that Stifle Competition," 5 Antitrust and Intellectual Property (Newsletter of the Antitrust Law Section of the ABA's Intellectual Property Committee) 36-37 (Fall 2004).

Symeonidis, George (1996), Innovation, Firm Size and Market Structure: Schumpeterian Hypotheses and Some New Themes, *OECD Economic Studies, 27,* 35-70.

Somaya D., & Teece D.J., "Combining Patented Inventions in Multi-invention Products: Transactional Challenges and Organizational Choices," Working Paper, August 2, 2001, pp. 15-17

Takalo, Tuomas (1998). Innovation and Imitation under Imperfect Patent Protection. *Journal of Economics (Zeitchrift fur Nationalokonomie), 67*, 229-41.

Takalo, Tuomas (2001). On the Optimal Patent Policy, 14 FINNISH ECONOMIC PAPER,1 , 33-40.

Takalo, T., & Kanniainen, V. (2000). Do Patents Slow Technological Progress? Real Options in Research, Patenting, and Market Introduction. *International Journal of Industrial Organization, 18*, 1105-27.

Tandon, P. (1982). Optimal Patents with Compulsory Licensing. *Journal of Political Economic, 90*(3), 470-486.

Tandon, P. (1983). Rivalry and the Excessive Allocation of Resources to Research. *Bell Journal of Economics, 14*, 152-165.

Tandon, P. (1984). Innovation, Market Structure, and Welfare. *American Economic Review, 74*, 394-403.

Teece D.J., Managing Intellectual Capital, New York, Oxford at 208-209 (2000).

Tirole, Jean (1994). *The Theory of Industrial Organization.*

Turner, D. F. (1984). Basic Principles in Formulating Antitrust and Misuse Constraints on the Exploitation of Intellectual Property Rights. *Antitrust Law Journal, 53*, 485-502.

U.S. Government Printing Office (2002). *The Economic Report of President.*

U.S. Department of Justice and Federal Trade Commission, "Antitrust Guidelines for the Licensing of Intellectual Property," April 6, 1995.

Utterback, James M., Innovation and the Diffusion of Technology, *Science, 183*, 4125, 620-626.

Van Cayseele, P.J.G. (1998). Market Structure and Innovation: A Survey of the Last Twenty Years. *De Economist, 146*, 391-417.

Villard, Henry H. (1958). Competition, Oligopoly and Research. *Journal of Political Economy, 66*, 483-97.

Vossen, R. W. (1999). Market Power, Industrial Concentration and Innovative Activity. *Review of Industrial Organization, 15*, 367-379.

Wahlroos, B., & Backstrom, M. (1982). R&D Intensity with Endogenous Concentration: Evidence for Finland. *Empirical Economics, 7,* 13-22.

Waterson, M. (1990). The Economics of Product Patents. *The American Economic Review, 80*(4), 860-869.

Whinston, M.D. (1987). Tying, Foreclosure, and Exclusion. *American Economic Review, 80*(4), 837-859.

Williamson, Oliver (1965). Innovation and Market Structure. *Journal of Political Economy, 73,* 67-73.

Yi, Sang-Seung (1999). Market Structure and Incentives to Innovate: The case of Cournot oligopoly. *Economics Letters, 65,* 379-388.

Ziedonis, Rosemarie Ham, (2004), Don't Fence Me In: Fragmented Markets for Technology and the Patent Acquisition Strategies of Firms, *Management Science*, 50, 6, 804-820.

Zizzo, D.J., 2002. Racing with Uncertainty: A Patent Race Experiment. *International Journal of Industrial Organization*, 20, 6, 877-902.

TABLE OF CASES

A

Automatic Radio Mfg. v. Hazeltine Research, 339 U.S. 827 (1950), 2, 213, 214, 414, 512

AVEKA L.L.C. v. Mizuno Corp., 243 F. Supp. 2d 418 (M.D.N.C. 2003), 394, 395

Avery Dennison Corp. v. Acco Brands, No. CV-99-1877DT(MCX), 2000 WL 986995 (C.D. Cal. Feb. 22, 2000), 356, 361, 387

Axis, S.p.A. v. Micafil, Inc., 870 F.2d 1105 (6th Cir. 1989), 299

B

Baker v. Selden, 101 U.S. 99 (1879), 25

Baker-Cammack Hosiery Mills v. Davis Co., 181 F.2d 550 (4th Cir. 1950), 236, 240

Baltimore Scrap Corp. v. David J. Joseph Co., 237 F.3d 394 (4th Cir. 2001), 361, 372

Barr Rubber Prods. v. Sun Rubber Co., 277 F. Supp. 484 (S.D.N.Y. 1967), *aff'd in part and rev'd in part*, 425 F.2d 1114 (2d Cir. 1970), 231

Barry Fiala, Inc. v. Arthur Blank & Co., No. 2:02cv2282, 2003 U.S. Dist. LEXIS 2609 (W.D. Tenn. Feb. 19, 2003), 347

Barry Wright Corp. v. ITT Grinnell Corp., 724 F.2d 227 (1st Cir. 1983), 48, 417, 504, 505

BASF Aktiengesellschaft v. Reilly Indus., 283 F. Supp. 2d 1000 (S.D. Ind. 2003), 394

Bateman v. Mnemonics, Inc., 79 F.3d 1532 (11th Cir. 1996), 79

Bauer v. O'Donnell, 229 U.S. 1 (1913), 72

Baxa Corp. v. McGaw, Inc., 996 F. Supp. 1044 (D. Colo. 1997), *aff'd without op.*, 185 F.3d 883 (Fed. Cir. 1999), 334, 335, 344

In re Baxter Int'l, 123 F.T.C. 947 (1997), 425

Baxter Int'l v. Abbott Labs., 315 F.3d 829 (7th Cir. 2003), 185

Baxter Int'l, v. McGaw, Inc., 149 F.3d 1321 (Fed. Cir. 1998), 336

Bayer AG v. Housey Pharms., 169 F. Supp. 2d 328 (D. Del 2001), *aff'd*, 340 F.3d 1367 (Fed. Cir. 2003), 496

Bayer AG v. Housey Pharms., 228 F. Supp. 2d 467 (D. Del. 2002), 215, 225, 234

Bayou Fleet v. Alexander, 234 F.3d 852 (5th Cir. 2000), 377, 390

B.B. Chem. Co. v. Ellis, 314 U.S. 495 (1942), 81, 198

B. Braun Med. v. Abbott Labs., 124 F.3d 1419 (Fed. Cir. 1997), 78, 176, 177, 218, 498, 502

Beckman Instruments v. LKB Produkter AB, 892 F.2d 1547 (Fed. Cir. 1989), 377

Becton, Dickinson & Co. v. Eisele & Co., 86 F.2d 267 (6th Cir. 1936), 173

Bela Seating Co. v. Poloron Prods., 297 F. Supp. 489 (N.D. Ill. 1968), 177

Bela Seating Co. v. Poloron Prods., 438 F.2d 733 (7th Cir. 1971), 220

Beltone Elecs. Corp., 100 F.T.C. 68 (1982), 188

Bendix Corp. v. Balax, Inc., 421 F.2d 809 (7th Cir. 1970), 334
Bendix Corp. v. Balax, Inc., 471 F.2d 149 (7th Cir. 1972), 234
Benger Lab. v. R.K. Laros Co., 209 F. Supp. 639 (E.D. Pa. 1962), *aff'd per curiam*, 317 F.2d 455 (3d Cir. 1963), 177
Berkey Photo v. Eastman Kodak Co., 603 F.2d 263 (2d Cir. 1979), 37, 195, 282, 433
Berlenbach v. Anderson & Thompson Ski Co., 329 F.2d 782 (9th Cir. 1964), 189
Besser Mfg. v. United States, 343 U.S. 444 (1952), 469, 470
Bethlehem Plaza v. Campbell, 403 F. Supp. 966 (E.D. Pa. 1975), 391
B&G Plastics v. E. Creative Indus., 269 F. Supp. 2d 450 (S.D.N.Y. 2003), 356, 361, 393
Binks Mfg. Co. v. Ransburg Electro-Coating Corp., 281 F.2d 252 (7th Cir. 1960), 231, 504
Biodex Corp. v. Loredan Biomed., Inc., 946 F.2d 850 (Fed. Cir. 1991), 453
Boggild v. Kenner Prods., 776 F.2d 1315 (6th Cir. 1985), 223
Bonito Boats v. Thunder Craft Boats, 489 U.S. 141 (1989), 64
In re Boston Scientific, 119 F.T.C. 549 (1995), 442
Boston Scientific v. Schneider Europe AG, 983 F. Supp. 245 (D. Mass. 1997), 239, 299, 376
Boulware v. Nev. Dep't of Human Res., 960 F.2d 793 (9th Cir. 1992), 376, 380
Bourns, Inc. v. Raychem Corp., 331 F.3d 704 (9th Cir. 2003), 344, 349
Bowers v. Baystate Tech., 320 F.3d 1317 (Fed. Cir. 2003), 234
Brenton Prod. Enters. v. Motion Media, No. 96-6044, 1997 WL 603412 (6th Cir. Sept. 30, 1997), 331
Bristol-Myers Squibb Co. v. Ben Venue Labs., 90 F. Supp. 2d 540 (D.N.J. 2000), 349, 351
Bristol-Myers Squibb Co. v. IVAX Corp., 77 F. Supp. 2d 606 (D.N.J. 2000), 326
Broad. Music v. CBS, 441 U.S. 1 (1979), 5, 45, 152, 169, 237, 238, 488, 515
Broadcom Corp. v. Qualcomm Inc., 2006 U.S. Dist. LEXIS 62090 (D.N.J. Aug. 31, 2006), 400
Brokerage Concepts v. U.S. Healthcare, 140 F.3d 494 (3d Cir. 1998), 194
Brooke Group v. Brown & Williamson Tobacco, 509 U.S. 209 (1993), 43, 263, 279
Brooks Furniture Mfg. v. Dutailier Int'l, 393 F.3d 1378 (Fed. Cir. 2005), 375, 385
Brotech Corp. v. White Eagle Int'l Techs. Group, No. Civ. A. 03-232, 2003 WL 22797730 (E.D. Pa. Nov. 18, 2003), 379
Brotech Corp. v. White Eagle Int'l Techs. Group, No. Civ. A. 03-232, 2004 WL 1427136 (E.D. Pa. June 21, 2004), 349
Brown Shoe Co. v. United States, 370 U.S. 294 (1962), 39, 52
Brownwell v. Ketcham Wire & Mfg. Co., 211 F.2d 121 (9th Cir. 1954), 172
Brulotte v. Thys Co., 379 U.S. 29 (1964), 8, 212, 215, 222, 224, 297, 494, 496
Brunswick Corp. v. Pueblo Bowl-O-Mat, Inc., 429 U.S. 477 (1977), 161, 348

580   *Intellectual Property and Antitrust Handbook*

Deere v. Heaston, 593 F.2d 956 (10th Cir. 1979), 334
Deering, Milliken & Co. v. Temp-Resisto Corp., 160 F. Supp. 463 (S.D.N.Y. 1958), *aff'd in part and rev'd in part*, 274 F.2d 626 (2d Cir. 1960), 175
Dehydrating Process Co. v. A.O. Smith Corp., 292 F.2d 653 (1st Cir. 1961), 195, 510
In re Dell Computer Corp., 121 F.T.C. 616 (May 20, 1996), 398
Denbicare U.S.A. v. Toys "R" Us, Inc., 84 F.3d 1143 (9th Cir. 1996), 450
Dentsply Int'l v. New Tech. Co., No. 96-272 MMS, 1996 U.S. Dist. LEXIS 19846 (D. Del. Dec. 19, 1996), 376
Digidyne Corp. v. Data Gen. Corp., 734 F.2d 1336, 1341-42 (9th Cir. 1984), 526
Digital Equip. v. Diamond, 653 F.2d 701 (1st Cir. 1981), 331
Digital Equip. v. Uniq Digital Techs., 73 F.3d 756 (7th Cir. 1996), 510
DiscoVision Assocs. v. Disc Mfg., 42 U.S.P.Q. 2d (BNA) 1749 (D. Del. 1997), 415, 512
D.L. Auld v. Chroma Graphics, 714 F.2d 1144 (Fed. Cir. 1983), 338
Doran v. Purdue Pharma, 324 F. Supp. 2d 1147 (D. Nev. 2004), 325
Douglas v. Wis. Alumni Research Found., 81 F. Supp. 167 (N.D. Ill. 1948), 461
Dow Chem. v. Mee Indus., 341 F.3d 1370 (Fed. Cir. 2003), 32
Dr. Miles Med. Co. v. John D. Park & Sons Co., 220 U.S. 373 (1911), 163, 503
DSC Communs. v. Pulse Communs., 170 F.3d 1354 (Fed. Cir. 1999), 79, 450
Dunhall Pharms. v. Discus Dental, 994 F. Supp. 1202 (C.D. Cal. 1998), 395
Duplan Corp. v. Deering Milliken, Inc., 444 F. Supp. 648 (D.S.C. 1977), *aff'd in part and rev'd in part*, 594 F.2d 979 (4th Cir. 1979), 218, 225, 231, 232, 238, 247
Duplan Corp. v. Deering Milliken, Inc., 540 F.2d 1215 (4th Cir. 1976), 397

E

Eastman Kodak Co. v. Goodyear Tire & Rubber, 114 F.3d 1547 (Fed. Cir. 1997), 349
Eastman Kodak Co. v. Image Technical Servs., 504 U.S. 451 (1992), 7, 37, 39, 192, 208, 287, 288, 292, 506
eBay Inc. v. Bidder's Edge Inc., No. C-99-21200 RMW, 2000 WL 1863564 (N.D. Cal. July 25, 2000), 362
E. Bement & Sons v. Nat'l Harrow Co., 186 U.S. 70 (1902), 67, 68, 69, 172, 184, 186, 296
Ecrix Corp. v. Exabyte Corp., 191 F.R.D. 611 (D. Colo. 2000), 462, 464, 465
Eden Hannon & Co. v. Sumitomo Trust & Banking, 914 F.2d 556 (4th Cir. 1990), 376
In re E.I. du Pont de Nemours & Co., 96 F.T.C. 653 (1980), 298
E.I. du Pont de Nemours & Co. v. Berkley & Co., 620 F.2d 1247 (8th Cir. 1980), 330
E.I. du Pont de Nemours & Co. v. FTC, 729 F.2d 128 (2d Cir. 1984), 155
Eldred v. Ashcroft, 537 U.S. 186 (2003), 18

J

K

L

M

Motion Picture Patents Co. v. Universal Film Mfg., 243 U.S. 502 (1917), 2, 71, 72, 196

Mozart Co. v. Mercedes-Benz of N. Am., 833 F.2d 1342 (9th Cir. 1987), 510, 511

In re Multidist. Vehicle Air Pollution, 367 F. Supp. 1298 (C.D. Cal. 1973), 246

N

Nabisco, Inc. v. PF Brands, 191 F.3d 208 (2d Cir. 1999), 34

Nartron Corp. v. STMicroelectronics, 305 F.3d 397 (6th Cir. 2002), 34

Nat'l Lockwasher Co. v. George K. Garrett Co., 137 F.2d 255 (3d Cir. 1943), 189

Nat'l Soc'y of Prof'l Eng'rs v. United States, 435 U.S. 679 (1978), 44, 152, 237

NCAA v. Bd. of Regents, 468 U.S. 85 (1984), 45, 153, 162, 163

N.C. Elec. Membership Corp. v. Carolina Power & Light, 666 F.2d 50 (4th Cir. 1981), 390

Nelson v. Miller, 227 Kan. 271, 607 P.2d 438 (1980), 374

Newburgh Moire Co. v. Superior Moire Co., 237 F.2d 283 (3d Cir. 1956), 166, 498

N.Y. Mercantile Exch. v. Intercont'l Exch., 323 F. Supp. 2d 559 (S.D.N.Y. 2004), 282

Nilssen v. Motorola, Inc., 203 F.3d 782 (Fed. Cir. 2000), 449

In re Nine West Shoes Antitrust Litig., 80 F. Supp. 2d 181 (S.D.N.Y. 2000), 392

Nitinol Med. Techs. v. AGA Med., 135 F. Supp. 2d 212 (D. Mass. 2000), 395

Nobelpharma AB v. Implant Innovations, 930 F. Supp. 1241 (N.D. Ill. 1996), *aff'd*, 141 F.3d 1059 (Fed. Cir. 1998), 377, 397

Nobelpharma AB v. Implant Innovations, 141 F.3d 1059 (Fed. Cir. 1998), 87, 86, 140, 298, 323, 324, 325, 327, 328, 329, 330, 332, 335, 336, 337, 338, 343, 344, 345, 351, 367, 369, 445, 452, 453, 463

Nobody In Particular Presents, Inc. v. Clear Channel Communs., 311 F. Supp. 2d 1048 (D. Colo. 2004), 281, 282

N. Pac. Ry. Co. v. United States, 356 U.S. 1 (1958), 75, 76, 192, 193, 207, 275

N. Telecom, Inc. v. Datapoint Corp., 908 F.2d 931 (Fed. Cir. 1990), 323, 326

Northlake Mktg. & Supply v. Glaverbel S.A., 861 F. Supp. 653 (N.D. Ill. 1994), 344, 345

Nw. Wholesale Stationers v. Pac. Stationery & Printing, 472 U.S. 284 (1985), 162

Novell, Inc. v. CPU Distrib., Civ. A. No. H-97-2326, 2000 U.S. Dist. LEXIS 9952 (S.D. Tex. May 12, 2000), 381

Novo Nordisk of N. Am. v. Genentech, Inc., 885 F. Supp. 522 (S.D.N.Y. 1995), 349

NYNEX Corp. v. Discon, Inc., 525 U.S. 128 (1998), 252

Nystrom v. Trex Co., 374 F.3d 1105 (Fed. Cir. 2004), 21, 24, 32

O

P

592   *Intellectual Property and Antitrust Handbook*

Potter Instrument v. Storage Tech., Nos. 79-579-A, 79-626-A, 79-993-A, 79-994-A, 79-995-A, 1980 WL 30330 (E.D. Va. Mar. 25, 1980), *aff'd on other grounds*, 641 F.2d 190 (4th Cir. 1981), 398
Practice Mgmt. Info. v. AMA, 121 F.3d 516 (9th Cir. 1997), 79, 189
Precision Instrument Mfg. v. Auto. Maint. Mach., 324 U.S. 806 (1945), 295, 320, 341
Premier Elec. Constr. v. Nat'l Elec. Contractors Ass'n, 814 F.2d 358 (7th Cir. 1987), 468
PrimeTime 24 Joint Venture v. NBC, 219 F.3d 92 (2d Cir. 2000), 182, 356, 359, 388
Proctor & Gamble Co. v. Paragon Trade Brands, 61 F. Supp. 2d 102 (D. Del. 1996), 247
Prof'l Real Estate Investors v. Columbia Pictures Indus., 508 U.S. 49 (1993), 13, 267, 315, 353, 354, 362, 366, 367, 368, 373, 374, 375, 376, 380, 381, 383, 384
Pro-Mold & Tool v. Great Lakes Plastics, 75 F.3d 1568 (Fed. Cir. 1996), 453
PSC Inc. v. Symbol Techs., 26 F. Supp. 2d 505 (W.D.N.Y. 1998), 217

Q

Q-Pharma, Inc. v. Andrew Jergens Co., 360 F.3d 1295 (Fed. Cir. 2004), 375, 381

R

Raines v. Switch Mfg., No. C-96-2648, 327
In re Rambus, Inc., FTC Dkt. No. 9302, (F.T.C. Aug. 2, 2006), http://www.ftc.gov/os/adjpro/d9302/060802commissionopinion.pdf, 401, 402, 403, 404, 405
In re Rambus, Inc., FTC Dkt. No. 9302 (F.T.C. Feb. 5, 2007), http://www.ftc.gov/os/adjpro/d9302/070205opinion.pdf, 404, 405
Rambus, Inc. v. Infineon Techs., 318 F.3d 1081 (Fed. Cir. 2003), 402, 403
Ransburg Elector-Coating Corp. v. Spiller & Spiller, Inc., 489 F.2d 974 (7th Cir. 1973), 235
Re-Alco Indus. v. Nat'l Ctr. for Health Educ., 812 F. Supp. 387 (S.D.N.Y. 1993), 321, 348
Rebel Oil Co. v. Atl. Richfield Co., 51 F.3d 1421 (9th Cir. 1995), 39
In re Recombinant DNA Tech. Patent & Contract Litig., 850 F. Supp. 769 (S.D. Ind. 1994), 189
In re Recombinant DNA Tech. Patent & Contract Litig., 874 F. Supp. 904 (S.D. Ind. 1994), 334
Record Club of Am. v. Capitol Records, 1971 Trade Cas. (CCH) ¶ 73,694 (S.D.N.Y. 1971), 410

S

Schering-Plough v. FTC, 402 F.3d 1056 (11th Cir. 2005)), *cert. denied*, 126 S. Ct. 2929 (2006), 11, 62, 144, 267, 268, 297

Schinzing v. Mid-States Stainless, Inc., No. 04-2535, 2005 U.S. App. LEXIS 14300 (8th Cir. July 15, 2005), 458

Schlegel Mfg. Co. v. USM Corp., 525 F.2d 775 (6th Cir. 1975), 236, 462

Schor v. Abbott Labs., No. 05-C-1592, 2005 WL 1653606 (N.D. Ill. July 12, 2005), 285, 308, 325

Schwarzkopf Dev. v. Ti-Coating, Inc., 800 F.2d 240 (Fed. Cir. 1986), 444

Schwinn Bicycle Co. v. Murray Ohio Mfg., 339 F. Supp. 973 (M.D. Tenn. 1971), 331

In re S.C. Johnson & Son, 125 F.T.C. 753 (1998), 425

SCM Corp. v. RCA, 318 F. Supp. 433 (S.D.N.Y. 1970), 175

SCM Corp. v. Xerox Corp., 463 F. Supp. 983 (D. Conn. 1978), 185

SCM Corp. v. Xerox Corp., 645 F.2d 1195 (2d Cir. 1981), 289, 290, 292, 308, 410, 415, 417

Scripto-Tokai Corp. v. Gillette Co., No. CV-91-2862-LGB(JRX), 1994 WL 746072 (C.D. Cal. Sept. 9, 1994), 330, 333

Sears, Roebuck & Co. v. Stiffel Co., 376 U.S. 225 (1964), 216

Seattle Audobon Soc'y v. Lyons, 871 F. Supp. 1291 (W.D. Wash. 1994), 456

In re Sensormatic Elecs. Corp., 119 F.T.C. 520 (1995), 425

Senza-Gel Corp. v. Seiffhart, 803 F.2d 661 (Fed. Cir. 1986), 200

Serv. Employees Int'l Union Health & Welfare Fund v. Abbott Labs., No. C 04-4203 CW, 2005 WL 528323 (N.D. Cal. Mar. 2, 2005), 284, 304

Shea v. Blaw-Knox Co., 388 F.2d 761 (7th Cir. 1968), 209

Sheet Metal Duct v. Lindab Inc., 55 U.S.P.Q. 2d (BNA) 1480 (E.D. Pa. 2000), 186

Shields Jetco v. Torti, 314 F. Supp. 1292 (D.R.I. 1970), 223

Shell Oil Co. v. Amoco Corp., 970 F.2d 885 (Fed. Cir. 1992), 346

Silva v. Mamula, Civ. No. 93-5618, 1994 WL 66070 (E.D. Pa. Feb. 24, 1994), 345, 350

Simpson v. Stand 21 S.A., 32 U.S.P.Q. 2d 1848 (S.D. Ind. 1994), 466, 467

Simpson v. Union Oil Co., 377 U.S. 13 (1964), 59, 252, 295, 311, 318

Sindell v. Abbott Labs., 607 P.2d 924 (Cal. 1980), 257

Six W. Retail Acquisition v. Sony Theater Mgmt., No. 97 Civ. 5499, 2004 U.S. Dist. LEXIS 5411 (S.D.N.Y. Mar. 30, 2004), 193

Skinder-Strauss Assocs. v. Mass. Continuing Legal Educ., 870 F. Supp. 8 (D. Mass. 1994), 378

Smith Int'l v. Kennametal, Inc., 621 F. Supp. 79 (N.D. Ohio 1985), 177, 186

SmithKline Beecham Corp. v. Apotex Corp., No. 99-CV-4304, 2005 WL 2436662 (E.D. Pa. Sept. 28, 2005), 396

Softview Computer Prods. v. Haworth, Inc., No. 97 Civ. 8815 KMWHBP, 2000 WL 351411 (S.D.N.Y. March 31, 2000), 397

In re Spalding Sports Worldwide, 203 F.3d 800 (Fed. Cir. 2000), 397

Spanish Int'l Communs. v. Leibowitz, 608 F. Supp. 178 (S.D. Fla. 1985), 391

T

Gender Equality and Public Policy

Despite formal United Nations and European Commission commitments to improving gender imbalances, progress towards gender equality in wealth and pay has progressed at a discouragingly slow pace in recent decades. European countries have been proactive in their support for corrective policies such as family leave and gender quotas for corporate boards, yet measuring the effectiveness of these policies has proven difficult. This book offers a close comparative analysis of gender-targeted policies in Europe, providing an in-depth overview of how public policy is shaping gender equality and how the presence of women in the economy and decision-making positions is itself shaping public policy. Paola Profeta bases her analysis on new data and an innovative interdisciplinary perspective for understanding the relationship between gender equality and public policy and their impact on the European economy and society, with lessons that resonate beyond Europe.

PAOLA PROFETA is Professor of Public Economics at Bocconi University, Italy.

Gender Equality and Public Policy

Measuring Progress in Europe

PAOLA PROFETA
Bocconi University

CAMBRIDGE
UNIVERSITY PRESS

CAMBRIDGE
UNIVERSITY PRESS

University Printing House, Cambridge CB2 8BS, United Kingdom

One Liberty Plaza, 20th Floor, New York, NY 10006, USA

477 Williamstown Road, Port Melbourne, VIC 3207, Australia

314–321, 3rd Floor, Plot 3, Splendor Forum, Jasola District Centre, New Delhi – 110025, India

79 Anson Road, #06–04/06, Singapore 079906

Cambridge University Press is part of the University of Cambridge.

It furthers the University's mission by disseminating knowledge in the pursuit of education, learning, and research at the highest international levels of excellence.

www.cambridge.org
Information on this title: www.cambridge.org/9781108423359
DOI: 10.1017/9781108525886

First published 2020

Printed in the United Kingdom by TJ International Ltd. Padstow Cornwall

A catalogue record for this publication is available from the British Library.

Library of Congress Cataloging-in-Publication Data
Names: Profeta, Paola, 1972– author.
Title: Gender equality and public policy : measuring progress in Europe / Paola Profeta.
Description: New York : Cambridge University Press, 2020. | Includes bibliographical references and index.
Identifiers: LCCN 2019042177 (print) | LCCN 2019042178 (ebook) | ISBN 9781108423359 (hardback) | ISBN 9781108525886 (epub)
Subjects: LCSH: Sex discrimination against women – Europe. | Women – Employment – Europe. | Women's rights – Europe. | Sex role – Europe.
Classification: LCC HQ1237.5.E85 P76 2020 (print) | LCC HQ1237.5.E85 (ebook) | DDC 305.42094–dc23
LC record available at https://lccn.loc.gov/2019042177
LC ebook record available at https://lccn.loc.gov/2019042178

ISBN 978-1-108-42335-9 Hardback
ISBN 978-1-108-43746-2 Paperback

Contents

Figures

Tables

Preface

We must have perseverance and above all confidence in ourselves. We must believe that we are gifted for something.

—Marie Curie

When the introduction of board gender quotas was first discussed in Italy a decade ago, those in favour of quotas relied on non-academic results from consultancy companies claiming that a higher share of women would 'lead' to substantially better performance. The arguments against gender quotas were dominated by the defense of 'meritocracy', arguing that quotas contravene meritocracy because they risk promoting less qualified individuals and thus reducing the quality of board members. I was puzzled. The argument in favour was not convincing, since it was based on a simple correlation, which is different from causality. The one against was misplaced: Why do we talk about the quality of women if the quality of men has never been an issue? Moreover, since highly qualified women are abundant, why should the promotion of women reduce quality? At that time, together with some co-authors, I contributed to the production of new evidence in the political sphere, showing in a *causal* way (i.e. using a rigorous analysis) that the introduction of gender quotas in candidate lists increased – rather than decreased – the quality of elected politicians. The rationale for gender quotas changed: policymakers stopped using unreliable correlations between female representation and performance to justify gender quotas and realized that gender quotas do not contravene meritocracy but rather enhance it.

This is only one example among many. This book is written to propose appropriate academic and scientific answers to real-world policy questions related to gender equality.

This book has its genesis in the confluence of three circumstances. First, in 2015, I created the Dondena Gender Initiative (DGI) within the Dondena Research Center on Social Dynamics and Public Policy at

Bocconi University. This new research section focuses on the topic of gender equality in the economic, political and social spheres with a particular reference to the role of public policy in promoting gender equality in Europe. During my years as coordinator of DGI, from 2015 to the present, I have organized seminars, conferences and workshops at Bocconi University on the topic of gender equality, which have been attended by students, academics, members of the business community and policymakers working on the topic of equality between men and women in the labour market, firms and governments. In particular, each year I organize a 'Gender Equality' conference at Bocconi University, jointly with the UniCredit Foundation, where academics, managers, policymakers and other experts on the topic present and discuss research related to gender equality issues. Young and senior scholars interact, present rigorous research and assess its impact on real-world decisions and suggest how to proceed towards the promotion of equality between men and women in the economic sphere.

Inspiring conversations with prominent international scholars at the many meetings concerning the Dondena Gender Initiative encouraged me to write a book that addresses the relationship between women and public policy by rigorously examining *all* the dimensions of the relationship, including the 'public economic' aspect (i.e. how family policy affects women's participation in the labour market), the 'political economy' aspect (i.e. how the presence of women in decision-making positions influences public policies) and the role of culture, among others.

As a second ingredient in the genesis of this book, at the same time that I established the DGI, I started teaching an undergraduate course at Bocconi University entitled 'Diversity Policy and Management' and a PhD course entitled 'Gender and Family Policy'. It was the first time that Bocconi University offered specific courses on these topics. I entered Bocconi University when I was eighteen for my undergraduate studies in economic and social sciences. I then earned my PhD in economics at Pompeu Fabra University in Barcelona. After several years of research and teaching experience in different places, I returned to Bocconi University. I have spent most of my professional life there, pursuing the study of public finance and gender economics. I consider the introduction of these new courses on gender, together with the overall greater attention that the university is now paying to the issue of equality between men and women, my most successful contribution to the Bocconi community.

During the preparation of my classes, I started to search for a *fil rouge* (guiding thread) to select and present the enormous evidence on gender equality and public policy in a convincing and coherent way. It was much harder than I expected – contributions are rarely rigorously organized, and evidence is sometimes unclear or contradictory. At the same time, despite the abundance of contributions, I found a clear weakness in the existing analyses: researchers have paid little attention to the twofold relationship between gender equality and public policy. While the relationship between women's empowerment and public policies or economic outcomes has often been addressed, most of the existing contributions show only associations and correlations between the two and cannot infer *causality*. This suggested to me that it was important to organize the existing material in a way that allowed me and other researchers to have immediate access to the existing results. In addition, this new, more organized approach to looking at the existing evidence allows me to produce new evidence and to provide a comprehensive, unified new approach to the study of gender and public policy.

The third essential ingredient in developing this book is my professional and practical experience in the field. In the past twelve years, I have been active in the policy debate on gender equality both in Italy and in Europe. I have met with policymakers, politicians, ministers, unions, CEOs of large corporations, women at the top of their business careers in different industries, professionals in international organizations and several professional women's associations to discuss the economic effects of gender quotas, paternity leaves and flexible work arrangements, among many other policies under debate worldwide. I have written articles for major Italian newspapers (*Corriere della Sera* and *Il Sole 24 Ore*); been interviewed by major international newspapers, including *The Economist*, the *Financial Times* and *The Wall Street Journal*, and major French, German and Spanish newspapers; and I have contributed articles on gender and policy to international blogs such as VoxEU, LSE Business Blog, and Oxford University Blog. These discussions encouraged me to write a clear, comprehensive and accessible book on the topic of women and public policy, based on rigorous evidence. This approach has allowed me to identify the direction of the relationship between gender equality and public policy and to propose new evidence on how women's empowerment influences outcomes.

During my experience with policymakers and business leaders, I realized that there is widespread confusion between *descriptive evidence*, which provides only *correlations* between gender equality and public policies, and *causal evidence*, which identifies how women's empowerment influences public policies and economic outcomes. Only causal evidence can be trusted to provide policy prescriptions. However, policymakers and public opinion leaders often base their knowledge and policies only on descriptive evidence and ignore the lessons from causal evidence. Part of this bias is due to the abundance of available descriptive evidence, mostly provided outside academia. This type of bias is not confined to the topic of gender, but it is especially pervasive in such studies. The bias is partly caused by the researchers themselves, who communicate the results of their studies in a sparse, inaccessible and sometimes incomprehensible way. Another difficulty is that many scholars do not communicate their results outside academia and 'proudly' remain far removed from the real world, where policies are decided. Although many prominent colleagues subscribe to this idea, I have always had difficulty understanding it. I believe that it is our responsibility to warn against the 'false myths' that start from the claims of non-academic researchers and often lead to decisions with unpredictable outcomes in the real world. Instead, I believe that academics should find ways to meet and speak with policymakers, decision makers and institutions and to collaborate with them to design policies that may improve real economic conditions.

Because gender gaps in all areas of society (the labour market, business and government) are still a serious concern in many countries worldwide, a joint effort by researchers and policymakers is urgently needed. I am also convinced that the contribution of women researchers in a male-dominated academic world can be particularly important in this direction. It will help reorient the discipline and link academia to the real world.

I truly hope this book will encourage researchers in all relevant disciplines to share the results of their rigorous academic research with a large audience with the purpose of supporting policy measures that may contribute to a more gender-balanced society and, ultimately, a better world for men and women.

The book reflects my background in both public economics and political economics. Public economics teaches how to design policies to improve gender equality throughout society and promotes the idea that women's empowerment follows the principle that government should intervene in the economy for equity and efficiency reasons. Political economics teaches that public policies themselves are the result of the aggregation of voters' preferences, thus suggesting a possible link between women's empowerment and public policy. My approach to the study of gender equality and public policy starts from the precise identification of each side of the analysis and elaborates a way to reach a unified synthesis.

In addition, I have incorporated into this book an essential feature of my research since I began: an interdisciplinary approach that includes insights and evidence from many disciplines. In addition to economics, my original field of study, I have been influenced by and have contributed to research in several disciplines, ranging from management to finance, political science, sociology, demography and public policy. All these disciplines have extensively addressed the topic of gender and public policy through specific lenses, and it is my goal to focus all these lenses on the issue of gender and policy.

Acknowledgements

I am indebted to the many people in the academic, policymaking and business communities with whom I have interacted intensively over the past twelve years. In different ways, they have all contributed to this book: they discussed my papers at conferences, taught me how difficult it is to implement policies even when the academic research recommends them and nurtured my passion for the analysis of gender gaps and female leadership and my passion for promoting policies to bridge those gaps.

Many inspiring ideas were shared with extraordinary women responsible for organizations such as Aldai Merito e Talento, Fondazione Bellisario, Fondazione Bracco, Fuori Quota, La 27esima Ora, 30% Club, Valore D, Insieme per le Donne, Professional Women Association, Inclusione Donna and 100 esperte. I have benefitted greatly from my frequent interactions with, among many others, Magda Bianco, Roberta Cocco, Marilisa D'Amico, Daniela Del Boca, Elsa Fornero, Alessia Mosca, Monica Parrella and Barbara Stefanelli. I also thank Francesca De Marco and Helga Gentry for inspiring conversations at Bocconi University and for their support during the project.

Various chapters were planned or written while I was visiting Nuffield College at Oxford University, the University of Edinburgh and Trinity College in Dublin. I thank these places for their warm hospitality.

Some of the thoughts expressed in the book are based on papers co-authored with Mario Amore, Marta Angelici, Audinga Baltrunaite, Piera Bello, Pamela Campa, Francesca Carta, Alessandra Casarico, José Ignacio Conde-Ruiz, Ester Fanelli, Giulia Ferrari, Valeria Ferraro, Juan José Ganuza, Salvatore Lattanzio, Donato Masciandaro, Chiara Pronzato, Davide Romelli, Giulia Savio, Lilach Trabelsi, Eleanor Woodhouse and Maurizio Zollo.

I also have to thank my young collaborators of the past five years: Marta Angelici, Lorenzo Demasi, Vittoria Di Candia, Ester Fanelli,

Valeria Ferraro, Giulia Giupponi, Annarita Macchioni, Smriti Ganapathi and Eleanor Woodhouse. Because the origins of this project can be traced back several years, some of them are already brilliant scholars in their own right! A special thank you to Carmela Accettura, who provided excellent research assistance for the chapters of this book. I would also like to thank Karen Maloney of Cambridge University Press for her initial inspiration and continuous support.

With the help of my husband, Vincenzo, I am still professionally active. My family and close friends know that I very rarely picked up my daughters at school when they were children. I am sorry for missing such precious time. However, we had wonderful times together, especially during our frequent travels. I truly hope the famous World Value Survey statement that 'when a mother works for pay, children suffer' is not true. I wish that Chiara (b. 2001) and Isabella (b. 2008) will be able to develop their professional careers in a more open-minded and gender-equal world than the one I have experienced.

1 | *Introduction*

The dramatic change in women's identities and their roles in family and society led to a substantial increase in the share of women in the workforce, which was the most significant change in labour markets during the past century. The changing role of women in the economy and society has major long-term consequences for individual choices (education, fertility, work and career) and firms' decisions (hiring and promotions). Culture and attitudes crucially shape the ongoing process, while they are challenged by the increasing participation of women in the workforce and decision-making processes. Public policies are continuously being adjusted as governments are asked to take action to meet the new needs and change accordingly.

Goldin (2006) uses the words 'quiet revolution' to characterize the emergence of a new economic role for women in the past century. Women shifted from being static passive actors, who took the income and time allocation of other family members as a given, to becoming active participants, who bargain in the household and in the labour market. They stopped being 'secondary workers', who accepted their husbands' labour market decisions as given to them and now make their labour force decisions jointly with their partners. Their labour market decisions are strictly linked to a change in human capital investment and have become part of a new long-term horizon: investment in education is the first step to perceiving that their lifetime labour force involvement will be long and continuous rather than brief and intermittent. Finally, women have moved from being agents who work because they and their families 'need the money' to those who are employed, at least in part, because occupation and employment define their fundamental identity, profession and career. The formation of identity occurs before, rather than after, marriage.

Despite this continuous evolution, economic gender gaps appear to be persistent and difficult to eliminate (see Chapter 2). The quiet revolution, which Goldin defines with reference to the United States, is still ongoing in many parts of the world. In Europe, while gender gaps in educational attainments have nearly disappeared in most countries, the quiet revolution lags behind, especially in the Mediterranean area, where substantial differences still exist in the participation of men and women in the labour force. The 'glass ceiling' – the invisible barriers that prevent women from reaching upper-level positions – is still a dominant phenomenon worldwide. The World Economic Forum calculates that economic gender gaps have been reduced by only 2.5 per cent since 2006 and claims that without substantial changes, it will take another 202 years before such gaps vanish (WEF, 2018). However, academic researchers, international organizations and policymakers agree that gender equality has beneficial effects for the economy and society (Duflo, 2012; IMF, 2016). The 2030 Agenda for Sustainable Development launched by the United Nations and adopted in 2015 includes the following fundamental goal: to '*achieve gender equality and empower all women and girls*'. Gender equality has attracted much attention in Europe: the *Manual for Gender Mainstreaming, Social Inclusion and Social Protection* policies, published by the European Commission in 2007, maintains that '*Gender equality is a fundamental right, a common value of the EU, and a necessary condition for the achievement of the EU objectives of growth, employment and social cohesion.*'

Public policy is advocated as a tool for accelerating progress towards gender equality. It includes childcare; maternity, paternity and parental leave; fiscal policies; affirmative action and gender quotas; labour market interventions; pension design; and flexible work arrangements (agile working, i.e. flexibility of time and space). In a continuously changing context, public policies are under pressure: they reflect the change in women's roles and their increasing empowerment and leadership in the decision-making process, and they face the challenge of redesigning adequate and sustainable institutions to address these major changes (Del Boca and Wetzels, 2001; Olivetti and Petrongolo, 2017). The role of public policy in connection with gender equality is an intense and dominant topic, particularly for European countries and in the European agenda. A crucial issue when addressing the role of public policies in connection with gender equality is whether gender gaps depend on *nature* – they have biological roots; on *nurture* – they are the outcomes of environmental influences or on both. If gender gaps depend on biological differences, then it is difficult to imagine how policies can play a relevant role in reducing them. If, instead, as many studies suggest, the cultural and societal contexts in which economic agents make their choices also matter, then institutions can play a more fundamental role.

The relationship between gender equality and public policy needs a thorough investigation. On the one hand, policies have a clear impact on gender gaps, particularly those related to motherhood and the labour market (Del Boca et al., 2009). Family policies or affirmative action may have a substantial effect on women's economic opportunities and thus on gender equality. I refer to this as the 'public economics' side of the relationship between gender equality and public policy. A clear example is childcare (i.e. provision of services and public day-car centers to children) a public policy that supports women's participation in the labour market, thus promoting gender equality.

On the other hand, women as economic agents may themselves have an impact on policies: this is the 'political economy' side of the relationship. A clear example is municipalities that randomly happen to be led by female mayors, who spend more resources on public policies (e.g. childcare) that contribute to reducing gender gaps. We expect the changing role of women in families and societies and their higher representation in decision-making positions to contribute to focusing and redirecting the policy agenda towards items that better correspond to women's needs (Chattopadhyay and Duflo, 2004) or preferences (Funk and Gathmann, 2015) with the final goal of reducing gender gaps.

Although several contributions to the literature of different disciplines, ranging from economics to sociology, political science, public policy and management, help describe the complex nature and main elements of the twofold relationship between gender and public policy, this has not been at the centre of research on gender thus far. The two sides of the relationship between gender equality and public policy have mostly been investigated separately. Their interactions and feedback effects have remained mainly unidentified. However, both public and political elements are at work in the gender and public policy relationship, and they both play an important role in the dynamic process of gender equality.

The public economics side of the relationship, that is, how public policies affect or reduce gender gaps, is present in the labour and public economics literature (see Chapter 3). Cross-country regressions are used to show that policies such as childcare, maternity leave, taxation design and labour market measures are related to gender equality. Micro-level analyses provide more careful assessments of the relationship, but they must limit their focus to a specific policy in a specific country. A major challenge for these analyses is to incorporate the role of policies into contexts in which cultural and historical determinants are a crucial component of gender gaps and their persistence.

The political economy side of the relationship, moving from gender equality and women's empowerment to public policies, is less investigated than the public economics side, though research in this area is increasing (see Chapter 4). Traditionally, research attempting to assess the causal role of women in setting the policy agenda and the consequent effects on economic outcomes has been concentrated on developing countries (see e.g. Chattopadhyay and Duflo, 2004 and Clots-Figueras, 2011, for India; Brollo and Troiano, 2016, for Brazil). For high-income countries, the political economy side of the relationship consists of scant and inconclusive evidence. Among others, Funk and Gathman (2015) find that women in Switzerland invest more in health and environmental issues, while Ferreira and Gyourko (2014) find no effects of the gender of local US politicians on the allocation of public expenditures. In parallel, gender equality matters in the business context: the presence of women in decision-making positions in firms may influence the firms' outcomes, such as profits, returns on equity and investment, assets, sustainability scores, international results such as openness to exports or international trade, and labour market policies such as recruiting and promotion (see Chapter 5).

Research on both sides of the relationship suffers from the major problem of *endogeneity* – understanding the *causal effect* between public policy and gender equality and between women's representation in decision-making positions and policy outcomes; disentangling the two sides is difficult. For instance, if we observe that countries with higher childcare expenditures have higher female labour force participation, can we conclude that childcare *leads* to gender equality? It could be the case that countries where more women work give more importance to childcare expenditure (*reverse causality problem*) or that both childcare and gender equality measures are driven by cultural or historical determinants (*omitted variable bias*). Similarly, if we observe a positive *correlation* between female mayors and higher local public expenditures on childcare, is the reason that women as policymakers invest more in childcare or that a larger amount of this expenditure helps women's work and empowerment and thus the likelihood that women become mayors? Or is the reason that both the composition of public spending and women's representation in decision-making are determined by different external drivers, such as culture or family background?

Recent developments in data analysis and methods of policy evaluations (see the Appendix) are useful for assessing causality and not confounding it with correlation. The availability of microdata and large datasets with detailed information on individual characteristics, intentions and behaviours makes it possible to use new and more precise techniques to identify causal relationships, including fixed effects panel data estimations, instrumental variables, difference-in-difference evaluation designs, difference-in-discontinuities and regression discontinuity analysis. Moreover, the development of psychological economics and behavioural science and the use in social sciences of experiments based on randomized trials also contribute to this direction. Indeed, experiments help understand the nature and nurture aspects and their interplay at the origin of gender gaps and the related role of policies. An additional opportunity is provided by the recent availability of historical data and large historical datasets, which, by making possible the measurement of initial conditions in the past, are useful for understanding the direction of the relationship between gender and public policy. Finally, it has been recognized that one of the most useful contexts for assessing the causal impact of women's empowerment on policies is one in which women hold decision-making positions independently of the policies that they support. This is the case, for example, with gender quotas, which impose higher female representation by law. Here, we can appropriately address how women in decision-making positions affect policies. This evidence, in turn, provides the rationale for policies promoting gender balance in decision-making. However, there may be instances in which gender does not matter in economic decisions and economic outcomes, thus limiting the role of policies designed to reduce gender gaps.

Understanding the twofold relationship between gender and public policy is crucial in our rapidly changing world. Demographic, socio-economic and technological changes can be both a risk and an opportunity for progress towards gender equality. The design of appropriate public policies is fundamental for turning these changes into opportunities to develop a sustainable growing economy and society that will improve gender equality even further (Chapter 6). We need, for example, to understand how the process of obtaining gender equality interacts with public policies to design measures that address demographic changes such as the ageing of the population and massive migration flows. Similarly, if women matter to economic outcomes and firms' performance, gender policies may play an important role in promoting sustainable economic growth in the context of modest growth and increasing inequality.

In spite of the previously described recent methodological developments, which allow us to better deal with causality concerns, the two sides of the research – public economics and political economics – have not thus far been explored as a central question in research on gender and public policy. Still lacking are a unified perspective and a comprehensive framework to take into account both the public economics and the political economics aspects of the relationship between gender and public policy while also exploring interactions and feedback effects. This book aims to fill the gap and provide such a comprehensive framework.

The book will answer the following fundamental questions: How does public policy affect gender equality? Which policies matter, and what is the mechanism that allows policy to influence women's involvement in the economy? Which policies are more effective? Once women are enrolled in decision-making positions in organizations, governments and companies (mainly due to the introduction of gender policies), how do they influence public policies? Do they support policies that favour female employment and gender equality, thus giving rise to a reinforcing mechanism that will increase the presence of women in the future? Do they influence broader policies, for example, by integrating gender concerns into them? Is there evidence of additional contributions or spillover effects of women's empowerment in the economic context?

To answer these questions, the book provides a comprehensive and in-depth examination of gender gaps, public policies and economic outcomes. It provides evidence on the dynamics of gender equality in connection to public policy. It delivers a stimulating picture of the status of women in setting a new agenda for the future, sustaining the success of the gender 'revolution' and contributing to a broader perspective – with gender equality as a fundamental value – when addressing economic policy. Finally, it provides new insights into how to interpret the major global challenges of our modern societies, such as ageing, globalization and technological changes, as opportunities for a more gender-balanced society. At the end of this journey, we will understand how public policies are a driving force for gender equality and how women in decision-making positions can make a difference in current and future economies.

1.1 Notes on the Approach Developed in the Book

It is important to clarify some limitations of the book. First, gender studies is a broad and continuously growing field that covers several disciplines. It would be impossible, and it is beyond the scope of this book, to consider all contributions and to cover all aspects. The book develops its own perspective on the study of gender and public policy, which is centred on the twofold relationship between gender and public policy. As already explained, the approach developed in this book is at the intersection of public economics and political economics. Pure labour economics studies, for example, those focused on measuring wage gaps, which represent an extensive part of the literature on gender economics, will not be covered. However, several interesting analyses related to this perspective, though clearly belonging to disciplines other than economics – such as demography, sociology, political science or management – will be taken into account.

Second, the book focuses on developed economies, mainly OECD countries and pays particular attention to Europe. Thus, apart from some notable exceptions that are useful for understanding the gender dynamics in which I am interested, the book will not cover the large number of studies related to gender in development economics. Regarding developed economies, the book focuses in several ways on Europe, an interesting laboratory of analysis with substantial activism in policies to promote gender equality. Compared to the US, Europe has been more open to policy intervention. The target of gender equality represents a fundamental pillar of the global European view, and gender equality and public policies are intertwined in different European contexts (including in new EU member countries). Moreover, the recent experiences of European countries have made them an important laboratory of analysis and a source of inspiration for other countries, including the United States, in terms of implementing policies to promote gender equality.

Finally, this book identifies gender equality with equality between men and women, although I am aware that the concept of 'gender' is not exclusively represented by the man-versus-woman categorization.

1.2 Organization of the Book

The book is organized in chapters. Each chapter has its own subject and can be read separately. The message of the book is, however, unitary and is centred on the complex double relationship between gender and public policy. This view can be fully captured by reading the entire book.

The chapters are organized as follows. Chapter 2 presents data and facts that provide a scenario of gender gaps along the three main dimensions of education, the labour market and politics and the main trends across countries and over time. It also explains the main determinants of gender gaps in the labour market. A crucial role in determining gender gaps is played by public policies, which are at the centre of the next analysis. Chapter 3 concentrates on the relationship between public policy and gender equality and discusses what policies may support gender equality, including maternity, paternity and parental leave; childcare; taxation; and measures in the labour market. Chapters 4 and 5 move the analysis to the relationship between women and outcomes: Chapter 4 addresses how the presence of women in policy-making positions affects public policy, examining policies designed to improve gender equality and more general outcomes, while Chapter 5 concentrates on the business context and analyzes how the presence of women in firms' top positions may influence firms' outcomes. Chapter 6 introduces the role of global challenges – classified as demographic, economic and technological changes – in the relationship between women, public policy and economic outcomes. Chapter 7 concludes the book. The Appendix contains a brief *ad hoc* explanation of the methodological tools used in the analysis contained in the book.

2 | The Scenario
Gender Gaps in Education, the Labour Market and Politics

Despite the reduction in differences between men and women in several dimensions of social and economic life, gender gaps are still a widespread phenomenon in OECD countries. Even within Europe, the scenario is quite complex and heterogeneous across countries and areas of the continent: common features suggest that gender gaps are higher in Mediterranean countries, followed by continental and Anglo-Saxon countries, while they are lower in Nordic countries. However, it is difficult to identify general clusters.

In this chapter, I provide an overall scenario of the current situation of gender gaps in OECD countries by focusing on three dimensions: education, the labour market and politics. For each dimension, after providing the most interesting evidence, the chapter uses results from the recent literature to discuss the determinants of the observed gaps, which include both the nature and nurture drivers and their interactions. I will spend more time on data and information that are of interest in regard to the development of the next analysis in the book, that is, the interaction between the public and political aspects of the relationship between women and public policy.

2.1 Education

No disadvantages for women compared to men arise any longer in educational attainment and in college performance (Goldin et al., 2006) in developed countries. Data on European countries show that gender gaps in education have been reversed, and women are now more educated than men. Women have experienced enormous gains in educational achievement everywhere in Europe: since around the year 2000 in most European countries, the share of female university graduates has outnumbered the share of males. Figure 2.1 highlights this trend by showing the evolution of the female-to-male ratio of tertiary education graduates.

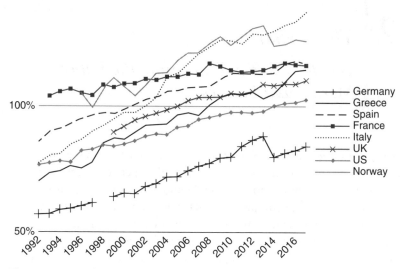

Figure 2.1 Female-to-male ratio of tertiary education graduates.
Source: Author's elaboration of OECD data, 2018.

Education is a powerful instrument to increase female labour market participation: in Europe, the employment rate for women graduates is approximately 80 per cent, while it is less than 40 per cent for women with primary or lower secondary education. Thus, there is a clear selection into employment, with more educated women more likely to be employed.[1]

The results on education do not imply that gender gaps are no longer an issue in the educational context. In fact, women still tend to prefer humanities and men scientific disciplines (Flabbi, 2012). The lowest percentages of female graduates are in the fields of engineering, manufacturing and construction and science, mathematics and computing. The scarcity of women in STEM (science, technology, engineering, mathematics) disciplines is considered a crucial dimension of current gender gaps. There is an urgent need to fill this gap, as these disciplines

---

[1] Interestingly, there may also be feedback effects from the labour market to education. In a paper with A. Casarico and C. Pronzato (Casarico et al., 2016), I show that across European countries, the number of working women with children aged younger than 5 and the share of women in managerial positions have an impact on the probability of girls enrolling in a university. In other words, by looking at other women, girls realize that there are more favourable contexts for mothers' occupation and women's careers, and they have more incentives to invest in education. The effect is null for men.

open better labour market opportunities and provide access to more rewarding jobs, leadership careers and empowerment. In fact, Altonjii et al. (2012) show that when considering the level of wages, the choice of major is as important as the choice of enrolling or not enrolling in graduate education. By comparing students near the admission thresholds for specific majors in Norwegian universities, Kirkeboen et al. (2017) show that the return on early income for business and engineering relative to humanities is substantial (on the order of $30,000 per year). Thus, part of the gender gap in the labour market may be accounted for by different college decisions (Blau and Kahn, 2017).

2.1.1 Why Are There Few Women in STEM Disciplines?

Research on the origins of gender gaps in educational fields is growing. Scholars have examined whether the choice of field is based on preferences, on abilities or on a context which does not favour the presence of women in scientific disciplines. It is very difficult to disentangle whether what we observe depends on nature, that is, biological differences between men and women, or on nurture, that is, the outcome of environmental influences, as the different factors interact and are difficult to isolate (Bertrand, 2011). The nature-based explanation derives from the different abilities of males and females, with males supposedly endowed with better mental flexibility and spatial skills (Gardner, 1983) that give them an advantage in geometry and math (Maloney and Beilock, 2012). In fact, gender disparities in math tests appear quite early. Across OECD countries, for example, the data of the Program for International Student Assessment (PISA) based on standardized tests of students aged 15 show that boys perform better than girls in mathematics in almost all countries, while girls perform better than boys in reading. These differences tend to be persistent over the life cycle: male students perform better than females in all standardized tests, such as the Scholastic Aptitude Test (SAT) and the Graduate Record Examination (GRE), particularly among high performers (Hedges and Nowell, 1995; Machin and Pekkarinen, 2008; Ellison and Swanson, 2009). The nurture-based explanation instead focuses on the role of culture and gender stereotypes that shape the environment in which students grow up and develop their abilities and their preferences: male and female students are perceived differently by teachers, parents and their own peers. Parents and teachers may influence the choice of majors by imposing gender-stereotyped specializations, that is, male-dominated majors (such as engineering) for boys and female-dominated majors (such as humanities) for girls. The stereotype that girls are not as good as boys at math becomes self-fulfilling, translates into preferences (Zafar, 2013) and induces girls to lose self-confidence. As a consequence, their performance in math worsens (Spencer et al., 1999), but their performance in the subjects in which they are expected to do better does not. The nurture-based explanation is supported by evidence that countries with more persistent stereotypes are associated with larger math gaps (Guiso et al., 2008; Hyde and Mertz, 2009; Pope and Sydnor, 2010; Reuben et al., 2014; Nollenberger et al., 2016). Isolating the role of stereotypes from that of innate abilities is difficult; thus, the puzzle between nature and nurture remains.

2.1.2 *Competitiveness and Risk Aversion*

The high level of competitiveness of math tests reinforces gender gaps in math (Niederle and Vesterlund, 2010; Jurajda and Munich, 2011; Ors et al., 2013), since men and women have different attitudes towards risk preferences and competition (see also Chapter 5 on that). A growing experimental literature suggests that women tend to perform worse in competitive environments and, as a consequence, to shy away from competition, whereas the performance of men may actually improve under such conditions (Gneezy et al., 2003; Gneezy and Rustichini, 2004; Niederle and Vesterlund, 2007). Coffman (2014) relates these different attitudes to gender gaps in math: according to her experimental study, female students do feel confident about competing in topics such as languages and arts, whereas male students are more at ease about competing in math and sports. Again, this may depend on their true ability and/or on cultural stereotypes. The ultimate consequence is that women self-select into other than mathematical fields, with consequences for their future careers and leadership outcomes. This is a quite general outcome: Bertrand et al. (2010) show that even among MBA students, women are less likely than men to take finance courses, which contributes to the gender gap in their lifetime earnings.

Where do gender differences in risk aversion and competitiveness come from? Again, it is difficult to disentangle nature from nurture. The differences in risk aversion may depend on the peer environment and composition of the class (Carrell et al., 2009; Carrell and Hoekstra, 2010): men increase their self-confidence in environments where they compete with other men, while women tend to become less confident under the pressure of competition with men (Bengtsson et al., 2005; Niederle and Vesterlund, 2011). Buser et al. (2014) find significant evidence that women choose mathematics-intensive and prestigious high school tracks less frequently than men in large part because they tend to shy away from highly competitive environments. This evidence, however, does not appear to apply to college choices: Reuben et al. (2017) find an impact of self-confidence on expected income but not on the choice of college major. Experimental evidence by Booth and Nolen (2012) and Booth et al. (2018) shows that while on average females are significantly less likely than males to make risky choices, those coming from a single-sex school behave similarly to males. This suggests that a part of the observed gender differences in risk aversion reflects social learning (nurture) rather than inherent gender traits (nature).

The peer environment matters. Using administrative data for Italian high schools, where students are randomly assigned to first-year classes, Anelli and Peri (2019) are able to identify the causal impact of the gender composition of peers on performance and choice of field study. They find no significant lasting effect of being exposed to a larger own-gender share of peers in high school on college major choice. Only male students graduating from classes with a very large majority of male peers (80 per cent or more) are more likely to choose 'prevalently male' college majors (economics, business and engineering). Classmates' gender has no effect on women's choices or on their academic performance in either the short or the long term, even when examining more extreme female-share classes (see also Stevenson, 2017). This is broadly consistent with some studies (Park et al., 2013) that found that same-gender environments in schools affect mainly male students (albeit in terms of academic performance) in the short term. Anelli and Peri (2019) argue that this differential effect may be due to boys forming a larger network when a large number of their peers are male compared to girls, who prefer smaller networks and are insensitive to a large number of females in their class (Stehlé et al., 2013). If peer networks affect choice through imitation and pressure, this may explain the differential effect of own-gender peers on choice for men and women.

The gender of siblings may also matter. Anelli and Peri (2015) consider families with at least two children ready to go to college.

They find that mixed-gender siblings are associated with a stronger gender-stereotypical specialization of males: boys with a sister are more likely to enrol in economics, business, medicine or engineering compared to those with only brothers. The effect is weaker and not significant for females. Same-gender siblings have a higher probability of making non-gender-stereotypical choices.

What policy implications can be drawn from these results? If nature is the dominant factor, very little can be done. However, as long as nurture plays a role, as research recognizes, many interventions can be effective in reducing gender gaps: they range from reducing time pressure during math exams or entry tests for college (Galasso and Profeta, 2018) to increasing single-sex schools, or at least entry groups (one class a week, for example), to enhance the confidence of women in targeted programmes for girls in STEM with the purpose of removing gender stereotypes.

2.1.3 Women in Science

Gender differences in educational fields are associated with the under-representation of women in science and research. A study from a decade ago by Ginther and Kahn (2009) in the United States, after providing evidence of the scarce presence of women in science, shows that having a child is a penalty for women in a scientific academic career, while it is an advantage for men.

In Europe, the situation of women in science resembles a 'leaky pipeline': according to the last 'She Figures' report of the European Commission (2015), women are on average more numerous than men among university students in all European countries, while they represent 47 per cent of PhD students, 45 per cent of assistant professors, 37 per cent of associate professors and only 21 per cent of full professors. The reduction in the share of women occurs for all disciplines, but it is stronger for science (only 8 per cent of full professors in engineering and technology are female). The report also shows a positive trend: a significant increase in the share of female professors, more than that of the male professors.

This positive trend needs to be monitored. A first alarm comes, for example, from the economics profession in the United States: the 2018 report by the American Economic Association (AEA) Committee on the Status of Women in the Academic Profession shows that the number of women in the academic economics profession is starting to decrease. How is it possible that women are increasingly present among students and researchers but are decreasing as a share of professors? This evidence seems to be at odds with the idea of a meritocratic academic selection process (see Chapter 5, Box 5.1). Moreover, the female voice in scientific disciplines matters. Regarding economics, female economists are more specialized than males in fields such as labour, education, family, gender and public policy: a higher presence of women could contribute to rebalancing the attention of policymakers, politicians and the economics field in general to these issues, which in turn are crucial to promoting gender equality. The scarce presence of women marginalizes these fields of study within the discipline. I will develop this line of argument in Chapter 4.

2.2 Labour Market

Employment rates by gender and over time show that the female employment rate has substantially increased in recent decades. In 2009, a famous cover of *The Economist* entitled 'We did it!' celebrated as a success the fact that women had reached 50 per cent of the labour force in the United States and the UK. However, there are still wide gender gaps. In contrast to education, the gender gaps in the labour market are still persistent. As shown in Figure 2.2, which highlights women's employment rate vis-à-vis that of men, large cross-country variations still dominate the picture, notwithstanding a remarkable improvement over time. Countries such as Italy and Greece lag far behind Scandinavian countries, which are persistently at the top of female employment rankings. Namely, Italy (in particular southern Italy) and Greece have not yet reached the Lisbon Agenda target, which recommended reaching a female employment rate of 60 per cent in all European countries by 2010. In contrast, Scandinavian countries have already met the new objective launched by the European agenda for 2020 of reaching an employment rate of 75 per cent for both men and women.

Mothers represent the most disadvantaged group of working women. Having a child represents a penalty for mothers in the labour market: female employment rates decrease with the presence of a child in all European countries. In some countries, the exit of women from the labour market after the birth of a child is often permanent: women do not return to the labour market when their children grow up. For

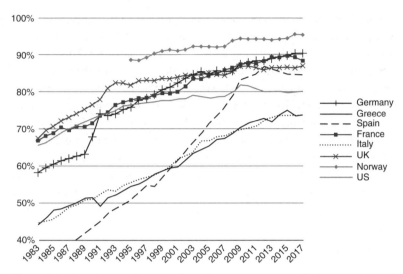

Figure 2.2 Female-to-male ratio of employment rates, populations aged 25–54.
Source: Author's elaboration of International Labour Organization (ILO) data,
2018.

working mothers, the penalty may be very high: mothers earn less than
non-mothers because of labour market interruptions, reduction in
working time and a shift to family-friendly jobs that are lower paid.
This motherhood gap increases as the number of children increases: in
Europe, it is substantial after the second and third child (see Grimshaw
and Rubery, 2015, for a review of the estimates of the motherhood
penalty).

When we investigate the quality of work, additional gender gaps
emerge. A fundamental one is the gender pay gap, which persists in
Europe. The raw gender pay gap provided by Eurostat shows an
average value difference of 16.2 per cent between male and female
wages in Europe. Italy has the lowest wage gap, while Estonia and
Austria show the highest wage gap. These raw data, however, must be
corrected for the selection effect, which may arise if fewer women work
and those who do earn a relatively higher average wage, as in the case of
Italy. In countries where less-educated women do not work, the average female salary corresponds to that of educated women, which is
typically higher and thus closer to the average male salary. Olivetti and
Petrongolo (2008) show that there is a negative correlation between

gender wage gaps and gender labour gaps: where the labour participation gap is higher, the gender wage gap is lower. They propose a correction of the gender wage gap for this selection effect. After this correction (Olivetti and Petrongolo, 2008), the gender pay gap in countries such as Italy is larger than the raw gender pay gap and is in line with the European average. In other words, a low gender pay gap does not necessarily mean a better result in terms of overall gender gaps in the labour market. Other studies have also shown that gender wage gaps increase with the number of children. Paull (2006) shows that in the UK, the wage gap jumps from 10 per cent to 33 per cent with the first child and continues to increase. For a sample of European countries, Davies and Pierre (2005) show that maternity is associated with a wage penalty that ranges between 2 per cent and 6 per cent for the first child and increases to up to 18 per cent when the third child is born.

A comprehensive study is provided by Kleven et al. (2019) who calculate the child penalty, that is, the impact of children on the labour market outcomes of women relative to men, in six European countries, using a uniform empirical approach, specification and sample selection. They consider two Scandinavian countries (Denmark and Sweden), two German-speaking countries (Germany and Austria) and two English-speaking countries (United Kingdom and United States). They analyze several labour market outcomes, including employment, hours worked and hourly wage. The study finds that child penalties emerge in all countries, although their magnitude is stronger in countries where gender norms are more traditional (see Section 2.2.3).

Other indicators of the quality of work are the number of temporary workers, among whom women have a higher presence than men in almost all European countries, and the share of women with part-time occupations. This share varies widely throughout Europe, from 2.5 per cent in Bulgaria to 75.4 per cent in the Netherlands. A large and increasing proportion of part-time work is involuntary, as suggested by the fact that in some countries, the share of middle-aged, part-time women is higher than that of mothers with young children.

The glass ceiling is a different phenomenon. Even in countries where the problem of access to the labour market for women has been substantially solved, women still encounter obstacles in careers and in reaching top positions. This is a fact in many fields. As reported during the Official Monetary and Financial Institutions Forum 2018, female representation in central banks is poor: worldwide, women represent

19 per cent of members of all key decision-making bodies, and the share increases to 21 per cent only when focusing on Europe. With respect to the judicial system, on the whole, it seems quite gender equal. However, the average hides fundamental differences that depend largely on the level of legal authority and keep women out of top positions. As of 2017, the Legal Affairs Committee of the European Parliament mapped representation by gender in legal professions across the European Union (EU) and reported that women represent 48 per cent of judges of courts of second instance, and the percentage decreases to 40 per cent and 36 per cent for court presidents and supreme court judges, respectively. I already mentioned the situation in the academic professions. Very few women are managers: the data in Figure 2.3(a), show that in all countries in 2016, women with a managerial position represent less than 10 per cent of the total number of females employed, and the gap between females and males is substantial in all countries. These values are quite stable over time or evolve very slowly.

The only exception is the presence of women on boards: Figure 2.3(b), shows the share of women on the boards of the largest publicly listed companies in Europe in 2003 and 2017. Several countries show a striking increase. Italy is the clearest example, being the country with the lowest share of women on boards in 2003 and among the top performers in 2017. It is an example of a substantial increase due to the introduction of mandatory corporate gender quotas. In Figure 2.3(c), I show the evolution of the share of women on the boards of Italian

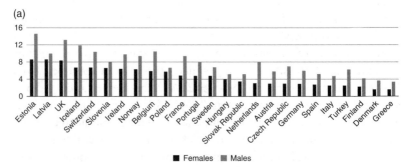

Figure 2.3 (a) Employed who are managers, by sex (%), 2016. (b) Women on boards of the largest publicly listed companies (%). (c) Women on corporate boards of Italian listed companies (%).
Source: Author's elaboration of OECD and Commissione Nazionale per le Società e la Borsa (CONSOB) data, 2018.

(b)

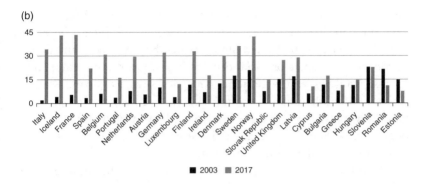

(c)

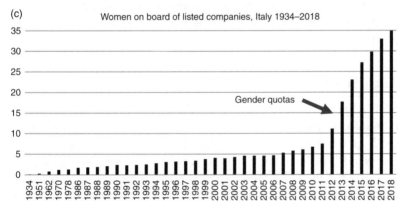

Figure 2.3 (cont.)

publicly listed companies from 1934 to 2018. While the evolution until 2010 was insignificant, in recent years, the share of women on boards has jumped from 6 per cent in 2010 to more than 30 per cent in 2018. This was possible as a result of the introduction of a gender quota law in 2011, to which I will return in Chapter 5.

Nevertheless, according to the *Egon Zehnder 2016 Global Board Diversity Analysis*, regional variation in the number of women in boardrooms is still present, and the report identifies three clusters of countries by level of board gender diversity attained. The cluster that has on average achieved the critical mass of three female board directors is labelled 'diversity champion'. In this cluster, there are countries of the Scandinavian regions, Canada and countries of Western Europe which have recently instituted ambitious quotas (as is the case for Italy). The second cluster contains regions where the number of women on boards ranges from two to one. These countries stagnate in bringing in more women; among them, the most notable laggard is the United States, which has not taken any direct action such as quotas or social benefits to support diversity in boardrooms. Ranking at the bottom, countries such as Japan, Russia, China and South American countries have been slow to progress in board diversity. In this group, women hold fewer than 10 per cent of board seats. Social, political and cultural challenges are the key determinants of that gender imbalance.

Why do women invest in education more than men but still lag in the labour market? Do gender gaps in the labour market depend on biological differences between men and women (nature) or on the environmental context shaped by culture (nurture)? Again, the answers are complex and not unique.

2.2.1 Maternity

Motherhood depends on nature, but the way motherhood is addressed in the labour market and society depends on nurture. Personality traits (such as risk love and power orientation) also differ by gender (see Chapter 5) and may contribute to explaining gender pay gaps, glass ceilings, and the lower presence of women in high-paying jobs or in highly competitive environments. However, it is unclear whether these traits depend on intrinsic differences between men and women or on cultural or historical components.

The traditional family was based on the principle of specialization (Becker, 1981): even though men and women are intrinsically identical, they gain from a division of labour between market and household activities. The traditional male breadwinner family model is characterized by an employed husband who provides economic resources and a wife who stays home and cares for the home and the children. This equilibrium arises because, according to specialization theory, men have a comparative advantage in working in the market and women in performing domestic and care work: it is a small but sufficient comparative advantage based on nature or biological characteristics to explain full specialization if there are no decreasing returns. When physical strength was a necessary attribute for working in the market, this was clearly what happened. However, economic development, technological innovations and the rise of the service sector have reduced the role of physical strength and thus the male comparative advantage in the market. Similarly, medical progress has reduced the risk of disease related to pregnancy and birth as well as the need for breastfeeding, thus reducing the comparative advantage of women in taking care of children. I will return to this argument in Chapter 6. Moreover, as long as women increase their investment in education, the opportunity costs of having children and renouncing the pursuit of a career increase, thus inducing an unavoidable evolution of the traditional model of the family.

There are still reasons why maternity – which differentiates men and women by nature – is proposed as a key determinant of gender gaps in the labour market. The evidence is quite complex. Maternity is indeed a penalty in the labour market. However, this is not due to women as mothers having specific inherent traits that enable them to work and have a career or limit their productivity at work. Rather, it is due to the influence of the environment. In fact, although there is still room for improvement, mothers' participation in the labour market has increased consistently over time in almost all countries. Moreover, in contrast to the past, and to the common intuition, there is no trade-off between fertility and female employment: starting in the mid-1980s, countries with high female employment rates also had high fertility rates (and vice versa).

A possible argument is that lower birth rates provide women with more time to fully participate in the formal labour market. However, this negative relationship between fertility and female labour force participation has been challenged by numerous studies (Del Boca and Locatelli, 2006), which argue that the gender revolution has led to the emergence of a new positive relationship in which working and having children go hand in hand (Engelhardt and Prskawetz, 2004). Working and earning her own income enlarge the set of possible choices for a woman, including the choice of having children. The literature has also stressed that this outcome emerges when the context in which the decisions are made, as shaped by normative, institutional, family and cultural variables, is favourable to the double role of women as workers and mothers. In particular, the availability of childcare services, a flexible labour market and a gender-equal intra-household division of family chores (Oppenheimer, 1994; Fuwa, 2004), in contrast to the within-household specialization theory formalized by Becker (1981), contribute to creating this positive association.

This positive relationship between fertility rate and female employment rate suggests that maternity *per se* cannot be responsible for gender gaps in the labour market. The context matters: in countries where policies support female employment and fertility (e.g. childcare and family policies; see Chapter 3), where the gender culture is favourable to the participation of women in the labour market and where men and women share childcare responsibilities, both the fertility rate and female employment are high. In contrast, countries where policies do not support the double role of women as mothers and workers and women bear the entire burden of family care are more likely to be trapped in an equilibrium that features low fertility and low female employment.

2.2.2 The Role of Men

Men play an important role in influencing women's participation in the labour market and thus in gender gaps. Gender equality at home can help women balance work and family, thus supporting women in working and pursuing their career ambitions.

Do fathers participate in childcare? Is the intra-household division of labour balanced? According to Burda et al. (2013), only in the rich non-Catholic European countries do men and women have the same amount of total work (at home and in the market); in the other countries, the total work of women is disproportionately larger than that of men. This burden on women contributes to their poor labour market outcomes.

In a recent paper with Fanelli (Fanelli and Profeta, 2019), we analyze the role of men in women's decisions to have children and work full time. Using longitudinal data from two successive waves of the Generations and Gender Survey, we show that higher fathers' involvement in housework and childcare (measured at the time of the first interview) – mainly fathers washing dishes and engaging in leisure activities with the children – increases the subsequent likelihood that the mother has a second child and works full time. We also show that fathers' involvement in housework is more important than fathers' involvement in childcare. We show that the effect is confirmed when we consider women who initially wanted a child and/or working women and when we consider women whose partner wants an additional child.

2.2.3 Culture

Culture matters: it plays a fundamental role in gender gaps in the labour market. Gender culture captures the view on women's and men's roles in society, on their responsibilities in the family and on their positions in the labour market (Pfau-Effinger, 2005). Gender culture depends on stereotypes that are well established among both men and women. They influence the extent to which men and women share the same responsibilities, in particular in domestic work and childcare, and in turn contribute to explaining gender gaps in the labour market.

Culture also matters when we assess the role of men: their attitudes and ideologies towards gender equality influence women's choices of working or not working. Moreover, consistency of gender equality in attitudes and in the actual division of housework (Aassve et al., 2015) within a couple has a positive impact on the probability that the woman works (Fanelli and Profeta, 2019).

Culture tends to be persistent, but it may also slowly change. Fogli and Veldkamp (2011) show that by observing nearby employed women of the previous generation, women may learn about the effects of maternal employment on children and realize that they can have both a job and a family at little (or no) cost to their children. As a result, they work more.

A growing strand of research uses survey data to measure attitudes and culture and to assess the influence of culture on gender gaps in employment (Fernández, 2007; Fernández and Fogli, 2009). The most explored sources of information are the World Value Survey and the European Value Survey for EU countries, which, among many others, contain questions for a representative sample of citizens in different countries to capture their attitudes towards gender roles and gender culture. Using factor analysis, I pooled survey data for a group of OECD countries to obtain a single index of 'gender culture'. Factor analysis is a mathematical technique that analyzes patterns of correlation between multiple 'indicator' variables (answers to the surveys) to infer their relationship to a third, unknown – and usually unknowable – variable, which in this case is the 'gender culture' variable, an index proxying citizens' attitudes towards gender roles and culture.

The survey questions under scrutiny are as follows:

- When jobs are scarce, men should have more right to a job than women.
- Men make better political leaders than women do.
- University is more important for a boy than for a girl.

- A preschool child suffers if the mother works.
- A job is the best way for women to be independent.
- Men make better business executives than women do.

The choice of the questions was not random: the Kaiser-Meyer-Olkin test, a measure of how well-suited data are for factor analysis, confirmed the sampling adequacy of the model. Each of these variables is indeed correlated with the others because there is a common correlation with the gender culture index. This pattern of correlation between the indicators is then used to determine the correlation coefficient between gender culture and the variables. Correlation coefficients are the weights used to create the index, which is an exact weighted linear combination of the scores from the indicators. The resulting gender culture, displayed in Figure 2.4, is an index scored from 0 to 3.5: the higher the value, the more gender equal and less role stereotyped the country is. Once again, we observe that the Scandinavian countries score high, as opposed to more culturally conservative countries such as Italy, Romania and Turkey.

Regarding intra-household decisions, although assortative mating is not directly related to the concept of culture, it is important to mention its role: many scholars have shown an increase in assortative mating, that is, educated women marrying educated men. The literature has shown that education gives women an advantage in the intra-household allocation of jobs: when education translates into a career, it shapes women's identity, which contributes to their position not only

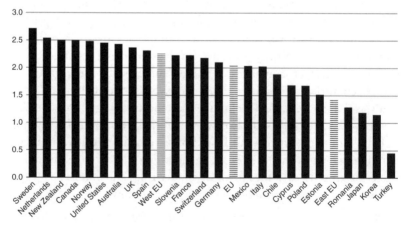

Figure 2.4 Gender culture score.
Source: Author's elaboration of World Value Survey data, 2010–2014.

in the labour market but also in the family (Chiappori et al., 2018). Investing in education may have returns that are not limited to labour market outcomes but also include the private sphere and bargaining power within the couple. This may in part explain why women's investments in education are larger than their labour market outcomes.

An extreme consequence of intra-household gender inequality is domestic violence against women, which I analyse in Box 2.1.

Box 2.1 Attitudes towards domestic violence

Eurobarometer surveys conducted in 2010 and 2016 measure perceptions of domestic violence against women across European countries. Both surveys contain questions related to the perception of the diffusion of domestic violence, its acceptability and its existence among both men and women close to the respondent.

Table 2.1 shows the results of the elaboration of the answers to the following questions, respectively labelled 'Perception', 'Acceptability' and 'Knowledge', for countries in Western and Eastern Europe:

- How common do respondents think domestic violence is in their country? The possible answers are 'very common', 'fairly common', 'not very common' and 'not at all common'. I pool the first two possible answers and show the percentage of people who think it is very common or fairly common.
- When do respondents think domestic violence is acceptable? The possible answers are 'acceptable in all circumstances', 'acceptable in some circumstances', 'unacceptable, but should not always be punished by the law' and 'unacceptable and should always be punished by the law'. I pool the first two options and show the percentage of people who think it is acceptable in all or some circumstances.
- Do respondents know a victim of domestic violence among family and relatives, immediate neighbours, or where they work or study? I show the percentage of people who declare they know of at least one case.

At the aggregate level, the trends show a slight decline in all three variables over the course of the six years for both men and women.

However, the phenomenon appears to still be consistent. Moreover, when comparing Eastern and Western European countries, we observe a reversing trend in the perception of the phenomenon from 2010 to 2016. In the more recent survey, Eastern European residents perceived the phenomenon more than their Western counterparts, and an increasing number of male respondents from the Eastern bloc claimed that they personally knew at least one victim of domestic violence. Nevertheless, as the surveys deal with self-reported information, caution should be exercised in interpreting the data. Indeed, the surveys may not necessarily indicate an increase in domestic violence over time in Eastern Europe but rather an increased consciousness of the phenomenon and a shift in the reference value of what can be regarded as an act of domestic abuse. As these measures of domestic violence are inherently subjective, they also capture attitudes towards domestic violence that may well differ from country to country. Indeed, and most strikingly, such differences are supported by the fact that Eastern women are persistently more prone to accept domestic violence than Western women are.

Table 2.1 *Perception, acceptability and knowledge of domestic violence*

	Perception				Acceptability				Knowledge			
	Men		Women		Men		Women		Men		Women	
	2010	2016	2010	2016	2010	2016	2010	2016	2010	2016	2010	2016
AT	54,8	63,4	69,6	75,2	4,4	5,8	3,0	3,4	27,0	24,4	38,4	30,8
BE	71,4	59,6	83,0	71,4	6,0	2,8	4,2	1,8	41,4	33,8	51,6	42,8
BG	46,2	41,8	63,4	59,0	2,6	2,6	1,0	1,4	21,4	19,2	34,4	37,0
CY	60,4	59,2	76,8	80,2	2,0	1,2	1,2	0,8	44,8	37,8	48,8	45,6
CZ	41,4	41,2	59,0	60,2	4,6	2,8	3,6	2,4	23,6	23,0	32,0	31,0
DE	54,8	60,4	72,4	72,8	2,2	1,8	0,8	1,0	23,8	26,8	29,6	33,8
DK	66,4	51,2	79,0	72,2	1,0	1,6	0,2	0,6	43,8	41,0	53,6	48,6
EE	52,6	49,6	78,8	72,8	3,4	2,2	3,2	0,8	46,4	29,2	56,6	44,8
ES	74,6	78,8	84,4	93,0	3,6	0,8	2,2	0,2	29,2	29,2	37,2	35,4
FI	68,4	53,0	80,2	68,2	0,6	1,6	1,2	0,6	41,4	35,2	57,0	50,2
FR	86,0	72,8	92,6	85,2	1,4	2,2	0,6	0,6	31,0	21,2	41,4	34,8
GR	66,4	57,2	82,8	79,2	1,8	2,0	2,4	1,2	35,8	27,0	48,6	39,8
HU	67,4	66,6	82,2	77,4	3,4	2,8	2,0	4,0	33,6	20,2	41,0	25,0
IE	67,0	73,0	85,6	84,4	1,8	2,4	1,4	1,2	29,2	31,4	47,0	41,2

Table 2.1 (*cont.*)

	Perception				Acceptability				Knowledge			
	Men		Women		Men		Women		Men		Women	
	2010	2016	2010	2016	2010	2016	2010	2016	2010	2016	2010	2016
IT	89,0	88,4	93,4	91,4	6,2	3,6	4,8	3,0	23,4	17,4	28,8	22,0
LT	68,4	73,8	90,0	91,0	4,4	4,0	2,6	2,2	51,0	35,8	68,2	50,0
LU	61,2	52,4	72,8	68,0	1,2	2,2	2,6	2,8	37,6	26,8	46,6	39,0
LV	60,4	40,6	83,0	74,2	3,8	3,0	3,4	2,0	49,4	37,8	65,8	55,6
MT	71,6	77,6	83,6	87,2	2,6	0,4	1,6	0,4	37,8	32,0	40,4	34,2
NL	73,2	67,4	87,4	84,8	0,2	0,6	0,8	1,4	45,4	42,0	57,8	56,6
PL	57,2	48,6	73,8	60,4	4,4	8,8	3,2	5,4	37,2	27,6	53,0	40,4
PT	84,8	91,2	87,8	94,0	3,8	1,4	5,4	1,6	30,0	20,4	36,8	30,8
RO	81,6	81,2	86,4	88,4	7,8	6,0	4,6	5,0	35,2	31,0	45,6	37,4
SE	64,4	62,6	84,8	81,6	1,2	0,4	1,6	0,2	44,6	48,2	64,0	64,4
SI	75,4	60,0	88,6	79,6	1,8	2,0	1,8	2,2	40,4	29,4	52,0	33,2
SK	73,8	56,8	83,6	68,8	5,2	6,8	5,2	4,0	30,6	26,6	46,8	30,0
UK	81,8	73,6	91,8	90,0	0,8	1,6	1,2	1,4	37,6	35,0	49,6	46,2

AVERAGE

	Men		Women		Men		Women		Men		Women	
	2010	2016	2010	2016	2010	2016	2010	2016	2010	2016	2010	2016
EU	67,4	63,0	81,4	78,2	3,0	2,7	2,4	1,9	36,0	30,0	47,1	40,0
WEST	70,4	67,2	82,8	81,1	2,4	1,9	2,1	1,3	35,5	31,2	45,7	41,0
EAST	69,4	68,6	82,4	82,0	2,4	1,9	2,3	1,4	34,5	31,4	44,7	40,1

Notes: The numbers represent the percentage of people, grouped by sex and country, who think domestic violence is *very* or *fairly common* in their country (PERCEPTION), acceptable in *all* or *some circumstances* (ACCEPTABILITY), and who declared to know at least one victim of domestic violence among family and relatives, immediate neighbours or where they work or study (KNOWLEDGE).

2.2.4 History

Gender gaps have historical roots. These roots can be traced back to the organization of the family and to traditional agricultural practices in the pre-industrial period, which influenced the gender division of labour, the role of women and the evolution and persistence of gender norms.

A seminal work by Boserup (1970) argues that differences in the role of women in societies are the consequences of different types of agricultural practices, mainly between shifting agriculture and plough agriculture. The first type uses tools such as the hoe and digging stick, while the second uses the plough. The plough requires physical strength and is not compatible with simultaneous childcare. Thus, in plough agriculture, men tend to specialize in agricultural work outside the home, while women specialize in activities within the home. This division of labour generates different norms and cultural beliefs about the role of women in society, which tend to persist. As summarized by Giuliano (2015), Alesina et al. (2013) show that this traditional agricultural practice affects the present-day participation of women in the economy through the transmission of culture.

Historical factors also matter for education gender gaps. Bertocchi and Bozzano (2015) show that the family structure – nuclear versus non-nuclear families – and the inheritance rule – the partition of inheritance versus primogeniture – explain part of the education gender gap in Italy during the period 1861–1901: after controlling for economic, institutional, religious and cultural factors, nuclear families characterized by equal partition of inheritance have a higher female-to-male enrolment rate ratio in upper primary schools.

2.2.5 Demand Side and the Notion of Discrimination

Firms' decisions and employers' attitudes and beliefs, that is, labour demand, are as important as individuals' incentives and choices in determining the gender composition of the workforce, female careers and the overall outcomes of gender gaps. Decades of research have shown that we should be careful in assuming discrimination when we observe gender wage gaps. We first need to take into account all observable factors that contribute to wage differences between men and women, such as education, experience, human capital accumulation, type of job and industry of occupation. Preferences of individuals for specific jobs also matter. For example, if men prefer jobs that are considered 'unpleasant' by women (because of time constraints, physical conditions of work, etc.), they need to be compensated with a higher wage (Filer, 1985). The institutional context also matters, for example, the way wages are set or the existence of a minimum wage. Only the residual difference, after accounting for all these factors, can be considered discrimination. However, the residual difference exists and is estimated to still be significant in European countries.

At least three types of discrimination exist (Eswaran, 2014): first, taste discrimination arises when employers prefer not to hire or promote women even if they are equally productive as men because they have a prejudice against women (Becker, 1957). However, in a perfectly competitive market, this type of discrimination will not survive: firms that use only male labour will incur higher costs (male wages are higher than female wages in equilibrium) than those that also use female labour; thus, they will exit the market.

Second, statistical discrimination arises when employers do not have full information about an individual's relevant work characteristics and use group statistics as a proxy. They may make errors in evaluating some individuals, but on average, these errors will cancel each other out. Statistical discrimination against women is easy to understand: if employers do not have information about the work value of the woman they have to evaluate, they attribute average characteristics to her. If they expect women to devote more time and effort than men to household and childcare activities – as is reasonable because it is what happens in reality – they will have more incentives to hire men, promote men and pay men more than women. In other words, being a woman may be a signal of lower effort and lower productivity than being a man. Thus, employers who are not adverse to women *per se*, because of their nature or characteristics, think that by hiring or promoting a woman, they will obtain, on average, a lower profit than by hiring or promoting a man (de la Rica et al., 2013). This generates gender pay gaps. At this point, within a couple, the woman will have fewer career opportunities and will earn a lower wage than a man. Thus, it will be more convenient for the couple to invest in the man's career and leave the woman responsible for care and household activities. The initial equilibrium becomes self-fulfilling and becomes a trap for women. Overall, on average, the incentives for women to invest in their careers will dramatically decrease.

The third type of discrimination is screening discrimination: the selection process itself is typically not gender neutral since employers are less able to evaluate the ability of workers from one group than from another (Aigner and Cain, 1977; Lundberg and Startz, 1983; see a review in Altonji and Blanck, 1999; on non-neutrality in the selection process, see also Chapter 5, Box 5.1). Research suggests the existence of a homo-accuracy bias; that is, males (females) more accurately evaluate males (females) (see Conde Ruiz et al., 2017). Cornell and Welch (1996) show that even when employers do not have preferences for people similar to themselves, they favour the promotion of people of the same type since they can better judge job applicants' unknown qualities when the candidates belong to the same group. In other words, they can better distinguish good and bad individuals in a population of similar people. As a consequence, the measurement error for a given evaluator is smaller when the considered people have a similar cultural background. Bagues and Perez-Villadoniga (2012) show that in a multidimensional framework of statistical discrimination where the accuracy of the evaluators depends on how knowledgeable they are in each dimension, candidates who excel in the same dimensions as the evaluator tend to be preferred. Evaluators can assess knowledge more accurately in those dimensions where they are more knowledgeable and thus will consider the signals in these dimensions more important. Lavy (2008) compares data on blind and non-blind scores that high school students receive on matriculation exams in their senior year in Israel and finds that the grades obtained in non-blind tests are sensitive to the characteristics of the evaluators. In the context of gender, Pinkston (2003) finds strong evidence that employers receive less accurate initial signals from women than from men, even when comparing men and women in the same job. The accuracy of evaluating candidates of a different gender may depend on the existence of gender-segregated networks, gender-segregated tasks in jobs or gender stereotypes. Although Bagues et al. (2017) find no evidence that these mechanisms are in action in the specific contexts of promotions in academia, the mechanisms may still be crucial in evaluations affected by unconscious bias towards unobservable dimensions of productivity. Accuracy may also depend on differences in language, communication style and perception that make it easier for a person to evaluate the personal skills and attitudes of people of the same gender as themselves and to believe that these characteristics are relevant for the position (Lang, 1986). This concept has been studied by a large sociolinguistic literature: differences in verbal and nonverbal communication style between groups of different races or genders may affect economic and social outcomes (Dindia and Canary, 2006; Scollon et al., 2011).

2.2.6 Public Policy

Finally, as I have already mentioned, public policies play a relevant role in explaining gender gaps and thus, potentially, in reducing them. If nurture matters, even considering biological differences, then policy interventions are important. Family policies, parental leave and formal childcare provisions may help support the female labour supply, while gender quotas may be useful in reducing the glass ceiling. The effectiveness of these policies in addressing gender gaps and how they are influenced by the presence of women as powerful decision makers will be investigated in depth in Chapters 3 and 4.

2.3 Politics

Women's representation in politics has remained scarce in many countries, although it shows an increasing trend. Figure 2.5 shows women's participation at the ministerial level across Europe: only Sweden and France have more female than male ministers, with a share slightly above 50 per cent. Regional heterogeneity characterizes the map, with northern countries ranking higher in terms of female representation. At the world level, no country has yet reached parity in a national parliament; at lower levels of government, the situation is no better, although

Figure 2.5 Share of female ministers, 2017.
Source: Author's elaboration of OECD data, 2018.

in some countries, there are specific affirmative action measures for increasing female participation in local politics.

2.3.1 Demand and Supply

The underrepresentation of women in politics is the result of both supply and demand: on the one hand, it depends on women's preferences and choices; on the other hand, it depends on the obstacles that they encounter in the process of political recruitment (Norris and Lovenduski, 1995). For education and the labour market, it is difficult to understand whether preferences and obstacles depend on the innate characteristics of women, which are not aligned with what is needed in the political arena, or on circumstances created by the political context. What we observe is the interaction of these components. In addition to demand and supply, another factor may explain the underrepresentation of women in politics: voters may be biased and not disposed to vote for women (Black and Erickson, 2003; Schwindt-Bayer et al., 2010). To what extent these preferences are intrinsic or are modifiable by the institutions is, again, an open question. Recent evidence seems to support the second factor (Baltrunaite et al., 2017).

Examining the supply side in more depth, scholars have argued that women may not be willing to compete or may not be interested in competing for political seats, for instance, due to time constraints associated with childcare duties (e.g. Schlozman et al., 1994) or due to their lack of self-confidence (Fox and Lawless, 2004) and competition aversion, which I have already mentioned. Women are 'election averse' because they are 'sensitive to the details of the selection process, whereas men are not' (Kanthak and Woon, 2015, 609) and because they expect that society at large and the media will not treat them as they treat their male counterparts (Kahn, 1992, 1994). In line with a general trait that differentiates men and women (see Chapter 5), women politicians also tend to be less conflictual than men and more risk averse. Similarly, women also tend to dislike personal exposure (Profeta and Woodhouse, 2018), which is fundamental in political races, especially in majoritarian systems.

In Chapter 4, I provide evidence in this direction based on the Comparative Candidate Survey data which covers candidates running for national parliamentary elections in different countries in the period 2005–2013. I estimate that women are significantly more likely than men to follow a party position when there is a conflict between the politician position and the party position and that women are less likely than men to run again in national elections after having lost an election (see Chapter 4).

On the demand side, parties, in their role as gatekeepers, may not put women forward as candidates (e.g. Kunovich and Paxton, 2005). This in turn depends on the level of political culture (Norris, 1985; Rule, 1987; Kenworthy and Malami, 1999; Reynolds, 1999; Norris and Inglehart, 2001; Yoon, 2004) and on the party ideology: left-wing and more environmentally conscious parties have been found to nominate more female candidates (Caul, 1999; Paxton and Kunovich, 2003; Kittilson, 2006).

2.3.2 The Context Matters

The context matters for both supply and demand: according to Julio and Tavares (2017), if the returns from political offices are higher, more high-quality women run for office. Low returns on the political market for women explain their absence from politics. Others have emphasized that women's likelihood of participating in politics is higher where female labour force participation is also higher (Norris, 1985; Rule, 1987; Matland, 1998). This is particularly true for professional, administrative and managerial occupations that commonly lead to political careers (Norris, 1985, 1987; Rule, 1987, 1988; Darcy et al. 1994). Moreover, given their risk aversion, women will be more ready to run in safe positions in which their chances of being elected are higher. Electoral rules matter: if the proportional system provides a higher number of safe seats for women, then they will run more often and have more chances of being elected than in majoritarian systems (Matland, 1993; Norris, 2006; Profeta and Woodhouse, 2018). In parallel, since the identity of the candidate is less relevant than in majoritarian systems, in proportional systems, parties have less incentive to choose the strongest candidate with high experience, who is more likely an incumbent (Norris, 1985, 2006). These arguments support the fact that typically more women are elected in proportional than in majoritarian systems. In addition to the electoral system, greater levels of party competition, measured in the number of parties, are found to increase the number of female candidates while not necessarily translating into higher rates of election (Inglehart and Norris, 2003).

The presence of targeted policy interventions such as gender quotas also matters (Krook, 2010; Krook and Mackay, 2011;

Freidenvall and Dahlerup, 2013): although the general effects of such interventions are under scrutiny (see Chapters 4 and 5), they have been shown to be effective in increasing female representation (De Paola et al., 2010; Casas-Arce and Saiz, 2015; Bagues and Campa, 2018).

An overall picture of political careers of women is presented in Box 2.2 for the Italian case.

Box 2.2 Women in political careers

Evidence on women in politics generally shows that they are under-represented compared to men at all levels and that they are more represented in local politics than at the national level. This seems, again, to support the evidence that a career for women in politics is difficult. To provide evidence in this direction, it is necessary to concentrate on a single country and understand the evolution of women's representation in politics over time and across levels of government. Some European countries are more interesting to investigate than others: where gender gaps are wide and obstacles to women's careers appear in several areas of the labour market, a stimulating question is whether political careers follow a similar pattern and whether the male and female patterns are different. Italy is one of these interesting countries.

The Italian Parliament is composed of the House and the Senate. The subnational levels of government are regional, provincial and municipal. In a recent paper with Woodhouse (Profeta and Woodhouse, 2018), we collect data for the universe of Italian politicians from all levels of government over the period 1987–2013. These data deliver a complete picture of the career paths of male and female politicians across the entire arc of their careers. Women are increasing at all levels of government: the number increased from 11 per cent of members of the Parliament in 1987 to 26 per cent in 2013, while the percentages for members of municipal councils were 7 per cent and 21 per cent, at the provincial level 7 per cent and 16 per cent and at the regional level 8 per cent and 17 per cent, respectively. The increase is not only numerical: elected women also show high quality when this is proxied by the level of education. At all subnational levels of government

---

(municipal, regional and provincial) and for the entire period under investigation, elected women were more educated than elected men. This is less clear for the national politicians, where the level of education was similar.

Despite having a higher level of education, women encountered more obstacles in their political careers. The share of women who were re-elected ranged from 20 per cent to 40 per cent over the considered period, while the corresponding numbers for men were 30 per cent and 60 per cent. Fewer than 3 per cent of women moved up to a superior level of government, while 5 per cent of men did so. The obstacles may also explain why elected women had less experience than men: women elected to the Parliament had on average over the entire period 4.33 years of subnational experience, while men had 5.73 years. Women were also significantly more represented than men in the category of 'parachuters' – politicians elected at the national level with no previous political experience.

Instead of being a positive signal, and in contrast to what was observed for men, subnational experience for women was itself an obstacle to their career: for example, in the 2013 national elections, elected women had, on average, 5.15 years of subnational experience (compared to 6.97 years for men), but non-elected women had, on average, 5.4 years of experience (compared to 6.55 years for men). Similarly, the level of education of non-elected women was higher than that of elected women, while for men, it was the opposite. In other words, a political career is more difficult for a woman than for a man, and part of the observed increase of women in the national Parliament was due to the election of parachuters, while female candidates with more experience and higher education remained outside the top level of politics. Good female candidates are still waiting for their turn.

2.4 Conclusions

This chapter has presented a long journey into gender gaps, starting from education and including the labour market and politics. The analysis has emphasized that in all contexts, there is no unique determinant of gender gaps, as they emerge as a result of complex interactions between innate traits (nature) and influential contexts (nurture) or are even historically determined, which shapes both women's preferences and choices (the supply side) and the recruitment and career process (the demand side). A crucial role is played by incentives: the context matters in terms of providing the right incentives for women to invest in their education and professional career.

The chapter has also drawn some initial policy implications for each dimension by referring to public policy and measures aimed at dealing with the obstacles and accelerating progress towards gender equality. This introduces our core analysis in Chapters 3, 4 and 5.

3 | From Public Policy to Gender Equality
Theory and Evidence

Public policies are important in promoting gender equality. Family policies, parental leave and formal childcare provisions may help support the female labour supply, while gender quotas may be useful in reducing the glass ceiling. Other provisions in the labour market, such as part-time and new forms of job flexibility in time and space, have also proved to play a relevant role. This chapter explores how these policies are effective in addressing gender gaps. As explained in Chapter 1, I refer to this side of the analysis as the *public economics* side: the impact of government intervention through specific policies on gender gaps is analyzed as a specific economic outcome.

I concentrate on the relationship between public policy and gender equality, taking into account how difficult it is to identify the effects of the presence of public policy and its impact on gender equality. I start from family policy and then move to taxation, to measures in the labour market and finally to pensions.

Family policies have been introduced in developed countries since the nineteenth century. They include support for maternity and childcare. As effectively reviewed by Olivetti and Petrongolo (2017), countries have first introduced support for maternity (mainly maternity and parental leave) and then childcare provisions. These policies have been shown to play a role in the promotion of female employment and the reduction in gender gaps in the labour market.

In this chapter, I present the theoretical arguments behind the relationship between family policies and gender gaps in the labour market. Then, I review the results of the empirical literature and provide new evidence in support of the different arguments. To this end, I assemble a dataset from OECD statistics that contains information on family policies for thirty-five OECD countries over the period 1970–2016. The dataset also contains OECD data on female employment (aged 15–65), employment gap (male minus female), employment of mothers with children aged younger than 14 and employment of mothers with small children (aged 0–2). The OECD data are complemented by more detailed institutional information about family policies in Europe based on Eurostat. The figures present evidence for the latest available year. Regression analysis then establishes whether family policies play a role in explaining female employment and in what direction.

3.1 Maternity, Parental and Paternity Leave

There are three types of leave when a child is born: maternity leave, parental leave and paternity leave. Maternity leave for employed women occurs around the time of childbirth (both during late pregnancy and after birth, depending on the country's legislation) or adoption during which they do not work. The length and generosity of the payment vary across countries, but it is typically substantial, funded by the social insurance system and covered by employee and employer social security contributions. Parental leave is an extended period of leave for working parents after childbirth, which can be enjoyed either by the mother *or* by the father and is typically paid as a percentage of the wage of the worker who takes the leave. Since women's wages are mostly lower than men's wages (see Chapter 2), parental leave is typically taken by women to maximize the income of the household. Finally, paternity leave is an exclusive period for fathers at childbirth: it is typically limited to a period of days or a few weeks and is fully paid. In some countries, maternity and paternity leave are mandatory; in others, they are a choice of the workers.

Figure 3.1 summarizes the main characteristics of maternity and paternity leave in Europe. It clearly shows how limited the periods of paternity leave are throughout Europe, while the periods of maternity leave are quite generous, though with some differences.

Maternity leave, parental leave and paternity leave are introduced to support women's employment when children are present, to rebalance the care burden of children between fathers and mothers (as the burden typically falls mostly on the mothers) and thus to support female participation in the labour market.

Theoretically, it is unclear whether longer and/or more generous maternity and parental leaves would support female employment: on the one hand, the leave allows women to stay in the labour market despite the temporary interruption of work, to keep their attachment to

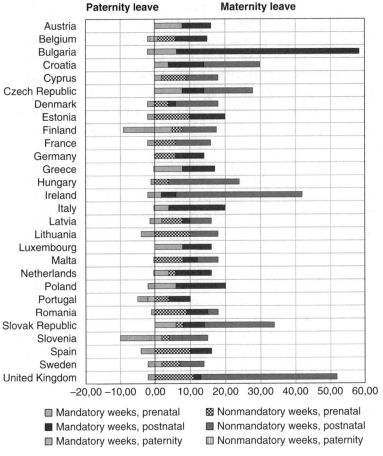

Figure 3.1 Paternity/maternity leave, weeks granted.
Source: Author's elaboration of Eurostat data, 2017.

work and to continue working. On the other hand, the leave may induce women to stay out of work for a long period; consequently, an effective re-entry to employment becomes more difficult, and their career prospects may be negatively affected. In a perfectly competitive labour market, generous leave periods may also induce an increase in wage gender gaps via a reduction in female wages. If wages are fixed by law, then we expect a decrease in female labour demand, which reduces female employment. Moreover, very generous policies may reinforce employers' expectations of women's specialization at home and in childcare, thus reinforcing statistical discrimination (see Chapter 2) and ultimately backfiring against gender equality.

Which effect dominates is thus an empirical issue. Cross-country evidence delivers a first answer to this question. Figure 3.2(a) shows a negative cross-country relationship between the gender gap in employment rates (individuals aged 25–54) and the maximum weeks of job-protected leave available to mothers. This means that in countries where maternity is more protected, the gender gap is lower, and women work more. Similarly, there is a positive relationship between the maximum weeks of job-protected leave available for mothers and female employment. However, this cross-country relationship disappears if, instead of the gender gap in employment, employment rate of mothers with a child aged 0–14 is considered (Figure 3.2(b)). This suggests that generous maternity leave is associated with neither higher nor lower employment of mothers. Interestingly, Figure 3.2(c) shows that if we concentrate only on mothers with small children (aged 0–2), the relationship even becomes negative; a generous maternity leave is associated with lower employment of mothers who are the beneficiaries of these leave policies.

Figure 3.2(d) shows that in contrast, the share of total paid leave available to fathers (as a percentage of the total paid leave for both parents) is weakly positively related to the employment rates of

(a)

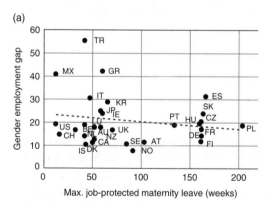

Max. job-protected maternity leave (weeks)

Figure 3.2 (a) Maternity leave and gender employment gap. (b) Maternity leave and mothers' employment, child aged 0–14. (c) Maternity leave and mothers' employment, child aged 0–2. (d) Paternity leave and mothers' employment, child aged 0–2.
Source: Author's elaboration of OECD data, 2018.

(b)

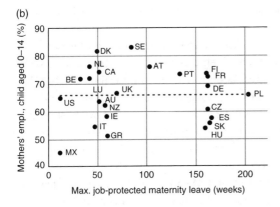

(c)

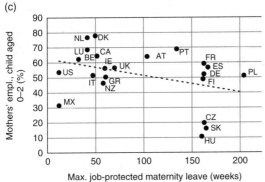

(d)

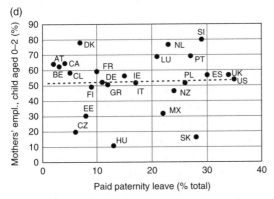

Figure 3.2 (cont.)

mothers with small children. These relationships suggest that sharing leave between mothers and fathers may play a positive role in women's employment. It is important to specify that paternity leave must be exclusive; it is lost if the father does not take it and cannot be given to the mother.

To better investigate the relationship between periods of leave, their length and generosity and female employment, I perform a regression analysis using data for OECD countries in the period 1970–2015. Table 3.1(a) presents OLS estimations at the country level for OECD countries using country and year fixed effects and with standard errors clustered at the country level. In this way, we concentrate on within-country variations. Column 1 shows that the number of maximum weeks of job-protected leave has a hump-shaped relationship with female employment rate (aged 25–54): a higher period of leave is associated with higher female employment up to a certain level, after which a further increase of the period of leave is related to lower female employment. The result is confirmed when I control for the payment – the percentage of total leave that is paid and the average payment rate (column 2). The two variables that capture the payment are, however, negatively related to female employment rate: a higher level of generosity does not seem to produce good results for female employment. Similar results apply when I consider the gender employment gap (difference in the male and female employment rate as a percentage) rather than the female employment rate (columns 4 and 5). The results are consistent, though less clear, when I consider the wage gap, that is, the difference between the median earnings of men and women relative to the median earnings of men (column 6; see also column 4 from panel b).

Several previous studies have found similar cross-country evidence. Most of them concentrate on maternity and parental leave: Ruhm (1998) and, more recently, Olivetti and Petrongolo (2017) find a similar nonlinear relationship between maternity (number of weeks of total paid leave available to mothers) and parental leave and female employment, with female employment increasing up to approximately fifty weeks of leave and then declining. Blau and Kahn (2013) find a positive relationship between parental leave and female employment and a negative relationship with the gender gap in employment. The relationship with wages is less clear and often not significant. Micro evidence for specific countries shows mixed results: Lalive and Zweimüller (2009) show that the extension of parental leave in Austria delays the return to work of mothers and reduces female employment for the first three years after birth, while it has a positive effect on fertility. Schönberg and Ludsteck (2014) find no effect on female employment of the extension of maternity leave coverage in Germany during the 1990s, while the 2007 reform increased female employment (Kluve and Tamm, 2013) and fertility (Raute, 2017). No impact on the female labour supply in the long term resulted in Norway after the expansion of maternity leave in 1992 (Dahl et al., 2016).

Paternity leave is a relatively new policy. Apart from graphical insights, it is still difficult to assess its impact on female employment due to a lack of research and data. As shown in Figure 3.1, only a few countries have a non-negligible period of paternity leave, thus making a similar analysis impossible. Parental leave, however, seems a promising policy for at least two reasons: it reduces the relative specialization of women in caring for children and thus can contrast with statistical discrimination, and it promotes equality between men and women in the household, which, as explained in Section 2.2.3, may result in a positive impact on gender equality in the labour market.

3.2 Childcare

The other group of policies relevant to reducing gender gaps is childcare. I refer here to public expenditures for childcare (early childhood and preschool education and care as a percentage of GDP); in the next section, I discuss tax provisions related to childcare.

As reported in Figure 3.3, across OECD countries, childcare expenditure as a percentage of GDP is negatively associated with the gender gap in employment (Figure 3.3(a)) and positively associated with the employment of mothers with children aged 0–14 (Figure 3.3(b)). A similar positive relationship emerges if I consider the female employment rate. In other words, when the expenditure on childcare is higher, women work more. Interestingly, as shown in Figure 3.3(c), the relationship is U-shaped when I consider mothers with small children (aged 0–2): in countries where childcare expenditure is low or high, mothers with small children work more than in countries with moderate expenditure. The results are similar if I consider public expenditure on families instead of childcare expenditure.

The nonlinearity of childcare policies that emerges when I consider the employment of mothers with small children deserves better investigation. Do working mothers with small children need more than the

(a)

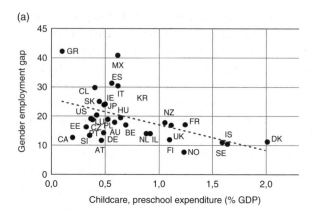

(b)

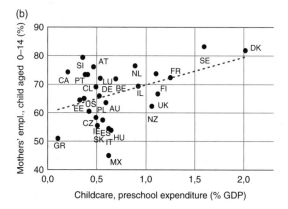

(c)

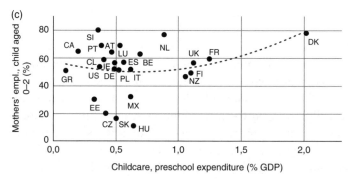

Figure 3.3 (a) Childcare/preschool expenditure and gender employment gap. (b) Childcare/preschool expenditure and mothers' employment, child aged 0–14. (c) Childcare/preschool expenditure and mothers' employment, child aged 0–2. Source: Author's elaboration of OECD data, 2018.

current childcare expenditure? Do they use different childcare provisions when the public expenditure is too low? Theoretically, this evidence resembles the case of 'no single-peaked preferences' in public good provision: a moderate public expenditure in childcare can represent a trap for many mothers, as it is not high enough to induce them to work but not low enough to incentivize the use of private alternatives. Countries such as Italy seem to be 'trapped' in this situation. Obviously, this simple graph does not allow any inference about the causes and consequences of the relationship between working mothers and childcare policies. The trade-off, again, must be empirically documented.

The regression analysis in Table 3.1(a) is expanded to include the role of childcare expenditure (column 5 from Table 3.1(a), columns 1, 2, 3, 5, 6 from Table 3.1(b)). I perform a regression analysis similar to the previous one. Table 3.1(b) shows that childcare expenditure is positively associated with female employment rate (column 1) and negatively associated with the gender gap in employment (column 3). When leave and childcare variables are considered together, the results are in line with our expectations (columns 2 and 5 from Table 3.1(a)).

A growing body of research assesses how early childcare is an important policy in supporting maternal employment and promoting child development. In addition to cross-country evidence, micro evidence confirms that the expenditure on early childcare is positively correlated with female employment. For the United States, small effects – mainly among low-skilled women – are found by Cascio and Schanzenbach (2013), while strong effects are found by Gelbach (2002) and Cascio (2009). Strong positive effects of childcare on maternal employment are detected by Lefebvre and Merrigan (2008) for Canada, while no effects are found by Havnes and Mogstad (2011) for Norway, Givord and Marbot (2015) for France, Bettendorf et al. (2015) for the Netherlands and Nollenberger and Rodríguez-Planas (2015) for Spain.

Identifying a causal relationship, however, is difficult: even in cases in which childcare is costly, maternal employment may be high if both childcare costs and female employment reflect a high general labour demand. To isolate the effect of childcare cost on maternal employment, Gelbach (2002) considers US mothers with children born just before and just after the cut-off date that determines free access to kindergarten and finds that mothers in the first group are more likely

Table 3.1 (a) *Employment, parental leave and childcare expenditure*

	(1) Fem. Empl. Rate	(2) Fem. Empl. Rate	(3) Empl. Gap	(4) Empl. Gap	(5) Empl. Gap	(6) Wage Gap
Max. weeks job-protected leave	0.109***	0.153***	0.084***	0.091***	0.122***	0.003
	(0.020)	(0.028)	(0.020)	(0.026)	(0.031)	(0.024)
Max. weeks squared/100	-0.059***	-0.077***	0.041***	0.038***	0.038**	0.001
	(0.011)	(0.014)	(0.011)	(0.013)	(0.016)	(0.013)
Percentage of total paid leave		-0.110***		0.116***	0.111***	
		(0.012)		(0.010)	(0.011)	
Average payment rate		-0.042***		0.020**	0.013	
		(0.012)		(0.010)	(0.016)	
Early childcare expenditure					-8.134***	
					(1.111)	
Constant	44.83***	38.92***	48.88***	53.25***	42.23***	35.95***
	(1.734)	(2.112)	(2.168)	(2.586)	(1.578)	(0.658)
Observations	1099	685	1099	685	477	597
R^2	0.894	0.910	0.913	0.937	0.932	0.939

Notes: OLS estimations at the country level. OECD countries. All specifications include country and year dummies. Data refer to full-time employees and self-employed employees. *Fem. Empl. Rate:* the employment/population ratio to men aged 25–54. *Empl. Gap:* the male-female difference in employment rates (%). *Wage Gap:* the difference between median earnings of men and women relative to median earnings of men. *Max. weeks job-protected leave:* maximum weeks of job-protected maternity, parental and home care leave available (and its squared version). *Percentage of the total paid leave:* total weeks of paid maternity, parental and home care payments available to mother (%). *Average payment rate:* mother's average payment rate. *Early childcare expenditure:* public spending on early childhood education and care (% GDP). Sample period: 1970–2016 (columns 1, 3, 6), 1970–2010 (column 2), 1980–2010 (column 5). *Source:* OECD. Robust standard errors in parentheses. *** $p<0.01$, ** $p<0.05$, * $p<0.1$.

Table 3.1 (b) *Employment, parental leave and childcare expenditure*

	(1) Fem. Empl. Rate	(2) Fem. Empl. Rate	(3) Empl. Gap	(4) Wage Gap	(5) Wage Gap	(6) Wage Gap
Max. weeks job-protected leave		0.175***		0.123***		-0.191***
		(0.034)		(0.029)		(0.032)
Max. weeks squared/100		-0.063***		0.039***		0.058***
		(0.017)		(0.014)		(0.017)
Percentage of the total paid leave		-0.124***		0.033**		0.021
		(0.013)		(0.016)		(0.013)
Average payment rate		0.050***		0.023*		-0.030
		(0.018)		(0.013)		(0.020
Early childcare expenditure	4.645***	9.768***	4.370***		4.160***	-2.119**
	(1.101)	(1.274)	(0.928)		(0.695)	(0.915)
Constant	53.55***	47.72***	37.83***	37.95***	19.03***	23.80***
	(1.902)	(1.644)	(2.014)	(0.905)	(1.651)	(1.804)
Observations	853	477	853	320	489	255
R^2	0.902	0.910	0.921	0.964	0.942	0.970

Notes: OLS estimations at the country level. OECD countries. All specifications include country and year dummies. Data refer to full-time employees and to self-employed employees. *Fem. Empl. Rate*: the employment/population ratio for men aged 25–54. *Empl. Gap*: the male-female difference in employment rates (%). *Wage Gap*: the difference between median earnings of men and women relative to median earnings of men. *Max. weeks job-protected leave*: maximum weeks of job-protected maternity, parental and home care leave available (and its squared version). *Percentage of the total paid leave*: total weeks of paid maternity, parental and home care payments available to mother (%). *Average payment rate*: mother's average payment rate. *Early childcare expenditure*: public spending on early childhood education and care (% GDP). Sample period: 1970–2010 (column 4), 1980–2014 (columns 1, 3, 5), 1980–2010 (columns 2,6). *Source*: OECD. Robust standard errors in parentheses. *** p<0.01, ** p<0.05, * p<0.1.

to work than mothers in the second group. Baker et al. (2008) explored the law that introduced universal access to childcare in Quebec as a quasi-natural experiment to investigate the impact of free childcare on maternal employment. The effects are positive, although not very large.

Despite its positive effects on gender equality, formal childcare is still scarcely used. A possible obstacle is the lack of information about the benefits to children of attending formal childcare. In a recent paper with Galasso, Pronzato and Billari (Galasso et al., 2017), we present a randomized experiment on 700 Italian women of reproductive age with no children. The pool of women is randomly selected into a group which is exposed to positive information about formal childcare through a text message or a video and another which receives no information. We find a positive effect on the intention to use formal childcare by high-skilled women who receive the information. Surprisingly, we find a negative effect on the intention to work among less-educated women. We explain this result by women's education reflecting their work-family orientation and their ability to afford formal childcare: since high-skilled women are work oriented and are able to pay for formal childcare, when they know that formal childcare is beneficial for their children, they declare that they will use it more. In contrast, because low-skilled women are less attached to their career and cannot afford formal childcare, when they receive information about the beneficial effects of early childcare, they decide to spend more time with their young children and provide the best possible care themselves.

3.3 Taxation

One of the basic lessons of economics is that individuals respond to incentives. Taxes are a powerful incentive; thus, individuals' behaviours respond to them. Mainly, taxes on labour income affect the labour supply. In the traditional work-leisure choice, theoretically, the effect of taxes is ambiguous: the substitution effect reduces labour supply because individuals prefer more leisure and less work if the after-tax wage decreases. The income effect instead leads to an increase in labour supply: workers are poorer if they have to pay taxes on wages and thus need to work more to reach the same level of income. The final effect of taxes on labour supply is thus ambiguous: if the substitution effect prevails, the labour supply decreases with taxes, while the opposite is true if the income effect dominates. Empirically, the literature has found different effects for primary earners – family members who are the main source of labour income for a household – and secondary earners – other workers in the family who are less attached to the labour force, mainly because they are in charge of other household activities (Blau and Kahn, 2007). More specifically, the literature has found that while the labour supply of primary earners is not very responsive to taxes, secondary earners are much more responsive to taxes, mainly on the extensive margin, that is, whether or not to work. Although the elasticity of the female labour supply is evolving over time (Goldin, 2006; Gelber, 2008), traditionally men were the primary earners and women the secondary earners because providing childcare was considered a natural alternative to outside work for women and not for men (see Chapter 2). Thus, taxes on the labour supply may play an important role in the females' decisions of whether or not to work.

The simple fact that the elasticity of the female labour supply is higher than that of the male labour supply suggests that following the Ramsey (1927) 'inverse elasticity rule' of optimal taxation, it would be efficient to tax women less than men (Rosen, 1977; Boskin and Sheshinski, 1983). Apps and Rees (2007) provide empirical support for this idea and show under what conditions it is optimal to tax males at a higher rate. Alesina et al. (2011) have proposed a gender-based taxation system. They show that the different labour elasticities across genders are endogenously determined by the intra-household bargaining process, which is the result of an unbalanced division of family chores across genders within families. Men receive higher wages, work more in the market, are at home less and have lower labour supply elasticity. The introduction of gender-specific taxes, mainly lower taxes for women than for men, changes the bargaining power, inducing a more balanced allocation of family chores within the household and ultimately increasing social welfare.

No country in the world has thus far introduced gender-based taxation, although some have discussed it. Several concerns have been raised. Among them is the possibility that gender-based taxation favours high-income women and penalizes low-income men. Moreover, it implies the unequal treatment of two single-parent families that are identical in income but different in the gender of the parents. Finally, it is based on the fact that female employment is always more elastic than male employment, while this may not apply universally – for example, it does not apply to single women with or without children (Saint-Paul, 2008). The main concern is – in my view – a political feasibility constraint: to keep the same revenue with gender-based taxation, if taxes for women are reduced, taxes for men should be increased. Although these changes can be internalized within each household at zero cost, it is not obvious how to reach this new equilibrium with the support of voters. Thus, it is unlikely that gender-based taxation will be adopted as a policy measure.

An additional disincentive to the labour supply of the secondary earner may arise in the presence of family-based or joint family taxation. If the government decides to tax the couple instead of the individual, the tax base will be the sum of the incomes of the individuals of the household (the family income). Since taxes on income are typically progressive, the couple will pay a higher tax than if the two incomes are considered separately. This is called a 'marriage tax', an increase in the total tax of two individuals simply from marrying. Most importantly, suppose the man works and earns 100 euros, while the woman has to decide whether to work. In the case of family-based taxation, the first euro earned by the woman is euro 101 of the couple; thus, in a progressive system, it is taxed more than the first euro would be in an individual taxation system. In other words, family-based taxation entails a disincentive for the secondary earner to work.

The French system ('quotient familial') belongs to this category: the gross income is the household total income divided by a coefficient that increases with the number of household components. The tax schedule is applied to this ratio and then multiplied by the coefficient to obtain the tax amount. While this system favours large families, by applying a progressive tax schedule to the joint family income, it may still contain a disincentive for the secondary earner to work: the marginal tax rate is not the individual one but depends on the partner's income. The empirical literature has investigated the disincentive to work for women in countries with joint taxation (see Buffeteau and Echevin (2003) for France, Steiner and Wrohlich (2004) for Germany) and has shown that a hypothetical shift from individual-based to family-based taxation would likely reduce the female labour supply (see Aassve et al. (2007) for Italy).

Individual-based taxation is instead neutral and is not subject to this distortion. However, it is not uncommon to provide a tax credit for a dependent nonworking spouse. This provision reintroduces a disincentive to work for married women (Colonna and Marcassa, 2015).

Alternative systems are based on tax credit, such as the American Earned Income Tax Credit (EITC) and the British Working Tax Credit (WTC). In these cases, the tax unit is the individual. However, households where both spouses are employed have the right to receive a tax credit, which increases with the size of the family and can even become a transfer. The empirical literature has shown that this system increases the employment rates of mothers (see Chote et al. (2007) for Great Britain, Eissa and Liebman (1996) and Ellwood (2000) for the United States).

The presence of children may reduce the time available to work and increase the cost. This is why the tax treatment of childcare, mainly tax credits related to children and/or childcare that reduce taxes for working parents, may be a stimulus for employment. Theoretically, the effect is similar to what was explained before: a reduction in childcare costs through taxes increases the net returns from working for working parents and thus leads to more work (substitution effect), while it increases the net income of the family and thus leads to less work needed for a given level of income (income effect). The empirical literature suggests that for secondary earners, the substitution effect dominates (Anderson and Levine, 1999). Thus, tax credits for childcare may induce secondary earners to work more.

OECD countries differ both in the unit of taxation (individual, family or any of the two at the choice of the taxpayer) and in the generosity of tax credits related to children. To provide an overall picture, I assemble the information on the unit of taxation from each OECD country fiche. Figure 3.4 shows for 2016 the unit of taxation (individual, family or choice) and the level of family expenditure for the countries for which both sets of information are available. The two datasets together provide, at least on an initial basis, information on how the tax system is potentially related to gender equality. As I argue, tax systems based on individual taxation are neutral towards the female labour supply; thus, if I concentrate on this group of countries, I expect that the higher the expenditures are, the higher the support of female employment.

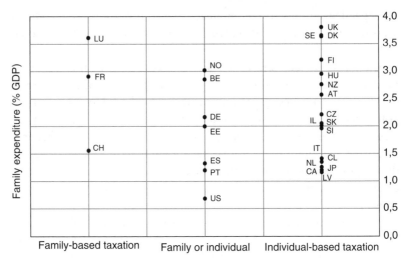

Figure 3.4 Unit of taxation and family expenditure (as % of GDP).
Source: Author's elaboration of OECD data, 2018.

3.4 Measures in the Labour Market to Promote Gender Equality

Female employment rates are also the result of how work is organized in specific contexts: part-time work and smart work have an impact on labour market outcomes that may be different for males and females. Pension design may also play a relevant role. Finally, when we discuss women's empowerment, we should consider gender quotas as a critical policy for promoting gender equality.

3.4.1 Part-time Work

Many mothers prefer to work part time to combine work and childcare. Del Boca (2002) shows that part-time opportunities have a positive impact on the probability of women participating in the labour market. The impact is stronger for mothers. However, part-time work among mothers plays a significant role in the gender pay gap: women are paid less than men, and their career opportunities dramatically decrease. Connolly and Gregory (2008) show that the pay penalty cost of working part time is increasing. This is mainly due to part-time jobs being polarized into low-paid occupations (Manning and Petrongolo, 2008).

However, many part-time workers in low-paid occupations are qualified for and have previously held higher-level, better-paid jobs: many women reduce their work hours substantially after childbirth, particularly at the arrival of the first child (Paull, 2008). This downgrading represents an underutilization of human capital. When examining satisfaction, a puzzle emerges: women prefer part-time work, but this does not translate into higher satisfaction. Women with children, in particular, report being more satisfied with life when working full time. This puzzle probably depends on the pay penalty attached to part-time workers and, more generally, on the way firms consider part-time workers. Traditionally, firms have not always been eager to employ part-time workers. At the same time, some existing part-time work is involuntary, especially at low skill levels: workers are forced to work fewer hours (and thus earn less) than they would prefer to do.

3.4.2 Smart Work

A different concept is 'smart work', a new way to organize work based on flexible time and space. Workers agree with their supervisors to work for a defined period of their job activity – for instance, one day per week – outside the company's physical workplace and with a personalized time schedule. This defined period places no precise constraints on the time or location of the work. Owing to the use of technological tools, workers may perform the same duties and activities as before and achieve the set targets and results. In contrast to part-time work, while supporting work-life balance, smart work does not produce a pay penalty. Thus, it may be a good alternative to solve the part-time puzzle of job satisfaction. However, a concern arises: if flexible work makes workers work longer (overtime) and more intensively (Clark, 2000), then smart work may be associated with higher performance but not with a reduction in work-family conflicts. Smart work not only targets women, but it also may prove to support female employment in particular to the extent that women have more duties related to childcare and elderly care and benefit more from flexible work organization.

The impact of smart work on gender equality at work is difficult to establish. It is a recent way to organize work, and, more importantly, it is difficult to assess the causal impact of smart work on economic outcomes. From a gender perspective, outcomes such as work-life balance are particularly interesting. As smart work relies on the use of technology, a major global challenge for our economies, I return to this discussion in Chapter 6.

3.4.3 Pensions

Labour market gaps translate into pension gaps. Pension rules themselves may help reduce gaps during retirement, but they should not be confounded with policies that support gender equality in the labour market. At the same time, the design of the pension system may influence gender gaps during work life if women anticipate their future pension.

How gender gaps in the labour market are prolonged into gaps during retirement depends on several factors: part-time work, occupations in less rewarding sectors, a discontinuous career and interruption of work after childbirth characterize female work more than male work and negatively affect pension rights.

The design of the pension system may have consequences for pension gender gaps. In a flat-rate system, contributions are proportional to earnings, and pensions do not depend strictly on the income of the worker. This system redistributes across income levels. In this case, as women are typically poorer than men, they benefit from the intra-generational redistributive component of pensions. Poverty in old age is reduced (Ginn, 2004). If the system is earning related, then pensions strictly depend on the contributions paid by each individual: if women contribute less than men or if their contributions are interrupted more over their working life, then the gender gaps after retirement are exacerbated. This second case applies in notional defined contribution systems, that is, systems in which the amount of a pension is determined on the basis of the contributions paid by the worker during the entire working life, such as the current Italian pension system. Another element of the design of pension systems that may generate pension gender gaps is the official retirement age, which in some cases is lower for women than for men. This is often seen as a way to compensate women *ex post facto* for their double burden as caregivers and workers in the labour market, and it may become very generous from the social security point of view, given that women have a higher life expectancy than men. For women, on the one hand, early retirement means that they can enjoy more leisure and exploit other opportunities outside the labour market, although it often means that they have more time to care for grandchildren and other members of the family, thus reinforcing the specialization trap discussed in Chapter 2. On the other hand, it may also represent a cost, as it implies a reduction in pension benefits (which depend on the years of contributions) and thus a higher risk of poverty in old age.

Men and women have different preferences for their retirement age, which may in turn translate into differences in pension benefits: women live longer than men, but they typically prefer to retire earlier, especially in geographical areas where adult children need the help of grandmothers for childcare. In many European countries, the availability of informal care by grandmothers is a crucial support for female employment (see, among others, Arpino et al., 2014). However, given their interrupted careers and average wages that are lower than those of men, women would need to retire later than men to reach a certain level of pensionable income. In redistributive systems, women may have an additional incentive to retire earlier if they can take advantage of this design (Ginn, 2004). Many authors argue that retirement is often a joint decision (e.g. O'Rand and Farkas, 2002) or that women tend to follow their spouse's decision.

The argument that the availability of retired grandparents, and more often grandmothers, is positively related to the female labour supply, especially when formal childcare is scarce – for example, in Mediterranean countries – makes the relationship between the design of pension systems and reforms and the level of the gender gaps more complex than what is generally considered. On the one hand, increasing retirement age is a way to reduce gender gaps by increasing the pension benefits of women in old age; on the other hand, it may reduce the availability of informal childcare with negative consequences for female employment. Joint policies, which support both formal childcare and pension reforms, are a way to avoid undesirable outcomes for gender gaps.

3.4.4 Gender Quotas

Finally, among policies that support female empowerment, gender quotas in the labour market play an important role. Gender quotas are a way to accelerate progress towards economic gender equality and to promote women's empowerment. In Europe, gender quotas have become a reality in some contexts. Norway pioneered the introduction of gender quotas for boards of directors in 2005. Italy, France and Germany, among others, followed suit (see Chapter 5 for a detailed description). Gender quotas are also used to promote the presence of women in politics (see Chapter 4).

However, gender quotas are controversial. The main argument in favour of the adoption of gender quotas is their effectiveness as a means of equalizing opportunity in specific areas where women face systematic barriers due to discrimination or persistent stereotypes (Holzer and Neumark, 2000). These policies may lead to a redistribution of jobs, positions, contracts or Parliament seats in favour of women and thus allow a fair distribution of rewards for good jobs. Moreover, if women who benefit from affirmative action are largely qualified to successfully perform the tasks to which they are appointed, the benefits do not remain within the group of women but spread to the entire economy. If women accumulate more human capital that raises their productivity, then these policies may even increase efficiency (Conde-Ruiz et al., 2017). Quotas are an instrument (often considered the only one) to break down masculine monopolistic power, which obviously does not lead to an equal outcome but probably also does not lead to an efficient one. Critics of affirmative action share the view that the under-representation of women is not due to discrimination but is merely the result of women's choices, especially those related to fertility and motherhood. Quotas, they argue, violate meritocracy: by equalizing outcomes rather than opportunities, quotas risk promoting less-qualified individuals, who are likely to perform poorly (Holzer and Neumark, 2000). For instance, if highly qualified women cannot be found, board gender quotas may produce negative effects on the performance of companies. Not only is there a risk of decreasing the average quality if there are not enough women with the appropriate qualifications to be appointed, but also a 'mismatch' may occur if women are allocated to positions in which they are unable to perform successfully. Studies have also doubted the effectiveness of quotas in reducing gender inequalities in specific contexts (e.g. Bagues and Esteve-Volart, 2010). Bagues et al. (2017) find that the gender composition of evaluation committees does not necessarily increase the chances for women to be promoted, thus limiting the effectiveness and desirability of gender quotas.

How to understand which effect dominates is again an empirical question. Gender quotas impose an exogenous increase of women and thus provide an excellent opportunity to identify the causal effects of the role of women in decision-making. I return to the empirical evidence on the introduction of gender quotas in Chapters 4 and 5.

4 | *How Women Affect Public Policy*

This chapter moves my analysis towards the *political economy* side – the analysis of how women's empowerment affects government intervention in the economy. I consider women politicians at all levels of government and analyze whether their presence influences the policy implemented, such as the size and allocation of public spending. The chapter answers the following questions: Are female politicians making different decisions than male politicians? Is a gender-balanced composition of policymakers influencing the level of public spending and the allocation among different items? Is it reorienting the priorities of politicians towards, for example, social or welfare expenditures?

Before analyzing the relationship between the gender of politicians and public policy outcomes, natural questions arise: Why should we expect any effect on public policies of the presence of female politicians? Why should women in politics matter, and why should the way they act as politicians matter? To provide a first answer to these questions, I propose a new analysis based on individual data from a rich dataset that contains answers from the 'Comparative Candidate Survey', which spans the separate periods 2005–2013 and 2013–2016 for a large set of countries. Politicians were asked several questions related to their views on general topics (economy, rights, environment, women's issues, migration, the role of Europe, etc.) and on their approach to making decisions (aligned with the party or with the voters, etc.). I analyze the individual answers and provide new evidence that politicians' gender matters: men and women differ in their answers, with women being more open to social issues, including migration, rights and the environment and less inclined to military intervention. These differences are established by controlling for individual characteristics, political orientation and country.

The new evidence that male and female political candidates have different preferences enriches what we know about the preferences of male and female voters and creates expectations for the political agenda. The chapter then investigates the emergence of a 'new agenda' when decision-making positions are gender balanced: Are the items proposed and implemented by women different from those typically proposed and implemented by men? In particular, do they reflect the more socially oriented preferences of women? I first present a new analysis using aggregate data at the country level, which shows interesting correlations between the share of women in parliament and some categories of public expenditures, such as childcare and family expenditures. In Chapter 3, I identified how specific public policies promote gender equality. I here ask whether gender equality *ex ante* can influence policy decisions *ex post*. Do women policymakers make different decisions than men? Do they care more about women's needs? Although suggestive, as we know well, this macro-level analysis may suffer from well-known endogeneity concerns; mainly, it is difficult to disentangle the impact of women policymakers on policies from the potential impact of policies on women's representation.

I therefore move to a microdata-based analysis focused on specific countries. A microdata-based analysis allows me to identify the impact of women in decision-making positions on public policy. Most studies focus on the share of women in political bodies (mainly at the local government level) and exploit the existence of gender quotas (or similar measures that create an exogenous increase of women in policymaking bodies) and discontinuities in their adoption. This means that, for example, they compare a group of municipalities subject to such quotas and another group with similar characteristics that is not subject to the quotas. Other studies, mainly those focused on mayors, exploit mixed-gender close races, that is, cases in which women won elections against men by a small margin; this implies that the election of the woman can be considered random. The chapter shows that, as a general result, the allocation of expenditure, rather than the total size, is responsive to the gender of politicians. Moreover, the results differ between developing and developed countries: in developing countries, we observe that, as expected, a higher share of women is associated with policies that are more oriented towards social issues, education and women's needs, whereas in developed countries, the evidence is much less conclusive. Finally, the chapter provides evidence of the impact of women in decision-making positions on a different dimension of public policy, such as monetary policy.

4.1 Male and Female Politicians

Other than the symbolic argument, by which increased female representation enshrines equal rights for women and men, a greater number of women in politics also has a substantive effect. Women can broaden the diversity of viewpoints, experiences, interests and expertise, thus enriching political debate and impacting the direction of public policy (Phillips, 1995; Mansbridge, 1999).

First, according to an extensive political science literature, in comparison to men, women politicians are more concrete in their action and more focused on problem solving and on real issues. They also have a lower rate of absenteeism and are more cooperative and less conflictual (see Epstein et al., 2005), as they tend to seek solutions rather than create conflicts (Footitt, 2002). They are also less corrupt (Dollar et al., 2001; Swamy et al., 2001): in Brazil, female mayors are less likely to engage in corruption and tend to hire fewer temporary public employees and to attract fewer campaign contributions when running for re-election than male mayors (Brollo and Troiano, 2016).

Second, as culture matters, having more women in political decision-making may be beneficial for the dominant culture of a country. The attitudes of voters and the general population towards women may change when more women are elected (Beaman et al., 2012). Female participation in politics may create role models for other women, who may decide to take an interest in politics, become active voters or pursue a political career (Atkeson, 2003; Wolbrecht and Campbell, 2007; Karp and Banducci, 2008; Gilardi, 2015). These effects are not confined solely to women but extend to male citizens as well, increasing their confidence in the political system and encouraging civic engagement (Schwindt-Bayer and Mishler, 2005; Espìrito-Santo, 2011).

Third, male and female politicians tend to behave differently. Several studies have emphasized that the identity of politicians matters for policies (Osborne and Slivinski, 1996; Besley and Coate, 1997). Gender is a fundamental part of individual identity; as such, it is expected to play an important role in politicians' decisions in addition to party affiliation (Levitt, 1996). Several authors have studied the decisions of members of the US Congress and found that, at least in the past, when they vote on issues of civil rights, gun control and abortion, they are less subject to party pressure and tend to vote more freely (Snyder and Groseclose, 2000; Ansolabehere et al., 2001).

Similarly, Hibbing and Marsh (1987) show that for UK politicians, personal characteristics such as religion, age, education and gender matter more than party affiliation when decisions on controversial issues are made.

Fourth, and related to the previous point, male and female politicians may have different agendas. Women are particularly attentive to important topics that are often not prioritized or addressed, among which are issues that disproportionately affect them (Thomas, 1994; Swers, 2002; Childs, 2004). Political scientists have analyzed the impact that women have on political outcomes, showing mainly that women politicians are more likely to introduce or pass bills dealing with women's issues (Haavio-Mannila et al., 1985; Thomas, 1991). For example, a higher presence of female legislators is associated with the approval of abortion legislation (Berkman and O'Connor, 1993). In the United States, women officeholders were found to be more likely to vote for nuclear disarmament and welfare programs (Stanwick and Kleeman, 1983). However, it is difficult to understand whether the association between the gender of the politician and the outcome depends on intrinsic traits and preferences that differentiate men and women or is the result of voters' preferences.

To gain an in-depth understanding of the main traits that differentiate men and women politicians and may translate into a different policy agenda, I perform a novel analysis based on the Comparative Candidate Survey (CSS) dataset. The CSS collects answers to survey questions posed to a sample of candidates running for the national parliaments of different countries in the periods 2005–2013 and 2013–2016. It also contains information about the background of the candidates, the constituency in which they are running and the political system under scrutiny.

The questions contained in the survey are useful for understanding both the view of male and female politicians on general topics and the style of political leadership. The dataset has not previously been used with reference to gender analysis.

For the same set of countries considered in previous chapters, I analyze the individual answers to the following CSS items:

(1) Immigrants are not required to adapt to the customs of the country
(2) The country should provide military assistance to the war on terror
(3) Stronger measures should be taken to protect the environment

(4) The country's membership in the EU is a good thing
(5) Women should be free to decide on matters of abortion
(6) Women should be given preferential treatment when applying for a job

The possible answers are in a range (-2 to 2), with a higher value indicating a higher level of agreement with the statement (-2 indicates strong disagreement, and 2 indicates strong agreement). At first glance, men and women differ in their answers to these questions: approximately 30 per cent of women agree with the first statement, while the corresponding percentage for men is only 25 per cent. Almost 45 per cent of women disagree with the statement on military assistance, while more than 40 per cent of men agree. The share of women who agree with the protection of the environment is larger than the share of men (83 per cent versus 75 per cent). Similarly, women tend to agree more than men with the statements on women's issues.

Since these simple descriptive statistics are obviously not fully informative, and omitted variables bias can be a crucial issue, I also perform a regression analysis to explain the answers to the questions. I include the following individual control variables: female (a dummy variable taking a value of 1 if the respondent is female and 0 otherwise), position of candidate's party on a left-right scale (based on the ParlGov database, where extreme left is 0 and extreme right is 10), year of birth, whether the respondent was born abroad, level of education (on a 1–8 scale, from none to university degree attainment), occupational status (employed, unemployed, retired), marital status (married, widowed, divorced), level of religiosity (on a 0–6 scale, based on church attendance from never to at least once a week), religion (Christian, Protestant, Islam, No religion, Others) and number of children in care divided into two age groups (aged 0–4 and 5–15). I also control for the year in which the survey was answered and for the country. Standard errors are clustered at the country level.

The results are provided in Table 4.1, which shows, for all considered questions, the significance of the coefficient of the variable capturing the gender of the respondent. Please note that 'Unemployed', 'Christian' and 'Married' values do not appear in the table because they are the reference values for the occupational status, religion and marital status variables.

Table 4.1 *Women in parliament, issues and policies*

	(1)	(2)	(3)	(4)	(5)	(6)
Female	0.042***	−0.099**	0.083***	0.034	0.103***	0.191***
	(0.009)	(0.040)	(0.018)	(0.027)	(0.023)	(0.039)
Left-right	−0.136***	0.154***	−0.103***	−0.019	−0.043***	−0.120***
	(0.012)	(0.024)	(0.016)	(0.079)	(0.011)	(0.017)
Birth year	0.005***	−0.004	0.002*	0.002	0.000	−0.005*
	(0.001)	(0.003)	(0.001)	(0.003)	(0.001)	(0.002)
Born abroad	−0.032	−0.056		0.112***		
	(0.078)	(0.062)		(0.026)		
Education	0.020	0.027**	−0.006	0.067	0.005	0.005
	(0.013)	(0.012)	(0.009)	(0.044)	(0.007)	(0.010)
Employed	−0.000	0.034	0.019	0.180**	0.060	−0.052
	(0.038)	(0.094)	(0.030)	(0.056)	(0.034)	(0.047)
Retired	−0.029	0.029	0.016	0.110*	0.066	−0.044
	(0.032)	(0.087)	(0.057)	(0.051)	(0.045)	(0.048)
Religiosity	−0.030***	0.048***	0.024**	0.029***	−0.132***	0.002
	(0.004)	(0.009)	(0.009)	(0.008)	(0.025)	(0.006)
Protestant	0.029	−0.120	−0.041**	0.025	−0.008	−0.040
	(0.022)	(0.099)	(0.018)	(0.030)	(0.029)	(0.028)
Muslim	−0.030	−0.281	−0.129	0.174	0.179*	0.095
	(0.088)	(0.259)	(0.168)	(0.107)	(0.082)	(0.161)
No religion	0.025	−0.137	−0.006	0.012	−0.021	−0.001
	(0.025)	(0.076)	(0.024)	(0.044)	(0.040)	(0.021)
Other religions	−0.140*	−0.491	0.014	0.050	−0.038	0.002
	(0.071)	(0.272)	(0.046)	(0.060)	(0.033)	(0.087)
Widowed	−0.037	0.089	−0.013	−0.090*	−0.088***	−0.015
	(0.046)	(0.062)	(0.030)	(0.045)	(0.022)	(0.035)
Divorced	−0.047**	0.006	0.001	−0.073*	−0.044*	−0.036
	(0.021)	(0.059)	(0.025)	(0.037)	(0.022)	(0.036)
Single	0.025	−0.143	−0.053*	−0.079**	−0.021	−0.018
	(0.028)	(0.204)	(0.026)	(0.027)	(0.038)	(0.039)
No. children aged 0–5	−0.012	0.002	−0.012	−0.035*	−0.021	0.008
	(0.029)	(0.014)	(0.010)	(0.019)	(0.019)	(0.023)
No. children aged 5–15	0.014	−0.008	−0.025*	0.007	−0.021**	0.007
	(0.010)	(0.028)	(0.014)	(0.022)	(0.008)	(0.007)
Country FE	Y	Y	Y	Y	Y	Y
Year FE	Y	Y	Y	Y	Y	Y

Table 4.1 (cont.)

	(1)	(2)	(3)	(4)	(5)	(6)
Observations	6,367	2,128	6,402	3,935	6,395	6,213
R^2	0.319	0.252	0.168	0.163	0.246	0.202

Notes: OLS estimations at the individual level. Candidates surveyed in Australia, Belgium, Canada, Czech Republic, Denmark, Estonia, Finland, Germany, Greece, Hungary, Iceland, Ireland, Italy, Netherlands, New Zealand, Norway, Portugal, Romania, Sweden, Switzerland and UK. Dependent variables capture agreement to statements (1) Immigrants are not required to adapt to the customs of the country; (2) Country should provide military assistance to the war of terror; (3) Stronger measure should be taken to protect the environment; (4) Country's membership in the EU is a good thing; (5) Women should be free to decide on matters of abortion; (6) Women should be given preferential treatment when applying for a job. All specifications include country and year dummies. Sample period: 2005–2016. *Source:* CSS, ParlGov for *Left-Right*. Robust standard errors in parentheses. *** p<0.01, ** p<0.05, * p<0.1.

Table 4.1 shows interesting significant results. Women are more favourable to having migrants not adapt to the customs of the country, which may translate into female politicians being more open to immigration. Female politicians are also less in favour of military intervention, which suggests that when empowered, they will allocate fewer resources to defence expenditures. They are also more favourable to measures for the protection of the environment, which may translate into female politicians being associated with larger expenditure on environmental policies. On the other hand, female politicians do not significantly show pro-European sentiment, while preferences related to women's issues go in the expected direction: female politicians are more sensitive to abortion rights and to preferential treatment of women when applying for a job.

The same dataset also provides additional questions that are useful for providing information about what I can call the 'female style of political leadership'. The questions are as follows, and the values in brackets are attached to voter/party/politician:

(1) If the opinion of voters (0) and party (1) differs, should a member of parliament follow the voters or the party?

(2) If own opinion (0) and voters' opinion (1) differ, should a member of parliament follow own opinion or the voters'?

(3) If own opinion (0) and party's opinion (1) differ, should a member of parliament follow own opinion or the party's?

(4) Members of parliament should be able to vote in parliament independently of their party's position.

The answers are based on a range (–1 to 1), with a higher value indicating a higher level of agreement (–1 indicates strong disagreement, and 1 indicates strong agreement).

Table 4.2 provides the results of a regression that explains the determinants of the answers to these questions, including the same individual, country and year variables used before. In addition, I account for a variable capturing whether the politician resides in the same constituency that she is running for; in that case, candidates are expected to be more aligned with their electorate and thus to stand more strongly in favour of policies benefiting the constituency.

Again, gender matters. Women believe that politicians should prefer voters' and party's opinions to their own, and they also maintain that parliamentarians should not vote independently of their party's position. On the other hand, women do not significantly take a stand when voters' and party's opinions are in conflict. Based on these results, it is possible to establish a ranking in which parties come first, followed by voters, and the politician places herself at the bottom. This trait may indicate a lack of self-confidence, higher risk aversion when the competition involves personal exposure and less conflictual attitudes in female politicians but also higher accountability to voters and difficulty dealing with pressure from the party. This evidence seems to support the view that female political leaders may be less successful than male political leaders in translating their identity into political action.

The analysis of the Comparative Candidate Survey shows that gender matters: men and women politicians have different views on general topics, with women being more open to immigrants, environmental issues and Europe and less open to defence. They also show a different leadership style, with women being more ready to sacrifice their opinions when they differ from the preferences of voters or parties. In Box 4.1, I analyze if these different traits of male and

Table 4.2 *Women in parliament, 'female style of leadership'*

	(1)	(2)	(3)	(4)
Female	−0.045	0.090*	0.115**	−0.114***
	(0.033)	(0.039)	(0.026)	(0.013)
Left-right	−0.013*	0.016	0.011***	−0.004
	(0.006)	(0.014)	(0.002)	(0.016)
Birth	0.002*	−0.000	0.001***	0.001
	(0.001)	(0.001)	(0.000)	(0.001)
Born abroad	0.197***	−0.051	0.055	−0.170
	(0.041)	(0.043)	(0.106)	(0.080)
Education	0.032**	−0.077***	−0.012	0.010
	(0.011)	(0.007)	(0.012)	(0.022)
Running for own	−0.013	0.047*	0.004	0.029
constituency	(0.014)	(0.019)	(0.024)	(0.027)
Employed	−0.003	−0.023	0.026	−0.017
	(0.036)	(0.014)	(0.027)	(0.089)
Retired	−0.060	−0.026	−0.021	0.050
	(0.048)	(0.022)	(0.032)	(0.068)
Religiosity	−0.002	−0.001	−0.000	−0.019*
	(0.004)	(0.009)	(0.005)	(0.009)
Protestant	0.038	−0.028	−0.023	0.001
	(0.030)	(0.029)	(0.030)	(0.070)
Muslim	−0.406***	0.031	−0.089	0.402***
	(0.032)	(0.113)	(0.091)	(0.078)
No religion	−0.018	−0.070*	−0.014	−0.002
	(0.010)	(0.032)	(0.034)	(0.053)
Other religions	−0.022	−0.046	−0.202***	0.075
	(0.031)	(0.045)	(0.024)	(0.162)
Widowed	−0.053	−0.011	−0.004	−0.048
	(0.034)	(0.037)	(0.027)	(0.032)
Divorced	−0.106**	−0.007	0.015	−0.107*
	(0.032)	(0.039)	(0.046)	(0.042)
Single	0.115	−0.114	0.128	−0.202
	(0.144)	(0.115)	(0.080)	(0.247)
No. children	−0.032	0.010	−0.007	0.034
aged 0–5	(0.040)	(0.012)	(0.033)	(0.033)

Table 4.2 (*cont.*)

	(1)	(2)	(3)	(4)
No. children	0.023	−0.015	−0.024	0.043***
aged 5–15	(0.014)	(0.009)	(0.014)	(0.007)
Country FE	Y	Y	Y	Y
Year FE	Y	Y	Y	Y
Observations	1,222	1,268	1,248	1,317
R^2	0.044	0.085	0.055	0.091

Notes: OLS estimations at the individual level. Candidates surveyed in Australia, Belgium, Canada, Czech Republic, Denmark, Estonia, Finland, Germany, Greece, Hungary, Iceland, Ireland, Italy, Netherlands, New Zealand, Norway, Portugal, Romania, Sweden, Switzerland and UK. Dependent variables capture answers to questions (1) If the opinion of voters (0) and party (1) differs, should a member of parliament follow the voters or the party? (2) If own opinion (0) and voters' (1) differs, should a member of parliament follow own opinion or the voters'? (3) If own opinion (0) and party' (1) differs, should a member of the parliament follow own opinion or the party's? (4) Members of parliament should be able to vote in parliament independently of their party's position. All specifications include country and year dummies. Sample period: 2005–2016. *Source:* CSS, ParlGov for *Left-Right*. Robust standard errors in parentheses. *** $p<0.01$, ** $p<0.05$, * $p<0.1$.

Box 4.1 Male and female voters

Men and women vote differently. There are some established regularities. First, women vote more for leftist parties. Second, women do not necessarily vote more for female candidates. Third, women prefer political candidates who conduct positive rather than negative campaigns.

Starting with the first element, the evidence that women vote more often for leftist parties (Edlund and Pande, 2002) may depend on the origin of the modernization of society and is a consequence of the instability of marriages and the increase in divorces. As the weaker partner in the couple, women need more protection and thus more social spending. Women are left alone with their children more often than men are and therefore need more assistance from the government. As leftist parties tend to protect weaker groups, this can easily explain why women have traditionally voted left more than men. According to Edlund and Pande (2002), when divorce rates increase, US Democrats lose votes among men but not among women.

Consistent with this behaviour is the fact that women's enfranchisement has been followed by a large increase in public spending (Lindert, 1994). This is particularly strong in countries where the divorce rate is high (Lott and Kenny, 1999). While the positive effect of women's enfranchisement on public spending in the United States is large (Lott and Kenny, 1999), for Europe, the result is weaker (Aidt et al., 2006; Aidt and Dallal, 2008; Bertocchi, 2011). It is also true that the relationship between women's enfranchisement and the level of public spending is stronger in societies with more progressive family cultures or when religion – especially the Catholic religion – is less strong (Bertocchi, 2011).

The increase in public spending related to women's enfranchisement is driven mainly by the increase in health, education and welfare expenditures. Aidt et al. (2006) use data from Western Europe from 1830 to 1938 to find that increased female suffrage had an effect (though not strong) on increasing public spending, mainly through health, education and welfare, especially where the culture is more progressive (see also Aidt and Dallal, 2008 and Bertocchi, 2011). In Switzerland, where women acquired the right to vote only in the 1970s, Abrams and Settle (1999) show that women's enfranchisement has increased the level of public expenditures for welfare.

Theoretically, a simple median voter model can explain the positive relationship between women's enfranchisement and the level of public spending. As women have on average a lower income than men, the enfranchisement of women changes the income level for the median voter, who becomes poorer; thus, a higher level of public spending emerges in equilibrium.

The second piece of evidence is that women do not necessarily vote for women. Several studies have documented the existence of a general voter bias against female candidates (Sanbonmatsu, 2002; Black and Erickson, 2003; Schwindt-Bayer et al., 2010). In many settings, voter bias is an explicit phenomenon, and male politicians use it to their advantage when setting rules. In France, Fréchette et al. (2008) highlight how an overwhelming majority of male incumbents approved gender quotas in order to run against a woman and exploit male bias to increase their likelihood of re-election.

In a recent study (Baltrunaite et al., 2019), we show that the introduction of double-preference voting conditioned on gender in Italian municipal elections increased the share of female councillors by 18 percentage points. This measure targets voters: voters can express two preferences instead of one if they vote for candidates of different genders. The effectiveness of the policy is an indirect proof of the existence of voter bias against women, which is not gender specific. This result seems, however, to be far from general: other studies have shown that gender bias exists among parties but not among voters (Iversen and Rosenbluth, 2010; Murray et al., 2012; Shair-Rosenfield and Hinojosa, 2014).

The third ingredient of the evidence on male and female voters is based on recent studies about how men and women voters react to political campaigns. Galasso and Nannicini (2018) perform a randomized experiment of two electoral campaigns in Italy (for the mayor of Milan and the mayor of Cava de' Tirreni, a midsize city in southern Italy) and analyze the effect of positive and negative campaigning on the turnout and voting behaviour of male and female voters. They find that a negative campaign increases male turnout by approximately 5 percentage points, while it has no effect on female turnout. They also find that when the opponent conducts a positive campaign, women vote more for the opponent (by 9 percentage points) and less for the incumbent (by 8 points), while the opposite is true for men. In other words, women prefer candidates who conduct a positive campaign, while men respond more to a negative campaign, that is, more aggressive behaviour. This result is in line with that of Fridkin and Kenney (2011), who use survey and observational data to show that women are less tolerant than men of negative campaigns, and that of Brooks (2010), who performs a laboratory experiment to show that negativity reduces women's intention to vote.

female politicians are consistent with documented differences between men and women as voters. Do these gender-specific traits translate into a different approach to decision-making? To what extent is this difference visible?

4.2 Male and Female Political Leaders and Expenditures: Aggregate Analysis

Figure 4.1 plots childcare and preschool expenditures in our sample of OECD countries (Figure 4.1(a)) and family expenditures (Figure 4.1(b)) over the share of women in parliament (as a percentage of total seats). As expected, the relationship is positive: countries with a higher share of women in parliament have higher family and childcare expenditures. Scandinavian countries, for example, rank high in both female

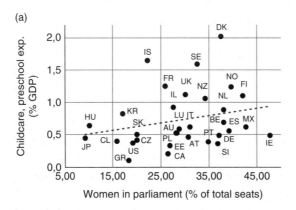

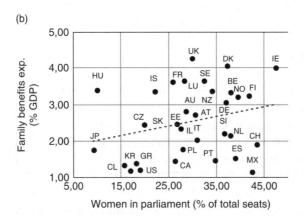

Figure 4.1 (a) Childcare/preschool expenditures and share of women in parliament. (b) Family expenditures and share women in parliament.
Source: Author's elaboration of OECD data.

representation in politics and such expenditures. Japan is on the opposite side of the graph.

The positive relationship between women in parliament and family/childcare expenditures is in part confirmed in Table 4.3, where I show the results of a cross-country regression with country fixed effects.

A large theoretical and empirical literature has analyzed the fundamental economic variables that play a crucial role in determining the level of public spending, as well as their composition (see Hinrichs, 1966; Tanzi, 1992). GDP plays an important role: according to Wagner's law (Wagner, 1883), economic development is associated with an increased demand for public expenditure (Tanzi, 1987). Additional socioeconomic variables that may have an impact on the level and composition of public outlays are the level of government debt, the share of agriculture in value added and the percentage of elderly people in the total population (Tanzi, 1992; Burgess and Stern, 1993; Ghura, 1998; Rodrik, 1998; Gupta and Mitra, 2004). Female labour force participation is also directly linked to family and childcare expenditure. I thus add the previously mentioned control variables in Table 4.3, columns 1–4. The share of women in parliament remains significant. The last column shows the results of the full specification when all control variables are included. In this case, the variable that captures the presence of women in parliament is no longer significant. However, the control variables appear to be highly correlated, thus reducing the validity of the last model.

The positive relationship suggests that more women in parliament can be associated with a higher level of attention to some items in the expenditure allocation that are typically difficult to promote because they benefit only a minority of voters. Early childcare, for example, is a policy that is unlikely to be supported by a large majority of voters because the group of beneficiaries is quite limited. It is difficult to consider women themselves a decisive group of voters because their interests are fragmented among different priorities, making it difficult for them to become a cohesive swing voter group. The fact that these policies may have a positive impact on female occupation (see Chapter 3) is not visible to voters and is often neglected.

Table 4.3 (a) *Family expenditure (as % of GDP) and share of women in parliament*

Public spending on families (% of GDP)	(1)	(2)	(3)	(4)
Seats held by women in national parliaments (%)	0.0143* (0.00701)	0.0130* (0.00762)	0.0144* (0.00748)	0.00392 (0.00485)
GDP per worker	−5.14e-06 (1.10e-05)		−5.23e-06 (1.13e-05)	−2.18e-05*** (5.38e-06)
Female labour force (%)		0.00139 (0.0156)	−0.00158 (0.0149)	−0.0166 (0.0329)
Government gross debt (% GDP)				0.00219 (0.00170)
Population aged 65+				0.0322 (0.0523)
Constant	2.598*** (0.917)	2.130*** (0.729)	2.686* (1.332)	4.546** (2.141)
Country FE	Y	Y	Y	Y
Year FE	Y	Y	Y	Y
Observations	184	184	184	159
R^2	0.035	0.030	0.035	0.150

Notes: OLS estimations at the country level, OECD countries. All specifications include country and year dummies. Sample period: 2005, 2007, 2009–2013.
Sources: OECD Social Expenditure Database, World Bank. Robust standard errors in parentheses. *** $p<0.01$, ** $p<0.05$, * $p<0.1$.

The simple correlations of Figure 4.1, as well as the results in Table 4.3, are suggestive and only partially informative, but they obviously say little about causal relationships. It may be the case that in countries where family expenditures are higher, more women are elected to parliament because gender gaps are smaller or because the country is characterized by a culture that is more open to gender balance in all dimensions.

The introduction of gender quotas in politics may be used to address this endogeneity problem: quotas exogenously increase the share of

(b) *Childcare expenditure (as % of GDP) and share of women in parliament*

Public spending on early childhood education and care (% GDP)	(1)	(2)	(3)	(4)
Seats held by women in national parliaments (%)	0.00732* (0.00366)	0.00647** (0.00314)	0.00576* (0.00317)	0.00195 (0.00221)
GDP per worker	1.70e-06 (7.60e-06)		3.22e-06 (6.44e-06)	−5.76e-06*** (2.06e-06)
Female labour force (%)		0.0284** (0.0117)	0.0299** (0.0123)	0.0207* (0.0107)
Government gross debt (% GDP)				0.000277 (0.000935)
Population aged 65+				0.0686** (0.0280)
Constant	0.350 (0.597)	−0.983 (0.616)	−1.308* (0.761)	−1.045 (0.652)
Country FE	Y	Y	Y	Y
Year FE	Y	Y	Y	Y
Observations	195	195	195	165
R^2	0.056	0.121	0.129	0.368

Notes: OLS estimations at the country level, OECD countries. All specifications include country and year dummies. Sample period: 2005, 2007, 2009–2013. *Sources:* OECD Social Expenditure Database, World Bank. Robust standard errors in parentheses. *** $p<0.01$, ** $p<0.05$, * $p<0.1$.

women. Political scientists have investigated whether quotas have been followed by subsequent changes in gender-related policies (Franceschet et al., 2012), for example, the promotion of women's rights (Franceschet and Piscopo, 2008; Barnes, 2012; Kerevel and Atkeson, 2013). However, the results are inconclusive (Franceschet and Piscopo, 2008; Htun, Lacalle, and Micozzi, 2013). In this direction, a recent study in political science adopts a cross-country approach to relate the existence of electoral gender quotas to subsequent budgetary priorities (Clayton and Zetterberg, 2018). The study considers 139 countries around the world during the period 1995–2012. By comparing countries that have experienced substantial quota shocks (i.e. those that significantly increase the presence of women in parliament) and others, the authors find that countries in the first category are associated with a subsequent increase in national health spending without significant changes in the total budget or expenditure on education and the military. The authors argue that this occurs because quotas may send cues about legislative priorities to all members of Parliament, they allow more opportunities for female members of the Parliament to include their preferences in budgetary priorities in different ways, and/or provide increased attention to the budgetary preferences of female citizens.

Although interesting, this type of cross-country study suffers from several drawbacks: first, it is difficult to exclude the possibility that the countries with and without substantial quotas may differ in other dimensions. Second, several public policies are implemented at the local rather than the central level of government, and the presence of female politicians at the local level may thus matter for public policies. Third, and most important, aggregate analysis cannot guarantee that the gender of politicians, rather than other individual characteristics or variables that determine their identity, is the unique driver of their effects on policies. Studies that use microdata are better able to identify the effects of the presence of women in political bodies on the policies implemented, though at the cost of concentrating on a unique country and thus reducing the general validity of the results.

4.3 Male and Female Political Leaders and Expenditures: Micro-level Analysis

When exploring whether the gender of policymakers matters, two major questions can be empirically investigated: first, whether the total expenditure decided by men and women is different, and second, whether men and women choose a different allocation of public budget across expenditures. I present the evidence related to developing and developed countries separately and try to understand why they differ.

4.3.1 Developing Countries

The first evidence comes from a group of studies focused on India, where the design of legislation allows a natural experiment to perform a causal analysis. Since 1993, Indian states have been required to decentralize a significant number of policy decisions to a three-tier system of local governance. The lowest tier is the village council, or Gram Panchayat, where villagers elect members of the village council and its leader. The law establishes that one-third of the leader positions should be reserved for women and that the reservation should be rotated between elections. In most cases, this system guarantees a random allocation of female leaders. The differences between reserved and unreserved villages can be exploited to assess the causal impact of female leadership on outcomes. The pioneering research by Chattopadhyay and Duflo (2004) shows that women allocate more resources to investments that support female needs, such as investment in fresh drinking water.

Again in India, Clots-Figueras (2011) uses close races between men and women to assess the causal impact of female politicians on policy outcomes. She shows that social position matters: women who obtain seats in places reserved for the lower caste invest more in health and education and favour redistributive policies, such as land reforms and laws in favour of women (e.g. the same inheritance rule for men and women). Those who hold seats reserved for higher castes have no impact on laws in favour of women; instead, they invest mainly in tertiary education and reduce social expenditures. In a different paper, Clots-Figueras (2012) finds that electing a female politician has a positive impact on educational outcomes in Indian urban areas.

As a result, in India, women in decision-making positions choose policies differently from male politicians; in particular, choosing policies that may support female needs suggests the existence of a virtuous circle: gender policies promote women's representation in decision-making positions, as described in Chapter 3, which, in turn, promotes more gender equality. A virtuous circle may start if female politicians favour public expenditures on services which promote female labour supply, which in turn increases the demand for certain services (Cavalcanti and Tavares, 2011).

4.3.2 Developed Countries

Funk and Gathmann (2015) analyze the direct democracy in Switzerland, where every citizen is a potential policy maker. Swiss citizens vote directly on several policy issues. Funk and Gathman analyze data from surveys held after the federal ballots since 1981. They argue that although some of the results trend in the same direction, their analysis is much more informative and less biased than results that can be derived from surveys. The reason is that they analyze the real vote rather than a hypothetical attitude.

They find large gender gaps. Controlling for the most important sociodemographic characteristics (age, education, income), they find that women are less likely than men to approve an increase in retirement age; are more likely to approve the allocation of funds to environmental protection; are less supportive of nuclear energy; and are more in favour of a healthy lifestyle, equal rights for men and women and more support for the disabled.

More precisely, when the authors consider the votes related to increases in government spending, taxes or debt, they find a small gender difference related to the decision on the total size of government (women are 2.5 percentage points more likely than men to approve projects that increase the size of government) but a large difference in the composition of the public budget. Women are 10 percentage points more likely to support spending for protection of the environment and 6 percentage points less likely to support agricultural or military spending.

In developed countries, in contrast to direct democracies such as Switzerland, research has concentrated on the gender of local politicians, mayors or municipal councillors and local public policies. To identify the causal effects of female politicians on local public policies, studies that focus on municipal councillors mainly use the introduction of gender quotas, which exogenously increases the share of female politicians. They analyze whether this exogenous increase is related to a change in the size and allocation of public expenditures. If the focus is on mayors instead, the identification of the effect is based mainly on the comparison of mixed closed races.[1] As long as the margin of victory is small, we can think of the results of these elections, that is, the

---

[1] Close mixed-gender races can also be used to analyze the role of municipal councilors; see Baskaran and Hessami (2018).

presence of a woman, as random and thus identify the effects of women on policies. In other words, these close races are a way to exclude the possibility that policies themselves induce the election of more women or that an external driver is responsible for a high share both of elected women and of certain types of policies.[2]

In this spirit, Ferreira and Gyourko (2014) study US mayoral elections from 1950 to 2005 and use a regression discontinuity design to compare short- and long-term outcomes across elections in which a woman barely loses against a male candidate. They find no impact of gender on outcomes such as the size of local government, the composition of municipal expenditures and municipal employment or local crime rate. This result suggests that the context and the institutional framework matter: local US politicians are responsive to the preferences of the median voter and have little space for changing redistributive policies. A slightly different result is obtained by Rehavi (2007), who finds that the increasing representation of women among legislators in the United States led to a modest increase of spending on health and correctional institutions.

The case of Italy has also been exploited. Gagliarducci and Paserman (2012) find no consistent effects of female mayors on local spending in Italy. In a more recent paper with Casarico and Lattanzio (Casarico, Lattanzio and Profeta, 2019), we analyze close mixed-gender elections of mayors in Italian municipalities in the period 2000–2015 and find that female mayors collect more revenues and spend more than male mayors, while the composition of both revenue and spending is not affected by gender. When constrained to make fiscal adjustments, female mayors reduce both expenditures and revenues more than male mayors do. Interestingly, again in Italy, gender differences in policymaking are significant when we consider the strategic component of the decisions, that is, the existence of political business cycles. The preliminary results of work with Accettura (Accettura and Profeta, 2019) show that male mayors act more strategically than female mayors. We consider mayors elected after a mixed-gender close race. This means that, as explained before, we can consider the gender of the mayor random. We find that male and female mayors allocate public spending differently only when they are near the election date: while female mayors do not change their decisions when the elections

---

[2] See the Appendix.

approach, male mayors spend more on tourism, territory and environment, social services, public education and especially transportation and road infrastructure. These spending items, given their high visibility and the clear and immediate benefits that they yield, generate widespread electoral consensus. For this reason, they figure among the instruments that are most preferred by incumbents for engaging in political manipulation and suggest that Italian male mayors are more likely to act strategically than their female counterparts.

No effect of female politicians on the allocation of public spending is found for Spain. Bagues and Campa (2018) analyze the introduction of gender quotas in 2007 local elections for municipalities with more than 5,000 residents. They use a regression discontinuity design to compare municipalities subject to the quotas (with more than 5,000 residents) and those not subject to them (below 5,000 residents), near the cut-off of 5,000 residents. First, they find that quotas increase the share of women in candidate lists. They then use this exogenous increase of female politicians to analyze whether the presence of female politicians has a causal impact on the allocation of public expenditures. To do so, they classify expenditures as 'female', 'male' and 'neutral' based on survey data on the policy preferences of a sample of 57,000 Spanish residents. The survey suggests that men care more about housing and urbanism, basic infrastructure and transport, agriculture, hunting and fishing and the environment (for the period 2010–2014), which are therefore classified as 'male' expenditures. Women care more about social security, protection (unemployment, pensions), education and health – which are therefore classified as 'female' expenditures. The other expenditures are 'neutral', neither female biased nor male biased. The authors do not identify differences in the budget allocation of expenditures of the three categories around the cut-off – municipalities with a different share of female politicians due to the quotas.

Again, for Spain, Carozzi and Gago (2018) study female mayors and use a fuzzy regression discontinuity design focused on mixed-gender electoral races for the 2007 and 2011 municipal elections. They find no evidence that female mayors are more sensitive to policies such as family policies, long-term care, preschool and work and family balance services. Instead, what matters in terms of the policies is the party. Once the party is controlled for, gender has no effect on the allocation of public spending.

A different conclusion is reached by a recent study conducted by Baskaran and Hessami (2018) in Germany. They focus on municipal councillors rather than on mayors. They use data for 250,000 candidates running in local council elections between 1996 and 2014 in the 2,056 Bavarian municipalities and exploit the fact that Bavarian local elections rely on open lists. Their identification strategy is based on close mixed-gender races for the last council seat that accrues to a given party. They show that a higher share of female council members has substantive consequences for a council's policy choices: more precisely, a higher share of female council members has a causal positive impact on the availability of childcare.

In summary, research suggests that in developing countries, the presence of women legislators influences the allocation of public spending, while the results are much less clear in developed countries. In this case, studies looking at the causal impact of municipal councillors tend to find slightly more significant results related to policy outcomes than studies concentrating on the causal impact of mayors.

Why do we observe these differences? I suggest the following possibilities. First, the preferences of men and women as voters are in the end not different, at least in mature democracies. However, in this case, it is difficult to explain the evidence described in Box 4.1. Second, politicians do not reflect voters' preferences because they are a selected group of people who are different from the average population. However, Section 4.1 describes documented gender gaps in preferences among politicians. While it is true that data from polls may be biased (Funk, 2016), there is evidence that these gaps remain in unbiased data (Funk and Gathmann, 2015). Third, elected politicians have limited power because of party pressure, which is stronger for women (as documented in Section 4.1); thus, real preferences do not translate into action. This seems to be the more plausible explanation.

4.4 Women and Monetary Policy

I finally analyze a different context, monetary policy. Monetary policy committees of central banks decide monetary policies, which are crucial for the economic situation of a country. For most central banks around the world, the main instrument of monetary policy is the short-term interest rate (Clarida et al., 1998). Central banks choose the level of the short-term policy rate. The decisions are made based on the current interest rate and on expected deviations of the inflation rate and the output gap. The nature of the decision reduces endogeneity concerns.

Does the presence of women matter in monetary policymaking? The question is interesting because a small but increasing number of women have risen to the top at central banks. As of June 2018, thirteen central banks were headed by women, on either an interim or a full-time basis, the most well-known of whom are Elvira Nabiulina in Russia and Karnit Flug in Israel, not to mention, in the recent past, Janet Yellen in the United States. However, little is known about the evolution and role of women on monetary policy committees around the world. The literature to date has focused on investigating how the composition of central bank committees can shape monetary policy outcomes, in particular the degree of activism – the level of dovishness/hawkishness. The existing literature has shown that the composition of these committees, including their level of diversity, seems to matter (Blinder and Morgan, 2005, 2008; Blinder, 2007). Gender is one of the dimensions of diversity that seems to be important. Chappell and McGregor (2000) were among the first to draw attention to gender. They study the voting behaviour of Federal Open Market Committee (FOMC) members over the period 1966–1996, ranking their dovishness/hawkishness. Of the seven women who served on the board during that period, six were ranked among the thirteen most dovish members. Bennani et al. (2018) look at the FOMC's monetary policy decisions over the period 1994–2008 and find that during the 121 meetings considered, female members appeared to have a high dissenting attitude. However, these recent findings on the role of gender in monetary policy are not very informative, as they are either limited to a single central bank or link inflation outcomes to board characteristics.

The question of whether women matter in monetary policy remains open. To answer this question, in a recent paper with Masciandaro and Romelli (Masciandaro et al., 2018), we construct a new dataset on the presence of women on central bank monetary policy committees for 103 countries over the period 2002–2016. Building a comprehensive dataset on the composition of central bank boards is a challenging task. Central bank directories are not available online; most of the time, they provide only the names of the board members without explicitly identifying their gender. Thus, individual name searches must be manually performed. Our final dataset allows us to provide a complete picture of the gender composition of central bank boards over time. Female representation is still very low: in 40 per cent of the countries, there were no women on boards in 2016. The average share of women on boards was 16 per cent in 2016. Since the average size of a board is seven, on average, there is only one woman per board. There is, however, high heterogeneity across countries: in Canada, Sweden, Serbia and Bulgaria, for example, boards have reached a share of 60 per cent women. We also show an overall increasing trend in the average share of women on boards, moving from 11 per cent in 2002 to 16 per cent in 2016. This increase was more pronounced after 2012. Moreover, this trend is not associated with an increase in the average size of the board, which remained almost unchanged at approximately seven members over the analyzed period. Similarly, the proportion of women who held the function of governor or deputy governor has also undergone a steady increase, from less than 9 per cent to approximately 16 per cent. If we focus on women governors in particular, this proportion was stable until 2012 and substantially increased afterwards.

We then use our new dataset to analyze the relationship between the presence of women on boards of central banks and monetary policy decisions. To isolate the effects of gender heterogeneity on policy decisions, we estimate a forward-looking Taylor rule that relates the target policy rate to deviations of expected inflation and output, and we augment the rule to include the share of women board members and the interaction of the share with the inflation rate. Our results show that for the same level of inflation, a higher share of women on the central bank board is associated with a higher interest rate. In terms of magnitude, an increase of one percentage point in inflation results in an interest rate that is 30 basis points higher in a central bank with a 50 per cent share of women board members than in a bank with a 10 per cent share of women board members. This suggests that women in central banks have a more hawkish attitude and are more aggressive in fighting inflation. The results are confirmed in both fixed effects ordinary least squares regressions and the generalized method of moments.

These results are in line with more general results of research in the business context (see Chapter 5), that is, that women are more risk-averse than men and make more conservative decisions. Note that very few studies can prove causality from women to outcomes and that, as we show in Chapter 5, the results are not always consistent. Thus, the monetary policy context is a great opportunity for advancing our understanding of the role of women in policymaking for at least two reasons: endogeneity is a weak concern, and we can explore whether the relationship between women and risk aversion applies to women in real decision-making positions.

4.5 Conclusions

Women's empowerment affects public policy. This chapter has presented new evidence on the different preferences between men and women politicians and policymakers, which creates the expectation of differences in the policies that they implement when elected. Aggregate-level analysis and micro-level analysis of developing countries confirm that the agenda of female politicians is more oriented towards education and social issues than the agenda of male politicians. However, studies on developed countries based on convincing identification of the causal effect of women politicians on public policy outcomes are less conclusive. I argued that this is because, as shown by my analysis of the surveys on political candidates, women tend to suffer party pressure more than men do; thus, they struggle to translate their identity into real outcomes. Interestingly, in the case of monetary policy, women seem to be successful in influencing the policy outcomes: the association between gender and policy decisions emerges as a general result when controlling for the specific characteristics of each country.

5 | *How Women Affect Firms' Outcomes*

This chapter focuses on women as decision-makers in business positions. It aims to answer the following questions: Are firms' outcomes, such as profits, returns on equity and investment, assets and sustainability scores related to the gender of the decision-making persons? Do women on boards, in CEO positions or in managerial positions affect the business and financial performance of companies? Do they influence social performance and sustainability outcomes, including environmental scores? Do they affect other firms' international outcomes, such as openness to exports or international trade? Do they influence the labour market policies implemented by the firms, such as recruiting and promotion policies – which affect the presence of women in managerial positions – or work organization (the use of part-time positions, for example)?

Before beginning the analysis, a natural question arises: Why should we expect any effect on firms' outcomes of the presence of women in leadership positions and gender-balanced leadership? More generally, why do women in corporate bodies matter, and why does how they act in such bodies matter?

A major source of gender differences, which may be important for firms' results, resides in the individual psychological attributes and preferences of men and women. These psychological attributes – which I will henceforth also refer to as 'individual traits' – include risk aversion, attitude towards negotiation and competition, time horizon, social preferences (such as sensitivity to fairness, justice, trust and altruism) and networking. In addition to individual traits, men and women generally interact with one another differently in teams. However, it is difficult to separate gender interactions from individual traits because groups tend to be endogenously formed. Overall, these factors help identify what I will call a 'style of leadership', which emerges as a complex combination of different individual psychological attributes and the way they are mixed in the dynamic and evolving exercise of power. These traits remain important even though the style of male and female leadership differs in different contexts and interactions with features of the organization.

Gender differences in individual traits have been explored by a large experimental literature (see Azmat and Petrongolo, 2014, for an extensive review). However, experiments are generally not performed on a sample of business women, thus raising concerns about the validity of their results when applied to a selected sample of women who have reached leadership positions (Adams and Funk, 2012). Findings from the laboratory are thus a useful guideline for what we should expect from female or male (or balanced) leadership, but they need to be verified in context.

In this chapter, I present evidence on gender-specific individual traits and their potential impact on firms' outcomes. For example, if a fundamental trait is that women are more risk averse than men, under the cautionary check that this trait characterizes not only the average population but also male and female leaders, the prediction is that firms led by women (or in which the share of women on boards is larger) will make less risky decisions. This chapter explains whether this prediction is confirmed by empirical evidence.

There are numerous analyses of the relationship between the presence of women in decision-making positions and business and financial outcomes, although only a small number of them are methodologically rigorous and reliable. Business and financial outcomes are generally not directly related to the promotion of gender equality, making the reverse causality argument less serious than that in Chapter 4. In fact, it is unlikely that firms increase profits to improve gender equality, while it is true that governments may decide to increase spending on family policy precisely because they want to improve gender equality. When the analyzed outcomes are instead labour policies, which may be considered particularly beneficial for women, though not necessarily targeting them, such as the diffusion of part-time positions, the reverse causality concern appears more serious. However, the omitted variable bias is a serious issue: given other correlated variables, firms with high profits may be more likely to hire or promote women than firms with low profits, similar to what occurs in governments with generous family policies.

In the second part of the chapter, I present an empirical analysis to test some of the predictions of the impact of female leadership on firms' outcomes using rigorous identification strategies. I organize the empirical analysis by outcome: firms' business performance, firms' social and sustainability performance, firms' international performance (export and trade) and labour market outcomes. I present a cross-country analysis with fixed effects as well as more detailed country analyses for two selected countries, Norway and Italy.

The chapter provides a guideline to navigate around the abundant existing evidence. It also coherently provides new contributions, mainly by concentrating on how to establish a causal relationship between women's leadership and firms' outcomes. This dramatically reduces the abundance of the existing contributions on the topics that are of interest in our analysis to a small set. In fact, as I argued in Chapter 4, for reliable results, the effect of gender on outcomes should be assessed without endogeneity concerns, mainly by ensuring that the presence of women does not itself depend on the measured outcomes or on a common determinant. Overall, the chapter delivers a picture of what it truly means to have women's leadership and gender balance in decision-making positions in the corporate world.

5.1 Why Should Women Matter for Firms' Outcomes?

I start by identifying the potential drivers of why we expect gender diversity to matter for performance, that is, individual traits that, on average, distinguish men from women and may have an impact on business performance by making the presence of both genders, as well as their interaction, significant for performance. If men and women were perfectly equal, there would be no reason for gender diversity to be associated with varied performance. Different psychological attributes and preferences, as well as a different way to interact in teams, may instead generate interesting implications for how gender matters in firms' decisions and performance.

As already reviewed in Chapter 2, it is difficult – if not impossible – to disentangle whether these different traits depend on nature or nurture or, more likely, a combination of the two. I thus abstain from attempting to understand the causes of these traits.

The section is organized by the following individual traits: risk aversion, competition, negotiation, altruism, long-term horizon and networking.

5.1.1 Risk Aversion

A major individual trait that differentiates men and women is risk aversion. An abundant literature tests the existence of gender differences in risk aversion by using laboratory experiments in which individuals are asked to solve real and hypothetical gambles. These studies assess whether men and women have different levels of willingness to gamble. They also study whether, when facing gambles with different expected returns and variances (riskier gambles have higher payoffs), men and women make different choices. Other studies are based on surveys. The general result of this literature is that women are more risk averse than men (see surveys by Eckel and Grossman, 2008 and Croson and Gneezy, 2009).

This evidence has been used to explain the scarce presence of women in high-risk jobs, for example, jobs with high earning volatility or in which the risk of job loss is substantial, which are typically rewarded by higher earnings. The scarce presence of women in such jobs implies that gender gaps in the labour market are wide and that some highly risky sectors, such as the financial sector, are male dominated. Sapienza et al. (2009) document that at the University of Chicago, approximately 36 per cent of female MBA students choose a risky career in finance (e.g. investment banking or trading), whereas 57 per cent of male students do so. They highlight the dependence of the male choice on biological factors, such as a high level of testosterone and low risk aversion.

However, a male-dominated financial sector may not be the ideal outcome. This became clear after the financial crisis under the pressure to find new ways to strengthen the financial system and re-establish the trust and confidence in financial institutions that had been lost. If women are more cautious and more careful in understanding and preventing risky situations, the contribution of women to the financial sector is both needed and recommended. This idea became clear in the words of Christine Lagarde (2008) of the IMF, who claimed, 'If Lehman Brothers had been a little bit more Lehman Sisters, the financial crisis would not have produced such disastrous consequences.' She then qualified this conclusion, suggesting that brothers and sisters together may be the ideal solution for better outcomes in the financial sector.

This intriguing idea, which, after Lagarde's words, became quite popular, needs to be tested. We will never know what would have happened in the case of 'Lehman Sisters'. However, we can try to understand whether the hypothesis behind this popular argument has any empirical foundation. Adams and Ragunathan (2015) provide evidence that partially undermines the Lehman Sisters hypothesis: they analyze 300 large publicly traded US banks and bank holding companies in a four-year period around the 2007–2008 financial crisis and find that listed banks with more female directors did not engage in fewer risk-taking activities around the crisis and had no less risk than other banks. This result, however, does not imply that women do not matter: using an instrumental variable regression, the authors find that banks with more diverse boards had better performances. In other words, gender diversity matters during the crisis and has a positive value, though the channel is not the reduction in risks.

Adams and Ragunathan (2015) explain that the failure of the Lehman Sisters hypothesis depends on the fact that experiments and survey-based research that have found that women are more risk averse than men are based on samples of college students or the general population, and managers, top executives and directors are obviously different from these groups. As a self-selected part of the population who have chosen risky careers in a risky context, female managers need not be more risk averse than men. Adams and Funk (2012) indeed provide evidence that generalizing from the population to the executive ranks may be misleading. In a survey of the population of directors in Sweden, they show that women on the boards of publicly listed firms are different both from women in the general population and from male directors in the values that they emphasize. Female directors are more open to change and less conservatively oriented than both their population and male director counterparts. Moreover, female directors are less risk averse than male directors in this sample. One explanation for these results is self-selection: women who choose a career that leads to a directorship may be very different from women who do not; they may be less risk averse than the general female population.

Another piece of evidence relates to gender and the financial crisis: during the period of the crisis, many women were asked to lead companies either after the failure or in highly risky situations (the so-called glass cliff hypothesis). If women are appointed to precarious leadership positions, they obviously face a higher risk of failure (see Haslam and Ryan, 2008); in contrast to what is predicted by experiments based on gender and individual traits, the correlation between female leadership and risk will appear positive instead of negative or zero. Again, we must be careful in distinguishing correlation from causality.

Financial studies have largely investigated whether there is a relationship between women's empowerment and stock market returns and volatility (see Adams and Ferreira, 2009). The evidence is inconclusive. Wolfers (2006) finds no differences in stock price performance between female-headed firms and other firms. Dobbin and Jung (2011) argue that women on corporate boards are more likely to adversely affect stock prices. How the stock market reacts to the appointment of a female director is also ambiguous: Chapple and Humphrey (2014) find no reaction in Australia, Adams et al. (2011) find a positive reaction and Lee and James (2007) find a negative reaction. Thus, whether women matter for firms' outcomes because of their different risk aversion remains an empirical question, and causality remains to be seriously addressed.

A side effect of risk aversion is the attitude towards monitoring and adopting caution and attention to the process and the performance. The evidence suggests that in comparison to men, women are more responsible, allocate more time and resources to monitoring (Adams and Ferreira, 2009) and tend to monitor employee feedback and development more intensively (Melero, 2011). However, it is difficult to establish whether these traits are due to their risk aversion or to the pressure and attention imposed on their performance, which is generally higher than those imposed on men's performance. As monitoring is a primary responsibility of a board, if women pursue this activity more than men do, we expect more women on boards to be associated with more effective boards (see the results of the meta-analysis of Post and Byron, 2014).

5.1.2 Competition

Another important trait that has been found to differentiate men and women is the attitude towards competition. Niederle and Vesterlund (2007) develop a laboratory experiment in which subjects can choose between a piece-rate incentive scheme (a compensation based on the number of correct answers) and a tournament (a higher amount only to the best performers). They found that women prefer the piece-rate compensation incentive scheme and that men prefer the tournament, that is, women shy away from competition. Women with high performance scores also prefer the piece-rate scheme, even more than low-performers men. This suggests that men are over-confident and women have low self-esteem. Gneezy et al. (2003) also show that men perform better than women in tournament schemes. Outside laboratory experiments, the fact that men are more competitive than women has been established by field experiments, such as one by Gneezy and Rustichini (2004) on children and running performance. The experiment was conducted by first recording each child's speed when running alone and then randomly assigning children to two subsamples, one in which they had to run by themselves and another in which they had to run in pairs. The results showed that in the no-competition group, there was no improvement in performance by gender, but when a boy had to compete with another boy, he improved his speed by a large margin, as opposed to girls competing with other girls.

If women are less competitive than men, we expect fewer female entrepreneurs than male ones. If this fundamental trait persists when we compare women and men in leadership positions, we expect firms with more women in top positions to be associated with less competitive decisions, for example, less exposure to the global market and less engagement in trade and export. Again, this is ultimately an empirical question.

5.1.3 Negotiation

Men and women have different negotiation skills. The general fact that 'women don't ask' – and this is one reason that they earn less than men – has been confirmed by laboratory experiments. Small et al. (2007) show that women are less likely than men to initiate a negotiation (for the payment of the experiment). Bowles et al. (2007) find that women are less likely than men to start a negotiation in the presence of a male evaluator and that, when they do, it generates a poorer evaluation than that received by men.

Evidence from ultimatum games may also be useful in understanding gender differences in negotiations. In these games, one of the two players makes a take-it-or-leave-it offer on the division of the amount of money between the two players, and the other player can accept or reject it. If he rejects it, both players obtain nothing. The evidence on gender differences in these games is inconclusive. Eckel and Grossman (2001) find that men and women make similar offers, but women are more likely to accept. Solnick (2001) shows that women demand higher offers when they play against a woman (see also Rigdon, 2012). In contrast, in dictator games, in which the respondent does not have the choice to reject the offer, women tend to offer more than men (Andreoni and Vesterlund, 2001).

If women negotiate less than men, we expect women to receive lower wages, even when they reach a leadership position. If firms run by women are in sectors and activities in which negotiations (with clients, other firms, etc.) are important for profits, these firms can have lower profits than those run by men.

5.1.4 Altruism

Men and women differ in their degree of altruism, fairness, trust and social preferences in general. Laboratory experiments using dictator and ultimatum games generally suggest that women are more altruistic than men. In an influential paper, Andreoni and Vesterlund (2001, 294–5) use a slightly modified version of the dictator game to show that 'when it is relatively expensive to give, women are more generous than men; however, as the price of giving decreases, men begin to give more than women. In addition, men are more likely to be either perfectly selfish or perfectly selfless, whereas women tend to be "equalitarian" and prefer to share evenly.' Thus, although women seem to be more altruistic than men, to what extent this trait shapes men and women and their behaviour is not obvious. Other types of experiments are also inconclusive: simple trust games find no gender differences in trust (see Croson and Buchan, 1999) or in contributions to the provision of public goods (Eckel and Grossman, 2008).

Altruism, defined in its broad sense as caring for other individuals' utility, may have important consequences for business outcomes. If women are more altruistic than men, we expect women in business leadership positions to be less likely than men to fire workers (or to make similar decisions) and more likely to propose measures that support the well-being of workers and respond to workers' needs.

As a related consequence, we also expect social preferences to shape the way in which women collaborate with other workers and with the workers they supervise, especially women, which in turn may affect gender equality in the workplace. In other words, women in top positions are expected to promote a more general process of gender gap reduction, which, in turn, may have an impact on performance. This process develops along different dimensions: first, women in leadership positions are expected to support other women and help them more effectively build their careers, acting as role models and contributing to developing mentoring and networking activities that are useful for other women's careers. Second, women at the top are expected to promote a more gender-neutral evaluation process and to be more likely than men to directly promote other women. More specifically, in the presence of an *ex ante* non-neutral selection process or discrimination against women (see Chapter 2), having more women in top positions may re-establish a gender-neutral, non-discriminatory selection process, which may ultimately be efficient for business outcomes.

A related aspect of altruism is the way men and women perceive their subordinates and interact with them. Altruism may generate a democratic style of interaction in which subordinates are encouraged to participate in the decision-making process, interpersonal channels of communication are more active (Melero, 2011), and employees find higher motivation to plan and develop their own careers. If women are more favourable to the promotion of female subordinates, this trait may generate a virtuous circle of female leadership and reduction in gender gaps. Overall, research has found that female leadership is generally associated with a reduction in gender gaps (Tate and Yang, 2015; Flabbi et al., 2019).

A large body of evidence, however, shows that women in top positions are not necessarily favourable to the career development of other women. In contrast, women who have reached top positions in a male-dominated world tend to penalize other women as a way of showing their exceptional and unique talent as successful women (the so-called "queen bee syndrome"). They make clear their neutrality towards gender issues to ensure that nobody can doubt that they adopt meritocratic criteria for selections – similar to those that were applied to them – and are not influenced by gender-based homophily biases. Unfortunately, this attitude is another way to perpetuate gender discrimination. These studies may, however, suffer from methodological problems, as emphasized by a recent study (Arvate et al., 2018) that reached different conclusions and cast doubts on the existence of the queen bee effect.

Box 5.1 summarizes evidence on gender non-neutrality in the selection process.

Box 5.1 Gender non-neutrality in the selection process

This mechanism relates to the concept of screening discrimination, which I introduced in Chapter 2. Discrimination may arise if a male-dominated evaluation committee is unable to correctly evaluate women and prefers to select similar, male people. Evidence on gender non-neutrality in the selection process is abundant. Goldin and Rouse (2000) find that moving to blind auditions in major American orchestras, where the sex of the musician cannot be observed by the evaluators, increases the likelihood that women will advance in the hiring process and that they will eventually be hired. In their examination of the factors that influence evaluators when reviewing curricula vitae, Steinpreis et al. (1999) find that both male and female evaluators have a gender bias towards male job applicants in the field of academic psychology. This discrimination against women may depend on the presence of stereotypes (Gorman, 2005) in the selection criteria, which often include masculine characteristics (see also Reuben et al., 2014 in an experimental setting). In other words, well-established biases influence the selection process, which are presumably difficult to remove without strong intervention. Non-neutrality in the selection process may also derive from individual homophily preferences: individuals may prefer people who are similar to them since they are able to better assess such people's characteristics, and this preference may result, for example, in male evaluators preferring male candidates. Non-neutrality may occur because it is generally easier for individuals to screen people of a similar background (Pinkston, 2003). As a result of this non-neutral selection process, male evaluators tend to prefer male candidates.

The direct evidence for this is, however, not fully conclusive (see Feld et al., 2016). In the context of academia, De Paola and Scoppa (2015) find that having a female evaluator increases women's chances of being selected, while Bagues et al. (2017) find that the gender composition of scientific committees does not affect either the quantity or the quality of female candidates. In the managerial context, Bell (2005) finds that female executives have significantly higher chances of promotion in firms with a female CEO or female board chair. Matsa and Miller (2011) find that having had women on a board of directors in previous years has a significant positive effect on the female share of top management.

In a recent paper with Conde-Ruiz and Ganuza (2017), we theoretically show that this non-neutrality of the selection process is inefficient. More precisely, the group that is most represented in the evaluation committee generates more accurate and less noisy signals (the 'homoaccuracy' bias) and consequently has a greater incentive to invest in human capital. Human capital does not refer to the level of education; rather, it is a comprehensive concept of investment in increasing productivity in several dimensions that are difficult to assess, such as steadiness, punctuality, responsiveness, leadership, effort in previous job experience or initiative. The reduction in incentives generates a discrimination trap. If, for some exogenous reason, one group is initially poorly evaluated (is less well represented in the evaluation committee), this translates into lower investment in the human capital of the individuals in that group, which leads to their lower representation in the evaluation committee in the future, generating a persistent discrimination process. Quotas may be effective in addressing this discrimination trap and increasing welfare as talented workers of the discriminated group decide to invest in human capital.

5.1.5 Long-term Horizon

The idea that women have a long-term horizon and perspective, while men tend to choose based on short-term consequences is old. As women give birth and invest in childrearing more than men, they are expected to be predisposed to long-term investments.

Studies show that women are more able than men to delay gratification and are more patient. Bjorklund and Kipp (1996) review experiments that test gender differences in delayed gratification using a simple procedure: participants are asked to choose between a small (or less preferred) immediate reward and a larger reward after some amount of time. They find that although the evidence may be less strong than expected, experiments confirm that women generally tend to be more patient and wait for the higher reward.

Patience may, however, also be related to other characteristics, such as risk aversion, as mentioned previously, and it is difficult to isolate one trait from another. In spite of these difficulties, if women are more able than men to plan their outcomes over a longer-term horizon, then we expect firms in which the share of women in top positions is higher to make decisions that are more oriented towards investments (e.g. by financing long-term debt) and long-term profits rather than towards short-term profits and short-term debts. We also expect women in decision-making positions to care more than men about policies with a clear long-term impact, such as those related to sustainability or environmental issues. Finally, we expect women to be more involved in innovative processes, growth-oriented plans for the future of the firm and the longevity of the firm than in fast growth (Bird and Brush, 2002).

5.1.6 Networking

Men and women differ in how they interact. These differences may be related to the psychological traits discussed earlier (e.g. different attitudes towards competition translate into different dynamics of the interaction process between candidates or colleagues), but they may also represent pure effects generated by the team dynamic context. While it is difficult to isolate the origin of the nature of interactions, it is clear that they may translate into different outcomes.

A widely investigated aspect is the way in which men and women establish connections with other members of the organization – their style of networking (Mengel, 2015; Beaman et al., 2018). Gender differences in networking may translate into different opportunities for jobs and careers. Several studies have found that while both men and women recognize that networking is fundamental for professional success, men focus more on connections with other men in the organization, while women focus more on a balanced mix of connections with other men and women. Mengel (2015) conducts an experiment to understand gender differences in networking. Participants are divided into groups of six and perform a (gender-neutral) task. After the task, they receive information about their performance, their rank and the overall group performance but not about others' performance. However, they can form links with other group members to share the information. After that, one group is selected as a 'decision-maker': the results show that both men and women tend to link to individuals of the same gender. However, men have a stronger tendency to favour their network neighbours. As long as men are more represented in powerful positions and in networks, and networking is important for earnings and careers, women have a clear disadvantage.

Another important gender difference in networking is described by Lindenlaub and Prummer (2014). They show that women tend to have smaller and tighter networks, while men have larger and looser networks. Tight networks promote trust and peer pressure among agents and reduce shrinking and free-rider problems because repercussions are perceived to affect the entire network. However, as the network becomes smaller and closer, the amount of information received by the members is limited. The authors build a theoretical model to show that loose male networks are more effective in work environments characterized by uncertainty and high returns, that is, the male network is more effective than the female network for business success in most jobs.

5.1.7 Style of Leadership

I interpret the primary traits described by the experimental literature and the way they shape interactions in the business context as fundamental ingredients of what I refer to as the 'style of leadership', more precisely, the male and female styles of leadership. Traditional management studies in organization and diversity have elaborated on a previous version of this concept. Eagly and Carli (2003) and Eagly et al. (2003), based on a previous meta-analysis and their own meta-analysis of the previous literature, summarize the fundamental female leadership traits as follows:

- Women have a democratic style of leadership, in which subordinates are encouraged to participate in decision-making, as opposed to the autocratic style of men;
- Women's leadership style is interpersonally oriented, as opposed to the task-oriented men's leadership style;
- Women are more future oriented than men (what they call 'a transformational leader') and more likely to exchange their self-interest for the satisfactory performance of their subordinates ('transactional leadership').

Defining what constitutes a style of leadership is complex. An enormous body of literature has studied which traits are effective, achieving results that are clear and unique. A gendered approach to leadership is even more complex, and there is little agreement in the existing studies on what are male and female styles of leadership. Survey evidence documents gender differences in corporate directors' preferences and values (Adams and Funk, 2012), which correspond, at least in part, to the individual traits I have discussed: according to these expectations, female directors are more benevolent but less power oriented than their male counterparts. My approach is therefore to refer back to the fundamental individual traits described earlier. From now on, I refer to 'leadership style' as the result of (several combinations of) individual traits and the way that individuals interact. In parallel, gender differences in terms of individual traits are the foundation of different styles of leadership between women and men.

Several studies have explored whether gender differences in leadership are associated with different performances of male and female leaders and of firms led by men or women. There is evidence that individual managers bring their own personal 'styles' to managing their firms (Bertrand and Schoar, 2003; Graham and Narsimhan, 2004; Bloom and Van Reenen, 2010; Malmendier et al., 2011). There is also evidence that gender matters in defining this personal style. Specifically the female style of leadership may drive a positive relationship between women in leadership positions and performance. This is probably because some of the traits summarized earlier seem to suggest an advantage of women's leadership over men's leadership. Many of these studies concentrate on the relationship between women on boards and firms' business and financial performance. The underlying hypothesis is that boards make relevant decisions in which the style of leadership matters; boards are not simply 'window dressing' (Helland and Sykuta, 2004). I return to this evidence in the next section.

Another way to understand the effectiveness and impact of women's style of leadership is to observe the creation of role models. The style is effective if women at the top become role models and thus promote and influence other women's careers. This result is, of course, stronger when women at the top are directly engaged in mentoring, motivating, stimulating and empowering their subordinates and helping them develop their potential and identify the ways in which they can contribute more effectively to their organization.

Overall, what I have called the 'style of leadership', which I have identified in this section, and the individual traits behind it may influence firms' outcomes. In the next sections, I focus on the following four groups of outcomes: business and financial performance, social and sustainability performance, international performance (trade and openness) and labour market results.

5.2 Women's Leadership and Business Performance

In this section, firms' outcomes are business and financial performance measured by profits, return on assets, return on investments and return on equity. Decision-makers are women in high-level business positions in firms – managers, CEOs and board members. Risk aversion and competition, as well as how they interact with others, are the individual traits that are expected to play a major role in the relationship between women's leadership and business performance.

Several decades ago, well-known consulting companies, such as McKinsey & Company, started to provide evidence of a positive relationship between the share of women in top positions of firms and the firms' performance. Shortly afterwards, financial institutions and other consulting companies, such as Catalyst, CONSOB, Credit Suisse and Egon Zehnder, followed suit. The general message of this evidence is that having more women leaders is associated with an increase in profits. As of 2012, McKinsey reported that mixed-gender boards in the United States outperformed all male ones; in 2011, Catalyst published a report that the Fortune 500 companies whose boards had the highest proportion of women performed significantly better than those whose boards had the lowest proportion. For Europe, CONSOB gathered data about listed companies in Italy, France, Germany and Spain and found a positive relationship between the presence of female executive directors and the return on assets of the firms they run. These reports suggest that this positive relationship depends on the abilities of women to deal with and solve conflicts, their aptitude to collaborate and make decisions with the agreement of partners and their capacity to pay attention to people and interact with them. Using interviews with general managers, CEOs and women on the boards of large companies, the reports conclude that these women's leadership traits are fundamental to the business success. This evidence is the start of the so-called business case for gender diversity – the view that diversity among board members increases performance. Promoting diversity becomes an issue of business in addition to equity and fairness considerations.

The literature of management and organization took a step forward and used quantitative tools to investigate whether the presence of women in the top positions of firms is correlated with better performance. The diversity literature developed the concept that what matters for business success is having both men and women in top positions: in a heterogeneous context, the perspectives are enlarged, discussions are more effective, innovation increases and the pool of talent is widened. Employees with a variety of qualifications are available, and the overall corporate image improves (Ingley and van der Walt, 2003; Rose, 2007). Competition among workers within the firm is also positively affected since workers know that they may reach top positions independently of their personal characteristics. Thus, this dynamic and constructive context is more stimulating for the population of employees. Overall, employees are more likely to make better decisions, with positive effects for the company as a whole.

Along these lines, much attention has been paid to women on boards and to performance. Early, non-causal research provides evidence of a positive correlation between women on boards and the performance of companies in several countries. To cite some studies, research on a panel of 2,500 firms in Denmark in the period 1993–2001 (Smith et al., 2006) finds that the share of women on boards is positively and significantly related to performance, even when controlling for the sector, the size and the age of the firm. This study also identifies stronger effects when women on boards have higher levels of education and when they do not belong to the family of owners. Similar positive relationships between women on boards and performance are obtained for samples from Australia (Nguyen and Faff, 2007), Spain (Campbell and Minguez-Vera, 2008) and various regions of the United States (Erhardt et al., 2003). A positive relationship between the presence of women on boards or in top management and firms' performance is also confirmed for two samples of Fortune 1000 and Fortune 500 American firms (Krishnan and Park, 2005; Carter et al., 2007). The literature is, however, mixed. When control variables for important aspects of firms (the type of governance, for example; see Gul et al., 2011 and Jurkus et al., 2011) are introduced, the relationship becomes weaker or even disappears. For specific samples (Adams and Ferreira, 2009), the relationship even becomes negative, suggesting that there is no clear understanding of the existence of a stable and robust relationship between female leadership and firms' performance.

To assess and try to explain the mixed results of the existing literature, Post and Byron (2014, 1546) perform a meta-analysis of studies of the relationship between women on boards and firm accounting performance. They statistically combine the results of 140 studies (92 published and the others unpublished) and examine whether the results vary by firms' legal/regulatory and sociocultural contexts. They find that the relationship is positive, especially in countries with stronger shareholder protections; in their view, the reason is that 'shareholder protections motivate boards to use the different knowledge, experience, and values that each member brings'. They also find that the relationship between women on boards and market performance is generally near zero; it becomes positive in countries with high gender equality and negative in countries with low gender equality because the gender equality of the country may influence investors' evaluations of the positive results of firms with more women on their boards. A different conclusion is reached by the meta-analysis of Pletzer et al. (2015), based on 20 studies on 3,097 companies that investigate the relationship between women on boards and performance. In contrast to Post and Byron (2014), Pletzer et al. (2015, 1) limit the meta-analysis to research that considers the relationship between the percentage of women on corporate boards, on one hand, and a firm's financial performance, measured by return on assets, return on equity and Tobin's Q, on the other hand. They conclude that the 'mere representation of females on corporate boards is not related to firm performance if other factors are not considered.' These factors include country development and income, which should be included as controls to obtain a (small) level of statistical significance of the relationship. Overall, it seems that the business case for diversity on boards has in general limited empirical support. The context matters. The mixed results may also be due to methodological concerns: as previously mentioned, most of these studies suffer from endogeneity concerns and cannot provide a rigorous assessment of whether and why the female leadership style has a positive effect on performance.

More recently, the role of female leadership on business outcomes has been analyzed using the most advanced econometric techniques in a new field of study at the intersection between corporate governance, labour economics, finance and management. The most rigorous studies take advantage of the introduction of mandatory corporate board gender quotas in selected European countries, which is described in Box 5.2.

As summarized in Table 5.1, Belgium, France, Germany, Italy, Iceland, Norway and Portugal are the European countries with hard gender quota laws for listed companies. These countries are the appropriate candidates for testing the causal effect of the presence of women on performance. In fact, the introduction of board gender quotas is an exogenous variation in the gender composition of boards and can therefore be used to assess the causal effects of women's leadership on performance by overcoming the endogeneity issues related to reverse causality and omitted variable bias. We can thus learn much about the relationship between women on boards and firm performance from analyses of these countries. Research has so far concentrated on Norway and Italy, as I detail in the following sections. As I have emphasized several times, the context matters. Thus, focusing on Norway and Italy is particularly interesting because it provides an opportunity to exploit two very different contexts: Norway ranks high in terms of gender equality indicators, while Italy performs very poorly.

5.2.1 Norway

In late 2003, a law was approved in Norway mandating at least 40 per cent representation of each gender on the boards of companies listed on its stock market. The Norwegian law imposed a dramatic and rapid transformation of the composition of boards of directors (Teigen and Engelstad, 2012; Huse and Seierstad, 2013) with an increase in women and young members as well as an increase in female directors with multiple positions (the so-called golden-skirt phenomenon; see Seierstad and Opsahl, 2011). What about firms' outcomes?

An influential study by Ahern and Dittmar (2012) analyzes 248 publicly listed Norwegian firms for the period 2001–2009 to show that the increase of women on boards in Norway imposed a significant cost on Tobin's Q, which measures the value of firms.

Box 5.2 Board gender quotas in Europe

Norway is the pioneer in the introduction of board gender quotas, with the 2003 requirement threshold of 40 per cent of each gender on the boards of companies listed on its stock market. The law established that existing firms must comply by January 2008, while new firms must comply by January 2006. Firms that did not comply by January 2008 were dissolved. Teigen and Engelstad (2012) and Huse and Seierstad (2013) develop a detailed description of the Norwegian law.

France adopted board gender quotas in January 2011, when the Parliament voted for the so-called Zimmermann-Copé law, which established the gradual introduction of board gender quotas in listed companies. Beginning in January 2011, if the board was unisex, a member of the non-represented gender had to be appointed once a seat became vacant. By 2014, each gender had to represent at least 20 per cent of directors. The threshold increased to 40 per cent in 2017. In 2012, the law was extended to public companies. Board gender quotas were thus introduced gradually. Noncompliance with the law implies nullification of the board appointments. Rebérioux and Roudaut (2016) provide a first assessment of the effects of the French law on within-board inequalities (who is appointed and in which role).

Shortly after France, Italy passed a similar law on board gender quotas for listed companies in July 2011. The so-called Golfo-Mosca law (known by the names of the two politicians who jointly proposed the law – Lella Golfo from the center-right coalition and Alessia Mosca from the center-left coalition) mandates gender-balanced representation on the boards of directors and statutory auditors of publicly listed companies. The Italian quotas are temporary and gradual (for details on the implementation of the law, see Ferrari et al., 2018). In fact, the measure will be in place for only three consecutive board elections. The required target of the representation of either gender is set at one-fifth for the first board election after August 2012 and increases to one-third for the following two board elections. Board elections occur on a specific date for each firm; thus, the quota is not introduced at the same time for all firms.

Belgium introduced board gender quotas for listed and state-owned companies in 2011. The law required that each gender make up at least one-third of the members of the executive boards of listed companies. The threshold increased to two-thirds by 2019. Listed companies have a transition period to comply (five years for large companies and eight for small ones), but this does not apply to state-owned companies. In case of noncompliance, only women can be appointed until the quota is reached. In the meantime, serving board members are not paid. After one year of noncompliance, the general meeting must elect a new board.

Germany started to promote gender equality in 2010 through the German Corporate Governance Code, which suggests that when filling managerial positions in the enterprise, the Management Board shall take diversity into consideration and, in particular, aims for an appropriate consideration of women and finally moved to quotas in 2015. The 'Act on Equal Participation of Men and Women in Leadership Positions in the Private and Public Sector' introduces a mandatory quota of 30 per cent for the underrepresented sex on nonexecutive boards (supervisory boards or, in a one-tiered board structure, administrative boards) of companies listed on the stock exchange. It also establishes a different criterion for a wider set of companies, that is, free determination of quotas: companies must establish their own initial set of quotas to be reached by June 2017. Noncompliance with gender quota requirements is sanctioned by empty board seats or administrative fines.

The last European country to introduce quotas is Portugal in 2018. The law applies to publicly listed companies, which are required to reach 33 per cent of each gender by 2020. If companies do not comply, the board election is nullified.

A slightly different case is Iceland, which in 2010 introduced board gender quotas for publicly traded, state-owned and private limited firms with at least fifty employees. The quota is fixed at 40 per cent and has to be reached by 2013. It is considered a hard law, although there are no sanctions in case of noncompliance.

Other countries have introduced 'soft' quotas – a threshold that does not penalize noncompliant companies, thus exerting less pressure for board gender balance. Spain and the Netherlands have this type of provision. Spain adopted a soft gender quota law in 2007: the Gender Equality Act recommends that all large public and private Spanish firms appoint a target of 40 per cent of each gender to serve as board directors by 2015. There is no penalty for noncompliance. However, there is an incentive to comply, as firms adopting the quota receive preference in the tendering of public contracts. Conde-Ruiz and Hoya (2015) document that the Spanish non-binding legislation was not able to increase the share of women on boards to the recommended threshold. However, as analyzed by de Cabo et al. (2017), due to the incentive that they contain, the soft Spanish quotas were effective in increasing the presence of women on the boards of firms whose activity is related to public contracts.

The Netherlands is following what is called the 'comply or explain' principle, which means there is a suggested target of 30 per cent female representation for large enterprises, and those that choose not to comply must explain their choice in their annual report and publish a specific action plan explaining what they are doing to achieve female representation in the boardroom.

The UK is promoting women on boards on a voluntary basis. The Women on Board Report (Davies, 2011) suggests that FTSE 100 companies should aim for at least 25 per cent of women on boards, but firms are still free to set their own goals at their own discretion. This recommendation is based on the estimate that at the current rate of change, it would take more than seventy years to achieve gender-balanced boardrooms in the UK. A stronger stance should thus be taken to encourage more active policies.

Finally, there is also a proposal for a EU directive on improving gender balance among directors and companies listed on stock exchanges. However, the process of approval of the proposal has been stalled since 2012.

Board gender quotas have recently been discussed outside Europe. A notable case is California, the first US state to approve in September 2018 a bill for the inclusion of women on the boards of directors of public companies.

Table 5.1 summarizes the main features of board gender quotas across European countries.

Table 5.1 *Board gender quotas in European countries*

Country	Year	Policy	Companies	Sanctions	Duration
Belgium	2011	*Hard quota* 33%	– Publicly traded – State Owned	– Nullification of new board election – Members of boards lose their benefits and compensation	6 years to reach the target (8 for SMEs)
France	2011	*Hard quota* 40%	– Publicly traded – Non-listed with >500 employees or revenues > € 50m	– Members of boards lose their compensation	Full compliance by 2017
Germany	2015	*Hard quota* 30%	– Publicly traded	– Fines – Nullification of board election	Full compliance by 2017
Iceland	2010	*Hard quota* 40%	– Publicly traded ≥ 50 employees – State-owned ≥50 employees – Private limited ≥50 employees	None	Full compliance by 2013
Italy	2011	*Hard quota* 33%	– Publicly traded	– Official warning – Fines – Nullification of board election	3 board elections

Country & Year	Quota type	Scope	Sanctions	Compliance deadline
Netherlands 2011	*Soft quota* 30%	– Publicly traded (+250 employees)	– Explanation for non-compliance – Action plan for achievement	
Norway 2003	*Hard quota* 40%	– Publicly traded – State owned	– Official warning – Fines – Dissolution	Full compliance by 2008
Portugal 2018	*Hard quota* 33%	– Publicly traded – State owned	– Nullification of board election – Noncompliance declaration by the Securities Market Authority (listed companies only)	Full compliance by 2020
Spain 2007	*Soft quota* 40%	– Publicly traded (+250 employees)	None, but gender diversity gives priority for public subsidies and state contracts	
UK 2011	*Voluntary quota* 25%	– Publicly traded	Recommendation only	

They estimate that a 10 per cent increase in women on boards due to the quota led to a 12.4 per cent decrease in Tobin's Q. The study is considered the pioneer of a rigorous methodological approach to prove the causal effects of women on boards on performance. Owing to the exogenous increase of women on boards due to the quota law, the authors build a convincing instrument for the exogenous change of the share of women on boards: they use the pre-quota cross-sectional variation in women's representation on boards as an instrument for exogenous changes to corporate boards following the quota. The underlying hypothesis is that firms that had a lower proportion of women on boards before the quota law faced a stronger constraint than firms that had a higher proportion of women. Constraints may in fact have negative effects on performance. This is true, however, as long as the initial status quo is optimal, that is, if the board composition and structure before the quota were chosen to maximize the firm value, a fact that may differ across different firms or countries and is difficult to generalize. According to Ahern and Dittmar (2012), the quota law acted as a binding constraint, which forced the appointment to boards of young and less expert members who performed poorly. In particular, these members changed the strategy of the boards by inducing more acquisitions, increasing leverage and reducing cash holdings, with negative effects on performance.

Ahern and Dittmar (2012) also conduct an event study of the stock price reaction to the announcement of the quota and find similar results: firms with a lower share of women on boards before the quotas had more negative effects than those with more women directors. The same result is obtained in comparing Norwegian firms with firms in the United States and other Scandinavian countries that are not subject to such quotas.

Several papers raise doubts about the conclusions of Ahern and Dittmar (2012). Nygaard (2011) shows that the negative effects on performance depend on asymmetric information between independent members of boards and the companies' managers (see also Ferreira et al., 2015). A recent paper by Eckbo et al. (2018) discusses the validity of the results of Ahern and Dittmar (2012) and shows that by using a more robust specification the negative market reaction in Norway becomes insignificant.

Thus, the analysis of Norway does not lead to a unique result. The methodology was not as perfect as initially thought (Eckbo et al., 2018), and the mechanism that is used by Ahern and Dittmar (2012) to rationalize the results hinges on a not uncontroversial hypothesis (namely, that the pre-quota status quo was optimal). The controversy on whether the presence of women on boards matters for performance remains open.

5.2.2 Italy

Italy introduced board gender quotas for listed companies in July 2011. As already mentioned, the Italian law is gradual (first threshold 20 percent, second threshold 33 per cent) and temporary (the target is required only for three consecutive board elections). Interestingly, the quota is not introduced at the same date for all firms since board elections happen every three years on different dates for each firm, and the quota was to be respected at the first board election after August 2012. Since elections are typically held between April and June, the election date with the first adoption of quotas, which is specific to each company, is a day in April–June 2013, a day in April–June 2014 or a day in April–June 2015.

In a paper with Ferraro, Ferrari and Pronzato (2018), I extensively analyze the effects of the Italian board gender quotas on performance. To perform the analysis, we manually collect individual data on all members of the boards of Italian listed companies in the period 2007–2014 (4,627 individuals), as well as firm-level data on the relevant outcomes of these companies (243 companies) and stock market prices. Using these data, we explore the selection effects of the introduction of the quotas – whether and how boards change. We use two alternative methodologies, which deliver similar results. First, we compare, within each firm, before reform and after reform changes in board member characteristics, such as gender, age and education, while controlling for time trends. To understand the method, consider the cohort of firms that had board elections in 2007, 2010 and 2013. In 2007 and 2010, elections occurred without the quotas, while in 2013, they occurred after the requested for the quotas. We can thus compute for each indicator (average age of board members, average education level, etc.) the change between 2010 and 2013 and compare it with the change between 2007 and 2010. The same exercise applies to the cohort with board elections in 2008, 2011 (without quotas) and 2014 (with quotas). The second methodology compares the level of every indicator for three groups of firms on the same date:

30 June 2013. On that date, there are three groups of firms, which are randomly selected, as the date of the elections depends on the past, and we ensure that the firm did not manipulate the date:

- First, a group that has a new board in place after recent elections in the period April–June 2013 subject to the quotas
- Second, a group with the board elected in 2012, when the quotas were approved but not yet adopted
- Third, a group with a board elected in the period April–June 2011, when the quotas were neither approved nor implemented.

A simple comparison of the average indicators in the three groups of firms, as well as a proper regression with dummies for each group, reveals the effect of the quotas on outcomes.

The results from both methodologies are similar: when gender quotas are enforced, firms show a higher share of women directors (well above the required threshold), higher average education levels of all members of the board (men and women) and fewer elderly members than before the quotas. Overall, we find that gender quotas trigger a more efficient selection process of the entire board. Moreover, despite boards' having to select more women, we do not find an increase in board members belonging to the families of firms' owners or a clear increase in the average number of positions held by each board member.

To assess the causal effect of gender quotas on firms' performance, we use the reform period, which is exogenous to firms' decisions, as an instrument for the share of female directors. Data on performance for the period 2011–2015 are collected from the AIDA, Datastream and Bankscope databases. We make a great effort to make the data homogeneous, as the available information is sparse and incomplete. Regressions are performed with instrumental variables and several specifications, of which the most demanding is the fixed effects specification at the firm level. The results show that to date, quotas in Italy have not been associated with different (e.g. worse, as in Norway) firm performance as measured by number of employees, assets, production, profits, ROA, Tobin's Q and debts. In other words, we are not able to identify significant effects of the share of women on boards, instrumented by the reform of the quota law, on the indicators of firm performance. This is probably due to the short time period after the introduction of gender quotas, which does not allow us to assess the long-term effects.

When we consider stock market performance, we show that gender quotas reduce the variability of companies' stock prices. These results are consistent with the fact that performance needs more time to adjust – and we will probably see effects in the coming years – while the stock market reacts immediately, and we are thus able to see changes.

We further investigate the stock market effects of the introduction of the quota law. In the same spirit as the study of Ahern and Dittmar (2012) for Norway, data collected on Italy are used to conduct an event study on two important dates related to the approval of the Italian law – 15 March 2011, the date of the approval by the Senate, and 28 July 2011, the date of the approval by the Parliament. We first check, using newspaper databases, that on these dates, the final approval of the law was difficult to anticipate. Then, we compare the stock market returns of Italian companies and Spanish companies listed on the Madrid Stock Exchange on these dates. As previously mentioned, in contrast to Italy, Spain adopted a voluntary approach and did not impose penalties for noncompliance with the recommended threshold, which weakens its request for a gender-balanced composition of boards. Our results do not identify significantly different effects between Italy and Spain on stock market returns on the day of the approval of the Italian law.

To provide a final assessment of the impact of gender quotas on stock market returns, we perform an event study on the day of board elections, which occurs on a different date for each firm. We find that the introduction of gender quotas in Italy is associated with better firm returns: companies with a smaller share of women in the pre-reform board composition (i.e. farther from the quota target) experienced better stock market results on the date of the first board election after the approval of the law than companies that were closer to the target. In other words, the renewal of the board associated with gender quotas has positive effects on stock market returns.

Clearly, it is difficult to compare Norway and Italy, as Norway is a champion with respect to gender statistics, and Italy is a poor performer (see Chapter 2). The gender cultures differ accordingly. The board gender quota law itself is different: the required threshold is much higher in Norway than in Italy and must be reached immediately, while gradualism of the threshold is an important feature of the Italian reform. However, the different results in two countries where quotas allow the implementation of a strong methodology is intriguing, and it leaves us without a clear answer to the following fundamental question: Do women on boards matter for good business?

5.3 Women's Leadership and Social/Sustainability Performance

Two of the identified individual traits play a crucial role in the relationship between women's leadership and social and sustainable performance: altruism and long-term horizon. As women are more altruistic and socially oriented than men, we expect the presence of women on boards to be associated with firms' engagement in socially responsible activities. However, the empirical evidence is again not uncontroversial. Post and Byron (2014) develop a meta-analysis of eighty-seven studies based on independent samples and confirm the existence of a positive relationship between women on boards and the social performance of firms. The relationship is particularly strong in countries with higher gender equality in the labour market and society: in these contexts, the distribution of power within the board may be more balanced. It is also stronger where boards are influenced by the resources brought by women directors, for example, in countries with stronger shareholder protections.

On a related note, as described earlier, women tend to have a longer-term horizon than men. Gender differences in social orientation, coupled with different long-term horizons, predict that women decision-makers will encourage more environmentally friendly policies (Diamantopoulos et al., 2003) and pay more attention to sustainability issues, which typically manifest in the longer term. More recent contributions have started to investigate whether these psychological differences between decision-making by men and women have direct implications for environmental decisions. The existing results generally confirm the prediction that the presence of women is associated with better environmental performance. Post et al. (2011) show that companies with three or more female directors perform better on one specific measure of environmental performance (although no relationship emerges for the other considered measures). Kimball et al. (2012) and Glass et al. (2016) study US companies in 2009 and find that those with women in their top management team and board of directors show better environmental performance, with a stronger effect coming from the board.

In a recent paper with Amore, Trabelsi and Zollo (2018), we provide a rigorous and comprehensive analysis of the relationship between women in top corporate positions and companies' social and environmental performance. We use data from Thompson Reuters' Asset4, a comprehensive panel database of environmental, social, corporate governance and economic (ESG) measures of public companies that disclose ESG-related data, belonging to all major industries for thirty-six countries of the world. We analyze the relationship between the percentage of women managers and the environmental score, a measure of a company's impact on the natural environment. This indicator measures how well a company uses best management practices to avoid environmental risks and capitalize on environmental opportunities to generate long-term value for shareholders and other stakeholders in a given year. A higher score indicates better environmental performance, which depends on (1) pollution of air, land and water and the impacts on biodiversity, climate change and related natural maladies; (2) the use of energy from nonrenewable sources, water, land, forests, minerals, etc., that influence the quality of both the natural and the social environments; (3) the production of waste in any form; and (4) new product development efforts to remedy or avoid any of these problems. Our panel OLS regressions with firm and year fixed effects show that a higher female presence in senior management or board positions is positively associated with environmental performance. We also explore the relationship of the presence of women with the social performance indicator and the sustainability program at the firm level.

5.4 Women's Leadership and Firms' International Performance

Trade and export policies are at the centre of the decision-making of companies and governments. The level of export is important not only for companies themselves but also for the country, as internationalization positively affects employment, economic growth and current account deficits. Export currently accounts for a huge and growing part of countries' GDP: for example, the World Bank reports that in

France, export accounted for 30 per cent of the GDP in 2015 compared to 14.4 per cent in 1960, while in the same period in the United Kingdom, the share of GDP represented by export increased from 20.2 per cent to 27.4 per cent.

What do we expect from women leaders when we consider exports and trade? Several individual traits identified in Section 5.1 may play a role. Risk aversion and competition matter. Export implies relationships with a foreign country, with different socioeconomic and cultural contexts. It involves more risk than domestic business. Trade entails more costs and uncertainty, related to dealing with information asymmetry, in relation to the need for financial capital. As women are less competitive and more risk averse than men and have greater difficulty in accessing financial capital, we expect women to be less involved in trade and export activities and firms led by women to be less open to trade. Attitudes towards negotiation also matter. As already discussed, women negotiate differently than men, in a less strategic way and by giving more importance to ongoing relationships involving personal feeling and emotions. This negotiation style is expected to reduce attitudes in favour of exporting products to distant markets, reduce proactivity in exploring distant markets and result in a more conservative and domestic strategy. Networking is also important for export activities, as relations with other people in different countries are an essential part of international business: gender differences in networking may therefore affect the relationship between women's leadership and trade performance. In contrast, women tend to be more 'open' to innovation and to interacting with others than men, suggesting an opposite channel through which the presence of women in decision-making positions is related to higher exports.

The relationship between gender and trade has been addressed with reference to women entrepreneurs. The evidence is mixed. Welch et al. (2008) study twenty Australian business owners and show that gender influences the export orientation of firms. Carter and Anderson (2001) show that in the UK, more than 40 per cent of women entrepreneurs intend to expand internationally. However, only 7 per cent actually do so. Beckton (2008) shows that in Canada, women entrepreneurs generate almost 40 per cent of their sales in foreign markets, and this value is increasing. However, women entrepreneurs declare that they encounter gender-specific export challenges.

All existing evidence seems to suggest that the context matters. Gender culture plays an important role, as export and trade activities imply relationships with different countries. If these countries show conservative attitudes towards gender equality, then women entrepreneurs and firms led by women may encounter obstacles in trade and export activities. It is therefore difficult to assess causal relationships by using cross-country analysis.

To assess the causal relationship between women's leadership in firms and trade, we can exploit the existence of board gender quotas. In a project in progress with Ghio, I focus on France and the UK and consider listed companies in the period 2006–2015. I choose these two countries because of both data availability and convenient comparability. As previously explained, France introduced gender quotas for the boards of listed companies in 2011, while the UK has no quotas but only a recommendation for gender balance on boards. Thus, the comparison of the two countries can deliver interesting insights. For these two countries, data on export revenues (and the share of export revenues on total operating revenues) are available for (some) listed companies in Amadeus (Bureau van Dijk). The final dataset includes 84 companies listed on the French stock exchange and 816 companies listed on the UK stock exchange. For each company and year, in addition to export revenues, we collect information on the number of employees, return on equity, total assets and operating revenues. French companies elect their boards every six years. Thus, not all French firms introduced board gender quotas at the same time: we also collect information on the year of the first implementation of the gender quota law in each firm. On average, English firms have higher exports than French firms, and export revenues are increasing in both countries.

Individual-level data are collected for board members in French and UK companies and for managers in UK companies. Manual collection of data from the websites of the firms is needed because Amadeus contains much missing data. The final dataset contains information on 1,100 French directors and their gender and 20,000 English directors and top-level managers. While both countries show an increasing trend in the share of women on boards, in France, the average share of women on boards was higher than that in the UK even before the

French quota law, and it jumped up substantially after the quota. In the considered period, the share of women on boards in France increased from 15.38 per cent (2006) to 31.45 per cent (2015), while the corresponding values for the UK were 6.5 per cent and 11.85 per cent.

Simple OLS regressions with country, year and firm fixed effects, which include controls for the number of employees, return on assets and operating revenues and sector of activity, show a positive and significant relationship between the share of women on boards and the (log of) export revenues (or share of export revenues on the total). The result is the same if we perform separate regressions for France and the UK.

As we know well, simple OLS regressions do not provide causal effects. On the one hand, it is still possible that specific firm variables that influence the export orientation of companies are not considered. On the other hand, reverse causality is a concern. We therefore exploit the introduction of board gender quotas in France, which produces an exogenous increase in the share of women on boards. We use the reform as an instrument for the share of women on boards and perform an instrumental variable analysis. More precisely, we construct a dummy variable, which takes the value of 1 for each (French) firm for all periods after the introduction of quotas and 0 otherwise. After checking that the dummy variable is a strong instrument, we perform instrumental variable regressions with firm fixed effects. The results show that the share of women on boards positively affects export performance. The size of the relationship is larger than that obtained with OLS.

We finally perform a difference-in-difference estimate, using UK firms as a control group and French firms after the introduction of quotas as the treated group. The results show that after the introduction of board gender quotas in France, the difference between the change in French firms' export performance after the quotas and that of UK firms is positive and significant. In other words, the introduction of board gender quotas, which exogenously increased the share of women on boards of French firms, has a positive impact on export performance. As the parallel trend assumption between French and UK firms is not clearly satisfied, we also perform semi-parametric difference-in-difference estimations (Abadie, 2005). In the considered period, not all French companies were yet subject to the gender quota law. This allows us to estimate the average effect of the treatment on the treated French firms by comparing changes over time in the (log of) export revenues across treatment groups, adjusting for differences between the treatment groups in the observable characteristics at baseline. The positive link between women on boards and export performance is confirmed.

5.5 Women's Leadership and the Labour Market

If men prefer other men (see Section 5.1.6 about networking), moving from male leadership to gender-balanced leadership is expected to reduce gender gaps. A gender-balanced board may matter for more than firms' performance. The board plays an active role in developing corporate strategy, objectives, goals and the future agenda. Thus, after an increase in the number of women on boards, important consequences for the labour market are expected. These include changes in the gender-balanced composition of the workforce of the firms subject to quotas or even a change in the gender composition of the overall workforce and a reduction in gender gaps if gender quotas generate cascade effects on the labour market.

These effects may arise through three possible channels:

(1) Women on boards of directors act as role models for other women; thus, quotas are expected to be related to an increase in the presence of women at all managerial levels;
(2) Women on boards directly support the hiring and promotions of women in top management positions;
(3) Women on boards influence the adoption of policies that support women's careers, including mentoring programs, flexibility of work, etc.

These effects may be the direct result of a different selection process followed by women on boards: they actively select managers with an agenda that is more in line with their style of leadership, or they influence existing managers, as shown by results based on surveys (see e.g. Demb and Neubauer, 1992). Evidence from specific countries will help us assess the existence and magnitude of these effects.

5.5.1 Norway

Research based on the adoption of board gender quotas in Norway shows that women on boards are associated with more women in managerial positions and fewer layoffs, that is, year-to-year net reductions in the size of the workforce (Matsa and Miller, 2011). Studies provide causal evidence of the relationship between female leadership and employment outcomes by comparing financial data for publicly listed firms in Norway (affected by the quota law) and a matched sample of unlisted firms in Norway and listed and unlisted firms in other Nordic countries (not affected by the quotas). They find that most corporate decisions were unaffected after women's board representation increased due to the quotas: revenues and non-labour costs were similar between firms affected and unaffected by the policy. However, they find significant differences in firms' employment policies. Norwegian firms affected by the quota undertook fewer employee layoffs, causing an increase in relative labour costs (but not in the average wage). Matsa and Miller (2011) estimate a large magnitude of the employment effects: the quota increased relative employment by almost 30 per cent. When they adjust for outliers, the estimates decrease by as much as two-thirds, but the results are qualitatively unchanged. The result is obtained under no evidence of pre-trends or differential employment patterns among listed Norwegian firms during the previous global recession. The authors argue that the reduction in layoffs cannot be attributed to general board dysfunction, as boards affected and unaffected by the quota appear equally willing to initiate mergers, acquisitions and joint ventures. They argue that 'to the extent that the effects of the quota reflect gender differences in corporate leadership, the findings align with prior research documenting gender differences in attitudes towards layoffs, such as Rubinstein's (2006) survey of business newspaper readers' Matsa and Miller (2011, 138). Rather, the results are based on a female style of leadership; specifically, they reflect a distinctive female leadership style in labour hoarding. This in turn reflects the female long-term strategy approach, or higher altruism, meaning women leaders' concern for workers' vulnerability to unemployment risk – two traits that I documented thoroughly in the previous section. However, this style of leadership does not translate into an advantage for firms, at least in the short term: Matsa and Miller (2011) find that the reduction in layoffs reduces firms' short-term profits. Whether in the long term the returns for the firms will become positive remains to be investigated.

The already mentioned golden-skirt phenomenon may also be responsible for the limited effectiveness of the new female leadership and its impact on outcomes. After quotas were introduced in Norway, there was not a sharp increase in the pool of female directors but rather the creation of a small élite group of women who increased their influence. If a critical mass of women is needed to create a visible impact of female leadership on outcomes (as I argued in Section 5.1), the emergence of the golden-skirt phenomenon helps explain why the effects of Norwegian quotas on outcomes are more limited than expected.

To what extent do more women on boards start a cascade process that increases the share of women in lower-level managerial positions? A recent influential paper by Bertrand et al. (2018) shows that the increase in women on the boards of Norwegian firms subject to the quota law has reduced the gender gap in earnings within boards and increased the representation of female employees at the very top of the earnings distribution (top five highest earners) within the same firms. However, there is no evidence that these gains at the very top trickled down. They find no statistically significant change in gender wage gaps or in female representation in top positions.

They also find little evidence that the reform has affected the decisions of women more generally, for example, by changing women's enrolment in business education programmes. As far as the work environments of the affected firms are concerned, again, no impact was found. Moreover, women with qualifications similar to those of women appointed to boards were also not affected. Thus, the effects of the quota law on the labour market remain quite limited.

5.5.2 Italy

Using data from the Italian Social Security Administration (INPS), Maida and Weber (2019) show the effects of the adoption of board gender quotas in Italy on gender gaps within firms. For 200 Italian listed firms in the period 2008–2016, they consider the following firm-level variables: gender composition of the management team (at different levels, including the CEO) and the employees, wage distribution by gender, part-time workers by gender and hiring and firing rates by gender. They consider the effect of the exogenous increase in the share of women on boards due to the quota law on the firm-specific indicators by comparing firms before and after the reform. They also compare each firm with a matched similar firm, chosen (using a propensity score) on the basis of similarity between the same indicators (wage distribution, part-time workers, etc.) in the four years before the reform.

The results are as follows: quotas are associated with the probability that a woman is the highest-paid worker of the firm, while there is no significant effect on the presence of women at the top level of the wage distribution of the firm (75th and 90th percentiles). A positive effect arises only for firms that already had at least 20 per cent of women directors before the implementation of the quota law, that is, where quotas were not binding.

There is also evidence that the increased share of women on boards due to the quota law is negatively associated with the presence of part-time workers, probably because part-time work in Italy is largely involuntary, and women in top positions may be more likely to reduce this undesired practice. It will be interesting to analyze the effects on the flexibility of working (see Chapter 6).

Again, the short time period after the reform, together with the gradualism of the reform itself, may have weakened the labour market effects of the reform. Alternatively, the role played by women directors may not be sufficiently important to produce changes, at least in the short term. Alternatively, there may be no consequences of the presence of women on boards on labour market outcomes.

5.6 Conclusions

Women and men are different according to several attributes, including risk aversion, attitude towards negotiation and competition, time horizon, social preferences (such as sensitivity to fairness, justice, trust and altruism) and networking. These attributes, which together define what I call the style of leadership, are likely to affect firms' performance: business and financial performance, social and sustainability performance, international performance (export and trade) and labour market outcomes. For example, the greater risk aversion and lesser competition of women are expected to translate into more stable financial performance but less international exposure. The greater altruism and longer-term horizon of women compared to men suggest higher social performance and more attention to sustainability and environmental issues. Moreover, if men prefer other men (homophily bias), moving from male leadership to gen-der-balanced leadership is expected to reduce gender gaps overall.

To prove that individual traits translate into firms' outcomes is challenging. The first issue is that individual traits are generally assessed by looking at the entire population rather than at women in leadership positions, who, as a selected subgroup of the population, may have different characteristics from those of the average popula-tion. A second concern is methodological: we need an exogenous increase of women in leadership positions to study the causal impact of women's leadership on outcomes and avoid reverse causality from outcomes to the presence of women. A third difficulty is that the context matters: gender culture (prejudices, stereotypes versus the role of men and women in society and jobs) plays a crucial role in the effectiveness of the female style of leadership. Firms' organization also matters: the gender composition of different hierarchies of leadership (management, directors, etc.) and the collaborative or conflictual envir-onment interact significantly with the presence of women in decision-making positions and jointly affect the outcomes.

Why do many studies find no significant differences in the effects on firms' performance of male and female leadership? Three elements must be considered: the need for a critical mass, the existence of pre-judicial evaluations and the emergence of conflicts.

First, the capacity or possibility of women to contrast with the male dominant style may be limited. If women in leadership positions adapt to male-dominant traits because the male-dominant network requires them to do so or because they find it convenient, the potential impact of women's style on performance is weakened. This argument is used by Rose (2007) to explain why, in a sample of Danish firms listed on the stock market in the period 1998–2001, there is no evidence that women matter for performance. Rose argues that women were simply forced to adapt to the male-dominant traits. That is the reason why, for female traits to become visible in action, a critical mass of women seems to be needed. This critical mass is therefore also needed for the positive association between women on boards and performance to become visible. Carter et al. (2007) find a positive relationship between return on sales, return on invested capital and return on equity and women's presence only when comparing high-commitment firms (three or more women on the board) to low-commitment firms (all men on the board). The importance of a critical mass of women has been emphasized by recent results. Using original data on the detailed minutes of 402 board and board committee meetings of a selected sample of companies in Israel, Schwartz-Ziv (2017) shows that companies with boards that had critical masses of at least three directors of each gender in attendance, performed better than those that did not. The first group of boards was approximately twice as likely both to request further information and to take initiative. As a consequence, the return on equity (ROE) and net profit margin are significantly larger in companies that have at least three female directors. Furthermore, boards that included a critical mass of female directors were more likely to experience beneficial CEO turnover when firm performance was weak. At the level of individual directors, both men and women were more active when at least three female directors were in attendance. Amore et al. (2014) also emphasize the role of the critical mass: using data on family-controlled Italian firms, they find that companies led by female CEOs perform significantly better, and this effect increases with the number of women on the board of directors.[1]

A second important element that may explain why the female style of leadership does not translate into gender-specific firm outcomes is prejudice in evaluations of women's competence as leaders, especially in masculine organizational contexts (Hoogendoorn et al. 2013). While individual traits and intrinsic characteristics are an advantage for performance, women suffer the disadvantage of being undervalued because of prejudice, stereotypes and biases against them as leaders. In such a context, women's style of leadership risks being ineffective (Eagly et al., 1995), especially if leadership positions are male dominated.

Finally, the absence of results and the impact of women's leadership may also be due to gender diversity being associated with both negative and positive effects. Studies have found that in diverse teams, interpersonal conflicts may increase, provoking delays in the decision-

---

[1] The critical mass of women on the board is crucial not only for performance but also for the company's organizational aspects. Konrad et al. (2008) highlight three aspects for which a minimum threshold of three women is pivotal: first, one or two women are not sufficient to break the gender stereotypes; second, more women allow change in the all-male communication dynamic, thus breaking up the 'old boys' club'; and third, a different group dynamic is enhanced, with different points of view being circulated. These changes in attitudes towards women on boards might then lead to a different approach for working women more generally.

making process, increasing the need for communication and reducing strategic consensus, with negative consequences for boards' effectiveness and performance (Van Knippenberg et al., 2004). Not only is there a risk that the introduction of new perspectives and diversity overall will be ineffective, but it may even backfire if conflicts are exacerbated and discussions become too demanding.

Nonetheless, the existing evidence is almost uncontroversial in associating women's leadership with a positive (or at least not negative) value for business, an improvement in social and sustainability performance, and a reduction in gender gaps, although to a limited extent. Moreover, a clear result is that the quality of leadership increases when women are more represented in top positions (education level, competence, monitoring activities, etc.). Finally, it is obvious that for equality reasons, gender-balanced leadership is preferred. Overall, the assessment of the beneficial effects of women's leadership in business cannot but be positive.

6 | Global Challenges, Gender and Public Policy

The World Economic Forum (2016) conducted a survey on a sample of 2,450 companies, including the 100 largest global employers in several industry sectors, the 50 largest national employers in several countries, and a number of leading, fast-growing, small and medium-sized companies. More than a quarter of the companies surveyed identify female talent as a key feature of future workforce strategy: 53 per cent of the respondents perceive promoting women's participation as a priority, and 58 per cent think that they have implemented measures that will lead to this result. Similarly, companies perceive women's rising labour force participation and economic power as consumers as key drivers of change across several industry sectors. Women will account for US$5 trillion in additional consumer spending and more than two-thirds of global disposable income over the next decade. Companies also share the view that women's participation in the labour market is one of the unambiguously positive trends in the current ambiguous labour market scenario.

How will this positive trend of women's participation in the labour market, empowerment and increasingly important role in the economy change under the ongoing transformation of jobs driven by demographic, socioeconomic and technological changes? How can gender equality evolve to guarantee stable progress in terms of economic and social sustainability?

This chapter considers some of the major global challenges and explains how they interact with gender equality and public policy. The relationships are complex, and it would be impossible to provide a full-fledged analysis of all of them. I therefore focus on the following three major drivers of global changes: demographic, socioeconomic and technological changes.

Demographic challenges such as the ageing of the population and migration flows will continue to increase in Europe. How does the increasing presence of women in the labour market interact with this global demographic change? For example, more women at work may imply a change in fertility rates, but in which direction? It may also be a good way to counterbalance the increase in the ratio between workers and retirees, which is a consequence of the ageing of the population, one of the most dramatic changes of recent decades. Similarly, migration flows may mitigate the consequences of the ageing process.

At the same time, there is a constant process of socioeconomic changes: the old European continent must face the challenge of modest economic growth and increasing inequality. More women at work may be a way to increase economic output, a crucial outcome in times of slow economic growth. A major challenge is how to promote growth sustainably. The United Nations established Sustainable Development Goals to be reached by 2030 to address the global challenges of economies, including poverty, inequality, climate change and protection of the environment. The role of women in contributing to achieving these goals is fundamental (see also Chapter 5). In fact, the UN included as goal number 5 to 'achieve gender equality and empower all women and girls ... as a necessary foundation for a peaceful, prosperous and *sustainable* world'. Sustainability also involves the social sphere: several authors have expressed concerns about the possible drawbacks of an increase in gender equality, mainly in terms of the happiness of women, families and children. Addressing these issues is fundamental for promoting gender equality in a sustainable and equal society.

In addition to demographic and socioeconomic drivers, technological changes have the potential to transform the global employment landscape. Again, a gender divide emerges. On the one hand, by making possible new forms of job organization, such as remote working, the digital revolution can create more work for women and enhance women's empowerment. On the other hand, it may represent a barrier for women who are less involved in STEM (science, technology, engineering, mathematics) educational disciplines and who therefore risk being less involved than men as primary actors in these transformations.

In the following sections, I provide new insights into the gender dynamic implications of global demographic, socioeconomic and technological changes.

6.1 Demographic Challenges

6.1.1 Fertility

One of the fundamental questions of demographic research is whether gender equality contributes to the decline in fertility that has been observed in all developed countries over time. The decline in fertility, together with the increase in life expectancy, translates into an overall ageing process, the major global demographic transformation of our century (see the next section). If more gender equality is related to lower fertility, a clear challenge for the future is how to continue progress towards gender equality without exacerbating the process of population ageing.

Demographers have emphasized that low fertility is driven mainly by postponement of parenthood (Kohler et al., 2002; Lesthaeghe, 2010), which is the result of the increased attention and time devoted to building individual identity and economic independence before the formation of the family. Individuals focus more than they did in the past on non-material needs, such as freedom of expression, self-realization and autonomy, and on their own happiness and freedom; this leads to the postponement or even rejection of choices and responsibilities, primarily marriage and parenthood.

As previously emphasized by Goldin (2006, see also Chapter 2), this change in perspectives and timing of choices greatly involves women: since the second half of the twentieth century, women have taken many steps towards independence and more gender-equal societies. However, the new roles of women as students, workers and politicians lead to a postponement of fertility choice. In addition to postponement, the falling demand for children may eventually translate into childlessness. According to Pritchett and Viarengo (2012), the social construction of gender roles suggests that women could play a 'role' in society solely by being good nurturers. However, when allowed to seek satisfaction in their economic lives, women started to invest in education and enter the public sphere, finding a source of life meaning and social validation outside their families. The intrinsic rewards from work and career contributed to the reduction in the overall fertility rate, thus suggesting that gender equality and fertility rate may have a negative relationship.

Other contributions challenge the negative relationship between gender equality and fertility rate (see also Chapter 2). Myrskylä et al. (2009) use cross-sectional and longitudinal analyses of total fertility rate and human development index (HDI) to show that the negative relationship between fertility and development became J-shaped as the population entered the twenty-first century. For an HDI lower than 0.85–0.9, the association remains negative; for higher levels, it becomes positive. They find that in eighteen countries with an HDI above 0.9, the downward trend in fertility rate has been reversed. This reversal trend may depend on the level of gender equality in the country vis-à-vis the level of gender equality within the family. According to McDonald (2000), at the beginning of the process towards gender equality, the improvement was based mainly on regarding women as individuals in society who are given equal rights in education and the labour market. However, gender inequality continues to dominate the private sphere, that is, the family context, with the result that women must bear the double burden of work and family. In such a context, working or having children is a trade-off for women, and the result is a decrease in the fertility rate. As the process of gender equality continues, even the private sphere is involved in the process: the division of family chores within a couple becomes more balanced, and men become involved in domestic and care work. Hofferth and Goldscheider (2010) define this phase characterized by men's increasing involvement in household activities as the natural completion of the gender revolution. As a consequence, the trade-off between working and having children for women has begun to relax, and fertility has started to increase together with gender equality, thus leading towards a new equilibrium in which couples share domestic and care work and both partners have a job (Esping-Andersen and Billari, 2015). Institutions and public policy measures also support the evolution towards this new equilibrium. As shown in Chapter 3, in Europe, the Nordic countries have already moved towards this new equilibrium, while other countries are still on their way.

Several studies have found a positive association between gender equality in household tasks and both fertility intentions (Tazi-Preve et al., 2004; Mills et al. 2008; Pinnelli and Fiori 2008) and behaviour (Oláh, 2003; Bailey et al., 2004; Mencarini and Tanturri 2004; Torr and Short, 2004; Cooke, 2008). The role of men's involvement in household activities in fertility has also been emphasized by Esping-Andersen (2009), Kan et al. (2011) and Pasqua and Mancini (2012).

Other scholars have stressed that what matters for fertility is not gender equality within the family but rather the mismatch between egalitarian attitudes and the actual behaviour of the couple. Gender attitudes may differ from actual behaviour: mainly, men tend to declare attitudes in favour of sharing care responsibilities and domestic work that are more egalitarian than their actual behaviour (Bernhardt et al., 2008). This inconsistency may crucially impact fertility: women build expectations of sharing responsibilities with their partners; if those expectations are not met, the natural reaction is a delay in childbearing (see Goldscheider et al., 2013, for Sweden). In this direction, Aassve et al. (2015) use Gender and Generations Survey data for five European countries to show that couples who are not consistently egalitarian in attitude and behaviour are less likely to have a second child than consistently egalitarian couples. In countries where men are increasingly involved in childcare and domestic work, as described in Box 6.1, we can therefore expect an increase in fertility.

Box 6.1 Sharing domestic work and childcare within couples

To understand asymmetries in domestic work and childcare within couples, I use data from the Generations and Gender Survey 2002–2013, which reports information about the division of housework and childcare tasks within cohabiting couples in twelve European countries. The countries considered can be divided into Western European (Austria, Belgium, France, Germany, the Netherlands and Sweden) and Eastern European (Bulgaria, the Czech Republic, Hungary, Poland, Romania and Russia) countries, with the two groups presenting slightly different characteristics. I consider cohabiting heterosexual couples in which the woman is younger than age 45. Only one partner in each couple is interviewed, and he/she reports information about the other partner.

Table 6.1(a) reports information about the sharing of housework activities and childcare (Table 6.1(b)). Data are reported for the entire sample of interviewed people (31,975 individuals) and separately for men (labelled 'M', 13,848 individuals) and women (labelled 'W', 18,127 individuals). The basic question is 'Please tell me who in your household does the following tasks?' For housework, four tasks traditionally performed by women are considered: preparing daily meals, doing the dishes, shopping for food and vacuuming the house. For childcare, six activities are considered: dressing children; putting them to bed; staying at home with them when they are ill; playing with them or taking part in leisure activities; helping with homework; and taking them to/from school, day care centre, babysitter or leisure activities. Only respondents with at least one child younger than age 14 were interviewed about childcare activities. The possible answers were on a scale from 0 to 4, where a higher value corresponds to greater participation of the man in household activities: a value of 0 means that the woman always performs the task, 1 that the woman usually performs the task, 2 that the woman and man perform the task equally, 3 that the man usually performs the task and 4 that the man always performs the task.

The average values for each country and task are reported. Then, an overall index of household cooperation is created from the sum of all the values of the different tasks. For housework, this index ranges from 0 to 16, with a midpoint of 8 corresponding to the perfectly egalitarian case in which the woman and man equally share the four housework tasks. For childcare, the index ranges from 0 to 24, with a midpoint of 12 corresponding to the perfectly egalitarian case in which the woman and man equally share the six childcare tasks considered.

In all the considered countries, women still perform many more household and childcare activities than men. The activity performed most often by women is preparing daily meals, while shopping for food and playing with children are tasks in which men are generally more involved in household and childcare activities, respectively. It is very uncommon for a man to stay home when children are ill. No country reaches the egalitarian threshold for housework or childcare activities. Eastern European countries show lower values than Western countries; they lag in terms of sharing duties between men and women, particularly for household activities and less for childcare. Sweden is the country with the highest sharing between men and women in both household and childcare duties, followed by Germany for household and Estonia for childcare. Bulgaria and Hungary are the most unequal in the gender division of housework tasks. Interestingly, in all the countries, men report higher values than women, that is, men tend to declare, on average, a higher level of sharing than that declared by women; they perceive their contribution to household duties as more significant than women perceive it.

Table 6.1 *Sharing activities within a couple*

(a) *Housework*

	AT	BE	FR	DE	NL	SE	West EU	BG	CZ	HU	PL	RO	RU	East EU	Tot.
Preparing meals	1.0	1.2	1.1	1.3	1.2	1.7	1.2	0.8	0.8	0.8	1.0	0.7	0.9	0.8	1.0
W	0.8	1.0	0.9	1.2	1.1	1.6	1.1	0.8	0.5	0.7	0.9	0.7	0.8	0.7	0.9
M	1.2	1.4	1.2	1.5	1.3	1.7	1.4	0.9	1.1	1.0	1.1	0.8	1.1	1.0	1.2
Doing the dishes	1.3	1.6	1.5	1.5	–	1.9	1.6	0.9	1.1	0.9	1.1	0.8	1.1	1.0	1.3
W	1.2	1.4	1.4	1.4	–	1.8	1.5	0.8	0.9	0.8	1.1	0.8	1.0	0.9	1.2
M	1.5	1.7	1.7	1.7	–	2.0	1.7	1.0	1.3	1.1	1.3	0.9	1.3	1.1	1.4
Shopping for food	1.3	1.4	1.3	1.5	1.4	1.8	1.5	1.5	1.3	1.5	1.5	1.6	1.4	1.5	1.5
W	1.1	1.3	1.2	1.5	1.3	1.6	1.3	1.4	1.1	1.4	1.4	1.6	1.3	1.4	1.3
M	1.5	1.6	1.5	1.7	1.6	2.0	1.7	1.6	1.3	1.7	1.6	1.7	1.6	1.6	1.6
Vacuum-cleaning the house	1.3	1.4	1.3	1.5	1.1	1.7	1.4	1.1	1.4	1.0	1.1	1.2	1.5	1.2	1.3
W	1.1	1.2	1.2	1.5	0.9	1.7	1.3	1.0	1.3	0.9	1.0	1.2	1.4	1.1	1.2
M	1.5	1.5	1.4	1.6	1.3	1.8	1.5	1.2	1.6	1.2	1.2	1.2	1.6	1.3	1.4
Sum [0;16]*	4.8	5.6	5.2	5.9	3.6	7.1	5.6	4.3	4.5	4.3	4.7	4.5	4.9	4.5	5.1
W	4.3	5.0	4.8	5.5	3.3	6.7	5.2	4.0	3.8	3.8	4.3	4.3	4.5	4.1	4.6
M	5.7	6.2	5.8	6.5	4.2	7.6	6.3	4.7	5.3	4.9	5.2	4.6	5.5	5.0	5.7

Notes: The numbers represent the average value of the answers to the question 'Please tell me who in your household does the following tasks?' The answers are on a scale from 0 to 4, where higher values are associated to a greater participation of the man in the household activities. For each task, data are reported for the entire sample of interviewed people, and separately for men M and women W. The last three rows capture an overall index of household cooperation, ranging from 0 to 16 (*12 for the Netherlands) with the midpoint 8 corresponding to perfectly egalitarian cases in which woman and man equally share the four housework tasks.

(b) *Childcare*

	AT	BE	FR	DE	NL	SE	West EU	BG	CZ	HU	PL	RO	RU	East EU	Tot.
Dressing children	1.1	1.2	1.1	1.3	1.3	1.5	1.3	1.1	1.1	1.3	1.1	1.1	1.0	1.1	1.2
W	1.0	1.0	1.1	1.2	1.3	1.4	1.2	1.0	0.9	1.2	1.0	1.0	0.8	1.0	1.1
M	1.3	1.3	1.2	1.5	1.4	1.6	1.4	1.2	1.5	1.4	1.2	1.1	1.2	1.3	1.3
Putting to bed	1.5	1.6	1.6	1.7	-	1.8	1.6	1.2	1.3	1.4	1.3	1.1	1.2	1.3	1.5
W	1.4	1.4	1.5	1.5	-	1.7	1.5	1.1	1.1	1.3	1.2	1.1	1.1	1.2	1.4
M	1.6	1.7	1.7	1.9	-	1.9	1.8	1.3	1.6	1.5	1.4	1.2	1.4	1.4	1.6
Staying with children when ill	0.9	1.3	1.1	1.3	1.3	1.7	1.2	0.8	0.8	0.8	1.0	0.9	0.8	0.9	1.1
W	0.8	1.1	0.9	1.2	1.2	1.7	1.1	0.8	0.6	0.7	0.9	0.9	0.6	0.8	1.0
M	1.0	1.4	1.2	1.5	1.5	1.7	1.4	1.0	1.1	1.0	1.2	0.9	1.0	1.1	1.2
Leisure activities	1.7	1.9	1.8	1.7	-	1.9	1.8	1.7	1.6	1.9	1.6	1.7	1.7	1.7	1.7
W	1.6	1.8	1.7	1.6	-	1.9	1.7	1.6	1.5	1.8	1.6	1.7	1.6	1.6	1.7
M	1.7	1.9	1.9	1.8	-	2.0	1.9	1.7	1.9	1.9	1.7	1.7	1.8	1.8	1.8
Helping with homework	1.2	1.4	1.4	1.4	-	1.8	1.5	1.4	1.4	1.4	1.3	1.4	1.4	1.4	1.4
W	1.1	1.3	1.3	1.3	-	1.7	1.4	1.3	1.2	1.2	1.2	1.4	1.3	1.3	1.3
M	1.4	1.5	1.5	1.7	-	1.9	1.6	1.5	1.7	1.5	1.3	1.5	1.5	1.5	1.6

Table 6.1 (b) (*cont.*)

	AT	BE	FR	DE	NL	SE	West EU	BG	CZ	HU	PL	RO	RU	East EU	Tot.
Transport	1.4	1.5	1.5	1.5	-	1.8	1.5	1.6	1.4	1.6	1.5	1.6	1.6	1.6	1.6
W	1.3	1.4	1.4	1.4	-	1.8	1.5	1.6	1.2	1.5	1.4	1.6	1.5	1.5	1.5
M	1.4	1.6	1.6	1.7	-	1.9	1.6	1.7	1.7	1.8	1.6	1.6	1.7	1.7	1.7
Sum [0;24]*	7.6	8.8	8.4	8.8	2.6	10.5	8.9	7.8	7.6	8.4	7.8	7.9	7.6	8.0	8.5
W	7.2	8.1	7.8	8.3	2.5	10.2	8.4	7.4	6.5	7.6	7.2	7.7	7.0	7.5	7.9
M	8.5	9.6	9.1	10.0	2.9	11.0	9.7	8.4	9.3	9.3	8.5	8.0	8.5	8.8	9.2

Notes: The numbers represent the average value of the answers to the question 'Please tell me who in your household does the following tasks?' The answers are on a scale from 0 to 4, where higher values are associated to a greater participation of the man in the childcare. For each task, data are reported for the entire sample of interviewed people, and separately for men *M* and women *W*. The last three rows capture an overall index of household cooperation, ranging from 0 to 24 (*18 for the Netherlands) with the midpoint 12 corresponding to perfectly egalitarian cases in which woman and man equally share the six childcare tasks.

These recent contributions seem to suggest that low fertility is not the necessary cost of increased gender equality; in contrast, gender equality may go hand in hand with fertility. However, to make this possible, the context matters. The attitudes and behaviour of men – sharing domestic and childcare work within the couple not only in declared attitudes but also in actual behaviour – are crucial in shaping a new equilibrium, which starts within the family. As I argued in Chapter 3, institutions and public policy may follow and reinforce this new equilibrium, thus turning gender equality into a positive factor, rather than an obstacle, in addressing the global challenge of decreasing fertility.

6.1.2 Ageing

All European countries are ageing: the proportion of the population aged 65 and older in Europe was 15.7 in 2000 and 17.5 in 2010, and it is expected to increase to 29.7 in 2050 (World Bank Population Estimates and Projections, 2016). Currently, Italy and Germany have the oldest populations on the oldest continent, Europe. The ageing process has an impact on the workforce and distribution of work: the proportion of the working population will decline unless reforms are implemented to change age-specific patterns of work and to maintain older individuals at work. Ageing will also affect the well-being of European citizens, pose questions about individuals' choices over the lifespan and their financial security in old age and require public policy reforms, mainly in social security and health care provision (see Feldstein and Liebman, 2002; Galasso, 2008; Vaupel and Kistowski, 2008; Christensen et al., 2009; Van Soest et al., 2010).

Few studies have addressed the relationship between ageing and gender gaps. Demographic and sociological research has focused mainly on older women (Arber and Ginn, 1995; Gibson 1996), a particularly disadvantaged group that faces the double challenge of being female as well as the vulnerability of the old (the 'double jeopardy' hypothesis of Chappell and Havens, 1980). The 'life course' perspective (Riley et al., 1972; Elder, 1975; Hatch, 2000) is used to analyze how changes in status and role as a person ages (such as from married to widowed or employed to retired) affect men and women differently. Other authors have recognized that the relationship between ageing and gender is complex, as well-being in older age is a multidimensional issue (Knodel and Ofstedal, 2003).

An important related strand of research has investigated the role of elderly women as grandmothers. In fact, in several European countries, grandmothers play an important role in supporting women's participation in the labour force and the dual-career model. They act as a substitute for scarce formal childcare services, the insufficient number of school hours and the inadequate access to part-time work (Del Boca et al., 2005; Keck and Saraceno, 2008). Grandparents' involvement in childcare is widespread, more intense when children are small and do not attend day care. There is large heterogeneity across countries. According to Share data, the percentage of grandparents who take care of grandchildren at least once per week is 45 per cent in Italy, 20 per cent in Sweden, and 30 per cent in France. The percentage of grandparents who take care of grandchildren every day is 30 per cent in Italy, 15 per cent in Germany, and 2 per cent in Sweden. They are mainly grandmothers. Obviously, this system is difficult to sustain under the ageing process, which requires an increase in retirement age in all countries to achieve sustainable pay-as-you-go (PAYG) pension systems (Galasso and Profeta, 2004). The increase in mother's age at first birth due to labour market obstacles and the desire to construct women's identity before having children (Goldin, 2006) will also make it problematic for grandparents to continue to provide childcare at a very old age. Geographical mobility is also increasing, and grandparents rarely move with their adult children. It is difficult to predict what will happen, but there is an urgent need to rethink policies to avoid undesirable outcomes under the pressure of demographic changes. An interesting recent study by Coda Moscarola et al. (2016) finds that the Italian 2011 pension reform, which forced a postponement of female retirement age, was associated with an increase in the sick leave of working grandmothers, likely to enable them to care for their grandchildren. In fact, this effect was stronger in regions with low childcare services. The authors interpret the use of sick leave as 'a response to the chronic lack of well-structured, high-quality care facilities, and the necessity for middle-aged women to compensate for them with informal care'. (Coda Moscarola et al. (2016,16))

The approach developed in the previous chapters suggests a new perspective for analysis. The ageing process is likely to affect both sides of the relationship between women and public policies. For a

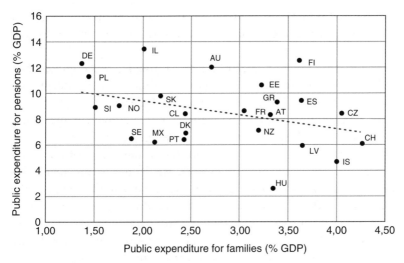

Figure 6.1 Expenditure on family policies and pensions (as % of GDP). Source: Author's elaboration of OECD data, 2018.

given level of ageing, on the one hand, the increase in female labour force participation may represent a way to rebalance the ratio between the working population and retirees, which is constantly decreasing due to the ageing process and is problematic for the sustainability of PAYG pension systems. On the other hand, if women influence the policy agenda (Chapter 4), having more women in decision-making positions may allow a more balanced distribution of resources across different items, mainly away from pensions (the dominant component of current welfare systems) and towards family policies, which are typically marginalized. This in turn may be positive for gender equality and for fertility, thus partially limiting the effects of the ageing process.

Figure 6.1 shows a negative relationship between public expenditure in family policies and in pensions (both as percentages of GDP) across European countries, which suggests the existence of a trade-off between the two components of public spending. Two interesting links emerge: on the one hand, female labour force participation is positively related to public expenditure in family policies and negatively related to public spending in pensions. A similar relationship appears if I consider the share of women in parliament. On the other hand, the dependency ratio (the ratio between population aged older than 65 and population between 15 and 64) is positively related to public expenditure in pensions and negatively related to public expenditure in family policies.

Overall, the reduction in gender gaps – through a higher presence of women in the labour market and in top positions – has the potential to mitigate the current 'male gerontocracy' in societies and in the allocation of expenditure within the welfare state (see Baltrunaite et al., 2014), which will be exacerbated by the ageing of the population. This will be particularly important for the sustainability of European welfare systems. It will also counterbalance the use of informal childcare by grandparents, which is under pressure due to the ageing of the population and the consequent pension reforms that postpone retirement. Similarly, a society, an economy and a political system open to the young will guarantee greater female representation as women are more represented among young workers and professionals.

6.1.3 Migration

Demographic challenges include the growing phenomenon of international migration. Migration may at least in part counterbalance the low fertility rate, which contributes to the ageing of the population and, thus, similar to the increase in female employment, may help reduce the pressure of ageing on PAYG social security systems. Migration also has a specific gender dimension. According to the OECD, almost half of all international migrants are women. The gender-specific nature of migration has been studied by several disciplines. Chant (1992) provides the first comprehensive empirical analysis of women and migration in developing countries. Many others follow, mainly empirical analyses and case studies. Kofman et al. (2000) focus on migration in Europe and show the evolution of the relationship between migration and gender roles. During the 1960s and 1970s, male migration was driven by labour reasons, while women followed as dependents, often without the right to work. This situation has changed, with many men now migrating as dependents and for family reunification reasons.

The relationship between gender and migration is complex. First, there are several juridical issues, such as discriminatory migration practices and unequal rights under the law in employment and mobility. Here, I focus on the economic factors, which are difficult to disentangle from other factors. Research has shown that gender relations affect the size, direction and composition of migration flows. In places with a strong intra-household division of labour, men migrate for employment and make autonomous decisions, while women migrate as dependents, following the family's decision, over which they do not have full control. In some cases, migrant women are not allowed to work outside the home. This means a risk that migration flows will exacerbate gender gaps. In many other cases, however, even though women enter as dependent spouses more often than men do, it would be misleading to conclude that migrant women do not work. This is a rather old and stereotyped representation of migration. It is true that a gender bias exists in migrant admissions systems, that careers are unequally prioritized within migrant couples and that migrant women encounter disproportionate difficulties in the labour market. However, migrant women also have great opportunities to work, for example, as domestic workers (Carling 2001). In this case, the gender relationship will change, mainly because migrant women can improve their status after migration if they become independent workers.

However, there is a dark side of the relationship between gender roles and migration strengthened by the evolution of women's role in the society of the receiving country. The opportunity for migrant women to work is strongly linked to the rise of a dual-career household model with the emergence of a new need for a person to care for the house and children while both parents work outside the home. This need is particularly strong in countries where childcare is scarce and where men's participation in domestic work and childcare is very limited – the intra-household division of labour is not gender balanced. In these places, the increase in female labour market participation, which contributes to the reduction in gender gaps, increases the demand for someone else, typically a woman, to perform domestic work and childcare. This means that the problem of the gender division of labour is not solved but rather is passed on to other women: grandmothers (as discussed in the previous section) and migrant women who work full time as domestic workers. This seems to be a reaffirmation of patriarchal values, with women employed in domestic work and childcare. Government intervention in the form of high-quality childcare services may help remove these new forms of gender stereotypes. Why are migrant women considered able to care for children at home but not in kindergartens, where they would also receive appropriate training before employment? Why is informal care a good substitute for a mother's employment? These questions remain unanswered.

A gender divide in migration studies also emerges because men and women migrants have a different propensity to remit their earnings: women are found to send a larger share of their earnings to their families in their home countries (Boyd, 1989). Finally, the way that men and women themselves think of their status as migrants is different: in a study of Barbadian migrant families, Chamberlain (1997) shows that although the circumstances of migration were quite similar for men and women, men described their migration as spontaneous, casual and independent, while women assigned more importance to the family context.

Another growing migration-related phenomenon, which has attracted the attention of international organizations such as the OECD, is the rapid increase in highly skilled migrant women: in the past decade, the number of tertiary-educated migrant women in OECD countries rose by 80 per cent; it rose by 60 per cent for men. However, despite their high social and human capital, skilled migrant women remain underrepresented among labour migrants. The reason is that even skilled women migrate mainly for marriage, family reunification and asylum-seeking reasons rather than for labour reasons. The OECD data also reveal that highly skilled migrant women continue to experience high levels of unemployment compared to their native-born counterparts. They are more exposed to risks and vulnerability than their male counterparts. Skilled women migrate because of gender-based discrimination in their country of origin, although emigration becomes more difficult when high levels of discrimination exist. As expected, women tend to migrate to countries with less discriminatory contexts (Ferrant and Tuccio, 2015), where their expectations at work are better realized.

It is difficult to predict how migration and gender will evolve in the future. In Europe, where international migration flows are increasing and gender roles show high variability across countries, the interplay between gender roles and migration is a promising area of research as well as an area that needs special attention from policymakers. The challenge is to turn the migration of women into an opportunity for gender equality and sustainable growth rather than an obstacle.

6.2 Socioeconomic Challenges

Recent decades have been characterized by modest economic growth in European countries. Except for the former Eastern bloc countries, whose growth rates lead the way (most notably, Romanian GDP grew by 6.9 per cent, followed by those of Slovenia, Estonia, Latvia and Poland), the figures are not impressive for the rest of the European Union, whose GDP in 2017 grew on average by 2.4 per cent. For some countries, the rate did not even reach 2 per cent, with Italy and Greece lagging behind and registering a GDP growth of 1.5 per cent and 1.4 per cent, respectively.

At the same time, inequality was exacerbated. The Gini index, which increased over the past two decades for many European countries, captures the phenomenon well. Namely, it escalated by 15 per cent in Sweden, 14 per cent in Spain and 10 per cent in both Germany and Greece. The trend was less dramatic for France and Italy, which, however, experienced a Gini index increase of 4 per cent and 1 per cent, respectively.

Can gender policies and gender equality boost economic growth, in particular 'inclusive economic growth' whose benefits reach everybody in society? In a period of a 'war of talent', better use of all talents, male and female, is necessary. As women are as educated as or more educated than men and have human capital, productivity and talent equal to those of men, their involvement in the economy could represent a driver of growth.

6.2.1 Economic Growth

Academic researchers, international organizations and policymakers agree that gender equality has beneficial effects for the economy and society (IMF, 2016). They emphasize that gender equality and economic development are strictly related: on the one hand, economic development is essential to reduce inequality between men and women through the reduction in poverty rates, the increase in public resources for weaker citizens and the increase in resources within the household. On the other hand, persistent discrimination against women is a clear obstacle to development (Duflo, 2012). Doepke and Tertilt (2009) develop a model to explain how women's economic and legal rights are endogenously extended over the process of economic development. International organizations also emphasize that gender equality and competitiveness are strictly related: promoting gender equality is a way to fully exploit talents that are essential for growth in a globally competitive world.

When we want to understand why gender equality matters, at least two approaches are possible: the first considers gender equality a value *per se*, and the second highlights the role of women in economic development and growth. Gender equality is a value *per se* for many disciplines, starting from equal rights and law. Even in economics, since the distribution of talents and abilities across men and women is the same, and women on average hold human capital and productivity no lower than those of men, female talent, which is generally not fully exploited, becomes a crucial element in the creation and management of performance and growth.

The second approach is centred on the role that women play in economic growth and development. I identify two ways to explore this relationship: the first passes through the direct contribution that women can make to economic growth when they work, when they are included in economic life and when they act as decision-makers both in the household and in the economy. The second passes through the indirect influence that women have on long-term choices and policies based on their different traits and preferences. This does not necessarily mean that women always make better decisions than men but rather suggests that it is not efficient to exclude the participation of women from most decisions.

Gender Equality, GDP and Growth: The Direct Impact

I start from the first channel – the direct impact of gender equality on economic growth. This is based on the empirical relationship between economic development – measured mainly by per capita GDP – and measures of gender equality, such as the global gender gap index built every year by the World Economic Forum or the Gender Empowerment Measure (GEM) constructed by the United Nations Development Program. Starting from this correlation, several international organizations have contributed to calculating the increase in GDP that would arise with more gender equality, that is, with a higher participation of women in the labour market (IMF, 2013). They have also emphasized the association of gender equality with macroeconomic stability (IMF, 2006). In a study for the IMF, Kinoshita and

Kochhar (2016) highlight that if female workers numbered the same as male workers, GDP would increase by a striking rate of 34 per cent in Egypt and 27 per cent in India. Even if less impressive, the conditional growth would also be substantial for more advanced economies: 11 per cent in Italy, 9 per cent in Japan, 6 per cent in Spain, 5 per cent in the United States and 4 per cent in both Germany and France.

The direct relationship between gender equality and economic growth has been studied in both developing and developed countries. However, there are differences between the two contexts. The level of development of a country matters. In poor countries, girls receive less education than boys, investment is lower in women's health than in men's health and women have weak legal rights and less political power than men. All these factors affect the relationship between gender equality and economic growth. Estimating a growth equation for a hundred countries during the period 1975–1990, Dollar and Gatti (1999) show nonlinearities in the relationship between economic growth and gender equality, which is measured by secondary attainment, wage gaps and proportion of women in parliament. When a very poor country becomes a lower- or middle-income country, there are no strong differences in terms of gender gap; while at higher stages of development, the relationship between income and gender equality becomes stronger. They relate this nonlinearity to the effect of female secondary schooling: when the level of female education is low, an increase in female education has a lower impact on growth than in cases where female education level is high.[1]

In developing countries, the relationship between gender equality and economic growth can be seen as the result of the dynamic among three dimensions (World Bank, 2006): household, market and society. In the household, gender equality is associated with changes in the allocation of expenditure: a larger share of resources is devoted to children's education and health, school enrolment for children including girls and better nutrition (World Bank, 2006). Mothers with better education will improve the living conditions of their children.

---

[1] From a historical perspective, the pioneering work by Boserup (1970) shows that economic growth and gender equality have a nonlinear relationship: as economies grow, gender gaps also increase because traditional household relationships change, mainly in the movement from agricultural to industrial societies. Then, there will be a point after which gender equality starts to increase, driven mainly by the improvement of women's education.

Moreover, gender equality increases the intra-household bargaining power of women, giving them more chances to work outside the home and to control their fertility decisions. In the market, gender equality means more equal access to land, credit, inheritance, property rights, financial resources and new production technologies.[2] In society, gender equality is associated with women's participation in civic and political life. All these dimensions have the potential to associate gender equality with economic growth.

In developed countries, instead, the positive association between gender equality and economic growth depends on the fact that women, who represent half of the population, are typically more educated than men and equally productive; thus, they contribute substantially to the value added of work in the market. Moreover, a virtuous circle may begin when more women work: the demand for services and consumption increases, and more jobs are created for both men and women. In other words, there is no substitution between male and female jobs, as the total number of jobs is not fixed but increases if more people work. Finally, women's participation in the labour market may play a positive role in fertility and household well-being.

Macroeconomists have tried to provide stronger evidence for the relationship between gender equality and growth and have developed new models to estimate the aggregate cost of gender inequality. The relationship between gender equality and long-term growth is studied in growth models. In Galor and Weil (1996), the link passes through fertility: economic development increases capital per worker and raises women's relative wages because capital is more complementary to women's labour input than to men's. This relatively higher female wage reduces fertility, which in turn raises the level of capital per worker, thus accelerating economic growth. Several macroeconomic growth models have focused on the role of female education as a driver of economic growth. Lagerlöf (2003) shows that higher female education reduces fertility and increases the human capital of children: both

---

[2] An extensive and important literature in development economics has analyzed the relationship between gender equality and economic outcomes at the micro level, often focusing on specific countries and/or specific mechanisms at work. As developing countries are not the focus of this book, in this chapter, we abstract from this literature and mention only how gender equality and economic outcomes may be linked at the macro level and/or using general results. For more details, see World Bank (2006).

channels positively affect growth. Others have found that female education has a greater impact on growth than male education (Abu-Ghaida and Klasen, 2004). Klasen (2002) finds that the direct and indirect effects of gender inequality in educational attainment account for 38 per cent of the 2.5 percentage points (pp) gap in growth rates between South Asia and East Asia, 17 per cent of the 3.3 pp gap between Sub-Saharan Africa and East Asia and 45 per cent of the 1.9 pp gap between the Middle East and North Africa and East Asia. Cuberes and Teignier (2016) focus on the gender gap in entrepreneurship in connection with the gender gap in employment. They calculate that the gender gap in entrepreneurship would lead to a loss in GDP of approximately 25 per cent with respect to the no-gender-inequality case, while the exclusion of women from the labour market would reduce income per capita by almost 40 per cent. This loss is due to an inefficient organization of production related to the obstacles to women's access to entrepreneurship: in the presence of gender discrimination, the threshold of talent decreases, and the entire talent distribution shifts to the left. When the most talented people (independent of their gender) are instead chosen to organize production carried out by others, they can spread their ability advantage over a larger scale. Cavalcanti and Tavares (2016) calculate the aggregate cost of gender inequality to GDP. They measure discrimination by the difference between female labour productivity and female wages. By calibrating their model to the US economy, they find that a 50 per cent increase in discrimination leads to a 35 per cent decrease in income per capita. They also calibrate the model for a large set of developed and developing countries, showing that higher discrimination leads to lower output (see also Hsieh et al., 2019).

A related argument that has been proposed to explain the direct association between gender equality and economic growth is that women control approximately two-thirds of consumer spending: they are a new 'emerging market'. Women control approximately 80 per cent of consumers' buying decisions, from healthcare and homes to furniture and food, but they also purchase more than 50 per cent of traditional male products, including automobiles and consumer electronics.[3] It has been estimated that women control more than US$20

---

[3] Kathy Matsui, chief strategist at Goldman Sachs in Tokyo, has calculated the benefits of women's purchasing power on a basket of 115 Japanese companies,

trillion in worldwide spending, and their purchasing power constantly increases. Women also control a substantial part of worldwide financial wealth, and they have overtaken men in financial planning decisions.

The fact that women's participation in the labour market may contribute to economic growth gained much attention during the period of the 2008 economic crisis. Data for European countries (ILO, 2009) show that female employment was less affected than male employment by the crisis, thus suggesting another beneficial role of greater participation by women in the labour market; that is, women provide *insurance* against the effects of a possible economic crisis. Several arguments have been used to understand whether and why a gender divide can be observed in the impact of the crisis. First, as the labour market is segmented, and men and women are employed in different sectors, if the sectors in which women are mainly employed – the public sector – are less damaged by the crisis than the financial or industrial sectors, which are more male dominated, female employment reacts better than male employment to the crisis. Second, women may have increased their participation in the labour market to compensate for the reduction in men's income due to the crisis. In times of crisis, it becomes clear that one income is not enough, and having two incomes in a household functions as insurance (Rubery, 1988). This fact is also consistent with the evidence on the increase in female entrepreneurs in several countries. From Global Entrepreneurship Monitor data, it is possible to observe that the female-to-male ratio of total early-stage entrepreneurial activity rose shortly after 2007 in most European countries. Finally, if women are paid less than men (see Chapter 2), in times of economic crisis, it may be convenient for firms to hire women instead of men.

These arguments about gender equality and economic growth have inspired the concept of 'womenomics': women are a powerful engine of global economic growth. It is, however, very difficult to identify the direct causal relationship between gender equality and economic growth, in both developing and developed countries, because of the well-known problem of endogeneity: gender equality increases growth, but faster development could also stimulate gender equality and reduce women's obstacles. In other words, they reinforce each other. Gender

including industries such as financial services, online retailing, beauty, clothing and prepared foods.

equality itself is an endogenous variable as I have shown in previous chapters: it is the result of culture, public policy and politics, and it is therefore impossible to isolate the impact of gender equality on economic outcomes. Many of these factors, such as the quality of institutions and governance or the cultural context, affect both gender equality and growth.

Before moving to the next approach, it is important to mention that GDP may not be the most appropriate measure of the wealth and well-being of a country (see Stiglitz et al., 2009). From this perspective, some researchers consider it misleading to measure women's contribution to the economy as an increase in GDP – as we have mentioned thus far – simply because GDP is not the appropriate measure of welfare and well-being. They suggest that gender equality may still be an issue of equity, but for the sake of efficiency, we need a different, more complex or less direct way to measure the potential contribution of women. This also leads towards the second channel.

Gender Equality and Growth: Indirect Impact
The second channel links gender equality and economic growth in a more complex and indirect way, which can, however, be tested more precisely. Since men and women have different traits and preferences, they may make different decisions. It is difficult and probably not very useful to try to understand whether women make *better* decisions than men (i.e. decisions that enhance growth) or vice versa. Not all women's empowerment initiatives increase growth (Doepke and Tertilt, 2016), but some likely do. What is more interesting is to explore where these differences emerge, to characterize them, to assess the complementarity/substitutability between men and women in decision-making and finally to draw conclusions about the possible efficiency gains of gender equality from this perspective.

In Chapters 4 and 5, I analyzed the causal impact of women in decision-making positions on public policy and firms' outcomes. What do we know about the connection between these outcomes and socioeconomic growth?

In developing countries, randomized field experiments and natural experiments are used to understand the causal impact of women's control of resources and their allocation. These studies show that women use old-age pension benefits, conditional cash transfers and loans from microcredit programs (Pitt and Khandker, 1998; Duflo,

2003; Rubalcava et al., 2004) differently than men and in a way that leads to the well-being of the younger generation and higher growth. Interestingly, Duflo (2003) exploits a natural experiment in which older adults were given pensions in South Africa and estimates that girls who live with a grandmother who receives pension benefits weigh more and are taller than those who live with a grandmother who is not eligible to receive pension benefits. Grandmothers' pensions translate into better nutrition. No effect of the pension is found for male receivers. The fact that women have preferences that are more in line with the objective of increasing growth and reducing poverty is also clear in microcredit institutions that explicitly target poor women (Rivero-Fuentes and McKernan, 2005): women use the money more for child schooling and child and maternal health than for tobacco, alcohol and recreation (Doss, 1996). It is also true that women are more vulnerable than men to negative shocks; thus, providing microcredit directly to them has higher value.

An extensive older literature concentrates on the benefits of diversity in the business context (see Chapter 5): having both men and women in decision-making roles expands the perspective, increases creativity and innovation, diversifies the pool of talents and competence, reduces the conflicts and improves the process of decision-making. The fact that women are less individually oriented (selfish) than men implies that they are expected to care more about the common good and less about their personal interests. This turns out to be particularly important in the political and institutional contexts: since a government works better if opportunistic behaviour is limited, women may contribute to the functioning of institutions. Dollar et al. (2001) examine the relationship between female participation in government legislatures and the level of perceived corruption in a sample of more than 100 countries. They find a strong, negative and statistically significant relationship between the proportion of women in a country's legislature and the level of corruption: women are less corrupted, more responsible and less absent than men. The final implication of this relatively old literature is that gender diversity is associated with better performance in both business and politics. However, these studies may suffer from endogeneity concerns.

More recent contributions concentrate on the relationship between gender equality and the performance of companies and try to identify causality. In fact, as I discussed in Chapter 5, a positive correlation between the share of women in companies (or in top positions) and the financial outcomes of the companies does not imply causality. To assess causality, we need to refer to an exogenous shock to the share of women in top positions, which has no direct relationship with the analyzed outcomes. I previously discussed the results of the introduction of board gender quotas in Norway in 2004 and in Italy in 2011 (see Chapter 5). Similarly, in the context of politics, recent papers try to establish the causal link between the presence of female politicians and the quality of action and/or the type of policies implemented, which may in turn have different relationships with economic growth (see Chapter 4). As we have seen, the results are not fully conclusive, thus making it difficult to claim that gender equality in decision-making has a clear positive impact on business and policy outcomes. However, it is important to emphasize that there is no causal evidence that gender equality has any negative impact! Whether this is enough to encourage gender equality on the normative side is outside the scope of this book. However, it is an interesting point to consider.

Other recent studies change the analysis perspective and examine the impact of gender equality on the selection process and the agenda of decision-making. I analyzed in Chapters 4 and 5 how female leadership in business and politics changes the selection process. It is important now to stress the potential link between these changes and growth. The selection argument is based on the fact that reducing gender gaps and, in particular, promoting women to top positions implies a dramatic change in the initial status quo dominated by male representatives. As competent and talented women are abundant, this change may induce a better selection process with positive effects on the quality of representatives. If the underrepresentation of women depends not on their lack of competence or qualifications but on forms of discrimination (see Chapter 2), an inefficient waste of talent arises, and reducing gender gaps will lead to a better outcome. Thus, it is a matter of efficiency. There is also a spillover effect: all candidates, women and also men, are better selected if the pool of candidates is enlarged and the competition is tougher. In fact, when not only men but also women are seriously considered among the pool of candidates, there is a rethinking of the entire group of representatives. If women are highly qualified, the standard of quality also increases for men. Thus, men themselves are better selected, and the overall quality increases. There is also an incentive effect: having more balanced leadership may induce more women to compete. In an expanded pool of talent, it is more likely that the appropriate candidate will be selected. Thus, a virtuous positive circle of quality may begin. Similarly, I emphasized in Chapters 4 and 5 that women contribute to the definition of a new agenda, including items that are typically neglected by men but may be related to better economic performance, such as firms' environmental policies and investments in education. These outcomes have a long-term perspective and are related to growth.

6.2.2 Inequality and Poverty Reduction

Gender equality is also associated with less inequality and poverty reduction. According to the ILO (Ernst and Berg, 2009), women's paid and unpaid work may be the single most important poverty-reducing factor in developing economies. Women's better access to the market and work increases their income, which leads to more consumption and directly reduces current poverty. At the same time, better control of household decisions by women improves the well-being of children, which increases their educational attainment and health as adults and thus reduces poverty in the future. More resources for women also translate into higher savings, which in turn reduce future poverty (Morrison et al., 2007).

It is challenging to establish an empirical relationship between gender equality and poverty reduction. First, gender equality plays a crucial role in alleviating the poverty of women as long as it increases their wealth, education, accumulation of human capital, access to financial markets and access to the labour market and to less risky jobs. Gender equality, the reduction in the disadvantages of poor women and economic growth are therefore likely to be related. In line with this argument, we expect female-headed households to be more likely to be chronically poor, while for male-headed households, poverty is typically a transition status. Promoting gender equality should also imply eliminating gender differences in poverty dynamics.

Second, economic growth and poverty reduction are associated through the same channels that link gender equality and economic growth, as described earlier. For example, higher investments of women in education and health contribute to explaining the association between gender equality and poverty reduction. Thus, more gender equality in resources such as education and access to employment can reduce the likelihood of a household being poor.

There is another interesting mechanism to consider: gender equality reduces risks and mitigates the negative effects of income shocks, which can easily lead to poverty. For example, when both partners in a household work, the household is better equipped to face the risk of one partner losing a job or having a negative income shock than a household in which only the man works. Female labour force participation plays a key role in keeping households from falling into poverty. This is particularly relevant in times of economic crisis. Overall, the evidence suggests that gender equality is a key ingredient for growth and poverty alleviation.

6.2.3 Sustainable Economy

Gender equality is not only related to economic growth but also may be fundamental to sustainable growth. As declared by the 2030 Agenda for Sustainable Development launched by the UN and adopted in 2015, a fundamental goal is to 'achieve gender equality and empower all women and girls'. Similarly, the European Commission claims that 'Gender equality is a fundamental right, a common value of the EU, and a necessary condition for the achievement of the EU objectives of growth, employment and social cohesion' (EU Commission).

The reasons are that women's empowerment increases environmental sustainability (as described in Chapter 5), helps reduce poverty (as explained earlier in this chapter), increases investments in education and social needs (as shown in Chapter 4) and reduces risky decisions. All these effects are fundamental pillars for sustainable growth.

6.2.4 Sustainable Society

Several studies have shown that gender equality may pose issues of social sustainability. Concerns about the consequences of gender equality in the social sphere must be taken into account if the goal is gender equality in a sustainable society. They mainly concern the stability of families, child development and the overall happiness and well-being of women themselves.

Divorce

Over recent decades, women's labour force participation and rates of divorce concurrently increased across all industrialized economies. However, this correlation is not enough to prove any causal effect of women's participation in the labour market on family instability. A first strand of literature, based on Becker's (1973) theory of marriage, hypothesizes that a higher level of female employment is not beneficial to marriage. As women cannot fully engage in home and childcare anymore, gains from the gendered specialization of tasks decrease, which creates tension within a couple (see Becker et al., 1977; Becker, 1981). These theories heavily rely on a classic breadwinner model; therefore, they are often regarded as outdated.

The improvement of gender equality and, in particular, the relative gains in women's labour market opportunities have the potential to challenge the traditional gender identity concept (Akerlof and Kranton, 2000). However, labour markets evolve more rapidly than social norms, which tend to be persistent and to change slowly. This creates a challenging situation. Either individuals modify their behaviour to fulfil gender roles, a fact that may threaten the gender revolution, or they must suffer the consequences of a misalignment of their behaviour with the dominant gender norms. The increase in divorces can be seen as a result of this case. As analyzed by Bertrand et al. (2015) for the United States, the well-established social norm that 'a man should earn more than his wife' explains why couples in which the wife earns (or potentially would earn) more than her husband have a higher probability of divorce or a high probability that the woman will stop working.

It would, however, be too simplistic to conclude that marital instability is the necessary cost of improvement in gender equality. Extensive sociological research has found that 'marital quality' is an important determinant of the relationship between divorce and women's employment: women's employment does not increase the risk of divorce in happy marriages, while it does so in unhappy ones (see Hobson 1990; Ruggles 1997; Schoen et al., 2002). More precisely, 'when men are not employed, either husbands or wives are more likely to leave. When wives report better than average marital satisfaction, their employment affects neither their nor their husbands' exits. However, when wives report below average marital satisfaction, their employment makes it more likely that they will leave' (Sayer et al., 2011). This means that it is not women's earnings that induce divorce but their unhappiness (Sayer and Bianchi, 2000) and that (dis)satisfaction with the marriage is a better predictor of divorce than women's economic independence.

Child Development

A major aspect of a sustainable society is child development. How does gender equality affect child development? Parents' education and income are important in child development, not only because of the genetic transmission of abilities but also because of the available resources that are fundamental to the social position of children. As emphasized by Heckman et al. (2013), the time spent by parents with children is also crucial not only for the development of children's cognitive abilities but also for their motivation and self-control, which are important for their success in the labour market. Nature is not the only determinant, as I have previously argued, and who our parents are is not the only factor that matters for our future. Parents' choices, including education, the choice of a partner and the time of birth, matter. Additionally, the school, the time spent on activities and the investment are important in creating and building abilities. School environment, peers and policies matter. Human capital development is a process with several steps: capacities influence the ability to invest further in the future and productivity, and effort matters. Investment at an early stage of life or even in utero is clearly important for child development (see Barker, 1990; Cunha and Heckman, 2007; Almond and Currie, 2011).

If the mother works, the income is higher, and so are the investment possibilities for the children. The more resources there are within the family budget, the more investment for children, as we know from Chapter 4. However, because working mothers must reduce their time spent with children, does more income compensate for the absence of the mother during the time of working? The answer is yes, as long as fathers participate actively in childrearing and high-quality childcare is available.

Fathers matter. Sociologists and psychologists have asked how the time devoted by parents to childcare affects children's development and how alternative care matters. In the United States, UK and Canada, where longitudinal data are collected, the evidence is mixed and inconclusive: some studies find that mothers' employment has positive effects on child development, others find negative effects and others find that the effects depend on the time of work and type of outcome. There is also an evolution over time: according to Cawley and Liu (2007), in the United States, when both partners work, working mothers spend less time on average on reading, doing homework and playing with their children, while fathers increase their time devoted to these activities, but only by a small amount. This is worrisome because it suggests that children with working parents spend less time on activities that are important for their development. I have already discussed how important the contribution of fathers to childcare is for fertility decisions in Europe. This is also crucial for child development. Paternity leave, which I discussed in Chapter 3, is an important policy to support gender equality in a sustainable society because it promotes fathers' sharing of childcare, which is essential for child development when mothers work. In the future, the discussion of gender equality will increasingly be more about parenthood than about motherhood.

The availability and quality of formal childcare also matter. According to Bernal and Keane (2011), when childcare is of good quality, maternal employment has no negative impact on child development. In particular, early childhood is crucial for children's future outcomes (Heckman et al., 2013). Day care attendance may have positive effects on children's educational outcomes, particularly for children from disadvantaged backgrounds. The results are, however, not uncontroversial (Havnes and Mogstad, 2011; Brilli et al., 2016). The importance of the quality of early care has relevant policy implications: formal care is generally of higher quality than informal care. More investments in formal care and more inclusion of current informal care in a formal system would be a good way to improve the quality of early childcare with beneficial consequences for future children's outcomes.

Happiness

An alarm has been sounded: gender equality reduces happiness, not only of children and families but also of women themselves. According to Stevenson and Wolfers (2009), there is a 'paradox' of declining female happiness: on the one hand, objective measures of well-being, such as gender wage gaps, labour market gaps and control of fertility show an improvement in the position of women in recent decades. On the other hand, the happiness of women, measured by subjective indicators (self-reported level of happiness and satisfaction with marriage, health, financial situation and job) is declining, both in absolute and in relative terms, compared to that of men. This trend applies to several countries and several cohorts, and it is confirmed by the use of several measures of happiness. Men are happier than women, and in spite of better conditions in the labour market and increased support from men compared to the past, women are less happy. Why? It is not easy to give an answer. A possible answer is that happiness is a relative status and depends on comparisons: as gender equality progresses, women stop comparing themselves with other women and start making comparisons with men, whom they see as always in a better position than they are in terms of higher pay, higher promotion rates and more leisure time. It is also possible that the expectations of changes in terms of gender equality were greater than what women were ultimately able to achieve, thus nurturing frustration. The way women have entered the labour market may also create ambiguous consequences in terms of well-being. Part-time work, for example, has allowed women to enter the labour market while maintaining the social norms of being 'good' mothers and spouses: the possibility of reconciling their role with the dominant social norms may be positive for their happiness but may also backfire. Women may realize that they ultimately have lower-quality jobs while maintaining the entire responsibility of the house and the care of children (Booth and van Ours, 2008).

Although often neglected, these concerns about the consequences of gender equality for social sustainability are part of the global challenges that our societies are facing. The risk is that we may have more gender-equal but less sustainable societies, with more divorce, lower child development and lower happiness. The opportunity is to transform the process towards gender equality in a way that achieves a more sustainable society. Again, the context matters in turning risks into opportunities, and this is where policies will play a fundamental role: protection in case of divorce, high-quality childcare services and the involvement of fathers in childcare (e.g. through paternity leave) are some examples.

6.3 Technological Challenges: The Future of Jobs

Technology is in continuous evolution and progress. The internet has changed the way we live, work, produce and consume. Recent developments in artificial intelligence, robotics, machine learning, biotechnology and big data as well as the rise of the sharing economy and smart systems are transforming the jobs of the future. According to the World Economic Forum 2016 Report on the 'Future of Jobs', 65 per cent of children currently entering primary school will ultimately work in completely new job types that do not yet exist. This is both a great opportunity and an enormous challenge. On the one hand, technology enlarges the potential for the growth and creation of new jobs; on the other hand, it may imply the disruption of current jobs and the rise of skills instability across all jobs. New skills are required, which need to be developed to avoid the risk of talent shortages. As the changes are very rapid, it is impossible to count only on a more appropriate education of the next generation of workers: what is needed is an instantaneous retraining of the current workforce and efforts by individuals to adapt to the new skills requirements, and by firms to manage the transition to the new technology-driven business. Government should also play an active role in creating a favourable environment to manage the current transition in labour markets. The changes will impact industries differently: for example, big data will have a stronger impact on information and communication technology and financial services than other sectors. In all industries, present-day actions will determine whether changes will result in the massive displacement of workers or the emergence of new opportunities.

These changes may have a strong gender divide, which I discuss here. A great challenge is how to exploit technological changes to further enhance gender equality. I identify three main channels through which technology changes and gender equality can reinforce each other.

First, the gender divide depends on gender segregation across jobs. This is crucial for understanding the gender impact of the ongoing transformations: women are less represented in fast-growing STEM jobs, and they are concentrated in low-growth or declining sectors, such as sales, business and financial operations, office work and administration. This implies that some of the gains towards gender equality that we have experienced in the past century will be reversed in the future. However, women are also less represented in sectors such as manufacturing and production, construction and extraction, which are expected to lose – mainly male – jobs. Sectors that are more able to employ and retain female workers will probably have an advantage in recruiting female talent to address their skills shortages. The dynamics of the industry gender gap under disruptive technological change will crucially affect the new employment scenario.

Second, technological changes have the potential to enable the narrowing of gender gaps in many industries. Washing machines, vacuum cleaners and refrigerators are labour-saving devices for work that is predominantly performed by women. When these technologies to deal with household work – a prevalently female responsibility – were introduced, they freed women's time from household tasks and improved their opportunities to invest in the labour market (Greenwood et al., 2005; Attanasio et al., 2008). This outcome was amplified by the marketization of home production: many household activities have close substitutes in the service sector, particularly in jobs where women have a comparative advantage. The expansion of the service sector reduces the cost of these activities, with the double result of promoting women's work outside the home and increasing (other) women's employment in these jobs in the service sector (Akbulut, 2011; Buera et al., 2019; Rendall, 2018). A virtuous circle starts: when more women work in the market, more jobs are created in the service sector, particularly in household activities and childcare, where women have a comparative advantage.

From a historical perspective, several authors have shown that progress in female participation in the labour market has occurred owing to medical progress, such as the introduction of a contraceptive pill (Goldin and Katz, 2002; Bailey, 2006), which reduced fertility and increased women's control over it. From the same historical perspective, Albanesi and Olivetti (2016) provide further evidence that technological progress has played an important role in supporting gender equality. They show that in the United States, medical progress in the period 1930–1960 was fundamental in promoting women's participation in the labour market by increasing maternal health and decreasing maternal mortality rate. Poor maternal health was a critical limit to the capacity of women to be employed. The availability of infant formula, developed in the mid-1920s, also played an important role for women who wanted to work.

Third, a given aspect of technological progress may strongly support female labour force participation, for example, by making it possible to organize jobs more flexibly. Goldin (2014) defines the changes in how jobs are structured and remunerated to enhance temporal flexibility as the 'last chapter' of the great convergence towards equality between men and women. According to the World Economic Forum (2016, Table 2, p. 6), 'New technologies are enabling workplace innovations such as remote working, co-working spaces and teleconferencing. Organizations are likely to have an ever-smaller pool of core full-time employees for fixed functions, backed up by colleagues in other countries and external consultants and contractors for specific projects.'

In 2015, approximately one in five workers in EU member states had access to flexible schedules (European Working Condition Survey, Eurofound). Major international organizations, such as the EC and the OECD, are promoting flexibility as a way to increase work-life balance and productivity. A survey by Eurofound-ILO (2017) shows that flexible work arrangements are appreciated by workers and can lead to increased productivity owing to the reduction in commuting time and the possibility of better organizing time based upon preference. There are also positive spillover effects for the environment owing to the reduction in CO_2 emissions related to decreased commuting.

In this context, an interesting new practice is 'smart work', a new way of working based on flexible time and flexible space. Workers agree with their supervisors to work for a defined period of their job activity, say one day per week, outside the company's physical workplace and with a personalized time schedule. During this defined period, there are no precise constraints on the time or location of work. Owing to the use of technological tools, workers may perform the same duties and activities that they perform in the workplace and achieve the set targets and results. Smart workers may decide to work from home or at other places, such as a library or a park: in contrast to the concept of traditional teleworking, which requires work at the domicile of the worker, smart workers may choose a workplace based on the activity to be performed and their personal needs. In some cases, the place of work itself becomes 'smart': offices become flexible spaces where workers perform part of their activity, without a fixed place but with free access to the necessary technological devices and with a new physical layout, that is, with concentration zones and areas for team work and communication. Workers also decide the time of work. These flexible work arrangements, sometimes referred also as 'agile working', have attracted the attention of workers, firms, policymakers and lawyers. This revolutionary new organizational model, made possible by the development of technology, promises not only to support work-life balance and promote the well-being of workers but also to meet employers' need for new ways to increase productivity and competitiveness – adapting to new technologies, optimizing the costs of work (including saving on office spaces and reducing absenteeism) and retaining talent within the organization. Moreover, given its flexible and modifiable nature, in contrast to teleworking, smart work can anticipate and adjust for the risk of isolation. However, if flexible working makes workers work longer (overtime) and more intensively (Clark, 2000), it may be associated with higher performance but not with a reduction in work-family conflict.

The effects of smart work have been analyzed by different disciplines, although they have only recently attracted rigorous studies. The introduction of smart work has clear substantial economic consequences, mainly captured by the potential changes in workers' productivity. Whether flexibility is good or bad for productivity is difficult to assess because it is difficult to measure productivity or to establish the causality of flexibility on productivity. Attempts to measure productivity based on objective measures such as absenteeism (Koopman et al., 2002) and output rates per hour (Golden, 2012) show a positive relationship with flexibility. Self-declared productivity is also positively related to flexibility (see Riedmann et al., 2006). As these works provide *ex post* descriptive evidence on the implementation of smart work, they suffer from well-known endogeneity concerns; mainly, they cannot control for other variables affecting productivity and cannot establish whether smart work increases productivity or whether places with high productivity are more likely to introduce smart work. Smart work may also affect productivity through changes in workers' well-being and work-life balance, which therefore are important to establish.

Flexibility also has consequences for well-being and work-life balance that may have a clear gender impact. Labour sociologists (Kelly and Moen, 2007; Schieman and Glavin, 2008) have studied the relationship between flexibility and work-life balance. As reviewed by Chung (2017), the evidence for this relationship is mixed: on the one hand, flexibility may reduce work-family conflict (Chung, 2011; Kelly et al., 2014); on the other hand, it can lead to spillovers from work to home, blurring the boundaries between the two and increasing the overtime hours of workers with negative results for work-life balance (Golden et al., 2006). This second effect is linked to the use of flexible working mainly by highly skilled workers in large companies, which also offer performance-related pay and other arrangements that motivate workers to work harder. Chung (2017) provides evidence of the emergence of a gender divide: while women use flexibility for family-friendly purposes, men use it for performance purposes. Women increase their chance to remain employed after the birth of their first child and their capacity to work when their family duties increase, thus enjoying better work-life balance. In contrast, men increase their work intensity and performance-related payments with no changes in family arrangements and obtain an income premium. Thus, flexibility is associated with a risk that traditional gender roles will be strengthened. These results, however, are obtained in studies that cannot establish the causality of flexibility on outcomes.

More recently, academic attention to the study of flexibility has developed in management (Leslie et al., 2012), mainly with a focus on performance outcomes: flexibility may increase performance if workers are 'happy' to control their own work schedule and work more effectively, with fewer days of sickness and absenteeism. Major companies across the world have been practicing smart work for at least a decade. They provide case studies for scholars in management, which offer descriptive evidence on how this practice is implemented and with what consequences. Again, case studies and surveys on the adoption of workplace flexibility and work-life balance practices cannot provide causal evidence.

An extended economic literature has studied how productivity differs between firms according to differences in management practices (see the literature from Walker, 1887; Leibenstein, 1966; Bloom et al., 2013; Syverson, 2011; Gibbons and Henderson, 2013). Few studies conduct randomized experiments that are able to identify the causality of management practices and productivity. Dutcher (2012) performs laboratory experiments on routine and non-routine tasks with and without remote monitoring and finds that more routine tasks were negatively affected by mimicking a home-based environment. He conjectures that the result depends on the lack of peer and manager effects, which have been shown to be important in low-level tasks in field environments by Bandiera et al. (2005), Falk and Ichino (2006) and Mas and Moretti (2009). Kelly et al. (2014) examine the impact of a work-life balance training program randomized across branches of a large firm, finding significant reductions in employee work-family conflict and improved family time and schedule control. Bloom et al. (2015) conduct a randomized experiment on a large Chinese firm, comparing a group of teleworkers and workers at an office within the same firm. They find that teleworkers have higher productivity than the others, but they feel isolated and when given the opportunity to choose again between teleworking or working in the office, they prefer to return to their workplace.

In a recent paper with Angelici (Profecta and Angelici, 2019), I study the causal impact of smart work on labour market outcomes, well-being and work-life balance. We develop a randomized field experiment conducted on a sample of workers in a large Italian company who have not practiced smart work before. Smart work is introduced for a randomly selected group of workers in the sample: in agreement with their supervisors, for nine months, these workers have the option to work 'smart' (i.e. with no constraints on the place and time) one day per week. The rest of the workers continue to work traditionally. As the company has never used smart work before, the possibility that the effects we test are derived from confounding factors is excluded. Italy is characterized by low flexibility in work organization and the very recent introduction of a law that provides a regulatory framework for the implementation of smart work by firms (Law 81/2017). The law includes specific provisions to encourage the use of smart work, including the protection of the health and safety of the workers and guarantees equal remuneration of workers. We follow the methodology of randomized experiments by selecting a sample of 310 workers who meet our interest and randomly divide them into two groups, one treated by the use of one day per week of smart work during a nine-month period (200 individuals) and the other (110 individuals) not having the option of smart work. We evaluate the effect of smart work on productivity, well-being and work-life balance. To do so, we administer a questionnaire to each worker and his/her supervisor before and after the experiment. The questions capture several dimensions of self-assessed well-being, productivity and work-life balance. We also use objective measures of workers' performance measured monthly by the firm. After collecting the data, we use a difference-in-difference methodology to identify the causal effect of smart work on outcomes. Workers treated with smart work show an increase in productivity, both objective and declared by the supervisor (efficiency, respect for deadline), compared to those who continue working traditionally. They are also more satisfied with their income, health, job, social life, leisure time and overall life. They declare that they are more able to concentrate, to appreciate their daily activities and to overcome problems. The effects are stronger for women and for individuals with children and/or family burdens.

6.4 Conclusions

In this chapter, I have described how the gender equality process interacts with global changes in our economies and societies. Demographic, socioeconomic and technological changes can be both a risk and an opportunity for progress towards gender equality. How to turn them into opportunities rather than risks depends on the context: culture, attitudes and public policy will play a fundamental role in developing a sustainable growing economy and society that will further improve gender equality.

7 | Conclusions

The relationship between gender and public policy is twofold. On the one hand, public policies are needed to promote gender equality in a context in which the under-representation of women in the economic and political spheres has negative consequences for both equality and efficiency. On the other hand, the constant progress towards a gender-balanced socioeconomic role for women and the process towards women's empowerment have the political capacity to reorient decisions related to public policies. This may in turn reinforce the link between policies and gender equality.

The previous chapters investigated the nature and development of this twofold relationship. Gender gaps in the economic and political dimensions are still widespread around the world: the evidence presented in Chapter 2 shows that they include low female labour force participation, differences in wages between men and women and lower career prospects for women than for men. They emerge as the result of complex interactions between innate traits (nature) and influential contexts (nurture) and are even historically determined, shaping both women's preferences and choices (the supply side) and recruitment and career processes (the demand side). Maternity plays an important role but cannot be considered uniquely responsible for gender gaps in the labour market.

Public policies matter: Chapter 3 showed how maternity, parental and paternity leave; public expenditure on formal childcare; labour market measures (such as flexible work arrangements); and the design of tax and pension systems may help support the female labour supply and reduce gender gaps. Trade-offs may arise: for example, highly generous maternity leave may protect working women when they have children and thus induce them to remain on the labour market, or they may be a disincentive for firms to hire and promote women. The final impact of family policies on gender equality outcomes must be determined empirically and often in a specific context.

Policies themselves are the outcome of a decision-making process in which the identity of the policymakers matters. Chapter 4 showed that gender is an important determinant of the identity of policymakers: women are more open to social issues, including migration, human and civil rights and the environment and less inclined to military intervention. These different preferences between male and female politicians translate into different decisions of male and female policymakers. Aggregate-level analysis, as well as micro-level analysis of developing countries, confirms that the agenda of female politicians is more oriented towards education and social issues. Women also make different decisions in monetary policymaking, opting for a higher interest rate. Some of the studies on developed countries based on convincing identification of the causal effect of women politicians on public policy outcomes are, however, less conclusive. This may be because women tend to experience party pressure more than men and thus struggle to translate their identity into real outcomes.

In parallel, women matter in the business context. Men and women have different traits, including risk aversion, attitude towards negotiation and competition, time horizon, and social preferences (such as sensitivity to fairness, justice, trust and altruism) and networking. These attributes, which together define what we call 'style of leadership', are likely to affect firms' business and financial performance, social and sustainability performance, international performance (export and trade) and labour market outcomes. It is not easy to prove how these individual traits translate into firms' outcomes. Chapter 5 proposed new evidence in the expected direction, similar to what has been found for political outcomes: women's leadership is at least not bad for business, as it improves social and sustainability performance and reduces gender gaps, although to a limited extent. Moreover, the quality of leadership increases when women are more represented in firms' top positions.

The gender equality process interacts with global changes in our economies and societies, which Chapter 6 classified as demographic, economic and technological changes. The participation of women in the labour force has the potential to counterbalance the increase in the ratio between workers and retirees, which is a consequence of the ageing of the population, one of the most dramatic changes of recent decades. It may also affect fertility: in contrast to what happened in the past and to the 'conventional wisdom' that working or having children are alternatives for women, recent evidence shows that the relationship between female employment rate and fertility has become positive in several contexts, thus reinforcing the positive role of gender equality in facing the ageing process. In times of slow and modest growth, female employment may also contribute positively to economic growth. Sustainable development is a major goal of our economies and societies. Chapter 6 provided evidence that gender equality may contribute in this direction. Technology is rapidly transforming the jobs of the future. As women are less represented in fast-growing STEM jobs and are concentrated in routine jobs in low-growth or declining sectors, there is a risk of decelerating the progress towards gender equality. How to use technological changes to support rather than prevent gender equality, for example, by promoting new and more flexible forms of labour organization, is a challenging opportunity.

7.1 Work in Progress in Europe

Most of the data and analyses developed in this book are based on evidence from European countries. Europe is a true laboratory of analysis: the evolution of female participation in the labour force and in the political sphere and the introduction of new policies such as gender quotas, paternity leave and flexible work arrangements contribute to making the gender equality process a major transformation in the European scenario and one that will characterize the future of Europe. In parallel, differences across European countries related to social norms, family organization and gender culture provide opportunities to explore the role of these contextual factors in the relationship between gender equality and public policies. Progress towards gender equality is still ongoing, and European countries are at different stages of development: countries lagging in the process may still learn from more advanced ones. A clear lesson is that policies may play an important role in shifting from a low to a high gender equality equilibrium. Obviously, if differences have historical and cultural roots, policies have a more difficult task. However, as long as differences between men and women are not genetic, there is room for policy action.

What Are the Most Effective Policies?

Family policies and, in particular, paternity leave have the potential to move towards a better equilibrium within a couple, which is the first step towards gender equality in the labour market. If care responsibilities (for children and the elderly) are shared between men and women, both the supply and demand of women's labour are positively encouraged: women have more time to work, and firms have less incentive to prefer male workers. This will nurture a balanced equilibrium between domestic/care work and the labour market within a couple. It may also encourage fertility, which is low in some European countries characterized by low female employment. There is clear room for improvement in this direction; in several EU countries, such as Italy, paternity leave is still very limited (number of days and level of benefits) and has not gained the attention it deserves.

Effective policies need not be gender specific: there is no need to explicitly target women. For example, childcare expenditures have proven to be important. The provision of early childcare, in particular, is an essential part of a welfare state that aims to support child development and equal opportunities. Given family and cultural contexts, childcare is particularly beneficial for female employment. Even in this case, there is space for improvement: while early childcare has high coverage in Scandinavian countries, it is still limited in southern European countries, where childcare is offered traditionally within the family or through informal arrangements.

New forms of job organizations, such as smart work, based on flexibility in space and time, may also have a substantial advantage for female employment, though they are not gender-specific policies.

Regarding the promotion of women to top positions, gender quotas, which impose a minimum representation of each gender, have proven to be effective in European countries, not only in increasing the number of women in decision-making positions (in both politics and business) but also in improving the quality of the representatives and the outcome of the selection. Although not the ideal policy, given their intrinsic constraining nature, gender quotas may be useful as a temporary measure to break down the male-dominated equilibrium of decision-making positions.

Having more women in decision-making positions, in both firms and politics, is not only a better outcome of the selection process but also implies different decisions. This is particularly promising as long as the decision outcomes of a gender-balanced leadership are in line with greater attention to the policies that turn out to have a positive effect on gender equality. In contexts in which the evidence shows that women in decision-making influence policies, promoting gender balance in leading positions should be a top priority. A reinforcing mechanism may arise that goes from gender balance in decision-making to policies that promote gender equality, which in turn may increase women's representation in decision-making and so on. The final message to European policymakers is to strongly favour conditions that may initiate this virtuous circle. All economic actors are then encouraged to take an active role in supporting the process. Only a comprehensive plan of action can be effective.

7.2 Future Development

Several important aspects of gender equality have remained outside the scope of this book or at the margin. For example, I have not analyzed gender-based violence, which is a widespread phenomenon and has an important relationship with gender equality: on the one hand, the process of gender equality has made women economically independent, which is important in preventing violence and a necessary condition to deal with it. On the other hand, there are contexts in which women's empowerment is associated with unjustified, violent reactions. Many of the elements that the book has addressed, such as family relationships, gender culture, stereotypes and laws and institutions, play an important role in shaping the relationship between the process of gender equality and violence against women. It will be interesting to apply the approach developed by this book to this context.

The book has also neglected developing economies. A large literature in development economics concentrates on gender, the role of women and the close relationship between economic development and gender equality. Chapter 6 briefly addressed this topic and presented some results, which are useful as a comparison. However, we still lack a deep understanding of what drives the major differences that we observe in the relationship between women's empowerment and policies between developed and developing countries (see Chapter 4). Analysis based on these comparisons is encouraged and must be further developed in the future.

Although the road to achieving equality between men and women in economics and politics is still long, there is no doubt that progress towards gender equality has been constant and continuous during the past decades. We are entering a new phase in which the risk of stopping this progress or even taking a step back is, for the first time, serious. The increase in female labour force participation has stalled in some countries: new policy measures are difficult to implement, likely because they are costly and unaffordable in slow-growing European countries, except for gender quotas – a zero-cost measure that is flourishing in Europe. Cultural progress seems to have come to a halt. The success of political populism, mainly radical right parties, has contributed to the slowdown of cultural evolution. Intuitively, women's reaction may play an important role in contrast to this potential slowdown. In fact, recent studies have shown that women vote less than men for radical right parties. However, the links between women and populism need further investigation along these lines.

The recent economic crisis, the increase in inequality and the rise of populism have dramatically challenged the current organization of our economies and societies. One may argue that the dominant economic, political and social élites bear serious responsibilities in this process. They did not appropriately recognize the new course or protect the weakest individuals. Women have never been part of these élites and therefore can hardly be blamed. Currently, there is a great opportunity for women to assume responsibility. We have learned that this new role of women may translate into a new leadership paradigm and a new decision-making process, which effectively contribute to building an economy and society in which current and future generations of men and women can live better. We have also learned that to enter and successfully develop this new phase, the context matters. Understanding how to deal with this delicate phase, how to design more appropriate public policies to promote gender equality and how to exploit the female potential in this direction is currently of the utmost importance.

Appendix

Useful Methods to Identify the Relationship between Gender and Public Policy

The presence of women in decision-making positions in the economy and in politics is regularly associated with the presence of public policies oriented towards education, health and women's needs. This simple correlation does not necessarily imply causality for two main reasons.

The first reason is reverse causality: Does the presence of women cause public policy (a certain level of expenditure, design of the policy and similar outcomes), or does the policy induce higher female representation in decision-making positions? Both arguments can be true.

The second reason is omitted variable bias: a third element may cause both an increase in women in decision-making positions and the emergence of specific policies. This element, for example, can be culture, income or the organization of the labour market.

To draw conclusions and make policy recommendations, we need to precisely identify the direction of the relationship. Several methodologies can be used to solve the so-called identification problem. This appendix briefly explains the techniques employed for the analyses developed in the book. I divide them between the macro-level and micro-level of analysis.

A.1 Macro-level

A first group of studies is based on aggregate data organized in panel data with observations across countries (or across firms or across parties) and over time. In this case, the following approaches are possible.

Pooled Linear Regressions with Fixed Effects

Suppose we want to test whether a variable X (independent variable) has an impact on a variable Y (dependent variable). For both variables, we have observations from a set of countries (or firms) and over years. The equation to be estimated has the following form:

$$Y_{it} = \alpha_i + \beta_t + \gamma X_{it} + \delta controls_{it} + \varepsilon_{it}$$

where Y_{it} is the dependent variable observed in country i at time t; α_i is country fixed effect; β_t is time fixed effect; X_{it} is the independent variable in country i at time t; *controls* is a vector of control variables, which may also affect the dependent variable; and ε_{it} is the error term. Since the error term might be serially correlated within countries (even after controlling for country fixed effects) and thus incorrectly inflates the precision of the estimates, it is recommended that the standard errors be clustered at the country level (see Bertrand et al., 2004).

This estimate exploits the within-country variation of the variable X over time and correlates it with the dependent variable Y of interest. If X is the share of women in a decision-making body and Y is a measure of outcome/decisions of the body, the estimated γ is a measure of how much a change in the share of women in this decision-making body in a country from one period to the next is related to a change in its outcome. The presence of fixed effects reduces the risks of omitted variables while not fully solving the problem of reverse causality. An alternative option is to introduce lagged values of the dependent variable (X_{it-1}).

Example: We want to estimate the impact of the share of women in politics on the generosity of family policies. We have information on the share of women in politics across countries and over time and on the extent and type of family policy across countries and over time. We concentrate on within-country variations of the share of women in politics and link them to within-country evolution of family policies. (Note that this approach does not prove causality.)

Historical Approach

An alternative method is to use historical variables, which involves the direct use of a historical variable as the independent variable X in the equation. Control variables are also measured at the historical time.

This method solves the problem of reverse causality since it is impossible for present-day outcomes to cause historical outcomes. However, it may still be the case that the historical independent variable influences the past value of the dependent variable, which in turn is related to the current value of the dependent variable. Alternatively, it may be the case that the historical independent variable influences the dependent variable through an external omitted variable.

Example: We want to estimate the causal impact of the share of women in politics on the generosity of family policies. We use a historical variable, such as past female literacy rate or the type of preindustrial agricultural practice that favoured women versus men (or vice versa), which is related to women's empowerment (and thus to the share of women in politics) but not directly to present-day female labour force participation.

Instrumental Variables

To overcome the issue of the endogeneity of variable X when assessing its impact on variable Y, instrumental variables can be used. An instrument is a Z variable that is related to X but not to Y. For Z to be a good instrument, it must satisfy two conditions: it is related to X (first stage), and it is related to Y only through X (exclusion restriction). The second condition is difficult to verify. After checking these conditions, the second stage of the regression implies estimating the following equation:

$$Y_{it} = \alpha + \beta \hat{X}_{it} + \gamma_i + \gamma \delta_t + \varepsilon_{it}$$

where $\hat{X}_{it}$ is the level of variable X in country i at time t predicted by instrument Z according to the function

$$X_{it} = \vartheta Z_{it} + u_{it}$$

Intention to treat is a variation of this approach in which the instrument (rather than the predicted value of the independent variable) is directly plugged into the regression.

Example: We want to estimate the causal impact of the presence of women on boards on the performance of firms. We have data for a sample of firms (indicated by i) and years (indicated by t). Since the share of women can be endogenous (for example, because an external market condition increases both the performance of firms and the

presence of women on boards), we use the introduction of manda-
tory board gender quotas as an instrumental variable for the share of
women on boards. (See Chapter 5.*)*

A.2 Micro-level

Micro-level studies are based on several techniques, for which a concise
description follows.

Difference-in-Difference

To estimate the causal impact of a policy on a specific outcome, we
exploit the fact that the policy does not affect all subjects that are indexed
by i (they can be individuals, firms, municipalities, etc.). We can identify
a treatment group, which is affected by the policy, and a control group,
which is not. The two groups must be separated and not confounded.
Belonging to one group or the other must be random, that is, not related
to other unobserved characteristics that affect the dependent variable.
We need to observe outcomes for both groups for different time periods.
The identification of the causal effect of the policy on outcomes is based
on the estimation of the difference between the outcome of the treatment
group and that of the control group before and after the policy.

To guarantee the validity of this estimation procedure, a parallel trend
assumption is required – the existence of common trends between the
two groups prior to the reform. Formally, we must assume that in the
absence of the policy, the difference in the outcome between the
treatment and the control group would remain the same:

$$E(\varepsilon_{it}|Treatment_i, After_t, X_{it}) = 0$$

where $Treatment_i$ is a dummy variable equal to 1 if subject i belongs to
the treatment group and 0 otherwise; $After_t$ is a dummy variable equal
to 1 if the outcome is observed after the introduction of the policy and 0
otherwise; X_{it} is a vector of control variable characteristics for subject
i at time t; and ε_{it} is an error term.

The baseline difference-in-difference estimator has the following form:

$$Y_{it} = \alpha + \beta Treatment_i + \gamma After_t + \delta Treatment_i * After_t + \theta X_{it} + \varepsilon_{it}$$

where Y_{it} is the outcome of interest for subject i at time t; *Treatment*
is the same dummy variable specified earlier, which allows us to

control for unobserved time-invariant characteristics that may differ across observations in the two groups; *After* captures the temporal trend common to both groups, and *Treatment$_i$ * After$_t$* is the interaction term between the two dummies that measures the treatment effect of interest; X_{it} is a vector of control variable characteristics for subject i and time t; and ε_{it} is an error term.

If the parallel trend assumption cannot be proven, a semiparametric difference-in-difference estimation model (Abadie, 2005) investigates the average effect of the treatment on the treated (ATT) by comparing variations over time in the measures of the outcome across treatment groups.

Example: We want to estimate the causal impact of the introduction of gender quotas for municipal electoral lists on the share of women elected. We exploit a quasi-natural experiment due to the staggered implementation of the policy, as not all municipalities voted with the quotas at the same time. The treatment group is municipalities that voted with the quota, while the control group is other municipalities. The dependent variable is the share of women elected. (See Chapter 4.)

Regression Discontinuity Design

Regression discontinuity design exploits the existence of a discontinuous variation in the institutional design of a policy, for example, based on the exogenous existence of a geographical discontinuity (e.g. municipalities above a certain threshold of residents are subject to the policy, and those below the threshold are not). If the discontinuity is exogenous, we can assume that observations are randomly allocated on the right and left sides of the threshold. A McCrary test (McCrary, 2008) can be used to check that there is no manipulation at the cut-off. Thus, comparing the outcomes of these two groups (treatment and control) near the threshold provides a causal analysis of the effect of the policy.

The estimated regression is as follows:

$$y_i = \alpha + \beta_{01}\widetilde{x}_i + \beta_{02}\widetilde{x}_i^{\,2} + \ldots\ldots + \beta_{0P}\widetilde{x}_i^{\,P} + \gamma Treatment_i$$
$$+ \beta_{11}\widetilde{x}_i * Treatment_i + \beta_{12}\widetilde{x}_i^{\,2} * Treatment_i + \ldots\ldots$$
$$+ \beta_{1P}\widetilde{x}_i^{\,P} * Treatment_i + \varepsilon_i$$

where y_i is the outcome variable of interest for observation i; $\widetilde{x}_i$ is the value of variable x for observation i centred at the threshold, where variable x is characterized by a threshold level such that observations with a value larger than the threshold belong to the treatment group and observations with a value below the threshold belong to the control group (or vice versa); p is the order of the control polynomial function $(p=1,2 \dots p)$; and *Treatment$_i$* is an indicator for observations with more than the threshold number of x. The coefficients of the polynomial terms are also indexed by 0 and 1 to allow for different polynomial coefficients on the two sides of the cut-off. The main coefficient of interest is γ, which estimates the local average treatment effect of the policy.

The previous equation is estimated using a polynomial of different orders for the entire sample of observations (parametric approach). Local linear regressions are also estimated by using one of the optimal bandwidth selectors: notably, see Calonico et al. 2014, Imbens and Kalyanaraman (2012) and Ludwig and Miller (2007) (nonparametric approach). Recently, one-common MSE-optimal bandwidth selector has been introduced by Calonico et al. (2017).

A difference-in-discontinuities design (Grembi et al., 2016) is recommended to check the validity of RDD results.

Example: We want to estimate the causal impact of the introduction of gender quotas for municipal electoral lists on the share of women elected (and policies implemented). We exploit the existence of a threshold in the number of residents, that is, quotas apply only to municipalities with more than a threshold number of residents. We estimate a polynomial function (of different orders) of the distribution of the share of women elected in different municipalities with a number of residents near the threshold (just above and just below the threshold, where municipalities are selected by different bandwidth selectors). (See Chapter 4.)

Randomized Control Trials
The experimental approach implies the design of a policy that is randomly attributed to one group of subjects in the sample (treated) and not to the other (control). By comparing the outcomes of the two groups before and after the policy, we estimate the causal impact of the policy.

Example: We want to estimate the causal impact of childcare on female labour force participation. We consider a sample of mothers with small children and divide them randomly into two groups: the first group receives free access to childcare, and the second group does not. We then observe the choices of the two groups in terms of labour supply, wages, career and so on.

Bibliography

Aassve, Arnstein, Giulia Fuochi, Letizia Mencarini, and Daria Mendola. 2015. 'What Is Your Couple Type? Gender Ideology, Housework Sharing, and Babies'. *Demographic Research* 32: 835–58.

Aassve, Arnstein, Maria Pazienza, and Chiara Rapallini. 2007. 'Does Italy Need Family Income Taxation?' *ECINEQ, Society for the Study of Economic Inequality*. Working Papers, January.

Abadie, Alberto. 2005. 'Semiparametric Difference-in-Differences Estimators'. *The Review of Economic Studies* 72 (1): 1–19.

Abrams, Burton, and Russell F. Settle. 1999. 'Women's Suffrage and the Growth of the Welfare State'. *Public Choice* 100 (3–4): 289–300.

Abu-Ghaida, Dina, and Stephan Klasen. 2004. 'The Costs of Missing the Millennium Development Goal on Gender Equity'. *World Development* 32(7): 1075–1107.

Accettura, Carmela, and Paola Profeta. 2019. 'Gender Differences in Political Strategies' Mimeo. Bocconi University.

Adams, Renée B., and Daniel Ferreira. 2009. 'Women in the Boardroom and Their Impact on Governance and Performance'. *Journal of Financial Economics* 94 (2): 291–309.

Adams, Renée B., and Patricia Funk. 2012. 'Beyond the Glass Ceiling: Does Gender Matter?' *Management Science* 58 (2): 219–35.

Adams, Renée B., and Vanitha Ragunathan. 2015. 'Lehman Sisters'. SSRN Scholarly Paper ID 2380036. Rochester, NY: Social Science Research Network.

Adams, Renée B., Stephen Gray, and John Nowland. 2011. 'Does Gender Matter in the Boardroom? Evidence from the Market Reaction to Mandatory New Director Announcements'. SSRN Scholarly Paper ID 1953152. Rochester, NY: Social Science Research Network.

Ahern, Kenneth, and Amy K. Dittmar. 2012. 'The Changing of the Boards: The Impact on Firm Valuation of Mandated Female Board Representation'. *The Quarterly Journal of Economics* 127 (1): 137–97.

Aidt, Toke, and Bianca Dallal. 2008. 'Female Voting Power: The Contribution of Women's Suffrage to the Growth of Social Spending in Western Europe (1869–1960)'. *Public Choice* 134 (3): 391–417.

172

Aidt, Toke, Jayasri Dutta, and Elena Loukoianova. 2006. 'Democracy Comes to Europe: Franchise Extension and Fiscal Outcomes 1830–1938'. *European Economic Review* 50 (2): 249–83.

Aigner, Dennis J., and Glen G. Cain. 1977. 'Statistical Theories of Discrimination in Labor Markets'. *Industrial and Labor Relations Review* 30 (2): 175–87.

Akbulut, Rahşan. 2011. 'Sectoral Changes and the Increase in Women's Labor Force Participation'. *Macroeconomic Dynamics* 15 (2): 240–64.

Akerlof, George, and Rachel E. Kranton. 2000. 'Economics and Identity'. *The Quarterly Journal of Economics* 115 (3): 715–53.

Albanesi, Stefania, and Claudia Olivetti. 2016. 'Gender Roles and Medical Progress'. *Journal of Political Economy* 124 (3): 650–95.

Alesina, Alberto, Paola Giuliano, and Nathan Nunn. 2013. 'On the Origins of Gender Roles: Women and the Plough'. *The Quarterly Journal of Economics* 128 (2): 469–530.

Alesina, Alberto, Andrea Ichino, and Loukas Karabarbounis. 2011. 'Gender-Based Taxation and the Division of Family Chores'. *American Economic Journal: Economic Policy* 3 (2): 1–40.

Almond, Douglas, and Janet Currie. 2011. 'Human Capital Development Before Age Five'. In *Handbook of Labor Economics*, Vol. 4, O. Ashenfelter and D. Card, eds. Amsterdam: Elsevier.

Altonji, Joseph, and Rebecca Blank. 1999. 'Race and Gender in the Labor Market'. In *Handbook of Labor Economics*, Vol. 3, O. Ashenfeher and D. Card, eds. Amsterdam: Elsevier.

Altonji, Joseph, Erica Blom, and Costas Meghir. 2012. 'Heterogeneity in Human Capital Investments: High School Curriculum, College Major, and Careers'. *Annual Review of Economics* 4: 185-223.

Amore, Mario Daniele, Orsola Garofalo, and Alessandro Minichilli. 2014. 'Gender Interactions within the Family Firm'. *Management Science* 60 (5): 1083–97.

Amore, Mario Daniele, Lilach Trabelsi, Maurizio Zollo, and Paola Profeta. 2018. 'Gender and Environmental Performance'. Working Paper. Bocconi University.

Anderson, S., M. Patricia, and Philip B. Levine. 1999. 'Child Care and Mothers' Employment Decisions'. Working Paper 7058. National Bureau of Economic Research.

Anderson, S., and S. Carter. 2001. 'On the Move: Women and Men Business Owners in the UK'. Washington, DC: National Foundation for Women Business Owners.

Andreoni, James, and Lise Vesterlund. 2001. 'Which Is the Fair Sex? Gender Differences in Altruism'. *The Quarterly Journal of Economics* 116 (1): 293–312.

174

Bibliography

Anelli, Massimo, and Giovanni Peri. 2015. 'Gender of Siblings and Choice of College Major'. *CESifo Economic Studies* 61 (1): 53–71.

2019 'The Effects of High School Peers' Gender on College Major, College Performance and Income'. *The Economic Journal* 129 (618): 553–602.

Ansolabehere, Stephen, James M. Snyder, and Charles Stewart. 2001. 'The Effects of Party and Preferences on Congressional Roll-Call Voting'. *Legislative Studies Quarterly* 26 (4): 533–72.

Apps, Patricia F., and Ray Rees. 2007. 'Taxation of Couples'. SSRN Scholarly Paper ID 1000899. Rochester, NY: Social Science Research Network.

Arber, Sara, and Jay Ginn. 1995. *Connecting Gender and Ageing: A Sociological Approach*. Open University Press.

Arpino, Bruno, Chiara Pronzato, and Lara Tavares. 2014. 'The Effect of Grandparental Support on Mothers' Labour Market Participation: An Instrumental Variable Approach'. *European Journal of Population* 30 (4): 369–90.

Arvate, Paulo Roberto, Gisele Walczak Galilea, and Isabela Todescat. 2018. 'The Queen Bee: A Myth? The Effect of Top-Level Female Leadership on Subordinate Females'. *The Leadership Quarterly* 29 (5): 533–48.

Atkeson, Lonna Rae. 2003. 'Not All Cues Are Created Equal: The Conditional Impact of Female Candidates on Political Engagement'. *The Journal of Politics* 65 (4): 1040–61.

Attanasio, Orazio, Hamish Low, and Virginia Sánchez-Marcos. 2008. 'Explaining Changes in Female Labor Supply in a Life-Cycle Model'. *American Economic Review* 98 (4): 1517–52.

Azmat, Ghazala, and Barbara Petrongolo. 2014. 'Gender and the Labor Market: What Have We Learned from Field and Lab Experiments?' *Labour Economics* 30(C): 32-40.

Bagues, Manuel, and Berta Esteve-Volart. 2010. 'Can Gender Parity Break the Glass Ceiling? Evidence from a Repeated Randomized Experiment'. *Review of Economic Studies* 77 (4): 1301–28.

Bagues, Manuel, and Pamela Campa. 2018. 'Can Gender Quotas in Candidate Lists Empower Women? Evidence from a Regression Discontinuity Design'. Discussion Paper No. 12149. CEPR.

Bagues, Manuel, and Maria J. Perez-Villadoniga. 2012. 'Do Recruiters Prefer Applicants with Similar Skills? Evidence from a Randomized Natural Experiment'. *Journal of Economic Behavior & Organization* 82 (1): 12–20.

Bagues, Manuel, Mauro Sylos-Labini, and Natalia Zinovyeva. 2017. 'Does the Gender Composition of Scientific Committees Matter?' *American Economic Review* 107 (4): 1207–38.

Bailey, Adrian J, Megan K. Blake, and Thomas J. Cooke. 2004. 'Migration, Care, and the Linked Lives of Dual-Earner Households'. *Environment and Planning A: Economy and Space* 36 (9): 1617–32.

Bailey, Martha J. 2006. 'More Power to the Pill: The Impact of Contraceptive Freedom on Women's Life Cycle Labor Supply'. *The Quarterly Journal of Economics* 121 (1): 289–320.

Baker, Michael, Jonathan Gruber, and Kevin Milligan. 2008. 'Universal Child Care, Maternal Labor Supply, and Family Well-Being'. *Journal of Political Economy* 116 (4): 709–45.

Baltrunaite, Audinga, Piera Bello, Alessandra Casarico, and Paola Profeta. 2014. 'Gender Quotas and the Quality of Politicians'. *Journal of Public Economics* 118 (C): 62–74.

Baltrunaite, Audinga, Alessandra Casarico, Paola Profeta, and Giulia Savio. 2019. 'Let the Voters Choose Women'. *Journal of Public Economics*. forthcoming.

Bandiera, Oriana, Iwan Barankay and Imran Rasul. 2005. 'Social Preferences and the Response to Incentives: Evidence from Personnel Data'. *The Quarterly Journal of Economics* 120 (3): 917–62.

Barker, D. J. 1990. 'The Fetal and Infant Origins of Adult Disease'. *BMJ (Clinical Research Ed.)* 301 (6761): 1111.

Barnes, Tiffany D. 2012. 'Gender and Legislative Preferences: Evidence from the Argentine Provinces'. *Politics & Gender* 8 (4): 483–507.

Baskaran, Thushyanthan, and Zohal Hessami. 2018. 'Does the Entry of a Woman into Political Office Affect Policy Choices?' mimeo. https://sites.google.com/site/zohalhessami/publications

Beaman, Lori, Esther Duflo, Rohini Pande, and Petia Topalova. 2012. 'Female Leadership Raises Aspirations and Educational Attainment for Girls: A Policy Experiment in India'. *Science* 335 (6068): 582–86.

Beaman, Lori, Niall Keleher, and Jeremy Magruder. 2018. 'Do Job Networks Disadvantage Women? Evidence from a Recruitment Experiment in Malawi'. *Journal of Labor Economics* 36 (1): 121–57.

Becker, Gary, Elisabeth M. Landes, and Robert T. Michael. 1977. 'An Economic Analysis of Marital Instability'. *Journal of Political Economy* 85 (6): 1141–87.

Becker, Gary. 1957. *The Economics of Discrimination*. Chicago : University of Chicago Press.

1973. 'A Theory of Marriage: Part I'. *Journal of Political Economy* 81 (4): 813–46.

1981. *A Treatise on the Family*. Enl. ed. Cambridge, MA: Harvard University Press.

Beckton, Clare. 2008. 'Strong Women, Strong World: By Involving Women in National Economic Policy, Canada Is Forging a Model for Empowering Women and Building the Strength of Domestic and Global Marketplaces'. www.questia.com/magazine/1G1-197801214/strong-women-strong-world-by-involving-women-in...

Bell, Linda A. 2005. 'Women-Led Firms and the Gender Gap in Top Executive Jobs'. SSRN Scholarly Paper ID 773964. Rochester, NY: Social Science Research Network.

Bengtsson, Claes, Mats Persson, and Peter Willenhag. 2005. 'Gender and Overconfidence'. *Economics Letters* 86 (2): 199–203.

Bennani, Hamza, Etienne Farvaque and Piotr Stanek. 2018. 'Influence of Regional Cycles and Personal Background on FOMC Members' Preferences and Disagreement'. *Economic Modelling* 68: 416–24.

Berkman, Michael B., and Robert E. O'Connor. 1993. 'Do Women Legislators Matter?: Female Legislators and State Abortion Policy'. *American Politics Quarterly* 21 (1): 102–24.

Bernal, Raquel, and Michael P. Keane. 2011. 'Child Care Choices and Children's Cognitive Achievement: The Case of Single Mothers'. *Journal of Labor Economics* 29 (3): 459–512.

Bernhardt, Eva, Turid Noack, and Torkild Hovde Lyngstad. 2008. 'Shared Housework in Norway and Sweden: Advancing the Gender Revolution'. *Journal of European Social Policy* 18 (3): 275–88.

Bertocchi, Graziella, and Monica Bozzano. 2015. 'Family Structure and the Education Gender Gap: Evidence from Italian Provinces'. *CESifo Economic Studies* 61(1): 263–300.

———. 2011. 'The Enfranchisement of Women and the Welfare State'. *European Economic Review* 55 (4): 535–53.

Bertrand, Marianne, and Antoinette Schoar. 2003. 'Managing with Style: The Effect of Managers on Firm Policies'. *The Quarterly Journal of Economics* 118 (4): 1169–1208.

Bertrand, Marianne, Esther Duflo, and Sendhil Mullainathan. 2004. 'How Much Should We Trust Differences-in-Differences Estimates?' *The Quarterly Journal of Economics* 119 (1): 249–75.

Bertrand, Marianne, Claudia Goldin, and Lawrence F. Katz. 2010. 'Dynamics of the Gender Gap for Young Professionals in the Financial and Corporate Sectors'. *American Economic Journal: Applied Economics* 2 (3): 228–55.

Bertrand, Marianne, Emir Kamenica, and Jessica Pan. 2015. 'Gender Identity and Relative Income within Households'. *The Quarterly Journal of Economics* 130 (2): 571–614.

Bertrand, Marianne, Sandra E. Black, Sissel Jensen, and Adriana Lleras-Muney. 2018. 'Breaking the Glass Ceiling? The Effect of Board Quotas on Female Labour Market Outcomes in Norway'. *The Review of Economic Studies* 86 (1): 191–239.

Bertrand, Marianne. 2011. 'New Perspectives on Gender'. In *Handbook of Labor Economics*, Vol. 4, 1543–90. O. Ashenfeher and D. Card, eds. Amsterdam: Elsevier.

Besley, Timothy, and Stephen Coate. 1997. 'An Economic Model of Representative Democracy'. *The Quarterly Journal of Economics* 112 (1): 85–114.

Bettendorf, Leon J. H., Egbert L. W. Jongen, and Paul Muller. 2015. 'Childcare Subsidies and Labour Supply – Evidence from a Large Dutch Reform'. *Labour Economics* 36 (C): 112–23.

Bird, Barbara, and Candida Brush. 2002. 'A Gendered Perspective on Organizational Creation'. *Entrepreneurship Theory and Practice* 26 (3): 41–65.

Bjorklund, David F., and Katherine Kipp. 1996. 'Parental Investment Theory and Gender Differences in the Evolution of Inhibition Mechanisms'. *Psychological Bulletin* 120 (2): 163–88.

Black, J. H., and L. Erickson. 2003. 'Women Candidates and Voter Bias: Do Women Politicians Need to Be Better?' *Electoral Studies* 22 (1): 81–100.

Blau, Francine, and Lawrence Kahn. 2007. 'Changes in the Labor Supply Behavior of Married Women: 1980-2000'. *Journal of Labor Economics* 25: 393–438.

2013. 'Female Labor Supply: Why Is the US Falling Behind?' *American Economic Review, Papers and Proceedings* 103(3): 251-256.

2017. 'The Gender Wage Gap: Extent, Trends, and Explanations'. *Journal of Economic Literature* 55 (3): 789–865.

Blinder, Alan S. 2007. 'Monetary Policy by Committee: Why and How?' *European Journal of Political Economy* 23: 106–23.

Blinder, Alan S., and John Morgan. 2005. 'Are Two Heads Better Than One? Monetary Policy by Committee'. *Journal of Money, Credit and Banking* 37 (5): 789–811.

2008. 'Do Monetary Policy Committees Need Leaders? A Report on an Experiment'. *American Economic Review* 98 (2): 224–29.

Bloom, Nicholas, and John Van Reenen. 2010. 'Why Do Management Practices Differ across Firms and Countries?' *Journal of Economic Perspectives* 24 (1): 203–24.

Bloom, Nicholas, Benn Eifert, Aprajit Mahajan, David McKenzie, and John Roberts. 2013. 'Does Management Matter? Evidence from India'. *The Quarterly Journal of Economics* 128(1): 1-51.

Bloom, Nicholas, James Liang, John Roberts, and Zhichun Jenny Ying. 2015. 'Does Working from Home Work? Evidence from a Chinese Experiment'. *The Quarterly Journal of Economics* 130(1): 165–218.

Boca, Daniela Del, and Cécile Wetzels. 2008. *Social Policies, Labour Markets and Motherhood: A Comparative Analysis of European Countries*. Cambridge University Press.

Boca, Daniela Del, Silvia Pasqua, and Chiara Pronzato. 2009. 'Motherhood and Market Work Decisions in Institutional Context: A European Perspective'. *Oxford Economic Papers* 61 (suppl_1): 147–71.

Booth, Alison L., and Jan C. Van Ours. 2008. 'Job Satisfaction and Family Happiness: The Part-Time Work Puzzle'. *The Economic Journal* 118 (526): F77–99.

Booth, Alison L., Lina Cardona, and Patrick J. Nolen. 2018. 'Do Single-Sex Classes Affect Achievement? An Experiment in a Coeducational University'. *Journal of Public Economics* 168: 109-126.

Booth, Alison, and Patrick Nolen. 2012. 'Choosing to Compete: How Different Are Girls and Boys?' *Journal of Economic Behavior & Organization* 81 (2): 542–55.

Boserup, Ester. 1970. *Woman's Role in Economic Development*. Allen & Unwin.

Boskin, Michael J., and Eytan Sheshinski. 1983. 'Optimal Tax Treatment of the Family: Married Couples'. *Journal of Public Economics* 20 (3): 281–97.

Bowles, Hannah Riley, Linda Babcock, and Lei Lai. 2007. 'Social Incentives for Gender Differences in the Propensity to Initiate Negotiations: Sometimes It Does Hurt to Ask'. *Organizational Behavior and Human Decision Processes* 103 (1): 84–103.

Boyd, Monica. 1989. 'Family and Personal Networks in International Migration: Recent Developments and New Agendas'. *The International Migration Review* 23 (3): 638–70.

Brilli, Ylenia, Daniela Del Boca, and Chiara D. Pronzato. 2016. 'Does Child Care Availability Play a Role in Maternal Employment and Children's Development? Evidence from Italy'. *Review of Economics of the Household* 14 (1): 27–51.

Brollo, Fernanda, and Ugo Troiano. 2016. 'What Happens When a Woman Wins an Election? Evidence from Close Races in Brazil'. *Journal of Development Economics* 122 (C): 28–45.

Brooks, Deborah Jordan. 2010. 'A Negativity Gap? Voter Gender, Attack Politics, and Participation in American Elections'. *Politics & Gender* 6 (3): 319–41.

Buera, Francisco J, Joseph P. Kaboski, and Min Qiang Zhao. 2019. 'The Rise of Services: The Role of Skills, Scale, and Female Labor Supply'. *Journal of Human Capital* 13(2): 157-187.

Buffeteau, Sophie, and Damien Échevin. 2003. 'Taxation, Marriage and Labor Supply: Evidence from a Natural Experiment in France'. Cahiers de recherche. CIRPEE.

Burda, Michael, Daniel Hamermesh, and Philippe Weil. 2013. 'Total Work and Gender: Facts and Possible Explanations'. *Journal of Population Economics* 26 (1): 239–61.

Burgess, Robin, and Nicholas Stern. 1993. 'Taxation and Development'. *Journal of Economic Literature* 31 (2): 762–830.

Buser, Thomas, Muriel Niederle, and Hessel Oosterbeek. 2014. 'Gender, Competitiveness, and Career Choices'. *The Quarterly Journal of Economics* 129 (3): 1409–47.

Calonico, Sebastian, Matias Cattaneo, and Rocio Titiunik. 2014. 'Robust Data-Driven Inference in the Regression-Discontinuity Design'. *Stata Journal* 14 (4): 909–46.

Calonico, Sebastian, Matias Cattaneo, Max Farrell, and Rocio Titiunik. 2017. 'rdrobust: Software for Regression-Discontinuity Designs'. *Stata Journal* 17 (2): 372–404.

Campbell, Kevin, and Antonio Mínguez-Vera. 2008. 'Gender Diversity in the Boardroom and Firm Financial Performance'. *Journal of Business Ethics* 83 (3): 435–51.

Carling, Jørgen. 2001. 'Aspiration and Ability in International Migration: Cape Verdean Experiences of Mobility and Immobility'. PhD thesis, Oslo: University of Oslo.

Carrell, Scott E., and Mark L. Hoekstra. 2010. 'Externalities in the Classroom: How Children Exposed to Domestic Violence Affect Everyone's Kids'. *American Economic Journal: Applied Economics* 2 (1): 211–28.

Carrell, Scott E., Richard L. Fullerton, and James E. West. 2009. 'Does Your Cohort Matter? Measuring Peer Effects in College Achievement'. *Journal of Labor Economics* 27 (3): 439–64.

Carter, Nancy M., Lois Joy, Henry M. Wagner, and Sriram Narayanan. 2007. 'The Bottom Line: Corporate Performance and Women's Representation on Boards'. Bottom Line. New York: Catalyst.

Casarico, Alessandra, Salvatore Lattanzio and Paola Profeta. 2019. 'Women, Local Public Finance and Fiscal Adjustments'. Working Paper 133 Dondena, Bocconi University.

Casarico, Alessandra, Paola Profeta, and Chiara Daniela Pronzato. 2016. 'On the Regional Labour Market Determinants of Female University Enrolment in Europe'. *Regional Studies* 50 (6): 1036–53.

Casas-Arce, Pablo, and Albert Saiz. 2015. 'Women and Power: Unpopular, Unwilling, or Held Back?' *Journal of Political Economy* 123 (3): 641–69.

Cascio, Elizabeth. 2009. 'Maternal Labor Supply and the Introduction of Kindergartens into American Public Schools'. *Journal of Human Resources* 44 (1).

Cascio, Elizabeth, and Diane Whitmore Schanzenbach. 2013. 'The Impacts of Expanding Access to High-Quality Preschool Education'. Working Paper 19735. National Bureau of Economic Research.

Caul, Miki. 1999. 'Women's Representation in Parliament: The Role of Political Parties'. *Party Politics* 5 (1): 79–98.

Cavalcanti, Tiago, and José Tavares. 2011. 'Women Prefer Larger Governments: Growth, Structural Transformation and Government Size'. *Economic Inquiry* 49(1): 155-171.

———. 2016. 'The Output Cost of Gender Discrimination: A Model-Based Macroeconomics Estimate'. *The Economic Journal* 126 (590): 109–34.

Cawley, John, and Feng Liu. 2007. 'Mechanisms for the Association between Maternal Employment and Child Cognitive Development'. SSRN Scholarly Paper ID 1032864. Rochester, NY: Social Science Research Network.

Chamberlain, Mary. 1997. 'Gender and the Narratives of Migration'. *History Workshop Journal* 1997 (43): 87–110.

Chant, Sylvia H. 1992. *Gender and Migration in Developing Countries.* Belhaven Press.

Chappell, Henry, and Rob Roy McGregor. 2000. 'A Long History of FOMC Voting Behavior'. *Southern Economic Journal* 66 (4): 906–22.

Chappell, Neena L., and Betty Havens. 1980. 'Old and Female: Testing the Double Jeopardy Hypothesis'. *The Sociological Quarterly* 21 (2): 157–71.

Chapple, Larelle, and Jacquelyn Humphrey. 2014. 'Does Board Gender Diversity Have a Financial Impact? Evidence Using Stock Portfolio Performance'. *Journal of Business Ethics* 122 (4): 709–23.

Chattopadhyay, Raghabendra, and Esther Duflo. 2004. 'Women as Policy Makers: Evidence from a Randomized Policy Experiment in India'. *Econometrica* 72 (5): 1409–43.

Cherlin, Andrew J. 1981. *Marriage, Divorce, Remarriage.* Harvard University Press.

Chiappori, Pierré-Andre, Monica Costa Dias, and Costas Meghir. 2018. 'The Marriage Market, Labor Supply and Education Choice'. *Journal of Political Economy* 126 (S1): S26-S72.

Childs, Sarah. 2004. *New Labour's Women MPs: Women Representing Women.* London: Routledge.

Chote, Robert, Carl Emmerson, Andrew Leicester, and David Miles. 2007. 'The IFS Green Budget: January 2007'. 31 January 2007. www.ifs.org.uk/green-budget/2007

Christensen, Kaare, Gabriele Doblhammer, Roland Rau, and James W. Vaupel. 2009. 'Ageing Populations: The Challenges Ahead'. *Lancet* 374 (9696): 1196–1208.

Chung, Heejung. 2011. 'Flexibility for Employers or for Employees? A New Approach to Examining Labour Market Flexibility across Europe Using Company Level Data'. In *Flexicurity and Beyond: Finding a New Agenda for the European Social Model*, 243–77. Copenhagen: DJØF Publishing.

2019. 'National-Level Family Policies and Workers' Access to Schedule Control in a European Comparative Perspective: Crowding Out or In, and for Whom?' *Journal of Comparative Policy Analysis: Research and Practice* 21 (1): 25–46.

Ciavarella, Angela. 2017. 'Board Diversity and Firm Performance Across Europe'. Quaderni di Finanza. CONSOB.

Clarida, Richard, Jordi Galì, and Mark Gertler. 1998. 'Monetary Policy Rules in Practice: Some International Evidence'. *European Economic Review* 42: 1033–67.

Clark, Sue Campbell. 2000. 'Work/Family Border Theory: A New Theory of Work/Family Balance'. *Human Relations* 53 (6): 747–70.

Clayton, Amanda, and Pär Zetterberg. 2018. 'Quota Shocks: Electoral Gender Quotas and Government Spending Priorities Worldwide'. *The Journal of Politics* 80 (3): 916–32.

Clots-Figueras, Irma. 2011. 'Women in Politics: Evidence from the Indian States'. *Journal of Public Economics* 95 (7–8): 664–90.

2012. 'Are Female Leaders Good for Education? Evidence from India'. *American Economic Journal: Applied Economics* 4 (1): 212–44.

Coda Moscarola Flavia, Elsa Fornero, and Steinar Strøm. 2016. 'Absenteeism, Childcare and the Effectiveness of Pension Reforms'. *IZA Journal of European Labor Studies* 5 (1): 1–18.

Coffman, Katherine Baldiga. 2014. 'Evidence on Self-Stereotyping and the Contribution of Ideas'. *The Quarterly Journal of Economics* 129 (4): 1625–60.

Colonna, Fabrizio, and Stefania Marcassa. 2015. 'Taxation and Female Labor Supply in Italy'. *IZA Journal of Labor Policy* 4 (1): 5.

Conde-Ruiz, J. Ignacio, and Carmen Hoya. 2015. '"Gender (in)Equality Act" and Large Spanish Corporations'. Policy Paper 2015–03. FEDEA.

Conde-Ruiz, J. Ignacio, Juan-José Ganuza, and Paola Profeta. 2017. 'Statistical Discrimination and the Efficiency of Quotas'. 2017–04. Working Papers. FEDEA.

Connolly, Sara, and Mary Gregory. 2008. 'Moving Down: Women's Part-Time Work and Occupational Change in Britain 1991–2001'. *The Economic Journal* 118 (526): F52–76.

Cooke, Thomas J. 2008. 'Gender Role Beliefs and Family Migration'. *Population, Space and Place* 14 (3): 163–75.

Cornell, Bradford, and Ivo Welch. 1996. 'Culture, Information, and Screening Discrimination'. *Journal of Political Economy* 104 (3): 542–71.

Croson, Rachel, and Nancy Buchan. 1999. 'Gender and Culture: International Experimental Evidence from Trust Games'. *American Economic Review* 89 (2): 386–91.

Croson, Rachel, and Uri Gneezy. 2009. 'Gender Differences in Preferences'. *Journal of Economic Literature* 47 (2): 448–74.

Cuberes, David, and Marc Teignier. 2016. 'Aggregate effects of gender gaps in the Labor Market: A Quantitative Estimate'. *Journal of Human Capital* 10 (1): 1–32.

Cunha, Flavio, and James Heckman. 2007. 'The Technology of Skill Formation'. *American Economic Review* 97 (2): 31-47.

Dahl, Gordon, Katrine Løken, Magne Mogstad, and Kari Vea Salvanes. 2016. 'What Is the Case for Paid Maternity Leave?' *The Review of Economics and Statistics* 98 (4): 655–70.

Darcy, R., Janet Clark, and Susan Welch. 1994. *Women, Elections, and Representation*. Rev, edn. University of Nebraska Press.

Davies, Evan Mervyn. 2011. 'Women on Boards'. *Women on Boards*. GOV. UK. https://assets.publishing.service.gov.uk/government/uploads/system/uploads/attachment_data/file/31480/11-745-women-on-boards.pdf

Davies, Rhys, and Gaëlle Pierre. 2005. 'The Family Gap in Pay in Europe: A Cross-Country Study'. *Labour Economics* 12 (4): 469–86.

De Cabo, Ruth, Siri Terjesen Mateos, Ricardo Gimeno, and Lorenzo Escot. 2019. 'Do "Soft Law" Board Gender Quotas Work? Evidence from a Natural Experiment'. *European Management Journal* 37 (5): 611-624.

De Paola, Maria, and Vincenzo Scoppa. 2015. 'Gender Discrimination and Evaluators' Gender: Evidence from Italian Academia'. *Economica* 82 (325): 162-188.

De Paola, Maria, Vincenzo Scoppa, and Rosetta Lombardo. 2010. 'Can Gender Quotas Break Down Negative Stereotypes? Evidence from Changes in Electoral Rules'. *Journal of Public Economics* 94 (5–6): 344–53.

Del Boca, Daniela. 2002. 'The Effect of Child Care and Part Time Opportunities on Participation and Fertility Decisions in Italy'. *Journal of Population Economics* 15 (3): 549–73.

Del Boca, Daniela, and Marilena Locatelli. 2006. 'The Determinants of Motherhood and Work Status: A Survey'. 2414. IZA Discussion Papers. Institute for the Study of Labor (IZA).

Del Boca, Daniela, Marilena Locatelli, and Daniela Vuri. 2005. 'Child-Care Choices by Working Mothers: The Case of Italy'. *Review of Economics of the Household* 3 (4): 453–77.

Demb, Ada, and Friedrich Neubauer. 1992. *The Corporate Board: Confronting the Paradoxes*. Vol. 26. New York: Oxford University Press.

Devillard, Sandrine, Wieteke Graven, Emily Lawson, Renée Paradise, and Sandra Sancier-Sultan. 2012. 'Women Matter: Making the

Breakthrough'. Women Matter. www.calstrs.com/sites/main/files/file-attachments/women_matter_2012_making_the_breakthrough.pdf

Diamantopoulos, Adamantios, Bodo B. Schlegelmilch, Rudolf R. Sinkovics, and Greg M. Bohlen. 2003. 'Can Socio-Demographics Still Play a Role in Profiling Green Consumers? A Review of the Evidence and an Empirical Investigation'. *Journal of Business Research* 56 (6): 465–80.

Dindia, Kathryn, and Daniel J. Canary. 2006. *Sex Differences and Similarities in Communication.* Taylor & Francis.

Dobbin, F., and J. Jung. 2011. 'Corporate Board Gender Diversity and Stock Performance: The Competence Gap or Institutional Investor Bias?' *North Carolina Law Review* 89 (3): 809–38.

Doepke, Matthias, and Michèle Tertilt. 2009. 'Women's Liberation: What's in It for Men?' *The Quarterly Journal of Economics* 124 (4): 1541–91.

2016. 'Families in Macroeconomics', in *Handbook of Macroeconomics*, chap. 23, John B. Taylor and Harald Uhlig, eds. Amsterdam: Elsevier.

Dollar, David, and Roberta Gatti. 1999. 'Gender Inequality, Income, and Growth: Are Good Times Good for Women?', Policy Research Report on Gender and Development Working Paper 1, World Bank Washington, DC.

Dollar, David, Raymond Fisman, and Roberta Gatti. 2001. 'Are Women Really the "Fairer" Sex? Corruption and Women in Government'. *Journal of Economic Behavior & Organization* 46 (4): 423–29.

Doss, Cheryl R. 1996. 'Testing among Models of Intrahousehold Resource Allocation'. *World Development* 24 (10): 1597–609.

Duflo, Esther. 2003. 'Grandmothers and Granddaughters: Old-Age Pensions and Intrahousehold Allocation in South Africa'. *World Bank Economic Review* 17 (1): 1–25.

2012. 'Women Empowerment and Economic Development'. *Journal of Economic Literature* 50 (4): 1051–79.

Dutcher, E. 2012. 'The Effects of Telecommuting on Productivity: An Experimental Examination. The Role of Dull and Creative Tasks'. *Journal of Economic Behavior & Organization* 84 (1): 355–63.

Eagly, Alice H., and Linda L. Carli. 2003. 'The Female Leadership Advantage: An Evaluation of the Evidence'. *Leadership Quarterly* 14 (6): 807–34.

Eagly, Alice H., Mary C. Johannesen-Schmidt, and Marloes L. Van Engen. 2003. 'Transformational, Transactional, and Laissez-Faire Leadership Styles: A Meta-Analysis Comparing Women and Men'. *Psychological Bulletin* 129 (4): 569–91.

Eagly, Alice H., S. J. Karau, and M. G. Makhijani. 1995. 'Gender and the Effectiveness of Leaders: A Meta-Analysis'. *Psychological Bulletin* 117 (1): 125–45.

Eckbo, Espen, Knut Nygaard, and Karin S. Thorburn. 2018. 'Board Gender-Balancing and Firm Value'. SSRN Scholarly Paper ID 2746786. Rochester, NY: Social Science Research Network.

Eckbo, Espen, and Karin Thorburn. 2016. 'Does Gender-Balancing the Board Reduce Firm Value?' ECGI Finance Working Paper No. 463/ 2016.

Eckel, Catherine, and Philip Grossman. 2001. 'Chivalry and Solidarity in Ultimatum Games'. *Economic Inquiry* 39 (2): 171–88.

Eckel, Catherine, and Philip Grossman. 2008. 'Men, Women and Risk Aversion: Experimental Evidence'. *Handbook of Experimental Economics Results*, C. Plott and V. Smith, eds. New York: Elsevier.

Edlund, Lena, and Rohini Pande. 2002. 'Why Have Women Become Left-Wing? The Political Gender Gap and the Decline in Marriage'. *The Quarterly Journal of Economics* 117 (3): 917–61.

Eissa, Nada, and Jeffrey B. Liebman. 1996. 'Labor Supply Response to the Earned Income Tax Credit'. *The Quarterly Journal of Economics* 111 (2): 605–37.

Elder, Glen H. 1975. 'Age Differentiation and the Life Course'. *Annual Review of Sociology* 1 (1): 165–90.

Ellison, Glenn, and Ashley Swanson. 2009. 'The Gender Gap in Secondary School Mathematics at High Achievement Levels: Evidence from the American Mathematics Competitions'. Working Paper 15238. National Bureau of Economic Research.

Ellwood, David T. 2000. 'The Impact of the Earned Income Tax Credit and Social Policy Reforms on Work, Marriage, and Living Arrangements'. *National Tax Journal* 53 (4): 1063–105.

Engelhardt, Henriette, and Alexia Prskawetz. 2004. 'On the Changing Correlation between Fertility and Female Employment over Space and Time'. *European Journal of Population/Revue Européenne de Démographie* 20 (1): 35–62.

Epstein, Michael, Richard G. Niemi, and Lynda W. Powell. 2005. 'Do Women and Men State Legislators Differ?' In *Women and Elected Office: Past, Present and Future*, 2nd ed., 94–109, Sue Thomas and Clyde Wilcox, eds. Oxford University Press.

Erhardt, Niclas L., James D. Werbel, and Charles B. Shrader. 2003. 'Board of Director Diversity and Firm Financial Performance'. *Corporate Governance: An international review* 11(2):102-111.

Ernst, Christoph, and Janine Berg. 2009. 'The Role of Employment and Labour Markets in the Fight against Poverty'. Geneva: International Labour Organization.

Esping-Andersen, Gøsta. 2009. *Incomplete Revolution: Adapting Welfare States to Women's New Roles*. Polity.

Esping-Andersen, Gøsta, and Francesco C. Billari. 2015. 'Re-Theorizing Family Demographics'. *Population and Development Review* 41 (1): 1–31. Espírito-Santo, Ana. 2011. 'The Symbolic Value of Descriptive Representation : The Case of Female Representation'. Thesis.

Eswaran, Mukesh. 2014. *Why Gender Matters in Economics*. Princeton University Press.

European Commission. 2007. *Manual for Gender Mainstreaming of Employment Policies* .

European Commission. 2015. *She Figures*. https://ec.europa.eu/research/sw afs/pdf/pub_gender_equality/she_figures_2015-final.pdf

Eurofound-ILO. 2017. 'Working Anytime, Anywhere: The Effects on the World of Work', Publications Office of the European Union, Luxembourg, and the International Labour Office, Geneva. http://eurofound.link/ef1658

Falk, Armin, and Andrea Ichino. 2006. 'Clean Evidence on Peer Effects'. *Journal of Labor Economics* 24 (1): 39–58.

Fanelli, Ester, and Paola Profeta. 2019. 'Fathers' Involvement in the Family, Fertility and Maternal Employment'. Working Paper 131. Dondena. Bocconi University.

Feld, Jan, Nicolás Salamanca, and Daniel S. Hamermesh. 2016. 'Endophilia or Exophobia: Beyond Discrimination'. *The Economic Journal* 126 (594): 1503-1527.

Feldstein, Martin, and Jeffrey Liebman. 2002. 'The Distributional Aspects of Social Security and Social Security Reform'. *International Journal of Social Economics* 30 (12).

Fernández, Raquel. 2007. 'Women, Work, and Culture'. *Journal of the European Economic Association* 5 (2–3): 305–32.

Fernández, Raquel, and Alessandra Fogli. 2009. 'Culture: An Empirical Investigation of Beliefs, Work, and Fertility'. *American Economic Journal: Macroeconomics* 1 (1): 146–77.

Ferrant, Gaëlle, and Michele Tuccio. 2015. 'South–South Migration and Discrimination against Women in Social Institutions: A Two-Way Relationship'. *World Development* 72 (C): 240–54.

Ferrari, Giulia, Valeria Ferraro, Paola Profeta, and Chiara Pronzato. 2018. 'Do Board Gender Quotas Matter? Selection, Performance and Stock Market Effects'. SSRN Scholarly Paper ID 3170251. Rochester, NY: Social Science Research Network.

Ferreira, Daniel, Emanuel Ornelas, and John L. Turner. 2015. 'Unbundling Ownership and Control'. *Journal of Economics & Management Strategy* 24 (1): 1–21.

Ferreira, Fernando, and Joseph Gyourko. 2014. 'Does Gender Matter for Political Leadership? The Case of US Mayors'. *Journal of Public Economics* 112: 24–39.

Filer, Randall K. 1985. 'Male-Female Wage Differences: The Importance of Compensating Differentials'. *Industrial and Labor Relations Review* 38 (3): 426–37.

Flabbi, Luca. 2012. 'Gender Differences in Education, Career Choices and Labor Market Outcomes on A Sample of OECD Countries'. World Development Report. World Bank.

Flabbi, Luca, Mario Macis, Andrea Moro, and Fabiano Schivardi. 2019. 'Do Female Executives Make a Difference? The Impact of Female Leadership on Gender Gaps and Firm Performance'. *The Economic Journal* 129 (622): 2390–423.

Fogli, Alessandra, and Laura Veldkamp. 2011. 'Nature or Nurture? Learning and the Geography of Female Labor Force Participation'. *Econometrica* 79 (4): 1103–38.

Footitt, Hilary. 2002. *Women, Europe and the New Languages of Politics.* Bloomsbury Academic.

Fox, Richard L., and Jennifer L. Lawless. 2004. 'Entering the Arena? Gender and the Decision to Run for Office'. *American Journal of Political Science* 48 (2): 264–80.

Franceschet, Susan, Mona Lena Krook, and Jennifer M. Piscopo. 2012. *The Impact of Gender Quotas.* Oxford University Press.

Franceschet, Susan, and Jennifer M. Piscopo. 2008. 'Gender Quotas and Women's Substantive Representation: Lessons from Argentina'. *Politics & Gender* 4 (3): 393–425.

Fréchette, Guillaume R., Francois Maniquet, and Massimo Morelli. 2008. 'Incumbents' Interests and Gender Quotas'. *American Journal of Political Science* 52 (4): 891–909.

Freidenvall, Lenita, and Drude Dahlerup. 2013. *Electoral Gender Quota Systems and Their Implementation in Europe.* European Union.

Fridkin, Kim L., and Patrick Kenney. 2011. 'Variability in Citizens' Reactions to Different Types of Negative Campaigns'. *American Journal of Political Science* 55 (2): 307–25.

Funk, Patricia. 2016 'How Accurate Are Surveyed Preferences for Public Policies? Evidence from a Unique Institutional Setup' *Review of Economic and Statistics* 98(3): 442–454.

Funk, Patricia, and Christina Gathmann.
2015. 'Gender Gaps in Policy Making: Evidence from Direct Democracy in Switzerland'. *Economic Policy* 30 (81): 141–81.

Fuwa, Makiko. 2004. 'Macro-Level Gender Inequality and the Division of Household Labor in 22 Countries'. *American Sociological Review* 69 (6): 751–67.

Gagliarducci, Stefano, and M. Daniele Passerman. 2012. 'Gender Interactions within Hierarchies: Evidence from the Political Arena'. *Review of Economic Studies* 79(3): 1021- 1052.

Gago, Andres, and Felipe Carozzi. 2018. 'Female Mayors and Gender Policies in a Developed Country'. Mimeo.

Galasso, Vincenzo. 2008. 'Postponing Retirement: The Political Effect of Aging'. *Journal of Public Economics* 92 (10): 2157–69.

Galasso, Vincenzo, and Tommaso Nannicini. 2018. 'Persuasion and Gender: Experimental Evidence from Two Political Campaigns'. Working Paper. IGIER.

Galasso, Vincenzo, and Paola Profeta. 2004. 'Lessons for an Ageing Society: The Political Sustainability of Social Security Systems'. *Economic Policy* 19 (38): 63–115.

Galasso, Vincenzo, Paola Profeta, Chiara Pronzato, and Francesco Billari. 2017. 'Information and Women's Intentions: Experimental Evidence About Child Care'. *European Journal of Population* 33 (1): 109–28.

Galligan, Yvonne, Renate Haupfleisch, Lisa Irvine, Katja Korolkova, Monika Natter, Ulrike Schultz, and Sally Wheeler. 2017. 'Mapping the Representation of Women and Men in Legal Professions Across the EU', www.europarl.europa.eu/RegData/etudes/STUD/2017/59680 4/IPOL_STU(2017)596804_EN.pdf

Galor, Oded, and David N. Weil. 1996. 'The Gender Gap, Fertility, and Growth'. *American Economic Review* 86 (3): 374–87.

Gardner, Howard. 1983. *Frames of Mind: The Theory of Multiple Intelligences*. Basic Books.

Gelbach, Jonah. 2002. 'Public Schooling for Young Children and Maternal Labor Supply'. *American Economic Review* 92 (1): 307–22.

Gelber, Alexander. 2014. 'Taxation and the Earnings of Husband and Wifes: Evidence from Sweden'. *Review of Economics and Statistics* 96(2): 287–305.

Ghura, Dhaneshwar. 1998. 'Tax Revenue in Sub-Saharan Africa: Effects of Economic Policies and Corruption'. SSRN Scholarly Paper ID 882694. Rochester, NY: Social Science Research Network.

Gibbons, Robert, and Rebecca Henderson. 2013. 'What Do Managers Do? Exploring Persistent Performance Differences among Seemingly Similar Enterprises'. In *The Handbook of Organizational Economics*, 680–731, Robert Gibbons and John Roberts, eds. Princeton: Princeton University Press.

Gibson, Diane. 1996. 'Broken down by Age and Gender: "The Problem of Old Women" Redefined'. *Gender and Society* 10 (4): 433–48.

188   *Bibliography*

Gilardi, Fabrizio. 2015. 'The Temporary Importance of Role Models for Women's Political Representation'. *American Journal of Political Science* 59 (4): 957–70.

Ginn, Jay. 2004. 'European Pension Privatisation: Taking Account of Gender'. *Social Policy and Society* 3 (2): 123–34.

Ginther, Donna K., and Shulamit Kahn. 2009. 'Does Science Promote Women? Evidence from Academia 1973–2001'. *Science and Engineering Careers in the United States: An Analysis of Markets and Employment*, June, 163–94. www.nber.org/papers/w12691

Giuliano, Paola. 2015. 'The Role of Women in Society: From Preindustrial to Modern Times'. *CESifo Economic Studies* 61 (1): 33–52.

Givord, Pauline, and Claire Marbot. 2015. 'Does the Cost of Child Care Affect Female Labor Market Participation? An Evaluation of a French Reform of Childcare Subsidies'. *Labour Economics* 36 (C): 99–111.

Glass, Christy, Alison Cook, and Alicia R. Ingersoll. 2016. 'Do Women Leaders Promote Sustainability? Analyzing the Effect of Corporate Governance Composition on Environmental Performance'. *Business Strategy and the Environment* 25 (7): 495–511.

Gneezy, Uri, Muriel Niederle, and Aldo Rustichini. 2003. 'Performance in Competitive Environments: Gender Differences'. *The Quarterly Journal of Economics* 118 (3): 1049–74.

Gneezy, Uri, and Aldo Rustichini. 2004. 'Gender and Competition at a Young Age'. *American Economic Review* 94 (2): 377–81.

Golden, Annis G., Erika L. Kirby, and Jane Jorgenson. 2006. 'Work-Life Research from Both Sides Now: An Integrative Perspective for Organizational and Family Communication'. *Annals of the International Communication Association* 30 (1): 143–95.

Golden, Lonnie. 2012. 'The Effects of Working Time on Productivity and Firm Performance, Research Synthesis Paper'. SSRN Scholarly Paper ID 2149325. Rochester, NY: Social Science Research Network.

Goldin, Claudia. 2006. 'The Quiet Revolution That Transformed Women's Employment, Education, and Family'. *American Economic Review* 96 (2): 1–21.

——— 2014. 'A Grand Gender Convergence: Its Last Chapter'. *American Economic Review* 104 (4): 1091–1119.

Goldin, Claudia, and Cecilia Rouse. 2000. 'Orchestrating Impartiality: The Impact of "Blind" Auditions on Female Musicians'. *American Economic Review* 90 (4): 715–41.

Goldin, Claudia, and Lawrence Katz. 2002. 'The Power of the Pill: Oral Contraceptives and Women's Career and Marriage Decisions'. *Journal of Political Economy* 110 (4): 730–70.

Goldscheider, Frances, Eva Bernhardt, and Maria Brandén. 2013. 'Domestic Gender Equality and Childbearing in Sweden'. *Demographic Research* 29 (December): 1097–126.

Gorman, Elizabeth H. 2005. 'Gender Stereotypes, Same-Gender Preferences, and Organizational Variation in the Hiring of Women: Evidence from Law Firms'. *American Sociological Review* 70 (4): 702–28.

Graham, John R., and Krishnamoorthy Narasimhan. 2004. 'Corporate Survival and Managerial Experiences during the Great Depression'. SSRN Scholarly Paper ID 489694. Rochester, NY: Social Science Research Network.

Greenwood, Jeremy, Ananth Seshadri, and Mehmet Yorukoglu. 2005. 'Engines of Liberation'. *Review of Economic Studies* 72 (1): 109–33.

Grembi, Veronica, Tommaso Nannicini and Ugo Troiano. 2016. 'Do Fiscal Rules Matter?' *American Economic Journal: Applied Economics* 8 (3): 1–30.

Grimshaw, D. and J. Rubery. 2015.'The Motherhood Pay Gap: A Review of the Issues, Theory and International Evidence', ILO Working Paper.

Guiso, Luigi, Ferdinando Monte, Paola Sapienza, and Luigi Zingales. 2008. 'Diversity. Culture, Gender, and Math'. *Science* 320 (June): 1164–65.

Gul, Ferdinand A., Bin Srinidhi and Anthony C. Ng. 2011. 'Does Board Gender Diversity Improve the Informativeness of Stock Prices?' *Journal of Accounting and Economics* 51 (3): 314–38.

Gupta, Indrani, and Arup Mitra. 2004. 'Economic Growth, Health and Poverty: An Exploratory Study for India'. SSRN Scholarly Paper ID 513451. Rochester, NY: Social Science Research Network.

Haslam, S. Alexander, and Michelle K. Ryan. 2008. 'The Road to the Glass Cliff: Differences in the Perceived Suitability of Men and Women for Leadership Positions in Succeeding and Failing Organizations', *The Leadership Quarterly* 19 (5): 530–46.

Hatch, Laurie Russell. 2000. *Beyond Gender Differences: Adaptation to Aging in Life Course Perspective*. Baywood Pub.

Haavio-Mannila, Elina, Drude Dahlerup, Maud Eduards, Esther Gudmundsdóttir, Beatrice Halsaa, Helga Maria Hernes et al. (eds). 1985. *Unfinished Democracy. Women in Nordic Politics*. Oxford: Pergamon Press.

Havnes, Tarjei, and Magne Mogstad. 2011a. 'Money for Nothing? Universal Child Care and Maternal Employment'. *Journal of Public Economics* 95 (11): 1455–65.

2011b. 'No Child Left Behind: Subsidized Child Care and Children's Long-Run Outcomes'. *American Economic Journal: Economic Policy* 3 (2): 97–129.

Heckman, James, Rodrigo Pinto, and Peter Savelyev. 2013. 'Understanding the Mechanisms through Which an Influential Early Childhood Program Boosted Adult Outcomes'. *American Economic Review* 103 (6): 2052–86.

Hedges, L. V., and A. Nowell. 1995. 'Sex Differences in Mental Test Scores, Variability, and Numbers of High-Scoring Individuals'. *Science* 269 (5220): 41–45.

Helland, Eric, and Michael E. Sykuta. 2004. 'Regulation and the Evolution of Corporate Boards: Monitoring, Advising or Window Dressing?' *The Journal of Law & Economics* 47(1): 167- 193.

Hibbing, John R., and David Marsh. 1987. 'Accounting for the Voting Patterns of British MPs on Free Votes'. *Legislative Studies Quarterly* 12 (2): 275–97.

Hinrichs, H. H. 1966. *A General Theory of Tax Structure Change during Economic Development*. Cambridge, MA: Law School of Harvard University.

Hobson, Barbara. 1990. 'No Exit, No Voice: Women's Economic Dependency and the Welfare State'. *Acta Sociologica* 33 (3): 235–50.

Hofferth, Sandra L., and Frances Goldscheider. 2010. 'Family Structure and the Transition to Early Parenthood'. *Demography* 47 (2): 415–37.

Holzer, Harry, and David Neumark. 2000. 'Assessing Affirmative Action'. *Journal of Economic Literature* 38 (3): 483–568.

Hoogendoorn, Sander, Hessel Oosterbeek, and Mirjam van Praag. 2013. 'The Impact of Gender Diversity on the Performance of Business Teams: Evidence from a Field Experiment'. *Management Science* 59 (7): 1514–28.

Hsieh, Chang-Tai, Erik Hurst, Charles Jones, and Peter Klenow. 2019. 'The Allocation of Talent and U.S. Economic Growth'. *Econometrica* 87 (5): 1439–1474.

Htun, Mala, Marina Lacalle, and Juan Pablo Micozzi. 2013. 'Does Women's Presence Change Legislative Behavior? Evidence from Argentina, 1983–2007'. *Journal of Politics in Latin America* 5 (1): 95–125.

Huse, Morten, and Cathrine Seierstad. 2013. 'Getting Women on to Corporate Boards: Consequences of the Norwegian Gender Balance Law'. *The European Financial Review* 2013 (December): 37–39.

Hyde, Janet S., and Janet E. Mertz. 2009. 'Gender, Culture, and Mathematics Performance'. *Proceedings of the National Academy of Sciences* 106 (22): 8801–7.

Ibarra, Herminia. 1992. 'Homophily and Differential Returns: Sex Differences in Network Structure and Access in an Advertising Firm'. *Administrative Science Quarterly* 37 (3): 422–47.

ILO 2009. Global Employment Trend for Women Report. www.ilo.org/glo bal/publications/WCMS_103456/lang–en/index.htm

Imbens, Guido, and Karthik Kalyanaraman. 2012. 'Optimal Bandwidth Choice for the Regression Discontinuity Estimator'. *Review of Economic Studies* 79 (3): 933–59.

IMF Annual Report 2006. International Monetary Fund.

IMF Annual Report 2013. International Monetary Fund.

IMF Annual Report 2016. International Monetary Fund.

Inglehart, Ronald, and Pippa Norris. 2003. *Rising Tide: Gender Equality and Cultural Change around the World.* Cambridge University Press.

Ingley, C., and N. van der Walt. 2003. 'Board Configuration: Building Better Boards'. *Corporate Governance: The International Journal of Business in Society* 3 (4): 5–17.

International Labour Office. 2009. *Global Employment Trends for Women: International Labour Office.* International Labour Office.

Iversen, Torben, and Frances Rosenbluth. 2010. *Women, Work, and Politics: The Political Economy of Gender Inequality.* Yale University Press.

Júlio, Paulo, and José Tavares. 2017. 'The Good, the Bad and the Different: Can Gender Quotas Raise the Quality of Politicians?' *Economica* 84 (335): 454–79.

Jurajda, Štěpán, and Daniel Münich. 2011. 'Gender Gap in Performance under Competitive Pressure: Admissions to Czech Universities'. *American Economic Review* 101 (3): 514–18.

Jurkus, Anthony F., Jung Chul Park, and Lorraine S. Woodard. 2011. 'Women in Top Management and Agency Costs'. *Journal of Business Research* 64 (2): 180–86.

Kahn, Kim Fridkin. 1992. 'Does Being Male Help? An Investigation of the Effects of Candidate Gender and Campaign Coverage on Evaluations of U.S. Senate Candidates'. *The Journal of Politics* 54 (2): 497–517.

1994. 'Does Gender Make a Difference? An Experimental Examination of Sex Stereotypes and Press Patterns in Statewide Campaigns'. *American Journal of Political Science* 38 (1): 162–95.

Kan, Man Yee, Oriel Sullivan, and Jonathan Gershuny. 2011. 'Gender Convergence in Domestic Work: Discerning the Effects of Interactional and Institutional Barriers from Large-Scale Data'. *Sociology* 45 (2): 234–51.

Kanthak, Kristin, and Jonathan Woon. 2015. 'Women Don't Run? Election Aversion and Candidate Entry'. *American Journal of Political Science* 59 (3): 595–612.

Karp, Jeffrey A., and Susan A. Banducci. 2008. 'When Politics Is Not Just a Man's Game: Women's Representation and Political Engagement'. *Electoral Studies* 27 (1): 105–15.

Keck, Wolfgang, and Chiara Saraceno. 2008. 'Grandchildhood in Germany and Italy: An Exploration'. *Comparative Social Research* 25: 133–63.

Kelly, Erin L., and Phyllis Moen. 2007. 'Rethinking the Clockwork of Work: Why Schedule Control May Pay Off at Work and at Home'. *Advances in Developing Human Resources* 9 (4): 487–506.

Kelly, Erin L., Phyllis Moen, J. Michael Oakes, Wen Fan, Cassandra Okechukwu, Kelly D. Davis, Leslie B. Hammer et al. 2014. 'Changing Work and Work-Family Conflict: Evidence from the Work, Family, and Health Network'. *American Sociological Review* 79 (3): 485–516.

Kenworthy, Lane, and Melissa Malami. 1999. 'Gender Inequality in Political Representation: A Worldwide Comparative Analysis'. *Social Forces* 78 (1): 235–68.

Kerevel, Yann P., and Lonna Rae Atkeson. 2013. 'Explaining the Marginalization of Women in Legislative Institutions'. *The Journal of Politics* 75 (4): 980–92.

Kimball, Amanda, Donald Palmer, and Christopher Marquis. 2012. 'The Impact of Women Top Managers and Directors on Corporate Environmental Performance'. SSRN Scholarly Paper ID 2211826. Rochester, NY: Social Science Research Network.

Kinoshita, Yuko, and Kalpana Kochhar. 2016. 'She Is the Answer'. International Monetary Fund. www.imf.org/external/pubs/ft/fandd/20 16/03/kinoshita.htm

Kirkeboen, Lars J., Edwin Leuven, and Magne Mogstad. 2017. 'Field of Study, Earnings, and Self-Selection'. *The Quarterly Journal of Economics* 131 (3): 1057–111.

Kittilson, Miki Caul. 2006. *Challenging Parties, Changing Parliaments: Women and Elected Office in Contemporary Western Europe.* Ohio State University Press.

Klasen, Stephan. 2002. 'Low Schooling for Girls, Slower Growth for All? Cross-Country Evidence on the Effect of Gender Inequality in Education on Economic Development'. *The World Bank Economic Review* 16 (3): 345–73.

Kleven, Henrik, Camille Landais, Johanna Posch, Andreas Steinhauer, and Josef Zweimüller. 2019. 'Child Penalties across Countries: Evidence and Explanations'. *American Economic Review Papers and Proceedings* 109: 122–26.

Kluve, Jochen, and Marcus Tamm. 2013. 'Parental Leave Regulations, Mothers' Labor Force Attachment and Fathers' Childcare Involvement: Evidence from a Natural Experiment'. *Journal of Population Economics* 26 (3): 983–1005.

Knodel, John, and Mary Beth Ofstedal. 2003. 'Gender and Aging in the Developing World: Where Are the Men?' *Population and Development Review* 29 (4): 677–98.

Kofman, Eleonore, Annie Phizacklea, Parvati Raghuram, and Rosemary Sales. 2000. *Gender and International Migration in Europe: Employment, Welfare, and Politics.* Psychology Press.

Kohler, Hans-Peter, Francesco C. Billari, and José Antonio Ortega. 2002. 'The Emergence of Lowest-Low Fertility in Europe during the 1990s'. *Population and Development Review* 28 (4): 641–80.

Konrad, Alison M., Vicki Kramer, and Sumru Erkut. 2008. 'Critical Mass: The Impact of Three or More Women on Corporate Boards'. *Organizational Dynamics* 37 (2): 145–64.

Koopman, Cheryl, Kenneth R. Pelletier, James F. Murray, Claire E. Sharda, Marc L. Berger, Robin S. Turpin, Paul Hackleman, Pamela Gibson, Danielle M. Holmes, and Talor Bendel. 2002. 'Stanford Presenteeism Scale: Health Status and Employee Productivity'. *Journal of Occupational and Environmental Medicine* 44 (1): 14–20.

Krishnan, Hema A., and Daewoo Park. 2005. 'A Few Good Women–on Top Management Teams'. *Journal of Business Research* 58 (12): 1712–20.

Krook, Mona Lena. 2010. *Quotas for Women in Politics: Gender and Candidate Selection Reform Worldwide.* Oxford University Press.

Krook, Mona Lena, and Fiona Mackay. 2011. 'Introduction: Gender, Politics, and Institutions'. In *Gender, Politics and Institutions: Towards a Feminist Institutionalism*, Mona Lena Krook and Fiona Mackay, eds., 1–20. Gender and Politics Series. London: Palgrave Macmillan.

Kunovich, Sheri, and Pamela Paxton. 2005. 'Pathways to Power: The Role of Political Parties in Women's National Political Representation'. *American Journal of Sociology* 111 (2): 505–52.

Lagarde, Christine. 2018. Ten years after Lehman: Lessons learned and challenges ahead. IMF blog. https://blogs.imf.org/2018/09/05/ten-years-after-lehman-lessons-learned-and-challenges-ahead/

Lagerlöf, Nils-Petter. 2003. 'Gender Equality and Long-Run Growth'. *Journal of Economic Growth* 8 (4): 403–26.

Lalive, Rafael, and Josef Zweimüller. 2009. 'How Does Parental Leave Affect Fertility and Return to Work? Evidence from Two Natural Experiments'. *The Quarterly Journal of Economics* 124 (3): 1363–402.

Lang, Kevin. 1986. 'A Language Theory of Discrimination'. *The Quarterly Journal of Economics* 101 (2): 363–82.

Lavy, Victor. 2008. 'Do Gender Stereotypes Reduce Girls' or Boys' Human Capital Outcomes? Evidence from a Natural Experiment'. *Journal of Public Economics* 92 (10): 2083–105.

Lazarsfeld, P. F., and R. K. Merton. 1954. 'Friendship as a Social Process: A Substantive and Methodological Analysis'. In *Freedom and Control in*

Modern Society, M. Berger, T. Abel and C. Page, eds., 18–66. Van Nostrand.

Lee, Peggy M., and Erika Hayes James. 2007. 'She'-e-Os: Gender Effects and Investor Reactions to the Announcements of Top Executive Appointments'. *Strategic Management Journal* 28 (3): 227–41.

Lefebvre, Pierre, and Philip Merrigan. 2008. 'Child-Care Policy and the Labor Supply of Mothers with Young Children: A Natural Experiment from Canada'. *Journal of Labor Economics* 26 (3): 519–48.

Leibenstein, Harvey. 1966. 'Allocative Efficiency vs. "X-Efficiency"'. *American Economic Review* 56 (3): 392–415.

Leslie, Lisa M., Colleen Flaherty Manchester, Tae-Youn Park, and Si Ahn Mehng. 2012. 'Flexible Work Practices: A Source of Career Premiums or Penalties?' *Academy of Management Journal* 55 (6): 1407–28.

Lesthaeghe, Ron. 2010. 'The Unfolding Story of the Second Demographic Transition'. *Population and Development Review* 36 (2): 211–51.

Levitt, Steven D. 1996. 'How Do Senators Vote? Disentangling the Role of Voter Preferences, Party Affiliation, and Senator Ideology'. *American Economic Review* 86 (3): 425–41.

Lindenlaub, I., and A. Prummer. 2014. 'Gender, Social Networks And Performance'. Cambridge Working Papers in Economics 1461, Faculty of Economics, Cambridge University.

Lindert, Peter. 1994. 'The Rise of Social Spending, 1880–1930'. *Explorations in Economic History* 31 (1): 1–37.

Lott, John R., Jr, and Lawrence Kenny. 1999. 'Did Women's Suffrage Change the Size and Scope of Government?' *Journal of Political Economy* 107 (6): 1163–98.

Ludwig, Jens, and Douglas Miller. 2007. 'Does Head Start Improve Children's Life Chances? Evidence from a Regression Discontinuity Design'. *The Quarterly Journal of Economics* 122 (1): 159–208.

Lundberg, Shelly, and Richard Startz. 1983. 'Private Discrimination and Social Intervention in Competitive Labor Markets'. *American Economic Review* 73 (3): 340–47.

Machin, Stephen, and Tuomas Pekkarinen. 2008. 'Assessment. Global Sex Differences in Test Score Variability'. *Science* 322 (5906): 1331–32.

Maida, Agata, and Andrea Weber. 2019. 'Female Leadership and Gender Gap within Firms: Evidence from an Italian Board Reform'. CEPR Discussion Paper DP13476.

Malmendier, Ulrike, Geoffrey Tate, and Jon Yan. 2011. 'Overconfidence and Early-Life Experiences: The Effect of Managerial Traits on Corporate Financial Policies'. *Journal of Finance* 66 (5): 1687–733.

Maloney, Erin A., and Sian L. Beilock. 2012. 'Math Anxiety: Who Has It, Why It Develops, and How to Guard against It'. *Trends in Cognitive Sciences* 16 (8): 404–6.

Manning, Alan, and Barbara Petrongolo. 2008. 'The Part-Time Pay Penalty for Women in Britain'. *Economic Journal* 118 (526): F28–51.

Mansbridge, Jane. 1999. 'Should Blacks Represent Blacks and Women Represent Women? A Contingent "Yes"'. *The Journal of Politics* 61 (3): 628–57.

Mas, Alexandre, and Enrico Moretti. 2009. 'Peers at Work'. *American Economic Review* 99 (1): 112–45.

Masciandaro, Donato, Paola Profeta and Davide Romelli. 2018. 'Do Women Matter in Monetary Policymaking?' Research Paper 2018–88. Baffi Carefin Centre Research.

Matland, Richard E. 1993. 'Institutional Variables Affecting Female Representation in National Legislatures: The Case of Norway'. *The Journal of Politics* 55 (3): 737–55.

1998. 'Women's Representation in National Legislatures: Developed and Developing Countries'. *Legislative Studies Quarterly* 23 (1): 109–25.

Matsa, David A., and Amalia R. Miller. 2011. 'Chipping Away at the Glass Ceiling: Gender Spillovers in Corporate Leadership'. *American Economic Review* 101 (3): 635–39.

2013. 'A Female Style in Corporate Leadership? Evidence from Quotas'. *American Economic Journal: Applied Economics* 5 (3): 136–69.

Matsui, Kathy. 2014. 'Womenomics 4.0: Time to Walk the Talk'. Goldman Sachs.

McClelland, Emma. 2004. 'Irish Female Entrepreneurs: Mapping the Route to Internationalisation'. *Irish Journal of Management* 25 (2): 92–107.

McCrary, Justin. 2008. 'Manipulation of the Running Variable in the Regression Discontinuity Design: A Density Test.' *Journal of Econometrics* 142 (2): 698–714.

McDonald, Peter. 2000. 'Gender Equity in Theories of Fertility Transition'. *Population and Development Review* 26 (3): 427–39.

McPherson, Miller, Lynn Smith-Lovin, and James M. Cook. 2001. 'Birds of a Feather: Homophily in Social Networks'. *Annual Review of Sociology* 27 (1): 415–44.

Melero, Eduardo. 2011. 'Are Workplaces with Many Women in Management Run Differently?' *Journal of Business Research* 64 (4): 385–93.

Mencarini, Letizia, and Maria Letizia Tanturri. 2004. 'Time Use, Family Role-Set and Childbearing among Italian Working Women'. *Genus* 60 (1): 111–37.

Mengel, Friederike. 2015. 'Gender Differences in Networking'. SSRN Scholarly Paper ID 2636885. Rochester, NY: Social Science Research Network.

Merluzzi, Jennifer. 2017. 'Gender and Negative Network Ties: Exploring Difficult Work Relationships within and across Gender'. *Organization Science* 28 (4): 636–52.

Mills, Melinda, Letizia Mencarini, Maria Letizia Tanturri, and Katia Begall. 2008. 'Gender Equity and Fertility Intentions in Italy and the Netherlands'. *Demographic Research* 18 (February): 1–26.

Morrison, Andrew, Dhushyanth Raju, and Nistha Sinha. 2007. 'Gender Equality, Poverty and Economic Growth'. Policy Research Working Paper 4349. World Bank.

Murray, Rainbow, Mona Lena Krook, and Katherine A. R. Opello. 2012. 'Why Are Gender Quotas Adopted? Party Pragmatism and Parity in France'. *Political Research Quarterly* 65 (3): 529–43.

Myrskylä, Mikko, Hans-Peter Kohler, and Francesco C. Billari. 2009. 'Advances in Development Reverse Fertility Declines'. *Nature* 460 (7256): 741–43.

Nguyen, Hoa, and Robert Faff. 2007. 'Impact of Board Size and Board Diversity on Firm Value: Australian Evidence'. *Corporate Ownership and Control* 4 (2): 24–32.

Niederle, Muriel, and Lise Vesterlund. 2007. 'Do Women Shy Away from Competition? Do Men Compete Too Much?' *The Quarterly Journal of Economics* 35.

———. 2010. 'Explaining the Gender Gap in Math Test Scores: The Role of Competition'. *Journal of Economic Perspectives* 24 (2): 129–44.

———. 2011. 'Gender and Competition'. *Annual Review of Economics* 3 (1): 601–30.

Nollenberger, Natalia, and Núria Rodriguez-Planas. 2015. 'Full-Time Universal Childcare in a Context of Low Maternal Employment: Quasi-Experimental Evidence from Spain'. *Labour Economics* 36 (C): 124–36.

Nollenberger, Natalia, Núria Rodriguez-Planas, and Almudena Sevilla. 2016. 'The Math Gender Gap: The Role of Culture'. *American Economic Review* 106 (5): 257–61.

Norris, Pippa. 1985. 'Women's Legislative Participation in Western Europe'. *West European Politics* 8 (4): 90–101.

———. 1987. *Politics and Sexual Equality: The Comparative Position of Women in Western Democracies*. Boulder, CO: Lynne Rienner Publishers.

———. 2006. 'The Impact of Electoral Reform on Women's Representation'. *Acta Politica* 41 (2): 197–213.

Norris, Pippa, and Ronald Inglehart. 2001. 'Cultural Obstacles to Equal Representation'. *Journal of Democracy* 12 (3): 126–40.

Norris, Pippa, and Joni Lovenduski. 1995. *Political Recruitment: Gender, Race and Class in the British Parliament*. Cambridge University Press.

Nygaard, Knut. 2011. 'Forced Board Changes: Evidence from Norway'. SSRN Scholarly Paper ID 1793227. Rochester, NY: Social Science Research Network.

O'Rand, Angela M., and Janice I. Farkas. 2002. 'Couples' Retirement Timing in the United States in the 1990s'. *International Journal of Sociology* 32 (2): 11–29.

Oláh, Livia Sz. 2003. 'Gendering Fertility: Second Births in Sweden and Hungary'. *Population Research and Policy Review* 22 (2): 171–200.

Olivetti, Claudia, and Barbara Petrongolo. 2008. 'Unequal Pay or Unequal Employment? A Cross-Country Analysis of Gender Gaps'. *Journal of Labor Economics* 26 (4): 621–54.

———. 2017. 'The Economic Consequences of Family Policies: Lessons from a Century of Legislation in High-Income Countries'. *Journal of Economic Perspectives* 31 (1): 205–30.

Oppenheimer, Valerie Kincade. 1994. 'Women's Rising Employment and the Future of the Family in Industrial Societies'. *Population and Development Review* 20 (2): 293–342.

Ors, Evren, Frédéric Palomino, and Eloïc Peyrache. 2013. 'Performance Gender Gap: Does Competition Matter?' *Journal of Labor Economics* 31 (3): 443–99.

Osborne, Martin, and Al Slivinski. 1996. 'A Model of Political Competition with Citizen-Candidates'. *The Quarterly Journal of Economics* 111 (1): 65–96.

Park, Hyunjoon, Jere R. Behrman, and Jaesung Choi. 2013. 'Causal Effects of Single-Sex Schools on College Entrance Exams and College Attendance: Random Assignment in Seoul High Schools'. *Demography* 50 (2): 447–69.

Pasqua, Silvia, and Anna Laura Mancini. 2012. 'Asymmetries and Interdependencies in Time Use between Italian Parents'. *Applied Economics* 44 (32): 4153–71.

Paull, Gillian. 2006. 'The Impact of Children on Women's Paid Work'. *Fiscal Studies* 27 (4): 473–512.

———. 2008. 'Children and Women's Hours of Work'. *The Economic Journal* 118 (526): F8–27.

Paxton, Pamela, and Sheri Kunovich. 2003. 'Women's Political Representation: The Importance of Ideology'. *Social Forces* 82 (1): 87–113.

Pfau-Effinger, Birgit. 2005. 'Culture and Welfare State Policies: Reflections on a Complex Interrelation'. *Journal of Social Policy* 34 (1): 3–20.

Phillips, Anne. 1995. *The Politics of Presence*. Oxford University Press.

Pinkston, Joshua C. 2003. 'Screening Discrimination and the Determinants of Wages'. *Labour Economics* 10 (6): 643–58.

Pinnelli, Antonella, and Francesca Fiori. 2008. 'The Influence of Partner Involvement in Fatherhood and Domestic Tasks on Mothers' Fertility Expectations in Italy'. *Fathering: A Journal of Theory, Research, and Practice About Men as Fathers* 6 (April): 169–91.

Pitt, Mark, and Shahidur Khandker. 1998. 'The Impact of Group-Based Credit Programs on Poor Households in Bangladesh: Does the Gender of Participants Matter?' *Journal of Political Economy* 106 (5): 958–96.

Pletzer, Jan Luca, Romina Nikolova, Karina Karolina Kedzior, and Sven Constantin Voelpel. 2015. 'Does Gender Matter? Female Representation on Corporate Boards and Firm Financial Performance – A Meta-Analysis'. *PLOS ONE* 10 (6): e0130005.

Pope, Devin G., and Justin R. Sydnor. 2010. 'Geographic Variation in the Gender Differences in Test Scores'. *Journal of Economic Perspectives* 24 (2): 95–108.

Post, Corinne, and Kris Byron. 2014. 'Women on Boards and Firm Financial Performance: A Meta-Analysis'. *Academy of Management Journal* 58 (5): 1546–71.

Post, Corinne, Noushi Rahman, and Emily Rubow. 2011. 'Green Governance: Boards of Directors' Composition and Environmental Corporate Social Responsibility'. *Business & Society* 50 (1): 189–223.

Pritchett, Lant, and Martina Viarengo. 2012. 'Why Demographic Suicide? The Puzzles of European Fertility'. *Population and Development Review* 38: 55–71.

Profeta, Paola, and Marta Angelici. 2019. 'Smart-Working: Does job flexibility work?'. Bocconi University. Mimeo.

Profeta, Paola, and Vincenzo Galasso. 2018. 'Gender Gaps in Math Tests: Women under Pressure'. Bocconi University. Mimeo.

Profeta, Paola, and Eleanor Woodhouse. 2018. 'Do Electoral Rules Matter for Female Representation?' SSRN Scholarly Paper Rochester, NY: Social Science Research Network.

Ramsey, F. P. 1927. 'A Contribution to the Theory of Taxation'. *The Economic Journal* 37 (145): 47–61.

Raute, Anna. 2017. 'Can Financial Incentives Reduce the Baby Gap? Evidence from a Reform in Maternity Leave Benefits'. Working Paper 23793. National Bureau of Economic Research.

Rebérioux, Antoine, and Gwenaël Roudaut. 2016. 'Gender Quota inside the Boardroom: Female Directors as New Key Players?' Working Papers hal-01297884, HAL.

Rehavi, M. Marit. 2007. 'Sex and Politics: Do Female Legislators Affect State Spending?' Unpublished Manuscript, University of Michigan 78.

Rendall, Michelle Petersen. 2018. 'Female Market Work, Tax Regimes, and the Rise of the Service Sector'. *Review of Economic Dynamics* 28: 269-289.

Reuben, Ernesto, Paola Sapienza, and Luigi Zingales. 2014. 'How Stereotypes Impair Women's Careers in Science'. *Proceedings of the National Academy of Sciences* 111 (12): 4403–8.

Reuben, Ernesto, Matthew Wiswall, and Basit Zafar. 2017. 'Preferences and Biases in Educational Choices and Labour Market Expectations: Shrinking the Black Box of Gender'. *The Economic Journal* 127 (604): 2153–86.

Reynolds, Andrew. 1999. 'Women in the Legislatures and Executives of the World: Knocking at the Highest Glass Ceiling'. *World Politics* 51 (4): 547–72.

Rica, Sara de la, Juan, J. Dolado, and Cecilia García-Peñalosa. 2013. 'On Gender Gaps and Self-Fulfilling Expectations: Theory, Policies and Some Empirical Evidence'. *Economic Inquiry* 51(3): 1829- 1848.

Riedmann, Arnold, Harald Bielenski, Teresa Szczurowska, and Alexandra Wagner. 2006. *Working Time and Work-Life Balance in European Companies: Establishment Survey on Working Time 2004–2005*. EF, 06,27. Office for Offical Publ. of the European Communities.

Rigdon, Mary L. 2012. 'An Experimental Investigation of Gender Differences in Wage Negotiations'. SSRN Scholarly Paper ID 2165253. Rochester, NY: Social Science Research Network.

Riley, Matilda White, Marilyn Johnson and Anne Foner. 1972. *Aging and Society: A Sociology of Age Stratification*. Russell Sage Foundation.

Rivero-Fuentes, M. Estela, and Signe-Mary McKernan. 2005. 'Gender and the Impact of Credit and Transfers'. Report number 34967. The World Bank.

Rodrik, Dani. 1998. 'Why Do More Open Economies Have Bigger Governments?' *Journal of Political Economy* 106 (5): 997–1032.

Rosa, William, ed. 2017. 'Transforming Our World: The 2030 Agenda for Sustainable Development'. In *A New Era in Global Health*. Springer Publishing Company.

Rose, Caspar. 2007. 'Does Female Board Representation Influence Firm Performance? The Danish Evidence'. *Corporate Governance. An International Review* 15(2): 404-413.

Rosen, Harvey. 1977. 'Is It Time to Abandon Joint Filing?' *National Tax Journal* 30 (4): 423–28.

Rubalcava, Luis, Graciela Teruel, and Duncan Thomas. 2009. 'Investments, Time Preferences and Public Transfers Paid to Women', *Economic Development and Cultural Change* 57 (3): 507–538.

Rubery, Jill. 1988. *Women and Recession*. London: Routledge.

Rubinstein, Ariel. 2006. 'A Sceptic's Comment on the Study of Economics'. *The Economic Journal* 116 (510): C1–9.

Ruggles, S. 1997. 'The Rise of Divorce and Separation in the United States, 1880–1990'. *Demography* 34 (4): 455–66; discussion 467–79.

Ruhm, Christopher. 1998. 'The Economic Consequences of Parental Leave Mandates: Lessons from Europe'. *The Quarterly Journal of Economics* 113 (1): 285–317.

Rule, Wilma. 1987. 'Electoral Systems, Contextual Factors and Women's Opportunity for Election to Parliament in Twenty-Three Democracies'. *The Western Political Quarterly* 40 (3): 477–98.

　　1988. 'Why Women Don't Run: The Critical Contextual Factors in Women's Legislative Recruitment'. *The Western Political Quarterly* 34: 60–77.

Saint-Paul, Gilles. 2008. 'Against "Gender-Based Taxation"'. SSRN Scholarly Paper ID 1140512. Rochester, NY: Social Science Research Network.

Sanbonmatsu, Kira. 2002. 'Gender Stereotypes and Vote Choice'. *American Journal of Political Science* 46 (1): 20–34.

Sapienza, Paola, Luigi Zingales, and Dario Maestripieri. 2009. 'Gender Differences in Financial Risk Aversion and Career Choices Are Affected by Testosterone'. *Proceedings of the National Academy of Sciences of the United States of America* 106 (36): 15268–73.

Sayer, Liana C., and Suzanne M. Bianchi. 2000. 'Women's Economic Independence and the Probability of Divorce: A Review and Reexamination'. *Journal of Family Issues* 21 (7): 906–43.

Sayer, Liana C., Paula England, Paul Allison, and Nicole Kangas. 2011. 'She Left, He Left: How Employment and Satisfaction Affect Men's and Women's Decisions to Leave Marriages'. *American Journal of Sociology* 116 (6): 1982–2018.

Schieman, Scott, and Paul Glavin. 2008. 'Trouble at the Border?: Gender, Flexibility at Work, and the Work-Home Interface'. *Social Problems* 55 (November): 590–611.

Schlozman, Kay Lehman, Nancy Burns, and Sidney Verba. 1994. 'Gender and the Pathways to Participation: The Role of Resources'. *The Journal of Politics* 56 (4): 963–90.

Schoen, Robert, Nan Marie Astone, Kendra Rothert, Nicola J. Standish, and Young J. Kim. 2002. 'Women's Employment, Marital Happiness, and Divorce'. *Social Forces* 81 (2): 643–62.

Schönberg, Uta, and Johannes Ludsteck. 2014. 'Expansions in Maternity Leave Coverage and Mothers' Labor Market Outcomes after Childbirth'. *Journal of Labor Economics* 32 (3): 469–505.

Schwartz-Ziv, Miriam. 2017. 'Gender and Board Activeness: The Role of a Critical Mass'. *Journal of Financial and Quantitative Analysis* 52 (2): 751–80.

Schwindt-Bayer, Leslie A., Michael Malecki, and Brian F. Crisp. 2010. 'Candidate Gender and Electoral Success in Single Transferable Vote Systems'. *British Journal of Political Science* 40 (3): 693–709.

Schwindt-Bayer, Leslie A., and William Mishler. 2005. 'An Integrated Model of Women's Representation'. *The Journal of Politics* 67 (2): 407–28.

Scollon, Ron, Suzanne Wong Scollon, and Rodney H. Jones. 2011. *Intercultural Communication: A Discourse Approach*. John Wiley & Sons.

Seierstad, Cathrine, and Tore Opsahl. 2011. 'For the Few Not the Many? The Effects of Affirmative Action on Presence, Prominence, and Social Capital of Women Directors in Norway'. *Scandinavian Journal of Management* 27 (1): 44–54.

Shair-Rosenfield, Sarah, and Magda Hinojosa. 2014. 'Does Female Incumbency Reduce Gender Bias in Elections? Evidence from Chile'. *Political Research Quarterly* 67 (4): 837–50.

Small, Deborah A., Michele Gelfand, Linda Babcock, and Hilary Gettman. 2007. 'Who Goes to the Bargaining Table? The Influence of Gender and Framing on the Initiation of Negotiation'. *Journal of Personality and Social Psychology* 93 (4): 600–613.

Smith, Valdemar, Nina Smith, and Mette Verner. 2006. 'Do Women in Top Management Affect Firm Performance? A Panel Study of 2,500 Danish Firms'. *International Journal of Productivity and Performance Management* 55 (7): 569–93.

Snyder, James M., and Tim Groseclose. 2000. 'Estimating Party Influence in Congressional Roll-Call Voting'. *American Journal of Political Science* 44 (2): 193–211.

Soest, Arthur van, Lans Bovenberg, and Asghar Zaidi. 2010. 'Ageing, Health and Pensions in Europe: An Economic Perspective'. In *Ageing, Health and Pensions in Europe*, Lans Bovenberg, Arthur van Soest and Asghar Zaidi, eds., 1–9. Palgrave Macmillan UK.

Solnick, S. J. 2001. 'Gender Differences in the Ultimatum Game'. *Economic Inquiry* 39 (2): 189–200.

Spencer, Steven J., Claude M. Steele, and Diane M. Quinn. 1999. 'Stereotype Threat and Women's Math Performance'. *Journal of Experimental Social Psychology* 35 (1): 4–28.

Stanwick, Kathy A., and Katherine E. Kleeman. 1983. Women Make a Difference: Report. Center for the American Woman and Politics.

Stehlé, Juliette, François Charbonnier, Tristan Picard, Ciro Cattuto and Alain Barrat. 2013. 'Gender Homophily from Spatial Behavior in a Primary School: A Sociometric Study'. *Social Networks* 35 (4): 604–13.

Steiner, Viktor, and Katharina Wrohlich. 2004. 'Household Taxation, Income Splitting and Labor Supply Incentives: A Microsimulation Study for Germany'. *CESifo Economic Studies* 50(3): 541- 568.

Steinpreis, Rhea E., Katie A. Anders, and Dawn Ritzke. 1999. 'The Impact of Gender on the Review of the Curricula Vitae of Job Applicants and Tenure Candidates: A National Empirical Study'. *Sex Roles* 41 (7): 509–28.

Stevenson, Betsey, and Justin Wolfers. 2009. 'The Paradox of Declining Female Happiness'. *American Economic Journal: Economic Policy* 1 (2): 190-225.

Stevenson, Megan. 2017. 'Breaking Bad: Mechanisms of Social Influence and the Path to Criminality in Juvenile Jails'. *The Review of Economics and Statistics* 99 (5): 824–38.

Stiglitz, Joseph, Amartya K. Sen, and Jean-Paul Fitoussi. 2009. 'The Measurement of Economic Performance and Social Progress Revisited: Reflections and Overview'. 2009–33. Sciences Po Publications.

Swamy, Anand, Stephen Knack, Young Lee, and Omar Azfar. 2001. 'Gender and Corruption'. *Journal of Development Economics* 64 (1): 25–55.

Swers, Michele L. 2002. *The Difference Women Make: The Policy Impact of Women in Congress.* 1st edn. University of Chicago Press.

Syverson, Chad. 2011. 'What Determines Productivity?' *Journal of Economic Literature* 49 (2): 326–65.

Tanzi, Vito. 1987. 'Quantitative Characteristics of the Tax Systems of Developing Countries'. In *The Theory of Taxation for Developing Countries*, D. M. G. Newbery and N. H. Stern, eds. Oxford University Press, Oxford for the World Bank.

—— 1992. *Financial Markets and Public Finance in the Transformation Process.* International Monetary Fund.

Tate, Geoffrey, and Liu Yang. 2015. 'Female Leadership and Gender Equity: Evidence from Plant Closure'. *Journal of Financial Economics* 117 (1): 77–97.

Tazi-Preve, I., D. Bichlbauer, and A. Goujon. 2004. 'Gender Trouble and Its Impact on Fertility Intentions'. *Yearbook of Population Research in Finland* 40: 5–24.

Teigen, Mari, and Fredrik Engelstad. 2012. *Firms, Boards and Gender Quotas: Comparative Perspectives.* Emerald Group Publishing.

Thomas, Sue. 1991. 'The Impact of Women on State Legislative Policies'. *The Journal of Politics* 53 (4): 958–76.

1994. *How Women Legislate*. Oxford University Press USA.

Torr, Berna Miller, and Susan E. Short. 2004. 'Second Births and the Second Shift: A Research Note on Gender Equity and Fertility'. *Population and Development Review* 30 (1): 109–30.

Van Knippenberg, Daan, Carsten K. W. De Dreu, and Astrid C. Homan. 2004. 'Work Group Diversity and Group Performance: An Integrative Model and Research Agenda'. *The Journal of Applied Psychology* 89 (6): 1008–22.

Vaupel, James W., and Kristín G. V. Kistowski. 2008. 'Living Longer in an Ageing Europe: A Challenge for Individuals and Societies'. *European View* 7 (2): 255–63.

Wagner, Adolph. 1883. *Finanzwissenschaft*. C. F. Winter.

Walker, Francis A. 1887. 'The Source of Business Profits'. *The Quarterly Journal of Economics* 1 (3): 265–88.

Washington, Ebonya L. 2008. 'Female Socialization: How Daughters Affect Their Legislator Fathers'. *American Economic Review* 98 (1): 311–32.

Welch, Catherine L., Denice E. Welch, and Lisa Hewerdine. 2008. 'Gender and Export Behaviour: Evidence from Women-Owned Enterprises'. *Journal of Business Ethics* 83 (1): 113–26.

Wolbrecht, Christina, and David E. Campbell. 2007. 'Leading by Example: Female Members of Parliament as Political Role Models'. *American Journal of Political Science* 51 (4): 921–39.

Wolfers, Justin. 2006. 'Diagnosing Discrimination: Stock Returns and Ceo Gender'. *Journal of the European Economic Association* 4 (2–3): 531–41.

World Bank. 2006. 'Equity and Development 2006'. World Development Report.

World Economic Forum (WEF) 2016. 'The Future of Jobs: Employment, Skills and Workforce Strategy for the Fourth Industrial Revolution'. Global Challenge Insight Report.

2018. *The Global Gender Gap Report*.

Yoon, Mi Yung. 2004. 'Explaining Women's Legislative Representation in Sub-Saharan Africa'. *Legislative Studies Quarterly* 29 (3): 447–68.

Zafar, Basit. 2013. 'College Major Choice and the Gender Gap'. *Journal of Human Resources* 48 (3): 545–95.

Index